ALLITERATIVE POETRY IN MIDDLE ENGLISH

THE DIALECTAL AND METRICAL SURVEY

ALLITERATIVE POETRY
IN MIDDLE ENGLISH

THE DIALECTAL AND METRICAL SURVEY

BY

J. P. OAKDEN

TWO VOLUMES IN ONE

" As hit is stad and stoken,
In stori stif and stronge,
With lel letteres loken,
In londe so hatȝ ben longe."
            Syr Gawayn and the Grene Knyȝt, l. 33 et seq.

ARCHON BOOKS
1968

Originally published 1930, 1935

Reprinted in one volume 1968
with permission of
Manchester University Press

Library of Congress Catalog Card Number: 68–11255
Printed in the United States of America

To

PROFESSOR W. J. SEDGEFIELD

THIS BOOK IS

GRATEFULLY DEDICATED

PREFACE TO THE 1968 EDITION

I am under a debt of gratitude to Archon Books for their suggestion of reprinting my *Alliterative Poetry in Middle English* in a single volume. After so many years of teaching and further research into these topics, the original volumes cannot express the totality of my present views and judgments, but a completely revised and rewritten edition would not be feasible on either financial or other grounds at this time. There are things I would have liked to do, in particular to revise the section entitled "Approach to Dialectal Questions" on which so much work has been done both in America by the compilers of the Middle English Dictionary and in this country too and in Sweden by so many distinguished scholars. Their work is not yet completed, however, and this kind of volume would not be the place to attempt a synthesis, even if I were capable of doing so. Middle English Dialects now form a field on their own, and the student who wishes to study dialectal questions in detail has vast material before him readily available. The sketch given here may still be of value and interest to the general student of Alliterative Poetry which is all that it ever attempted to be. Of the Alliterative works themselves, much work has been done on *Piers Plowman* and the *Gawain* poet where advance has been steady. I need but mention such studies as M. Borroff's *Sir Gawain and the Green Knight: A Stylistic and Metrical Study*, New Haven, 1962, which I had the pleasure of reviewing for *Medium Aevum*, and J. A. Burrow's *A Reading of Sir Gawain and the Green Knight* which must prove most rewarding to the student and indicate the lines of still further understanding and appreciation. My original volumes gave some impetus to alliterative studies in Middle English, the results of which can easily be followed in the appropriate bibliographical works both literary and linguistic which are the stand-by of every serious student. I shall be only too happy if the reader still finds here raw material for study and a general guide to sympathetic judgments upon this large body of works from Western England in the Fourteenth Century.

J. P. O.

THE UNIVERSITY OF ST. ANDREWS,
March, 1967

PREFACE.

THIS work forms Part I of a survey of Middle English Alliterative Poetry. Part II will deal with problems of a literary and semi-literary nature and will show how the linguistic and literary sides of the problem are bound up with each other. The theories advanced are often of a controversial kind, especially in the metrical section, but this is largely due to the fact that the Middle English alliterative poetry has not received the attention it un-doubtedly deserves. It is hoped that the present work will arouse further interest in the difficult questions involved.

My best thanks are due to Professor W. J. Sedgefield, my teacher, without whom the work could never have been accomplished; to him I owe a debt which cannot be repaid; he has watched over the work during the years of its preparation and has always been ready with his help and advice; I have also to thank him for reading the proofs.

I am also indebted to Miss F. E. Harmer for suggestions regarding the matter of Appendix 2; to Dr. A. Mawer for advice about certain minor details; to Dr. O. K. Schram for bringing to my notice several important matters when the work was in the proof-stage; and to Mr. Idris Bell, the Deputy-Keeper of the MSS. in the British Museum, for help in the dating of certain MSS. I am greatly indebted to Miss M. Campbell for continued help in checking the statistics, arranging the material and preparing the typescript for the press. To Mr. H. M. McKechnie, the secretary of the Manchester University Press, I am grateful for help and advice as the book passed through the press; it is owing to him that it was possible to present the material in so convenient a manner.

Lastly, I have to thank the Manchester University Press for undertaking the publication of the work, and the administrators of the Ward Bequest for bearing a portion of the expense.

J. P. O.

MANCHESTER,
July, 1930.

TABLE OF CONTENTS.

TABLE OF ABBREVIATIONS.

acc. . . = accusative.
adj. . . = adjective.
adv. . . = adverb.
A.N. . . = Anglo-Norman.
Beib. Angl. . = Beiblatt Anglia.
c. . . . = circa.
Chet. Soc. N.S. . = Chetham Society, New Series.
Chet. Soc. O.S. . = Chetham Society, Old Series.
C.W. Midl. . = The Central West-Midland Dialect of Middle English.
C.S. Midl . . = The Central South-Midland Dialect of Middle English
doc. . . = document.
E.E.T.S. . . = The Early English Text Society, Old Series.
E.E.T.S. E.S. . = The Early English Text Society, New Series.
E. Midl. . . = The East-Midland Dialect of Middle English.
Eng. Stud. . = Englische Studien.
fem. . . = feminine.
Gaw. . . = *Sir Gawayn and the Green Knight* (used in statistics).
gen.. . . = genitive.
indic. . . = indicative.
infin. . . = infinitive.
l. . . . = line.
M.E. . . = Middle English.
Midl. . . = The Midland Dialect of Middle English.
M.L.G. . . = Middle Low German.
Mn.E. . . = Modern English.
Mod. Lang. Rev. = The Modern Language Review.
N.E. Midl. . = The North-East-Midland Dialect of Middle English.
nom. . . = nominative.
Nth. . . = The Northern Dialect of Middle English.
N.W. Midl. . = The North-West-Midland Dialect of Middle English.
O.E. . . = Old English.
O.Fr. . . = Old French.
O.M. . . = Old Mercian.
O.N. . . = Old Norse.
p. . . . = page.
Pat. . . = *Patience* (used in statistics).

pers. . . = person.
Piers Plowman . = *The Vision of William concerning Piers the Plow-
                  man.*
pl. . . . = plural.
pres. . . = present.
pres. part . = present participle.
pret. . . = preterite.
Prl. . . = *Pearl* (used in statistics).
Pt. . . . = Point (*The Dialectal Points* on page 10).
Pubs. Mod. Lang. Ass. of America
                = Publications of the Modern Language Association
                  of America.
Pur. . . = *Purity* or *Cleanness* (used in statistics).
sb. . . . = substantive.
S.E.E. Poems . = *Select Early English Poems*, edited by Sir Israel
                  Gollancz.
S.E. Midl.. . = The South-East-Midland Dialect of Middle
                  English.
sg. . . . = singular.
S. Midl. . . = The South-Midland Dialect of Middle English.
Sth. . . = The Southern Dialect of Middle English.
S.T.S. . . = The Scottish Text Society.
str. syll. . . = stressed syllable.
S. Western . = The South-Western Dialect of Middle English.
S.W. Midl. . = The South-West-Midland of Middle English.
wk. . . . = weak.
W. Midl. . . = The West-Midland Dialect of Middle English.

All other abbreviations explain themselves.

INTRODUCTION.

In recent years no group of Middle English poets has excited such interest as that of the writers of alliterative poetry. Almost without exception these authors remain unknown, despite repeated efforts to discover their identity. For the searching hand of criticism has swept away once-cherished theories, and in the inevitable reaction that has followed, attention has been concentrated upon other problems, the study of which has proved more profitable. Fanciful theories concerning the author of *Sir Gawayn and the Green Knight, Pearl, Patience,* and *Purity,* are no longer fashionable, and where these have been based solely on the individual interpretation of certain supposedly biographical details in the poems, the reaction is surely to be welcomed. We are not justified in refusing to consider the possibility of discovering historical references to an author's life, but are clearly right in suggesting that it is always dangerous to argue solely from internal evidence. No one will deny that Layamon was the author of *The Brut* or that he was a secular priest serving a village church at *Ernleye* on the bank of the Severn in Worcestershire, for these facts are unmistakably set forth in the opening lines of his poem ; but such unequivocal details are very seldom found. The difficult problems of authorship of the Middle English poems which come within the scope of the present survey are only touched upon in Appendices 1 and 2. In the first of these we have endeavoured to use the data afforded by a study of the metre as a test for common authorship. This seems to be a more reliable test than that afforded by minute parallels of identical phraseology, since the latter may be due either to conscious borrowing or to the fact that many phrases were the stock-in-trade of all the writers. The same difficulty does not arise with regard to the metrical evidence, and it is noticeable that the metre of *Sir Gawayn and the Green Knight, Patience,* and *Purity,* when closely examined, plainly indicates the common authorship of the three poems. The other groups of poems treated give the same result, for an alliterative poet unconsciously reveals his identity in his manipulation of the verse.

The problems of authorship relating to *The Vision of William concerning Piers the Plowman* are not treated in this volume, nor have we considered those centred round *Huchown of the Awle Ryale*. In Appendix 2 we have merely recorded the results of an attempt to identify the castle of the Green Knight in the light of the dialectal evidence. There is no desire to press the arguments unduly, but to some scholars they may not appear unreasonable.

The second great group of problems arising out of a study of the Middle English alliterative poems is the dialectal one. It was not long after the commencement of this work that it was realised how difficult a task this was. The poems in question had been assigned to a western dialect because of the absence of eastern forms rather than owing to the presence of western ones. Indeed, the more closely we studied the " character- istics " of the western dialect actually accepted by scholars, the clearer did it become that these had been gathered from a study of some of the alliterative poems themselves. It seemed that the whole foundation was falling to pieces, and it is true that we are only at the beginnings of dialectal study. If the conclusions reached are in the main orthodox, that is because the original guess-work of the early scholars happened to be correct, though they advanced no proofs for their statements. In not a few cases, however, they were certainly wrong. The study of genuine western texts by scholars such as Professor Menner and Miss Serjeantson, and of place-name records by the latter and Professor Wyld, has enabled us to speak more authori- tatively on problems of dialect. Often we have felt compelled to disagree with many present-day opinions, either because of some new evidence which has come to light, or because of a different interpretation of the same material. In all cases, therefore, we have started at the beginning, and have en- deavoured not to utilise evidence which cannot be substantiated.

The scope of the dialectal survey is indicated at the beginning of Part I., but it may be necessary to add at this stage that we are not concerned with the localisation of the extant MS. in each case, but of the original one. The methods used are thus somewhat removed from those of Miss Serjeantson. This is because there has been an attempt to keep in mind the poets as a group, and consequently problems of a more literary nature have come within the scope of the work. Therefore, in certain cases where there are signs of dialectal corruption we have merely relied on those points which can be proved to have been original by a study of the rhyme and alliteration. At the same time, these methods incidentally help in the localisation of the copy.

The study of the metre cannot be undertaken altogether apart from that of the dialect. For this reason the poems have been divided into five groups, which are examined in chapters 2 to 6. Chapters 7 to 11 correspond with the same divisions. The first four of these groups treat of all the purely alliterative poems in Middle English. Of the poems dealt with in chapter 6, those with ornamental alliteration, only the more important have been dealt with, though all have been examined from a metrical point of view. Economy of space has demanded the suppression of many dialectal statistics which would otherwise have been included.

To those who care little for dialectal investigations the metrical problems may prove more interesting. The survival or revival of the alliterative long line has long been a subject of controversy. In this section the aim has been to view the problem historically. All the fragments of alliterative poetry which are extant from the close of the Old English period until the fourteenth century have been dealt with, and because these, when chronologically arranged, appear to indicate a continuous evolution of the Old English verse, it has been concluded that the alliterative tradition never died, certain intermediary stages having been lost. The history of the long line between the two periods is fascinating, and we shall not be inclined to grumble at the absence of literary merit in the fragments which occur in the long gap. The causes of the decay of the alliterative metre are also revealed by a patient study of the last products of the school. In dealing with the metre we are indebted to the work of many German scholars, notably to that of Kaluza, Luick, Schumacher, and Trautmann.

The subjects treated in the appendices will indicate that the work is meant to go outside the usual enquiries of the philologist.

The study of the dialect and metre of these alliterative poems has incidentally revealed great poetic value in some of the more neglected ones.

The study of the vocabulary, phraseology, and style opened up such a wide field of enquiry that it was deemed necessary to reserve this section of the work for a second volume.

PART I.

THE DIALECTAL SURVEY.

CHAPTER I.

A METHOD OF APPROACH TO THE DIALECTAL QUESTIONS.

THERE are few alliterative poems in Middle English whose dialect can be localised from internal evidence; for local references are infrequent, and authors usually anonymous. The problem becomes still more complicated when we remember that most of the longer alliterative poems are unrhymed, a fact which involves the possibility of scribal alteration, not readily detected.

Despite these real difficulties, scholars have not hesitated to assume that most of the alliterative poems were written in the west of England.

Dr. R. Morris[1] assigned the *Early English Alliterative Poems* to Lancashire because of : the use of " schin," the neuter genitive as " hit," the 2nd. pers. sg. wk. pret. in -*es*, the pres. indic. sg. in -*es*, and the pl. in -*en*. His views were unquestioned until 1921, when Hulbert[2] attacked the traditional view and conclusively proved that each of Morris' dialectal tests was untrustworthy. His criticism was throughout destructive, and some of his statements were far from accurate. But his attack on the traditional view was justifiable. We may recall that Bateson[3] had followed Morris in his edition of *Patience*, as did Sir Israel Gollancz when editing *Pearl*. Professor Wyld alone had attempted to tackle the problem seriously; by the use of place-name statistics

---

[1] *E.E.T.S.*, 1, 1864.
[2] *The West-Midland of the Romances*, Mod. Phil., xix, p. 1, 1921.
[3] *Patience*, 2nd. edit., 1915, Manchester.

(5)

he sought to find a new basis for dialectal study.[1] His methods are too well-known to need any restatement here. His work represents a new attempt to handle what will always remain a difficult problem, namely, the settling of dialectal boundaries. We may not always agree with the methods he employs, but it is true that he has opened up a new line of enquiry. It was not, however, entirely his own idea. Pogatscher[2] had made a beginning, but Brandl, Ekwall, Jordan, Reaney and Miss Serjeantson have all shown the importance of Professor Wyld's work by what they themselves have accomplished after him. The work is all the more valuable inasmuch as few admittedly western texts are known from which the dialectal characteristics could be discovered. It is precisely on this point that scholars have gone astray. Luick, Morsbach and even Wyld himself have, in their study of Middle English grammar, drawn up lists of " western dialectal features," based on the study of texts not proved to be western, such as the *Early English Alliterative Poems*. Hulbert is hardly fair to these scholars on this point, as Menner[3] pointed out, but now that Morris' tests for the western dialects have been proved inconclusive, the later grammarians' statements about these dialects must be questioned. An alternative method of approach is necessary, and this is to be found in the employment of genuine western texts, if such exist.

The employment of genuine localised texts and documents is of vital importance, and if these can be obtained for the western areas, they are bound to throw light on the problem before us. While recognising that dialectal boundaries are very far from being clear-cut, we hope to show that it is nevertheless possible to indicate on a map the approximate boundaries. We shall see that there were often causes for such boundaries—geographical, political and ecclesiastical. Thus the Ribble in Lancashire seems to have divided that county into two distinct dialectal areas.[4]

A very important beginning along such lines was made

[1] *O.E. y̆ in the Dialects of the Midlands*, Eng. Stud., 47, 1-58, 145-166, 1913.   [2] Anglia 34, p. 302, 1901.

[3] *Sir Gawayn and the Green Knight*, Pub. Mod. Lang. Ass. of America, vol. 37, p. 503, 1922.

[4] E. Ekwall, *Ortsnamenforschung ein Hilfsmittel für das engl. Sprachgeschichte-Studium*, Germ. Rom. Monatsschrift, 1913, pp. 592-608.

by R. J. Menner,[1] who replied to Hulbert in 1922. He called attention to the fact that Myrc and Audelay were Shropshire writers, and from a study of the works of these two authors he showed that West-Midland was essentially different from East-Midland, examples of which he took from such works as *The Norfolk Guilds, Havelock the Dane* and *Handlyng Synne.* For the west he also consulted eight original local documents, which afforded further indications of the characteristics of the western dialects. The documents are, however, late, so that their value is not so great as it might otherwise have been. Menner concludes that Hulbert was incorrect in saying that it was impossible to distinguish between East and West-Midland, and he gives the following tests for the latter dialect :—

1. O.E. $\bar{y}$ > $\ddot{u}$.
2. O.E. $\breve{e}$o > a rounded vowel.
3. O.E. $\breve{a}$ + n > *on.*
4. The use of *ho* for the 3rd. sg. fem. pers. pron. nom.
5. The use of the endings *-us, -ud* for *-es, -ed.*
6. The i-mutation of O.E. $\breve{a}$ + 1 + Cons. as $\breve{a}$.

Menner does not assign *Sir Gawayn and the Green Knight* to Lancs, but merely to the North-West-Midland dialect.

Menner's short article was the most important contribution towards the solution of the problem that had so far appeared. Since then, however, Miss Serjeantson has published the results of her studies in the same field.[2] She begins by quickly reviewing the statements of the leading scholars who have concerned themselves with the West-Midland dialect, revealing how inadequately the problems have been treated.

She then gives a list of literary documents useful in ascertaining the characteristics of the western dialects : *The Worcester Fragments, The Brut, Lyrics of the Harley MS.* 2253, *Poems of Herebert,* the works of *Myrc* and *Audelay, Robert of Gloucester's Chronicle,* and *Trevisa's Translation of Higden's Polychronicon.* She examines these along with short historical documents and the place-names of the western counties. From this evidence she divides the west into three

---

[1] R. J. Menner, *Sir Gawayn and the Green Knight* (see p. 6).

[2] M. S. Serjeantson, *The Dialects of the West-Midlands,* Rev. of Eng. Stud., vol. 3, 1927 : no. 9, pp. 54-67, no. 10, pp. 186-203, no. 11, pp. 319-31.

linguistic groups : the north-western, the central-western and the south-western. Each of these areas, she says, has its own " dialect-complex," but all are united by a combination of features especially distinctive of the whole area. All these features are subsequently enumerated, but the statistics are unfortunately omitted through lack of space. The relevant portion of the present work, however, had already been finished before Miss Serjeantson's results were published, so that our investigations are based on a separate examination of⸱ what are often the same texts.

We have sometimes felt compelled to differ from Miss Serjeantson in the use of place-name statistics. Hulbert rightly criticised Wyld's methods on this point. He suggested that Wyld argued solely from proportions in the development of O.E. ў as i, $ü$, and e, a method which had led Wyld to locate Myrc's poems in Lancs, and Audelay's in Derby, whereas both of these writers can be proved to have written in Salop. Does not Professor Wyld also assume that every recorded instance of a particular place-name has survived, or at any rate that sufficient records have survived to enable us to say that one development was slightly more common than another? Again, is he not assuming that writers such as Myrc were so speech-conscious that they employed two developments in a certain ratio because they were more familiar with the one than with the other ? The followers of Professor Wyld, with the notable exception of Professor Ekwall, have fallen into the same error. Lastly, Professor Wyld is not always careful in ascertaining the region in which a particular place-name was written down, thus making no allowance for possible scribal alteration. Ekwall, on the other hand, pays great attention to this possibility, for place-name spellings are often apt to be traditional. Thus, though the M.E. *heȝe* may have been written *hiȝe*, if still recognised as the ordinary word, local scribes may have continued to write *heȝe*.

In compound names, however, the pronunciation may or may not have been changed. It is as a result of her failure to realise this that Miss Serjeantson locates the MS. of *Sir Gawayn and the Green Knight* in Derby instead of in Lancs, because M.E. $ē$ȝ is not raised to $ī$ȝ in the place-names of the latter county.

It is for these reasons that we think place-name evidence

is not being used with sufficient caution. Thus if both the *ü* and *i* developments are found for the O.E. ͯȳ in the records of a particular county, that merely indicates that both developments were current for some reason or other. If, on the other hand, one development is almost unknown, that is sufficient to indicate the trend of phonological development in that county. Most counties are predominantly of one type, whereas in the case of two counties in which both developments occur in equal proportions in the place-name statistics, it is surely important to remember that county boundaries are not dialectal ones. Thus in the case of Derby and Lancs, each county can be divided into two dialectal areas, and these counties must not be treated as single dialectal areas.

It is a failure to observe these things that has led scholars to attach too much importance to place-name statistics. In this book, therefore, they will be treated as of secondary, and genuine texts as of primary, importance.

The study of modern dialects has also proved to be an additional help in trying to localise the dialectal boundaries ; here again, however, care has to be taken in drawing conclusions from the evidence gleaned from this source.

We shall now give a list of the points which have been found to be of some dialectal value in localising texts, and particularly those of the fourteenth century. Subsequently, it will be possible, by the methods outlined above, to indicate on a map the approximate boundaries of these features, or " isoglotts," if we may be allowed to coin a new term. The map may then be used as a key for localising a document of a particular period with a considerable degree of accuracy. In particular, such a map would also show how in a given place certain features were to be expected in a group. This method must naturally be used with caution, and actual dialectal conditions always kept in mind, together with the qualifications to be attached to certain of the isoglotts.

While giving every credit to Professor Wyld and Miss Serjeantson for their pioneer work, we have for the purposes of the present study submitted all the literary texts, historical documents, and most of the place-names to an independent investigation.[1]

---

[1] Prof. Wyld in his 3rd. edition of *A Short History of English*, 1927, has modified some of his earlier views on these points. See especially pp. 88-90.

The Dialectal Points in Middle English.

(1) O.E. ă + nasal as *a* or *o*.

(2) O.E. ă + l + Cons. mutated as *a* or *e*.

(3) O.E. '-ănd' as '-*and*' or '-*ond*.'

(4) Is M.E. '-ŏng' retracted to '*ung*'?

(5) O.E. ў as *ü, i, e*.

(6) O.E. ā as *a* or *o*.

(7) O.E. āw as *aw* or *ow*.

(8) O.E. āg, āh as *aw* or *ow* (*aʒ* or *oʒ*).

(9) O.E. ō as *o* or *ü*.

(10) Do *ai, ei, oi* appear for *ā, ē, ō*?

(11) Does M.E. ou appear as *au*?

(12) O.E. ǣ[1] as tense or lax *ē*.

(13) Is O.E. ǣ[2] before d, t, s, n, l, r tense *ē*?

(14) O.E. čo as *e* or a rounded vowel (*oe, u, ue*).

(15) O.E. ča + Cons. mutated as *e* or *ü*.

(16) Is O.E. ēa when shortened, *a* or *e*?

(17) Is M.E. ēʒ from O.E. *ēag, ēah*, raised to *īʒ*?

(18) O.E. ǣ̆ as *a* or *e*.

(19) O.E. hw as *wh, w* or *qu*.

(20) O.E. cw, O. Fr. qu as *qu* or *wh*.

(21) Any initial voicing of *f, s*?

(22) Does ' sc- ' in unstressed positions appear as ' *s-* '?

(23) Does the spirant ' -ht ' appear as ' -ght,' ' -ht,' ' -ʒt,' etc. ?

(24) Do ' -us,' ' -ud ' occur for ' -es,' ' -ed '?

(25) Are there any noun ' -en ' plurals?

(26) Is the form of the plural of " this " found as *thire* or *these*, etc. ?

(27) The form of the 3rd. pers. sg. fem. pron. nom. (she).

(28) The form of the 3rd. pers. pl. pron. nom. (they).

(29) The form of the 3rd. pers. pl. pron. acc. (them).

(30) The form of the 3rd. pers. pl. pron. gen. (their).

(31) Is the adj. and adv. ending ' -ly ' or ' lich(e) '?

(32) The infinitive termination.

(33) Does the ' -i- ' of the 2nd. class of O.E. wk. verbs survive?

(34) Does the ' i- ' verbal prefix survive?

(35) The pres. part. termination.

(36) The pres. indic. sg. terminations.

(37) Any syncopated forms in the pres. indic. sg. ?

(38) The pres. indic. pl. terminations.

(39) The form of the pres. indic. pl. of the verb ' *to be.*'

(40) The imperative terminations.

(41) The 2nd. pers. sg. wk. pret. termination.

(42) Is the final ' -ed ' of the wk. pret. and past part. unvoiced ? (excluding the cases where it occurs in connexion with voiceless sounds) ?

(43) Is this final ' -d,' ' -t ' ever lost ?

(44) Are the contracted forms of *take* (ta), *make* (ma) ever found ?

(45) Are the forms ' quilke,' ' swilke ' found rather than ' whiche,' ' swiche ' ?

Note.—O.E. ĕar is not treated, for in the fourteenth century it was mostly *ar.*

Similarly we have found that for the alliterative poems, the development of O.E. ǣld is unimportant, usually being ' *-old.*'

Each of the points will now be treated and the results of the investigations given. Unfortunately, space forbids the inclusion of much material that is important. However, references will be given wherever there might arise any controversy. The place-names cannot be given save in exceptional cases.

In most cases it will be possible to indicate a boundary on the map, which appears facing page 38.

First, it is necessary to give the literary texts which will be used for the various dialects.

West-Midland.—*Audelay's Poems* [1] [R. W. Chambers, Mod. Lang. Rev., 5 (473-91), 6 (69-82), and Percy Soc., vol. 14, 1846]. Audelay wrote in 1426 in the monastery of Haghmond, Salop, and his rhymes afford a test against scribal alteration. (See *Die Sprache John Audelay's*, J. K. Rasmussen, 1914): *Myrc*, who about 1400 wrote *The Instructions for Parish Priests* in rhymed verse and *The Festial ;* he was a canon of Lilleshall in Salop : *Trevisa*, vicar of Berkeley and canon of Westbury, both in Glos, who finished his translation of *Higden's Polychronicon* in 1387 : *William Herebert*, a friar of the Hereford Convent, where he died in 1333, who wrote

---

[1] Audelay, Robert of Gloucester, etc., are printed in this chapter in italics, since we are referring to their works, and not to the writers. In this way *Audelay* can be referred to as a W. Midl. text.

religious poems (edited by C. Brown in *Religious Lyrics of the Fourteenth Century*, 1924) : *Layamon*, a secular priest, serving a village church at King's Areley in N. Worcs, who wrote *The Brut* not earlier than 1155, when Wace finished his *Brut*, and not later than 1207, judging from certain references (*Layamon's Brut*, Madden, 1847 ; J. Hall, 1923) : *The Coventry Plays*, dated 1430-50 : *The Coventry Leet Book* (the entries from 1420 to 1450 only, E.E.T.S., 134-5, pp. 22-255) : *The 15th Century Chester Plays ; Robert of Gloucester*, who saw the Battle of Evesham in 1265 and inserts a reference to 1297 in his *Chronicle*, which has numerous references to Glos.   The above works are for the most part rhymed, so that we can gather from them the leading features of the speech of the West-Midlands at certain periods.   It will be noticed that there are no literary documents for the north-west, but there are historical documents.

Southern (including Kentish).—*Michael of Norgate*, who wrote his *Ayenbite of Inwyt* in 1340 and was a monk of St. Augustine's, Canterbury ; the surviving copy is an autograph one : *The London Petition to Parliament*, 1386 : *The English Proclamation* of Henry III., 1258 : *Adam Davy*, who wrote his *Dreams* in London from 1307 to 1327 : *Gower*, a Londoner, who wrote his *Confessio Amantis* from 1390 to 1393.

Some little evidence may be derived from *The Owl and the Nightingale*, written in Dorset or Surrey about 1220.

East-Midland.—*Richard Rolle*, who was born about 1300, at Thornton-Le-Dale, near Pickering, Yorks, and died at Hampole in 1349.   *The Prose Treatises* (E.E.T.S., 20) are unquestionably his, and probably some of the rhymed religious lyrics attributed to him are his also : *The Guilds of Lynn and Norwich*, made in 1389 by order of Parliament (See *Die Sprache d. E. Guilds*, E. Schultz, 1891) : *Robert Mannyng*, born at Brunne (now Bourn) in Lincs, who completed his *Chronicle* in 1338, and began his *Handlyng Synne* (in rhyme) in 1303 : *The York Plays*, ranging from 1360 to 1579 (the main early dialect stands out clear) : *The Towneley Plays*, collected by the Towneley family and originally connected with Wakefield about 1388, though the language in which they are preserved for us is much later : *Chaucer*, whose dialect is that of S.E. Midl. of the second half of the fourteenth century : *The Ormulum*, probably written in Lincs about 1210.   Some little information is to be derived from a

study of *Wiclif's* genuine works ; a Yorkshireman by birth,
educated at Oxford, he settled down at Lutterworth in Leics
from 1374 to 1384, when he died.   Many works have been
assigned to him wrongly, but the *De Officio Pastoralis* is
certainly his own work.

Northern.—*Barbour's Bruce* is the only northern text we
have which can definitely be proved to be northern.   It was
written in 1375 by Barbour, the Archdeacon of Aberdeen.
The Cursor Mundi is certainly a northern work, but the MSS.
differ so considerably that it is not possible to form any accurate idea of the original dialect.   Fortunately we have many
N.E. Midl. texts which fill up the gap.   For the N.W. Midl.
dialect we have to rely on local documents ; and the counties
of Lancs and Ches are richer in this respect than most others,
for documents in English are very rare, Latin being the usual
medium.   Menner [1] was the first to call attention to the existence of these local documents for the north-west ; he discovered eight such documents and to these a few more are
here added :—

A. *The Dukenhalgh Deeds* (Whalley, S. Lancs).   Chet. Soc.,
    N.S., vol. 80, 1921, p. 33 (1430), p. 35 (1452-53 and 1465),
    p. 88 (1455).
B. *The Coucher Book of Furness Abbey*.   Chet. Soc., vol. 78,
    N.S., pt. 2, p. 773 (1424) and p. 788 (1430-31) : *Duchy
    of Lancaster Deeds.*
C. *The Leigh Documents* (S. Lancs).   *Public Declarations in
    Leigh Parish Church*, 1429-30 and 1435 ; *Local Gleanings,*
    J. P. Earwaker, pp. 146, 147-8, 148-9.
D. *Wills and Inventories from the Ecclesiastical Courts*, Chester,
    1517 to 1538.   Chet. Soc., O.S., 33 and 54.
E. *The Dutton Family of Cheshire*, 1432.   *Local Gleanings,*
    J. P. Earwaker, p. 69.
F. *1456 : Sir Geoffrey Mascy*, an Eccles Doc., vol. 30, 1896.
    Record Soc. for the pub. of Orig. Doc. relating to Lancs
    and Ches.
G. (a) *1485*, at Leigh, pp. 22-3 of the same volume.
    (b) *1486*, near Manchester, pp. 23-7.
H. *1407 : Sir John Bold of Bold*, S. Lancs, pp. 203-4 of the
    same volume.
I. *1431 :* Hale, Ches ; Hist. Soc. of Lancs and Ches, 1851
    vol., p. 105.

[1] See p. 6, n. 3.

J. 1413 : Hale, Ches ; pp. 106-7 of the same.

K. 1417-18 : Lancaster Document in the same volume, p. 107.

L. 1439 : N. Staffs Doc. in the *William Salt Archæological Journal,* vol. 7, N.S., pp. 50-51.

M. 1478 : N. Derby Doc., Derby Arch. Journal, vol. 24, pp. 42-3.

N. 1419 : Whitchurch, Salop ; Mod. Lang. Rev., vol. 22, p. 74, 1927.

O. 1467 : The Ordinances of Worcester, E.E.T.S., 40 ; 1870.

As the date of these documents is late, great care must be exercised in arguing from evidence found in them about the dialect of the north-west before 1400.

The modern dialectal forms are taken from Wright's *English Dialect Dictionary* as well as from personal acquaintance with the dialect of certain of the W. Midl. areas.

Concerning the use of place-names, certain reservations have been added above. The most important book of all has been Ekwall's *Place-names of Lancashire,* Manchester, 1922, especially with regard to early forms written down locally. The chief works used in connexion with place-names have been those listed in Ekwall's *River Names* or in *Place-names of Lancashire* (Bibliography).

(1) **O.E.** $\breve{a}$ + **nasal, O.N.** $\breve{a}$ + **nk,** may appear as *a* or be rounded to *o.* The rounding has been recognised as western by Morsbach, Luick, Jordan, Wyld and Menner. There is not the slightest trace of any such rounding process in the Nth. or E. Midl. texts ; of the Sth. texts only *The Owl and the Nightingale* has *o*-forms (*a* and *o*-forms in equal proportions) ; but this text was probably written in Dorset.

In W. Midl. texts the rounding is common ; both forms occur about equally in *The Coventry Plays ; Herebert* and *Layamon* have *o* throughout. *The Late Coventry Leet Book, The Chester Plays* and *Trevisa* have *a* practically throughout with a few forms such as *mon, mony,* which are exceptional, the latter being, of course, common in Nth. ; *Robert of Gloucester* has ' *a : o :* : 5 : 1.' All the MSS. of *Piers Plowman* have both *a* and *o*-forms. *Audelay* has *o* practically throughout, and *Myrc* has ' *a : o :* : 1 : 5.' In a S. Lancs Lay Subsidy Roll of 1332 (Lancs Rec. Series, 31) there are eleven examples of *bonk* and thirteen of *mon* for *man ;* Docs. *A, C, E, F, G, H, I, J, K* (all S. Lancs) have *a* and *o,* even at so late a period. Doc. *B* (the Furness doc., N. Lancs) has *a* only ; Docs. *N,* and *O*, which are very late, have *a* with *o* very rarely.   Doc. *L* (Staffs) has *a* and *o*.

In modern dialects, excluding the word " *mon*," the rounded forms are current in Lancs, south of the Ribble, Ches, Staffs, the extreme N.W. Derby, N. War, Worcs and Salop, but not in E. Midl. counties.   The feature is still W. Midl.

In the place-names, confining ourselves to the north and west, though the other areas have been investigated, there is no rounding in those of Notts, Derby, Yorks, Cumb, etc. ; for Lancs north of the Ribble, there are eleven examples of *an* in local spellings, but none of *on* ; south of the Ribble there are four examples of *an* and nine of *on* ; this confirms the evidence of the Lay Subsidy Roll.   Salop and Staffs are decidedly *on* areas.   There was no material available for Ches.

The evidence agrees on all sides, and the boundary on the north is the Ribble (which we shall see to have been a very important geographical boundary), excluding S.W. Yorks, skirting Derby, including Staffs, Worcs and Glos.   The only conflicting evidence is *The Owl and the Nightingale*, whose exact place of composition is not known, but which may have been N. Wilts, and at any rate is of early date, when the south-west was still in the " rounded " area.   *Trevisa*, on the other hand, shows no rounding, perhaps because he lived on the other side of the Severn.

In dealing with this dialectal feature we have to remember that we must not expect a given text to have solely one development or the other ; thus Lancs, south of the Ribble, has both types ; the mixture of forms is probably due to the influence of the standard dialect, which possibly accounts for the *a*-forms in *Myrc*.   The later the document is, the more likely will it be that the unrounded forms will have ousted the rounded ones ; it may thus often be that if a text has only a few *o*-forms it is precisely these that will supply a clue to the dialect of the work ; it is only complete absence of the rounded forms that argues against composition in the west.

(2) **O.E.** $\check{a}$ + 1 + **Cons. mutated.**—This point has been thoroughly investigated by Ekwall in *Contributions to the History of O.E. Dialects*, 1917, where he collects the available material from the place-names in all the counties.   He is able to show conclusively that the development in West Mercian was different from that in the other Anglian dialects,

being *ă* in the former but *ĕ* in the latter; the two areas are carefully worked out on the map from these statistics, the boundaries of the *ă*-area being the Ribble Valley, Mid-Derby, Staffs and the Severn Valley. In East Derby ·there are no examples, but numerous ones in the west.

The evidence from our texts is in complete agreement; there are no *ă*-forms in any Sth., E. Midl. or Nth. texts; the late *Coventry Plays* and *Leet Book* have *ĕ*, either because they are late documents, but more probably in this case because Coventry was outside the *ă*-area; *Myrc* has *wallen*, *wallyng* and *walle* beside the standard *welle;* *Audelay* has *ĕ* only, but his work is very late (*c.* 1426); *The Chester Plays* have often *walle* beside *welle;* *Layamon* has only *ă* (*walme*, l. 22,124, O.E. wïelm; *walle*, l. 21,334, O.E. wïell, *falle*, O.E. fïellan; etc.); *Herebert*, *Trevisa* and *Robert of Gloucester* have *ĕ*. With regard to the word *well*, it was natural that at a very early date the standard form with *ĕ* ousted the western form with *ă*; for this reason absence of *ă*-forms is no argument against a text being western, owing to the rapid encroachment of the *ĕ*-forms; in addition the number of words in which the feature occurs is very small. Ekwall [1] has found many cases in the place-names of this same encroachment of the non-western forms.

(3) **O.E. '-ănd' as '-and' or '-ond.'**—This point is obviously quite distinct from Pt. 1. O.E. ă before a nasal, with which it has often been confused.

The following texts have '-and' only: *Barbour's Bruce*, *Orm.*, *Rolle*, *The Towneley* and *York Plays*. *Mannyng of Brunne* has '-and : -ond :: 3 : 1'; *The Guilds of Norfolk* have both developments, about equally, as is the case in *The Owl and the Nightingale*, and in the late *Coventry Leet Book*; '-and' forms are rare in *Chaucer*, *Wiclif*, *The Ayenbite*, *Adam Davy*, *Myrc*, *Audelay*, *Trevisa*, *Layamon* and *The Coventry Plays*. *The Petition to Parliament*, *The Proclamation*, *Herebert* and *Robert of Gloucester* have '-ond'; the late *Chester Plays* usually have '-and.' All the documents have '-ond,' with '-and' very rarely.

The place-names confirm the evidence of the texts and documents. South of a line drawn through N. Salop and

---

[1] *Note.*—On the map, the ï-development in Devon and the ŭ-development in Dorset have been purposely omitted. See Ekwall.

S. Lincs, ' -ond ' forms are usually found in local names with rare ' -and ' forms due to late shortening. N. Derby, Notts and Lincs have usually ' -and,' but Ches and S. Lancs have ' -ond ' as the prevailing form. This agrees with Jordan's statement [1] that ' -and ' is found much farther south in the east than in the west ; the S. Lancs documents agree with this and *Mannyng* has ' -and : -ond : : 3 : 1 ' ; the explanation is probably that the rounding before the nasal in the west caused rounding in this combination also ; the line that therefore appears on the map is by no means a rigid one, but indicates that no ' -ond ' forms are found north of it, at any rate in the west, whereas ' -and ' forms are common in varying degrees south of the line.

(4) **Is M.E. ' -ŏng ' raised to ' -ŭng ' ?**

This point will at least in one case prove to be of considerable importance, but the evidence for the change in various districts is very small, since it is never recognised in spelling. There is, therefore, no place-name evidence and none to be gathered from prose texts ; rhymes such as ' *longe* : *tonge* ' are our most certain guide. Unfortunately such rhymes are very rare ; of the localised texts the change has been found in the rhymes of both *Myrc* and *Audelay*, but of no other writer ; it did not occur in the dialect of *Mannyng*, judging solely from the rhymes.

There is the evidence of modern dialects, from which we learn that the retraction is found in northern counties as far south as Ches, N. Staffs, N. Derby, Notts and Lincs. The feature is therefore not N.W. Midl., as Tolkien suggests in his edition of *Sir Gawayn and the Green Knight*. Possibly the use of it in a certain text may indicate an area north of a line drawn through N. Salop and the Wash. A dialectal feature of this kind, supported mainly by evidence from modern dialects would, of course, mean nothing at all by itself, but may be useful as corroborative evidence.

(5) **O.E. ȳ as i, ü, e.**—With regard to this point the pitfalls mentioned on page 8 et seq. must constantly be borne in mind. A careful examination of the texts has impressed upon us the danger of arguing from proportions of the varying forms either in texts or in place-names ; it is always necessary to ask in combination with what sounds does the

---

[1] *Die mittelenglischen Mundarten,* Germ. Rom. Monats., 2, p. 130.

rounding or unrounding occur. It has often been observed that unrounding of $\overset{\vee}{y}$ occurs before or after palatals : e.g. *king, drihten ;* the process of unrounding began in O.E. and seems to have been complete in certain dialects by the M.E. period, whereas in the west it was not complete by the end of the M.E. period ; but three things were happening in the " *rounded* " area. Firstly, the standard forms were rapidly spreading and ousting the local forms ; this can be seen from a careful examination of the place-names and texts ; thus ' *-hill* ' becomes more and more frequent, while ' *-hull* ' only occurs sporadically. Secondly, the unrounding process seems to have proceeded more quickly in certain areas than in others. Thirdly, the labials when preceding the $\overset{\vee}{y}$ seem to have been the most resistant of all consonants.

As for place-names, when allowance has been made for these points, and certain counties, for example Derby, have been recognised as being in two distinct dialectal areas, the theory of proportions as propounded by Wyld seems to be erroneous ; most counties are predominantly of one type, with sporadic forms of the other two occasionally occurring.

The evidence from the texts.

Nth. *The Bruce* has *i* with a few *e*-forms in such words as *bery, besyly,* etc.

E. Midl. *ü*-forms are only found in the following texts : *The Guilds of Norwich* have the forms *furst* and *suster ;* the former may represent a mixed vowel, due to the preceding labial *f,* as the word has in Mn.E. ; the latter has probably developed from O.E. *swĕoster* > *swuster* > *suster,* rather than from O.N. *sy̆stir.*

In *Chaucer* all three developments meet ; Reaney has examined two long passages with the following results : *ü, i, e*—3, 19, 4, and *ü, i, e*—8, 6, 3 respectively. No other E. Midl. texts have *ü*-forms.

Sth. *The Ayenbite* has *e* throughout ; *Adam Davy* has 8 *i*-forms only ; *The Petition* has 8 *ü* and 5 *i* ; *The Proclamation* has 3 *ü* and 1 *e* ; and *The Owl and the Nightingale* has *ü* in 33 words and *i* in 4.

W. Midl. The late *Chester Plays* have ' *i : ü* : : 5 : 1,' showing the unrounding process still going on ; *The Coventry Plays* have mostly *i,* but not infrequently *ü* and *e* (*rysshes, ressys, ruysshes :* O.E. ry̆sc) ; In *Layamon* O.E. ȳ > *ü* through-out (e.g. *fuyre,* O.E. fȳr), and $\overset{\vee}{y}$ > *ü,* except before palatals

(*king, driht*, etc.) ; *Herebert* has *ü* throughout, except for the
rare *sinne* beside *sunne*, O.E. sўnn.   *Robert of Gloucester* has
the *ü* development practically throughout, but occasionally
i and *e*-forms.   *Trevisa* has all three developments, though the
Cotton MS. has *ü* throughout.   *Audelay* has *ü* in more words
than he has *i*, but the *i*-forms are more frequently found, when
the totals are added ; *Myrc* has both *i* and *ü* in rhymes, and
in *The Festial* he has *ü* in 17 words and *i* in 24 words, and in
The Instructions for Parish Priests he has *ü* in 10 words and
i in 8 words ; in addition he has *euele* throughout, O.E. ўfel.
The documents are late and the sound y̆ is of rare occurrence,
but some little evidence is afforded by them ; Docs. *B*, *E*,
H, *I*, *K*, *N* offer no evidence ; *A*, *J*, *L* (S. Lancs and N. Staffs)
have both *i* and *ü* ; *D* (*The Chester Wills*) have rare *ü*-forms,
and *O* (*The Worcester Ordinances*) have *u*, *uy*, but *i* rarely,
even at so late a period.   *C* (Leigh) and *F*, *G* (S. Lancs) and
M (Derby) have *i* only.   These documents, though late,
show that S. Lancs had still traces of the *ü*-form left.

Nth. and E. Midl. have thus only *i*, but Sth. and W. Midl.
clearly retained *ü* for some time, and in the fourteenth century
the *i*-forms were fast prevailing over the *ü*-forms, due largely
to the process of unrounding, reinforced by spreading from
the standard dialect.   In the case of the London dialect, all
three developments seem to have met ; for the history of
y̆ in this dialect see the articles by Reaney mentioned in
the Bibliography.

The place-name evidence.—Here it is important to take
into account the date of the various documents used, as well
as the locality in which they were written down.   Concerning
proportions of forms we have to be particularly careful to
enquire to what the proportions are due : to the spreading
of standard forms, to the unrounding process or to the fact
that the county-boundary is not the dialectal-boundary ;
Wyld was quite illogical on these points, locating the *Early
English Alliterative Poems* in Derby where the place-names
show '*ü* : *i* : : 2 : 1,' but the *Alliterative Poems* '*ü* : *i* : : 1 : 3' ;
Wyld has surely been led astray because he has considered
the whole of Lancs and the whole of Derby as two separate
dialectal areas, complete in themselves.   The only point
that matters is whether a county or area has *ü*-forms in any
considerable numbers.   Wyld divides the country up into
ü/*i*, *ü*—*i*, *i*—*e*, *ü*/*e*, etc. areas, but such nice distinctions do

not mean much.   The country will divide itself up into three large areas as Wyld first suggested,[1] without further sub-divisions :—

(1) a *ü-area* where *i* and *e*-forms are either completely absent or quite the exception in varying degrees ; here in late records the *i*-forms rapidly come in through the unrounding process ;

(2) an *i-area* where *ü* and *e*-forms are practically unknown ;

(3) an *e-area* where *e*-forms predominate, but where *i* and *ü* are also often found.

Most counties are practically pure *i* or *ü*-areas.   Derby has both *i* and *ü* about equally and it is only reasonable to suppose that the boundary line cut across Derby ;   indeed a careful enquiry into the locality of the forms will show that this is so ;   the boundary has been carefully worked out and indicated on the map.   The unrounding process that started in Devon, and has been fully discussed by Wyld, hardly concerns us.   Concerning Lancs, we have the valuable work done by Ekwall,[2] who has had access to very early forms ; Lonsdale north of the Sands is a pure *i*-area, but all the county south of the sands has *ü*-forms in varying proportions.   Ekwall concludes that the Ribble was originally the rough dividing line, and that *ü*-forms spread a little northward.   There is conclusive proof that S. Lancs was a *ü*-area.

There is naturally no evidence to be gathered from a study of modern dialects, but the evidence from the place-names does agree entirely with that of the texts examined.   Any work with a considerable number of *ü*-forms (especially when after labials and kindred sounds) must be located in the *ü*-area ;   and the later the text is, the fewer will be the number of *ü*-forms to be expected.

(6) **O.E. ā as** *a* **or** *o* ; **(including O.N. á).**—All the Sth. texts have *ǭ*, except *The Owl and the Nightingale*, which has *ā*, due to the early period at which the work was written. The Nth. *Bruce* has *a*.   With the exception of *Layamon*, again a very early writer, all the W. Midl. texts have *ǭ*, but *Myrc*, *Audelay* and *Robert of Gloucester* occasionally have ' *hame*,

---

[1] *Eng. Stud.*, 47, p. 46.

[2] *Ortsnamenforschung ein Hilfsmittel für das engl. Sprachgeschichte-Studium*, 1913.

mare' as a concession to rhyme (O.E. hām, māre) ; the N.W. Midl. documents all have $\bar{\varrho}$.

The E. Midl. texts : the following have $\bar{\varrho}$ only : *The Guilds of Norwich and Lynn, Chaucer* and *Wiclif ; Robert Mannyng* has usually $\bar{\varrho}$, and this form is well attested by his rhymes, but $\bar{a}$ is also occasionally used as a concession to rhyme both in *Handlyng Synne* and *The Chronicle. The Towneley Plays* have '$\bar{a}$: $\bar{\varrho}$: : 2 : 3' (both developments occur in rhyme), and *The York Plays* '$\bar{a}$: $\bar{\varrho}$: : 5 : 2.' Rolle has $\bar{a}$ practically throughout with a few $\bar{\varrho}$-forms, which are probably scribal.

From a study of modern dialects we learn that O.E. ā has given rise to many varieties of sound, divisible into two great classes :—

(1) a fronted vowel found in northern counties as far south as the Ribble Valley in Lancs and the Aire Valley in Yorks.

(2) a back vowel everywhere south of this line. This is in agreement with the evidence from the texts.

Coming to the place-name evidence, we find that Northumb., Dur, Cumb, Westmor, all retain *a* in local spellings, e.g. *Halieland, Sadelyngstanes ;* south of Lancs and Yorks, *o* is the only development. With regard to Lancs, Prof. Ekwall[1] has shown that the boundary in that county was the Ribble Valley. North of that valley we get *scale* (O.N. skáli), *wra* (O.N. vrá), *Har* (O.E. Hār), etc., but south of it *schǫle*, etc.

Turning to the county of Yorks, we find a similar situation ; there the dividing line is the Aire valley ; *scales* abound north of that river, but only *scholes* south of it.

This agrees with Ekwall's theory that N. Lancs was peopled by Northumbrians and S. Lancs by a Mercian-speaking people.[2] He adduces linguistic evidence, and name-types ; there were also geographical, political and ecclesiastical divisions between the two areas. In S. Yorks the Mercians apparently extended as far as the Aire Valley approximately ; the Mercians in S. Yorks may have spread from S. Lancs.

Myrc, Audelay and *Mannyng* all have *a* as a rare concession to rhyme ; this is very peculiar, but indicates that the other form was known. It is not our intention to enter into the

[1] See p. 20, n. 2.
[2] *The Place-names of Lancashire,* Manchester, 1922.

difficult question as to the exact nature of the northern *a*
and as to when it actually became fronted.

(7) **O.E. āw,** and (8) **O.E. āh, āg.**—These two points can
be treated together because the development is the same
in each case ; the result is either " *au, aʒ* " or " *ow, oʒ.*"
The boundaries of these two developments are not co-terminous with those of O.E. ā, discussed above.

The Bruce has *au, aw ; Orm, Layamon* and *The Owl and the
Nightingale* have *aw, au* simply on account of the early period
at which the works were written. *The Ayenbite* has *aw, aʒ,*
being a Kentish document. The W. Midl. texts have *ou,*
except *The Chester Plays* which have *au.* The E. Midl. texts
vary ; *Rolle* and *The York Plays* have *au* only ; *The Towneley
Plays,* ' *au* : *ou* : : 3 : 2,' but all the other E. Midl. texts
have *ou.*

The Lancs Docs. *A, C, D* have *aw* and *ow,* whereas *L, M,
N, O* have *ow* only.

In modern dialects O.E. āw, āh, āg appear as some variety
of *ou, o,* in Ches, Staffs, Derby and all counties to the south,
but as some variety of *au, a* in Scotland and northern counties
as far south as Lancs and Yorks inclusive. On the whole,
the place-name evidence agrees with this ; there are no local
forms with *aw* south of Derby and Notts and very few south
of Lancs and Yorks, that is to say, in the M.E. period proper,
excluding early forms. Putting all the evidence together we
might say that the approximate line above which no *ow*-
forms are found, runs through Mid-Ches, Mid-Derby and
Lincs ; the boundary is very far from being rigid. It should
be noted that neither *Myrc* nor *Mannyng* shows any *aw*-forms.
Kentish probably retained *aw, au.*

(9) **O.E. and O.N. ō as *o* or *ü*.**—In all the Sth. and W. Midl.
texts *ọ̄* is the only form ; and of the E. Midl. texts the *ü*
development only occurs in *The York Plays* ('*o* : *ü* : : 2 : 3 '),
and in *Rolle,* who has *ü* as the universal form. *The Bruce*
has the *ü*-form throughout.

In the local documents, *ü* only occurs three times : *gude*
occurs twice in *The Chester Wills* and once in *The Dukenhalgh
Deeds.*

The study of modern dialects affords us no help owing to
the rapid spreading of the standard form.

In local place-names, *ü* never occurs south of Lancs and
Yorks, but is frequent north of the two latter counties.

Examples are very scattered in Lancs and Yorks records, but on the whole the O.E. ō seems to remain. However, *Rolle* and *The York Plays* afford us sufficient evidence for an approximate boundary line ; it was very probably the same as the $\bar{a}/\rho$ boundary—the *Ribble-Aire* Valleys. The evidence of the texts in the east also seems to bear this out ; the *ü* was the Northumbrian and the ρ the Mercian type.

It should be noted that the word *gude*, O.E. gōd, often appears in a text which otherwise has only ρ-forms ; it is certainly not necessary to regard it as scribal in such a text ; thus it is frequent in the Cotton MS., Nero A.X.

(10) **Do ai, ei, oi occur for ' ā, ē, ō ' ?**—Such spellings only occur in the following texts : occasionally in *The York* and *Towneley Plays*, but not in *Rolle ; ey* occurs rarely for $\bar{e}$ in *Mannyng*, possibly due to scribal interference, but there are no examples of *ay, oy*.

The spellings are very common in *The Bruce*, for the feature was Scottish and extreme Nth., but is not of very great importance for our purpose.

(11) **Does M.E. *ou* (of whatever origin) appear as *au* ?**—This is a feature found in certain alliterative poems and is therefore important for us. It is, however, very rare and only found in three texts : in the Kentish *Ayenbite of Inwyt*, which also retains O.E. āw ; on rare occasions in the late *Coventry Plays*, e.g. *trawþe ;* and in one of the S. Lancs documents there is one *faurthe* form.

In place-names the feature has only been found in Lancs, where Ekwall[1] has found *Rawcliffe* for *Routhclif* in the Amounderness Hundred, and *Rawtinstall* for *Routonstall* in the Blackburn Hundred, and the O.N. *ou > au, aw* in the Amounderness and Lonsdale Hundreds. It is quite impossible to localise the boundaries of such a feature, but we have evidence to show that it was known in Lancs.

(12) **O.E., æ[1] (W. Gmc. ā) appears in M.E. as ' ē ' or ' ę̄.'**—The former is the Anglian development. Pogatscher, Ritter, Jordan and Brandl have all done valuable work with place-name studies on the basis of străt—strĕt. From their work it would appear that the boundary line runs by the Severn valley, S. War, Mid. Northants, Mid. Camb and N.W. Norfolk (excluding the Kentish ę̄-area). Hulbert would overthrow

---

[1] See p. 20, n. 2.

the whole of this evidence, saying that the ă-forms are nearly always found alongside ĕ-forms. We disagree with Hulbert's extreme scepticism, for he has surely not kept apart the local spellings from those copied from non-local documents.

In the texts, however, Hulbert is right ; we have examined the alliterative poems for the shortened forms, but the evidence has proved to be so contradictory that it was felt wiser to suppress it altogether ; on the whole, ĕ is the Anglian development, but the two developments are hopelessly confused. The rhymes are the only secure test ; *Adam Davy, Trevisa, The Owl and the Nightingale, Robert of Gloucester* all have ę̄ in rhymes, whereas *Barbour's Bruce, Myrc, Audelay, The Chester Plays, Herebert, Mannyng, The York* and *Towneley Plays* all have ẹ̄ in rhymes. *Chaucer* has both the tense and slack ē in rhymes, but according to ten Brink the tense ẹ̄ is more usual.

The evidence agrees fairly well with that from the place-names. This point can, however, only be used for rhymed works, for the shortening of the sound needs a much more thorough investigation than it has yet received ; the forms in M.E. texts need a new examination.

(13) **Is O.E. ǣ² tense before d, t, s, n, l, r ?**—This point, like the former, remains very obscure ; here our best guide is undoubtedly the rhymes, but careless poets often rhyme tense and slack ē together ; in *The Bruce* this ē is tense before the above consonants, but otherwise slack ; in *The York* and *Towneley Plays, Mannyng, Myrc* and *Audelay* there are examples in rhyme to prove that it was tense before dentals ; in *Chaucer, Herebert* and *The Owl and the Nightingale* it is always slack. The evidence of the development of the sound, when shortened, whether occurring in place-names or in texts, is very contradictory, and on this point it cannot be trusted. Thus we can prove that in *Sir Gawayn* O.E. ǣ² was tense before *d, t* in rhymes, but when shortened is ă.

Judging solely from the rhymes it would appear that the tense form extended as far south as *Myrc, Audelay* and *Mannyng*, but how much further we cannot say ; probably it was approximately the line running from Mid-Salop to the Wash. It is not very important for alliterative poems which are usually unrhymed.

(14) **O.E. ĕo** appears either as ĕ̆ or as a rounded vowel, written *eo, ue, oe*, etc. The Nth. and E. Midl. texts all have *e*,

except *Orm*, who, owing to the early period at which he was writing, has *eo*. The W. Midl. texts : *The Coventry Plays* and *Leet Book*, and *The Chester Plays* all have *ĕ*, possibly owing to the late date of these compositions, as is the case in all the documents except *N*, *The Whitchurch Letter*, in which the form *hure* (O.E. heora) is found. *Herebert* has the rounded development throughout, the spellings being *eo*, *oe* : e.g. *oerþe*, O.E. ĕorðe ; in *Layamon* *ĕo* remains in spelling with also a few *u* spellings, and the sound in both cases is probably the rounded vowel (*ö*). *Trevisa* has *ĕ* rarely, having usually *o*, *eu*, *u*, *eo* ; *Myrc* and *Audelay* have both *e* and *u*, the latter occurring particularly in certain words : *urþe* beside *erþe* : *bun* (O.E. bēon) ; *duply* (cf. O.E. dēope) ; etc. In *Robert of Gloucester*, O.E. ĕo appears as *e*, but the long form, ēo, usually as *u* ; e.g. *huld* (O.E. hēold).

All the Sth. texts have *e* except *The Owl and the Nightingale*, which has *eo*, which at such an early period may represent either the unrounded or rounded form.

Professor Wyld and Miss Serjeantson have independently collected the place-name material.[1] The latter concludes by saying that the rounded forms occur rarely in the place-names of Derby, Ches, Salop, Staffs and War : not infrequently in Lancs, Hereford, Worcs, Glos, of the same period (fourteenth and fifteenth centuries) ; Professor Wyld [2] says that the *u*-forms occur strangely enough in Lancs, but that he has not found any in Ches ; Miss Serjeantson, however, has presumably had access to more forms. The rounded form also occurs in the place-names of Devon, Dorset, Hants, Wilts, Berks and Somerset.

This evidence corroborates that of the texts and the boundary has been drawn accordingly ; the feature was obviously western and south-western. We must, however, beware of assuming that a text is not western because it only contains a few rounded forms ; in the fourteenth century this is precisely what we should expect for any text. It would seem that the encroachment of the standard forms in this point was more frequent than in the case of *i* for O.E. ў ; if only a few rounded forms occur, as in the case of the place-names, it is an indication that the text is western ; it is quite

[1] Wyld, *Place-names and Linguistic Study*, 1924 (Place-Name Soc., vol. 1) ; Miss Serjeantson, English Studies, 1922, vol. 4, p. 231.
[2] Wyld, Essays and Studies, vol. 6, p. 113.

impossible to argue from proportions of rounded and unrounded forms in this feature.

(15) **O.E. ĕa Cons. mutated as ' e ' or 'ü.'**—The e development is found in all the Nth. and E. Midl. texts and in most of the W. Midl. ones, but *Robert of Gloucester* has both forms about equally, whereas *Trevisa* has usually *ü* with rare *e*-forms. Miss Serjeantson has investigated this point very thoroughly in the article just mentioned, and shows that the counties south of the Thames, with the exception of Kent, Sussex and Surrey, have *ü*; the place-names and the texts agree on this point. Few alliterative poems, however, show any rounded forms in the texts. For further details, see Miss Serjeantson, Rev. of Eng. Stud., vol. III, no. 10, p. 186, Point 11.

(16) **O.E. ēa when shortened is either ' ă ' or ' ĕ.'**—This point has proved to be of some small value, but the evidence for a boundary between the two developments is very conflicting.

The Nth. and E. Midl. texts have *ĕ* with the exception of *Wiclif*, who seems to prefer *ă*; of the W. Midl. texts, *Audelay* and *The Chester Plays* have *ĕ* only; *The Coventry Plays*, *Robert of Gloucester* and *Trevisa* have both *ă* and *ĕ*; *Layamon* has only *ă*, and *Myrc* has usually *ă*, but also *ĕ*: e.g. *aster*, O.E. ēastre. The documents offer no evidence.

It would thus appear that the *ă* development was originally western, but that the *ĕ*-forms were undoubtedly spreading very rapidly; the place-names confirm this view, for the E. Midl. counties have *ĕ* in local documents, but Notts, Staffs and Derby have both *ă* and *ĕ*, whereas Salop has consistently *ă*; Lancs has mostly *ă*, as far as the meagre evidence goes (e.g. *Radcliffe*, O.E. rēad-). Therefore no boundary can be located but an abundance of *ă*-forms in a text is an indication of western composition.

(17) **M.E. ēȝ, from O.E. ēah, ēag.**—Sometimes *ēȝ* remains, but often is raised to *īȝ*, while other areas show a diphthongal form *eiȝ*.

Miss Serjeantson has recently published a new study of this point in Middle English place-names : *The Development of O.E. ēah, ēag in M.E.*, Journal of English and Germanic Philology, xxvi, pp. 198-230, and 350-400. See also the two articles by Miss Serjeantson already mentioned. She comes to the conclusion that the diphthonging of *ēah*, *ēag* to *eiȝ* is not dialectal in M.E., but the raising to $\bar{\imath}$ʒ, which she finds only in the Central Midlands and Central South from Derby to Hants, is.   The area includes Derby, Notts, Leics, Staffs, War, Northants, Herts, Bucks, Oxon, Wilts, Berks, Hants and parts of Surrey and Sussex ;   Ches has only 1 *i*ʒ to 310 *eh*, *ei*ʒ-forms and Lancs only 4 in 850 *ei*, *eh*, etc. forms, whereas Derby shows 20 in 403 *eh*-forms, which would be equivalent to 42 in 850 forms.

The evidence from the texts is not in complete agreement ; the Sth. texts show no trace of raising ; E. Midl. : *Rolle*, *Orm* and *The Guilds* have *e*ʒ, *egh*, *eh* only ; *The York* and *Towneley Plays* have *igh* with rare *egh*-forms ; *Chaucer* has *eigh* and *eye*, with rare *ȳe*-forms, which occur even in rhymes ; *Wiclif* has *e*ʒ and *ei*ʒ, and *Mannyng* has *i*ʒ and *e*ʒ, both occurring in rhymes.

W. Midl. texts : *Myrc* has *e*ʒ in *The Instructions*, but *i*ʒ and *e*ʒ in *The Festial*.   *Trevisa* and *Robert of Gloucester* have *e*ʒ and *ei*ʒ.   *Herebert* has *ei*ʒ ; *Layamon* *æ*ʒ, *e*ʒ, *ei*ʒ ; *The Coventry Plays* and *Leet Book* and *The Chester Plays* all show the raising complete.   *Audelay* has usually *i*ʒ, rarely *e*ʒ.   Of the documents only *N*, *The Whitchurch Letter*, offers any evidence, having the form *hye*, O.E. hēah.

In trying to weigh up the evidence we must exclude all later works.   *Mannyng of Brunne*, *c.* 1330, shows from his rhymes that in his dialect the raising had taken place or was in the process of doing so, since both *i*ʒ and *e*ʒ occur in rhymes ; but Miss Serjeantson has only found one example in the place-names of Lincs.   Similarly *Chaucer*, outside the raising-area, shows *ȳe* in his rhymes ;   Miss Serjeantson assigns *Sir Gawayn* to Derby, instead of to Lancs, on the grounds that the place-names of the latter county only show four examples of the raising ;   it would most certainly seem that the place-names are apt to be influenced by tradition in this matter, though Derby has examples as early as 1255 ;   probably if an area has any of the *i*ʒ spellings at all, the change had in that locality taken place ;   also Miss Serjeantson is treating the boundary between Lancs and Derby as quite rigid dialectally.   Therefore, on the map we must accept the boundary from the place-name evidence, but it must be interpreted in accordance with the above statements ;   in addition we have come to the conclusion that in MSS. in which all three developments are found, we must not assume that all three pronunciations were current ; writers seem to have been very traditional with regard to this point, and rather slow to recognise the change.

(18) **O.E. ǽ was either retracted to ǎ or raised to ě.**—This point hardly affects an investigation of the dialect of alliterative poems, so that we may rely mainly on Miss Serjeantson's [1] statements, which have long been accepted as true : The Midl. and Nth. dialects retracted ǽ to ǎ, whilst Kentish and the extreme S. Midl. and the Sth. dialect raised the sound to ě ; but after the beginning of the fourteenth century, the ě-form disappears, being ousted by the Midl. form.

(19) **O.E. hw as *wh*, *w*, or *qu*.**—Here we have to recognise that the spellings may be scribal ; but in the alliterative poems it is, however, usually possible to test the phonological development by the alliteration.

The Sth. texts all have *wh*, *hw*, or *w*, as have all the W. Midl. texts except *Myrc*, who has in addition three *qu*-forms, which may be scribal.

In E. Midl. texts *qu* spellings are rare, only occurring occasionally in *The Towneley Plays*, but not in *Rolle*, and a few of *The Norfolk Guilds* have *qu* only, such as *The Peltyers' Guild of Norwich ;* the two spellings are never mixed in any guild ; *The Bruce* has *quh* only ; of the documents, the following have *wh* only : *A, B, C, D, E, F, L, M, N, O,* but *J* and *I* have both *qu* and *wh* well represented ; *G, H* (S. Lancs), and *K* (Lancaster) have nearly always *qu*. In modern dialects the χw aspirated form is heard as far south as Lancs, north of the Ribble· and the North Riding of Yorks. The place-names of the counties below Lancs and Yorks do not show *qu* spellings in local documents, but north of those two counties they are very plentiful. In Lancs *qu*-forms were only written down north of the Ribble, as Tolkien observes : " The local names originally beginning with *hw*, written down at Cockersand in Furness are spelt *qu*, whereas such local names south of the Ribble are spelt *wh*, *w*." The evidence is very slight in Yorks, but *qu* hardly ever occurs except in the North Riding.

The evidence from all sides agrees and the *approximate* line which divides the two developments is the *Ribble-Aire* valleys.

---

[1] *The Dialects of the West Midlands*, English Studies, 1922, and Rev. of Eng. Stud., vol. III, No. 10, p. 186, 1927.

(20) **O.E. cw, O. Fr. qu, as** *qu* **or** *wh.*—The former spelling is practically the only one found, but *wh* is liable to occur in those areas where O.E. *hw* > *qu*, so that the two spellings became interchangeable. Thus it is occasionally found in the place-names of the northern counties.

(21) **The initial voicing of f, s.**—This is very rare in the texts examined : *The Owl and the Nightingale* shows the consistent voicing of *f* to *v*, but *s* remains. *The Ayenbite* voices both *f* and *s* consistently ; *Layamon, Herebert* and *Robert of Gloucester* usually have *v* for *f* initially ; *Trevisa* has *v* for *f* sometimes.

In modern dialects the initial voicing is found in most of the counties south of the Thames, Glos and Mid-Hereford ; hence the absence of the voicing of initial *f* is no argument against a southern dialect, but the occurrence of it is an argument the other way ; the initial voicing of *s* was evidently less frequent in the M.E. period.

(22) **O.E. ' sc- ' in unstressed positions sometimes becomes ' s-.'**—This change only occurs in *The Bruce, Rolle* and *The York Plays*, where it is consistently used ; there is one *sal* form in *The Guilds of Lynn* (O.E. sceal). All the other texts have *schal, shall, ssal* (= šal) ; only Doc. *B* (Furness Abbey, north of the Ribble) has *sall ;* therefore the boundary stretched from Nth. as far south as *Rolle* (but not *The Towneley Plays*) in the east, and as far as the Ribble in the west ; this is again the *Ribble-Aire* valleys boundary.

(23) **Does the spirant appear spelt as ' -ght,' ' -ht,' or ' -ʒt ' ?**—This point is not very important for our purpose, since it can only help occasionally in the localisation of the manuscript, not the original text ; the Scottish spelling was usually ' -cht,' and in the fourteenth century ' -ght ' was no longer dialectal, but ' -ʒt ' still remained non-Nth. ; *Mannyng, Myrc* and *Audelay* use it, whereas it is not to be found in *Rolle ;* it was slightly more common in the west than in the east. No boundary is needed on the map.

(24) **The forms ' -us,' ' -ud,' for ' -es,' ' -ed.'**—This form of the weak vowel is very rare in the texts examined ; there is one example in *The Guilds of Norwich* and a few in the works of *Wiclif ;* in the writings of *Myrc,* such spellings are common, especially in *The Festial ;* in *Audelay* ' *is* : *us* : *es* : : 5 : 3 : 1 ' ; The ' -*u*- ' spellings are also found rarely in *Robert of Gloucester.* In the Staffs, Derby and Worcs documents, the feature is

found, and also very frequently in the late Lincs documents ;
in the M.E. period proper, such spellings may have been typically W. Midl., but were not exclusively so.

(25) '-en' noun plurals, excluding the non-dialectal
fossilised form *eyen ;* ·these are not exclusively Sth., being not
infrequently found in *Chaucer,* occasionally in *Wiclif* and
Mannyng, and quite frequently in *The Guilds of Norfolk ;
The York* and *Towneley Plays* have a few ; *Audelay* has them
in rhymes, but they are rare in *Myrc ; Trevisa* and *Robert
of Gloucester* have them frequently, and *Herebert* has a few ;
Layamon, being early, has numerous examples. It is therefore obvious that ' -en ' noun plurals were common in Sth.
and S. Midl., but their presence in a more northernly
document need not surprise us.

(26) **Is the plural of " this " found as** *thire* **or** *these ?—
The Bruce* has *thire* and *these ; Rolle* has þire, and the *York
Plays* have þer, þir, *these.* No other works have the form
thire ; thire is therefore Scottish and northern but the other
form is not dialectal.

(27) **The form of the 3rd. pers. sg. fem. nom. pronoun,
" she."**—The forms in the various texts are very numerous ;
we are chiefly concerned with the fourteenth century ; *she,
sche* is liable to occur in both East and West Midl. in the
fourteenth century ; it is more common in the east, but in
the west is found in *Myrc* and occasionally in most of the
writers ; it is not found in Sth. or Nth.

scho is found in *The Bruce, Mannyng* (rarely), *Rolle, The
York* and *Towneley Plays, The Chester Wills* and in *Myrc,*
where in *The Instructions* it is common. Therefore, though
scho occurs over a fairly wide area, it is important to notice
that it did not occur south of the *Salop-Wash* line, and probably its use extended farther south in the west than in the
east. Of course *scho* very easily lends itself to scribal altera·
tion to *sche.*

There are various forms with ' *h-* ' in M.E. : *hoe, hue, he,
heo, ho, hoo.* Such forms do not occur in the Nth. and E.
Midl. texts, but only in the Sth. and W. Midl. ; and the
first·four forms given above are liable to be found anywhere
in the two latter dialects ; *ho,* however, only occurs in *Robert
of Gloucester,* and then only rarely, but in *Myrc* not infrequently.
Audelay has *heo* with rare *s(c)he* forms, which do actually
occur in rhymes ; *ho* also occurs in *The Owl and the Nightingale,*

but probably with a different pronunciation [*hö*](?), whereas the western form is [*hō*](?).

The documents offer no evidence. From mod. dialects we observe that O.E. *hēo*, M.E. *hō*, survives as [*ū*] in S. Lancs, Ches, Staffs, Derby, Notts, Glos, and parts of S.W. Yorks. Lindkvist [1] similarly shows that the Sth. dialect had [*hē*] phonetically, the S. Western *hue*, [*hö*] or [*hφ*] and the W. Midl. [*hō*]; the latter form is certainly non-Nth. and non-E. Midl.

A boundary can be located on the map for this Western development, as approximately stretching from S. Lancs to Glos in the west; Lindkvist also says, " at an early date *scho* appears to have spread far beyond the boundaries of the northern dialectal area into the adjoining regions of the Midlands ; in these parts *scho* was soon in current use, alternating with the corresponding forms that were peculiar to the N. Midl. dialects, *sche* in the east and *ho* in the west."

See also Miss Serjeantson's statistics, point 19, *The Dialects of the West Midlands*, Rev. of Eng. Stud., vol. III, p. 186.

(28) **The form of the 3rd. pers. pl. nom. personal pronoun, " they."**—The two groups of forms are (1) *þay, thay, þey, they*; (2) *hi, he*, etc. *They* or some orthographical variant occurs in all the E. Midl. and Nth. texts. Of the W. Midl. texts, *Trevisa* has *þei*, but also *hy, hey* in certain MSS. ; *Robert of Gloucester* has *hi* ; *Herebert, hoe* ; *The Chester* and *Coventry Plays, Myrc* and *Audelay* have *they*, etc. *Layamon, c.* 1200, has *hi*.

The Sth. texts have *hi, ho, heo*, except *The Petition* and *Gower* with *they*, representing London English. Thus the *thay* forms in the fourteenth century extended as far south as London in the east and as far as *Trevisa*, but not *Herebert*, in the west. The approximate boundary is, therefore, the Thames valley to N. Glos and S. Hereford.

(29) **The acc. form, " them."**—This appears as ' *them*,' ' *thaym*,' ' *theym* ' or ' *hem*,' ' *hom*.'

Theym is found in *The Bruce* as *thayme* ; *The Plays* have *theyme*, as have *Rolle* and most of the late documents ; *Orm* has *hemm* and *þeȝȝm*, probably due to his acquaintance with the Danish population. All the other texts have *hem, hom* or *ham* ; thus Docs. *J, H (Hale* in Ches.) have *ham, hom* only.

As all the other texts have no trace of *th*-forms, we may

---

[1] H. Lindkvist, *The Origin and History of the Pronoun " she,"* 1919.

say that the dividing line *th/h*, in the fourteenth century, was approximately the *Ribble-Aire* valleys. *Mannyng, Myrc* and *Audelay* did not have the *th*-forms ; after that time the Scandinavian form spread rapidly.

The form *hom* is usually supposed to be western ; it is not infrequently found in *Audelay*, in *Myrc's Festial*, but not in *The Instructions ; Robert of Gloucester*, where it is the usual form, the Hale Doc. (*J*), in *The Owl and the Nightingale* beside *heom*, and occasionally in *Mannyng* in rhyme (with *martyrdom*) ; though appearing to be chiefly a western feature, it is evidently not exclusively so. No boundary is possible.

(30) **The gen. form, " their."**—As in the former case, there are either forms with *th*- or *h*- ; and the boundary between the two is the same. The form with *th*- is only found in *The Bruce, The Plays* and *Rolle ;* there are also isolated cases : one instance in *The Guilds of Lynn*, occasional examples in *Wiclif*, and *Mannyng* (found in rhymes : e.g. *þeires*) and *Orm* has *þeʒʒre, here* and *heore ;* there is no trace of the Scand. form in *Myrc* and *Audelay*. Docs. *A, B, D, F, G, L, M, N, O*, being late, have *th*-forms, but the S. Lancs Docs. *C, H, J, K* have *h*-forms only. The *English Dialect Dictionary* and the *English Dialect Grammar* (J. Wright) tell us that Lancs still has *her* for ' their.' Hence we may assume that the approximate boundary in the fourteenth century was the *Ribble-Aire* valleys, though ·isolated examples may be expected south of that line, as in the case of *Robert Mannyng* in Lincs.

The form *hor* is usually considered western ; it is found in *Myrc's Festial*, but not in *The Instructions*, and on rare occasions in *Audelay ; Robert of Gloucester* has *hor* beside *her(e). The Owl and the Nightingale* has ' *hore*,' ' *heore*,' ' *here*,' ' *eore*,' ' *hire*,' forms which may indicate [hǿr], not like the western form [hōr].

It is also found in the Lancs and Ches documents *C, H, J, K*. From this evidence it would appear that the boundaries of *hor* were co-terminous with those of ' *an/on*,' extending from S. Lancs to N. Glos. *hor* is exclusively western, but most western writers also use *her*, for example *Audelay*, either occasionally or as the sole form.

(31) **The adv. and adj. ending ' -ly ' or ' -lich(e).'**— From the texts it is seen that the form ' -ly ' was in the fourteenth century current in all dialects except Sth. On

the other hand, ' -lich(e) ' forms are used in varying degrees south of the *Ribble-Aire* valleys, i.e. the line below which, according to Ekwall,[1] O.E. c was palatalised. Hence we may assume that this line was the northern limit of the ' -lich(e) ' form ; the latter form is, for example, very common in *Myrc* and *Robert Mannyng*, but less frequent in *Audelay*.

(32) **The infinitive termination.**—The loss of the final ' -n ' seems to be as much a question of date as of dialect ; in *Orm* and *Layamon* it is naturally retained. In all the documents, plays, *Rolle*, *The Bruce*, *Trevisa* and *Robert of Gloucester*, it is lost. In *Audelay*, *c.* 1426, it is retained as a concession to rhyme 8 times, and quite often in *Mannyng ; Myrc*, *Wiclif*, and *The Guilds of Norfolk* and *Chaucer* have ' -en ' and ' -e ' quite arbitrarily. *Herebert* usually retains the ' -en ' ; from this evidence it is clear that the complete retention is not to be expected in any fourteenth-century text except in Sth. ; on the other hand, it may be retained in any Midl. text as a concession to rhyme or to avoid hiatus before *h*.

(33) **Does the ' -i-' of the 2nd. class of O.E. wk. verbs survive ?**—This ' -i- ' is lost in all the documents, Nth. and E. Midl. texts, except in *Wiclif*, who retains it on rare occasions, In W. Midl. it is more persistent ; in *Audelay*, *The Chester* and *Coventry Plays* it is lost, but it survives in the words *wony*, *louy* (O.E. wunian, lufian) in *Myrc*, and in *Trevisa*. In *Robert of Gloucester*, *Herebert* and *Layamon* it is usually retained ; in all the Sth. texts it is consistently retained except in *The Petition*. Therefore, in the fourteenth century it was lost, except in Sth. and S.W. Midl., but in the words *louy*, *wony* does survive in W. Midl. proper to a much later period.

(34) **Does the ' i- ' Prefix survive in the Past Participle ?**— In all the documents and in *The Bruce* it is lost, and is only found in the following E. Midl. writers : *Chaucer* usually retains it, and it is found in *The Guilds of Lynn* once ; *Mannyng* uses it occasionally for metrical purposes.

Of the W. Midl. texts, it is only found in *Herebert* and *Layamon*, who use it consistently ; in *Trevisa* and *Robert of Gloucester*, who mostly retain it ; in *Myrc* it is consistently retained, and in *Audelay* quite often, appearing as ' y- ' or

---

[1] Ekwall, *The Place-Names of Lancashire*, 1922.

3

' e- ' : e.g. *eslayn, ydrawyn.* From such evidence we cannot localise the boundary exactly for the fourteenth century, but we might say that the consistent absence of the prefix points to an area north of the *Salop-Wash* line ; at the same time isolated examples might occur anywhere between this line and the *Ribble-Aire* valleys.

(35) **The Pres. Part. Termination** : **' -ande,' ' -ende,' ' -inde ' or ' -inge.'**—*The Bruce, Rolle, The York Plays* and *Mannyng* have ' *-ande* ' only ; *The Towneley Plays* have ' *-ande* ' : ' *-ing* ' : : 4 : 3,' the latter forms being due to the late period. The Nth. form therefore involved the N.E. Midl. dialect. *Orm* has ' *-ende* ' only ; *The Guilds of Lynn* have ' *-ende* ' with rare ' *-and,*' ' *-inde,*' ' *-inge* ' forms ; and *The Guilds of Norwich* ' *-ande* ' with rare ' *-ende,*' ' *-yng* ' forms. *Chaucer* and *Wiclif* have ' *-yng* ' only.

Of the Sth. texts, *The Ayenbite, The Owl and the Nightingale* and *The Proclamation* all have ' *-inde,*' but *The Petition* has ' *-yng.*'

Of the W. Midl. texts, *The Chester Plays, Herebert, Trevisa, Myrc* and *The Coventry Plays* all have ' *-yng(e)* ' only. *Robert of Gloucester* has both ' *-yng(e)* ' and ' *-inde,*' *Audelay,* ' *-ing,*' except for three ' *-and* ' forms, and *Layamon,* ' *-inde,*' ' *-ende,*' ' *-inge,*' about equally. The documents, being late, have ' *-yng* ' practically throughout, but *A* and *J* have ' *-ande* ' as well as ' *-inge,*' thus showing that at so late a period the dialects of Ches and S. Lancs both had the form ' *-ande.*'

There are also a few place-name forms which are valuable ; ' *-ande* ' forms are found in Northumb. and Yorks, and in Lancs, where *Hanging Chadder*, near Middleton, occurs five times in M.E. records and always with ' *-ande* ' ; also in Norfolk, Lincs and Staffs.

It would seem that the southern limit of the ' *-ande* ' form was the *Salop-Wash* line, since both *The Guilds* and *Audelay* have it ; the boundary, however, is very approximate.

On the other hand, ' *-ing* ' was in the fourteenth century scarcely dialectal, save that it was not found in Nth. The ' *-ende* ' form evidently extended from the Thames to the *Salop-Wash* line, though isolated instances may be expected farther north. The western limit of the ' *-ende/-inde* ' forms is very uncertain ; at an earlier period it would seem to have run through Worcs, and Miss Serjeantson's statistics confirm this view ; she also finds ' *-ande* ' forms in Derby and Staffs place-names; this agrees with the evidence from the texts.

(36) **The Endings of the Pres. Indic. sg. 2nd. and 3rd. persons.**—The Sth. texts have '-est,' '-eth,' '-(e)þ.' Of the E. Midl. texts, the following have '-est,' '-ist,' '-st,' and '-eth,' '-ith': *Chaucer, Orm* and *Wiclif*. *The Guilds of Lynn* have '-es,' '-etʒ' with '-ith,' '-eth' rarely; *The Guilds of Norwich*, '-est,' '-eth' with '-etʒ' in one guild only. *Rolle, The York* and *Towneley Plays* have '-es' only. *Mannyng* has '-es,' '-ys,' and also a few '-est' forms for the 2nd. pers., but no '-eth' forms for the 3rd. pers.

Of the W. Midl. texts *Robert of Gloucester, Herebert, Trevisa* and *Layamon* all have '-est,' '-eth'; *The Coventry Plays* have rare '-is' forms, whereas *The Chester Plays* have both types about equally. *Myrc* has both '-eth' and '-es' in rhyme, but the latter form is rare, being chiefly a concession to rhyme; *Audelay* has for the 2nd. pers. '-is,' '-ys' 11 times and '-ist,' '-yst,' '-ust' 16 times, and for the 3rd. pers. 24 '-is,' '-ys,' '-us' forms and 22 '-yth,' '-uth,' '-eth,' '-th' forms. Docs. *A, D, G,* have '-eth,' '-es,' and '-ys'; *B, J, I, K, L,* '-es,' '-ys' only; *N* and *O*, '-eth,' '-uth' only.

It becomes impossible to draw a dividing line between the two forms, but it is possible to say that '-es' is not found south of the *Salop-Wash* line (*Myrc, Audelay* and *Mannyng*); this is a limit for the south, but '-eth' forms may be expected north of that line.

(37) **Syncopated forms in the Pres. Indic. sg.**—These are only found in the following: rarely in *Orm* and *Mannyng* (in the latter even in rhymes); quite often in *Chaucer*, and regularly in *Layamon;* rarely in *Robert of Gloucester;* frequently in *The Ayenbite* and *The Owl and the Nightingale;* once in *The Proclamation*, but not in *The Petition, Myrc* or *Audelay*, etc. No boundary is possible, but isolated examples may be expected in Midl.

(38) **The Pres. Indic. pl. Terminations**: *' es,' ' en,' ' eth,'*—The '-es' form is only found in *The Bruce, Rolle* (who has also '-en' forms occasionally); *The York* and *Towneley Plays*, which have either no ending or '-e,' but occasionally '-es,' '-ys'; *Mannyng*, who has '-es : -en :: 1 : 5'; Docs. *B* and *F* (the Furness and Eccles documents) which have '-es' and '-en': Hence *the Sth. limit of the '-es' form.*

is approximately a line passing through Ches and Mid-Lincs (*Myrc* and *Audelay* being excluded).

On the other hand, we have ' -en ' as far north as *Mannyng* in the east and as the S. Lancs documents in the west, including *Myrc* and *Audelay*, etc. ; (*Audelay* has ' -(y)th ' 11 times, ' -un,' ' -on,' ' -yn,' ' -n ' 33 times, and ' -e ' 15 times ; *Myrc* has ' -en : -eth : -e : : 4 : 3 : 1 '; the S. Lancs documents, other than the two mentioned above, have ' -yn,' ' -en,' ' -n,' ' -e.' Therefore *the Nth. limit of the ' -en ' form* seems to be the *Ribble-Aire* valleys.

The Sth. limit of the ' -en ' form is naturally the Thames valley, south of London and passing through Mid-Glos in the west, for *The Ayenbite* and *The Owl and the Nightingale* have no ' -en ' forms, whereas the three London texts have.

The Nth. limit of the ' -eth ' form, when legal documents are excluded, would seem to run north of London in the east, but as far north as *Audelay* (Salop) in the west. These boundaries are quite approximate, but serve as a general guide.

Note.—Miss Serjeantson [1] has found one ' -es ' form in *Robert of Gloucester*, two in Myrc's *Instructions* and a few in *Audelay*.

(39) **The form of the Pres. Indic. pl. of the verb ' to be.'**—Speaking generally, *are* seems to be ˌthe Nth. form, *arne* and *ben* the Midl. forms and *beth* the Sth. The last three forms naturally occur according to the rules of the previous point, for the endings are the same (in *Myrc* with *ben*, *beth*, etc). *are*, *ere*, *er* are found (sometimes alongside other forms) in *The Bruce, The Plays, Rolle, The Guilds, Mannyng* and *Chaucer;* also rarely in *Myrc, Herebert* and *The Coventry Leet Book* ; from this evidence it is quite clear that *are*, once Nth., was no longer so in the fourteenth century ; it was merely non-Sth.

(40) **The Imperative in ' -es ' or ' -eth '.**—The form ' -e ' is not dialectal. In the Sth. texts, where there is any evidence, the ending is ' -eth ' such as in *The Owl and the Nightingale* and *Adam Davy ;* in *Chaucer, Orm, The Guilds of Lynn* and *Wiclif*, the form is ' eth,' ' -e,' etc. ; *Manyng* has ' -es,' ' -eth ' equally ; *Rolle* and *The Plays* have ' -ys ' (-is) or ' -e ' ; the boundary in the east would, therefore, appear to have

---

[1] Miss Serjeantson, Rev. of Eng. Stud., vol. III, p. 186, April, 1927ˏ

been the Wash. There are no ' -es ' forms south of *Myrc*, who himself does not have it, but *Audelay* has 3 ' -yth ' to 16 ' -ys,' ' -is,' ' -us ' forms ; in the fourteenth century the boundary would appear to be N. Salop in the west ; there is no evidence available in the documents.

(41) **The Termination of the 2nd. pers. sg. wk. pret.**— Sth. texts, in which there is any evidence (*The Ayenbite* and *The Owl and the Nightingale*) have ' -est.' Of the E. Midl. texts, *Rolle, The York Plays* and *Mannyng* have ' -es,' '-is,' '-e ' ; *Orm* and *Wiclif* have ' -est ' and ' -e ' ; there is no evidence in *The Guilds ; Chaucer* has ' -est ' and ' -e,' and *The Towneley Plays* have ' -es,' ' -ys ' except for a few ' -yst ' forms, due to modernisation of the text. S. Lincs thus seems to be the southern limit of the ' -es ' form in the east ; in the west *Myrc* alone has the ' -es ' form, in addition to ' -est,' ' -ist,' ' -st,' '-e,' whereas *Audelay* has no ' -es ' forms. Thus the approximate boundary passes through the Wash and Salop ; ' -est ' might be found north of the line, but probably no ' -es ' forms south of it.

(42) **The unvoicing of the final ' -d ' of the wk. pret. and past part.**—In modern dialects this is found in northern counties and N. Midl. districts, but not so consistently as in the dialect of the southern counties of Scotland. In the Sth. and E. Midl. texts it is only found in one or two of *The Guilds of Lynn*.

It is found consistently in *The Bruce*, occasionally in *Audelay*, but frequently in *Myrc ;* also consistently in the Docs. *B* and *J*, and not infrequently in *C, D, F, H, M*. From this evidence it would appear that the feature was Nth. and W. Midl. as far south as Salop, but not an E. Midl. one at all ; north of this line plenty of texts may not, of course, unvoice the final ' -d.'

(43) **The total omission of this ' -d '** is sometimes found. It occurs in none of the texts examined, but is well evidenced in modern dialects as far south as Lancs and Yorks. A point supported by modern dialectal study only is of little value by itself, but in one poem will prove to be of some importance.

(44) **The use of the forms *ta*, *ma*, for " take, make."**— Only the following texts use these forms (alongside the usual ' take ' and ' make ') : *The Bruce, Rolle, The Plays, Myrc*, who has the form *wythtan* once, and *Audelay*, who has *tane* on rare occasions. The documents never have these forms.

In modern dialects they are found as far south as N. Salop and the Wash. This agrees with the evidence from the texts, for *Mannyng* has no examples, and *Audelay* has only a few.

(45) **The forms " quilke, swilke " or " whiche, siche " with loss of ' l.'**—*Layamon* has 'swilke,' which can be accounted for by the early period at which he was writing. *The York Plays* have ' swilke,' etc., but neither *Rolle* nor *The Towneley Plays* shows such forms ; in *The Guilds of Lynn* there are a few ' swilke ' forms ; in *Orm* they are due to the early period at which he was writing.

In all probability the loss of the ' l ' coincided with the palatalisation of the O.E. c, which according to Ekwall took place below the Ribble valley in Lancs, and presumably the Aire valley in Yorks : see Pt. 31 above. Isolated forms may be expected south of the line, but the examples in one or two of *The Guilds of Lynn* seem rather due to the fact that there may be northern scribal influence in those particular guilds.

Note on Map with Key to Letters.

All the boundaries are to be interpreted in accordance with the statements made above in dealing with each point ; certain notes are here appended for the more complex problems.

All the boundaries are approximate and some more so than others, as stated in the text.

Pt. 3. *-and/-ond,* meaning that the latter forms do not occur north of the line, while *-and* is found below the line occasionally.

Pt: 4. M.E. *-ong* is retracted to *-ung* only north of the line, though *-ong* doubtless occurred north of the line as well.

Pt. 17. *ē3/ī3* must be interpreted strictly in accordance with the statements made on page 27.

Pt. 21. *f/v ;* when the initial voicing is found in the fourteenth century it will be below this line, but need not, however, be expected at all.

Pt. 27. There are two boundaries : *-/ho ;* and the Sth. limit of *scho.*

Pt. 28. *thay/hi,* etc. ; this only holds for the fourteenth century.

Pt. 31. *-/lich(e) ;* *-ly* forms are not dialectal.

Pt. 36. The pres. indic. sg. *-es/-eth ;* this takes no account of later legal documents.

Pt. 38. The pres. indic. pl. ; here there are four lines :—

    (*a*) The Nth. limit of the *-en* form.
    (*b*) The Sth.   ,,   ,, *-es* ,,
    (*c*) The Sth.   ,,   ,, *-en* ,,
    (*d*) The Nth.   ,,   ,, *-eth* ,,

Pt. 44. *ta/-* ; *take, make* are not dialectal.

No boundaries are, of course, added for those points which are dialectally too vague to be localised.

It will be observed that though topographical and racial divisions have not been taken into consideration in the construction of the map, yet the main dialectal boundaries do approximately coincide with these, such as the Ribble Valley in Lancs, the watershed of the Midlands, and the Thames Valley in the south ; also, despite the shifting of the original invading nations, their ancient colonies are still to be discerned from the dialectal evidence.

A.—Pt. 5. i/ü, etc.

B.—Pt. 6. ā/ǭ ; Pt. 9. ü/ō ; Pt. 10. ai/ā ; Pt. 19. qu/wh ; Pt. 22. s-/sch- ; Pt. 29. theym/hem ; Pt. 30. theyre/her. Pt. 31. -/-lich ; Pt. 45. quilke/whiche.

C.—Pt. 14. e/ü.

D.—Pt. 3. -and/-ond ; Pt. 38a. The Nth. limit of the -en form for the Pres. Indic. pl.

E.—Pt. 1. ăn/ŏn ; Pt. 2. ălCj/ĕlCj ; Pt. 27. ho ; Pt. 30. hor.

F.—Pts. 7 and 8. āw/ōw ; Pt. 38b. The Sth. limit of the -es form for the Pres. Indic. pl.

G.—Pt. 4. -ung/- ; Pt. 13. O.E. $\bar{æ}^{2}$ as ẹ̄ ; Pt. 27. The Sth. limit of " scho " ; Pt. 34. -/i- (Verbal prefix) ; Pt. 35. -ande/-ende (Pres. Part.) ; Pt. 36. -es/-eth (Pres. Indic. sg.) ; Pt. 40. -es/-eth (Imperative) ; Pt. 41. -es/-est (2nd. pers. wk. sg. pret.) ; Pt. 44. ta/take.

H.—Pt. 38d. The Nth. limit of the -eth form for the Pres. Indic. pl.

I.—Pt. 42. -t/-d (Unvoicing of the final -d of the wk. pret.).

J.—Pt. 21. f/v ; Pt. 28. þay/hi ; Pt. 32. -(e)/-n (infinitive) ; Pt. 35. -ende/-inde (Pres. Part.) ; Pt. 38c. The Sth. limit of the -en form for the Pres. Indic. pl.

K.—Pt. 15. ĕaCj.

L.—Pt. 12. O.E. $\bar{æ}^{1}$ as ẹ̄/ę̄.   M.—Pt. 17. ī3/ē3.

CHAPTER 2.

POEMS IN THE ALLITERATIVE LONG LINE FROM THE CLOSE
OF THE O.E. PERIOD TO *c.* 1300.

IN this chapter we shall examine dialectally the few remnants
of alliterative verse that survive during the above-mentioned
period. There is little need to add any metrical justification
for including them at this stage. The poems discussed are
not, of course, metrically uniform, and rhyme is often added.

The works have been arranged as nearly as possible in
chronological order.

A Description of Durham, an early M.E. poem, consisting
of 21 alliterative long lines without rhyme, preserved in the
MS. Camb. Univ. Lib. Fl. 1, 27, dated the twelfth century, of
northern origin, found at the end of *The Chronicle of Simeon
of Durham,* and edited by T. Wright and J. O. Halliwell in
Reliquiæ Antiquæ, vol. 1, p. 159, 1845. There is naturally little
dialectal evidence in so short a poem.

Pts. 6 and 9. O.E. ā and ō remain : e.g. *stanas,* l. 2, O.E.
stān, *domes,* l. 21, O.E. dōm.

At this very early period these afford no dialectal
evidence. Likewise Pt. 5. O.E. y̆ is preserved in spelling
and possibly also in sound : e.g. *kyn,* l. 5, O.E. cynn, *yðum,*
l. 4, O.E. ȳð.

Pt. 14. O.E. ĕo remains in spelling at any rate : *deope,*
l. 8, O.E. dēope.

Pt. 1. *monige,* l. 7, *monia,* l. 19, O.E. mănig, probably
represent the Nth. dialect, since they are not W. Midl. in this
text.

Pt. 29. The 3rd. pers. pl. pron. acc. is *heom,* l. 14, ðem
ll. 7, 18, 19. The latter form probably owes its initial ' ð- ' to
Scandinavian influence, which would not be felt except in
Nth. and N. Midl. dialects.

The verbal inflexions are scarcely worth recording, since
(40)

they are entirely traditional. There is no other relevant evidence. Therefore there is no proof of Nth. origin, but the internal evidence is sufficient to prove that the poem was written in the locality of Durham, and judging from the language we may date the text *c.* 1100 ; the writer, probably a monk, was conservative both in his language and metre.

Wenne, Wenne, Wenchichenne, a charm in 13 alliterative verses in the MS. Royal 4. A. xiv., edited by F. Holthausen in Beib. Angl., vol. 19, p. 213, 1908.

The evidence for the dialect is very meagre indeed, but we may note the following : Pt. 6. O.E. ā is consistently retained, owing to the early date of composition : e.g. *alswa,* O.E. ealswā ; *hond,* 1. 12, is non-Nth., as are also *scealt,* ll. 2, 3, and *sceal,* 1. 5.

The following verbal forms are indicative of the early period at which the charm was written : *timbrien,* 1. 2, *habben,* 1. 2.—infinitives : *geweornie,* 1. 7, but *weorne,́* 1. 10—2nd. cl. of O.E. wk. vbs. ; the ' ge- ' verbal prefix is retained 4 times : e.g. *gewurþe,* ll. 11, 12, 13.

J. E. Wells [1] describes the piece as S.W. Midl., but there is no real evidence for this ; the retention of the verbal prefix may indicate a Sth. or S. Midl. work, though this is by no means certain. The points which might prove that the dialect was western are not found. The date cannot be later than about 1150.

The Grave, consisting of 25 alliterative verses of the twelfth century, preserved in the Bodl. MS. 343, dated 1150-75, edited by A. Schroer in Anglia, vol. 5, p. 289, and in Archæologia, 17, 174.

The Nth. dialect is ruled out by the following points : Pt. 3. O.E. ' -ănd ' as ' -*ond* ' ; Pt. 32. The retention of the ' -n ' of the infinitive ; Pt. 33. The retention of the ' -i- ' of the 2nd. cl. wk. vbs. ; Pt. 34. The retention of the ' i- ' verbal prefix ; Pt. 37. Syncopated forms in the pres. indic. sg. ; Pt. 38. The pres. indic. pl. in ' -eð.' Other points could be adduced to prove that the dialect was Nth.

The Sth. dialect is indicated by the following : Pt. 18. O.E. ǽ usually as *e* : e.g. *wes,* 1. 1, O.E. wǽs ; Pt. 38. The pres. indic. pl. in ' -eð,' already noted above, is probably Sth. at this period.

---

[1] *A Manual of Middle English Writings,* Yale, 1916.

There are many points found alike in Sth. and S. Midl. : Pt. 32. The infinitive in ' -n ' ; Pt. 34. The retention of the ' i- ' verbal prefix ; Pt. 33. The retention of the ' -i- ' of the 2nd. cl. of wk. vbs. ; Pt. 31. Two examples of ' -lich(e) ' ; Pt. 36. The pres. indic. sg. in ' -st,' ' -ð ' ; Pt. 37. Two syncopated forms in the pres. indic. sg. (it will be recalled that such forms are found in Layamon).

There is only 1 ' -en ' noun plural, *fronden*, l. 17, O.E. frēond, a fact which does not, however, speak very strongly for the Sth. dialect.

Pt. 14. O.E. ĕo as *eo, o* definitely suggests the west : *fronden*, l. 17, O.E. frēond, *broste*, l. 10, O.E. brēost, *eorð*, l. 15, O.E. ĕorðe ; Pt. 5. O.E. ў̆ remains in spelling and probably also in sound, for *i* is here exclusively reserved for O.E. ῐ̆, and *y* for O.E. ў̆ ; if the latter had become *i*, then the two symbols would have been interchangeable. This points to the western area. Pt. 6. O.E. ā retained throughout, is, of course, due to the early period.

It is difficult to assign this poem either to the S. Western, or S.W. Midl. dialect, since the two points (18 and 38) mentioned above are at this early period found in Layamon, who did not write in the Sth. dialect. We have little evidence for the date other than that afforded by the MS. (1150-70) and the archaic nature of the language ; we may place it *c.* 1150.

The First Worcester Fragment, preserved in the Worcester Cathedral Library MS. 174, consisting of 23 alliterative long lines, and edited by J. Hall in *Early Middle English*, 1920, p. 1, and also by Carlton Brown in *Religious Lyrics of the 14th Century*, 1924, p. 237. The MS. is dated by Hall *c.* 1180, and from internal evidence he is able to date the composition *c.* 1170.

The Nth. dialect is ruled out by 9 different points : Pt. 5. O.E. ў̆ as *u,* e.g. *Canterburi*, l. 14 ; Pt. 6. O.E. ā as *o* ; Pt. 30. *heore*, not *theire ;* Pt. 34. The retention of the verbal prefix ; Pts. 36, 38. The pres. indic. sg. and pl. in ' -þ ' ; Pt. 31. The use of ' -liche ' ; Pt. 25. Four noun ' -en ' plurals surviving.

A western area would seem to be indicated by Pt. 5 (above), and very probably by Pt. 30 (*heore*) and by Pt. 14. O.E. ĕo, which remains in spelling, and very probably in sound represents a rounded vowel, as in western dialects ; on the other hand, Pts. 34, 36, 38 (mentioned above) might point to the

Sth. dialect, though scarcely at this period. The dialect is probably that of Worcs in the twelfth century.

The Departing Soul's Address to the Body, from the same MS., *c.* 1180. It consists of 349 alliterative long lines and has been edited by Th. Phillips in *Fragments of Aelfric's Grammar,* 1838, 5, by S. W. Singer, *The Departing Soul's Address to the Body,* 1845, and by G. Buchholz, *Die Fragmente der Reden der Seele an den Leichnam,* Erlanger Beiträge, 2. 6, 1890.

The date is presumably the same as that of the 1st. Fragment —*c.* 1170. The text is very corrupt indeed, but this does not matter greatly in a study of the dialect, though when the metre is examined it occasions considerable difficulty.

The Nth. dialect is again excluded by 27 points, which need not be enumerated here, but the following may be noted : Pt. 5. O.E. $\check{y}$ appears as *u* throughout: e.g. *fure,* l. 305, O.E. f$\bar{y}$r, *sunne,* l. 134, O.E. s$\check{y}$nn, etc. ; Pt. 1. O.E. $\check{a}$ + nasal appears as *o* : e.g. *mon,* l. 5, etc., O.E. m$\check{a}$nn, etc. ; Pt. 19. O.E. hw as *wh* and alliterating with O.E. w ; these and many other points prove that the dialect is not Nth.

The E. Midl. dialect is excluded by Pts. 1 and 5, as given above ; Pt. 27. The 3rd. pers. sg. fem. pers. pron. nom. as *heo,* ll. 613, 619, etc. ; Pt. 28. The 3rd. pers. pl. pron. nom. as *heo,* ll. 132, 227, etc. ; Pt. 30. The gen. form of the same, as *hor(e),* e.g. ll. 466, 500, etc. ; Pt. 14. O.E. $\bar{e}$o normally remaining in spelling, probably indicating the rounded vowel, characteristic of the west : e.g. *freonden,* l. 454, O.E. fr$\bar{e}$ond, *eorthe,* l. 191, etc., O.E. $\bar{e}$orðe.

Of the above points, 1, 5, 14 and 30 definitely point to a western region, including possibly the south-west ; the latter area is required in preference to W. Midl. proper, by Pt. 35. the pres. part. in ' *-inde* ' or ' *-iende* ' throughout : e.g. *weopinde,* l. 17, *woniende,* l. 18 ; Pts. 38 and 39. The pres. indic. pl. in '-eth,' '-ieth,' '-th'; Pt. 37. Syncopated forms in the pres. indic. sg. ; and finally by Pt. 25. The large number of ' -en ' noun plurals, both historical and analogical. On the other hand, Pt. 15. O.E. $\check{e}$a + Cons. mutated as *e* throughout, is scarcely in keeping with the Sth. dialect proper.

This study has included all the relevant points, and it would appear that the dialect has to be limited to extreme S.W. Midl. of the twelfth century. Hall prefers the Middle-South because he believes that the scribe lived at Winchester, but

Pts. 1, 15 and 30 do not confirm this view; the dialect seems to be rather S.W. Midl.

The Proverbs of Alfred, in the MS. Jesus College, Oxf., 29 (c. 1275, 456 lines), and in the MS. Trinity Coll. Cbg., B. 14, 39 (beginning of the thirteenth century, 709 lines). The Jesus is the better copy, and the best edition is that by J. Hall in *Early Middle English*, p. 18, with notes on p. 285. The editor finds the metre to have been corrupted by the scribe and writes thus : " . . . a considerable time and several copies must have intervened between the original and the present form of the poem. The composition of that original should, I think, be placed somewhere about 1180 A.D."

Since so much has been written about the dialect, no new investigation is attempted here. Hall,[1] who has made a very careful investigation of the dialect, says, " Dialect : Sth., free from South-Eastern influence. The wavering in the representation of *a* before nasals points to Middle-South, but ' ihure, ihurd ' are South-Western."

The Death Fragment, from the MS. Trinity Coll. Cbg., B. 14, 39, of the twelfth century, edited by T. Wright in *Latin Poems attributed to Walter Map*, p. 322, Camden Soc., vol. 16, and by G. Kleinert, Anglia, 3, p. 577. The fragment consists of 24 half-lines with rhyme and alliteration ; the date is probably c. 1160-80. There is naturally little evidence to offer concerning the dialect. The Nth. dialect is ruled out by Pt. 6. O.E. ā as *o* throughout, and by many of the inflexions, which will be noted below. On the other hand, the Sth. dialect is ruled out by Pt. 22. O.E. ' sc- ' in unstressed positions as ' s- ': 1. 21, *salt* (*scealt*) ; and by Pt. 41. the 2nd. pers. sg. wk. pret. in ' -is,' *neldis*, l. 15.

A western dialect seems to be indicated by Pt. 1. O.E. ă + nasal as *o* : e.g. *con*, l. 4, *mon*, l. 1 ; and by Pt. 5. O.E. y̆ as *u* in *hude*, l. 20, O.E. hȳdan beside *sinful*, l. 12, O.E. sȳnn. The remaining points are natural over the whole of the Midl. area at this early period ; such as Pt. 6, which is mentioned above; Pt. 32. The infinitive in ' -en '; Pt. 34. The retention of the ' i- ' verbal prefix.

The form *salt*, already discussed, may point to N. Midl., as may also the consistent unvoicing of the final ' -d ' of the wk. pret. and past part.: e.g. *legget*, l. 7, *prickit*, l. 6, etc.

[1] J. Hall, *Early Middle English*, 1920, p. 292.

Hence it is probable that the dialect, as it now stands, is N.W. Midl.

Layamon's Brut, from the MS. Cotton Caligula A., ix., dated *c.* 1200-25, and the MS. Cotton Otho C., xiii., 50 years later. The former MS. is the better representative of the original. *The Brut* was one of the works used in chapter I as representing the dialect of Worcs. Hall [1] says: "What the professional scribes, who copied them, contributed to the divergencies from the original text was mainly graphic and in a great measure due to the clash of native spelling with the French scribal methods to which they were accustomed." Concerning the question of date, Hall [2] says, "it is perhaps safest to say that Layamon wrote between 1189 and 1207 and nearer to 1189 than to 1207. . . ."

There have been numerous studies on the language of Layamon, for which see the Bibliography in Wells' *Manual of M.E. Writings*.

The Bestiary, from the Arundel MS. 292 Brit. Mus., *c.* 1275. The dialect of this work has been discussed many times and agreement reached sufficiently for our purpose. First, Hall, in *Early Middle English*, p. 579, makes an important contribution to the problem ; on p. 590 he says : "The author of the *Bestiary* lived in East-Anglia, sufficiently near its northern border to account for such rhymes as ' loð : sloð,' ' gast : stedefast ' ; the large Scandinavian element also points to the northern part of East Anglia " ; secondly, Wyld,[3] in an important article says : ". . . . the above indications taken together go to show that the dialect was more southernly than S.E. Lincoln and more northernly than that of Suffolk ; Norfolk and rather to the north of the county seems the most probable area, taking all things into consideration." The date is usually considered to be *c.* 1200-50.

A Satire against the Blacksmiths, from the Arundel MS. 292, in a late addition by a hand dated *c.* 1400-25 ; edited by K. Sisam in *Fourteenth Century Prose and Verse*, p. 169. The date is very difficult to decide, but we might suggest the early fourteenth century, *c.* 1300-25, but the copy itself is late. The Nth. dialect is excluded by at least 10 points, such

[1] The same, p. 463.

[2] J. Hall, *Selections from Layamon's Brut*, 1924.

[3] Wyld, *South-Eastern and S. Midl. Dialects in M.E.*, Essays and Studies, vol. 6, pp. 113-45.

as Pt. 6. O.E. ā as *o* throughout, or Pt. 36, the pres. indic. sg. in ' -eth.'

Sth. is ruled out by such points as No. 38, the pres. ind. pl. in ' -en,' ' -yn ' 13 times. W. Midl. is excluded by Pt. 14. O.E. ĕo as *e*; Pt. 1. O.E. ă + nasal as *a* throughout; and Pt. 5. O.E. ў as *e* in *den*, l. 2, O.E. dўn, and as *i* in *dyntes*, l. 2, O.E. dўnt; the former development may point to the S.E. Midl. dialect. This is corroborated by Pt. 36. above—the pres. sg. in ' -eth,' '-ith.' All the remaining points appear with the forms which would be expected in E. Midl., such as Pt. 29. *hem* and Pt. 30. *here*, etc.

These ten survivals of the alliterative metre will prove to be interesting metrically. It will be noticed that they occur in all the dialects : Nth., Sth., S. Western, N.W. Midl., N.E. Midl. and S.E. Midl. ; the importance of which will be seen later.

CHAPTER 3

PòEMS IN THE ALLITERATIVE LONG LINE FROM *c.* 1300 TO
THE END OF THE MIDDLE-ENGLISH PERIOD.

THERE are 28 alliterative poems to be treated in this chapter;
with one exception there are no clues, other than the alliteration and occasionally some purely circumstantial evidence,
to indicate to us the nature of the poet's own dialect. This
means that we shall not, as in chapters 2, 4, 5 and 6, be able
to rely solely on points that can be proved original; however,
we shall see that the task is by no means hopeless.

Alexander A (*Alisaunder*), from the MS. Greaves 60,
Bodl. of the sixteenth century, edited by Skeat for the
E.E.T.S., E.S., I, p. 177. Trautmann[1] considered *Alexander
A* and *B* to be two fragments of one poem, the bulk of the
poem having been lost; we may later be able to adduce
new evidence to corroborate this theory. Skeat described
Alisaunder as the oldest existing specimen of English alliterative verse unmixed with rhyme since the Conquest.
The date *c.* 1340 is usually accepted, and with this we would
agree for dialectal and metrical reasons; also in point of view
of literary art, the poem would be considered early.

We have found nothing conflicting in the dialectal evidence,
a fact which, in general, indicates that the dialect has not
to any great extent been tampered with by a scribe.

The Nth. dialect is ruled out by at least twenty different
dialectal features, such as the retention of O.E. ọ̄; O.E.
ā as ọ̄; O.E. hw as *wh*; etc.

Equally certain is it that the Sth. dialect must be ruled
out: because of such points as the pres. part. sometimes in
'-*and*'; the pres. indic. pl. in '-en'; or the pres. indic. sg.
in '-es' as well as '-eth'; and many other similar points.

---

[1] See Appendix I, p. 247.

The dialect is assuredly Midl., but we may be able to narrow down this extensive area.

The E. Midl. dialect is altogether unsuitable for the following reasons : Pt. 1. O.E. ă + nasal as *o* and *a* ; *o* occurs in 6 different words (*blonke*, l. 435, etc., *on*, l. 17 (O.E. ănn—ŭnnan), *ronke*, *bygonne*, *con*, *gon*) and *a* in 8 words (*many*, *man*, *gan*, *bank*, *can*, *manlich*, *byganne*, *an* (O.E. ănn)) ; it will be remembered that such proportions of *a* to *o*-forms are common in western writers ; though it is possible that some of the latter forms are scribal, yet the development in the copy was western not eastern. This is corroborated by Pt. 5. O.E. ў as *ü* and *i* ; *ü* in 6 words (*gurden*, *burth*, *burde*, *beurde*, *buyld*, *brutned*, *burye*, and possibly *suster*, O.N. sȳstir, not O.E. swēoster) ; *i* in 33 words (such as *mirth*, *mirie*, *kid*, *dint*, *stint*, *tint*, *kyll*, *gilt*, *first*, *biggen*, *birth*, etc.) ; the forms, it will be seen, do not occur haphazard, but according to plan ; generally speaking, the development is *ü* after the labial *b*, which is usually the case in western writers, whilst the sound is not so persistent after *k*, *t*, *st*, *g*, *d*, etc. On the whole, this point indicates a late copy in W. Midl. of an originally western text.

Pt. 2. O.E. ă + 1 + Cons. mutated, has the western development *a*, so far as the evidence goes : *alder*, l. 22, O.E. ïeldra, *aldust*, l. 27, O.E. ïeldest ; these forms are found in genuine western texts.

Pt. 27. The form for ' she ' is *hue* 13 times with two *she* forms both occurring in l. 723 ; we need have little hesitation in considering these scribal, though, of course, *she* is found in the west (see chap. 1, Pt. 27). Given that the text is Midl., *hue* forms must be western. Pt. 30. The form of the 3rd. pers. pron. pl. gen. is *hur* 39 times, *her* twice (ll. 271, 387), and þeir 11 times ; the latter forms in the middle of the fourteenth century would not occur in a Midl. text, and we need not hesitate to regard them as scribal of a later period than that at which the poet wrote. The usual form, *hur*, is definitely western, not eastern. Pt. 29. The acc. form is *hem* with 9 examples of þem, which must likewise be scribal. Lastly Pt. 14. O.E. ĕo as *e* and *u*, the former development being found in 21 words and being the usual form ; on the other hand, there are many significant western forms in the text : *chused*, l. 140, *dupe*, ll. 1132, 1156, *buern*(*es*), 16 times, *lued*, *lud*, 24 times, *hue*, etc. ; the *e*-forms are not found in these words, but in such words as *sterne, erth, free,* etc. ; the exception is in the word *bern(es)* beside *burn(es) ;* the development is therefore typically western, see chapter I, Pt. 14.

Pt. 24. There are 2 examples of the ending ' -us,' but none of ' -ud ': *frotus,* l. 1174, *cairus,* l. 623.

These points afford ample proof of the fact that the dialect is W. Midl. and not E. Midl.

In the next place, it is easy to prove that the dialect does not lie south of the *Salop-Wash* line : Pt. 35. The pres. part. ends in ' -and ' 6 times and in ' -yng ' 8 times ; this would not suggest an area south of Salop. Pt. 36. The pres. indic. 3rd. pers. sg. ends in ' -es ' 113 times, in ' -us ' twice, in ' -eth ' 13 times ; the 2nd. pers. ends in ' -st ' 9 times and in ' -es ' 3 times. The ' -es ' form is evidently the true one, and does not occur south of Salop, but if both forms were used as in Myrc and Audelay, then it is possible that the dialect of *Alexander A.* was similarly a border one.

Pt. 25. Only three ' -n ' plurals are found, and all occur in the word *fone,* O.E. gefā.

Pt. 40. There are two imperatives : l. 591 *kennes,* l. 563 *kares,* which would hardly be found south of Salop.

The remaining points indicate a place not too near the north :—

Pt. 3. O.E. ' -and ' is ' -ond ' 43 times and ' -and ' 9 times only; Pt. 19. O.E. hw alliterates with *w,* ll. 153, 1071; Pt. 44. No contracted forms of ' take,' ' make '; Pt. 32. The infinitive retains the final ' -n ' not infrequently; Pt. 33. The ' -i- ' of the 2nd. cl. of wk. vbs. survives 5 times; Pt. 34. The verbal prefix is often retained in the past part.; Pt. 36. The few ' -eth ' forms in the pres. indic. sg. ; and Pt. 41. The 2nd. wk. pret. sg. ends in ' -st,' when there is any ending.

All these points suggest a place not very far above the *Salop-Wash* line ; indeed there is hardly any difference between the language of this poem and that of Myrc and Audelay. The dialect was that of Salop, or, to speak more broadly, C.W. Midl.

All the significant points have been covered in the above survey, except that O.E. ēa when shortened is ă, which may be the western development ; see chapter I, Pt. 16 ; and O.E. ēah, ēag, M.E. ēʒ is raised to īʒ in the copy, but we cannot assume that the raising had taken place in the original ; if

4

it had taken place, it would indicate the dialect of Salop rather than that of Ches.

Hence there are clues to indicate that the original dialect was C.W. Midl. ; as *Alexander B* is from a different MS., we shall be able to see whether this assumption is correct, for both poems were by one author.

Alexander B (*Alexander and Dindimus*), from the MS. Bodl. 264, fifteenth century, edited by Skeat, E.E.T.S., E.S. 31. At once we may observe that there have been some scribal alterations by a Sth. copyist who added a sentence of his own, quoted by Skeat on page viii ; the sentence contains the 3rd. pres. sg. in ' -eth ': *fayleþ*; *lasteþ*, pl. imperatives in ' -eth ': *turneþ*, *bygynneþ*; and a past part. : *ywrete*.

Skeat says : " These point strongly to a Sth. dialect or a Midl. dialect strongly marked by Sth. forms. . . . It seems fair to assume that the numerous western forms in the poem, such as the use of the suffix -us, are not due to the scribe, but to the original which he had before him." Hence the few extra Sth. forms to be found in *Alexander B* are to be put down to this Sth. scribe ; this may account for the following small differences in the language of *Alexander B* as distinct from that of *Alexander A :* the pres. part. in ' -ynge,' ' -inge ' throughout ; 1 example of the pl. imperative in ' -eth,' the remaining examples ending in ' -es,' ' -us '; 2 examples of syncopated forms in the pres. indic. sg. ; more frequent retention of ' -i- ' in the 2nd. cl. of O.E. wk. vbs. and of the verbal prefix, especially in the case of wk. past part. ; a much greater number of ' -en ' noun plurals ; and lastly, the pres. indic. sg. 2nd. pers. ends in ' -est ' throughout, and the 3rd. pers. in ' -eth ' 71 times to ' -es,' ' -us,' 28 times ; this is just the opposite to what we find in *Alexander A*.

All these things are quite obviously due to this Sth. or S. Midl. scribe, who fortunately added the above sentence in the MS. Otherwise the differences between *Alexander A* and *B* are only two :—

First, the ending ' -us,' only found twice in *Alexander A*, is here very common, especially in nouns, but also found in verbs ; this feature was C.W. Midl., and was probably in the original MS.

Secondly, O.E. ă before a nasal is *a* throughout ; this would appear scribal, and may be due to the S. Midl. or Sth.

scribe, whose alterations were not great, but very marked in character.

Otherwise the language of the two poems does not differ, and this is surely a remarkable fact, when we remember that the poems are preserved in different MSS. To illustrate this it may be interesting to add one or two details ; the form for ' she ' in *Alexander B* is *hue* as in *Alexander A*, with one *sche* form, l. 309 ; the form for ' their ' is *hur(e)* 30 times to *here* 4 ; cp. *Alexander A* : *hur* 39 times, *her* twice, and 11 þ*eir* forms, obviously scribal. Pt. 5. O.E. y̆ as *i* and *ü* ; *i* in 44 words and 135 instances (chiefly after *k, h, m, s, d,* etc.) ; *ü* in 12 words and 28 instances (chiefly after *b, f,* etc., as in *Alexander A*) ; this again is similar to the development in the former fragment ; the unrounding process is still going on, but probably represents a stage further than that actually reached in the original.

Note.—The two forms for the 3rd. pl. pres. indic. of the verb ' to be ' are *ben* and *arn* and both these forms were original, as is indicated by the alliteration :—

l. 904 : " For as **b**estes ȝe **b**en   **b**y no skile reuled."
l. 506 : " Sire **e**mperour **A**lixandre   þis **a**rn oure lawes."

There is also proof that the þ*em* forms in *Alexander A* are scribal and not due to the poet himself :—

l. 996 : " þat I was **h**olpe by **h**ym   **h**em too distrie."
l. 396 : " ȝif þei ne haue none **h**elp   þem to auenge."

þ*em* must be emended to **h**em to alliterate correctly.

The originality of the form *hue* can likewise be proved :—

l. 190 : " **H**upes had **h**ue faire,   and **h**ih was **h**ue þan."

Thus there is almost proof that the poet's dialect was C.W. Midl.

The Parlement of the Thre Ages, from the MS. Brit. Mus. Addit. 31042, of the fifteenth century ; the same MS. contains the companion poem *Wynnere and Wastoure.* These two poems until recently have been ascribed to the same author, and there is certainly a very clôse connection between the two. Wells sums up the former discussion by saying : " The date of the poems is fixed at about 1350 by two allusions in *Wynnere*, one to the 25th year of Ed. III. (l. 206), the other to William de Shareshull as chief Baron of the Exchequer (l. 317) ; this dating would seem to indicate the indebtedness of *Piers Plowman* to the two poems or at least to one of them. The three pieces have the vision form; there is remarkable similarity between the openings of *The Parlement* and *Piers Plowman*; and there are striking parallels in lines of *The Parlement* and *Wynnere* on the one hand and *Piers Plowman* on the other." [1] The matter is further discussed in Appendix I.

In dealing with the dialect we have to remember that the present text is very corrupt and shows considerable modernisation of the language. The best edition is by Gollancz, S.E.E. Poems, 1915. Pt. 19. O.E. hw always as *wh* or *w*, and usually alliterating with itself only, as in l. 294, etc., but *wh* alliterates with *qu* at least three times : l. 626 **wh**are and **qu**ene ; so also ll. 233, 234 [2] ; in *Wynnere* it only alliterates with itself, thus giving us no clue as to the original form.

Another point to be tested by alliteration is Pt. 2. O.E. ă + 1 + Cons. mutated ; the development is *a* in *aldeste*, l. 300, but *e* in *eldest*, l. 464 ; when we reach the metrical examination we shall see that the poet was in the habit of alliterating identical vowels together :

    l. 464 : " **A**reste was Sir **A**rthure and **e**ldeste of tyme."
    l. 300 : " The firste was Sir **E**ctor and **a**ldeste of tyme."
The poet may, therefore, have used both forms.

The development was western, and hence in these two points we have proof that the dialect was N.W. Midl., not far away from the Ribble boundary, yet still in the west. *The Destruction of Troy* alliterates O.E. hw and cw, whereas *Sir Gawayn* does not ; alliterative poems were evidently written near the Ribble boundary.

Let us now assume that the text is a true representation of the original dialect, though not preserving the original spelling ; we at once see that the pronouns are in agreement : *scho*, the form for ' she,' only occurring once, l. 540 ; the forms for ' them,' ' their' being *thaym* (*þam*) and *thaire* (*theire*) ; these are exactly the forms we should expect in N. Midl. near to the Nth. boundary.

Similarly O.E. ō remains except in the word *gude* throughout, O.E. gōd, and sometimes in the word *tuke, toke*, O.N. tōk ; these forms are probably not scribal, but merely N. Midl. ; O.E. ā appears as *o* except in the word *halde*, O.M.

---

[1] Wells, *A Manual of Middle English Writings*, p. 242.
[2] L. 626, " **W**hare es now Dame Dido   was **qw**ene of **C**artage." l. 233, " & **qu**opes thaym to the **qu**errye   that **qu**elled hym to dethe," (O.E. hwopan ?) ; see also l. 234. Additional proof is to be found in the fact that *hw* never alliterates with *w*.

hāldan ; again a N. Midl. development, for it is not uncommon
to find in N. Midl. MSS. and texts O.E. ā as *o* with the solitary
exception of this word.

Pt. 22. There is one *sall* form in the poem, l. 168, whereas
elsewhere the development is ' *sch-* ' etc. ; this suggests N.
Midl.

Pt. 38. The pres. indic. pl. ends in ' -en,' ' -yn ' 23 times,
in ' -es ' 4 times and in ' -e ' 3 times ; we shall find that this
same mixture of forms is to be found in *Sir Gawayn*, and is
not uncommon in N. Midl. texts generally ; there is no need
to reject any of the forms as scribal.

With Pts. 7 and 8 there is a strange admixture of forms :
O.E. āw, āg, āh, as *aw*, *ow* in almost every word in which the
sound occurs : e.g. *knawen*, l. 458, *knowe*, l. 168, O.E. cnāwan ;
such a confusion is possible in a border district, but would
not appear too probable.

The dialect is thus not Nth., but extreme N. Midl., as all
these points go to show. There are other points which are
N. Midl. in general : the pres. indic. sg. in ' -es,' ' -is,' ' -ys ' ;
the imperative pl. sometimes in ' -es ' ; the final ' -d ' of the
wk. past part. often unvoiced to ' -d,' but it would be difficult
to say whether this point occurred in the original or not.

Most of the remaining points are of little importance as
they fall within the N. Midl. area, such as the complete loss
of the verbal prefix and of the ' -i- ' of the 2nd. cl. of wk.
vbs., no syncopated forms in the pres. indic. sg., no examples
of the endings ' -us,' ' -ud,' O.E. ĕa + Cons. mutated as *e*,
O.E. ' -and ' as both ' -ond ' and ' -and.'

In addition the following points should be noted : the
final ' -n ' of the infinitive is retained 13 times, usually to
avoid hiatus ; this, it will be remembered, is also found in
Mannyng in Lincs, so that the feature is not impossible in
extreme N. Midl.

The pres. indic. pl. of the vb. ' to be ' is *ben(e)* and *are*, the
usual forms in Midl. ; the pres. part. only occurs 3 times,
once in ' -ande,' and twice in ' -ynge ' ; the ' liche ' ending
is only found once : *egheliche*, l. 28. Pt. 17. M.E. ē₃ is
not raised to ī₃.

There are three more difficult points remaining : O.E. ĕo
as *e* throughout ; O.E. ă + nasal as *a* except for 3 *o*-forms :
blonke, l. 111, O.E. blănca, *donkede*, l. 10, cp. O.N. dökk,
homelyde, l. 90, O.E. hămelian ; O.E. ў̆ as *i* almost throughout

though there are a few *ü*-forms : *lure*, l. 323, O.E. lўre, *cruche*, l. 165, O.E. crўcce, *schutt*, l. 585, O.E. scўttan, *schurtted*, l. 661, O.E. scўrtan ; *i*-forms occur elsewhere : *birde*, ll. 390, 453 (woman) always occurs as *burde* in alliterative poetry, and is never found with *i* ; it is therefore almost certain that this form is scribal, as are possibly also many of the other *i*-forms. The scribe was evidently N.E. Midl., and left the 3 *o*-forms mentioned above and the few *ü*-forms, but altered most of the western forms ; this theory is corroborated by the previous statements concerning the western form *aldeste*, which the scribe left in l. 300, but possibly altered to *eldeste* in l. 464. The poem was therefore written in extreme N.W. Midl., but the scribe was N.E. Midl. ; this agrees with Miss Serjeantson's results from a different line of enquiry ; she says [1] that the copy is in the dialect of Notts. The poet himself, however, probably wrote in S. Lancs.

Wynnere and Wastoure, from the same MS. The text is exceedingly corrupt and this corruption was not by any means entirely due to the scribe of the present copy. See Gollancz's edition in S.E.E. Poems, 1920, p. 1 ; the editor has made a careful comparison of these two Thornton texts and arrives at the conclusion that the copy of *Wynnere* has passed through more hands than that of *The Parlement ;* despite this, the dialect stands out very clear, and there are few differences between the language of the two poems.

O.E. hw as *wh* is only found alliterating with itself, as in l. 181 ; but since it never alliterates with *w*, this surely suggests that such alliteration was not phonetically possible in this dialect as in the case of *The Parlement ;* there is no proof, but good grounds for the assumption that both poems are alike in the development of this sound.

The two poems do not differ dialectally except for the following points ; elsewhere, the reader may assume that there is no difference at all.

(1) While *The Parlement* has only *halde* as the *a* development of O.E. ā, *Wynnere* has in addition *mare*, l. 305, O.E. māre, and *wate*, l. 389, O.E. wāt ; these are clearly of no importance.

(2) In addition to the usual form *thaire*, *Wynnere* has *hire*, l. 14, and *hir*, l. 16, O.E. hĭera ; it would be impossible

---

[1] Rev. of Eng. Stud., vol. 3, pp. 319-31.

to say whether these two forms are scribal or not, but they are possible in a genuine N. Midl. text.

(3) There is one contracted form of 'take' in *Wynnere*, but none in *The Parlement: tast*, l. 445 (takest), a form which does not indicate a different dialect.

(4) The pres. indic. sg. in *The Parlement* ends in ' -es,' ' -is,' but in *Wynnere* these endings are found 64 times to the ' -ist,' ' -eth ' (2nd. and 3rd. pers.) 29 times ; this point is quite different from the three former ones ; it is the only point of serious disagreement between the two texts, and suggests scribal alteration ; in an otherwise extreme N. Midl. text, it is obvious that the ' -eth ' forms must be scribal, due either to a S. Midl. scribe, or to the spreading of these forms at a later period.

(5) O.E. ēah, ēag, normally not raised to ī₃, either in *The Parlement* or *Wynnere*, occurs as ī₃ twice in the latter poem : *hye*, ll. 246, 372, O.E. hēah ; this, however, only concerns the scribe and probably does not apply to the original. There are no other points of difference.

It may, however, be interesting to note the following : O.E. ĕo as *e* in both poems ; O.E. ȳ as *i*, but with a few *ü* forms in both poems (*Wynnere, full*, ll. 217, 367, O.E. fȳllan, " to fill " : *sturte*, l. 265, of uncertain origin : and a few other forms ; as in *The Parlement* these have been left by the scribe) ; similarly, O.E. ă + nasal is *a* with a few *o*-forms in both poems ; 3 in *The Parlement*, and 2 in *Wynnere : bonke*, ll. 33, 109, O.N. banki. Miss Serjeantson, in the article referred to above, has found 1 *bonke* form in *The Parlement*. All the remaining points in the same way show identical treatment. We need, therefore, have no hesitation in saying that the dialect of the two poems is the same, and we have evidence that the original dialect was the same. Hulbert, in suggesting that *Wynnere* was originally of more southern origin than *The Parlement*, has surely been misled by the ' -eth ' forms of the pres. indic. sg. to which we have referred above. Dialectally there would be no objection to assigning both poems to one author, but see Appendix 1 for further details.

William of Palerne, from the MS. King's College, Camb 13 (*c.* 1350), edited by Skeat for the E.E.T.S., E.S. 1. The poem has rightly been considered one of the earliest of the alliterative romances, not merely on account of the references to Sir Humphrey De Bohun, Earl of Hereford, who died 1361, but also on account of the literary style and metre. The date is certainly not much later than 1350.

This poem presents the most difficult dialectal problem of all the alliterative poems owing to the peculiar mixture of forms. However, the more accurate localisation of the dialectal boundaries does help matters considerably. The confusion of forms may be explained as due to scribes, or as Hulbert suggested,[1] to a S. Midl. poet who was trying to imitate a Nth. dialect, as being more suitable with regard to literary tradition; we may leave this theory for the present.

To begin with, the internal evidence, such as it is, seems to indicate the S.W. Midl. dialect in the neighbourhood of Hereford or Glos, since the author tells us that he wrote at the command of the Earl of Hereford ; there are points in the dialect of the text that bear this out, but there are others that do not.

Pt. 19. O.E. hw as *wh*, alliterating with *w* very frequently : e.g. l. 15 or 2830, etc. ; this rules out the Nth. dialect, as do the majority of the points.

(1) Midl. Features. Pt. 9. O.E. ō remaining throughout. Pt. 6. O.E. ā as *o*, except occasionally in the form *halde* beside *holde*. Pts. 7, 8. O.E. āw, āh, āg as *ow*, except in the word *saules*, which might be scribal. Pt. 3. O.E. ' -and ' as ' -*ond* ' throughout. Pt. 22. Absence of *sall* forms. Pt. 44. No contracted forms of ' take,' ' make.' Pt. 45. Absence of *swilke*, *qwilke*, etc. Pts. 29, 30. The pronouns *hem*, *here ;* all these points may be either Midl. or Sth., but as the pres. indic. pl. never ends in ' -eth,' we may assume that they are Midl. Specifically Midl. is the pres. indic. pl. in ' -en,' ' -un ' 129 times with ' -es ' 27 times only ; the latter forms we shall leave for the moment.

(2) From this point we meet with a few features which are decidedly N. Midl. : the *saules* and *halde* forms, mentioned above ; the 27 ' -es ' forms of the pres. indic. pl. (these three forms are rather extreme N. Midl.) ; the imperative pl. in ' -eth ' : ' -es ' : : 1 : 4, the latter forms being N. Midl. ; the pres. indic. sg. 2nd. pers. ' -est ' : ' -es ' : : 2 : 1, but for the 3rd. pers. ' -eth ' : ' -es ' : : 1 : 2 ; both N. Midl. and S. Midl.

---

[1] J. R. Hulbert, *The West Midland of the Romances,* Mod. Phil., xix., p. 1.

forms are therefore found ; the pres. part. in ' -ande ' 29 times, in ' -ende ' 16 times, in ' -inde ' 5 times, and in ' -inge ' 31 times ; there is one *þaim* form, l. 5407, besides the usual *hem*.

Thus we have these N. Midl. features, and because some of them are extreme N. Midl., we must assume that they come from a copy in that area.

(3) Alongside these we have a number of S. Midl. features, which could not have been found in the N. Midl. dialect : the imperative pl. sometimes in ' -eth ' (see above) ; the pres. indic. sg. sometimes in ' -eth ' ; the pres. part. in ' *-ende*,' ' *-inde* ' (the latter forms might be found in the S.W. Midl. dialect of Glos or Hereford) ; the ' -i- ' of the 2nd. wk. cl. of verbs is preserved occasionally ; the ' i- ' verbal prefix in the wk. pret. and past part. is sometimes found ; the infinitive not infrequently retains the final ' -n ' ; the 2nd. pers. wk. pret. sg. ends in ' -est ' or ' -e ' ; O.E. ĕa + Cons. mutated, is *e* except in *hure*, l. 3270, O.E. hīeran, which elsewhere appears as *here*, etc. ; this form might be scribal, but is possible in S.W. Midl.

We have thus so far a poem with a Midl. basis and N. Midl. and S. Midl. features. In addition there are a few western features : the pres. part. ending in ' *-inde* ' 5 times is certainly S.W. Midl. and not S.E. Midl. O.E. ĕo as *u* and *e* ; the development on this point is typically western, the *u*-forms being found in such words as *burne, lude, bihuld, furþe*, etc., which are the natural forms in western dialects.

O.E. ă + nasal is both *o* and *a* ; the latter forms are about three times as numerous as the *o*-forms, but the development is typically western, as the rounded forms are particularly found before *nk*.

O.E. ў̆ appears as *ü* in 30 words and 104 forms, as *i* in 28 words and 94 forms, and as *e* in 15 words and 36 forms ; *i* and *ü*-forms occur after the same consonants—*k, l, f, h, b, m, g, st, s, þ* ; thus we have *fur, fir*, O.E. *fȳr, kudden, kidden*, O.E. cȳ̆ðde, etc. ; such a medley of forms occurs in no other alliterative poem and doubtless there has been much scribal alteration by a non-western scribe.

The ending ' -us ' occurs once in every 150 lines, and -ud ' in about every 250 ; these are at this period probably western.

These western features are typically south-western, rather than north-western, because of the slowness with which the unrounding process was taking place in this dialect, being much more rapid in the north. In addition the ' -inde ' endings of the pres. part. confirm this view.

The forms for ' she ' are *sche, che, ʒhe*, forms which obviously belong to the N. Midl. group of characteristics, and not to the S.W. Midl. ones.

As we have good reasons for believing that the poet lived in Hereford or Glos, we naturally assume that these S.W. Midl. forms represent the poet's own dialect, and that the N. Midl. forms are due to a scribe ; the dialectal confusion in the text is thus not so great as might be imagined, since the features divide themselves into two distinct groups ; there is no need for Hulbert's ingenious theory of a poet imitating the northern alliterative writers ; the confusion of forms would have been far greater if that had been the case. Miss Serjeantson, in the same article previously referred to, says that it is possible that *William of Palerne* is a Leics copy of an original written on the borders of Glos and Oxon. The original dialect was, we think, a little more northern than she asserts.

Note.—The following unimportant points have not fallen in the above survey : there are no syncopated forms in the pres. indic. sg. ; few ' -en ' noun plurals ; no initial voicing of *f* or *s* ; no *h*-forms for the pronoun ' they ' ; the forms for the pres. indic. pl. of the vb. ' to be ' are : *aren, arn, ben, bene* with rare *ar* forms ; all these are typically Midl. The adv. and adj. endings ' -ly ' and ' -lich(e) ' are both found and in the proportion of 2 to 3 respectively ; the final ' -d ' of the wk. pret. and past part. is unvoiced to ' -t ' on 6 occasions. There are only 2 examples of M.E. *ēʒ* from O.E. ēah, ēag, being raised to *īʒ* ; it is impossible to say whether these are scribal or not, and hence we cannot explain them.

Joseph of Arimathie, from the Vernon MS. 1370-80, edited by Skeat for the E.E.T.S., 44, 1871. The poem is usually recognised to be an early composition and it has literary affinities with *Alexander A* and *B*, and *William of Palerne ;* we shall also see later that metrically it falls in the early period of the so-called *Alliterative Revival*. The date is probably *c.* 1350-60.

The dialect is not Nth. as is revealed by the fact that O.E. hw appears as *wh* and alliterates freely with *w* : e.g. ll. 237, 658. This is confirmed by such points as : Pt. 6. O.E. ā as *o* throughout; Pt. 9. O.E. ō as *o* throughout; Pts. 7, 8. O.E. āw, āg, āh, as *ow, ou;* Pt. 3. O.E. '-and' as '-ond' throughout; Pt. 22. No examples of *sall;* Pt. 45. Use of *whuche,* etc. All these points are simply non-Nth.

Similarly the Sth. dialect is ruled out by the following points : Pt. 28. The pron. " they " as *þei* with one exception in *heo,* l. 97, which may be scribal; Pt. 33. The '-i-' of the 2nd. cl. of wk. vbs. is completely lost; Pt. 36. The pres. indic. sg. normally ends in '-es'; Pt. 38. The pres. indic. pl. normally ends in '-en.'

The dialect is thus obviously Midl., and the S. Midl. dialect would seem to be indicated by the following points : Pt. 35. The pres. part. ends in '-inde' 4 times and in '-ynge' 8 times : this would indicate extreme S. Midl. of Glos and neighbourhood (see the map). Pt. 32. The '-n' of the infinitive often survives : " -en : -e :: 2 : 5." Pt. 34. The verbal prefix is retained 34 times, though normally lost. Pt. 41. The 2nd. pers. sg. wk. pret. ends in '-est' with one exception in '-es': *souȝtes,* l. 431 ; cf. *souȝtest,* l. 4 (the '-es' form may be scribal). Pt. 25. '-en' noun plurals are not uncommon. Pt. 39. The pres. indic. pl. of the verb 'to be' is *ben, beon, aren,* as the prevailing forms with *beþ,* l. 409, and *beoþ,* l. 331 ; if these last two forms are not scribal, they support the theory of a S. Midl. dialect. Pt. 38. The pres. indic. pl. normally ends in '-en,' but there is one example in '-es,' *bydes,* l. 468, and two in '-eþ,' *clepeþ,* l. 379, *goþ,* l. 386 ; see also Pt. 39 above. Skeat regards these forms as scribal, but it seems to us more probable that the '-es' form is scribal. Pt. 40. The imperative pl. ends in '-es' twice : *holdes,* l. 492, *þinkes,* l. 493 ; and in '-eþ' once : *foleweþ,* l. 245 ; it is difficult to believe that both forms were used by an obviously S. Midl. poet ; we shall return to the point later. Pt. 44. No contracted forms of 'take,' 'make.'

The dialect is obviously S. Midl., and if we may trust the evidence regarding Pts. 38 and 39, the dialect was extreme S. Midl., in which case the solitary example of *heo* for 'they' would probably be original. Pt. 35 is also extreme S. Midl.— the pres. part. in '-inde.' Pt. 36. The pres. indic. sg. 2nd. pers. ends in '-est' with only two exceptions : *ȝemes,* l. 316, *wendes,* l. 320, but *berest,* l. 40, etc. ; in the 3rd. pers. the ending is '-es,' '-is' with 4 exceptions of '-eþ': e.g. *ledes,* l. 32, *bereþ,* l. 396 ; see also ll. 6, 196, 347 ; this seems an odd confusion of forms, especially when we remember that the poem seems to have been written in extreme S. Midl. In that region the ' -es ' forms are impossible ; we think they are scribal along with the isolated ' -es ' pres. pl. form, the 2nd. sg. wk. pret. in ' -es,' and the two examples of the imperative plural in ' -es ' ; all these we may attribute to a N. Midl. scribe.

The following features are western : Pt. 27. The form of the 3rd. sg. nom. pers. pron. is *heo* 9 times and *he* once, l. 831. Given that the dialect is not Sth., these forms are W. Midl. and certainly not E. Midl. Pt. 24. There are 3 examples of ' -us ' for ' -es,' *gultus*, l. 249, *noskunnus*, l. 219, *Augrippus*, l. 19 : these may be western in origin at this period. Pt. 2. O.E. ă + 1 + Cons. mutated is *a* once and *e* once : *fallen*, l. 558, *fel*, l. 569, O.E. fïellan : the former is certainly a western form. Pt. 1. O.E. ă + nasal is *o* throughout, with no *a* forms : e.g. *nome*, l. 10, O.E. năma, etc. Pt. 5. O.E. ў appears as *ü* with only 7 exceptions in *i* : *pinkes*, l. 157, etc., O.E. pўncean, *lift*, l. 41, *vpliftes*, l. 584, O.N. lўfta, *sinful*, l. 638, O.E. sўnn, *brimme*, l. 458, O.E. brўmme ; elsewhere the forms are with *ü* : *huirenes*, l. 13, O.E. hўrne, *cülles*, l. 545, O.E. cўllan, etc. The western forms have not been tampered with by the scribe.

Pt. 14. O.E. ĕo as *eo*, *u* with 3 isolated *e* forms ; probably all the remaining ones are rounded forms, typical of the west ; *dere*, l. 37, O.E. dĕore or dīere ; *bernes*, ll. 414, 472, beside *burnes*, ll. 501, 708, O.E. bĕorn ; *huld*, l. 504, etc., O.E. hĕold ; *heold*, l. 113, etc. Pt. 29. *hem* 56 times to *heom* 3 times only, ll. 130, 367 (2). Pt. 30. *heore* 12 times and *here* only in l. 30 ; these forms are all common in the S.W. Midl. dialect of the fourteenth century.

There are two other points : Pt. 17. M.E. ēʒ is only raised to īʒ once (l. 254), and this is what we should expect in the south-west. Pt. 42. The final unvoicing of consonants is so common as to suggest that it was phonetically universal in this dialect : e.g. *wynt*, l. 658, for *wynd* ; *iugget*, l. 251, *fondet*, l. 12, etc.

This may have been typical of the S.W. Midl. dialect, but is probably due to the N. Midl. scribe.

This text is one of the best examples of a western work and the main dialect is unmistakable ; there have been, however, a few marked alterations by a N. Midl. scribe ; his dialect was probably N.W. Midl. in view of the fact that he tampered with none of the western forms as far as we are able to judge.

The Vision of William concerning Piers the Plowman.— It is not our intention to attempt to investigate the dialect of this work afresh, partly because of the magnitude of such an undertaking and also because little might be gained for our purpose ; at best it would only be possible to localise the dialect of the various MSS. ; whereas our aim is to arrive at the original dialect, which in this case may well be considered a difficult task in view of the controversy that rages around the questions of authorship of the poem. We agree with the theory of single authorship, largely because of the metrical evidence. If this theory is correct, the author knew London and at some time lived in the locality of the Malvern Hills ; other alliterative poets such as the author of *St. Erkenwald*, also knew London but wrote in their native dialect. " Was the poet's original dialect western ? " is the main question to be answered. The most important article on this problem is by R. W. Chambers, *The Three Texts of Piers Plowman and their Grammatical Forms*, Mod. Lang. Rev., 14, p. 129.

The reader is referred to this article, as it throws great light on this problem ; among other things he shows that both *she* and *heo* occur in alliteration in all three texts, the latter form being a W. Midl. and certainly not a London form ; he also says that the scribes of *A*. and *B*. show a tendency to substitute *she* for *heo*, but that the best MSS. preserve traces of the *heo* form ; Chambers is able to show that there are western provincialisms in all texts which the scribes were continually eliminating. He uses this evidence to show that all three texts were by one poet, but it also shows that the poet was a western man ; that is perhaps as far as we can go in our present imperfect state of knowledge ; in the metrical section we shall accept the *A*. text as *c*. 1362-63, *B*. as 1376-77, and *C*. as 1393-98 ; the metrical results are not, of course, affected by any theory of authorship we happen to hold.

Chevelere Assigne, from the Cotton MS. Brit. Mus., Caligula A. 2, edited by H. H. Gibbs for the E.E.T.S., E.S. 6, 1868.

The dialect in its present state is E. Midl., but scholars, following Morris, have assumed a western original ; Gibbs quotes Morris' opinion on page xvii of his Introduction : " The dialect in its present form is East Midlànd.   But as we do not find (other) East Midland writers adopting alliterative measures in the fourteenth century, I am inclined to think that the original English text was written in the north or north-west of England, and that the present copy is a mere modified transcript."

This kind of argument is exceedingly dangerous, as it presupposes that all alliterative poems were written in the west.

Let us therefore examine the copy as it stands.

The Nth. dialect is obviously ruled out by such points as : Pt. 6. O.E. ā as *o* throughout; Pts. 7, 8. O.E. āw, āg, āh as *ow*; Pt. 9. O.E. ō as *o* ; Pt. 19. O.E. hw as *wh* alliterating with *w* : e.g. l. 1 (this point rules out Nth. for the original as well as for the MS.) ; Pt. 3. O.E. ' -and ' as ' -*ond* '; Pt. 22. Absence of *sall* forms ; Pt. 45. Use of *swiche*, etc.

The Sth. dialect is ruled out by such points as :

Pt. 28. The use of *they* instead of forms with ' *h-* '; Pt. 34. Complete loss of the verbal prefix ; Pt. 33. The loss of the ' -i- ' of the 2nd. cl. of wk. vbs ; Pt. 38. The pres. indic. pl. in ' -en.'

The dialect is obviously Midl. and the western portion of this dialect is excluded by the following : Pt. 5. O.E. ў as *i*; Pt. 14. O.E. ĕo as *e* throughout; Pt. 1. O.E. ă + nasal as *a* except in the word *mony* beside *many;* Pt. 2. O.E. ă + 1 + Cons. mutated is *a* in *fallethe,* l. 310 (*felled*), O.E. fĭellan : *e* in *wellede,* l. 166, O.E. wĭellan ; the former is a western development; Pt. 27. The form for ' she ' is *she,* not *ho,* etc.; Pts. 29 and 30. The forms for ' them,' ' their,' are *hem* (with one exception in *ham,* l. 152) and *her*(*e*) respectively.   All these points exclude W. Midl.

Confining ourselves to the E. Midl. dialect, the southern portion is undoubtedly required by the following : Pt. 35. The pres. part. always in ' -*ynge* '; Pt. 36. The pres. indic. sg. normally in ' -est,' ' -eth,' with only the following exceptions : 2nd. pers., one example in ' -es,' *fyndes*, l. 305 ; 3rd. pers., five examples in ' -es,' ' -is,' *lykes*, l. 134, *wendis*, ll. 155, 178, *launces*, l. 323, *formerknes*, l. 362 ; these forms may not be due to this scribe at all.

Pt. 17. O.E. ēah, ēag is raised to *ī*ȝ throughout, which

would rather indicate the central portion of the country, i.e. C.S. Midl.

Note.—There are also the following points which are not relevant : No contracted forms of ' take,' ' make ' ; the final ' -n ' of the infinitive is occasionally retained to avoid hiatus before *h* or a vowel; the pres. indic. pl. of the verb ' to be ' is *ar*, l. 82, *ben*, l. 353; the final ' -d ' of the wk. pret. and past part. is never unvoiced ; O.E. ĕa + Cons. mutated is *e* ; these points are all natural in S.E. Midl. except *ar*, l. 82.

There is one exception to the pres. indic. pl. in ' -en ' : l. 72, *hem that it deservethe ;* the scribe has obviously taken *it* as the nom. ; incidentally, this tells us that the scribe's form of the pres. indic. sg. was ' -eth ' ; unless he was accustomed to the use of both forms, the few ' -es ' forms were not his.

Let us sum up the strange forms : 6 examples of ' -es ' in the pres. indic. sg. ; the western form *fallethe* (see above), whereas *wellede* would be natural in any dialect owing to the spreading of the standard form ; isolated examples of *mony* and *ony ; ar*, l. 82, for *arn ;* the first two and the last points are Nth. or N. Midl. ; the 2nd. is western ; as a group they are N.W. Midl.

What we have to ask ourselves is whether we have an E. Midl. poet with a N.W. Midl. copyist, or a N.W. Midl. poet with an E. Midl. copyist. We have no hesitation in accepting the latter theory, because no other alliterative romances are found in the east and we have evidence of corruption either one way or the other ; here was obviously an eastern scribe who forgot to alter these forms in a N.W. Midl. poem.

Note.—Pt. 16. O.E. ēa shortened is ă in *byrafte*, ll. 199, 351, O.E. rēafian. See chapter I, Pt. 16 ; this *a* is possibly a western form ; if so, it has also been left by the scribe.

Morte Arthure, from the Thornton MS., Lincoln Cathedral, *c.* 1430-50. Robert Thornton was a native of Oswaldkirk, Yorks, and was Archdeacon of Bedford in the diocese of Lincoln about the middle of the fifteenth century ; we therefore know the dialect of the scribe. This is important, because in the copy itself there is considerable confusion of dialectal forms. The best edition is that by E. Björkman, 1915, but see also E.E.T.S., 8, 1865, G. G. Perry. Both the Sth. and S. Midl. dialects are ruled out by such points as the following : the pres. indic. sg. and pl. normally in ' -es ' ; O.E. ā normally remaining, and many other similar points.

There are Nth. forms and Midl. ones, though many overlap.

(1) **Nth. Points** (and extreme N. Midl.) : Pt. 3. O.E. ' -and ' remains except for about 39 ' -ond ' forms in the whole of the poem ; this would suggest extreme N. Midl. ; Pt. 6. O.E. ā appears as $a : o :: 5 : 1$; the development is, therefore, usually Nth. ; Pts. 7 and 8. O.E. āw, āg, āh as *aw, au* with only one exception : *beknowe*, l. 3867, O.E. becnāwan ; Pt. 9. O.E. ō as *u* with very rare *o*-forms ; Pt. 27. The form for ' she ' is *scho, cho ;* Pts. 29 and 30. The pronouns for ' them,' ' their ' are *theme* (and *þem*) and *theire* (and *thayre*) ; Pt. 22. O.E. ' sc- ' in unstressed positions is ' s- ' almost throughout (' *sch-* ' is found about 32 times) ; Pt. 38. The pres. indic. pl. normally ends in ' -es,' but ' -en ' forms are not infrequent ; Pt. 26. The pl. of ' this ' is occasionally *thire*, *þir* (4 times, ll. 993, 3179, 1161, 2359) ; lastly, Pt. 19. O.E. hw normally appears as *wh*, but also as *qu, quh* 24 times ; the alliteration affords us some evidence regarding this point, but is, however, conflicting and the text should be con- sulted ; see ll. 948, 3231, 3261, 3389, 3810, 2189, 2103, 1788, 1736 :

> l. 3261 : " ouer**wh**elme all **qw**ayntely   þe **wh**ele as cho scholde."
>
> l. 2103 : " **Qw**arells   **qw**ayntly   **qw**appeȝ thorowe knyghteȝ."

qwappe corresponds to " *whap* " (Mn. E.) ; the MS. has *swappeȝ* which is obviously wrong.

> l. 1736 : " I walde be wellyde all qwyke   quarterde in sondre."

This is obviously an *aab/b* type, not *aaa/a ;* see chapters 7 and 8.

> l. 2189 : " grete **w**ele my ladye þe qwene   ȝif þe **w**erlde happyne."

This is an *ax/ax* type. Thus O.E. hw definitely alliterates with *qu-*.

There are two lines which seem to contradict this :—

> l. 948 : " To **w**ette of þe **w**arlawe   **wh**are þat he lengeȝ."
>
> l. 3231 : " that I ne **w**iste no **w**aye   **wh**edire þat I scholde."

The poet certainly seems to have used both forms ; this may indicate that he lived near to the border between the two dialects, i.e. the *Ribble-Aire* line.

The number of Nth. forms in the poem are therefore considerable ;   let us see how many Midl. forms there are, and since S. Midl. has been ruled out as unsuitable, we may call them N. Midl.

(2) **N. Midl. Points.**—Many points correspond to those above :—

Pt. 3. The few ' *-ond* ' forms ;   Pt. 6. The few *o*-forms for O.E. ā ;   Pt. 9. The rare *o*-forms for O.E. ō ;   Pt. 38. The pres. indic. pl. in ' -en ' occasionally ;   Pt. 22. The few ' *sch-* ' forms for O.E. ' sc- ' in unstressed positions.

Also : Pt. 35. The pres. part. in ' *-ande* ' with only one exception, *chawngynge*, l. 3267 ;   Pt. 44. Frequent contracted forms of ' take,' ' make ' ;   Pt. 32. The final ' -n ' of the infinitive is preserved about a dozen times to avoid hiatus ;   Pt. 36. The pres. indic. sg. 2nd. and 3rd. persons ends in ' -es,' and the 1st. pers. ends in ' -es ' twice : *dyghttes*, l. 2625, *gretis*, l. 3338 ;   Pt. 40. The imperative pl. usually ends in ' -es ' ;   Pt. 31.   Though the ' -ly ' ending is almost universal, the ' -liche ' ending is found not infrequently ;   Pt. 45. Both *swilke* and *swyche* forms are found in about equal proportions.

Of the above points, Nos. 35, 36, 40, 44 are Nth. as well as N. Midl., but the remaining points are here non-Nth.

All the above forms might be possible in a border dialect between Nth. and N. Midl. ;   in that case the dialect of the poet was chiefly Nth. with a few Midl. peculiarities.

(3) **Notes on a few irrelevant forms.**—Pt. 41. The 2nd. pers. wk. pret. sg. ends in ' -e ' ;   Pts. 42 and 43. There is no loss or unvoicing of the final ' -d ' of the wk. pret. or past part. : this does not rule out N. Midl., as the feature did not occur over the whole area ;   Pt. 34. Complete loss of the verbal prefix ;   Pt. 33. Loss of the ' -i- ' of the 2nd. cl. of wk. vbs. ;   Pt. 25. There are a few ' -en ' noun plurals (not peculiar even in a N. Midl. text) ;   Pt. 15. O.E. ĕa + Cons. mutated is *e* ;   Pt. 39. The pres. indic. pl. of the verb ' to be ' is " *are, er, be, beȝ, ben,*" the latter form only occurring once—l. 2850 ;   these are typically N. Midl. forms and agree with the evidence concerning the pres. indic. pl.—Pt. 38. (See above.)

(4) **Western Points.**—Pt. 24.   There are no examples of

'-us,' '-ud'; Pt. 2. O.E. ă + 1 + Cons. mutated is *e* throughout; Pt. 14. O.E. ĕo is *e* throughout; Pt. 5. O.E. ў is *i* with a few significant *ü* and *e* forms : *thursse*, l. 1100, O.E. þỹrs or more probably O.N. þurs ; *brustils*, l. 1095 (bristles) (a derivative of O.E. bỹrst). The *e*-forms are somewhat peculiar, but are confined to the usual words such as *merry*, *bery* (vb.), etc. ; the development is not W. Midl. Pt. 1. O.E. ă + nasal as *a* with a good number of *o*-forms, especially before *nk* (*wlonke*, *blonke*, etc.) ; O.N. banki is *banke* throughout ; O.E. blanca is usually *blonke*, but *blanke*, ll. 1799, 1860 ; these two forms are very suspicious, for this word is never found with *a*, even in Scotland.

Generally speaking, there is therefore no evidence for a western dialect except in this one doubtful case.

Finally, Pt. 17. M.E. *ē3* is very rarely raised to *ī3*; these few forms may indicate C.N. Midl.

We have therefore N. Midl. and Nth. features ; it is difficult to believe that such a confusion of forms is due to the poet himself ; it seems much more probable that the Midl. forms are due either to a Midl. scribe or to a Midl. original ; Morris believed that a Midl. scribe copied the text before it came into the hands of Thornton, who transcribed it as it stood ; this is very hypothetical ; Thornton was a Yorkshireman, and we know that the dialect of S. Yorks was a border one, so that he might employ mixed forms. S. O. Andrew, in an important article has recently [1] brought forward some very useful evidence ; he points out that in l. 3064 a form for ' she ' with *h-* is required by the alliteration ; also that *g-* initially is the rule in alliteration, but that 3- is admitted, if it suits ; in l. 3154 that the scribe has mistaken an infinitive in ' -en ' for a pres. indic. pl. and has altered it to ' -es.' These points very strongly suggest a Nth. scribe and a Midl. poem ; The fem. pronoun in *h-* points unmistakably to W. Midl. and not to E. Midl. ; this agrees with the theory of the alteration of *blonke* to *blanke* in two instances ; the scribe, a Nth. man, has altered the dialect to Nth. almost completely, leaving, however, a number of Midl. forms and a few W. Midl. ones. The fact that O.E. hw alliterates with *qu* and with *w* indicates that the dialect is extreme N.W. Midl.

Wells dates the poem *c.* 1350-1400 and these limits are

---

[1] *The Dialect of Morte Arthure*, Rev. Eng. Stud., vol. 4, pp. 418-23.

sufficiently broad ; formerly the date was considered to be *c.* 1440, but judging from the metrical evidence we would suggest that this date is far too late ; the poem has also literary affinities with others of an early date.

The Gest Historiale of the Destruction of Troy, from a MS. dated *c.* 1450 in the Hunterian Museum in the University of Glasgow ; this lengthy work is edited by Donaldson and Pantin for the E.E.T.S., 39, 56 ; the date of the poem is usually considered to be *c.* 1350-1400 ; these limits are sufficiently broad, but there is little evidence to assist us in dating the poem other than general considerations of style and metre.   There are three points which can be proved by a study of the alliteration to have been original : Pt. 19. O.E. hw alliterates with O.E. cw : e.g. l. 2649, **wh**erfore alliterating with **wh**eme (O.E. hwǣr and gecwēme), or l. 3028, **qw**eme alliterating with **wh**ite (O.E. gecwēme and hwīt) ; many similar examples can easily be found in the poem. This point indicates the Nth. dialect as far south as the *Ribble-Aire* valleys.

Pt. 27. There is an example of *ho* for ' she ' in alliteration : l. 3089, " So he **h**edit þat **h**ynde,   and **h**o hym agayne." The other forms used, *scho, sho, she*, never occur in alliteration ; the poet's form was therefore the western form *ho*.

Pt. 29. The form for ' them ' is *hom* almost throughout the text, but there are a few þaim forms ; these are probably scribal because the form **h**om not infrequently occurs in alliteration : e.g. ll. 2774, 2769, 2594, 13255, etc. ; this means that the original form was either *hom* or *hem*, the latter not occurring in this text ; the form was obviously *hom*, since we know that *ho* was original, which is a western form.   Putting these three points together we are able to prove that the dialect was extreme N.W. Midl., farther north than that of *Sir Gawayn*, which alliterates O.E. hw and w ; the dialect is not Nth., but N. Midl. near the Ribble boundary.   We shall see later that many alliterative poems were written near this border.

Let us see whether the remaining evidence is in agreement ; the few þaim forms mentioned above need not necessarily be scribal in a border dialect ; *ho* for ' she,' we have seen, was the poet's own form, but other forms occur : *ho : sho : she* : : 8 : 3 : 3 ; *sho* might also have been used by the poet, but this is not likely, because *sho* only occurs as *scho* three times : ll. 12148, 12150, 12152 ; these three forms, occurring together, give rise to suspicion, and we need have little hesitation in saying that the poet used only the *ho* form. The forms for the gen. pl. pers. pronoun are *hor* and *þere* (*þaire*), the latter being the more common; neither form is found in alliteration, but since we know that the poet used *hom*, we may naturally assume that the poet used *hor* and not *þere*.

The confusion in the pronouns is very great as may be seen from the fact that *hor* and *þere* both occur in l. 9501; also *she* and *ho* in l. 12736; the form for the nom. pl. is of course *þai*.

The following points would be natural in Nth. and N. Midl. alike.: Pt. 44. Numerous contracted forms of 'take,' 'make.' Pt. 32. The loss of the final '-n' of the infinitive; Pt. 33. The loss of the '-i-' of the 2nd. cl. of O.E. wk. vbs.; Pt. 34. The loss of the verbal prefix; Pt. 40. The imperative sg. or pl., when not ending in '-e,' ends in '-es'; Pt. 42. The '-d' of the wk. pret. and past part. is often unvoiced to '-t'; Pt. 31. The complete absence of the '-liche' ending; Pt. 25. '-en' noun plurals are confined to such words as *children*, etc.; Pt. 15. O.E. ĕa + Cons. mutated is *e*.

All these points are found in common in the Nth. and N. Midl. dialects.

The following are Nth.: Pt. 10. There are occasional examples of *ai* for ā, and of *ei* for ę̄, but there are no examples of *oi* for ō. Pts. 38 and 39. The pres. indic. pl. normally ends in '-es,' '-ys,' except when immediately preceded or followed by a personal pronoun, in which case the ending is '-e'; but there are many forms in '-en'; these Midl. forms are very significant; similarly with regard to the pl. pres. indic. of the verb 'to be,' the usual form is *bese*, but there are rare examples of *bene*, whereas the form *are* is fairly common; now it is possible, but not probable, that in the border district the poet used mainly '-es'; rather it would appear that the same scribe who altered the pronouns, also altered the verbs in the direction of the Nth. dialect.

Then there are two distinctive Midl. features: Pt. 22. O.E. 'sc-' in unstressed positions never appears as 's-,' but only as '*sch-*'; and Pt. 9. O.E. ō remains throughout; remembering this, we would scarcely hesitate to say that the above Nth. forms are scribal.

Further scribal confusion is found with regard to the following points: Pt. 6. O.E. ā occur mostly as *o* but with rare *a*-forms as well, the latter being probably scribal. Pts. 7 and 8. O.E. āw, āg, āh appear as *aw*, *ow* quite indiscriminately in the same word, the former type being, however, more common.

Pt. 36. The pres. indic. sg. ends in ' -es,' ' -is ' with rare ' -eth ' forms, which are quite impossible in a N.W. Midl. text; they must be due to a S. Midl. scribe. Similarly, with regard to Pt. 41, the 2nd. pers. sg. wk. pret. ends either in ' -e ' or in ' -es,' but on very rare occasions in ' -est '; these must be likewise due to this S. Midl. scribe.

We have thus reached the position of having a N.W. Midl. poem copied by a Nth. scribe, and previously copied by a S. Midl. scribe.

There yet remain the usual tests for a western dialect. (1) We have already seen that the poet used the western pronouns *ho*, *hom* and probably *hor*. (2) Pt. 24. There are a few examples of the ending ' -us ' scattered throughout the whole of the poem, which may be western forms surviving from the original. (3) Pt. 1. O.E. ă + nasal is both *a* and *o* indiscriminately ; every word in which the sound is possible has both *a* and *o*-forms, except the word *blonke* which always appears with *o* in accordance with alliterative custom ; probably the original had *o* very much more consistently, being a western poem. (4) Pt. 5. O.E. ȳ usually appears as *i*, but mostly after labials appears as *ü* ; there has been some scribal alteration on this point, though to what extent it is impossible to say. (5) Pt. 14. O.E. ĕo appears as *e* except for occasional forms in *u* : *buerne*, l. 1177, etc., *stuerne*, l. 538, etc., *hur*, l. 716, etc., O.E. hĕore, and a few other rounded forms. (6) Pt. 2. O.E. ă + l + Cons. mutated is *a* in *aldeste*, ll. 2753, 11055, etc., beside *eldeste*, l. 394, etc., O.E. ĭeldest ; but *felle*, l. 6512, etc., O.E. fĭellan ; the first of these three forms, which is of frequent occurrence, is western. (7) Pt. 3. O.E. ' -and ' is ' -ond ' practically throughout ; this, we think, is due to the fact that in the west the ' -ond ' form extended right up to the Ribble, on account of the rounding before the nasal, whereas in the east the boundary was farther south. This accounts for the fact that the pres. part., which normally ends in ' -ande ' (very rarely in ' -yng '), often appears as ' -onde ' (' -ounde ') ; this is certainly due to the western rounding of ă before the nasal.

Pt. 17. M.E. ēȝ is not raised to īȝ in this work ; this

may be explained by the fact that the region near the Ribble does not show any raising in the place-name forms in the fourteenth century.

Lastly, Pt. ii. M.E. *ou* appears both as *ou* and *au* indiscriminately; thus *fawre*, l. 12317, O.E. fēower, *trauthe*, l. 1749, *trouthe*, l. 3802, O.E. trēowþ. See chapter i, Pt. ii, where it is shown that this peculiar change has yet been found only in Lancs and Kent. This is a very significant fact in a poem, which we can prove to have been written in the N.W. Midl. dialect.

The Destruction of Jerusalem, from various MSS. : Ashburnham 130, *c.* 1390-1400 ; Cotton Caligula A. ii., fifteenth century ; Cotton Vesp. E. xvi., fifteenth century ; Laud 656, fifteenth century ; Brit. Mus. Addit. 31042, *c.* 1450 ; Camb. Univ. Lib. Mm. V. 14, fifteenth century. Of these, the Laud MS. alone is complete and has been edited by G. Steffler, Marburg, 1891, but there are no notes or glossary. The E.E.T.S. have an edition of this poem at the press which will possibly make the study of the poem easier. The language is dialectally uniform, despite a few stray forms.

The Nth. dialect is definitely excluded by such points as : Pt. 6. O.E. ā as *o* throughout ; Pts. 7 and 8. O.E. āw, āg, āh as *ow, ou* ; Pt. 9. O.E. ō as *o* ; Pt. 19. O.E. hw as *wh* and alliterating with *w* : e.g. l. 346, " Eche **w**(h)iȝt in a **wh**ite scherte & no **w**ede ellys." Pt. 27. The form for 'she' is *ȝo*, ll. 99, 112—the only examples ; such a form is not Nth. Pts. 29 and 30. The forms for 'them,' 'their' are *hem, her.* Pt. 22. O.E. ' sc- ' in unstressed positions is never ' *s-*.' Pt. 31. The ' -ly ' ending is rare, the usual one being ' -lich(e).' Pt. 44. There are no contracted forms of 'take,' 'make.' Pt. 45. The forms *swilke, quilke* are not found. These points are sufficient to exclude the Nth. dialect.

On the other hand, the Sth. dialect is excluded by : Pt. 28. The form for 'they' is *þei* ; Pt. 33. The ' -i- ' of the 2nd. cl. of O.E. wk. vbs. is not retained ; Pt. 38. The pres. indic. pl. normally ends in ' -en ' ; many other points corroborate the statement that the dialect is non-Sth.

The S. Midl. dialect is indicated by the following points : Pt. 32. The infinitive often ends in ' -en ' ; ' -en ' : ' -e ' : : i : 3. Pt. 34. The verbal prefix is occasionally retained, though not frequently. Pt. 40. The imperative pl. oc-

casionally ends in ' -eþ,' ' -yþ,' the S. Midl. and Sth. form.
Pt. 38. The pres. indic. pl. normally ending in ' -en,' ' -yn,'
has 8 exceptions in ' -eþ '; unless these are scribal, they also
point to a S. Midl. dialect. Pt. 36. The pres. indic. sg.
2nd. and 3rd. pers. ends in ' -est ' and ' eth ' 63 times, and
in ' -es ' 9 times; the latter may be scribal. Pt. 39. The
pres. indic. pl. of the verb ' to be ' is *ben* with one exception
in *beþ*, l. 363, which may be scribal. Pt. 44. No contracted
forms of ' take,' ' make.' All these points are an indication of
a S. Midl. dialect, with either a N. Midl. or Sth. scribe; if
the 9 examples of the pres. indic. sg. are genuine, then the
' -eþ ' forms of the pres. indic. pl. are scribal, and vice versa.
Pt. 35. The pres. part. ends in ' -ande ' as a rule, but there
are 7 exceptions in ' -yng '; also one example in ' -inde ':
walynde, l. 463, a Sth. form, which is probably scribal. Pt. 15.
O.E. ĕa + Cons. mutated is *e* with one exception in *u* : *hure*,
l. 1093, O.E. hīeran; this may be by the same Sth. scribe.
Pt. 42. The final ' -d ' of the wk. pret. and past part. is
unvoiced to ' -t ' on 6 occasions only; these would not be
unnatural as far south as the *Salop-Wash* line where the
9 examples of the pres. indic. sg. in ' -es ' were written; if
these two features were original, then the dialect was a border
one near the above boundary and the scribe was responsible
for the isolated Sth. features.

There are certain western points :—
Pt. 5. O.E. ў̆ appears usually as *ü*, but also as *i* ; the
ü-development is found after *b*, *f*, *l*, and the *i*-development
after *k*, *g*, *s*, *d*, *m*, *þ* : *burde*, *brused*, *fur*, *luþer*, *kynde*, *synful*,
girdell, *dyntes*, etc. ; we should expect to find this in a western
text of the fourteenth century.

Pt. 1. O.E. ă̆ + nasal is *a* except before *nk*, when it appears as *o*. The alliterative word *blonke* naturally has *o*
throughout, O.E. blănca ; O.N. bănki appears as *bonke* with
one exception, *banke*, l. 71 ; *bonked*, l. 661, formed from the
same O.N. word ; finally, *donked* from O.N. dǫkk, Swedish
dialectal *dänka ;* elsewhere the text has *a*.

We have strong suspicions of scribal interference, but
western forms are certainly found in the text, and the
development is similar to that in the works of Myrc and
Audelay. Pt. 2. O.E. ă̆ + l + Cons. mutated, is both *e*
and *a*, but there is naturally little evidence available ; *fellen*,
l. 1109, O.E. fīellan, *eldres*, l. 106, O.E. ĭeldren, *walynde*, l. 463,

O.E. wĭellan, *walwyþ*, l. 732, O.E. wĭelwan or possibly wĕalwan; also *waltreþ*, l. 732, from a form *wieltran* or *wealtran ;* the Mn. E. *welter* would favour the former derivation. The development may be western. Pt. 24. There are no examples of '-us,' '-ud' for '-es,' '-ed.'

Pt. 14. O.E. ĕo as *e* except in two words : *burne(s)*, ll. 269, 367, etc., and there are only 4 examples with *e* (*berne*, l. 73, etc.) ; *sulf*, ll. 2, 149, etc., O.E. sĕolf, but *self*, l. 1044. These are genuine western forms, but it is probable that the scribe has interfered with the original forms.

There are only two points remaining : Pt. 3. O.E. '-and' appears as '-*ond*' 24 times, and as '-*and*' 6 times ; this is natural in W. Midl. Pt. 17. M.E. *ē3* is not raised to *ī3*; if the poem were written in the west and near the *Salop-Wash* line, Staffs would be ruled out by this last point, and one would rather suggest Salop, where the raising definitely did not take place.

There has undoubtedly been some scribal alteration ; the text as it stands is C.W. Midl. near the border between N. Midl. and S. Midl. ; we have no reason to suspect that there has been a radical alteration of the original dialect and the isolated stray forms make it appear that a Sth. scribe inserted them ; they were : 1 *hure* form, 1 pres. part. in '-*ynde*,' 1 *beþ* form ; and 8 examples of the pres. indic. pl. in '-eth.' The remaining forms are consistent and were found in Salop ; indeed the dialect very closely resembles that of Myrc and Audelay. The above Sth. forms could not have been used by a writer who also used the pres. part. ending '-*ande*.'

The dialect was that of C.W. Midl., for all points are found there, even *hem* and *her* as well as *hom* and *hor*.

When the new edition is published with the other MS. readings, it will probably be possible to locate the poem more accurately. The date is about 1370-90, the latter limit being fixed by the date of the Ashburnham MS.

Sir Gawayn and the Green Knight, Pearl, Patience and **Purity,** from the MS. Cotton Nero A. X. These four poems are usually attributed to the same author for many reasons. The first two poems contain rhymes, thus giving a valuable clue to the poet's dialect, and we hope to adduce evidence to show that these two poems were originally written in exactly the same dialect. The other line of argument is usually concerned with the vocabulary, style, phraseology and parallel passages found in all four poems. The best and most recent exposition of the theory of common authorship is that by Menner in the Introduction to his edition of *Purity*[1] (*Cleanness*). We feel, however, that a still surer test is the metrical one, which is sketched in Appendix I, for common phraseology may be due to imitation of one poet by another.

We therefore include *Pearl* in this chapter, though its proper place would be in chapter 6. The editions used are as follows : *Pearl*, Gollancz, Mediæval Library, 1921 ; *Patience*, Bateson, 2nd. edition, 1915 ; *Sir Gawayn and the Green Knight*, Tolkien and Gordon, 1925 ; *Purity*, Menner, 1920. We venture to use the title *Purity* in this book, partly because of the use of Menner's edition, but also because we consider the title is more applicable to the poem than *Cleanness*.

We have carefully noted all differences in the language of the four poems, but will reserve discussion of these until the examination of the four has been made together.

The Language.—Pt. 1. O.E. ă + nasal (*an, ank*) is *a* and *o* in all poems ; *Pat.* has *o* in 9 different words and a total of 19 occurrences : *a* in 6 words and 8 occurrences ; *Pur.* has *o* in 13 words and 71 occurrences : *a* in 9 words and 24 occurrences ; *Prl.* has *o* in 7 words and 68 occurrences : *a* in 7 words and 17 occurrences ; *Gaw.* has *o* in 9 words and 115 occurrences, but *a* in 5 words and 8 occurrences only [*can* (2), *ran, bygan, schankeȝ, answare* (3)]. Thus the treatment in the first three poems is the same, and the two developments are usually found in the same word ; *Gaw.* has more occurrences of *o*, but this might be quite accidental. A rhyme is found in *Prl.* to prove that the rounding is due to the poet : *wlonk*, l. 903, O.E. wlănc, rhyming with *amonc*, O.E. onmăng > *among* in M.E.

In addition, O.E. ă before a nasal in open syllables sometimes appears as $\bar{\varrho}$ beside $\bar{a}$: e.g. *wane*, *Gaw.* 493, O.E. wăna ; *nome*, O.E. năma, occurs in *Prl.* 872 and in *Gaw.* 5 times, beside *name* twice. So *schomely*, *Pat.* 128, *schome*, *Gaw.* 2372, beside *schame*, ll. 317, 2504, O.E. scămu ; *tone* (taken), *Gaw.* 2159, rhyming with *grone*, O.E. grănian ; *tane* (*Gaw.* 1396), etc. Having examined all these forms in *Gaw.* and the other poems, we feel convinced that the rounding was just as frequent in that poem as in the other three.

---

[1] p. xiii et seq.

Pt. 2. O.E. ă + l + Cons. mutated is normally *a* except in the common word *welle*, in which we expect *e*. *aldest*, O.E. ïeldest, *Prl.* 1042, *Pur.* 1333 ; *alder*, O.E. ïeldra, *Prl.* 621, *Gaw.* 948, 972, 1317 ; *malte*, O.E. mïeltan, *Prl.* 224, *Pur.* 776, 1566 (cp. *malt*, pret. of *mĕltan*, *Prl.* 1154) ; *welle*, *Prl.* 365, 649, *Pur.* 439 ; *welle-hedes*, *Pur.* 428, but *walle-heued*, 364 ; this latter form is a very valuable testimony to the western development ; *bale*, *Gaw.* 1333, O.E. bïelg ; *elde*, O.E. ïeldu, *Gaw.* 844, 1520, *Pat.* 125. There are in addition a few doubtful forms : *wallande*, *Prl.* 365, *Gaw.* 1762, O.E. wïellan or wĕallan ; *overwalt*, *Gaw.* 314, O.E. -wieltan (?) ; *walt*, *Gaw.* 1336, *Pur.* 364, 501, 1037 ; *walter*, *Gaw.* 684, *Pat.* 142, *Pur.* 414, 1027 ; *walterande*, *Pat.* 247. It is most significant that Mn.E. has "welter" ; the development in the four poems is certainly western ; there are no rhymes to attest the poet's form, but since he has other western features in rhyme we may conclude that this was also original.

Pt. 3. O.E. '-ănd ' as '-*and* ' and '-*ond*.' *Pat.* has *a* in 3 words and 3 occurrences : *o* in 7 words and 8 occurrences ; *Pur.* has *a* in 5 words and 11 occurrences : *o* in 12 words and 32 occurrences ; *Prl.* has *a* in 5 words and 9 occurrences : *o* in 5 words and 9 occurrences ; *Gaw.* has *a* in 3 words and 4 occurrences : *o* in 10 words and 55 occurrences. There are no differences in the statistics which are not purely accidental. Both forms are proved original by rhymes : *londe*, *Prl.* 148, rhyming with *byʒonde*, O.E. begĕondan ; *hande*, *Gaw.* 1203, rhyming with a pres. part. *laʒande ;* or *stande*, *Prl.* 867, rhyming with *farande ;* the pres. part. hardly ever ends in '-*onde* ' in M.E.

Pt. 4. M.E. '-*ong* ' is retracted to '-*ung* ' as is seen by the following rhyme : *stronge*, *Gaw.* 34, O.E. străng, strŏng, rhyming with *tonge*, O.E. tŭnga.

Pt. 5. O.E. ȳ as *i*, *ü*, *e*. Scholars such as Wyld, Hulbert and Osgood have not realised how many *ü*-forms there are in the poems ; space forbids the giving of references, but the following statistics have been very carefully worked out : *Pat.*, *i* in 37 words and 47 occurrences : *ü* in 20 words and 35 occurrences ; *e* in 5 words and 5 occurrences ; *Pur.*, *i* in 64 words and 211 occurrences : *ü* in 32 words and 142 occurrences : *e* in 8 words and 12 occurrences ; *Gaw.* has *i* in 77 words and 265 occurrences : *ü* in 35 words and 116 occurrences : *e* in 5 words and 18 occurrences ; *Prl.* has *i* in 51 words and

128 occurrences: *ü* in 16 words and 54 occurrences: *e* in 2 words and 3 occurrences.

The *e* forms are, of course, not "Kenticisms" in this dialect, but are due to the lowering of M.E. *ĭ* to *ĕ*, which is not seldom found in this MS., e.g. *swefte*, *Prl.* 354, *Pat.* 108, O.E. swĭfte, *schemered*, *Gaw.* 772, O.E. scĭmerian, and many other examples in all four poems; similarly we have found 13 examples of the raising of M.E. *ĕ* to *i* in this MS. Neither change is dialectal, so far as we can judge from place-name evidence collected.

Taking the poems together, *i*-forms occur in 111 different words and *ü* in 65 different words, a proportion of *ü*-forms far greater than Wyld asserted; the reader will observe a decrease of *ü*-forms in *Prl.* and *Gaw.*, especially when the calculation is made on the occurrences. The explanation of this may be the increased spreading of the standard forms, either as the scribe continued his copying, or more probably in the dialect of the author himself; this would agree with the plausible theory that the homilies preceded the rhymed poems in order of composition. After careful examination of the *ü*-forms occurring in the four poems, we observed that the forms do not occur haphazard, but that the *ü* development is found after *r*, *m*, *n*, *l* almost without exception. In *Prl.* and *Gaw.*, *m*, *b*, *f* are much less resistant than in the homilies; the unrounding process had progressed further. To argue from proportions without taking these things into account is foolish. The *i* development is attested by rhymes: *wynne*, *Gaw.* 15, 1765, O.E. wўnn, rhyming with *perinne*, O.E. þǣrĭnne; *hille*, O.E. hўll, *Prl.* 678, rhyming with *tylle*, O.N. tĭl. There are no examples of the *ü* development in rhymes because of the difficulty of finding suitable rhyming words. The development in the poet's dialect was western of a late period.

Pt. 6. O.E. ā appears as *o* with few exceptions; this naturally excludes shortening; in *Pat.* there are no *a*-forms; in *Pur.* there are three possible *a*-forms: *wlate* (2), O.E. wlātian (this word is very rare in M.E., and its form in other dialects is not ascertainable), *wham*, l. 259, may have a long vowel, as the usual M.E. form is *whōm*, but on the other hand the vowel may be short. In addition, there are three very doubtful forms from O.N. ā: *are* (2) adv., O.N. ār, though it may be a shortened form of O.E. ǣr; *braþ*, l. 916, O.N.

bráþr, beside broþe (2), broþely (3) ; the vowel in braþ may be short.

Gaw. has *ā* in 4 words and 8 occurrences : *hame*, l. 1534, O.E. hām, is purposely used to provide a rhyme with *schame*, O.E. scămu ; so *hame*, l. 2451, to rhyme with *name*, O.E. năma ; *bade*, l. 1699 (not for rhyme), O.E. bād, preterite of bīdan, but elsewhere the form *bode* is used ; *laþe*, l. 2507 (not for rhyme), O.E. lāþ ; *þare*, O.E. þāra, l. 463, to rhyme with *bare*, O.E. bær ; also at l. 1889, rhyming with *are*, O.E. ǣr ; also at l. 2173 and l. 2508 for no apparent reason ; O.N. ā appears as *a* in *waþe*, l. 2355, O.N. vāði, to rhyme with *ta* *þe* (O.N. tăka) ; also *braþ*, l. 1909 (see above) ; and *are* (3) ; the *a*-forms in *Gaw.* are partly a concession to the needs of rhyme, as in Myrc, Audelay and Mannyng.

Prl. has *a* in 8 words and 10 occurrences : see the rhymes in lines 138, 145, 151, 388, 502, 617, 830, 1021, 1027 ; all these contain examples of O.E. ā retained for the purposes of rhyme ; *wham*, l. 131, is the same peculiar form found in *Pur.* From O.N. ā, there is *brathe*, *braþes* (for which see above), and *are-þede*, O.N. ār or O.E. ǣr.

The poet's usual form was, of course, *o* : e.g. *more*, *Prl.*, l. 180, O.E. māra, rhyming with *yuore*, O.Fr. ivorie, or *Gaw.* 2281, rhyming with *restore*, O.Fr. restorer. *Gaw.*, l. 967, *brode*, O.E. brād, rhyming with *Gode*, O.E. gŏd. The poet evidently lived in the N. Midl. area, and hence allowed himself the liberty of using the Nth. development to meet the exigencies of rhyme.[1]

Pts. 7 and 8. O.E. āw, āg, āh. The development is both *aw* and *ow*, and there is good reason to suspect scribal interference ; little importance can, therefore, be attached to the proportions of forms occurring. *Pat.* has 2 *aw* and 8 *ow*, *o3*, etc. ; *Pur.* 25 *aw* and 17 *ow* ; *Prl.* 15 *aw* and 14 *ow* ; *Gaw.* 31 *aw* and 24 *ow* forms. This excludes the forms *nau3t*, *nou3t*, *nawther*, *nouther*, etc., from variant forms in O.E., such as *nāht*, *nōht*, etc.

Two rhymes will prove that the poet used *aw* as the development of O.E. āw, āg, āh : *knowe*, *Gaw.* 1647, O.E. cnāwan, rhyming with *lawe*, O.E. lăgu from O.N., and with

---

[1] Anglian -*āld* normally appears as -*old*, but often as -*ald* in what must have been a truly fossilised form *halde* ; in this word *Pat.* has *a* 5 and *o* 2 ; *Pur.* has *a* 13 and *o* 2 ; *Gaw.* *a* 18 and *o* 14 ; *Prl.* *a* 4 and *o* 1. In addition *Gaw.* has *bald(e)ly* twice, O.E. bĕaldlice, băldlice.

drowe, O.E. drăgan, which must be emended to *drawe*, just as *knowe* must be emended to *knawe*. *Prl.* 461, *sawle*, O.E. sāwol, rhyming with *gawle*, O.E. găgl, and with *nawle*, O.E. năfela. Elsewhere O.E. āw rhymes with itself. The poet obviously lived in the area where O.E. āw remained.

Pt. 11 is best treated at this stage ; M.E. *ou* becomes *au* : *Gaw.*, 2238, *trawe*, MS. *trowe*, O.E. trēowian, rhyming with *snawe*, O.E. snāw. Since we know that the poet wrote *snawe*, we know that he must also have written *trawe ;* this was natural, since the scribe altered *aw* from O.E. āw to *ow ;* again the proportions of forms are useless, but both spellings are well-represented : *Gaw.* 373, *trow ; Gaw.* 626, *trawþe ; Gaw.* 1564, *bawemen*, O.E. bŏgamann ; *Prl.* 282, *trawe ; Prl.* 933, *trowe ; Pur.* 950, *fawre*, O.E. fēower ; *Pur.* 360, *stawed*, beside *stowed*, l. 113, O.E. stōwigian ; *flawen*, *Pat.* 214, O.E. flōwen ; *baweline*, *Pur.* 68, 417, *Pat.* 104, O.N. bōgalina.

Pt. 9. O.E. ō does not become *u* ; there is one rhyme to prove this : *wolde*, *Gaw.* 2478, O.E. wǫlde, rhyming with *cǫlde*, O. Anglian cāld. This imperfect rhyme affords conclusive proof that the development was ǫ.

Pt. 10. *ai*, *ei*, *oi* are not used to express M.E. ā, ē, ō.

Pt. 12. O.E. ǣ¹ is tense *ę* as the rhymes indicate : *Gaw.* 320, *were*, O.E. wǣron, rhyming with *lere*, O.E. hlēor ; or *Prl.* 739, *were* rhyming with *dere*, O.E. dēore, etc.

Pt. 13. O.E. ǣ² is tense *ę* before *d*, *t*, *s*, *n*, *l*, *r ; Gaw.* 146, *clene*, O.E. clǣne, rhyming with *grene*, O.E. grēne ; or *Prl.* 409, *lede*, lǣdan, rhyming with *schede*, O. Anglian scēdan.

Pt. 14. O.E. ĕo is normally *e* ; *dere*, *Prl.* 733, O.E. dēore, rhyming with *clere*, O.Fr. cler ; but there are scattered examples of rounded forms ; O.E. ĕo + r + Cons. is usually *u* ; *Pat.* has 3 *u*-forms, *Pur.* 34 *u*-forms, *Prl.* 9 *u*-forms and *Gaw.* 37 *u*-forms ; (*rurd, burne, brurd, urþe, nurne* (?)). Both *e* and *u*-forms occur in the word *erthe*, *urthe*, O.E. ĕorðe. Only *e*-forms are found in such words as *herte, fer, lerne, kerve*, etc. The occurrence of the rounded forms is, therefore, in accordance with the general rules given in chapter 1, Pt. 14.

Similarly with regard to O.E. ēo, the rounded forms are confined to words in which the vowel is, as a general rule, preceded by *l* or *r* : *Pur.* has *ludisch* and *ludych* beside one *ledisch* form (O.E. lēod = people), while O.E. lēod = man gives *lede* throughout, as is the case in *Pat.* *Prl.* has *lede* throughout, but *drury*, l. 323, O.E. drēorig, and *furþe*, l. 1005, etc., O.E. fēorþa. *Gaw.* has *leude,* l. 1124, rhyming with ȝede, O.E. ge-ēode ; *lede* (2), " people." *Gaw.* has also *leudleȝ, leude, lude* beside *lede* for O.E. lēod = man.

The above rhyme surely indicates that these *leude*-forms are scribal ; it does not necessarily mean that the examples of rounded forms of O.E. ĕo + r are scribal, for this is phonologically different. The latter examples are very probably original.

Pt. 15. O.E. ĕa + Cons. mutated is *e* ; the only apparent exception is in the word *firre, Gaw.* 411, 1304, etc., *Prl.* 103, etc., *Pat.* 116, etc., *Pur.* 131, etc. ; *ferre* forms are also found, O.E. fïerra ; it is just possible that the *firre* forms are scribal, but more probable that they are due to some phonological variant.

Pt. 16. O.E. ēa shortened is ă ; e.g. *grattest, Pur.* 1645, *Gaw.* 1326, etc., O.E. grēat- ; *rafte, Pur.* 1142, etc., O.E. rēafian, etc.

Pt. 17. M.E. *ēȝ* is raised to *īȝ* as seen by the rhymes : *Gaw.* 2087, *hyȝe,* O.E. hēah, rhyming with *by,* O.E. bī ; or *yȝe,* l. 228, O.E. ēage, rhyming with *studie,* O.Fr. studier. In the four poems the *eȝ* spellings are only half as numerous as the *iȝ* ones, but this is unimportant, because the former ones are either scribal or due to the fact that the change is often not recognised in spelling.

Pt. 18. O.E. ǣ is naturally *a* in these poems, except in a few cases which admit of other explanations ; these are words such as *when, then,* etc., and *festen* due to O.N. festa, etc. ; see Knigge under ǣ.

Pt. 19. O.E. hw appears as *wh, w, qu ; Pat.* has 48 *wh,* 1 *w,* 5 *qu* spellings ; *Pur.* 97 *wh,* 5 *w,* 14 *qu* spellings ; *Gaw.* 82 *wh,* 3 *w,* 82 *qu* spellings ; *Prl.* 44 *wh,* 4 *w,* 36 *qu* spellings. It will be noticed that the homilies contain less *qu*-forms than do the other two poems ; the alliteration shows that the *qu* spellings are scribal, for *hw* alliterates with *w,* not with *qu* from O.E. cw., as in *The Destruction of Troy.*

> *Pur.* 1120, " þat **w**ynnes **w**orship   abof alle **wh**yte stones."
>
> *Pat.* 246, " a **w**ylde **w**alterande **wh**ale,   as **w**yrd þen schaped."
>
> *Gaw.* 1573, " **wh**ettes his **wh**yte tusches ;   **w**ith hym þen irked."
>
> *Prl.* 15, " þat **w**ont watȝ **wh**yle de**u**oyde my **wr**ange."

The scribal *qu* spellings often obscure the alliteration with *w* : e.g., *Prl.* 1102, " Depaynt in perles and **w**ede3 **qw**yte." *Gaw.*, 225, " and **qu**at-so þy **w**ylle is,   **w**e schal **w**yt after." See also lines 257, 1186, 1227.

Pt. 20. O.E. cw, O.Fr. qu appear as *wh* 3 times, but these forms are scribal, obscuring the alliteration : *Gaw.* 877, " **wh**yssynes vpon **qu**eldepoyntes   þat **k**oynt were boþe." l. 2494, " þe **k**yng **k**ysses þe **k**ny3t,   and þe **wh**ene alce." l. 74, *whene*, O.E. cwēn, not in alliteration. In the dialect of the scribe who was responsible for these three forms, O.E. hw and cw had become identical in sound ; this was not so in the poet's dialect.

Pt. 21. There is no initial voicing of *f, s*.

Pt. 22. O.E. ' sc-' in unstressed positions never appears as ' *s*-'

Pt. 23. The spelling of the spirant is of little interest owing to the possibility of scribal alteration ; '-3t ' is the usual form, only one '-ght ' spelling being found : *laght, Gaw.* 127, but there are 52 examples of '-gh ' in such forms as *burghe, Prl.* 980, etc.

Pt. 24. The ending '-ud ' is not found, but '-us ' is found 8 times : *Pur.* 31, *flemus ; Pur.* 1579, *exorsismus ; Gaw.* 2522, *Arthurus ; Gaw.* 456, *behoueus ; Gaw.* 93, 95, 491, *Pur.* 456, *auenturus ;* there are no examples in *Pat.* or *Prl.*   It is impossible to say whether these are scribal.

Pt. 25. '-en ' noun plurals, excluding the non-dialectal *y3en*, are rare ; there are only three, and they occur in *Pur.:* l. 127, *poueren*, an adj. used as a plural noun ; l. 1402, *sturnen*, a real adj. qualifying *trumpen*, itself showing an analogical '-en.' " stu**rn**en trumpen strake   steuen in halle—aywhere by þe wowes   wrasten krakkes." The obvious explanation is that the scribe's eye caught the other two '-*en* 's ; hence he accidentally added '-en ' to the noun and adj., and judging from the example in l. 127, where an infinitive *chaufen* occurs in the next line, the same theory would hold for the other '-en ' plural.

Pt. 26. There are no *thire* forms.

Pt. 27. The form for ' she ' is *ho* with six exceptions of *scho : Prl.* 758, *Gaw.* 969, 1259, 1550, 1555, 1556 ; the last three examples occurring so close together suggest scribal inter- ference.

Pt. 28. The form for ' they ' is *þay* : e.g. *Gaw.* 1450,

where it rhymes with *baye*, O.Fr. abai.   There are two exceptions in *Pur.*, 62, 657, with *he*-forms which look as if they were scribal.

Pt. 29. The form for ' them ' is normally *hem ;* there are a few exceptions in *hom*, none occurring in *Pat.* or *Prl.*, and one very doubtful example in *Pur.*, 1715 ; in *Gaw.* the form occurs 8 times, l. 99, etc. These forms may be dialectal.

Pt. 30. The usual form for ' their ' is *her ;* but *þayr* occurs *Gaw.* 1359 and 1362 ; *þayres*, *Gaw.* 1019, rhyming with *repayres*, and also in *Pur.* 1527 ; these isolated forms with ' þ-' were therefore original.   In addition, *hores* occurs in *Pat.* 14, 28 only, and *hor* occurs in *Pur.* 1524, and in *Gaw.* 18 times, but not in *Prl.*

That the ' *h-*' forms were original can be proved by the fact that they occur in alliteration : *Pat.* 14, " For **h**ores is þe **h**euen-ryche   to **h**olde for euer " ; this does not prove the originality of the form *hores*, but of the ' *h-*' alone.

Pt. 31. The usual ending is '-ly,' but '-lych ' occurs in a few adjectives, though not in adverbs, *Gaw.* having 29 examples, *Pur.* 20 examples, *Pat.* 7 examples, but *Prl.* none. Whether these examples were in the original, we cannot say.

Pt. 32.   The infinitive ends in '-en ' only 24 times, and of these, 13 are used to avoid hiatus before *h* or a vowel, 6 to provide rhymes, and 5 for the rhythm at the end of the line : e.g. *Pat.* 3, *aswagen hem ; Pur.* 128, *chaufen her ; Gaw.* 1254, *colen her ; Prl.* 1032, *meten hit ; Prl.* 68 and 69, *dyscreuen, leuen*, to rhyme with *sweuen*, O.E. swefn.   See also *Prl.*, lines 45, 820, 914, 1196, for similar instances ; examples of the '-en ' retained for the rhythm are all to be found in *Gaw.* : e.g. *lyþen þe*, l. 1719.

The retention of the '-en ' was a concession only, but indicates N. Midl., as in Nth. the '-en ' was lost ; e.g. *Gaw.* 367, *roun*, rhyming with *croun*, sb. ; or *Prl.* 88, *forȝete*, rhyming with *grete*, pl. adj.

Pt. 33. The '-i-' of the 2nd. cl. of O.E. wk. vbs. is retained 37 times, of which 4 are infinitive forms : *Prl.* 284, *wony*, O.E. ŵunian ; *Pat.* 462, *wony ; Pur.* 1066, *louy*, O.E. lufian ; *Pur.* 1720, *styry*, O.E. styrian.   In *Pat.* there are 3 examples, in *Prl.* 5, in *Gaw.* 9, and in *Pur.* 20 ; but the examples are mostly confined to the words *wony, louy, livy*, etc.

A few analogical forms are found in Fr. words : e.g.

enfaminied, Pur. 1194; *stonyed, Gaw.* 1291. It is difficult to say whether these forms are scribal or not, but it will be remembered from the statistics in chapter 1 that N. Midl. did occasionally retain the '-i-' in these fossilised words.

Pt. 34. The 'i-' verbal prefix is only retained twice: *Prl.* 904, *ichose*, a past part., and *Pur.* 1693, *ibrad*, a pret. form.

Pt. 35. The pres. part. normally ends in '*-ande*': e.g. *Prl.* 1207, *laʒande*, rhyming with *hande;* the same rhyme occurs in *Gaw.* 1207. There are in addition 5 examples of the termination '*-yng*': *Prl.* 1175, *sykyng* (see Gollancz's interesting note on the early confusion of the two forms in this verb); *Gaw.* 611, *pernyng*, l. 753, *sykyng*, l. 1334, *forlancyng*, l. 2126, *gruchyng;* these 5 forms are probably not scribal, and at any rate would not be dialectally impossible in this area.

Pt. 36. The pres. indic. sg. 2nd. and 3rd. pers. ends in '-es,' '-eʒ': e.g. *Prl.* 125, *hales*, rhyming with *bales*, sb. pl.; *Gaw.* 2327, *falles*, rhyming with *halles*, sb. pl.

The 1st. pers. sg. usually ended in '-e,' proved by *sitte*, *Gaw.* 1531, rhyming with *witte*, sb.; but the poet also knew the Nth. '-es' ending, which he used as a concession to rhyme in *Prl.* 568, *byswykes*, rhyming with *mykes*, sb. pl.

' *wons*,' *Pur.* l. 326, is probably a scribal error for *wones*, *wonis*. The above '-es' ending occurs as '-us' twice and '-is,' '-ys' three times.

Pt. 37. There are no syncopated forms in the pres. indic. sg.

Pt. 38. The pres. indic. pl., except when immediately preceded or followed by a personal pronoun, normally ends in '-en,' '-yn'; but the '-es,' '-eʒ' ending is found: *Prl.* has '-en' 42 times, '-es' 10 times, '-e' 12 times; *Gaw.* '-en' 61 times, '-es' 11 times, '-e' 27 times; *Pur.* '-en' 41 times, '-es' 14 times, '-e' 13 times; *Pat.* '-en' 22 times, '-es' 8 times, '-e' 6 times. Both the '-en' and '-es' endings were original: *Prl.* 64, *meuen*, rhyming with *sweuen*, O.E. swefn; *Prl.* 573, *pykes*, rhyming with *mykes*, sb. pl.; *Gaw.* 1351, *hyʒes*, rhyming with *þyʒes*, sb. pl.

The poet must have lived in a border-dialectal area, but so far as we can judge, neither form was used purely as a concession to rhyme.

Pr. 39. The pres. pl. of the verb 'to be' is *ar(e)*, *arn*, *ben;* *ar* is found for all three persons, as are the other two forms. *Prl.* uses *bene*, l. 785, for a rhyme with *quene*, etc.

6

Pt. 40. The imperative sg., except when without ending or simply with '-e,' ends in '-es': *Prl.* 1 example, *Pur.* 1 example, *Pat.* 0 examples, *Gaw.* 3 examples, including *slokes*, l. 412, rhyming with *cnokes*, 2nd. pers. sg. pres. indic.; the ending was therefore original. There are more examples in the plural: *Prl.* 4 examples, *Pat.* 5 examples, *Pur.* 29 examples, *Gaw.* 9 examples. There are no examples of the plural in rhyme, but the example for the singular in rhyme given above is sufficient to prove the originality of the form.

Pt. 41. The 2nd. pers. wk. pret. sg. ends in '-es': e.g. *lantes*, *Pur.* 348; *diptes*, *Pat.* 308; *trauayledes*, *Pat.* 498. There is one exception in '-est': *myntest*, *Gaw.* 2274, which may be scribal.

Pt. 42. Probably the final unvoicing of consonants in this MS. was originally universal and was not confined to verbs of the weak class. *Prl.* 700, *justyfyet*, rhyming with *hyt;* l. 905, *amonc*, O.E. onmang, rhyming with þonc, O.E. þancian; l. 170, *fonte*, O.E. fundian, rhyming with *frount*, sb.; see also l. 1163, *bycalt*, l. 591, *rert*, both in rhyme; *dresset*, *Pur.* 1477; *naylet*, *Gaw.* 599; *lont*, *Pat.* 322, etc.; as a result we find such spellings as *captyuide*, *Pur.* 1612; *coumforde*, *Prl.* 369, etc.

Pt. 42. The loss of the '-d' of the wk. pret. and past part. Miss Day, Mod. Lang. Rev., xiv., pages 413-15, found 30 examples of this omission of the '-d,' of which 21 occur before a vowel or an unstressed *h*, or voiced *th*, the stems of the verbs in question ending in *l, n, r;* e.g. *Gaw.* 1928, " he *were* a bleaunt of blwe "; there is one example in *Prl.* in a rhyme: *outfleme*, l. 1177, rhyming with *queme*, adj.; in this case and in others, the editors tend to add the '-d,' which is needless and incorrect.

Pt. 44. Contracted forms of 'take,' 'make' are common: *Gaw.* 2357, *ta þe* ("take thee"), rhyming with *waþe*, O.N. vāði; l. 2159, *tone* (taken), rhyming with *onĕ*, O.E. ān; *boȝ*, *Pur.* 687; *bos*, *Prl.* 323; *byhode*, *Gaw.* 717; *Prl.* 928; O.E. behofian. Such contracted forms occur in the same dialectal region as the former ones.

Pt. 45. There are no traces of such forms as *quilke*, *swilke*, etc.

The Dialect.—With the following exceptions, all the dialectal points have been proved to be original by the study of rhyme and alliteration: Pt. 1. O.E. ă + nasal as *a* is not found in rhymes, but *o* is found; both forms are probably original. Pt. 2. O.E. ă + 1 + Cons. mutated as *a*. Pt. 14.

O.E. ĕo + r + Cons. as *u*, and Pt. 16. O.E. ēa as *a* when shortened. Pts. 21, 22, 23, 24, 25, 27, 29, 31, 33, 34, 39, 41, 45, being quite simple, need not be recorded.

Let us therefore approach the dialectal question, neglecting these uncertain points.

(1) A place south of the *Ribble-Aire* line is required by the following: Pt. 6. O.E. ā as *o*; Pt. 9. O.E. ō as *o*; Pt. 1. O.E. ă + nasal as *o*; Pt. 19. O.E. hw alliterating with *w*; Pt. 30. The form for 'their' beginning with '*h-*'; Pt. 38. The pres. indic. pl. normally in '-en,' and by many of the other points also.

(2) A place north of the *Salop-Wash* line is required by the following: Pt. 4. M.E. '-ong' retracted to '*-ung*'; Pts. 7, 8. O.E. āw, āg, āh as *aw*, not as *ow*; Pt. 13. O.E. ǣ[1] as tense *e*; Pt. 35. The pres. part. in '*-ande*'; Pt. 36. The pres. indic. sg. in '-es'; Pt. 40. The imperative in '-es'; Pt. 42. The final unvoicing of consonants; Pt. 43. The occasional loss of '-d' of the wk. pret. and past part.; Pt. 44. Many contracted verbal forms.

The reader will see that all the proved points are found between the *Ribble-Aire* and *Salop-Wash* lines.

(3) The W. Midl. dialect is indicated by Pt. 1. O.E. ă + nasal as *o*; Pt. 5. O.E. ў as *i*, *ü*.

The other western points cannot be proved original by rhymes, but there is no reason to suspect Pt. 2. O.E. ă + l + Cons. as *a* (in view of Pts. 1, 5), or Pt. 27. The use of *ho*, since it occurs practically throughout.

(4) How can we further subdivide this western area ?

Pts. 7, 8. O.E. āw, āg, āh as *aw* point to an area not below S. Ches. Pt. 38. The pres. indic. pl. ends in '-en' and in '-es'; since the poet used both forms, he probably lived near the border-line, where both were current. In chapter I, Pt. 38, the boundaries of these were worked out; as the Sth. limit of the '-es' form passes through S. Ches., and the Nth. limit of the '-en' form is the Ribble valley, these four poems must fall between the two lines.

Pt. 1. O.E. ā as *a* when required by rhyme, is found in Myrc and Audelay and hence is natural in this area. . The same applies to the rare retention of the '-n' of the infinitive.

Pt. 36. An example in rhyme of the pres. indic. sg. in '-es' suggests a region very near to the Nth. dialect.

Pt. 17. M.E. ē3 raised to ī3. This change did not take

place in Ches, very rarely in Lancs, but frequently in Derby, though not in the place-names of the north-west of that county, which is the only one within our area. Miss Serjeantson assigns the poems to Derby rather than to S. Lancs, but her argument is scarcely convincing for the reasons stated in chapter I. Mannyng shows the change in rhymes when the place-names of his county do not, and there is likewise no *a priori* reason for assigning the poems to Derby rather than to Lancs.

We have thus far relied on points which can be proved original; if the remaining features are universally found, there is no reason why they should not be treated as original. Pts. 21, 22, 25, 39, 45 obviously need no comment. Pt. 41. The 2nd. wk. pret. sg. in '-es' is obviously original, since the pres. indic. sg. ends in '-es.' Pts. 29, 30. *hem*, *her*, are quite possible in the north-west in the fourteenth century, and were probably the poet's forms; however, the forms *hor*, *hom* occasionally used, may be original; similarly the few *scho* forms may have been used in the N.W. Midl. dialect.

Pt. 16. O.E. ēa shortened to ǎ is western. Pt. 14. O.E. ĕo + r + Cons. as *u* as well as *e* is very probably original, and, if so, is a further indication of a western dialect.

The remaining isolated features may possibly be scribal :—

1. The 8 examples of '-us' for '-es' in *Pur.* and *Gaw.* only.
2. There are 6 examples of '-is,' '-id,' for '-es,' '-ed,' in *Prl.* and *Gaw.* only.
3. The few '-gh-' spellings for the spirant in all poems.
4. The 3 '-en' noun plurals in *Pur.*
5. The use of the Nth. relative pronoun *at*, *Prl.*, 536 only.
6. The retention of the verbal prefix once in *Prl.* and once in *Pur.*
7. The rare survival of the '-i-' of the 2nd. cl. of wk. verbs.
   These rare forms are probably not scribal, in view of the artificial rhymes in *Prl.*: *streny*, *pleny*, to rhyme with *peny*, l. 501.
8. The few '-lich' endings in *Pur.*, *Pat.*, *Gaw.*
9. The 6 pres. parts. in '-yng' in *Prl.* and *Gaw.*

10. The 6 examples of *scho* in *Prl.* and *Gaw.*, but cp. *þayres*, twice only, yet occurring in rhymes.

11. The forms *hor*, *hores* in *Pat.*, *Pur.* and *Gaw.*

12. The two *he*-forms for ' they ' in *Pur.* are probably scribal.

13. The 8 *hom*-forms in *Gaw.*

14. The sole example of the 2nd. pret. sg. in '-est ' in *Gaw.*

There is no reason why any of these should not have been used by the poet, except Pt. 12 and probably Pt. 4.

We have shown above that the following are scribal :—

(1) The *qu* spellings of O.E. hw (all poems).

(2) The 3 *wh* spellings of O.E. cw, O.Fr. qu.

(3) The *eu* spellings for O.E. ēo are probably scribal.

(4) Where O.E. āw is spelt *ow*, this is due to the scribe.

(5) M.E. ou as *ou* is scribal, the poet writing *au*.

(6) Similarly there are 5 examples in *Prl.* of *w* as *v*, lines 249, 772, 785, 976 (2 examples) ; at lines 249 and 772 the alliteration is obscured by this spelling, which must therefore be scribal.

(7) Also 17 instances of *v* as *w*, found in all poems, and in *Gaw.* 1518, the only instance in alliteration, obscuring the alliteration with *v*.

Therefore in those points which can be tested by rhyme, there is no indication of any dialectal differences in the four poems ; it is only in these minor isolated ones that there is any difference ; these differences are possibly scribal. In order not to complicate matters at this stage, the problems raised by these slight differences are left until Appendix 3.

The dialect seems, therefore, to be that of the area comprising S. Lancs and N.W. Derby with no preference for either. The latter is not, however, sufficiently to the north for the poet to have used the form *þayres*. More important, however, is the change of M.E. *ou* to *au* in this MS. and also in the poet's dialect ; this was a Lancs change, for which see chapter I, Pt. II.

In order to make a still more extensive survey of the dialect, the vocabulary was examined in detail ; the percentage of O.N. words in these poems is so great as to suggest a dialect where Scandinavian influence was strong. This would rule out Ches, and S. Lancs shows a much stronger Scandinavian element than does Derby.

The percentage of O.N. words in the poems is as follows : *Gaw.* 10·3 per cent. ; *Prl.* 9·2 per cent. ; *Pur.* 7·6 per cent. ; *Pat.* 9·4 per cent. Myrc has about 1 per cent., and Audelay 2·5 per cent. ; the only writer who has such a high proportion is Orm with 11·5 per cent.

Then from a study of the words that survive in modern dialects much can be learned. Excluding those which survive in all parts, there are 76 words used which survive in the dialects north of the *Salop-Wash* line ; by a process of elimination it was discovered that 29 of these occur only in an area comprising S. Lancs, S.W. Yorks, N.W. Derby and Ches. It would perhaps be dangerous to narrow the area further, but actually the only place where all are now found is a strip of land composed of S.E. Lancs, extreme N.W. Derby and extreme S.W. Yorks. It is the dialect of Rossendale and district rather than that of the Peak. We must beware of attaching too much importance to such a line of enquiry, but it is useful in the case of these works which contain so many words which were dialectal in the M.E. period.

We feel convinced that Derby is excluded because O.E. '-and ' does not, as far as we know, occur consistently as '-*ond*,' and also rounding before the nasal in other positions is absent there. Professor Wyld assigns the poems to Derby on the proportions of *ü* to *i*-forms for O.E. $\bar{y}$; with this we have already disagreed. Miss Serjeantson assigns them to Derby on the change of *ēʒ* to *īʒ* ; this appears to us insufficient evidence, for the place-name statistics are untrustworthy ; and there are other points which distinctly favour S. Lancs. Miss Serjeantson states that she is referring to the MS. only, adding, " whatever the dialect of the original may have been " ; the study of the rhymes and alliteration, however, proves that the original dialect was N.W. Midl.

It is at present impossible accurately to fix the date for any of the poems. Gollancz in his edition of *Cleanness*, page xiv, tries to show that the author knew of *The Book of the Knight of La Tour Landry*, compiled in 1371-72 ; on this basis he thinks that the earliest date that can be assigned to *Cleanness* is 1373 ; Menner, however, in his edition of the poem does not think that any more approximate date can be given than 1360-1400 ; the same applies to *Patience*, for everything turns upon the relation of these poems to *Piers Plowman*.

It is equally difficult to date the other two poems ; the editors of *Sir Gawayn and the Green Knight* say that the latter poem was not composed after 1400, and not before the last quarter of the fourteenth century. All the poems may, however, be earlier.

St. Erkenwald, from the MS. Harley 2250, Brit. Mus., of the fifteenth century. The standard editions are those by Sir I. Gollancz, S.E.E. Poems, 1922, and by L. Savage, Yale, 1926. The poem has frequently been attributed to the author of *Sir Gawayn and the Green Knight,* and the evidence presented by Savage is certainly very convincing ; concerning the dialect, there are few points of difference, and these may well be due to a scribe. O.E. hw appears as *qu* throughout, but this is scribal, because the sound alliterates with *w*, as is the case in *Sir Gawayn and the Green Knight.*

We may therefore summarise the points of difference :—

1. M.E. *ou* is nowhere written *au*.
2. O.E. ĕo is *e* throughout.
3. M.E. *ē*ʒ is never raised to *ī*ʒ.
4. The '-us ' ending is not found.
5. There are no examples of '-liche.'
6. There are no examples of *scho,* only *ho.*
7. The use of *hor, hom* instead of *her, hem.*
8. The final '-d ' of the wk. pret. and past part. is never lost.

In addition there are three purely scribal points :—

1. '-tʒ ' is not found finally for the voiceless *s*.
2. '-ed ' is spelt '-id ' 107 times and '-ed ' only 10 times.
3. O.E. hw as *qu* is scribal : l. 185, " Sithin we **w**ot not **qu**o þou art **w**itere us þi selwen " ; see also l. 186.

The reader may assume that all the remaining points are exactly as they occur in the four poems of the Cott. MS. Nero A. x. ; but for convenience, points of special interest are appended :—

Pt. 1. O.E. ă + nasal as *o* practically throughout ; there is *wan,* l. 301, O.E. wănn, *name,* O.E. năma, ll. 28, 195, while *nome* occurs 3 times : ll. 16, 18, 318.

Pt. 2. O.E. ă + l + Cons. mutated as *a* in *malte,* l. 158, O.E. mïeltan, the only example that occurs.

Pt. 3. O.E. '-and ' as '-*ond,*' except in the cj. *and.*

Pt. 5. O.E. $\breve{y}$ as *ü* after *b* and *g*; *i* after *f, k, th*; after *l, m* it is both *ü* and *i*. The development is western.

Pt. 6. O.E. ā as *o*, but there are the same *a*-forms in the word *halde* as in the other four poems.

Pts. 7 and 8. O.E. āw, āg, āh as *aw* 5 times and as *ow* 12 times.

Pt. 34. The verbal prefix is lost.

Pt. 38. The pres. indic. pl. ends in '-en' 5 times, in '-es' 3 times, and in '-e' twice; the proportions are very similar to those in the other four poems.

Pt. 39. The pres. indic. pl. of the verb 'to be' is *are* 4 times and *arne* once, l. 304.

Pt. 44. There is one contracted form of 'take': *bitan*, l. 28 (betaken).

Therefore the only serious differences among the eight points enumerated above are Nos. 2, 3, 6, 7. The remainder are quite ·trivial and are probably scribal. Pt. 6. There are only 6 examples of *scho* in the other four poems, and the absence of such a form here does not indicate a different dialect, and in the other four poems the form is probably scribal. Pt. 7. *hor* and *hom*. These are found rarely in the other four poems, the usual forms being *her, hem*. However, the western forms *hor, hom*, do not necessitate a dialect different from that in which the other four poems were written. Pt. 2. O.E. ĕo as *e* is not western, and even in Ches, despite Miss Serjeantson's assertions, we should expect a few rounded forms. Nevertheless, she is right in her supposition that if the poem is north-western on other grounds, Ches is more likely than Lancs. Pt. 3. M.E. ē3 remaining, would be more natural in the dialect of Ches than in that of either Derby or Lancs.

Miss Serjeantson assigns the poem in its present form to Ches. We disagree with this because we know that the scribe altered *wh* to *qu* consistently; he was, therefore, writing in a place more to the north than was the author of *Sir Gawayn and the Green Knight;* if this area was just near the Ribble boundary, everything in the MS. of *St. Erkenwald* would be in agreement: O.E. ĕo as *e*, but $\breve{y}$ as *ü, i*, and ē3 as *e3*. Naturally from the dialectal evidence we can scarcely say anything concerning the common authorship of all the five poems, since we know that a scribe has altered at least one point.

Savage in his edition makes some interesting remarks concerning the dialect of the poem, and arguing along quite different lines tries to show that the dialect was originally N. Midl., irrespective of possible scribal alterations.

Concerning the date of the poem Savage says: " It is in honour of *St. Erkenwald* that the poem must have been composed. The outstanding date in connexion with the observance of the feast-days of the saint was the year 1386." This is now well-accepted, and we may therefore assume that the poem was written *c.* 1386. The author obviously knew London, but there is no trace of any influence of the London dialect; hence we may assume that the poet was writing in his native dialect for the local people.

Pierce the Ploughman's Crede, preserved in the MS. Royal 18 B. xvii., dated *c.* 1520, in the Trinity College Camb. MS. R. 3. 15, dated after 1600, and lastly in Wolfe's edition of the poem in 1553. The Trinity MS. is the best representative of the original.

The Nth. dialect is ruled out by the following points :—

Pt. 6. O.E. ā as *o*; Pts. 7 and 8. O.E. āw, āg, āh as *ow*; Pt. 9. O.E. ō as *o*; Pt. 3. O.E. '-and' as '-ond' with 2 exceptions of '-and'; Pt. 19. O.E. hw as *wh*, though there are no examples in alliteration; Pt. 22. O.E. ' sc-' in un-stressed positions as ' *sch-*'; Pt. 27. The 3rd. sg. nom. fem. pers. pron. is *ho*; and many other similar points.

Likewise the following points rule out N. Midl. : Pt. 25. '-en' noun plurals are very common; Pt. 32. The infinitive usually ends in '-en'; Pt. 34. The ' i-' verbal prefix is extremely common; Pt. 35. The pres. part. ends in '-*inge*,' '-*ynge*' with one exception in '-*ande*': *styncande*, l. 649; Pt. 36. The pres. indic. sg. 2nd. and 3rd. pers. end in '-est,' '-eth' respectively; Pt. 41. The 2nd. pers. sg. wk. pret. ends in '-est.'

We are thus reduced to S. Midl. and Sth. dialects. The latter dialect is ruled out by Pt. 33. The '-i-' of the 2nd. cl. of O.E. wk. verbs being consistently lost; Pt. 38. The pres. indic. pl. usually in '-en'; Pt. 21. No initial voicing of *f, s.*

All the points are in the fourteenth century to be found in the S. Midl. dialect. The extreme portion of this dialect is, however, suggested by one or two points: Pt. 38. The pres. indic. pl. in '-en' 127 times and in '-eth' 79 times; similarly, Pt. 39. The pres. indic. pl. of the verb 'to be' as *ben* 39 times and *beth* 9 times; also the imperative pl. occasionally in '-eth' (Pt. 40). If both endings were original, this would indicate an area near to the Thames valley, and rather to the west than to the east, for the boundary between Sth. and Midl. was much less rigid in the west. Pt. 37. There is one example of a syncopated form of the pres. indic. sg.— *halt*, l. 345 (holdeth); Pt. 28. The form for 'they' is both *þei* and *he, hy:* possibly both forms were in the original.

Finally there are a few points to indicate that the poem or copy is written in a western dialect: Pt. 27. The form of the 3rd. pers. sg. fem. nom. pron. is *ho*, except for *he* at l. 703; the former is definitely western, whereas the latter would rather appear to be Sth. Pt. 2. O.E. ă + 1 + Cons. mutated is *a* in the only example in which the combination occurs: *baly*, l. 736, O.E. bĭelg. Pt. 5. O.E. ў̆ appears as *i* with the exception of four examples of *ü*, which appear after *f, b, st* in the words " *furste, sturen, ybuld, buldeþ* "; these are genuine western forms and, remembering the late date of the copies, may represent the last stage of the spreading of the standard forms in the early fifteenth century.

Pt. 24. There are no examples of '-us,' '-ud' for '-es,' '-ed.' Pt. 1. O.E. ă + nasal is *a* only. Pt. 14. O.E. ĕo is *e* only. These last three points are not western as they stand, but at so late a period may in the south-west be due to the spreading of the standard forms; this we believe to be the explanation, and the other western forms together with the forms *hy, he* for 'they' and the pres. indic. pl. in '-en' and '-eth,' all suggest the west rather than the east. Such a peculiar mixture of inflexional forms we have already met with in the writers of Glos.

The forms for the pronouns 'them,' 'their' are *hem, her(e)*, respectively and these forms, it will be remembered, are usual at this period in the south-west.

Note.—M.E. ē3 as *ey, ei3*, but very rarely as *i3*, would suggest S.W. Midl., rather than C.S. Midl., but it is not safe to generalise from this point, one which seems to be particularly liable to scribal interference; on the whole, the dialect of the copy seems to be S.W. Midl., and there is no good reason for suspecting that this does not also apply to the dialect of the original. The solitary example of the pres. part. in '-ande' is probably scribal.

Concerning the date of the poem, Wells says, p. 268: "Mention (l. 657) of the persecution of Walter Brute fixes the date after the latter part of 1393; and the allusion to flattering kings (ll. 364-5) may indicate composition before the death of Richard II. Skeat accepts the date 1394. The author was a Wycliffite. The general plan of the poem would seem derived from *Piers Plowman*—particularly from the Prologue to Vita de Dowel." Richard II. died in 1399; hence we may date the poem 1393-99.

The best edition is that by Skeat for the Oxford Press, 1906; the same editor has also an edition in the E.E.T.S. 30, 1867.

Skeat is incorrect in saying that there are no traces of western forms, and that the dialect is that of London. There may be traces of the influence of London English, particularly with regard to the spreading of the standard forms, but Skeat has been led away by the differences of poetic style and vocabulary; we may, however, leave these points until volume 2.

Richard the Redeles, from the MS. Camb. Univ. Lib. L. 1, iv., dated *c.* 1450, edited by T. Wright for the Camden Society, 1838, and by Skeat, E.E.T.S. 54, p. 460, and in his Oxford edition of *Piers Plowman*, vol. 1, p. 603. The date of the poem can easily be fixed, thus Wells says, p. 269: "Lines 23-9 of the Prologue indicate composition after Richard was taken prisoner on Aug. 18th, 1399, and before the receipt of the news of his deposition Sept. 18th, 1399. There is also an allusion to the execution of Scrope at Bristol, July 29th, and to the release of the Earl of Warwick just before Aug. 25th."

The poem is divided into a prologue and four passus, and the references below are made accordingly; thus 3.7 means "Passus 3, line 7."

With regard to the dialect, Nth. is ruled out by Pt. 6. O.E. ā as *o*; Pts. 7, 8. O.E. āw, āg, āh as *ow*; Pt. 9. O.E. ō as *o*; Pt. 3. O.E. '-and' as '-ond' with 2 exceptions of '-and'; Pt. 36. The pres. indic. 3rd. sg. in '-eth,' '-ith; and Pt. 19. O.E. hw as *wh*, alliterating with *w*; e.g. 2.189, þat **wh**ere so þey **w**alkid, þey **w**altrid down-**w**ardis." This point is conclusive in its evidence.

N. Midl. is ruled out by the following points: Pt. 32.

The infinitive ends in '-e' with only 3 exceptions in '-en';
Pt. 34. The 'i-' verbal prefix is frequently retained; Pt.
35. The pres. part. ends in '-ynge,' '-inge' only; Pt. 36.
The pres. indic. sg. 2nd. and 3rd. pers. end in '-est' ('-ist')
and '-eth' ('-ith') respectively; Pt. 40. The imperative
pl. usually ends in '-eth'; Pt. 41. The 2nd. pers. sg. wk.
pret. ends in '-ist.' All these points indicate a place of
composition south of the *Salop-Wash* line, leaving us with the
Sth. and S. Midl. dialects. The former of these is ruled out
by: Pt. 33. The loss of the '-i-' of the 2nd. cl. of O.E. wk.
verbs; Pt. 28. The form of the pronoun 'they' is *þei*, a
non-Sth. form; Pt. 37. The absence of syncopated forms
in the pres. indic. sg.; Pt. 25. There are only 3 '-en' noun
plurals; Pt. 21. O.E. *f*, *s* are not voiced initially.

We are thus left with the S. Midl. dialect, and on close
examination all the points are found there in common.
Several comments are, however, necessary. Pt. 38. The
pres. indic. pl., excluding the examples immediately preceded
or followed by a personal pronoun, ends in '-en,' '-yn' 20 times
and in '-eth' 33 times; similarly Pt. 39. The pres. indic.
pl. of the verb 'to be' is *ben* 4 times and *beth* 7 times. As
in *Pierce the Ploughman's Crede*, the occurrence of both types
may not be due to scribal interference, but to the fact that
the author may have lived in the extreme S.W. Midl. dialectal
area; this seems extremely probable, and is supported by the
fact that the 3rd. sg. fem. pers. pron. nom. is *hue*, 3.50 (the only
example); this form is not E. Midl., and is S.W. Midl. rather
than C.W. Midl.

Regarding the western forms which occur, we may note
the following: Pt. 24. The ending '-us' occurs 5 times,
and '-ud' once, forms which may be western. Pt. 1. O.E.
ǎ + nasal is usually *a*, but there are 2 examples of *o*: *mony*,
4.37, O.E. mănig, *monside*, 3.105, O.E. mănsian; in addition
the word *ony* for *any* might be included here; the development
is therefore comparable to that in the same point in *Pierce
the Ploughman's Crede*. Pt. 2. O.E. ǎ + l + Cons. mutated
is *a* twice: *walmed*, 3.114, O.E. wĭelman, *walwed*, 1.27, O.E.
wĭelwan; there are also 2 *e*-forms: *elderne*, 1.65, O.E. ĭeldran,
and *elde*, Pr. 70, O.E. ĭeldu, a word in which *a* never occurs.
The *a*-forms look like genuine western types.

Pt. 5. O.E. ŷ is *i*, and there are no genuine *ü*-forms;
it will be remembered that a few *ü*-forms are found in *Pierce*

the Ploughman's Crede, but it should also be noticed that those words in which these *u*-forms occur are absent from *Richard the Redeles,* i.e. words in which *y* is preceded by labials. That accounts for the complete absence of *u*-forms in this poem, which was written at a late period when the spreading of the standard forms was almost complete.

Pt. 14. O.E. ĕo is *e* except in the word *burne* twice, beside *berne* once ; this was a word frequently found in alliterative poetry, and hence may have survived in its original western form. Pt. 16. O.E. ēa when shortened is *ă* ; this may also be western.

Thus we have, as in the case of *Pierce the Ploughman's Crede,* a poem connected with London, but probably written in the west, for there are traces to show that this is so ; at the same time in both cases it may be that a London copy of the poem has been preserved for us ; this would account for the comparative rarity of western forms.

Note.—The above survey has included all the important points, but the following may also be mentioned : Pt. 15. O.E. ĕa + Cons. mutated is *e* throughout, as we should expect. Pt. 17. M.E. *ēȝ* is raised to *īȝ, ī ;* if this change had taken place in the original, it would suggest that the poem originated in Oxon and neighbourhood rather than in Glos ; or the feature might be due to the non-western copy, if such it was. Pts. 29 and 30. The forms for ' them,' ' their ' are *hem, her* respectively ; as we have pointed out above, these forms were common in the S.W. Midl. dialect of the late fourteenth century.

Skeat suggested that *Richard the Redeles* was written by the author of *Piers Plowman ;* whatever truth there may be in the theory, the dialectal evidence does lend support to such a view ; the dialect may have been that of the locality of the Malvern Hills. This theory of common authorship is, however, subjected to a metrical test in Appendix I.

The ABC of Aristotle, found in 9 E. Midl. MSS. of 1450-1500, and there are only minor differences in the dialect of these. The MSS. Harley 541, f. 213, and 1304, f. 103, and Lambeth 853, f. 30, have introductions of 12, 10, 13 verses respectively, differing considerably from each other in expression ; the Harley 5086 and the Lambeth 853 are edited in E.E.T.S. 32, page 9 and 11 respectively, and the Harley 1304 in the E.E.T.S., E.S. 8, page 65. The following examination of the language is based on the Lambeth MS., which is probably more consistent than the other.

The Nth. dialect is ruled out by Pt. 6. O.E. ā as *o*; Pts. 7, 8. O.E. āw, āg, āh as *ow*; Pt. 9. O.E. ō as *o*; Pt. 19. O.E. hw· as *wh* (no examples in alliteration); Pt. 22. O.E. ' sc-' in unstressed positions as ' *sch-*.'

Similarly the Sth. dialect is ruled out by Pt. 32. The infinitive ending in '-e '; Pt. 33. The loss of the '-i-' of the 2nd. cl. of O.E. wk. verbs; Pt. 34. The loss of the verbal prefix; Pt. 15. O.E. ĕa + Cons. mutated as *e*.

The W. Midl. dialect is excluded by Pt. 1. O.E. ă + nasal as *a*; Pt. 5. O.E. ў as *i*; and Pt. 14. O.E. ĕo as *e*; Pt. 24. No examples of '-us,' '-ud.' We are thus left with the E. Midl. dialect, and it is the southern portion of this dialect which is required by Pt. 36. The pres. indic. sg. in '-eth '; Pt. 40. The imperative pl. in '-eth '; Pt. 35. The pres. part. in '-*ing*,' '-*inge* '; Pt. 42. The final '-ed ' of the weak pret. and past part. not unvoiced.

The Harley 5086 is also in the E. Midl. dialect, but has the western form *mury ;* similarly the Harley 1304 has the form *oƿus*, whereas the other MSS. have *ooƿis ;* it has also *hure* twice for the pronoun ' their.' It is possible that these scattered western forms, which occur in various other MSS. also, may indicate a western original ; the poems being short, we have no evidence regarding several important points.

It is very difficult to suggest a date more definite than does Wells himself, who suggests—" 1400-1450, or perhaps 1350-1400."

Jacke Upland, and the Reply of Friar Daw Thopias, and the Rejoinder of Jacke Upland.—The three poems are edited by T. Wright in *Political Poems*, vol. 2, pp. 16-114, 1861. *Jacke Upland*, a Wycliffite attack on the friars, was composed in 1401 or 1402, and this was followed by *The Reply of Friar Daw Thopias*. The text is so utterly corrupt and modernised that it is extremely difficult to make any observations concerning the dialect of the original works. It seems probable that the dialect is S. Midl., but whether to the east or to the west we cannot say, owing to the modernised forms of possibly original western points.

Pts. 38 and 39. The pres. indic. pl. ends in '-en,' but the sg. in '-eth ' (Pt. 36) ; N. Midl. would have '-es,' even at so late a period.

Pts. 29 and 30. The forms for ' them ' and ' their ' are usually *hem* and *her* respectively ; these are genuine Midl. forms.

Perhaps there are no other points whose dialectal evidence can be trusted, so that we shall have to be content with describing the copy as ' probably S. Midl.' The works belong to the *Piers Plowman* group of alliterative poems, and may have originated in the south-west also.

The Wars of Alexander, from the MSS. Ashmole 44, and Dublin, Trinity College D. 4, 12, the former dated *c.* 1450, and the latter *c.* 1500 ; both were edited by Skeat for the E.E.T.S., E.S. 47 ; the Dublin MS. is incomplete, and its language is less uniform than that of the Ashmole. The alliteration is very useful in trying to discover the original dialect.

Pt. 19. O.E. hw as *qu*, alliterating with O.E. cw, and with O.Fr. qu : e.g. l. 3303, " Lo so þe **qu**ele (wheel) of **qw**istsumnes my **qu**alite has changid " ; or l. 4511, " For hem was **qu**artirs of **qw**ete   um**qw**ile out of nombre " (O.E. hwǣte). This means that the poem was written either in Nth. or very near the *Ribble-Aire* valley.

Pt. 2. O.E. ă + l + Cons. mutated is *e* in the Ashmole, but often *a* in the Dublin, and this latter was probably the poet's form, because he usually alliterated identical vowels together, and the *e* in this case often spoils the alliteration, whereas the Dublin MS. restores it by retaining the western form with *a* ; e.g.

l. 1619, " Syn him **a**doured **a**ll men,   **e**ldire and ȝongir "
            (Ashmole) ;
        " Syn him **a**doured **a**ll men,   **a**lder and yonger "
            (Dublin).
or
l. 2844, " His **e**ldirs and his **a**ncestris,   **a**ls he remembris "
            (Ashmole) ;
        " His **a**lders and his **a**ncestris,   **a**ls he remembris "
            (Dublin).

The Dublin has surely the correct reading ; see also ll. 1619, 2319, 2727. The poem was definitely written in the west, and putting these two points together we arrive at the conclusion that the original dialect was the extreme N.W. Midl. near the *Ribble* valley.

Pt. 28. The 3rd. pl. nom. pers. pronoun is þai, and the form occurs in alliteration : l. 3675, "and þe thinnest was a nynche thicke,   quen þai were þurȝe persed."

Pt. 29. The form of the acc. is þaim (þam), and there are two apparent examples in alliteration : l. 1323, "Quare althare-thickest was þe thrange,   þurȝe þaim he rynnes." (The alliteration may be on the pronoun) : l. 1829, "Takes þam with him to his tent,   and þam at ese makis "; this is faulty alliteration, but probably proves the originality of the Nth. pronoun ; there are no examples of þaire (þar) in alliteration, but this latter was obviously original if the form for the acc. was þaim ; these would be the natural forms near the *Ribble* valley.

Pt. 27. The form for ' she ' is scho, but there is evidence that the original may have had ho: l. 257, " Be it hee, be it scho, haly þare werdes " ; the original probably had ho, for the alliteration seems to require a form with h ; if this was so, this is a further indication of the western dialect.

Lastly, remembering that the poet usually alliterates identical vowels together, l. 2263 may indicate rounding before the nasal :—

" þan answars þam þaire ald gode, and osses on þis wyse " (Ashmole) ;
" thus answers þaim þis old god, and ossus on þis wyse " (Dublin).

Is it possible that the original had " onswers," the western form ? The ending '-us ' is also noticeable.

We may further ask whether the remaining evidence is in general agreement with the above points, which can be proved original. Pt. 32. The infinitive in '-(e).' Pt. 33. The loss of the '-i-' of the 2nd. cl. of O.E. wk. verbs. Pt. 34. The loss of the ' i-' verbal prefix. Pt. 35. The pres. part. in '-ande.' Pt. 36. The pres. indic. sg. in '-es,' '-is.' Pt. 40. The imperative pl. in '-es,' '-is,' '-s.' Pt. 44. Frequent contracted forms of ' take,' ' make.' Pt. 3. O.E. '-and ' as '-and ' throughout. Pt. 31. The '-lich(e) ' ending never occurring. All these points are quite natural in the N.W. Midl. dialect.

Certain Nth. points would also be natural in this dialect ; thus we have Pt. 6. O.E. ā remaining. Pts. 7, 8. O.E. āw, āg, āh as aw, au. Pt. 9. O.E. ō as u as well as o (the

Dublin prefers *u*). Pt. 22. O.E. ' sc-' in unstressed positions as ' *s-*.' Pt. 38. The pres. indic. pl. ending in '-es,' '-is,' though the Dublin occasionally has '-en.' Pt. 39. The same form for the verb ' to be ' being *er(e)* with rare *ben* forms in the Dublin. Pt. 26. The consistent use of *þir(e)*. All these points would be possible in a border dialect such as that in which this poem was written.

Finally, O.E. ĕo is *e* throughout, even in the word *berne* instead of *burne ;* O.E. ȳ is *i*, even in the word *birde*, which, as we know, always appears as *burde ;* this makes us inclined to believe that these points were western in the original ; the same would apply to Pt. 1. O.E. ă + nasal as *a* with rare *o*-forms in the words ' *blonke*,' ' *mony*,' and ' *con*.' The Ashmole MS. evidently originated farther to the north than the poem itself, and the Dublin may be a better representative of the original.

The Crowned King, from the Douce MS. 95, of the middle of the fifteenth century, consisting of 144 long lines ; this " early imitation of *Piers Plowman* " is edited by Skeat in E.E.T.S. 54, pages 523-34, *Piers Plowman C. Text and Crowned King*. Fortunately the date and dialect of this poem are known from internal evidence ; see Skeat's edition, page cxxiv, ". . . written at Southampton, probably in June, 1415, and addressed to Henry V. shortly before his famous campaign." An examination of the language confirms the statement that the dialect is Sth.

Pt. 19. O.E. hw as *wh* alliterating with *w*: e.g. l. 7 ; this indicates that the poet wrote in a non-Nth. dialect.

An area south of the *Salop-Wash* line is required by the following points : Pt. 36. The pres. indic. 2nd. and 3rd. pers. sg. end in '-est,' '-eth,' respectively. Pt. 38. The pl. form in '-eth ' and '-en.' Pt. 41. There is one example of the 2nd. pret. wk. sg., which ends in '-est ' : *didest*, meaning " didst die." Pt. 35. The pres. part. ending in '-yng ' is probably S. Midl. or Sth. at this period.

We have to remember the date of the composition, so that the boundaries on the map facing p. 38 will not always hold ; hence Pt. 32. The infinitive in '-en,' l. 84 (elsewhere '-e '), is at this date Sth., as is Pt. 33. The '-i-' of the 2nd. cl. of wk. vbs. surviving once : l. 3, *heried*, O.E. herian, and also Pt. 34. The ' i-' verbal prefix retained twice.

Pt. 5. O.E. ȳ as *i* throughout, seems to exclude the western

7

dialect, as does Pt. 14. O.E. ĕo as *e*, and Pt. 1. O.E. ă + nasal as *a*, except in *thonke*, 1. 48, *ponke*, 1. 96.

There are three other relevant points : Pt. 17. M.E. *ē̄ȝ* raised to *ī̄ȝ* consistently, would appear to point to the middle-south rather than to the south-east ; Pt. 39. The pres. indic. pl. of the verb ' to be ' as both *are* and *be(e)n ;* so Pt. 38. The pres. indic. pl. in '-eth ' and in '-en,' '-yn '; these two points would appear rather to be S. Midl. than Sth. It is, however, possible that a scribe has been responsible for the forms in '-en ' ; the internal evidence is sufficient for our purpose.

All the remaining points are in general agreement, such as O.E. ā as *o*, O.E. āw, āh, āg as *ow*, O.E. ō as *o*, O.E. '-and ' as '-*ond*,' and the use of the pronouns *thei, hem, here* for ' they,' ' them,' ' their,' respectively ; the details of these need not be given.

The Prophecies ascribed to à Becket, from the MS. K. k. I, 5, Camb. Univ., in a fifteenth century hand. The work is edited by J. R. Lumby, E.E.T.S. 42, page 23, 1870. The subject-matter seems to bear upon the events of the reign of Henry V., and the date is usually fixed about 1420.[1] Like *The Scottish Prophecies* of about the same date, these prophecies were written in Scotland, where this type of literature evidently flourished at that period.

There is little need to labour the point about the dialect, for the Scottish dialect is easy to detect ; O.E. hw usually appears as *quh, qwh*, though there are no examples in alliteration ; the pres. indic. sg. and pl. end in '-is,' '-ys '; the final '-d ' of the wk. pret. and past part. is not infrequently unvoiced to '-t '; O.E. ā appears as *a*, and O.E. āw, āg, āh as *aw, au* ; O.E. ' sc-' in unstressed positions as ' *s-*' ; the pronouns *tham(e)*, *par(e)* occur for ' them,' ' their '; and many other similar points. There has probably, however, been some slight alteration in the direction of the Midl. dialect by a Midl. scribe. The internal evidence regarding the dialect is nevertheless quite sufficient for our purpose.

The Scottish Prophecies are also edited in the same volume ; the first, on pages 18-22, is 139 lines long, and the second, on pages 32-4, is 71 lines long.; they are also found in the same MS.

Lines 66-8 of the 2nd. Proph. indicate the Scottish origin of the works :—

[1] But see Wells, p. 226.

" Busk ye wyell, Berwyk ! be blith of þis wordis
þat Sant Bede fande in his buk of þe byg bergh,
þe trew toune upon Twede, wytht towrys fayre."

The spelling is typically Scottish throughout ; thus the spirant is frequently spelt '-cht' as well as '-ght' ; and O.E. hw as *qwh*, as well as *wh*, *w*, but there are no examples in alliteration. In addition all the points mentioned above in connexion with *The à Becket Prophecies* are also true of these *Scottish Prophecies*. There are the same traces of a Midl. scribe as in the former work. The date assigned to *The Scottish Prophecies* is usually *c*. 1400-50.

We shall see later that these prophecies are metrically quite distinct from the alliterative romances composed in W. Midl.

Death and Life, from the Percy Folio MS., *c*. 1650 ; edited by Skeat, *The Percy Folio MS.*, vol. 3, p. 49, 1868. A far better edition is that by J. H. Hanford and J. M. Steadman, Jr., in *Studies in Philology*, vol. 15, p. 221, 1918.

The language has been considerably modernised ; thus Hanford, p. 223 : " Unfortunately the text of *Death and Liffe* is corrupt beyond the powers of a modern editor to restore, or even in some cases to explain. Originally written in the archaic diction affected by writers of the alliterative school, the piece was copied by a scribe or scribes to whom many of the expressions were unintelligible. The latest copyist, moreover, was very careless, and as a result the MS. is a chaos of modernisation and sheer blunder."

Hence it is very difficult to form any definite opinion concerning the original dialect in which the poem was written ; it is possible, however, to make some general observations upon the dialect of the present copy.

(1) The Nth. dialect is ruled out by Pt. 6. O.E. ā as *o* ; Pts. 7, 8. O.E. āw, āg, āh as *ow*, *ou* ; Pt. 9. O.E. ō as *o* ; Pt. 35. The pres. part. in '-*ynge*' ; Pt. 38. The pres. indic. pl. in '-en.'

(2) The following point rules out the Sth. dialect : Pt. 38. The pres. indic. pl. in '-en.'

The remaining evidence is negligible at so late a period. Thus the pronouns *she*, *they*, *them*, *their*, are hardly dialectal in the fifteenth century ; likewise, the infinitive without ending, the loss of the verbal prefix, O.E. hw as *wh*, and O.E. '-and' as '-*and*.'

Similarly the tests for a western dialect are no longer valid : O.E. ă + nasal is *a* ; O.E. ӯ is *i* (except where Mn. E. has *u*, as in *busy*, etc.) ; O.E. ĕo is *e* ; and O.E. ă + 1 + Cons. mutated is *e*.

Pt. 36. The pres. indic. sg. is interesting : the 2nd. and 3rd. pers. sg. end in '-es ' 12 times, and in '-est,' '-eth ' (respectively) 69 times ; similarly the 2nd. pers. wk. pret. sg. ends in '-est.' This might suggest S. Midl. even at so late a period, but not necessarily so ; it is, moreover, impossible to say which of the two types was the more common in the original.

Therefore, it is scarcely possible to describe the dialect as anything but Midl. The absence of western forms is, at such a late period, no evidence that the poem was not originally written in the west. The statements of Hanford and Steadman are very hypothetical and of little value dialectally, since they do not appear to us to be based on genuine dialectal study.

The editors have presented very weighty evidence to disprove the theory of the common authorship of *Death and Life* and *Scottish Field*. This makes the dating of the poem much easier, for there is no longer need to postulate such a late date. The author must have read *Piers Plowman*, which sets a limit in one direction. Luick dates the poem *c.* 1450, and judging from the metre, viewed in its historical setting, we are inclined to agree with him in this matter. But naturally the dating remains largely guesswork ; we may safely assume that the poem was written *c.* 1450-1500, thus allowing sufficiently broad limits.

The Twa Mariit Wemen and the Wedo, by William Dunbar, who was born *c.* 1460 and probably died after 1513. The date of the poem is generally considered to be *c.* 1500, and as the work was written in the dialect of the Lowlands of Scotland, no linguistic examination is needed.

Scottish Field, from the Percy Folio MS., *c.* 1650, edited by Skeat in vol. I, p. 199, 1867. The poem was written after Flodden, since it sets forth the glories of the House of the Stanleys, and of its achievements at Bosworth Field and Flodden. Summing up the evidence regarding the date, Skeat says, p. 210 : " The poem was composed some two or three years after the battle (Flodden). Vv. 285-91 seem to speak of the death of the Bishop of Ely as a recent event, and he died in March, 1515. But the present edition may be of much later date. The confusion of Maxwell with Horne seems to place it after 1542." The difficulty regarding the dialect of *Death and Life* is also found here, for the date, both of the present copy and of the original composition, is late.

Again, it is true that as the poem stands, the dialect in which it is written is Midl. We have examined the forms in this poem, and for each of the points examined there is no difference of treatment in the two poems, so that the remarks made concerning the language of *Death and Life* hold for *Scottish Field* also. We might notice, however, that concerning the pres. indic. sg., the treatment is again similar ; there are 29 '-eth ' forms and 10 '-es,' '-s ' forms. But the spreading of the standard forms had extended so far at this time that it is impossible to describe the poem as anything but Midl. generally.

Note.—The traditional alliterative word *burne* occurs in both poems. In *Scottish Field* it appears in the form *bearne(s)*, ll. 178, 375, but as *burne*, ll. 21, 65 ; in *Death and Life* the latter spelling occurs once only—l. 411, whereas elsewhere the spelling is *bearne*.[1] It is just possible that *burne* is a traditional alliterative spelling, surviving from the original copies written in a western dialect. The present copy is, unfortunately, too corrupt to enable us to localise the dialect in either case.

In conclusion it may be noted that these poems in the unrhymed alliterative long line range in date from 1340 to 1515, though few such poems were written after 1400 ; the tradition lingered for over a century after this, yet it was little more than a mere tradition, as we shall see when we come to the metrical investigation. These late survivals were chiefly in Scotland. The poems of the M.E. period proper were, as we have seen, written in the W. Midl. dialect ; in one or two cases we have met with poems in other dialects, but there have invariably been indications that the original dialect was western ; thus *Chevalere Assigne* and *The ABC of Aristotle*, though preserved in E. Midl., can be shown to have originated

---

[1] Owing to confusion between O.E. *bearn* and *beorn* both in form and meaning.

in the west, owing to the presence of certain dialectal forms ; there are also a few poems which, in their present state, are northern rather than western, but in these the alliteration has revealed the alteration of pronouns, etc., from their western forms to northern ones.

In dealing with the works treated in this chapter, there were no rhymes to help us except in the case of the *Sir Gawayn* poet ; but it should also be noticed that we are extremely fortunate in having other evidence available ; the alliteration is often of considerable help, and in addition the scribe has in many places left traces of his alteration of original dialectal points. Hence we are now more certain that the poems were actually written in the west, wherever the present copies may have originated.

CHAPTER 4.

POEMS IN THE ALLITERATIVE LONG LINE WITH END-RHYME.

THE poems treated in this chapter are written in the ordinary alliterative long line with end-rhyme. No dialectal survey is included for : (1) *The 1st. Rolle Lyric,* since the other seven lyrics come within the scope of chapter 6 ; the dialect is that of S. Yorks, *c.* 1350-70. (2) *The Harley* 2253 *Lyrics* 1 *and* 4, since the other nine are treated in chapter 6.

On God Orison of Our Lady, from the MS. Cotton Nero, A. 14, Brit. Mus., dated 1200-25. The poem consists of 171 long lines, rhyming *aabbcc,* etc. ; the latest and best edition is that in Hall's *Early Middle English,* 1920, p. 132, with notes on p. 531. The important linguistic forms are collected by Hall, but it is quite certain that the dialect of the present MS. does not represent that of the original. Hall says : [1] " The Orison in its present form agrees substantially with the copy of the Ancren Riwle in the same manuscript ; both are in the dialect of the scribe, that of the Middle-South. But the Midl. *i* for *y* is attested by the spoilt rhymes . . . ; there is nothing else in the rhymes to help to a nearer localisation of the author ; it can only be said that his dialect was Midland."

schrude, l. 139, O.E. scrȳdan, rhymes with *wide,* O.E. wīde. This and many other similar rhymes show that the original dialect was not western or south-western. Hall is therefore wrong in saying that we can only describe the dialect as Midl. The dialect was obviously E. Midl. Also the infinitive ends in '-en ' : e.g. *understonden,* l. 31, rhyming with *honden,* a wk. pl., and if all the noun plurals of the latter type are likewise original, these two points indicate S.E. Midl. in preference to N.E. Midl. The date of the composition is presumably about 1200.

On Serving Christ, from the MS. Jesus Coll., Oxf. 29,

---

[1] P. 535.

f. 258 (c. 1275), consisting of 78 alliterative verses, edited by Skeat for the E.E.T.S. 49, *An Old English Miscellany*, p. 90. A non-Nth. dialect is indicated by such points as 19. O.E. hw as *hw*, alliterating with *w*, e.g. l. 26; or Pt. 28. *heo* for 'they.'

The Sth. dialect would seem to be required by the following points in particular: Pt. 28. *heo* for 'they'; Pt. 34. The retention of the verbal prefix; Pt. 35. The pres. part. in '-*ynde*'; Pt. 38. The pres. indic. pl. in '-eð'; Pt. 39. The pres. indic. pl. of the vb. 'to be' as *beoð*; and Pt. 21. The voicing of initial *f* to *v*. Most of the other points are in the form which we should expect in the Sth. dialect, but the following need comment: Pt. 38. The pres. indic. pl. ends in '-eð,' but there are also two forms in '-en' which are, however, probably scribal; Pt. 30. *heore* is S. Western, as also are Pt. 1. O.E. ă + nasal as *o* throughout, and Pt. 5. O.E. ȳ as *ü* with two exceptions—the words *king*, and *fyr*, l. 26 (O.E. fȳr), but also *fur*, l. 42 ; elsewhere the form is *ü* : e.g. *monkunnes*, l. 30, *sunfulle*, l. 25, etc.

Pt. 14. O.E. ĕo appears as *eo*, a spelling which is not infrequently an attempt to represent a rounded vowel. These three points would seem to indicate the west. Pt. 12. O.E. ǣ[1] appears as tense *e*, judging from the rhymes in ll. 11 and 17 ; this in the south-west would indicate a county as far north as Glos. We may therefore assume that the dialect is that of the latter county, c. 1250.

Two Scraps of Love-Songs, from a MS. in the College of Arms, marked E.D.N. 27, written in a small illegible hand of the time of Ed. II., edited by T. Wright and J. O. Halliwell in *Reliquiæ Antiquæ*, vol. 2, 19, 1845.

(1) *A levedy and my love leyt*, 11 lines.

(2) *As I stod on a day*, 32 lines. The text is exceedingly corrupt, and we can only date the scraps by saying that they are not later than 1320, the latest date at which the MS. could have been written.

The Sth. dialect is ruled out by such points as 32. The infinitive ending in '-e,' proved by rhymes, e.g. l. 9. Pt. 12. O.E. ǣ[1] as tense *e*, proved by rhymes, e.g. l. 39, *rede*, O.E. rǣdan, and *spede*, O.E. spēdan. The Nth. dialect is also unsuitable because of Pt. 19. O.E. hw, which appears as *w*, *wh*, alliterating with O.E. *w*, l. 10 ; and because of many other points which cannot be proved to have been original.

Thus we are limited to the Midl. dialect, and W. Midl. is excluded by Pt. 5. O.E. y̆ as *i*, proved by rhymes : *hille*, l. 5, O.E. hyll, rhyming with *stille*, O.E. stĭlle ; by Pt. 1. O.E. ăn as *ăn*, though there are no rhymes to prove this ; Pt. 14. O.E. ĕo as *e*, proved by rhymes ; Pt. 28. The use of *sche*, not *ho* ; and Pt. 2. O.E. ă + l + Cons. mutated is *e* in *welle*, O.E. wĭell, rhyming with *belle ;* this rhyme would be of no proof in itself, but there is ample evidence that the writer wrote in E. Midl.

In addition, all the points are to be found in E. Midl., but not over the whole area, the following pointing to N.E. Midl. : the infinitive in '-e,' proved by rhymes, the loss of the '-i-' of the 2nd. wk. cl. of O.E. verbs, the complete loss of the verbal prefix, the pres. indic. sg. 2nd. and 3rd. pers. in '-is,' which requires a place of composition north of the *Salop-Wash* line, and also the O.E. ǣ[1] as tense *e*, proved by rhymes. There is thus conclusive proof that the dialect was N.E. Midl., of presumably *c.* 1300.

The Song of the Husbandman, from the MS. Harley 2253, f. 64, *c.* 1310, consisting of 72 alliterative verses, edited by T. Wright, *Political Songs*, Camden Soc., 1839, p. 149. The dialect, as it stands, is certainly Sth., as may be seen from a study of the following points :—

Pt. 28. *he* for ' they ' ; Pt. 37. Syncopated forms for the pres. indic. sg. ; Pt. 38. The pres. indic. pl. in '-eth ' ; Pt. 39. The pres. indic. pl. of the verb ' to be ' as *beth, buth*. Most of the remaining points occur in the form naturally to be expected in the Sth. dialect ; such as Pt. 29. *hem ;* Pt. 30. *here.* But the south-western dialect rather than the south-eastern is required by Pt. 1. O.E. ăn as *on* throughout ; Pt. 5. O.E. y̆ as *u*, e.g. *hude*, l. 22, O.E. hȳdan ; and possibly by Pt. 14. O.E. ĕo as *eo, u*, spellings which probably represent the rounded vowel ; also Pt. 2. *sulle*, ll. 44, 46, 54, O.E. sĭellan, is probably S. Western at this period.

But Pt. 12. O.E. ǣ[1] as tense *e* (see the rhyme of l. 64), would seem to indicate a county as far north as Glos, and the rest of the evidence is not at variance with this ; thus the infinite ends in '-e ' 24 times, and in '-en ' 3 times, but the former termination is proved original by the rhymes. Yet it is impossible to tell what the poet's dialect was from the evidence available. The date of the poem is probably *c.* 1300.

The Harley Lyrics, 1 and 4, for which see chapter 6, p. 122.

The Rawlinson Strophic Pieces, from the MS. Rawl. Poetry, 175 Bodl., edited in Anglia 27, p. 283, by W. Heuser: 1. (*Luke*, 48 lines) ; 2. (*Math.*, 48) ; 3. (*Mark*, 30) ; 4. (*John*, 30). The date of the MS. is *c.* 1350 and we can only date the pieces accordingly, since there is no internal evidence ; we might therefore date the composition *c.* 1300-40. The dialect is undoubtedly Nth., judging from the following points : Pt. 35. The pres. part. in '*-and*' throughout. Pt. 7. O.E. āw, āg, āh as *au*, the development which is proved original by the rhymes : *knaw*, O.E. cnāwan, *law*, O.E. lăgu, *sawe*, O.E. săgu, and *raw*, O.E. rāw. Pt. 6. O.E. ā as *a* and *o*, though the rhymes indicate that the former was the poet's form : *fase* (foes), O.E. gefā, rhyming with *case*, *trace* (Fr. words). Thus there is absolute proof that the dialect is Nth.

Nth. also are þir, used consistently ; 'er' as the pl. pres. indic. of the verb 'to be' ; and the use of þam : þair : scho : sall (for "schall"), etc. ; in addition, the remaining points occur in the Nth. forms, such as O.E. ȳ as *i*, and O.E. ăn as *an* throughout.

Both the text and the copy are therefore in the same dialect.

The Poems of Lawrence Minot, from the MS. Cotton Galba E. ix., f. 52*a*, dated *c.* 1425. They have been edited by W. Scholle, 1884, and by J. Hall, 1914. Poems 2, 5, 9, 10, 11 are written in the alliterative long line, and the others have alliteration of the stressed syllables. As the events dealt with in the poems range from 1333-52 we may assume that the poet wrote within the same limits, since the works are topical in tone. Hall says concerning the dialect:[1] ". . . it follows from the above remarks that the grammar of the poems is in its main features northern. . . . Accidence, Vocabulary, Phonology . . . ; the dialect, then, is in its basis Northern, but with a slight admixture of Midland forms, due to the poet himself. We may therefore infer that the poet lived on the borderland between the Northern and Midland areas and to the east rather than to the west." From the other poems in the MS., Hall thinks that the scribe was of the Nth. dialect. ". . . Probably Minot was a Norfolk man and the scribe had a Midland copy before him."

The area north of the *Salop-Wash* line is required by the

[1] Hall, p. xvi.

following points, all proved to be original by the rhymes :
Pt. 4. M.E. '-ong ' retracted to '-ung,' proved by l. 20, Poem
3 ; Pt. 35. The pres. part. in '-ande '; Pt. 6. O.E. ā as *a* ;
Pt. 44. Contracted forms of ' take ' in rhymes ; Pt. 36.
The pres. indic. sg. in '-es ' ; e.g. *hetes*, l. 26, Poem II, rhyming
with *stretes*, sb. pl ; Pt. 38. The pres. indic. pl. in '-es,' e.g.
betes, l. 28, Poem 2 ; and many other points which cannot,
like these, be tested by rhymes, such as the use of *sall*, *þam*,
þaire, *whilk*, *þire*. However, the dialect is not Nth. but N.E.
Midl., near the border, between the two dialects, because of :—
Pt. 6. O.E. ā *also* occurs in rhymes as *o*, e.g. *sore*, l. 53,
Poem 7, O.E. sār, rhyming with *forlore*, O.E. forlŏren ; and
other similar rhymes. Pt. 32. The '-n ' of the infinitive
is retained on four occasions for purposes of rhyme : *slaken*,
l. 49, Poem 9, rhyming with *taken* (past part.), etc. ; this
is exactly as in Mannyng of Brunne, who retains '-en ' as a
concession to rhyme. Thirdly, though the pres. indic. pl.
ends in '-es,' except when ending in '-e ' because of an
immediately preceding or following personal pronoun, there
are yet two examples in '-n,' both of which occur in rhymes :
lien, *gapin*, l. 135, Poem 7, rhyming with *wapin* (sb.) ; the
Midl. form was, therefore, known, though it was not Minot's
usual form. These points indicate a border area, and we
would suggest Mid-Lincs rather than Norfolk, with Hall, for
the language is much more northern than that of *The Norfolk
Guilds*, even when confining ourselves to those points which
can be tested by rhymes.

   The Preface to Rolle's Commentary on the Psalter, edited
by Bramley in 1884 for the Oxford Press, is 60 lines long.
The Psalter is generally accepted as Rolle's, but *The Preface*
was not written by him. There has been some scribal
alteration in the text, but the dialect is the same as that of
Rolle, who was born at Thornton in Yorks, and died at
Hampole 1349.

   Like Rolle, the author retained O.E. ā, though the scribe
altered it to the Midl. *o* : e.g. *hold*, O.E. hāldan, rhyming
with *cald*, l. 3, meaning ' called,' O.N. kalla. But O.E. hw
alliterates with *w*, which indicates a place of composition
south of the Aire valley. O.E. ȳ appears as *i*, as we should
naturally expect in N.E. Midl.

   These are the only relevant points which can be tested
by rhymes, but they are sufficient to show that the place of

composition was near the N.E. Midl. border, which was the home of Rolle himself. The other points need not trouble us. The date would be *c.* 1340-50. The language and dialect of **The 1st. Rolle Lyric** are discussed in chapter 6, p. 126.

The Lament of the Monk, from the Arundel MS. 292, of the late thirteenth century, edited by T. Wright and J. O. Halliwell in *Reliquiæ Antiquæ,* vol. i, p. 291. The lament consists of 52 alliterative long lines. Pt. 6. O.E. ā remaining *a,* indicates the Nth. dialect: e.g. *wa,* l. 43, O.E. wā, rhyming with *ta* (take), and other similar rhymes; Pt. 36. The pres. indic. 3rd. sg. ends in '-es' in rhymes: *talmes,* l. 34, rhyming with *salmes,* sb. pl.; the 2nd. pers. ends in '-es' 6 times and in '-est,' '-ist' 6 times, though probably the latter forms are scribal. Pt. 44. *ta* for *take* occurs once, l. 44, rhyming with *wa,* O.E. wā. These are the only three rhymes that afford us any help, but they indicate a place of composition north of the *Salop-Wash* line, and in the case of Pt. 6, the Nth. dialect itself or extreme N. Midl.

The remaining points agree, and if we may trust the evidence, the dialect is N.E. Midl., not N.W. Midl., because Pt. 1. O.E. ăn remains throughout, and Pt. 5. O.E. ў as *i* throughout.

The pres. indic. pl. ends in '-en' twice, and in '-es' 4 times; and if these are original, they confirm the view that the dialect was bordering on Nth.; the scribe was probably more southern than the writer. The MS. is dated *c.* 1375-90 (i.e. the hand responsible for this poem), and we can only conjecture the date of composition as *c.* 1350-80.

The 1st. Burlesque, from a MS. in the Advocates' Library, Edinburgh, fifteenth century, consists of 49 lines and is edited in *Reliquiæ Antiquæ,* vol. i, p. 81. The text is very corrupt and has been considerably modernised. There are only four points in rhymes which can help us: Pts. 12 and 13. O.E. $\bar{æ}^{1\,\&\,2}$ both as tense *e*; Pt. 32. The infinitive without ending in rhymes; Pt. 36. The pres. indic. sg. in '-es': *makes,* l. 43, rhyming with *stakes,* sb. pl. Taken together, these rhymes indicate a place of composition north of the *Salop-Wash* line.

If the present copy be a true representation of the original dialect, despite the modernisation, then the Nth. dialect is excluded by such points as *hom,* ll. 24, 29, 31; O.E. '-and' as '-*ond*'; O.E. ā as *o* throughout. On the other hand, the western area is indicated by *hom*, occurring 3 times to *them* once. The form *mony*, the only example of Pt. 1, need not be western, and Pt. 5 O.E. ў is *i*, probably on account of the late period.

This dialectal survey confirms the evidence offered by a consideration of the references in the text itself to the Bishop of Chester. The dialect is undoubtedly N.W. Midl. of a late period, which we may guess to have been *c.* 1400, judging from the style, metre and language.

The 1st. Chester Play, The Fall of Lucifer, contains 32 alliterative long lines, edited by Deimling for the E.E.T.S., E.S., 62 ; the language represents the speech of Chester of 1450-1500, and since the text was examined in chapter 1, there is no need for any further investigation here.

The works treated in this chapter range in date from 1200 to 1500, that is, over the whole of the M.E. period. Concerning the dialect, each is represented from Nth. to S. Western. After the metrical examination it will be possible to generalise further regarding the above facts.

CHAPTER 5.

POEMS IN RHYMED ALLITERATIVE STANZAS.

THE alliterative stanzas in the poems to be treated in this chapter are of various kinds, but in all cases there is a number of alliterative long lines followed by a number of shorter rhymed lines.

A Satire against the Pride of Ladies, from the MS. Harley 2253 (*c.* 1310), edited by T. Wright in *Political Songs*, Camden Soc., 1839, p. 153, and from the reign of Ed. I. (1272-1307).

We have already seen that the poems in this MS. are in the S. Western dialect, wherever their original place of composition may have been. In some of the poems there are references to Hereford, etc. ; hence the poems were probably composed in the south-west.

We have here the following rhymes : Pt. 32. The infinitive usually ends in '-e,' but 3 times in '-en,' and both forms occur in rhymes : e.g. *to hude*, l. 14, rhyming with *prude* (sb.) ; *eren*, l. 23 (sb. pl.), rhyming with *beren* (infinitive) ; this would suggest S. Midl. rather than Sth. Pt. 25. '-en ' plurals are found, though these need not necessarily be Sth., but S. Midl. Similarly Pt. 12. O.E. $\bar{æ}^1$ as tense *e* in a rhyme (l. 3) would indicate S.W. Midl. rather than Sth. or S.E. Midl. The remaining evidence cannot be tested by rhymes, but is in complete agreement : such as O.E. $\breve{y}$ as *u* throughout (rhyming naturally with itself only) and O.E. ăn as *on* (both these points are western) ; the pronouns for *she, they, them, their* respectively are *he* and *heo, he, hem, here ;* the pres. indic. sg. and pl. end in '-eth,' and the pres. part. in '-*ynde* ' in l. 24, the only instance of that verbal form.

Thus if we may trust this evidence, and there is no reason why we should not, it corroborates that afforded by the points which can be tested by the rhymes. The date of composition must fall within the reign of Ed. I., 1272-1307.

Old Age, from the MS. Harley 913, of the beginning of the

(110)

fourteenth century, edited in *Reliquiæ Antiquæ*, vol. 2, p. 210. The text affords very little evidence of the original dialect, but apart from the possibility of scribal alteration, is obviously S. Western. The only rhyme that affords any evidence is *more*, l. 15, O.E. māre, rhyming with *gore*. O.E. y̆ as *u* throughout, and O.E. ǎn as *on* are both western, as may also be the form *heordmon*, O.E. hĕord-.

The pres. indic. sg. and pl. end in '-eth,' '-ith,' which indicate Sth. or S.W. Midl. in this text. The form for ' them ' is *ham*, l. 29, the only instance. From this meagre evidence it is not possible to say whether the dialect is S.W. Midl. or S. Western.

There is no clue as to the date of the composition other than that afforded by the date of the MS. itself ; presumably it would be *c.* 1300.

A Satire on the Consistory Courts, from the MS. Harley 2253, f. 70 (*c.* 1310), edited by T. Wright in *Political Poems*, p. 155 ; and by G. Sampson in *The Cambridge Book of Prose and Verse*, p. 393.

Again, the poem, as it stands, is in the S.W. Midl. dialect, as may be seen from the fact that O.E. y̆ appears as *u* ; O.E. ǎn as *on* ; the pres. indic. sg. and pl. in '-eth ' ; the pres. part. in '-*inde* ' ; and the forms for the pron. ' they ' being *he, heo*. These and many other similar points indicate the nature of the dialect of the present copy. In the case of *A Satire against the Pride of Ladies*, the rhymes indicate a S. Western original, but here there is conclusive evidence that the dialect was originally N. Midl. Pt. 5. O.E. y̆ as *u*, but note *hure*, l. 19, O.E. hȳr, rhyming with *sire*, O. Fr. sire, which indicates that the scribe has altered the original *i* to *u* ; this is the only conclusive instance. Pt. 38. The pres. indic. pl. in '-eth ' 17 times, in '-en ' once and in '-es ' 3 times, but the rhymes show that the latter forms are the poet's : *gredes*, l. 9, rhyming with *redes* (sb. pl.), and *biledes* also rhyming with the same word ; this indicates the Nth. or N. Midl. dialect. Pt. 19. O.E. hw as *wh, w*, and alliterating with *w*, l. 17, definitely rules out the Nth. dialect, leaving us with N. Midl. Pt. 12. O.E. ǣ[1] as tense *e* is the development which we should expect in the latter dialect. Pt. 5 above would indicate N.E. Midl., and not W. Midl. at this period.

Lastly, Pt. 32. The infinitive ending in '-e,' proved by many rhymes, but once ending in '-en,' *breven*, l. 23, rhyming with *sleven*, sb. pl. ; it will be remembered that Robert Mannyng in N.E. Midl. occasionally retains the final '-n ' of the infinitive as a concession to rhyme, but here it is quite possible that the poet wrote *sleves—breves*.

The evidence from the remaining points is irrelevant, because of the possibility of scribal alteration ; but the main dialect is obviously N.E. Midl., despite the copy which is S. Western. The poem again falls in the reign of Ed. I., 1272-1307.

The Pistill of Susan, from the Vernon MS. 317, dated 1370-80, and from the Cotton Caligula A. ii., Brit. Mus. Addit. 22283, dated 1380-1400. It has been edited by F. J. Furnivall in *Minor Poems of the Vernon MS.*, E.E.T.S. 117, 1901, p. 626 ; and by F. J. Amours in *Scottish Alliterative Poems*, 1897, S.T.S., vol. 27 ; and there are also other editions.

The texts differ considerably and neither is a correct representation of the original dialect, which fortunately can be rediscovered by a careful study of the rhymes ; all other points are irrelevant.

Pt. 6. O.E. ā as *a* : e.g. *sare*, l. 222, O.E. sār, rhyming with *care*, O.E. căru ; the MS., however, has *sore ;* and there are many similar rhymes. Pt. 5. O.E. ў as *i* in rhymes, whereas within the line the scribal *u*-forms remain : e.g. *fyre*, l. 193, O.E. fўr, rhyming with *schire*, O.E. scīr. Pt. 32. The infinitive usually in '-en,' but, however, in rhymes only in '-e' : e.g. *to bide*, l. 147, rhyming with *tyde*, sb. Pt. 36. The pres. indic. sg. in '-es' : e.g. *comes*, l. 36, rhyming with *domes*, sb. pl. ; and many other similar rhymes. Pt. 38. The pres. indic. pl. in ' -es ' : e.g. *glees*, l. 84, rhyming with *trees*, sb. pl. ; in the MSS. the form is usually '-en,' but not always. Pt. 12, 13. O.E. ǣ¹ & ² are tense *e* in this poem, judging by the rhymes ; finally, Pt. 7. O.E. āw, as *aw* : e.g. *iknawen*, l. 238, O.E. cnāwan, rhyming with *drawen, dawen*, O.E. drăgen, dăgas.

This is all the evidence available, since we are not concerned with locating the MSS. themselves, but are trying to ascertain the dialect of the original composition, which is probably Nth. Pts. 6, 7, 38 in particular show this, and the other points (5, 12, 13, 32, 36) occur in the forms which we should expect in the Nth. dialect. It is quite possible, however, that the poem was N.E. Midl., but not probable. We will say nothing at this stage concerning the supposed author of this poem—"Huchown of the Awle Ryale," since this matter does not fall within the scope of this volume. Dialectally there would be no objection to assigning the poem to a Nth. writer. The date usually assigned to the poem is 1350-60.

The Awntyrs of Arthure at the Terne Wathelyne, from the famous Thornton MS. in Yorks, dated 1430-40 from the Douce MS. 324 Bodl. and finally from the Ireland MS. of Hale. The three texts differ considerably. Miss Serjeantson [1] has examined the Ireland MS. dialectally and concludes by saying, " There seems to be no good reason for doubting that the MS. originated in Lancs, where it still remains.'' The Ireland MS. is edited in *Three Metrical Romances*, Robson, Camden Society, 1842, and all three MSS. by F. J. Amours in *Scottish Alliterative Poems*, S.T.S., vol. 27, 1897. The poem naturally centres round Cumberland, and the author certainly shows a close acquaintance with the places he describes, such as Inglewood Forest and Tarn Wadling, whereas his notions of the south of England are very confused ; thus there is internal evidence for assigning the poem to the north of England.

As the Thornton MS. seems to be a more accurate representation of the original dialect, the study of the dialect is taken from that MS. Only the points that can be tested by rhymes are, however, included. Pt. 5. O.E. $\ddot{y}$ as i: e.g. *hydes*, l. 125, O.E. hȳdan, rhyming with *bydis*, O.E. bīdan ; and many other similar rhymes. Pt. 6. O.E. ā as a: *mare*, l. 199, O.E. māre, rhyming with *care*, O.E. cǎru : or *more*, l. 100, rhyming with *bare*, O.E. bǽr (showing scribal alteration). Pt. 9. O.E. ō as $\ddot{u}$: e.g. *fure*, l. 712, O.E. fōron, rhyming with *Arthüre*. Pt. 19. O.E. hw alliterates with O.E. cw: e.g. l. 144, **Q**wene was a **wh**ilome (O.E. cwēn and hwīlum). Pt. 36. The pres. indic. sg. ends in '-es,' '-is ' : e.g. *glydis*, l. 118, rhyming with *sydis*, sb. pl. Pt. 38. The pres. indic. pl. ends in '-es,' '-is,' except when immediately preceded or followed by a personal pronoun : e.g. *rydys*, l. 332, rhyming with *hydis*, sb. pl., O.E. hȳd. Pt. 12. O.E. ǣ[1] is tense *e* in many rhymes.

Of the above points, 6, 9, 19, 38 are exclusively Nth., and Pts. 5, 12, 36 occur in the forms which they would be expected in the Nth. dialect ; so that there is proof that the

[1] *The Dialects of the West Midlands*, Rev. Eng. Stud., vol. 3, p. 319, 1927.

poem was written in Nth., but it is not possible to particularise further. The internal evidence is, however, sufficient to locate the poem near Carlisle, or at least the county of Cumberland, and the date is the latter part of the fourteenth century. **The Quatrefoil of Love,** from the Brit. Mus. Addit. MS. 31042, dated 1430-50, edited by Sir I. Gollancz in *The Furnivall Miscellany*, p. 112 ; it is also found in the Bodley Addit. MS. A. 106, but this is not a good text. There is no evidence of any scribal alteration, yet it is best to rely mainly upon the evidence afforded by the rhymes. The following points are important : Pt. 6. O.E. ā as *a* : e.g. *gane*, l. 145, O.E. gān, rhyming with *tane*, O.N. tăka ; *sare*, l. 26, O.E. sār, rhyming with *care*, O.E. căru, cĕaru ; *one*, l. 85, O.E. ān, rhyming with *trone* (O. Fr.) would, however, seem to indicate that the poet lived near to the border between Nth. and Midl. Pt. 32. The '-n ' of the infinitive is lost : e.g. *to synge*, l. 5, rhyming with *playing*. Pts. 12 and 13. O.E. ǣ¹ ᵃ ² as tense *e* (the latter before d, t), proved by rhymes : e.g. ll. 41, 60, 195. Pt. 44. Contracted forms of 'take' occur : *tane*, l. 144, rhyming with *gane*, O.E. gān. Pt. 5. O.E. y̆ as *i* : e.g. *syn*, l. 495, O.E. sўnn, rhyming with *begyne*, O.E. begĭnnan, or *fyre*, l. 419, O.E. fȳr, rhyming with *syre*, O. Fr. sire. Lastly, Pt. 17. O.E. ēah, ēag, M.E. ẹ̄ raised to ị̄ : e.g. *hey*, l. 183, O.E. hēah, rhyming with *crye*, O. Fr. crier : *hye*, l. 586, O.E. hēah, rhyming with *gentry*.

Of the above points, No. 6 indicates the Nth. dialect or extreme N. Midl., and this is confirmed by Pt. 17, which, as may be seen from the map, appears as ị̄ in Derby and the immediate neighbourhood, but as ẹ̄ in the Nth. dialect. The consistent raising in the rhymes suggests N. Midl. rather than Nth. proper. The remaining points occur in their Nth. and N. Midl. forms, and Pt. 5 would indicate N.E. Midl., rather than W. Midl. There are many other points which would corroborate this, but which cannot be tested by rhymes : The pres. part. in '-ande ' ; the use of *scho*, *þam*, *þaire*, *thire* (1 example) ; the pres. indic. sg. and pl. in ' -es,' '-is ' ; O.E. ăn as *an*; O.E. ĕo as *e*. These and other similar points are also quite natural in N.E. Midl.

It is very difficult to date the poem except by general considerations of metre, which incline us to suggest c. 1350-1400 ; these limits are probably sufficiently broad.

St. John the Evangelist, from the Thornton MS. dated 1430-40, edited by G. G. Perry, E.E.T.S. 26, 1867, p. 88. This is also a Nth. work, and the fact is well attested by the rhymes.

Pt. 6. O.E. ā as *a* and *o*, though the rhymes show that the former was the original form : e.g. *mare*, l. 27, O.E. māre, rhyming with *fare*, O.E. făru ; or *sare*, l. 70, O.E. sār, rhyming with *bare*, adj. O.E. bǣr. Pt. 5. O.E. ў̆ as *i* in rhymes : e.g. *syn*, l. 65, O.E. sўnn, rhyming with *virgyn* (O. Fr.). Pt. 38. The pres. indic. pl. ends in '-(e)s ' in rhymes and also within the line, except in connexion with personal pronouns : e.g. *mase* (makes), l. 34, rhyming with *face*. The same rhyme indicates that the poet was familiar with the contracted form of the word *make*, Pt. 44. Pt. 32. The infinitive has lost the final '-n ' : e.g. *to wende*, l. 163, rhyming with *fende*, sb. Pts. 12 and 13. O.E. ǣ¹ ᵃⁿᵈ ² as tense *e* (under the usual conditions) ; see the rhymes in ll. 111, 263, etc., which prove this.

These are the only points which can be proved by rhymes.

Pts. 6 and 38 require the Nth. dialect, or extreme N. Midl., and the remaining points agree with this, though Pt. 5 would rule out N.W. Midl. The other points in the text, which cannot be proved original by the study of the rhymes, corroborate the above statements ; thus the pronouns are *scho*, *þay*, *þam* or *thayme*, *thaire*, etc. (Pts. 27-30) ; Pt. 22. O.E. ' sc-' in unstressed positions as ' *s*-' ; Pt. 36. The pres. indic. sg. in '-es ' ; Pts. 7 and 8. O.E. āw, āg, āh as *aw*, *au* ; Pt. 14. O.E. ĕo as *e* ; Pt. 35. The pres. part. in '-*ande* ' ; Pt. 1. O.E. ăn as *an*, except in the word *mony*, a form common in Nth. and N.E. Midl.

There is one last point—Pt. 19. O.E. hw appears as *wh* and alliterates with *w* : e.g. l. 24, " For thi **w**erkes ay **w**hare " (O.E. wĕorc, hwǣr). This indicates a place of composition south of the *Ribble-Aire* line ; hence we have to choose the extreme N.E. Midl. dialect instead of the Nth. dialect proper. This is also corroborated by the development of O.E. ō, which appears as *u* usually, but also as *o*, though never in the same word, indicating that both forms were used by the poet himself, who lived on the border area (*buke*, *tuke*, *gude*, etc. ; *sone*, *mode*, *forsothe*). The date usually assigned to the poem is *c.* 1375-1400, and judging from metrical considerations we would say that the earlier date is more likely to be correct ;

we can, however, only conjecture the date in works of this kind.

The 2nd. Burlesque, from the same MS. as that of *The 1st. Burlesque*, discussed on p. 108, in the Advocates' Library, Edinburgh, of the fifteenth century, and edited in the same volume, p. 84. It is only 29 lines long. *The 2nd. Burlesque*, like *The 1st. Burlesque*, is written in the dialect of Chester ; the evidence for the dialect in this short poem is very scanty, but we may notice *hom* (for ' them '), ll. 23, 25, as in *The 1st. Burlesque ;* also the endings '-us,' '-ur ' are extremely common. The remaining points are the same as in the other poem.

An Alliterative Poem on Fortune, from the MS. Laud. 108 Bodl., early fifteenth century, edited in *Reliquiæ Antiquæ*, vol. 2, p. 7. The present copy is full of very contradictory evidence, and represents a mixture of forms not possible in any dialect ; also the number of rhymes which help us is very small.

Pt. 5. O.E. $\bar{y}$ as *u* usually, but also as *i* and *e* : e.g. *kith*, l. 113, O.E. cȳðð, rhyming with *with ;* but from such a rhyme we cannot generalise and conclude that the development was *i* throughout, because we should expect *i* after *k* even in the west ; the development is *u* in the text after *r, m, l, g, b* (*rugge*, l. 7, O.E. hrȳcg, *murthe*, l. 15, O.E. mȳrgð, *gurte*, l. 45, O.E. gȳrdan, etc.) ; on the other hand, *mynde, litel, tynt, kynde, kysed*, etc., which occur, are natural (see chapter 1) ; the only form that suggests scribal alteration is *birde*, l. 47, beside *burde*, l. 58 ; the latter form is the usual one in alliterative poetry, but the former with *i* is hardly ever found. Therefore, on the whole the development is western ; the forms *merthes*, l. 120, O.E. mȳrgð, *merye*, l. 37, O.E. mȳrig, *meriere*, l. 73, *denede*, l. 13, O.E. dȳnian—these are not unusual. The point is worth dealing with at length, for in the absence of rhymes it affords some evidence regarding the dialect. Pt. 19. O.E. hw appears as *wh* and alliterates with *w*, e.g. ll. 42, 60 ; this rules out Nth. ; and Pt. 32. The infinitive has lost the final '-n ' : e.g. ʒede, l. 16, rhyming with *drede*, sb. Pt. 12. O.E. $\bar{æ}^1$ as tense *e*, proved by many rhymes. These two last points seem to indicate an area at least as far north as Glos (see map) ; and if we may trust the evidence for Pt. 5, the dialect was W. Midl. ; this in fact is almost certain.

Most of the remaining points corroborate this : The pres. indic. pl. in '-en,' but the sg. in '-eth ' (S. Midl.) ; the pres. part. in '-inde ' twice and in '-inge ' four times (this is not impossible in Glos) ; the form of the 3rd. pers. pl. nom. pron. is *they*, but there are no examples of the acc. and gen. forms ; the 3rd. sg. nom. fem. pron. is *ȝe*, l. 42, a form also found in Glos at this period.

There is no means of dating the poem except by a consideration of the language and metre ; the former is a very dangerous path to take, whereas the latter inclines us to place the poem rather late, *c.* 1400, for reasons which will appear obvious when the metrical examination has been made.

Golagrus and Gawain (G), The Houlate (H), and Rauf Coilȝear (R), three Scottish poems, edited by F. J. Amours in *Scottish Alliterative Poems*, S.T.S., vols. 27 and 38, 1897 ; the 1st. p. 1, the 2nd. p. 47, and the 3rd. p. 82.

Golagrus and Gawain is from a text of 1508 preserved in the Advocates' Library, Edinburgh. The date usually assigned to the poem is 1450-1500, and the general atmosphere is that of Scotland, though there are no local references.

The Houlate is from the MS. Asloan, *c.* 1515, and from the Bannatyne MS. in the Advocates' Library, Edinburgh, dated 1568. In the last stanza the author tells us that his name was Holland and that *The Buke of the Houlat* was written at Darnaway for Eliz. Dunbar, Countess of Moray, who died 1455 ; an approximate date would be *c.* 1450.

Rauf Coilȝear is from a text printed by Robert Lepreuik in 1572. As the poem is referred to by Douglas in 1503 and by Dunbar before 1500, it is not reasonable to put back the date of composition before the latter part of the fifteenth century, 1480-1500 ; there are no references to Scottish places, but there are many descriptions of true Scottish scenery.

It is unnecessary to examine the dialect of these three poems, which are obviously, from internal evidence, Scottish in origin.   But one or two conclusive points may be given.

Pt. 6. O.E. ā as *a*, *ai* : e.g. *sair*, l. 727 G., O.E. sār, rhyming with *cair*, O.E. căru ; or *rair*, l. 826 H., O.E. rārian, rhyming with *fair*, O.E. fæger. Pt. 9. O.E. ō as a rounded vowel *ü* : e.g. *fure*, l. 79 H., O.E. fōr, rhyming with *sure*, O. Fr. sur, sëur ; and many other similar rhymes in all three poems. Pt. 38. The pres. indic. pl. ends in '-ys,' '-is ' :

e.g. *dwellis*, l. 537 R., rhyming with *bellis*, sb. pl. Pt. 7. O.E.
āw as *aw* : e.g. *knawin*, l. 155 G., O.E. cnāwan, rhyming with
drawin, O.E. drăgen, etc.
Further rhymes are unnecessary to demonstrate the fact
that the poems are northern in origin.
    Sum Practysis of Medecyn, by Robert Henryson, *c.* 1430-
1506 (?). This short alliterative poem, in fact Henryson's
only alliterative poem, belongs to his first literary period, and
would therefore fall between the dates 1450 and 1462 ; it
may be found on p. 229 of the edition of his works,
edited by W. M. Metcalfe, 1917. The poem was written in
Scotland.
    The Ballad of Kynd Kittock, by William Dunbar, who wàs
born *c.* 1460, and died soon after 1513 ; the poem consists
of three stanzas, and was written in Scotland *c.* 1500. It can
be found in H. B. Baildon's edition of Dunbar's works, p. 23.
    The Prologue of the 8th. Book of the Aeneid, by Gavin
Douglas, who was born 1474 and died 1522 ; the poem was
completed in 1513, and this prologue may be found in Small's
edition of the works of Douglas, vol. 3, p. 142.
    A Pleasant Satire upon the Estates, by Sir David Lyndsay,
who was born *c.* 1490 and died 1555—a long poem written
c. 1553. His works are edited by D. Laing, 1879, in three
volumes.
    Thus, these poems in rhymed alliterative stanzas range
in date from *c.* 1280 to *c.* 1550, a very extensive period, but
from 1300 onwards the works mostly appear in Nth. or Low-
land Scotch.

CHAPTER 6.

POEMS WITH ALLITERATION OF THE STRESSED SYLLABLES.

IN this chapter we shall examine a number of poems not always metrically uniform, but linked together by the fact that the writers used alliteration very frequently as an additional ornament in ordinary rhymed syllabic verse. The long line has disappeared, but alliteration remains. Some of the texts treated in chapter 2 also fall under this heading.

The Proverbs of Alfred, which contain some verse of the kind described above. Remarks on the dialect have already been given on p. 44, and no further statement is necessary here.

The Hymns of St. Godric, from the MS. Harley 322, of the twelfth century. The three hymns of St. Godric do not contain much alliteration, but are included here on account of the early period at which they were written. St. Godric died 1170 and his poems are roughly to be dated *c.* 1160-70. They are edited by J. Hall, *Early Middle English*, 1920, p. 5, with notes on p. 241. St. Godric was the hermit of Finchale, near Durham. The dialect is Nth., and though there is little evidence of this in the text, Hall points out three features which are Nth. : Pt. 6. O.E. ā as *a*; Pt. 22. The use of *silde*, l. 10, O.E. scyldan ; and lastly the extreme simplification of the inflexions at so early a date.

The fact that we know he lived near Durham as a hermit is sufficient.

The Departing Soul's Address to the Body, already discussed on p. 43, contains some purely syllabic verse with ornamental alliteration, as does **Layamon's Brut,** discussed on p. 45 ; whether Layamon consciously used syllabic verse will be a matter for discussion later.

(—)idde Huve with milde Stevene, from the MS. Cotton Cleopatra B. vi, f. 201 v. (*c.* 1250) ; edited in *Reliquiæ Antiquæ*, vol. I, p. 22.

The *Pater Noster*, the *Hail Mary*, and the *Creed* follow,

written in the same dialect. There is no real evidence as to
the nature of the original dialect, but only of the dialect of
the surviving copy. Pt. 9. O.E. ō as *o* : *don*, l. 16, O.E.
dōn, rhymes with *kingdom*, O.E. cynedōm, but we cannot
argue from this that the dialect was not Nth., because of the
early period at which the poem was written. Pt. 5. O.E.
ў̆ as *i* in *mankinde*, l. 9, rhymes with *finde*, O.E. fĭndan,
though again we cannot generalise from such a rhyme on
account of the different development of O.E. ў̆ after certain
consonants. The same rhyme, however, proves that the '-n '
of the infinitive was lost, since *finde* is an infinitive form,
ruling out the Sth. dialect at this early period.

The dialect would, however, appear to be Nth. in view of
Pt. 6. O.E. ā as *a*, except in the word *fro*, O.N. frá, but
fra, l. 22 ; Pt. 29. The use of *þam* once to *ham* twice—ll.
6, 8 ; Pt. 36. The pres. indic. sg. in ' -es '; Pt. 38. The
pres. indic. pl. in '-e ' twice and in ' -n ' twice. If these
points are original, they would require us to locate the poem
in extreme N.E. Midl. The date is probably *c*. 1200-50, but
not later, because the MS. itself is not later than 1250.

The Bestiary, already described on p. 45 in chapter 2.
This work, like its Latin original, is written in a variety of
metres.

The Debate Between the Body and the Soul, from six
different MSS. The earlier ones are : Laud 108 f. 200 (*c*.
1290) ; Auchinleck, f. 31 (*c*. 1330-40) ; Vernon, f. 285 (1370-
80). The Laud MS. is probably the best representation of
the original. Since the texts differ considerably it is essential
to adduce as evidence only those points which can be proved
original by the rhyme-study. The Laud MS. is edited with
the Vernon by T. Wright for the Camden Soc., vol. 16, *The
Latin Poems of Walter Map*, p. 334 ; but is erroneously
printed in long lines.

Pt. 2. O.E. ă + l + Cons. mutated : *wal*, l. 219, O.E.
wĭellan, rhyming with *smel*, O.E. smĕl ; this rhyme is clearly
very important because it shows that the scribe used the
western form (see the map) with *a*, although the poet himself
used the non-western form with *e*. Pt. 5. O.E. ў̆ as *i* :
pride, l. 211, O.E. prȳto, rhyming with *side*, O.E. sīd : *schride*,
l. 139, O.E. scrȳdan, rhyming with *biside*, O.E. sīd ; this latter
rhyme is important because the usual form expected in the
west would be *schrude*, not *schride ;* the poet did not live in

the west. Pt. 6. O.E. ā as *o* ; this is proved by one rhyme : *þro*, l. 55, O.N. *þrár*, rhyming with *to, do*, O.E. tō, dōn ; this rhyme, though a false one, gives us the clue to the poet's form. Therefore, we are so far reduced to E. Midl. and Sth. Pt. 32. The infinitive without '-n ' : e.g. *to singe*, l. 173, rhyming with *þinge*, sb. ; at such an early period this would rule out the Sth. dialect. This is confirmed by Pt. 41. The 2nd. sg. wk. pret. in '-es,' though '-est' also occurs : *leddes*, l. 14, O.E. lǣdan, rhyming with *beddes*, sb. ; also *edest*, l. 101, O.E. ge-ēode, rhyming with *medes*, sb. pl. This means that the poem was originally written in the N.E. Midl. dialect, not below the *Salop-Wash* line ; unfortunately we cannot particularise further, owing to lack of evidence. The date usually assigned to the poem is *c.* 1250, the middle of the thirteenth century.

A Disputison bitwene childe Jesu and maistres of the Lawe of Jewus, from the Vernon MS., leaf 300, 1370-80, and from the Brit. Mus. Addit. 22283, 1380-1400, edited by J. Furnivall, E.E.T.S., 117, pp. 479-84, 1901. The date usually assigned to the poem is *c.* 1275-1300. The poem has always been considered to be in the Kentish dialect, and the evidence afforded by the rhymes corroborates this view.

Pt. 5. O.E. y̆ as *e*, almost throughout : *knet*, l. 132, O.E. cny̆ttan, rhyming with *set*, O.E. sĕttan ; *fulfelle*, l. 200, O.E. fulfy̆llan, rhyming with *dwelle*, O.E. dwĕllan ; of course, this *e*-development should be described as S.E., rather than Kentish, for which see the map. The remaining points indicate a Sth. dialect, such as : Pt. 6. O.E. ā as *o* : e.g. *lore*, l. 168, O.E. lār, rhyming with *bore*, O.E. bŏren.

Pt. 12. O.E. ǣ[1] as tense *e* : e.g. *were*, l. 13, O.E. wǣron, rhyming with *manere*, A.N. manẹre ; such a rhyme in a text which has been proved to be southern indicates the Kentish neighbourhood.

Pt. 15. O.E. ĕa + Cons. mutated is both *e* and *u* : *hure*, l. 61, O.E. hīeran, rhyming with *süre, mesüre* (O. Fr.) ; this proves that the dialect was Sth. ; but there is also *heere*, l. 161, O.E. hīeran, rhyming with *deore*, O.E. dēore ; evidently both forms were current. The remaining forms in the copy agree with the evidence forthcoming from the above rhymes, and there is no further proof needed for the statement that the poem was written in the Kentish dialect ; the verbal forms do not occur in conclusive rhymes.

Certain Alliterated Lyrics in the MS. Harley 2253, *c.* 1310, edited by T. Wright in *Specimens of Lyric Poetry composed in England in the reign of Ed. I.*, Percy Soc., 1842, there are 17 alliterated ones :

1. *Mon in þe mone*, p. 110.
2. *Ichot a burde in boure bryht*, p. 51.
3. *Lenten ys come*, p. 43.
4. *Ichot a burde in a bour*, p. 25.
5. *Mosti ryden by Rybbesdale*, p. 33.
6. *In a fryht as y con fare*, p. 36.
7. *A wayle whyt ase whalles bon*, p. 38.
8. *In may hit murgeth*, p. 45.
9. *Weping haveþ myn wonges wet*, p. 30.
10. *Middelerd for Man*, p. 22.
11. *Heʒe louerd*, p. 47.
12. *Bytwene mershe and averil*, p. 27.
13. *With longyng I am lad*, p. 29.
14. *Of a mon Matheu thohte*, p. 41.
15. *I syke when y singe*, p. 85.
16. *Mayden moder milde*, p. 97.
17. *God, that al this myhtes may*, p. 99.

These poems are not all the work of one poet and there are not sufficient rhymes in each poem to enable us to localise the dialect in each case. Miss Serjeantson, in her study of the W. Midl. dialect, takes these lyrics as representative of the speech of Hereford and neighbourhood, because of the references to Hereford saints, and undoubtedly the bulk of the lyrics are from that district, though there are others which may be N.E. Midl. ; the point is not very important for our purpose since these lyrics are mainly poems with ornamental alliteration, a type found in all dialects.

Pt. 6. O.E. ā as *o*: e.g. *sore*, l. 72, No. 11, O.E. sār, rhyming with ʒore, O.E. gēara ; or *non*, l. 29, No. 4, rhyming with *Iohon ;* this rules out Nth. Pt. 9. O.E. ō as *o*: *mone*, l. 31, No. 4, O.E. mōna, rhyming with *trone*, O.Fr. Pt. 1. O.E. ă + nasal as *o*: e.g. *mon*, l. 43, No. 7, O.E. mănn, rhyming with *on*, O.E. ŏn ; the same rhyme occurs at l. 64, No. 9. This might indicate a western dialect, though the form *mon* is of course common in Nth., a fact which would not, however, apply in this case ; within the line the form is *o* consistently. Pt. 5, O.E. ẙ as *u* but also as *i* ; the only conclusive rhyme

in the poems is *cusse*, l. 27, No. 7, O.E. c̄yssan, rhyming with
wisse, O.E. wïsse. The original must have had *kisse*, the form
we should naturally expect even in W. Midl., though *cusse*
is, of course, found ; however, we cannot generalise from this
word concerning O.E. y̆ after other consonants. The remaining rhymes are inconclusive in their evidence, such as : l. 48,
No. 6, *cluppe, asluppe, huppe, luppe*—all rhyming together ;
all these words occur in M.E. with *i* and *u*, so that the poet
might have written all four words with *i* ; however, since
u is the main form, it would seem that O.E. y̆ was retained,
the dialect being western. Pt. 19. O.E. hw as *wh* alliterating
with *w* : e.g. *whuch*, l. 42, No. 8, O.E. hwylc, alliterating with
worldes, O.E. weoruld ; and many other similar examples.
This corroborates the previous evidence that the dialect is
non-Nth. Pt. 32. The infinitive ends in '-e' in rhymes :
e.g. *deme*, l. 30, No. 3, rhyming with *breme*, adj.; see also No. 11,
l. 21 ; No. 4, l. 42 ; No. 10, l. 6, etc. When the ending '-en'
is found, it is used to avoid hiatus before *h* or a vowel : e.g.
l. 14, No. 3, *dutten* (is) ; l. 100, No. 11, *heryen* (him), etc.
Pt. 36. The pres. indic. sg. in '-eth,' rhyming with the '-eth'
ending of the pres. indic. pl. (Pt. 38) ; *shereth*, l. 4, No. 1,
rhyming with *totereth*, a pres. indic. pl. ; *semeth*, l. 28, No. 5,
rhyming with *spredeth* (pl.), and with *ledes* (sg.) ; this and
similar forms are surely scribal, because the plural could not
end in '-es' in a dialect which had all the above points in
common. This is confirmed by the fact that there are examples of syncopated forms in the 3rd. sg. pres. indic. : e.g.
byt (biddeth), l. 42, No. 9, rhyming with *wyt*, sb. Pts. 7 and 8.
O.E. āw, āg, āh, as *ow, ou* : e.g. *wowes*, l. 5, No. 8, O.E. wāg
(wall), rhyming with *bowes*, O.E. bŏga.

Pt. 12. O.E. ǣ[1] is tense *e*, as proved by many rhymes ;
this point would, in the west of the country, indicate an
area not below W. Glos.

These are the only points in the rhymes that help us,
but they are sufficient to indicate that the original dialect
of the bulk of the lyrics was S.W. Midl. ; the pres. indic.
pl. in '-eth' indicates Glos and neighbourhood rather than
any area further to the north. The MS. as a whole is undoubtedly in the SW. Midl. dialect. The poems were
written *c.* 1300.

On the Retinues of the Great, from the same MS. f. 124,
a satire in all probability written before the death of Edward I.

(1307), and edited by T. Wright in *Political Songs*, Camden Soc., 1839, p. 237, and by G. Sampson in *The Cambridge Book of Prose and Verse*, p. 404. The present copy is S. Western, but from the study of the rhymes we can only learn that the '-n ' of the infinitive was lost : e.g. *spelle*, 1. 74, rhyming with *felle*, sb. ; for the remaining points, we have to rely on the copy. Western features are : O.E. y̆ as *u* throughout (only rhyming with itself ; this, however, may be an indication that O.E. y̆ did remain, for otherwise it would have been found rhyming with *i*) ; O.E. ă before a nasal as *o*.

Sth. features are the pronouns for 'they,' 'them,' 'their'— *hue, hem* and *huem, here* and *huere* respectively; the pres. indic. sg. and pl. in '-eth '; the extreme frequency of '-en ' noun plurals. These points, taken together, require S. Western or extreme S.W. Midl. ; judging from O.E. y̆ as *u*, the original was western also.

The Enemies of Man, from the MS. Auchinleck 303, dated 1330-40 ; it has been edited many times, but the best editions are those by C. Brown, *Religious Lyrics of the 14th Century*, p. 32, and by C. Bullock in the Rev. of Eng. Stud., vol. 18, p. 186, 1929. The poem was composeᴄ in the early fourteenth century. The copy is Nth. or N. Midl., and there are rhymes to prove that the original was also in the same dialect.

Pt. 6. O.E. ā as *a* : e.g. *agas*, 1. 5, O.E. gān, etc., rhyming with *tas* (takes), O.N. tăka ; or *mare*, 1. 22, O.E. māre, rhyming with *care*, O.E. căru. Pt. 38. The pres. indic. pl. ends in '-es ' : e.g. *fiʒtes*, 1. 8, rhyming with *wiʒtes*, sb. pl. ; these two points are proof of a northern dialect in themselves. Pt. 7. O.E. āw retained, is only found in Nth. and N.E. Midl. : e.g. *lawe*, 1. 48, O.E. hlāw, rhyming with *wawe*, which never appears as *wowe* in M.E., being equated with M.L.G. *wage;* the evidence of the rhyme is therefore conclusive. Pt. 36. The pres. indic. sg. ends in '-es ' : e.g. *bites*, 1. 20, rhyming with *sites*, sb. pl., and three other similar rhymes. Pt. 32. The infinitive ends in '-e ' : e.g. *mete*, 1. 96, rhyming with *fete*, sb. pl., O.E. fēt. Pt. 5. O.E. y̆ as *i* : *sites*, 1. 24, O.N. sýt, rhyming with *bites*, O.E. bītan. All these points are only found in common in Nth. and extreme N.E. Midl. ; unfortunately there are no examples of O.E. hw in alliteration to enable us to decide between these two areas.

The remaining points, which cannot be tested by the rhymes, seem to favour N.E. Midl. : O.E. '-and ' as '*-ond* ';

O.E. ō retained ; O.E. sc· as '*sch-*'; the occasional survival of the verbal prefix ' y-'; the use of *hem, her* for ' them,' ' their ' respectively ; these features may be scribal, and the point must be left open.

Minot's Poems, *Nos. 1, 3, 4, 6, 7, 8.* The dialect of these and of the remaining poems by Minot has already been discussed in chapter 4, p. 106 ; no further statement is necessary here.

Lady Fortune and Her Wheel, a rhymed quatrain from the MS. Camb. Univ. Otho 7, 32, edited by C. Brown in *Religious Lyrics of the 14th Century,* p. 56, No. 42 ; the editor places it among the lyrics of the mid-century, *c.* 1350.

Pt. 19 is alone conclusive in the evidence it affords : O.E. hw as *wh* alliterating with *w* : l. 4, *whel,* O.E. hwēol and *wele* (weal) ; O.E. wĕla. There is also *man,* l. 4, O.E. mănn ; O.E. ā as *o* throughout ; *che,* l. 3 (she) ; the 3rd. sg. pres. indic. : *turneȝ, makit, turnet.* If these points were original,we might suggest E. Midl. as the most suitable dialect.

Falsenesse and Couetys er feris, from the Merton Coll., Oxf. MS. 248, edited by C. Brown, *Religious Lyrics of the 14th Century,* p. 54, No. 39, and described as a lyric of the mid-century, i.e. *c.* 1350.

There is very little evidence regarding the dialect, save for Pt. 36. The pres. indic. sg. in '-es ' : *leris,* l. 5, rhyming with *feris,* sb. pl. ; this is Nth. and N. Midl. If we may trust the remaining evidence, the former dialect is the more suitable because of : þem (them) ; *sall* instead of ' shall ' ; Pt. 39. The pl. pres. indic. of the vb. ' to be,' as *er, ar, are ;* Pt. 5. O.E. ȳ as *i* ; Pt. 1. O.E. ăn as *an.*

Pt. 6. O.E. ā̆ as *o* throughout, is either scribal or indicates the extreme N. Midl. dialect.

Ave Maris Stella, from Bishop Sheppey's Collection, *c.* 1360 ; this lyric is also edited in the above volume, p. 55, No. 41.

Pt. 6. O.E. ā retained as *a* : e.g. *gast,* l. 9, O.E. gāst, rhyming with *chaste,* O.Fr. chaste ; this requires a Nth. dialect and the fact is corroborated by the other points : *sall* instead of *schall;* the pres. part. in '-ande '; O.E. ȳ as *i* ; O.E. ă + nasal as *a* ; and the pres. indic. sg. in '-us.' The dialect is obviously Nth. or N. Midl.

A Strophic Version of Old Testament Pieces, from the Bodl. Selden Supra 52 (beginning of the fifteenth century) ; Wells in describing this lengthy work says : " The work is probably of 1350-1400 and was originally written in Northern ; . . . only the De Matre, the De Arithiaco and the first 48 lines of Genesis have been printed."[1] Since this was written, Kalen has published an edition of 6000 lines, M.E. *Paraphrases of the O. Test.*, Götesborgs Högskolas Årsskrift, 28.5 ; unfortunately this has not been accessible ; Kalen is said to have dated the work *c.* 1400 or 1410 and located it in Yorks.

There has been a good deal of scribal alteration in the copy ; we therefore rely on a few significant rhymes in the portion available, that is, in the three sections mentioned above, edited by W. Heuser in Anglia, 31, 1908.

Pt. 32. The infinitive without the final '-n ' : e.g. *knaw*, G. 3, rhyming with *law*, sb., and many other similar rhymes. Pt. 35. The pres. part. in '-and ' ; e.g. M. 17, *lastand*, rhyming with *land* (sb.). Pt. 36. The pres. ind. sg. in '-(e)s ' : e.g. *socours*, M. 18, rhyming with *honours* (sb. pl.). Pt. 38. The pres. ind. pl. ends in '-es,' but there are no examples in rhyme.

Pt. 30. The form of the 3rd. pers. pl. pron. gen. is *þayrs*, A. 9, rhyming with *heirs*, O.Fr. heir. These and many other similar points, such as O.E. ǣ[1] as tense *e*, seem to prove that the Nth. or N. Midl. dialect was that in which the poet wrote ; the latter dialect, however, is seen to have been the original one by the fact that O.E. ā is sometimes retained and sometimes not : *lathe*, M. 29, O.E. lāð, rhyming with *scath*, O.N. skăði, and many similar rhymes ; but *sore*, M. 28, O.E. sār, rhyming with *before*, O.E. befŏran ; both types are equally common. This would suggest a border dialect between Nth. and N. Midl., and N.E. Midl. is required rather than N.W. Midl., by the fact that O.E. ȳ appears as *i* in rhymes throughout : e.g. *fyre*, M. 10, O.E. fȳr, rhyming with *desyre*, O. Fr. desyre. Hence Kalen is correct in saying that the work was written in Yorks.

The Lyrics of the School of Richard Rolle, from the MS. Camb. Univ. Dd. 5, 64, iii (late fourteenth century). " *Luf es lyf* " is generally accepted as Rolle's own composition and other lyrics are obviously inspired by him ; they are to be found in *Religious Lyrics of the 14th Century*, C. Brown, 1924, Nos. 79-86. After a careful examination of the language of these eight lyrics, and a study of the rhymes, we are con-

---

[1] Wells, *A Manual of Middle English Writings*, p. 398.

vinced that the dialect in which they are written is exactly the same as that of the county in which Rolle wrote his works—S. Yorks. As we have assumed in chapter I that Rolle's dialect was that of Yorks, there is no need to submit further forms from these poems, which, if not by Rolle himself, owe their inspiration directly to him. The date assigned to the bulk of them is *c.* 1350-70.

Friar Henry's Little Sermon, from the Vernon MS. (1370-80), edited in *Minor Poems of the Vernon MS.,* E.E.T.S. 117, 1901, p. 476 ; the date of the sermon is usually considered to be *c.* 1370-80. As the poem is only 80 lines in length, it is not very easy to test for the original dialect. The only helpful rhymes are : Pt. 6. O.E. ā as *o* : e.g. *mo,* l. 24, O.E. mā, rhyming with *slo,* O.E. slōh ; Pt. 2. *wellan,* l. 8, O.E. wĭellan, rhyming with *dwellen,* O.E. dwĕllan ; however, from such a common form as *welle,* it is unsafe to conclude that the dialect was non-western. Similarly Pt. 14. O.E. ĕo as *e* in the following rhyme is scarcely conclusive in its evidence : *stere,* l. 70, O.E. stĕoran, rhyming with *here,* O.E. hēr ; hence we have to rely on the copy itself.

The Nth. dialect is obviously ruled out by Pt. 6. O.E. ā as *o* in rhymes. Sth. is also ruled out by the fact that the pres. indic. pl. ends in '-en,' the Midl. form, and by the loss of the ' i-' verbal prefix with only one exception—*iharied,* l. 77. At the same time N. Midl. is excluded by the fact that the pres. indic. sg. ends in '-est,' '-eth,' and by the use of *heo* for ' they ' ; taken together, these points indicate the extreme S. Midl. dialect. The western portion is indicated by the fact that O.E. ȳ appears as *u* practically throughout, and O.E. ă before a nasal as *o* with only one exception ; this feature can be tested by a rhyme : *mon,* l. 80, O.E. mănn, rhyming with *non, gon,* O.E. nān, gān. Thus there is almost absolute proof that the dialect is S.W. Midl.

Þurgh Grace Growand in God Almyght, from the MS. Harley 1022 (*c.* 1380-1400), edited by L. Horstmann in *Yorkshire Writers,* vol. I, p. 161 ; the poem is a short lyric of 52 alliterated verses.

There are only three points which can be proved by rhymes : Pt. 6. O.E. ā as *o* : e.g. *holygost,* l. 12, O.E. hālig-gāst, rhyming with *lost,* O.E. lŏsian ; *one,* l. 37, O.E. ān, rhyming with *Iōne* (John) ; similarly, Pt. 9. O.E. ō retained : e.g. *sone,* l. 17, O.E. sōna, rhyming with *trone,* O.Fr. trone ; these two

rule out Nth; Pt. 32. The infinitive is without ending : e.g.
to spryng, l. 2, rhyming with *syng* (infinitive).

For the other points we have to rely upon the evidence
in the text : N. Midl. are the pres. part. in '*-and* '; the use
of *þaim;* the pres. indic. sg. in '*-us* '; O.E. hw as *qu* (no examples in alliteration). The pres. indic. pl. in '*-en* ' is also
Midl.

O.E. ў as *i* and O.E. ăn as *an,* rule out the west, leaving
us with N.E. Midl. as the dialect of the copy and presumably
of the original as well. The date is probably *c.* 1370-90.

Pearl, which has already been discussed in chapter 3,
p. 72, because of its affinity with the other three poems of
the same MS.

The Vernon-Simeon Lyrics, from the Vernon MS. (1370-80),
and in the Simeon Brit. Mus. Addit. 22283 (1380-1400).
They are thirty in number, all edited in the E.E.T.S. 117,
p. 658, *The Minor Poems of the Vernon MS.* Twenty-four
of them are also edited by C. Brown, *Religious Lyrics of the
14th Century,* 1924, 125-205. As the poems have suffered
in transcription it is essential to rely only on those points
which can be attested by the rhymes. The pieces are
obviously not all by one poet, but probably originated in the
same dialect, with certain exceptions.

Pt. 6. O.E. ā as *o* : e.g. *mo,* l. 80, No. 1, O.E. mā, rhyming
with *do,* O.E. dōn ; or *wo,* l. 18, No. 13, O.E. wā, rhyming
with *misdo,* O.E. mis-dōn. Incidentally this proves that O.E.
ō did not become *u* in this dialect.

The Nth. dialect is ruled out, for Pt. 19. O.E. hw as *wh*
alliterates with *w* freely. Pt. 35. The pres. part. in '*-yng* ' :
e.g. *standyng,* l. 46, No. 1, rhyming with *þing,* sb., and there
are many similar rhymes. Pt. 8. O.E. āw as *ow* : e.g. *knowe,*
l. 12, No. 6, O.E. cnāwan, rhyming with *trowe,* O.E. trēowian.
All the above points are merely non-Nth.

There are, however, other points which seem to rule out
Sth. : Pt. 12. O.E. ǣ[1] as tense *e* : e.g. *misdede,* l. 51, No.
1, O.E. mis-dǣd, rhyming with *fede,* O.E. fēdan. Pt. 13.
O.E. ǣ[2] is also tense before dentals, etc. : e.g. *lede,* l. 145,
No. 1, O.E. lǣdan, Gothic laidjan, rhyming with *hede,* O.E.
hēd ; there are such rhymes in most of the lyrics. Pt. 38.
The pres. indic. pl. ends in '-e,' when immediately preceded
or followed by a pers. pron., but otherwise ends in '-en ' :
No. 15, l. 25, *bene,* rhyming with *wene* O.E. wēnan ; the evi-

dence from this rhyme is conclusive. These last three points rule out the Sth. dialect, leaving us with Midl. Pt. 36. The pres. indic. sg. ends in '-es' and in '-est,' '-eth'; both types are represented in rhymes, and often in the same poem : e.g. l. 22, No. 4, *whoso geþ* rhyming with *Nazareth;* l. 30, No. 9, *he fedes* rhyming with *dedes*, sb. pl. ; the area near the *Salop-Wash* line would be most suitable in view of the use of both types. Pt. 32. The infinitive ends in '-e,' except when the '-n' is retained to avoid hiatus before *h* or a vowel : e.g. *to ateyne*, l. 2, No. 9, rhyming with *peyne*, sb. Pt. 44. Contracted forms of *take, make* appear, indicating an area not too near the south : e.g. *he tas*, l. 59, No. 18, rhyming with *was*, vb. ; it is the only example in rhyme and such forms are very rare.

Lastly, the dialect would appear to be E. Midl., rather than W. Midl., because of the following : O.E. y̆ as *i*: e.g. l. 13, No. 1, *muynde*, O.E. gemy̆nd, rhyming with *bynde*, O.E. bĭndan : *muynde* is obviously scribal ; l. 28, No. 2, *kinne*, O.E. cy̆nn, rhyming with *inne*, O.E. ĭnne ; l. 22, No. 12, *druyȝe*, O.E. drȳge, rhyming with *Fantasȳe* (O.Fr. ī). There are many other similar rhymes, showing that the dialect was non-western.

O.E. ăn is usually *an* : e.g. l. 2, No. 20, *man*, O.E. mănn, rhyming with *Satanne;* however, No. 16, l. 28, has the rhyme *mon—Ion* (John) ; this may indicate that this particular lyric was western ; the main development was *an* ; O.E. ĕo as *e*: *beone*, l. 103, No. 15, O.E. bĕon, rhyming with *wene*, O.E. wēnan, a rhyme which affords no absolute proof. Yet the other points are quite sufficient to indicate that the dialect was E. Midl., though it may not be possible to say whether the original dialect was N.E. Midl. or S.E. Midl. The date of the lyrics is usually considered to be *c.* 1380-90.

On the Battle of Agincourt, from the MS. Cott. Cleop. C. iv., and edited in *Political Poems*, vol. 2, p. 125, by T. Wright. The poem is only 64 lines long. It occurs in a London Chronicle, and must have been written after 1415, though not necessarily very much later. There are only three significant points occurring in rhyme : Pt. 6. O.E. ā as *o* : *foon*, l. 53, O.E. gefā, rhyming with *schone* (shoes) ; Pt. 25. '-en' noun plurals are common : *foon*, l. 53 (above) rhyming with *one*, O.E. ān ; Pt. 32. The infinitive has lost the final '-n' : e.g. *fele*, l. 4, rhyming with *stele*, sb.

The other points which cannot be tested by rhymes are in agreement: O.E. ꝺ̆ is *i*; O.E. ăn is *an*; O.E. ĕo is *e*; O.E. '-and' is '*-ond*'; the pronouns are *they, hem, her(e)*; there are no examples of the pres. indic. sg. or pl. in the poem.

There are indications that these points would be natural in the London dialect, but the internal evidence is sufficient.

Thus the poems treated in this chapter range over the whole of the M.E. period to 1420, and there is no dialect unrepresented.

We do not intend to add anything by way of conclusion to Part I at this stage, because adequate conclusions can only be drawn when we have noted the various metrical differences, even within the groups themselves, as well as amongst the the groups.

It is, however, interesting to note that our study does not lend support to the theory that the alliterative writers used an artificial dialect; rather it would seem that each poet used the dialect of the locality in which he lived with all its dialectal peculiarities, so that the dialect of few alliterative poems is alike. What may have been artificial was the vocabulary, which included many words not used in ordinary current speech; also the phraseology, which had become the stock-in-trade of all the writers; these problems, however, fall within the scope of volume 2.

PART II.

THE METRICAL SURVEY.

CHAPTER 7.

THE SURVIVAL OF THE ALLITERATIVE LONG LINE TO *c.* 1300.

BEFORE beginning our survey of the metre of the M.E. alliterative poems, it is necessary to point out a few characteristics of the O.E. metrical system, and what we shall assume concerning it.

1. There were five rhythmical types, according to Sievers :—

$$A. \ / \times \ / \times \quad (/ \times \times \ / \times),$$
$$B. \ \times \ / \times \ / \quad (\times \times \ / \times \ /),$$
$$C. \ \times \ / / \times \quad (\times \times \times \ / / \times),$$
$$D. \ / / \searcap \times \quad (/ / \times \searcap),$$
$$E. \ / \searcap \times \ / \quad (/ \searcap \times \times \ /).$$

There were slight variations in addition to those contained in the brackets ; also extended half-lines, or " Schwellvers," which, when occurring in the 1st. half-line, seem to have had three main stresses instead of the normal two ; but when occurring in the 2nd. half-line were usually the *A.* type ' mit auftakt ' :—

$$(\times \ \times) \ \times \ \times \ \times \ / \ \times \ / \ \times.$$

These extended half-lines are thought to occur in solemn passages, and this is often true, but in later poems, such as *Genesis B.*, they become more frequent, and at the same time of a cruder type. Luick divided these extended half-lines into groups, classifying them according to his theory of joint-types ; thus he has *A.* + *B.*, *B.* + *C.*, etc. We do not wish to dispute such a theory at this stage, for the lines can be recognised as extended ones, whatever theory we hold as to their composition and origin.

2. The cæsura does not cut across a phrase-group, but enjambement is frequent. There are, however, no stanzas, and the paragraphs are of irregular length.

3. The usual alliterative combinations in the line were $a\,a\,/\,a\,x$ and $a\,x\,/\,a\,x$. The type $x\,a\,/\,a\,x$ was not uncommon; and this also is true of *Transverse Alliteration*, $a\,b\,/\,a\,b$, which occurs in *Beowulf* 71 times: e.g. l. 282. *Introverted Alliteration*, $a\,b\,/\,b\,a$ is much less common. The following are later licences: $a\,a\,/\,x\,a$, $a\,x\,/\,a\,a$, $a\,a\,/\,a\,a$, and $a\,a\,/\,b\,b$, *Double Alliteration*. These types are to be found in such poems as *The Battle of Maldon*.

4. Vocalic alliteration, which was very common in O.E., was practically always on different, not identical, vowels. Thus *Beowulf* has only one example of alliteration on identical vowels, l. 836, *ea, ea, ea*, whereas according to Lawrence [1] there are 493 examples of vocalic alliteration in the poem, that is, 15·48 per cent. of the lines have vocalic alliteration. We shall find that this is contrary to the practice in M.E.

5. The various consonantal sounds usually alliterate with themselves only, but the palatal and velar *g*'s and *k*'s alliterate together; *h* does not alliterate with vowels except in the later poems, such as *Judith*. The groups *sp, sc, st* only alliterate with identical groups. In later poems various licences begin to creep in, such as *s, st* alliterating together. It should be noted that *w, wr* alliterate together, as do *sw, s : br, b: sn, s: c, cn: c, cw: c, cn, cw*.

6. Rhyme is very rarely found. There are 18 examples in *Beowulf*, 5 of which serve to link the two half-lines together, whereas the remaining 13 examples serve no such purpose, and may be more or less accidental. In the later poems rhyme becomes more frequent, particularly in *Judith, The Battle of Maldon, Be Domes Dæge*, and in *The Phœnix*, which has several rhymes. Cynewulf's *Elene*, ll. 1236-50, is rhymed, and lastly there is *The Rhyme Poem*, in which the rhyme and alliteration together prove a little too much for an ambitious poet.

We have only mentioned these six points, because they are the sole ones which are of prime importance for the study

---

[1] J. Lawrence, *Chapters on Alliterative Verse*, p. 65, London, 1892,

of M.E. alliterative verse; other minor points will be
mentioned in due course.

THE LAST REMNANTS OF THE O.E.
ALLITERATIVE VERSE.

The latest specimens of the O.E. alliterative verse are to
be found in *The Anglo-Saxon Chronicle*, in which there are the
following entries written in the correct O.E. versification :
under 937 (73 lines), under 942 (13 lines), under 973 (20 lines),
under 975 (35 lines), and lastly under 1065 (34 lines).[1] If the
reader will consult these entries, he will observe how correctly
the tradition had survived.   Thus in the 1065 entry there
is the usual enjambement, and the metrical types are still
employed : ðæs þéodkýngces—a *C.* type.

Concerning the alliteration, 13 lines are of the traditional
aa/ax type, 16 of the *ax/ax* type, 3 of the *xa/ax* type,
and 1 of the *ab/ab* type ; all these were the ancient types.
There is only one exception, an *ax/xa* type, a late licence.
The old poetic compounds have disappeared and with them
the *D.* and *E.* types, but otherwise the metre remains the
same.   Here there is testimony to the survival of the O.E.
metre up to the Conquest.   From this we cannot, of course,
generalise and say that the knowledge of the technique was
widespread; possibly it was largely confined to the monasteries.

At the same time there were many examples appearing
in O.E. at a late period, which were not so accurate as those
occurring in *The Chronicle*, such as the christianised *O.E.*
Charms; the licences employed in these poems are very
numerous.   Hence it seems probable that a correct knowledge
of the metrical system existed chiefly in the monasteries ;
but amongst the people, and in many monasteries also, the
tradition had become vaguer.   Changes were taking place
in the length of vowels at this period, and quantity became
neglected in the writing of the verse.   The rhythm became
purely accentual ; this was not because it would not have
been metrically possible to readjust the line in accordance
with the linguistic changes, but because the knowledge of the
tradition had become confused, and quantity neglected.

[1] See the edition by Plummer-Earle, Oxford, 1892.

The results of this were, however, very far-reaching, and led not merely to the rhythm becoming purely accentual, but also to an increase in the number of unaccented syllables.

THE EMERGENCE INTO LITERATURE OF A POPULAR KIND OF VERSE.

We are well aware that alliterative rhythmical prose was very popular in late O.E. times ; both Ælfric and Wulfstan made use of it in their homilies and other religious works, and doubtless it was also used in lays and stories of a popular kind. Professor Sedgefield has scanned some of it in his *Anglo-Saxon Prose Book*, p. 373 ; see also his *Anglo-Saxon Verse Book*, pp. 122-4. Remarkable examples are to be found in *The Chronicle* in the entries under the dates 959, 975, 979, 1011, 1036, 1057, 1067, 1075, 1076, 1086. It is often very difficult to know whether these entries should be printed as verse or not. They extend over a hundred years, and show remarkable metrical development. Let us briefly look at them.

959. On his dagum hit godode georne . . . wide and side. The passage consists of 29 lines (as printed) of irregular length. The rhythm is exactly of the type to be found in Wulfstan's *Address to the English*, or in Ælfric's *Lives of the Saints;* alliteration is plentiful, but not in any way systematic ; there are occasional rhymes, and assonance is not uncommon. Here is a crude poetry of a different and more popular tradition than that of the alliterative poetry.

975. Her Eadgar gefor, 18 short lines. Each line has two main stresses with liberty as to the number and arrangement of the unstressed syllables. There are 5 lines with alliteration, 2 with assonance, and a rhyming couplet : " Næs se flota swa rang, ne se here swa strang." In this poem there is greater regularity in the rhythm.

A few lines farther on in the Worcester MS. (D), there are 20 short lines similar to those above, beginning, " *On his dagum for his iugoðe. . . .*" Alliteration is practically absent, but there is more assonance.

979. Ne wearð Angelcynne nan wersa dæd gedon, 25 lines. This scrap is of a very crude type, and ought to be printed as prose. Alliteration and assonance are plentiful, but the rhythm is quite irregular.

1011. Wæs ða ræpling, 6 lines of the same crude type.

1036. Ac Godwine hine þa gelette, 40 lines. This represents an advance and consists mainly of rhymed couplets, and alliteration is also common. The result is a crude form of couplet with a distinct, but rather irregular rhythm.

1057. Her com Eadward, 19 lines of the same crude type as those occurring under the year 959. Alliteration is more common, but the piece remains little more than rhythmical prose.

1067. And cwæð þ heo hine ne manne habban wolde, 5 lines similar to the above, but there is sometimes medial assonance and medial rhyme. It shows some influence of the O.E. alliterative metre, for there is a distinct medial pause in 3 of the lines, and some of the half-lines are linked by alliteration ; rhyme has become well established.

1075. the couplet, " *þaer wes þ bryd eala, mannum to beala*," is a combination of rhyme and alliteration.

Under the same year there is also an entry of 4 lines, *sume hi wurdon ablænde*, with some alliteration and assonance.

1076. Sume hi wurdon geblende, 5 lines, which are ultimately from the same source as the preceding entry ; there is no alliteration, but rhyme and the same popular rhythm.

1086. Castles he let wyrcean, 25 lines in which rhyme is well established, and in which alliteration is also common. The result is a mixture of long lines and rhymed couplets, the latter being fairly regular.

These entries are very important, because they are sufficient to show that popular rhythms did exist, and subsequently developed along certain lines, until rhyming couplets were evolved. All this took place before French influence could have been felt, and it is almost equally certain that the use of rhyme was not due to the influence of the Latin Hymns of the Church, but to popular tradition. There are a few instances of what appears to reflect the influence of the O.E. alliterative long line with its two half-lines linked by alliteration.

Rankin [1] makes out a very good case for the existence of

---

[1] *Rime and Rhythm before the Conquest*, Pub. Mod. Lang. Ass., vol. 36, p. 401.

an O.E. popular kind of rhymed verse before the Conquest. Some of his arguments may be weak, but the general hypothesis seems sound. In the second volume we shall bring forward further illustrations from the vocabulary and phraseology to show that there existed a popular literature before the Conquest, no longer extant.

EARLY MIDDLE ENGLISH ATTEMPTS AT THE O.E. METRICAL SYSTEM.

A Description of Durham, *c.* 1100, in the dialect of Durham, 21 lines. The metre of this poem is of the traditional type and shows no sign of decay. There is the usual enjambement; there are 6 lines with vocalic alliteration, always on different vowels; *st* still alliterates with itself; there is no excess of unstressed syllables; and the alliterative groups are mainly traditional. Thus 14/21 lines are of the *aa/ax* type: e.g. l. 2, "**st**eppa ge**st**aðolad **st**anas ymbutan." Ll. 6, 10, 21 are of the *ax/ax* type, and l. 19 of the *ab/ba* type. All these are the traditional O.E. types. L. 17, *aa/xa*, and l. 15, *aaa/ax*, are examples of licences, quite common in late O.E. verse. L. 11, the only exception, is probably corrupt.

With regard to the rhythmical types, the practice is again a continuance of the O.E. system. There are 15 *A.* types, 1 *B.* type, 13 *C.* types, 4 *D.* types, and 1 *E.* type; in addition, 4 *A.* types 'mit auftakt,' and 1 extended half-line.

e.g. l. 4*a* " éa ýðum strònge "—*D.* type.

l. 1*a* " Is ðeos búrch bréome "—*C.* type.

The style and theme of the poem are thoroughly O.E., and the work is surely by a monastic, who remembered the old tradition very well. It affords conclusive proof of the continuity of the alliterative metre into the early M.E. period.

Wenne, wenne, wenchichenne, *c.* 1150, in the S. Midl. dialect, a charm of 10 lines. The metre of this poem is quite as good as that of the former poem or of any late O.E. verse, but there are a few signs of change. There is now no enjambement, and *h* alliterates with a vowel in l. 4, but there is still no excess of unstressed syllables in the line. There are only 4 types of alliteration used, and these are all of the traditional types : *aa/ax* 3 lines, *ax/ax* 5 lines, *xa/ax* 1. 5 only, and *ab/ba* 1. 2 only.

e.g. 1. 2, " **h**er ne scealt þu **t**imbrien   ne nenne **t**un **h**abben."

Concerning the rhythmical types used, the practice is again strictly traditional, there being 12 examples of the *A.* type, 2 of the *B.* type, 3 of the *C.* type, and 3 of the *A.* type ' mit auftakt.' ·The *D.* and *E.* types are not found, owing to the disappearance of the poetic compounds.

The preservation of this charm is important, because it carries us right into the M.E. period, and shows that a knowledge of the older tradition was still surviving in the monasteries of the south, unless the poem be a copy of a non-extant O.E. charm.

The Grave, *c.* 1150, in the S.W. Midl. dialect, is a similar poem of the same date.   A few signs of change are manifest to the keen observer.   There is again no enjambement, and only one example of vocalic alliteration in the 25 lines ; but the same consonants still alliterate together as in O.E., and none of the later alliterating combinations have yet appeared ; there is no excess of unstressed syllables.   Regarding alliterative types, the practice is strictly traditional, except in four lines : 1. 9, of the *ax/xa* type, and ll. 18-20 of the *xa/xa* type.   The remaining lines have the following types : *aa/ax* 3 lines, *xa/ax* 13 lines, *ax/ax* 1 line, and *ab/ba* 1 line.   In addition two lines, ll. 11 and 23, are without any alliteration.   In l. 11 there is possibly an example of assonance : *molde—calde*, and in l. 23 of a rhyme : *hæfet—biræued.* The rhythmical types are quite traditional, there being 20 *A.* types, 13 *B.* types, 3 *C.* types, and 14 *A.* types ' mit auftakt.'

e.g. 1. 2. " ðe wes **m**ólde ímýnt   er ðu of **m**óder cóme."

This short poem, thoroughly O.E. in tone and atmosphere, is a further testimony to the survival of the long line in M.E., being free from any traces of the popular metre that was developing at the same time.

THE FUSION OF THE TRADITIONAL AND POPULAR
FORMS OF VERSE.

This is to be seen in the next poem we are to consider :—
The 1st. Worcester Fragment, *c.* 1170, in the S.W. Midl.
dialect, a poem patriotic and anti-Norman in tone. We
should, therefore, naturally expect such a writer to employ the
older type of verse, if such were surviving. This is precisely
what we find, but unfortunately the author was not able to
write these 23 lines in the correct O.E. versification. Ll. 11-
14 are ordinary prose, and 3 lines have no alliteration at
all, but a syllabic rhythm, e.g. l. 16, " næs deorc heore liht,
ac hit fæire gold." Of the remaining 16 lines, 10 are of the
traditional types (*aa/ax, ax/ax, xa/ax*), while the other 6 are the
usual licences found in such poems as *The Battle of Maldon*,
etc. (*aa/xa, ax/aa, xa/xa*), except for l. 19, an example of the
abb/aa type.

Thus with regard to alliterative types the author remembered sufficient to be able to write tolerable verse, but
he had completely forgotten the rhythmical types. With
seven exceptions only, the type he uses is the *A.* ' mit auftakt,'
which we may call " Rising-Falling Rhythm," because
historically it developed from the *A.* type, but ceased to
be recognised as such. The popularity of this new rhythm
is, we think, entirely due to the influence of the popular verse,
which was discussed above. With this writer the influence
was probably unconscious, as he did not employ any rhymes.
He was attempting to write the traditional verse, but his
knowledge of the technique had become vague and uncertain.
The tradition had not died, however, for there is still one *C.*
type, and a few *A.* and *B.* types. The historical importance
of this fragment cannot be over-estimated.

The Departing Soul's Address to the Body, *c.* 1170, S.W.
Midl., represents a further stage in the development of the
English metre. Fortunately, the work runs to 342 long lines,
so that we can obtain a better idea of the changes which were
taking place.

There are 292 alliterative long lines without either rhyme
or assonance ; 21 alliterative long lines with medial rhyme
or assonance, and in which it is easy to see the effect of the
syllabic verse on the rhythm of the line ; 29 syllabic couplets,

21 of which have alliteration, and in 15 of the latter the alliteration serves to link the two halves of the couplet together. This is clearly due to the influence of the O.E. tradition. This couplet is not, of course, a conscious product. It is due to the encroachment of rhyme and assonance from the popular poetry. The effect is to be seen in the rhythm. It is important to notice that the poet makes little use of rhyme; ll. 350-61 in Singer's edition are all rhymed, but this is the only example of a continuous succession of rhymed lines.

The examples of rhymed couplets we shall leave until chapter 11, for reasons which will appear obvious later. This couplet has nothing to do with the French couplet, nor with the metre of the Latin hymns, but has evolved from the O.E. metre, which had come into contact with the popular verses, which had had a separate evolution.

This poem has 292/342 lines of the same type as those found in *The 1st. Worcester Fragment*, and they are easy to keep apart from those in which rhyme or assonance is added ; in the latter lines there is discernible a tendency in the direction of syllabic verse and in 29 cases a couplet has resulted.

Let us compare the unrhymed lines with those of *The 1st. Worcester Fragment*, remembering that the MS. is very corrupt, and may not preserve the poet's system intact. In general the practice of enjambement has gone, but there are a few examples of run-on lines to be found by the careful reader. Vocalic alliteration is still on different vowels, but there are only 6 examples in the poem ; see Singer's edition, ll. 31, 163, 196, 264, 318, 475. This means that vocalic alliteration is falling into disrepute, a tendency evident in most of the works we have so far examined.

Concerning the peculiarities of alliterating sounds, there are signs of a neglect of O.E. rules ; *st* is still a group, l. 186, but *sc* alliterates with *s* and with *sk;* new groups to emerge are *gr, sw, fl, cl,* but there are many examples where this is ignored. As a rule the poet avoids the alliterating together of groups.

With regard to the alliterative types, 165 lines have the original O.E. types : *aa/ax* 43 lines, *ax/ax* 37 lines, and *xa/ax* 79 lines, *ab/ab* 3 lines, and *ab/ba* 3 lines. This is rather remarkable, and is a testimony to the survival of the long line. 67 lines are made up of the various licences to be found in late O.E. verse, such as *ax/aa, ax/xa, xa/xa, aa/aa.* The remaining

lines have either alliteration in one half-line only, or no
alliteration at all, but merely the rhythm of the long line—
a fact which is, however, probably due to corruptions in the
text. The scribe had little, if any, knowledge of the technique
of the alliterative poetry.

The observations already made concerning the rhythm of
The 1st. Worcester Fragment are equally applicable to this
work. The usual rhythm of the half-line is the *Rising-
Falling* type : × × × / × × / ×, in both half-lines.
Occasionally the descendants of the *A.*, *B.*, and *C.* types are
found. We may call these *Falling*, *Rising*, and *Clashing
Rhythms* respectively. There are 20 examples of the *Clashing
Rhythm* found, e.g.

l. 548. " So theo béc séggeth."

The importance of this work lies in the fact that it shows
the historical development of the O.E. alliterative long line
coming into contact with the popular rhymed verse. The
former holds its own as a rule, but on those occasions when
it succumbs to the influence of the latter, the result is a crude
syllabic couplet.

THE GRADUAL EMERGENCE OF A NATIVE
COUPLET.

The gradual emergence of this couplet is very apparent in
The Proverbs of Alfred, *c*: 1180, again in S.Western. As
Hall points out in his edition of the Jesus MS. in *Early Middle
English*, 1920, the text is corrupt beyond restoration. On
page 293 he classifies the various errors as follows :—

1. Archaic and uncommon words are rejected.
2. Older forms and constructions are modernised.
3. Words are rearranged mostly in a prose order, spoiling
   rhyme and rhythm.
4. Lines and parts of lines are transposed.
5. Padding is freely used.
6. The rhymes may, in some cases, have been spoiled by
   the substitution of alien dialectal forms.

Hall [1] describes the metre as " a mixture of native alliter-

---

[1] J. Hall, *Early Middle English*, p. 292.

ative verse, loosely constructed and rhyming couplets; the latter are bound together by perfect, imperfect and even inflectional rhymes and assonances."

The following statistics are as accurate as possible, but the corrupt nature of the text must be borne in mind in drawing conclusions from them. There are :

1. 129 alliterative long lines without rhyme,
2. 11 alliterative long lines with rhyme or assonance.
3. 100 lines in couplets without alliteration.
4. 46 lines in couplets with alliteration.
5. 11 lines utterly corrupt, e.g. l. 68, " he may beon on elde wenliche lorþeu."

The 73 couplets in 3 and 4 are discussed in chapter 11. They are again in no sense an imitation of the French couplet, but a by-product of the O.E. alliterative metre, as shown above. The couplet remains quite irregular and crude.

The poet would seem to have preferred the long line without any rhyme ; otherwise a syllabic couplet with or without alliteration, but usually without. It would therefore appear that the poet considered alliteration or rhyme sufficient in itself, and did not mix the two as a general rule. We shall see later that this was an important factor in the development of the metre in the thirteenth century.

Let us briefly examine the 140 long lines. There are very few run-on lines ; only 6 examples of vocalic alliteration occur, and there is a tendency apparent to alliterate on identical vowels, anticipatory of the later M.E. practice. There is now a certain amount of irregularity with regard to the number of unstressed syllables, and the line is generally much longer than in O.E. This is due to the more frequent use of the *Rising-Falling-Rhythm*. This type of rhythm is the most common one used, whereas the other three are rare. The *Clashing-Rhythm* is found on few occasions ;

e.g. l. 81a, " and þ **g**old **g**reowe."
l. 184b, " ne so wyn drunke."

The rhythm is thus rather crude and formless ; indeed the character of the O.E. rhythms has become completely transformed.

Regarding the alliterative types, there is much the same confusion. The older types are not more frequently used than the later licences. As a rule each half-line has one alliterating sound only. The type *aa/ax* is used in 15 lines, but *xa/ax* in 44 lines. This latter is the most popular type. *ab/ab* occurs in 4 lines and *aa/bb*, a later type, in 2 lines. There are 4 lines of the *aa/xx* type, and 4 of the *xx/aa* type, both of which are failures.

From a careful study of all the lines, we come to the conclusion that the choice of types is not arbitrary, but that there was a distinct tradition still surviving.

The Proverbs of Alfred are thus metrically very interesting despite the corrupt state of the texts ; they represent a stage beyond that reached by *The Departing Soul's Address to the Body*. Rhyme is struggling with alliteration, but the latter still holds the upper hand.[1]

Layamon's Brut, 1189-1207, written in the dialect of N. Worcs. This lengthy work is very important for our purpose. Unfortunately, it is rather long and we have therefore carefully examined the 1885 long lines edited by Hall for the Oxford Press in 1924. These representative selections should yield quite satisfactory results. Of the 1885 lines, 860 have either rhyme or assonance linking the two half-lines together ; that is 45·5 per cent. of the lines, a very high percentage. Of these only 277 have " rich rhyme," the rest having imperfect rhymes and assonances. However, the correct rhymes are not very varied in their quality, the following occurring very frequently : *riht, miht; londe, sonde,* etc. ; *hende, sende;*

---

[1] **The Death Fragment,** 1170-85, N.W. Midl., exists in a very corrupt state. The poem consists of 12 long lines, or 24 half-lines with rhymes or assonances as follows : - - *aa* - - *bcbbccdd* - *cee* - - - *dd* -. It will be observed that sometimes the rhymes are medial and sometimes not. The disintegrating effect of the rhyme and assonance upon the rhythm is very marked. Some of the lines are like the O.E. ones, such as, " wormes to cheuen," l. 11b, but they are usually longer.

With regard to alliteration we may notice that 7 lines have none at all, whereas the remaining lines have alliteration without any apparent system, e.g. l. 2, " nou is mon hol and soint and huvel him muit in mund." The fragment is not very important because it has been preserved in a formless state, and it is not sufficiently long to enable us to draw any conclusions from it. It is interesting in that it comes from a different dialectal area from that of the compositions we have previously examined.

care, fare; long, strong; king, þing. The lines can be divided into the following types :—

1. 1170 lines with the two halves linked by alliteration only.
2. 226 lines with the two halves linked by alliteration and also with rhyme or assonance as a mere ornament.
3. 192 lines of the same structure, but already showing in varying degrees the disintegrating effect of rhyme in their wavering rhythm.
4. 462 lines with a regular syllabic rhythm.
5. 56 corrupt lines, having neither rhyme nor alliteration.

Illustrations of these types may be found in Hall's edition, p. xv. The rhymes in Layamon are not an imitation of French rhyme, but of the type found in alliterative prose and popular poetry.

The couplets are discussed in chapter 11, and we may therefore confine ourselves to the lines in the first three groups.

Run-on lines are practically absent, and vocalic alliteration is rare, as there are only some 50 examples in the 1885 lines. Occasional examples are found of alliteration on identical vowels, as in l. 53, but this is rarely the case.

Concerning the peculiarities of alliterating sounds, we observe that the practice of Layamon is not traditional ; thus the groups *sp, st, sc, sk* often alliterate with the same group, but frequently this rule is broken, so that *s, st: sk, k: sc, st: sp, s,* etc., alliterate together. New separate groups are *br, tr, gr,* though these frequently alliterate with *b, t, g* respectively ; *sm, sw,* are sometimes treated as alliterative groups. The poet was not, however, careful in his use of such groups.

The number of unstressed syllables in the line varies considerably, some half-lines being quite short and others extremely long ; however, as a rule they are fairly even in length.

Layamon remembered the traditional metre more accurately than did the author of *The Proverbs of Alfred,* or of *The Departing Soul's Address to the Body.* This is seen from a study of his rhythms and alliteration.

Layamon uses in each half-line five different types of rhythm. In the 1st. half-line the types are divided up as follows :—*Falling-Rhythm* in 132 half-lines ; *Rising-Rhythm* in 274 ; *Rising-Falling-Rhythm* in 870 ; *Clashing-Rhythm,*

$\times$ $\times$ / / $\times$—in 29, and $\times$ $\times$ / $\times$ / $\times$ with the weak -*e* in between the two main stresses, in 59 half-lines ; in addition, the type " / $\times$ $\times$ ($\times$) / " is found in 32 half-lines.

e.g. *C.* " þat þas bóc rǽde," l. 31.

" séilien ouer sǽ," l. 1078,

is an example of the last type.

The rhythm is thus more varied than in the earlier poems with which we have dealt.   In the 2nd. half-line the proportions do not differ very much.   The *Falling-Rhythm* is found in 242 half-lines, and the *Rising-Rhythm* in 107 only ;   this is as we should expect in the 2nd. half-line, where the ending " /$\times$" became more and more common.   The *Rising-Falling-Rhythm* is found in 933 half-lines, and the *Clashing-Rhythm* in 33 half-lines, when no weakly-stressed -*e* comes between the two main stresses, and 62 examples when this is the case. There are 19 examples of the / $\times$ $\times$ $\times$ / type.

Perhaps the greater regularity in Layamon is due to the fact that his work is preserved in a better state than are *The Proverbs of Alfred* and similar poems.   This may account for something, but at the same time it seems evident that Layamon had a greater feeling for the O.E. rhythms ;   he may have been in touch with a more accurate tradition, which may account for the fact that his work is not so popular in theme and manner of execution as *The Proverbs of Alfred* and *The Departing Soul's Address to the Body.*

The alliterative types used by Layamon are those found in late O.E. verse ;   the later licences are now quite as common as the .earlier types.   Thus each half-line has usually one alliterating letter only.   *ax/ax* is found in 245 lines, and *xa/ax* in 343 lines (these two types are used in O.E. verse of all periods) ;   *xa/xa* is found in 275 lines, and *ax/xa* in 122 lines. The other five simple types are these :—

aa/xa in 95 lines ;   *aa/xa* in 59 lines ;
aa/aa in 41 lines ;   *ax/aa* in 50 lines ; ·
xa/aa in 59 lines.

These figures show that Layamon is not absolutely conservative in his use of alliteration.   *Transverse Alliteration—ab/ab*—is found in 51 lines, and *Introverted Alliteration—ab/ba*

—in 50 lines; both these types were common in O.E., but *aa/bb* only begins to occur in very late poems; this type is only found in 18 lines, showing that Layamon recognised it as feeble, for it fails to join the two half-lines together. The same is also true of two other types used by Layamon—*aa/xx* and *xx/aa*. The former is found in 95 lines, and the latter in 43 lines. Some of these examples may be put down to the carelessness of the copyist, but not the majority of them.

We have carefully examined all the examples where rhyme or assonance is added to the alliteration, and have found that Layamon paid the same attention to the alliteration in these lines as he did in the others, and there is no difference of treatment.

The historical importance of Layamon's verse is that it shows alliteration still stronger than rhyme. The new couplet which was evolved from the long line, as described before, has become syllabic and fairly regular. There are 462 lines of this kind, but we may mention the important fact that in these only 36 have alliteration, whereas in the case of the alliterative long lines 1170 are without rhyme, and only 428 with rhyme.

The obvious conclusion is that the poet is coming to consider alliteration or rhyme to be sufficient in itself, and is averse to mixing the two. In the rhymed couplet, alliteration is very rare, and only ornamental. This couplet is thus approximating to the French octo-syllabic couplet, while the alliterative long line is still vigorous in its rhythm and alliteration.

The Bestiary, *c.* 1200-1250, is interesting in coming from the N.E. Midl. dialectal area, a testimony to the fact that the long line persisted in other parts of the country than the west. The author was a conscious metrist, imitating his Latin source, and even used several metres in the same passage. The metres can be classified as follows :—

1. The Alliterative long line—174 examples.
2. The Octosyllabic couplet—272 examples.
3. Verses of three measures—119 lines.
4. Common metre—39 lines.
5. The Latin septenary—32 lines.
6. Verses of two measures—4 lines.

The last five of these types are foreign metres, and ornamental alliteration is added. This is discussed in chapter II.

It must be remembered that the couplet in section 2 is a direct imitation of the French couplet, and is not derived from the crude couplet which developed from the O.E. long line.

We are here only concerned with the 174 alliterative long lines. With regard to this part of the poem we have to take into account the fact that the text is very corrupt, and a scribe, unaccustomed to the traditional metre, has made the same blunders as did the scribes of *The Proverbs of Alfred*. Hall says concerning this point in his edition of the poem in *Early Middle English*: " The parts written in alliterative verse are in a much worse state than the rest of the text, probably because the scribe's ignorance of the technique of the native metre gave him greater scope for alteration." Therefore, the following attempt to divide the alliterative lines into the usual groups can only be tentative :—

1. 107 long lines with the two halves linked by alliteration only.

2. 24 lines similar to these, but having rhyme as an ornament ;

   e.g. l. 134, " atte **k**irke dure   ðar ðu **c**ristned were."

   The rhythm of these lines is the same as those under 1.

3. Lines similar to those under 2, but showing the disintegrating effect of rhyme upon the rhythm. Three lines are undoubtedly of this type—ll. 24, 112, 138.

   e.g. l. 24, **M**árie bi náme   ðe him bár to **m**ánne fráme.

4. 7 lines are purely syllabic in their structure, giving rise to seven rhymed couplets—ll. 12, 116, 118, 305, 306, 362, 381.

5. 33 lines are without rhyme or alliteration, and are probably corrupt. Often the whole half-line seems to have been lost.

   e.g. l. 22, " hu he dun come. . . ."

It will be observed that the poet preferred alliteration without any additional rhyme. The great decrease in the number of rhymed alliterative verses is remarkable. The O.E. long line is slowly recovering from the effects of rhyme ; a native couplet has been evolved, which was subsequently absorbed by the French couplet. The latter, as used in *The Bestiary* and other poems, is not so strict as in French poetry, for the freer nature of the O.E. long line has had its inevitable effect upon the regularity of the French form, and the couplet of native origin has fallen in with the French form. Thus there are only 7 of these crude couplets left, the rest having become indistinguishable from the verses of three measures, and couplets under which they are included. In these alliteration is merely ornamental, and of very rare occurrence.

Let us examine the alliterative lines to compare them with those of *The Brut* and *The Proverbs of Alfred*.

Vocalic alliteration is very rare, being only found in ll. 139 and 308 ; in both cases the alliteration is on identical vowels.

With regard to the peculiarities of alliterating sounds, it should be noted that the poet is not conservative. It is true that *h* alliterates with itself only and not with vowels, but the older groups are no longer preserved except accidentally ; *sp, sw: s, st: s, sk:* etc., all alliterate together. *st* is occasionally a separate alliterating group, and two new groups are found—*sm, cr*. Hence his knowledge of the older rules is not very accurate.

The rhythm is in both half-lines chiefly of the *Rising-Falling* type, as in the case of *The Proverbs of Alfred*. The *Falling* and *Rising-Rhythms* are both rare, as is the *Clashing-Rhythm* :

$$\text{e.g. l. 5, “ alle hise } \acute{\text{fet}} \acute{\text{steppes}}.”$$

The rhythm of the few lengthened half-lines that are to be found is as follows :—

$$(\times \ \times) \ / \ \times \ \times \ / \ \times \ \times \ / \ (\times \ \times).$$

$$\text{e.g. l. 6, “ dra}\acute{\text{ge}}\check{\text{ð}} \ \acute{\text{dust}} \text{ with his } \acute{\text{stert}}.”$$

On the whole, the rhythm of the long lines of *The Bestiary* is simpler than that of those in Layamon, but the types found are the same. The latter writer shows more variety probably because the text of his work has been preserved in a better condition.

Concerning the alliterative types, the writer of *The Bestiary* shows himself to have been in contact with the older practices, for the licences common in O.E. are rare. Thus *aa/ax* is found 44 times, *ax/ax* 17 times, *xa/ax* 10 times, *ab/ab* 5 times, and *ab/ba* 3 times. e.g. l. 161, "fast at tin herte ðat tu firmest higtes." These five types were the usual ones in O.E. verse. The later licences are not so common : *aa/xa* 14 lines, *aa/aa* 12 lines, *ax/aa* 4 lines, *xa/aa* 4 lines, *xa/xa* 4 lines, *ax/xa* 4 lines. These types are obviously not so common, and *aa/bb* is not found at all. *aa/xx* is found 6 times, and *aaa/xx* once, but these are probably due to scribal alterations.

In the 1st. half-line there are 10 examples of lengthened lines : *abb/aa*, l. 11 ; *aab/ab*, l. 6 ; *aab/b*, 4 lines, e.g. l. 126 ; *aba/b*, l. 308 ; *aaa/xx*, l. 8 ; *aaa/ax*, 2 lines, e.g. l. 369.

e.g. l. 6, "drageð dust with his stert ðer he dun steppeð."

Therefore the decay of the O.E. long line was not so complete when we come to examine in detail the various remnants that have been preserved for us. The texts are often poor ; yet despite this fact, the old alliterative types still stand out. Great changes have come about and we have been able to trace the effect of these upon the rhythm, which has become purely accentual. The evidence for the survival of the line to *c.* 1250 is thus existent, and the last example, *The Bestiary*, does not show us the long line in its last stage of disappearance, ·but still strong, though greatly changed.

Here we may mention a feature of O.E. verse which is seldom commented upon. We refer to the practice of linking together consecutive lines in the following way :—

The Wanderer, 28-9 :

" oþ   mec freondleasne   frefran wolde, wc ᵻan mid wynnum.   Wat se þe cunnað."

The last stressed syllable of the 1st. line sets the alliteration for the 2nd. line. Lest anyone should think this to be accidental, we may add that the feature occurs in a succession of lines in various poems. It is, of course, rare, especially in *Beowulf*, but see ll. 22-3, 36-7, 88-9, 92-3 ; or *Exodus*, ll. 40-1, 41-2, 43-4, 47-8, 52-3, which surely form a noticeable succession of examples ; *Widsith*, ll. 36-7 ; *The Wanderer*, ll. 26-7, 28-9, 35-6 ; *The Seafarer*, ll. 54-5, 65-6 ; *Riddle No.* 3, ll. 19-20, 25-6 ; *Cynewulf's Crist*, ll. 229-30, etc.

These examples will be sufficient to show that the feature was common among all poets. It is remarkable that it should also survive into the M.E. period, and be found in all the alliterative romances, as we shall see later.   It is also common in these earlier works.   *A Description of Durham* has 3 examples, *Wenne* 1 example, *The Grave* 4, *The Departing Soul's Address to the Body* 13, *The Proverbs of Alfred* 5, the selections from *The Brut* have 59 examples in 1885 lines, and *The Bestiary* has 9 examples.   This seems a remarkable testimony to the survival of the long line.   *The Brut*, which in many respects is metrically more conservative than the other poems we have discussed, shows a large number of examples of this feature.

A second method of joining consecutive lines together in O.E. verse was to have two lines together with the same alliterating letter.   This is very rare in *Beowulf*, though examples are found, e.g. ll. 1520-1 *hh*.   See *The Battle of Maldon*, ll. 7-8 *hh*; *The Seafarer*, 1-2 *ss*, 85-6 *dd*; *The Wanderer*, 36-7 *ww*, 64-5 *ww*.   It is especially common in later poems such as *Judith*, e.g. ll. 220-1 *ff*, ll. 249-51 *hhh*.

In the early M.E. alliterative poems there are a few sporadic examples as in O.E.   Thus, *The Grave* has ll. 12-14 *ddd*, ll. 24-5 *ff*; *The Departing Soul's Address to the Body*, ll. 13-14 *ss*; *The Proverbs of Alfred*, ll. 21-2 *ww*; *The Brut*, ll. 201-2 *ll*, etc.   The practice is equally rare in O.E. and early M.E. poetry.

A third testimony to the historical survival of the line is the continuance of the *C*. type, as we have seen.   The disappearance of the poetic compounds resulted in the loss of the *D*. and *E*. types, and often of the *C*. type, when the latter was due to a compound with level stress; however, the *C*. type, when consisting of two separate stressed words coming together, is found continuously in all the works we have examined.

The last poem to be discussed is **The Satire against the Blacksmiths,** *c*. 1300-25 in the S.E. Midl. dialect.   The satire has only 22 lines, but is a very vigorous poem, the alliteration being skilfully employed to imitate the blows of the smith.

There is no rhyme in the poem, yet metrically it continues the development of the long line, as last seen in *The Bestiary*. It is not connected with the alliterative romances from the west.   We observed that in *The Bestiary* the long line had given rise to a couplet which was absorbed by the French couplet, and that the long line itself had almost shaken rhyme off altogether. In this satire we find the process complete. Rhyme has gone, leaving the long line with its accentual rhythm. The poem is short but we may notice the following points : Vocalic alliteration is not found at all ; the poet treats *sp*, *st*, *sch* as alliterating groups, and in l. 1 has *sw, sm, sm, sm, sm*, and l. 9, *gn, gn, gr, g*. The most remarkable feature of the metre is, however, the excessive alliteration. The type *aa/aa* is found in 12 out of 22 lines ; *aaa/aa* ll. 1 and 14 ; *aa/aaa* l. 5 ; *aa/bb* ll. 12 and 15 ; *ab/ab* l. 7 ; *ab/ba* l. 11 ; *aabb/aaaa* l. 19 ; *ax/ax* l. 21, and *aa/xx* l. 22.

Here the poet, in his desire to imitate the hammer of the smith, has disregarded rules, if indeed he knew them, and has merely crowded in as much alliteration as possible.

In his use of rhythmical types he does not differ from the writer of *The Bestiary*. He has the *Rising-Falling-Rhythm* in 31 half-lines, *Falling-Rhythm* in 2 half-lines only, but no examples of *Rising-Rhythm*. The *Clashing-Rhythm* is found in 5 half-lines, always with the weak *e* between the two main stresses, e.g. l. 10*b*, " with here hárde hámers."

L. 19 has probably 8 stressed syllables, but is quite artificial.

" tik ! tak ! hic ! hac ! tiket ! taket ! tyk ! tac ! "

The alliterative metre is skilfully handled, but this satire is a signpost, indicating the trend of the alliterative metre ; alliteration once structural, is becoming more and more ornamental.

To sum up the main points in this chapter, we may say that in some parts of the country there were monks who maintained the true alliterative tradition until about 1150. They lived in the *Old English* world and were averse to new French ideas. Others equally patriotic tried to keep the national verse alive, but were powerless to do so.

Meanwhile, the popular poetry developed rapidly, ultimately finding its way into literature ; it comes face to face with the traditional verse, and leaves unmistakable signs upon it. Sometimes the long line breaks up and a couplet is formed, which inevitably becomes more and more syllabic, until it is written side by side with the French couplet and becomes indistinguishable from it. The long line, however, still persists, and when rhyme is not added, shows little signs of becoming syllabic in its rhythm.   Finally it shakes rhyme and assonance off altogether.   At the beginning of the fourteenth century it was still existent in some areas where presumably the national feeling had always remained strong.

Judging from the pieces which have survived, the tradition would seem to have been stronger in S. Western and S.W. Midl. counties.   Layamon, in particular, affords weighty evidence in favour of the continuance of the alliterative tradition in the west.   Though a long period intervenes between the date of composition of his chronicle and that of the first M.E. romance, this is no argument against the theory of the continuance of the tradition in the intervening period, since in other parts of the country examples of the alliterative metre are to be found in this same interval.

A Note on Alliterative Prose.—We have already seen that alliterative rhythmical prose was popular in late O.E. times.   There is evidence of its use particularly in homiletic writings, and judging from some few examples contained in *The Anglo-Saxon Chronicle*, it was not confined to religious works.   Possibly lays of a popular kind were made in this loose type of verse, for O.E. poetry was distinctly "high-brow," and would be unintelligible to the lower classes.

However, it is interesting to notice that the tradition of the alliterative rhythmical prose survived into the M.E. period, affording an important link between the two eras.

There is first a group of pieces, from the south-west, of 1200-50. They are all religious, being prayers addressed either to Jesus Christ or the Virgin Mary.

On Lofsong of Ure Lefdi, 750 words, E.E.T.S., 34, p. 205, is a translation of the Latin *Oratio Ad Sanctam Mariam* of Archbishop Marbod of Rheims (A.D. 1035-1128).

On Lofsong of Ure Lauerde, 1200 words, E.E.T.S. 34, p. 209.

On Ureisun of Oure Louerde, 1200 words, E.E.T.S. 34, p. 183, is an earlier, but incomplete version of **On wel swuðe God Ureisun of God Almihti,** 1350 words, E.E.T.S. 34, p. 200.

The Wohunge of Ure Lauerd, 3500 words, E.E.T.S. 34, p. 269.

These works are very closely allied, but a careful study will reveal that they are not the work of a single author.   The first piece has more alliteration than any of the others, being alliterated throughout in the following manner :   " **m**aue **m**eiden ouer alle **m**eidnes, þat **b**ere ðat **b**lisfule **b**ern - - þene **d**eouel a**d**un and **h**eriede **h**elle."

The second group consists of the well-known works in exaltation of virginity.   They are in the same dialect and of the same date as the pieces of the first group.

Hali Maidenhed, E.E.T.S. 18, a long homiletic treatise on the above subject, and different in style from the three works that follow.

Juliana, E.E.T.S. 51, a romantic treatment of the famous legend, translated from the Latin, with no dependence on the O.E. poem.

Seinte Marherete, E.E.T.S. 13, and **Saint Katherine**, E.E.T.S. 80, again translated from the Latin. These two works are written in the same alliterative rhythmical prose, but as Hall suggests, not in "rhymeless Layamonic verse," as Einenkel and others have tried to prove.[1]

The above-mentioned works are very important for a study of the phraseology and vocabulary of the M.E. alliterative poets, and of considerable help in tracing the origin of the literary habits of early M.E. poets.

The Sawles Warde, edited by R. Morris, *Old English Homilies*, pp. 244-67, is also a translation from the Latin, and is of approximately the same dialect and date as the above pieces, and has likewise been erroneously treated as verse rather than prose.

Though these works have a prose punctuation and were intended to be prose, it is possible that the popular alliterative verse, as found in such works as *The Proverbs of Alfred*, has had some effect upon the prose-rhythm.

A third important group of works, written in the same kind of alliterative prose, is associated with the name of *Rolle*. His prose-work entitled **The Form of Perfect Living** is rhythmical and alliterative. It is edited in *Yorkshire Writers*, I, 3.

There is also the work on **Prayer**, in *Yorkshire Writers*, I, 295, consisting of 3000 words of the same type of alliterative prose. Also associated with the name of *Rolle* is the work entitled **A Talkyng of the Love of God**, in *Yorkshire Writers*, 2, 345, made up chiefly of alliterative long lines with rhymed couplets, tirades, and strophes, but written and punctuated as prose. The work has, however, never been metrically investigated.

This northern group of prose-works offer a further testimony to the lasting popularity of alliterative rhythmical prose, especially in religious exhortation and devotional literature. We have but to study the religious lyrics of the " School of Rolle " to realise how popular alliteration was in an area in which no purely alliterative poems were written.

[1] See Hall, *Early Middle English*, pp. 504-5, and 526.

CHAPTER 8.

The Alliterative Revival.

The alliterative poems which we shall now consider are at least remarkable in their bulk. Previously, with the exception of *Layamon's Brut*, we have only had to deal with fragments and short poems. We have now, however, a continuous succession of lengthy alliterative poems, in time extending over a hundred years. This is in itself sufficient to justify the use of the above title for this chapter, whatever theory we hold as to the history of the long line during the early M.E. period.

The Alexander Fragments A and *B*, dated *c.* 1340, are probably the earliest poems of the period. The last important poem is *Alexander C* (*The Wars of Alexander*), which was written not later than 1450. By that time decay was apparent, and alliterative poetry almost dead. Excluding the minor Scottish poems, which were written after the close of the fourteenth century, the alliterative poems were nearly all composed in W. Midl. This applies to *Cheuelere Assigne*, which has been preserved in an E. Midl. copy. *The Crowned King*, a very short poem written in the early fifteenth century, is in the dialect of the Middle-South, but is clearly unimportant. It remains true that the Alliterative Revival arose in the west and flourished there.

This is in agreement with the evidence which presented itself in the previous chapter. There it was seen that in the south-west and western areas more specimens of alliterative verse have survived than from any other part of the country. This is unlikely to be a matter of pure accident. It is also from the same districts that the alliterative prose homilies originated. *Layamon's Brut* is the most obvious link between the two groups of alliterative poems. It is a chronicle in form, but the elements of romance contained in its pages are very extensive. From a purely literary point of view, it has close affinity with the alliterative romances, and in its vocabulary and phraseology shows remarkable points of contact with the later poems. In this chapter, however, we shall concentrate our attention upon the proofs afforded by a study of the metre. Let us see what points these later poems have in common with the earlier ones, which we considered in chapter 7.

On page 148 we discussed a metrical practice, found in O.E. poetry, which survived in the alliterative poems in early M.E., thus indicating the continuity of the tradition. This practice of allowing the last unalliterated stressed syllable in the long line to set the alliteration for the next line is as common in the romances as it was in the earlier poetry. This is proof of the continuity of the tradition. Let us examine the statistics.

Alexander A has 49 examples in 1249 lines, i.e. 4 per cent. of its lines are thus linked. *Alexander B* has 77 examples in 1139 lines, i.e. almost 7 per cent. *William of Palerne* has 350 examples in 5540 lines, i.e. 6·2 per cent. *Joseph of Arimathie* has 27 examples in 709 lines, i.e. almost 4 per cent., but this work has extensive grouping of a similar kind.[1] *The Destruction of Jerusalem* has 69 examples in 1332 lines, i.e. 5·2 per cent. The feature is therefore quite common in the group of poems from the C. and S.W. Midl. areas. It is often found in consecutive lines; e.g. ll. 474-5 *k*, 475-6 *r*, *The Destruction of Jerusalem*. *The Parlement of the Thre Ages* has 36 examples in 665 lines, i.e. 5·5 per cent., and *Wynnere and Wastoure* has 28 examples in 503 lines, i.e. 5·5 per cent. also. This fact is rather remarkable, unless the two poems are by the same author, since there are so many points of similarity between the metre and style of these two alliterative works. *Piers Plowman* (B text) has 371 examples in 7089 lines, i.e. 5 per cent., and the feature is equally common

---

[1] There would appear to be a very intricate system of grouping in this poem, as may be seen by the following instances :—

ll. 97-8, "Bote þorwʒ þe grace of himself   gete him heo ne miʒt,
His moder ay with him fleih   forþ into Egipte."
or ll. 385-6 "and þe fend of his bodi   fleyʒ to þe lufte
þenne þei leuen him þer   and goþ touward oþure."

It would be almost impossible to attempt to classify the various devices used by this poet.

throughout the poem. *Pierce the Ploughman's Crede* has 64 examples in 850 lines, i.e. 7·5 per cent. *Richard the Redeles* has 47 examples in 857 lines, i.e. 5·5 per cent. *The Crowned King* has 6 examples in 150 lines, i.e. 4 per cent. The poems of this group do not, therefore, differ materially one from another.

Patience has 27 examples in 531 lines, i.e. 5 per cent. *Purity* has 78 examples in 1812 lines, i.e. 4·3 per cent. *Sir Gawayn and the Green Knight* has 112 examples in 2025 lines, i.e. 5·5 per cent. *St. Erkenwald* has 16 examples in 352 lines, i.e. 4·5 per cent. Remarkable consecutive groups can be found in these last four poems.

Cheuelere Assigne has 11 examples in 370 lines, i.e. 3 per cent. *The Destruction of Troy* has 788 examples in 14,044 lines, i.e. 5·5 per cent. *Morte Arthure* has 204 examples, i.e. 4·5 per cent. *The Wars of Alexander* has 316 examples in 5677 lines, i.e. 5·5 per cent. *The Scottish Prophecies* are too short to enable us to draw conclusions from the statistics, but the feature is found 4 times in *The 1st. Prophecy* and 3 times in *The 2nd. Prophecy*. *The Prophecies ascribed to à Becket* have 5 examples. *The Twa Mariit Wemen and the Wedo* has 24 examples in 530 lines, i.e. almost 5 per cent. *Death and Life* has 21 examples in 459 lines, i.e. 4·5 per cent. *Scottish Field* has 8 examples in 482 lines, i.e. under 2 per cent.

Therefore, on the whole, the various poems do not differ greatly in the use of this device, one which must have been handed down continuously from O.E. times. Other devices of a similar type are found in *Joseph of Arimathie*, and to a less extent in *Cheuelere Assigne*. We shall see later that these two poems are metrically very poor, the writers being largely a law unto themselves.

The alternative method of grouping consecutive lines together was by identical alliteration in two or more lines. This was rare in O.E. verse, though nevertheless a conscious device. In the early M.E. alliterative poems, the feature is equally common, though still comparatively rare. In the alliterative works treated in this chapter the feature is still surviving and in some cases its use is greatly extended. This affords a second proof of the continuance of the alliterative tradition. Let us glance at the statistics. Groups of two, three, or four such lines, we may call " twos," " threes," and " fours " respectively.

Alexander A has 35 twos, and 1 three, ll. 619-21 *sss.*
Alexander B has 39 twos, but no threes. (It is a curious
fact that 18 of the twos are on the letter *l.*) *The Parlement
of the Thre Ages* has 34 twos, and 5 threes. Ll. 332-40
contain a remarkable succession of examples, the alliteration
for these lines running as follows : *ss vv kk ggg. Wynnere
and Wastoure* has 36 twos, and 2 threes, ll. 495-7 *www*, and
ll. 248-50 *www.* In *William of Palerne* the feature is quite rare.
In the first 100 lines there are no examples at all : from
l. 1000 to 1100 there are only 3 twos, and 1 three : from l. 2000
to 2100 there are 5 twos, and 1 three: from l. 3000 to 3100
there are 6 twos : from l. 5000 to 5100 there are 1 two and
1 three. *Joseph of Arimathie* has 51 twos, 5 threes, and 1 four,
ll. 9-12 *ffff.* Remembering the length of the poem, it will
be observed that the poet has employed the device very
frequently. *Piers Plowman* has the device very rarely,
isolated twos being found occasionally. *Cheuelere Assigne*
has 15 twos, but no threes. *Morte Arthure* has more frequent
examples than any other alliterative poem to be treated in
this chapter. The most notable example found in the poem
is a group of 10 lines, each having *f* as its alliterating sound :
ll. 2483-92. There are 6 consecutive lines with alliteration
on *vowels:* ll. 1591-6 ; and 6 with alliteration on *h* : ll. 1082-7.
The feature is equally common throughout the work, and
some idea of the frequency of its occurrence may be seen in
the fact that from l. 1000 to 1200 there are 86 lines linked
in this manner. *The Destruction of Troy* shows hardly any
grouping of this kind. In the first 100 lines there are 2 twos,
and from l. 2000 to 2100 there is only 1 two. The feature
is rarely used in any part of the poem. *The Destruction of
Jerusalem* has 52 twos, 10 threes, and 1 group of 5 : ll. 655-9
bbbbb. Patience has 32 twos, and 4 threes. *Purity* has
83 twos, 6 threes, and 1 four. (Note ll. 1109-13 *kk ss mm.*)
Sir Gawayn and the Green Knight has 100 twos, and 7 threes.
St. Erkenwald has 16 twos, and 1 three. *Pierce the Ploughman's Crede* has 39 twos, and 4 threes. *Richard the Redeles*
has 43 twos, and 2 threes. (*Note*, Passus 2, ll. 106-11 *kk
pp dd.*) There are no examples in *The ABC of Aristotle*,
since each line of necessity has a different alliterating sound.
The Wars of Alexander shows numerous examples of the
device in its first 200 lines, after which very few occur. The
poet evidently tried to add this popular feature, but found

the task too difficult. *The Crowned King* has 14 twos, 1 three, and 1 four, ll. 130-3 *kkkk*. *The Scottish Prophecies* have 9 twos, and 2 threes. *The Prophecies ascribed to à Becket* have 27 twos, and 5 threes. *The Twa Mariit Wemen and the Wedo* has two-thirds of its lines linked in this way. Thus 17 out of the first 20 lines are linked. This poem is in this respect closely akin to the Scottish poems treated in chapter 10. *Death and Life* has 17 twos only, and *Scottish Field* has 13 twos and 2 threes.

To sum up, the device was employed by all poets, but by some much more extensively than by others. The feature had survived from early times, and its use was preserved and extended.

The third proof of the continuance of the O.E. tradition is afforded by the survival of the *C.* type : $(\times) \times / / \times$.

In the previous chapter we traced the *C.* type, or the *Clashing-Rhythm*, from the earliest M.E. fragments right up to *The Bestiary*. The same type is found in all the alliterative works now under discussion. There are two varieties, both of which are common. The first is the simple *C.* type :

$$\times \times / / \times.$$

      e.g. *Alexander A*, l. 65*b*, " þat his kíth ásketh."

The second form differs in that a weakly stressed syllable, usually the final -*e*, is found between the two stressed syllables :

$$(\times) \times / \times / \times.$$ e.g. *Morte Arthure*, l. 1849 *b*, " with his kýdde cómpanye."

Often it is quite impossible to decide to which of the two types a given half-line conforms, owing to the loss of the final -*e* in the MS. Thus *Morte Arthure*, l. 3200, " And this róye róyall," but l. 3206, " than this róy róyall." At the moment, however, we are only concerned with the fact that the *C.* type survived, and was still used in *Scottish Field*, a poem written after the Battle of Flodden.

These three points are sufficient to prove that the alliterative tradition had never died in the west of England. We shall now proceed to discuss the development of those tendencies which were already apparent in the alliterative poems written in the early M.E. period.

1. The practice of enjambement, usual in O.E. poetry, became very rare in the early M.E. poems, such as *The Proverbs of Alfred, Layamon's Brut,* and *The Bestiary*. Only very occasional examples are to be found in the poems of the Alliterative Revival, and of these we have found most in *Piers Plowman*. The cause of the change probably lies in the fact that the bulk of early M.E. poetry had end-rhyme, which tended to make each line a unit in itself.

2. We saw in the previous chapter that vocalic alliteration in O.E. poetry was usually on different vowels, but in *The Brut* and *The Bestiary* there is manifest the tendency to alliterate on identical vowels. This is anticipatory of the practice in the later alliterative poems, and affords further proof of the continuity of the tradition. J. Lawrence, in *Chapters on Alliterative Verse*, Oxford, 1892, examined the vocalic alliteration in *Morte Arthure, The Destruction of Troy, William of Palerne, Alexander, Sir Gawayn and the Green Knight, Cleanness, Patience, Piers Plowman*.

His statistics are quite reliable, though his conclusions are hardly acceptable to-day, since they are built upon the theory of the " glottal catch " in O.E. Accordingly he condemns the vocalic alliteration in the fourteenth century as feeble, compared with the O.E., which he looks upon as vigorous.

Schumacher, in *Studien über den Stabreim in der mittelenglischen Alliterationsdichtung*, Bonn, 1913, p. 44, made a valuable study of vocalic alliteration in the fourteenth century. He treats those works which Lawrence omitted, and works out the percentage of lines with vocalic alliteration. The average percentage of such lines is 3 per cent., and the first poem, *Alexander A*, and the last poem, *Scottish Field*, have 3 per cent. and 3·25 per cent. respectively. This represents a marked decrease, as compared with the O.E. practice, for *Beowulf* has vocalic alliteration in 15·5 per cent. of its lines. This decrease was, however, already apparent in *The Brut* and the other early alliterative poems. There is no need to comment upon those poems in which the percentage of lines with vocalic alliteration is from 2·5 per cent. to 3·5 per cent.

Wynnere and Wastoure has only 2 per cent., whereas *The Parlement of the Thre Ages* has 7 per cent., a remarkable fact if the two poems were written by the same author. *Alexander A* has 3·7 per cent. and *Alexander B* has 5 per cent., a difference not so wide as in the former case. The three texts of *Piers Plowman* have 3·6 per cent., 3·8 per cent., and 3·9 per cent. respectively, a fact which does not suggest plurality of authorship.

Poems from the south-west have on the whole a much smaller percentage of lines with vocalic alliteration than the works from the north-west. *Alexander A* and *B* have been given above; in addition *William of Palerne* has only 2·36 per cent., *The Destruction of Jerusalem* 2 per cent., *Joseph of Arimathie* 3 per cent., *Pierce the Ploughman's Crede* 3 per cent., *Richard the Redeles* 1 per cent., *The Crowned King* 2 per cent., and *Death and Life* 3·2 per cent. On the other hand, *Patience* has 5 per cent., *Purity* 6 per cent., *Sir Gawayn and the Green Knight* 4·8 per cent., *The Destruction of Troy* 5 per cent., *Morte Arthure* 6 per cent., *Cheuelere Assigne* 5·67 per cent., and *The Wars of Alexander* 7 per cent. The difference is noticeable. *St. Erkenwald* has only 1·43 per cent., but we have to remember that the poem is only 352 lines long, and that it is therefore dangerous to lay too much stress on the low percentage of such lines occurring in this poem. Similarly, *The ABC of Aristotle* has 10 per cent., but this is probably accidental. The Scottish poems are short, but *The Twa Mariit Wemen and the Wedo*, a longer poem, has 2·5 per cent. Vocalic alliteration is therefore not so common in the four-teenth-century alliterative verse as in O.E. poetry. However, the poems coming from the north-western region show a much higher percentage of vocalic alliteration than the other important group of poems coming from the south-west.

In chapter 7 we mentioned the fact that in O.E. verse it was not usual to allow the alliteration to fall on identical vowel-sounds. In *The Brut* and *The Bestiary* we found the tendency to alliterate on identical vowels already manifest, but in these works vocalic alliteration is very rare. In the works now under discussion the above tendency is still more apparent. The theory of the glottal stop in O.E. has been well-nigh abandoned, so that the older explanation of this change with regard to vocalic alliteration no longer holds. May it not be that the change was due to the fact that alliteration in general was becoming ornamental, and appealing to the eye as well as to the ear ? We shall see that the M.E. alliterative poets often alliterated an unstressed verbal prefix, a practice contrary to O.E. custom. This may have been likewise due to the fact that alliteration was becoming as important for

the eye as for the ear.   It would account for the tendency to
alliterate on identical vowel-sounds.   Let us glance at the
statistics of such alliteration in the later M.E. poems :—

(1) The following poems have only an occasional example
of such alliteration : *The Scottish Prophecies, The
Prophecies ascribed to à Becket* and *The Twa Mariit
Wemen and the Wedo.*   However, in all these poems
vocalic alliteration is very rare.

(2) The following English poems have likewise only
occasional examples of the tendency : *Joseph of
Arimathie* has only one example out of 22 instances
of vocalic alliteration.   The writer of this poem is
very exceptional in this respect.   There are two other
poems in which vocalic alliteration is also so rare
as to make it unwise to generalise from the statistics.
The Crowned King has one such example out of
3 lines with vocalic alliteration, and *Wynnere and
Wastoure* one example out of 11 lines.

(3) The remaining poems, all of which exhibit the tendency
in some measure, may be classified as follows :
(" threes " stands for a line with three identical
vowels in alliteration, " twos " for a line with two
such vowels, and " all-different " for lines where
none of the alliterating vowels are alike).

A. Poems in which the " threes " are greater than the
" twos," and the " twos " than the " all-different " :
Alexander A: 29 " threes " ;   10 " twos " ;   0 " all-
different."
Alexander B: 27 " threes " ;   26 " twos " ;   4 " all-
different."
William of Palerne: 66 " threes " ;   39 " twos " ;
28 " all-different."
The Wars of Alexander: 44 " threes " ;   27 " twos " ;
1 " all-different."
In these poems the tendency is very marked, and it
will be observed that the first three belong to the
south-western group.

B. Poems in which the " twos " are greater than either
of the other two groups :
The Parlement of the Thre Ages: 9 " threes " ;   29
" twos " ;   10 " all-different."

Cheuelere Assigne: 1 " three "; 5 " twos "; 15 " all-
different."

The Destruction of Jerusalem: 7 "threes"; 11 " twos ";
9 " all-different."

Pierce the Ploughman's Crede: 3 " threes "; 10
" twos "; 9 " all-different," and also 3 " fours."

The Destruction of Troy (from the 6000 lines examined
by Lawrence) : 64 " threes "; 176 " twos ";
50 " all-different."

Piers Plowman, in which the rule is that usually
there are two idéntical vowels, though the other
two types are quite common.

Scottish Field: 4 " threes "; 6 " twos "; 4 " all-
different."

This is the largest group, and the fact suggests that
most poets were content with two of the three
vowels identical.

C. In this group the order is the reverse of that in *A.,*
i.e. the largest number is the " all-different " :

Morte Arthure: 12 " threes "; 87 " twos "; 158 " all-
different."

Patience: 1 " three "; 9 " twos "; 18 " all-different."

Purity: 9 " threes "; 36 " twos "; 67 " all-different."

Sir Gawayn and the Green Knight: 3 " threes "; 24
" twos "; 75 " all-different."

St. Erkenwald: 1 " three "; 2 " twos "; 2 " all-
different."

Death and Life: 1 " three "; 6 " twos "; 8 " all-
different."

Morte Arthure is surely the most noticeable poem in
this group. *Richard the Redeles* does not fall within
the above groups, having 3 " threes," 1 " two," and
5 " all-different."

The ABC of Aristotle in most of the MSS. always has
vocalic alliteration on identical vowels, and the actual proportion of lines with vocalic alliteration is 10 per cent. The
probable explanation of the above fact is that the poem was
written to appeal to the eye, and if the vocalic alliteration
had not been on identical vowels, the whole visual pattern
would have been destroyed. Though different poets have
different tastes in this respect, yet the tendency to alliterate

on identical vowels was universal in M.E. If we may be allowed to make dialectal distinctions, the poets of the south-west had a greater fondness for the device than had the poets of the north-west.

The last point with regard to vocalic alliteration is the practice of allowing *h* to alliterate with a vowel. The exact statistics on this point can easily be obtained from the studies of Lawrence and Schumacher mentioned above, and we do not propose to add them here. We have, however, ventured to classify the poems into four groups, as follows :—

> *A.*, in which the tendency is to alliterate *h* with itself only, but in which occasional examples of the alliteration of *h* with vowels are found. Within this group fall *Alexander A* and *B*, *The Destruction of Jerusalem*, *The Wars of Alexander*, *The Crowned King*, *Death and Life*, *Scottish Field*, and *The Twa Mariit Wemen and the Wedo*.
>
> *B.*, in which there are more examples of *h* alliterating with vowels, but in which the usual tendency is to alliterate *h* with itself. Within this group fall *Cheuelere Assigne*, *Morte Arthure*, *St. Erkenwald*, and *Joseph of Arimathie*, *Pierce the Ploughman's Crede*, *Richard the Redeles*.
>
> *C.*, in which the rule is to alliterate *h* with vowels, though *h* is found alliterating with itself. Within this group fall *William of Palerne*, *Piers Plowman*, *Patience*, *Purity*, and *Sir Gawayn and the Green Knight*. Of these the most notable are *Piers Plowman* and *Sir Gawayn*, with, respectively, 74·3 per cent. and 62·2 per cent. of the examples of vocalic alliteration containing an *h*.
>
> *D.*, in which *h* alliterates with itself only. Within this group fall *The Parlement of the Thre Ages*, *Wynnere and Wastoure*, *The Destruction of Troy*, and *The ABC of Aristotle*.

Thus the practice in M.E. alliterative poetry is in sharp contrast to that in O.E. poetry, where *h* alliterates with itself only. In the early M.E. alliterative poems, however, despite the rarity of vocalic alliteration, it is not difficult to find examples of *h* alliterating with vowels. Numerous examples can be found in *The Brut*, and a few in *The Proverbs of Alfred*.

The later M.E. poems are therefore continuing a practice already found in earlier poetry. For an interesting discussion of these points, the reader is referred to Schumacher's dissertation, mentioned above, pp. 81-94, *h : vokal.*

3. The third point of contact between the earlier and later M.E. alliterative poems is the treatment of alliterative groups, that is to say, of the consonantal groups that alliterate together. It will be remembered that in O.E. poetry single consonants alliterate with like consonants only, and that the groups *st, sp, sc* are treated as single consonants for the purpose of alliteration. In M.E. alliterative poetry there is a tendency to form additional groups for this purpose.

In the first place, however, the alliterating together of certain consonants is largely a question of dialect. Under this heading come *s, z: f, v: v, w: wh, w:* and *wh, qu.* The alliterating together of *s* and *z*, we have only found in three poems : in *Purity*, l. 1169, in *Sir Gawayn and the Green Knight* occasionally, e.g. l. 517, and in *The Destruction of Troy* at least 4 times, e.g. ll. 3723, 10,630. But clearly in these poems the point is of no dialectal significance, being a licence of the poets in question.

The alliterating together of *f* and *v* is usually dialectal, though again it may be a licence allowed himself by the poet. The point is treated by Schumacher in his dissertation on p. 62. The feature is found in all poems except *Alexander A* and *B*, *The Parlement of the Thre Ages, Cheuelere Assigne, Pierce the Ploughman's Crede, The Crowned King, The Scottish Prophecies, Death and Life, Scottish Field,* and *The Twa Mariit Wemen and the Wedo.* In the remaining poems it is found occasionally, but only in *Piers Plowman* is it particularly noticeable. In this poem the feature is probably dialectal, as it was in *The Brut.* The same might apply to some of the other works from the south-west, but in *Morte Arthure* and other poems from the north-west, the feature is merely a metrical licence.

The alliterating together of *v* and *w* is only found very occasionally, and in northern and Scottish poems is undoubtedly dialectal. In poems such as *William of Palerne, Alexander A,* and *Piers Plowman*, it is a metrical licence, and is of no dialectal importance. The feature has been investigated by Schumacher in his dissertation on p. 68, and as the details can be consulted in that work, no further comment is necessary here.

wh, w or *wh, qu* alliterating together is a purely dialectal feature, and has already been of considerable help to us in our attempt to ascertain the dialect of the various works. The statistics in each poem on this point can be consulted in Part I. Schumacher has examined the alliterative poems for this dialectal feature, but his statistics are not always reliable. However, where they are inaccurate we have been careful to quote the references to the lines. In addition, it is essential to take into account the possibility of scribal influence.

In the second place, there are groups of consonants that are treated as single consonants for alliterative purposes. In O.E. there were only three such groups : *st, sp, sc.* In early M.E. the first two of these groups are strictly observed, except in *The Brut* and *The Bestiary.* In the former poem the careful reader will observe examples of *s* alliterating with *st* and with *sp,* though Layamon usually treats *st* and *sp* as separate alliterating groups. In *The Bestiary* we have found *s* alliterating with *st,* and *sp* with *sw.* But otherwise the two groups are preserved. The later M.E. alliterative poems continue the same practice. *Sp* is preserved as a group except in *Scottish Field,* in which it is only found alliterating with *p.* On the other hand, *st* is treated as a group in all the alliterative poems, in which it occurs in alliteration. Though *st* and *sp* are treated as groups, yet isolated examples of *s, sp* and *s, st* alliterating together are found in not a few poems. The former licence is found in the following : *Joseph of Arimathie* (l. 209), *St. Erkenwald* (l. 132), *The 2nd. Scottish Prophecy* (l. 47). *P, sp* are found alliterating together in poems whose authors are careless in these matters : *Pierce the Ploughman's Crede* (l. 264, etc.), *The 1st. Scottish Prophecy* (l. 83), *Sir Gawayn and the Green Knight* (l. 544), *Joseph of Arimathie* (ll. 123, 314). *Sp, sm* alliterate together in *The Crowned King* (l. 116), and *sp, sh* in *Cheuelere Assigne* (l. 315). *S, st* is found in *Purity* (l. 999), *St. Erkenwald* (l. 2), *Pierce the Ploughman's Crede* (l. 255, etc.), *The 1st. Scottish Prophecy* (l. 14). Also there is *sh, st: Cheuelere Assigne* (l. 326), and *Pierce the Ploughman's Crede* (l. 550) ; *sl, st: Death and Life* (l. 285) ; *sk, st:* l. 370 of the same poem. Hence one would say that the M.E. poets generally adhered to ancient custom with regard to *st, sp* as separate alliterating groups. The authors of *Cheuelere Assigne* and of *Joseph of Arimathie* are the most notable offenders, but we shall see that in many respects they were both regardless of precedent in metre. *Sk* is a fairly stable group, but *sch* is seldom treated as a group consistently. Exceptions to the former are found in the following poems : *Alexander B* has *sk, k,* 1. 81 ; *Purity* has *sk, s,* 1. 523 ; *The Destruction of Troy* has *sk, sch,* ll. 5973, 9511 ; *William of Palerne* has *sch, sk,* 1. 2749, and *sk, k,* 1. 1680 ; *Wynnere and Wastoure* has *sk, s,* 1. 443 ; *Cheuelere Assigne* and *Scottish Field* never treat *sk* as a group. *sch* would not appear to be considered an alliterating group by the authors of the following poems : *Cheuelere Assigne, St. Erkenwald, Pierce the Ploughman's Crede, Richard the Redeles, The Scottish Prophecies*, and *Death and Life*. The remaining poems as a general rule show alliteration of *sch* with itself, but the authors concerned do not hesitate on occasion to allow it to alliterate with *s*. Some poets were, however, more careful than others.

Lastly, though in O.E. poetry no other groups were observed, we have already seen that in early M.E. alliterative poetry new groups emerged. Thus *The Brut* has the following : *sp, st, sc, sm, br, sw, gr,* but *The Bestiary* and *The Proverbs of Alfred* have even more groups, such as *cl, fl,* etc. This does not mean that the above groups are invariably treated as units, for exceptions are numerous.

The same tendency to form new groups is found in the later M.E. alliterative poems. Schumacher, on pp. 40 to 44 of his dissertation, gives the results of his researches on this point, which are worthy of close study. *Sl, sn, sm, sw* are common groups, and the number of exceptions in which any one of these is allowed to alliterate with *s* is not great. This was probably due to the influence of the older groups inherited from O.E. poetry—*st, sp.*

Cr, wr, pr, þr, cl, fl, str, tw, fr, bl are groups concerning which there is no unified treatment. Some poets completely ignore them, but the majority employ certain of them. The third section consists of *br, tr, gr,* the first two of which were very popular groups, but a poet who might be very careful concerning uniformity of treatment with regard to the other groups, did not seem to hesitate to treat *tr,* etc., as groups in one line, and not as such a few lines below.

There was, therefore, no uniformity among the alliterative poets in M.E. in their treatment of these newer groups which gradually emerged and became popular. They followed no recognised rule. Some were more careful and consistent than others, and some took advantage of these devices to produce a more sonorous effect. The authors of *Cheuelere Assigne*, and of *Joseph of Arimathie* were the most careless in the use of alliteration. They even alliterated *g* and *k* together, as well as *k* and *ch*.

With the exception of the author of *Scottish Field*, it is not true to say that the later poets were careless with regard to the use of alliterative groups. Dunbar, in *The Twa Mariit Wemen and the Wedo*, is particularly careful, as were all the Scottish poets. *Scottish Field* is, however, metrically very poor, and shows the alliterative metre in its last stage of dissolution.

4. A fourth point, common to the earlier and later M.E. alliterative poems, is the increased length of the long line as compared with O.E. practice. This lengthening of the line is not to be found in *A Description of Durham, Wenne,* or *The Grave*. It appears, however, in *The 1st. Worcester Fragment*, and in *The Departing Soul's Address to the Body,* in which it is probably due to the increased use of the ' auftakt ' in both half-lines. In *The Proverbs of Alfred, The Brut* and *The Bestiary* it is possible to trace the gradual lengthening of the line, which is partly due to the use of the above feature, and also to the increased number of unstressed syllables in the line. This last point is probably to be accounted for by the fact that the rhythm had become purely accentual, and quantity neglected. The result was that the length of the line became less rigid. Despite this fact, it was still possible to keep the lines fairly even in length, avoiding that irregular movement produced by allowing short lines to follow longer ones, and vice versa. In the following poems, the lines are even in length and the number of unstressed syllables in the line is not excessive : *Alexander A* and *B, The Parlement of the Thre Ages, Wynnere and Wastoure, Patience, Purity, Sir Gawayn and the Green Knight, The Wars of Alexander, The Crowned King, The Destruction of Troy,* and *The ABC of Aristotle*. In the case of *The Destruction of Troy* this regularity is very apparent.

In the following poems there is considerable irregularity, and the effect produced is not harmonious : *Piers Plowman, Morte Arthure, Pierce the Ploughman's Crede, The Destruction of Jerusalem,* and *Richard the Redeles.* But in the last group of poems the irregularity is so apparent that all metrical balance is lost : *Joseph of Arimathie, Cheuelere Assigne, William of Palerne, The Scottish Prophecies, Death and Life, Scottish Field,* and *The Twa Mariit Wemen and the Wedo.*

e.g. *Alexander A,* " Arisba in exile euer was after," l. 240.
   The Destruction of Troy, " Maistur in mageste maker of alle," l. 1.
   Joseph of Arimathie, " þou schewest on symple skil, quaþ þe kyng ofscutered þou semest," l. 71.

The difference is very noticeable, and such lines as the latter are crude. The only excuse that can be brought forward for them, is that there is a large conversational element in *Joseph of Arimathie,* which seems to necessitate a freer treatment of the long line. However that may be, the effect upon the development of the line was unfortunate. Metrical restrictions are often helpful to a poet, but some of the alliterative poets, noticeably the authors of *Cheuelere Assigne* and *Joseph of Arimathie,* took little heed of metrical precedent, with the result that the alliterative verse in their hands became crude and well-nigh intolerable. It represents the extreme antithesis of the polished verse of their great contemporary Chaucer.

5. The fifth important point of contact between the earlier and later M.E. alliterative poems is the use of identical alliterative types. We may divide the types used into four groups :—

1. **Types used in O.E.** (in *Beowulf,* etc.) : *aa/ax, ax/ax, xa/ax, ab/ab,* and *ab/ba.* Statements regarding the relative frequency of each of these types will be found on p. 132.

2. **Types used in late O.E. :** *aa/xa, xa/aa, aa/aa, ax/aa, aa/bb, ax/xa, xa/xa.* Some of these are, however, very rare.

3. **Types with excessive alliteration :** *aaa/a(a),* and *aab/ab,* etc. These begin to appear in late O.E. verse with the lengthening of the line.

4. **Types which are failures :** *aa/xx, xx/aa, aaa/xx,* and *lines with no alliteration at all.* In these the two half-lines are not bound together.

It will be remembered from our treatment of the early M.E. alliterative poems in the last chapter that in general the later licences became more common, but were always rarer than the historic alliterative types. *The Description of Durham* and *Wenne* were traditional in this respect, whereas the other poems favoured the newer types in varying degrees of frequency.

Secondly, there was a marked tendency in the direction of excessive alliteration, reaching its climax in the last poem, *The Satire against the Blacksmiths.*

Coming to the alliterative poems of the later period,[1] we at once discover that all the four groups are used by practically all writers, and the same tendencies are apparent. The oldest type in O.E. was probably the *aa/ax* type, and this was certainly the most frequently used. It is therefore not accidental that in the poems now under discussion, this type is still the most popular, with a few notable exceptions. Let us glance at the percentage of lines in each case with the *aa/ax* type :—

	Per cent.
Alexander A	90·4
Alexander B	96
The Parlement of the Thre Ages	84·9
Wynnere and Wastoure	90
William of Palerne	71·1
Joseph of Arimathie	9
	(only 64/709 lines)

Piers Plowman—A. 65·2 per cent. ; *B.* 70·3 per cent. ; *C.* 72·1 per cent.

Cheuelere Assigne	12·2
	(only 50/370 lines)
Morte Arthure	75·9
The Destruction of Troy	99·9
The Destruction of Jerusalem	86·1
Sir Gawayn and the Green Knight	75·65
Purity	79·63
Patience	83·8
St. Erkenwald	76
Pierce the Ploughman's Crede	61·125
Richard the Redeles	72

[1] Analysis of the alliterative types used in each poem will be found at the end of this chapter, to which references will be made.

	Per cent.
The ABC of Aristotle	53
The Wars of Alexander	86·61
The Crowned King	64·8
The Prophecies ascribed to à Becket . .	45·3
The Scottish Prophecies	49
Death and Life	74·7
The Twa Mariit Wemen and the Wedo . .	70
Scottish Field	65·64

These statistics reveal the fact that there was a tendency to
excessive alliteration in M.E. as compared with O.E. practice,
in which the type *ax/ax* was much more common than in M.E.
In the above poems, the *aa/ax* type is very common except
in *Joseph of Arimathie*, and *Cheuelere Assigne*, which are very
lax in metre. At the other extreme is *The Destruction of
Troy* with 99·9 per cent. of its lines of the *aa/ax* type, but this
excessive regularity produces an effect of monotony. In the
remaining poems, however, there is a remarkable similarity
of treatment.

The frequency of the *aaa/a(a)* type is due to the same
tendency to excessive alliteration, a tendency already discernible in some of the earlier M.E. poems. The statistics
relating to this point will be left until the rhythm of the
extended lines is discussed later in the chapter.

Most of the poems differ somewhat regarding the remaining types. It is interesting to observe how many poets are
apt to repudiate the types *ax/xa* and *xa/xa*, which never
achieved the same prestige as *ax/ax*, *xa/ax*—the traditional
types. *Alexander A* and *B* have the former group only once ;
The Parlement of the Thre Ages, *Wynnere and Wastoure*, and
The Destruction of Troy, not at all. In most of the poems
it may be noticed how rarely these late licences are employed.
Thus *Morte Arthure* has *ax/ax* in 287 lines, and *xa/ax* in
257 lines, but *xa/xa* in 16 lines only, and *ax/xa* in 14. The
same preference is to be found in most of the poems. This is
even true of *Joseph of Arimathie*, which is metrically one of
the most untraditional of alliterative poems. This affords
sufficient proof, if indeed proof were needed, that the
alliteration is not placed haphazard, but according to a definite
rule.

The following poems use few types, and seldom make use

of the later licences: *Alexander A* and *B*, *The Parlement of the Thre Ages*, *Wynnere and Wastoure*, *St. Erkenwald*, and *The Destruction of Troy*, the latter being the most simple and regular of all the alliterative poems.

In the second group there is not the same monotonous regularity, but a pleasing diversity in the use of types: *Patience, Purity, Sir Gawayn and the Green Knight, The Wars of Alexander, The Destruction of Jerusalem*, and *The Twa Mariit Wemen and the Wedo*.

In the third group the diversity is greater still: *Morte Arthure, Pierce the Ploughman's Crede, Richard the Redeles*, and *The Crowned King*.

In the fourth group there are distinct signs of carelessness as well as diversity: *William of Palerne, Piers Plowman, Scottish Field, Death and Life*.

The poems in the last group are extremely crude and lawless: *Chevelere Assigne, Joseph of Arimathie, The à Becket*, and *Scottish Prophecies*. In these poems we find not merely diversity, but many lines which are failures, i.e. lines of the *aa/xx*, *xx/aa* types, or lines with no alliteration at all.

It is worthy of note that *The Twa Mariit Wemen and the Wedo* is metrically regular, despite the late period at which it was written. A knowledge of the traditional usages was still existent at the close of the period, though apparently in the west it was less accurate than in certain parts of Scotland. There were, however, individual writers, both in the west and in Scotland, who either cared little for ancient custom or knew nothing of it. A careful study of poems such as *Joseph of Arimathie* reveals that some poets, while knowing the rules, deliberately flouted them. Despite these facts, there is a central uniformity in all the alliterative poets. We have been able to trace the survival and development of the alliterative types from the close of the O.E. period right to the close of the M.E. period, and have found continuity throughout.

6. The rhythm of the long line is naturally important for a study of the evolution of the alliterative metre. In the first place, there are the extended half-lines; these, it will be remembered, occurred in O.E. poetry, and became more frequent in later verse. In the early M.E. alliterative poems they are rare. One example is found in *The Description of Durham*, 10 in *The Bestiary*, and 4 in *The Satire against the*

Blacksmiths. They are thus not very common, but are by no means absent. In the poems of the Alliterative Revival the examples become more frequent, even when allowance has been made for the greater length of the poems.

The Destruction of Troy has 23 first half-lines with three alliterating syllables, but as none of these have three stresses, they can hardly be classed as " Schwellvers " (see p. 131). The following poems have under 4 per cent. of the lines " extended " :—

	Per cent.
Alexander B	3·9
Joseph of Arimathie	3
Cheuelere Assigne	1·7
Richard the Redeles	2·85
The ABC of Aristotle	3·3
The 1st. Scottish Prophecy . . .	·25
The 2nd. Scottish Prophecy . . .	·75

The remaining poems have over 4 per cent. :—

Alexander A	8
The Parlement of the Thre Ages . . .	10·9
Wynnere and Wastoure	9·3
William of Palerne	11
Piers Plowman	9
The Destruction of Jerusalem . .	12
Morte Arthure	4·3
Sir Gawayn and the Green Knight . .	15·3
Purity	15·8
Patience	13·7
St. Erkenwald	17·5
Pierce the Ploughman's Crede . .	7
The Wars of Alexander	9·66
The Crowned King	4·7
The Prophecies of à Becket . .	5·8
Death and Life	10·8
The Twa Mariit Wemen and the Wedo .	10
Scottish Field	7·4

These statistics will show that extended lines became more popular in the middle of the period, being somewhat infrequent in the earlier part. The frequency of the type illustrates the tendency to excessive alliteration so common at this period. Though these half-lines have three alliterating syllables, it is not always certain that there are three main stresses. Thus in *Alexander A* (l. 212), " **B**ut **b**ring that **b**lisfull . . .," the alliteration on " **B**ut " is surely ornamental. Examples of this type may be found occasionally in most of the alliterative poems. In many cases it is very difficult to decide whether the half-line ought to be read with three stresses or with two. On the other hand, there are examples of lines with two alliterating syllables only and three stressed

syllables ; e.g. *Alexander A*, l. 187, " **H**óndes **h**óndely wroúght

. . ." or *Sir Gawayn and the Green Knight*, l. 21, " **B**ólde

brédden perínne. . . ." Such first half-lines surely have three stresses.

The rhythm of all the extended half-lines is of two main types. The first comprises four distinct varieties :—

$$\times \times / \times \times / \times \times / \times \times, \ \times \times / \times \times / \times \times /, \ / \times \times / \times \times / \times \times,$$
$$/ \times \times / \times \times /.$$

All these are but varieties of the first type :

$$(\times \times) / \times \times / \times \times / (\times \times),$$

and were clearly not distinct in the poet's mind ;
e.g. *Patience*,

l. 104, " **S**prude **s**pak to þe **s**prete . . ."

l. 10,   " How **M**atthew **m**elede þat his **M**ayster . . ."

Further illustrations need not be given of such lines, which occur in any poem which might be selected. This type is the more frequent of the two, and the second type is not found at all in some poems. This is of two varieties :—

$$\times \times // \times \times \times \times / \times, \ \text{or} \ \times \times / \times \times \times // \times ;$$

e.g. *William of Palerne*,

l. 185, " þat **b**old **b**arn wiþ his **b**owe . . ."

$$// \times \times /$$

is occasionally found, and is a further variety of the above type ;

e.g. *Patience*, l. 44, " Múch máugre his mún . . ."

The use of this type gives us a clue to the structure of the extended half-line ; for in the second type there is an example of the *Clashing-Rhythm*, combined with an example of *Rising* or *Falling-Rhythm*. The poet begins with one of these rhythms and passes into another before the end of the half-line is reached.

For the *Clashing-Rhythm*, both varieties are found, i.e. either

$$\times \times // \times \times \quad \text{or} \quad \times \times \times / \times / \times \times \times ;$$

e.g. *William of Palerne*,

l. 401, " A dére damisele to douȝter . . ."

All these varieties of rhythm for the extended half-lines may be reduced to the following scheme :—

$$(\times \times \times)/(\times)(\times \times)/(\times)(\times \times)/(\times \times \times).$$

The $// \times \times /$ type of rhythm is not, like the other two, found in all poems. Apart from isolated examples occurring in several poems, it is only found in any considerable number of examples in *Sir Gawayn and the Green Knight*, *Purity*, and *Patience*, in which this shortest variety of the rhythm of the extended half-lines is a noticeable feature ;

e.g. *Purity*,

l. 401, " lúf lókeȝ to lúf . . ."

Sir Gawayn and the Green Knight,

l. 76, " Smál séndal besídes . . ."

The extended half-lines which have only two alliterating syllables, conform in their rhythm to the above types ;

e.g. *The Destruction of Jerusalem*,

l. 243, " ló lórdlynges hér . . ."

or *Purity*,

l. 23, " Krýst kýdde hit hymsélf . . ."

These are found rarely in most poems, but the peculiar rhythm in the two examples quoted is not common, being only found in *Sir Gawayn and the Green Knight*, *Purity*, *Patience*, and *The Destruction of Jerusalem*, except for isolated examples occurring in a few of the remaining poems, such as *St. Erkenwald*, *Alexander A* and *B*, *William of Palerne*, etc. The extended half-lines have become much more common than in late O.E. verse, being now a regular feature of the metrical system.

Concerning the rhythm of the normal half-lines much might be said. Let us, however, endeavour to trace the development throughout the period. It will be recalled that in the last chapter we discussed the changes which took place in late O.E. verse, including the gradual disappearance of the *D.* and *E.* rhythmical types, owing to the loss of the poetic compounds. This loss often involved the *C.* type in those cases where the latter consisted of a compound with level stress, as in the following: "hwǽt we Gárdéna"; but in those cases in which this was not so, the *C.* type would naturally remain :
e.g. " on béarm scípes." *D.* and *E.* types are found in *The Description of Durham*, *c.* 1100, but not in any of the later pieces of early M.E. alliterative poetry. The *C.* type, however, is found in all the alliterative poems subsequent to 1100, as illustrated on p. 140. There is absolute continuity in rhythm from the O.E. period to the close of the M.E. period, despite a few important changes.

The first of these was the above-mentioned one, which was not in any way deliberate, but inevitable.

The *A.*, *B.*, and *C.* types survived, as we have already seen in the last chapter, but in all probability ceased to be recognised as such ; we have therefore called them the *Falling-*, *Rising-*, and *Clashing-Rhythms* respectively. The essential difference lies in the gradual increase in the number of weakly stressed syllables, resulting in a much longer half-line. Not infrequently the *C.* type has a final *-e* between the two main stressed syllables.

The third change is the increased use of the ' auftakt ' with the *Falling-Rhythm*, producing a new type—

$$\times \times / \times \times / \times \times,$$

i.e. *Rising-Falling-Rhythm.* This is found in late O.E. verse, but in the early M.E. alliterative poems became, as we have already seen, the most frequently used of all the types. This is likewise true of all the poems of the Alliterative Revival.

As a result of these changes, the O.E. rhythmical types in their changed form have come nearer to one another, and as they are all reducible to one type, viz.

$$(\times \times \times) \quad / \quad (\times)(\times \times) \quad / \quad (\times \times).$$

any given portion may be omitted at the discretion of the poet. This system is obviously much simpler than the O.E. one with its rigid types. Indeed, the chief differences between the rhythmical structure of the long line of the various M.E. alliterative poems is the amount of regularity or irregularity in the line, as discussed on p. 166. Some poems are so regular as to be monotonous, among which we may mention *The Destruction of Troy* as a typical example, whereas others, such as *Joseph of Arimathie*, are so irregular as to be formless and crude. Most poets, however, succeed in avoiding both extremes.

The last type of rhythm used in the alliterative poems is $/ \times \times \times /$. This is only another variant of the above type. It is found in all MSS., but in many cases its use is only apparent, owing to the loss of the final -*e* at the end of the line. In these cases, the poet may actually have used the $/ \times \times \times / \times$ type ;

e.g. *Patience,*

l. 372*b*, " doúred in hért(e)."

but *The Destruction of Jerusalem,*

l. 289*a*, " Soúȝte ouer þe sé."

Therefore, though in many instances the type only accidentally occurs, there are genuine examples of its use in the original MSS. This merely indicates that, as suggested above, all the types of rhythm go back to the archetype previously given. To these may be added the rhythms of the extended half-lines, which give us the following scheme :—

$$(\times \times \times) \quad (/) \quad (\times)(\times \times) \quad (/) \quad (\times)(\times \times) \quad (/) \quad (\times \times \times).$$

Such a scheme may appear complicated on the surface, but when analysed is quite simple, and the poet's ear would be a sufficient guide, whereas in O.E. poetry it may be doubted whether this was possible.

Space forbids the printing of the statistics of the rhythm in the various poems. There are naturally minor differences, but a general uniformity is discernible from a minute examination of the results. This may be expressed by the following table :—

	1st. half-line.	2nd. half-line.
$/\times\times/\times\times$	fairly common	quite common
$\times\times\times/\times\times/$	common	rare
$\times\times\times/(\times)/\times\times$	very rare	quite common
$\times\times/\times\times\times/\times\times$	the usual type	the usual type
$/\times\times\times$	rare	rare

The *C.* type is much more common in the 2nd. half-line than in the 1st. However, the increased number is in the examples of the *C.* type with the *-e* between the two stressed syllables, and not in the pure *C.* types.

The *Rising-Rhythm* is not common in the 2nd. half-line, largely because the ending " $/\times$ " had become so popular. With the loss of the final *-e* in the MS. on many occasions, this feature is not always so apparent. In the later poems, such as *Scottish Field*, in which the final *-e* had been lost long before the time of writing, a change has inevitably taken place ; the line frequently ends in " $\times/$," and the *C.* type is always of the simple variety : $\times\times\times//\times\times$.

Because there was continuity in the rhythmical system of the alliterative verse, it follows that we cannot assume that the line in M.E. had 7 stressed syllables, and that the O.E. had only 4. Hence in this book we make no references to the " 7-beat theory " regarding the M.E. alliterative long line. For an interesting discussion of the theory the reader is referred to studies by Kaluza, Leonard, Stewart, and others mentioned in the Bibliography. We do not attempt to discuss these theories here, because they are based on the belief that the metre of the alliterative poems in M.E. is an imitation either of " Otfridian verse " or of the Latin septenary, and is not derived from O.E. poetry. We have seen that there is no evidence for this.[1]

[1] Many of the German dissertations listed in the Bibliography contain numerous examples of the scansion of M.E. alliterative verse.

There are three points which remain to be discussed in this chapter, and which are illustrative of new tendencies which arose in the poems of the Alliterative Revival, and not to any great extent in the earlier period.

The first is the occasional use of a stanzaic form. *Sir Gawayn and the Green Knight* is divided into paragraphs of irregular length, each concluding with the rhymed " bob and wheel." This shows an affinity with the poems in rhymed alliterative stanzas, to be treated in a later chapter. The author of this poem made a daring experiment, and was successful, though apparently he had no imitators. Each paragraph is a unit, and the mind is soothed by the rhymed bob and wheel, which have usually no important facts to convey, but serve to round off the stanza.

The quatrain-form has been discovered in *Patience, Purity*, and *St. Erkenwald*, details of which may be found in the editions of these poems by Sir Israel Gollancz in *Select Early English Poems*. There are no marginal marks in the MS. of *St. Erkenwald*, as there are in those of the other two poems, but the quatrain is undoubtedly found. Sometimes a stanza has five lines instead of the normal four, in which case the next stanza often has only three lines. Thus in *St. Erkenwald* every stanza has four lines except the following : ll. 117-21, and 150-4 form two individual stanzas of five lines each ; ll. 177-84 consists of 5 + 3 ; ll. 163-8 form a separate stanza of 6 lines, and ll. 309-16 form a single stanza of 8 lines. The same qualifications apply to the other two poems, and especially to *Purity*. According to Gollancz the same quatrain arrangement is found in *The Sege* or *Destruction of Jerusalem*. The effect produced is quite happy, and, as Sir Israel Gollancz says, " A stanzaic arrangement renders a poem altogether more vivid, and lighter in structure." It can scarcely be denied that the stanzaic arrangement used in these poems is in keeping with the subject-matter, whereas in a pure romance it would probably have a disintegrating effect upon the movement of the poem as a whole.

The second point is the tendency for poets to bear in mind alliteration for the eye as well as for the ear. We have already met with this tendency in a different form in dealing with vocalic alliteration in the fourteenth century. It was suggested that the alliterating together of identical vowel-sounds, which is contrary to O.E. practice, may have been due to the desire to allow the alliteration to make its appeal to the eye as well as to the ear. This theory is supported by the facts which we are now going to consider. In O.E. verse, an unstressed prefix is never allowed to alliterate, and in general the early M.E. alliterative poems continue the same tradition. However, in *The Proverbs of Alfred* (l. 25) may be found an example of an unstressed pronoun in alliteration :—

> " **M**ildeliche ich **m**unye   **m**yne leoue freond."

A few such licences are to be found in *The Departing Soul's Address to the Body*, in which an auxiliary verb or the second element of a compound sometimes take the alliteration. These licences are not found in *The Bestiary*, but are not infrequent in *The Brut*. Thus a verbal prefix occasionally alliterates : e.g. **b**iswiken, l. 729 ; a pronoun in several cases : e.g. l. 170, **h**eo ; similarly an auxiliary verb : e.g. "**w**as," l. 68, etc. ; and finally the second element of a compound quite often : e.g. boc**f**elle, l. 26, mete**b**ordes, l. 403. Layamon, therefore, does not hesitate to violate the laws of natural stress when it suits his purpose.

Though the licences became more common in the poems of the Alliterative Revival, the tendency was not one which originated in the middle of the fourteenth century ; it had begun in early M.E., but its use became greatly extended. It is, however, another point of contact between the two periods, though not a very important one. We may divide the poems now under discussion into three groups :—

1. Poems in which no violations of the stress occur for the sake of alliteration : *The Parlement of the Thre Ages, Wynnere and Wastoure, The ABC of Aristotle,* and *The Crowned King.*

2. Poems in which such violations are very common : *Alexander A* and *B, William of Palerne, Piers Plowman,* and *Death and Life.*

3. In all the remaining poems, which need not be enumerated, rare examples are to be found, the poets not hesitating, when it appears needful, to violate the laws of stress for the sake of the alliteration.

E.g. *Alexander A.*

1. on a prefix : **r**eceiuen, l. 63 ; **m**isproude, l. 312 ; **f**orthoughten, l. 446 ; **b**eganne, l. 457 ; **b**ehelde, l. 1191, etc.

2. on an unaccented preposition : **to**, ll. 469, 673, etc. ;
   with, ll. 1065, 929 ; **by**, l. 689, etc.
3. on an auxiliary verb : " **w**as," l. 725, etc.
4. on pronouns : **h**em, l. 996, etc.
5. on the second element of a compound : wher**f**ore,
   l. 1050 ; sea**f**oule, l. 811, etc.

The same extensive liberties are found in *Alexander B* and *William of Palerne*.

In *Joseph of Arimathie* and *Cheuelere Assigne* the licences are very rarely found, contrary to expectation. The explanation seems to be that the poets concerned were not greatly anxious to make their lines regular and uniform. The author of *Alexander A* is willing to allow these licences, in order that the poem may appear metrically correct to the eye as well as to the ear.

In *Sir Gawayn and the Green Knight, Purity*, and *Patience*, all the five types of licence are found, and are very marked. Illustrations may be found in Schumacher's dissertation, pp. 26-8. The alliteration of the unstressed verbal prefix is especially common, and there are indications that the poet allowed himself this licence without any hesitation.

The third point is the tendency to excessive alliteration, which we have previously noted in our study of the alliterative types. There were traces of such a tendency in the early M.E. poems, but it was only in the later *Satire against the Blacksmiths* that it became marked. However, in the poems of the Alliterative Revival we have seen that the *aa/ax* type becomes the one most frequently used, the *ax/ax* type becoming comparatively rare. Also, owing to the increased number of extended half-lines, the *aaa/ax, aaa/aa* types become a noticeable feature of the verse, and with these may be included the complex types *aab/ab, abb/ba*, etc. This increase in the actual amount of alliteration used is indicative of the direction which the alliterative poetry was taking. Alliteration was destined to become more and more ornamental, and less and less structural. Incidentally this is part of the larger tendency we have already discussed, for the alliteration to make its appeal to the eye as well as to the ear. In *Sir Gawayn and the Green Knight*, for example, we find many lines with superabundant alliteration of a purely ornamental kind.

The aim of this chapter has been to demonstrate that there

was no historical break between the Old English and Middle English alliterative poetry. In particular, sufficient documents have survived in early Middle English to indicate to us the happenings of the intervening period. It is from these documents that we are enabled to trace the development of the Old English rhythms and use of alliteration with all its peculiarities. There is change, but continuity. Even in the minor details, such as the linking of lines together by means of elaborate devices, there is the same continuity.

Though there may be a whole century from which nothing has survived, it is nevertheless reasonable to suppose that the tradition lingered in the west, as the dialectal evidence goes to show. It is probable that in Worcs there was considerable literary activity, and the thirteenth century may not have been so great a blank as we are apt to imagine. There was certainly no learned revival of the Old English metrical system.

What were the causes of the literary revival in the west, if such it may be called, we can never know. That there was a revival of literary activity cannot be doubted. The new enthusiasm may have spread rapidly to the other parts of the western dialectal area, but it would seem that there were few outside imitators until after the close of the century. Strangely enough, a few feeble attempts are found in Scotland in the early years of the fifteenth century, but only Dunbar, writing a century later still, can produce tolerable verse. *The Crowned King* is but an off-shoot from the *Piers Plowman* literature in the south-west. There was considerable uniformity in metrical practice amongst these poets ; yet certain liberties were allowed themselves by most writers, so that the final impression is not one of rigid uniformity. The subjects treated were of no narrow range. There were romances dealing with the " matter of Troy and of Britain " ; satires, political, moral and religious ; and purely didactic poems. The resulting literature is remarkable both in bulk and merit. The cause of the eventual decay of this literature does not altogether lie in the metre itself, but in the decline of literary power. The inspiration having disappeared, the alliterative metre died a lingering death.

Note.—**Jacke Upland, The Reply of Friar Daw Thopias and Jacke Upland's Rejoinder.** (1401 S. Midl.) The metre of these poems is so corrupt and crude that the usual investigation is quite impossible.

In its present state the work is more like alliterative prose. Thus in *Jacke Upland* about one-sixth of the lines have two alliterating syllables, whereas the rest have no alliteration. A few lines will illustrate :

" been grounded on Goddis law."

" weeden ne reapen."

" and if thou thinkest to be on Christes side. . . ."

" For whom oweth walking and deceiving Christ's Church. . . ."

The metre of *The Reply* and of *The Rejoinder* is not quite so formless, alliteration being found in a third of the lines of the former poem, and in a quarter of those of the latter poem. Some accurate half-lines can be found, such as " to wailen and to wepyn."

Beneath the formlessness can be observed the older system, but the decay is complete.

THE STATISTICS.

Alexander A.

1. aa/ax—1127/1249 lines, a very high percentage ; e.g. l. 2 :
   " Beurnes, or bachelers   þat boldely thinken."
2. aa/aa—4 lines ; e.g. l. 978 :
   " whan hee is fare fro fight   his folke for to feaste "
   (' fro ' and ' for ' are unstressed, and only accidentally alliterate.)
3. aaa/ax—80 lines ; e.g. l. 20 :
   " and long ladden hur life   in lond togeder."
   aaa/aa—2 lines : ll. 190 and 263 ; e.g. l. 263 :
   " þough Philip fared with folke   ferefull in fyght."
4. ax/aa—3 lines : ll. 351, 557, 895 ; e.g. l. 351 :
   " The Lacedemonieins   lowe laide were."
   xa/aa—2 lines : 741, 1064 ; e.g. l. 1064 :
   " that ilk for to see   hee sayed, ' I desyre '."
5. ax/ax—11 lines ; e.g. l. 40 :
   " In the formest yere   that hee first reigned."
   xa/ax—4 lines ; e.g. l. 99 :
   " And thus sought hee his lond   with loðelike dyntes."
   xa/xa—l. 1075 only :
   " Euyll it is of syght   the walles besyde."
6. aa/bb—2 lines : ll. 58, 1077 ; e.g. l. 1077 :
   " Joyfull Jupiter   myrthfull Mercurie."
   aaa/bb (?)—l. 172 :
   " I karp of a kid king   Arisba was hote."
7. ab/ab—4 lines : 109, 407, 491, 950 ; e.g. l. 491 :
   " Artasarses þe kyng   and armed knightes."
8. ab/ba (?)—l. 240 :
   " Arisba in exile   euer was after."
9. aa/xx—3 lines, which are probably corrupt ; e.g. l. 231 :
   " mani a lud of þe lond   raid hi to grounde."
   aaa/xx—l. 417 only :
   " With grim graiþed gomes   of Lacedemonie."
10. aab/ab—ll. 904 and 998 :
    l. 904 : " þe king kiþes his grim   too keueren him gate."
    l. 998 : " þe dragon dreew him awaie,   with drift of his winges."

The alliteration is thus of a very simple kind, 1127 lines being of the *aa/ax* type, 80 of the *aaa/ax* type, only leaving 41 lines for all the other alliterative types.

Alexander B.

1. aa/ax—1092/1139, a very high percentage ; e.g. l. 14 :
   " Hurde þiþinge telle   and toknynge wiste."
   aa/xa—2 lines : ll. 31, 728 ; e.g. l. 31 :
   " For what richesse, rink   vs miȝht þou bireue."
2. aa/aa—3 lines : ll. 303, 674, 997 ; e.g. l. 303 :
   " And when we faren to fed   we finde no faute."
3. aaa/ax—28 lines ; e.g. l. 324 :
   " For littil lengure a lud   liueþ þan an oþir."
   aaa/aa—l. 544 only :
   " miche maugre ȝe maken   among many kingus."
5. ax/ax—3 lines : ll. 588, 782, 815 ; e.g. l. 782 :
   " for ȝif ȝe seggus ȝour lif   soþli biþenke."
          (Skeat, we think, rightly suggests " ȝourself.")
   l. 11 : " þe proude genosophistiens   were þe gomus called,"
          is surely a scribal mistake, for cf. l. 23 : " þe gentil geno-
          sophistiens   þat goode were of witte."
   xa/xa—l. 302 only :
   " For to refe þe brod   of briddus heuene."
          (Skeat is probably correct in suggesting that the original
             had " bruten " instead of " refe.")
8. ab/ba—l. 774 :
   " For þei schulle in þis word   wirche for sinne."
          (The original probably had " wulle ".)
9. aaa/xx—l. 1065 :
   " And euyl endid on erþe   and wrout ful foule."
          (The reading is probably corrupt.)
10. abb/a—l. 290 :
   " Bute as we simpleliche our lif   sostaine mowe."
   aba/bb—l. 6 :
   " Of bodi wente þei bar   wiþoute any wede."
   aba/ab—ll. 34 and 229 ; e.g. l. 34 :
   " nouht welde we now   but naked we wende."
   abb/ba—l. 45 :
   " þat he wolde fare wiþ his folke   in a faire wise."
          l. 695 is possibly corrupt, " ȝe holden hure a goodesse
             god   þaȝ haþ for to kepe."

The regularity of the alliteration is very noticeable.

The Parlement of the Thre Ages.

1. aa/ax—562/662 lines ; e.g. l. 194 :
   " Than the gome alle in grene   greued full sore."
   aa/xa—l. 639 only :
   " Vanitas vanitatum   et omnia vanitas."
2. aa/aa—5 lines ; e.g. l. 70 :
   " And I s(clis)te hym at þe assaye   ˙ to see how me semyde."

3. aaa/ax—59 lines ; e.g. l. 40 :
   " I waitted wiesly the wynde   by waggynge of leues."
   aaa/xa—ll. 184 and 338 ; e.g. l. 184 :
   " For alle fantome and foly   that thou with faris."
   aaa/aa—ll. 372, 606 ; e.g. l. 606 :
   " Merlyn was a meruayllous man   and made many thynges."
   aaaa/xa—l. 610 :
   " Thies were the wyseste in the worlde of witt   þat euer
      ȝit were."
4. ax/aa—3 lines ; e.g. l. 513 :
   " Sir Godfraye de Bolenn   siche grace of God hade."
   ax/a(a)a—l. 479 :
   " Mordrede & Bedwere   men of mekyll myghte."
5. ax/ax—3 lines ; e.g. l. 478 :
   " Sir Perceualle de Galeys   þat preued had bene ofte."
   xa/ax—3 lines ; e.g. l. 300 :
   " The firste was Sir Ector   and aldeste of tyme."
6. aa/bb—3 lines ; e.g. l. 626 :
   " Whare es now Dame Dido   was qwene of Cartage."
   aaa/bb—ll. 382, 389 ; e.g. l. 382 :
   " And fledden faste of the felde   and Alexandre suede."
7. ab/ab—2 lines : ll. 420, 423 ; e.g. l. 420 :
   " With alle the iles of the see   appon iche a syde."
8. ab/ba—None.
9. aa/xx—4 lines ; e.g. l. 238 :
   " lowppes in thaire lesses   thorowe vertwells of siluere."
   aaa/xx—4 lines ; e.g. l. 371 :
   " And brayde owte the brighte brande   owt of the kynges
      hande."
10. aab/ab—ll. 425, 497 ; e.g. l. 425 :
    " And renkes þat rede kane   Regum it callen."
    abb/a—l. 50 :
    " Bot gnattes gretely me greuede   and gnewen myn eghne."
    aa/bab—l. 344 ; aba/ba—l. 652.
    (Ll. 642, 645, and 647 are written in Latin without alliteration.)

Wynnere and Wastoure.

1. aa/ax—451/503 lines ; e.g. l. 56 :
   " For he was worthiere in witt   than any wy ells."
2. aa/aa—None.
3. aaa/ax—40 lines ; e.g. l. 74 :
   " A lighte lebarde and a longe   lokande full kene."
   aaaa/ax—l. 378 :
   " Late lordes lyfe als þam liste,   laddes as þam falles."
4. ax/aa—l. 103 only :
   " Thynke I dubbede the knyghte   with dynttis to dele."
   xa/aa—l. 212 :
   " And sayde, welcome heres,   as hyne of oure house bothen."
5. ax/ax etc.—None.
6. aa/bb—None.

7. ab/ab—ll. 346, 476 ; e.g. l. 346 :
> " Noghte bot worttes with flesche,   without wilde fowle."
> ("with " and "without " may also alliterate.)

8. ab/ba—None.

9. aa/xx—None.

10. abb/ab—ll. 159, 356 ; e.g. l. 159 :
> " Thies are Sayn Franceys folke,   þat sayen alle schall fey worthe."

aab/ab—ll. 30, 336, 414, and possibly 339 ; e.g. l. 336 :
> " Chewettes of choppede flesche,   charbiande fewlis."

The regularity of the alliteration is such as to produce a monotonous effect.

11. l. 79 has no alliteration, but is probably corrupt :
> " And two out of ynglonde   with sex grym bestes."

The same probably applies to l. 429 :
> " Aftir hir faire chere   to forthir hir herte."

The ax/ax type not being found elsewhere, suggests scribal alteration.

William of Palerne.

1. aa/ax—4325/5540 lines ; e.g. l. 22 :
> " And leued ful louely   þat lent grete schade."

aa/xa—69 lines ; e.g. l. 1016 :
> " þat hire maistres and þat man   no schuld hire nouȝt misse."

2. aa/aa—89 lines ; e.g. l. 51 :
> " cloped ful komly   for ani kud kinges sone."

3. aaa/ax—392 lines ; e.g. l. 90 :
> " he fond þe feute al fresh   where forþ þe herde."

aaa/aa—17 lines ; e.g. l. 2098 :
> " And swowned sixe siþe   for sorwe and for schame."

4. ax/aa—15 lines ; e.g. l. 3905 :
> " As fersli as þei nade   fouȝt nouȝt bifore."

xa/aa—12 lines ; e.g. l. 2087 :
> " þemperour ful kenely   ded kalle kniȝttes fele."

5. ax/ax—98 lines ; e.g. l. 2065 :
> " Alisaundrine for þat cas   was sorwful in herte."

xa/ax—104 lines ; e.g. l. 2022 :
> " Hire were leuer be weded   to a wel simplere."

xa/xa—11 lines ; e.g. l. 4715 :
> " Quite þe þe tenþe del   in al mi lif time."

6. aa/bb—30 lines ; e.g. l. 2033 :
> " On on þe boldest barn   þat euer bistrod stede."

7. ab/ab—18 lines ; e.g. l. 108 :
> " I wol ȝou telle as swiþe   trewely þe soþe."

8. ab/ba—51 lines ; e.g. l. 4740 :
> " I ne wilne noþing but þi suster   to be samen wedded."

9. aa/xx—99 lines ; e.g. l. 2037 :
> " And þat brouȝt ȝou out of bale   wiþ his cler strengþe."

aaa/xx—120 lines ; e.g. l. 62 :
> " þe cherl ful cherli þat child   tok in his armes,"

10. aab/ab—ll. 32, 2017, etc. ; aab/ba—l. 4769, etc. ; aba/ab—l. 4767,
etc. ; aba/ba—l. 1069 ; such combinations are to be found
in 81 lines ; e.g. :
   l. 32 : " þe couherdes hound þat time   as happe bytidde."
   l. 4767 : " now forto munge forþer   as þe mater falles."
11. No alliteration in 9 lines ; e.g. l. 166 :
   " þe king edwardes newe   at glouseter þat ligges."
   (These lines are probably corrupt.)

Joseph of Arimathie.

1. aa/ax—64/709, a very small percentage ; e.g. l. 79 :
   " To a maiden ful meke   þat Marie was hoten."
   aa/xa—27 lines ; e.g. l. 44 :
   " And Ioseph walk in þe world   and preche myne wordes."
2. aa/aa—21 lines ; e.g. l. 16 :
   " And þus þei ladden þe lyf   and lengede longe."
3. aaa/ax—3 lines : ll. 508, 510, 664 ; e.g. l. 508 :
   " Meeten miʒtful men   mallen þorw scheldes."
   aaa/xa—5 lines : ll. 12, 17, 503, 558, 569 ; e.g. l. 12 :
   " Siþen he fette his fader   with a ferde and aʒeyn fondet."
   xa/aaa—l. 13 only :
   " þer þei bosked hem out   þat hudden hem in huirenes."
   (This line is more likely to be an example of the " xa/aa "
   type, however.)
   aaa/aa—3 lines : ll. 71, 501, 647 ; e.g. l. 71 :
   " þou schewest on symple skil, quaþ þe kyng,   ofscutered
   þou semest."
   (Such crude lines are common in this poem.)
4. ax/aa—26 lines ; e.g. l. 41 :
   " whon þe lust speke with me   lift þe lide sone."
   xa/aa—9 lines ; e.g. l. 35 :
   " And come to a forest   with flowers ful feire."
5. ax/ax—115 lines ; e.g. l. 10 :
   " In þe nome of þe fader   Ioseph him folewede."
   xa/xa—62 lines ; e.g. l. 26 :
   " In þe morwe he was sone boun   don as he biddes."
   ax/xa—55 lines ; e.g. l. 51 :
   " And alle turne to þi mouþ   holliche atenes."
   xa/ax—116 lines ; e.g. l. 2 :
   " þenne alle lauhwhen an heiʒ   þat herden his wordes."
6. aa/bb—9 lines ; e.g. l. 109 :
   " Sire seide Ioseph   þou hiʒtest me to heere."
7. ab/ab—28 lines ; e.g. l. 54 :
   " þei ferden to a cite   faste bisyde."
8. ab/ba—17 lines ; e.g. l. 133 :
   " Bote as hit com heom to mouþ   and meleden þe wordes."
9. aa/xx—24 lines ; e.g. l. 134 :
   " Holliche euere he heold   for þat diʒede neuere."
   xx/aa—14 lines ; e.g. l. 151 :
   " þe kyng biheold on his face   and on his limes lowore."

10. abb/a—ll. 159, 607 ; e.g. l. 159 :

> " þe tale is heiȝ in himself   þat þou of tellest."

aab/ba—l. 504 ; a/bba—l. 261 ; aab/b—ll. 430, 509, 668 ; e.g. l. 509 :

> " Harde hauberkes toborsten   and þe brest þurleden."

11. No alliteration in 113/705 lines ; e.g. l. 105 :

> " þenne seis þe kyng,   my wit may not leeue."

The alliteration in this poem is of a very crude type, and almost a sixth of the lines have none at all.

Piers Plowman.

The proportion of lines with alliteration of a certain type varies somewhat in the three versions. Miss Deakin investigated the point in Mod. Lang. Rev., 4, 478, finding that certain types increased in frequency in the later versions. The following percentages are based on a separate examination. Since the versions differ in length, it was deemed necessary to give percentages rather than the number of lines.

1. aa/ax—A 65·2 per cent. ; B 70·3 per cent. ; C 72·1 per cent. ;
   e.g. Pr. 2 :

> " I schop me in shroudes   as I a shepe were."

aa/xa—A 1·58 per cent. ; B 1·65 per cent. ; C 1·72 per cent.

2. aa/aa—A 7·45 per cent. ; B 7·57 per cent. ; C 8·9 per cent. ; e.g.
   Pr. 1 :

> " In a somer sesun   whon softe was the sonne."

3. aaa/ax or aaa/xa—A 8·08 per cent. ; B 8·2 per cent. ; C 8·9 per cent.;
   e.g. Pr. 4 :

> " Wende I wydene in this world   wondres to here."

aaa/aa—A ·8 per cent. ;   B ·9 per cent. ;   C 1 per cent. ;
   e.g. Pr. 105 (A) :

> " Goode gees and grys   gowe dyne, gowe."

4. ax/aa and xa/aa—A 1·1 per cent. ; B 1·1 per cent. ; C 1·02 per
   cent. ; e.g. Pr. 106 :

> " Tauerners to hem   tolde the same tale."

5. ax/ax—A 2·32 per cent. ; B 1·6 per cent. ; C 1·32 per cent. ;
   xa/ax—A 2·6 per cent. ; B 1·9 per cent. ; C 1·82 per cent. ; e.g.
   Pr. 11 :

> " Thenne gon I meeten   a meruelous sweuene."

6. aa/bb—A 1·93 per cent. ; B 1 per cent. ; C 1 per cent. ; e.g.
   Passus 1, 1 :

> " What þis mountein bemeneþ   and þis derke dale."

7. ab/ab—A ·3 per cent. ; B ·2 per cent. ; C ·2 per cent. ; e.g.
   Passus 2, 101 :

> " & meede is a juweler   a mayden ful gent."

8. ab/ba—A ·1 per cent. ; B ·09 per cent. ; C ·07 per cent. ; e.g.
   Passus 1, 106 :

> " & ouer his meyne   made hem archaungelis."

9. aa/xx—A 4·5 per cent. ; B 3·4 per cent. C 2·1 per cent. ; e.g.
   Passus 3, 98 (A) :

> " with myrthe & with mynstrasye   thei pleseden hir ychoone."

10. Complex groups such as aab/ab—A 2·42 per cent. ; B 1·2 per cent. ; C ·7 per cent. ; e.g. Pr. 63 :
> " But holychirche biginne   holde bet togedere."
> (Much of the alliteration in these groups is purely ornamental.)

11. No alliteration : A ·8 per cent. ; B ·7 per cent. ; C ·9 per cent. ; e.g. in Passus I (C), ll. 95-124, there are 8 examples ; e.g. l. 110 :
> " & noȝt chased hem therof   & wolde not rebukie hem."

Cheuelere Assigne.

1. aa/ax—50/370 lines, a very small percentage ; e.g. l. 147 :
> " Thay stoden alle stylle   for stere þey ne durste."
aa/xa—30 lines ; e.g. l. 4 :
> " Nere þe hyȝnes of hym   þat lengeth in heuene."

2. aa/aa—4 lines ; e.g. l. 360 :
> " He bote hymself with his bylle   þat alle his breste bledde."

3. aaa/xa—3 lines : ll. 42, 91, 239 ; e.g. l. 42 :
> " Sex semelye sonnes   & a douȝter þe seueneth."

4. ax/aa—37 lines ; e.g. l. 17 :
> " But to be lordeles of his   whenne he þe lyf lafte."

5. ax/ax—52 lines ; e.g. l. 10 :
> " For she sette her affye   in Sathanas of helle."
xa/ax—36 lines ; e.g. l. 5 :
> " For this Isaye by a lorde   was lente in an yle."
ax/xa—40 lines ; e.g. l. 150 :
> " And he takethe vp þe cheynes   & to þe courte turnethe."
xa/xa—16 lines ; e.g. l. 55 :
> " Whenne he herde þat tale   hym rewede þe tyme."

6. aa/bb—10 lines ; e.g. l. 111 :
> " And cryede ofte vpon cryste   for somme sokour hym to sende."

7. ab/ab—5 lines ; e.g. l. 110 :
> " Whenne he come before hem   on knees þenne he felle."

8. ab/ba—6 lines ; e.g. l. 90 :
> " And mony a fayre orysoun   vnto þe fader made."

9. aa/xx—20 lines ; e.g. l. 59 :
> " Whenne his moder matabryne   browȝte hym tydynge."
xx/aa—7 lines ; e.g. l. 117 :
> " And she kepte hem þere   whylle our lorde wolde."

10. aab/b—3 lines : ll. 241, 228, 287 ; e.g. l. 241 :
> " That styged styffe in here brestes   þat wolde þe qwene brenne."

11. No alliteration in 35 lines ; e.g. l. 21 :
> " The kynge loked adowne   & byhelde under."

The alliteration in this poem is extremely irregular, and there is no adherence to traditional usage in the matter.

Morte Arthure.

1. aa/ax—3297/4346 lines ; e.g. l. 2 :
> " And the precyous prayere   of his prys modyr."
aa/xa—136 lines ; e.g. l. 138 :
> " Thow arte þe lordlyeste lede   þat euer I one lukyde."

2. aa/aa—68 lines ; e.g. l. 226 :
        " To feede ʒow with syche feble   as ʒe before fynde."
3. aaa/ax—181 lines ; e.g. l. 32 :
        " Scathyll Scottlande by skyll   he skyftys as hym lykys."
    aaa/aa : 3 lines—ll. 322, 2097, 3015 ; e.g. l. 322 :
        " In west Walys iwysse   syche woundyrs þay wroghte."
4. ax/aa—11 lines ; e.g. l. 391 :
        " Redy wayes to make   & rennkes ful rowme."
    xa/aa—12 lines ; e.g. l. 693 :
        " Nowe he takeʒ hys leue   & lengeʒ no langere."
5. ax/ax—287 lines ; e.g. l. 636 :
        " In þe paleʒ of Ʒorke   a parlement he haldeʒ."
    xa/ax—257 lines ; e.g. l. 50 :
        " Mad of his cosyns   kyngys ennoyntede."
    xa/xa—16 lines ; e.g. l. 658 :
        " And þat in þe seson   whene grees es assignyde."
    ax/xa—14 lines ; e.g. l. 634 :
        " Wythin sexten dayes   hys fleet was assemblede."
6. aa/bb—7 lines ; e.g. l. 2144 :
        " That iche a furthe in the firthe   of rede blode rynnys."
7. ab/ab—23 lines ; e.g. l. 4189 :
        " I see þe traytoure come ʒondyr   trynande full ʒerne."
8. ab/ba—25 lines ; e.g. l. 1019 :
        " Bot luke nowe for charitee,   þow chasty thy lyppes."
9. aa/xx—4 lines (probably all corrupt) ; e.g. l. 3409 :
        " þe toþer Ector of Troye   the cheualrous gume."
    xx/aa—l. 3437 only :
        " Ne siche myschefe dreghe,   when trewthe sall be tryede."
10. aab/ab—l. 2704 :
        " A fyole of fyne golde,   thay fande at his gyrdill."
    aab/ba—l. 77 :
        " Mad in myd wynter   in þe waste marchys."
    aba/ba—l. 210 :
        " Sexty cowpes of suyte   fore þe Kyng seluyn."
    aba/b—l. 3136 :
        " Grete sommes of golde   sexti horse chargegid."
11. No lines without alliteration.

The alliteration is thus very careful, and is in strict accordance with traditional usage ; it is significant that the two types most frequently used are the two O.E. ones : *aa/ax*—3297 lines, and *ax/ax*—287 lines.

In section 5, it will be observed that the two late O.E. licences— *ax/xa* and *xa/xa*—are very rarely found.

The Destruction of Troy.

1. aa/ax—13,999/14,044 lines, a very high percentage ; e.g. l. 1 :
        " Maistur in mageste   maker of alle."
    aa/xa—7 lines : 2046, 2091, 2290, 2600, 2655, 2823, 3844 ; e.g. l. 2600 :
        " Into Grece for to go   and hom to greme."

2. aa/aa—6 lines : 4109, 4122, 4945, 6194, 8236, 9416 ; e.g. l. 4109 :
   " Rufirus the ryche   raght fro his Rewme."
5. ax/ax—5 lines : 2985, 3727, 5908, 6609, 9681 ; e.g. l. 5908 :
   " þat he fell of his horse   flat to þe ground."
   xa/ax—15 lines ; e.g. l. 453 :
   " Hir ene as a trendull   turned full rounde."
6. aa/bb—2 lines : ll. 11,847, 12,938 ; e.g. l. 11,847 :
   " Prayd to Priam   for a great vow."
7. ab/ab—3 lines : ll. 3466, 7345, 12,944 ; e.g. l. 7345 :
   " Ffore to þere Innes   & þus the fight endit."
8. ab/ba—4 lines : ll. 503, 6376, 6665, 8963 ; e.g. l. 6376 :
   " With twenty auntrid   abill men two."
9. aa/xx—l. 9225 only :
   " On suche couenaund to kepe   yf þat dere wold."
       (This line is probably corrupt.)
10. aab/ab—2 lines : ll. 2649, 2756 ; e.g. :
    l. 2649 : " Wherefore wheme kyng !   for what þat may
       come."
    l. 2756 : " Bowne on hor best wise   in hor bright wedis."

       Note.—There are in addition 23 lines which look like
          examples of the " aaa/ax " type, but as it is almost
          certain that the first half-line in each case has only
          2 stresses, the type may be accidental ; e.g.
    l. 5870 : " þat his wedis wex wete   of his wan teris."
       See also lines 2074, 2271, 5838, 6870, 11,069, etc.

The alliteration in this poem is therefore extremely regular, and it
is possible that in the original there were still more examples of the
aa/ax type.

The Destruction of Jerusalem.

1. aa/ax—1147/1332 lines, a very high percentage ; e.g. l. 1 :
   " In tyberius tyme   þe trewe emperour."
   aa/xa—2 lines : l. 1061, 1210 ; e.g. l. 1061 :
   " And of þe tene in þe toune   wer hard for to telle."
2. aa/aa—12 lines ; e.g. l. 76 :
   " And he fraynes how fer   þe flode hadde yferked."
3. aaa/ax—110 lines ; e.g. l. 63 :
   " þe schip scher vpon schore   schot froward rome.
   aaa/xa—l. 891 only :
   " Peter apostlen prince   & seint poule."
   aaa/aa—l. 636 only :
   " Geten girdeles and ger   gold & goode stones."
4. ax/aa—l. 1148 only :
   " þo pried he hadde jofophus   to preche þe peple."
   xa/aa—6 lines ; e.g. l. 411 :
   " And on eche pomel   wer pyȝt penseles hyȝe."
5. ax/ax—13 lines ; e.g. l. 34 :
   " And Waspasian was called   þe waspene bees after."
   xa/ax—13 lines ; e.g. l. 286 :
   " Sprad on þe brod se   aboute four myle."

6, aa/bb—3 lines ; e.g. l. 51 :
    " An heye setteþ þe sayl   ouer þe wode water."
7. ab/ab—2 lines ; e.g. l. 1229 :
    " And þan þey deuysed hem   & vengaunce hit helde."
8. ab/ba—2 lines ; e.g. l. 1162 :
    " Toren euereche a gome   & þe gold taken."
9. aa/xx—12 lines ; e.g. l. 402 :
    " þer britned to be   or þe toun wynne."
10. aaa/bb—l. 878 :
    " Marchals maser men   þat he to trustiþ."
   aab/bb—l. 253 :
    " þe kerchef carieþ fram alle   & in þe eyr hangyþ."
   abb/a—2 lines : ll. 941, 112 ; e.g. l. 941 :
    " seuen monþes þes man   hadde septre on hande."
   Excessive alliteration is found in l. 1221 :
    " Voys from est & from west   & from þe four wyndis."
11. No alliteration in 2 lines : ll. 1166, 1253 ; e.g. l. 1253 :
    " þe clerkes hadde none oþer lyʒt   whenne þat þey dede
    ryse."

Sir Gawayn and the Green Knight.

1. aa/ax—1532/2025 long lines ; e.g. l. 63 :
    " þe chauntre of þe chapel   cheued to an ende."
   aa/xa—23 lines ; e.g. l. 161 :
    " And alle his vesture verayly   watʒ clene verdure."
2. aa/aa—70 lines ; e.g. l. 179 :
    " Wel gay watʒ þis gome   gered in grene."
3. aaa/ax—239 lines ; e.g. l. 47 :
    " Dere dyn vpon day   daunsyng on nyʒtes."
   aaa/xa—4 lines : ll. 983, 1133, 2143, 2197 ; e.g. l. 983 :
    " Hent heʒly of his hode   & on a spere henged."
   aaa/aa—14 lines ; e.g. l. 595 :
    " Lacheʒ lufly his leue   at lordeʒ & ladyeʒ."
4. ax/aa—6 lines ; e.g. l. 1406 :
    " þat chaunce so bytydeʒ   her cheuysaunce to chaunge."
   xa/aa—4 lines ; e.g. l. 461 :
    " Neuer more þen þay wyste   from queþen he watʒ wonnen."
5. ax/ax—40 lines ; e.g. l. 93 :
    " Of sum auenturus þyng   an uncouþe tale."
   xa/ax—59 lines ; e.g. l. 134 :
    " For uneþe watʒ þe noyce   not a whyle sesed."
    (It is possible that the n of " uneþe " may alliterate here.)
    or l. 644 :
    " & quere-so-euer þys mon   in melly watʒ stad."
6. aa/bb—2 lines ; e.g. l. 939 :
    " & he hym þonked þroly   ayþer halched oþer."
7. ab/ab—10 lines ; e.g. l. 663 :
    " þus alle with red golde   upon rede gowleʒ."
8. ab/ba—5 lines ; e.g. l. 90 :
    " & also anoþer maner   meued him eke."
9. aaa/xx—2 lines : ll. 971, 1906 ; e.g. l. 1906 :
    " þe lorde lyʒtez bilyue   & cacheʒ hym sone."

10. aab/ab—ll. 370, 1331 ; abb/a—ll. 60, 541, 656 ; abb/ba—ll. 111,
 263 ; abb/ab—l. 427, 568 ; aba/b—l. 1440 ; aba/ab—
 l. 123 ; abab/ab—l. 1097 ; e.g. l. 1351 :
 " **Sch**aued wyth a **sch**arp **kn**yf   & þe **sch**yre **kn**itten."
Excessive ornamental alliteration is not infrequently found ; e.g.
 l. 1445 :
 " & þay halowed hyghe ful hyȝe   & hay ! hay ! "
Very rarely do the lines of the " wheel " have three alliterating
 sounds, but occasionally this is the case : e.g. l. 1661 :
 " Bot he **n**olde **n**ot for his **n**urture."

Patience.

 1. aa/ax—442/531 lines ; e.g. l. 4 :
 " For ho **qu**elles vche a **qu**ed   & **qu**enches malyce."
 2. aa/aa—8 lines ; e.g. l. 269 :
 " He **gl**ydes in by þe **g**iles   þurh **gl**aym ande **gl**ette."
 3. aaa/ax—68 lines ; e.g. l. 104 :
 " **Sp**rude **sp**ak to þe **sp**rete   þe **sp**are bawe-lyne."
 5. ax/ax—4 lines ; e.g. l. 238 :
 " To oure **m**ercyable God   on **M**oyses wyse."
 xa/ax—5 lines ; e.g. l. 526 :
 " For he þat is to **r**akel   to **r**enden his cloþeȝ."
 8. ab/ba—l. 463 only :
 " On **h**eȝe vpon **E**ffraym   oþer **E**rmonnes **h**illes."
 10. aab/ab—ll. 319, 438 ; e.g. l. 319 :
 " þe **p**ure **p**oplande **h**ourle   **p**layes on my **h**eued."
 aba/b—l. 66 only :
 " **N**ym þe **w**ay to **N**ynyue   **w**ithouten oþer speche."
The use of alliteration is therefore quite regular with a distinct
preference for the older types.

Purity.

 1. aa/ax—1442/1812 lines ; e.g. l. 17 :
 " He is so **c**lene in his **c**orte,   þe **k**yng þat al weldeȝ."
 2. aa/aa—52 lines ; e.g. l. 158 :
 " **D**epe in my **d**oungoun   þer **d**oel ever **d**welleȝ."
 3. aaa/ax—263 lines ; e.g. l. 51 :
 " As **M**athew **m**eleȝ in his **m**asse   of þat **m**an ryche."
 aaa/aa—9 lines ; e.g. l. 903 :
 " **f**oundeȝ **f**aste on ȝor **f**ete,   bi**f**ore ȝor **f**ace lokes."
 5. ax/ax—10 lines ; e.g. l. 427 :
 " Of **s**ecounde monyth,   þe **s**evenþe day ryȝtez."
 xa/ax—5 lines ; e.g. l. 105 :
 " For certeȝ, þyse ilk **r**enkeȝ   þat me **r**enayed habbe."
 6. aa/bb—3 lines ; e.g. l. 1573 :
 " Out**t**aken bare **t**wo,   and **þ**enne he þe **þ**rydde."
 7. ab/ab—4 lines ; e.g. l. 237 :
 " **A**dam ino**b**edyent   ordaynt to **b**lisse."
 8. ab/ba—3 lines ; e.g. l. 608 :
 " Hit is **e**þe to leve   by þe last **e**nde."
 9. aa/xx—ll. 28, 63 ; e.g. l. 28 :
 " For he schal loke on our **L**orde   with a bone chere."

10. aab/ab—5 lines (ll. 11, 493, 782, 951, 1776) ; aab/ba—l 657 ;
        aab/b—ll. 299, 345, 1655 ; aba/ab—3 lines, e.g. l. 476 ;
        abb/ab—3 lines, e.g. ll. 20, 538 ; abb/ba—l. 1720 ;
e.g.   l. 493 : " Myryly on a fayr morn,   monyth þe fyrst."
        l. 299 : " Sem sothly þat on ;   þat oþer hy3t Cam."

As in *Sir Gawayn and the Green Knight*, and in *Patience*, we meet
with lines having excessive alliteration of a purely ornamental type ;
e.g. l. 676 :

" wyth wroþe wolfes to won and with wylde asses."

St. Erkenwald.

1. aa/ax—268/352 lines ; e.g. l. 3 :
      " Ther was a bischop in þat burghe   blessyd and sacryd."
2. aa/aa—14 lines ; e.g. l. 179 :
      " Now lykhame, þat þus lies   layne þou no lenger."
3. aaa/ax—51 lines ; e.g. l. 39 :
      " mony a mery mason   was made þer to wyrke."
   aaa/xa—l. 328 :
      " And þe relefe of þe lodely lures   þat my soule has levyd
      in."
   aaa/aa—3 lines : ll. 46, 61, 213 ; e.g. l. 213 :
      " The bolde Breton Ser Belyn,   Sir Berynge was his
      brothire."
   aaaa/ax—l. 143, a line with excessive alliteration :
      " þe maire with mony ma3ti men   & macers before hym."
4. xa/aa—l. 214 :
      " Mony one was þe busmare   boden hom bitwene."
5. ax/ax—l. 247 :
      " Alle menyd my dethe,   þe more and þe lasse."
   xa/xa—l. 19 :
      " þat ere was of Appolyn   is now of Saynt Petre."
   xa/ax—l. 122 :
      " þoghe I be unworthi,   al wepande he sayde."
6. aa/bb—3 lines ; e.g. l. 92 :
      " As he in sounde sodanly   were slippide opon slepe."
9. aa/xx—l. 192 :
      " þurghe sum lant goste lyfe   of hym þat al redes."
10. aab/ab—ll. 34, 61, 77 ; aab/ba—l. 124 ; abb/ba—l. 308 ; aaab/ba—
      l. 326 ; e.g. :
      l. 34 : " At love London toun   & þe laghe teches."
      l. 308 : " Longe er ho þat soper se,   oþer segge hyr to
      lathe."
      l. 77 : " Araide on a riche wise   in rialle wedes."
         An example of a line with excessive ornamental alliteration
         is the following :—
      " Quat wan we with oure wele-dede   þat wro3tyn ay ri3t."

The alliteration is thus simple in that few types are usually found,
but there is also manifest a tendency towards excessive ornamental
alliteration.

Pierce the Ploughman's Crede.

1. aa/ax—520/850 lines ; e.g. l. 3 :
   " And þoruȝ þe speciall spirit   þat sprong of hem tweyne."
   aa/xa—37 lines ; e.g. l. 11 :
   " þe lengþe of a lenton   flesh mot I leve."
2. aa/aa—30 lines ; e.g. l. 8 :
   " Bot all my kare is to comen   for I can noȝt my crede."
3. aaa/ax—36 lines ; e.g. l. 19 :
   " And fulliche folweth þe feyþ   and feyneþ non oþer."
   aaa/xa—l. 82 only :
   " Wiþ sterne staues & stronge   þey ouer lond strakeþ."
   aaa/aa—3 lines ; e.g. l. 391 :
   " A masse of us mene men   is of a more mede."
   aaaa/ax—ll. 536, 668 ; e.g. l. 536 :
   " Fynd foure freres in a flok   þat folweþ þat rewle."
   aaaa/xa—l. 442 :
   " þe sely man siȝede sore & seide,   children beþ stille."
4. ax/aa—2 lines ; e.g. l. 26 :
   " Hollich on þe grete God   & holden alle his hestes."
   xa/aa—4 lines ; e.g. l. 64 :
   " Sikerli y can nouȝt fynden   who hem first founded."
5. ax/ax—50 lines ; e.g. l. 4 :
   " And alle in on godhed   endles dwelleþ."
   xa/ax—58 lines ; e.g. l. 43 :
   " þei ben but iugulers   & iapers of kynde."
   xa/xa—8 lines ; e.g. l. 387 :
   " For all þe soules & þe lyves   þat we by lybbeth."
   ax/xa—10 lines ; e.g. l. 98 :
   " Alas frere, quaþ I þo,   my purpos is ifailed."
6. aa/bb—5 lines ; e.g. l. 493 :
   " Eft he seyde to hemselfe   wo mote ȝou worþen."
7. ab/ab—10 lines ; e.g. l. 14 :
   " And also Iesu hymself   to the Iewes he seyde."
8. ab/ba—5 lines ; e.g. l. 60 :
   " þan suen any god liife ;   but lurken in her selles."
9. aa/xx—32 lines ; e.g. l. 69 :
   " And no obedience bere   but don as hem luste."
   xx/aa—l. 617 only :
   " And perfore of þat blissinge   trewlie as y trowe."
   aaa/xx—2 lines ; e.g. l. 499 :
   " And wilneþ worschipes of þe werlde   & sitten wiþ heye."
   xx/aaa—l. 280 only :
   " Alas, quaþ þe frier,   almost y madde in mynde."
10. aab/ba—4 lines, e.g. l. 282 ; aa/abb—l. 78 ; abb/a—2 lines,
    e.g. l. 569 ; aab/b—2 lines, e.g. l. 272 ; aba/ab—l. 210 ;
    aba/b—2 lines, e.g. l. 40 ; aaa/bb—2 lines, e.g. l. 559 ;
    aab/ab—2 lines ; e.g. l. 829 :
    " Knowen cristes pryuitee   þat all kynde passeþ."
11. No alliteration in 10 lines ; e.g. l. 42 :
    " Houȝ schulde þei techen þe God   þat con not hem-selue "
    The tendency to excessive alliteration is very noticeable.

Richard the Redeles.

1. aa/ax—619/857 lines ; e.g. Pr. 1 :
   " And as I passid in my preiere   ther prestis were at masse."
   aa/xa—32 lines ; e.g. Pr. 8 :
   " So sore were the sawis   of bothe two sidis."
2. aa/aa—33 lines ; e.g. 1. 13 :
   " By pillinge of ȝoure peple   ȝoure prynces to plese."
3. aaa/ax—21 lines ; e.g. 2. 40 :
   " Lieges that loued ȝou the lesse   for her lither dedis."
   aaa/xa—2. 45 only :
   " To sette siluer in signes   that of nouȝt serued."
4. ax/aa—3. 84 only :
   " that he hem ffede shulde   & ffostre fforther."
   xa/aa—8 lines ; e.g. 1. 103 :
   " All that they moued   or mynged in that mater."
5. ax/ax—21 lines ; e.g. 1. 84 :
   " Of maters that I thenke   to meve for the best."
   xa/xa—7 lines ; e.g. 3. 141:
   " & ffordoth the coyne   & many other craftis."
   ax/xa—1. 98 only :
   " They made ȝou to leue   that regne ȝe ne myȝte."
   xa/ax—64 lines ; e.g. 1. 10 :
   " Wherby it standith   & stablithe moste."
6. aa/bb—2 lines : 1. 15 and 2. 77 ; e.g. 1. 15 :
   " Or be tallange of ȝoure tounes   without ony werre."
7. ab/ab—3 lines : 1. 73, 2. 133, and 3. 130 ; e.g. 3. 130 :
   " With gyuleris, Ioyffull   ffor here gery Iaces."
8. ab/ba—5 lines ; e.g. Pr. 11 :
   " Henri was entrid   on the est half."
9. aa/xx—20 lines ; e.g. Pr. 28 :
   " Whedir god wolde ȝeue him grace   sone to amende."
   xx/aa—2. 112 only :
   " that neuere weren to truste   so god saue my saule."
   aaa/xx—4 lines ; e.g. 2. 153 :
   " And gaderid gomes on grene   ther as they walkyd."
   xx/aaa—4. 21 only :
   " And no thing ylafte   but the bare baggis."
10. aab/b—1. 58 ; abb/a—1. 21, 2. 121 ; e.g. 1. 21 :
   " miche nede is it not   to muse theron."
11. No alliteration in 8 lines ; e.g. 1. 97 :
   " More than for wurschipe   that they to ȝou owed."

The ABC of Aristotle (the two versions from the MS. Harl. 1304).

1. aa/ax—25 lines ; e.g. l. 4 :
   " And it is councell to clerkis   & knightis a thousand."
   aa/xa—3 lines ; e.g. l. 14 :
   " Dred god and do well   þan nede þe not dowte."
2. aa/aa—15 lines ; e.g. l. 13 :
   " Care for þi conscience   & kepe it ay clene."
3. aaa/a(a)—8 lines ; e.g. l. 2 :
   " Lett hym lerne one letter   & loke on anoþer."

6. aa/bb—1 line ; l. 36 :
    " A coward & contacowre   manhod is þe mene."
7. ab/ab—1 line ; l. 31 :
    " þus rede we in bokys   & rollis abowte."
9. aa/xx—4 lines ; e.g. l. 32 :
    " Thus god is begynnere   & former of alle thyng."
   xx/aa—1 line ; l. 34 :
    " And mesure he taughte vs   in alle his wise werkes."
11. No alliteration—1 line ; l. 38 :
    " For to moche of on thynge   was neuer holsome."

The Wars of Alexander.

1. aa/ax—5026/5803 lines ; e.g. l. 4 :
    " Sum is leue to lythe   þe lesing of Sayntis."
   aa/xa—12 lines ; e.g. l. 212 :
    " Bot will ȝe herken hende   now sall ȝe here."
2. aa/aa—18 lines ; e.g. l. 134 :
    " Vn-wetandly to any wel   þat wont in his wanes."
3. aaa/ax—578 lines ; e.g. l. 152 :
    " To laite þar lord at was lost   with latis vnblythe."
   aaa/aa—7 lines ; e.g. l. 2165 :
    " þan standes in stede noght of a stra   all our styffe stedes."
4. ax/aa—None.
5. ax/ax—29 lines ; e.g. l. 41 :
    " He was wyse enoȝe   wirdis to reken."
   xa/ax—26 lines ; e.g. l. 351 :
    " As erly as þe riche qwene   was resyn fra slepe."
   xa/xa—3 lines ; e.g. l. 3672 :
    " þat ware as semely   quen þai ware samen."
   ax/xa—3 lines ; e.g. l. 4081 :
    " & on þe ferre halfe of þe bourne   was wemen on hors."
6. aa/bb—15 lines ; e.g. l. 42 :
    " When he þe hauyn beheld   of ledes opon lyfe."
7. ab/ab—3 lines ; e.g. l. 2048 :
    " Sike scoures were of blude   of schondirhed bernes."
8. ab/ba—2 lines ; e.g. l. 1993 :
    " Or any wee to acounte   vndire þe clere welkyn."
9. aa/xx—51 lines ; e.g. l. 67 : .
    " Of slik a naue is noy   to here or to tell."
   aaa/xx—15 lines ; e.g. l. 270 :
    " My frely fode, quod þe freke,   noȝt bot þe werdes."
10. aab/ab—l. 4385 :
    " þe swoȝing of þe swift wynde   & of þe swete wellis."
   aab/b—l. 390 and 829 ; e.g. l. 390 :
    " þus begylid he this gude wyfe   & makis hire to wene."
   aba/b—ll. 26, 1742 ; e.g. l. 26 :
    " þe sise of all þe grete see   & of þe grym wawys."
   aaa/bb—l. 5476 :
    " þat ferly faire ware of face   with haare to þaire heelis."
11. No alliteration in 10 lines ; e.g. l. 503 :
    " þen come þarin a litill brid   into his arme floȝe."

Note.—The two MSS. do not agree metrically, the Dublin being much more regular than the Ashmole. We have therefore taken the Dublin MS. as the basis of study for the above statistics, but where the text is missing we have to rely on the Ashmole. Where the two texts are found side by side, the Ashmole reading is often unmetrical. We are able to correct this from the Dublin MS., where this exists, but where only the Ashmole exists we may be right in suspecting metrical corruption. Thus the 10 lines without alliteration, and the 66 lines of *aa/xx* and *aaa/xx*—the only deficient lines—are from passages where only the Ashmole MS. exists ; e.g.

Ash. l. 2404 : " þat þai nere liȝt as belyue   at the kyngis tentis."
Dub.   " & lyȝt all belyue   at the lordis tentis."
Ash. l. 2601 : " þare I rede, quod þe kyng,   oure bakis neuer to turne."
Dub.   " þarfore I breke, quod þe berne,   oure bakkeȝ neuer to turne."

The original was probably very simple in its use of metrical types.

The Crowned King.

1. aa/ax—101/150 lines ; e.g. l. 3 :
    " With þi halwes in heuen   heried mote þu be."
   aa/xa—5 lines ; e.g. l. 62 :
    " Take hit for a tresour   of hem that are true."
2. aa/aa—13 lines ; e.g. l. 2 :
    " And art comfort of all care   þow kynd go out of cours."
3. aaa/a(a)—5 lines ; e.g. l. 29 :
    " Swythe y swyed in a sweem   þat y swet after."
4. ax/aa—l. 109 only :
    " Loke þou haue siche a man   that loueth not to lye."
   xa/aa—6 lines ; e.g. l. 107 :
    " Suche þou shuldest comfort   be cours of þy kinde."
5. ax/ax—3 lines ; e.g. l. 41 :
    " This ordinaunce he made   in ease of his peple."
   xa/ax—3 lines ; e.g. l. 53 :
    " Yif þou be chief Iustice   Iustifie the truthe."
   xa/xa—l. 126 only :
    " Rather þou shalt yeve hem   þat fele hem agreved."
   ax/xa—l. 103 only :
    " That for his doughtynesse   men mowe hym drede."
6. aa/bb—3 lines ; e.g. l. 132 :
    " This is corage out of kinde   when mukke is his maistre."
7. ab/ab—3 lines ; e.g. l. 15 :
    " Ones y me ordeyned   as y haue ofte don."
8. ab/ba—2 lines ; e.g. l. 138 :
    " Of all the seyntes in heven   that for hym deth suffred."
9. aaa/xx—l. 50 only :
    " To stonde and sey what hym semed   and knele no lenger."
10. aab/bb—l. 135 :
    " My liege lord of this mater,   y meve you no more."

10. abb/ba—l. 51 :
"Than he seid, 'Sir crowned kyng,   thou knowest well
þy-self.'"

In view of the late date of the work, the alliteration is regular,
and the usage according to tradition.

Fragment of an Alliterative Poem containing Thomas à Becket's Prophecies.

1. aa/ax—116/256 lines ; e.g. l. 6 :
"Love barnes, quod beket,   go bye me ane oþer."
aa/xa—20 lines ; e.g. l. 9 :
"Forthy wende we on oþir ways   and hime no more wroth."
2. aa/aa—18 lines ; e.g. l. 5 :
"All for faurte of a faþer   sall fele folk dye."
3. aaa/ax—7 lines ; e.g. l. 15 :
"And gat vp a glowe full of that grunde   with glayde hartis."
aaa/xa—l. 242 only :
"To wend out our the wan watterys,   as þar none ware."
aaa/aa—2 lines ; e.g. ll. 182, 185 ; e.g. l. 182 :
"þar beys na byerde wytht twa bekis,   nor best þat hede
berys."
4. ax/aa—2 lines ; e.g. l. 87 :
"At yhon secunde cross   þat I of say schall."
5. ax/ax—13 lines ; e.g. l. 10 :
"For all þar wroke sall ende   wyght þam selwne."
xa/ax—15 lines ; e.g. l. 1 :
"And redy his schippis,   he that the soth tellys."
xa/xa—2 lines ; e.g. l. 134 :
"In quhyte sande the ledene sal be,   no houss lewyde."
ax/xa—5 lines ; e.g. l. 12 :
"Twelff days Iurnay,   as the buke tellys."
6. (a)aa/bb—3 lines ; e.g. l. 17 :
"Be my saule, he sayde, þat war a selly,   þat ar riall and
rewme."
7. ab/ab—2 lines ; e.g. l. 42 :
"For ony way that mycht happine,   on yon west halfe."
8. ab/ba—2 lines ; e.g. l. 137 :
"a noyntede kynge   sall come fro the North."
9. aa/xx—20 lines ; e.g. l. 183 :
"So hardy to lyght on þat lande,   þar the ber restis."
xx/aa—l. 89 only :
"And preloettis of haly kyrke,   sall þar lyffis loss."
aaa/xx—4 lines ; e.g. l. 13 :
"At the last he landes in ane noþer lande,   þar Avyoune
standis."
10. aab/b(b)—4 lines ; e.g. l. 61 :
"Der lady, latte me witt,   and thy wille were."
11. No alliteration in 11 lines ; e.g. l. 211 :
"For he sall lewe his trouth   on crystis owyne grawde."

The Scottish Prophecies.—1st. Prophecy.

1. aa/ax—31/139 lines ; e.g. l. 25 :
"þen sall dulefull destany   drive to þe nyghte."

1. aa/xa—11 lines ; e.g. l. 40 :
   " The busment of brykhyll   þer with sall breke."
2. aa/aa—17 lines ; e.g. l. 139 :
   " Scho has closede him in a cragge   of cornwales coste."
3. aaa/ax—l. 21 :
   " Wycht balde bernese in bushment   þe batell sall mete."
4. ax/aa—4 lines ; e.g. l. 101 :
   " þe gayt buke þat mayde   þe greyfe is þen ner gon."
   xa/aa—5 lines ; e.g. l. 18 :
   " And sadilles horse & a bore   wygh bernyse so brycht."
5. ax/ax—l. 49 :
   " Then þe sonn & þe mone   sall shine full bricht."
   xa/ax—5 lines ; e.g. l. 50 :
   " þat mony longe day   full dirke has beyne."
   xa/xa—l. 85 :
   " And þe abbays trewly   þat standis on twede."
   ax/xa—4 lines ; e.g. l. 63 :
   " In comforte   of a yhong knyght."
6. aa/bb—10 lines ; e.g. l. 7 :
   " Then shall the lyonne be lousse,   þe baldest and best."
7. ab/ab—l. 104 :
   " And mony on sall tyne   þir lyff in the mene tyme."
8. ab/ba—2 lines : ll. 6, 124 ; e.g. l. 6 :
   " In a clowde als blak   as the bill of a crawe."
9. aa/xx—15 lines ; e.g. l. 3 :
   " þan shall fortune his frende   þe ʒattis vpcaste."
   xx/aa—l. 69 :
   " Fyftyne dayis   Iornay fro Ierusaleme."
11. No alliteration in 22 lines ; e.g. l. 4 :
   " And rychte shall haue   his free entre."

2nd. Prophecy.

1. aa/ax—30/71 lines ; e.g. l. 10 :
   " Fully nynty ande nyne,   nocht one wone."
2. aa/aa—5 lines ; e.g. l. 8 :
   " Bothte knychtis & knawys   clede in on clethinge."
3. aaa/ax—ll. 43 and 68 ; e.g. l. 43 :
   " Shall fande flowrys to fange   in þat fyrste sesoun."
   aaa/aa—l. 45 :
   " To bynde bandis vnbrokyne   þat salbe furthe broucht."
4. xa/aa—l. 3 :
   " Betuix three & sex,   who so wolde vnderstande."
5. ax/ax—3 lines ; e.g. l. 17 :
   " And everyche lorde   shall austernly werk."
   xa/ax—7 lines ; e.g. l. 15 :
   " Betweyne þe cheyff of the somer   & the sad winter."
   ax/xa—l. 6 :
   " Lychory is ryffe,   and theffis has haldin þar lyff."
6. aa/bb—l. 18 :
   " þen shall Nazareth noy   welle a while."
8. ab/ba—l. 29 :
   " þen Albanattus þe kene,   kynde kyng offe erthe

9. aa/xx—9 lines ; e.g. l. 5 :
　　" When pryde is most in price,　　ande wyt is in covatyse."
　　aaa/xx—l. 55 :
　　" And trow tytylle of trouth　　þat þe strenth haldis."
10. ab/aab—l. 2 :
　　" Ande the prest haffys　　the poppys power in hande."
11. No alliteration in 7 lines ; e.g. l. 12 :
　　" þan shall dame fortowne　　turne hir whell."

Death and Life. (Hanford and Steadman have worked out the
　　number of lines conforming to each type. The figures are
　　reproduced here.)

　1. aa/ax, aa/xa—343/459 lines.
　2. aa/aa—l. 122 only.
　3. aaa/a(a)—41 lines.
　4. ax/aa—7 lines.
　5. ax/ax, xa/ax, xa/xa—16 lines.
　6. aa/bb—11 lines.
　7. ab/ab—ll. 95, 160 only.
　8. ab/ba—l. 285 only.
　9. aa/x or aaa/x—15 lines.
10. No alliteration—6 lines.
　　Vocalic alliteration—11 lines (aa/ax—10 lines ; and aa/bb—l. 276).

The Twa Mariit Wemen and the Wedo.

　1. aa/ax—386/530 lines ; e.g. l. 5 :
　　" Quhairon ane bird, on ane branche,　　so birst out hir notis."
　　aa/xa—3 lines ; e.g. l. 102 :
　　" Than ma na sauyne me save　　fra that auld Sathane."
　2. aa/aa—19 lines ; e.g. l. 11 :
　　" I hard vnder ane holyn　　hewinlie grein hewit."
　3. aaa/ax—48 lines ; e.g. l. 9 :
　　" I drew in derne to the dyk　　to dirken efter mirthis."
　　aaa/aa—2 lines : ll. 39, 69 ; e.g. l. 39 :
　　" Thay wauchtit at the wicht wyne,　　and warit out wourdis."
　　(l. 349 shows excessive alliteration :—
　　" Thair micht na mollat mak me moy,　　nor hald my mouth
　　　　in ")
　4. xa/aa—l. 201 only :
　　" I wend I had chosin and jeme,　　and I haue ane geit
　　　　gottin."
　5. ax/ax—25 lines ; e.g. l. 1 :
　　" Apon the Midsummer ewin,　　mirriest of nichtis."
　　xa/xa—3 lines ; l. 231 :
　　" I wend ane tendir peronall,　　that micht no put thole."
　　xa/ax—26 lines ; e.g. l. 12 :
　　" Ane hie speiche, at my hand,　　with hautand wourdis."
　6. aa/bb—No lines.
　7. ab/ab—l. 259 only :
　　" Be constant in ȝour governance,　　and counterfit god
　　　　maneris."

8. ab/ba—4 lines ; e.g. l. 376 :
     " That I held mair in dantie,   and derrar be full mekill."
9. aa/xx—5 lines ; e.g. l. 58 :
     " It is agane the law of luf,   of kynd, and of nature."
10. aab/b—3 lines : ll. 136, 158, and 228 ; e.g. l. 136 :
     " His purse payis richelie   in recompense efter."
   aa/bab—l. 18 :
     " All grathit in to garlandis   of fresche gudlie flouris."
11. No alliteration in l. 34 :
     " And marbre tabile coverit   wes befoir thir thre ladeis."
   In view of the lateness of this work, the alliteration is extremely
regular and traditional.

Scottish Field. (N.B.—The figures given by Steadman [1] for this poem
        are totally inaccurate ; the aa/ax type is found 277 times, not
        123 as he states.)
1. aa/ax—277/422 lines ; e.g. l. 2 :
     " That I may say or I cease   thy seluen to plese."
   aa/xa—16 lines ; e.g. l. 122 :
     " And enter into England   & weld it for ever."
2. aa/aa—17 lines ; e.g. l. 91 :
     " Bende the toune of turwin   our tents doune we telden."
3. aaa/ax—26 lines ; e.g. l. 308 :
     " Grant, gracious god,   graunt me this time."
   aaa/aa—2 lines ; e.g. l. 22 :
     " A more maniful man   was not of this mold maked."
4. ax/aa—3 lines ; e.g. l. 131 :
     " Till all his bright armour   was all bloudye beronen."
5. ax/ax—12 lines ; e.g. l. 44 :
     " To the celestiall blisse   with saints enowe."
   xa/ax—19 lines ; e.g. l. 7 :
     " Henri the seaueneth   that soveraigne Lord."
   ax/xa—3 lines ; e.g. l. 98 :
     " When he heard how vnkindly   his townes were halched."
6. aa/bb—9 lines ; e.g. l. 75 :
     " Calleth to his councell   to witt their wille."
7. ab/ab—2 lines ; e.g. l. 228 :
     " They were tenants to the booke   that tended the bishoppe."
8. ab/ba—4 lines ; e.g. l. 321 :
     " Heavenly was theire Melody   their mirth to heare."
9. aa/xx—25 lines ; e.g. l. 7 :
     " Toke prisoners prest   & home againe wenten."
   aaa/xx—l. 113 :
     " He bad buske him & boune him   to gye on his message."
10. abb/ba—ll. 72, 344 ; aa/abb—ll. 270, 389 ; aab/ab—l. 76 ; e.g.
        l. 72 :
     " And many a sellcoth saylor   where seene on their masts."
11. No alliteration in 1 line : l. 330 :
     " Then betid a checke   that the shire men fledden."

[1] J. H. Hanford and J. M. Steadman, Jr., Studies in Philology, vol. 15,
p. 221.

CHAPTER 9

THE ADDING OF RHYME TO THE ALLITERATIVE LONG LINE.

THE twelve documents to be discussed in this chapter are
united by one common feature, being written in the alliterative long line of the same type as previously found, but having
in addition end-rhyme. The earliest document, *On God
Orison of Our Lady*, was composed *c.* 1200 in E. Midl., and the
latest document, a portion of *The 1st. Chester Play*, was composed towards the close of the fifteenth century in N.W.
Midl. In the intervening period, documents are found in
several parts of the Midland-area, and particularly in N.E.
Midl. Hence it is not improbable that the type flourished
in certain parts of the Midland-area, at least throughout the
fourteenth century. Before attempting to theorise concerning this type of alliterative verse, we shall examine some of
its prominent features.

1. Some sort of stanzaic arrangement is found in most of
the works.

On God Orison of Our Lady is written in rhyming couplets,
without any grouping of the lines into stanzas.

On Serving Christ has a crude stanzaic arrangement, since
the rhymes follow the scheme : *aaa* (8 lines), *bbb* (16 lines),
ccc (8 lines), *ddd* (10 lines), *eee* (8 lines), *fff* (6 lines), *ggg* (8
lines), *hhh* (14 lines). The poet was evidently feeling his way.

The 1st. Love Scrap consists of 11 lines, rhyming
aaa–babab– –.

The 2nd. Love Scrap has 3 irregular stanzas, rhyming
aabcb–bcddd, *ababababaccc*, and *ababababcc* respectively. There
is here some sort of attempt to evolve a stanza-form. The
text is, however, extremely corrupt.

The Song of the Husbandman has a simple stanza-form,
abababab or *abab*.

The Harley Lyric No. 1 is written in the same stanza as
the preceding poem, and *The Lyric* No. 4 has stanzas of 10
lines rhyming *aaaaaaaabb*.

The Rawlinson Strophic Pieces are written in stanzas of 6 lines, rhyming *aaaaaa*.

Minot's Poems, Nos. 2, 5, 9, 10, 11, have as their normal stanza 6 lines rhyming *aaaabb;* in addition there are two stanzas of 8 lines, rhyming *aaaaaabb* (a natural development of the normal stanza), and 7 stanzas of 4 lines, rhyming *aaaa*.

The Preface to Rolle's Commentary on the Psalter is written in rhyming couplets with no stanzaic arrangement.

The Rolle Lyric No. 1, " My trewest tresoure," is written in quatrains, rhyming *abab*.

The Lament of the Monk is written in quatrains, rhyming *aaaa, bbbb*, etc.

The 1st. Burlesque is written in couplets, rhyming *aabb*, etc.

The 1st. Chester Play (the alliterative portion) is written in stanzas of 8 lines, rhyming *abababab*. .

From a study of these, it is possible to trace the gradual evolution of a stanza-form. At first using the rhyming couplet, poets seem to have endeavoured to create some sort of stanza-form. Their efforts were not very successful, and there is little variety in the types of stanza employed. After 1300, poets do not seem, however, to hesitate to use any of the newer forms.

2. Enjambement is naturally not found in these poems, but the cæsura is very marked.

3. Violations of the natural stress for the sake of alliteration are rare, for the shortness of the poems does not put the same strain upon the writer. The licences are usually confined to the alliterating of an unstressed verbal prefix, and are only found in *On God Orison of Our Lady, On Serving Christ, The Rawlinson Strophic Pieces, Minot's Poems, The Preface to Rolle's Commentary*, and *The 1st. Chester Play*. In the last work alone, however, does the unaccented verbal prefix alliterate frequently.

4. Grouping of Consecutive Lines by Identical Alliteration. —Owing to the extreme shortness of the poems, we should scarcely expect a considerable number of examples of this feature. But it is important to observe that examples are found. There are 5 " twos " in *On God Orison of Our Lady*, 1 " two " and 1 " three " in *On Serving Christ*, no examples in *The Two Scraps of Love-Songs*, 3 " twos " in *The Song of the Husbandman* (and in addition 6 other " twos " due to the " repetition " between the stanzas, for which see below), no examples in *The two Harley Lyrcs*, 2 " twos " in *The Rawlinson Strophic Pieces*, 11 "twos" in *Minot's Poems*, no examples in *The Preface to Rolle's Commentary*, none in *The 1st. Rolle Lyric*, 2 "twos" in *The Lament of the Monk*, but none in *The 1st. Chester Play*.

Though the examples are few, they are nevertheless sufficient to show that the device was still used. The alternative method of grouping, discussed on p. 148, is also found. There are 4 examples in *On God Orison of Our Lady*, 1 in *On Serving Christ*, 2 in *The Song of the Husbandman*, 4 examples in *Minot's Poems*, but none in the remaining poems.

The examples are so few that it would seem unlikely that the device was consciously used. If an explanation were needed, there is a sufficient one in the fact that the poems come from areas where the traditional alliterative poetry was not generally written, that is, chiefly in the N.E. Midl. area in the fourteenth century.

5. The ending " $/\times$ " for the second half-line is not so common in these poems as in the poems written in the rhymeless alliterative long line. The explanation of this fact is that there are many monosyllabic rhymes employed, necessitating the use of the termination " $\times/$ ".

6. Vocalic alliteration is found in these poems, with the exception of *The Song of the Husbandman, The 1st. Rolle Lyric*, and *The Two Scraps of Love Songs*. Thus there are three examples in *The 1st. Chester Play*, including one example of " Transverse Alliteration " : *o a / o a*, l. 24.

Owing to the shortness of the poems, it is somewhat difficult to ascertain whether there was a general tendency to alliterate identical vowels together. In *The Harley Lyric* No. 4, l. 14, there is an example of three identical vowels alliterating together, but the usual practice in most poems is to have two of the vowels identical, e.g. *The Lament of the Monk*, l. 39 : " *e e a*."

H is usually found alliterating with itself, but occasionally with vowels. *Minot* stands apart with his practice of consistently alliterating *h* with vowels, thus recalling the *Gawayn* poet. Indeed, vocalic alliteration is only found in his poems in conjunction with *h*. Hence, so far as the scanty evidence goes, these poets did not differ from those of the earlier groups regarding the use of vocalic alliteration.

7. The Use of Alliterative Groups.—The traditional groups are as a rule consistently observed. *St* is preserved as a group in *On God Orison of Our Lady*, in *The Harley Lyrics*, and in *The 1st. Rolle Lyric*. In *The Song of the Husbandman, st, sp* are preserved, and *sw* is added. In *The Rawlinson Strophic Pieces* we find *st, sp, sch ;* in *Minot's Poems st, sp;* in *The 1st. Burlesque st, sp, sk, sch.*

Sch is not in these poems usually treated as a group, but, as in the rhymeless alliterative verse, alliterates freely with *s*. *The Preface to Rolle's Commentary* is most lax, the writer alliterating *st* and *s ; st, sp* and *s ; sl* and *s ;* etc.

Despite the shortness of the poems, there is evidence to show that the poets concerned treated alliterative groups in the same manner as did the alliterative poets of the west.

8. The Use of " Repetition " to link the Stanzas together.— This device, found more frequently in the poems to be treated in the next chapter, is only found in three of the works here examined.

1. *The Song of the Husbandman*, in which the last line of a stanza is carried on by a phrase into the first line of the next stanza. This is found between stanzas 1 and 2, 2 and 3, 3 and 4, 4 and 5, 8 and 9, 9 and 10, 10 and 11, 11 and 12.

2. In *Minot's Five Poems* there is " medial repetition " throughout, that is, between the 4th. and 5th. lines of each stanza, which rhymes *aaaa bb*.

3. *The Harley Lyric* No. 4 has likewise " medial repetition " throughout. The origin of stanza-linking is still a matter of controversy.[1]

9. The Alliterative Types.—The statistics are added in the pages that immediately follow, and it will be observed that the actual types used are the same as those in the poems written in the alliterative long line. The difference lies in the relative frequency of certain types, as compared with former practice.

[1] For an interesting discussion of " repetition " or " iteration," as it is sometimes called, see *Stanza-linking in M.E. Verse*, by M. P. Medary, Romanic Review, vol. 7, p. 243, 1916.

Also *On the Origin of Stanza-linking in English Alliterative Verse*, by A. L. C. Brown, on p. 271 of the same volume.

THE STATISTICS.

Owing to lack of space, the quotations will not be given as in the case of the poems treated in the last chapter, but merely the references, except for Minot's poems, which will serve the purposes of illustration.

On God Orison of Our Lady.

1. aa/ax—6 lines ; e.g. l. 60.
   aa/xa—3 lines ; e.g. l. 1.
2. aa/aa—4 lines ; e.g. l. 148.
5. ax/ax—7 lines ; e.g. l. 71.
   xa/ax—14 lines ; e.g. l. 6.
   xa/xa—12 lines ; e.g. l. 3.
6. aa/bb—6 lines ; e.g. l. 61.
7. ab/ab—2 lines : ll. 101 and 151.
8. ab/ba—3 lines ; e.g. l. 130.
9. aa/xx—25 lines ; e.g. l. 8.
   xx/aa—13 lines ; e.g. l. 44.
   aaa/xx—3 lines ; e.g. l. 37.
11. No alliteration—57 lines ; e.g. l. 10.

There are only 171 lines in the poem, so that the percentage of lines without alliteration is high.

On Serving Christ.

1. aa/ax—10 lines ; e.g. l. 39.
   aa/xa—1 line : l. 47.
2. aa/aa—6 lines : e.g. l. 71.
3. aaa/ax—1 line : l. 4.
4. ax/aa—3 lines ; e.g. l. 1.
   xa/aa—7 lines ; e.g. l. 9.
5. ax/ax—8 lines ; e.g. l. 21.
   xa/ax—17 lines ; e.g. l. 2.
6. aa/bb—2 lines ; e.g. l. 74.
7. ab/ab—1 line : l. 7.
8. ab/ba—1 line : l. 3.
9. aa/xx—9 lines ; e.g. l. 18.
   xx/aa—2 lines ; e.g. l. 13.
11. No alliteration—9 lines ; e.g. l. 19.

Two Scraps of Love Songs.

The 1st. Scrap, consisting of 11 lines, is very crude in form, the aim apparently being to have three alliterating syllables to the half-line. Two lines will illustrate :—

l. 1 : " A levedy ad my love leyt   the bole bigan to belle."
l. 11 : " I swar be the leves, let her ches,   were sche wel love or bene."

The 2nd. Scrap, consisting of 32 lines, is more consistent:—

1. aa/ax—2 lines ; e.g. l. 3.
   aa/xa—1 line : l. 13.
2. aa/aa—3 lines ; e.g. l. 28.

5. ax/ax—2 lines ; e.g. l. 1.
   xa/xa—3 lines ; e.g. l. 14.
6. aa/bb—5 lines ; e.g. l. 6.
9. aa/xx—6 lines ; e.g. l. 5.
   xx/aa—3 lines ; e.g. l. 29.
   aaa/xx—1 line : l. 8.
11. No alliteration—3 lines ; e.g. l. 18.

In addition there are 3 shorter lines, which may be corrupt. Most of the lines, however, are quite normal ; e.g. l. 28 :

" Ther most a balder byrd   billen on the bow."

The Song of the Husbandman.

1. aa/ax—6 lines ; e.g. l. 14.
   aa/xa—5 lines ; e.g. l. 19.
2. aa/aa—15 lines ; e.g. l. 9.
3. aaa/aa—1 line : l. 15.
4. ax/aa—5 lines ; e.g. l. 55.
   xa/aa—11 lines ; e.g. l. 35.
5. ax/ax—1 line : l. 38.
   xa/ax—4 lines ; e.g. l. 41.
   ax/xa—2 lines ; e.g. l. 47.
   xa/xa—3 lines ; e.g. l. 10.
6. aa/bb—5 lines ; e.g. l. 30.
   aaa/bb—1 line : l. 16.
7. ab/ab—3 lines ; e.g. l. 36.
9. xx/aa—1 line : l. 29.
   aaa/xx—1 line : l. 17.
11. No alliteration—1 line : l. 8.

The Harley Lyric No. 1.

1. aa/ax—1 line : l. 37.
   aa/xa—1 line : l. 36.
2. aa/aa—1 line : l. 7.
4. xa/aa—2 lines : ll. 2 and 40.
5. ax/ax—4 lines ; e.g. l. 39.
   xa/ax—2 lines ; e.g. l. 31.
   xa/xa—7 lines ; e.g. l. 19.
6. aa/bb—5 lines ; e.g. l. 1.
8. ab/ba—1 line : l. 15.
9. aa/xx—4 lines ; e.g. l. 5.
   xx/aa—3 lines ; e.g. l. 14.
11. No alliteration—7 lines ; e.g. l. 3.

The Harley Lyric No. 4.

1. aa/ax—6 lines ; e.g. l. 12.
   aa/aa—27 lines ; e.g. l. 1.
3. aaa/aa—4 lines ; e.g. l. 26.
4. ax/aa—1 line : l. 14.
   xa/aa—1 line : l. 26.
5. ax/ax—1 line : l. 40.
6. aa/bb—7 lines ; e.g. l. 3.
   aaa/bb—3 lines ; e.g. l. 27.

(The tendency to excessive alliteration is noticeable.)

The Rawlinson Strophic Pieces.

1. aa/ax—16 lines ; e.g. Luke 1.
   aa/xa—9 lines ; e.g. Luke 13.
2. aa/aa—32 lines ; e.g. Luke 3.
4. ax/aa—3 lines ; e.g. Matt. 46.
   xa/aa—18 lines ; e.g. Luke 18.
5. xa/ax—9 lines ; e.g. Luke 15.
   xa/xa—8 lines ; e.g. Luke 45.
6. aa/bb—22 lines ; e.g. Luke 4.
   aa/bbb—1 line : Luke 29.
7. ab/ab—1 line : Luke 27.
8. ab/ba—3 lines ; e.g. Luke 24.
9. aa/xx—14 lines ; e.g. Luke 33.
   xx/aa—15 lines ; e.g. Luke 20.
11. No alliteration—3 lines ; e.g. John 9.

Minot's Poems, Nos. 2, 5, 9, 10, 11 (taken as a group.)

1. aa/ax—14 lines ; e.g. 10. 7 :
   " þai sailed furth in þe **Sw**in   in a **s**omers tyde."
   aa/xa—22 lines ; e.g. 11. 22 :
   " Sone þaire **d**iner was **d**ight   & þaire wald þai **d**ine."
2. aa/aa—44 lines ; e.g. 10. 3 :
   " þat now er **d**riven to **d**ale   & **d**ed alle þaire **d**ede."
3. aaa/ax—no lines.
   aaa/xa—4 lines ; e.g. 10. 5 :
   " **F**ele **f**issches þai **f**ede   for all þaire grete **f**are."
   aaa/aa—3 lines ; e.g. 10. 20 :
   " & **s**one **s**et þe to **s**chriue   with **s**orow of þi **s**in."
4. ax/aa—7 lines ; e.g. 5. 41 :
   " þe **d**uc of Lankaster   was **d**ight for to **d**riue."
   xa/aa—13 lines ; e.g. 5. 16 :
   " I pray Ihesu **s**aue þam   fro **s**in and fro **s**chame."
5. ax/ax—8 lines ; e.g. 5. 29 :
   " ȝit **t**rumped þai & daunced   with **t**orches full bright."
   xa/ax—10 lines ; e.g. 5. 21 :
   " þan had he no **l**iking   **l**anger to dwelle."
   xa/xa—6 lines ; e.g. 5. 10 :
   " All Flandres to **b**rin   & mak it al **b**are."
   ax/xa—4 lines ; e.g. 11. 40 :
   " þat he **m**ay at his ending   haue heuin till her **m**ede."
6. aa/bb—27 lines ; e.g. 10. 4 :
   " þai **s**ail in þe **s**ee-gronde   **f**isches to **f**ede."
   aaa/bb—2 lines : 2. 28 and 5. 42 ; e.g. 2. 28 :
   " Bot **f**one **f**rendes he **f**indes   þat his **b**ale **b**etes."
7. ab/ab—1 line : 9. 28 :
   " For at þe **N**euil **c**ros   **n**edes bud þam **k**nele."
8. ab/ba—2 lines ; e.g. 10. 12 :
   " Of gold & of **s**iluer,   of **sk**arlet & grene."
9. aa/xx—24 lines ; e.g. 10. 6 :
   " It **w**as in þe **w**aniand   þat þai come þare."
   xx/aa—27 lines ; e.g. 2. 16 :
   " Bot at þe last sir Edward   **r**ifild þaire **r**out."

10. aab/bb—1 line : 10. 28 (?) :
      " When ye wald in Ingland   lere of a newe lare."
11. No alliteration—38 lines ; e.g. 10. 18 :
      " And þat þai bifore reued   þan most þai tyne."
There are altogether 260 lines in the five poems.

The Preface to Rolle's Commentary on the Psalter.

1. aa/xa—1 line : l. 23 :
2. aa/aa—4 lines ; e.g. l. 25.
4. ax/aa—3 lines ; e.g. l. 22.
5. ax/ax—1 line : l. 20.
  xa/ax—2 lines ; e.g. l. 33.
  xa/xa—2 lines ; e.g. l. 3.
6. aa/bb—5 lines ; e.g. l. 2.
9. aa/xx—4 lines ; e.g. l. 1.
  xx/aa—8 lines ; e.g. l. 6.
10. Excessive alliteration : aa/bbb—l. 58 ; aaa/bbb—l. 60 ; aaa/aa—
    l. 46 ; aabb/aacc—l. 47.
11. No alliteration—22/60 lines.
    Thus in a few lines there is excessive alliteration, whereas in a third
of the lines there is no alliteration at all.

The 1st. Rolle Lyric.

1. aa/xa—1 line : l. 3.
2. aa/aa—20 lines ; e.g. l. 2.
5. xa/ax—1 line : l. 10.
6. aa/bb—2 lines : ll. 4 and 14.
7. ab/ab—1 line : l. 18.
9. aa/xx—2 lines : ll. 22 and 23.
  xx/aa—1 line : l. 11.

The Lament of the Monk.

1. aa/ax—5 lines ; e.g. l. 17.
  aa/xa—3 lines ; e.g. l. 42.
2. aa/aa—6 lines ; e.g. l. 2.
3. aaa/aa—1 line : l. 38.
4. ax/aa—1 line : l. 36.
5. xa/xa—1 line : l. 22.
  ax/ax—1 line : l. 10.
  ax/xa—2 lines ; e.g. l. 11.
6. aa/bb—6 lines ; e.g. l. 9.
8. ab/ba—1 line : l. 29.
9. aa/xx—6 lines ; e.g. l. 7.
  xx/aa—4 lines ; e.g. l. 14.
11. No alliteration—13 lines ; e.g. l. 12.

The 1st. Burlesque.

    The metre is so crude and formless that it is very unlikely that the
author consciously used any of the types. There is merely an attempt
to link the two half-lines together.

    1. In 18 out of the 49 lines there is no alliteration, but the usual
        rhythm ; e.g. l. 4 :
      " Then wax I as pore as the bischop of Chestur."

2. In the remaining lines the poet employs 2, 3 or even 4 alliterating syllables :

There are 13 " twos " ; e.g. l. 1 :

" Herkyn to my tale that I schall to yow schew."

10 " threes " ; e.g. l. 31 :

" Tho breme went round abowte & lette hom all blode."

8 " fours " ; e.g. l. 39 :

" There was pestells in porres & ladul in lorres."

The 1st. Chester Play.

1. aa/ax—2 lines ; e.g. l. 7.
   aa/xa—3 lines ; e.g. l. 11.
2. aa/aa—10 lines ; e.g. l. 13.
3. aaa/aa—6 lines ; e.g. l. 14.
   aaa/xa—2 lines ; e.g. l. 5.
4. xa/aa—1 line : l. 49.
5. xa/ax—1 line : l. 15.
6. aa/bb—1 line : l. 18.
   aaa/bb—2 lines ; e.g. l. 12.
9. aa/xx—2 lines ; e.g. l. 46.
   xx/aa—1 line : l. 6.

The most striking difference between the use of the alliterative types in these and in the former poems is the comparative infrequency of the *aa/ax* type. Owing to the extreme shortness of the poems, percentages do not give an exact representation of the facts, but only a general impression.

		Per cent. of the lines.
On God Orison of Our Lady has the type in		3·5
On Serving Christ	,, ,,	14
The Song of the Husbandman	,, ,,	8·3
The 2nd. Love Scrap	,, ,,	6·25
The Harley Lyric No. 1	,, ,,	2·6
The Harley Lyric No. 2	,, ,,	12
The Rawlinson Strophic Pieces	,, ,,	10·2
Minot's Poems	,, ,,	5·3
The Preface to Rolle's Commentary on the Psalter	,, ,,	0
The 1st. Rolle Lyric	,, ,,	0
The Lament of the Monk	,, ,,	9·6
The 1st. Chester Play	,, ,,	6·25

The poems written in the alliterative long line without rhyme usually have from 60 per cent. to 80 per cent. of the

lines of the *aa/ax* type.   It is, however, important to remember
that *Joseph of Arimathie* has only 9 per cent., and *Cheuelere
Assigne* 12 per cent.   Some poets were, therefore, lax, and
abandoned traditional rules to achieve more variety in their
use of alliteration.   The same applies to the poets now
concerned.   Their poems were short, and their actual knowledge of traditional practice may have been small ; however,
they may also have consciously striven after variety.   It
will be observed that this variety in the use of alliterative
types is found in all the poems, a fact which is surely not
accidental.   The result is that as a general rule no one type
is noticeably more common than another.

The types *ab/ab, ab/ba,* and *aa/bb* are not less common than
they were in the rhymeless alliterative verse.   However, the
complex types, such as *aab/ab,* etc., are only found in *Minot's
Poems.*

Though in some poems a preference is shown for the types
ax/ax, xa/ax as opposed to *xa/xa, ax/xa,* there is nevertheless
in general no preference shown for the traditional types.

There is also manifest the same tendency to excessive
alliteration.   This is particularly noticeable in *The Song of
the Husbandman* with more than half its lines of four alliterating syllables : *The Harley Lyric* No. 4, in which the same holds
good ; *Minot's Poems,* in which a sixth of the lines are
written in the *aa/aa* type, and in which the following types
also occur : *aaa/a(a), aaa/bb, aab/bb ; The Preface to Rolle's
Commentary,* in which the excessive alliteration is illustrated
on p. 208 ; and lastly in *The 1st. Chester Play,* in which the two
most frequently used types are : *aa/aa,* and *aaa/aa.*

The lengthened lines of the *aaa/a(a)* type are not very
common, and often the 1st. half-line has only two stresses
instead of the usual three.   To this point, however we shall
return later.

Hence the poets were indifferent as to their choice of
alliterative types, perhaps owing to the fact that they considered that rhyme compensated for the comparative weakness
of the alliteration.   This may also account for the fact
that in some poems there are many lines to be found without
any alliteration, the most noticeable examples being *On
God Orison of Our Lady* with 57/171 lines, i.e. 30·4 per cent. ;
On Serving Christ with 9/78 lines, i.e. 11·5 per cent. ; *The
Harley Lyric* No. 1 with 7/40 lines, i.e. 17·5 per cent. ; *Minot's*

Poems with 38/260 lines, i.e. 15 per cent.; *The Preface to Rolle's Commentary* with 22/60 lines, i.e. 36·6 per cent.; and *The Lament of the Monk* with 13/52 lines, i.e. 25 per cent.

In the same class are instances of the use of the types *aa/xx* and *xx/aa*, which are found frequently in the following poems: *On God Orison of Our Lady* in 41/171 lines, *Minot's Poems* in 51/260 lines, and *The Lament of the Monk* in 10/52 lines.

To sum up, it may be said that some of these poets were careful concerning the employment of alliterative types though at the same time holding no brief for traditional practice; yet the majority of them did not hesitate to consider rhyme sufficient in itself, when difficulty was encountered regarding the alliteration. In addition, they must have had confused notions about the traditional alliterative verse, for the simple reason that they lived in areas in which the rhymeless alliterative verse was not apparently written.

10. The number of unstressed syllables in each line is on the whole constant throughout a poem. The lines may be short, as in *Minot's Poems*, or long, as in *The Rawlinson Strophic Pieces*, but the approximate regularity is the same. The only noticeable exception is *On God Orison of Our Lady*, which will be discussed later.

The explanation of this regularity may be that the use of rhyme has approximated the verse to the French syllabic metres. We have already seen that in *The Brut* rhyme had the effect of disintegrating the rhythm of the alliterative long line. The same is naturally true of these poems, but it must be added that there is always great freedom exercised in the arrangement of the main stresses, as we shall see when discussing the rhythm.

In *On God Orison of Our Lady* the rhyme is merely ornamental, the alliteration being the important thing; in *The Two Scraps of Love Songs* the rhythm is still of the alliterative type. But in most of the remaining poems the rhyme seems more important than the alliteration. *The Preface to Rolle's Commentary* is very rugged in its rhythm, and its lines are so long as to suggest that the author possibly had in mind the Latin *septenary*. In *The 1st. Burlesque* the line is even more unwieldy.

A few illustrations will make these facts clear :—

On God Orison of Our Lady :

l. 130 : " For þin is þe **w**urschipe   ȝif ich **w**recche wel iþeo."

l. 44 : " ne weopen ne murnen   ne helle **st**enches **st**inken."

The Preface to Rolle's Commentary :

l. 23 : " Glosed the **s**auter that **s**ues here   in englysch tong **s**ykerly."

The illustrations from *Minot's Poems*, given on p. 207, will indicate the average type of line in these poems.   Taken individually the lines do not differ from those in the rhymeless alliterative verse, but there are less violent transitions from one type to another, and greater control is exercised in the matter of unstressed syllables.

11. The Rhythm.—In the first place, extended half-lines are very rare, there being 3 examples in *The Song of the Husbandman*, 7 in *The Harley Lyric* No. 4, 10 in *Minot's Poems*, and 8 in *The 1st. Chester Play*.   In the last work, however, it is unlikely that 3 stresses were intended ; e.g. *The 1st. Chester Play*, l. 12 :

" As **g**od gre᷄atest & gló᷄rious."

But in the other three poems, the half-lines in question seem to have the 3 stresses ; e.g. *The Harley Lyric* No. 4, l. 36 :

" When **d**érne **d**éde is in **d**aýne."

Or *The Song of the Husbandman*, l. 17 :

" The **w**ódeward **w**áiteth us **w**ó."

The same is true of the isolated examples in a few of the other works.

In general, the type of rhythm used does not include the *Clashing-Rhythm*, so that the half-lines conform to the following type :—

$$(\times\ \times)/\times\ \times/\times\ \times/(\times\ \times).$$

An apparent exception is to be found in *On Serving Christ*, l. 4 : " **C**rist **k**undeliche **k**yng "—$//\times\ \times\ \times/$.

The comparative infrequency of the extended half-lines

is probably to be explained by the fact that apparently the poets had a desire for smoothness and regularity, as previously mentioned. The extended lines, when followed by normal ones, inevitably produce an effect of irregularity, and seem to have been avoided by most poets.

In the second place, the rhythms of the normal half-lines are simple. The usual type in both half-lines is, as in the rhymeless alliterative poems, the *Rising-Falling* type : $\times \times / \times \times \times / \times \times$; e.g. *The 1st. Rolle Lyric*, l. 2 :

    " Sa bítterly bóndyn wyth býtand bándes."

The *Rising-* and the *Falling-Rhythms* are, however, by no means uncommon, and the former are found frequently in the second half-line, owing to the use of monosyllabic rhymes.

The *Clashing-Rhythm* is just as frequently employed as in the rhymeless alliterative verse, both in the first and second half lines. These facts may be illustrated by the statistics of the rhythm in a normal poem, such as *On Serving Christ*.

	The 1st. half-line.	The 2nd. half-line.
Falling-Rhythm.	10	12

    e.g. l. 5*a* : " Ríhtwise lóuerd."

       l. 37*b* : " wárlawes wóde."

Rising-Rhythm.	18	22

    e.g. l. 1*a* : " Hwi ne sérve we críst."

       l. 1*b* : " and sécheþ his sáuht."

Rising-Falling-Rhythm.	45	24

    e.g. l. 11*a* : " þer þe crýsmechild for súnnes."

       l. 9*b* : " And dúten ure déden."

Clashing-Rhythm.	2	9

    e.g. l. 35*a* : " þayh we hér hóppen."

       l. 63*b* : " he þet líf sólde."

The " $/ \times \times \times /$ " type, here due to the loss of the final -e in the MS.

	2	11

    e.g. l. 16*a* : " léue we this for sáyn."

       l. 74*b* : " mákeþ her món."

The proportions are roughly the same as in any other poem that might be selected, with the exception of the following, which call for special treatment :—

1. *On God Orison of Our Lady.*—Various theories have been advanced concerning the metre of this early work, Schipper and others believing it to be a mixture of *septenaries, alexandrines,* and *alliterative verse.* It has been pointed out, however, that such a mixture of native and foreign metres is very unnatural and improbable. Kaluza regarded the poem as written throughout in the *septenary,* but as Hall suggested, this involves such a straining of the native stress-rules, that the theory becomes impossible. Alliteration is found in so many lines that it is difficult to avoid suggesting that there is an attempt to write the alliterative long lines in rhyming couplets. This is the opinion of Hall, who, on p. 530 of his *Selections from Early Middle-English* says : " It is very doubtful whether the poet meant to write syllabic verse at all. Rather the metre exhibits the alliterative long line in the last stage of its dissolution, in which systematic rhyme has largely displaced the older and once essential elements of verse ; if lines occur which can with some violence be forced into the moulds of purely syllabic verse, they are not of the author's express purpose."

The regularity found in the later poems is not to be found here, for the long line approximates more closely to that of *The Brut* and *The Bestiary.* The influence of the foreign metres is still very small.

2. The rhythm of *The 1st. Love Scrap,* as already suggested on p. 205, is very crude, there being considerable irregularity both with regard to the number of stressed and unstressed syllables. The text is, however, very corrupt.

3. *The Preface to Rolle's Commentary* has lines of such a length as to suggest that the author may have also had in mind the Latin *septenary.* But however this may be, the writer knew little of either system, and the result is that the rhythm of all his half-lines is simply according to the following scheme : $\times \times / \times \times \times / \times \times \times / \times \times \times$. All attempt at regularity is absent.

4. *The 1st. Burlesque,* as illustrated on p. 208, has some few lines of the normal types, but usually the rhythm is crude and the lines unwieldy.

We have seen that metrically the poems treated in this

chapter do not differ to any great extent from those written in the rhymeless alliterative verse, especially when the shortness of the works is borne in mind. There are two points worthy of mention, the first being the comparative infrequency of the extended half-lines, and the second the greater variety in the use of the alliterative types. We have tried to explain these two points above, as due to the influence of the syllabic metres, and to inaccurate knowledge of the traditional practices.

These writers of religious and satirical songs form an important group of poets, and illustrate for us the different historical developments of the O.E. alliterative verse. We have already traced the long line from the close of the O.E. period, observing it coming into contact with popular influences, and finally freeing itself altogether from the rhymed couplet.

There was obviously, however, a second line of development. The early M.E. alliterative long line, usually without any medial rhyme, sometimes adopted end-rhyme, giving rise to a couplet of four stressed syllables, with liberty as to the number of unstressed syllables, and with a strong medial pause. It is noticeable that the first specimen extant, *On God Orison of Our Lady*, was written in the E. Midl. dialectal area, far removed from the western district where the alliterative tradition was stronger. Other examples must have followed in N.E. Midl., but frequent examples are only found subsequent to 1300 : *The Rawlinson Strophic Pieces*, *Minot's Poems*, *The Lament of the Monk* and other works. The apparent blank from *c*. 1275-1340, thus becomes partly filled. The alliterative long line was still being correctly written in the north-eastern counties, while apparently in the west this was not the case, if we were to judge solely from extant documents. This gap is, however, filled by *The Song of the Husbandman, c.* 1300, *The Harley Lyrics*, 1 and 4, *c*. 1300, all from S.W. Midl. There are few examples after the middle of the fourteenth century, but the type did not die, and reappears later in *The 1st. Burlesque*, and *The 1st. Chester Play*.

Judging from the comparative scantiness of the extant documents representing this metrical development, we might conclude that it never became very popular. We have, nevertheless, the testimony afforded by *Minot's Political*

Songs, which are of a popular type. Alliterative verse in N.E. Midl. seems to have come into contact with foreign metres, and as a result we find the alliterative line of the orthodox type in many varieties of stanza-forms. The poets sought to effect a compromise between the older and newer systems ; some were remarkably successful, whereas others were remarkably unsuccessful.

CHAPTER 10

The Use of Stanzas in Alliterative Poems.

In the last chapter we saw that the alliterative long line with end-rhyme was found in simple stanza-forms. The poems to be treated in this chapter are likewise written in stanza-forms, but of a different type, the distinguishing feature being the addition of shorter lines at the end of the stanza, which may or may not have alliteration. The " bob and wheel " is the most common type of termination of this kind.

The general scheme involves a number of alliterative long lines of the usual type, followed by some shorter lines of two or three stresses. We have (**a**) a stanza of 9 alliterative long lines, followed by four short lines of two accents, the rhyme-scheme being: *ababababc dddc*. This type is found in *Golagrus and Gawain, Rauf Coilȝear, The Houlate, Awntyrs of Arthure, The Prologue to the 8th Book of the Aeneid* (which has, however, the first three short lines of 3 accents, but the fourth of 2 only), and *Sum Practysis of Medecyn*.

(**b**) A stanza of 8 alliterative long lines, followed by the " bob and wheel," with the same rhyme-scheme : *ababababab cdddc*. This type is found in *The Pistill of Susan, The Quatre-foil of Love, Fortune, The Ballad of Kynd Kittock*, and *A Pleasant Satire upon the Estates* (1st. stanza).

The stanza-form of *St. John the Evangelist* is of approximately the same pattern, having 8 alliterative long lines, followed by 6 short lines of 2 stresses.

With the exception of the poem *Fortune*, written in S.W. Midl., the works are either Nth. or Scottish, and in date range from *c.* 1350 (*The Pistill of Susan*) to *c.* 1553 (*A Pleasant Satire*). The stanza-forms were evidently very popular in these districts at the time when in the west the alliterative long line without rhyme was at the height of its popularity There is thus evidence to indicate that there was a revival in the north as well as in the west, though of a different type.

It will be observed that the poems written in the north were either pure romances, or works of a romantic cast, even when dealing with religious themes. The most interesting point of contact between the two " revivals " is the romance of *Sir Gawayn and the Green Knight* with the " bob and wheel " at the end of each stanza—a stanza which consists of an indefinite number of unrhymed alliterative long lines. This daring experiment would seem to suggest that the two schools of alliterative poetry were antagonistic, and that this poem represented an attempt to effect a compromise between the traditional alliterative writers, and the group of more polished writers, who had themselves effected a compromise along different lines.

The alliterative poem *Fortune, c.* 1400, S.W. Midl., is indicative of a similar tendency in the south-west. It is written in the normal stanza-form, as described above. There are, however, two other poems of a similar kind, also from the south-west.

(*a*) *A Satire against the Pride of Ladies, c.* 1272-1307, written in a stanza of 7 lines, rhyming *aaaa bbb*, the first four being alliterative long lines, l. 5 of one stress, l. 6 of two stresses, and l. 7 of three. This was a most novel experiment by an ambitious writer. In the first four long lines there are also medial rhymes at the cæsura. The final appearance is that of 4 " Layamonic " long lines with medial and end-rhyme, followed by 3 shorter lines of varying length. The resulting form is more pleasing to the eye than to the ear.

(*b*) *Old Age, c.* 1300, the third and last poem from the south-west, is metrically very weak. It consists of 7 irregular stanzas. Lines 1-8 are alliterative long lines with medial and end-rhyme, the remaining lines being shorter, and usually having two alliterating syllables. The poem is exceedingly crude, and is little more than a metrical exercise.

It would therefore appear that in the south-west there were experiments similar to those in the north, but complicated alliterative stanzas never became popular, and gave rise to no school of poetry as in the north.

The 2nd. Burlesque, c. 1400, from the north-west, a poem of 29 lines, represents a crude attempt at a stanza-form. There are 22 long lines without rhyme, followed by 7 short lines of 3 stresses, rhyming *abbacca*. The fragment is of no importance, save to indicate that isolated attempts at such stanza-forms are found in unexpected places.

A Satire on the Consistory Courts, c. 1272-1307, N.E. Midl., is written in a stanza of 18 lines, divided into two parts, the 1st. consisting of 12 lines, rhyming *aab ccb ddb eeb;* the *b* lines are of 2 stresses, whereas the others are normal alliterative long lines. The 2nd. part consists of 5 lines of 3 stresses, and a sixth of 2 stresses. This exceedingly complicated stanza-form is again an isolated experiment of little historical importance.

To conclude, we may say that in the north alone did a " school of poets " arise, as a result of the experiments made in this type of versification. In other areas there were similar efforts, but owing to lack of poetic power in the authors concerned, no body of literature was produced, as far as the evidence of the documents goes.

In our examination of the metre of these poems, we may treat the various points to be considered, under two main headings : points of similarity between these poems and the unrhymed alliterative works, and points of difference between the two groups.

Points of Similarity.

1. Enjambement is naturally absent, as in the case of the poems treated in the last chapter. The cæsura is equally marked.

2. Violations of the natural stress for the sake of alliteration are not common in the shorter poems, and indeed in most of them do not occur. In *The Quatrefoil of Love* there are two examples of the alliteration of an unstressed prefix : stanza 6, l. 4, " **wi**thine and **wi**thoute." There are a few violations in *St. John the Evangelist*, such as " **d**efouled," l. 60, " **b**ecome," l. 233. Even in the northern group, including *Golagrus and Gawain*, etc., there are comparatively few violations. It would therefore appear that these poets did not allow themselves as much liberty in this respect as did such writers as the author of *Sir Gawayn and the Green Knight*.

3. The Use of Alliterative Groups.—In the shorter poems there is naturally little evidence available, but in general the groups *st, sp* are preserved, whereas *s(c)h, sk*, and other groups, are neglected. However, confining our attention to the longer poems, in which there is more evidence available, we discover that these poets were usually as careful as the western writers. The only notable exception is the author of *St. John the Evangelist* who alliterates *sp* with *s*, or *st*, etc., at will. *Tr* appears as a group in l. 89, but otherwise no groups are observed. *The Prologue to the 8th. Book of the Aeneid* exhibits similar licences, but in this and the other works, *sp*, *st* are nearly always observed as alliterative groups. *Sk*, *sw*, and sometimes *sl*, *tr*, *gr*, *br*, are preserved. There is usually the same laxity about *s*, *sch*. Indeed, the tendency in most of the Scottish poems is to exercise greater care concerning these things, possibly because the poets were, as we shall see, more interested in, or at any rate attentive to, the more ornamental features of alliterative verse.

4. Vocalic alliteration is naturally rare in the shorter poems, and in four, there is none at all : *A Satire against the Pride of Ladies, Fortune, The Ballad of Kynd Kittock,* and *A Pleasant Satire upon the Estates.*

In the following poems, vocalic alliteration is rare and always on different vowels : *Old Age* (2), *A Satire on the Consistory Courts* (2), *St. John the Evangelist* (2), *Sum Practysis of Medecyn* (4), and *The Prologue to the 8th. Book of the Aeneid* (1). From such scanty material it is impossible to generalise. In *The Quatrefoil of Love*, vocalic alliteration is rare, but apt to be on identical vowels ; e.g. stanza 31, l. 2, and 35, l. 5.

In the five longer poems, *Golagrus and Gawain, The Houlate, Rauf Coilȝear, Awntyrs of Arthure,* and *The Pistill of Susan*, vocalic alliteration appears in the following percentages of the lines :

G. 2·4 per cent. ; H. 2·5 per cent. ; R. 1·6 per cent. ; A. ·8 per cent. ; P. 2·4 per cent.

In these the general tendency is for 2, 3, or even 4 of the vowels to be identical ; e.g. *P*. 15 :

" Heo was **E**lches douȝter, **e**ldest and **e**yre."

Some poets alliterate *h* with vowels, whereas others alliterate *h* only with itself. Thus the author of *The Quatrefoil of Love* never alliterates *h* with a vowel ; e.g. stanza 24, l. 4, *hhhh*. The five poems just mentioned usually alliterate *h* with itself, but isolated examples of *h* alliterating with vowels can easily be found.

Hence, with regard to vocalic alliteration, viewed from

all its aspects, these writers did not differ from those who wrote rhymeless alliterative verse in the west.

5. Grouping of Consecutive lines by identical alliteration is an important link between these poems now under discussion and those written in the alliterative long line without rhyme. In the south-western group of poems—*A Satire against the Pride of Ladies, Old Age,* and *Fortune*—there are no examples of the tendency, but in the more important northern group of poems, the feature is found very frequently.

In examining the statistics, it is always necessary to remember that accidental " twos " are liable to occur in a poem in which " repetition " is frequent. These have, therefore, been omitted. In the small poem, *A Satire on the Consistory Courts*, there are no examples of " grouping."

The Pistill of Susan has " grouping " only rarely, having 2 " threes," e.g. ll. 144-6, *sss* ; and 27 " twos," e.g. ll. 13-14, *ss*.

Golagrus and Gawain has an intricate system of " grouping." 48 of the 105 stanzas begin with a couplet of 2 lines with identical alliteration ; e.g. stanza 1, etc. Three stanzas have the first 6 lines joined into three couplets by the same method ; e.g. stanza 88. Altogether there are 106 " twos " in 1362 lines, and 2 " threes " : ll. 121-3, *fff* ; and ll. 1343-5, *rrr*.

The Awntyrs of Arthure has the same intricate system. 33 out of 55 stanzas begin with a couplet of this type ; e.g. stanzas 1-8, and 6 stanzas begin with 3 couplets : stanzas 3, 4, 8, 17, 34, 45. Altogether there are 79 " twos," 5 " threes," and 2 " fours " ; e.g. ll. 370-2, *kkk* ; and ll. 150-3, *kkkk*.

Rauf Coilȝear has 80 " twos " in 791 lines. The most notable instances are :—

stanza 38. *aabbccdd* – – – – –
,, 39. *aabb–ccdd* – – – –
,, 40. *aabbccdd* – – – – –
,, 62. *aa – – bbcc* – – – – –
,, 63. *aabbccdd* – – – – –

The Houlate has 59 " twos " and 1 " three " in 767 lines. Thus stanza 1 begins *aabb*, and stanza 36 *aabbccdede*.

These northern writers, being conscious artists, greatly extended the use of this ancient metrical device, and employed it more skilfully.

The Quatrefoil of Love has 19 " twos," but no " threes " in 520 lines.

St. John the Evangelist has the most intricate system of "grouping" of any of the poems treated in this chapter. All the stanzas, with the exception of 4, 13, 15, begin with four couplets, i.e. with 8 lines, but only 4 alliterating letters. Stanza 4 has the scheme *aab – – cdd* instead of *aabbccdd*, but has only 12 lines instead of the normal 14. Stanza 13 has *aabb – – dd*, and stanza 15 has *aabbcc – –*.

The 2nd. Burlesque, a very short poem, has only 1 "two": ll. 12-13, *hh*.

Sum Practysis of Medecyn, a short poem, has only 2 "twos."

The Ballad of Kynd Kittock has 1 "two," but the poem is likewise short.

The Prologue to the 8th. Book of the Aeneid has in its 14 stanzas, 10 "twos" and 1 "three": ll. 27-9, *lll*.

A Pleasant Satire upon the Estates (1st. stanza) has 3 "twos."

Hence it would seem that in the north the alliterative writers used the device as frequently as possible.

Points of Difference.

The points which fall under this heading are not in general features not found in other alliterative works, but the same features found in a different form.

1. The Alternative Method of Grouping, as described on p. 148, is not common in these poems. It is naturally not found in the shorter poems, but even in the longer poems is very rare; an adequate explanation, however, is not far to seek.

The poem *Fortune* has 5 "twos," and *The Prologue to the 8th. Book of the Aeneid* has 3 "twos"; e.g. ll. 54-5, *p*.

Coming to the longer poems, we look almost in vain for examples of this device. Let us take *St. John the Evangelist*, in which the first 8 lines of every stanza are linked by the normal method of grouping, as previously explained. Remembering that the most common "alliterative type" is *aa/aa*, we can understand how it was impossible for the poet to allow the last stressed syllable of a line to set the alliteration for the next line. This accounts for the complete absence of the device of the alternative method of grouping in some of these longer poems, and for the rarity of the device in others. Thus *Rauf Coilȝear* has only 8 examples (e.g. ll. 250-1, *w*), and *St. John the Evangelist* has none.

However, we shall see later that the alliterative type *aa/bb* is fairly common in the alliterative poems now under discussion, and that the poets employ a slightly different type of " grouping." Thus two consecutive lines may have the following alliterative scheme :—

1st. line : *aa/bb*   *aa/bb.*
                 or
2nd. line : *bb/cc*   *bb/bb.*

e.g. *The Houlate,* ll. 420-2 :

> " Off metallis and colouris   in tentfull atyr
> It war tyrefull to tell,   dyte or address,
> All thar deir armis   in dewlye desyre."

or ll. 80-1 :

> " Quha is fader of all foule,   pastour and pape ;
> That is the plesant Pacok,   preciouss and pure."

This interesting device is found rarely in the longer poems, but rather frequently in *The Quatrefoil of Love.*

But of the normal device of allowing the last stressed syllable of a line to set the alliteration for the next line, there are at least 7 examples in *The Houlate ;* e.g. ll. 592-3 :

> " The armes of the Dowglass, thairof was I fayne,
> Quhilk oft fandit with force, his fa till offend."

This ancient device was evidently known amongst these poets, but circumstances prevented them using it frequently. Both systems of " grouping " could not be extensively used at the same time, and the normal type proved the more attractive.

2. As in the case of the poems treated in the last chapter, these alliterative poems with end-rhyme show the substitution of the ending " ✕ / " for " / ✕," owing to the use of monosyllabic rhymes. This is even more frequently found in Nth. and Scottish poems owing to the loss of the final *-e* in the middle of the fourteenth century.

3. The use of " Repetition," which we met with in a few poems in the last chapter, is found more frequently in these poems. It is not found in *The Quatrefoil of Love,* or in many of the shorter poems. *A Satire on the Consistory Courts* has " medial repetition," that is between the 12th. and 13th. lines in each stanza.

St. John the Evangelist has " medial repetition " between

the 8th. and 9th. lines in all stanzas except the 16th., and "final repetition" between stanzas 1 and 2, and between 10 and 11.

Fortune has "final repetition" throughout.

The Pistill of Susan has "final repetition" between stanzas 6 and 7 only. *Golagrus and Gawain* has no "repetition."

Rauf Coilȝear has "repetition" between stanzas 3 and 4, between 11 and 12, between 39 and 40, and between 45 and 46.

The Houlate has 22/77 of its stanzas linked by "final répetition," and *Awntyrs of Arthure* has "final repetition" except between 8 of the 55 stanzas, and it is certain that the author intended the device to be used throughout. In these last two poems there is also an attempt to link the two parts of the stanza together by "medial repetition," and the device is carried out fairly consistently.[1]

"Repetition" was one of the ornamental devices popular amongst these alliterative poets of the north.

4. The Alliterative Types.—The statistics are given at the end of the chapter. These naturally include only those portions of the stanzas which are written in the long line. We may conveniently discuss the poems in groups.

> (a) *The early S. Western Poems.*—*A Satire against the Pride of Ladies*, and *Old Age* are metrically crude, and there is no acquaintance with traditional practice. In the former poem the tendency to excessive alliteration is very marked, for 12/20 of the lines are of the *aa/bb* type. The use of this type is mainly due to the presence of medial rhymes. There is merely a desire to crowd into the lines as much alliteration as possible.
>
> (b) *Fortune*, the late S.W. Midl. poem, is equally crude with regard to the use of alliterative types; 27/69 lines are of the type: *aaa/(a)(a)*; and 32/69 are of the type: *aa/aa*. The author is mainly concerned with adding as much alliteration as possible, and there is apparently no acquaintance with traditional practice.
>
> (c) *A Satire on the Consistory Courts*, c. 1300, N.E. Midl., exhibits the same tendency to excessive alliteration but to a less marked degree. There is again no

[1] See J. Amours, *Scottish Alliterative Poems*, p. lxxxv.

preference shown for the traditional types as opposed to the newer licences.

These short poems are not important, but serve
to indicate the lack of knowledge of the technique
of the older verse in many areas.

(d) *The Northern Group of Romances and Religious Poems.*
—In these longer poems we observe the tendency to
excessive alliteration. The type *aa/aa* has become
the most popular type used, as the following statistics
will show :—

	aa/ax, *aa/xa*	*aa/aa*	*aaa/(--)*
	Per cent.	Per cent.	Per cent.
Golagrus and Gawain	22	45·7	14·9
The Houlate . .	31·5	30·2	13·9
Rauf Coilȝear . .	29·9	16·6	6·6
Awntyrs of Arthure .	26·7	48·6	6
The Pistill of Susan .	33	46	6·2

If the first two columns were added together, the
resulting percentages would be approximately the
same as those for the *aa/ax* type in the unrhymed
alliterative poems. This gives us the clue to the
difference of treatment. These poets endeavoured
to have four or five stressed syllables with alliteration
in each line, that is every stressed syllable in the
line. It will also be observed that there is a slight
increase in the number of extended half-lines, and
each of these has practically always three alliterating
syllables.

Secondly, a careful analysis of the alliteration
in these five poems will reveal that the types *ax/ax,*
xa/ax are not more frequently employed than the
types *xa/xa, ax/xa,* no special preference being shown
for either group. The practice is, therefore, not
slavishly traditional.

Thirdly, the types *aa/bb, ab/ab,* and *ab/ba* are
commonly found, and in particular the first type,
which, it will be remembered, is a very late licence.

Lastly, reference to the statistics will indicate
how frequently in these poems the types *aa/xx,*
xx/aa, and lines with no alliteration at all, are
allowed. *Rauf Coilȝear* is the most notable example

15

of this with the type *aa/xx* in 10·6 per cent. of the lines, and 12·9 per cent. of the lines with no alliteration at all. Amours suggested that this weakness might be due to the ·fact that the conversational element in this romance is large, and it is principally in these sections that lines without alliteration ·occur. The other four poems exhibit a more careful treatment. But the fact does remain that these poets in the north were not as careful regarding the use of alliterative types as were the poets in the west.

The above statements equally apply to *The Quatrefoil of Love,* of which the most noticeable feature is the use of the *aa/bb* type in 8·6 per cent. of the lines. We have already observed that the poet did this in order to carry out an elaborate system of " grouping " of the lines together.

St. John the Evangelist is interesting in that the tendency to excessive alliteration is abundantly manifest, for the type *aa/aa* is found in 56 per cent. of the lines.

The later Scottish poems exhibit a similar treatment, and are not important, but special attention may be drawn to *The Prologue to the 8th. Book of the Aeneid,* in which there are no lines with less than 3 alliterating syllables, and in which 76 per cent. of the lines have 4 or 5 alliterating syllables. This late work is a landmark in the history of the metre ; alliteration is added to such an extent that the ancient versification has been reduced to a mere " jingle " of sounds. Two lines will illustrate this :—

l. 93 : " **B**aill has **b**anist **b**lythnes,   **b**ost gret **b**rag **b**lawis."

l. 18 : " **B**ailfull **b**yssynes **b**ayth **b**lys   and **b**lythnes can **b**ost."

5. The length of the lines is somewhat more constant than in the poems written in the rhymeless alliterative verse. This is similar to the poems treated in the last chapter, in which it was seen that the rhyme had the effect of making the rhythm more even and the number of unstressed syllables more constant. This is in general true of these poems. There are less violent contrasts between the length of consecutive lines.

6. The Rhythm.—The rhythm in these poems does not materially differ from that of the rhymed alliterative poems treated in the last chapter.   In the early poems from the south-west, the *Clashing-Rhythm* is not found, the rhythm always conforming to the type : $(\times \times)/\times \times/(\times \times)$.

A Satire on the Consistory Courts, however, has the usual alliterative rhythms, including lines with *Clashing-Rhythm*, and one of the peculiar type found before :—

$//\times \times /$–l. 38a : " **M**ys **m**otinde **m**en."

The same is true of the northern group of alliterative poems. The *Clashing-Rhythm* is usually of the type without the -*e* between the two main stresses, but this is only accidental, because by the time of the composition of these poems the final -*e* had been lost.   It was this fact which helped to dis-integrate the alliterative rhythm.   The older types as a result became unrecognisable.

E.g. *Rauf Coilȝear*, l. 17b : " in mony d́eip d́ell."

The rhythm of *Rauf Coilȝear* is more rugged and crude than that of any other of the Scottish poems.

The inevitable tendency was for the rhythm of each half-line to conform to the type $\times \times / \times \times /$, owing to the loss of the final -*e*.   It is often quite impossible to detect whether a half-line of the $aaa/(--)$ type has 3 stresses or only 2.   The actual number of extended half-lines is considerable, and it would be rather unnatural if these had only 2 stresses as Amours asserts.   Comparison with the rhymeless alliterative poems becomes somewhat difficult, but an early poem—*A Satire on the Consistory Courts*—may serve to illustrate the similarity.

	1st. half-line.	2nd. half-line.
$/\times \times /\times \times$	6	14

e.g. l. 40a : " **h**yrdmen hem **h**atieth."
l. 1b : " **L**ibben in londe."

$\times \times /\times \times/$	13	8

e.g. l. 56a : " Ant **h**at out an **h**eh."
l. 5b : " Ant **l**urnen huere **l**ay."

$\times \times /\times \times /\times \times$	18	14

e.g. l. 11a : " On **a**lle maner **o**thes."
l. 22b : " with honginde sleven."

$\times \times //\times$	0	3

e.g. l. 56b : " that al the **h**yrt **h**erde."

A comparison of these statistics with those in the table on p. 176 will show that in general there is no difference of treatment between the rhythms in the two groups of poems.

The alliteration and rhythm of the " wheel " part of the stanzas have not been discussed in the foregoing enquiry. Little would be gained by adding statistics concerning the number of alliterating syllables in each short line, since there is no uniformity of practice. In general there are only two alliterating syliables in the line, but not infrequently three. However, in many poems there are lines without alliteration.

To sum up the results of this chapter, we may say that in the north there arose a group of poets who had inherited the alliterative tradition, though it must be acknowledged that it reached them in a mangled form ; these poets were conscious artists, copying French forms, and effecting a marvellous compromise between the older and newer systems of verse. They made extensive use of " repetition," and " grouping," and added as much alliteration as possible. The resulting school of poets seems to have flourished for at least two centuries.

There were, however, many points of difference between the versification of this northern school of poets and that of the western school. The former made light of tradition, whereas the latter remained faithful to it, in so far as the actual knowledge of it had survived.

THE STATISTICS.

The actual quotations will not be given, but the references. Illustrations will be added from *The Quatrefoil of Love*.

A Satire against the Pride of Ladies.

1. aa/ax—None.
   aa/xa—1 line : l. 8.
2. aa/aa—1 line : l. 10.
3. aaa/aa—1 line : l. 1.
4. xa/aa—1 line : l. 15.
6. aa/bb—12 lines ; e.g. l. 4.
9. aa/xx—2 lines ; e.g. l. 3.
11. No alliteration—2 lines ; e.g. l. 17.
   The proportion of lines under type 6 is very high.

Old Age.

1. aa/ax—1 line : l. 6.
2. aa/aa—1 line : l. 7.
4. xa/aa—4 lines ; e.g. l. 1.
7. ab/ab—1 line : l. 8.
9. xx/aa—1 line : l. 2.

A Satire on the Consistory Courts.

1. aa/ax—5 lines ; e.g. l. 22.
   aa/xa—2 lines ; e.g. l. 77.
2. aa/aa—8 lines ; e.g. l. 1.
3. aaa/aa—1 line : l. 46.
4. xa/aa—9 lines ; e.g. l. 4.
5. xa/ax—4 lines ; e.g. l. 61.
   xa/xa—1 line : l. 43.
6. aa/bb—8 lines ; e.g. l. 5.
   aaa/bb—1 line : l. 38.
7. ab/ab—2 lines ; e.g. l. 62.
9. xx/aa—2 lines ; e.g. l. 80.
10. aaba/b—1 line : l. 74.
11. No alliteration—1 line : l. 19.

Golagrus and Gawain, The Houlate, Rauf Coilȝear, Awntyrs of Arthure, and The Pistill of Susan.

F. J. Amours, on p. lxxxvi of his edition of these works, recorded the percentages of the various types, and his statistics are appended here for reference. They are, however, brought into line with the scheme here adopted.

1. aa/ax and aa/xa—G. 22 per cent. ; H. 31·5 per cent. ; R. 29·9 per cent. ; A. 26·7 per cent. ; P. 33 per cent.
2. aa/aa—G. 45·7 per cent. ; H. 30·2 per cent. ; R. 16·6 per cent. ; A. 48·6 per cent. ; P. 46 per cent.
3. aaa/ax and aaa/xa—G. 4·3 per cent. ; H. 6 per cent. ; R. 3·1 per cent. ; A. 2·2 per cent. ; P. 1·3 per cent.
   aaa/aa—G. 10·6 per cent. ; H. 7·9 per cent. ; R. 3·7 per cent. ; A. 3·8 per cent. ; P. 4·9 per cent.
4. ax/aa and xa/aa—G. 6·4 per cent. ; H. 6·2 per cent. ; R. 7·5 per cent. ; A. 8·7 per cent. ; P. 7·5 per cent.
5. xa/xa, ax/xa, xa/ax—G. 2·8 per cent. ; H. 5 per cent. ; R. 9·1 per cent. ; A. 5·1 per cent. ; P. 4·9 per cent.
6-8. aa/bb, ab/ab, ab/ba—G. 3·7 per cent. ; H. 8·2 per cent. ; R. 3·7 per cent. ; A. 3·8 per cent. ; P. 1 per cent.
9. aa/xx—G. 2·5 per cent.; H. 1·7 per cent.; R. 10·6 per cent.; A. 5 per cent. ; P. 1·3 per cent.
   xx/aa—G. 5 per cent.; H. 2·2 per cent. ;· R. 1·9 per cent. ; A. o per cent. ; P. o per cent.
11. No alliteration—G. 1 per cent. ; H. 7 per cent. ; R. 12·9 per cent. ; A. 5 per cent. ; P. o per cent.

The *Rauf Coilȝear* statistics have been checked from the text, and the results are given in terms of lines, to make comparison with other texts easier.

1. aa/ax — 81 lines.
   aa/xa — 73 ,,
2. aa/aa —121 ,,
3. aaa/ax — 16 ,,
   aaa/xa — 5 ,,
   aaa/aa — 27 ,,
   aaa/aaa— 1 ,,
   xa/aaa — 2 ,,

4. ax/aa — 17 lines.
   xa/aa — 24 ,,
5. ax/ax — 17 ,,
   xa/ax — 15 ,,
   xa/xa — 17 ,,
   ax/xa — 14 ,,
6. aa/bb — 33 ,,
7. ab/ab — 5 ,,
8. ab/ba — 2 ,,
9. aa/xx — 72 ,,
   aaa/xx — 6 ,,
   xx/aa — 21 ,,
10. Complex Groups such as aab/bb, abb/ab, aba/bb, etc.—11 lines.
11. No alliteration—92 lines.

The Quatrefoil of Love.

1. aa/ax—77 lines ; e.g. l. 1 :
      " In a moruening of Maye   whenne medowes salle spryng."
   aa/xa—11 lines ; e.g. l. 21 :
      " Som sight of þat selcouthe   þat I hafe lange soughte."
2. aa/aa—23 lines ; e.g. l. 6 :
      " And bowes for to burgeone   & belde to þe boures."
3. aaa/ax—3 lines ; e.g. l. 15 :
      " For I walde wiste of his wille   & of his wilde thoghte."
   aaa/xa—2 lines ; e.g. l. 110 :
      " And bere hir blythe bodworde   of hir wille I be borne."
   aaa/aa—1 line ; l. 46 :
      " Brighte birde of þi blee   my balis may þou bete."
4. ax/aa—12 lines ; e.g. l. 17 :
      " Wrange scho hir handis   & wrothely scho wroghte."
   xa/aa—10 lines ; e.g. l. 7 :
      " Was I warre of a maye   þat made mournyng."
5. ax/ax—18 lines ; e.g. l. 29 :
      " Alle my wylle & my thoghte   walde I þe telle."
   xa/ax—28 lines ; e.g. l. 16 :
      " Rafe scho hir kerchefs   hir kelle of hir hede."
   xa/xa—15 lines ; e.g. l. 66 :
      " Whare þou fyndis grewande   a trewlufe grysse."
   ax/xa—8 lines ; e.g. l. 119 :
      " And alle þe bale of þis werlde   in þe salle be bett."
6. aa/bb—45 lines ; e.g. l. 28 :
      " Thi carpyng es comforthe   to herkene & here."
7. ab/ab—6 lines ; e.g. l. 124 :
      " Fulle hally in thi seruyse   es my hert sett."
8. ab/ba—9 lines ; e.g. l. 106 :
      " For his lufly handwerke   þat þan he hade lorne."
9. aa/xx—45 lines ; e.g. l. 3 :
      " Als I went by a welle   on my playing."
   aaa/xx—4 lines ; e.g. l. 40 :
      " Thou faire foulle, fulle of lufe,   so mylde and so swete."
   xx/aa—21 lines ; e.g. l. 97 :
      " Toke þam þat appille   to stirre mekille stryue."

9. xx/aaa—1 line ; 1. 301 :
> " He ʒode to his discypilles   & taughte þame trewthe trewe."

10. Complex Groups : aab/bb—1. 254 ; aab/ab—1. 184 ; ab/abb— 1. 343 ; aaa/bb—3 lines ; e.g. 1. 98.
> 1. 254 : " Wende away with þi myrthe   þou makis me alle made."

11. No alliteration—1. 105 :
> " þane bigane þe firste lefe   to morne for vs alle."

St. John the Evangelist.

1. aa/ax—18 lines ; e.g. l. 2.
   aa/xa—10 lines ; e.g. l. 83.
2. aa/aa—84 lines ; e.g. l. 4.
3. aaa/ax—3 lines ; e.g. l. 139.
   aaa/aa—6 lines ; e.g. l. 243.
4. ax/aa—6 lines ; e.g. l. 244.
   xa/aa—10 lines ; e.g. l. 61.
5. xa/xa—1 line : l. 214.
6. aa/bb—6 lines ; e.g. l. 90.
9. aa/xx—5 lines ; e.g. l. 45.

The 2nd. Burlesque.

1. aa/ax—17 lines ; e.g. l. 3.
2. aa/aa—3 lines ; e.g. l. 6.
5. ax/ax—1 line : l. 5.

Fortune.   (Lines 1-8 of each stanza.)

2. aa/aa—32 lines ; e.g. l. 1.
3. aaa/ax—1 line : l. 3.
   aaa/xa—1 line : l. 46.
   aaa/aa—17 lines ; e.g. l. 7.
   aa/aaa—9 lines ; e.g. l. 4.
   aaa/aaa—8 lines ; e.g. l. 14.
4. ax/aa—1 line : l. 2.

Sum Practysis of Medecyn.

1. aa/ax—9 lines ; e.g. l. 21.
   aa/xa—14 lines ; e.g. l. 16.
2. aa/aa—22 lines ; e.g. l. 6.
3. aaa/ax—1 line : l. 66.
4. ax/aa—2 lines ; e.g. l. 85.
   xa/aa—3 lines ; e.g. l. 87.
5. ax/xa—2 lines ; e.g. l. 3.
   xa/xa—4 lines ; e.g. l. 8.
6. aa/bb—3 lines ; e.g. l. 70.
   aaa/bb—1 line : l. 55.
9. aa/xx—1 line : l. 56.

The Ballad of Kynd Kittock.

1. aa/ax—1 line : l. 21.
   aa/xa—2 lines ; e.g. l. 6.
2. aa/aa—2 lines ; e.g. l. 4.

3. aaa/xa—1 line : l. 3.
   aaa/aa—1 line : l. 2.
4. ax/aa—1 line : l. 17.
5. ax/xa—4 lines ; e.g. l. 16.
   xa/xa—1 line : l. 32.
6. aa/bb—1 line : l. 30.
9. aa/xx—6 lines ; e.g. l. 29.
   xx/aa—3 lines ; e.g. l. 19.
11. No alliteration—1 line : l. 18.

The Prologue to the 8th. Book of the Aeneid.

1. aa/ax—25 lines ; e.g. l. 48.
   aa/xa—3 lines ; e.g. l. 147.
2. aa/aa—41 lines ; e.g. l. 1.
3. aaa/ax—12 lines ; e.g. l. 15.
   aaa/xa—3 lines ; e.g. l. 17.
   aaa/aa—34 lines ; e.g. l. 4.
   aa/aaa—1 line : l. 95.
   aaa/aaa—3 lines ; e.g. l. 93.
   aaaa/aa—1 line : l. 18.
9. aaa/xx—1 line : l. 152.

A Pleasant Satire upon the Estates.   (The 8 long lines.)

1. aa/ax—1 line : l. 8.
2. aa/aa—3 lines : ll. 1, 3, 6.
6. aa/bb—2 lines : ll. 4, 7.
9. aa/xx—2 lines : ll. 2, 5.

CHAPTER 11

ALLITERATION AS AN ORNAMENT.

WE have already seen that alliteration, once structural, has become more and more ornamental. Various devices of an ornamental kind, such as increased " grouping " together of lines by identical alliteration, and excessive alliteration, are added.

Again, in the rhythmical lyrical prose in late O.E. and early M.E., alliteration was an important feature, yet nevertheless not structural but purely ornamental. Alliterative prose must have been exceedingly popular in M.E., and it was natural that poets, when writing in French forms, should not hesitate to add alliteration of the stressed syllables. Sometimes a line may have all four stressed syllables alliterated, but usually only two or three. The alliteration falls indiscriminately on the first, second, third, or fourth syllable.

A. We may divide the works under discussion into two groups. The first deals with those written in the alliterative long line in early M.E. and having also some purely syllabic verse.

In **The Proverbs of Alfred,** as stated on p. 141, there are 50 couplets without alliteration, and 23 couplets with ornamental alliteration. The couplet is very crude, and owes nothing to the French form. It is noticeable, however, that the poet usually considered rhyme to be sufficient without the added alliteration.

In **The Departing Soul's Address to the Body** there are 29 couplets of a similar type. Eight of these couplets have no alliteration ; for example, ll. 27-8 :

> " For heui is his greoning
> and sorhful is his woaning."

In 21 of the couplets there is in addition ornamental alliteration. In 15 of these examples the alliteration also

serves to link the two halves of the couplet together ; e.g.
ll. 239-40 :

> " Lowe beoth the **hel**e**w**ewes,
> Un**hei**ʒe beoth the sid**w**owes."

The author is hesitating between the two systems, and his
alliteration in such lines is not purely ornamental.

Layamon's Brut has 462 couplets of a syllabic type, for
which see p. 143.   Alliteration in these couplets is very rare,
being only found in 36.   Of these, 25 have two alliterating
syllables in one half of the couplet, whereas in the remaining
ones, the alliteration also serves to link the two halves together.

E.g. l. 1556 : " **B**rien hafde muchele care ; **B**rien **b**onnede his
fare."
l. 733 : " Ah **n**auest þu **n**æuere **n**anne mon, þe cunne
awiht þeron."

Layamon, therefore, did not usually add ornamental alliteration in his couplets ; evidently he considered rhyme and
rhythm sufficient.

B. The second group of poems consists of all those written
in the ordinary syllabic metres with ornamental alliteration
of the stressed syllables.   In this group the earliest example
is **The Hymns of St. Godric,** *c.* 1170, Nth. His rhythms are
taken from the Latin hymns, and there is a little ornamental
alliteration ; e.g. l. 3 :

> " At þi **b**urth, at þi **b**are."—3rd hymn.

Hall, in his edition of the hymns in *Selections from Early
Middle English*, says : " In Godric's verse the strict syllabic
principle, with its consequent abandonment of alliteration,
save for ornament, and its consistent attempt at end-rhyme,
has obtained a complete mastery, whilst in most of the
contemporary poetry it is still struggling with the traditional
alliterative metric."

( )**idde huve with milde stevene,** 1200-50, N.E. Midl., is
an interesting fragment, consisting of 6 irregular couplets,
rhyming *aabbcc*, etc.   There are usually 4 stresses to the line,
but occasionally even 6.   Four lines have no alliteration at
all, e.g. l. 2 :

> " Til ure fader þe king of hevene."

The remaining lines have alliteration of 2, 3, or 4 stressed syllables. There is one example of *ab/ab*, one of *aa/bb*, and one of *ab/ba*, e.g. l. 4 :

"For þe laverd of þis **h**us & al **l**ele **h**ine."

The rhythm is only partially syllabic, and has been greatly influenced by the O.E. stress-rhythms. It is an interesting relic, showing the transition from the older to the newer type.

The remaining poems are usually those written in the ordinary metres of M.E., such as the couplet, common metre, septenary. The statistics regarding the works discussed in chapter 6 are given at the end of the chapter.

These works are found, it will be remembered, from 1200 to 1420, and every dialect is represented in the examples chosen. The statistics will, in general, speak for themselves, and only a few special comments are necessary.

1. The Enemies of Man has alliteration in all its lines, and the poem stands somewhat apart from the remaining works. The author is careful to observe the alliterative groups, and there is some grouping of consecutive lines by identical alliteration ; thus ll. 7-10, *ffff*; 67-9, *lll*; 97-100, *ffff*, and in addition 17 "twos." It is often very difficult to ascertain whether a given line has two or three stressed syllables. As a general rule, all the stressed syllables of the line alliterate. There is great liberty as to the number of unstressed syllables.

2. Pearl, apart from its intricate stanza-linking devices, is interesting in its rhythm. There are four stresses to the line, and liberty as to the number of unstressed syllables. There is also a medial cæsura of a very definite character, and the influence of the rhythm and structure of the alliterative long line is discernible. In 33 per cent. of the lines there is no alliteration. The author shows complete mastery over this unique metrical form.

The practice of "repetition," which we have already met with in earlier poems, is also to be found in some of these :—

(a) In 4/10 of the stanzas of *Friar Henry's Little Sermon.*
(b) In the *Harley Lyrics* Nos. 2, 3, 5, 8, 9, 10, 11.
(c) In *Minot's Poems*, Nos. 1, 6, 8.
(d) In the *Vernon-Simeon Lyrics*, 3 and 6. (These lyrics usually have a refrain instead of "repetition.")
(e) In *Pearl*, which has the most intricate system of "repetition" in the whole range of M.E. literature.

There are 101 stanzas, though probably intended for 100, grouped in 20 sections of 5 stanzas (except the 15th, which has 6 stanzas). The last line of each stanza of a section is a refrain for that section. Section is bound to section and stanza to stanza by " repetition," and the last line of the poem is reminiscent of the first—also a noticeable feature of *Patience*, and *Sir Gawayn and the Green Knight*.

The works treated in this chapter, and of which the statistics are added, were chosen either as representatives of the various dialects, or because they served to illustrate some special aspect of the use of ornamental alliteration in the various stanza-forms. But there are in addition many other important works in M.E. with some alliteration of the stressed syllables. These have usually less than 33 per cent. of the lines with such alliteration. There are certain short poems, such as *The Five Thornton Lyrics*, edited in " Yorkshire Writers," vol. 1, pp. 363-4, with 25 per cent. of the lines alliterated ; *A Lutel Soth Sermon*, *c.* 1230, S. Midl., with 23 per cent. of its lines alliterated ; *Mary and the Cross*, *c.* 1350, S.W. Midl., with 83 per cent. of its lines alliterated.

Many of the romances, written in rhymed stanzas, have some ornamental alliteration. Thus *King Horn*, the earliest romance, has alliteration in 9 per cent. of its lines ; *Horn Childe and Maiden Rimenhilde* in 17 per cent. ; *The Lay of Havelock the Dane* in 17 per cent. ; and *The Story of Joseph*, *c.* 1300, in 42 per cent.

Other works with alliteration in varying degrees are : *Genesis and Exodus*, *c.* 1250, S.E. Midl. ; *Trentalle St. Gregory*, 1300-50, Sth. ; *Ywan and Gawain*, 1300-50, Nth. ; *The Tale of Gamelyn*, *c.* 1350, E. Midl. ; *The Avowynge of Arthure*, *c.* 1350, N.W. Midl. ; *Sir Firumbras*, 1375-1400, Sth. ; *Sir Percyvell of Galles*, 1350-1400, N.E. Midl. ; *The Song of Roland*, *c.* 1400, S.W. Midl. ; *The Laud Troy Book*, 1400, N.W. Midl. ; *Le Morte Arthure*, 1400, N.W. Midl. ; *The Earl of Toulouse*, *c.* 1400, N.E. Midl. ; *The Turke and Gawin*, *c.* 1450, Nth.

In addition many alliterated passages will be found in *The York, Towneley, Coventry*, and *Chester Plays*.

Purely ornamental alliteration was thus very popular throughout the M.E. period in all parts of the country. This fact, however, shows how great a change alliteration had undergone ; once an essential part of the verse, it had become reduced to a mere ornament.   It is in this tendency that the cause of the ultimate decay of the alliterative metre is to be found.

THE STATISTICS.

1. **The Bestiary.**   (References are to Hall's edition in *Selections from Early Middle-English.*)

   (a) *Common Metre* (alternate octosyllabic and three-bar lines, arranged in stanzas of 4 lines, rhyming *abab*).

   39 lines.   In 25 lines, *no alliteration ;*   e.g. l. 78.
   In 13 lines, 2 *str. syll. alliterate ;*   e.g. l. 86.
   In 2 lines, 3 *str. syll. alliterate ;*   e.g. l. 512.

   (b) *Verses of three measures.*

   115 lines.   In 82 lines, *no alliteration ;*   e.g. l. 61.
   In 30 lines, 2 *str. syll. alliterate ;*   e.g. l. 28.
   In 3 lines, 3 *str. syll. alliterate ;*   e.g. l. 277.

   (c) *The Octosyllabic Couplet.*

   272 lines.   In 161 lines, *no alliteration ;*   e.g. l. 596.
   In 94 lines, 2 *str. syll. alliterate ;*   e.g. l. 541.
   In 15 lines, 3 *str. syll. alliterate ;*   e.g. l. 326.
   In 2 lines, 4 *str. syll. alliterate ;*   e.g. l. 618.

   (d) *Verses of two measures*—ll. 317, 449, 452, 460, but none of these has alliteration.

   (e) *The Septenary.*

   32 lines.   In 4 lines, *no alliteration ;*   e.g. l. 576.
   In 21 lines, 2 *str. syll. alliterate ;*   e.g. l. 591.
   In 6 lines, 3 *str. syll. alliterate ;*   e.g. l. 215.
   In 1 line, 4 *str. syll. alliterate :*   l. 294.

Thus there is plenty of ornamental alliteration in *The Bestiary*, and this fact is not remarkable, when we recall that the author could also write the alliterative long line.   61 per cent. of the lines have, therefore, alliteration.

2. **The Debate Between the Body and the Soul.**

   The poem consists of 61 stanzas of 8 lines, rhyming *abababab*, with four stresses to the line.

   In 190 lines, *no alliteration ;*   e.g. l. 6.
   In 256 lines, 2 *str. syll. alliterate ;*   e.g. l. 2.
   In 30 lines, 3 *str. syll. alliterate ;*   e.g. l. 7.
   In 12 lines, 4 *str. syll. alliterate ;*   e.g. ll. 3, 89 :
   l. 3 :   " Forsoþe I sauȝ a selly siȝt " ;
   l. 89 :   " **W**an I þe **w**olde **t**eme and **t**eche."

61 per cent. of the lines have, therefore, alliteration.

3. **A Disputison bitwene childe Ihesu and Maistres of the lawe of Jewus·**

The poem consists of 215 lines in stanzas of 8 lines, rhyming
ababab.

In 112 lines, *no alliteration ;* e.g. l. 11.
In 53 lines, 2 *str. syll. alliterate ;* e.g. l. 35.
In 36 lines, 3 *str. syll. alliterate :* e.g. l. 6.
In 14 lines, 4 *str. syll. alliterate ;* e.g. l. 5.

48 per cent of the lines have, therefore, alliteration.

4. **Selected Harley Lyrics.** (For the titles, see p. 114.)·

Lyric No. 2—10 stanzas of 8 lines, rhyming *aaabcccb, b* having 3
stresses, whereas the remaining lines have 4 stresses.

(Lines *a* and *c.*) In 11 lines, *no alliteration ;* e.g. l. 27.
In 30 lines, 2 *str. syll. alliterate ;* e.g. l. 2.
In 13 lines, 3 *str. syll. alliterate ;* e.g. l. 1.
In 6 lines, 4 *str. syll. alliterate ;* e.g. l. 10.
(Lines *b.*) In 1 line, *no alliteration :* l. 52.
In 16 lines, 2 *str. syll. alliterate ;* e.g. l. 8.
In 2 lines, 3 *str. syll. alliterate ;* e.g. l. 4.

The statistics for the remaining lyrics may be given in a shorter
form.

Lyric No. 3 has alliteration in 95 per cent. of the lines.

,,	No. 5	,,	,,	92	,, ,, ,,
,,	No. 6	,,	,,	91	,, ,, ,,
,,	No. 7	,,	,,	79	,, ,, ,,
,,	No. 8	,,	,,	70	,, ,, ,,
,,	No. 9	,,	,,	94	,, ,, ,,
,,	No. 10	,,	,,	100	,, ,, ,,
,,	No. 11	,,	,,	94	,, ,, ,,
,,	No. 12	,,	,,	62·5	,, ,, ,,
,,	No. 13	,,	,,	77·5	,, ,, ,,
,,	No. 14	,,	,,	87·5	,, ,, ,,
,,	No. 15	,,	,,	27	,, ,, ,,
,,	No. 16	,,	,,	87·5	,, ,, ,,
,,	No. 17	,,	,,	55·5	,, ,, ,,

5. **On the Retinues of the Great.**

The poem consists of 10 stanzas of 8 lines, rhyming -*a-a-a-a*, that
is, the alternate lines alone are rhymed. There are only
2 stresses to the line.

In 23 lines, *no alliteration ;* e.g. l. 70.
In 56 lines, 2 *str. syll. alliterate ;* e.g. l. 1.
In 1 line, 3 *str. syll. alliterate :* l. 33.

71·25 per cent of the lines have, therefore, alliteration.

6. **The Enemies of Man.**

The poem consists of 7 stanzas of 16 lines, rhyming
aaabcccbdddbeeeb.

In 75 lines, 2 *str. syll. alliterate ;* e.g. l. 112.
In 21 lines, 3 *str. syll. alliterate ;* e.g. l. 9.
In 3 lines, 4 *str. syll. alliterate ;* e.g. l. 13.

100 per cent of the lines have, therefore, alliteration.

7. The Poems of Minot (1, 3, 4, 6, 7, 8).

Poem No. 1 consists of 11 stanzas of 8 lines, rhyming *abababab*, except the twelfth stanza of 4 lines, rhyming *abab*.

> In 16 lines, *no alliteration;* e.g. l. 6.
> In 55 lines, 2 *str. syll. alliterate;* e.g. l. 3.
> In 20 lines, 3 *str. syll. alliterate;* e.g. l. 9.
> In 1 line, 4 *str. syll. alliterate*—l. 10:
>   " For derne dedes þat done me dere."

The statistics for the remaining poems of Minot may be given in a shortened form.

Poem No.	3 has alliteration in 42 per cent. of the lines.					
,,	No. 4	,,	,,	57·3	,,	,,	,,
,,	No. 6	,,	,,	87	,,	,,	,,
,,	No. 7	,,	,,	77	,,	,,	,,
,,	No. 8	,,	,,	81	,,	,,	,,

8. Lady Fortune and Her Wheel.

The poem is a quatrain of four lines, rhyming *aaaa*.

> " þe leuedi fortune is boþe frend and fo
> Of pore che makit riche, of riche pore also.
> Che turneȝ wo al to wele, and wele al into wo,
> Ne triste no man to þis wele, þe whel it turnet so."

There appear to be from 5 to 7 stresses in the line, and a distinct medial pause.

9. Falsenesse and Couetys er feris.

The poem consists of 20 lines, rhyming *ababababccdd eeee ffgg*.

> In 10 lines, *no alliteration;* e.g. l. 9.
> In 10 lines, 2 *str. syll. alliterate;* e.g. l. 3.

50 per cent. of the lines have, therefore, alliteration.

10. Ave Maris Stella.

The poem consists of 34 lines in rhyming couplets.

> In 20 lines, *no alliteration;* e.g. l. 8.
> In 14 lines, 2 *str. syll. alliterate;* e.g. l. 10.

41 per cent. of the lines have, therefore, alliteration.

11. A Strophic Version of O.T. Pieces.

This lengthy work, of which only a small part has been printed, has a stanza-form, unique in M.E., consisting of 12 lines, rhyming *abababab cdcd*, each of the first eight lines having 4 stresses, and each of the last four lines 3 stresses.

Judging from the text available, the proportion of lines with alliteration is as follows :—

No allit. : 2 *str. syll. allit. :* 3 *str. syll. allit. :* 4 *str. syll. allit. : :* 1 : 5 : 2 : 1. That is to say, there are usually two alliterating syllables to the line, the lines of 3 stresses seldom having more than two alliterating syllables.

12. The Rolle Lyrics. (2-8).

2. *A Prayer to Jesus.* There is only alliteration in l. 8. The poem consists of 3 stanzas of 4 lines, rhyming *abab*.

3. *When Adam delf & Eue span.*

The poem consists of 6 stanzas of 6 lines, rhyming *aaaabb*. There are 6 or 7 stresses to the line, and a medial pause. It might be possible to divide the line into two distinct halves, but medial rhymes are practically absent.

> In 6 lines, *no alliteration ;* e.g. l. 5.
> In 12 lines, 2 *str. syll. alliterate ;* e.g. l. 4.
> In 8 lines, 3 *str. syll. alliterate ;* e.g. l. 1.
> In 6 lines, 4 *str. syll. alliterate ;* e.g. l. 25.
> In 2 lines, 5 *str. syll. alliterate ;* in 1 line, 6 *alliterate ;* and in 1 line, 7 *alliterate (a a b b b b b)* : l. 32 :

" þi ble so bright, þi mayn, þi myght, þi mowth þat miri mas."

5. *Ihesu, God Son, Lord of Mageste.*

The poem consists of 48 verses of the same type as in the previous poem, and there is alliteration of 2, 3, or 4 stressed syllables in 71 per cent. of the lines.

4. *Mercy es maste in my mynde.*

The poem consists of 4 stanzas of 12 lines each, rhyming *abababcdcdcd.* It will be recalled that this is the stanza in which *Pearl* is written.

> In 27 lines, *no alliteration ;* e.g. l. 11.
> In 17 lines, 2 *str. syll. alliterate ;* e.g. l. 3.
> In 4 lines, 3 *str. syll. alliterate ;* e.g. l. 6.

6. *Luf es lyf þat lastes ay.*

The poem consists of 192 lines of 3 or 4 stresses, with rhymes *abababab* or *ababcbcb*.

> In 127 lines, *no alliteration ;* e.g. l. 2.
> In 55 lines, 2 *str. syll. alliterate ;* e.g. l. 3.
> In 10 lines, 3 *str. syll. alliterate ;* e.g. l. 1.

7. *Heyle Ihesu, my creatowre.*

The poem consists of 56 lines of the same type, with alliteration in 41 per cent. of the lines.

8. *Thy ioy be ilk a dele.*

The poem consists of 72 lines of the same type, with alliteration in 36 per cent. of the lines.

13. **Friar Henry's Little Sermon.**

This poem consists of 10 stanzas of 8 lines, rhyming -*a-a-a-a*, with the exception of the 1st. stanza, which has the following rhyme-scheme : -*a-abb-b*.

> In 17 lines, *no alliteration ;* e.g. l. 18.
> In 40 lines, 2 *str. syll. alliterate ;* e.g. l. 45.
> In 17 lines, 3 *str. syll. alliterate ;* e.g. l. 50.
> In 3 lines, 4 *str. syll. alliterate ;* e.g. l. 66.

In addition l. 12 has the type *abab*, l. 41 the type *abba,* and l. 52 the type *aabb ;*

e.g. l. 12 : " We haue no Borwes heer to be."

79 per cent. of the lines have, therefore, alliteration.

14. **Þurgh Grace Growand.**

The poem consists of 5 stanzas of 8 lines, rhyming *ababcdcd*.
> In 6 lines, *no alliteration ;* e.g. l. 12.
> In 20 lines, 2 *str. syll. alliterate ;* e.g. l. 3.
> In 5 lines, 3 *str. syll. alliterate ;* e.g. l. 26.
> In 9 lines, 4 *str. syll. alliterate ;* e.g. l. 27.

85 per cent. of the lines have, therefore, alliteration.

15. **Pearl.**

Pearl consists of 101 stanzas of 12 lines, rhyming *abababbcbc*.
> In 397 lines, *no alliteration ;* e.g. l. 430.
> In 504 lines, 2 *str. syll. alliterate ;* e.g. l. 342.
> In 232 lines, 3 *str. syll. alliterate ;* e.g. l. 330.
> In 57 lines, 4 *str. syll. alliterate ;* e.g. l. 61.
> In addition the type *aabb* occurs in 19 lines ; e.g.
> l. 106 :
> > " As fyldor fyn her bonkes brent " ;
> the type *abba* in 3 lines ; e.g. l. 439 :
> > " Sir, fele here porchasez & fongez pray."

63·7 per cent. of the lines have, therefore, alliteration.

16. **The Vernon-Simeon Lyrics.** (See p. 128, for references.)

Since there are 30 of these lyrics, the statistics are given in a
shortened form.

The stanza-form is usually *ababbcbc*.

In No. 1, 56 per cent. ; No. 2, 68 per cent. ; No. 3, 62½ per cent. ;
No. 4, 12½ per cent. ; No. 5, 75 per cent. ; No. 6, 52 per
cent. ; No. 7, 52 per cent. ; No. 8, 85 per cent. ; No. 9,
52 per cent. ; No. 10, 69 per cent. ; No. 11, 50 per cent. ;
No. 12, 68 per cent. ; No. 13, 75 per cent. ; No. 14, 35 per
cent. ; No. 15, 49 per cent. ; No. 16, 71 per cent. ; No. 17,
54 per cent. ; No. 18, 94 per cent. ; No. 19, 48 per cent. ;
No. 20, 31 per cent. ; No. 21, 92 per cent. ; No. 22, 49 per
cent. ; No. 23, 27 per cent. ; No. 24, 65 per cent. ; No. 25, 32
per cent. ; No. 26, 20 per cent. ; No. 27, 87 per cent. ; No.
28, 45 per cent. ; No. 29, 17 per cent. ; No. 30, 27 per cent.

The percentage of lines with alliteration varies considerably.

17. **On the Battle of Agincourt.**

The poem consists of 8 stanzas of 8 lines, rhyming *ababbcbc*.
> In 25 lines, *no alliteration ;* e.g. l. 64.
> In 22 lines, 2 *str. syll. alliterate ;* e.g. l. 30.
> In 10 lines, 3 *str. syll. alliterate ;* e.g. l. 1.
> In 6 lines, 4 *str. syll. alliterate ;* e.g. l. 2.

60·3 per cent. of the lines have, therefore, alliteration.

CONCLUSION.

It remains to summarise the conclusions already reached. There is evidence available to demonstrate that the O.E. alliterative long line was still being written in its correct form at the time of the Norman Conquest. Certain entries in *The Angle-Saxon Chronicle* of a late date are written in a metrical form which would have been considered correct in the days in which *Beowulf* was written. Other small fragments are to be found until as late as 1150.

Though we cannot infer that knowledge of the metrical system was widespread, the fact that perfect specimens have survived is in itself important.

Meanwhile popular alliterative rhythmical prose was being written in homiletic works. Wulfstan, Aelfric, and doubtless others, used this medium, and the extent of its popularity can scarcely be exaggerated. It is not difficult to imagine what effect this metrical prose had on the native poetry, especially when we remember that the knowledge of the traditional metrical system must have become very vague amongst the people. Some of the so-called metrical entries in *The Anglo-Saxon Chronicle*, as we have already seen, are indistinguishable from ordinary prose, whereas in others there is in varying degrees an approximation to rhymed syllabic couplets ; the metre in these entries consists of a combination of assonance with the rhythm of the alliterative prose. In very few of the entries, however, is there discernible any trace of the influence of the traditional alliterative long line.

Nevertheless, it was inevitable that the metrical currents should converge. *The 1st. Worcester Fragment, c.* 1170, is the first extant document to indicate that this convergence had taken place. The alliterative line has become longer, and the rhythm is of the popular type ; there is as yet no assonance. *The Departing Soul's Address to the Body* reveals the process completed, the native assonance having secured a firm footing in the structure of the verse, its function being to link the two half-lines together, especially when the poet fails to do this by means of alliteration. Beneath all the crudities of the verse can be seen the alliterative long line, still strong and vigorous, though struggling against the encroachment of the popular forms of verse.

The Proverbs of Alfred, The Brut, and *The Bestiary* carry on this fascinating story. A couplet of undoubtedly native origin has been evolved; at the same time the alliterative long line still continues with no break in tradition. Eventually the two streams flow apart once more, the long line continuing its separate existence and shaking off rhyme altogether, while the crude couplet shows alliteration reduced to a mere ornament and no longer structural. Finally the modified French couplet seems to have absorbed the native couplet.

It will be recalled that proof of the continuity of the alliterative tradition has been afforded in the foregoing pages; there was no break, and the changes that occurred were largely due to knowledge of the metre becoming obscured. Judging from the works which have survived, the alliterative tradition was strongest in the S.W. Midl. dialect.

The second chapter in the history of the Alliterative Versification deals with the group of poems written in the rhymeless alliterative long line from *c.* 1340 to *c.* 1450 in the W. Midl. dialect. Twenty poems of varying lengths yield a rich harvest of poetry. Our dialectal investigations have proved that the centre of this particular form of literary activity was the west, embracing the extreme north and south-west. After 1400, however, several poems were written in Scotland.

The versification of these western poems is not a copy of that in which the Old English poems were written; the differences are precisely those found in the post-Conquest alliterative poems. There is historical continuity even in the minor metrical features, some of which may have been unconsciously used.

The intermediate stages of the process have been lost, but it is significant that the extant specimens, both in the earlier and later stages, come from the west. There were few imitators, however, outside the western area, except at a later period in Scotland, and their compositions were insignificant. Eventually decay set in, poetic inspiration declining, and the metre becoming more and more formless. Yet the body of literature produced during the two centuries in which these western writers lived is by no means inconsiderable, and is worthy of closer study than it has received.

There had been, however, a second line of development in the early M.E. period. In the south-west and in certain other parts of the country, end-rhyme rather than medial-rhyme had been added. The earliest example of this is *On God Orison of Our Lady*, *c.* 1200, in which the alliterative long line is extremely crude. It is probable that end-rhyme was adopted in imitation of the Latin septenary. The scattered examples in the south-west are written in the same long line with the same peculiarities as are found in the non-rhyming alliterative verse. No school of writers, however, arose, and the last extant specimen is *c.* 1300. But in the north-east, many important poems were written in this metre, and the type flourished in the fourteenth century.

This continuance of the same alliterative tradition in non-western areas is interesting, for it shows that the long line had in these areas survived, though undergoing change. The bulk of literature produced was small in comparison with that produced in the west, but the long line with end-rhyme was not a suitable medium for longer poems, being ideally suited to lyrical verse.

In the mid-fourteenth century a school of poets arose in the northern counties and Scotland which flourished for two centuries. These writers were evidently accustomed to the alliterative long line with end-rhyme, as used in lyrical verse. They desired, however, to write longer poems and possibly recognised the unsuitability of the poetic medium at their disposal. The simple stanza of eight or more metrically uniform lines did not prove very attractive, and this difficulty was obviated by the use of the *bob and wheel* or of the *wheel* alone. The resulting stanza-forms became very popular in the north, but never in the west and elsewhere.

The experiment was not unsuccessful, yet looking back we are able to see the danger involved. It was the desire for ornament that led these poets to overcrowd their lines with alliterating sounds, and to employ so many metrical devices. In its last stages the long line is a mere jingle of sounds.

Possibly the northern and western schools of alliterative

poets were rivals.   We have already made a detailed comparison of the two, and have suggested that the intrinsic
difference lies in the fact that the northern school made light
of tradition, whereas the western school was faithful to it,
in so far as the actual knowledge of it had survived.

The two schools flourished and both passed away.   Alliteration, once structural, had become more and more ornamental, until finally the verse became chaotic and ceased to
be a worthy vehicle of what little poetic inspiration survived.

APPENDIX I.

The Common Authorship of Certain Poems.

As stated in the Introduction, when dealing with problems of common authorship, the metrical test is likely to be more reliable than that afforded by minute parallels of identical phraseology, since style and general literary characteristics may be a matter of imitation. Hence the metrical test is valuable, but must be used with care. In the poems here discussed, the conclusion can only hold if other things, such as date, vocabulary, and phraseology, are also in agreement.

1. Alexander A and **B.** Trautmann[1] and Skeat[2] regarded these two incomplete works as fragments of the same poem. They reached this conclusion from a study of the vocabulary, phraseology and general characteristics of style. A study of the metre amply confirms their views.

> (a) *The Alliterative Types* (see pp. 167-9).—The *aa/ax* type is found in *Alexander A* in 90·4 per cent. of the lines, and in *Alexander B* in 96 per cent., a remarkably high percentage in both, only paralleled in one other poem, *The Destruction of Troy*. Secondly, the untraditional type *xa/xa* is only found once in each poem, and the type *ax/xa* is not found in either. Thirdly, the complex types, such as *aab/ab*, are found in both. Fourthly, the *aaa/a(a)* type is found in both fragments, but roughly twice as frequently in *A* as in *B*. This is, however, a matter of little importance. The regularity of the alliteration is very noticeable in both.
>
> (b) *The Rhythm.*—Here there is the same similarity. The rhythm of the extended half-lines is similar in

---

[1] M. Trautmann, *Über verfasser und entstehungszeit einiger alliterirender gedichte des altenglischen,* Halle, 1876.

[2] W. Skeat, *Alexander and Dindimus,* E.E.T.S., E.S., 31.

both poems, the type "$// \times \times \times \times \times \times$" being found in both poems in the first half-line. The actual percentages of lines having the various types of rhythm are almost identical.

(c) *Violations of the natural stress for the sake of alliteration* are more common in these two fragments than in any other alliterative poem (see p. 178). The alliteration is very frequently found on the unstressed verbal prefix.

(d) *Vocalic Alliteration.*—*Alexander A* has vocalic alliteration in 3·7 per cent. of its lines, and *Alexander B* in 5 per cent. See also p. 160, where it may be seen that the tendency to alliterate identical vowels together is very strong in both these fragments, *Alexander A* having 29 "threes," and *Alexander B* 27 "threes." Similarly it may be seen from the study on p. 162 that the author of these two fragments generally alliterates *h* with itself, and not with vowels.

(e) *Alliterative Groups.*—Concerning these, the poet was extremely careful, *sp, st, sk, s(c)h* being practically always treated as groups for the purposes of alliteration. New groups, which are less consistently employed, are: *sl, sw, dr, br, gr, tr, pr, wr*, all of which are found in both fragments.

(f) *Grouping of Lines by Identical Alliteration.*—*Alexander A* has 35, and *Alexander B* 39 examples of two consecutive lines with identical alliteration. Regarding the alternative method of grouping lines, discussed on p. 148, *Alexander A* has 49 examples and *Alexander B* 77 examples.

(g) Lastly, there is a close resemblance in minor details, such as the comparative shortness of the line, as compared with many other poems, and a certain regularity and manipulation of the verse common to both fragments.

It would therefore appear certain that the two fragments are by the same author.

2. Skeat [1] also assumed that **William of Palerne** had been written by the same poet, as however, not only are there

---

[1] E.E.T.S., E.S., I, *William of Palerne* and *Alisaunder*.

very noticeable differences in style and general treatment of the theme, but also in the metre.

Thus the *aa/ax* type is only found in 71 per cent. of the lines as compared with 90 and 96 per cent. in the other two poems ; the *ax/ax* type is of much more frequent occurrence, and the number of lines with the *aaa/a(a)* type is almost 11 per cent. The rhythm is approximately the same, and violations of the natural stress are common. Vocalic alliteration is not so common, the percentage being only 2·36 per cent., and the tendency to alliterate on identical vowels is not so strong (see p. 160). A still more noticeable difference is the frequent alliterating of *h* with vowels, a practice quite contrary to that of *Alexander A* and *B*. Alliterative groups are very much less common, and are not consistently employed. Lastly, the grouping of consecutive lines by identical alliteration is quite rare. For these reasons, it seems unlikely that *William of Palerne* was written by the same author as the *Alexander* Fragments.

3. The Parlement of the Thre Ages and **Wynnere and Wastoure.**—These two poems have been ascribed to one author by Sir Israel Gollancz and other scholars of repute. Steadman (Mod. Phil., 21, 7-14) has adduced certain evidence which is said to render the theory of a common authorship dubious.

The metrical evidence may afford some help towards a solution of this difficult problem.

(*a*) *The Alliterative Types.*—The *aa/ax* type is found in *The Parlement of the Thre Ages* in 84·9 per cent. of the lines, and in *Wynnere and Wastoure* in 90 per cent. The slight difference is obviously of no importance.

Secondly, the *ax/xa* and *xa/xa* types are not found in either poem.

Thirdly, the complex types, such as *aab/ab*, are found in both poems.

Fourthly, the type *aaa/a(a)* is found in *The Parlement of the Thre Ages* in 10·5 per cent. of the lines, and in *Wynnere and Wastoure* in 9 per cent. The statistics given on p. 171 will illustrate the close similarity between the two poems, especially in view of the fact that there has been considerable scribal corruption of the texts.

(b) *The Rhythm.*—A careful study of the types of rhythm used, both in the simple half-lines and in the extended ones, does not reveal any differences. The actual number of extended half-lines used does not differ very much in the two poems.

(c) *Violations of the natural stress for the sake of alliteration,* it will be remembered, do not occur. Most poets seem to have allowed at least a few such violations.

(d) *Vocalic alliteration* is found in 7 per cent. of the lines of *The Parlement of the Thre Ages*, but only in 2 per cent. of those of *Wynnere and Wastoure.*

Secondly, with regard to the alliterating together of identical vowels, *The Parlement of the Thre Ages* has 9 " threes," 29 " twos," and 10 " all-different," whereas *Wynnere and Wastoure* has 1 " three," 7 " twos," and 3 " all-different."

These differences may be only accidental, but in themselves give rise to some suspicion.

Thirdly, *h* never alliterates with a vowel in either poem.

(e) *Alliterative Groups.*—*Sp, st* are always treated as alliterative groups consistently in both poems. *Sl, sw* are likewise invariable groups and do not alliterate with *s.*

Sk, tr, gr, br are much less stable groups.

(f) *Grouping of Lines by Identical Alliteration.*—The grouping of consecutive lines by means of identical alliteration is equally common in both poems ; there are in *The Parlement of the Thre Ages* 34 " twos," and 5 " threes," and in *Wynnere and Wastoure* 36 " twos," and 2 " threes."

The alternative method of grouping, discussed on p. 148, is found in 5·5 per cent. of the lines in each poem.

The similarity of treatment is noticeable.

Thus the two poems are metrically in almost complete agreement. The only point of difference is in the amount of vocalic alliteration used, but this may well be a matter of accident. Other things being equal, the two poems would seem to come from the same hand. The question is therefore, " Are Steadman's objections of sufficient weight to disprove the theory of common authorship ? "

4. Richard the Redeles and **Piers Plowman.**—Skeat was of the opinion that Langland was the author of *Richard the Redeles* as well as of *The Vision concerning Piers the Plowman*. In view of the possibility of the composite authorship of the latter work, the problem becomes more complicated. However, there seems sufficient evidence to disprove Skeat's theory, owing to the following points of difference :—

1. Grouping of consecutive lines by identical alliteration is much more common in *Richard the Redeles* than in *Piers Plowman*.
2. Vocalic alliteration is only found in 1 per cent. of the lines of *Richard the Redeles*, but in 3·8 per cent. of the lines of *Piers Plowman* (*B* text).
   Also the alliteration of *h* with vowels is more common in *Piers Plowman*. In arguing from these two characteristics, the differing length of the two poems should be borne in mind.
3. The percentage of lines of the *aaa/a(a)* type in *Richard the Redeles* is 2·8 per cent. only, whereas in *Piers Plowman* it is roughly 9 per cent. The difference is surely not a mere coincidence.

There are other minor points of difference, but in view of the differing length of the two works, it would be unwise to press them. It seems unlikely that *Richard the Redeles* was written by the author of *Piers Plowman*. If there were several authors' work in the latter composition, the above statements will not, of course, hold.

5. Sir Gawayn and the Green Knight, Purity, and **Patience.**— The three poems have repeatedly been ascribed to one poet, and the parallels of vocabulary, phraseology, literary style, and general outlook are so strong that there remains little doubt concerning the common authorship. The evidence has been set forth many times, but the most convincing presentation of the case is that by Professor Menner in his edition of *Purity* (1920).

The metrical test corroborates the theory in a remarkable manner.

(*a*) *The Alliterative Types* (see pp. 167-9).—The *aa/ax* type is found in *Gaw.* in 75·65 per cent. of the lines, in *Pur.* in 79·63 per cent., and in *Pat.* in 83·8 per cent. The similarity is sufficiently strong.

Secondly, the types *ax/xa* and *xa/xa* are not found in any of the poems, which is in remarkable contrast to the custom in most poems, since there are very few poets who reject them completely.

Thirdly, the complex types are common in all three poems, and the tendency to excessive alliteration of a purely ornamental kind is more plentiful in these poems than in any other alliterative work of the fourteenth century.

Fourthly, the percentage of lines with the *aaa/a(a)* type is exceptionally high : *Gaw.* 15 per cent. ; *Pur.* 15 per cent. ; *Pat.* 13·5 per cent. Reference to p. 171 will reveal how remarkable these statistics are ; in *St. Erkenwald* alone is there a similar state of affairs, most poems having under 10 per cent.

The alliteration is not merely regular, but shows a strong preference for the traditional types, and a marked tendency towards excessive alliteration.

(*b*) *The Rhythm.*—The percentage of extended half-lines is very high in all poems, as just indicated, but the most noticeable feature concerning the rhythm is the greater use of certain types, as mentioned on p. 172 ; these are $\times // \times \times \times \times / \times$, $\times / \times \times \times \times // \times$, $// \times \times \times /$, and $// \times \times \times \times$. The last two are of frequent occurrence in these poems only, being found sporadically in the other poems. The three poems are thus not only similar in the choice of rhythmical types, but in this respect stand out clearly from other poems of the alliterative school.

(*c*) *Violations of the natural stress for the sake of alliteration* are very marked, especially with regard to the unstressed verbal prefix. Schumacher on pp. 26-8 of his previously mentioned dissertation called attention to this fact. The poet did not hesitate to allow himself this liberty when he deemed it necessary.

(*d*) *Vocalic Alliteration.*—The actual amount of vocalic alliteration used is similar in all three poems : *Gaw.* 4·8 per cent. ; *Pur.* 6 per cent. ; and *Pat.* 5 per cent.

A second remarkable point is the absence of the tendency to alliterate on identical vowels. These facts are illustrated on p. 161. *Morte Arthure* is the only poem in which there is a parallel to this.

Thirdly, the tendency to alliterate *h* with vowels is very strong. It will be remembered that such a licence is only found consistently in these three poems, *William of Palerne*, and *Piers Plowman*. In *Gaw. h* enters into the alliteration of vowels 69 out of 102 times, in *Pur.* 50 out of 101 times, and in *Pat.* 24 out of 27 times. These facts speak for themselves.

(*e*) *Alliterative Groups.*—*Sp, st, sk* are consistently treated as groups, but *sch* is allowed to alliterate freely with *s*. There are many other groups found, but these are not so consistently employed, numerous exceptions being allowed. Among these groups we may mention in particular *sw, sn, sl*.

(*f*) *Grouping of Lines by Identical Alliteration.*—The statistics are given on p. 156, where it will be seen that the grouping of the type indicated is very marked. *Gaw.* has 100 " twos," *Pur.* 83, and *Pat.* 32.

The alternative method of grouping the lines together, which is described on p. 148, is equally common. *Gaw.* has 5·5 per cent., *Pur.* 4·3 per cent., and *Pat.* 5 per cent.

In view of the collective evidence afforded by these points, it seems certain that the three alliterative poems, found in the same MS., and traditionally ascribed to the same poet, were by the same gifted author. When the non-metrical evidence is also taken into account, the theory of common authorship becomes unassailable.

6. St. Erkenwald and the Group of Poems ascribed to the Gawayn Poet.—*St. Erkenwald* has frequently been ascribed to the author of the poems just treated. In England, Sir Israel Gollancz has demonstrated the plausibility of such a theory, and Mr. L. Savage in his new edition of the poem has presented the evidence afforded by a study of the vocabulary, phraseology and style in a most convincing manner. It is possible that a study of the metre may throw some light on the problem.

It is important, however, to remember that the poem is short, having only 352 lines ; hence it is more dangerous to argue from percentages.

(a) *The Alliterative Types* (see pp. 167-9).—The *aa/ax*
type is found in 76 per cent. of the lines, as compared
with 75·65 per cent. in *Gaw.*

Secondly, there is only one example of an *xa/xa*
type.

Thirdly, there is the same use of complex types
and a typical example of a line with excessive
alliteration is given on p. 192. The use of purely
ornamental alliteration is an important link between
the *Gawayn* poems and *St. Erkenwald.*

Fourthly, the percentage of lines of the *aaa/a(a)*
type is high, as in the other poems, being 17 per cent.
No other poem has so high a percentage, and the one
immediately below it is *Pur.* with 15 per cent.

In the use of alliterative types there is therefore
a remarkable similarity.

(b) *The Rhythm.*—Under this heading must be mentioned
the high percentage of extended half-lines, and
the same use of the types: $\times // \times \times \times \times / \times$,
$\times / \times \times \times \times \times // \times$, $// \times \times \times \times /$, and $// \times \times \times \times$.

Hence, as far as we can judge, there is no
difference in the rhythm of the four poems, but a
close similarity not found in any other alliterative
poem of the fourteenth century.

(c) *Violations of the natural stress for the sake of alliteration*
are just as common as in the other three poems.
They are marked and deliberate, and especially
common in the case of the unstressed verbal prefix.

(d) *Vocalic Alliteration.*—*St. Erkenwald* has only 1·43 per
cent. of its lines with vocalic alliteration, but two
considerations have to be borne in mind, the first
of which is the shortness of the poem, so that the
percentage may be largely a matter of accident;
the second is the more important fact that in this
poem, as in the other three, there are in addition
many examples of *h* alliterating with vowels. The
total number of instances in which this occurs is
11, i.e. over 3 per cent. of the lines. This is a very
important point of similarity between the *Gawayn*
poems and *St. Erkenwald.* In the latter poem there
is only one example of 3 of the vowels alliterating
together being identical, and two of 2 being identical,

which is proportionately the same as in the other three poems.

(e) *In respect of alliterative groups* there is similar treatment. *Sp, st, sk* are practically always consistent groups, but *sch* is not usually a group. The poet is, however, careless regarding the remaining groups.

(f) *Grouping of Lines by Identical Alliteration.*—The first method of linking of consecutive lines by identical alliteration is found in 16 " twos," which is roughly the same percentage as that in *Gaw.*

The alternative method is found in 4·5 per cent. of the lines, which is approximately the same percentage as in the other three poems.

(g) Lastly, there is the quatrain arrangement found in this poem as in *Pur.* and *Pat.*, and though the marginal marks are not found in the MS., it is possible that the original one had them.

When the metrical evidence is considered in conjunction with the evidence afforded by other points, such as the style, vocabulary, phraseology, and similar passages, it seems probable that the theory of Horstmann, which was accepted by Trautmann, Knigge, Luick, Brandl, Osgood and Gollancz, is correct.

7. It has been suggested that **The Destruction of Troy** and **The Wars of Alexander** may possibly have been written by the same author. S. O. Andrew has, however, recently pointed out important differences of style between the two poems.[1]

The metrical evidence is wholly against the theory of common authorship. A glance at the important points of difference will be sufficient.

1. The *aa/ax* type is found in 99·9 per cent. of the lines in *The Destruction of Troy*, but only in 86·61 per cent. of the lines in *The Wars of Alexander*.

   The *aaa/ax* type is found in 578/5803 lines of *The Wars of Alexander*, but only in 23/14,044 lines of *The Destruction of Troy*, and it is doubtful whether any of the latter have three stresses in the first half-line.

[1] *The Wars of Alexander and the Destruction of Troy*, S. O. Andrew, Rev. of Eng. Stud., p. 267, 1929.

2. The most important difference regarding the rhythm is the greater frequency of the extended half-lines in *The Wars of Alexander*, 9·66 per cent.

3. In the examples of vocalic alliteration, *The Destruction of Troy* usually has two of the vowels identical, whereas *The Wars of Alexander* has three rather than two (see p. 160).

3. *h* never alliterates with vowels in *The Destruction of Troy*, but several examples can be found in *The Wars of Alexander*.

4. *The Destruction of Troy* has very few examples of consecutive lines linked by identical alliteration, but *The Wars of Alexander* has numerous examples in the first 200 lines, though after that the device becomes extremely rare.

These are important differences for which it would be difficult to account if the two poems were by the same author. It has likewise been suggested that *The Wars of Alexander* may have been written by the author of *Morte Arthure*, but such a theory is untenable even when judged solely on the metrical evidence. The most important characteristic of the metre of *Morte Arthure* is the excessive grouping together of consecutive lines by identical alliteration ; on one occasion ten successive lines alliterate on *f*. Such grouping is rare in *The Wars of Alexander*. Also the author of *Morte Arthure* tends to alliterate unidentical vowels, which is contrary to the practice of the author of *The Wars of Alexander*.

It is equally impossible that *Morte Arthure* was written by the author of *The Destruction of Troy*, for in the latter poem there is no such grouping as in the case of *Morte Arthure*.

8. Death and Life, and **Scottish Field.**—These two late alliterative poems were ascribed to the same author, but as previously stated, Hanford and Steadman in their new edition of the former poem have shown that such a theory is no longer tenable. A few metrical points may, however, be given to corroborate their views.

1. The *aa/ax* type is found in 74·7 per cent. of the lines of *Death and Life*, but only in 65·64 per cent. of those of *Scottish Field*.

Secondly, the *aaa/a(a)* type is found in 10·8 per cent. of the lines of *Death and Life*, but only in 7·2 per cent. of those of *Scottish Field*.

Thirdly, the complex types are not apparently found in *Death and Life*, but are occasionally found in *Scottish Field*.

2. The alternative method of grouping consecutive lines together is only found in 2 per cent. of the lines of *Scottish Field*, but in 4·5 per cent. of those of *Death and Life*.

3. The amount of vocalic alliteration actually used is similar, but in *Death and Life* the tendency is to alliterate on different vowels, whereas in *Scottish Field* the reverse is true.

There are many other minor points of difference which also demonstrate that the two poems were not written by a single author.

APPENDIX 2.

THE LOCALITY OF THE GREEN KNIGHT'S CASTLE AND CHAPEL.

Sir Gawayn and the Green Knight is one of the few alliterative works which contain local references which appear to be genuine.

In l. 698 the hero, Sir Gawayn, is described as passing into North Wales, leaving on his left the isles of Anglesey, presumably Anglesey, Holy Island, and Puffin Island. " The fords by the promontories at the Holy Head " are still unidentified, though as Tolkien and Gordon have suggested, these may refer to the crossing of the river Conway or of the river Clwyd near Foryd. We are then told that Sir Gawayn passed into the wilderness of the Wirral, and the author's description of the latter place seems to reveal a certain acquaintance with the district. A journey of some distance is then indicated, but not necessarily as far north as Cumberland. Nor is it necessary to resort to the latter country for scenery such as is described in the poem.

In our dialectal investigations we have gathered certain evidence which indicates that the poem was written not far from the Pennine Chain, probably near the Ribble Valley, so that it is not unreasonable to enquire whether there be any existing castle in the locality which might fit the description of Bercilak's castle.

Any castle which might be considered must date back to at least the fourteenth century. The only castle of importance in this locality at that period was the one at Clitheroe near the Ribble.

Though the castle is in ruins, much may be learned from a study of the site and of the actual remains. The elaborate architectural features which are described in the poem are, needless to say, no longer existent. Indeed, it may be doubted whether all the features which are described so carefully could actually have existed in any one castle of that period, since many of them were the most recent fashions in architectural design. At the same time the author doubtless had in mind some actual castle, which served as a nucleus around which he could build this ideal castle.

Certain features bear a striking resemblance to those in the poem. The castle is similarly situated on a high hill, surrounded with many trees and a vast park. From the keep of Clitheroe Castle it is possible to survey the country for two or three miles to the south, but the castle itself is still surrounded with many trees, and stands on an isolated limestone hill. An adequate description of the remaining keep, the square tower, the bailey, and outer wall, may be found in the Victoria History of Lancashire, vol. 2, p. 523, and vol. 6, p. 362. It is interesting to observe that the castle contained the extra-parochial chapel of St. Michael, which was maintained until the Civil Wars.

The owner of the castle in the poem must have possessed extensive facilities for hunting in the neighbourhood, and it is significant that the forest lands annexed to Clitheroe Castle were the most extensive in the north of England, and included the forests of Pendle (12,962 acres), Trawden (6,808 acres), Rossendale (22,000), and Bowland (25,247 acres). These lands have been described as the last retreat of the wolf and wild boar.

Clitheroe Castle was probably built in the late eleventh century, and belonged to the Lacy family. Edmund de Lacy, a friend of Edward I., died in 1310, leaving a daughter Alice, who married Thomas Plantagenet, Earl of Lancaster, who was beheaded by Edward II. in 1321. Thus the honor became united to the earldom of Lancaster. In 1327 life tenure was granted to Queen Isabella, but before her death the Duke of Lancaster succeeded to the honor of Clitheroe and the hundred of Lancaster by virtue of entail. In 1360, his son, John of Gaunt, succeeded to them, holding them until his death in 1398. Hence at the time of the composition of the poem Clitheroe Castle belonged to John of Gaunt.

It will be recalled that there recently appeared an article entitled *The Pearl and its Jeweller*.[1] In the first part of this article the writers endeavour to prove that ' Pearl ' was the grand-daughter of Edward III. On p. 108 they state: "*The Pearl* is an elegy written on the death of Margaret, grand-daughter of Edward III., not by her father but by some-one closely connected with her father and the court, and (possibly as guardian) with the little girl herself. This would explain the unfilial, unpaternal language, the epithets (such as *ryal*) used in descriptions, and since the earldom of the girl's father was Pembroke, the use of a western dialect by the poet, who, even though born in Wales, might well have employed West Midland English." The general argument is convincing, and it seems highly probable that the identification of Pearl is correct, but it is hardly necessary to point out that " West Midland English " was not a uniform dialect spoken throughout the west of England. The author of *Pearl* and *Sir Gawayn and the Green Knight* was surely writing in a local dialect for local people, though he may have been to court, a place which was not, however, his usual abode. The writers of the article suggest the possibility that a certain John Prat, the King's minstrel, was the child's guardian, and author of *Pearl* and *Sir Gawayn*.

The author of *Pearl*, though grieved at the death of the little girl, may nevertheless have written the poem by command. He may have been some one closely associated with Clitheroe Castle, since it can scarcely be doubted that *Pearl* and *Sir Gawayn* are by one author. Margaret died in 1369, and *Pearl* may have been written in that year. It is likewise possible that *Sir Gawayn* may have been written for an occasion, and there are indications that the poem is con-nected with the Order of the Garter, which was itself founded in 1346, a date too early, however, to have been the occasion

---

[1] Oscar Cargill and Margaret Schlauch, Pub. Mod. Lang. Ass. of America, vol. 43, p. 105, 1928.

of the poem. It is, nevertheless, significant that John of Gaunt, the uncle of Margaret, was admitted to the Order in 1370. Is it not possible that the poem was written to celebrate this occasion ?

Lastly, there are certain clues to the situation of the chapel of the Green Knight. In l. 1078 we learn that the chapel was not more than two miles away from the castle, and the description of the journey to it begins in l. 2077. There were banks, cliffs, brooks, and a wood, until a high hill was reached. If the castle were Clitheroe, the knight would obviously go north, in the opposite direction to the route by which he arrived at the castle. Going in that direction, he would approach Salt Hill, having the lofty Pendle Hill on his right. Then he would be forced to cross the brook before reaching Greenhow and Warsaw Hill, which overlook the village of Downham. On the right is the village of Worston and Angram Green. Greenhow may be the high hill mentioned in l. 2087. The *rake* which is then referred to may have been the ancient path along Downham Green, which leads over Downham Hill. The lower stages of this path are known as *Green Lane*. The path brings us to Downham Mill and Mill Wood, which belonged to the honor of Clitheroe in the fourteenth century. The present mill occupies the site of an ancient mill, which in the fourteenth century was worth 26s. a year ;[1] the mill is situated on Ings Beck, which in winter-time is a very turbulent stream and might answer the description in l. 2174 of the poem. Ll. 2202-3 mention a *gryndelston and water at a mulne*.

From the description in the poem, it is not easy to make out the exact situation, though it may have been that the Green Knight was on the bank at the mill, and that the old cave around which Sir Gawayn went was over the stream. There are plenty of rocks, barrows, and overhanging crags, but no trace of the cave is surviving. The ancient mill may have been on the other side of the bank in former days. The construction of the modern mill and farm would have led to the inevitable removal of the peculiar mound. The watercourse is broad and the Green Knight would need his axe to assist him to hop over, as is indicated in l. 2232.

The general features of the place fit the description in the

[1] The Vict. Hist. of Lancs, vol. 6, p. 553.

poem, though it is probable that the imaginative poet may
have elaborated the scene and made it more *wysty* than it
really was.   At the same time local people might recognise
Downham Mill near Downham Green, where superstitions
concerning a green knight and " *the devil saying his matins
about midnight* " may have been prevalent.

It has been suggested that *Pearl* and *Sir Gawayn and the
Green Knight* were written by command.   The poem *St.
Erkenwald*, which was itself a poem written for an occasion,
is probably the work of the same man.[1]   It seems not unlikely
that the author of the three works may have written them
all by command ; and there is some evidence to suggest that
he was connected with John of Gaunt's household and the
castle at Clitheroe.

APPENDIX 3.

The Scribes of the Poems of the Cotton MS. Nero A. X.

On pages 84-5 were enumerated certain features found in the
poems of the Cotton MS. Nero A. X., which may be scribal.
These fourteen points are not found in each of the four poems,
but a given feature may only occur in one of the poems.   In
addition there were enumerated seven other features which
can be proved to have been scribal.   These cases of scribal
alteration may not all be due to one scribe, for each of the
poems may have passed through several copies.

The Cotton MS. Nero A. X. is full of scribal errors, but
as we have already seen, they are usually non-dialectal.   These
errors have been classified by Sir Israel Gollancz on p. 40 of
his edition of the facsimile of the MS.,[2] in which he divides the
errors into 23 classes with many subdivisions.   The editor
only gives selected examples, a fact which must be borne in
mind when drawing conclusions from his statistics.   It has,
therefore, been necessary to collect *all* the scribal errors.

Examining the occurrences of the 21 linguistic points and
of the 23 types of error, we discover that they arrange themselves into groups in the following manner :—

[1] See p. 253.   [2] E.E.T.S., 162.

1. Features occurring in all poems.
2. Features occurring only in *Pearl*.
3. Features occurring only in *Sir Gawayn and the Green Knight*.
4. Features occurring only in *Purity*.
[5. No features occurring only in *Patience*.]
6. Features occurring in *Sir Gawayn and the Green Knight* and *Pearl*.
7. Features occurring in *Sir Gawayn and the Green Knight*, *Purity*, and *Pearl*.
8. Three features occurring in *Sir Gawayn and the Green Knight* and *Purity*.
9. Two features occurring in *Sir Gawayn and the Green Knight*, *Purity*, and *Patience*.
10. One feature occurring in *Sir Gawayn and the Green Knight*, *Patience*, and *Pearl*.
11. One feature occurring in *Purity* and *Pearl*.

The last four groups are not important and will be disposed of later. If we neglect them for the moment, we might suggest that each of the four poems was copied by à different scribe, that subsequently *Pearl* and *Sir Gawayn and the Green Knight* were recopied by a fifth scribe, that a sixth scribe recopied the last two poems and added *Purity*, and finally that a seventh scribe gathered the four poems together.

This theory is supported by the results obtained from working out the proportion of errors in the text of each poem.

1. *Patience* has 31 errors in 531 lines, i.e. 1 error in 18 lines.
2. *Purity* has 165 errors in 1812 lines, i.e. 1 error in 11 lines.
3. *Sir Gawayn and the Green Knight* has 178 errors in 2025 long lines and 505 short lines, which we may reckon as 250 long ones, making a total of 178 errors in 2275 lines, i.e. 1 error in 13 lines.
4. *Pearl* has 170 errors in 1212 lines, which are roughly equivalent to 808 long lines, i.e. 1 error in 5 lines.

This would seem to suggest that *Pearl* and *Sir Gawayn and the Green Knight* are relatively in a more corrupt state than the other two poems, and have therefore passed through more hands.

Let us now dispose of the features in sections 8 to 11 above, which seem to upset the proposed scheme.

AUTHOR'S COPY OF PATI[ENCE]
copied by **SCRIBE A.**, who pro[...]
made a faithful transcript o[...]
author's copy.

PEARL,
o belonged
area, and
, probably
few '-lich '
ut the few
e any. He
in a line
eviation of
the wrong
may have
pronoun *at*

of *Pearl*,
lings to *qu*.
pellings for
one in the

SCRIBE F, who[...]
was very perplexed
abbreviation 4 tim[...]
different word 7 ti[...]
for the two instance[...]

ive times ;
lacing the
stituting a
responsible
r Gawayn.

SCRIBE G, who copied **F**'s c[...]
very careless indeed, adding 20 [...]
stressed word 20 times ; substi[...]
wrote similar letters 46 times ; [...]
8 times, just as he doubled unstr[...]
r in the combinations *tr*, *er*, *re* 11[...]
é and *ie* still more complicated ; [...]
forms for the poet's rare doublets[...]
ings of the spirant, for the few i[...]
forms of all origins to *ow*, and m[...]

, and was
small un-
mes ; mis-
l syllables
; omitted
-*y* for Fr.
e common
gh ' spell-
poet's *aw*

Note.—The scribal errors assig[...]
some of the minor errors occurrin[...]
nevertheless extremely careless.
It is not impossible that the [...]
The former would be responsible [...]
more northernly area. Scribe [...]

However,
scribe was
scribe *H*.
me from a

8. Three features in *Sir Gawayn* and *Purity* only :+—

   (*a*) There are 8 '-us ' spellings, but these are extremely
        rare and may have come from the original western
        copy.

   (*b*) The pronoun *hom* occurs once in *Purity*, but the
        reading is very doubtful.   In *Sir Gawayn*, how-
        ever, the form occurs 8 times.

   (*c*) The loss of an initial consonant 5 times is surely
        a scribal error, likely to be made by any careless
        scribe.

9. Two features in *Sir Gawayn, Purity,* and *Patience* only :—

   (*a*) The pronoun *hores* occurs in *Patience* twice, and the
        form *hor* in *Purity* once, and in *Sir Gawayn* 18
        times.   The scribe who copied *Sir Gawayn* was
        obviously responsible for the *hor* forms in that
        poem.   The forms in the other two poems may
        have survived from the original western copy.

   (*b*) The absence of '-lich ' forms in *Pearl* may be due
        to the scribe who copied that poem, since it is
        highly probable that the poet used a few '-lich '
        forms.

10. One feature in *Sir Gawayn, Patience,* and *Pearl :*—

    There are 8 examples of short syllables doubled :   e.g.
        nonoper.   This error is almost identical with the
        repetition of an unstressed word, an error found
        in all four poems.

11. One feature in *Purity* and *Pearl :*—

    The ' i-' verbal prefix is retained once in each poem.
        A feature of such rare occurrence may be due
        to the scribe who copied *Sir Gawayn, Purity,*
        and *Pearl.*

Hence there is no need to presuppose additional scribes
to account for these minor points.   The seven scribes we have
previously postulated are sufficient to account for all the errors
which are found in the final MS.   We may represent these
errors in the form of a table.[1]

---

[1] The scribal errors in the rhymes of *Sir Gawayn* and *Pearl* are examined by O. F. Emerson in *Some Imperfect Lines in Pearl and Gawain,*
Mod. Phil., xix. p. 131.

BIBLIOGRAPHY.

EDITIONS.

THE best and most recent edition of each of the alliterative poems has been given in Part I. as the works first appeared ; in those cases where older editions are still of considerable value, these are also enumerated.

LANGUAGE AND DIALECT.

Articles and dissertations of little importance are mentioned in the text itself and are not recorded here.

H. Bateson, *Patience*, " Dialect," pp. xxxii-xxxvii, Manchester, 1915.
E. Björkman, *Zur dialektischen Provenienz der 'nordischen Lehnwörter im Englischen*, Halle, 1900.
E. Björkman, *Scandinavian Loan Words in Middle-English*, Halle, 1900-2.
A. Brandl, " Zur Geographie der Altenglischen Dialekte," *Abhandlungen der Konigl. Preuss. Akad. der Wissensch., Phil. Hist. Klasse*, Nr. 4, pp. 1-77, 1915.
M. Day, " The Weak Verb in Sir Gawain," *Mod. Lang. Rev.*, vol. 14, pp. 413-15, 1919.
E. Ekwall, " Contributions to the History of O.E. Dialects," *Lund Universitetet*, vol. 12, 1917.
E. Ekwall, " Ortsnamenforschung ein Hilfsmittel für das engl. Sprachgeschichte-Studium," *Germ. Rom. Monats.*, 1913, pp. 592-608.
E. Ekwall, *Scandinavians and Celts in the North-West of England*, Lund, 1918.
W. Fick, *Zum Mittelenglischen Gedicht von der Perle*, Kiel, 1885.
I. Gollancz, *Facsimile of the Cotton MS., Nero A. X.*, E.E.T.S., 162, 1923.
J. Hall, *Early Middle English*, Part 2, Notes, Oxford, 1920.
J. R. Hulbert, " The West-Midland of the Romances," *Mod. Phil.*, xix., p. 131, 1921.
R. Jordan, " Mittelenglischen Mundarten," *Germ. Rom. Monats.*, 2, p. 130, 1910.
R. Jordan, *Handbuch der Mittelenglischen Grammatik*, Heidelberg, 1925.
A. Knigge, *Die Sprache des Dichters von Sir Gawain, etc.*, Marburg, 1885.
H. Luick, *Historische Grammatik der Englischen Sprache*, Leipzig, 1914.
R. J. Menner, " Sir Gawayn and the Green Knight," *Pub. Mod. Lang. Ass. of America*, vol. 37, p. 503, 1922.
R. J. Menner, *Purity*, " Language and Dialect," pp. lviii-lxii, Yale, 1920.
L. Morsbach, *Mittelenglische Grammatik*, Halle, 1895.

A. Noreen, *Altnordische Grammatik*, Halle, 1903-4.

A. Pogatscher, " O.E. æ/ē," *Anglia*, 34, p. 302, 1901.

P. H. Reaney, " The Dialect of London in the 12th and 13th centuries,"
Eng. Stud., vol. 59, p. 321, and vol. 61, p. 9, 1925-26.

O. Ritter, " O.E. æ/ē," *Anglia*, 37, p. 269, 1913.

E. Schwahn, *Die Conjugation in Sir Gawayne, etc.*, Strassburg, 1884.

M. S. Serjeantson, " The Dialects of the West Midlands," *Rev. of Eng.
Studies*, vol. 3, Nos. 9, 10, 11, 1927.

M. S. Serjeantson, " Dialectal Distribution of Certain Phonological
Features in Middle English," *English Studies*, vol. 4, p. 231, 1922.

M. S. Serjeantson, " The Development of O.E. ēag, ēah in Middle
English," *Journal of English and Germanic Philology*, vol. 26,
pp. 198 and 350, 1927.

K. Sisam, " The Language of the Fourteenth Century," *Fourteenth
Century Verse and Prose*, p. 265, Oxford, 1921.

J. R. Tolkien and E. V. Gordon, *Sir Gawain and the Green Knight*,
pp. xxii-xxiv, and pp. 122-32, Oxford, 1925.

M. Trautmann, *Über verfasser und entstehungszeit einiger alliterirender
gedichte des altenglischen*, Halle, 1876.

A. Wall, " The Scandinavian Element in English Dialects," *Anglia*, 20,
pp. 45-135, 1898.

H. C. Wyld, *A Short History of English*, London, 1927, 3rd edition.

H. C. Wyld, *A History of Modern Colloquial English*, London, 1920.

H. C. Wyld, " O.E. ȳ in the Dialects of the Midlands," *Eng. Stud.*,
vol. 47, pp. 1-58, 145-66, 1913.

H. C. Wyld, " South-Eastern and South-Midland Dialects in Middle
English," *English Essays and Studies*, vol. 6, pp. 113-45, 1920.

H. C. Wyld, " Linguistic Studies and Place-Names," vol. 1, p. 133,
Place-name Society, Cambridge, 1924.

METRE.

F. J. Amours, " Scottish Alliterative Poems," p. lxxxv. of vol. 27,
Scottish Text Society, 1897.

E. Björkman, *Morte Arthure*, pp. xxiv-xxvi, "Metrik," Heidelberg, 1915.

R. Buchholz, " Die Fragmente der Reden der Seele an den Leichnam,
Metrik des Textes von Worcester," p. lxii, *Erlanger Beiträge*,
2, 6, 1890.

The Cambridge History of English Literature, vol. 1, chapter xviii.

M. Deutschbein, *Zur Entwicklung des Englischen Alliterationsverses*,
Halle, 1902.

J. Fischer, " Die Stabende Langzeile in den Werken des Gawain-
dichters," *Bonner Beiträge zur Anglistik*, 2, pp. 1-64, Bonn, 1901.

J. Fuhrmann, *Die Alliterierenden Sprachformeln in Morris' Early
English Alliterative Poems und in Sir Gawayne and the Green
Knight*, Hamburg, 1886.

J. Hall, *Layamon's Brut*, pp. xv-xix, " Prosody," Oxford, 1924.

J. Hall, *Early Middle English*, vol. 2, notes, Oxford, 1920.

J. Hanford and J. M. Steadman, " Death and Life," p. 255, *Stud. in
Phil.*, xv, 1918.

M. Kaluza, *A History of English Versification*, London, 1911.

M. Kaluza, " Strophische Gliederung in der Mittelenglischen rein
    alliterierenden Dichtung," *Eng. Stud.*, vol. 16, pp. 169-80, 1891.
B. Kuhnke, " Die alliterierenden Langzeile in der mittelenglischen
    ↓Romanze Sir Gawayn and the Green Knight," *Studien zum Ger-
    manischen Alliterationsvers*, vol. 4, Berlin, 1900.
J. Lawrence, *Chapters on Alliterative Verse*, London, 1893.
W. E. Leonard, " Scansion of Middle English Alliterative Verse,"
    University of Wisconsin Studies in Language and Literature, 2, 1920.
K. Luick, " Die Englische Stabreimzeile im XIV., XV., und XVI. Jahr-
    hundert," *Anglia*, 2, pp. 392-443, 553-618, 1880.
K. Luick, " Zur Metrik der mittelenglischen Reimenalliterierenden
    Dichtung," *Anglia*, 12, p. 437, 1889.
R. J. Menner, *Purity*, p. liii, " Metre and Alliteration," Yale, 1920.
L. Pilch, *Umwandlung des Ae. Allit. Verses in den Me. Reimvers*,
    Königsberg, 1904.
J. W. Rankin, " Rhythm and Rhyme before the Norman Conquest,"
    Pubs. Mod. Lang. Ass. of America, vol. 36, p. 401, 1921.
K. Regel, " Die Alliteration in Lajamon," *Germanistiche Studien*,
    1, 171, Wien, 1872.
F. Rosenthal, " Die Alliterierende Englische Langzeile im 14 Jahr-
    hundert," *Anglia*, 1, pp. 414-59, 1878.
L. Savage, *St. Erkenwald*, " Metre and Alliteration," p. xliii, Yale, 1926.
J. Schipper, *Englische Metrik,* Bonn, 1881.
J. Schipper, *Grundriss der Englischen Metrik*, Wien, 1905.
J. Schipper, *A History of English Versification*, Oxförd, 1910.
K. Schumacher, " Studien über den Stabreim in der Mittelenglischen
    Alliterationsdichtung," *Bonner Studien zur Englischen Philologie*,
    vol. 11, Bonn, 1914.
W. J. Sedgefield, *An Anglo-Saxon Verse Book*, pp. 125-130, Manchester,
    1922, and *An Anglo-Saxon Prose Book*, p. 134.
W. Skeat, " Essay on Alliterative Poetry," *Percy Folio MS.*, vol. 3,
    p. 1, London, 1868.
G. R. Stewart, " The Metre of Piers Plowman," *Pubs. Mod. Lang. Ass.
    of America*, vol. 42, pp. 113-28, 1927.
J. S. P. Tatlock, " Laȝamon's Poetic Style and its Relations," *The
    Manly Anniversary Studies*, p. 3, Chicago, 1923.
J. Thomas, *Die Alliterierende Langzeile des Gawayn-Dichters*, Coburg,
    1908.
J. R. Tolkien and E. V. Gordon, *Sir Gawain and the Green Knight*,
    pp. 118-20, Oxford, 1925.
M. Trautmann, " Zur Kenntniss und Geschichte der Mittelenglischen
    Stabzeile," *Anglia*, 18, pp. 83-100, 1896.

LIST OF TEXTS EXAMINED.

THE following is a list of the works examined, seventy-one in all, with the pages of this book on which a study of their dialect and metre may be found ; the first reference in each case is to the dialect, other references being to the metre.

GENERAL INDEX.

ADDENDUM.

A new edition of *Alexander A* and *B*, by Prof. F. P. Magoun, was published in 1929, too late to be considered in the present volume. The author cites two metrical features (visual alliteration and the alliteration of consonantal groups) which, because of their *differing* frequency in one poem as compared with the other, lead him to reject the theory of common authorship. To this we may reply that the poet might have improved his technique in the interim (which the present writer believes to be the case), and that the points of similarity mentioned on pp. 247-248 above afford *positive* rather than *negative* evidence in support of the theory of common authorship.

ALLITERATIVE POETRY IN MIDDLE ENGLISH

A SURVEY OF THE TRADITIONS

ALLITERATIVE POETRY
IN MIDDLE ENGLISH

A SURVEY OF THE TRADITIONS

BY

J. P. OAKDEN

WITH ASSISTANCE FROM

ELIZABETH R. INNES

"But whanne we meuen our mynde mirþe to here,
We raiken to oure romauncus and reden þe storrius
þat oure eldrene on erþe or þis time wroute."
Alexander and Dindimus, 466–468.

FOREWORD.

THIS companion volume to the author's earlier work is offered as a further contribution towards the study of that important group of alliterative works in Middle English which never fails to interest the student of our early literature, for when we have located the poems dialectally so far as our present state of knowledge enables us, we have only reached the fringe of the vast subject which opens before us. The study of the metre might well have been included under the sub-title of the present volume, for it demonstrated the existence of a continuous metrical tradition from the earliest times. The reader is therefore asked to bear in mind this section of the former volume and the resultant conclusions, when studying this work.

The heart of the volume will be found in Chapter 5, which some may prefer to read first. In that chapter, which takes the place of the customary introduction, the results of many years' study have been gathered together into a comprehensive whole. In the first four chapters an attempt has been made to survey the literary worth and historical value of the various alliterative poems which for that purpose are treated in what is approximately their chronological order within the various literary categories. In this section the needs of the student who may have little first-hand acquaintance with many of the alliterative poems have constantly been borne in mind, and the indulgence of the scholar is craved for dealing with some points which may seem to him trivial. Yet it is important to examine critically the works of the school as a whole, if we are to view the Alliterative Revival in its right perspective.

The study of the vocabulary, phraseology and style is fairly exhaustive in its treatment, and there is no need to anticipate the results at this stage. Throughout there has been an endeavour to treat the material from the historical point of view. The importance of this in regard to the vocabulary is obvious enough, but the study of Old English phraseology has proved well worth while, for it has shown the continuity of the alliterative tradition even in small points. It is hoped that the lists of phrases may be felt by some to have an intrinsic value of their own apart from the important conclusions which are drawn in the several introductory paragraphs. Lack of space must account for the suppression of much material, especially in the vocabulary, which the author would have preferred to include. If something is gained by the resultant arrangement, there need, however, be no regrets. Of the many loose ends which inevitably remain, some, it is hoped, will be dealt with in article form at a later date.

It is a pleasure to be able to express my sincere thanks to the following for their assistance at some period in the preparation of this work : Dr. Allen Mawer, who so far back as 1929 guided me in drawing up a scheme of study and suggested lines of enquiry which proved most fruitful ; Dr. O. K. Schram, for friendly advice when I was in Liverpool ; Professor Wyld, for permission to quote from his article on *Laȝamon ;* Dr. Mabel Day, for granting access to the text of *Mum & Sothsegger*, without which this work would have been most incomplete ; Miss E. R. Innes, my former research student, for help with Chapter 8 ; Professor E. V. Gordon, who has kindly read through the typescript and made most helpful suggestions ; the University of Liverpool, for the William Nobel Fellowship which in the first instance made the work possible ; the Carnegie Trustees for the Universities of Scotland, for a most generous grant towards the cost of publication ; and Sir James Irvine, the Principal of the University of St. Andrews, for his kindly interest and help in securing the same ; the Manchester University Press, for undertaking the publication ; Mr. H. M. McKechnie, the Secretary to the Press, for his never-failing help and advice ; and to Miss Mary Campbell, for continuous help with the classification and arrangement of the material.

J. P. O.

Whitsuntide, 1934.

TABLE OF CONTENTS.

The survival of the Old English homiletic, popular and heroic traditions—the importance of Laȝamon's *Brut*—the renewal of poetic vitality and inspiration—the thoroughly English quality of the works of the Revival — the alliterative metre — the dialectal boundaries of the school—the identity of any of the alliterative authors—Huchown—theories of common authorship —the importance of the metrical test, especially in its negative aspect—the problems of dating—the chronological order of composition known with some degree of certainty—the inter-relationship of the alliterative poems—familiarity with London life—the external causes of the rise of the alliterative school— Professor Hulbert's interesting hypothesis—the literary types

b

BIBLIOGRAPHY.

REFERENCES to editions of alliterative poems have already been given in Section I and are not repeated here, and the numerous articles dealing with special problems which have been discussed (such as the theories concerning the interpretation of *Pearl*) are likewise omitted, since the index gives ready access to them. This bibliography is chiefly concerned with dissertations on alliterative phraseology and vocabulary.

Brink, A., *Stab und Wort im Gawain*, 1920.

McClumpha, C. F., *The Alliteration of Chaucer* (undated), Leipzig.

Ellinger, J., " Zur Alliteration in der modernen eng. Prosa-dichtung," *Eng. Stud.*, vol. 19, pp. 360-80, 1894.

Fuhrman, J., *Die alliterierenden Sprachformeln im Morris' Early English Poems und im Sir Gawayn and the Green Knight*, Kiel diss., 1886.

Gerould, G. H., " Abbot Aelfric's Rhythmic Prose," *Mod. Phil.*, vol. 22, pp. 353-66, 1925.

Gillespy, F. L., *Laȝamon's Brut : a Comparative Study in Narrative*, California, 1916.

Gröger, O., *Die althochdeutsche und altsächsische Kompositionsfuge*, diss., Zürich, 1910.

Heyne, M., *Formulae alliterantes ex antiquis legibus lingua Frisica conscriptis extractae*, Halle, 1864.

Höfer, P., *Alliteration bei Gower*, diss., Leipzig, 1890.

Hoffmann, O., *Reimformeln in Westgermanischen*, diss., Freiburg, 1885.

Lindner, J., " Chaucer's Alliteration," *Jahr für rom. und eng. Sprache und Literatur*, vol. 14, p. 311.

Olszewska, E. S., "Illustrations of Norse Formulas in English," *Leeds Studies in English*, vol. 2, pp. 76-84.

Petzold, E., *Über Alliteration in den Werken Chaucers mit Ausschluss der Canterbury Tales*, Marburg, 1889.

Prick van Wely, F. P. H., " Apt Alliteration's Artful Aid," *Eng. Stud.*, vol. 47, p. 185.

Regal, K., " Die Alliteration im Laȝamon," *Germ. Stud.*, vol. 1, pp. 171-246.

Reiche, C., *Untersuchungen über den Stil der me. allit. Gedichte Morte Arthure, The Destruction of Troy*, etc., Königsberg, 1906.

Schwarz, M., *Alliteration im eng. kulturleben neuerer zeit*, Greifswald, 1921.

Seitz, K., *Zur Alliteration in Neuenglischen*, 1883.

Seitz, K., *Die Alliteration im Englischen vor und bei Shakespeare*, 1875.

Tatlock, J. S. P., "Laȝamon's Poetic Style and its Relations," *The Manly Anniversary Studies*, p. 3, Chicago, 1923.

Tatlock, J. S. P., "Epic Formulas in Laȝamon's *Brut*," *P.M.L.A.*, vol. 38, p. 494.

Willert, H., *Alliter. Bindungen in der ne. Bibelübersetzung*, 1897-8.

Willert, H., *Die alliterierenden Formeln der englischen Sprache*, Halle, 1911.

Wyld, H. C., "Studies in the Diction of Laȝamon's *Brut*: Points of Difference between the Earlier and Later Text," *Language*, vol. 6, p. 1, 1930.

Zeuner, M., *Die Alliteration bei neuenglischen Dichtern*, Halle, 1880.

PART I.

THE POEMS AS LITERATURE.

CHAPTER I.

THE EARLY MIDDLE ENGLISH ALLITERATIVE POETRY.

THE earliest fragments of Middle English alliterative poetry are not distinguished for their literary worth, but are of interest as serving to bridge the gulf between Old and Middle English literature generally. Such works as the *First Worcester Fragment* and the *Death Literature* testify to the continuance of the homiletic tradition, while the proverbs and short satires find parallels in some late Old English verse. These short popular satires of the thirteenth century, though later than the majority of the poems here discussed, have no definite literary connection with the Alliterative Revival, and are rather to be grouped with these early poems since, in a large measure, they continue the same tradition as is found in them.

A DESCRIPTION OF DURHAM,[1] the first extant Middle English alliterative poem, was written by a monastic who remained unaffected by the influences of the new age. The 21 lines yield an interesting description of Durham, strangely reminiscent of several descriptive passages in Old English poetry, especially of *A Woman's Complaint*, and the poem is similarly tinged with a feeling of the transitoriness of all earthly things and the need for reliance upon God. On the purely external side it is as traditional in vocabulary and phraseology as in metre,[2] and as a link with the past it is naturally of exceptional interest.

WENNE, WENNE, WENCHICHENNE,[3] a charm of the Old English type, may be a transcript of an earlier poem, though direct evidence

[1] Edited in *Reliquiæ Antiquæ*, vol. I, p. 159.
[2] See vol. I, p. 136.
[3] Edited by F. Grendon, *The Old English Charms*, Journal of American Folk-lore, p. 105, 1909, revised 1930.

I

of this is lacking. The work is typically Old English in spirit and in form, and like some of its antecedents, abounds in superstition and heathen lore :

> e.g. " He þe legge leaf et heafde,
>   Under fot uolmes, under ueþer earmes,
>   Under earmes clea ". ll. 5–7.

Yet there are differences between this and genuine Old English charms, as Grendon points out : " It is a quaint charm, quite unlike any other in the *A* group ; it lacks the epic passage and heroic style characteristic of the poetic incantations. The prayer includes a series of six similes, whose force rests on sympathy between the respective similes and the desired extinction of the wen." [1]   It is an imaginative and truly poetic poem, written in the traditional metrical form.

Further indication that charms were written till a late period is afforded by the survival of three other poems of a similar type : THE NAMES OF A HARE,[2] a charm equally pagan, is extremely crude in form and execution. The first 10 lines state that when a man meets a hare, he must lay earth on whatever he is carrying and say a prayer in worship of the animal. Then follow 44 lines, consisting of names of the hare, evidently to be recited in order to lay its power. The date of this poem is about 1250.

Two CHARMS FOR TOOTH-ACHE,[3] of the late fourteenth century, are but crude attempts to christianise the same popular stream of superstition. The invocations are now made to the Virgin Mary, St. Katherine, St. Margaret and to other saints, and the atmosphere breathes the mysticism of the school of Richard Rolle, but the poems have little poetic value.

These three non-alliterative charms are thus distinct from the alliterative *Wenne, Wenne, Wenchichenne*, which reflects the genuine Old English poetic tradition ; they are merely a later popular crystallisation of local superstitions.

THE FIRST WORCESTER FRAGMENT [4] is a short poem in which " some English patriot laments the wholesale substitution of foreign prelates for English under William the Conqueror ".[5]   It was

---

[1] *The Old English Charms*, Journal of American Folk-lore, p. 216.

[2] Edited in *Reliquiæ Antiquæ*, vol. 1, p. 133 ; and by A. S. C. Ross in Proc. Leeds Phil. Soc., *Lit. and Hist.*, vol. 3, June, 1935.

[3] Edited in *Yorkshire Writers*, vol. 1, p. 375, and in *Reliquiæ Antiquæ*, vol. 1, p. 126.

[4] Edited by J. Hall, *Early Middle English*, p. 1.

[5] *Ibid.*, p. 224.

evidently written by a monk who yearned for a return to the glories of the time of the Venerable Bede and of Ælfric (Alcuin) ; and in ll. 11–14 he gives a list of English teachers who " lærden ure leodan on englisc ". A study of the phraseology shows that the writer knew nothing of the Old English poetic tradition, but was steeped in the ecclesiastical and homiletic language of the Church.[1]

The importance of this fragment, however, lies in the fact that it offers evidence for the survival of the Old English metrical form without traces of the influence of the older poetic diction.[2]

" THE DEATH LITERATURE."

THE DEPARTING SOUL'S ADDRESS TO THE BODY (Worcester Cathedral MS.) is an important poem in this group of alliterative works dealing with one of the most popular of mediæval themes. In Old English it has two antecedents : *The Speech of the Lost Soul to the Body* and *The Speech of the Saved Soul to the Body*, the former representing the more usual type, that in which the lost soul upbraids the body for the evil deeds which it has committed. The Old English poem is restrained, austere and dignified, and is unaffected by the more material crudities of contemporary continental religious literature. There is also extant a homily by Wulfstan, based on a Latin version.[3]

The Departing Soul's Address to the Body [4] is reminiscent of the Old English *Speech of the Lost Soul to the Body*, and actual dependence on the latter is not impossible. The argument is the same though the atmosphere is notably different. The following similar passages suggest a close affinity between the two works :—

(O.E. poem) : 30, " & þe gebohte blode þy halgan
                & þu me mid þy heardan hungre gebunde
                & gehæftnedest helle witum ".
(M.E. poem) : 139, " swuth deor ðurðe lac licame cristes,
                þurh þære þu wære alesed from helle wite
                and mid his reade blode þat he on ȝeat on rode ".
(O.E. poem) : 33, " Eardode ic þe on innan ; "
(M.E. poem : 124, etc., " þeo hwile ic was innen þe ".

---

[1] See Hall's notes on lines 5 and 16.
[2] Vol. 1, p. 138.   [3] Ed. Napier, 140, 1.
[4] Edited by S. W. Singer, 1845, and by G. Buchholz, *Erlanger Beiträge*, 2, 6, 1890.

Lines 52–56 of the Old English poem correspond very closely to lines 164–81 of the Middle English poem, and lines 57–74 of the Old English poem to lines 186–201 of the Middle English poem.

Hall is probably correct in saying : " Our author may indeed have been acquainted with the Old English version and have drawn thence the leading ideas for his poem. If so, he treated them with much originality, for there is a wide difference between the austere simplicity and concentrated energy of the older composition and his diffuse and picturesque style which reflects the influence of the new literature imported from the Continent." [1] It is this difference in atmosphere that gives us the clue to the weakness of the Middle English poem. The stress on physical horror and the conscious attempt to instil religious fear detract from the value of the composition. The most effective passage in the work is that which describes the fading beauty of the body in the tightly locked chest to which Death alone possesses the key. Yet, while there runs through the poem real feeling, much of the language and phraseology is conventional. The " ubi sunt " formula found in l. 96, *hwar is nu . . . ? ;* l. 98, *hwar beoð nu ?* does not indicate borrowing from Old English poems such as *The Wanderer*, since it was almost universally known at that time, and recurs in many other Middle English poems.

The interesting little fragment, *The Grave*,[2] also bears testimony to the popularity of the theme in the twelfth century. Every important phrase in it can be paralleled in the longer poem, and it is evident that the author borrowed from the older work :—

e.g.   *Gr.* 9, "ðe helewaʒes beoð laʒe, sidwaʒes unheʒe ".
    Dep. 239, "lowe beoð þe helewewes, unheiʒe beoð þe sidwowes".
or   *Gr.* 10, " þe rof bið ibyld þire broste ful neh ".
    Dep. 241, " ðin rof liið on ðin breoste ful nei ".
or   *Gr.* 13, " Dureleas is þæt hus ".
    Dep. 171, " on durelease huse ".
or   *Gr.* 14 and *Dep.* 510, " & deað haueð þe keiʒe ".
or   *Gr.* 16, " þer þu scealt wunien & wormes þe todeled ".
    Dep. 235, " þet þu scoldest mid wurmen wunien in eorþan ".

THE DEATH FRAGMENT [3] is interesting as presenting further evidence of the popularity of the theme, but it is so short and the text so corrupt that the work is of no great value. The following

---

[1] J. Hall, *Early Middle English*, p. 233.
[2] Edited by A. Schroer in *Anglia*, vol. 5, p. 289.
[3] C. Brown, *Thirteenth Century Lyrics*, no. 20, p. 31, *Shroud and Grave*.

parallels between certain of its phrases and others occurring in *The Departing Soul's Address to the Body* will show that the poem is written in the same vein as the preceding works :—

         13, " þenne sait þe soule to þe licam ".

Dep. 87, " þonne bisihð þeo soule sorliche to þen lichame ".

         14, " Wey ! þat ic ever in þe com ".

Dep. 91, " ic wunede inne þe ".

Dep. 486, " walawa ! & wa is me þat ic æfre com to þe ! "

         21, " þu salt in horþe wonien & wormes þe to-cheuen ".

Dep. 254, " þe sculen nu waxen wurmes bisiden ".

These are the only three alliterative poems in Middle English on this theme, but there are other works which demonstrate the popularity of the subject throughout the thirteenth century.

THE DEBATE OF THE BODY AND THE SOUL,[1] a poem of the thirteenth century with much ornamental alliteration, is the first example in English of the *Dialogus inter Corpus et Animam*, i.e. of the Debate-form. In this work the body retorts to the soul, and the ensuing debate is skilfully managed, but there are still further developments from the outlook of the earlier poems. The author is more concerned with Hell than with the grave ; a thousand devils, whose behaviour and aspect are graphically described, appear and apply the usual tortures, but the soul cries out for mercy when it is too late. There are a few phrases which are also found in *The Departing Soul's Address to the Body*, such as—

  9 (Wright's edition), " þow þat were woned to ride heyre on
                     horse in and out ".

Dep. 193, " ne þearft þu næffre onȝean cumen reowliche riden ".

       17, " ȝwere ben þi murðli wedes ? "

Dep. 107, " hwar beoth nu þin wæde ? "

The poem represents the transition from the older treatment of the theme to the later one which is reflected in three other works : *The Signs before Judgment, c.* 1300,[2] *Sinners Beware, c.* 1250,[3] and *Death,* also *c.* 1250,[4] all of which are crude poems of admonition.

It seems likely that the influence of the Continental literature was felt early in the transition period between Old and Middle English, and that there was genuine continuity with the past, though eventually a complete transformation. The study of the

---

[1] Edited by G. Wright, Camden Soc., vol. 16, p. 334, *The Latin Poems of Walter Map.*   [2] Edited E.E.T.S., 49, p. 163.
   [3] *Ibid.*, p. 72.   [4] *Ibid.*, p. 168.

phraseology and vocabulary shows that there was likewise historical continuity with the diction of Old English poetry, but that the influence of Ælfric and Wulfstan was also definitely apparent.

"PROVERBS IN EARLY MIDDLE ENGLISH."

Proverbs were not common in Old English literature, Skeat [1] finding but three, two of which had been taken from the Vulgate direct. Though the majority of Middle English proverbs can be traced to the Bible, the Classical authors, and to the Fathers of the Church, there remain not a few which were probably current in Old English times among the ordinary people, but which never found their way into literature.

Despite the rarity of proverbs in Old English, however, " precepts " were common. Moralising passages are to be found in many poems, and *A Father's Advice* and other gnomic verses afford specially good examples of the stereotyped precept.

THE PROVERBS OF ALFRED [2] contains much religious admonition and popular wisdom as to conduct. The author begins by quoting as his authorities, Alfred and Ælfric (the names are significant), and then passes on to give a eulogy of Christ ; here follow seven stanzas (3–9) of worldly wisdom and advice, stanza 10 returning to the homiletic strain to remind the reader of death and judgment. In stanzas 11–13 the two strains fall together, but stanzas 14–20 are mainly occupied with further worldly wisdom. This latter section is very similar in tone to *The Proverbs of Hendyng*, and is equally bitter. The work consists of " the cautious wisdom of the common people varied by reflections of a higher strain on the favourite mediæval theme of the shortness and uncertainty of life ".

The poem looks back, however, not so much to the Old English poetry as to the late homiletic literature and to the popular literature of the type discussed in vol. 1, p. 134, a type which for obvious reasons did not appear in writing until the late Chronicle fragments. In Part III we shall see that this is borne out by a study of the phrases. The number of otiose " tags " used, such as *vppen eorþe, buen eorþe,* is remarkable. There is also much padding, and all the elements of popular poetry are found. An interesting stylistic feature is the presence of a sort of kenning :—

[1] *Early English Proverbs*, W. Skeat, Oxford, 1910.
[2] Edited by J. Hall, *Early Middle English*, p. 18.

e.g. 6, "Ealured, englene hurde"; 7, "Ealured engelene durlyng";[1]
19, "Ealured, englene frouer"; 37, " Ealured, englene urouer ";
27, "Crist, louerd of lyf"; 118 (Dryhten), "doweþes louerd";
etc.[2]

Such a feature can hardly have been inherited from the Old English
poetry. The ascription of the proverbs to Alfred is significant, for
he was certainly in no sense responsible for any portion of the work
as we now have it. Possibly some of the worldly wisdom may have
originated with him, but the majority of the precepts and some of
the proverbs are evidently derived from popular lore. The ascription to Alfred, however, indicates that the work is representative
of the older streams of influence; he is still the popular hero.
The Proverbs ascribed to Hendyng mark a new age when Alfred's
popularity has waned.

MEMENTO MORI,[3] a short piece of admonition, was inspired by
stanzas 10 and 21 of The Proverbs of Alfred, from which are
borrowed many of its ideas and phrases. It is significant that
there is more religious moralising than worldly wisdom, and there
is an interesting reference to feasting in the hall :

" nys king ne quene þat ne schal drynke of deþes drench ;
mon er þu falle of þi bench, þyne sunne þu aquench ".

The phrases are mostly derived from the homilies of the Church,
which is not surprising when we consider that the work was written
by an ecclesiastic.[4]

THE PROVERBS OF HENDYNG [5] is a much later work, dated
c. 1250, and the ascription to Hendyng rather than to Alfred is an
indication of the decline of the latter's popularity. The poem is
more artistic than The Proverbs of Alfred, the argument being less
disconnected and the language less ornate. The tone of the poem
is sometimes thought to be more worldly and bitter than that of
the earlier collection, but both seem equally caustic.

There are two kennings : Ihesu crist, al folkes red and Ihesu
crist, heuene kyng, but these are clearly unimportant. The proverbs
and precepts quoted are often alliterative in form, but the writer's

---

[1] Laȝamon has englelondes deorling, 6316 ; also Bruttene . . . Irisce
. . . monnen deorling, etc.
[2] Cp. duguþa Dryhten, Elene 81, Crist 782, Andreas 698. The Ureison
of oure Louerde has englene quene and lifes louerd.
[3] Edited by J. Hall, Early Middle English, p. 29.
[4] For parallels see Hall, pp. 310-11.
[5] Edited Reliquiæ Antiquæ, vol. 1, 109.

discontent with the past is seen in the fact that his poem is written in rhymed stanzas and not in alliterative measures ; ornamental alliteration is almost entirely due to the presence of certain traditional expressions and phrases such as : *gredy is the godles, weder after wille, treye and tene, wit and wisdom,* etc. Three of the proverbs have been taken directly from the earlier collection and four others in a modified form. The collection is of great interest in showing the changes which had taken place in popular writings of this type. .

THE ABC OF ARISTOTLE may be conveniently discussed at this point, for though later in composition it falls within the same category. It is a collection of wise saws, one for each letter of the alphabet. The change of title is again significant, for the ascription to Aristotle reflects the anti-traditional feeling already found in *The Proverbs of Hendyng.*

There are two versions of the *ABC*,[1] the first definitely pagan and worldly, the second Christian ; " as contrasted with the first version which urges pagan and worldly virtue, the second version urges especially Christian notions, with less stress on temperance and more reliance on devotion to God and Christian conduct ".[2] It is an interesting fact that in the first version the traditional and popular sentiments found in the earlier collections of proverbs also occur here ; and the fact that the poem is written in the alliterative form, suggests that in the fourteenth century precepts were still popular among the ordinary people in an alliterative form or jingle. The poem has clearly no connection with the " Alliterative Revival " of the West at the same period.

Proverbial literature in Middle English literature is thus usually written in an alliterative form, though isolated proverbs are found in many works, as pointed out by Skeat in his collection, to which we have already referred. It is surprising that Laʒamon's *Brut* should have but twelve examples, whereas of Chaucer, Skeat writes : [3] " The proverbs quoted by Chaucer out-number all the preceding ones in the present collection, which gives all such as can be readily found in the works of his predecessors and contemporaries ". It remains significant that in Middle English times popular lore and superstition have been crystallised for us in alliterative verse.

[1] For details of editions see vol. i, p. 93.
[2] J. E. Wells, *A Manual of M.E. Writings,* p. 382.
[3] Skeat, *op. cit.,* p. 57.

" THE PHYSIOLOGUS LITERATURE."

The Middle English BESTIARY,[1] written about the middle of the thirteenth century, is a translation of Tebaldus' Latin *Bestiary*. The Old English *Physiologus*, which consists merely of the Panther, Whale and Partridge, was obviously unknown to the Middle English writer, whose work is wholly removed from Old English poetry, both in spirit and in outlook.   The translation from the Latin was made into the homiletic language of the Church, and the phraseology can be paralleled in the Vulgate and in the Old and early Middle English homilies.   The vocabulary is not archaic and poetic, but like that of *The Owl and the Nightingale* is notable for its many local and conversational words.

Regarding the style two points are especially worthy of mention, the first being the abundant use of similes, a feature in itself contrary to Old English poetic style.   These similes are mostly of a commonplace type, such as the following :—

> ll. 540–1, " ðanne remen he all a rem,
> so hornes blast oðer belles drem ".

The whole conception of a Bestiary is a comparison in the form of a simile ; some religious person, idea or force is likened to an animal or bird.   Unfortunately, too often would it seem that the writer started from the *Signification* and worked backwards to the *Nature* (of the animal), and in so doing was led to ascribe to the animal certain characteristics which it does not possess.   This is allegory at its lowest, and judged artistically the work has little intrinsic value.   It is, however, interesting since it shows that the ecclesiastical writers (almost the only writers at this time) had at least some regard for literary form and execution.   The *Nature* and *Signification* of the *Dove* are apparently original, and indicate that the writer was able to maintain the standard of Tebaldus' work.

A second feature of the English writer's style is his use of otiose tags and phrases and the repetition of the same idea by means of the simple addition of another word : *heil & sund*, 279, 402 ; *nip & win*, 244 ; *golsipe & giscung*, 245 ; *warsipe & wisedom*, 324 ; *same & sendinge*, 339, etc., a feature typical of the diffuseness of the author's style.

[1] Edited by J. Hall in *Early Middle English*, p. 176.

" Short Popular Satires."

From about the middle of the thirteenth century onward there were many short popular satires written in England in English, Latin and in French. They are not satires in the strict sense of the term, but rather poems written in a satirical vein, being out-bursts against abuses of the time, such as excessive taxation, corruption in the courts, simony and luxury. It is therefore literature with a purpose—that of correction through ridicule and exposure. That such poems possess any merit is incidental, but despite this many of them have a distinct artistic value apart from their great historical interest.

Quite a number of these poems are written in alliterative measures, usually in combination with rhyme and often in a definite stanzaic form, details of which have already been given in the former volume.

THE SONG OF THE HUSBANDMAN,[1] a poem of 72 lines in a stanzaic form, is a passionate protest against the taxation imposed upon the lower classes for the wars of Edward I. The writer tells of his hardships and oppression ; more than ten times has he to pay his tax, and " that er werede robes, nou wereth ragges ". With much bitterness does he describe the approach of the beadle who demands a feast when he comes to collect : " cometh the maister budel brust as a bore, Seith he wole mi bugging bringe ful bare " ; and " He us honteth ase hound doth the hare ". It is useless to work thus, it would be better to die.

The little poem one feels is alive with its passionate despair and sincerity of utterance ; in diction and style it is extremely crude, but the poem did not come from a literary artist—it came from a simple peasant.

ON THE RETINUES OF THE GREAT,[2] a poem of ten alliterative stanzas, is a somewhat humorous exposure of the pages, grooms and attendants who follow the rich as they ride on their horses ; they ape the fashions and manners of their betters and will only eat the best food. The writer sums up the whole matter by enquiring whether the reader knows why Christ when on earth would not ride, the answer being that He did not want a groom to ride by His side. Finally, the poet warns them of Hell. Much of the poem is somewhat obscure owing to the use of colloquial words

---

[1] Edited by T. Wright in *Political Songs*, p. 149, Camden Soc., 1839, and in Böddeker, *Altenglische Dichtungen des MS. Harl.* 2253, 1878, p. 100.

[2] Edited *ibid.*, pp. 237 and 134 resp.

and expressions. It is a work of little merit, but is interesting in its testimony to the popularity of such satirical alliterative writing.

Of much more value is a SATIRE ON THE CONSISTORY COURTS,[1] a poem in five complicated alliterative rhyming stanzas. It purports to be a satire on the Consistory Courts of the period, dealing especially with the resultant vexation to the peasantry. The picture drawn is exceedingly unfavourable, and when one considers that the writer plays the rôle of culprit for immorality, we soon realise that his picture is a biased one. However, we are not concerned with the faithfulness of the picture, but with the forcefulness with which it is drawn. The scene is very vividly sketched ; there is the judge and the clerks, the priest and the court-crier who is very realistically portrayed :—

> l. 55 *et seq.*, " Ther stont up a ȝeolumon, ȝeȝeth with a ȝerde,
> Ant hat out an heh that al the hyrt herde,
> Ant cleopeth Magge ant Malle ;
> Ant heo cometh bymodered ase a morhen,
> Ant scrynketh for shome, ant shometh for men,
> Uncomely under calle ".

The writer achieves his aim, which was to expose the oppression of the peasants rather than the moral corruption of the courts ; and he did this by sketching vividly a typical trial. Crude in style and abusive in tone, it nevertheless affords a striking example of popular satire, and it is very significant that it is written in a complicated alliterative form ; there is no question of the popularity of alliteration among the lower classes even as early as the reign of Edward I.

A SATIRE AGAINST THE PRIDE OF LADIES,[2] a short poem of five alliterative stanzas, is " an intense outburst against the vanity of women of the middle and lower classes in their efforts to deck themselves in the elaborate garb made the mode in the latter half of the thirteenth century ".[3] It is a religious, though anti-clerical attack, based on strong moral feeling ; its tone, however, is so narrow that the piece would scarcely be effective. As Wells suggests, something in a lighter vein would have had more point.

These four social satires are all from the reign of Edward I.

---

[1] Edited by T. Wright in *Political Songs*, p. 155, Camden Soc., 1839, and in Böddeker, *Altenglische Dichtungen des MS. Harl.* 2253, 1878, p. 107.

[2] Edited *ibid.*, p. 153, and p. 105 resp.

[3] J. E. Wells, *A Manual of M.E. Writings*, Yale, 1916, p. 229.

THE LAMENT OF THE MONK,[1] a poem of 52 alliterative long lines with end-rhyme, is the work of a monk who experienced great difficulty in learning the church music. The writer with considerable effort describes in humorous fashion his difficulties and the angry chidings of his teacher :—

l. 21 *et seq.*, " Wey the, leve Water, thu werkes al to wondre,
        Als an old cawdrun bigynnest to clondre ;
        Thu tuchest nowt the notes, thu bites hem on sonder ".

The metre is crude and rugged, but the poem has great incidental interest, for it gives a realistic picture of contemporary monastic education.

A SATIRE AGAINST THE BLACKSMITHS[2] is a similar poem, though unrhymed, and affords another valuable proof of the popularity of alliterative verse in Middle English. Wells has very aptly described this vivid and charming poem thus : " The twenty-two alliterative lines voice the author's wrath at the noise made by the smiths. The alliteration is used to mimic the crash of the hammers. The onomatopoetical representation of the rattle and clatter of smaller hammers, the clang of the sledges, the roaring of the bellows, and the shout of the men, is admirable. The scene with its hurry and noise, and its gaunt leathery-skinned actors is strikingly real, and gives an excellent picture of the activity of smiths before an expedition in the days when armor was worn generally. For all time is the indignation of the disturbed poet, from the beginning, ' Swarte smekyd smethes smateryd wyth smoke Dryue me to deth wyth den of here dyntes,' to the end ' Cryst hem gyue sorwe ! May no man for brenwateres a nyght han hys rest ! ' "[3] The poem is the most delightful of the alliterative short pieces.

The alliterative poems of early Middle English are thus considerable in number, especially when the relatively small output in the vernacular at this period is borne in mind. Leaving aside Laȝamon's *Brut*, which in a remarkable manner serves to bridge the gulf between Old English poetry and the works of the Alliterative Revival, we have other important contacts with Old English. The homiletic tradition is continued in many of the poems, and is not seldom combined with the native popular streams of influence.

---

[1] Edited in *Reliquiæ Antiquae*, vol. I, p. 291, 1845.
[2] Edited by K. Sisam in *Fourteenth-Century Verse and Prose*, p. 169, 1925.   [3] J. E. Wells, *A Manual of M.E. Writings*, p. 235.

In *The Proverbs of Alfred* and *The Bestiary* we have such an interesting combination, while in " The Death Literature " the homiletic tradition is more subtly grafted on to the older poetic forms current in late Old English times.   *The ABC of Aristotle* and *A Satire against the Blacksmiths*, both in unrhymed alliterative verse of the fourteenth century, attest the popularity of the alliterative metre right throughout the period, and it is highly probable that they would have been written even if there had never been an Alliterative Revival.

The poem *Fortune* or *Somer Soneday*,[1] the south-west midland poem of the early fourteenth century (1327–50), in rhymed alliterated stanzas, written upon the theme of Edward II's death, while a little later than many of the short popular satires, must also be considered a valuable link between them and the poems of the Alliterative Revival.   Its points of contact with earlier English and Anglo-Norman works are obvious, but its introductory hunting setting and its allegorical treatment of Fortune and her wheel, have left their mark on several alliterative poems, notably on *Morte Arthure*.

The popular satires, such as *The Song of the Husbandman*, a poem which the Cambridge History of English Literature describes as one of the most remarkable poems of the Revival [2]—a rather exaggerated estimate, it is true—frequently written in orthodox alliterative long lines with the simple addition of rhyme, suggest that alliterative forms were still the natural mode of expression among the peasant class.   The writers were in no case conscious artists, but aggrieved men who sought an outlet in these spontaneous utterances.   It is therefore not surprising that the author of *Piers Plowman*, essentially the representative of this class, should write in the alliterative form.   In so doing, he knew that his words would find an echo in the hearts of the poor.

The two *Scraps of Love Songs* [3] may be interesting survivals of popular love songs in alliterative verse, while the *Lament of the Monk* [4] of the middle of the fourteenth century is definitely popular.   In religious lyrics ornamental alliteration is always common, especially in those which come from the south-western areas.   Hence it would seem that alliterative measures, particularly in the west and north, had remained popular from Old English

[1] See vol. 1, p. 116 : edit. C. Brown in *Studies in English Philology in Honour of Fr. Klaeber*, pp. 362-74, 1923.

[2] Vol. 1, p. 370.   [3] See vol. 1, p. 104.

[4] Edited in *Reliquiæ Antiquæ*, vol. 1, p. 291.

times. The northern writer of *The Enemies of Man* in the early fourteenth century was not slow to rise to the occasion and do the best he could with this popular metre, and between the years 1333 and 1352 Lawrence Minot wrote five of his eleven poems in alliterative long lines that are not lacking in vigour, even though they are somewhat unmusical.

There is thus external evidence that alliterative long lines, both rhymed and unrhymed, were being used in popular verse on the eve of the Alliterative Revival. In secret places the measure had served the lowly ends of popular writers. But a new literary inspiration had been born and this much-despised form was to be the vehicle of its expression to mankind.

CHAPTER 2

THE EARLY MIDDLE ENGLISH ALLITERATIVE PROSE.

THE early Middle English alliterative prose is extremely important because it affords conclusive evidence of the popularity of alliteration and of rhythmical prose in the dark period, A.D. 1000–1250, since the works now to be considered are closely allied to the late Old English alliterative prose works.

The group of short pieces listed on page 151, vol. 1, consists of lyrical and fervent rhapsodic hymns, either to Jesus Christ or to the Virgin Mary. By far the best of these is ON LOFSONG OF URE LEFDI,[1] a translation of the Latin *Oratio ad Sanctam Mariam* of Archbishop Marbod of Rheims (A.D. 1035–1128), which is entirely free from that morbid and carnal atmosphere so prominent in two of the three remaining pieces now under discussion. It is genuine and passionate, though restrained, but its most remarkable feature is the concreteness of the pictures presented, which is admirably illustrated by the litany of Christ's death :—[2]

" bi his deaðfule grure and bi his blodie swote, bi his eadie beoden in hulles him one, bi his nimunge and bindunge, bi his ledunge forð, bi al þet me him demde, bi his cloðes wrixlunge, nu red, nu hwit him on hokerunge, bi his scornunge, and bi his spotlunge and buffettunge and his heliunge, bi þe þornene crununge, bi ðe kineȝerde of rode him of scornunge, bi his owune rode on his softe schuldres so herde druggunge, bi þe dulte neiles. . . ."

Though the rendering is a free one, these excellences are largely due to the original writer, and not to the English translator.

It strongly recalls the poem, ON GOD ORISON OF OUR LADY,[3] which in all probability is also a translation from some earlier Latin version. In this work of 171 long lines there is reflected the same love of colour and concreteness, and the feeling is equally passionate. The writer, after singing the praises of the Blessed

---

[1] Edited by R. Morris in *Old English Homilies*, E.E.T.S., 34, p. 205.
[2] *Ibid.*, p. 207, l. 2.
[3] Edited by J. Hall, *Early Middle English,* p. 132.

Virgin, entreats her pity, mercy and love. These two songs to the Virgin should be considered in conjunction with the great body of Middle English lyrics addressed to the Virgin ; all are connected with the Virgin-cult, and are ultimately derived from the *Ave Maria*.

The remaining short pieces are hymns to Jesus Christ ; there is On Lofsong of Ure Lauerde [1] and On Ureisun of Oure Louerde,[2] which is an earlier but incomplete version of *On wel swuðe God Ureisun of God Almihti*.[3] Wells [4] aptly describes the latter as " a notable prayer of passionate realisation of the sweetness and softness and brightness of Christ and of beseeching for purification and union with the Heavenly Lover. In its ardour the piece largely loses the spiritual in the physical." The two pieces are scarcely distinguishable one from the other, for both are equally fulsome yet also equally passionate. They represent a perversion of the inspiration of *Jesu Dulcis Memoria*.

The Wohunge of Ure Lauerd [5] is a longer treatment of the same theme, running to about 3500 words. Christ is described as being so beautiful that the sun is pale in comparison with Him, and the pains which He endured make Him more beloved. His agony and death are described in the fullest detail and with sympathetic understanding, the piece ending with a passionate plea for Christ's aid against the wiles of the devil.

The style is graphic and the treatment sympathetic, making the work extremely readable, and the personal feeling which was the inspiration of the piece is admirably reflected in the following passage :—

" a hwat schal i nu don ? . . . A nu mon ledes him forð to munte caluarie to þe cwalmstowe. A lo he beres his rode upon his bare schuldres. . . . A hu þat ha nu driuen irnene neiles þurh þine feire hondes in to þe hard rode þurh þine freoliche fet . . . henges dun his heaued and sendes his sawle . . ." [6]

The second group of alliterative prose works consists of the well-known pieces in exaltation of virginity, which are difficult for the present-day reader to appreciate, since modern ideas on the theme are so far removed from those current in the Middle Ages, so that the reader may tend to become wearied, though, granted a sympathetic understanding of the period, he might conclude that in some ways the pieces are remarkable.

[1] E.E.T.S., 34, p. 209.   [2] *Ibid.*, p. 183.   [3] *Ibid.*, p. 200.
[4] J. E. Wells, *A Manual of M.E. Writings*, p. 258.
[5] E.E.T.S., 34, p. 269.   [6] *Ibid.*, p. 283.

HALI MEIðHAD [1] is by general opinion the least interesting of the four works, so far as material is concerned, and it is difficult to believe that its author wrote any of the other three pieces, which are stylistically quite distinct from it. There is not, as in them, a story to illustrate the sermon, the author preserving his homily from any external embellishment.

Wells [2] aptly summarises its contents thus : " It dwells intemperately on the thraldom, the vexations and the miseries of marriage ; the baseness of carnal desires, and the avoidance of any incentive to such ; the woes of childbirth ; the troubles that children bring, and the troubles of the wedded who have no children. It urges a mystic marriage with Christ with its offspring of virtues, and a resolution to remain a maiden as if the opposite were Hell."

Its chief interest, however, lies in its style, the work being undoubtedly a powerful piece of writing. In vocabulary and phraseology it has much in common with the *Ancren Riwle*, many words and phrases being found only in these two works ; but the theory that they are by the one author is hardly tenable, though they probably originated in the same locality.

SAINT JULIANA [3] bears the stamp of a different author. It was probably translated from the Latin, though no original has as yet been found. Careful comparison with the Old English *Juliana* would convince anyone that the Middle English writer knew nothing of the older poem. The subject-matter is again the exaltation of virginity, but the author achieves his purpose by means of a romantic treatment of a popular legend, and the story is in itself not uninteresting.

Juliana, the daughter of Africanus, is promised to Eleusius, the friend of Maximian the emperor, but she declares that her suitor must first become the High Reeve, yet when he has gained this office she informs him that he must become a Christian, which request he refuses. She is beaten many times, boiling brass being poured over her, and she is thrown into prison, where a devil, disguised as an angel, informs her that she has suffered enough ; with her never-failing wisdom, however, she soon detects the deceit, and starts to beat this devil after extracting from him an account of the methods he uses in seducing mortals to sin ; Juliana is tied to a wheel, which is destroyed by an angel, whereupon she utters a long oration against the Reeve, and even the executioners

[1] Edited E.E.T.S., 18.
[2] *A Manual of M.E. Writings*, p. 272.
[3] Edited E.E.T.S., 51.

2

are converted to the Christian faith. She is thrown into a fire, but the fire is straightway quenched ; finally, she is boiled in pitch, but this ordeal does not harm her. Having endured all these trials, she dies a martyr's death, and the pursuers, including· Eleusius, who seek to capture the maiden's body which is being taken away, are drowned.

The tale would be extremely interesting to its hearers, and from the religious and ecclesiastical point of view would achieve its purpose. From our point of view it becomes a romantic tale and little more. Judged as such, it is a rapidly moving narrative, free from all digressions, and when viewed historically has its place in the development of religious stories in Middle English. In the latter period, however, there was nothing produced to equal the Old English lives of the saints, such as *Andreas* and *Guthlac*.

Having described in detail *Juliana*, there is no need to say much about *St. Marherete*[1] and *St. Katherine*.[2] ST. KATHERINE is perhaps nearest in spirit, form and phraseology to Ælfric's *Lives of the Saints ;* the amount of alliteration used is far more considerable than in the others, and the compounds, archaic words and phrases are more numerous, as a glance at the statistics in Part II will reveal. St. Katherine is a more attractive and gracious figure than Juliana. Her theological knowledge is far greater, but her disposition is more pleasant. More space is devoted to argument, for fifty wise men are brought to confound her reasonings, who are, however, convinced by her logic and become converted, and even the queen turns to the Christian faith. Finally, only the executioners and the emperor remain heathen. The author takes no interest in recording details of the torments, and the emphasis is rather on the Christian character of the maiden who wins all the people to her side. These merits of the story are, however, chiefly due to the Latin writer, and not to the English translator.

ST. MARHERETE is nearer to Juliana in form and in spirit ; there is an even stronger emphasis on horror and the maiden is so boastful that her character becomes repellant. Her prayers are unnatural and rhetorical, and the piece is undoubtedly the least attractive of the three. There were in Middle English later treatments of these legends, some of which have not yet been printed. The theme of virginity is also reflected in A LUUE RON, *c.* 1250, and OF CLENE MAYDENHOD, fourteenth century ; in these the treatment of the subject is more romantic and the phraseology has nothing akin to

Edited E.E.T.S., 13.   [2] *Ibid.*, 80.

that of the alliterative works. They serve, however, to illustrate the popularity of the theme throughout the period.[1]

The last remaining piece of early Middle English alliterative prose is SAWLES WARDE,[2] one of the most pleasing of the homilies written in the period. It is a sermon, based on the parable of the man who guarded his house against the thief, and is written in an allegorical form which is admirably sustained to the end. The soul is the treasure in the house which is perpetually besieged by the Vices; the Five Senses are the servants, and the Four Cardinal Virtues are God's daughters; Wit is the husband and Will his wife. Fear is a messenger from Hell, and Mirth another from Heaven. Not merely is this allegorical framework well maintained, it lends itself to a convincing dramatic treatment, and even the minor figures stand out as real persons. It is short, and is not conceived on a large scale, but it is not unworthy of comparison with Bunyan's *Pilgrim's Progress*, for there is the same simple dramatic quality and pictorial effect. The descriptions of Hell and of Heaven are unconventional; and referring to Christ the author says:

" ant ȝet ich iseh etsceñe þe studen of his wunden and hu he schaweð ham his feader to cuðen hu he luuede us and hu he wes buhsum to him þe sende him swa to alesen us and bischeð him a for moncunnes heale "

Similarly Fear's address to Hell :—

" O helle, deaðes hus, wununge of wanunge, of grure ant of granunge; heatel ham ant heard wan of alle wontreaðes; buri of bale and bold of eauer euch bitternesse, þu laðest lont of alle, þu dorc stude ifullet of alle dreorinesses. Ich cwakie of grisle ant of grure, and euch ban schokeð me ant euch her me rueð up of þi munegunge . . . ."

Seldom do we find homilies invested with such realism and power. " The piece is a rendering with considerable variations, additions and elaborations of Hugo de St. Victor's *De Anima et Ejus ad Sui et ad Dei Cognitionem et ad Veram Pietatem Institutione Libri Quatuor*, chapters 13 to 15." [3]

These compositions written in alliterative prose serve to connect the Old English *Lives of the Saints* with the later lyrical alliterative prose of the school of Richard Rolle. The rhapsodical hymns to Christ and the Blessed Virgin of the early Middle English period are repeated with greater intensity and fervour in the writings of Rolle and his disciples. There is thus an unbroken continuity in the alliterative prose tradition.

[1] See *A Note on the Authorship of the Katherine Group*, R. M. Wilson, in Leeds Studies in English, I, pp. 24–7. [2] Edited E.E.T.S., 34, p. 245. [3] J. E. Wells, *A Manual of M.E. Writings*, p. 273.

CHAPTER 3

LAȝAMON'S *BRUT*.

LAȝAMON'S BRUT is the one work in early Middle English which above all others recalls the Old English heroic poetry. The dominant note is no longer the homiletic or the popular ; here is great poetry born of a vivid imagination and written for its own sake, without any ulterior ecclesiastical motive, as is so often the case in the early post-Conquest literature.

Professor Wyld [1] has recently sought, quite justifiably, to restore to Laȝamon his rightful place in the history of early English literature. Needless to say, that place is a high one. Professor Wyld's main thesis is that Laȝamon is essentially an *English* poet —a thesis which he is able to demonstrate most convincingly. [2] Laȝamon loves the history of England—her heroes, her customs, her scenery and the associations that surround the hall, the chase and the field of battle. He understands the English temperament, and is always thoroughly human in his treatment of individuals.

It was most fitting that Laȝamon should employ the traditional alliterative metre rather than the French couplet of Wace. The form as known to Laȝamon may have been somewhat corrupt, but it remains essentially English, and one has to read Laȝamon for a long time before perceiving how suitable this metrical form is to his matter and spirit. From a mere external point of view, it emphasises for us the traditional nature of the work, but not unfairly so, because the spirit of the past breathes through the diction, through the poetic treatment of the landscape and warfare, and through the lofty tone and dignity with which the poet never fails to treat his material.

Laȝamon's phrases, both alliterative and non-alliterative, call up the past. A man does not die—' he makes a *fæisiþ* ' ; sailors

[1] H. C. Wyld, *Laȝamon as an English Poet*, Rev. of Eng. Stud., vol. 6, p. 1, 1930, an article from which its author has given the present writer permission to quote freely.

[2] See the quotation with which this chapter closes.

'*liþen into londen*'. All this is not due to an attempt to return to
the past; it is no literary affectation, but issues quite simply
from the poet's imagination. Never does *The Brut* fall to the level
of an academic exercise in archaisms. Laȝamon is always simple
and direct; thoughts are born and the poetical language comes
naturally and without strain; the emotions and the diction fit each
other perfectly.

The same is true of the ancient poetic compounds in which the
poem abounds. The list of such words given in chapter 6 is a
sufficient testimony to the archaic nature of Laȝamon's diction.
A large proportion of the vocabulary consists of words which are
charged with heroic association; they come from the past, but
live once more in the pages of Laȝamon, almost as fresh as ever
they were.[1]

Professor Wyld speaks appreciatively of the essential poetical
character of the diction. " Laȝamon's language is not merely the
ancient speech of Englishmen, almost free, at least in the older
text, from foreign elements, it is the language of their old poetry.
. . . Laȝamon is thus in the true line of succession to the old poets
of the land. His vocabulary and spirit are theirs. His poetry
has its roots, not merely in the old literary tradition, but also,
like theirs, in the essential genius of the race. . . . His copious,
varied and picturesque vocabulary, so rich in association, and often
so suggestive of mysterious beauty, gives his work a lasting value
possessed by no other Middle English poetry before Chaucer,
disfigured as so much of this is by an unredeemed flatness, insipidity
and matter-of-factness in thought and expression."

Should the reader have any doubts concerning Laȝamon's
originality, he need but to consider the poet's treatment of his
source, though it is generally agreed that he used a later version of
Wace's *Brut* than the one we possess. In the matter of actual
additions, Professor Wyld singles out from Madden's two-page list
of original episodes as one of the finest, the description of the
hunting down of Childric, in which the fugitive king is compared
to a fox pursued by hounds.[2] The whole passage is especially
valuable both for its poetical quality and for its descriptive interest.
Similarly, in varying degrees, all Laȝamon's additions and expan-
sions are never without poetic value.

Professor Wyld then considers *The Brut* in its descriptions of
natural scenery, and draws some striking though apt parallels with

---

[1] See chapters 6 and 7 for further details on this point.
[2] See Madden's edition, vol. 2, pp. 445–54.

Old English poetry. Especially noteworthy is the resemblance between Laȝamon's description of Loch Lomond and the Beowulf poet's account of Grendel's mere ; many of the words and phrases are identical and the atmosphere in both is similar.

There is the same delight in wild animals as is found in Old English literature, but Laȝamon's descriptions of the chase are rather anticipations of the same element which is so striking a feature of *Sir Gawayn and the Green Knight* and of *The Parlement of the Thre Ages*. Indeed, a close comparison of the hunting scenes in *The Brut* with those in the two later works suggests that we have here an important link with the Alliterative Revival. In both cases the interest is genuine, and the poets were familiar with the scenes they describe.

Other points of contact with Old English are Laȝamon's interest in the sea and in warfare, topics which reappear in the works of the Alliterative Revival. The arming of Arthur reminds us of the arming of Sir Gawain, as well as of the armour of Beowulf. Laȝamon can describe a battle with vigour and vividness and with an attention to detail only equalled by the authors of such poems as *Morte Arthure* and *The Destruction of Troy*.

The aim of this chapter is not to give a literary estimate of *The Brut*, but to emphasise those points of contact between the poem and Old English poetry which are often ignored, and to suggest that it is a valuable link between the poems of the Alliterative Revival and the old heroic works such as *Beowulf*. It will not, however, be unfitting to conclude with the final estimate of Laȝamon's work given us by Professor Wyld :—

" The more we read *The Brut* the more are we impressed by the versatility of the author. Laȝamon is gifted with an inexhaustible flow of poetical language ; he has a powerful and beautiful imagination, a tender and graceful fancy, a never-failing vigour and gusto, a wide sympathy with, and enjoyment of, every phase of life and action. He never fails to interest the reader, whether his theme be drawn from his rich stores of legendary lore, from his own observation of nature, or whether it be a battle or a banquet.

" Laȝamon is essentially an English poet. He is strongly moved by the old romantic stories of his native land. He loves her mountains and moors, her woods, her streams ; he is in intimate touch with the wild life that stirs within them. He enters as keenly as any of his countrymen into the excitement of the chase ; he loves horses, hawks, and hounds. He knows how to invest his description of battles and pageants, of ceremonies and feasts and minstrelsy, with the glow and splendour of chivalry, and the glamour of romance. The colours seem as fresh to-day as when the pictures were painted. When the poet chooses to exhibit the feelings and emotions of his characters in relation to the situation in which they find themselves he does it simply, naturally and with a noble dignity and restraint, witness the scene where Cordelia hears of her father's sorrows and his arrival in France, or the reconciliation of Brennus and Belyn, or the passage where Arthur learns that he is the son of Uther Pendragon :—

" ' For dead is Uther Pendragon, and thou art Arthur his son. Dead also is that other, Aurelien, his brother. Thus they told him the news, and Arthur sat silent. For a while he grew pale, and weak in all his body ; for a while he was flushed, and sorrowed much in his heart. At last his thoughts broke from him—it was well that he spoke.' " (ii, 411, 1–11.)

" We have in *The Brut* an intensely vivid world of external nature, of human action, and of human joys and griefs ; we find an untiring interest in the earthly life and affairs of men. Of strong religious and devotional feeling, or of solicitude concerning the future state of man, and his relation to eternity, we find small trace in this poem. Such a spirit, or attitude of mind, is not perceptible even as a background of the poet's thought. But if there is no expression of specific religious belief, and no avowedly moral intention, the whole atmosphere of the poem is lofty, chivalrous, and noble. Nor do we ever doubt that the writer is a man of a high and generous nature, with a true reverence for whatsoever things are lovely and of good report, and rich in every human quality which goes to make a man and a poet."

CHAPTER 4.

THE POEMS OF THE ALLITERATIVE REVIVAL.

THE poems of the Alliterative Revival, both rhymed and unrhymed, group themselves naturally into three main groups—romances, religious poems and allegorical works. The romances are of two distinct types, the chronicle and the pure romance, a division which is particularly helpful in dealing with the alliterative works.

I. CHRONICLES IN THE EPIC MANNER.

To some this heading may seem strange and inapt, but bearing in mind that the alliterative poems dealing with the legends of Troy and of Alexander the Great are not romances in the ordinary sense of the word, and that the central figures are never mediæval knights representative of the spirit of chivalry, but heroic supermen of the epic type, the reader may feel less impatient. Thus THE DESTRUCTION OF TROY deals with essentially epic material in the epic manner, and while there is no conscious attempt to write a literary epic, the result is a sort of chronicle poem exhibiting the main characteristics of heroic poetry.

ALISAUNDER and THE WARS OF ALEXANDER are very similar poems ; Alexander himself is superhuman and remote ; the love element is merely incidental, and the treatment is lofty and dignified. There are no other alliterative poems of the same type as these, written with such disregard for the romantic and with such apparent concern for historical accuracy ; it is these features that mark the group off from the romances, and even from those poems written around such historical themes as *Joseph of Arimathie* and *The Destruction of Jerusalem*.

ALEXANDER A and B, by general opinion, were written at the beginning of the Alliterative Revival 1340–50, whereas *The Wars of Alexander* and *The Destruction of Troy* belong to end of the century, though no direct evidence of date in any of the four works is available.

ALEXANDER A (or ALISAUNDER),[1] though a mere fragment of a much longer poem, is yet sufficiently long to afford some opportunity of estimating the author's powers as a writer. The "matter" he took firstly from the Latin chroniclers—Orosius, Rudolphus and others, and secondly from the *Historia Alexandri magni regis Macedonie de Preliis*. The matter taken from the former source includes the early conquests of Philip, his marriage with Olympias (ll. 1-451); Thermopylæ and Philip's cruelty to the Thebans (ll. 900-55), and the beginning of the Siege of Byzantium (ll. 1202-49). None of this is in *The Wars of Alexander* or in *Kyng Alisaunder*. In this section the narrative proceeds rapidly and without digression, and the work invites criticism as a chronicle. The author keeps his audience well in mind, and tells the story with gusto and zest, nowhere pausing to moralise. The conquests of Philip follow in such rapid succession that the poet achieves his purpose, the exciting narration of events in the life of a veritable superman, stripped of all human qualities. The king marries Olympias, but straightway leaves her at home, while he himself goes on further expeditions. The character of this superman is well set forth in the account of his obtaining Erubel's sister to wife, l. 201, *et seq.* :—

> " Philip þe free king that ferse was of myght.
> For þe beurde so bryght was of blee scheene,
> He had his liking ilaide þat Ladie too wedde.
> Too Molosor with his menne hee meeued in haste,
> Craued soone at þe kyng þat comelich beurde,
> For too welde too his wife as hee will hadde.
> þe king was full curtais and coflich hym grauntes,
> For had hee werned þat wyght, wo had hee suffred,
> For þat freelich fode Philip wolde eles
> Haue geten hire with grim stroke of grounden tooles."

After the enumeration of Philip's warlike deeds, the author wisely turned to his second source, *Historia de Preliis*. Nectanabus, the King of Egypt, is introduced at this stage to prepare for the birth of Alexander, since the poem was intended to set forth the exploits of the latter, and not those of Philip. The transition from one section to the other is skilfully managed, and no real break is caused. It is but the painting of another part of the vast canvas the author has unrolled before our eyes.

[1] Edited by Skeat, E.E.T.S., E.S., I, and by F. P. Magoun, *The Gestes of Alexander*, 1929.

This section is in the nature of a romance rather than of a chronicle, but the same rapid movement continues. The narration of these events occupies ll. 452–899, at which point we are brought back to Philip, who is still conquering in distant lands. The author's purpose is to unite the two themes more closely, and so prepare for the birth of Alexander. The magician Nectanabus, in the shape of a dragon, causes Philip in his dream to see things that will come to pass. After the birth of Alexander, Philip can thus be brought back to the scene of action.

Though the narrative is equally interesting throughout, certain passages inevitably stand out in picturesqueness and in poetic worth. In the chronicle portion the best sections are the description of Olympias (175–99), the Siege of Methone (255–310), and the attack on the Thebans (329–451).

The method employed in the description of Olympias is the piling up of detail, leading up to the final rhapsodical exclamation,

196–199, " Where is þer lengged in lond a Lady so sweete ?
þer sprong neuer spicerie so speciall in erþe,
Ne triacle in his taste so trie too knowe,
As that Ladie, with loue too lachen in armes ! "

The adjectival epithets employed in the course of the description are, in common with most alliterative poetry, usually vague and of little definite meaning, merely laudatory, such as *lufsum*, *blisfull*, *gracious*, *louely*, etc. ; but over against such as these might be mentioned *rose-red* (178), *glisiande as goldwire* (180), *liliwhite* (195).

The descriptions of the Siege of Methone and of the attack on the Thebans are almost Virgilian in their vigour and concreteness. Here we find the same love of picturesque detail as is found in the author of *Sir Gawayn and the Green Knight ;* the arrows are described thus :—

Grim arowes & graie with grounden hedes (270).
A schaft with a scharp hed shet oute his yie (277).
Gainus grounden aryght gonne they dryue (292).

It is especially in these descriptions of implements of war and of battles that this characteristic is revealed. In the Nectanabus section there are several excellent descriptive passages, and in particular the witchcraft of the King of Egypt offers scope for the writer's powers. His use of earthen pots filled with rain-water, his brass tablet, set in ivory and decked with gold, his ivory box with seven stars shining in it, his herb-juice, and wax ships, all add the element of colour that makes this section memorable.

Hence the work has certain decided merits, particularly of description, quite apart from those which are due to the original. However, in the matter of technique the translator shows himself somewhat unpractised, and evidently experienced considerable difficulty in writing alliterative verse.   It is interesting to examine in some detail his methods of constructing the verse.   We have seen how he strained the laws of stress by allowing the accent to fall frequently on the unstressed verbal prefix.   Similarly, he strains the meaning of words by forcing them into his somewhat rigid metrical scheme.   This is seen particularly in his adjectives, which are generally vague and colourless.

In the first half-line the word *Philip* is of very frequent occurrence, necessitating numerous adjectives with the sound *f* to fill out the half-line.   Thus *Philip the free* occurs eight times—47, 79, 98, 108, 201, 222, 330, 866.

It is the exigencies of alliteration that result in the use of rather hackneyed adjectives.   Thus 143 (first half-line) has *dulfull dint*, whereas 147 (second half-line) has *careful dintes*, since a different alliterating sound is required.   So *selcouthe dintes* (130), *lopelike dintes* (99), etc.   In the second half-lines, such absurdities are found as *On his merie slepe* (821), *In a ferce place* (659).   While many later alliterative poets share this weakness, none reveals so unpractised a hand.

ALEXANDER B (*Alexander and Dindimus*) [1] is possibly a second fragment of the same poem based on *Historia de Preliis*.   It is an interesting survival because, though dealing with Alexander's conquests, it contains no martial element.   Wells [2] gives a brief summary of the contents of *Alexander B* in these words : " Having slain Porus in single combat, Alexander comes to the country of the Oxydracæ, who in reply to his offer of peace on submission, bid him give them everlasting life.   Alexander sees trees that disappear at sundown, and which are guarded by birds which spit deadly fire.   At the Ganges, passable only in July and August, he corresponds with Dindimus, the king of the people on the other side of the river.   The rest of the piece consists of the five letters between the kings, really an episode added by an ecclesiastic for a moral purpose.   Alexander erects a pillar to mark his farthest progress and turns homeward."

The aim is to instruct, and no attention is paid to the unsuitability of many of the arguments put into the mouths of the two

---

[1] Edited by W. Skeat, *Alexander and Dindimus*, E.E.T.S., E.S., 31.
[2] J. E. Wells, *A Manual of M.E. Writings*, p. 104.

kings. " There are two leading ideas in the poem, both of them theological. The former is the common and favourite contrast between the Active and the Contemplative Life, which so often meets us in mediæval literature ; and the latter, the contrast between the Christian life and that of the heathen worshippers of idols. The arguments are so managed that the bias of one counteracts that of the other. We are led, on the one hand, to favour the Active Life as being more useful than the Contemplative ; but, lest the scale should preponderate in its favour, it is linked with Heathenism as opposed to Christianity. The life of Dindimus, in so far as it is assimilated to that of a Christian, is preferable to that of Alexander, in its Active aspect, enlists our sympathy rather than that of Dindimus. The author of this ingenious arrangement rather strove for oratorical effect than sought to inculcate a lesson. To regard the various arguments in this light is to regard them rightly. It is merely a question of seeing what can be said on both sides." [1]

The *Alexander B* fragment is of interest in a study of the debate form in Middle English. It shows points of contact with *The Debate between the Body and the Soul* on the one hand, and with *The Owl and The Nightingale* on the other. The moral point of view is dominant throughout, and little space is afforded for narrative. The description of the trees that disappear at sundown whose fruit is guarded by birds spitting deadly fire (113–36) is memorable, though its excellences are largely due to the Latin original. There is thus little in common between *Alexander A* and *B*. Whether *Alexander B* appears as a fragment by accident or design it is impossible to say. As a poem it is roughly complete in itself, but as an episode to a longer Alexander poem it would become an unfortunate digression tending to interrupt the flow of the narrative. In technique it is superior to *Alexander A*. There is a greater control over the metre and less use of tags to fill out the lines ; there are fewer otiose adjectives and the epithets are in general not so vague and colourless.

THE WARS OF ALEXANDER [2] (or *Alexander C*, as it is sometimes erroneously called, since it is not a third fragment of the early alliterative poem of which *Alexander A* and *B* form parts) is a long poem of 5788 lines, translated from *Historia de Preliis*. The ground covered includes the Nectanabus sections of *Alexander A*, and the contents of *Alexander B* relating to Dindimus ; hence, a comparison of the two alliterative versions is possible.

---

[1] Skeat, p. xviii.   [2] Edited by Skeat, E.E.T.S., E.S., 47.

Looking at the work broadly, we behold a vast drama played before our eyes ; vast, because the stage is the whole " then-known " world ; vast, because the work is so lengthy ; and vast, because the actors are protagonists, the mightiest men the earth has ever known—Philip, Alexander, Darius.   The rapid change of scene greatly increases the impression of vastness, instead of producing a disjointed effect.   We never question the actual possibility of armies conquering such mighty distances ; everything becomes natural when the actors are supermen.   The work is a drama because there is the element of conflict in it ; the story arises from the clash between the mighty personality of Alexander and the rest of the world.

The work is a drama in chronicle form—a rapid narration of events, centred around a mighty hero, Alexander the Great.   But the work is more than a chronicle-drama—it is a mediæval tragedy, the story of a man of high degree fallen to low estate.   Alexander is raised to as great an eminence as possible so that his fall may be the greater ; not that the author did this consciously, for the end was inevitable to the mediæval thinker.

The work is a study in the superman, and must be judged accordingly.   The centre and controlling force of the action is always Alexander, and digressions are not admitted ; there is an unadorned narration of the world's greatest superman, comparable to that of Marlowe's Tamburlaine, and there is nothing " romantic " about the descriptions, which are singularly free from folklore and supernatural adventures.   On the other hand, there are few references to the classical deities, for Alexander is sufficiently powerful to control the world without their assistance.

No attention is paid to dramatic possibility, but we accept the impossible feats of Alexander, simply because he is a veritable superman.   At Alexander's birth the earth quakes, and there is thunder and lightning ; stones fall from the sky, and all the world is warned, omens which form a fitting prelude to his great career. When but twelve years old he tames the mighty horse Bucephalus, and when insulted by Nicholas he easily defeats him in battle. After Philip's death Alexander becomes king, and soon conquers Europe and Africa.   He builds Alexandria, and subsequently goes to Egypt, Syria, Damascus and Tyre.   At this stage his men begin to grow weary and complain, and even Alexander is in great difficulties, but eventually takes the city of Tyre and proves himself to be the mightiest man on earth.   The Jews, with the bishop at their head, come to terms with Alexander without any strife, and this lengthy passage affords considerable relief from the warlike struggles with which the author has previously dealt. Darius is the next personage on the scene, and at once creates interest by sending Alexander a ball to play with, a golden head-piece and a hat made of twigs, indicating that at last a serious rival has appeared ;. Alexander dramatically replies that the ball signifies the world which he shall conquer, the head-piece that he shall be head, and the hollow hat that all shall give way to him. Subsequently, Alexander takes the city of Thebes and many other Grecian cities, and eventually comes into open conflict with Darius. After many struggles Alexander vanquishes his foe and becomes king of the Persians. He then marries Roxana, but soon leaves her to conquer other countries, including India, where he hears of Dindimus. He learns that he is to die by poison, but dramatically conceals the secret, though finally the prophecy comes true. In the English version the actual ending has been lost, but the original ending is interesting for our purpose, paraphrased by Skeat in these words : " Alexander was of middle height, with a long neck, bright eyes, and ruddy cheeks. The days of his life were thirty-two years and seven months. He began to war at eighteen, and in seven years subdued all the barbarian nations. . . . Alexander's tomb was of gold. It was visited by philosophers, of whom the first said : ' Alexander has made his treasures of gold '. The second said : ' Yesterday all the world was not enough for him ; to-day four ells of it suffice him '. The third : ' Yesterday he ruled the people, to-day the people rule him '. The fourth : ' Yesterday he could deliver many from death, to-day he could not deliver himself '. The fifth : ' Yesterday he led an army out of the city, to-day he is led by it to his burial '. The sixth : ' Yesterday he pressed the ground, to-day the ground presses on him '. The seventh : ' Yesterday all nations feared him, to-day they despise him '. The last : ' Yesterday he had both friends and enemies, to-day all men are alike to him.' "

The ending is typical of the mediæval conception of tragedy, though it cannot be denied that in this case it is awkwardly tacked on to an exciting chronicle of the conquests of a superman. The interest lies in the narration of the events rather than in the tragic design of the whole work. The story moves very rapidly, the only serious digression being the conversations between Alexander and Dindimus, which, though interesting in themselves, greatly retard the progress of the narrative. With this one exception, however, the interest in the story is well maintained, and the long attack on Tyre (1143 *et seq.*), of which a most realistic description is given, is one of the most notable passages in the poem. At first Alexander is not able to take the city, and it is significant of the dramatic outlook of the work that he does not win by superhuman devices, but by the building of stronger towers and earthworks. It is precisely such skilful manœuvring that makes Alexander an acceptable figure.

The description of Alexander's approach to Jerusalem is of a different order ; the bishop has been instructed by an angel to accept Alexander peacefully, and the excellence of the passage lies in the wealth of the description of the ecclesiastical display, of the costly vestments, censers, candlesticks, and relics. In all this the translator was assisted by his obvious love of mediæval ceremony. The attention paid to colour-effect is found in many of the poet's descriptions of battles, but most of all in the long descriptive passages towards the close of the book (3790, etc.), just before Alexander's combat with Porus. All sorts of mythical ogres and beasts are met with, and even the colour of the dragon's eyes are mentioned. Another descriptive passage especially worthy of mention is that which immediately follows Alexander's visit to the Brahmans (4175). There are trees of the sun and moon, and the Valley of Darkness in which he and his men are engulfed nine days, the diamond-covered cliff with its twenty-five hundred steps, at the top of which is a palace and a temple, where Alexander learns his·fate. Such descriptions are a relief from the military expeditions and redeem the poem from monotony.

When Darius realises himself defeated, Alexander in a characteristic way pities him, for he is at several points represented as a human person, capable of mercy and pity. The reply of Darius is, of course, nothing more than the moralisings of an ecclesiastic, but in a certain way serves to make the whole work what it was intended to be—a tragedy. Darius tells the story of his pride which has been the cause of his fall and warns Alexander in gentle terms that he may meet with the same fate. The irony of the passage justifies its existence in the poem. .

Of interest is the description of the Persian throne, with its seven steps made of different stones ; the seventh is of earth, and is to remind a king that he is of earth. Each step has an allegorical meaning, and the passage is somewhat reminiscent of the description of the pentagle in *Sir Gawain and the Green Knight.*

Space forbids further remarks about the general excellences of *The Wars of Alexander,* a poem in some ways remarkable. Despite its length it never lacks interest, and there are few dull passages. The work is a unity in itself, the study of a superman in a dramatic form.   The English version sustains the dramatic interest throughout, and is a worthy representation of the original.   The translation is often too close, and opportunities of poetic embellishment are missed, but, on the other hand, the faults of verbosity are avoided. The work deserves closer study than it has yet received, for it has a right to be regarded as one of the greater products of the alliterative school of poetry.

THE DESTRUCTION OF TROY[1] is the longest of the Middle English alliterative poems, a fact in itself a disadvantage for the reader, the work inevitably becoming wearisome.   A careful study of the poem certainly repays the amount of effort needed, for it is a work full of energy and poetic power.

The author speaks contemptuously of Homer, chiefly on the score of the latter's " trifles " about the gods fighting in the field as men, and, like other poets of the Middle Ages, he prefers the account of the Trojan War as given by Guido de Colonna, who based his story on the work of Dares and Dictys, the historians. He tells us that he chooses to follow Guido because his account is true ; and it is this attempt to convey historical truth that the reader has to keep in mind when trying to assess the value of the work.   The poet's imagination has been fired by the Trojan War, and it is the clash between the Greek heroes and the Trojan heroes that forms his theme.   He is attempting to rewrite the ancient epic, that great song of national heroes.

The account begins with the story of Jason and the Golden Fleece, of the setting out for Colchis in the Argo, and of his meeting with Medea.   This part is vividly sketched, and the subsequent account of Medea's passion and her deceit toward her father leaves little to be desired.   The poet understands the passionate Medea and traces the feelings of her heart in an arresting manner ; his imagination is caught by this tragic figure until he steps on to the scene himself and rebukes Jason in bitter terms (714, etc.).   On Medea's subsequent tragedy he remains silent, and leaves us with a feeling of disappointment.   He then passes on to the sacking of the First Troy by Hercules and Jason, a passage in which the poet first reveals his true genius, the power to describe battles.   They live for him ; he watches every movement, every blow dealt and every corpse that falls lifeless to the ground :—

[1] Edited by D. Donaldson and G. Pantin, E.E.T.S., 39, 56.

e.g. 1193–99, " With stithe strokes and store, strong men of armys
      Shildes throgh shote shalkes to dethe ;
      Speires vnto sprottes sprongen ouer hedes,
      So fuerse was the frusshe when þai first met.
      All dynnet þe dyn the dales aboute,
      When helmes and hard stele hurlet to-gedur ;
      Knightes cast doune to þe colde vrthe."

Then follows a detailed description of the New Troy which is somewhat long and wearisome in parts, but reveals in the poet an eye for colour and a developed power of visualisation seen in the wealth of detail presented. This part serves to sketch the truly epic background to the picture and at the same time to give rest to the mind of the reader after the first epic fight.

Following this we have Priam's dramatic speech to the council and Antenor's visit to the Greeks, which is vividly described. On the return journey he encounters a violent storm at sea which lasts for three days. The poet, in common with several other Middle English alliterative poets, had a rare gift for describing storms at sea :—

1983, etc., " There a tempest hom toke on þe torres hegh :—
      A rak and a royde wynde rose in hor saile,
      A myst & a merkenes was meruell to se ;
      With a routond rayn ruthe to beholde,
      Thronet full throly with a thicke haile ;
      With a leuenyng light as a low fyre,
      Blaset all the brode see as it bren wold.
      The flode with a felle cours flowet on hepis,
      Rose vppon rockes as any ranke hylles.
      So wode were the waghes & þe wilde ythes,
      All was like to be lost, þat no lond hade.
      The ship ay shot furth o þe shire waghes,
      As qwo clymbe at a clyffe, or a clent hille,—
      Eft dump in the depe as all drowne wolde."

Priam then holds a council of war and the debate, one of the most remarkable things in the poem, not unworthy of comparison with the one in *Paradise Lost*. Priam's speech, a good piece of oratory completely devoid of argument, is merely an ardent appeal for war. Hector follows, seeming to accept this point of view, his sole purpose being to defeat it later ; he is cautious and shrewd and skilfully seeks to persuade the others. Paris, in a like

3

manner, reveals his character in his speech ; he is passionate and impulsive, swayed by emotion and unaffected by reason. He relates his vision of the three goddesses, and by it completely wins over his audience. Deiphobus thereupon expresses his agreement with Paris, and says that there must be no hesitation. After this Helenus endeavours to dissuade the audience from war, but offers no argument to combat the counsel of Paris, merely adopting a prophetic strain. This he does so well that the king is puzzled, and knows not what to think. Troilus, the rationalist, seizes his opportunity, and at once war is decided upon. In vain does Protheus appeal to the king and tell him that his father predicted disaster if Paris should ever pass into Greece ; the people mock him, and Cassandra alone bewails the coming doom of Troy, spreading a tragic gloom over the final scene.

As the poet approaches the subject of Helen he avails himself of an opportunity to rail upon the shamelessness of women, against whom he is always biased. After this harangue (1920–82) he makes a bitter attack upon Helen herself. Such passages, besides being inartistic, impede the progress of the narrative.

The Eighth Book introduces the Greek heroes. Menelaus is somewhat dejected, but Agamemnon, who is to lead the expedition, bids him think of the sword. While in pursuit of the Trojans, Castor and Pollux are drowned, the poet giving us a fine description of a storm at sea, even more striking than the one already mentioned. The Greek ship is at length dashed upon the rocks, the alliteration used to describe this being " torrential ". Two somewhat artless digressions follow, the first on the kings of Greece and the second on the princes of Troy. The portraits of the former are better than those of the latter, and while many of the figures are without life, others are real. We select one at random :—

> 3768–73, " Tantelus the tore kyng was a tulke hoge,
> Borley of brede, and of big strenght ;
> Wele colouret by course, clene of his face,
> Rede roicond in white, as þe Roose fresshe ;
> With grete ene and gray, gleyit a litill ;
> Meke of his maners, and manly in werre."

The subsequent battle on the Trojan shore is powerfully described ; but it is in the next fight that the poet rises to greater heights. The account occupies some three hundred lines, 5672–6014 ; it is a truly epic fight, conveying to us the might of the protagonists.

Nowhere in the whole range of Middle English alliterative poetry is there such a presentation, not merely in its details, but in the sense of the sublime which it conveys.

The slaying of Hector by the ignoble Achilles raises the poet's anger and indignation, and in the sulkiness of the Greek hero in his mad love for Polyxena the author is able to bring out the character of Achilles. In 10,312, etc., he reproves Homer for representing Achilles as a noble knight, and the Trojans' treacherous slaying of Achilles is represented as a legitimate and pardonable act of revenge. But the inevitable is happening ; continued treachery and internal conflicts are combining to turn the dignified epic fighting into a despicable " scrap ". It is the tragic women figures at the end that alone redeem the story ; to a certain extent the dignity of the lofty epic has become the sublime pathos of the tragedy.

Had the poet ceased at this point, his work would have been a much more artistic creation, but he must play with other classical themes, such as the murder of Clytemnestra and Ægisthus by Orestes, without having the ability to lift his subject to the heights of tragedy. To this is rather clumsily added an account of the wanderings and death of Ulysses, with which the poem is drawn to a close.

The movement of the work is thus clear ; swift action, vividly and realistically presented, passes before a truly epic background, and the rapid succession of heroic events lends weight and dignity to the whole work. In short, the possibilities in the epic material at the poet's command are fully realised, despite the fact that a uniform level of excellence is not maintained ; it could hardly have been otherwise, but the unfortunate digressions, usually of a moral nature, which frequently impede the course of the narrative, cannot be excused. Yet the whole work is knit together as an epic. It is not a romance, but a chronicle conceived and executed in the epic manner.

MORTE ARTHURE [1] is more seriously historical in outlook than the usual Arthurian Romance. Like its predecessors, Geoffrey of Monmouth's *Historia Regum Britanniæ* and Laȝamon's *Brut*, it is a chronicle in form and incidentally much more epic in quality than a mediæval romance can ever be. This epic quality was recognised by no less a scholar than W. P. Ker.[2] *Morte Arthure*

---

[1] Edited by E. Björkman, 1915, and E.E.T.S., 8, 1865.

[2] *English Literature : Mediæval,* p. 143.

differs, however, from the Troy and Alexander poems in that its central figure is much less of a superman than Alexander, the conqueror of the world. Arthur does not defy the universe, nor does he dwarf all other warriors. The poet tries to make up for this deficiency by giving at the outset a long list of the countries which Arthur has conquered, but the effect is not the same. Alexander is like Tamberlaine, in comparison with whom Arthur becomes weak and at times feeble. Yet Arthur is a hero of sufficient vitality and importance to form the pivot of the whole poem. He dominates the scene and gives to the work a notable artistic unity. His figure is thrown into sharp relief by contrast, first with Lucius, the emperor of Rome, and secondly with the treacherous Modred. The encounter with the giant, a purely romantic element in the story, also serves to display Arthur's prowess and skill.

The poem is extremely simple in design. At the beginning Arthur is already conqueror of the bulk of Western Europe, so that it only remains for him to curb the power of the Roman Emperor. The events described in the work form the dramatic climax to Arthur's career, and inevitably issue in tragedy. Arthur's lust for power and territory has been his own undoing, a danger of which the author of *The Awntyrs of Arthure* uttered warning. The endings of Arthur and Alexander are strikingly alike. The heroes must fall from their high estate, but in the case of Arthur the issue is more truly tragic and the outcome more logical.

Such a subject offered wide scope to an alliterative writer, particularly to one who was steeped in the heroic traditions of the past. Battles and warlike encounters were the unfailing inspiration of such a poet, and *Morte Arthure* is without doubt the greatest achievement in martial poetry in the alliterative school. The poet is thrilled with the glamour and energy of fighting, and he can put his experiences into alliterative verse which is alive and throbbing with the warrior's spirit. The metre is always his servant, never his master, and with its aid he can make any encounter, whether on the sea, on the plain, or in the mountains, live for us in its vividness and in its intensity.

The poet's treatment of his originals is very free. He has taken material from various sources and adapted it according to his needs. Among the definitely original passages Wells would put " the vivid scene of the Roman envoys terror-stricken before Arthur's anger, Guinevere's grief at her separation from Arthur, the vivid description of the dragon of Arthur's dream, Arthur's fight with the second giant, and much of the dream of Fortune and her wheel ".[1]

The poem becomes a vivid succession of memorable scenes, described in the minutest detail and with an eye for the picturesque. Wherever there is a dramatic possibility in a situation it is made the most of. Human feelings are never forgotten, though not allowed to delay the action. Especially notable is the terror of the ambassadors, the anger of Arthur at the emperor's rude demands, the grief of Gawain over the dying warriors, Arthur's sorrow for Gawain's death, and the last scene of all when Arthur and Modred come face to face. No one can doubt the reality of Arthur's grief when he finds Gawain's dead body :—

l. 3949, " Than gliftis the gud kynge, and glopyns in herte,
              Gronys fulle grisely with gretande teris ;
              Knelis downe to the cors, and kaught it in armes,
              Kastys vpe his vmbrere, and kyssis hyme sone,
              Lokes one his eye-liddis, that lowkkide ware faire,
              His lippis like to the lede, and his lire falowede !
              Than the corownde kyng cryes fulle lowde,—
              ' Dere kosyne o kynde, in kare am I leuede !
              ffor nowe my wirchipe es wente, and my were endide !
              Here es the hope of my hele, my happynge of armes ! ' "

The same refinement of feeling and emotional reaction to the scenes of distress is always found whenever these situations arise.

The poem abounds in graphic descriptions, and only the most important ones can here be noticed. Of these, the most memorable are the noble feast prepared for the Roman ambassadors, the sailing of the fleet from Sandwich, the horrible appearance of the dragon in the dream, the arming of Arthur for his fight with the giant, the description of the monstrous giant and his encounter with Arthur (which is strongly reminiscent of Beowulf's fight with Grendel, though not in its actual details).

l. 1110, " The kynge castes vp his schelde, and couers hym faire,
              And with his burlyche brande a box he hyme reches ;
              ffule butt in the frunt the fromonde he hittez,
              That the burnyscht blade to the brayne rynnez ;
              He feyede his fysnamye with his foule hondez,
              And frappez faste at hys face fersely ther-aftyre ! "

[1] *A Manual of M.E. Writings*, p. 36.

l. 1124, " Thane he romyede and rarede, and ruydly he strykez
ffule egerly at Arthure, and one the erthe hittez
A swerde lenghe with-in the swarthe, he swappez at ones,
That nere swounes the kynge for swoughe of his dynttez !
Bot ȝit the kynge sweperly fulle swythe he by-swenkez,
Swappez in with the swerde that it the swange brystedde ;
Bothe the guttez and the gorre guschez owte at ones,
That alle englaymez the gresse, one grounde ther he
standez ! "

Similarly, the scenes on the battlefield, increasing in intensity as
they follow one another, until the emperor himself is slain, the
description of Lady Fortune at her wheel, so oriental in its dazzling
colours and splendour, the naval battle between Arthur and his
enemies, and the final encounter in which Gawain is slain by
Modred and Arthur himself is killed—all these pictures, and many
more besides, are drawn by a masterly hand and presented
artistically. Everything is to the poet a historical fact. The
giants are dreadful realities and the accounts of the battles read
as if they had come from an eye-witness.

The poem is one of the most notable achievements of the
alliterative school. The extracts which have been quoted show
the author's ability to use the long line effectively and to make it
an instrument for lending strength and vigour to the poetry. The
work is a sustained effort, and if the poet lacked the consummate
skill of the author of *Sir Gawayn and the Green Knight*, his actual
achievement can be set beside that noble poem without fear that
it will suffer in comparison.

II. ROMANCES.

In this section an attempt will be made to indicate the chief
characteristics of the alliterative romances of the revival and to
estimate their relative worth. The order in which they are discussed is not altogether chronological, for the Arthurian romances
are better treated as a single group, since they differ widely in
spirit and in conception from the semi-historical group which
includes such poems as *Joseph of Arimathie* and *The Destruction of
Jerusalem*.

WILLIAM OF PALERNE [1] is possibly the earliest of the alliterative
romances, since the reference to Sir Humphrey de Bohun fixes the

---

[1] Edited by W. W. Skeat, E.E.T.S., E.S., 1, 1867.

date of composition somewhere about 1350. It is also the only important example among the alliterative poems of a romance of the conventional type, which is usually characterised by wild improbabilities in action and by the dominance of the love theme. Apart from its external form, vocabulary, phraseology and metre, the work has little affinity with the alliterative romances, but rather recalls the numerous rhymed love-stories of the south and east. It may, indeed, be doubted whether the alliterative metre was a suitable medium for the French original, and the smoothness of the couplet would have been more in keeping with the polish of such courtly romances.

The reader need not therefore expect to find the somewhat stern realism of the Arthurian romances in *William of Palerne ;* instead, he will find a pleasant world of wild improbabilities in which the miraculous is bound to produce the desired happy issue of the tangle. Nor is there much ingenuity in the plot ; the adventures of the werwolf and of William and Melior are in essence commonplaces of mediæval romance, though the various episodes are not unskilfully linked together ; yet as a story it is trifling and only remotely interesting.

Again, the work has little vigour, for it is long-drawn-out, and some passages are definitely wearisome ; the story lags, partly because of the introspective tendencies of Melior, resulting in long soliloquy and meditation, and partly because the war episodes, though considerable, are merely incidental (William must have opportunities to display his prowess, therefore suitable wars and champions have to be provided) ; lastly, there are numerous minor delays in the narration of the events, a failure to come to the point at issue while interest is still aroused, and the insertion and repetition of much unnecessary detail.

Yet the romance as a whole is not unattractive. The reasons for this are, perhaps, the restrained sentimental vein which runs throughout ; our interest in the fate of the fugitive lovers is well maintained, and we fully share their anxieties and fears. Then there is the homeliness of some of the scenes, such as those at the dwelling of the cowherd and his wife, the extraordinary devotion of the werwolf and the dramatic quality of some of the scenes of recognition. But the possibilities of such a romance are not great. No true characterisation or realistic drama is possible. Nevertheless, within these narrow limits the poet has written a romance which can equal the average of the rhymed romance of the period—sentimentally attractive, sufficiently connected in plot to carry the reader along, and human enough to compel sympathetic interest. One feels, however, that the alliterative poets were generally wiser to concentrate on more imaginative and more realistic themes.

Though the battle scenes cannot compare with similar episodes in other alliterative poems, the author is able to describe warlike adventures with sufficient vigour and detail. The following passage describing William's attack upon the steward's nephew is worthy of the best alliterative tradition :—

l. 3438,   " At þe a-coupyng þe kniʒtes (speres) eiþer brak on oþer,
          Swiftli wiþ here swerdes swinge þei to-geder,
          & delten duelful dentes deliuerli þat stounde.
          & william was þe wiʒtere & wel sarre smot,
          & set so hard a strok sone after on þat oþer,
          þurth helm & hed hastili to þe brest it grint.
          þe swerd swiftili swenged þurth þe bode euen,
          þat tit ouer his hors-tail he tumbled ded to grounde."

Yet, when the battle scenes are considered as a whole, it has to be confessed that there is not the same concentrated visualisation of minor details which is perhaps the secret of the alliterative writers' power of description.

William of Palerne remains eminently readable, but falls far short of the French courtly romances. The lightness of touch, the polish and grace, the elaborate play of rhetoric and emotion lie beyond the power of the English translator to copy.

CHEUELERE ASSIGNE,[1] the solitary example in English literature before the fifteenth century of the legends of Godfrey of Bouillon, is a piece of crude melodrama showing no regard for dramatic possibilities, whether of action or of character. The whole story is woven around the villany of Matabryne, the king's mother, who when his wife gives birth at one time to six sons and a daughter, orders her man Marcus to drown the babes, and substitutes seven new-born whelps. She accuses the queen to the king, and has her imprisoned with threat of burning.

The only other character to play any important part in the action is the child Enyas, who though but twelve years old, is able to defeat the forester Malkedras in single combat. Marcus, moved by the helplessness of the babes he has been ordered to kill, spares them, but this is only part of the rôle he is obliged to play. The

[1] Edited by H. H. Gibbs, E.E.T.S., E.S., 6, 1868.

work is a folk-tale in which there is naturally no attention paid to probability. Resort is made to supernatural agencies in order that the plot may be worked out ; an angel appears the night before the queen is to be burned and tells the hermit the history of the child Enyas and of the part he is to play in the vindication of his mother's honour ; and again, as Malkedras slanders the cross of Enyas, an adder comes out of it and strikes him, so enabling the boy to strike off the head of his foe. The story is not, however, written from a romantic, but from a moral point of view, which is set forth in the opening lines and reinforced at frequent intervals throughout the poem. Hence the evil deeds of Matabryne and of Malkedras are punished with full poetic justice, and the author, in carrying this out, makes effective appeals to moral indignation and pity.

The work as a whole has little value, and there are few passages of interest save the one which deals with the boy's questions addressed to the hermit (208 *et seq.*) :—

> " Soone whenne þe day come to þe chylde he seyde,
> ' Christe hath formeþ þe sone to fyȝte for þy moder '
> He asskede hymm þanne what was a moder.
> ' A womman þat bare þe to man, sonne, & of her reredde.'
> ' ȝe, kanste þou, fader, enforme me how þat I shalle fyȝte ? '
> ' Vpon a hors,' seyde þe heremyte, ' as I haue herde seye.'
> ' What beste is þat ? ' quod þe chylde, ' lyonys wylde ?
> ' Or elles wode or watur ? ' quod þe chylde þanne.
> ' I seyȝe neuur none,' quod þe hermyte ' but by þe mater of
>   bokes
> They seyn he hath a feyre hedde and foure lymes hye ;
> And also he is a frely beeste, for-thy he man serueþe.' "

—a passage strangely reminiscent of Ælfric's *Colloquy*.

JOSEPH OF ARIMATHIE,[1] obviously an early work, though no definite dating is possible, is not primarily a romance, but a religious story in which certain romantic elements have been incorporated ; there is warfare and fighting, and improbable things happen, yet the interest does not lie in these things, but in the devotional setting into which they are put ; the real centre is Joseph's faith and devotion. The first hundred lines of the poem have been lost, and with them the account of Joseph's imprisonment. At the opening of the fragment Joseph, on being released, tells how the forty-two

---

[1] Edited by W. Skeat, E.E.T.S., 44, 1871.

years he has spent in prison seem but as three nights. A voice
bids him leave Jerusalem, whereupon he departs the next day;
whenever Christ speaks to him, he answers with the same simple
faith. With his people he comes to Sarras, where he feels it his
duty to endeavour to convert the king (l. 67) :—

> " ' Wolde ȝe herkene to me, icholde ow bi-heete,
> He þat is mi foundeor may hit folfulle,
> þat was ded on þe cros and bouȝte us so deore ;
> I am worþi to seyn moni of his werkes.'
> ' þou schewest a symple skil,' quaþ þe kyng, ' ofscutered þou
>   semest
> To speke of a ded mon ; what may he don þer-ate ? '
> ' I schal sei ou ', quod Ioseph, ' & ȝe wol vndurstonde ; '
> ' Tel on,' seis þe kyng, ' þi tale wol I here.' "

The long account that follows is remarkable for its simplicity and
reverence, and the conversation is perfectly natural. The king is
perplexed by the doctrine of the Trinity and of the Virgin Birth,
but is always reverent in his questionings. The truth is revealed
to him by a vision of three trees with equal stems, and of a child
coming through a door. Behind all this there is the didactic
purpose of the author.

To Josaphe, the son of Joseph of Arimathie, is granted the
mystic vision of the sacred relics of the Cross and of Christ's death.
This passage is extremely well done, both in the actual description
of the relics, and in the fitting language in which the mystical
thoughts are clothed ; Josaphe is consecrated bishop by Christ
himself.

We are then brought to the third section, dealing with the
attack of Tholomer, the king of Babylon, upon Evelak, the king of
Sarras. The purpose of this is to test the faith of the newly converted Evelak, and a further opportunity for instructing the
hearers is afforded the author. The king's clerk is denying the
doctrine of the Trinity, when Josaphe prophesies that Tholomer
will take the king and kill him ; thereupon the clerk disputes
further, but his eyes fly out of his head. Evelak, on asking whether
there is any remedy for the oncoming disaster, is told to ask the
idols ; Apollin, being dumb, is broken to pieces by Joseph. A
messenger arrives in haste telling of Tholomer's victories.

Evelak is forced to answer the attack, and the episode that
follows is not unlike the war-episodes in such poems as *The Wars
of Alexander*, except that the supernatural plays a great part.

Josaphe makes a cross of red cloth on Evelak's shield, which in the hour of his capture he with prayer uncovers, whereupon a white knight comes to his rescue and slays Tholomer. Hence the battle is not fought out as a human contest, but as one in which the deciding factor is the divine aid given to those who have faith in God. ·Evelak's people are converted to the faith, and Joseph's people leave Sarras, having fulfilled their mission.

The story is thus clearly set forth, and is an episode in Joseph's career to provide an opportunity for teaching doctrine, and for strengthening religious faith. As such it would fulfil this function admirably in the Middle Ages, and, judged by the standards of art then current, is an excellent piece of work, for interest is sustained throughout the story ; the general tone is reverent and never trivial, and the work is suffused with the mystical experience of the writer.

The romance element is small, but extremely noteworthy, especially the account of the warfare. In this the most remarkable qualities are the realism and the economy with which the events are described ; a few masterly strokes without any added ornamentation are the secret of the poet's power (e.g. l. 531) :—

> " He mette a gome on a hors with a gret route,
> He hente vp his hachet and huttes him euene,
> Al to-hurles þe helm and þe hed vnder."

Many similar passages might be quoted, but the one that most clearly brings out the author's powers, his terseness of expression, the pictures his latent imagination conjured up, and the masterliness of his style, is the one describing Seraphe's spirited attack (l. 498 et seq.) :—

> " Whon Seraphe seiȝ þat men, þei miȝte iseo sone
> His polhache go and proude doun pallede.
> In þe þikkeste pres he preuede his wepne,
> Breek braynes abrod, brusede burnes,
> Beer bale in his hond, bed hit aboute.
> He hedde an hache vppon heiȝ wiþ a gret halue,
> Huld hit harde wiþ teis in his two hondes ;
> So he frusschede hem with and fondede his strengþe,
> þat luyte miȝte faren him fro and to fluiȝt founden.
> þere weore stedes to struien, stoures to medlen,
> Meeten miȝtful men mallen þorw scheldes,
> Harde hauberkes to-borsten and þe brest þurleden."

Such a description recalls many a similar passage in Laȝamon's *Brut*, a poem also remarkable for its descriptions of battles.

Sufficient has been said to show that *Joseph of Arimathie*, though one of the early alliterative romances, is of extraordinary power. Its author was no mere translator of the French *Grand Saint Graal*; he transformed his somewhat prosaic material into poetry.

He made little use of the stock alliterative phrases, and employed no artificial devices in the construction of his verse. We have already observed that there was little that was traditional about his metre; indeed, it is crude and lawless. The sudden transitions from one metrical type to another and the uneven length of the lines jar on the ear that has become accustomed to the cadences of the alliterative poetry. Yet, despite these faults and the general lack of polish, there is a certain vigour and strength in the alliterative lines which is all too seldom met with in the later poems.

THE DESTRUCTION OF JERUSALEM [1] (or *The Sege of Jerusalem*, as it is sometimes known), though probably of much later date than *Joseph of Arimathie*, has several points of contact with that poem; both deal with semi-religious themes and in both the romance element is incidental; both profess to have a historical subject, and in both the moral aim is abundantly evident. Yet in *Joseph of Arimathie* the atmosphere is more mystical and more purely religious, whereas in *The Destruction of Jerusalem* it is mainly anti-Jewish. The manifest aim of the author is not the narration of an exciting tale, but to pour scorn upon the Jews.

In the earlier part of the poem dealing with the Passion of Christ, the healing of Titus and his father of their diseases by means of St. Veronica's veil, there is naturally more of the devotional spirit present, and this section is often reminiscent of *Joseph of Arimathie*. The story is graphically told, and the manner in which it is executed is simple, reverent and dignified. The main body of the work, however, proceeds along different lines, resulting from the use of different material which evoked a peculiar response in the mind of the poet.

Titus and Vespasian, his father, after their baptism, swear vengeance against the Jews, and the bulk of the poem is occupied with a detailed account of the subsequent siege of Jerusalem. In common with many other alliterative poets, the author revels in

[1] Edited by E. Kölbing and Dr. M. Day, E.E.T.S., 188.

describing battles, sieges and the like, and it cannot be said that he had not the power to narrate graphically and vividly. The account of the Jews fleeing into the town, the plundering of the slain for their gold and precious stones, the repeated assaults on the city and the final surrender, all these episodes attest the ability of the poet to describe successfully military attacks as well as warfare in general. Every detail is visualised, and by the exercise of restraint upon his imagination the poet gives us a most realistic picture.

It is this zest which sweeps the reader along, and it is only occasionally that the anti-Jewish feeling becomes uppermost, as when we are told :

" þe fals Jewes in þe felde fallen so þicke
    As hail froward heuen, hepe ouer oþer " (ll. 597–8).

Or, " Comeþ, caytifes, forþ, ȝe þat Crist slowen,
    Knoweþ hym for ȝour kyng, or ȝe cacche more " (ll. 767–8).

It is therefore as a story that we must regard *The Destruction of Jerusalem ;* as such, it is told realistically, though it is marred by several faults. The author takes delight in gruesome detail, a tendency apparent in many parts of the poem, e.g. (ll. 699–702) :—

" Corres and cattes with claures ful scharpe
    Four kagged and knyt to Cayphases þeyes,
    Twey apys at his armes to angren hym mor,
    þat renten þe rawe flesche vpon rede peces."

At lines 822 *et seq.*, 941–2, and 1078 *et seq.*, we have similar descriptions of the sufferings of the wounded, and occasionally the effect is nauseating.

The account is seldom interrupted by conversations ; there are occasional dramatic incitements to battle, and there are deliberations concerning the plan of attack, but little space is afforded to argument. Nor is this a flaw, for any serious interference with the progress of the narrative might have ruined the whole poem.

The work remains a semi-historical narrative ; there is no attempt at delineation of character ; Titus and Vespasian are mere crusading knights, who though newly converted to Christianity, display not the slightest trace of Christian character ; it is true that Titus on two occasions " weeps for woe " at the sufferings of the Jews, whom he thereafter attacks more fiercely than before. All the persons introduced are mere puppets.

A striking feature is the absence of divine intervention in the action of the story such as occurs in *Cheuelere Assigne* and in *Joseph of Arimathie*. No such intervention was necessary in *The Destruction of Jerusalem*, but the author was in any case more concerned to give a realistic picture, and it cannot be asserted that any of the details are innately improbable. The poem is a historical romance worked out with logical consistency and inherent probability, and though equalling any other like poem in Middle English, cannot be acclaimed a great achievement.

Yet the poet's ability to write with vigour and interest is sufficient to redeem the work from much of its artlessness; "it is the tumult of battle, whether of men or of the elements, that interests our author; with the metre of the old pre-conquest poets he has inherited much of their spirit ".[1] His picture of a storm (ll. 53–70) recalls similar accounts in *Patience* and in *The Destruction of Troy*, and the descriptions of the siege itself are equally vivid. Since the bulk of the poem is occupied with these details, the work becomes essentially readable.

Dr. Day has noted many points of similarity between *The Destruction of Jerusalem* and *The Destruction of Troy*, and proves to the satisfaction of the present writer that the former work is indebted to the latter. In consequence of this indebtedness, Dr. Day is able to date the poem in the last decade of the fourteenth century, since *The Destruction of Troy* was written after Chaucer's *Troilus and Cressida* (*c.* 1382–85), and since the earliest manuscript of *The Destruction of Jerusalem* is dated *c.* 1400. This is a most important discovery for our attempt to trace the growth of the alliterative school as a whole.

The merits of SIR GAWAYN AND THE GREEN KNIGHT are sufficiently appreciated by students and scholars alike to call for no restatement here. Among the English romances it must be accorded the highest place, on account of its admirable construction and freedom from serious digressions and from the customary incoherence of such works, and for the poet's realistic imagination revealed in the vivid descriptions of the feasting in the hall, of the Green Knight's appearance, of the arming of Sir Gawayn, of the wild winter journey, of the castle, of the hunting of the hart, the boar and the fox, and of the scene at the Green Chapel. " He caught, and makes us feel, the very spirit of nature in her wilder aspects, the biting winter, the icy rain, the dreary forest, the rugged

[1] Dr. M. Day, *op. cit.*, p. xix.

rocks, the snow-covered country, and the cold hills lost in mist—
all this he makes us not so much see as feel ; he inducts us into
the atmosphere of the very scene." [1]   This remarkable attitude to
nature is in very sharp contrast to the conventional scenery of so
many romances, and reveals a poet of rare gifts and of warm
feeling.   The details he enumerates in such quick succession are
never in the nature of a catalogue ; the whole scene, whether it be
a knight in armour, a castle, a hunting scene or the cutting up of
a beast—all is visualised as a complete picture, and the poet dis-
closes the details effectively and with a natural feeling for literary
grace and form.

It is this same gift for realism that makes the obvious absurdities
of the story vanish ; we accept the impossible as real and having
once accepted it, the author never relaxes his hold upon us.   We
are carried along with the same sense of reality until the final
dénouement.   The thinly-veiled moral purpose of the author adds
further weight to the poem, and emphasises the essential unity
that exists between this romance and *Purity*.

THE AWNTYRS OF ARTHURE [2] is, like *Sir Gawayn and the Green
Knight*, concerned much more with Gawayn than with Arthur.
Like its counterpart the poem is written with a moral purpose in
view, though the methods employed are singularly different.   The
author of *Sir Gawayn and the Green Knight* does not need to
point the moral of his story ; it is self-evident and self-revealing.
In *The Awntyrs of Arthure* the poet had two sins to give warning of
—incontinence as found in Guinevere, and covetousness as seen in
Arthur's desire for further conquests and in the dispute over lands
between Gawayn and Galleroune.   To exhibit these vices in their
proper colour in a single poem based on Arthurian material would
tax the powers of the best of alliterative poets, and it cannot be
said that the result is too happy from the point of view of form
and construction.   The appearance of the horrible apparition to
Guinevere and Gawayn under the laurel-tree, and the combat
between Galleroune and Gawayn in the second section could not
be a complete artistic unit ; it is disjointed and unconvincing in its
effect.

But, as Andrew [3] has convincingly argued, there is more connection than has generally been supposed.   " In the first part the
ghost has warned Gawayn of the consequences of Arthur's bellicose

[1] J. E. Wells, *A Manual of M.E. Writings*, p. 57.
[2] Edited by F. J. Amours, S.T.S., 1897.
[3] S. O. Andrew, *Huchown's Works*, Rev. Eng. Stud., vol. 5, p. 17, 1929.

covetousness, and in the second the strange knight appears to fight for his possessions which Arthur has won in war and awarded to Gawayn." [1]   There still remains the fact, however, that the two main episodes are unconnected and inculcate different lessons. The last stanza stating that the Queen ordered a million masses to be said for her mother is the only reference to the theme of the first " fitte ".

Despite the artlessness of the framework, the work reveals a poet of no mean ability.   Though he could not, or did not choose to, construct, he can describe vividly and imaginatively.   The opening hunting scene, the breaking of the storm as Gawayn and Guinevere rest beneath the laurel-tree, the ghostly apparition of the Queen's mother, the banquet and the appearance of the strange prince and his lady, and the duel—all are alike described with minute detail and an eye for colour.   The hunting scene is strangely reminiscent of the parallel passages in *The Parlement of the Thre Ages* and *Sir Gawayn and the Green Knight*, and though much less detailed is equally spirited.   The appearance of the apparition, which called for delicate and imaginative description, is efficiently set forth and the horror is suggested by the effect on the animals and the birds as well as upon Guinevere herself ;   it is a remarkable study in psychological description (cp. l. 118) :—

" Alle glowede als gledis the gaste whare scho glydis,
Vnbyclede in a clowde, with clethynge vn-clere,
Cerkelytt withe serpentes, þat satt by hir sydes ;
To telle þe dedis þer one my tonge were to tere.
The beryn brawndeche owte his brande, and the body bydis.
There fore þat cheualrous knyghte thoghte it no cherebydis
The hundes are to hillys, and þaire hedes hydes,
For þat grysely gaste made so gryme bere.
The grete grewhundes were agayste for that grym bere ;
The birdis one the bewes,
þat one that gaste gewes,
Thay clyme in the clewes,
That hedows whene þay here."

Whatever the poet sets out to describe, he does it with the same power and vividness.   His work in this respect upholds the best alliterative tradition.

The aim of the author of GOLAGRUS AND GAWAIN,[2] while not so

[1] S. O. Andrew, *Huchown's Works*, Rev. Eng. Stud., vol. 5, p. 17.
[2] Edited by F. J. Amours, S.T.S., 1897.

definitely moral or religious as in the case of *The Awntyrs of Arthure*, is nevertheless a conscious one—to set forth Sir Gawain as the model of courtesy and of knightly prowess. His successful request for provisions from Sir Spinagros' castle is contrasted with Sir Kay's ill-mannered behaviour in his attempt to obtain supplies, while in the combat with Golagrus Sir Gawain is set forth as the ideal knight. This ulterior aim is, however, kept well in the background, and the interest of the poem is not upset by moralisings.

As a story, the poem reveals the same weakness of construction as *The Awntyrs of Arthure ;* it is similarly divided into two rather unconnected episodes. The only formal connection is that Sir Spinagros, the owner of the castle in the first episode, after providing Arthur and his knights with food and troops, himself joins the pilgrimage and acts as guide. The besieging of the castle of Golagrus has a vital connection with the first episode, but save for the fact that it does describe a pilgrimage, the poem is lacking in unity.

Out of these two episodes, the author finds material for 105 stanzas of thirteen lines, resulting in a much longer work than one might reasonably have expected. This unnecessary elaboration is partly accounted for by the speeches, particularly those of Sir Spinagros, " who as a sort of expositor from time to time explains the history, nature, motives and probable behaviour of Golagrus ". These speeches perform a useful function, but by their excessive length delay the narrative.

A second reason for the elaboration of the story lies in the poet's love of description. He sees things vividly and, like other alliterative writers, can describe with vigour and imagination, particularly when there is an opportunity for dealing with a battle or a combat. Indeed, the fighting scenes are as good as anything in *Morte Arthure ;* they are vivid and graphic, and effectively convey the stress of the battle (cp. l. 999) :—

> " Thai gyrd on sa grymly, in ane grete ire,
>   Baith schir Gavine the grome, and Gologras the knight,
>   The sparkis flew in the feild, as fagottis of fire,
>   Sa wndir frely thai frekis fangis the fight ;
>   Thai luschit and laid on, thai luflyis of lyre.
>   King Arthur Ihesu besoght, seymly with sight."

Occasionally the reader wearies of these details, particularly when the issue is long delayed, but the exhilarating spirit that breathes through the work is sufficient to redeem its undoubted faults; and the picturesqueness of the gleaming banners of Arthur's men, as they pass through the mountains, the discerning of the city with its towers and high walls, the richly decorated hall where Sir Kay sees the dwarf roasting birds on a spit, the castle of Golagrus on the Rhone valley, the various combats so graphically described are things which leave a memorable impression.

RAUF COILƷEAR,[1] the late fifteenth-century Scottish work, is the only example among alliterative works of a romance of the Charlemagne cycle, but its connection with that cycle is merely superficial. While the scene is ostensibly in France, the atmosphere is typically Scottish, with its wild storms and murky mountains, described with the customary realism of the alliterative poets (l. 14) :—

> " And as that Ryall raid ouir the rude mure,
>   Him betyde ane tempest that tyme, hard I tell ;
>   The wind blew out of the Eist stiflie and sture,
>   The deip durandlie draif in mony deip dell ;
>   Sa feirslie fra the Firmament, sa fellounlie it fure,
>   Thair micht na folk hald na fute on the heich fell.
>   In point thay war to parische, thay proudest men and pure,
>   In thay wickit wedderis thair wist nane to dwell.
>   Amang thay myrk Montanis sa madlie thay mer."

This romance, while definitely connected with chivalry and the court, seems nearer to the humorous folk-tale.   Rauf, the charcoal-burner, who unwittingly entertains Charlemagne, becomes the model of courtesy, though this does not prevent him from using violence in his endeavours to teach the king good manners.   The scene in the cottage is most vividly described, and presents a realistic picture of Scottish life and manners.

The rest of the story, describing Rauf's appearance at court by the king's own orders to sell his merchandise there, his discovery of the king's identity, his knighthood for his action in saving the king's life, and his subsequent adventures with Sir Roland and the Saracen, is told vividly and dramatically, and without waste of words.   The narrative moves freely and rapidly and with a zest which is all too rare in mediæval literature.   The simplicity and freedom from stiffness is echoed in the skilfully though not subtly drawn character of Rauf himself.   He is at all times hearty and naïvely genuine. The poem represents a reaction (whether conscious or unconscious) against the conventional romance, though the traditional Scotch temperament undoubtedly accounts in part for

[1] Edited by F. J. Amours, S.T.S., 1897.

the absence of the more obvious absurdities of the romances. As a result, the poem is unusually sane and strong.

Its humour has led some to believe that the second episode is a burlesque on the chivalry romances, but this view has been generally abandoned.

III. Satire and Allegory.

From about the middle of the fourteenth century we find several alliterative poets turning their attention to the social, political and economic problems of the day. Their aim is generally satirical, as might be expected, and the form most frequently employed is the debate, often allegorical and not seldom set in the dream-framework borrowed from the *Roman de la Rose*. Allegory came naturally to the mediæval mind, and the habit of controversy fostered by the discipline of the schools tended to throw the allegory into the debate form. While there are some points of contact between these poems and those which we have already considered, the line of demarcation is very definite.

As we have seen, political and social satire had flourished from the middle of the thirteenth century onwards, and as social and religious abuses became more rampant, it is not surprising that the alliterative poets turned their attention to these questions of the hour.

WYNNERE AND WASTOURE [1] is admittedly the earliest poem in this group of allegorical works, for it can definitely be dated 1352–53. It is true that the evidence for this as presented by Sir Israel Gollancz in his edition of the poem was not entirely conclusive, largely because the essential arguments had been confused by the admission of other somewhat doubtful points. Professor Hulbert,[2] with his customary acumen and scholarlike scepticism, was able to seize upon these weaknesses in Gollancz's argument, and thereby arrived at the conclusion that " any date between 1351 and 1366 would accord with the references in *Wynnere and Wastoure* ". J. R. Steadman, Jr.,[3] however, has gone over the whole ground most carefully, and has proved beyond any possible doubt that the poem was written 1352–53, and incidentally has

---

[1] Edited by Sir Israel Gollancz, S.E.E.P. (revised edition), 1931.

[2] The problem of authorship and date of *Wynnere and Wastoure*, Mod. Phil., vol. 18, pp. 31–40, 1920.

[3] The date of *Winnere and Wastoure*, Mod. Phil., vol. 19, pp. 211–19, 1921.

revealed how irrelevant much of the satire would be if it had been composed in any other year ; " if we assume any other date, the purpose of the allegory, the definite references to topics of the day, in short, the timeliness of the poem and its significance as a pamphlet of the hour are at once considerably weakened, if not rendered quite meaningless ".[1]

The poem thus becomes a precursor of *Piers Plowman*, and our earliest specimen of political satire in the Alliterative Revival. It has the conventional dream-framework with the poet wandering along the bank of a stream in the heat of the day, resting under a hawthorn tree, and towards night falling asleep. This dream-framework was already to hand, but our poet may well have set the fashion so far as alliterative poetry was concerned and prepared a model for a genius infinitely greater than himself.

The poem is interesting rather than intrinsically valuable, for it is local and essentially topical ; it achieves its purpose, namely, the satirising of the greed of the friars, the papal methods of raising money, the prevalent luxury in dress, eating and drinking, the profiteering in wheat, and just complaint of the distressing social conditions, prices, wages and the scarceness of food.

To appreciate such a work, it is manifestly necessary for the reader to acquaint himself in detail with the social conditions described, and to read the poem as belonging to a bygone age, and not as a timeless work of art. It is then that one can agree with Gollancz [2] when he says, " this poem is in fact a topical pamphlet in alliterative verse on the social and economic problems of the hour, as vivid as present-day discussions on like problems ".

There can be no doubt of the effectiveness of the work when judged in this light ; the poverty on the one hand and the luxury on the other so vividly set forth, and Wynnere and Wastoure, both servants of the king's household, the chief figures of the drama.

That the poet should choose as his medium the popular debate form is not surprising, for it so aptly suited his purpose ; and though as a debate it is not comparable with many other like works in Middle English it is nevertheless skilfully managed and dramatically enacted. The poet's personal bias is kept well in the background, and the presentation of the two points of view makes the poem a serious contribution in argument to the burning economic, social and political problems of the day. Though he has a certain power

[1] The date of *Winnere and Wastoure*, Mod. Phil., vol. 19, p. 219.
[2] Preface, p. 6.

of giving point to his satire, his work is yet rather in the nature of a complaint against the evils of the time.

Steadman has observed the poet's discriminating perception of colour in the ornate setting (somewhat conventional, one must admit) and in the picturesque scene of the two armies with the various heraldic banners. Yet of true poetry little is to be found in the work ; in style it is plain and unadorned, and the range of vocabulary is not wide. The poet, evidently a western man (see lines 8 and 32), was, like the author of the C-text of *Piers Plowman*, well acquainted with London and with London life, a fact to which we shall have reason to refer later. The poem remains strong, alive and convincing, a valuable forerunner of *Piers Plowman*, a work in which the purely local and temporary was to be broadened into a world-wide vision of life.

THE PARLEMENT OF THE THRE AGES [1] is in some respects typical of the Alliterative School as a whole, and many of the most noticeable features of several poems seem gathered together in this charming composition. The outlook is serious and moral, as in so many of the alliterative poems, and the author in the opening prologue shows from the striking description of slaying the deer the same interest in hunting as does the gifted author of *Sir Gawain and the Green Knight ;* his detailed descriptions of nature, which are far from being conventional, recall the same poet, as does also his delight in colour. The three men in green, in gray and in black, representing Youth, Middle Age, and Old Age, are sketched in a charming manner, the author evidently recalling his earlier days in the joyous picture of the gay young knight with his love of the hunt and the hall. Yet his ostensible sympathy is with Old Age, who warns the others as they dispute together concerning their respective outlook on life (ll. 290–4) :—

> " Makes ʒoure mirrours bi me, men, bi ʒoure trouthe ;
> This schadowe in my schewere schunte ʒe no while.
> And now es dethe at my dore that I drede moste ;
> I ne wot wiche daye, ne when, ne whate tyme he comes,
> Ne whedir-wardes, ne whare, ne whatte to do aftire ; "

Old Age reinforces his point of view by telling his juniors of the Nine Worthies and of the heroes of romance, all of whom Death has claimed. The little sketches that follow form very pleasant reading, and judging from the extant works in which the Nine

---

[1] Edited by Sir I. Gollancz, S.E.E.P., 1915.

Worthies are treated,[1] might prove exceedingly popular. But these pictures, delightful as they are, upset the whole balance of the poem and one surmises that by the end Youth and Middle Age would have forgotten the reason why Old Age was thus addressing them. The author's point of view is lost for the time being, and only recovered at the end when Old Age says :

 " Dethe dynges one my dore, I dare no lengare byde "

Then the dreamer awoke as the sun was setting ; so he turned towards home, invoking Christ and the Blessed Virgin.

Though faulty in construction, the poem is pleasing in its parts. The hunting scenes,[2] the dream-framework, the bright colours and and the didactic theme call up associations with many other poems of the Alliterative Revival, and one feels that the work was written with such poems as *Piers Plowman* and *Sir Gawain and the Green Knight* in mind. There are only two alternatives, either that the author of *The Parlement* had read the afore-mentioned works, or that the authors of these works were themselves indebted to *The Parlement*.[3]

Our answer to this question turns *partly* on whether with Professor Hulbert[4] and Dr. Steadman[5] we reject the common authorship of *Wynnere and Wastoure* (1352) and *The Parlement*. Sir Israel Gollancz's arguments in favour of this hypothesis were indeed somewhat unconvincing—such as occurrence in the same manuscript, and use of the dream-framework and the presence of many parallel and identical passages ; on the tests of language and metre, he is, however, probably on firmer ground.[6] Dr. Steadman objects to the ascription of the two poems to the same author on general grounds, but more especially on " differences in rhetoric, syntax and vocabulary," which he amplifies in detail. With all due deference to so great a scholar, we feel that the point is still *sub judice ;* difference of subject may require a different style and different vocabulary, as Dr. Steadman himself admits, and an interval of a good number of years may work havoc with a

---

[1] See Gollancz, p. 3, and Appendix.

[2] See R. L. Savage, M.L.N., xliii, pp. 177–9.

[3] The opening lines of *The Parlement* and *Piers Plowman* are extremely similar.   [4] *Op. cit.*, p. 51.

[5] J. M. Steadman, Jr., The authorship of " *Wynnere and Wastoure* " *and* " *The Parlement of the Thre Ages* " *: a study in methods of determining the common authorship of Middle English Poems,* Mod. Phil., vol. 21, p. 7, 1923.   [6] See vol. 1, p. 249.

poet's " rhetoric, syntax and vocabulary ".[1]   It is just *possible*
that *The Parlement* was written later than *Piers Plowman* and
Sir Gawain and the Green Knight, but it is more probable [2] that the
author was also the poet who wrote the early satire *Wynnere and
Wastoure* that gave the writer of *Piers Plowman* his first inspiration.

Assured that *Wynnere and Wastoure* is correctly dated 1352–53,
we need not hesitate to assert the indebtedness of PIERS PLOWMAN
to the former work.   The similarity in form and setting, and the
striking verbal parallels in several passages have frequently been
commented upon by scholars, and need no further elaboration here.
Nevertheless, this indebtedness is largely confined to the choice of
the dream-framework and of the vision as a suitable medium for
political and religious satire in allegorical form ; mere evidences of
having read the earlier poem are not so important.   The author
of *Piers Plowman*, realising the scope which this form offered him,
may have been fired in his imagination by the intimate picture of
fourteenth-century luxury and poverty afforded him in *Wynnere
and Wastoure*.

The limits of this book preclude all but the merest reference to
the authorship-controversy which rages around *Piers Plowman*.
It had seemed that Dr. Day, in her valuable researches [3] into the
problem, had certainly achieved something solid and definite
amid the welter of arguments that have from time to time been
adduced.   But Professors Chambers and Gratton,[4] after their long
and painstaking study, have felt constrained to point out " firstly,
that if we wish to argue from the textual problems of A, B and C
as to the authorship of the different versions, we *must* (italics theirs)
go back to the MSS. ; secondly, that, when we have done so, we
shall find the evidence so complicated as to discourage any hasty
dogmatism," [5] and again, " no final textual results can be reached
without further investigation of the MSS ". [6]   It is in the light of
these facts, supported by very detailed evidence, that Chambers
and Gratton find little to corroborate Dr. Day's theories.

Hence it is unlikely that the bases of discussion can be available
for many years to come, and meanwhile we must content ourselves
with such work as has been done by A. H. Bright [7] along different

---

[1] The weakness of Dr. Steadman's thesis is indicated in a note by the
present writer in R.E.S., vol. 10, pp. 200–2, 1934.

[2] See *infra*, p. 97.

[3] M.L.R., xvii, pp. 403–9, 1922, and M.L.R. xxiii, pp. 1–27, 1928.

[4] M.L.R., xxvi, pp. 1–51, 1931.

[5] *Ibid.*, p. 21.   [6] *Ibid.*, p. 23.

[7] *New Light on Piers Plowman*, Oxford, 1928.

lines, though it is not impossible for provisional study to be carried out on Skeat's texts.[1]

Of *Piers Plowman* as a poem (the work will obviously remain as it is, whatever the final verdict upon the authorship-question may be) sufficient has already been written to justify but the merest mention here. Yet it is important that its place in the alliterative school as a whole should be realised, for it is not an isolated work. It had, as we have seen, at least one precursor, and called forth several imitations, none of which were worthy of comparison with it, for *Piers Plowman* is not a poem dealing merely with contemporary social and political problems ; its stage is the world and it concerns the great issues of life and death in a manner applicable to any age.

The poet's wide sympathy with the poorer classes is manifest on every side, and the poem has rightly been acclaimed ' the only adequate representation of the evils and the sufferings and the aspirations of the common life of the times '.[2] This stark realism makes the work a striking succession of pictorial episodes drawn from real life and enables the author to escape from the abstract in his allegorising, a fault to which most mediæval writers were especially prone ; ' the general is always exhibited in the individual, the abstract is vivified in the concrete—all is objectivised, is seen in action '.[3] His allegorical figures are flesh and blood individuals, seldom abstractions ; indeed, in a few cases they become so concrete that the general is completely lost sight of, and the poet is not even afraid to introduce to us simple human beings. Here is indeed a realistic picture of fourteenth-century life.

Yet the author has an immediate purpose in all this ; the poem becomes in a most vivid sense a reviewing of the ' field full of folk ' and of the relations in which folk stand to one another. He is concerned with conditions of labour ; he shows his impatience with those who will not work, whom he would fain discipline with hunger ; he is indignant against those who exploit the poverty of the poor, and is vehement against all that was insincere in fourteenth century England, whether in the manifold aspects of church life or in the affairs of the state, society and industry. All these evils of

---

[1] See vol. I, p. 61. A detailed metrical study in statistical form of Skeat's texts by the present writer *seems* to favour the theory of single authorship, but in view of the above criticism of Dr. Day's own metrical study, it is very doubtful whether such work is of any value.

[2] J. E. Wells, *A Manual of M.E. Writings*, p. 265.

[3] *Ibid.*

the time he exposes ruthlessly and none escapes the whip of his satire ; he has no use for kindly humour, only for indignation and wrath.

The spirit of the poet who thus saw his own age so realistically, was yet so white-hot with the fire of imagination that his own personal experiences became transmuted into poetry of the highest order. Thoughts are expressed as they are born, spontaneous, glowing and impulsive. This is why the work lacks the neat and tidy external form due to conscious literary effort, for the poet has no time to concern himself with such things. There is no subtly worked-out allegory, part of a great central design ; indeed, the poem is lacking in form, judged by conventional standards, though there is probably more order in it than has sometimes been suspected.[1] What order there is has been evolved while the work grew into shape in the poet's mind. Allegory follows allegory in a most careless manner, and there are many apparently needless interruptions and violent transitions, all of which make the work difficult to read. Yet there are no subtle allegorical fancies of the usual mediæval kind indulged in, for the poet is intent on making his meaning plain, and has no interest in such trivialities.

The result of this imaginative process is not a number of visions loosely strung together, but a unified structure in vision form. Without striving for literary effect, the author has produced a poem in which the issues of life and death, of good and evil, are worked out with dramatic intensity and logical consistency. The force that welds the poem together is the personality of Piers Plowman himself, that strange figure who appears as the representative of so many types of mankind, and of Christ Himself. He is a complex personality, but as Professor Troyer[2] has recently argued in a most convincing way, to the mediæval mind this combination of humanity and divinity would be perfectly natural. Piers is Christ as man, in whose armour, that is, in whose flesh and blood, the Son of God fought. " May not the applicability of Piers as a symbol of Christ be then his humanity ?   In his human essence he was blood brother to the laborer, the plowman, the king and the pope, and alike reducible to the common denominator of man. The unity of the Piers symbol lies . . . in the humanness of all its variants, Piers is man." [3]   " Piers is a multifold symbol.

[1] H. W. Wells, *The Construction of Piers Plowman*, P.M.L.A., vol. 44, pp. 123–40.

[2] H. W. Troyer, *Who is Piers Plowman ?*, P.M.L.A., vol. 47, p. 368, June, 1932.   [3] *Ibid.*, p. 371.

He is allegorically man the race. He is sometimes an individual man, who is in his integrity a picture of moral perfection in the functions of society which the race has developed. And he is also the great God-man, the highest achievement of the race in the figure of its own redeemer. This interpretation has a significance for us in the title of the poem itself. . . . It is as we see the organic unity of the Piers symbol uniting all its variants, that we see the significance of the title *Visio Wilhelmi de Petro le Plowman*, for with the symbol standing for man, for humanity, the work becomes entitled for what it is—a vision concerning man in this life, in his attainment of economic and political well-being, and in his attainment of salvation and a free access to heaven, through the medium of the Son of God, who became man to save man. In this sense the poem is truly a vision concerning Piers Plowman." [1]

To the author the true origin of many of the evils from which the people suffered appeared to him to lie in the defects of human nature, which are only amenable to spiritual remedies. But man, sharing the humanity of Jesus Christ, may set out on the eternal quest for truth, which for the poet is no less than God himself. For him the quest is not for the ' rose of love '—the age of chivalry for him has already passed—but for truth, and the truth is God, and the guide is ' Jesus Christ of Heaven, who in poor man's apparel pursueth us ever '. He is no pessimist, and is confident of the inherent goodness of human nature ; nor is he a foolish optimist, for he sees that the end is not yet ; the gladness and triumph of the Easter morn must give way to the Antichrist. Life is to be a pilgrimage through unknown and unexplored territory, but the hope is in man himself, who claims his relationship with Jesus Christ.

The more we read the poem, the more we feel that Langland is a great thinker, constructive and intense. We need to become absorbed in his work, to accustom ourselves to his strange methods of thought, his intuitive insight into the heart of things, whence he comes back with visions of the eternal realities, before we can realise what a mighty work he has left us, an allegory without its equal in the English language.

PIERCE THE PLOUGHMAN'S CREDE,[2] dated by Skeat, 1394,[3] is perhaps our earliest extant imitation of *Piers Plowman* in alliterative verse. That the work is indebted to *Piers Plowman* goes

---

[1] H. W. Troyer, *Who is Piers Plowman ?*, P.M.L.A., vol. 47, p. 384.
[2] Edited by Skeat, Oxford, 1906.   [3] See vol. I, p. 91.

without question ; the author clearly had in mind the prologue to *Vita de Dowel*, in which the dreamer in his quest meets two Minorite friars whom he questions as to the whereabouts of *Do-wel*. The work is a Wycliffite attack on the four Orders of the friars. There is no dream-framework, but the poet himself, knowing only his *Pater Noster* and *Ave Maria*, wanders in search of one who may be able to teach him his Creed. This is chiefly a device for showing up the friars, but instead of the poet describing indirectly his interviews with representative friars, he employs the method of direct discourse, which makes the attack more effective ; the friars are condemned out of their own mouths. He first meets with a Minorite (Franciscan) friar, who makes a clever attack on the Carmelites (White Friars) and subsequently proceeds to applaud the doings of his own Order ; to the poet's request to be taught his Creed, he replies that his absolution will be sufficient and assures him of the intercession of St. Francis on his behalf, if only he will pay to have a church window glazed.

The poet in disappointment goes next to the Dominicans (Black Friars), and describes in exquisite detail their abode (155–215)—a mere objective account which serves to satirise admirably the luxury and love of fine buildings for which these friars were so well known. The particular friar he chances to meet is (221)—

> " A greet cherl and a grym, growen as a tonne,
> Wiþ a face as fat as a full bledder
> Blowen bretfull of breþ and as a bag honged
> On boþen his chekes, and his chyn wiþ a chol lollede,
> As greet as a gos ey, growen all of grece ; "

Failing to derive any satisfaction from this source, with a righteous rebuke he takes his leave and seeks an Augustine friar who can do nothing better than attack the Minorites and offer to absolve the poet, assuring him that his creed is of no importance. Subsequently, he finds two Carmelites in a tavern who, having attacked the Dominicans, likewise offer to absolve the poet for money or goods.

The excellency of the dramatic satire is at once apparent ; the four Orders have condemned themselves, and are further shown up by contrast with the poor ploughman whom the poet next meets. Piers, all in tatters, hard at work in the field, his ill-clad wife walking with bleeding feet and their three wailing infants form a most realistic picture of poverty (421–42). Piers' harangue against the friars and defence of Wycliffite teaching is well written, and well thought out, but is rather too long, and too infrequently interspersed with comment by the poet, who finally learns the creed from the lips of Piers.

The poem is a vigorous and skilfully-planned attack upon the friars, and, though indebted to *Piers Plowman* for its general inspiration, has decided merits of its own.   Its vivid descriptions, dramatic form and vigorous conversation make it a true satire, effective regarding its purpose and incidently artistic in its quality.

JACKE UPLAND [1] (1401 – 2), THE REPLY OF FRIAR DAW THOPIAS,[2] and THE REJOINDER OF JACKE UPLAND,[3] though chronologically coming after *Richard the Redeles* (1399), are more conveniently treated here, for they are nearer akin to *Pierce the Ploughman's Crede.*

Jacke Upland is a virulent attack on the friars by a Wycliffite, and is entirely lacking in poetic form and inspiration.   The author violently rebukes the friars for their vices, their luxury and gluttony, their love of money, their neglect of the poor and their pursuit of the rich and indifference to the ideals of St. Francis, and their many other sins of omission and commission.   The poem is entirely formless, and though it becomes more heated in tone as the attack proceeds, it is never inspired.

The Reply of Friar Daw Thopias has more external marks of poetry than *Jacke Upland ;* its lines are fairly regular and there is some attempt at metrical form.   It is a more reasoned attack on the Lollards, accusing them of schism and heresy, the worst of all sins.   They are in league with the Antichrist, and due punishment will be meted out to them at the Judgment Day.   In accusing Jacke of the sin of Pharisaism, the author reveals considerable skill in argument, and the work, though needlessly long, is interesting to read and follow ; it is energetic and vigorous.

The Rejoinder of Jacke Upland is written in a better metrical form than his earlier attack, probably under the influence of *The Reply*, with its greater metrical regularity.   It is more skilful in its arguments and there are more appeals to Biblical precedent, but the work is marred by repetition and mere invective and, like its predecessors, is lacking in poetic quality.

RICHARD THE REDELES,[4] an early imitation of *Piers Plowman*, was dated 1399 by Skeat, who placed its actual time of composition

---

[1] Edited by T. Wright, *Political Poems*, vol. 2, p. 16, 1861.

[2] *Op. cit.*, p. 39.   [3] *Op. cit.*, p. 39.

[4] Edited by Skeat in his edition of *Piers Plowman*, 2 vols., Oxford, 1886, p. 603.

between 18th August when Richard was taken prisoner and before the receipt of the news of his deposition on 18th September in that year. The ascription of the poem to the author of *Piers Plowman* by Skeat and others is not however tenable.[1]   Professor Manly dismissed this hypothesis as fantastic many years ago, and there is no doubt that tests of metre and style tell heavily against such an assumption.   Moreover, the later poem has not the dream-frame-work or the vision-form, and its methods are singularly different from those employed by the author of *Piers Plowman*, as anyone who has made a close and sympathetic study of the poem is aware.

The prologue briefly relates in terse and plausible language the circumstances of the composition of the work—an appeal to King Richard to accept the advice contained in the poem.   The four passus (the last incomplete) treat of the errors and wrongs of Richard's rule—the folly of the court favourites, the crimes of the retainers, the extravagance of the court, and the corruptions of the Parliament.

The open attack on Richard and his policies in Passus I and IV is quite effective, because it is straightforward and to the point, while the more allegorical method employed in the middle portions of the work with the veiled references to Bolingbroke and Richards' retainers under the forms of the eagle and the white harts respec-tively give the author an opportunity for more biting satire and more pointed comment, an opportunity he was not slow to utilise. The work reveals a writer exceptionally alert to the political and national bankruptcy of the moment ; a power of expression suffi-cient to portray the situation in its true colours and a satirical vein which could make the darts carry.   But the poem is essentially topical—a pamphlet of the hour, and apart from its historical interest, has little permanent value.   The breadth of vision, the imaginative insight, and the moral force revealed in *Piers Plowman* are strangely lacking here.

MUM AND SOTHSEGGER,[2] the recently discovered alliterative poem, consisting of 1751 long lines, is in all probability some sort of continuation of *Richard the Redeles*, as suggested by Mr. Steele, who is also of the opinion that about a hundred and fifty connecting lines have been lost.

While (at the time of writing) the poem has not received the study it demands, an examination of the text in some detail suggests that the work, though as a whole lacking in artistic quality

[1] See vol. 1, p. 251.
[2] See *Brit. Mus. Quarterly*, iii, Mar., 1929, pp. 100–2.

and poetic inspiration, is well written, and has a few passages of special charm and vitality. The earlier portion of the poem, consisting chiefly of a discussion of the abuses of the court, arising from the fact that nobody tells the king the truth, is rather confused, unduly prolonged and uninspired. The argument is, however, well-conducted, and the ideas for which Mum stands are illustrated with sufficient detail and comment. The poet's journeyings to various representatives of mankind in the ensuing section, where he discovers that Mum holds sway everywhere, afford the writer an opportunity of giving little miniatures of fourteenth-century life; his delightful sketches of the university, the friary, the abbey, the monastery, the cathedral, etc., are terse and excellently drawn, and the satire is keen without being bitter.

In the poet's dream-vision which follows, l. 871 *et seq.*, there is much detailed description of the landscape and general setting which is among the finest things in the poem, and is in parts reminiscent of the similar setting of *The Parlement of the Thre Ages*. The method is much the same, a piling up of detail and an attention to colour, light and shade.

The allegory of the bees and drones told to the poet by the old man in the vision is long-drawn-out, excessively sermonising and undramatic. But the advice to follow Sothsegger, who presides in his own court, the heart of man, is by no means ineffectively given. The largely disconnected admonition, moralising, and attacks on evils and abuses of the time with which the work ends, differ greatly in quality, and form a rather odd conclusion to the work. Though these booklets (all beginning with either *Yit is there a . . .* or *There is a . . .*) are quite effective in their own way, they add little to the value of the work.

The insertion of a vision in the middle of the poem detracts from the value of the composition as a whole. A greater poet would have cast his subject into the form of a vision-debate, after the style of *Wynnere and Wastoure* or of *The Parlement of the Thre Ages ;* but this writer is too fond of moralising and admonishing ; the method of *Richard the Redeles* is more to him than that of *Piers Plowman* and its precursors. He can effectively discern the weaknesses and abuses of the day, and set these forth in their true colours, but beyond this he has neither desire nor power to go.

Mr. Steele suggests that the reference to the hanging of the friars at Tyburn is to be connected with the execution of the friars in 1402, so that the date of composition cannot be much later than that.

THE CROWNED KING,[1] " written at Southampton, probably in June, 1415, and addressed to Henry V, shortly before his famous campaign," is a later imitation of *Piers Plowman*. A short poem (only 144 lines in length), it has the customary dream-framework, but in the baldest terms imaginable ; there is no attempt to paint a conventional natural setting in brilliant colours ; the prosaic writer must needs tell us that the place was six or seven miles out of Southampton, and that the time was *Corpus Christi Eve*.[2]

Apart from the mere framework, the poem is more reminiscent of *Richard the Redeles* than of *Piers Plowman ;* its historical allusions are many, some of which are admittedly obscure ; there is the usual regard for the nation's welfare. The king asks the multitude of commons which he beholds in the deep dale for a subsidy for his wars ; a clerk kneels down and urges the king to rule with reason and with due regard for his people, to beware of flatterers and evil counsellors, and to resist avarice.

The poem is like *Richard the Redeles*, a pamphlet of the hour, and as such is direct and convincing, but its claim to poetry is small. The work abounds in terse and witty remarks such as :—

" The wittyest and wylyest and worthiest in armes,
    All is but wast wele and he wronge vse,
    And vnsemely for a souerain (So saue me our lord) " (81–3) ;

Or : " As a brokour to go borowe pore mennes wittes " (118).

It is these flashes of native wit that give the poem its point and vigour, but the work, while of interest, is of no permanent value. As in the case of *Richard the Redeles,* an effective imitation of·*Piers Plowman* has been produced, but it remains a faint echo of a greater poem ; it is topical, *Piers Plowman* is timeless.

DEATH AND LIFE [3] is one of the late Middle English poems which is quite obviously indebted to *Piers Plowman ;* Skeat in his edition first called attention to the presence of some very striking parallels between the two poems and later editors have been able to elaborate Skeat's suggestions very considerably. In *Piers Plowman* (C. xxi), the main source of inspiration, however, Jesus is to joust with Satan in a sort of tournament, whereas in *Death and Life* the

---

[1] Edited by Skeat, E.E.T.S., 54, *Piers Plowman C-Text and The Crowned King*, pp. 523–34.

[2] The dating of visions by reference to a religious feast is not uncommon ; cp. *Pearl*, etc.

[3] Edited by J. H. Hanford and J. M. Steadman in *Studies in Philology*, vol. 15, p. 221, 1918 ; also by Sir I. Gollancz, S.E.E.P., 1930.

struggle takes on the form of a debate ; this and several other points of difference in treatment indicate that the author of the later poem had some originality. The neglect which has attended this poem until quite recent years is unfortunate, but explicable ; the hopelessly corrupt manuscript belongs to the seventeenth century and the author's work is marred throughout by the aimless repetition of stock alliterative and non-alliterative phrases borrowed from earlier poets.

Despite a superficial lack of originality, the poem is by no means devoid of merit and certainly no apology need be made for it. We cannot, however, agree with the remarkable tribute paid to the poem by Dr. Steadman,[1] who says, " There are few finer things in the whole range of Middle English poetry. The author has brought to his didactic theme a lofty imagination and a sense of poetic phrase which make *Death and Life* rank high even among the most powerful productions of the alliterative school. Its noble solemnity and religious fervour are touched with a romantic grace, and the subject is handled with the artistry of a poet bred in the traditions of such matchless works as *Gawain and the Green Knight* and *The Pearl*."

After a short prologue consisting of an invocation to Christ and of a warning to man, the poet makes use of the conventional dream-framework to introduce to us his vision ; (strangely enough there is no reference to a May morning). The scene in the dream is extremely simple and fitting ; it was something the poet had visualised for himself and to appreciate it we must visualise it also. There are the natural surroundings which form an admirable background and the people of all classes from king to peasant. The whole picture is reminiscent of the ' field full of folk '. Without any waste of words the figure of Lady Life is introduced in what is perhaps the finest passage in the poem, l. 60, etc., the beauty consists not so much in the description of the figure of Lady Life, as in her effect upon the surrounding scene ; everything seems to experience a kind of *joie de vivre*, even the birds in the trees and ' the fishes in the flood '. Lady Life has in her train of allegorical knights and ladies—Sir Hope and Dame Mercy and all the rest ; but these are merely enumerated and no effort is made to clothe them in flesh and blood ; in the same manner Death has her train of allegorical knights.

[1] Edited by J. H. Hanford and J. M. Steadman in *Studies in Philology*, vol. 15, p. 223.

The introduction of the figure of Death gives the poet an opportunity for a study in constrast, which he makes use of by a few graphic strokes rather than by great attention to detail ; the picture is gruesome, almost causing the dreamer to faint.   Death slays one thousand five hundred kings and queens at a blow, and many children in their cradles, and succeeds in casting a gloom over the whole scene ; it is only when Lady Life has successfully appealed to the high king of Heaven that Death reluctantly stays her hand.   This is the signal for the debate to begin and Lady Life seizes the opportunity of exposing Death, accusing the latter of killing the innocent grass and green trees, and man, the handiwork of God himself ; Death subtly defends her actions by reference to the disobedience of Adam and Eve, to which Lady Life replies that Death's cruel deeds must be those of the Devil.

From this point onward Death alters her tactics and assumes a double rôle, namely that of the enemy of physical life but also the servant of God.   She it is who restrains men from excessive wickedness ; she it was who killed Adam and Eve, the patriarchs, Alexander, Hector, Arthur, Gawain, and even ' Jesu of Heaven ' :

345,   " Haue not I justed gentlye with Jesu of heauen ?
          He was frayd of my fface in ffreshest of time,
          Yett I knocked him on the crosse and carued throughe his hart."

Apparently remembering that she is the servant of God, Death kneels low in adoration at the name of Jesus, followed by Lady Life and by every one in Heaven, in Earth and in Hell.   Lady Life then tells Death that having uttered such ' witless ' words she has sealed her own doom, and in very striking terms tells how Death came like a traitor and beat Jesus on the cross so that the blood ran down from the rood ; she thought Him dead, but on dis-covering her mistake had run in haste to warn Satan to bolt the gates of hell quickly ; but Jesus had followed and ' harrowed hell '.   So Lady Life turns to her ' barnes ' and encourages them, for she has won the victory ; having identified herself with Ever-lasting Life, she brings back to life all those whom Death had slain, making them fairer than before.   The dreamer would have followed Lady Life, but he awoke and closes the account with a prayer to Jesus.

The poem has thus a simple unity of form and structure ; the speeches are well balanced, and though the debate as such is not brilliant, it is not unskilfully designed.   As already observed, both figures have a double rôle, a fact which threatens to upset

5

the stability of the work ; yet the poet successfully prevents this by emphasising the essential unity of this double rôle. We leave Death kneeling at the foor of the cross, the servant not the enemy of God ; likewise all life appears as one, natural and supernatural. In this way the poet is worthy of comparison with the author of *Piers Plowman ;* he keeps his gaze steadfastly upon life's realities and his imaginative vision, though not powerful, is nevertheless clear and discerning.

While the poem is obviously indebted to *Piers Plowman*,[1] the work is strongly reminiscent of *Wynnere and Wastoure* and of *The Parlement of the Thre Ages.* In all three we have the allegorical debate, the dream-framework and the usual accompanying devices. Professor Hanford [2] has also noted the strong resemblance in actual details in all three poems in the opening vision-scenes, and an essential kinship in the principal figures in the three debates. Not merely are *Wynnere* and *Wastoure* parallel to *Life* and *Death*, *Old Age* in *The Parlement* is the messenger of Death. Another interesting point mentioned by the same authority is the predilection for romance shared by the authors of *Death and Life* and *The Parlement.*

" From this comparison it will appear that in its general structure *Death and Life* approximates very closely to *Wynnere and Wastoure*, while in its essential theme and in details of expression it is rather nearer to *The Parlement.* The resemblances in either case are too striking and fundamental to be the result of accident." [3] The author of *Death and Life* was certainly acquainted with the three earlier poems, and further was steeped in the alliterative traditions, as a study of his phrases and vocabulary will show.

Luick would date the poem *c.* 1450, and in this Dr. Steadman is in general agreement, who says, " the poem is before 1450 rather than after that date " ; though direct means of dating the poem are entirely lacking, yet everything points to the middle of the fifteenth century as the period of composition. The poem is a fitting epilogue to the great allegorical work of the alliterative school, and through *Piers Plowman* looks back to the earliest example *Wynnere and Wastoure.*

---

[1] The extent and limits of this indebtedness have been very thoroughly investigated by Professor Hanford ; *op. cit.*, pp. 246–8.

[2] *Op. cit.*, p. 252.   [3] *Op. cit.*, p. 252.

IV. Religious Poetry.

The poets of the alliterative school are characterised by their " high seriousness " and loftiness of purpose, notes which are reflected in the allegory of *Piers Plowman* and also in the later imitations which it called forth.   So the gifted author of *Pearl*, *Purity* and *Patience* paraphrases the Scriptures and seeks to relate them to human life, and even the shorter religious poems here discussed are marked by the same lofty outlook.   Fate has preserved to us few alliterative religious poems, but those we have are not unworthy of any age.

Patience,[1] whether classified as a paraphrase of the Scriptures or as a homily, must occupy a high place in either category of Middle English works.   Perhaps the most striking feature of the poem is its artistic unity ;   it is a perfect whole.   In the short prologue the writer introduces to us his *theme*—the virtue of Patience, which he says may often be displeasing at the time but in the end brings its reward ;   his *text*, the Beatitudes, then follows with a special stress upon Patience as underlying the whole of the Christian life.   His *sermon* illustrating this virtue takes the form of a recounting of the story of Jonah the prophet, and the version given is as simple and severe as that in the Vulgate.   It is, of course, much fuller, for the poet had a vivid imagination which made of the storm a mighty tempest visualised in its every detail and which pictured the interior of the whale realistically.   The poet loved to narrate his story, and had also the ability to write with power.

He was equally successful in his portraying of human nature ; the character of Jonah was fully developed in his original, but the poet has given us delightful sidelights on the hero ;   the reader does not easily forget Jonah's musings to himself against God or his ponderings as he sits in a nook of the whale's entrails.   The largeness of the poet's heart is admirably reflected in the final speech of God to the prophet which brings the work to its dramatic climax ; it is the poet who speaks through the mouth of God and appeals for the little children who never did any wrong, for many who cannot discern between their right hand and their left and for all the dumb beasts who know not how to sin.   Out of a single verse of the original the poet has made a speech of thirty lines throbbing with human sympathy.   No long moral is appended—the story

[1] Edited by H. Bateson, Manchester, 1918, and by Sir I. Gollancz, S.E.E.P., 1913.

must speak for itself—and the poet wisely draws his poem to a close, leaving us a masterpiece both in construction and in execution.

PURITY [1] is certainly not the equal of *Patience*, either in design or in execution ; the poet's method is more rambling and his style far less concise than in *Patience*. The theme is the virtue of purity, but the poet was unable to find a single passage of Scripture equal in power and suitability to the Book of Jonah which he paraphrased to illustrate the virtue of patience. His material was less suitable and definitely more intractable.

After a somewhat discursive paraphrase of the parable of the Marriage Feast, accompanied by moralising and admonition, the poet treats in great detail of the Fall of the Angels, the Flood, the Destruction of Sodom and Gomorrah. After pointing the moral of the Scriptural passages, the writer should have brought his poem to a close, but instead of doing so, he tells us of ' the purity of Christ and of the Virgin and their potency for man's salvation,' and then passes on to adduce further examples of impurity from the Book of Daniel with God's judgment upon the wickedness of Nebuchadnezzar and Belshazzar ; in design therefore the work is not remarkable.

In atmosphere the two poems also differ considerably ; in *Patience* the emphasis is on God's mercy and magnanimity and the poet shows a corresponding human sympathy. In *Purity*, however, much more space is devoted to direct moralising and great stress is laid upon the severity and justness of God, the poet displaying the same harshness of spirit. Alone in the beautiful passage dealing with the purity of Christ do we get the sympathetic tenderness found so repeatedly in *Patience ;* here he goes so far as to say that God is merciful, and though man may have sinned grievously, he may nevertheless through penance become a pearl. The whole passage, l. 1113 *et seq.*, likening the reformed sinner to a pearl should be read carefully in connection with any attempt to interpret *Pearl ;* to this point we shall, however, return later.

It is impossible not to believe that *Purity* was an early work of the poet, probably earlier than *Patience*. It is less finished in every way but, though we miss the vividness of *Patience*, we have, as has often been pointed out, many spirited descriptions, such as those of the Flood, the Destruction of the Cities and the spoiling of the Temple, to mention only a few, which are not merely delightful in

[1] Edited by R. J. Menner, Yale, 1920, and by Sir I. Gollancz, S.E.E.P., 1921.

themselves, but indicative of what the poet could accomplish in the way of description.

PEARL [1] has been the subject of much controversy in the present century, and little agreement concerning its nature has been reached. Dr. Morris, the first editor of the poem, regarded the work as an elegy, and his view was endorsed by Sir I. Gollancz, Professor Carleton Brown, Professor Osgood and by Mr. Bateson. It was, however, most unfortunate that Gollancz, Osgood, and Bateson in particular, should have attempted such a minute reconstruction of the poet's life ; imaginary details of the poet's boyhood, manhood, married life and status were given for which there was no solid foundation ; it was a fanciful pastime. But allowing for these extravagances, their views regarding *Pearl* as an elegy are eminently sensible ; any one reading the poem for the first time would inevitably regard it as such a lament.

This view of *Pearl* as an elegy prevailed until Professor Schofield wrote an article entitled *The Nature and Fabric of the Pearl*,[2] in which he declared that the poem was not an elegy, that the child had never lived, and that Pearl was the symbol of ' clean maidenhood '. This article is now little more than a literary curiosity, for its arguments have been ably refuted more than once. Dr. Coulton was the first to do this in his rejoinder, *In Defence of Pearl*,[3] in which he pointed out that certain of the clergy were allowed to marry, that Boccaccio's daughter Violante lectures her father in exactly the same unnatural way as does Pearl, that the poet specifically refers to the child's corpse, and most important of all that if Pearl were simply maidenhood, in what manner could the author's lost maidenhood now be safe in heaven.

Professor Schofield was naturally obliged to defend himself against this not unjustifiable attack and did so in an admirable article entitled *Symbolism, Allegory and Autobiography in the Pearl*.[4] In this article, however, he does not answer the criticisms which had been raised against his view of Pearl as the symbol of pure maidenhood, and it is indeed quite obvious that Mr. Coulton's objections on this score are valid. This does not mean that the article is of no value ; the reverse is the case ; but this *specific* interpretation of the poem is not proved.

It is perhaps for this reason that Professor Schofield seems less anxious to gain acceptance for his specific interpretation of the

[1] Edited by Sir I. Gollancz, 1921, and by C. G. Osgood, 1906.
[2] P.M.L.A., 19, 154.　　　[3] M.L.R., 2, 39.　　　[4] P.M.L.A., 24, 585.

poem, as for his general interpretation of the poem as an allegory of some kind, and not as an elegy. Herein lies the value of his work ; he has studied the poem line by line—not always, however, with very stimulating results, to be sure—and is successful in throwing over many of the far-fetched autobiographical details discovered in the poem by Gollancz and Osgood. To do this was to perform a great service to scholarship. Thus he showed that numerous passages in which the translators had seen veiled references to the maiden, were simply allusions to the symbol ' pearl '. But the article does not take us very far, for its writer is so anxious to minimise and in fact to dispose of the personal element that he oversteps the bounds of common sense and probability. In the first place, if Pearl is allegorical, it is essential to state what the symbol means, for it must be something which the poet lost, mourned and could recover by the grace of God, strengthened by partaking of the Blessed Sacrament ; for this Professor Schofield can suggest nothing better than ' clean maidenhood '. Secondly, the clue to the allegory must be something which the poet could simultaneously represent as a pearl and as a dead maiden of two years old ; it follows that this must be something dear to him, and not any abstract virtue such as chastity.

The view of Professor W. H. Garrett [1] that Pearl is an intricate allegory upon the Eucharist has rightly been criticised and rejected both by Professor Carleton Brown [2] and by Sister Madeleva.[3] Professor Garrett (as suggested by his frontispiece) holds that the poet was inspired to write the allegory from seeing the Sacred Host elevated for the adoration of the faithful, which being round in shape reminded the poet of a pearl. In mediæval allegories we find pearls symbolising almost everything except the Blessed Sacrament, and in the poem itself there is no suggestion of such a comparison ; the text does not in the least lend support to his view. Again, as Sister Madeleva points out, Professor Garrett has little idea of the construction of the Mass as celebrated in the Western Church, for he states that the principal events of the Mass are ' the Pro-Anaphora, the Canon, the Agnus Dei and Adoration,' whereas the chief stages in the Mass are the Offertory and the Canon, consisting of the Consecration and Communion. Since much of Professor Garrett's interpretation turns on his incorrect analysis of the Mass, it is obvious that the argument falls to the ground. Many of the

---

[1] *The Pearl : An Interpretation*, Univ. of Wash. Pubs. 4, no. 1, Seattle, 1918.   [2] M.L.N., vol. 34, p. 42.

[3] *Pearl : A Study in Spiritual Dryness*, p. 18.

Eucharistic parallels are taken from the Eastern Orthodox Liturgies, details of which would be unknown to a Middle English poet, lay or clerical.

Sister Madeleva is hardly fair to Professor Garrett in saying that in the Orthodox Church the Sacred Host used for Adoration is square, representing redemption as extending to the four corners of the Earth, and that he ought not to have inferred that when the poet described the pearl as round, he was alluding to the roundness of the Host, because in the Eastern Church it happened to be square ; for Professor Garrett drew parallels from the Western Church whenever he could. She is also quibbling when she says that the Sacret Host is circular and a pearl spherical. Clearly, however, Professor Garrett's suggestion is untenable.

Professor Fletcher's view [1] is interesting. Believing that the poet was using the pearl to symbolise the Blessed Virgin Mary, Professor Fletcher was evidently confronted with the difficulty of explaining numerous passages in the poem which had no obvious connection with the supposed allegory. He then concluded that the poem was an elegy as well as an allegory, and that the poet was presenting his daughter in the image of the Virgin ; " the poet paints his glorified maiden in the very colours of the symbolised portrait of Mary ".[2] Professor Fletcher bases all his argument upon the parallels he has been able to find in the *De Laud. B. Mar. Virg.* of Albertus Magnus ; but as the latter states, the Blessed Virgin was " figured " in nearly every person or thing mentioned in Scripture, and moreover, as Schofield stated, the explanations of the ' pearl of great price ' were exceedingly numerous, and it is not usual to find the pearl symbolising the Blessed Virgin, despite the fact that Albertus Magnus had written an intricate allegory of that kind. Professor Fletcher rightly lays great stress on the couplet (ll. 743–4) :—

> " *I rede þe forsake þe worlde wode*
> *And porchase þy perle maskelles.*"

Taking this to refer to the Virgin-cult, he is led to interpret the poem accordingly. But not only is there no warrant for such an interpretation of the couplet, the allegory has to be forced by the critic upon the poem in a most unnatural way ; nor does Professor Fletcher attempt to interpret the poem line by line in the light of his own suggestion.

[1] Fletcher, *The Allegory of the Pearl*, J:E.G.P., vol. 20, p. 1.
[2] *Ibid.*, p. 7.

Sister Madeleva [1] of the Congregation of the Holy Cross has exceeded all previous critics in the ingenuity with which she has interpreted the poem. She calls Pearl *A Study in Spiritual Dryness*, and sees in it the autobiography of a great mystic cast in allegorical form. To her there is no suggestion of any child ; the poet's loss is the displacement of the early raptures of spiritual joy, or what is called " consolation "—by interior desolation—an experience well known to the religious and well evidenced by all the saints ; she is able to quote many parallels, from Richard Rolle, Blessed Juliana of Norwich, St. Teresa, and many others ; in this she is of course treading familiar ground, and it might have been wiser to quote only such parallels as were directly relevant to the discussion of Pearl as an allegory.

Sister Madeleva explains the allegory line by line, and it is to her credit that none of the passages which would appear to make her theory improbable are carefully omitted, but the difficulties are faced. Sister Madeleva comes through without any apparent difficulty ; it is to her so simple that it seems strange that no one should have thought of it before. The mystic mourned the loss of interior joy in a state of utter desolation, but face to face with his previous joy in a mystical vision, he realised that through the grace of God and participation in the Blessed Sacrament, he could recapture it ; the poem ends therefore on a note of joy.

One or two extreme examples will illustrate her method ; the poet says that the child was only two years old when she died, and did not know the PATER NOSTER or the CREED ; this Sister Madeleva does not interpret literally but as meaning that the mystic was but recently become a religious and scarcely knew the rudiments of spiritual life. Or again the maiden tells the dreamer that what he lost was but a rose that flowered and failed according to nature ; this is interpreted as the withering of ' sensible ' devotion which does not affect the root of devotion ; to a religious, God encourages the soul at first by spiritual joy, but causes this to wither lest devotion should prove too easy.

Sister Madeleva interprets Pearl as a spiritual autobiography in the light of the experience of Catholic mysticism as found in the writings of the Saints, and from her own spiritual growth as a religious. From this point of view only a religious is capable of criticising her interpretation ; evidently to her the poem is *The Mystic's Progress*, for she sees in the allegory her own

[1] *Pearl : A Study in Spiritual Dryness*, New York, 1925.

experience; in much the same way Professor Klaeber suggests that Beowulf is intended to represent the figure of Christ. An allegory can be read into anything, for one may see in some picture or other what to one is the perfect expression of something to which one is very attached. This may be the case with Sister Madeleva's interpretation of *Pearl*; if not, then *Pearl* becomes the greatest piece of Catholic mysticism ever known.

But there is a second line of criticism, and it has been stated so admirably by Professor Menner that his words may be quoted : " In every case Sister Madeleva's explanation might be regarded as possible in varying degrees ; but in every case, also, a strained and curious interpretation is substituted for the natural one, and the total impression is not favourable to the author's thesis ".[1] It is quite evident throughout that Sister Madeleva is determined to see allegory everywhere and to allow personal allusions nowhere ; and this is the chief reason why her views are unacceptable.

Again, would it not be true to say that *Pearl* would become the most artificial poem of the Middle Ages ? for behind it there would be a poet who had darkly concealed in almost every line some truth about his inward spiritual experience without leaving any definite clue to the meaning of it all. This is not the way of mystics ; scarcely ever do they use allegorical forms, and amid all the parallels quoted by Sister Madeleva there is no such one as this ; the mystics relate their experiences and visions in a more straight-forward manner.

Professor W. K. Greene,[2] in a brief article, takes the discussion of the doctrine of divine grace and the exposition of the parable of the workers in the vineyard as the central theme of the poem and concludes that the aim of the poet was to illustrate this doctrine, and that he used the allegorical figure of a child who died in infancy to express his own views. He is careful to state that the child was merely a literary fiction ; " in its purpose the *Pearl* is probably no less homiletic than *Cleanness* and *Patience*, though it is cast in the form of a vision and is warmed by emotion ".[3] He objects to the elegiac view as being unwarranted by the text, and to Schofield's allegorical view as being improbable in ' converting the maiden into so cold and impersonal a thing as pure maidenhood '. Professor Greene's many objections to the elegiac view are not very plausibly stated, and he never gets down to realities. What he is

---

[1] M.L.N., 41, p. 413.
[2] *The Pearl—a New Interpretation*, P.M.L.A., 40, p. 814.
[3] P. 815.

perfectly right in doing is to reject the detailed fabrications concerning the poet's life constructed by Morris, Gollancz, Osgood and Bateson.[1]

His criticism of Professor Schofield's views is sound; he rightly observes that Schofield's solution of the Pearl as pure maidenhood neglects the fact that ' literary art alone, without the emotion of the mystic, could never have produced the poem,' [2] and also that Schofield failed to explain away the poet's mourning and loss which are certainly in the poem and which cannot be explained merely by being ignored.   This constitutes the most valid objection to Schofield's theory.

When Professor Greene concludes from all this that the figure of a child lost in infancy is employed, then, as a literary device to impart the spiritual lesson of divine grace, it is difficult to see the connection.   Granted that there is a considerable amount of theological discussion in the poem, can we thereby conclude that this gives us the clue to the poet's purpose?   Professor Greene agrees that *Patience* and *Purity* are by the same author as *Pearl;* if he is correct in this supposition, why did not the poet give us another homily without this unnatural literary fiction of a dead child?   not merely is this unlike the habit of a mediæval poet, and especially of the author of *Purity* and *Patience*, it reduces the poem to an artificiality and makes the poet's loss—which Professor Greene is so intent in defending as genuine—quite unreal.

From a criticism of these views certain facts have come to light. In the first place, as Professor Menner in his criticism of Sister Madeleva's work has suggested, it is a mistake to regard allegory and elegy as incompatible, or that an elegy must be mournful throughout; there is much in Milton's LYCIDAS which is not pure elegy.   The critics on both sides are so intent on interpreting the poem either as an elegy or as an allegory that they weaken their case very considerably.   There is much in the poem that is definitely symbolical; the poet is mourning the loss of a pearl which he later identifies with the maiden.   Both the pearl and the maiden *may* be symbols of something dear to the poet, but they must be something which the poet can gain, for the child advises him to purchase his pearl.   Moreover, she describes herself as a pearl,

---

[1] Professor Greene is surely a little premature in suggesting that most critics admit the poet's indebtedness to Boccaccio's *Fourteenth Eclogue* and to Dante's *Divine Comedy !*   Dogmatic statements of this kind occur frequently throughout the article.   [2] P. 823.

is adorned with pearls, wears a large pearl on her breast, and both the pearl and the maiden are without spot.

A child who had died is in the poem, and must either be historical or a literary fiction ; impressionistic views may be despised, but they are sometimes essential as here, and we confess personally that we feel here is a poet trying to get over to us and win our sympathy in his loss ; and again, when the work is viewed without any preconceptions, the most obvious theme of the poem is seen to be the death of the child, without quibbling about the poet's relationship to her.   But the child is to the poet something more than a child ; she symbolised something that also suggested to him a pearl, and it was presumably this which the maiden urged the poet to purchase.   Moreover, she gained it by innocence through the rite of baptism, whereas he can only gain it by the grace of God.   If the poem is a genuine elegy, then the thing symbolised is most likely to be ' the childlike innocence ' of the maiden which he realises as the goal of his spiritual quest ; this is the pearl of great price which he is advised to purchase, as the child herself suggests in stanzas 61 and 62 ; she has been telling him how Christ had blessed the little children, and had declared that unless a man possessed their spirit he could not enter the Kingdom of Heaven.   This (l. 729), she says, is the pearl of great price sought by the jeweller, and it is at this point (l. 743) that she advises him to purchase the pearl of great price.

In other words, the child became the occasion of something infinitely wider in scope.   Critics have surely neglected the passage in *Purity* which deals with the pearl, ll. 1115 *et seq.*, in which the poet says that though a man be foul by his sins, yet because of God's mercy, through shrift and penance he may become a pearl, which though she lose her colour yet by being washed in wine regains her former brightness ; so may the sinner regain his former innocence.   Here, if anywhere, is surely to be found the poet's intention in *Pearl;* if it be the same poet whose heart in deep human sympathy went out to the innocent children and cattle in Nineveh, and to the unbaptised pagan judge, may it not have been that also in *Pearl* his heart went out to the little child who though baptised had not had time to accomplish much in the vineyard, only to discover by meditating upon these things that she had become a pearl, and that also in his case the same thing might happen, not by merit, but by the grace of God in the Blessed Sacrament.   In so doing, he allied himself with St. Thomas Aquinas and not with St. Bonaventura and others who believed that children lacked personal merit.

We cannot imagine the author of *Purity*, *Patience*, and even of *Sir Gawain* writing a poem in which he did not enunciate some sort of moral truth, and it is unmistakably there. But through a personal loss the poet's sympathies had become wider than when he wrote *Purity*, for he had learned that the grace of Christ was great enough to restore to him that former state of innocence, the loss of which had so been brought home to him by the loss of the innocent child ; but, as in the other three poems the stress is on the ethical rather than on the mystical side.

The poem is in many ways one of the most remarkable in Middle English ; it is admittedly a metrical and stylistic triumph ; its pictures when minutely and carefully visualised are found to be exceedingly beautiful ; and as Wells has admirably said [1]: ' It exhibits to us a true poet and true man—a person of high refinement, of extensive cultivation, of great and elevated imagination, of warm response to physical beauty, of fine artistic sense, of intense feeling, deeply religious, absolutely sincere, devout, strong, sound, sane, thoroughly human '.

St. Erkenwald [2] belongs to the group of Middle English writings dealing with legends of the saints ; there are extant many collections of such legends as well as isolated lives, and the stories enjoyed immense popularity. *St. Erkenwald* has, however, little of the popular ' cheapness ' usually found in this type of work ; it is a most artistic composition, compact and graphic in style. It relates how the grave of a judge was found in the crypt of St. Paul's Cathedral during excavations made when St. Erkenwald was Bishop of London ; the body was as if it had only just been buried, and when addressed by the Bishop on his arrival after celebration of High Mass, relates how it is the body of a pagan judge in ' New Troy ' many centuries before, who not being a Christian was compelled to remain in Limbo until such time as he might be baptised. The saintly bishop's tears fall on the corpse, whereupon the judge is baptised, his soul immediately passing to Heaven, and his body turning into dust while all the bells in the city ring forth a joyous peal.

The story is simple enough, and is clearly not calculated to generate either interest or excitement ; though if it be true, as seems not unlikely,[3] that the poem was written for the St. Erkenwald celebration in 1386, the work would have more point

---

[1] J. E. Wells, *A Manual of M.E. Writings*, p. 583.
[2] Edited by Sir I. Gollancz, S.E.E.P., 1922 ; R. L. Savage, Yale, 1926.
[3] Savage, p. lxxv.

and on that account arouse more interest. In any case, the poet makes the most of his material, imparting to this bare outline a wealth of graphic detail, yet nevertheless subordinating it to the careful unfolding of the narrative. In construction it will bear comparison with *Sir Gawain and the Green Knight,* and the dénouement in both is similar, the solution being carefully concealed until the end. This capacity to afford the reader surprise is likewise manifest in many of the purely descriptive parts of the poem ; perhaps the most suitable illustration of this gift is afforded by the account of the body in lines 77–92, a passage reminiscent of the picture of the Green Knight. It will be recalled that the fact that both the knight and his horse are green is reserved until near the end ; in the same way, the fact that the corpse is undecayed is not disclosed until the picture was well-nigh complete. As an example of the poet's descriptive power we quote four lines from the passage just mentioned (ll. 89–92) :—

> " And als freshe hym þe face and the fleshe nakyde,
> Bi his eres and bi his hondes þat openly shewid
> With ronke rode as þe rose, and two rede lippes,
> As he in sounde sodanly were slippide opon slepe."

In the same way throughout the poem the writer shows a keen eye for the picturesque, even to the most trivial detail ; in no instance, however, does the detail have the appearance of an insertion for its own sake, but remains part of a larger design. The poet is eager to tell us that when the body was found, the bishop happened to be away in Essex, and a little later how the door was opened when the procession reached the tomb (ll. 140–1) :—

> " Men unclosid hym þe cloyster with clustrede keies ;
> Bot pyne wos with þe grete prece þat passyd hym after."

Sometimes the poet achieves his effect by the use of a crisp simile, as in the account of the sudden decay of the body (ll. 343–4) :—

> " And alle the blee of his body was blakke as þe moldes,
> As roten as þe rottok þt rises in powdere."

Yet a further characteristic of his descriptive power is the ability to convey by words the effect which a situation has had upon the mind of some one ; so we have the effect of the speaking-corpse upon the people, remarkably similar to that of the Green Knight's challenge upon the frightened knights (ll. 217–19) :—

> " Quil he in spelunke þus spake, þer sprange in þe pepulle
> In al þis worlde no worde, ne wakenyd no noice,
> Bot al as stille as þe ston stoden and listonde."

The poet has successfully enshrouded his simple narrative in a mystical and religious atmosphere, partly by the use of description and partly by the breathing of his own personality into the work. We may be quite sure that he was not concerned about the validity of baptism by tears, or about the theological difficulties involved in the final salvation of a pagan who had died unbaptised ; it was the pity of his large and generous heart that went out in sympathy to the judge, as Savage has aptly reminded us,[1] " Theologians before the time of Aquinas had been fairly well agreed that the lot of those who did not hold the faith was eternal damnation. Against this dark background of ecclesiastical opinion the poet's warm and ready sympathy for struggling humanity shines out the more brightly. His reaction, as Osgood has said, is nearly always personal, and thus it comes about that he feels more for the poor dumb beasts and the innocent women and children of Nineveh than for the prophet of God, more for the little girl who had gone to dwell in heaven than for the angelic orders therein, more for the pagan judge than for the saintly bishop of ' love London toun '."

Tests of vocabulary, metre, style and artistic merit appear to justify the theory that the author of *St. Erkenwald* also wrote the poems of the Cotton MS. Nero A.X., but it is not insignificant that all five poems are indelibly stamped with the same distinctive personality.

THE PISTILL OF SUSAN [2] was evidently a popular poem, judging by the number of copies that have survived. Translated from the *History of Susanna*, contained in the Old Testament *Apocrypha*, it is not a slavish translation of the original ; at times it becomes a mere paraphrase ; sentences are omitted and passages are added. The description of the garden is the most obvious example of this, though the result is not particularly happy. It is too much of a mere catalogue of trees, fruits and birds, compared with which the similar description in *Pearl* seems quite original. There is little emphasis on colour such as one might have expected.

Occasionally a human touch is added by the poet, as when Susan, having requested to see her husband, proclaims to him her innocence :—

---

[1] *St. Erkenwald*, p. lxxiv.
[2] Edited by F. J. Furnivall, E.E.T.S., 117, p. 626, 1901 ; F. J. Amours, S.T.S., vols. 27 and 38, p. 189, 1897.

> " And euere he cussed þat swete,
> ' In oþer world schul we mete ' ;
> Seid he no mare."

Indeed, one could rightly say that the poet had succeeded in humanising the story ; he feels for the wronged Susan and makes us share his sympathy. It is perhaps this which gives the work its value, for its style is not distinctly attractive ; it is lacking in terseness and mere catch phrases are frequently employed for the sake of rhyme and alliteration, as in the following couplet :—

> " þis word we witnesse for ay,
> Wiþ tonge and wiþ toþ."

More than one critic has observed that the verse is particularly melodious ; there is a marked lilt, and it has been suggested that the poem may have been intended to be sung. At any rate, the poet had realised the immense possibilities in the rhyming alliterative stanza so popular in the north ; he avoided excessive ruggedness on the one hand and excessive regularity on the other.

St. John the Evangelist [1] is not a noteworthy poem. In the course of 264 lines the author treats of the birth of the apostle and of the chief incidents of his career, including his miracles at Ephesus. Most of the legends current in the Middle Ages concerning St. John are enumerated in a way that recalls Ælfric's treatment of the same theme in his *Lives of the Saints*. The poem gains nothing by being in the form of an address to the apostle, especially when one considers its purely descriptive character, and the impassioned appeal to the saint for assistance and intercession which one might have expected is completely absent.

The lack of originality is not redeemed by the unfortunate style ; for the poem abounds in absolutely conventional phrasing, both alliterative and otherwise ; the artless repetition of such phrases as *bouxom and bayne, ffaythefull and frendely, wise and witty* is typical of the author's lack of poetic insight. He was a good versifier, but though he accomplished his metrical feat of writing in a complicated rhyming stanza with excessive alliteration,[2] he was never able to transmute his material into poetry.

The Quatrefoil of Love [3] is the title happily supplied by Sir Israel Gollancz to a religious poem of the fourteenth century contained in the MSS. Brit. Mus. Add. 31042 and Bod. Add. A. 106.

[1] Edited by G. G. Perry, E.E.T.S., 26, p. 88, 1867.
[2] See vol. 1, pp. 217, 226, 231.
[3] Edited by Sir I. Gollancz in *An English Miscellany*, p. 112.

Doubtless designed as a piece of religious instruction, it has none
of the formlessness and 'set purpose' of the usual didactic verse.
The framework is conventional—a May morning with the opening
flowers and the singing birds, but the poet does not linger over these
details ; he does not even fall asleep and dream, but as he walks
along he hears a maiden complaining to a turtle-dove of her failure
to find a true love and asking for counsel.   The bulk of the poem is
occupied with the counsel of the turtle-dove, consisting of a terse
and picturesque account of the Incarnation, Passion, Death,
Resurrection and Ascension of Our Lord, followed by a description
of the Doom.   Especially noteworthy are the passages dealing with
Christ's death, 196, etc., which are characterised by extreme
simplicity and restraint, and with the Doom, 378, etc.   Much
space is devoted to the latter theme, which forms the climax of the
poem.   It is a mixed company that gathers together—kings and
kaisers, bishops and barons, earls and emperors, priests and prelates,
and lords and ladies, whose manner of dress is most picturesquely
described.   But what gives the passage its value is the fact that
no place is afforded to sensational bodily fears and tortures ; it is
the mental fears and anxieties that the poet seeks to convey to his
audience.

The author's point of view is set forth in the final verse, a point
of view frequently suggested throughout the poem—it is the need
for reliance upon the Blessed Virgin Mary for her intercession with
her Son :—

510, " Vnto þat ilke ferthe lefe I rede þat we praye,
            þat scho wille bere oure message with a mylde mode,
            And þat scho speke for oure lufe bifore þat laste day
            Vnto þase ilke iij leues þat we may wyne with mode
            þat grace grauntede grete gode þat dyede on gud fryday
            Vnto þat ilke ferthe lefe gracyouse and gude."

There is no other poem which is relatively so packed with alliterative phrases, but the poet has such control of his material and
of his metre that the style is strangely fresh and pleasing.

These are practically all the religious poems that can be claimed
for the Alliterative School or Schools ; they form pleasant reading
and are singularly free from prosaic moralising and admonition.
There are no other paraphrases of the Scriptures to equal *Patience*
and *Purity ;* there is no other Saint's legend to equal *St. Erkenwald ;*
and apart from lyrics there are no religious poems which can
approach those of the Alliterative School.

As a matter of principle, we have excluded THE ENEMIES OF MAN, but nevertheless in spirit and possibly also in form (it is regularly alliterated throughout), it can be claimed by the Alliterative School ; in its vigour and sincerity it belongs there.   Religious themes are always difficult to handle, but these Western and Northern poets avoided many of the common pitfalls.

V. MISCELLANEOUS LATER WORKS.

Among the poems of the Alliterative Revival which have not been discussed in one of the four preceding groups, THE HOWLAT and SCOTTISH FIELD are the most important.   The former work, a Scottish poem of *c.* 1450, is an imitation of Chaucer's PARLEMENT OF FOULES, and its chief connection with the Alliterative Revival lies in its metrical form—the alliterative stanza which in different varieties was so popular in the North of England and in Scotland. Like SCOTTISH FIELD, a late English work, written after Flodden Field, 1515, it is also a panegyric.   In method, however, the two poems are dissimilar.

THE BUKE OF THE HOWLAT [1] was composed—as the author tells us in the last stanza—at Darnaway for Elizabeth Dunbar, the Countess of Moray, whose first husband was one of the Douglas family that perished in the struggle with James II of Scotland. The internal evidence is sufficient to date the poem as between 1447 and 1455, since there are references to the arms of Pope Nicholas V, while the death of the Earl of Moray in 1455 must have occurred after the poem was written.   The probability, therefore, is in favour of 1450.[2]

The main idea of the poem—the assembly of the birds and their appeal to Dame Nature—came undoubtedly from Chaucer's *Parlement of Foules*, but the indebtedness does not extend much beyond the general framework ; in detail this is an original work. The reader seeks to discover some recondite meaning in the poem, but it seems quite certain that none was intended ; the humorous story is clearly meant to be taken at its face value.   Little skill was needed to describe the owl's dissatisfaction with his appearance, his subsequent appeal to the peacock, the Pope of birds, against Dame Nature, and the outcome of his petition.   Nor did such a framework present great opportunities.   The poem is somewhat lacking in interest, and some strain is put upon the reader's attention by the lengthy description of the woodpecker's coat-armour

---

[1] Edited by F. J. Amours, S.T.S., 1897.   [2] *Ibid.*, p. xxvii.

which contains among other insignia the lion rampant of Scotland and the arms of Douglas, whose doughty deeds are extolled in the course of fourteen stanzas—XXXI–XLIV—an interpolation which greatly impairs the artistic value of the work.   The merits of the piece, however, are such as to counteract these shortcomings.   The verse is extremely vigorous and the difficulties of working the names of sixty-four species of bird into alliterative lines are easily overcome.   The danger of mere cataloguing is not in this case always avoided, and the same weakness manifests itself again in the list of musical instruments (st. LIX).   Yet the author shows considerable humour and ingenuity in assigning the various parts to the various birds ; the peacock becomes the Pope, the cranes with their red hats the cardinals, and the white swans bishops.   The Pope's retinue is picturesquely described, and the emperor's retinue, while not so distinguished in itself, affords the poet an opportunity for vigorous writing which he is not slow to take advantage of.

The passages which leave a more memorable impression on the mind are undoubtedly the picture of the owl gazing at his shadow in the lake, as he soliloquises upon his ugliness, the account of the emperor's feast, the choir of minstrels singing in honour of the Virgin Mary, the juggling jay performing his tricks for the company's entertainment, and the rook babbling his unintelligible Gaelic (ll. 794-9) :—

> " Sa, come the Ruke with a rerd and a rane roch,
> A bard owt of Irland with Banachadee !
> Said : ' Gluntow guk dynyd dach hala mischy doch ;
> Raike hir a rug of the rost, or scho sall ryiue the.
> Mich macmory ach mach mometir moch loch ;
> Set hir dovne, gif hir drink ; quhat Dele alis the ? ' "

The final degradation of the owl leads the poet to warn his readers of the dangers of pride, but in putting the moralising into the mouth of the owl he shows that he had some regard for the artistic success of the poem which he was sending to the Countess of Moray.   The work is strong and full of life and energy, a worthy specimen of the later alliterative works whose death-knell had already been rung.

SCOTTISH FIELD,[1] written soon after 1515, is a panegyric of a different sort, and while it cannot be denied that the poem, especi-

---

[1] Edited by J. W. Hales and F. J. Furnivall in *Bishop Percy's Folio Manuscript*, vol. I, p. 199.   A new edition of this poem by the present writer will be published by the *Chetham Society* in their volume for 1934.

ally in the state in which it has come down to us, is very crude, it forms a fitting epilogue to the Alliterative Revival in England. It is marred throughout by the constant repetition of stock phrases and tags, and leaves the impression of a mosaic derived from earlier works, for quite half the poem consists of phrases of all types which can easily be paralleled in other alliterative poems.

The praises of the Stanleys are extolled by the simple method of relating their achievements at Bosworth and Flodden in the form of a chronicle. The earlier events dealing with the Battle of Bosworth, the reign of Henry VII, the invasion of France by Henry VIII, are passed over very rapidly, and the bulk of the poem deals with the Battle of Flodden itself. The poet has an eye for the picturesque and can describe a fight with vigour and realism, but when he descends to details he soon relapses into conventional phrasing which is reminiscent of the fourteenth-century alliterative war poems (ll. 324-9) :—

" Archers vttered out their arrowes, and egerlie they shotten ;
They proched vs with speares & put many over
That they blood out brast at there broken harnish.
Theire was swinging out of swords & swapping of headds ;
We blanked them with bills through all their bright armor
That all the dale dunned of their derfe strokes."

The poem is thoroughly conventional albeit not destitute of life, for the author had inherited some of the vigour and zest of the earlier alliterative writers.

THE PROPHECIES ASCRIBED TO À BECKET and the two SCOTTISH PROPHECIES [1] are important as attesting the popularity of alliterative verse in the north, though they are extremely crude in metre and possess little intrinsic literary value. Read in connection with the whole body of political prophetic writing of the Middle English period from the eleventh century onward, they are, however, extremely interesting documents, though no discussion of the problems arising from a study of them is possible within the limits of this book. All three works are obscure in places and the animal symbolism so frequently employed does not help to make the meaning clearer. On the stylistic side, it should be noted that the metrical structure shows the complete decadence of the alliterative long line.

[1] Edited by J. R. Lumby, E.E.T.S., 42, 1870 ; Von Dr. R. Haferkorn, *When Rome is Removed into England : Eine politische Prophezeiung des 14. Jahrhunderts*, Leipzig, 1932.

The later fifteenth and sixteenth century Scottish poems in alliterative verse, both rhymed and unrhymed, are important links in the chain of popular alliterative verse in Scotland, for " these burlesque pieces in Henryson, Dunbar and Douglas, and later in Lyndsay (in each case a single and disconnected effort) appear to have been of the nature of experiments or exercises in whimsicality, perhaps as a relief from the seriousness or more orderly humour of the muse ".[1]

Of these, Dunbar's THE TWA MARIIT WEMEN AND THE WEDO is perhaps the most sustained effort in alliterative verse, but even this is in the nature of a literary exercise or *tour de force*.   Nor is the alliterative prologue to the eighth book of Douglas' *Ænied* without suspicion of burlesque intention.   These poets write with vigour and with no little metrical skill, but the fact that the alliterative form is no longer a living poetical medium cannot be disguised.

The crude burlesques [2] similarly afford a sufficient testimony to the survival of popular alliterative verse in England to a late period.   These attempts have little, if indeed anything, in common with the works of the Alliterative Revival, for such a jingle of rhymes and alliteration could only have come from a purely popular source.

[1] G. Gregory Smith, *The Scottish Chaucerians*, Camb. Hist. Lit. 2, p. 249.
[2] See vol. 1, pp. 108 and 116.

CHAPTER 5

THE ALLITERATIVE SCHOOL.

HAVING thus surveyed in some detail the works of the Alliterative Revival and the types of poetry that were developed by their authors, we are in a better position to understand the rise of the school, its divisions, its achievements and subsequent decay. At the close of the first chapter the points of continuity between Old English and early Middle English literature were emphasised. Throughout the dark age which followed the eclipse of Old English civilisation, coinciding with the ascendancy of French as the official language, English literature is at a low ebb. The homiletic tradition survives and joins hands with the popular influences which had been at work in Old English times, but which naturally find scanty representation in extant literature. Yet the influence of the Old English literary tradition still lingered, and, if we may particularise, it was especially in the west that it was most felt. *The Departing Soul's Address to the Body* is one of the most important early Middle English embodiments of this spirit. It seems likely that its author had read *The Speech of the Lost Soul to the Body* in the Exeter Book, and though the homiletic and didactic attitude is very apparent in its lines, the poem represents a true survival of the older spirit. It is significant that one of the earliest interests in the poems of the revival was the Alexander and Dindimus debate theme, which affords a very close parallel to the earlier poem.

It is in Laȝamon's *Brut*, however, that the Old English heroic tradition has survived, though in a changed form. Laȝamon has inherited the diction, the vocabulary and phraseology of the older poetry, its interest in battles, in heroic customs, and in everything characteristically Germanic. He is so obviously in contact with the past that the point needs no further labouring.

It is not unlikely that the Laȝamon tradition lived on in the west, and that other works of a like kind were written which are no longer extant. At all events, the alliterative *Morte Arthure* is extremely similar both in spirit and outlook. Its author un-doubtedly borrowed from Laȝamon several details, and he assuredly inherited from him some of the zest for describing battles, and that heroic fire with which Laȝamon's pages abound. Save in diction, *Morte Arthure* is not far removed from *The Brut*. Neither is romantic in treatment or to any real extent affected by the French romances and there is a strength and vigour which is not found in the rhymed works of the period.

The homiletic tradition reappears in *Purity* and *Patience*, and in *The Enemies of Man*, while the popular tradition still lingers in the *ABC of Aristotle*, so reminiscent of *The Proverbs of Alfred*, and in *The Lament of the Monk*, *The Scraps of Love Songs*, and the *Burlesques*. The early popular satires as found in *The Song of the Husbandman*, form a vital link with *Piers Plowman*. Hence on the purely literary side there is no real gap in continuity from Old English times. At least three streams of influence, the heroic, the homiletic and the popular, had never died, but were destined to make their influence felt at the revival. At various points they come into touch with foreign influences, but at heart the works of the Alliterative Revival are traditional.

While there is no break in literary tradition, there is in a real sense a revival, a renewed poetic vitality and inspiration. Doubt-less something may have been lost between Laȝamon's *Brut* and the earliest alliterative poems of the fourteenth century, but there cannot have been anything very extensive. About 1350 there is in the west a renaissance, a new outburst of feeling, a new interest in poetry. Doubtless the inspiration had spread from the south and east. The French material stirred the hearts of poets and " imaginative poetry found a new home in the west-midlands. As before, poets turned to French for their subjects and often contented themselves with free adaptations of French romances. They accepted such literary conventions as the Vision, which was borrowed from the *Roman de la Rose*, to be the frame of *Wynnere and Wastoure* (1352) and *The Parlement of the Thre Ages*, before it was used in *Piers Plowman* and *The Pearl* and by *Chaucer*. But time and distance had weakened the French influence, and the new school of poets did not catch, as the southern poets did, the form and spirit of their models." [1]

The alliterative metre was already to hand.[2] It had survived through a long and curious development, so that when it emerges

---

[1] K. Sisam, *Fourteenth Century Verse and Prose*, p. xviii.
[2] See vol. 1, Part II, and Mod. Lang. Rev., vol. 27, p. 233, 1933.

into literature once more, it is in a strange disguise, but has become a metrical form better adapted to the needs of the changed language. The spirit which these poets had inherited from the past likewise called for the old alliterative metre. The wit and brilliance of the French made no appeal to the western writers, and when they do try to imitate the French, as did the author of *William of Palerne*, they are not very successful. The heroic spirit, the ' high seriousness ' which came to them so naturally, found its only suitable embodiment in alliterative verse.

This new alliterative school is confined to the west and north. Various scholars, working along different lines, have arrived at the same conclusions. From the south-west midland area come the political group of poems of the *Piers Plowman* type, *William of Palerne* and *Joseph of Arimathie*, while *Alexander A* and *B* come from central-west midland. The bulk of the remaining unrhymed works are from north-west midland, itself a wide area. There is now little doubt that *Morte Arthure*, *The Wars of Alexander* and *The Destruction of Troy* are not northern works, but were originally written in north-west midland, whatever their present form may be. This point has been abundantly demonstrated by Andrew,[1] and the same scholar, in his discussion of Huchown's works (see *infra*) has shown that *The Awntyrs of Arthure* and *The Pistill of Susan* were written in the same dialect as *Morte Arthure*—north-west midland. The alliterative poems of Scotland—*Golagrus and Gawain*, *Rauf Coilȝear* and *The Howlat* are later compositions of the fifteenth century when the voice of the west is silent. The home of alliterative poetry in the fourteenth century is the west, though there was doubtless some activity in the north and certainly a keen interest in alliterative poetry which resulted in the preservation of many poems there which might otherwise have disappeared. The works written in the north were probably shorter and more popular, such as Minot's poems, written in the alliterative long line.

Concerning the identity of any of the alliterative authors, little need be said in this book, for nothing can be stated with any degree of certainty. Leaving aside William Langland and his connection with *Piers Plowman*, we have only the mysterious *Huchown of the Awle Ryale* to whom any of the alliterative poems might be ascribed.[2]

[1] S. O. Andrew, *The Dialect of Morte Arthure*, Rev. Eng. Stud., vol. 4, p. 418, 1928 ; *The Wars of Alexander and the Destruction of Troy*, Rev. Eng. Stud., vol. 5, p. 267, 1929.

[2] The theory that Strode was the author of *Pearl* is admitted by Sir Israel Gollancz to be ' mere conjecture,' and the same is true of the suggestions concerning the identity of the author of *Sir Gawain* which have recently been brought forward.

The theories of Neilson [1] and other early scholars whereby a great number of the alliterative works was assigned to Huchown, were finally disposed of by MacCracken's able study of the whole question. [2] Wyntoun's statement that Huchown " . . . made the *Gret Gest of Arthure* and the *Anteris of Gawane* (and) the *Epistill als of Suete Susane* " must be taken at its face value, and as such the evidence for identifying the first two mentioned works with any pieces that have come down to us is rather slight. MacCracken allows that *The Pistill of Susan* is likely to be the work referred to by Wyntoun, but rejects Huchown's authorship of *Morte Arthure* and of *The Awntyrs of Arthure*.

Andrew [3] has recently examined the whole question again, but there are still doubts whether his arguments, whereby he assigns all the three poems to Huchown, are conclusive. Probably in our present state of knowledge we cannot say. The tests of rhyme, alliteration and rhythm, which Andrew employs, are of rather uncertain value, while the tests of words and phrases found in two or more of the texts are by no means conclusive. That Andrew has brought forward plausible evidence that all three poems were originally written in the north-west midland dialect cannot be denied, but the fact in itself proves nothing except that, as he himself rightly says, there is a *prima facie* case for an enquiry into the question of the unity of authorship. When it has further to be admitted that the last leaf of Wyntoun's copy of *Morte Arthure* must have been missing in order to account for his statement that he knows of no poem which deals with Arthur's death, our confidence is further shaken. It would therefore appear that until we know to what extent the alliterative poets borrowed from each other's work, the real basis of discussion will not be available. Meanwhile we shall do well to accept MacCracken's position, but at the same time be prepared to discover that Andrew's arguments may hold when further evidence is available.

The problems that are involved in theories of common authorship are many and varied. Proofs based solely upon a study of vocabulary, phraseology and style are obviously dangerous, since it is usually very difficult to distinguish between mere imitation and identical authorship. Professor Menner was fully alive to these dangers in his admirable treatment of *Purity*, and the parallels

---

[1] *Huchown of the Awle Ryale*, 1902.

[2] *Concerning Huchown*, P.M.L.A., vol. 25, p. 507, 1910.

[3] S. O. Andrew, *Huchown's Works*, Rev. Eng. Stud., vol. 5, pp. 12–21, 1929.

which he adduces between that poem and the other pieces of the same MS. are cumulatively so striking that the theory of common authorship becomes unquestionable. In this case the points of vocabulary, alliteration, phraseology and style shared by the four poems are so astonishing in their actual details that mere imitation of one poet's work by another is ruled out, and as we have already suggested there is a noticeable literary and moral affinity among the four works.

The same method of procedure will not, however, solve all the problems of common authorship, and the metrical tests are particularly valuable when, as in this case, they corroborate evidence gathered from other sources. Metrical peculiarities are less likely to be due to conscious or unconscious borrowing than is any other feature, whether of style or phraseology. When applied to the poems of the Cotton MS. Nero A.X., the metrical test is quite conclusive in its evidence.[1] Similarly, *St. Erkenwald* would seem on this basis to have come from the author of *Purity*. *Wynnere and Wastoure* and *The Parlement of the Thre Ages* on the one hand, and *Alexander A* and *B* on the other, appear to be the work of identical authors, though it does not follow that the two poems in either case were written at approximately the same time. *The Parlement of the Thre Ages* may have been separated from its companion piece by a good number of years.

The special value of the metrical test lies, however, on the *negative* side. When two poems are *notably* distinct in several of these unconscious metrical peculiarities, even though the phraseology and vocabulary may have points in common, there need be no hesitation in dismissing the theory of common authorship. In the light of such tests it becomes abundantly clear that *The Destruction of Troy*, *Morte Arthure*, *The Wars of Alexander*, and *The Destruction of Jerusalem* are by different authors. In fact, the only works for which a common authorship can be claimed are those mentioned above. The problems of Huchown cannot, of course, be settled by the application of the metrical test because the metre of rhymed poems is noticeably different from that of the unrhymed alliterative poems.

A careful examination of the alliterative phraseology contained in Part III will show how completely Neilson went astray in his study of parallel expressions, and it will also be realised that the mere use of traditional alliterative phrases in two poems does not

---

[1] See vol. I, pp. 247-57.   [2] *Ibid.*, pp. 255–6.

warrant a theory of borrowing. When poets draw from a common stock of catch phrases we have to be wary about forming hasty conclusions. On the other hand, the parallel passages here listed, while occasionally containing alliterative phrases, are in every case so strikingly similar that imitation or common authorship can safely be inferred. In the case of the poems of the Cotton MS. Nero A.X., the parallels have to be considered in the light of the other points of similarity already alluded to.

PURITY *and* SIR GAWAIN AND THE GREEN KNIGHT.[1]

Pur. 10, reken wyth reverence
Pur. 1318, rekenly wyth reverens
Gaw. 251, and rekenly hym reuerenced

Pur. 43, a boffet, paraunter
Gaw. 2343, a boffet, paraunter

Pur. 97, layteȝ ȝet ferre
Gaw. 411, layt no fyrre

Pur. 114, ay þe best byfore
Gaw. 73, þe best ay abof

Pur. 115, þe derrest at þe hyȝe dece
Gaw. 445, þe derrest on þe dece

Pur. 333, of uche best þat bereȝ lyf
Gaw. 1229, with alle þat lyf bere

Pur. 484, hit watȝ nyȝe at þe naȝt
Gaw. 929, hit watȝ neȝ at þe niȝt

Pur. 544, In devoydynge þe vylanye
Gaw. 634, voyded of vche vylany

Pur. 706, stylle stollen steven
Pur. 1778, stelen stylly þe toun or any steven rysed
Gaw. 1659, with stille stollen countenaunce

Pur. 855, he wonded no woþe of wekked knaveȝ
Gaw. 488, for woþe þat þou ne wonde

Pur. 735, tatȝ to non ille
Gaw. 1811, tas to non ille

Pur. 749, and he hit gayn þynkeȝ
Gaw. 1231, gayn hit me þynkkeȝ

Pur. 1459, enbaned under batelment wyth bantelles quoynt
Gaw. 790, enbaned vnder þe abataylment

Pur. 805, and þay nay þat þay nolde neȝ no howseȝ
Gaw. 1836, and he nayed þat he nolde neghe in no wyse

[1] Where the phrases have been previously noticed, this is acknowledged.

Pur. 832, þe trestes tylt to þe woȝe an þe table boþe
Gaw. 1684, þenne þay teldet tableȝ on trestes alofte

Pur. 854, boweȝ forth fro þe bench into þe brode ȝates
Gaw. 344, bid me boȝe fro þis benche and stonde by yow þere

Pur. 943, lest ȝe be taken in þe teche of tyraunteȝ
Gaw. 2488, he watȝ tane in tech of a faute

Pur. 1089, And ȝif clanly he þenne com ful cortays þerafter
Gaw. 653, his clannes and his cortaysye

Pur. 1376, þat to neven þe noumbre to much nye were
Gaw. 58, hit were now gret nye to neuen

Pur. 1383, troched toures bitwene
Gaw. 795, towres telded bytwene, trochet ful þik

Pur. 1408, pared out of paper
Gaw. 802, pared out of papure
　　　　　　　　　　—(All the above phrases from Menner.)

Pur. 201, he neuer so sodenly soȝt vn-soundely to weng
Gaw. 1438, and he vnsoundly out soȝt seggeȝ ouer-þwert—(Gollancz).

Pur. 1413, and ay þe nakeryn noyse notes of pipes
Gaw. 118, nwe nakryn noyse with þe noble pipes

Pur. 948, to wakan wedereȝ so wylde þe wyndeȝ he calleȝ
　　　　　and þay wroþely upwafte and wrastled togeder
Gaw. 525, wroþe wynde of þe welkyn wrasteleȝ with þe sunne [1]

PURITY *and* PATIENCE.

Pur. 9, they teen unto his temmple and temen to hymselven
Pat. 316, efte to trede on þy temple and teme to þy seluen

Pur. 24, þer as he hevened aȝt happeȝ and hyȝt hem her medez
Pat. 11, aȝt happes he hem hyȝt and vche on a mede

Pur. 381, bot al watȝ nedleȝ her note
Pat. 220, bot al watȝ nedleȝ note

Pur. 574, þe venym and þe vylanye
Pat. 71, vilanye and venym

Pur. 1294, hereȝ of Israel þe hyrne aboute
Pat. 178, herȝed out of vche hyrne to hent þat falles

Pur. 1013, þis watȝ a vengaunce violent þat voyded þise places
Pat. 370, þe verray vengaunce of God schal voyde þis place
　　　　　　　　　　—(All by Menner.)

Pur. 947–50, to be compared with Pat. 131–9—(Gollancz).

Menner also notes the following parallels which are less significant : Pur. 1675 and Pat. 392 ; Pur. 1294 and Pat. 178 ; Pur. 24 and Pat. 11 ; Pur. 256 and Pat. 260 ; Pur. 499 and Pat. 63.

[1] These are only a fraction of the striking parallels between these two poems.

PEARL *and* PURITY.

Pearl 726, wythouten mote oþer mascle
Pur. 556, wythouten maskle oþer mote—(Menner).

Pearl 980, blusched on þe burghe
Pur. 982, ho bluschet to þe burȝe

PEARL *and* PATIENCE.

Pearl 59, I slode vpon a slepyng-slaȝte
Pat. 192, in such slaȝtes of sorȝe to slepe so faste

PEARL *and* SIR GAWAIN AND THE GREEN KNIGHT.

Pearl 231, no gladder gome heþen into Grece
Gaw. 2023, þe gayest into Grece

Pearl 153-4, I schulde not wonde for wo[þe]
Gaw. 488, for woþe þat þou ne wonde
              Cp. Pur. 855 quoted above—(Gollancz).

Pearl 57, I felle upon þat floury flaȝt
Gaw. 507, falleȝ upon fayre flat, flowreȝ þere schewen

PATIENCE *and* SIR GAWAIN AND THE GREEN KNIGHT.

Pat. 89, þenne he ryses radly and raykes bylyue
Gaw. 1735, þe lady . . . ros hir up radly, rayked hir þeder

Pat. 141, þe wyndes on þe wonne water so wrastel togeder
              þat þe wawes ful wode waltered so hiȝe
Gaw. 525, wroþe wynde of þe welkyn wrasteleȝ with þe sunne.

SIR GAWAIN AND THE GREEN KNIGHT *and* ST. ERKENWALD.

Gaw. 789, of harde hewen ston
Erk. 40, harde stones for to hewe—(Savage)

Gaw. 2250, þat me gost lante
Erk. 192, þurghe sum lant goste

PATIENCE *and* ST. ERKENWALD.

Pat. 164, bot vchon glewed on his god
Erk. 171, bot glow we alle opon Godde

Pat. 316, efte to trede on þy temple and teme to þy seluen
Erk. 15, he turnyd temples þat tyme þat temyd to þe deuelle

PURITY *and* ST. ERKENWALD.

Pur. 294, ful redy and ful ryȝtwys and rewled hym fayre
Erk. 245, and for I was ryȝtwis & reken & redy of þe laghe

Pur. 195, þat þat ilk proper Prynce þat paradys weldeȝ
Erk. 161, towarde þe providens of þe Prince þat Paradis weldes

Pur. 987, wyth ly3t love3 uplyfte þay loved hym swyþe
Erk. 349, þenne was louynge oure lorde with loves up-haldene

Pur. 241, bot þur3 þe eggyng of Eve he ete of an apple
      þat enpoysened alle peple3 þat parted fro hem boþe
Erk. 294, dwynande in þe derke dethe, þat dy3t vs oure fader,
      Adam, oure alder, þat ete of þat appulle
      þat mony a ply3tles pepul has poysned for euer
        Cp. Pur. 241–8 and Erk. 294–8.

The arguments which support the theory that the author of
St. Erkenwald was the *Gawain* poet have already been discussed
from several angles, both in the last chapter and in the earlier
volume,[1] and scholars are agreed that the close similarity between
this poem and the works of the *Gawain* poet can only be explained
either by a theory of common authorship or as due to a conscious
imitation by a sympathetic disciple. The parallels in phraseology
are *not* sufficient to enable us to decide definitely in favour of either
of these two theories, for they are not nearly so numerous (*St.
Erkenwald* is admittedly very short) or so significant as in the case
of the four poems themselves. One scholar may read *St. Erkenwald*
and find in it a spirit different from that in *Purity* and *Patience*,
while another may find it aglow with the same spiritual intensity.
The problem must be left where it is for the present with perhaps
a new emphasis upon the close connection that undoubtedly exists
among the five poems.

Leaving aside the poems of the Cotton MS. Nero A.X., parallel
phraseology seems to the present writer to be in every other case
inadequate to prove a theory of common authorship. For this
reason, unless one is convinced by the *cumulative* evidence for
ascribing *St. Erkenwald* to the *Gawain* poet, it is doubtful whether
scholarship can take us much further in settling the problem. The
same holds for *The Parlement of the Thre Ages* and *Wynnere and
·Wastoure*, in which the metrical similarity must especially be borne
in mind. We have elsewhere endeavoured to show the weakness
of the objections which Dr. Steadman has raised,[2] and it may be
argued that there is no evidence left to *disprove* the theory of common
authorship ; the only question is whether the positive evidence in
favour is sufficiently distinct as to remove all uncertainty.

For obvious reasons the case must still remain *sub judice*, as it
must also with regard to *Alexander A* and *B*, wherein we find the
same metrical similarity, with certain minor differences in other
fields, which may be due to an interval of time in composition.

      [1] P. 78, *and* vol. i, p. 253.   [2] See p. 54.

We are therefore compelled to leave the problem of common authorship in a somewhat unsatisfactory state, though we can say with certainty that there are only four cases in which common authorship is at all possible,[1] whereas with regard to the other poems, such as *The Destruction of Troy*, *Morte Arthure*, *The Destruction of Jerusalem*, and *The Wars of Alexander*, we can assert that the metrical dissimilarity is so great as to show that there is not even a case for further enquiry.

Coming to the problem of the interrelationship of Middle English Alliterative poetry, we have to bear in mind that the number of alliterative writers was by no means small, and that the dating of the various works and the placing of them in chronological order is most important for a complete understanding of the " school ".

The earliest group of poems is undoubtedly that from central and south-west midland—*Alexander A* and *B*, *Joseph of Arimathie*, and *William of Palerne* (*c.* 1350). All these works, especially *Joseph of Arimathie*, show a marked metrical uncertainty and immaturity. There is little, if indeed any, influence exerted by these writings on the later alliterative works, and beyond the stock phrases which had been largely inherited from the past there are few points of contact between the two groups.

Wynnere and Wastoure and *The Parlement of the Thre Ages* form another early group of poems, and while there is no evidence of date regarding the latter work, there is good reason for dating *Wynnere and Wastoure* 1352–53. We know that this poem served as a model for the author of *Piers Plowman*, and that *The Parlement of the Thre Ages* seems to have been known by the majority of the later alliterative poets. The political group of poems—*Piers Plowman* (*c.* 1362–*c.* 1398), *Pierce the Ploughman's Crede* (1393–99), *Richard the Redeles* (1399), *Mum and Sothsegger* (*c.* 1402), and *The Crowned King* (1415)—forms a school quite apart from the alliterative romances of the north-west, though it seems likely that *Piers Plowman* was known to some of the writers.

The north-western school of alliterative writers is more difficult to date, but sufficient is known of the dependence of one poem upon another to arrive at a more or less chronological order of composition. Miss Day [2] has shown that *The Destruction of Jerusalem* is dependent upon *The Destruction of Troy*,[3] which was

[1] I.e. excluding the question of Huchown.

[2] *The Siege of Jerusalem*, p. xxvi.

[3] Dr. Day has shown conclusively that the *borrower* was the author of *Jerusalem* and not *vice versa*.

written after Chaucer's *Troilus and Cressida* (1382–85), so that *The Destruction of Jerusalem* must have been written between 1385 and 1400, the date of the earliest MS. Miss Day likewise suggests that the author borrowed from *Patience*, and that if this is correct, the latter poem cannot have been written after 1390, and that *Purity* must be approximately of the same date. *St. Erkenwald* is reasonably connected with the year 1386, and *Sir Gawain and the Green Knight* must belong to the last quarter of the fourteenth century.[1]

A study of the phraseology shows that *The Parlement of the Thre Ages* was probably known to the authors of *The Wars of Alexander*, *The Destruction of Jerusalem*, and *Death and Life*. The author of *The Wars of Alexander* knew of *Purity*, *Patience* and *St. Erkenwald*, while the author of *Death and Life* seems to have been influenced by a great number of earlier alliterative poems.[2] Thus the main lines of chronology are quite clear. Excluding *Death and Life* (early fifteenth century) and *Scottish Field* (1515), the last important poem of the revival is *The Destruction of Jerusalem*, which was written before 1400. The bulk of the alliterative poetry was therefore compressed into the period of about fifty years, a remarkably short space of time.

These connections are set forth in tabular form so that the reader may see at a glance what can reasonably be inferred, and the parallels are arranged so as to illustrate the truth of the inferences. The dependence of *Piers Plowman* upon *Wynnere and Wastoure*, and of the imitations of *Piers Plowman* upon that poem need no further demonstration here, since the facts are so well known. A single line indicates borrowing, whereas a double line is used to convey unity of authorship. (See diagram, p. 96.)

As we have already suggested, there exists little connection between the earliest group of alliterative works and any of the later groups, but there are a few points of similarity which do not seem to be altogether due to a common tradition.

e.g. Alex. B 823, þe aþel king . . . þat noble is and namekouþ
    Alex. B 1079, þe emperour . . . þat noble is and namekouþ
    Troy 2630, A ! nobill kyng and nomekouthe

    Will. of Pal. 2352, summe þat bere hem now brag
    Pierce the Ploughman's Crede, 706, beren hem bragg

---

[1] J. R. R. Tolkien and E. V. Gordon, *Sir Gawayn*, p. xxi.
[2] Savage, *St. Erkenwald*, p. li ; Menner, *Purity*, p. xxiii ; Gollancz, *Death and Life*, p. xv.

Other examples might be given of the same kind but little would be gained by giving an exhaustive list

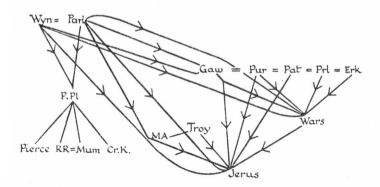

(1) The following parallels between *The Parlement of the Thre Ages, Wynnere and Wastoure* and the *Gawain* poems are clear evidence of borrowing :—

Parl. 80, cuttede corbyns bone and kest it awaye
Gaw. 1355, and the corbeles fee thay kest in a greve—(Neilson).

Parl. 7, als I habade one a banke be a bryme syde
Gaw. 2172, bi a bonke þe brymme bysyde

Parl. 453, for Bersabee . . . was alle that bale rerede
Gaw. 2419, ... Barsabe that much bale tholed—(Neilson).

Parl. 254, with coundythes and carolles
Gaw. 1655, as coundutes of Krystmasse and caroleȝ newe—(Neilson).

Parl. 646, to schryue ȝow full schirle and schewe ȝow to prestis
Gaw. 1880, þere he schrof hym schyrly and schewed his mysdedeȝ

Parl. 24, and als I lokede to a launde a littill me be-syde
Gaw. 2146, þenne loke a littel on þe launde on þi lyfte honde
    Cp. Gaw, 2171.

    Cp. Parl. 109–15 with Gaw. 136–44, two parallel descriptive passages.

Wyn. 338, if this were nedles note
Pat. 220, bot al watȝ nedles note

Wyn. 49, one a loueliche *lande* þat was ylike grene,
         þat lay *loken* by a *lawe* the lengthe of a myle
Gaw. 765, abof a *launde* on a *lawe loken* under boȝeȝ
Gaw. 2171, sone, a lyttel on a *launde*, a *lawe* as hit were.

Cp. Wyn. 109–14 *with* Gaw. 575–82 and 2014–17, passages which are too lengthy to transcribe here but which show conclusively that the author of *Gawain* was indebted to the author of *Wynnere* (1352–53). This is important because there is no doubt who was the borrower, and because it then becomes most unlikely that *Parlement* is indebted to *Gawain;* indeed, if the *Gawain* poet borrowed from *Wynnere,* as there seems no doubt that he did, it follows in the light of the above parallels that he also borrowed from *Parlement,* a fact which seems to decide the question of the priority of the latter poem.

Of later writers who also borrowed from these two early companion poems, the authors of *The Wars of Alexander, The Destruction of Jerusalem,* and *Death and Life* are the most important and details concerning their indebtedness will be found below. There is also evidence that *Morte Arthure* is indebted to *The Parlement of the Thre Ages,* as the following parallels suggest :—

Parl. 444, the grete grym Golyas he to grounde broghte
      and sloghe hym with his slynge and with no sleghte elles
M.A. 3419, for he slewe with a slynge be sleyght of his hands
      Golyas the grette gome grymmeste in erthe—(Neilson).

Parl. 247, with ladys full lovely to lappyn in myn armes
M.A. 3293, and ladys me lovede to lappe in theyre armes—(Neilson).

Parl. 574, and that cite he assegede appone sere halfves
M.A. 1979, forsette them the cite appon sere halfeȝ—(Neilson).

In view of the above evidence, it seems certain that the indebtedness is on the side of *Morte Arthure.*

(2) The parallels between *Morte Arthure* and *The Destruction of Troy* are quite numerous, but we have no clue as to who was the borrower, though it is not impossible that the problem may be settled later :—

Troy 5939, slit hym down sleghly thurghe the slote ewyn
M.A. 2957, sleghly in at the slotte slyttes hym thorowe

Troy 1248, the bourden of his basnet brestes in sonder
M.A. 4211, the bordoure of his bacenett he bristes in sondire

Troy 1307, & siket full sore with syling of teris
Troy 2680, all in siking & sorow with syling of teris
M.A. 1297, 3794, and thane syghande he said with sylande terys
      Cp. Troy 2608–12 with M.A. 144–51—(Donaldson and Pantin).

Troy 1089, skairen out skoute-wacche for skeltyng of harme
M.A. 2468, skayres þaire skottefers & theire skowtte-waches
    Cp. Purity 838, as a scowte-wach scarred, so þe asscry rysed—(Neilson).

The connection between the two poems is indisputable.

Similarly, there are interesting points of connection between *Purity* and *Morte Arthure* on the one hand, and *Purity* and *The Destruction of Troy* on the other, but they are not so striking. Cp. Pur. 1193 and Troy 9376 ; Pur. 1777 and Troy 4751 ; Pur. 1452 and M.A. 211 ; Pur. 1689 and M.A. 1078 ; Pur. 1411 and M.A. 3355 ; Pur. 716 and M.A. 3986. There is naturally in these cases no evidence as to who was the borrower.

(3) The author of *The Wars of Alexander* borrowed from several alliterative works, notably from *Purity*, as R. J. Menner is able to prove. The most striking parallels are here appended :—

THE WARS OF ALEXANDER *and* PURITY.

W. Alex. 415, how he myȝt compas and kast þe kynge to begyle
W. Alex. 1361, now compas kenely þe kyng and castes in hys mynd
Pur. 1455, for to compas and kest to haf hem clene wroȝt

W. Alex. (Dub.) 1368, sterne stevyn vpon stroke straked trompettes
Pur. 1402, sturnen trumpen strake steven in halle—(Menner).

W. Alex. (Ash.) 1393, and þai ȝapely aȝayne and ȝildis þam swythe
Pur. 665, I schal ȝeply aȝayn and ȝelde þat I hyȝt—(Menner).

W. Alex. 1489, I bringe þe bodword of blis, ser bischop, he said
Pur. 473, bryng bodworde to bot blysse to vus alle

W. Alex. 2979, þe pepill of þe palais . . . rusches vp in a res . . .
Pur. 1782, þenne ran þay in on a res on rowtes ful grete

W. Alex. 2981, with hard hattis on þaire hedis hied to þaire horsis
Pur. 1209, hard hattes þay hent and on hors lepes—(Menner).

W. Alex. 3725, ȝoure saule sa ful of sapient
Pur. 1626, of sapyence þi sawle ful

W. Alex. 4292, þat is to say all þe syn at solp may þe saule
Pur. 1135, sulp no more þenne in synne þy saule þerafter

W. Alex. 5297, It ware a daynte to deme for any duke oute
Pur. 1046, as any dom myȝt device of dayntyeȝ oute

The connections with other *Gawain* poems are not so numerous, but are equally interesting :—

W. Alex. 2574, I am noȝt gilty of þis gile be all þe grete gods
Pat. 285, thaȝ I be gulty of gyle as gaule of prophetes

W. Alex. 778, striden to stelebowe startyn upon lofte
Gaw. 435, steppeӡ into stelbawe strydes alofte—(Neilson).

W. Alex. 2458, sparrethis spetous to spend
Gaw. 209, a spetes sparþe to expoun in spelle

W. Alex. 5504, a grete glauir and a glaam of grekin tongis
Gaw. 1426, such a glauer ande glam of gedered racheӡ

W. Alex. 3796, as ai stremande sternes stared all þaire wedis
Pearl 115, as stremande sterneӡ . . . staren in welkyn

W. Alex. 334, þe liӡt lemand late laschis fra þe hewyn
Erk. 334, liӡtly lasshit þer a leme loghe in þe abyme—(Savage).

It follows from these parallels that the author of *The Wars of
Alexander* was undoubtedly acquainted with the works of the
Gawain poet. There is likewise good evidence for assuming that
he had also read *The Parlement of the Thre Ages* and *Wynnere and
Wastoure*, as the following parallels suggest :—

THE WARS OF ALEXANDER *and* WYNNERE AND WASTOURE.

W. Alex. 1403, Now a sparthe, now a spere and sped so hys mighteӡ
Wyn. and Wast. 238, a sparthe and a spere sparrede in ane hyrne

W. Alex. 2981, With hard hattis on þaire hedis hied to þaire horsis
Wyn. and Wast. 51, harde hattes appon hedes . . . —(Menner).
    Cp. Pur. 1209 *supra.*

W. Alex. 4955, clad all in clene gold kirtill and mantill
Wyn. and Wast. 90, comliche clade in kirtill and mantill
    Cp. Death and Life 83, comelye cladd in kirtle and mantle.

THE WARS OF ALEXANDER *and* THE PARLEMENT OF THE THRE AGES.

W. Alex. 792, Than strenys he hys steropes and streght up sittes
Parl. 116, He streghte hym in his steropis and stode up rightes—(Neilson).

W. Alex. 1538, With riche rabies of golde railed bi the hemmes
    (*rabies* is probably a mistake for *rybans*, the reading of Dub. MS.)
Parl. 128, With full rich rubyes raylede by the hemmes—(Neilson).

(4) We have already referred to the extensive borrowing by the
author of *The Destruction of Jerusalem*, but in view of the fact that
his work was written after the bulk of the alliterative poems had
been composed, this indebtedness is not surprising. The indebtedness to *The Parlement of the Thre Ages* and to *The Destruction of
Troy* is the most significant.

JERUSALEM *and* MORTE ARTHURE.

Jerus. 280, a grete dragon of gold
Morte Arthure 2026, dragone of golde—(Day).

Jerus. 285, þer wer floynes a flot farcostes many
Morte Arthure 743, In floynes and fercosteȝ—(Neilson).

Jerus. 286, cogges and crayers
Morte Arthure 738, coggeȝ and crayers

Jerus. 599, so was þe bent ouer brad blody by-runne
Morte Arthure 1863, The bente and þe brode felde alle one blode rynnys
                                                                    —(Day).
Jerus. 753, The glowes of gray steel that wer with gold hemyd
Morte Arthure 912, his gloues gaylyche gilte and grauen at the hemmes
                                                                —(Neilson).

JERUSALEM *and* THE WARS OF ALEXANDER.

Jerus. 560, & goutes fram gold wede as goteres þey runne
W. Alex. 4796, As gotis out of guttars in golnand wedres—(Day).

Jerus. 666, Schoten vp scharply to þe schene walles
W. Alex. 1391, Schotis vp scharply at shalkis on þe wallis—(Day).

JERUSALEM *and* SIR GAWAYN AND THE GREEN KNIGHT.

Jerus. 1122, þat fur out flowe as of flynt stonys
Gaw. 459, þat þe fyr of þe flynt flaȝe fro fole houes—(Day).

JERUSALEM *and* PATIENCE.

Jerus. 70, starke stremes þrow yn stormes & wyndes
Pat. 234, styffe stremes and streȝt—(Day).
      (In each case the line is the last descriptive touch of the storm.)

JERUSALEM AND PURITY.

Jerus. 99, & ȝo a mayde vnmarred þat neuer man touched
Pur. 867, þat ar maydeneȝ unmard for alle men ȝette—(Menner).

Jerus. 525, loude clarioun cry
Pur. 1210, Cler claryoun crak—(Day).

Jerus. 1261, Bassynes of brend gold and oþer bryȝt ger
Pur. 1456, For þer wer bassynes ful bryȝt of brende golde clere—(Menner).

JERUSALEM *and* THE PARLEMENT OF THE THRE AGES.

Jerus. 83-4, Me wer leuer at þat londe lengede þat y wer
                 þan alle þe gold oþer good þat euer god made
Parl. 199, 206, me were leuere one this launde lengen a while
                 Than alle the golde and the gude that thoue gatt euer
                                                                    —(Day).
Jerus. 199, & heyly y a-fowe
Parl. 178, and heghely I a-vowe—(Day).

Jerus. 782, ȝif ȝe as dogges wol dey þe deuel haue þat recche
Parl. 447, And he was dede of that dynt the deuyll hafe that reche
—(Neilson).

Jerus. 887, Ride to þe reuer and rer vp þe foules
Parl. 208, 217, And ryde to a reuere . . . to rere vp the fewles—(Neilson).

Jerus. 974, Tille me þe ȝates ben ȝet & ȝolden þe keyes
Parl. 398, 575, While hym the ȝates were ȝete and ȝolden the keyes
—(Day).

Jerus. 1005, Fayn as the foul of day . . .
Parl. 15–16, And iche foule in that frythe faynere than other—(Neilson).

Jerus. 1119–20, Brunyes and briȝt wede'blody by-runne
and many segge at þat saute souȝte to þe grounde
Parl. 62-3, The breris and the brakans were blody by-ronnen
And he assentis to þat sewte and seches hym afture—(Day)
N.B.—The general sense is quite different.

Jerus. 1286, morter ne mode walle bot alle to mulle fallen
Parl. 433, In manere of a mode walle that made were with hondes
—(Neilson).

JERUSALEM *and* WYNNERE AND WASTOURE.

Jerus. 489–90, Her nys king noþer knyȝt comen to þis place,
Baroun, ne burges, ne burne þat me folweþ
Wyn. and Wast. 327–8, Ne es nothir kayser, ne kynge, ne knyghte þat the
folowes
Barone, ne bachelere, ne beryn that thou loueste
—(Day).

JERUSALEM *and* THE DESTRUCTION OF TROY.

Jerus. 55, þe racke myd a rede wynde roos on þe myddel
Troy 1984, A rak and a royde wynde rose in hor saile—(Neilson).

Jerus. 235, þe mahound and þe mametes to-mortled to peces
Troy 4312, Bothe mawhownus and maumettes myrtild in peces—(Day).

Jerus. 247–8, . . . wryngyng of hondis
with loude dyn and dit for doil of hym one
Troy 8679–80, . . . wringyng of hond
The dit and the dyn was dole to behold
Troy 1347, 11946, the dyn and the dite was dole for to hear
—(Neilson).

Jerus. 1189, Was noȝt bot dyn and dyt as alle deye scholde
Troy 5788, of the dit and þe dyn þat to dethe went

Jerus. 290, Hadde byr at the bake and the bonke lefte
Troy 1902, Hade bir at his bake and the bankes levyt—(Neilson).

Jerus. 551, spakly her speres on sprottes they ȝeden
Troy 1195, Speires unto sprottes sprongen ouer hedes—(Neilson).

Jerus. 590, chair and chaundelers and charbokel stones
Troy 3170, chaundelers full chefe and charbokili stones—(Neilson).

Jerus. 613–17, Ledes lepen to a-non louken þe ȝates,
                Barren hem bigly with boltes of yren
                Brayden vp brigges with brouden chaynes
                & portecolis with pile picchen to grounde.
                þei wynnen vp whyȝtly þe walles to kepe
Troy 10462–4, þai wan in wightly, warpit to þe yates
                Barrit hom full bigly with boltes of yerne
                Braid vp the brigges in a breme hast—(Day).

Jerus. 657, brenten and beten doun þat bilde was wel þycke
Troy 11931, brentyn and betyn doun all the big houses

Jerus. 666, schoten up scharply to the schene walles
        838, dryven dartes a doun ȝeven depe woundes
Troy 4739–41, schottyn up sharply at the schene walles . . .
        .   .   .   .
                dryven up dartes gyffen depe woundes—(Neilson).

Jerus. 532, As þonder and þicke rayn þrowolande in skyes
Troy 12496, A thoner and a thicke rayne þrublet in the skewes—(Day).
Jerus. 725–35 was imitated from Troy—(Day).

(5) The author of *Death and Life* borrowed from many poems, and only the more striking parallels are here recorded :—

DEATH AND LIFE *and* WILLIAM OF PALERNE.

Death and Life 74, breme birds on the boughes busilye did singe
Will. of Pal. 23, briddes ful bremely on þe bowes singe

DEATH AND LIFE *and* WYNNERE AND WASTOURE.

Death and Life 13, If thou haue pleased the Prince þat paradice weldith
Wyn. and Wast. 296, It es plesynge to the Prynce þat paradyse wroghte
                                    —(Gollancz—D.L. edit.).

Death and Life, 83, comelye cladd in kirtle and mantle
Death and Life 445, comelye cladd in [kirtle] and mantle
Wyn. and Wast. 90, comliche clade in kirtill and mantill
        Cp. W. Alex. 4955, as quoted above.

DEATH AND LIFE *and* THE PARLEMENT OF THE THRE AGES.

Death and Life 9, But all wasteth away and worthes to noght
Parl. 637, me thynke þe wele of this werlde worthes to noghte
                                    —(Gollancz—D.L. edit.).

Death and Life 24, The red rayling roses, the richest of fflowers
Parl. 119, Raylede alle with rede rose richeste of floures
                                    —(Gollancz—D.L. edit.).

DEATH AND LIFE *and* PIERS PLOWMAN.

Death and Life 49, me a fferlye beffell soe fayre it me thought
P. Pl. B Pro. 6, me byfel a ferly of fairy me thou3te

Death and Life 16, Thou shalt byterly bye or else the booke ffalseth
P. Pl. A iii, 236, Thei schullen a-bugge bitterly or the bok ly3eth
—(both from Gollancz—D.L. edit.).

Death and Life 197, and the ffishes in the fflod ffaylen to swimme
P. Pl. C vi 149, Right as fisshes in flod when hem faileth water

DEATH AND LIFE *and* PURITY.

Death and Life 205, Merry maydens on the mold shee mightilye killethe
Pur. 1267, And alle þe maydens of þe munster ma3tyly he kyllen—(Menner).

Death and Life 248, Waxe fforth in the word and worth vnto manye
Pur. 521, Bot waxe3 now and wende3 forth and worþe3 to monye—(Menner).

DEATH AND LIFE *and* MORTE ARTHURE.

Death and Life 312, If the dint of my dart deared them neuer
Morte Arthure 3611, That no dynte of no darte dere theme ne schoulde

Death and Life 157, The ffoulest ffreke that formed was euer
Morte Arthure 718, the foulleste of fegure that fourmede was euer
Morte Arthure 1061, the fulsomeste freke that fourmede was euere

The introduction of Morte Arthure, 1–11, corresponds closely to the introduction of Death and Life, 1–21—(Gollancz—D.L. edit.).

The dependence of *Scottish Field* upon *Death and Life* and upon other poems is sufficiently well known, but attention may be called to the use in that poem of the periphrasis for God. The style of alliterative poetry is so lacking in individuality that it does not usually help us in deciding questions of interrelationship, but in this case it is of enormous help. Full details are given on page 394 where it will be seen that the feature was first found in *Wynnere and Wastoure*, from whence it passed into *Richard the Redeles* and *Mum and Sothsegger* on the one hand and into the works of the *Gawain* poet·on the other. At a much later period it passed from *Purity* into *Death and Life* and thence into *Scottish Field*. It will be seen that this theory of interrelationship is amply corroborated by the study of the parallel phraseology and general questions of date. A study of Part IV will show how dangerous it would be in our present state of knowledge to attach any great importance to other points of style for assistance in settling the problems of imitation. Vocabulary calls for still greater care and discrimination, and though there are some twenty odd cases (exclusive of the *Gawayn* poems) in which there would seem to be evidence of definite borrowing, the problem is much too complicated to admit of any easy solution ; accordingly, the corroborative evidence which it seems to supply has been purposely withheld.

The relationship between the rhymed alliterative works and unrhymed poems calls for a new investigation which naturally falls outside the scope of this volume, and beyond what has already been said, nothing more will here be added except to say that there is no doubt for example that the author of *The Awntyrs of Arthure* modelled his hunting-scene on the one he found in *Sir Gawayn and the Green Knight*. Further, the parallels which exist among *Morte Arthure*, *The Awntyrs of Arthure* and *The Pistill of Susan* [1] are so striking that common authorship or conscious imitation must be inferred, and it is hoped that the question may soon be settled, for upon it will depend our final understanding of the Alliterative Revival.

Returning to the alliterative writers as a whole, it can fairly be said that they were for the most part widely read. They were familiar with the French romances and the *Roman de la Rose*, the Latin Vulgate and many mediæval Latin works. The authors of *Sir Gawayn and the Green Knight* and of *The Parlement of the Thre Ages* had very intimate and technical knowledge of hunting. A number of the poets were familiar with London life, and must have been frequent visitors to the capital, though their works can scarcely have been intended for London folk. Sir Israel Gollancz has noted the parenthetical statement of the *St. Erkenwald* poet on the custom of visiting the metropolis in those days (134–5) :—

> " Mony a gay grete lorde was gedrid to herken hit
>   As þe rekenest of þe reame repairen þider ofte."

It is possible that the poet was himself of this class. He was not, however, the only alliterative poet who visited London. The author of *Wynnere and Wastoure*, though a western man, had an intimate knowledge of London life, and the author (or authors) of *Piers Plowman* had shared the same experience.

The question naturally arises in our minds as to what could have been the external circumstances that gave rise to the alliterative school of poets. The author of *Sir Gawayn and the Green Knight*, *Pearl*, *Patience* and *Purity*, whether a priest or layman, was probably of high birth, and certainly well-educated, and the author of *William of Palerne* was in some way connected with a person of

---

[1] A very complete list will be found in Amours' edition.

rank. On the other hand, the writer of *Piers Plowman* cannot have been directly patronised by anyone belonging to the landed classes. Professor Hulbert's interesting *Hypothesis Concerning the Alliterative Revival* [1] is an attempt to answer these questions, and to the present writer his solution seems the only one so far brought forward which takes full account of the circumstances of the situation. He lays down three requirements: (1) "an audience as courtly and as wealthy as any in England "; (2) "the deliberate choice of a form of English unlike that of London and full of archaisms "; (3) " the choice of a metre not used by poets of the royal court ". Professor Hulbert finds these requirements met by a theory of baronial opposition for which there is abundant historical evidence. The alliterative poems must have been written for refined and cultured audiences, and it is significant that the works are English in spirit and tone rather than French. Professor Hulbert admits that there is a difficulty with regard to *Piers Plowman*, but suggests that it may be " the culmination of a popular literature which had kept the tradition of the alliterative long line through the centuries; it may be that its authors adopted their verse-form from the first poems of the alliterative revival; it may be that the barons were clever enough to foster a poetry which would arouse people to thought about political conditions and moral betterment, and so gain aid for the baronial opposition in any attack on the corruptions and usurpations of the royal house ". The baronial setting of the Arthurian alliterative romances is also alluded to, and it is suggested that the Mortimers, Bohuns, and Beauchamps were the most probable patrons of the alliterative poets because baronial opposition was a tradition in their families. The dialectal objection to Professor Hulbert's hypothesis is not a serious one, since there may have been other barons in opposition in the north-western area as well as in the south-western. It is not unlikely that further evidence may eventually be brought to light which will substantiate the hypothesis put forward, but in the meantime it serves to account for many of the facts which do require some explanation.

The chronological groups do not altogether coincide with the literary types of work produced. The allegorical and political group is different in spirit and in conception from the romance group, but if *The Parlement of the Thre Ages* is by the same author as *Wynnere and Wastoure*, it forms an interesting link with *Sir Gawayn and the Green Knight*. The author shows the same interest in hunting and in romance, though his sympathy is ostensibly with

[1] P.M.L.A., vol. 28, pp. 405–22, 1931.

the sterner side of life, symbolised by the figure of Old Age. *Death and Life*, a late imitation of *Piers Plowman*, was written by a man who had read the bulk of the alliterative romances, judging from the fact that his work is indebted to them for much of its phraseology. Hence the political and romantic poems are not so distinct as might be imagined, and at any rate a few poets were in sympathy with the aims of both " schools ". The religious works originate chiefly in the north-west and north, and frequently show points of resemblance to the romances. The author of *Purity*, *Patience* and *Pearl* was also the writer of the greatest of the alliterative romances. The seriousness or earnestness of purpose which is so manifest in the allegorical and religious works, also runs through the romances. In the bulk of them there is a definite moral purpose which is in varying degrees thrust upon the reader. The alliterative writers are at heart one. They are united by their vision of life, though they look at it through different eyes and from different spheres of action. Rich or poor, high or low, their intent is equally serious.

The contributions which these alliterative writers made to Middle English literature are both considerable and noteworthy. If we exclude the works of Chaucer, their writings form an important part of the literature, though in actual bulk they are not nearly so extensive as the non-alliterative works. In the romance-form the results are on the whole much more successful than the attempts of their southern and eastern predecessors and contemporaries. The treatment is more realistic, and more definitely English. There is no attempt to imitate the peculiarly French features of the romances, such as the elaborate analysis of feeling, the numerous digressions, and the extreme sentimentality. The works are, however, not so popular in tone as many of the non-alliterative romances. At their best they excel in vigour and realistic treatment, though, in common with all romances, they deal with life ' in a heightened degree '. They are not afraid to introduce giants and all the stock-in-trade of the romance, but the final impression is that of a chronicle, especially in the group which we have ventured to call " *Chronicles in the Epic Manner* ". Miss Everett has rightly called attention to this point in her excellent study of the romances. She says, " One romance, the alliterative *Morte Arthure*, on a theme which roused more patriotic enthusiasm in an English poet than the doings of Charlemagne and his peers ever could, comes very near to claiming a place among heroic poems in English ".[1] In the pure romances,

---

[1] *A Characterization of the English Medieval Romances*, in *Essays and Studies by Members of the English Association*, vol. 15.

The Destruction of Jerusalem and *Joseph of Arimathie* have certainly something of the same quality.

In general, the French themes made little appeal to their imagination. The Arthurian, the Troy and Alexander subjects offered more scope for the description of battles and encounters, for which these poets had a special aptitude. The strength of the alliterative romance-writers lies in the original treatment of their material. They made no compromise with the French attitude, but adapted as freely as possible, and have left us a number of works distinguished by their humanity, their realism, their vigour and their refinement.

In the allegorical form the contribution made by the alliterative writers was no less considerable. They were more fitted by temperament to write allegory on serious themes. Schooled in the allegorical interpretation of the Scriptures and doubtless familiar with such homiletic works as *Sawles Warde* and *The Bestiary*, they saw the opportunities inherent in *The Roman de la Rose*, the storehouse of mediæval allegory, which gave new life to more traditional forms. *Piers Plowman* is the great English counterpart of the French poem. Differing widely in externals, there is yet a fundamental kinship. Each is the story of a quest, though of a distinctive kind. 'Langland' has transformed his material into a vision of life embracing all the activities of mankind. He has achieved the highest in the allegorical form, the portraying of life's realities through the medium of the shifting movements of time and space. *Piers Plowman* remains one of the highest achievements of Middle English alliterative poetry. Alongside it can, however, be put the works of the *Gawain* poet. Totally different in style, manner and execution, the four poems of the Cotton MS. Nero A.X. are a permanent contribution to our literature. They possess a value of their own, and however unconnected they may be with the later streams of poetic influence, they are worthy of the best traditions in our literature.

Like the Old English poets, the Middle English alliterative writers could describe with consummate skill. Their methods, however, are singularly different. The Old English descriptions are vague and allusive, whereas the Middle English descriptions are detailed and definite. The earlier poets are etchers, the later ones are painters. The Beowulf poets tells us little about Heorot ; it towers up high and its glittering gold shines far and wide, but beyond these mere details nothing further is disclosed. Of more significance to the poet is the fact that it awaited " the battle surges of the hostile flame ". In comparison with this vague shadowy hall, the Green Knight's abode appears before our eyes as an elaborate castle, visualised in its smallest detail. The other alliterative poets adopt the same method though their achievements may not be so distinguished.

Whatever parallel figure or scene we might study in the earlier or later alliterative poetry, the same broad distinction holds. The figure of Grendel reminds us of the first giant in *Morte Arthure*. No physical details of the Grendel monster are given, but he emerges from the darkness as a vague shadow, all the more impressive on that account. He is introduced to us as a ' fierce spirit,' ' grim and greedy,' ' savage and cruel,' who stalks across the misty moors and fens which he rules as his domain. He is a dark death-shadow, a monster, a horrible solitary roamer, who in the dark night goes on his secret journeyings. When he comes to Heorot for the last time he is pictured as a prowling figure emerging from the hill-slopes. As he moves across the floor an unholy light flashes from his eyes, and surveying the sleeping warriors he laughs. Of the details of the subsequent fight little is given. The poet wonders how the hall was able to withstand the battling foemen. Fear falls upon the warriors when they hear the agonising and despairing cries of God's adversary. Aware of his approaching end, Grendel departs once more into the darkness.

The Beowulf poet concentrates upon psychological reaction rather than upon detail. The impression left is one of vagueness and mystery, and the reader's imagination is given free rein. The description of Arthur's fight with the giant in *Morte Arthure* is almost an exact parallel to the Grendel episode. The giant is horrible, because he is monstrous in shape and repulsive in behaviour. When Arthur finds him, he is picking the thigh of a man. The giant's appearance is sketched in such detail, that the reader can visualise the figure completely, and the fight which follows is graphically described. The result is a brilliant picture dazzling in its colour and objective detail, but lacking in the finer subjective qualities of Old English poetry. The *Gawain* poet avoids crudities of this kind, but his method is always the same—the piling up of detail, which is often quite irrelevant in itself. The Middle English alliterative writers have left the intensity of Old English poetry for the more vivid surface of things, the sensuous appeal of the French romances.

The alliterative poets had inherited from the past a delight in describing warfare which partly explains why so much of their work

is reminiscent of Laȝamon's *Brut*   In the earliest alliterative poem
—*Alexander A*—the assault of Methone (264–307) and the wars
between the Thebans (337–54) are throughout vividly and dramatically described, as the short quotation on page 25 shows.   In an
early work this is at least surprising.   The battle scenes in *William
of Palerne* are on the whole more conventional, and the poet misses
many opportunities, but he writes with gusto and enthusiasm.
The author of *Joseph of Arimathie*, however, writes in a more concentrated manner ;   the battle described in lines 498–604 (see
p. 43) is brought vividly before our eyes, and its every detail is
visualised by the poet.   In the later alliterative poetry the note of
conventionality is frequently apparent, and as in *The Destruction
of Troy* a long succession of battle-scenes is apt to be wearisome.
Nevertheless, the battles in *The Destruction of Jerusalem* (530–578,
798–840, 1176–1210) are well described in the best alliterative
tradition, and the naval battle in *Morte Arthure* (3659–3703) is the
finest scene of warfare in the whole range of alliterative poetry.
The descriptions in *The Wars of Alexander* and *The Destruction of
Troy*, of which examples have already been given, are frequently
below the average, but on occasion do equal the best that is to be
found in Laȝamon's *Brut*.   The last alliterative poem—*Scottish
Field*—in which one might have expected some vivid description,
has merely one conventional picture consisting of traditional expressions loosely strung together (see p. 83).

Descriptions of storms are less frequent, but reveal the same
power.   The storm in *Patience*, ll. 137–56, is sketched with graphic
detail and like the corresponding passage in *The Destruction of
Jerusalem*, ll. 53–70, gains in effectiveness from its human setting.
The poet is concerned with Jonah, the cause of the tumult in
nature, and the lot of the helpless sailors is woven into the scene,
adding a human interest.   The storm passages in *The Wars of
Alexander*, 551–68 and 4140–50, and in *The Destruction of Troy*,
1983–2006, 3687–708, 4625–35, 7618–29, 12494–517, are all excellent in themselves, as the quotation on page 33 indicates, but
they are largely pieces of description for its own sake, often
unnecessary so far as the story is concerned.   They indicate, however, that the alliterative poets had always an eye for the realistic.

Attempts to describe nature are for the most part unsuccessful ;
even when the poet shows some original observation, he mars
the picture by the use of conventional phrasing.   The author
of *Sir Gawayn and the Green Knight* is the only writer to get completely away from the conventional in describing nature, but it is

not to be expected that lesser poets could achieve what such a master of description and observer of life achieved. Of descriptive methods in general abundant illustrations have already been given, especially in connection with *St. Erkenwald*. The attention to the minutest detail inevitably leads to the cataloguing type of description which unless carefully handled gives disastrous results. In *Wynnere and Wastoure* the effect is wearisome, whereas in *Purity* and *Sir Gawayn and the Green Knight* it is redeemed by the sheer brilliance of the details. The fact remains that the alliterative poets are, on the whole, successful in description—whether it be an allegorical figure as Youth in *The Parlement of the Thre Ages* or of Gluttony in *Piers Plowman*, a landscape as in *Death and Life*, or a castle, a convent, a hunting scene, a battle, a storm, or a scene of ecclesiastical or social splendour—they are always equal to the occasion. .The results differ widely, but the opportunity to paint a picture of some sort is seldom lost. That a few of these pictures are admittedly masterpieces should not prevent us from appreciating those which are undoubtedly of less worth.

The remaining parts of this volume treat of the style and diction of the alliterative poems. In dealing with the vocabulary an attempt will be made to trace the growth and development of the diction, the gradual decay of the nominal poetic compounds, and the survival of the Old English poetic diction in Laʒamon and through him to the poetry of the Revival. It will be seen that the older poetic diction like the metre is gradually transformed until it is no longer recognisable. A distinctive alliterative vocabulary is evolved, based largely, though not exclusively, on native foundations, enriched by all the purely poetical words available to Middle English poets in general. The vocabulary is saturated with local and dialectal forms and steeped in the poetic and archaic traditions of the past, until out of this welter of conflicting influences there emerges a diction adequate to the genius of the alliterative poets.

Though armed with so rich and varied a vocabulary, these writers were not masters of style. Just as the inheritance of an older poetic diction through such poets as Laʒamon yielded a valuable instrument which in able hands helped to produce masterpieces of poetry, so it seems that the penalty for receiving this gift was the forced acceptance of the stock phraseology which in mechanical hands produced work without a seeming spark of originality. The better poets moulded this traditional phraseology to their own ends, but most of the alliterative poets too readily yielded to the temptation to write fluent verse by the aid of all sorts of tags and phrases.   The demands of alliterative verse were admittedly great, yet the vocabulary was rich in synonymous words and phrases which came to the poet's rescue, often to his own undoing.   Except in the case of the 'Gawayn' poet no distinctive style is evolved and the literary inspiration behind the Revival died before the point of maturity was ever reached.

PART II.

THE VOCABULARY.

CHAPTER 6.

A STUDY OF THE NOMINAL POETIC COMPOUNDS.

ONE of the most noticeable features of Old English poetry is the extensive use made of nominal poetic compounds which are not found in ordinary prose. In *Beowulf* there is an average of one compound in every three lines, and this poem does not differ from any other that might be selected. Even in the latest specimens of versification found in *The Chronicle* there is a surprisingly large number of such words. In the 975 poetical entry we have : *beah-gyfa, cræftgleawe, cynerice, deormod, eðeltyrf, gamolfeax, higegleaw, rimcræft, soðboran, stiðferhþe, tirfæst, wordsnottor.* In the last entry, 1065, only one year before the Conquest, there are seven compounds : *bliðemod, hagesteald, heahþungen, kyneþrymme, soðfæst, þeodkynyng, wræclast.* There is, however, a noticeable decline in the number used and also in the actual type of compound, but there is much more than a vestige of the older practice remaining.

In the popular metrical entries discussed in vol. 1, p. 134, a few compounds are found : e.g. E. 975, l. 4, *mundbora ;* l. 18, *cynestol ;* E. 1075, l. 2, *brydeala ;* E. 1086, l. 7, *landleode.* The material is scanty and suggests that in the more popular forms of Old English verse compounds were little used ; this is indeed as we might expect.

In making a study of literary origins in early Middle English alliterative poetry, one naturally looks for the presence or absence of the older compounds ; two things must, however, be borne in mind : firstly, that writers do not in their works furnish us with a complete collection of all the compounds with which they are acquainted ; the result will be a mere selection from the poet's stock ; secondly, many compounds which in Old English were in no sense " poetic " may in Middle English times have become archaic and distinctly poetic.

Little would be gained, and probably something lost, in giving a complete list of all the nominal compounds found in the Middle English alliterative works. Purely prose compounds such as *freoman, godspel, holiwatere, cynedom,* etc., are not important for our purpose, and in addition to making the list unduly large, are also likely to convey a wrong impression. On the other hand, certain prose compounds are added for reasons which will appear obvious later.

Whereas in Old English poetry there is one poetic compound in every three lines (though a few poems have an average of one compound per line), in Laȝamon's *Brut* the average is one in forty lines ; in making a comparison, however, it must be remembered that *The Brut* is a poem of 16,000 long lines, so that the average number of compounds per line might naturally be less. While making no attempt to minimise the fact that there was an important decrease in the number of compounds used, it is desirable to collect the evidence to judge whether there has been a failure to realise Laȝamon's connection with the past in this matter. Before passing on to *The Brut* we shall, however, examine the earlier alliterative prose and poetry in Middle English ; in these works we should not expect to find many compounds, for the compositions are connected with the Old English homilies and popular verse rather than with Old English epic poetry ; hence, if any examples are found, they will offer strong evidence in favour of a survival, though modification, of Old English poetic traditions.

NOMINAL COMPOUNDS IN EARLY MIDDLE ENGLISH ALLITERATIVE WORKS, EXCLUDING LAȝAMON'S *Brut.*

Certain abbreviations are necessary owing to the length of some of the titles of the works :—

A Description of Durham	Dur.	ref. by line.
Wenne, Wenne, Wenchichenne . . .	W.W.	,,
The 1st Worcester Fragment . . .	Worc.	,,
The Grave	Gr.	,,
The Departing Soul's Address to the Body .	Dep.	,,
The Death Fragment	D.F.	,,
The Proverbs of Alfred	Alf.	,,
Memento Mori	M.M.	,,
The Proverbs of Hendyng	Hend.	,,
The Bestiary	Best.	,,
A Satire against the Blacksmiths' . . .	Blc.	,,
The Debate between the Body and the Soul .	Deb.	,,
On God Orison of Our Lady . . .	Lady	,,

On Lofsong of Ure Lefdi	.	.	.	.	Lef.	ref. by page.
On Lofsong of Ure Lauerde	.	.	.	.	Lou.	,,
On Ureisun of Oure Louerde		.	.	.	Ur.	,,
The Wohunge of Ure Lauerd		.	.	.	Woh.	,,
Hali Meiðhad	.	.	.	.	.	H.M.	ref. by line.
Juliana	.	.	.	.	.	Jul.	ref. by page.
St. Marherete	.	.	.	.	.	Mar.	,,
St. Katherine	.	.	.	.	.	Kath.	ref. by line.
The Sawles Warde	.	.	.	.	S.W.	ref. by page.

In the first column the word itself is given, followed by the reference; the meaning of the word is generally given in brackets immediately below the word.

The derivation of the word is given in the next column; if the word is not extant either in O.E. or in O.N., the constituent elements are recorded in brackets.   Underneath are recorded any other Germanic parallels that can be found; in certain cases these may indicate that the word, though not extant in O.E., was in all probability current.

If the word is peculiar to M.E., i.e. not found in O.E., [I] indicates this in the first of the narrow columns; if the word is unique in the given instance the same indication is given in the next column; if the word is not poetic in M.E., this is indicated by Pr. in the next column; if the word is also found in *The Brut*, [I] indicates the fact in the next column, and if the word is found in the later M.E. alliterative works, [I] indicates this in the last narrow column.   Any remarks or comments necessary are made in the final column.

Exclusive of a considerable number of ordinary prose compounds already mentioned, there are here recorded 223 nominal compounds found in these works.   Of these, 136 occur in the alliterative prose, and are not found in the Early Middle English alliterative poems with which we are dealing; on the other hand, 70 compounds occur in the poems which are not found in the prose works; 17 compounds alone are found in both.   It is doubtful whether, when all things have been considered, any safe conclusion can be deduced from these statistics owing to the varying length and differing character of the various pieces.

Of the 223 compounds, 154 are in Middle English 'poetic,' i.e. not in ordinary prose usage, so far as our evidence goes; this leaves 69 'prose' compounds, which suggests that a large proportion of the nominal compounds were literary and probably somewhat archaic.   We find 82 of the compounds extant in Old English literature of which 15 were then 'poetic' and 67 'prose'; this might at first sight suggest that there was no continuity of tradition at all, but we have to remember that among the survivals are included four very significant words : *eorðhus, forðsið, balewsiþes* and *goldfohne ;* also that the works themselves are scrappy and popular rather than epic ; for this latter type we have to rely on Laȝamon, and we shall later find that ' poetic ' compounds are found very frequently in his work. The fact that any of this type are to be found in these homiletic rather than epic works is some testimony to the continuity of tradition.

Many of the compounds for which Old English forms are not extant may nevertheless be traditional ; in 117 cases both elements of the compound derive from Old English, and in 11 cases a cognate is found in some other Germanic language such as Old Norse *glóðrauðr* corresponding to M.E. *gledred ;* in 17 cases the compound exists both in Old English and in one or more other Germanic language, such as O.E. *goldfæt*, O.S. *goldfat.* We have also odd examples of a compound consisting of an O.E. element with either an Old Norse or an Old French element, such as *brenwaterys, luuelettres,* or *nail-knife.*

It is interesting to observe that of the 139 compounds for which no Old English form is extant, many are distinctly poetic ; in particular we may mention *baledrinch, cwalmhus, girreblod, helle-dogges, luftfugeles, soulehus, wasið.* Equally remarkable is the fact that in 99 cases the words are in Middle English found only in the one work in question ; in a few cases this *may* mean that the writer coined a particular compound ; for instance there are 7 apparently new compounds with *helle*, but here the writer would have numerous compounds of the same type already in existence ; in a similar manner we still create new forms to-day. In numerous cases, however, the Middle English writer had no such model before him.

Of the 223 compounds here recorded, 49 also occur in *The Brut* and 25 in the later Middle English alliterative works.

Word and Reference.	Origin.	Peculiar to M.E. (?).	Unique (?).	Prose or Poetic (?).	Also in *The Brut* (?).	Also in later M.E. allit. works (?).	Remarks.
andweorke, Dep. 561 (substance)	andweorc Pr	X	I	P	X	X	
arfesta, Dur. 10 (dutiful)	ārfæst Pr	X	I	P	X	X	
axtreo, Jul. p. 56 (axle-tree)	(*eax* + *trēo*) cp. O.N. öxulltre	I	X	Pr	X	X	a rare M.E. prose word
balebondes, Mar. p. 13 (cruel bonds)	(*bealu* + **band*)	I	I	P	X	X	
baledrinch, Woh. p. 283 (deadly drink)	(*bealu* + *drinc*)	I	I	P	X	X	
baliduntes, Woh. p. 281 (mortal blows)	(*bealu* + *dynt*)	I	I	P	X	X	
baleusypes, Alf. 189, Ur. p. 185, Mar. p. 23 (misfortunes)	beaulusīð P	X	X	P	I	X	an early M.E. poetic word
barm-fellys, Blc. 11 (skin apron)	(*bearm* + *fell*)	I	I	Ṗ	X	X	
barnteam, H.M. 453 (offspring)	bearntēam Pr	X	X	P	X	I	
blamon, Mar. p. 10 (negro)	(**blā(w)* + *mann*) O.N. blámaðr	I	X	Pr	I	X	found also in A.R. the Brut, C.M., Trev.[1]
blodrune, Lof. p. 207 (issue of blood)	blōdryne Pr	X	I	P	X	X	
bocfelle, Mar. p. 23 (parchment)	bōcfell Pr. O.H.G. bouhfel	X	X	Pr	I	X	found elsewhere only in Laȝamon
bodisunnen, Lou. p. 189 (sins of the body)	(*bodig* + *synn*)	I	I	Pr	X	X	
bokilered, Alf. 2, 39 (book-learned)	cp. *bōclǣr* (*bōc* + *lǣran*)	I	X	P	I	I	found also in Pur. 1551
bolehyde, Blc. 11 (skin of a bull)	(**bula* + *hȳd*) O.N. boli +	I	X	Pr	I	X	
Breotenrice, Dur. 1 (the Kingdom of Britain)	Breotenrice Pr (very rare)	X	I	P	X	X	
brenwaterys, Blc. 22 (a burn-water, i.e. a smith)	(+ *wæter*) O.N. brenna	I	I	P	X	X	a nonce word; not in N.E.D.

[1] In addition to the abbreviations of alliterative works regularly used throughout this work, the other abbreviations employed in this column are those used in Stratman's *M.E. Dictionary* : *A.R., C.L., Frag., Hom. I and II, Misc., Pr. C., Pr. P., P.S.* and *Rob.*

Word and Reference.	Origin.	Peculiar to M.E. (?).	Unique (?).	Prose or Poetic (?).	Also in The Brut (?).	Also in later M.E. allit. works (?).	Remarks.
brestatter, Best. 121 (poison of the breast)	(brēost + āttor)	I	I	P	X	X	there were many compounds with brēost in O.E.
brestfilde, Best. 160 (breast-filth)	(brēost + fylð)	I	I	P	X	X	cp. brēostbān
breosteholke, Kath. p. 251 (hollow of the breast)	(brēost + hulc)	I	I	P	X	X	
briht-blikinde, Mar. 13 (shining brightly)	(briht + blīcan)	I	I	Pr	X	X	
broke-rugget, H.M. 374 (broken-backed)	(brocen + hrycg)	I	I	Pr	X	X	
brudgume, Mar. p. 19, etc. (bridegroom)	brȳdguma Pr	X	X	Pr	X	I	a common M.E. word
burdeboldes, Kath. 139 (hereditary mansions)	(gebyrd + bold)	I	I	P	X	X	
burdtid, Dep. 48, Woh. p. 277 (birth-time)	gebyrdtīd Pr	X	X	Pr	X	X	
burhȝetes, Kath. 2174 (castle-gates)	burhgeat Pr	X	X	P	I	X	found elsewhere only in Laȝamon
burhmen, Kath. 1473, etc. (citizens)	burhman Pr	X	X	Pr	I	I	a rare M.E. word
burhreve, Kath. 1904 (town-reeve)	burhgerēfa Pr	X	I	Pr	X	X	
buriboldes, Kath. 439 (palaces)	(burh + bold)	I	I	P	X	X	
cleiclot, Dep. 69 (a clot of clay)	(clǣg +) cp. M.Du. clot	I	X	P	X	X	a very rare M.E. word
clopemerys, Blc. 21 (smith)	(clāð + miere)	I	I	P	X	X	i.e. clothes-horse, a nonce word for the smith
cwalmhus, Woh. p. 273, Mar. p. 4, etc., Kath. 1547, 1807 (torture-house)	(cwealm + hūs)	I	X	P	X	X	found elsewhere only in A.R. 140
cwalm-stowe, Woh. p. 283 (place of execution)	cwealmstōw Pr	X	X	P	X	X	found elsewhere only in A.R. 106, except in place-names

Word and Reference.	Origin.	Peculiar to M.E. (?).	Unique (?).	Prose or Poetic (?).	Also in *The Brut* (?).	Also in later M.E. allit. works (?).	Remarks.
deadbote, Woh. p. 249, H.M. 186, 302 (penance)	dǣdbōt Pr	X	X	P	X	X	an early M.E. word
drakeliche, Mar. p. 12 (a dragon's form)	(*draca* + *līc*)	I	I	P	X	X	
dreampurles, Dep. 440 (breaking of a dream)	(*drēam* + *þyrel*)	I	I	P	X	X	
drihtfare, Jul. p. 32, Kath. 1832 (retinue)	(*driht* + *faru*)	I	X	P	X	X	
durewart, S.W. p. 247 (door-keeper)	duruweard Pr	X	X	P	I	X	a very rare M.E. poetic word
duuelrihtes, Kath. 1599 (vertically)	cp. M.L.G. dovel + O.E. rihtes	I	I	Pr	X	X	
earfepsiþ, Dep. 80, 84 (calamity)	earfoðsīð P	X	I	P	X	X	
eauraskes, S.W. 251 (water-frogs)	(*ēa* + *frox*)	I	X	P	X	X	found also in Hom. I. 326
eawbruche, H.M. 625 (adultery)	ǣbryce Pr	X	X	Pr	X	X	
edmodnesse, Lady 79 (humility)	ēadmōdness Pr	X	X	Pr	I	X	an early M.E. homiletic word
eypurl, Mar. p. 8 (eye-hole)	ēagþyrl Pr	X	X	P	X	X	an early M.E. homiletic word
elheowet, S.W. p. 249 (foreign-coloured)	(*ēl* + *hēow*)	I	I	P	X	X	
eorðhus, Gr. 15 (earth-cave)	eorðhūs P	X	X	P	I	X	found elsewhere only in Laȝamon
erðchine, Best. 308 (a cleft in the ground)	(*eorðe* + *cinu*)	I	X	P	X	X	cp. O.E. *eorðgræf*
eðell-þeowe) H.M. 464 (a paternal slave)	(*eðel* + *þēow*)	I	I	P	X	X	
eðluke, Jul. 70 (easy to lug)	(*ēaðe* + *lūcan*)	I	I	P	X	X	the only instance
eðsene, Kath. 381, etc., S.W. p. 259 (easily seen)	(*ēaðe* + *gesīene*)	I	X	Pr	X	X	found only in early M.E.
fæderhus, H.M. 585 (ancestral house)	(*fæder* + *hūs*)	I	I	P	X	X	
famon, Jul. p. 24, Mar. p. 8 (foe)	fāhman Pr	X	X	Pr	X	X	a common M.E. word

Word and Reference.	Origin.	Peculiar to M.E. (?).	Unique (?).	Prose or Poetic (?).	Also in *The Brut* (?).	Also in later M.E. allit. works (?).	Remarks.
feorþsiþ, Dep. 50 (journey from life)	(*feorh* + *sīð*) (*forð* + *sīð*)	I	I	P	X	X	cp. late O.E., *forðsīð*
fet-steppes, Best. 5	(*fōt* + *gesteppa*)	X	X	Pr	X	I	
fleschtimber, Kath. 1188 (corporeal matter)	(*flǣsc* + *getimbru*)	I	I	P	X	X	
fon(t)stone, Dep. 647, Mar. p. 19	(*font* + *stān*)	I	X	Pr	X	X	
forðfeder, Mar. p. 4, Kath. 94	forðfæder Pr	X	X	Pr	X	X	found only in these alliterative prose works
funt-fat, Best. 93 (font-vessel)	(*font* + *fæt*)	I	I	Pr	X	X	
ʒarewborh, Jul. p. 72 (ready bail)	(*gearu* + *borh*)	I	I	Pr	X	X	
ʒein-cleppes, Kath. 128 (counter-strokes)	(*gegn* + cp. M. Du. *klappe*)	I	I	Pr	X	X	
ʒein-turn, Kath. 2087 (counter-turn)	(*gegn* + *turnian*)	I	X	P	X	I	found elsewhere only in Will. of Pal. 3552
ʒimstones, H.M. 327, Kath. 1647, Lady 55, Mar. 3, etc. (gem-stones)	gimstān Pr	X	X	P	I	I	a common M.E. word
girreblod, Jul. p. 28, Woh. p. 281	(*gyre* + *blōd*)	I	X	P	X	X	found elsewhere only in A.R. 204
gled-red, S.W. 249, 253 (gleed-red)	(*glēd-rēad*) O.N. glóðrauðr	I	I	P	X	X	
gleobeames, Lady 62 (music)	glēobēam P	X	I	P	X	X	
goddeden, Ur. p. 187 (good deeds)	goddǣd Pr M.H.G. guottât	X	X	P	I	X	an early M.E. compound
goldfæten, Dep. 102 (gold vessels)	goldfæt P O.H.G.golt-faz, O.S. goldfat	X	I	P	X	X	
goldhorde, Mar. p. 17	goldhord P	X	X	P	X	X	an early M.E. poetic word
goldfohne, Dep. 188 (gold-decorated)	goldfāh P	X	X	P	I	X	found elsewhere only in Laʒamon
iʒraueston, Mar. p. 22 (stone coffin) [1]	(*græf* + *stān*)	I	X	P	X	X	also found in Pr. P. 208

[1] Or ' engraved stone ' : *ʒe-graven*.

Word and Reference.	Origin.	Peculiar to M.E. (?).	Unique (?).	Prose or Poetic (?).	Also in *The Brut* (?).	Also in later M.E. allit. works (?).	Remarks.
grundwal, Jul. p. 72 (foundation)	grundweall Pr	X	X	P	X	X	a rare M.E. poetic word
halewi, Best. 612, H.M. 199, Kath. 1692, Mar. p. 14, Woh. p. 269 (balm)	*hǣlewǣg* O.N. heilvágr	I	X	Pr	I	X	
hamcume, H.M. 459 (home-coming)	hāmcyme P	X	X	P	X	I	a rare M.E. poetic word
heauedponne, Dep. 288 (skull)	hēafodpanne P	X	X	P	X	X	rarely in M.E. poetry
heauedþౖ*awes,* S.W. 247, 267 (chief virtues)	(*hēafod + þēaw*)	I	X	Pr	X	X	found also in C.L. 799
hehengel, Kath. 710	hēahengel Pr	X	X	Pr	X	X	a common early M.E. homiletic word
Hehfeder, Kath. 661	hēahfæder Pr	X	X	Pr	X	X	
hehseotel, Jul. p. 50 (throne)	hēahsetl Pr	X	X	Pr	X	X	found also in Laȝamon
helewowes, Dep. 239, Gr. 9 (end walls)	(+ *wāh*)	I	X	P	I	X	cp. O.E. *helian,* to cover
helle-barnes, Woh. p. 281 (children of hell)	(*hell + bearn*) M.H.G. hellebarn	I	I	P	X	X	cp. O.E. *hellcniht*
helle-dogges, Woh. p. 273	(*hell + docga*)	I	I	P	X	X	
helle-houndes, Deb. 311	hellhund Pr M.H.G. hellehunt	X	X	P	X	X	not uncommon in rel. works
helle-hus, Woh. p. 273	hellhūs P	X	I	P	X	X	
helle-pine, Best. 638, Lady 104, etc.	(*hell + pīn*) M.H.G. hellepîne	I	X	P	X	X	found also in Hav. 405, Orm 12060
helle-sihðe, S.W. p. 267 (the sight of hell)	(*hell + gesīhð*)	I	I	P	X	X	
helle-stenches, Lady 44	(*hell + stenc*)	I	I	P	X	X	
helle-wa, Mar. p. 15 (hell-torment)	(*hell + wā*)	I	X	P	X	X	found also in Orm 10011
helleware, Mar. p. 9 (hell-dwellers)	hellwaru Pr	X	X	P	X	X	an early M.E. word
helle-wel, Deb. 482 (the pit of hell)	(*hell + welle*)	I	I	P	X	X	cp. O.S. *hellesēaþ*

Word and Reference.	Origin.	Peculiar to M.E. (?).	Unique (?).	Prose or Poetic (?).	Also in The Brut (?).	Also in later M.E. allit. works (?).	Remarks.
helle-wite, Dep. 142 (hell-torture)	hellewīte Pr O.N. helvíti O.L.G. helliwîti	X	X	P	X	X	found also in Hom. I. 109, 229
helle-wurmes, S.W. p. 251	(*hell* + *wyrm*)	I	I	P	X	X	
heorte-blisse, Lady 5	(*heorte* + *bliss*)	I	I	P	X	X	
heorte-blod, Lady 157, S.W. p. 271	(*heorte* + *blōd*) M.H.G. herzebluo|t	I	X	P	I	X	a M.E. poetic word
heouen-kinge, Lady 86	heofoncyning P	X	X	P	X	X	an early M.E. word
heuen-louerd, Best. 170	(*heofon* + *hlāford*)	I	I	Pr	X	X	
heouen-riche, Best. 18, etc., Jul. 24, etc., Kath. 1627, etc., Lady 24, 150, Mar. p. 15, 22 (Kingdom of Heaven)	heofonrīce Pr O.S. hebanrīki cp. O.H.G. himil-rîchi	X	X	P	X	I	a common M.E. poetic word
hetefeste, Mar. p. 12 (securely)	(*hete* + *fæst*)	I	X	Pr	X	X	an early M.E. homiletic word
hetelifaste, Woh. p. 281 (cruelly fast)	(*hete* + *fæst*)	I	I	P	X	X	
heuel-bed, H.M. 297, etc. (bed with canopy)	(*hefel* + *bedd*)	I	I	Pr	X	X	
hirdmen, H.M. 456, Kath. 2215 (servants)	hīredmann Pr	X	X	P	I	I	a common M.E. poetic word
hondwhile, H.M. 134, etc.,Kath.1617,etc. (moment)	handhwīl Pr M.H.G. hantwile	X	X	Pr	X	I	a very common M.E. word
huselauerd, S.W. p. 245, 246 (house-lord)	(*hūs* + *hlāford*)	I	I	P	X	X	an original compound
huslewe, Woh. p. 277 (house-shelter)	hūshlēow Pr	X	I	P	X	X	
inouhreðe, Lou. p. 215, Jul. p. 12 (soon enough)	(*genoh* + *hræð*)	I	X	Pr	X	X	
kinebearn, Woh. p. 273, Mar. p. 4, etc. (royal offspring)	cynebearn Pr	X	X	P	I	X	an early M.E word
kineburh, Kath. 1860 (royal castle)	(*cyne* + *burh*)	I	I	P	X	X	

Word and Reference.	Origin.	Peculiar to M.E. (?).	Unique (?).	Prose or Poetic (?).	Also in *The Brut* (?).	Also in later M.E. allit. works (?).	Remarks.
kineʒerde, Lef. 207 (sceptre)	cynegerd Pr	X	X	P	X	X	found also in Orm 8182
kinemede, Kath. 398 (royal reward)	(*cyne* + *mēd*)	I	I	P	X	X	
kinemerke, Dep. 656 (mark of royalty)	(*cyne* + *mearc*)	I	X	P	X	X	found also in Hav. 604
kinemot, Kath. 1954 (royal council)	(*cyne* + *gemōt*)	I	I	P	X	X	
kineriche, H.M. 250, Kath. 179, etc. (kingdom)	cynerīce Pr O.N. kynríkr O.H.G. chune-rīche	X	X	P	I	X	
kinering, Kath. 408 (royal ring)	(*cyne* + *hring*)	I	I	P	X	X	
kinescrud, Lady 34 (royal dress)	(*cyne* + *scrūd*)	I	I	P	X	X	
kineseotle, Kath. 45, 722 (throne)	cynesetl Pr	X	X	P	X	X	found also in Hom. I. 115
kinestol, Lady 25 (throne)	cynestōl Pr cp. O.S. kuning-stōl O.H.G. chuning-stuol	X	X	P	I	X	found elsewhere only in Laʒa-mon
ladþeow, Jul. p. 33 (leader)	lādþēow Pr	X	X	Pr	X	X	an early M.E. homiletic word
laʒefen, Mar. p. 14, H.M. 468, 477 (marsh)	(*lagu* + *fenn*)	I	X	P	I	X	
lanhure, H.M. 268, etc., Mar. pp. 13, 22 (immediately)	(*lā* + *huru*)	X	X	Pr	X	X	
larspel, Kath. 385 (doctrine)	lārspel Pr	X	X	Pr	I	X	a common early M.E. word
laðer-clut, H.M. 553 (lather-cloth)	(*leaðor* + *clūt*)	I	I	Pr	X	X	
leirwite, M.M. 708 (punishment of un-chastity)	legerwīte Pr	X	X	Pr	X	X	found also in Trev. II. 97
lendbon, Best. 273 (loin-bone)	lendenbān Pr O.H.G. leutenbein	X	I	Pr	X	X	
leoðebeie (*limen*), Jul. p. 16 (easy bending limbs)	(*lið* + *bēgan*) * *liðubēʒ*	I	X	P	X	X	found elsewhere only in Rel. I. 188

Word and Reference.	Origin.	Peculiar to M.E. (?).	Unique (?).	Prose or Poetic (?).	Also in *The Brut* (?).	Also in later M.E. allit. works (?).	Remarks.
licwurðe, H.M. 146, S.W. p. 265 (pleasing)	līcwyrðe Pr	X	X	Pr	X	X	an early M.E. homiletic word
lifdawes, Dep. 25 (the days of life)	lifdæg P O.N. lifdagar	X	X	P	I	X	a common early M.E. word
lifhali, Jul. p. 2 (holy of life)	(*līf* + *hālig*)	I	X	P	X	I	found in early M.E. works
lif-leouie, Kath. 1674 (lifelong lover)	(*līf* + *lēof*) cp. O.H.G. liubi	I	I	P	X	X	
lifsiðe, H.M. 656, 667, S.W. p. 249 (lifetime)	(*līf* + *sīð*)	I	I	P	X	X	
lof(t)song, Lady 8, 14, S.W. p. 261, etc. (song of praise)	lofsang Pr	X	X	P	I	I	a common M.E. poetic word
luftfuheles, Kath. 2245 (birds of the air)	(*lyft* + *fugol*)	I	I	P	X	X	
luue-lettres, S.W. p. 283	(*lufu* + O. Fr. *lettre*)	I	I	Pr	X	X	not recorded again till Shakespeare
luue-runes, Kath. 109 (love-talk)	(*lufu* + *rūn*)	I	I	P	X	X	
luuewurðe, Jul. p. 17, Woh. p. 269, etc.	(*lufu* + *wyrðe*)	I	I	Pr	X	X	an early M.E. homiletic word
marbrestan, Kath. 1479	marmastān Pr	X	X	Pr	I	I	
marheʒeue, H.M. 582, 592 (morning-gift, dowry)	morgengifu Pr O.H.G. morgangebe O.N. morgungjöf	X	X	P	I	X	found elsewhere only in Laʒamon, but common in fieldnames
mapemete, Dep. 585 (food for worms)	(*maða* + *mete*)	I	I	P	X	X	
melseotel, Mar. p. 11 (seat at table)	(*mǣl* + *setl*)	I	I	P	X	X	
mereminne, Kath. 1490 (mermaid)	meremen Pr O.H.G. meriminni M.L.G. merminne	X	X	P	I	I	found elsewhere only in Laʒamon
middelerd, Best. 352, Lady 78 (the earth)	cp. middeneard Pr	I	X	P	I	I	a common form in M.E. poetry
midside, Deb. 405 (the middle of the side)	(*mid* + *sīd*)	I	X	Pr	X	X	

Word and Reference.	Origin.	Peculiar to M.E. (?).	Unique (?).	Prose or Poetic (?).	Also in The Brut (?).	Also in later M.E. allit. works (?).	Remarks.
mildeu, Woh. 269 (honey-dew)	meledēaw Pr O.H.G. militou	X	X	Pr	X	X	
mildheortnesse, Lady 78, etc.	mildheort Pr	X	X	Pr	I	I	
moder-bern, Mar. p. 2 (mother's child)	(*mōdor* + *bearn*) M.H.G. muoter-barṅ	I	I	P	X	X	
moderburh, Kath. 46 (capital)	(*mōder* + *burh*)	I	I	P	X	X	cp. *mother-country, mother-tongue*
mondream, Kath. 2019 (joys of man)	mandrēam P	X	X	P	I	X	an early M.E. word found elsewhere only in Laȝamon
monquellers, Woh. p.279	(*man* + *cwellan*)	I	X	Pr	X	X	a very rare M.E word
monslahe, Mar. p. 11, 12 (man-slayer)	manslaga Pr	X	X	P	X	X	an early M.E. homiletic word
monsware, Dep. 371 (perjured)	mānswara Pr	X	X	P	I	X	found elsewhere only in Laȝamon
monþewes, Alf. 312 (virtues)	manþēaw Pr	X	I	P	X	X	
morðdeden, Dep. 408 (deeds of cruelty)	morðdǣd Pr M.H.G. morttât	X	I	P	X	X	
morweslep, Dep. 284 (morning sleep)	(*morgen* + *slǣp*)	I	X	P	X	I	found elsewhere only in the Crowned King 10
neil-cniues, Jul. p. 56 (nail-knife)	(*nægl* + O. Fr. *canif*)	I	I	P	X	X	an original compound (?)
nomecuðe, Kath. 537 (renowned)	namcūð Pr	X	X	P	X	I	a rare M.E. poetic word
nowcin, Kath. 2395, Mar. p. 1, S.W. pp. 255, 275 (distress)	O.N. nauðsyn	I	X	P	X	X	a rare early M.E. word
orleas, Dep. 230, etc. (despairing)	*ārlēas or *or-lēas	I	I	P	X	X	
ouergart, Mar. p. 11, etc. (arrogant)	(*ofer* + ?)[1]	I	X	P	X	X	found also in Orm 8163

[1] See *N.E.D.*

Word and Reference.	Origin.	Peculiar to M.E. (?).	Unique (?).	Prose or Poetic (?).	Also in The Brut (?).	Also in later M.E. allit. works (?).	Remarks.
ouerhohe, H.M. 637, 650 (contempt)	(*ofer* + *hoga*)	I	X	P	X	X	found also in A.R. 276
ofermete, Dep. 347 (excessive)	*ofermēttu* Pr	X	X	P	X	X	found also in A.R. 296
ouerprute, Alf. 194 (pride)	(*ofer* + *prȳto*)	I	I	P	X	X	
ouerwene, Best. 247 (pride)	(*ofer* + *wēn*) O.H.G. ubarwâni	I	I	P	X	X	cp. O.S. *ofer-wenian*
oðerhwiles, H.M. 500, etc. (sometimes)	(*ōðer* + *hwīles*)	I	X	Pr	X	I	a common M.E. word
pleiferen, Jul. p. 56 (play-fellows)	(*plega* + *gefēra*)	I	X	Pr	I	X	found also in Laȝamon
qualeholde, Dep. 174 (dead carcass)	(*cwalu* + *geheald*)	I	I	P	X	X	
querfaste, Woh. p. 285 (transversely)	(O. Fr. *esquare* + *fæst*)	I	I	Pr	X	X	
raketehe, Jul. p. 46, S.W. p. 249 (chain)	racentēag Pr	X	X	Pr	I	X	a common M.E. word
rædewise, Mar. p. 13	(*rǣd* + *wīs*)	I	I	Pr	X	X	
readmen, Kath. 574 (counsellors)	(*rǣd* + *man*) Cp. M.H.G. râtman	I	I	Pr	X	X	
rihtbileafde, Kath. 2317 (true believers)	(*riht* + *bilīefan*)	I	I	Pr	X	X	
rode-mercke, Mar. p. 16 (rood-mark)	(*rōd* + *mearc*)	I	I	P	X	X	
rode-taken, Mar. p. 10 (sign of the cross)	(*rōd* + *tācn*)	I	I	P	X	X	
rode-tre, Hend. st. 1	(*rōd* + *trēo*)	I	X	P	X	X	an early M.E. homiletic word
salmwruhte, Lou. p. 115, H.M. 3 (psalm-writer)	(Lat. *psalmus* + *wyrhta*)	I	X	Pr	X	X	
sea-stream, Mar. pp. 9, 25	sǣstream Pr O.S. sêostrôm	X	X	P	I	X	found elsewhere only in Laȝamon
se-grund, Best. 401, etc.	sǣgrund Pr	X	X	P	I	X	a very rare M.E. poetic word
selcuðes, Best. 441, Woh. p. 281 (marvels)	seldcūð Pr	X	X	Pr	I	I	

Word and Reference.	Origin.	Peculiar to M.E. (?).	Unique (?).	Prose or Poetic (?).	Also in *The Brut* (?).	Also in later M.E. allit. works (?).	Remarks.
sidwaʒes, Gr. 9, Dep. 240 (side-walls)	(*sīd* + *wāh*)	I	X	P	X	X	the only two instances of the occurrence of this word
skinbon, Best. 272 (shin-bone)	(*scinbān*) O.H.G. schinebein	X	X	Pr	X	X	found elsewhere only in Trev. viii, 15
snawhwite, Mar. p. 18, Kath. 2443	snāwhwīt Pr	X	X	P	I	X	found also in A.R. 314
sondesmon, Kath. 517 (messenger)	(*sand* + *mann*)	I	X	Pr	I	I	
sorimod, Dep. 410 (sad of heart)	sārigmōd P	X	X	P	I	X	an exclusively early M.E. word
soðcnawes, H.M. 353, Kath. 1079, Jul. p. 54 (well-assured)	(*sōð* + *cnāwan*)	I	X	Pr	X	X	the only instances of the occurrence of this word
soulebote, Hend. st. 37 (remedy)	(*sāwol* + *bōt*)	I	I	P	X	X	
souledeað, Lef. p. 205, Lou. p. 211	(*sāwol* + *dēað*)	I	X	P	X	X	found only in these two places
souledrink, Best. 158	(*sāwol* + *drinc*)	I	I	P	X	X	
sawlefon, Lef. p. 205, Woh. pp. 273, 284 (soul-foes)	(*sāwol* + *gefā*)	I	X	P	X	X	the only instances
sawle-heale, Ur. p. 183, S.W. p. 267 (healing)	(*sāwol* + *hǣl*)	I	X	Pr	X	X	an early M.E. homiletic word
soulehus, Dep. 40	(*sāwol* + *hūs*)	I	I	P	X	X	
souleliht, Lady 5	(*sāwol* + *lēoht*)	I	I	P	X	X	
soulenedes, Deb. 97	(*sāwol* + *nied*)	I	I	P	X	X	
soulespuse, Best. 587	(*sāwol* + O. Fr. espus)	I	I	P	X	X	
speatewile, H.M. 347 (inclined to spit)	? (*spittan* + *gewill*)	I	I	P	X	X	cp. *swetewil*
stalewurðe, Kath. 702, etc., Mar. p. 15, etc., Woh. p. 273	stǣlwyrðe Pr	X	X	Pr	I	I	
storesmon, Mar. p. 20, etc. (steersman)	cp. O.E. stēormann Pr M.H.G. stiurman	X	X	Pr	I	I	
steortnaket, Kath. 1537 (stark-naked)	(*steort* + *nacod*)	I	X	Pr	X	X	

Word and Reference.	Origin.	Peculiar to M.E. (?).	Unique (?).	Prose or Poetic (?).	Also in *The Brut* (?).	Also in later M.E. allit. works (?).	Remarks.
sunegild, H.M. 660 (female sinner)	(*synn* + *gylt*)	I	I	P	X	X	
sunnegleam, S.W. pp. 259, 265	(*sunne* + *glǣm*)	I	I	P	X	X	
sunnen-atri, Lou. p. 187 (sin-poison)	(*synn* + *āttor*)	I	I	P	X	X	
swetewil, Kath. 1690 (as sweet as you will)	(*swēte* + *willan*)	I	I	P	X	X	
swireforð, H.M. 342 (neck forward)	(*swīra* + *forð*)	I	I	P	X	X	
trotevale, Deb. 291 (idle talk)	(*origin unknown*)	I	X	P	X	X	found also in Rbt. Mannyng
unwine, Kath. 1221 (enemy)	unwine Pr	X	X	P	X	X	found elsewhere only in A.R. 178, Orm 19838, Laȝamon 1628
uorð-siðe, Lady 117 (departure)	forðsīð P	X	X	P	X	X	found elsewhere only in Hom. I. 197
walmhat, Jul. p. 68 (boiling hot)	(*wælm* + *hāt*)	I	I	P	X	X	
wankel-stede, Best. 446 (unstable position)	(*wancol* + *stede*)	I	I	Pr	X	X	
wa-sið, Dep. 592, H.M. 538 (time of woe)	(*wā* + *sīð*)	I	X	P	I	X	a rare early M.E. poetic word
waterbulge, H.M. 517, 527 (water-bottle)	(*wæter* + O. Fr. *boulge*)	I	I	Pr	X	X	
watergrund, Best. 277	(*wæter* + *grund*)	I	I	P	X	X	
walawa, wailawei, Dep. 486, Deb. 13, M.M. 17, etc., Mar. p. 6	wā lā wā Pr	X	X	Pr	X	I	
wedlowe, Dep. 370 (pledge-breaker)	wedloga Pr	X	I	P	X	X	
weimeres, H.M. 300 (lamentation)	cp. Gothic *waja-mērei* (blasphemy)	I	I	P	X	X	
welcweme, Kath. 1728 (well-pleasing)	(*gewill* + *gecwēme*	I	I	P	X	X	
wellegrund, Best. 58 (bottom of the well)	(*wylla* + *grund*)	I	I	P	X	X	cp. O.E. *wylle-strēam*

Word and Reference.	Origin.	Peculiar to M.E. (?).	Unique (?).	Prose or Poetic (?).	Also in *The Brut* (?).	Also in later M.E. allit. works (?).	Remarks.
welsprung, Lady 72	(*wylla* + *springe*)	I	X	P	X	X	found also in Gen. and Ex. 1243
weorld-witti, Kath. 488	(*weoruld* + *wittig*)	I	I	Pr	X	X	
wildedeor, Dur. 7, Mar. p. 10	wildedēor Pr	X	X	Pr	X	X	
wilȝeoue, Mar. p. 16 (free gift)	(*wil* + *giefu*)	I	X	P	X	X	found elsewhere only in A.R. 368
wyndrunke, Alf. 184 (drunk with wine)	wīndruncen Pr M.H.G. wînt-runken	X	X	P	I	X	a very rare M.E. poetic word found also in Laȝamon
wyperblench, M.M. 12 (attack)	(*wiðer* + *blenc*)	I	I	P	X	X	
wiðerlahen, Mar. p. 5 (infidels)	(*wiðer* + O.N *lagu*) O. Fris. witherlaga O.S. wiðarlaga	I	X	P	I	X	found elsewhere only in Laȝa-mon
wiðerwinnes, Best. 645, Lef. p. 205, Kath. 1191, etc. (foes)	wiðerwinna Pr	X	X	P	I	X	not uncommon in M.E. poetry
wondraðe, Kath. 624 (suffering)	O.N. vandráði	I	X	Pr	I	X	a common loan-word in early M.E.
worldmen, Kath. 485, 879 (worldly men)	weoruldmann Pr	X	X	Pr	I	X	found elsewhere only in Laȝa-mon
wraðerheale, Deb. 458, Jul. p. 42, etc., Mar. p. 10 (sorrow)	to wrāðre hæle Pr	X	X	P	I	X	common in early M.E.
wurðmunt, Kath. 216, etc.	wēorðmynd Pr	X	X	P	I	X	a common but archaic early M.E. word

9

THE NOMINAL COMPOUNDS IN LAȝAMON'S *BRUT*.

As in the case of the compounds treated in the previous section, much the same system of classification has been followed. The words are arranged in alphabetical order, and the reference by volume and page has been given in the second column; in those cases in which the word occurs more than twice, " *etc.*" has been added after giving the first occurrence of the word. In the third column as with the earlier poems the derivation is given in the same manner with the Germanic parallels in the fourth column.

If the word is peculiar to Middle English, i.e. not found in Old English [I] indicates this in the first of the narrow columns; if the word is unique in the given instance the same indication is given in the next column; if the word is not poetic in Middle English, this is indicated by Pr in the next column; if the word is found in the later Middle English alliterative works this is indicated in the last narrow column.

In the next large column the readings of the second MS. of *The Brut* are given, unless the word is retained, and in the final column any further remarks necessary. The readings of the second MS., where these differ from those of the Cotton Caligula MS., are most important, because the scribe of the Otho MS. was copying at least half a century after the composition of the original, and possibly much later; in addition to this fact, the later scribe was more prosaic than the earlier one. This gives us a clue as to the possible archaic nature of many of the compounds even in Laȝamon's day.

In the following lists we have included all the nominal compounds to be found in Laȝamon's *Brut* except, of course, those which were no longer recognised as compounds in any real sense of the term. This was because the number of " prose " compounds was so small. There are altogether 411 nominal compounds used by Laȝamon; even when the length of the poem is taken into account the number is small as compared with Old English practice; but it is sufficiently great to suggest that Laȝamon was in the direct succession of the English and Germanic alliterative poets; 135 of these compounds occur more than once and not a few several times. Only 93 of the 411 are " prose " compounds, though some of these might be considered archaic; this leaves 318 poetic compounds, and it is unnecessary to point out that Laȝamon did not consciously sprinkle these compounds about in his work; they were his inheritance and are but a selection. Doubtless if he had been asked to write out a complete list he would have furnished us with at least three times as many " poetic " compounds ; such was not, however, the case.

The poetic compounds used by Laȝamon are, on close examination and analysis, seen to differ from the Old English stock of such words. Many of the expressions have become colourless, and appear more as fossils. It is evident that several of them conveyed no more meaning than the simple word would have done ; accordingly the scribe of the Otho MS. in many cases substituted the simple word for the compound. The same sort of thing was doubtless true of many of the compounds in Old English literature, in particular those used for " warrior " such as : *drihtguma, herekempa,* etc. ; but there is nothing in Laȝamon's work to correspond to such beautiful compounds as *æppelfealu, beadoleoma, fætedhleor, scadenmæl, sigewæpen, wighafola,* etc. The only ones of the same type in Laȝamon are : *dæpsið, eorðhus, fæiesið, feðerhome, forþfare, goldfah, hokerleoð* (an original compound ?), *leirstow, lifdæȝen, morðspelle* (an original compound ?), *nailsax, qualesið* (an original compound ?), *siȝecræft* (an original compound ?), *sorhsið* (an original compound ?), *wadæi, writrune.* These are particularly noticeable and supply an unassailable proof that Laȝamon had inherited the Old English alliterative tradition.

The majority of Laȝamon's compounds are of the type which consists of a simple word preceded by a descriptive adjective or noun as in the above examples. It is not surprising that compounds of such a type as the O.E. *ȳðful,* which are virtually kennings, are not to be found in *The Brut.* Just as there are hackneyed compounds in Old English poetry, so there are in Laȝamon ; the latter employs ʊ compounds with *burh-,* 9 with *here-,* 8 with *hired-,* 11 with *kine-,* 15 with *leod-,* 6 with *lond-,* 9 with *mon-,* 14 with *sæ-,* 7 with *weorld-,* 11 with *wiðer-* and 11 with *wunder-.* Alongside this we might mention that in *Beowulf* there are 19 compounds with *sǣ-,* 14 with *here-,* 30 with *guþ-* and 24 with *wæl-.*[1]

Of the 411 compounds, 183 are found alike in Old English prose and poetry ; of these, 131 were in Old English prose words, though often occurring in poetry also ; the remaining 52 compounds were exclusively poetic. By Laȝamon's time so many of the Old English prose words had become poetic that only 93 of the 411 of the compounds used are " prose ".

Not only, however, did Laȝamon inherit many of the Old English

[1] F. P. Magoun, Jr., *Recurring First Elements in Different Nominal Compounds in Beowulf and the Elder Edda,* The Klæber Anniversary Studies, 1929, pp. 73-8.

poetic compounds, he used 228 compounds not found in Old English. Of these, 6 were Old Norse words and 5 contained an Old Norse first or second element, leaving us with 217 compounds whose first and second elements are both of native origin, but which are not found conjoined in Old English poetry. It would be ridiculous to suggest that Laȝamon created all these, but Germanic parallels to these words can only be found in 17 cases, such as *wiðerlaȝen* (O.S. *wiðerlaga*, O. Fris. *witherlaga*) and *wadæi* (M.H.G. *wētac*), etc.[1] We may assume that these words existed in Old English, though never recorded, and the same must also apply to many others. Yet having granted this, it is not likely that Laȝamon used 200 compounds (the majority of them poetic) which existed in Old English, but which were never recorded ; it seems certain that Laȝamon created many of them himself. If this was the case, the alliterative tradition must have been very much alive ; some compounds had in the course of time passed out of existence, but new ones had been created to take their place.

It is also worthy of note that Laȝamon used 261 compounds which are not used by any other Middle English writer ; the majority of these are not found in Old English poetry—a further indication of the poet's originality. In addition, the majority of the remaining 150 compounds are found only outside Laȝamon in the early Middle English alliterative verse and prose, and in the *Ancren Riwle*.

A good deal can be learned from a study of the readings of the second MS., the Cotton Otho :—

(1) In 15 cases the MS. has been damaged, so that we cannot ascertain the attitude of the later scribe ; this excludes those words for which another reference is available, so revealing the attitude of the later scribe.

(2) In 203 cases the word is retained in the second MS., and as the scribe in question was critical, it seems likely that he recognised these words or at any rate that they were intelligible to him. Here there is evidence to show that as late as 1275 the alliterative tradition was by no means dead ; the poetic compounds may still have been the stock-in-trade of alliterative poets.

(3) In 63 cases (excluding those instances· in which another reference is available) the word or the passage is omitted ; this is usually to be interpreted as a definite rejection by the scribe ;

---

[1] *furbrond, heorteblod, ifurndaȝen, leodfolc, nutescalen, onfreond, richedomr stangraffen, sweordbroper, tæuelbrede, wadæi, wilspel, winschence, wiðe-, laȝen, wunderfeole, wundergod, wunderkene.*

among such rejections are : *elþeod, frumræs, herefeng, hokerleoð, lichraste, siʒecraft.*

(4) In the remaining 130 cases the scribe of the second MS. makes some alteration.   The changes which resulted may be classified as follows :—

A. *The expression is brought up to date—*
　　e.g. ælmesmon > þore men—2.400
　　　　bocilærde men > clearkes wel wise—3.16
　　　　leirstowe > on erþe—2.538

B. *The first element is omitted—*
　　e.g. burhfolc > folc—1.416
　　　　dugeðecnihtes > cnihtes—1.433
　　　　dugeðekinge > kinge—3.30
　　　　feondslæhtes > slæhtes—2.265

C. *The passage only dimly intelligible to the scribe—*
　　e.g. fiede on bocfelle > wrot mid his honde—1.3
　　　　þat leodscopes singeð > many men seggeð—2.542

D. *The passage wholly unintelligible to the scribe—*
　　e.g. balufehte > mochele fihte—1·253
　　　　blæðfæst > rihfolle—1.430
　　　　on heora breostþonke > inne þisse liue—1.82
　　　　þe cuðen dweomerlakes song > after wittie an wise—1.12
　　　　liðende mon > soþemen—1.133

In this study we have naturally assumed that though the Otho MS. was not copied directly from the Caligula MS. there was nevertheless sufficient connection (due to a common relationship with the original) to justify the assumption that the Caligula MS. was for all practical purposes similar to the lost MS. from which the Otho MS. was made.

These illustrations are sufficient to show that some of Laʒamon's compounds were so archaic as to be unintelligible by 1275 ; yet allowing for the fact that this later scribe was distinctly prosaic, it is surprising how many of Laʒamon's poetic compounds were still intelligible at so late a date.

THE COMPOUNDS IN LAȜAMON'S BRUT.

	Ref.	O.E. Derivation.	Other Gmc. Parallels.	M.E. not O.E. Word.	Unique in Laȝamon (?).	P. or Pr. (?).	Found in Later M.E. Alliterative Works.	2nd MS. Reading.	Comments.
ēaðmēden (humility)	1.427, etc.	ēaðmēdu Pr.	= O.H.G. ōtmuotī = O.L.G. ōdmōdi	X	I	Pr	X	O has the form edmode	
æhsenen (eyesight)	1.131, etc.	cp. O.E. ēageseung Pr.	= O.H.G. ougsiuni	X	X	Pr	X		The compound is of no significance
æieleste (fearlessness)	2.386	cp. O.E. egelēas Pr.	= O.N. agalauss	I	I	P	X		The adj. eȝeles is found both in Orm and in Gaw.
ælmesmon (almsman)	2.400 401	(O.E. ælmesse + mann Pr.)	[Gk. ελεημοσυνη]	X	X	P	X	2.400 C an almes-monnes wise O in pore men guyse 2.401 O passage omitted	
ærdeden (offences)	1.373	ārdǣd Pr.		X	X	Pr	X		Found elsewhere only in Hom. II. 153
ærendrake (messenger)	1.28	ārendraca Pr.	O.N. erindreki	X	X	Pr	X		A word found in early M.E. religious prose
ærwene (presumptuous)	3.97	orwēne Pr.		X	I	P	X	O passage omitted	
ærwitte (unwise)	2.503	cp. O.E. or-(wene)		I	I	P	X	O passage omitted	Apparently an original compound, formed on the analogy of the previous one
æstende (east end)	3.131	ēastende Pr.		X	X	Pr	I		Not uncommon in M.E.

Compound (gloss)	Etymology	Ref.					Variant readings (C / O)	Cognates	Remarks
æsthalue	æasthalf Pr	3.173	X	I	Pr	X	O passage destroyed		Possibly an original compound modelled on the two preceding ones
æstside	(ēast + sīd)	2.491	I	I	Pr	X	O eastende		
æðelmod (noble-minded)	(æðele + mōd)	2.554	I	I	P	X	C æðelmod / O edmod		
æventime (eventide)	æfentima Pr	2.112	X	I	P	X	C æventime / O evetime		
aldeyfæder (ancestor)	ealdefæder Pr	3.204	X	X	Pr	I	O passage destroyed	O.H.G. altfater / O. Fris. aldafeder / O. Fris. aldirmon	
aldormon	ealdormann Pr	1.60	X	X	Pr	I	C aldermon, O man		
balufihte (deadly fight)	(bealu + feoht)	1.253	I	I	P	X	C balufehte		Both original poetic compounds
baluwæs (deadly attack)	(bealu + rǣs)	3.29	I	I	P	X	O mochele fihte		
balusiðe (evil fate)	bealusīð P	1.25, 28, etc.	X	X	P	X	1.25 O passage destroyed / 1.28 omitted		An archaic survival found also in Mar. and homilies
baluwis (wicked)	(bealu +)	2.294	I	I	P	X	O passage omitted	O.N. bôlviss / O.S. baluwîso / M.H.G. baruoz / O. Fris. berfôt	
barfot	bærfōt Pr	1.377	X	X	Pr	I			
bermannen (porters)	bērmann Pr	1.141, etc.	X	X	P	X			Found elsewhere only in Hav. 868. A rare M.E. compound
biscopstol (eccles. see)	bisceopstōl Pr	2.340, 598	X	X	Pr	X			
blæðfæst (famous)	blǣdfæst P	1.298, etc.	X	I	P	I	1.298 C seoððen was Bledon his sune and blæðfæst King; > O after him com his sone Bledo ihote. 1.430 blæðfæst > rihfolle	cp. O.H.G. plât	The word is distinctly archaic

THE COMPOUNDS IN LAȜAMON'S *BRUT* (*continued*).

	Ref.	O.E. Derivation.	Other Gmc. Parallels.	M.E. not O.E. Word.	Unique in Laȝamon (?).	P. or Pr. (?).	Found in Later M.E. Alliterative Works.	2nd MS. Reading.	Comments.
blamon (negro)	3.6	+ mann	O.N. blámaðr	I	X	Pr	I		A rare M.E. word
bliðemod (happy)	3.191	bliðemód P. & Pr.		X	I	P	X	O passage destroyed	
blodȝute (shedding of blood)	1.27, etc.	blódgyte Pr		X	I	P	X		
blodstremes	3.62, 133	(blód + stréam)	Germ. blūtström	I	I	P	X	3.62 C blodstrennes, O blodie stremes 3.133 O passage omitted	
bocfelle (parchment)	1.3	bócfell Pr	O.H.G. buohfel	X	X	P	I	C & fiede on bocfelle O & wrot mid his honde	The expression evidently not understood by the second scribe Found elsewhere only in Mar. 23
bocilærde	2.284, etc.	(bóc + gelǣred)		I	X	P	X	3.16 C & bocilærde men O & clearkes wel wise	Elsewhere the second scribe either omitted the passage or the MS. happens to be defaced A rare M.E. poetic word
bocrunen (letters)	1.192	(bóc + rún)		I	I	P	X	C stille bocrune	Plenty of compounds have bóc- in O.E.
bocspællen (story)	2.309, etc.	(bóc + spell)		I	I	P	X	O one deorne lettre	

Word (gloss)	Ref.	Compound	Cognates					Citations	Notes
bocstauen (letters)	1.326	bōcstæf Pr	O.S. bōkstaf / O.N. bókstafr / O.H.G. buohstab / O.N. boli	X	X	P	X		Found also in Orm 4308
bolehyde (bull skin)	2.169	(+ hȳd)		1	X	Pr	X		Very rare word in M.E. extant works
breostþanc (mind)	1.82	breōstgeþanc P	O.S. briostgithâht	X	1	P	X	C on heora breost-þonke / O inne þisse liue	
Brutlond	1.93	(+ land)		1	1	Pr	X		
burccnihte (chamberlains)	2.327, etc.	(būr + cniht)		1	1	P	X		Cp. O.E. būrþegn
burhcnauen (town lads)	2.227	(būr + cnapa)		1	1	P	X		Cp. O.E. būrþegn
burhfolc	1.416, etc.	(burh + folc)		1	X	P	X	C ah þet burhfolc wes war / O ac þat folc was wel war	Found elsewhere only in Hom. II. 89
burhmon	2.94	burhman Pr		X	X	P	X		Found elsewhere only in A.R. 350
burhwalles	2.504	burhweall Pr		X	1	P	X	3.133 C burhweren, O bormen / 3.134 O passage omitted	Found elsewhere only in Mat. xx. 10
burhweeren (burghers)	3.133, etc.	burgwaru Pr		X	X	P	X		
burhzate	2.317	burhgēat Pr.		X	X	P	X		
buvlutlen (bower maidens)	3.237	(būr + lytling)		1	1	P	X	O passage destroyed	Found elsewhere only in Kath. 1679
burward (guardian of the bower)	2.381	(būr + weard)		1	1	P	X		Cp. O.E. burhweard
burnehode (helmet)	2.267, etc.	(beorn + hōd)		1	1	P	X	C burnehode / O bruniehode	
burðeine	2.219, etc.	būrþegn Pr		X	1	P	X	2.149 C burðeines, O folke / 2.219 C burðeines, O riche þeines / 2.413 O passage omitted	

THE COMPOUNDS IN LAȝAMON'S BRUT (continued).

Word	Ref.	O.E. Derivation.	Other Gmc. Parallels.	M.E., not O.E. Word.	Unique in Laȝamon (?).	P. or Pr. (?).	Found in Later M.E. Alliterative Works.	2nd MS. Reading.	Comments.
candel-liht	2.575	candel leoht Pr		X	X	P	I		
cantel-cape (cope)	3.193	cantelcapa Pr		X	I	Pr	I		
castelburi	1.286	(O.Fr. castel+O.E. byrig)		I	I	P	X	O passage omitted	
castelȝat	2.359, 394	(O.Fr. castel + O.E. geat).		I	I	Pr	X		
chepmon	2.49, etc.	cēapmann Pr	O.H.G. choufman	X	X	Pr	I		
cheues-boren (born of a concubine)	1.185	(cefes + geboren)	O.H.G. chebisa	I	I	P	X		The first element is found in Mar. 3
chirche-grið (church-peace)	2.514	ciricgrið Pr		X	X	Pr	X		Found also in A.R. 174
chiriclond	2.197	(ciric + land)		I	I	Pr	X	O passage omitted	A not uncommon M.E. word
cnauechild	2.226	(M.E. cnave +O.E. cild)		I	X	Pr	X	C cnihtbærn, O cnaveehild	Cp. O.E. cnihtcild
cnihtbærn (male child)	2.226	(cniht + bearn)		I	I	P	X	C cnihtbærn, O cnauechild	
cnihtweored (a troop of lads)	3.65	(cniht + weorod)		I	I	P	X	O passage omitted	
craftmonnen	3.158	(craft + mann)		I	X	P	X	O passage omitted	Found elsewhere only in Ch. C.T.A. 1899
cunnesmon	1.115 etc.	(cynnes + mann)		X	X	Pr	I	O passage omitted	A common M.E. word
dæþsið (death journey)	1.271, 280	(dēaþ + sīð)		I	I	P	X		
dæiliht	1.241, etc.	(dæg + lēoht)		I	X	Pr	I		

Headword	Ref.	Form / Derivation	Cognates						Passage	Remarks
deorfriþ (deer-chase)	1.61	déorfrið Pr		X	I	P	X	X		
deorwurðe	1.86, etc.	déorwyrðe Pr		X	X	Pr	X	X		
domesdai	2.236, 597	dómdæg Pr	O.N. dómsdagr O.S. dómdag, etc.	X	X	Pr	I	X		
drakenhefd (dragon's head)	2.341	(draca + héafod)		I	X	P	X	I		Found in A.R. 246. Cp. O.E. dracanblód
drihtfolce (dependants)	1.59, etc.	drihtfolc P	O.S. druht-folk	X	I	P	X	X	1.59 C drihtfolce, O gode folke; 2.270 C drihtfolce, O folke; 1.359 passage omitted	
drihtmonnen	2.191	(driht + mann)		I	I	P	I	I	C mid al his drihtmonnen O mid hæþene folke	
drinc-hail (drink-health)	1.158, etc.	(drinc +	O.N. heill)	I	I	P	I	I		The word became fairly common in M.E.
duʒeðe-cnihtes (retainers)	1.433	(duguð + cniht)		I	I	P	I	I	C duʒeðe-cnihtes O cnihtes	
duʒeðe-kinge	3.30	(duguð + cynyng)		I	I	P	I	I	C duʒeðe-kinge O kinge	
duʒeðe-monnen	2.164	(duguð + mann)		I	I	P	I	I	O passage omitted	
dureward (keeper of the door)	2.317	duruweard Pr		X	X	P	X	X		A very rare M.E. word
dweomercraften (magic craft)	3.230	(dweomor + cræft)		X	I	P	X	X	O passage destroyed	
dweomerlakes (magic)	1.12, etc.	(dweomor + lác)		X	X	P	I	X	1.12 C þe cuðen dweomer-lakessong O after wittie an wise; 2.47 passage omitted	Only found in alliterative poetry in M.E.

THE COMPOUNDS IN LAȜAMON'S *Brut* (*continued*).

Word.	Ref.	O.E. Derivation.	Other Gmc. Parallels.	M.E., not O.E. Word.	Unique in Laȝamon (?).	P. or Pr. (?).	Found in Later M.E. Alliterative Works.	2nd MS. Reading.	Comments.
edmod (humble)	2.518	ēaðmōd Pr		X	X	Pr	X	C ædmode / O mildliche	
elreordi (speaking a foreign tongue)	3.17	elreordig Pr		X	I	P	X	C elreordi feond / O wel lopliche feond	
elþeod (foreign people)	1.98	elþēod P	O.H.G. elidiotig / O.S. elithiodig	X	I	P	X	passage omitted	Cp. early M.E. *elþeodi*
endedæie	1.158	endedæg P		X	X	P	I	C endedæie / O lifues (h)ende	
eorðe-itilie (tillage)	1.427	cp. O.E. eorðtilð		X	X	P	X	C eorðeitilie / O erþetilie	*erþetilþe* is used by Wiclif
eorðe-tilien (earth-tillers)	2.505	eorðtilia Pr		X	X	P	X.	O erþetilie	A rare M.E. poetic word
eorðhus (cave)	1.100 etc.	eorðhūs P		X	X	P	X		Found elsewhere only in the Grave l. 15
erendesmon (messenger)	2.622	(ǣrende + man)		I	I	Pr	X	C erendesmon / O herendrake	
fæie-sið (death)	1.14, etc.	(fǣge + sīð)		I	I	P	X	1.120 C faiesið þes kinges, / O Rudibras his deaþe / 1.14 C feiesið makede, / O phrase misunderstood and avoided / 2.444 C faiesih worhten / O folle to grunde	

Word	Line	Compound	Cognate					MS notes	Remarks
feondrǽse (attack of the enemy)	2.584	fēondrǽs P		X	I	P	X		
feondscaðe (enemy)	3.34	fēond + scaða P		X	I	P	X		
feondslæht (slaughter of foes)	2.256	(fēond + slæht)		I	I	P	X	C feondslæhtes / O slæhtes	
feonddewes (evil conduct)	1.25	(fēond + þēaw)		I	I	P	X	O passage omitted	
feower-noked (four-nooked)	2.500	(fēower + M.E. nōk)		I	I	P	X		
feðer-home (wings)	1.122, 3.26	feðerhama P	O.S. feðar-hamo	X	X	P	X		Found also in Rob. (W), E. 2 and Hom. I. 81
fohselcunne (volatiles)	1.346	fugelcynn P		X	X	P	X		A rare early M.E. word
folckinge	1.405, 1.106, etc.	folccyning P	O.S. folk-kuning	X	I	P	X	O passage omitted	
forþfare (death)		forþfaru P		X	I	P	X		Cp. *forðfore*, Gen. and Ex. 3158
freokinge	1.135, etc.	(frēo + cyning)		I	I	P	X		
freoman	2.228, etc.	frēoman Pr		X	X	Pr	I		A common M.E. word
frumwæs (a first onset)	1.369	(fruma + vǽs)		I	I	P	X	O passage omitted	Word not understood by the second scribe
furbrond (firebrand)	3.15	(fȳr + brand)	Ger. feuerbrand	I	X	P	I		Found also in King Alisaundir 6848 and in Pr. C. 7421
genecusti (liberal)	1.207	(giefan + cystig)		I	I	P	X	O passage omitted	
glæsfat (glass vessel)	2.319	glæsfæt Pr	O.H.G. glasfaz	X	I	P	X	C glæsfæt / O vrinal	
gleocræften (art of music)	1.299	gleocraft Pr		X	I	P	X	C of alle gleo-cræften / O of alle cræftes	

THE COMPOUNDS IN LAȝAMON'S *BRUT* (continued).

	Ref.	O.E. Derivation.	Other Gmc. Parallels.	M.E. not O.E. Word.	Unique in Laȝamon (?).	P. or Pr. (?).	Found in Later M.E. Alliterative Works.	2nd MS. Reading.	Comments.
gleodreme (song)	1.77	gleodrēam P		X	I	P	X		A fairly common M.E. word
gleoman	1.298, etc.	gleoman Pr		X	X	Pr	I		
godcunde, sb. (divinity)	2.627	godcund Pr	O.S. godkundi / O.H.G. gotchundi	I	I	P	X		
godcunde, adj. (divine)	1.432, etc.		O.S. godkund / O.H.G. gotschund	X	X	Pr	I		Found also in Orm 5873
goddede (a good deed)	2.461	goddǣd Pr	M.H.G. guottät	X	X	Pr	X		An early M.E. compound
goddspell	3.182, etc.	godspell Pr		X	X	Pr	I		A common M.E. compound
goldfah	1.417, etc.	goldfāh P		X	X	P	X		Found elsewhere only in the Dep. Soul's Add. to the Body, 188
•*goldwive*	1.300	(gold + wīv)		I	X	Pr	I		A rare M.E. word confined to poetry, but in no sense a poetic word
grasbedde	2.585	(grǽs + bedd)		X	I	P	X	C grasbedde / O gras	
gristbat (gnashing of teeth)	1.80	(grist + bāt)		X	I	P	X	O passage omitted	O.E. has, gristbitian, gristbātian, and gristbitung ⎱ Found also in Misc. 230 and Hom. I. 33
gristbatinge	1.221	(grist + bāt)		I	X	P	X		

Compound	Ref.	Composition	Cognates					MS. variants	Notes
grundfulled (thoroughly filled)	1.46	(grund + fyllan)		I	I	P	X	C mid gode grund-fulled / O mid gode þe siþes ifulled	
grundhat (quite hot)	1.242	(grund + hāt)		I	I	P	X	C grundhat / O hot	
grundladen (full laden)	1.47, 264	(grund + hladen)		I	I	P	X	C wel afulleð / O al grundlade	
hæfedbon (skull)	1.62	heāfodbān Pr	O.N. hǫfuð-bein	X	I	P	X		
hæfedwunde (head-wound)	1.325	hēafodwund Pr	Ger. hauptwunde / O.S. hoƀid-wunda	I	I	P	X		
hēzeburh		hēahburh Pr		X	I	Pr	X		
hēzemen	3.192	(hēah + mann)		I	X	Pr	X	C heȝemen / O heȝecunne	
hēhsetle (throne)	2.253	hēah-setl Pr	O.H.G. hōhsedal	X	X	P	X		Found also in Hom. I. 113 and Jul. 50
halfsuster	1.359	(healf + sweoster)		I	X	Pr	I		Found also in Gaw 2464
hæluendale (the half part)	1.142, etc.	(healf + gedāl)		I	I	Pr	X	O passage omitted	
halfzearu (half-ready)	1.369	(healf + gearu)		I	I	Pr	X		
heard-iheorted	2.75	(heard + heorte)		I	X	Pr	X	O passage omitted	Found also in A.R. 400
haleweie	2.546, etc.	*hǣlewǣg	O.N. heilvágr / M.H.G. heilwǣge	I	I	Pr	X		
halidom	2.218	hāligdōm	O.H.G. heiligtuom	X	X	Pr	X		
halimot (assembly)	3.287	(heall-gemōt)		I	X	P	I	O passage destroyed	Found elsewhere only in P.S. 154
halle-dure	2.457, 3.210	(heall + duru)		I	X	P	I		
halle-wah (hall-wall)	3.27	(heall + wāh)		I	I	P	X	C hallewah / O hilewoþ	Cp. helewowe in N.E.D. (O.E. helian + wāh)
heor-lochede (hoary locked)	3.25	(hār + locc)		I	I	P	X		

THE COMPOUNDS IN LAȝAMON'S *BRUT* (continued)

	Ref.	O.E. Derivation	Other Gmc. Parallels.	M.E. not O.E. Word.	Unique in Laȝamon (?).	P. or Pr. (?).	Found in Later M.E. Alliterative Works.	2nd MS. Reading.	Comments.
heorteblod	2.239	(*heorte + blōd*)	M.H.G. herzebluot	I	X	P	X		Found rarely in M.E. poetry
heortne-gnaning (sorrow)	2.322	(*heorte + gnānung*)		I	I	P	X	O passage omitted	
hereberȝe (shelter)	2.78, etc.	O.N. loan word	O.H.G. heriberga O.N. herbergi	I	X	P	I		A very common M.E. word
herebyrne (armour)	2.584	herebyrne P		X	I	P	X		
heredring (warrior)	1.366, etc.	(*here + dreng*)		I	I	P	X		
herefeng (plunder)	2.64	(*here + fēng*)		I	I	P	X	O passage omitted	
heregong (invasion)	2.329	heregang Pr	O. Fris. heregong	X	X	P	X	O passage omitted	Common in early M.E. poetry
heregumen (warriors)	2.184, etc.	(*here + guma*)		I	I	P	X	2.380 C heregumes, O hiredgomes; 2.426 C heregumes, O kene gomes; 2.184 O passage omitted	
herekempen (warriors)	2.441, etc.	(*here + cempa*)		I	I	P	X	2.441 C Cherekempen, O deorworþe kempes; O passage omitted in other cases	

Word (meaning)	Line	Etymology	Cognates	1	2	3	4	5	C / O variants	Notes
heremærken (standards)	2.368	(here + mearc)		I	I	I	P	X	C heremærken / O hire marke	
herescrud (war-dress)	1.216	(here + scrūd)		I	I	I	P	X	O passage omitted in each case	
heretoȝe (leader)	2.357, 1.251 etc.	heretoga Pr	O.S. heritogo, O.N. hertogi, O.H.G. herizoho	X	X	X	P	X	1.251 C heretoȝe, O cheutaine / 1.246 C heretoȝe, O heuedling	Found elsewhere only in Frag. 2 and Hom. I. III
hereword (fame)	2.72 etc.	hereword Pr		X	X	X	P	X	C hereword	Found elsewhere only in A.R. 148 and Hom. II. 83
herdswein	1.241	(heorde + O.N. sveinn)		I	I	I	P	X	C herdswein / O swein	
hindercraft (deceitful craft)	2.12	(hinder + cræft)		I	I	I	P	X	C hindercraft / O luper crafte	
hirdcniht (attendant)	1.184 etc.	hiredcniht Pr		I	I	X	P	X		
hirdfolc (retainer)	1.275	(hired + folc)		I	I	I	P	X	C hirdfolc / O folc	Few compounds with hīred in O.E.
hirdiferen (courtiers)	1.283	(hired + gefēra)		I	I	I	P	X	C hirdiferen / O ivere	
hirdchildren	2.269	(hired + cildru)		I	I	I	P	X	C hiredchildren / O heredmen	
hiredcnaue (attendant)	1.241 etc.	(hired + cnapa)		I	I	I	P	X	O passage in every case omitted	Cp. O.E. hīrēdcniht
hiredgume (courtier)	2.88, 380	(hired + guma)		I	I	I	Pr	X		
hiredmon (courtier)	1.99 etc.	hiredmann Pr		X	X	X	P	I		A rare M.E. poetic compound
hiredpleie (court-play)	2.181	(hired + plega)		I	I	I	P	X	O passage omitted	
hokerleod (song of mockery)	3.155	(hōcor + lēoþ)		I	I	I	P	X	O passage destroyed	Cp. hokerlahter, Hom. I. 283
hokerword (scornful language)	2.398	(hōcor + word)		I	I	I	P	X	C hokerword / O hokere wordes	Cp. O.E. hocorwyrde, adj.

10

THE COMPOUNDS IN LAȜAMON'S BRUT (continued).

	Ref.	O.E. Derivation.	Other Gmc. Parallels.	M.E. not O.E. Word.	Unique in Laȝamon (?).	P. or Pr. (?).	Found in later M.E. Alliterative Works.	2nd MS. Reading.	Comments.
hondfæst (pledge)	1.95	O.N. loan word	O.N. handfesta	1	X	Pr	X	C hondfæst	Cp. O.E. handfestan
hondsæx (dagger)	1.276	handseax Pr		X	1	P	X	O treoþe ipliȝt; O passage omitted	
horsbere (horse-litter)	2.398	horsbǣr Pr		1	X	Pr	X		A rare word in M.E.
horsleden (horsemen)	2.544	(hors + lēod)		1	1	P	X	O passage omitted	Cp. O.E. horscniht
husebonda	3.285	hūsbonda		X	X	Pr	I		A fairly common word
huxword (taunt)	2.487	huscword P	O.S. hoskword	X	1	P	X	C huxword; O hokere wordes; O passage destroyed	
ifurndaȝen (former days)	3.295	(gefyrn + dæg)	O.S. forndagos	1	1	P	X	O passage omitted	
ifurnȝer (former year)	2.634	(gefyrn + ȝēar)		1	1	P	X		
inȝeong (entrance)	3.133	ingang Pr		X	X	Pr	I		A common M.E. word
kineærde (royal land)	2.392	(cyne + eard)		1	1	P	X	C kineærde; O kinerþe	
kinebenche	1.413	(cyne + benc)		1	1	P	X	C an his kinebenche; O mid his winsenche	
kinebearn	1.9, etc.	cynebearn Pr		X	X	P	X		Found also in Mar. 4 and Hom. I. 273, and II. 47, 49
kinedom	1.260, etc.	cynedōm Pr	O.N. konung-dómr; O.H.G. cuningdómr	X	X	Pr	I		A common M.E. word
kinehelm (crown)	1.288, etc.	cynehelm Pr		X	X	P	X	C kinehelm; O croune	A rare M.E. poetic word

Compound	Line	Form	Etymology					MS. notes	Notes
kinelauerd, (cyne + land)	1.106, etc.	cynehláford Pr		X	I	P	X		
kinelond	1.9, etc.	(cyne + land)		I	I	P	X		
kineriche (kingdom)	1.26, etc.	cynerice Pr	O.N. kynríkr Cp. O.H.G. kuning-ríchi	X	I	P	X		
kinestole (royal throne)	1.192	cynestól Pr		X	X	P	X		Found elsewhere in M.E. only in Hom. I. 191
kinwurðe (royal)	2.35, etc.	(cyne + weorþ)		I	X	P	X		Found also in Kath. 567 and in C.L. 14
kineþeode (kingdom)	1.125, etc.	(cyne + þeod)		I	I	P	X		
læchecræfte	1.325, etc.	læccecræft Pr		X	X	Pr	I		A common M.E. word
lædesmen (steersmen)	1.266	ládmann Pr		I	I	P	X	C ledesmen / O lodesmen	
larspel (doctrine)	1.433, etc.	lárspel Pr		X	X	Pr	X		A common early M.E. word
larspelundre (preacher)	3.183	lárspel Pr		I	I	P	X	O passage destroyed	
laðspel (evil tidings)	2.449	láðspel Pr		X	I	P	X	O passage omitted	
laȝefen (swamp)	2.536	(lagu + fenn)		I	X	P	X		An early M.E. compound found also in A.R. 328, H.M. 33 and Mar. 14. Many compounds with lagu in O.E.
lauerdswike (traitor)	2.506, 622	hláfordswica Pr		X	X	P	X		Found elsewhere only in Chr. E. 1033 and in P.S. 220
leirstowe (cemetery)	2.287, 538	legerstów Pr		X	I	P	X	2.287 O passage omitted / 2.538 C leirstowe, O on erþe	

THE COMPOUNDS IN LAƷAMON'S BRUT (continued).

	Ref.	O.E. Derivation.	Other Gmc. Parallels.	M.E. not O.E. Word.	Unique in Laʒamon (?).	P. or Pr. (?).	Found in Later M.E. Alliterative Works.	2nd MS. Reading.	Comments.
lodcniht (guide)	3.21	(lād + cniht)		I	I	P	X		Cp. O.E. lādmann
leodealder (a chief)	1.58	(lēod + ieldra)		I	I	P	X	O passage omitted	Many compounds with lēod existed in O.E.
leodcnihtes (knights)	1.318	(lēod + cniht)		I	I	P	X	C leodcnihtes / O cnihtes	Cp. O.S. liudi-barn
leodferde (folk-army)	1.36, etc.	(lēod + ferd)		I	I	P	X	1.242 C leodferde, O strong ferde / O passage omitted in the other cases	
leodfolc (people)	1.86, etc.	(lēod + folc)	O.S. liudfolc	I	I	P	X		
leodkempen (warriors)	1.257	(lēod + cempa)		I	I	P	X	C leodkempen / O kempes	
leodking (king of the people)	1.22, etc.	lēodcyning P		X	I	P	X		
leodquide (national speech)	1.123	(lēod + cwide)		I	I	P	X	C leodquide / O ure speche	
leodrunen (discourse)	1.389, 2.184, 225	lēodrūn Pr		X	I	P	X		
leodscome (national shame)	3.45	(lēod + sceamu)		I	I	P	X	C leodscome / O schame	
leodscop (national poet)	2.542, 3.229	(lēod + scōp)		I	I	P	X	2.542 C þat leod-scopes singeð, O many men seggeð / 3.229 O passage destroyed	

Word (meaning)	Ref.	Formation	Cognate					Notes	Comments
leodspellen (traditional tales)	2.236, etc.	(lēod + spel)		I	I	P	X		
leodswike (national treachery)	1.32, etc.	(lēod + swicu)		I	I	P	X		
leodþeauwe (servant of the people)	1.87, 3.296	lēodðēaw Pr		X	I	P	X	O passages omitted	
leodþeines (national servants)	1.284	(lēod + þegn)		I	I	P	X	C leodþeines / O cnihtes	
leodwise (national custom)	1.303, 2.507	(lēod + wīse)		I	I	P	X		
lichraste (burial place)	2.298	licrest Pr		X	I	P	X	O passage omitted	
lifdæzen (life-days)	1.123, etc.	lifdæg P	O.N. lif-dagar	X	X	P	I		A very common early M.E. word
limmele (piecemeal)	3.16	limmālum Pr		X	X	Pr	X		A common M.E. prose word
lideudemon (seafarers)	1.133, 1.176	(līðan + mann)		I	I	P	X	1.133 Cliðendemon, O sopemen / 1.176 O passage destroyed	Cp. O.E. liðend, a sailor
lofsonge (song of praise)	1.4, 2.188	lōfsang Pr		X	X	P	X		
lohiboren (lowly born)	2.502	(O.N. lāgr + O.E. geboren)		I	I	Pr	I	O passage omitted	A common M.E. poetic word
londcnihtes (people)	2.414	(land + cniht)		I	I	P	X	C londcnihtes / O riche cnihtes	
londfolc (natives)	1.22, etc.	landfolc Pr	O.H.G. lantvolc	X	X	P	X		Found also in O. and N. 1158 and Rob. 173 and C.M. 9752
londgauel (land-tax)	1.319, 332	landgafol Pr		X	I	P	X	O passages omitted	

THE COMPOUNDS IN LAȜAMON'S BRUT (continued).

	Ref.	O.E. Derivation.	Other Gmc. Parallels.	M.E. not O.E. Word.	Unique in Laȝamon (?).	P. or Pr. (?).	Found in Later M.E. Alliterative Works.	2nd MS. Reading.	Comments.
londriche (kingdom)	3.15, 208	landric Pr		X	I	P	X		
londsorȝe	2.562	(land + sorh)		I	I	P	X	C londsorȝe / O mochele sorȝe	
londtilie (labourer)	2.197	(land + tilia)		I	I	P	X	O passage omitted	
luȝing (love-token)	1.8	(lufu + ðing)		I	I	P	X	O passage destroyed	
Lundeneburh	1.183	Lundenburh		X	I	P	X	O Lundene	
mæinclubbe (heavy club)	2.216	(mægen + O.N. klubba)		I	I	P	X	C mæienclubbe / O mochele club	
mætecun (kind of food)	1.40	(mete + cynn)		I	I	P	X	C mætecun / O beste tun	
maidechild	2.177	mægdencild Pr		X	X	P	X	C maidechild / O maide	Found in Orm 7897
marmeston (marble)	1.325	marmanstān ᴿ		X	X	Pr	X	O maide	A common M.E. word
meteburdes (food-tables)	1.54	(mete + bord)		I	X	P	X		Found also in Trev. 367
mereminne (siren)	1.57	meremen	O.H.G. meriminni / M.L.G. merminne	X	X	P	X		Found also in Kath. 1490
metecusti (liberal)	1.15, etc.	(mete + cystig)		I	I	P	X	C meterum	
meterum (moderation)	1.279	(mete + rūm)		I	I	P		O mete hende	Cp. rumhende Laȝ; 1.279, where the 2nd scribe again substitutes mete-hende

Word	Ref.	Compound	Cognates					Notes	Remarks
middeleard (the middle earth)	2.41, etc.	Cp. O.E. middan-geard		X	X	P	X	O has *middelerþe* throughout	A common form in M.E. poetry
middeneard (the middle earth)	2.619	Cp. O.E. middan-geard		X	X	P	X	C middenerde / O worle riche	A rare form in M.E.
midewinter	2.539	midwinter Pr		X	X	Pr	X		
midfesten (middle of a fast)	3.511	midfæsten Pr		X	I	Pr	I	O passage omitted	
milc-hwit	2.243	meolchwit Pr		X	X	P	I		Not infrequent in later alliterative poetry
mildheorte	2.280	mildheort Pr		X	X	P	X	O passage omitted	Found also in Hom. II. 121
milslide (merciful)	2.197	(milts + līðe)		X	X	P	X	O passage omitted	
modkare (sorrow)	1.132	môdcearu P	O.S. môdkara / O.H.G. môdkara	X	I	P	X	O passage omitted	
môdsorhʒe	1.370, 3.217	môdsorh P		X	I	P	X	1.370 C modsorʒe, O sorrow / 3.217 O passage destroyed	
moncun	1.19, etc.	mancynn Pr	O.N. mannkyn / O.H.G. mancunni	X	X		I		
mondrem (shout of men)	2.583	mandrêam P		X	X	Pr	X	C mandrem / O mannes drem	Found also in Kath. 2046
monferde (army of men)	2.22, etc.	(mann + fierd)		I	I	P	X		
monqualm (mortal disease)	1.166, 172	manncwealm Pr		X	X	P	X		A very rare M.E. religious word
monrædene (homage)	1.18, etc.	mannrǣden Pr		X	X	P	I		A common M.E. poetic word
monslæht (manslaughter)	3.110	mannslyht Pr	O.S. manslahta / O.H.G. manslaht	X	X	P	I		A common M.E. poetic word
mânsware (perjurer)	1.177, 2.506	mânswara Pr		X	X	P	X		Found elsewhere only in The Dep. Soul's Address to the Body

THE COMPOUNDS IN LAƷAMON'S *BRUT* (*continued*).

	Ref.	O.E. Derivation.	Other Gmc. Parallels.	M.E. not O.E. Word.	Unique in Laʒamon (?).	P. or Pr. (?).	Found in Later M.E. Alliterative Works.	2nd MS. Reading.	Comments.
monweorede (troop)	2.23, etc.	mannweorod Pr	O.S. manwerod O.H.G. manwerod	X	I	P	X	2.23, 432 and 3.139 C monweorde; O manferde; 2.615 O cnihtes; 2.587 O men; O elsewhere passage omitted or destroyed	A word of frequent occurrence, always rejected by the 2nd scribe
morƷenne	2.422	(mōr + fenn)	O.H.G. morgan-lioht	I	I	P	X	O passage omitted	Cp. O.E. mórhǣþ, etc. Also used by Wiclif
morƷenliht	2.328	morgenliht P	O.N. morgungiöf	X	X	P	X	O passage omitted	Found elsewhere only in H.M. 582, 592
morƷeue (nuptial gift)	2.178, 3.249	morgengifu Pr	O.H.G. morgangebe Dan mergengave	X	X	P	X	O passage omitted	
morðgomene (murder)	2.539	(morð + gamen)		I	I	P	X	O passage omitted	
morðspelle (tidings of destruction)	2.401	(morð + spell)		I	I	P	X	C morðspell; O morpre spell	
munec-child (young child)	2.129	(munuc + cild)		I	I	Pr	X	O passage omitted	
munec-clades (monk's robes)	2.118	(munuc + clāþ)		I	I	Pr	X	O passage omitted	
munnec-lif (monastic life)	3.191, etc.	munuclif Pr		X	X	Pr	X	3.191 C muneclif, O abbey; 3.296 O passage destroyed	Found also in Orm 6292

Word	Ref.	Form	Cognate					Readings	Notes
nailsax (nail-knife)	3.228	negelseax Pr		X	X	P	X		Found also in Frag. 5
neowcumen (newly come)	1.365	niwecumenum Pr		X	X	Pr	X	C neowcumene, O neuwe	Not uncommon in M.E.
nute-scalen (nut-shells)	3.172	(hnutu + sciell,)	M.H.G. nuzschal	I	X	Pr	X	O passage destroyed	Found also in Trev. IV. 141
oflonged (filled with long-ing)	2.366, 375	oflangod P		X	X	Pr	X		A common early M.E. word
onfreondes (enemies)	1.240, etc.	(un + frēond)	cp. M.H.G. unvriunt	I	I	P	X	1.241 C feondes, O onfrendes 1.364 C dædliche iuan, O onfrendes 2.314 C feonden, O onfrendes	A word peculiar to the 2nd scribe
picforchen	2.483	(pīc + forc)		I	X	Pr	I		Found also in Pr. P. 397
plaʒe-ineren (playmates)	2.230	(plega + gefēra)		I	X	P	I		
pratwrenchen (guileful tricks)	1.226	(prætt + wrenc)		I	I	P	I	C praetwrenchen, O felle wrenches	
quale-hus (house of tor-ture)	1.31, 160	(cwalu + hūs)		I	I	P	I		
qualesið (mortality)	3.283	(cwalu + sīð)		I	I	P	I	C qualesið, O wowe	
raketeʒe (chain)	2.278, etc.	racentēag Pr		X	X	Pr	X		A common M.E. word
richedom	1.141, etc.	ricedōm Pr	O.L.G. rikidōm O.H.G. richetuom	X	X	P	X		Elsewhere found only in H.M. 3, until early Mn.E.
Romeburh	1.228	Romeburh Pr		X	X	Pr	X		Found also in Orm 7110 and Mannyng Chr. 12665

THE COMPOUNDS IN LAȝAMON'S BRUT (continued).

	Ref.	O.E. Derivation.	Other Gmc. Parallels.	M.E. not O.E. Word.	Unique in Laȝamon (?).	P. or Pr. (?).	Found in Later M.E. Alliterative Works.	2nd MS. Reading.	Comments.
Romeleode (the Romans)	1.241	(Rome + lēod)		I	I	Pr	X		
Rompeode	1.386	(Rome + þeod)		I	I	Pr	X		
Romware	1.329, 2.585	Romewaru Pr		X	I	Pr	X	1.339 C Romeware, O Romanisse 2.585 O the word omitted	
Romwisen (wise men of Rome)	2.41	(Rome + wīsan)		I	I	Pr	X	C Romwisen O þe wise of Rome	
rumhende (liberal)	1.279	(rūm + hende)		I	I	P	X	C rumhende O metehende	
runstauen (letters)	1.425	(rūn + stæf)		I	I	P	X	O passage omitted	
sæbrimme (sea-shore)	1.272, etc.	(sǣ + brymme)		I	I	P	X		
sæcliua (sea-cliffs)	1.29, etc.	sǣclif Pr		X	X	Pr	X		
sæfisca	2.524	sǣfisc Pr	O.N. sǽ-fiskr	X	I	Pr	X		Found also in Trevisa 1.335
sæflode (sea)	1.1111	sǣflōd Pr		X	I	Pr	X		
sæflot navy	1.193	sǣflota P		X	I	P	X	C sæflot O flote	
sægrunde (the bottom of the sea)	1.173	sǣgrund Pr		X	X	P	X	—	Found elsewhere only in Best., C. Mundi, 20,953, and Minot, X. 4

sǣliðende (seafarers)	1.334	sǣliðend Pr	O.S. sēoliðandi	X	X	P	X	O passages omitted	
sǣmen	1.80, etc.	sǣman		X	I	Pr	X		
sǣoure	3.250	(sǣ + ār)		I	I	P	X	C sæoure / O oare	
sǣrime (the edge of the sea)	1.265, 274	sǣrima Pr		X	I	P	X		
sǣside	3.18	(sǣ + sīd)		I	X	P	X		Very rare in M.E.
sǣwerie	1.197, 265	sǣwērig P		X	I	P	X		
sǣstreme	1.15	sǣstrēam P	O.S. sēostróm	X	X	P	X		Found elsewhere only in Mar. 9
sǣstrond	1.394	sǣstrand Pr	O.N. sævarströnd	X	X	P	X		A rare M.E. poetic word
sarimod	3.187, 195	sǣrigmōd P.		X	I	P	X		An early M.E. poetic word
sceldtrume (body of troops)	1.493, etc.	scildtruma Pr		X	X	P	X		A not uncommon M.E. compound
scidwal (a wall of stakes)	2.6	scideweall Pr		X	I	P	X		
scaðedede (harmful deed)	3.186	(scaða + dǣd)		I	I	P	X	O passage omitted	
scaðewerc (harm)	1.66	(scaða + weorc)		I	I	P	X	C scaðewerc / O harm	
scipfierde (ship-army)	1.309, etc.	scipfierd Pr;		X	I	P	X		
scipgumen (sailors)	1.194	(scip + guma)		I	I	P	X	C scipgumen / O sipmen	
scipmen	1.46, etc.	scipmann Pr		X	X	Pr	I		A common M.E. word
Scotleode	2.418	(+ lēod)		I	X	Pr	X		
Scotþeode	2.433	(+ þēod)		I	I	Pr	X		
sibman (relative)	1.58	(sibb + mann)		I	I	P	X	C passage omitted	

THE COMPOUNDS IN LAȜAMON'S BRUT (continued).

	Ref.	O.E. Derivation.	Other Gmc. Parallels.	M.E. not O.E. Word.	Unique in Laȝamon (?).	P. or Pr. (?).	Found in Later M.E. Alliterative Works.	2nd MS. Reading.	Comments.
sibbefreond (kindred, friends)	1.103	(sibb + frēond)		I	I	P	X	C sibbefreond / O frendes	
sibelaȝe (law of affinity)	1.18	(sibb + lagu)		I	I	P	X	O passage omitted	
siȝecræften (magic)	2.225	(sīge + cræft)		I	I	P	X	O passage omitted	
snau-white	2.608	(snāw + hwīt)		X	X	P	X	C snau-white / O wite	Found also in A.R. 314 and Mar. 18
somrune (colloquy)	1.233	(sām + rūn)		I	I	P	X		
sondmon (messenger)	2.107	(sand + mann)		I	I	P	X		
sorhsiðes (misfortunes)	2.38	(sorh + sīð)		I	I	P	X	C & heore sorhsiðes / O on hii lore hadde	The 2nd scribe failed to understand the meaning of the compound
soðqvide (a true saying)	1.406	(sōð + cwide)		I	I	P	X	C soðquides / O wordes soþe	Cp. O.E. soðword, O.S. soðword
speresceaft	2.193	speresceaft Pr		X	X	P	X		Found also in Wiclif and in Trevisa
stæncunne (class of stone)	1.121	(stān + cynn)		I	I	P	X		
stalfeht (strong conflict)	1.78, etc.	(steall + feoht)		I	I	P	X	2.11 C stalfeht, O fihte	

Word	Ref.	Etymology	Cognate						Notes
stangraffen (stone pits)	3.282	(stān + græf)	O.S. stēngraf	I	I	I	P	X	C stangraffen / O greaues
stanwal (stone wall)	2.239, etc.	stānweall Pr		X	I	I	P	X	
stelboȝe	2.581	(style + boga)		I	I	I	P	X	C Arthur stop a stelboȝe / O Arthur leop pare
steoresmon	1.57, etc.	steormann Pr		X	X	X	Pr	I	
stepmoder	2.179	stēopmoder	O.N. stiupmoðir	X	X	I	Pr	I	
stepsune	3.293	stēopsunu	O.N. stiupsonr	X	X	I	Pr	I	
stiþþiwalled (strongly walled round)	3.233	(stīð + be + weall)		I	I	X	P	X	
stipimained (strong in might)	3.24	(stīð + mægen)		I	I	I	P	X	
stiðemoded (stiff minded)	2.467, 3.192	stiðemōd Pr		X	X	I	P	X	O passage omitted / 3.192 C stiðemoded, / O swipe modi men
sundervune (private conversation)	3.262	(sundor + rūn)		I	X	X	P	X	O passage destroyed
sunnelihte	2.325	(sunne + liht)	O.H.G. sunnanlioht	I	X	X	Pr	X	O passage omitted — Found also in Hom. II. 29
sudende	1.143	(sūð + ende)		I	I	I	Pr	X	Cp. O.E. sunnebēam
suðȝeat (south gate)	3.114	(sūð + geat)		I	I	I	Pr	X	
sweordbroþer (comrade in arms)	3.225	(swēord + brōþor)	M.H.G. swert-bruoder	I	I	I	P	X	O passage omitted
tæuelbrede (draught-board)	1.347	(tæfel + bred)	O.H.G. zabelbret	I	I	I	Pr	X	C tæuelbrede / O tauel
treowerkes (woodwork)	2.539	(trēo + weorc)		I	I	I	P	X	
þeinesmon	2.201	(þegn + mann)		I	I	I	P	X	C þeinesmen / O sweines

THE COMPOUNDS IN LAƷAMON'S BRUT (continued).

	Ref.	O.E. Derivation.	Other Gmc. Parallels.	M.E. not O.E. Word.	Unique in Laȝamon (?).	P or Pr. (?).	Found in Later M.E. Alliterative Works.	2nd MS. Reading.	Comments.
þeodfolke (national people)	3.53	(þēod + folc)		I	I	P	X	C þeodfolke	
þolemode (patient)	1.133	þolemōd Pr		X	X	Pr	X	O Romleode	Found also in Hom. I. 49
þrælwerkes (servitude)	1.20	O.N. loan-word	O.N. prælverk	I	X	P	X		
þrumferde (troop)	1.58	(þrymm + fierd)		I	I	P	X	C þrumferden / O ferde	
utlaȝe (outlaw)	2.15, etc.	ūtlaga Pr	O.N. útlagi	X	X	Pr	I		A common M.E. compound
uoregenglen (progenitors)	2.632	(fore +)	O.H.G. gengil	I	I	Pr	X	O passage omitted	
uostermoder (nurse)	3.28	fostormōdor Pr		X	X	Pr	I		
wadæi (day of woe)	1.373	(wā + dæg)	M.H.G. wêtag	I	I	P	X	C wadæi / O dai	
wamed (angry)	1.271	(wā + *mēde from mōd = angry)		I	X	P	X	O passage destroyed	Found elsewhere only in Hickes I. 167
wæisið (death)	3.25, 3.126	(wā + sið, O.N. vei)		I	X	P	X	3.25 C weop for hire weisið, O wepe wel sore 3.126 C weisið, O swikedom	Found only in early M.E. works
wæiwitere (guide)	2.112	(weg + witere)		I	I	P	X	C wæiwitere / O weiwittie	

Word	Line ref.	Derivation	Cognate					MS. variants	Notes
wæld-scaðe (savage monster)	1.275, 3.26	(*weald* + *scaþa*)		I	I	P	X	1.275, O passage omitted; 3.26 C wældscaðe, O wodescape	
wælkempe (mighty warrior)	1.25, etc.	(*wæl* + *cempa*)		I	I	P	X	1.25 C wælkempen, O gode cniptes; 1.93 C wælkempan, O cniptes; 2.577 C wælkempe, O bald kempe	
wælslahte (slaughter)	1.58	wælsleaht Pr		X	I	P	X	C wælslahte	
wænslahtes (slaughter)	1.406	(E.M.E. *wǣne* + O.E. *slæht*)		I	I	P	X	O bitere slahtes	
walle-stream (well-stream)	1.121	wyllestrēam Pr		X	I	P	X	O passage omitted	
wandreðe (misery)	2.97		O.N. vandrǽði	I	X	Pr	X	O passage omitted	A common loan-word in early M.E.
wansiðe (destruction)	1.23, etc.	(E.M.E. *wǣne* = misery + *sīð*)		I	I	P	X	C wansiðe	
wæþmoncun (male kind)	1.22	(*wǣþmann* + *cynn*)		I	X	Pr	X	O mochele harme	Found also in Orm 4092
wæþmon (man)	1.79, etc.	wǣþmann Pr		X	X	Pr	X	C wapmoncun	Common in early M.E. prose and poetry
waritreo (gallows)	1.243	(L.O.E. waritrēo) (*wearg* + *trēo*)	O.S. warag-treo; O.N. vargtré	I	X	P	X	O moncun	*waritreo* is found in O.E. and M.E. p. n. forms
waterscenc (draught of water)	2.403	(*water* + *scenc*)		I	I	P	X		A rare early M.E. word
wedbroþer (brother by baptism)	2.181, etc.	wedbrōþer Pr	O.N. veðbróðir	I	I	P	X		An archaic word found also in Horn (H.) 295

The Compounds in Laȝamon's *BRUT* (*continued*).

	Ref.	O.E. Derivation.	Other Gmc. Parallels.	M.E., not O.E. Word.	Unique in Laȝamon (?).	P. or Pr. (?).	Found in Later M.E. Alliterative Works.	2nd MS. Reading.	Comments.
weien-laten (crossways)	2.225	weggelǣte Pr (*wegena + gelǣðe*)		X	X	P	X	C weien-laten / O weynleates	See N.E.D. under *way-leet*; a rare M.E word
weldede (good deed)	1.1.134	weldǣd P		X	X	P	I	C weldeda / O wilninge	Found also in Hom. I. 33 and in P.Pl. A, iii, 62
wellestream	1.121	wylle-strēam Pr		X	X	P	X		Rarely in M.E. poetry
wellewater	2.407	wiellewæter P		X	X	P	X		A rare M.E. word
weorcman	2.6, etc.	weorcman Pr		X	X	Pr	I		Found also in A.R. 404 and P.Pl. B, xiv, 137
weored-strencðe (army)	1.22	(*weorod + strengþu*)		I	I	P	X	C mid his weorod-strencðe / O mid heni cunnes ginne	
weoruldkinge	1.270	weoruld cynning Pr	O.S. & O.H.G. weroldkuning	X	I	P .	X		
weoruldlifen	3.290	weoruldlif Pr		X	X	P	X	O passage destroyed	Found also in Orm 2978
weorldmonne	3.123	weoruldman Pr		X	X	P	X	C weorldmonne / O worle-þinge	Found also in Kath. 486
weorldriche (kingdom)	2.296	weoruldriche Pr	O.S. werold-riki / O.H.G. „ „	X	X	P	X	C weorldscome	Found also in Orm 11,800
weorldscome	1.355	(*weoruld + sceamu*)		I	I	P	X	O worliche same	

Word	Ref.	Compound	O.H.G.						Notes
weorldseli (happy in the world)	2.36	(weoruld + sēlig)		I		P	I	X	O passage omitted
weoruldwise	2.149, 225	(weoruld + wīs)		I		P	I	X	
westhalfe	3.173	westhealf Pr.	O.H.G. wësthalba	X		Pr	I	X	O passage destroyed
whalesbone	1.100	(hwæl + bān)		I		P	I	X	1.67, C wiæx, O gisarme
wi-ax (battle-axe)	1.67, etc.	(wīg + æsc)		X		P	X		1.196 and 3.119 C wiax, O ax 1.286 C wiax, O wepne; 3.8 = the only case where wiax is retained
wifðing (wedding)	3.251, etc.	wifðing Pr.		X		P	I	X	Word unintelligible to the 2nd scribe — 1.189 O passage destroyed 3.31 C wifðing, O wifinge 3.251 C þe wes wifðing riche and vnimete blisse, O þar was mid iwisse onimete blisse
wicenares (attendants)	2.338, 1.286	wīcnere Pr.		X	X	P	X	X	An archaic early M.E. word — 1.286 C wikenares, O cnihtes 2.338 O passage omitted
wildaʒes (welcome days)	1.76	wildagas P		X		P	I	X	O passage omitted
wilgomen (pleasure)	2.455	(wil + gamen)		I		P	I	X	O passage omitted

THE COMPOUNDS IN LAƷAMON'S BRUT (continued).

	Ref.	O.E. Derivation.	Other Gmc. Parallels.	M.E. not O.E. Word.	Unique in Laȝamon (?).	P. or Pr. (?).	Found in Later M.E. Alliterative Works.	2nd MS. Reading.	Comments.
wilspel (welcome news)	1.57, etc.	(wil + spell)	O.L.G. wilspel	I	I	P	X	1.57 O word simply omitted; 2.315 O passage omitted; 3.240 O passage destroyed	
wiltidende	2.292	(wil + O.N. tīdendi)		I	I	P	X	O passage omitted	
windræsen (assaults)	1.394, 3.238	windræs P		X	I	P	X	C windræsen; O bittere reses	
windruncen (drunk with wine)	1.347	windruncen Pr	M.H.G. wintrunken	X	X	P	X	C weoren wind-runken	
winemæies (loyal kinsmen)	1.248, etc.	winemǣg P		X	I	P	X	O dronge of wine; 1.248 C winemæies, O gode cnihtes; O passage is elsewhere omitted	
winschenche (a draught of wine)	1.150, etc.	(wīn + scenc)	M.H.G. wīnschanc	I	I	P	X		The word very probably existed in O.E.
wintunnen (wine-tuns)	3.232, etc.	wintun Pr	O.N. vintunna	X	I	P	X		
wilene-imot (assembly of counsellors)	2.57	(witena + gemōt)		I	I	Pr	X	O passage omitted	

Word (meaning)	Reference	Compound	Cognates					Notes	
wiðercraft (magic)	1.12, 42 2.400	(wiðer + cræft)		1		P	X		There were many compounds of *wiðer* + noun in O.E.: *wiðercwida, wiðer-lēan*, etc.
wiðerdeden (hostile deeds)	2.401, etc.	(wiðer + dǣd)		1	1	P	X		
wiðerfeht (hostile attack)	3.146	(wiðer + feht)		1	1	P	X	O passage omitted	Cp. O.E. *wiðerfeoh-tend*, 'an adversary', Found in Hom. II. 51
wiðerful (bold, hostile)	2.16, etc.	(wiðer + full)		1	1	P	X		
wiðergome (contest)	2.615	(wiðer + gamen)		1	1	P	X		
wiðerhappes (conflicts)	1.18	(O.E. wiðer + happ)		1	1	P	X		
wiðeriwinne (cruel foe)	1.179, etc.	(wiðer + gewinna)		1	1	P	1		*wiþerwinn*, 'contest,' is found in O.E. Cp. O.E. *wiðerwinna*, 'a foe'. Found also in Mar. 5
wiðerlaʒen (evil laws)	2.32	(wiðer + O.N. *lagu*)	O. Fris. witherlaga O.S. wiðarlaga	1	1	P	X		
wiðersaka (adversary)	1.77 2.102	wiðersaca	O.S. wiðarsako O.H.G. wiðarsacco	X	1	P	X		
wiðerræs (hostile attack)	2.632	(wiðer + rǣs)		1	1	P	X	C balu reses O wiðerræs	
wiðerside (opposite side)	2.74	(wiðer + sīd)		1	1	P	X		
wodeburʒe (a grove of trees)	1.92	wudubearu P		X	1	P	X	C þurh wodeburʒe O in wode oper in borewe	
wodelande	1.72	wuduland Pr		X	X	P	X		
woderime (edge of a wood)	1.32	wudurima Pr		X	1	P	X	C passage omitted	

THE COMPOUNDS IN LAȝAMON'S BRUT (continued).

Ref.	O.E. Derivation.	Other Gmc. Parallels.	M.E., not O.E. Word.	Unique in Laȝamon (?).	P. or Pr. (?).	Found in Later M.E. Alliterative Works.	2nd MS. Reading.	Comments.
1.20	(wudu + O.N. rót)		I	I	P	X		
2.481, 3.90	(wudu + sceaga)		I	X	P	X	2.481 C ut ofwude scaȝe, O vt of wode 3.90 C wudescaȝe, O wodesaye	
3.26	(wudu + sceaða)		I	I	P	X	C waldscaðe O wodescaðe	
1.21, 3.185	to wrāðre hǣle		X	X	P	I		A common early M.E. word
1.245	(gewrit + rūn)		I	I	P	X	O passage destroyed	
3.13	(wunder + blīþe)		I	X	P	I	O passage omitted	Found also in Will. of Pal. 1895
1.49	wundorcræft P.	M.H.G. wunderkraft	X	I	P	X		
1.49	(wundor + cræftig)		I	I	P	X		In O.E. wundor is usually compounded with a noun—wundorgifu, wundor-tācn, etc.
2.539	(wundor + fela)	M.H.G. wundervil	I	I	P	X	C wunder feole craftes O mani wonder-craftes	

woderoten (wood-roots)
wodescaȝe (thicket of a wood)
wodescaðe (wood-monster)
wraðerehele (injury)
writrune (letter)
wunderbliþe (very happy)
wundercraft (magic)
wundercrafti (skilled in magic)
wunderfeole (very many)

Word (meaning)	Ref.	Etymology	O.H.G. / M.H.G.					Readings	Notes
wundergod (very good)	3.10	(*wunder + gōd*)	O.H.G. wunterguot	I	I	P	X	C wunder god / O swipe god	
wunderkene (very bold)	1.310	(*wundor + cēne*)	M.H.G. wunder-küene	I	I	P	X		
wundermere (very glorious)	2.231	(*wunder + mǣre*)		I	I	P	X	C wundermere / O wonderliche	
wundermuchel (very much)	2.632	(*wundor + mycel*)		I	X	P	X	C wundermuchele / O mochelere	Found also in Orm 7284
wunderriche (very powerful)	3.2	(*wundor + rīce*)		I	I	P	X		
wunderstrong (very strong)	1.74	(*wundor + strang*)		I	I	P	X	O passage omitted	
wunderweorc (a marvellous work)	2.304	wundorgeweorc Pr	M.H.G. wunderwërc	X	X	P	X	C seolkuð werc / O wonderworc	
wunfolc (joyous people)	1.59	(*wynn + folc*)		I	I	P	X	C wunfolke / O gode folke	
wunsele (mansion)	2.233, 314	(*wynn + sele*)		I	I	P	X	O passage omitted in each case	
wurðmunt (honour)	2.367	weorðmynd Pr		X	X	P	X	O passage omitted	An early M.E. word
ȝætessel (gate-bolt)	2.373	(O.E. *geat* + O. Fr. *aissel*)		I	I	P	X	O passage destroyed	
ȝæteward (gate-keeper)	2.373	geatweard P (?)		X	I	P	X		
ȝeoldæie (Yule-Day)	2.532	(*ȝēol + dæg*)		I	X	Pr	X	C ȝeoldæie / O holy day	A rare M.E. word
ȝimston	2.464	gimstān Pr		X	X	Pr	I		A common M.E. poetic word

NOMINAL COMPOUNDS IN THE UNRHYMED ALLITERATIVE POEMS.

The actual number of nominal compound words in these alliterative poems is 880; even when divided among the twenty-six poems, the number is still remarkable. But of these the majority are nothing more than ordinary prose compounds consisting of a combination of two concrete words, such as : *cake-brede, chaumbre-flor, sea-foule, much-quat*, etc. These in themselves are of no value, but the actual number of them is somewhat astonishing ; there seems to be a certain fondness for compound words unequalled in other Middle English writers ; whether this was due to a tradition handed down from Old English times is a matter on which it would be idle to speculate.[1]

In these works there are about 210 nominal compounds which are in varying degrees " poetic ". The decrease in number as compared with the number of poetic compounds used by Laȝamon is particularly noticeable and the importance of the fact must not be underestimated. Nevertheless, though such compounds are rare, the fact that some are found surviving from Old English literature, and that others are found modelled on the same type is a sufficient proof of continuity despite change. The reader will naturally attach greater significance to certain compounds than to others, but the following are worthy of special notice : *baleangur, balestour, balwetre, demerlayk, dragonhame, fetherhame, flyȝtlomes, lacchedrawers, mysthakel, schroudehous, stelewede.*

It is scarcely necessary to record all the 210 poetic compounds, but the more important will be given ; these will be sufficient to illustrate the various types of compound used.

agayncome, W. Alex. 2890 (see *gayncome* infra).
agayntote, Pur. 931 (not found elsewhere).
agaynturn, Will. of Pal. 4182 (not found elsewhere).
baleangur, Troy 6648 (not found elsewhere).
balededis, Wynn. and Wast. 292 (not found elsewhere).
baledethe, Troy 2234 (not found elsewhere).
balefyre, Chev. 233, 344, Morte Arthure 1048, W. Alex. 562, 2658 (not found elsewhere).
balestour (death-pang), Pat. 426 (not found elsewhere).
balowe-tymbre, Chev. 317 (not found elsewhere).
balwe-tree, Jerus. 152 (not found elsewhere).

---

[1] It may be mentioned in passing that a prolonged search through non-alliterative works and Stratmann-Bradley's *Middle English Dictionary* confirms the impression that *poetic* compounds are entirely absent from the non-alliterative writers. Alone in early M.E. works is anything of this type to be found.

bale-chest (belly), W. Alex. 423 (not found elsewhere).
belly-joy (delight in food), P. Pl. B vii, 118 (not found elsewhere).
boklered, Pur. 1551 (found also in Laʒamon, see supra).
brayne-pan, W. Alex. 2499 (found also in Mand. 234).
brethemen (trumpeters), Morte Arthure 4107 (not found elsewhere).
cairweidis, Twa Mariit Wemen 422 (not found elsewhere).
careman, Morte Arthure 957 (not found elsewhere ; cp. O.N. *karlmaðr*).
chynwedys, Wynn. and Wast. 24 (not found elsewhere).
dayraw, Pur. 893, W. Alex. 392 (a common M.E. poetic word).
dedes-stoundes, Alex. A. 1069 (not found elsewhere).
dedethrawe, Morte Arthure 1150 (a common M.E. word).
demerlayk (magic), Pur. 1561, W. Alex. 414 (only found elsewhere in
    Laʒamon 12, etc.).
dragonhame, W. Alex. 487 (not found elsewhere).
egge-tol, Will. Of Pal. 3755, P. Pl. C iv, 479 (found also in Gower).
fetherhame (winged body), W. Alex. 380, etc., Jerus. 679 (found also in the
    Brut. and Hom. 1.81).
fir-hill (fire of hell (?)), Alex. B. 1069 (not found elsewhere).
fliʒtlomes (wings), W. Alex. 2710 (not found elsewhere).
gaynecome, Troy 2026 (found also in the Ancren Riwle 234, etc., and in
    the Cursor Mundi 8382).
gledfur, Jerus. 1252 (not found elsewhere).
goldbeten, Pierce 188 (not found elsewhere in M.E.).
helle-hole, Death and Life 386, Erk. 291, 307, Pur. 223.
hell-hous, Pierce 559 (not found elsewhere).
herewedis, Parl. 201, W. Alex. 1010 (not found elsewhere). [Beowulf 1897.]
hernepanne, Morte Arthure 2229, Troy 8775, etc., W. Alex 1713.
hevenglem, Pur. 946 (not found elsewhere).
ketill-hatte (helmet), Morte Arthure 2993 (not found elsewhere within the
    M.E. period).
knightewede (knightly armour), Alex. A. 544 (not found elsewhere).
lacche-drawers, P. Pl. C ix, 288 (found also in Jacob's Well).
ladisman (pilot), Pat. 179, Pur. 424, W. Alex. 2341 (not found elsewhere).
land-leperes, P. Pl. B xv, 207 (not found elsewhere in M.E.).
lof(t)-briddes (birds of the air), Alex. B 956 (not found elsewhere).
londriche, Alex. A 1219 (not found elsewhere in M.E.).
luflowe (flame of love), Pur. 707 (not found elsewhere).
lyffdaies, P. Pl. B i, 27, Richard the Redeles, iii, 175, Will. of Pal. 17, etc.
myst-hakel, Gaw. 2081 (not found elsewhere).
schottemen, Morte Arthure 2467 (not found elsewhere).
schroude-hous, Pur. 1076 (not found elsewhere).
sonnerist (East), Alex. A 791, etc. (not found elsewhere).
spille-tyme (waster of time), P. Pl. C vi, 28 (not found elsewhere).
stele-wede (armour), Parl. 200, Troy 9634, and Sc. Field 363 (not found
    elsewhere).
trodgate (beaten path), W. Alex. 2988 (not found elsewhere).
warlaʒes (traitors), Morte Arthure 613, etc., Pat. 258, Pierce 783, Pur. 1560,
    Troy 303, etc., W. Alex. 3795, etc. (a not uncommon M.E. poetic
    word).
wyderwyne (enemy), Morte Arthure 2045 (a not uncommon M.E. compound,
    inherited from O.E.).

winnehalle (joy-hall), Gaw. 2456 (cp. M.E. *wunsele ;* not found elsewhere).

wodwose (satyr), Gaw. 721, W. Alex. 1540 (cp. O.E. *wudu-wāsa* ; the word
     was very common in the fourteenth century).

wodwyse, Morte Arthure 3817, etc., Wynn. and Wast. 71 (a form of the
     above word, not found elsewhere).

wonyngestede, W. Alex. 3734 (see infra).

wo-stund, Pat. 317 (not found elsewhere).

NOMINAL COMPOUNDS IN THE RHYMED ALLITERATIVE WORKS.

In the groups of alliterative poems written in various forms of
rhymed stanzas compounds are extremely rare ; even the ordinary
prose compounds are of infrequent occurrence, as compared with
those in the unrhymed alliterative poems. A careful search for
poetic and archaic compounds of whatever type has yielded but a
mere handful ; these are here recorded :

agayne-cumyng, Gol. and Gaw. 271.

bale-ire, Fortune 47.

batallwricht (a battle maker, a warrior), The Houlat 916.

bokelered, Awntyrs of Arthure 707 (see supra).

brane-wod, The Houlat 811.

dayglem, Pearl 1094.

heuenkyng, The Rawl. Strophic Pieces, John 4.

heuenryke, Luf es Lyf 15, Pearl 719.

kynryk, Gol. and Gaw. 407.

lyhtburne (light-burning one, Lucifer), The 1st Chester Play 45.

midelerd, Minot's Poems 1.5, On Serving Christ 52, The Quatrefoil of Love
     72, etc.

seegronde, Minot's Poems 10.4 (cp. Bestiary 401, etc.).

warlawes, On Serving Christ 37.

wonyngstedes, Minot's Poems—App. 11.45, edit. J. Hall.

Of these, *batallwricht* and *lyhtburne* are the most significant ;
but the above facts speak for themselves ; poetic compounds are
dead and the ancient tradition has been completely broken, only a
few vestiges remaining. This supports the contention made in the
metrical section, namely that the writers of the rhymed alliterative
poems were much further removed from the ancient traditions than
were the writers of unrhymed verse in the west.

CHAPTER 7.

THE VOCABULARY OF THE EARLY MIDDLE ENGLISH
WORKS.

A DESCRIPTION OF DURHAM, *c.* 1100, is far too early in date to
offer much evidence concerning early Middle English vocabulary.
The whole poem is an echo of a former age, and in phraseology,
both alliterative and non-alliterative, it harks back to Old English
poetry and prose. But it is an isolated poem and is not connected with later Middle English works. Its vocabulary is naturally
entirely native in origin.

The same is true of WENNE, WENNE, WENCHICHENNE, *c.* 1150, a
poem apart from the main streams of development in early Middle
English literature. There are but two words that might be considered archaic at this time : *ambre* 10, ' a pail,' O.E. *amber*, and
weorne 10, *geweornie* 7, ' wither, dwindle,' O.E. *weornian.*

The importance of these two early poems lies rather in the fact
that they represent late survivals of the alliterative metre.

THE GRAVE, *c.* 1150, is, owing to its shortness, inevitably
restricted in its vocabulary ; yet though negative evidence in
these early fragments is of no value whatever, such positive evidence
as presents itself must not be ignored. In this poem there are no
French or Old Norse words ; *bidytt* 14 and *forscedan* 24, though
very rare in Middle English in these forms, are common enough
when uncompounded. The three poetic compounds already noted
are in fact the only words of significance in the poem ; of these,
eorðhus 15 is an early Middle English poetic form found also in
The Brut, and comes down from Old English times, whereas
helewaȝes 9, and *sidwaȝes* 9 are of less significance, and only occur
elsewhere in the companion poem, *The Departing Soul's Address
to the Body.* For the most part the poet relied on the current
vocabulary of his time.

THE 1ST WORCESTER FRAGMENT, *c.* 1170, is likewise of little
importance. Anti-French as the author was, he yet employed
two French words—*questiuns* 4 (presumably the first recorded

169

instance of this word in the language), and *feþ*. Of poetic and archaic words there are none. The vocabulary is essentially that of the bulk of early Middle English homiletic work, though none of the words is peculiarly homiletic. Only two words call for comment : *lorþeines* 19, where we might have expected O.E. *lāreow* or *lārðeow*, and *losiæþ* 19, used intransitively, meaning ' to perish,' a usage of O.E. *losian* rare in Middle English, and generally confined to early homiletic works with the notable exception of its use in *Pearl*, 907.

THE DEATH FRAGMENT, *c.* 1170, an extremely short poem, has nothing in its vocabulary calling for comment.

THE DEPARTING SOUL'S ADDRESS TO THE BODY, *c.* 1170, is the earliest Middle English alliterative work of such a length as to offer much evidence concerning the survival of distinctively poetic words. The reader may have already observed that this poem is rich in nominal poetic compounds ; of these, nine are especially worthy of note : *earfeþsiþ* 80, 84, *feorþsiþ* 50, *goldfæten* 102, *goldfohne* 188, *lifdawes* 25, *maþemete* 585, *sarimod* 410, *soulehus* 40, *wasiþ* 592. *Goldfohne* is perhaps the most important in this group.[1]

Turning to uncompounded forms, there are a few words which are apparently not recorded elsewhere in Middle English. The majority of these were evidently archaic, and their absence from Laȝamon's *Brut* is noticeable. These are not essentially Old English poetic words, being normal prose words, but their reappearance in the second half of the twelfth century attests the continuity of tradition in these poetical fragments : *afursed* 390, 453, " removed," O.E. *afeorsian ;* [2] *brostnien* 396, " decay," O.E. *brosnian ; fakenliche* 619, " treacherously," O.E. *fācenlic* (the adj. *faken* is a rare early Middle English word and occurs in this poem at l. 611) ; *forscutted* 455, " shut up," O.E. *forscyttan ; luti*(ȝ) 92, 332, " cunning," O.E. *lytig*. There are two other late survivals in *idol* 9, " separation," O.E. *gedāl*, and in *sæþe* 259, " pit," O.E. *sēað*, which apparently only survives elsewhere in Laȝamon's *Brut*.

The remaining words used by this interesting early Middle English poet, exclusive of normal native forms which survive right throughout the Middle English period, are often rare and in all probability archaic ; such are *bedæled* 122, *fuse* 119, *loc* 227, " an offering," O.E. *lāc*, and *siðian* 479, all of which are rare early Middle English words.

----

[1] For full details see the preceding chapter.
[2] *Fursien* without the prefix is a well-attested early M.E. word.

THE PROVERBS OF ALFRED, *c.* 1180, a much more popular work, has no distinctively poetical words of any kind ; *baleusyþes* 189, which has already been noted, may be poetic, but as an isolated word is of little significance.   Nevertheless, there are a number of archaic words, two of which do not occur elsewhere in Middle English : *forswunke* 200, " exhausted with toil," and *iauhteþ* 171, " reckon," O.E. *geeahtian*.   In addition, there are a few words which are extremely rare in early Middle English, but which are not necessarily archaic.   Of such is *egleche* 3, " valiant " O.E. *ǣglǣca*.

Similarly, the vocabulary of THE BESTIARY, 1200–50, is not poetic, even in origin.   The work is popular, and it is not surprising that dialectal words are found in it, such as *fikeð* 532.   Certain rare early Middle English words occur, it is true, such as *bilirten* 308, *flerd* 351, *forbroiden* 108, *golsiþe* 245, *skemting* 332, *wiþeren* 367, etc., but whether these were archaic it is impossible to say. All that is important for our purpose is the fact that there are no traces of any survival of O.E. poetic diction such as we find in *The Departing Soul's Address to the Body*, a poem which has its poetic counterpart in Old English, whereas there is nothing corresponding to the popular compositions such as *The Proverbs of Alfred* and *The Bestiary*, except the O.E. Physiologus which is quite unlike the M.E. poem.

The vocabulary of the early Middle English alliterative prose works would form a complete study in itself.   There are many obscure words, and a considerable group occurring only in one or more of these works and in the *Ancren Riwle*.   Another list might be drawn up consisting of words common to these works and Laȝamon's *Brut*.   Such a task, though interesting in itself, does not fall within the scope of the present study.   It must here suffice to say that the vocabulary of these alliterative prose works is of wide range and chiefly of the early Middle English homiletic type, which has its roots in the Old English homiletic prose, though not of course exclusively so.   Of such are *aþrusmeþ*, S.W. 251, A.R. 40, " suffocate," O.E. *aþrysman ; diveren*, Kath. 619, Mar. 16, etc., " tremble " ;   *dult*, Kath. 1268, A.R. 292, etc., " blunt ". Words of the less homiletic type are such as *siȝe*, Jul. 10, " victory," O.E. *sige*, a word beloved of Laȝamon.

In our endeavour to trace survivals of Old English poetic diction, we inevitably turn to the nominal compounds used in these works rather than to uncompounded words.   In the last chapter it has been shown that these early Middle English alliterative prose

Works are rich in compounds of this type. Many are to be associated merely with prose in general, but others are definitely poetic, that is to say, they are either inherited from or modelled on the Old English poetic compounds which are so striking a feature of Old English poetry. In particular, we can point to such words as : *baledrinch, burdeboldes, cwalmhus, fleschtimber, girreblod, laȝefen,* and *neil-cniues.* It is in view of these facts that we can rightly conclude that even in these alliterative prose works there are traces of the survival of Old English poetic diction.

THE VOCABULARY OF LAȜAMON'S *BRUT.*

Laȝamon's *Brut* is the earliest post-Conquest poem of any bulk or importance ; add to this the fact of it being written in the traditional alliterative metre, and it does not become a matter for surprise that here we find a work with a vocabulary almost entirely native in origin and exceedingly archaic in form. The poem, therefore, offers the best scope for a study of the survival of the Old English poetic diction in early Middle English times.

In the first place, the foreign element is very small. Madden [1] discovered less than fifty French words in the C text, of which he says ' the latter text retains about thirty, and adds to them rather more than forty, which are not found in the earlier version '. Professor Wyld does not say how many French words he has found in C, but says that there are twenty French words common to C and O, and that O substitutes fifty-two additional French words for English or Scandinavian used by C.[2] Similarly, the Scandinavian element is small, there being not more than thirty words of Norse origin in both C and O. Hence the vocabulary is almost entirely native in origin.

In the second place, many of Laȝamon's words are both archaic and poetic, that is to say, they represent survivals of words which even in Old English times were largely confined to poetry. The fact is obvious in itself, and calls for no proof, but the existence of the later MS. throws considerable light on the nature of Laȝamon's archaisms. The second scribe alters the reading of C in some 1200 places, in about 1100 cases of which he substitutes another English word less archaic than the earlier reading. In a large number of the remaining cases he substitutes a French word for an English

---

[1] P. xxii.
[2] H. C. Wyld, *Studies in the Diction of Layamon's Brut :* 1. *Points of Difference between the Earlier and Later Text,* 23–4, 1930.

one. This does not mean that every native word thus rejected is of necessity archaic ; a close study of the two passages in question is always essential, but with the exercise of due care we are able to discover the reasons for the rejection of a reading in almost every case.

The second scribe was evidently much more matter of fact than that of C, and was not afraid to modernise wherever he deemed it necessary for the understanding of the poem. He therefore rejects without hesitation archaisms whether of word or of phrasing. Professor Wyld, in the article already referred to, has made a study of some 138 words, thus rejected in O ; this of course represents only a selection, but includes most of the interesting examples.

Thus, regarding French words in O, *cri* replaces *grure*, *lude*, *rop* and *weop ; hostage* replaces *gisel*, and so on.   *Uul*, O.E. *full*, ' a cup,' in 14,337, an extremely archaic word, was misunderstood by the later scribe, as explained by Professor Wyld.[1] Other similar archaisms of great interest are *holm, madmes, scucke, uðen, weored*— words found only in C and always rejected in O.   Similarly, many of the nominal poetic compounds were, as we have seen, misunderstood and rejected by the scribe of O, such as *breostpanc, wælkempen*, etc.

Hence there is no need to give further illustrations of the archaisms in Laȝamon's *Brut*. The survival of archaic words and phrases is remarkable. What will, however, be of value for our future study is a brief list of archaic words in Laȝamon rejected by the later scribe, but reappearing in the poems of the Alliterative Revival, though not occurring in non-alliterative fourteenth-century works. This may enable us to judge how far the vocabulary of the later alliterative poets was an inheritance from earlier times.

ærde, O.E. *eard*, which occurs only in C, is always replaced by *erþe ;* the
    word was unintelligible to the scribe of O.
æðel, O.E. *eðel*, similarly occurs only in C and is replaced by *feld* in 4744.
æðel, adj., O.E. *æðel*, a word of frequent occurrence in C, is replaced by
    bold, god, hendest, mild, murie, riche, stalewurðe, strong, wisest.
baiȝes, O.E. *beah*, is replaced by *porses* in 5927.
blanken, O.E. *blanca*, a word found only in C, is replaced by *horse*(s), 894,
    5863.
burne, O.E. *byrne*, 9283, is replaced by *seine* (banner).
duȝeðe, O.E. *duguð*, is generally avoided in O (see Prof. Wyld, p. 6).
uæx, O.E. *feax*, a word found only in C, is replaced by *her* (hair).
flit, O.E. *flit*, only found at 24,966, is replaced by *strif*.

[1] H. C. Wyld, *Studies in the Diction of Layamon's Brut :* 1. *Points of Difference between the Earlier and Later Text,* p. 9.

fræine, O.E. *fregnan*, is always rejected by the later scribe.

frið (1) a park, O.E. *frið*, is usually replaced, whereas (2) peace, in the phrase *in griðe and in friðe* is always replaced, the substitute usually being *pais.*

fulste(n), O.E. *fylstan*, is generally replaced by *helpe.*

gare, O.E. *gār*, is on three occasions replaced by *spere.*

ȝeddien, O.E. *geddian*, is replaced by *seide*, and occurs only in C.

ȝeomere, O.E. *gēomor*, a word found only in C, is always replaced or avoided in O.

grure, O.E. *gryre*, occurring in 27,716, is replaced by *cri.*

hæleþ, O.E. *hæleþ*, which occurs only in C, is always replaced or avoided in O.

hired, O.E. *hīred*, when uncompounded is always rejected in O, the substitutions being *ferde, folk, heap, men.* For the compound forms see supra.

leoðien, O.E. *līðan*,[1] a word occurring only in C, is always replaced ; in 4775 by *griðie*, in 12,042 by *softi*, and in 21,922 and 23,346 by *slake.*

sæhtnien, cp. O.E. *sæht, sahtnyss, sehtian*, is always replaced in O.

segg, O.E. *secg*, is a word apparently unknown to the later scribe.

All these words were undoubtedly archaic at this time, and their reappearance a hundred and fifty years later is significant. Other examples might be given of rare fourteenth-century words occasionally rejected by the later scribe of Laȝamon's *Brut.* These may, however, be more conveniently discussed as the need for further evidence arises.

We have endeavoured to show that Laȝamon's vocabulary is archaic and poetic by a comparison of the earlier and later texts, but it must not be forgotten that the modernising scribe of MS. *Otho* allowed many of the old words to remain. In fact, his version is in many ways extremely archaic. However much of the original diction he retained without question, it seems certain that in the west of England there was a traditional poetic diction surviving as late as 1275. Many words which may have been meaningless in the east, may have still been available to poets in the west.

[1] or *līðian, leoðian.* See B.T.

CHAPTER 8.

THE VOCABULARY OF THE POEMS OF THE ALLITERATIVE REVIVAL.

A COMPLETE study of these poems would naturally call for much more space than can be devoted to the subject in a volume such as this. Moreover, the elucidation of the problems of interpretation that arise during a detailed reading of many of the alliterative poems, is more conveniently discussed as these poems are studied individually and are being gradually re-edited in a manner worthy of the interest which they arouse. Realising that many of these problems are at present incapable of an easy solution, it is essential that we should concentrate upon the major questions, such as the nature of the vocabulary generally employed and differences within the ' school ' as to the use of poetic and dialectal words. The difficulty at the outset is the inadequacy of our material. Until we possess a new and complete Middle English Dictionary (which happily we have reason to hope will soon be an accomplished fact) we are handicapped, and must needs state with great caution what might otherwise have been stated as fact. Indeed, however, in the matter of vocabulary we can only rely on positive evidence, for there is always the possibility of a word being used in an area from which there is no record of the fact. Hence we cannot go further than say that a given word is *chiefly alliterative,* meaning thereby that it is found but rarely or even not at all, outside the alliterative poems. There are obvious cases in which a word popularised by the alliterative poets was borrowed by a late fourteenth-century rhyming romance-writer ; the word does not thereby cease to be *alliterative.* Again, a few instances of the word early or late do not disguise the fact that the word is chiefly alliterative. It is with these dangers and pitfalls in view that we must approach the discussion of the vocabulary of these poems.

I. THE USE OF " CHIEFLY ALLITERATIVE " WORDS.

Any reader of Middle English alliterative poetry is aware that the texts before him abound in words not generally found elsewhere.

The impression gained is probably a little misleading, for while the facts which here follow indicate the great extent to which this is true, it is surprising how frequently the average reader may be misled. In this section the poems are arranged in more or less chronological groups based on similarity of outlook, such as the early romances and the political poems. In this way it is hoped that differences within and among the groups may stand out clearly.

A. The Early Romances.

Alexander A and *B, William of Palerne, Joseph of Arimathie,* and *Cheuelere Assigne.*

Alexander A [1] : *blonkes* O.E. *blanca* (horses) 435—a poetic word occurring chiefly in alliterative verse ; *burd*—see N.E.D. (lady) 715, *beurde(s)* 202, 228, etc.—chiefly in Nth works, and especially in alliterative verse ; *carpe,* O.N. karpa (to speak), 11, etc.—chiefly in Nth poetry and alliterative verse ; *lud,* O.E. lēod (knight, man, prince), 231, etc.—chiefly in alliterative verse, *leedes* 12 (MS. leethes) ; *rink,* O.E. rinc (man), 105, 480, *rinkes* 341, 354—chiefly alliterative ; *segge,* O.E. secg (man), 232, *segges* 286—chiefly alliterative ; *proliche,* O.N. þráliga (eagerly), 215—chiefly in Nth and alliterative works ; *weie,* O.E. wiga (man, person), 777, *weih* 1184, *weies* 164, 653—chiefly in alliterative verse.

Alexander B : *apel,* O.E. æðele (adj. noble), 822—chiefly alliterative ; *burde* 418, *burdus* 893 ; *carpe(n)* 166, 230, etc. ; *ferke,* O.E. fercian (hasten, go), 300—in this intransitive sense ' to move quickly, go ' it is chiefly alliterative ; *hapel,* see N.E.D. (man, knight), 219, etc. (common)—chiefly in alliterative verse ; *lud* 18, etc. (common) ; *note,* O.E. notu (usefulness), 849—in later Middle English chiefly in alliterative verse (see under *The Wars of Alexander*); *rink* 21, etc. ; *schalk,* O.E. scealc (man, knight), 20, etc.—chiefly in Nth and alliterative verse; *seg* 27, etc. (eleven times); *weiȝ* 69, etc. (common).

William of Palerne : blonk 3326, etc. ; *burde* 683, etc. ; *carpe* 503, etc. ; *ferde* (army) 386, 5326 ; *keuered* (went away) 3625 ; *lud* 453, etc., *ledes* 195, etc., *ludes* 390, etc. ; *rink* 1193, etc., *renkes* 1153 ; *seg(ge)* 226, etc. ; *spakly,* O.N. spakliga (adv. *well,* in several loose senses), 19, etc. (frequent)—this adverb is especially common in alliterative verse ; *pro,* adj. O.N. þrár (vehement), 3264, 3564 ;

---

[1] The meaning, origin and description when once given will not thereafter be repeated. Except where the meaning is absolutely dependent upon the context, quotations cannot be given.

þroly, adj. 612, etc. ; *þroly*, adv. (vehemently), 127, etc. ; *weiʒ* 281, etc. (in various spellings) ; *wlonke*, O.E. wlanc (proud, stately), 80, etc.—conventional epithet in alliterative verse.

Joseph of Arimathie: blusch, from O.E. blyscan (*sb.* a glance), 657—exclusively alliterative (for the verb, see below) ; *carpe* 175, 440, 615 ; *ferde*, O.E. ferd (army), 12—chiefly alliterative after the middle of the fourteenth century ; *keueren*, O. Fr. couvrer (to make one's way, get to), 27—a favourite sense in alliterative verse, but not exclusively alliterative ; *leodes*, O.E. lēod, lēode (people), 168, 585 ; *schalkene* (gen. pl.), 510 ; *schinder*, see N.E.D. (shiver in pieces), 513—exclusively alliterative (?) ; *þroly* (impetuously) 91.

Cheuelere Assigne is peculiar in that its vocabulary is essentially non-alliterative ; especially striking is the absence of the alliterative synonyms for ' man '.   *spynnethe* 331, in the modern dialectal sense of ' rush quickly ' is found also in *The Wars of Alexander*, 3033, in the same sense.   These two examples would scarcely justify the description of this sense of the word as alliterative.

In this early group of works from Central and S.W. Midland the number of " chiefly alliterative " words is small, the synonyms for " man " namely *lude, rink, schalke, segge, weih* being the most noticeable words in question.   Of these *lude, segge* and *weih* were confined to verse in Old English, and in Middle English all six were poetic and archaic, *segge* being one of the words rejected by the later scribe of Laʒamon's *Brut*.   It would therefore appear that at the very commencement of the Alliterative Revival certain traditional archaisms, handed down from Laʒamon's time, were still current.   These formed the nucleus of the characteristic diction of the alliterative poets.

B. Satire and Allegory.

(*a*) *Wynnere and Wastoure* and *The Parlement of the Thre Ages.*
Wynnere: birdis (ladies) 426 ; the *blusche* of the belt (shining appearance) 187 ; *carpe* 218, 452 ; *ferdes* 123 ; *hathell* 68 ; *hightle*, see N.E.D. (put in order), " hightilde up ʒour houses," 438, cp. Purity 1290 and W. Alex. 1541, etc.—an alliterative word ; *lede*(*s*) (man) 29, 88, 108, 466, *lede* (people) 369, 469 ; *note* (work, employ-ment) 338 ; *renke* 23 ; *schalkes* 317, 432 ; *segge* 89 ; *throly* (keenly) 37 ; *tryne*, O.Swed. trina (to go) 122—chiefly in alliterative verse ; *wy* (man) 8, 120, 136, 201.

The Parlement: athell (adj. noble) 499 ; *balghe*, cp. O.E. belg (rounded) 112—chiefly in alliterative verse ; *birde* (lady) 390, 453 ;

blonke 110; *carpe* 462; *douth*, O.E. duguþ (noble company), 348—
a survival chiefly in alliterative verse, especially in the fourteenth
century; *ferde* (army) 330, 480; *ferkes* (hastens) 659; *hathelle*
111, 170; *lede* (man) 152, 393, *ledys* (people) 106; *renke* 137, etc.;
segge 471; *thro* (adj. bold) 104; *throly* (adv. eagerly) 14, 133; *tulke*,
O.N. tulkr (man), 313—peculiar to alliterative verse; *wy* (man)
193, etc.

These two poems thus add to the list of chiefly alliterative words
nothing of any great interest except *douth*, a very archaic word,
rejected by the later scribe of Laȝamon's *Brut;* and *trine* and *tulke*,
both of Scandinavian origin. For the rest, the striking number of
words common to the two groups so far considered shows how the
various poets inherited the same common tradition, since there is
no evidence of any borrowing between the two groups.

(*b*) The *Piers Plowman* Group.

Piers Plowman (since the words are of such frequent occurrence,
no references are given except where essential): *birde* (spelt also
berde, burde, buirde, buyrde), *carpe, lede* (man or people, nation),
renk, segge, þroly and *weye*. In addition, there is *spaklich*, adv.
(quickly), B, xvii, 81, *spakliche*, adj. (sprightly), B, xviii, 12, and
manside, O.E. amānsumian (excommunicated), C, iii, 41, etc.—a
form chiefly alliterative.

Pierce the Ploughman's Crede: there are no alliterative words
other than *mansede* 718.

The Crowned King: carped 42, and *leedes* (people) 134.

Richard the Redeles: carpen, ii, 29, iv, 41; *ferkyd* (went), iii,
90; *leode*, iii, 255; *leodis* (men), ii, 2; *monside* (cursed), iii, 105;
wy, iii, 288.

Mum and Sothsegger: carpe 1408, 1460; *ferkid* (went) 392,
622, 788; *renke*(*s*) 1211, 1635; *segge*(*s*) 71, 1143; *wye* 1294;
wies 306.

The range of alliterative words used in the political group is
thus very narrow, all the examples (except *mansid*) being found in
the earlier poems. It seems likely that the author of *Piers Plowman*
from his reading of *Wynnere and Wastoure*, and possibly other works,
acquired a number of these poetic and archaic words. His imitators,
however, were largely out of touch with this tradition, so that most
of the purely alliterative forms are not found in their poems.
Their work forms an offshoot from the alliterative school in which
the old traditions are considerably weakened.

C. The Gawain group, including St. Erkenwald.

apel (adj. noble), Gaw. 5, etc., Pur. 207, etc.

balȝ (adj. rounded), Gaw. 967, 2032, 2172.

blonke, Gaw. 434, etc., Pur. 87, 1392, 1412, Erk. 112.

blusch (sb. gleam) Gaw. 520, *a blysful blusch of þe bryȝt sunne.*

blusche, O.E. blyscan, see N.E.D. (look at), Gaw. 650, 793, Pur. 904, 980, 982, 998, 1537, Prl. 980, 1083, Pat. 117, 343, 474—chiefly in alliterative verse ; cp. *blusschande bemeȝ*, Gaw. 1819.

blysne, see N.E.D. (vb. intrans. to shine), Prl. 163, 197, 1048, Pur. 1404, Erk. 87.

broþly, see N.E.D. (adj. vile), Pur. 848, (adv. basely), Pur. 1256—the adj. and adv. have this sense only in alliterative verse ; in Gaw. 2377 and Pat. 474 *broþely* has its normal meaning of ' violently,' a sense not peculiar to alliterative poetry.

burde (lady), Gaw. 613, etc., Pur. 80, etc., Pat. 117, 507.

carpe, Gaw. 263, etc., Pur. 74, 1591, Prl. 381, etc., Pat. 118, 415 (as sb.), Erk. 317, Gaw. 307, 704, 1013 (as sb.).

ceuer, keuer (make one's way to), Gaw. 2221, Prl. 319.

douth, doupe, Gaw. 397, etc., Pur. 270, etc., Prl. 839.

ferke (intrans. sense of ' hasten, go '), Gaw. 173, etc., Pur. 133, 897, Pat. 187.

frunt, O.Fr. fronter (trans. to strike), Pat. 187—found only here and in *The Destruction of Troy.*

gleme, cp. O.E. glǣm (to shine), Gaw. 598, Prl. 70, 990.

gleme, O.E. glǣm (sb. splendour), Gaw. 604, Pur. 218, Prl. 79—both sb. and vb. are rare except in alliterative verse—N.E.D.

glam, O.N. glam (word or noise), Gaw. 1426, 1652, Pur. 499, 830, 849, Pat. 63—only in alliterative verse.

glette, O.Fr. glette (venom), Pur. 306, 573, Pat. 269, Prl. 1060, Erk. 297 (MS. glotte)—almost exclusively in alliterative verse.

glewe, O.E. glēowian (in the sense of ' call upon '), Pat. 164, *vchon glewed on his god*, and Erk. 171, *glew we alle opon God* (MS. glow)—in this sense only in alliterative verse.

gremed, O.E. gremian (intrans. to become angry), Pur. 139—the intrans. use occurs chiefly in alliterative verse.

hapel (knight, man), Gaw. 221, etc., Pur. 27, etc., Pat. 217, Prl. 676, Erk. 198.

honyse, O.Fr. honiss (to ruin, destroy), Pur. 576—chiefly in alliterative verse.

hyȝtle, see N.E.D. (adorn), Pur. 1290, *þe hous and þe anournementes he hyȝtled togeder*—chiefly in alliterative verse.

lede, leude (man), Gaw. 675, etc., Pur. 347, etc., Pat. 168, etc., Prl. 542, Erk. 146.

loȝe, loghe, O.Nth. luh (water, sea), Pur. 366, 441, 1031, Pat. 230, Prl. 119 —chiefly in alliterative verse.

mansed (pp. cursed), Pur. 774 (pret. threatened), Gaw. 2345.

maskle, see N.E.D. (spot), Pur. 556, Prl. 725, 823—an alliterative word.

note, O.E. notu—see N.E.D. for its use in alliterative verse (business, affair, etc.), Gaw. 358, 420, 599, Prl. 155, 922, Pur. 381, 727, 1233, Pat. 220, Erk. 38 (piece of work), 101 (toil)—see W. Alex. *infra.*

nurne, norne, obscure (announce, propose, etc.), Gaw. 1661, etc., Pur. 65, 669, 803, Erk. 101, 152, 195—occurs in no other poem.

obeche, O.Fr. obeiss (to bow to), Pur. 745, Prl. 885—a usage chiefly in alliterative verse.

overwalte, O.E. oferwæltan (trans. to overflow), Gaw. 314, Pur. 370—occurs chiefly in alliterative verse.

picchit, piȝt, O.E. piccan, pp. set (with gems), Prl. 217, 247, Erk. 79—in this poetical sense chiefly alliterative.

reken, O.E. recen (adj. noble, a word of very lax application), Pur. 10, etc., Prl. 5, etc., Erk. 135, 245 ; *rekenly* (adv.), Gaw. 39, 251, 821, Pur. 127, 1318—both adj. and adv. chiefly in alliterative verse.

renk, Gaw. 303, etc., Pur. 7, Pat. 216, 351, 431, Erk. 239.

ronk, O.E. ranc (abundant), Gaw. 513, Prl. 844, 1167, Pat. 490, Erk. 91, Pur. 233, etc. (in varying senses—see R. J. Menner's edition)—occurs chiefly in alliterative verse.

ruche, ryche, O.E. *ryccan (to arrange, prepare), Gaw. 360, 599, etc. (in varying senses), Pat. 101 (?)—this word occurs only in alliterative verse).

runisch, adj. obscure, see N.E.D. (strange), Gaw. 457, Pur. 1545, *renischche* Pur. 96, *roynysche* Erk. 52, cp. Gaw. 457 note (Oxford Press).

runischly, adv. (fiercely), Gaw. 304, 432, Pat. 191—peculiar to alliterative verse, both adj. and adv.

schalke, Gaw. 160, etc., Pur. 762, 1029, Pat. 476.

schynder (burst asunder), Gaw. 424, 1458, 1594.

segge, Gaw. 96, etc., Pur. 93, Pat. 301, 409, Erk. 189.

skelten, see N.E.D. (intrans. ' to hasten,' trans. ' to scatter, spread '), Pur. 1186, 1206, 1554, Erk. 278—only in alliterative verse.

spakly (quickly), Pur. 755, Pat. 338, Erk. 312, 335.

swey, sweȝe, O.N. sveigja (intrans. 'to move,' trans. to 'cause to move'), Gaw. 1429, 1796, Pur. 87, 788, 956, Pat. 72—chiefly in alliterative verse.

þroly, adv. (fiercely), Pur. 180, 504 ; (heartily), Gaw. 939.   As sb. cp. Gaw. 1713, adj. 645, 1751.

þryvande, from O.N. þrífask (p.ple. adj. excellent), Gaw. 1980, Pur. 751.

þryvandely (adv.), Gaw. 1080, 1380, Erk. 47—chiefly in alliterative verse.

tryne (to go), Pur. 132, 976, Pat. 101, Prl. 1113.

tulke, tolke, Gaw. 3, etc., Pur. 498, etc., Erk. 109.

wlonk (adj. beautiful), Gaw. 515, etc., Pur. 606, etc., Pat. 486, Prl. 122, etc.

wyȝe (man), Gaw. 249, etc., Pur. 280, etc., Pat. 111, 397, 492, Prl. 71, etc., *wehes*, Erk. 73, 96.

This list excludes those words (except *nurne*) which occur solely in one or more of these poems, and which will be discussed at a later stage.   Nevertheless, all the " alliterative " words previously used are to be found in the list, together with many interesting additions.   These words (many of them of frequent occurrence) show that a distinctive alliterative vocabulary has come into being, derived largely from traditional sources, but not exclusively so. In particular, older poetic senses of native words and specialised senses of French words are markedly present, as are words of

obscure origin. These words circulated among the various alliterative writers, partly through a common tradition and partly through
imitation, but they never gained the same popularity among non-
alliterative writers, except occasionally in the north.

D. The Later Romances.

(a) *The Destruction of Jerusalem :* athel (adj. noble) 46 ; *blonke* 271,
521 ; *burde* 100, berde 1087 ; *carpe* 196, 357, 730 ; *ferde* (army) 479,
etc. ; *ferke* (go) 873, 1042 ; *lede* 98, 242, *ledis* 495, 519 ; *mansed* (accursed)
154 ; *note* (work) 797, 800 ; *at þis note* (in these circumstances) 501 ;
ouerwalte 1207 ; *pyȝt* 413 (in the alliterative sense, whereas normally in
this poem the word has the usual sense of *fixed, placed,* e.g. 9, 393) ; *renk(e)*
606, 839, 954 ; *schalke* 1118 ; *segge* 680 ; *pryuande* (adj. excellent) 433 :
wye (man) 204, etc. ; *wlonk* 294 ; *wlonful* = wlonkful 394.[1]

(b) *Morte Arthure :* atheliste (adj.) 1593, *hathelle* (adj.) 1659, 1662,
hathelest 988, *hathelieste* 2109 ; *byrde*, etc. (lady) 999, etc. ; *blonke* 453, etc. ;
blyschit (looked) 116 ; *carpe* 132, etc. ; *ferke* (go) 933, etc. ; *hathelle* (knight)
358 ; *lede* 138, etc., *ledes* 195, etc. ; *notte*, O.E. notu (business) 1816 ;
pighte (set with stones) 212, etc. ; *ran(n)ke* (adj. strong) 1474, etc., *rekeneste*
(readiest) 4081 ; *renke* 17, etc. ; *schalke* 1098, etc. ; *segge* 134, etc. ; *spakely*
(quickly) 2063 ; *swey* (intrans. to go) 57, 1467, 4273 ; *thra, thro* (adj. eager,
vehement) 249, 3259 ; *throly* (adv.) 1150, 2217, 4332 ; *tryne* (to go) 1757
etc. ; *wlonke* (adj.) 3154, 3338 ; *wye* (man) 164, etc.

(c) *The Destruction of Troy :* haithill (adj. noble) 38 ; *blonke* 2371, etc. ;
blusche (vb. to look at) 1316, etc., (intrans. to shine) 4665 ; *burde* 483,
etc. ; *carpe* 829, etc. ; *ferke* (to go) 1036, 11259 ; *frunt* (vb. to kick, strike)
6923, 8327 (see *Patience* supra), (intrans.) 6887, 6890 ; *gleme* (vb. to shine)
3943 ; *gleme* (sb. a light) 3067, 10971 ; *greme* (vb. to become angry) 1006,
(trans. to provoke) 12153 ; *hapel* 3857, etc. ; *lede* (man) 62, etc., *lede*
(people) 1326, etc. ; *note* (affair etc.) 284, etc. ; *ouerwalte* (overturned)
8155 ; *renke* 814, etc., *rink* 7131, etc., *ronke* (adj. strong) 4783, (' noted
of books ') 5544 ; *ricche* (vb. to adjust, etc.—various meanings) 1231,
1258, etc. ; *shalke* 72, 89, etc. ; *segge* 9979, etc. ; *skeltyng* (spreading) in
the phrase *skeltyng of harme* 1089, 6042—see *Purity* supra ; *sweyt* (into
swym as he swelt wold) (vb. to fall), 9454—see *Gawain,* etc., supra ;
throly (adv. fiercely) 208, 1987, etc. ; *thro* (adj. bold) 147, etc. ; *thrivand*
(adj. excellent), 1482, etc. ; *tulke* 63, etc. ; *wegh, wee* (man) 23, etc. (—a
lady) 3356.

(d) *The Wars of Alexander :* athel (adj.) 242, etc. (very frequent) ;
hathill (adj.) 447, etc. ; *balgh* (swollen) 4923 ; *birdis* (ladies) 595, etc. ;
blische (vb. to look at) 872, etc. ; *blisch* (sb. glance) 606, 5435 ; *blonk* 767,
etc. ; *carpe* (vb.) 8, etc. ; *carpe* (sb.) 748, etc. ; *couert* (pret. of ' made their
way ') 4815 ; *douth* 1647, etc. ; *ferd* (army) 5577 ; *ferkys* (goes) 766 (Dub.),
926 (Ash.) ; *glaam* (clamour) 5504 ; *gleme* (sb.) 2044, 4817 ; *glett* (clay)
4490 ; (mud) 4516 ; *hathill* (sb.) 84, etc. ; *hiȝtild* (vb. pt. sg. and pp. ornamented, set in order), 1541 (Ash.), 4540, 4969, 5126—see *Purity* supra ;

[1] *cariep* 255, ' goes,' is evidently O.N. *keyra,* influenced by O.N.Fr.
carier.

honyshyd, O.Fr. honiss (put to shame) 3004, *honest* 3791 ; *lede* (man) 96, etc., *lede* (people, nation) 240, etc. ; *loʒe* (lake) 3899 ; *mascles* (spots) 4989, 5138 ; *note*, O.E. notu (numerous senses—see Skeat's glossary —a word of very wide and indefinite meaning, often used in specialised senses) 76, etc. (of very frequent occurrence) ; *obesche* (bow to) 1620, etc. ; *piʒt* (ornamented) 194 ; *rekinly* (adv. quickly) 2329, etc. ; *renke* 21, etc. ; *renysche* (adj. furious) 2943, *renyst* (adj. passionate) 387, *renyschly* (adv. vigorously) 4931 ; *richis* (prepares) 5056 ; *ronke* (abundant) 1762 ; *ranke* (luxuriant) 3060, *rankest* (thickest) 1319 ; *schalk* 469, etc. ; *segge* 111, etc. (very frequent) ; *spakly* (swiftly) 786 ; *spynnes* (rush along) 3033 ; *swey* (trans. to drive) 3970, (intrans. to fall) 2057 (Dub.) ; *thraly* (adv. eagerly) 371, 2090 ; *thra, thro* (adj. bold, etc.) 1246, etc. ; *thra* (sb. struggle) 2259, etc. ; *thryfandly* (adv. prosperously) 3747 ; *trine* (go) 5171, 5195, 5231 ; *tulke* 752, etc. ; *wlonk* (adj. goodly) 5089 ; *wy, wee* (man) 134, etc.

These romances, while exceedingly rich in the " chiefly alliterative " words previously discussed, add little that is new. It would seem that in the central period the alliterative diction has become firmly established and shared by all writers, so that there is a monotonous uniformity in the use of these forms in all their works.

E. The Rhyming Alliterative Works.

The Quatrefoil of Love : *birde* 25 ; *carpe* 475 (vb.).

St. John the Evangelist : *byrde* 142 ; *lede* (man) 20, 243, *lede* (people) 115, 211 ; *thraly* (boldly) 114 ; *segge* 142.

The Pistill of Susan : *carpe* 249 ; *renke* 4, 198 ; *segge* 146, 254 ; *trine* (to go) 225 ; *wlonkest* 26, 186.

The Awntyrs of Arthur : *blonke* 29, 499 ; *birde* 29, etc. ; *carpe* 360, etc. ; *ferde* (host) 186 ; *gleme* (vb.) 15, etc. ; *greme* (intrans. to become angry) 524 (Douce) ; *hathill* (sb.) 130, etc. ; *lede* (man) 433, *lede* (people) 83 ; *note* (work) 375 ; *renke* 460 ; *ronke* (strong) 604 (Douce) ; *shindre* (to shiver to pieces) 501, 503 (Douce) ; *segge* 359 ; *wlonkeste* 9, 347 ; *wy* (man) 365, etc.

Rauf Coilʒear : *blonke* 563, 797, 807 ; *byrdis* 533 ; *carpe* 44, etc. ; *carping* (sb. talk) 728[1]; *glemis* (sb.) 456 ; *glemand* 667 ; *leid* (man) 395, 591 ; *picht* (adorned) 467 ; *renkis* 819 ; *seigis* (men) 713 ; *thra* (sb. haste) 801 ; *thraly* (adv. violently) 657, 701 ; *wy* 578, etc.

The Houlate : *athill* (adj.) 279, 314, 682 ; *gleme* (vb.) 412 ; *hathill* (sb.) 846 ; *leid* (man) 188, etc. ; *renkis* 624 ; *rank* (strong) 216 ; *thraly* (adv. strongly) 489, 918, 941 ; *wlonk* 533 ; *wy* (man) 513, etc.

Golagrus and Gawain : *blonk* 551, 560, 921 ; *birde* 134, 351, etc. ; *carpe* (vb.) 46, etc. ; *gleme* (vb.) 21 ; *hathill* (sb.) 900, etc. ; *leid* (man) 70, etc. ; *note* (business, etc.) 501, etc. ; *ranke* (abundant) 30, (heavy) 691 ; *renk* 11, etc. ; *schalk* 599, etc. ; *sege* (man) 90, etc. ; *thra* (adj. bold) 60 ; *thriuandly* (adv. prosperously) 435 ; *wy* (man) 57, etc.

The results in this section are according to expectations. The more stereotyped alliterative words are well known and widely used by these poets who do not, however, seem to be acquainted with many of the rarer forms found in the non-rhyming romances.

F. The Later Alliterative Works.

Death and Life: *bird* (MS. *birth*) (lady) 234, *birds* 81 ; *blushe* (to look at) 191, 388 ; *carpe* 231 ; *leed* (man) 315, *leeds* 339.

Scottish Field: *carpe* 5, 74, 83, etc. ; *hattell* = *hathell* 237 ; *leede* (knyght) 58, *leed(e)s* 109, etc. ; *ring* = *rink* 303 [1] ; *sege* 12 ; *seege(s)* 142, etc. ; *wye* 341, 414, *way(e)* 200, etc.

Scottish Prophecies and *à Becket*: *blonk* B 4 ; *hathell* B 193, *hatel* B 110 ; *lede* I. 128, *ledys* (pl.) I. 113, II. 20, etc. ; *renk* B 143 ; *wy(e)* B 57, etc.

In these late poems there are naturally but few traces surviving of the older alliterative words.

2. POETIC WORDS.

Much of the alliterative vocabulary is " poetic " in the sense that it is essentially different from that of ordinary prose texts. There is a large number of words entirely confined to poetry, including practically all the " chiefly alliterative " words. Furthermore, many of these words have a distinct poetical value, and belong essentially to poetry.

(1) Prominent among these poetic words are the synonyms for *man, knight*. In addition to the alliterative forms—*hapel, lede, renk, schalk, segge, tulke, wye*—there are the non-alliterative but poetic synonyms *berne*, O.E. beorn ; *freke*, O.E. freca ; *gome*, O.E. guma. Of these *berne* (in various spellings) is found in all the purely alliterative poems (excluding the short poem, *The Crowned King, Chev.* and *Pierce*), *freke* in all except *Chev., Joseph, Richard the Redeles*, and *Pierce*, and *gome* in all except *Chev., Sc. Field* and *Sc. Proph.* In the Northern rhyming alliterative works these words are equally common.

(2) Of the numerous synonyms to express movement—to *bowe, cayre, chese to, fare, ferke, founde, glyde, raike, schake, seche to, stràke* (see *Pur.* 905, *Pierce* 82), *strike, tryne, wade, walke, wawe, wende, win—bowe, cayre, ferke, glyde, schake, strike, tryne, wade* and *wawe* are definitely poetic ; *ferke* and *tryne* have already been discussed under the heading of alliterative words. For the rest, *cayre* (O.N. keyra) is the most popular synonym for ' go ' ; it occurs in *Alex. A* 623, *Alex. B* 48, etc., *Will. of Pal.* 2714, etc., *Wyn. and Wast.* 210, etc., *Parl.* 246, *P. Pl.* B, Pro. 29, etc., *Richard*

---

[1] Cp. Gaw. 1817, 1827 where *rynk* = 'ring'

the Redeles, iii, 302 (carieth), *Gaw.* 43, etc., *Prl.* 1029, *Pur.* 85, etc., *Morte Arthure* 243, etc., *Troy* 280, etc., *W. Alex.* 859, etc., *Death and Life* 47, etc., *Sc. Field* 154, etc. The other synonyms are, however, of more poetic value : *strike* in the sense of ' go ' (a sense surviving in modern dialects) is found in *Jerus.* 761, *Chev.* 229, *P. Pl.* C, viii, 224, etc., *Prl.* 570, 1186, *Morte Arthure* 755, 2086, 3659 and *W. Alex.* 826* (the only example in this sense) ; *schake* in *Wyn.* 403, *Morte Arthure* 1213, 1992, *Jerus.* 315, and *Troy* 2921, etc. ; *wade* in *P. Pl.* C, xv, 126, and *W. Alex.* 4141 (*wade* has its normal meaning in *Prl.* 143, 1151, etc.) ; *wawe* (O.E. wagian) in *Jos.* 52, *P. Pl.* C, viii, 158, etc., and *Troy* 13542 ; *bowe*, in the sense of ' go,' is of more frequent occurrence—*Chev.* 265, *Jos.* 294, etc., *Wyn.* 208, *Parl.* 370, 395, *P. Pl.* A, vi, 56, *Gaw.* 344, etc., *Pur.* 45, etc., *Prl.* 126, etc., *Erk.* 59, *Jerus.* 765, 817, *Morte Arthure* 69, 2310, *Troy* 362, etc., and *W. Alex.* 1312, etc. ; *glyde* in *Alex. A.* 279, *Prl.* 1105, *Pur.* 296, etc., *Gaw.* 748, etc., *Pat.* 63, 204, *Morte Arthure* 1371, 2972, *Troy* 2996, etc., *W. Alex.* 358, and *Death and Life* 28. Doubtless the use of so many synonymous words is to be explained partly by the exigencies of alliteration, but not wholly so. There is an evident desire for variety and poetical effectiveness.

(3) *Poetic Words for Natural Features.*—There is likewise under this heading the same twofold phenomenon—the exigencies of alliteration combined with true poetic feeling. *Molde*, a poetic word for ' *earth* ' is usually found in the phrase . . . *on molde*, and occurs in almost every alliterative poem. The references to the word are listed under the phrases and tags on pages 293 and 390, and need not be recorded here. It is a genuine instance of the survival of an O.E. poetic word, though the constant repetition of the word makes it hackneyed. *Folde*, O.E. folde, another word for ' earth,' is similarly bound up with the phrase *freke on folde* (see pp. 282 and 389, where practically all the examples may be found) ; *bent*, O.E. beonet, ' the open plain,' occurs generally in connection with the phrase . . . *on bent* (see pp. 268 and 389). The word is of very frequent occurrence, both in the rhymed and unrhymed alliterative poems.

There are, however, many words for natural features which are not bound up with stock phrases and tags : *flod*, O.E. *flōd*, is a notable poetic word for the *sea* or *water*. In *Pat.* 221 it has its normal meaning of ' flood,' but it occurs in its poetic sense in *Prl.* 736, etc. ; *Gaw.* 13 ; *Pur.* 538 ; as also in *Alex. A.* 532 ; *Alex. B.* 531, 1023 ; *Parl.* 216 (' waters ') ; *P. Pl.* B, x, 295 ; *Jerus.* 78,

479 ; *Morte Arthure* 773, 803, 1189 ; *Wyn.* 386 ; *Troy* 278, etc. ; *W. Alex.* 56, etc. (very frequent) ; *Quatr.* 331 ; and *Gol.* 302. Other poetic words connected with ' water ' are *brymme*, O.E. brim, an old poetic word for the ' sea ' ; in Middle English it is used for water simply or in a specialised sense, such as ' river '—*Gaw.* 2172 (water—perhaps a confusion between O.E. brim and and O.E. brymm) ; *Parl.* 7 (stream) ; *W. Alex.* 4080 (river) ; *brok. Pat.* 145, ' sea,' is apparently the only example of the poetic use of the word as applied to the open sea ; similarly *borne*, O.E. burna, ' a stream,' is used for ' sea ' in *Pur.* 482, " *Noe on anoþer day nymmeȝ þe do(wv)e and byddeȝ hir bowe over þe borne efte bonkeȝ to seche* ".

Troy 12,523 has *buerne* in the same sense : *(shippes) were brent in the buerne with the breme low.* *Pat.* uses *breþe*, O.E. brǣþ, in the poetical sense of ' wind '—107, 138, 145 ; *Troy* 3697 shows exactly the same specialised meaning.

(4) *Descriptive Adjectives.*—Under this heading it is only necessary to record the most important examples, for almost all the Middle English poetic adjectives make their appearance in alliterative verse. Especially common are the stock adjectives of compliment, such as *fre, frely, frelych, hende, lele, schene* and *wale*, which is much more frequent in alliterative than in rhymed verse. Of ordinary adjectives used in a specialised technical sense, a good example is *borelich*, which is generally applied to persons, but is poetically applied to things in the sense of ' massive,' e.g. *Gaw.* 766, 2225, *Pur.* 1488 ; this usage is extensively found in alliterative verse.

Under this heading must be noted the poetical use of the adjective as a substantive. Already in O.S. (and once in Old English) we find *frī* (neut. adj.) used in the sense of ' woman '. In M.E. *fre* and *frely* are both used absolutely as synonyms for 'person,' but presumably starting from this model its use was widely extended so that almost any descriptive personal adjective in alliterative poetry can yield a new poetical synonym : *þat comely, þat louely, þat semly*, etc. A complete list of these forms will be found in the chapter on *style*, p. 394, and it suffices to mention here that this poetical usage is largely confined to alliterative verse with certain well-defined exceptions.

(5) *Examples of Poetical Nouns.*—Of poetical nouns, except those coming under sections 1 and 3, there are numerous examples. There are several of the very common nouns, such as *bale, ble* (hue), *erde* (dwelling), *lere* (face), and *wone* (dwelling), which are of

so frequent occurrence in alliterative verse that no reference need be given. Of poetical synonyms for ' sword ' there is the common word *bronde*, with *egge*, O.E. ecg, in *Pur.* 1104, 1244, *Gaw.* 2392 ; for ' horse,' *caple* and *coursour*, both of which are poetical in Middle English. Of personal nouns, excluding the synonyms for warrior, the frequent use of *fode*, O.E. fōda, in the specialised poetical sense of ' person, child ' should be noted : *Pur.* 466, *Morte Arthure* 3776, *Alex. A.* 209, *W. Alex.* 270, etc. ; *here* (lord), O.E. herra, O.S. hêrro in *Gaw.* 59, *Troy* 1046, *W. Alex.* 1920, 3160 ; *may* (cp. O.N. mæ̂r) maiden, in *Gaw.* 1795, *Prl.* 435, etc., *P. Pl.* A, xii, 111, *Will. of Pal.* 659, *Parl.* 623, etc.

(6) *Verbs Chiefly Confined to Poetry*—Excluding the verbs indicating ' movement,' the alliterative writers make full use of the numerous poetical forms in M.E. : *layte*, ' seek,' O.N. leita, and *lenge* ' dwell,' ' tarry,' O.E. lengan, are commonplaces of alliterative verse, and these are merely typical of a large number of such words.

Of more interest, however, is such a word as *deme*, O.E. dēman, used in the sense of ' say ' ; cp. O.N. dœ́ma in poetry with the same meaning. This is a survival of an O.E. poetical usage of *dēman ;* it occurs in *Will. of Pal.* 151 ; *W. Alex.* 1231 ; *Gaw.* 1332, 2183 ; *Pat.* 119, 386 ; *Prl.* 361, 1183 ; *Pur.* 1021, 1161 ; this sense is exclusively poetic. *Sile*, O.N. sila (Sw. and Norw. dial.), ' to fall or sink,' frequently used of the sun, e.g. *Parl.* 658, but also of ' tears,' etc., is a typical example of an O.N. borrowing which never found its way into ordinary prose, but remained in poetry, and especially in alliterative verse. It is found in *Parl.* 658 ; *Pur.* 131 ; *Morte Arthure* 1297, 3794, 4340 ; *W. Alex.* 3043 ; *Troy* 1973, etc. ; and *Gol.* 524. *Witer*, O.N. vitra, ' to inform,' *Pur.* 1587, *Erk.* 185, *Jos.* 466, similarly failed to gain currency in prose. *Blykke*, O.N. blikja, O.E. blīcan, ' to shine,' in *Alex. B.* 411, *Pur.* 603, *Gaw.* 305, etc. ; and *drepe*, O.E. drepan, ' to kiH,' in *Parl.* 379, 456, *Pur.* 246, *Gaw.* 725, *Troy* 929, etc., and *W. Alex.* 867, are typically interesting examples of poetic verbs common to the alliterative writers.

(7) *Compound Words.*—These have been treated fully in chapter 6, and are mentioned here solely because they illustrate the poetic nature of the alliterative diction. These compounds are not merely words unknown in prose ; they are themselves full of poetic power. They are not as a rule archaisms, but new creations based on the older models, and show that some of the poets had a true feeling for poetic diction. Such forms are not extensive and do not form a typical feature of Middle English alliterative poetry.

3. Archaic Words.

Poetic words are frequently archaic, and it is clear that if no alliterative poetry had been written, or had come down to us, the majority of the " chiefly alliterative " words would not have been recorded after about the middle of the thirteenth century. Taking the second manuscript of Laȝamon's *Brut* as a fairly reliable criterion of what is archaic, we find that *athel* (adj.), *blonke, douthe* and *segge* are rejected by the later scribe. It is therefore certain that alliterative poetry gave renewed life to many archaic words. Whether there was a conscious attempt to keep alive old words and affect an archaic diction it is impossible to say.

In addition to these alliterative archaic words, however, there are other forms occurring isolatedly which are mere survivals. While such survivals are found in most groups of Middle English poetry, the archaisms in alliterative poetry seem to the present writer to be far more numerous. A complete list of these archaisms cannot be given here, but representative selections will serve to illustrate the range and nature of the forms collected :—

(1) *Selected Examples.*

aisliche (adv. timidly), Pierce 341, O.E. egeslice—no example in N.E.D. after 1200.

axles (shoulders), Parl. 113, O.E. eaxl—definitely archaic in the fourteenth century.

drem, in the phrase *dragounes drem*, Alex. A 781, 982—' droning noise ' —archaic sense : O.E. drēam.

galede (sang), Morte Arthure 927, O.E. galan—the latest survival of this O.E. verb.

pester (vb. to grow dark), Jos. 235, O.E. þēostrian—the last example of this verb.

wate deeds (brave deeds), Sc. Field 287, O.E. hwæt ; the Lyme MS. has, however, *wale ;* if *wate* be the correct form, it is a very archaic word at this period (1515).

were (man), Parl. 581, and *weris* (men), W. Alex. 1300, O.E. wer ; 1250 is the last example in N.E.D. with the meaning ' man ' and 1275 with the meaning ' husband '.

(2) *The Gawain Group.*

In some poems these archaisms are scarce, whereas in other poems they are plentiful. Thus *Piers Plowman* has relatively few such forms ; on the other hand, the works of the ' Gawain ' poet are comparatively rich in them. The chief archaisms in *Patience* are *hyȝt* 219, O.E. hyht (hope)—no example later than the thirteenth century in N.E.D. ; *lof* 448, O.E. lof (value)—1205 last example in

N.E.D. ; *waymot* 492, O.E. wēamōd (sad) ; *wyþer* 48, O.E. wiþerian (to strive)—1225 the last example in N.E.D.   *Purity* has also many examples, of which perhaps the most interesting is *wlateʒ* 305, 1501, O.E. wlātian (impers. to cause loathing), a very rare word in the early fourteenth century.   Among the numerous archaic words in *Pearl* the most striking is *gele* 931, O.E. gǣlan (tarry), this being the only Middle English quotation given in N.E.D., which marks the verb *rare*.   *Gawain* has perhaps not quite so many archaisms as the other poems of the MS., but there are several interesting examples, such as *hersum* 932 (devout), O.E. hērsum.   Indeed, with frequent study of the poems of this group, the reader is apt to become so familiar with them that he forgets how archaic and strange are many of their forms.   To a certain extent this is true of the whole body of alliterative verse.   Only by frequent reading of non-alliterative texts can one appreciate the archaic diction of these Western poets.

4. THE USE OF TECHNICAL WORDS.

The alliterative poets were well acquainted with the technical dialects of their day.   Through reading, culture, wide experience and travel they made themselves familiar with details of the new architectural fashions, with the technical terms associated with hunting and falconry, and with details of dress.   These writers, such as the ' Gawain ' poet or the authors of *The Parlement of the Thre Ages* and *Morte Arthure*, do not refer to these details as if they were things with which they had only a second-hand acquaintance. The internal evidence goes to show that they were well-educated and belonged to the upper classes.

(1) *Hunting and Falconry Terms.*—In the introductory setting of *The Parlement of the Thre Ages*, with its vivid description of a hunting scene there occur many technical hunting terms, several of which are paralleled in *Sir Gawain*, e.g. *assaye* 70, O.Fr. assai, ' a trial of grease of a deer ' ; *beme* 26, O.E. beam, ' the trunk of a stag's horn ' ; *chyne* 89, O.Fr. échiner ' to cut along the backbone,' cp. *Gaw.* 1354 ; *corbyns bone* 80, O.Fr. corbin, ' the bone given to the crows,' cp. *Gaw.* 1355; *fourche* 88, 91, O.Fr. fourche, 'the hindquarters of a deer,' cp. *Gaw.* 1357 ; *laners* 220, O.Fr. lanier, ' female falcon ' ; *lanerettis* 220, O.Fr. laneret, ' male falcon ' ; *soure* 34, O.Fr. sor, ' a fourth year buck ' ; *troches* 67, O.Fr. troche, ' tines,' cp. *Gaw.* 795 ; and *Pur.* 1383, p.p. *trochet*, ' furnished with pinacles '.   *Sir Gawain*, in its various hunting passages,

reveals the same detailed knowledge of hunting terms, and even in works such as *Richard the Redeles* there are isolated examples, e.g. *rascaile*, ii, 119, 129, ' the lean deer . The same poem has also several falconry terms : *bate*, ii, 102 ; O.Fr. batre, ' to beat the wings,' " than bated he boldelyche as a bird wolde ". *plewme*, ii, 163, O.Fr. plumer, ' to pluck the feathers ' ; or *reclayme*, ii, 182, O.Fr. reclaime, ' the recalling of a hawk '.

(2) *Architectural and Heraldic Terms* are well illustrated by the large number of such words in *Sir Gawain* and in *Purity* : e.g. *bastele, Pur.* 1187, *Gaw.* 799, O. Fr. bastille, ' tower ' ; *brutage, Pur.* 1190, A.Fr. brutesche, ' a temporary parapet ' ; *carnel, Pur.* 1382, *Gaw.* 801, O.N.F. carnel, ' embrasure ' ; *fylyole, Pur.* 1462, *Gaw.* 796, O.Fr. filloele, ' turret,' etc. The author of *Pierce the Ploughman's Crede*, in his description of the friaries, also uses some interesting architectural and heraldic terms, such as *armede* 183, O.Fr. armer, ' adorned with heraldic devices ' ; *crochettis* 174, O.Fr. crochet, ' small ornamental leaves ' ; *pomels* 562, O.Fr. pomel, ' ornamental knobs on pillars or towers,' etc. Two heraldic terms are used in *Wynnere and Wastoure; besantes* 61, O.Fr. besan, ' roundels,' and *chechun* 116, O.Fr. escuchon, ' badge '.

(3) *Law Terms* are plentiful in alliterative poetry, not merely in such works as *Piers Plowman*, but in simple romances and religious poems, e.g. *deraine, Alex. A* 124, 356, O.Fr. deraisnier, ' to vindicate a right ' ; *iustifiet, Erk.* 229, O.Fr. justifier, ' to administer justice,' etc.

(4) *Miscellaneous Terms, Armour, Dress, Wine, etc.—Morte Arthure* is in several places difficult to read, owing to the extensive use of technical terms. There are many names of wines (*maluesye* 236, *vernage* 204, 3166, etc.), and various dishes (*cretoyne* 197), of armour and weapons (e.g. *anlace* 1148, *avawmbrace* 2568, *bacenett* 906, etc., *chapes* 2522, *coutere* 2567, etc., *qwarelles* 2103, etc.), of nautical terms (*bonetteȝ* 3656, *dromowndes* 3615, *krayers* 738, 3666) nearly all of which are words of French origin.

(5) *Ecclesiastical and Homiletic Terms.*—Such words are found chiefly in *Purity, St. Erkenwald* and *Piers Plowman*. Of these, *St. Erkenwald* affords the most interesting and typical examples : *cenacle* 336, O.Fr. cenacle, is used of the Upper Room in which the Lord's Supper was held, and is rare in Middle English ; *herghedes* 291, O.E. hergian, is used in its specialised homiletic meaning, ' harrowing (of hell) ' ; *martilage* 154, ' a register of martyrs,' derived from Med. Latin *martilogium ; reuestid* 139, p.p. robed in vestments, O.Fr. revestir. Such technical words would scarcely be used in

their correct senses by a poet who was not trained in theology and acquainted with the formal details of mediæval religious life. These groups of technical words are meant to suggest how cultured were many of the alliterative writers. Their learning was often wide and their interest in contemporary life always keen.

5. OLD NORSE WORDS.

Regarding the mere number of Old Norse words found in the various poems there is a wide divergence, dependent largely on dialectal differences. The early works, chiefly from the south and central west-midlands, show a relatively small number of Old Norse words, their place of composition being removed from the strongly Scandinavianised areas. Thus *Wynnere and Wastoure* has 73 and *The Parlement* 82 Old Norse words, the bulk of these forms being in general circulation in the fourteenth century. The political poems have similarly few Old Norse words—*Piers Plowman* 180, *Pierce the Ploughman's Crede* 32, and *Richard the Redeles* 31. For higher percentages than these we have to go to the ' Gawain ' group, which has a total of 560 distinct Old Norse words, 238 in *Gaw.*, 195 in *Pur.*, 130 in *Prl.*, 103 in *Pat.*, and 83 in *Erk.* The romances from the north-west have by comparison much fewer examples, the average percentage being only slightly higher than that of *The Parlement.* In the case of the ' Gawain ' poet, some fact, probably beyond our ascertaining, lies behind this remarkable number of Old Norse loan words.

In the earlier poems the words are uniformly the usual Scandinavian forms of any Middle English poem of average length, such as *brenne, busk, calle* or *caste.* Exceptions are of course found : *Alex. A, shoutes* 484, cp. M.Du. schûte, ' flat bottomed boats '—a very rare Middle English word. *Alex. B, raiken* 467, O.N. reika, ' to go '—one of the rarer Old Norse loan words.[1] *Joseph* has the word *witer* 466, O.N. vitra, a poetic word which has already been discussed. In *Wyn. and Wast.* there are only three fairly uncommon forms : *goullyng* 359, O.N. gaula, ' howling,' cp. ȝaule ; *ridde* 57, O.N. ryðja, ' to part, combatants,' cp. *Gaw.* 2246 ; *slabbande* 411, ' trailing in mud '—a rare word of apparently Old Norse origin—see N.E.D. *The Parlement* is richer in the more unusual forms, *donke* 10, *nayte* 607, *naytly* 108, *skayle* 383, *syle* 658, being the most important ; these are words which are generally more popular in the alliterative than in the rhymed verse.

[1] Cp. *Gaw*, 1076, 1727, 1735.

Similar lists could be drawn up in connection with *Piers Plowman* and the other political poems, but would not serve any useful purpose. The types of more unusual Old Norse words in *Piers Plowman* are some "chiefly alliterative" words such as *carpe*, *keyre*, etc., some poetic words such as *tike*, C, xxii, 37, O.N. tík (a bitch), ' a low fellow '. In addition, there are several doubtful Scandinavian forms, such as *kete*, A, xi, 56—see N.E.D. A list of the rarer Old Norse words in *Piers Plowman* would number about thirty.

The Scandinavian element in the works of the ' Gawain ' poet is of special interest, partly because it is so extensive,[1] and partly because of its peculiar nature.[2] The number of Old Norse words suggests an area of composition in a dialectal region in which the Scandinavian element was very marked, but owing to the wide circulation in the west of typical Norwegian test-words such as *caple*, it is impossible to say whether the author was in touch with the West-Scandinavian settlements in the north-west of England. Many of the words are dialectal, such as *ryge*, *Pur.* 354, O.N. hregg, ' storm,' and in a list of words confined to these poems will be found many words of Old Norse origin. As Professor Gordon suggests, " it is evident that many of the Old Norse words (in these poems) have been called into play by the needs of alliteration," and there are even a few examples (such as *mynne*) of " survivals of Scandinavian literary tradition ".

What is true of the ' Gawain ' poet will be found true, though to a much smaller degree, of the lesser romance writers such as the author of *Morte Arthure*. There are in these north-western poems fewer Old Norse words than in *Sir Gawain*, but there are likewise in them numerous Scandinavian forms, not merely because the local dialect was rich in them, but because the needs of the alliterative technique demanded it.

6. DIALECTAL WORDS.

Under this heading we have to distinguish between words which survive in modern dialects and words which are themselves already dialectal in Middle English. The former class, by far the larger, may be of some value in determining the original dialect of a particular poem, but it is of little interest in a literary survey of Middle

[1] For the percentages see vol. 1, p. 86.
[2] See J. R. Tolkien and E. V. Gordon, *Sir Gawain and the Green Knight*, pp. 125–8.

English alliterative poetry. The second class is important because it shows that the alliterative poets drew largely upon their native dialects for their vocabulary. Until we possess a reliable Middle English Dictionary we cannot say with certainty whether any given word is strictly dialectal, but there are words which can be described as " chiefly northern," etc. Most alliterative poems are rich in such local words which are frequently of obscure origin. Thus, in *Cheuelere Assigne* there is *pele* 303 : *Thenne plukke out þy swerde and pele on hym faste.* The etymology of *pele* is quite obscure, but the E.D.D. records a word *pail* in the sense of ' to beat ' which would fit here. *Wynnere and Wastoure* has ' local ' words such as *daderinge* 97 (trembling), *dadillyng* 44 (chattering), *hurcle* 14 (to crouch) found also in *Pur.* 150, and *W. Alex.* 504, or *slabbande* 411 (trailing in mud), all of which survive locally in various modern dialects. There are also some chiefly northern words—*blesande* 168, O.E. blæse (sb.) ' bright,' *flakerande* 92, cp. O.E. flacer, ' fluttering,' *happede* 298, obscure, ' wrapped up,' found also in *Pur.* 626, *Pat.* 450, *Gaw.* 864, 1224, and *Troy* 9198, 12,627, *hodirde* 298, see N.E.D. ' covered up,' and *raxillyng* 436, ' stretching in sleep,' cp. *Prl.* 1174 and *W. Alex.* 4930.

These illustrations are given to show the ' local ' nature of much of the alliterative vocabulary. *The Parlement of the Thre Ages* has some twenty-two dialectal words of the same type, *Cheuelere Assigne* and *Joseph of Arimathie* three each. Of works which are particularly rich in dialectal words, *Piers Plowman*, the ' Gawain ' poems, and *Morte Arthure* should be specially noted, while the Scottish poems, *Rauf Coilȝear*, *The Houlate* and *Gologrus and Gawain* have many examples of Old Norse and French dialectal words confined to early Scottish literature. This extensive use of dialectal words by the alliterative poets would doubtless make its appeal to the audience to whom their works were addressed, but it is most unlikely that a London audience for example would have comprehended such a poem as *Sir Gawain*, owing to the large number of Scandinavian and local words with which they would be unacquainted.

7. RARE AND OBSCURE WORDS.

The alliterative poems abound in rare and obscure words, a fact which is partly explained by the use of technical terms, archaic, Old Norse and dialectal words, many of which are of very infrequent occurrence in Middle English. Numerous instances of such forms have already been given in the previous sections.

In *Pearl* alone there are twenty accepted cruxes in vocabulary which have not so far been satisfactorily explained. This poem is admittedly exceptional, but there is no alliterative work which is wholly free from obscure words. Kullnick, in his *Studien über den Wortschatz im Sir Gawayne*, p. 50, gives various lists of words common to *Sir Gawain* and other alliterative works, including a list of 115 words found only in *Sir Gawain*. This list is reduced to about 100 by the references in N.E.D., but the number is remarkable. It testifies to the wealth of the alliterative diction, which in its range and variety is unsurpassed in Middle English. That it is so frequently obscure is perhaps not to be wondered at, for the poets drew their vocabulary from humble local dialects as well as from the French and Latin writings with which they were so familiar.

PART III

THE ALLITERATIVE PHRASES.

CHAPTER 9.

THE ALLITERATIVE PHRASES IN OLD ENGLISH POETRY AND PROSE.

THE lists of phrases are arranged historically in groups, and in order that the past references to a given phrase may be recalled, the abbreviations to the various groups are used to indicate where a particular phrase has previously been found. In this way the reader may see at a glance whether the phrase is traditional or not. The Old English references are to the left, and the Middle English to the right, while the statistical table will be found at the end of Part III.

Owing to the confusion in Middle English between c and k, all words beginning with these letters are listed under c. The phrases are placed in alphabetical order as far as possible, but where a given phrase such as *hele and hide* can be reversed, the details are listed under the more usual form of the alliterative phrase. It was the author's intention to give the meanings in all cases, but this proved impracticable; the loss is not, however, great, because the meaning of a phrase is usually stereotyped; where this is not the case, the meaning has been given.

Before the alliterative phrases occurring in Middle English poetry had all been collected and arranged, it became evident that it would also be necessary to collect the alliterative phrases occurring in Old English poetry if any light was to be thrown upon the question of origins. The necessary labour involved has been rewarded with a rich harvest of data, and has afforded a proof of the historical continuity of poetic tradition only paralleled by that gleaned from a study of the metre and of the poetic compounds.

The phrases have been gathered into two groups, the first including those found in the heroic poems and in the secular verse generally, the second group including those from the religious and purely didactic verse. No hard and fast division into these two sections is possible, and to some the choice may in certain cases appear arbitrary. A ' heroic ' alliterative phrase which is also found in the religious verse is prefixed by " R," and a ' religious ' alliterative phrase which is also found in the heroic verse is prefixed by " H " ; in this way a simple comparison of the two groups becomes easier. Every effort has been made to ensure completeness, but despite this, it is possible that there have been some omissions. The abbreviations employed are such as will be readily intelligible to the student of Anglo-Saxon literature.

In the ' heroic ' poetry 174 different alliterative phrases are found, a phrase occurring in more than one passage being counted only once. Bearing in mind that the actual amount of heroic poetry in Old English is by no means large, the number of alliterative phrases found is surprising. The majority of these occur in *Beowulf*, though most poems show a fair sprinkling. We must not, however, suppose that the employment of stock alliterative phrases was characteristic of the Old English heroic poets. Nevertheless, a minute examination will show that the majority of these phrases were not mere everyday alliterative expressions, and it is noticeable that only eighteen of them occur also in the homiletic prose, and only twenty-one in the Alfredian. A few of the 174 phrases are undoubtedly mere everyday expressions, such as *feallan fæge, feallan to fotum, ferdon forþ, habban ond healdan, wer ond wif, word ond weorc*. Phrases such as these are to be found in Old English prose and in Middle English alliterative and non-alliterative poetry generally.

There remain, however, a large number of Old English ' heroic ' phrases, such as *synn ond sacu, wordum wrixlan*, which are not of the foregoing type ; and it is interesting to note how a number of these survive in Middle English poetry. *Stræt . . . stig, Beowulf* 320, reappears in Laȝamon's *Brut* 16,366, *bi stiȝen and bi straten*, and in Emare 196, 543 ; *ord ond ecg, Beowulf* 1549, Maldon 60, survives in Laȝamon's *Brut* 5202, and in Lib. Dis. 1923 ; in addition, such phrases as *blood and bones, game and glee, lond and leoden*, are of frequent occurrence in Middle English poetry. Still more interesting survivals are afforded by *folde and flode, Pearl* 736, with which should be compared *flode ond foldan*, Rid. V, 9, and also by *sutell and sene*, Ormulum 18,862, with which should be compared *sweotol ond gesyne*, a phrase found both in heroic and in religious Old English poetry.

Sixty-six of the 174 phrases occur also in the religious and didactic verse.   These naturally include the mere everyday alliterative phrases, such as *word and weorc*, but also many essentially poetic phrases such as *burh ond beagas*, and *wlitig ond wynsum*.   A phrase such as the former may have been borrowed by the author of Exodus ; and in any case it becomes clear that no hard and fast line can be drawn between the ' heroic ' and ' religious ' phrases, whatever may have been the extent to which the later religious writers modelled themselves on the older poets.

The phrases are not all of one type, but in fifty-four cases we have two complementary and parallel nouns in apposition, such as *adl ne yldo*, or *earm ond eaxle*, but never two nouns of identical meaning ; there is no idle repetition.   In nineteen cases we have pairs of adjectives employed in a similar manner, such as *fus ond fæge*, or *idel ond unnyt;* in a number of cases, however, the two adjectives appear to convey an identical meaning, such as *gifre ond grædig, sweotol ond gesyne*.   In the case of *leof ne laþ* we have perhaps the finest example of a ' complementary ' alliterative phrase.

In the religious and didactic verse there occur 346 separate alliterative phrases.   This is not proportionately greater in number than the 174 in the heroic poetry, for the religious poetry is much greater in bulk.   For the 174 phrases there are 243 instances, of which no less than 135 occur in *Beowulf*.   For the 346 religious phrases there are 657 instances, a fact which indicates that alliterative phrases were more popular among the ' religious ' poets than among the ' heroic ' poets.

In formation these religious phrases do not differ from those in the heroic poetry ; thus there are seventy-two cases of two nouns side by side, such as *eard ond eþel, hlæwas ne hlincas*, in every case expressing two distinct objects or ideas.   There are also instances of purely complementary nouns, such as *freonde ne feonde, welan ond wawan*.   There are forty-two cases of adjectives side by side, and as in the case of the heroic poems, we find pairs of adjectives identical in meaning : *scir ond scyne, snel ond swift*.   In several cases we have pairs of verbs which are sometimes identical and sometimes not identical in meaning : *cleopaþ ond cigeþ, habban ne healdan, tydran ond tyman, þolian ond þafian*.

Many of the religious phrases are undoubtedly not traditional, having come into being as a result of Christianity.   Among such might be mentioned *heah ond halig, heofon ond hel, leoht ond lif, scand ond sceamu, synn ond sacu, wop ond wanung, wuldor ond wyrþmynt.* In these and many other cases we may be sure that the phrases are not traditional. The requirements of metre would probably lead to the unconscious creation of new phrases, and these would in time become stereotyped ; this process may have continued throughout the Old English period, and from a study of the phrases which occur in the latest Old English poems it is evident that it was still possible to create new ones.

Of the 346 religious phrases, forty-eight are also to be found in the homiletic prose, forty-nine in the Alfredian, and twelve in the legal. If the reader will examine the phrases in the legal prose, he will discover that those which occur also in the Old English religious poetry are not specifically religious phrases, but the mere everyday alliterative phrases which find their way into poetry as well as prose ; these are of no significance. Those found in the homiletic and Alfredian prose are partly in the same category, but not exclusively so. Both King Alfred and the homiletic writers, such as Aelfric and Wulfstan used alliterative phrases which may in the first instance have originated with the religious poets. Of this type are *earm ond eadig, frofor ond fultum, man ond morþor, woþ ond wanung, wyrhta and wealdend,* etc. These are not only of frequent occurrence in all the homiletic writings, but are also found in the Old English version of Bede's *Ecclesiastical History* and in King Alfred's translation of *Boethius.* These, together with the commonplace phrases found both in prose and poetry generally, account for the element common to both the Old English religious phrases and those occurring in the prose.

A glance at the table of phrases on page 378 will reveal that the alliterative phrases found in Old English religious poetry have not all disappeared by the Middle English period ; a fifth of Laȝamon's alliterative phrases are represented in the older verse—a surprisingly large proportion, and the same is in a certain measure true of most of the other groups of phrases in Middle English. Details of these will be given in dealing with each section ; but even at this stage no proof is needed to establish the case for continuity of tradition —the facts speak abundantly for themselves. One or two illustrations must suffice ; the interesting phrase contained in the O.E. *biholene ond behydde, Phoenix* 170, appears as *hudden and heleden, P. Pl.* C, xiv, 114, and as *hele and hide,* Minot 6. 16, or the *Quatrefoil of Love* 476–7, and in numerous metrical romances. The O.E. *scir ond scyne, Phoenix* 308, reappears in *Pearl* 42 as *schyre and schene ;* similarly, the O.E. *beorht ond bliþe,* Crist 877, reappears in *Golagrus and Gawain* 378 as *blyth and bricht.*

Hence, though it is true that a vast number of the Old English alliterative phrases found in the poetry did not survive into Middle English—and there are reasons why this was so—it is a fact that large numbers of such phrases did survive and are represented in Laȝamon and in the later alliterative poetry also.

A. In the Heroic and Kindred Verse.[1] [O.E.P. H.]

R. *ādl nē yldo,* Beow. 1730.
bǣle ond bronde, Beow. 2322.
bēaga bryttan, Beow. 35, 352, 1487.
bearnum ond brōðrum, Beow. 1074.
beddum ond bolstrum, Beow. 1240.
beorn in burgum, Beow. 2433.
gebiden in burgum, Seaf. 28, Beow. 2452.
bill ond byrnan, Beow. 40 and 2621.
R. *blǣd in burgum,* Rid. 93, 6.
R. *blǣd ond blysse,* Rune 24.
R. *blisse in burgum,* Rid. 6, 6.
R. *blōd nē bān,* Rid. 37, 18.
bord ond byrnan, Beow. 2524.
bord to gebeorge, Mald. 131.
brād and brūnecg, Mald. 163, Beow. 1546.
brōgan on burgum, Rid. 1, 81.
būgan to bence, Beow. 327, 1013.
R. *burh ond bēagas,* Beow. 523.
R. *ceare cwīþan,* Wand. 9.
R. *clyppe ond cysse,* Wand. 42.
cyningas ne cāseras, Seaf. 82.
R. *cyning on corpre,* Beow. 1153.
of denum ond of dūnum, Rid. 25, 3.
drēamum (drēame) bedǣled, Beow. 721, 1275.
eafoð ond ellen, Beow. 602, 902, 2349.
eard ond eorlscipe, Beow. 1727.
earm ond eaxle, Beow. 835, 972, Rid. 30, 6, Rid. 84, 6.
eorl on eorðan, Mald. 233.
fǣge . . . feallan, Beow. 1755, Mald. 105, Brun. 12.
fǣge to gefeohte, Brun. 28.
fǣge ond geflȳmed, Beow. 846.
R. *fǣgne flǣschoman,* Beow. 1568.
fǣhðe ond fyrene, Beow. 137, 879, 2480. *fyrene ond fǣhðe,* Beow. 153.
fāh ond fǣted, Beow. 2701.
fāne gefyllan, Beow. 2655 : cp. *feond gefylde,* Beow. 2706.
faran ofer feldas, Rid. 30, 8.
faran on flotweg, Husb. 59.

---

[1] The Riddles are taken from *Die altenglischen Rätsel,* M. Trautmann, 1915.   The numbering of the other poems is the same as in any standard edition.   The meaning of the phrases is always so fixed and definite that it scarcely needs to be appended.

R.   *fēoll on foldan*, Beow. 2975.
R.   *æt fōtum fēoll*, Mald. 119.
fen ond fæsten, Beow. 104.
ferdon forð, Beow. 1632.
R.   *fēt ond folme*, Rid. 29, 7, Rid. 37, 10, Beow. 745.
Cp. **R.**   *þurh flānes flyht*, Mald. 71.
flōde ond foldan, Rid. 5, 9.
R.   *folc and foldan*, Mald. 54.
folc oþðe frēoburh, Beow. 693.
folces gefylled, Brun. 67.
R.   *folcum gefrǣge*, Beow. 55, Rid. 93, 3.
frēogan on ferhþe, Beow. 948.
frōd on forðweg, Beow. 2625.
frōfre ond fultum, Beow. 698, 1273.
fūs ond fǣge, Beow. 1241.
fūs and forðgeorn, Mald. 281.
Cp. **R.**   *fūs forðweges*, Rid. 28, 3.
afylled on foldan, Chron. 975, 8.
R.   *fēond gefylde*, Beow. 2706.
gamen ond glēodrēam, Beow. 3021.
gārum agēted, Brun. 18.
geatolic ond goldfāh, Beow. 308.
R.   *geond in geardum*, Beow. 13.
gidd ond glēo, Beow. 2105.
giest in geardum, Rid. 41, 2.
gold on geardum, Rid. 90, 4.
R.   *gierede mid golde*, Rid. 24, 13.   *golde gegyrede*, Beow. 553, 1028, Rid. 65,
    14.   *gold gearwade*, Rhyme Poem 36.   *golde gegirwan*, Wald. 39.
R.   *gīfre ond grǣdig*, Seaf. 62, Rid. 82, 31.
glād (glīdan) ofer grundas, Brun. 15.
golde on grunde, Beow. 2765.
R.   *goldwine gumena*, Beow. 1171, 1476, 1602.
R.   *gomban gyldan*, Beow. 11.
grim ond grǣdig, Beow. 121, 1499.
guman to gūþe, Mald. 94.
forgyteð ond forgȳmeð, Beow. 1751.
R.   *habban and healdan*, Mald. 236.
R.   *hæle hildedeor*, Beow. 1646, 1816, 3111.
R.   *hæleð on healle*, Mald. 214.
hæleð under heofenum, Beow. 52.   Cp. M.E. *haþel under heuen.*
hafalen hȳdan, Beow. 446.
R.   *hār hilderinc*, Mald. 169, Beow. 1307, 3136.
on hēafde helm, Beow. 2973 ; cp. Beow. 1030.
R.   *hēah hlifian*, Beow. 81, 2805.
R.   *heort oððe hinde*, Chron. 1086, 11.
honda ond hēafod, Wand. 43.
hord ond hāmas, Brun. 10.
hord ond hleoburh, Beow. 912.
þær wearð hrēam ahafen, Mald. 106.
hrēoh ond heorugrim, Beow. 1564.
hrēow on hreðre, Beow. 2328.

hringum hæfted, Rid. 2, 2.
on hyge hycge, Husb. 28.
hȳnðu ond hrāfyl, Beow. 277.
hyssas æt hilde, Mald. 123.
R. *īdel ond unnyt*, Beow. 413.
R. *innan ond ūtan*,[1] Beow. 774, etc.
R. *lācan on lyfte*, Rid. 57, 8.
lǣne on londe, Seaf. 65-6.
R. *lǣnan līfes*, Beow. 2845 ; *līf þis lǣne*, Chron. 975, 4.
lāð ond longsum, Beow. 134, 192.
hyre lōf lengede geond londa fela, Wids. 99.
R. *lēof nē lāð*, Beow. 511 ; *lēofes and lāðes*, Beow. 1061, 2910.
R. *lēoht ond līf*, Wids. 142.
R. *lēoman to lēohte*, Beow. 95 ; *lēohtan lēoman*, Rid. 38, 57.
leomum ond lēafum, Beow. 97.
līf forlǣtan, Mald. 208.
līf forlēosan, Wald. 10.
R. *land ond leode*, Chron. 1065, 25.
Cp. **R.** *lond ond lēodbyrig*, Beow. 2471.
R. *mǣgð ond mǣcgas*, Rid. 48, 7.
mēara ond māðma, Beow. 2166. *mēara ne māðma*, Husb. 62.
    R. *mēarum ond māðmum*, Beow. 1048, 1898.
mildust ond monþwǣrost, Beow. 3182.
mon on middangearde, Beow. 2996.
R. *man on moldan*, Chron. 975, 5.
ord ond ecg, Beow. 1549, Mald. 60.
ord ond īren, Mald. 253.
rēaf and hringas, Mald. 161.
recen and rǣdfæst, Wald. 58.
Cp. **R.** *receda under roderum*, Beow. 310.
rēoc ond rēþe, Beow. 122.
rodera Rǣdend, Chron. 975, 23.
R. *gesǣgd sōðlice*,[2] Beow. 141, 273, 2899. *secgan (tō) sōð(e)*, Beow. 51,
    590, 1049.
R. *secggende wæs lāðra spella*, Beow. 3028-9. *singan and secgan spell*,[3]
    Wids. 54. *spell gesecgan*, Rid. 2, 12.
sang ond swēg, Beow. 1063.
R. *sāres ond sorge*, Rune 23.
scuccum ond scinnum, Beow. 939.
secg on searwum, Beow. 249, 2530, 2700.
R. *secgum ond gesīþum*, Husb. 51.
R. *sinc ond symbel*, Beow. 2431. *sinc æt symle*, Beow. 81.
R. *sinc ond seolfre*, Rid. 18, 10, Rid. 65, 15, Ruin 36.
sinþecgo ond swyrdgifu, Beow. 2884.
R. *sīþas asettan*, Rid. 7, 11.
sīþas secgan, Seaf. 2.
R. *sorg ond slǣp*, Wand. 39.
sorh is me to secgan, Beow. 473.

[1] A common phrase throughout O.E. and M.E.
[2] Cp. O.N. *segir þu et sannasta*, etc.
[3] Cp. O.S. *singan endi seggean*.

strǣt (wæs stānfāh), stīg . . ., Beow. 320.

R. *swǣsra ond gesibbra*, Rid. 24, 22.

swǣse gesīðas, Beow. 29, 1934, 2040, 2518.

R. *sweordum aswefede*, Beow. 567, Brun. 30.

R. *swēotol ond gesyne*, Rid. 11, 4, Rid. 37, 3.

R. *synn ond sacu*,[1] Beow. 2472.

wǣfre ond wǣlfus, Beow. 2420.

wǣpen ond gewǣdu, Beow. 292.

wǣpna gewealdan, Beow. 1509, Mald. 168, 272.

wǣpnum geweorðad, Beow. 250.

wæter under wolcnum, Beow. 1631. **R.** *wan under wolcnum*, Beow. 651. *wēold under wolcnum*, Beow. 1770. **R.** *wēox under wolcnum*, Beow. 8. *wōd under wolcnum*, Beow. 714. *won to wolcnum*, Beow. 1374.

R. *weaxað ond wrīdað*, Beow. 1741.

wenian mid wynnum, Wand. 29.

R. *wer ond wīf*, Wids. 130, Beow. 993, Rid. 28. 6.

wicga ond wǣpna, Beow. 1045.

wigum ond wǣpnum, Beow. 2395. *wigan mid wǣpnum*, Mald. 126.

wigan to wīge, Mald. 235.

wigan on gewinne, Mald. 302.

wīg ond wīsdōm, Beow. 350.

R. *wintra on worulde*, Chron. 973, 19.

wīs ond gewittig, Beow. 3094.

wīs wordcwida, Beow. 1845.

wīsfæst wordum, Beow. 626.

wlanc under wǣdum, Rid. 40, 4.

wlonc bi wealle, Wand. 80.

wlonc ond wīngāl, Seaf. 29, Ruin 35.

R. *wlītig on wāge*, Rid. 15, 15 ; cp. Beow. 1662, *ic on wāge geseah wlītig hangian.*

R. *wlītig ond wynsum*, Rid. 82, 21, Chron. 975, 3.

R. *word ond worc* [2] (in various forms), Beow. 289, 1100, 1833.

R. *wordum wrixlan*, Beow. 366, 874, Husb. 10.

R. *wuldres waldend*, Beow. 17, 183.

R. *wulf on wealde*, 65.

R. *wyrceð his willan*, Rid. 61, 7.

yldo ne adle, Rid. 41, 4 ; cp. Beow. 1736, *ādl nē yldo.*

B. IN THE RELIGIOUS AND KINDRED VERSE.[3] [O.E.P. R.]

H. *ādl nē ȳldo*, Exeter Maxims I. 10.

bald in burgum, Elene 412. **H.** *blǣd in burgum*, Gen. 2583. **H.** *blis in burgum*, Crist 530. *blīþe in burgum*, Guth. 1914.

H. *bān ond blōd*, Guth. 351, The Last Judgment 40.

beald in brēostum, Phnx. 158. *bitre on brēostum*, Gen. 803. *blis in brēostum*, Guth. 927. *blīð on brēostum*, Gen. 656, 751, Saints' Calendar 98.

---

[1] Cp. O.S. *saca endi sundia.*

[2] Cp. O.S. *mid uuordun endi mid uuercun.*

[3] The numbering of the poems in the Junius MS. and in the Vercelli Codex is taken from the collective edition by G. P. Krapp, Columbia, 1931-2.

beald byrnwiggende, Jud. 17.
bēam on bearwe, Gen. 902.
beorht on blædum, Dan. 499.
beorhte blīcan, Andr. 789, Crist 701, Gen. 811, Phnx. 599.
beorht ond blīpe, Crist 877.
bīdan in bendum, Crist and Satan 49, Crist 147.
ic bidde eow bēnum, Be Domes Dæge 33.   *he his bēna bebēad,* Be Domes
   Dæge 60.
bisceopas ond bōceras, Andr. 607.
bitres (in ðæs) beala, Crist and Satan 273.
H. *blǣdes ond blissa,* Crist 1256, Guth. 1348.   *mid bledum and mid blisse,*
   Rood 149.   *blǣd mid blissum,* Crist 1346.
blǣdum blōwan, Ways of Creation 34.
blāwað bȳman, Crist 881-2.   *ne bȳman ablāwep,* Be Domes Dæge 110.
   beman blawan Crist and Satan 601.
blōde gebohtest, Hymn 26.
blostum geblōwen, Phnx. 21.
bodiað ond brēmað, Crist 483.
pine bodu brǣcon, Paternoster 109.
bogan bendeð, Ps. lvii, 6.
bord for brēostum, Jud. 192.
borda gebrec, Elene 114.
brēostum onbryrded, Phnx. 550.
brēost mine bēate (I beat my breast), Be Domes Dæge 30.
bringeð blisse, Crist 68.
brūcan blīðnesse, Be Domes Dæge 304.
burga ne bōlda, Crist and Satan 139.
H. *burh ond bēagas,* Exod. 557.
H. *ceare cwīpan,* Crist 1285, Guth. 194.
cempan in ceastre, Dan. 706.
cēne and craftig, Boet. x, 51.
clǣne ond cræftig, Gloria 16, 53.
cleopað ond cīgað, Gen. 1013.
clypiað . . . cwepað, Paternoster 12.
H. *cyningas on corðre,* Exod. 191, 466.
cyninga cyningc, Oratio Poetica 19.
H. *cyston hie ond clypton,* Andr. 1016.
dǣda dēmend, Ways of Creation 36, Jul. 725.
dǣdbōte dō, Be Domes Dæge 85.
dēaðe gedǣlan, Andr. 955, 1217, Guth. 343.
gedēmed to dēaðe, Jud. 196, Guth. 521.
todǣleð and todēmeð, Be Domes Dæge 20.
dalum gedǣled, Guth. 25, Bad Character 22.
dēme . . . dōmas, Ps. lxxxi, 1 and 2, cxviii, 154.
nē dene nē dalu, Phnx. 24.
on þæt dēope dæl,[1] Crist 1532.   *on pā dēopan dala,* Gen. 305, 421.
dimme ond deorce, Crist and Satan 104, 453.   *deorc ond dimhiw,* Be Domes
   Dæge 106.
drēames ond drihtscipes, Gen. 485.

[1] Cp. O.N. *i djúpa dala* ; O.S. *an ênum diapun dala.*

drēogan dēað, Guth. 607.
drihtna drihten, Gen. 638, Crist 405, Andr. 874, 1151.
drihtnes dōmas, Crist and Satan 505, 553, Dan. 32, 744, Gen. 2571, 2581, Crist 1021.
drincendra drēam, Fates of Man 79.
druncon ond drȳmdon, Gen. 2781.
dugoða dēmend, Andr. 87, 1189.
duguða Dryhten, Elene 81, Crist 782, Andr. 698.
dumb ond dēaf, Jul. 150, The Lost Soul to the Body 65.
dyrne ond dēgol, Crist 640, The Ways of Creation 62 ; cf. Beow. 1357.
ēadge mid englum, Phnx. 677.
eard ond epel, Dan. 611, 637, Fates of the Apostles 113, Gen. 962, Phnx. 158, Christian Life 59, 62, Boet. xxiv, 50.
earm ond ēadig, Be Domes Dæge 162.
ēce mid englum, Andr. 1722.
englum ond ældum, Crist 582.
fācen ond fyrene, Gen. 1941.
fæges feorhhord, Andr. 1182, Phnx. 221.   **H.**   *fæges flæschoman*, Andr. 154, Guth. 1004.   *fægra flæschaman*, Andr. 1085.
fægere on foldan, Gen. 1487, Saints' Calendar 143.
fæger ond frēolic, Gen. 1722.
fægre gefrætewod, Crist and Satan 307, Phnx. 585, Be Domes Dæge 275.
fægrum frætwum, Phnx. 610.
fæst under foldan, Exod. 537.
fāh ond frēondlēas, Elene 924.
H.   *feallan to* (or *on*) *foldan*, Rood 43, Crist and Satan 531, 543, Jud. 280, Phnx. 74, Andr. 918, The Fates of Men 26.
Cp. **H.**   *fēollan on foldan, ond tō fōtum*, Crist and Satan 531.
H.   *fēt ond folme*, Elene 1065, Crist 1456.
on flōd faran, Gen. 832.
færeð æfter foldan, Crist 983.
nē feax nē fel, Jul. 591.
feoh ond frætwa, Gen. 2130.
feoh on foldan, Crist 807.
H.   *fēondas gefyllan*, Rood 38.   *hiora fȳnd fylde*, Ps. lxxx, 13.   *fylde fēond*, Gen. 2071-2.
fēondrǣs gefremede, Gen. 900.
firena fremman, Gen. 19, A Father's Advice 17.
fīrum gefrǣge, Phnx. 3.
fiscas and fuglas, Azar 140.   *ne fuȝel ne fisc*, Sal. and Sat. 420.   *fugel oppe fisc*, The Lost Soul to the Body 79.
flǣsce befangen, Phnx. 535, The Lost Soul to the Body 34, Guth. 967, A Bad Character 48.
Cp. **H.**   *flēogan flāna* [1] *scūras*, Jud. 221.
flēogan ofer foldan, Crist and Satan 263.
H.   *folc ond foldan*, Crist and Satan 685.
folce to frōfre, Elene 502, Exod. 88.   *folcum to frōfre*, Andr. 606, Crist 1421, Elene 1142, Saints' Calendar 228.   *fuglum to frōfre*, Jud. 297.

---

[1] Cp. O.N. *fljúganda fleini*.

H. *folcum gefrǣge,* Guth. 792.
forht on ferðe, Crist 924, Jul. 328, Phnx. 504.
forð faran, Gen. 543.
fōron to gefeohte, Jud. 202.
fōtum afyllan, Guth. 256.
frecne ond ferðgrim, Jul. 141, The Whale 5.
frecne on ferhðe, Gen. 870.
frōd on ferhþe, Elene 463, 1163, Exod. 355.
gefrēode ond gefreopade, Crist 588, Jul. 565.
frēonde nē fēonde, Boet. xxv, 16.
friðes ond fultomes, Fates of the Apostles 91.
frōfre findan, Crist 801.
gefrugnen mid folcum, Crist 225.
fyrd wæs gefȳsed, Exod. 54.
fȳsan to gefeohte, Jud. 189.
Cp. **H.** *fūs on forðweg,* Exod. 129, Guth. 773, 918, Saints' Calendar 218.
fūs on forðsīþ, Guth. 1121 ; cp. *afȳsed on forðsīþ,* Guth. 911, *afȳsed on forðwege,* Rood 125.
fyll ond feorhcwealm, Gen. 1103.
H. *gīfre ond grǣdige,* Crist and Satan 191, Phnx. 507, The Lost Soul to the Body 74. *grǣdige ond gīfre,* Crist and Satan 32, Gen, 793.
H. *giong in geardum,* Phnx 355, 647, Crist 201.
goldes ond gimma, Boet. xiv. 3, Gifts of men 59. *golde geglenged, gimmes lixtan,* Elene 90. *golde geglengde ond gimcynnum,* Boet. xv. 4. *gegyred mid golde, gimmas hæfden,* Rood 16. *golde gegerede ond gimcynnum,* Boet. xxv, 6. *æfter golde and æfter gimcynnum,* Boet. viii, 57. *golde beweorcean and gimcynnum,* Elene 1023.
H. *goldwine gumena,* Elene 201, Jud. 22.
H. *gomban gieldan,* Gen. 1978.
begoten mid golde, Rood 7.
in gramra gripe, Andr. 951.
grennade ond grīstbitade, Jul. 596.
grim and gealgmōd, Dan. 229.
grimme grundas, Crist and Satan 258, Gen. 408, Crist 1527.
H. *gyredon mid golde,* Rood 16, 77. *golde gegerede,* Boet. xxv, 6.
H. *habban ne healdan,* Dan. 198.
hālig under heofenum, Elene 975. *hrēoh under heofenum,* Phnx. 58. *hālig ond heofonbeorht,* Dan. 340. *hālig ond heofonlic,* Elene 739. *hālig of heofonum,* Dan. 533, Guth. 657, 1257.
H. *hār hilderinc,* Christian Life 56.
hāt ond heorugrim, Crist 1524, Guth. 952.
H. *hæle hildedeor,* Andr. 1002, Elene 935.
H. *hæleð in healle,* Dan. 728.
hæleða helpend, Dan. 402.
hæleð under helmum, Jud. 202.
H. *hēa hlifiað,* Phnx. 32.
hēah ond hālig, Crist 378.
hēah to heofonum, Phnx. 521, Exod. 493, Gen. 97, Ps. lxxvii, 25. *hēah ofer heofonum,* Phnx. 641.
hēah heofoncyning, Gen. 463. *heofona hēahcyning,* Gen. 50, 1025, 2165, Crist 150, 1339, Andr. 6, Dan. 407, 625, The Creed 51, The Paternoster ii, 15, etc.

hēah ofer hrōfas, Phnx. 590.
heard ond heorogrim, Crist 1613.
heard ond hetegrim, Andr. 1395, 1562.
helle ond hinsīð, Gen. 718, 721.
helpe and hǣlo, Guth. 862.
helpend ond hǣlend, Jul. 157.
heofon ond hel, Crist 1591.
heofona hlāford, Rood 45.
H. *heortas ond hinda,* Boet. xix, 17.
hergas on helle, Exod. 46.
hlǣwas nē hlincas, Phnx. 25.
hlifian under heofenum, Rood 85.
hlifiað ofer hēafde, Phnx. 604.
hlūde for hergum, Elene 110, 406.
hlūde hliehhan, Gen. 73.
biholene and behȳdde, Phnx. 170. Cp. M.E. *hele and hide.*
āhōn ond āhebban, Jul. 228.
horsc ond hreðerglēaw, Exod. 13.
hūs under hrōfe, Crist 14.
hwīt ond heofonbeorht, Crist 1019.
hwīt ond hīwbeorht, Crist 1018, Elene 73, Gen. 266.
H. *īdel ond unnyt,* Gen. 106.
H. *innan ond ūtan,* Gen. 1322, Phnx. 301, etc.
H. *lācan on lyfte,* Fates of Men 23, Gen. 448, Phnx. 316.
ālǣded of līce, Jul. 670.
H. *lǣne līf,* Exod. 268, Phnx. 481, Ps. lxii, 3.
lǣne under lyfte, Elene 1270, Guth. 91.
H. *land ond lēode,*[1] Andr. 1321.
H. *land ond lēodweard,* Exod. 57, Gen. 1180, 1196.
lēof lēodfruma, Exod. 354.   *lēofes lēodfruma,* Gen. 1246.
līfes lēohtfruma(n), Andr. 1413, Boet. xi, 72, Dan. 408, Gen. 175, 926,
   1410, 1792, 2423, Guth. 565, 581.
H. *lēofum gē lāðum,* Crist 846.
H. *lēohtes lēoma,* Guth. 631, Phnx. 116.   *lēoht(n)e lēoman,* Azar. 78,
   Boet. v, 5, Crist and Satan 467, Jud. 191.
H. *lēoht ond līf,* Exod. 546.
lēoðcræft onlēac, Elene 1250.
libban on þys/þam lande,[2] Gen. 805, 878, 1940.
līc ond leomu, Guth. 1149.
nē līc nē leoþu, Jul. 592.
līf alifde, Be Domes Dæge 63.
lifian in lisse, Phnx. 672.
līfes ne lissa, Guth. 806.
lisse on lande, Gen. 1486.
lufan ond lisse, Boet. i, 59, Dan. 339, Gen. 2332.   *lufum ond lissum,* Gen.
   1949, 2737.   *lufena ond lissa,* Guth. 1049.
lufsum ond līðe, Crist 914.
līðe ond lōfsum, Gen. 468.
mægn ond mōdcræft, Elene 408.

---

[1] Cp. O.H.G. *liut unde lant ;* O.S. *ia land ia liudi.*
[2] Cp. O.S. *libbean an thesum landa.*

mægen ond mildse, Gloria 3.
H. *māgðum ond mæcgum*, Gen. 1123, Guth. 833.
māre ond mōdig, Dan. 105.
mærðum ond mihtum, Elene 15. *miht ond mærðo*, Fates of the Apostles 7.
mæst ond mærost, Dan. 692, Exod. 395.
mæton mīlpaðas, Exod. 171, Elene 1262.
H. *man on moldan*, Andr. 594, 1484, Dan. 566, Gifts of Men 9, Guth. 962, Phnx. 496. *men ofer moldan*, Boet. xx, 281, Guth. 1203, Rood 12, 82. *monnes ofer moldan*, Crist 421.
mān ond morður, Boet. ix, 7, Crist and Satan 320.
H. *mēarum ond māpmum*, Exeter Maxims ii, 88.
metod mancynnes, Andr. 69, 172, 357, 446, Crist and Satan 64, 457, 513, 667, Gen. 459, 1947, 2923.
meotudes mihte, Andr. 658, 694, Crist and Satan 164, 352, Dan. 537, 647.
metodes miltse, Dan. 334.
micel ond māre, Fates of the Apostles 121. *micelne ond mārne*, Jul. 26.
micel ond mihtig, Gen. 605.
miht ond mund, Paternoster 48.
mihtig on mōde, Gen. 342, 559.
milde on mōde, Gen. 2757. *milde mode*, Guth. 711.
mildse ond mihta, Paternoster 77.
milde mōdsefan, Jul. 235.
mōde and mægne, Boet. iv, 27, Guth. 1059, Ps. lxx, 8.
mōd ond mihte, Dan. 14.
in mōde and in mūpe, A Father's Advice 35, Ps. lxx, 7.
mōdig ond mægenrōf, Exod. 275.
muntas ond mōras, Sal. and Sat. 340. *nē munt nē mōr*, Sal. and Sat. 422.
murnan on mōde, Exod. 536, Gen. 735, Jud. 154. *murnende mōd*, Andr. 1667.
from orde oð ende, Elene 590. *ord ande ende*,[1] Dan. 162. Cp. *oor & ende*, Andr. 647 (quoted by Onions).
Cf. **H.** *ræd under roderum*, Elene 918. *rēc under roderum*, Elene 803. *rēde under roderum*, Elene 1234. *reorde under roderum*, Gen. 1344. *rīce under roderum*, Elene 13, 147, 631, Dan. 639. *rincas under roderum*, Elene 46. *rūme under roderum*, Gen. 1243, Phnx. 14.
āreccan mid ryhte, Crist 222.
reste on recede, Gen. 1584.
(dōmas synd) rihte ond rūme, Paternoster 15.
rōd (wæs) arēred, Andr. 967, Crist 1064–5, Elene 887.
H. *rodera rædend*, Andr. 627, 816.
rodera rīce, Phnx. 664.
rodera ryhtend, Crist 798.
sæce ond sorge, Elene 1030.
H. *sār ond sorge*, Gen. 75, Guth. 1063.
mid sorgum ond mid sargung, Be Domes Dæge 245.
sārum geswenced, Guth. 1110.
gesæt pa tō symble, Dan. 700. *sittap æt symble*, Bad Character 15.
sāwul on sīðfæt, Jul. 700.
scand ond sceamu, Ps. lxx, 12.

---

[1] See *ord and ende*, C. T. Onions, M.L.R. 24, p. 389, and *word and ende* in Leeds Studies in English, II, p. 66, E. S. Olszewska.

scerp ond scūrheard, Andr. 1133.
scīr and scȳne, Phnx. 308.
secgan oððe singan, Boet. ii, 17. **H.** *singan ond secgan*, Crist 667.
singe sōðlīce ond secge ēac, Ps. ciii, 31.
sægde him tō sorge, Guth. 447.
H. *secgan tō sōðe*, Gen. 570, etc. *sōðlīce secgan*, Elene 317, etc. (of very
    frequent occurence in O.E. poetry and in various forms).
sægde him unlȳtel spell, Gen. 2405. *on spellum sægdon sōðlīce*, Ps. cxviii,
    85.
H. *secgas and gesīðas*, Jud. 201, Gen. 2067.
sēoc ond sorhful, Crist and Satan 274.
H. *sinc ond seolfre*, Dan. 60.
singað and swinsað, Phnx. 140, Crist 884. *swinsað and singeð*, Phnx. 124.
sittað sorgende, Crist 26.
H. *sīð asettan*, Fates of the Apostles 111.
snel and swift, Phnx. 317.
snotor ond sōðfæst, Dan. 736.
song on swegle, Crist and Satan 45, 142.
H. *sorg nē slǣp*, Phnx. 56.
stīð ond stæðfæst, Crist 980.
H. *stōp on strǣte, stīg wīsode*, Andr. 985.
strang ond stīðmod, Crist and Satan 246, Rood 40 ; cp. Ps. lx, 2, cxvii, 14.
H. *swǣsum ond gesibbum*, Gen. 1612.
sweart ond gesworcen, Be Domes Dæge 105.
swefan on slǣpe, Andr. 849.
sweord ond sceld, Ps. lxxv, 3.
H. *sweordum aswebban*, Andr. 72.
H. *swēotul and gesȳne*, Saints' Calendar 129, Gen. 2806, Gloria 50.
swiðmōd in sefan, Dan. 605.
H. *synn ne sacu*, Phnx. 54.
in synna sēað, Jul. 413.
synnum gesargod, The Lost Soul's Address 67.
tēamum ond tūdre, Gen. 1535. *tȳdran ond tȳman*, The Ways of Creation 48,
    Boet. xiii, 39. *tȳmað ond tīedrað*, Gen. 1512.
torht ofer tunglas, Crist 107. *torht mid tunglum*, Crist 235, 969.
tregan ond tēonan, Gen. 2274.
þafað in geþylde, The Gifts of Men 71.
þēnað ond þīowað, Boet. xxix, 77.
geþēon on þēode, Crist 377.
þegne on þēode, Guth. 1204, Bad Character 79.
þolian ond þafian, Jul. 466.
þrēatum and þrymmum, Jud. 164.
geþungen on þēode, Phnx. 160.
wǣdum geweorðode, Rood 15.
wǣpen æt wigge, Elene 1188.
waldend ond wyrhta, Boet. xxx, 14.
Cf. **H.** *wand ofer wolcnum*, Exod. 80. **H.** *wann under wolcnum*, Rood 55,
    Andr. 837, Guth. 1254. **H.** *weaxan under wolcnum*, Gen. 1702 (see
    under *wintra*).
wēan ond wītu, Crist and Satan 184, 335, 713.
weard ond wīsa, Gen. 1157, Dan. 565.

H. *weaxað and wrīdað,* Gen. 1532.

welan ond wāwan, Gen. 466.

gewended to wuldre, Elene 1047.

weoroda waldend, Crist and Satan 187, 251, 563, Elene 751, 1084, Dan. 331, Andr. 388, Crist 1569, Guth. 566.

weoroda wuldorcyning, Dan. 308, Gen. 2, Exod. 548, Crist 161, Boet. xx, 162.

weoroda wuldorgyfa, The Creed 48.

H. *wuldres waldend,*[1] Andr. 193, 539, Crist and Satan 24, Dan. 13.

geweorðod in wuldre, Elene 822. *wuldre geweorðad,* Phnx. 551.

H. *wer ond (oððe) wīf,* Boet. xvii, 4, Christ 101, Domesday 60, Elene 236, 508, 1221, Exeter Maxims 24, Fates of Men, 2, Gen. 1574, 1738, Phnx. 394, Saints' Calendar 186.

wīf . . . wer, Paternoster 87.

weras on wonge, Gen. 1882.

werede mid wǣdum, The Lost Soul's Address 127.

wesan on worulde,[2] Gen. 470 (see *wurde on worulde*).

wīc weardiað, Jul. 92, Phnx. 448, The Whale 26.

wīdle and womme, Jud. 59.

wīf ond wǣpned, Gen. 195, 2745.

wigena weard, Elene 153.

wind ond wolcna, Gloria 7.

wind under wolenium, Boet. vi, 9, vii, 26.

windig ond wynsum, Dan. 346.

windas ond wǣges, Andr. 456.

H. *wintra on worulde,* Gen. 1231.

wintra under wolcnum, Gen. 1231. *gewītaþ under wolcnum,* Elene 1273. *geworden under wolcnum,* Crist 226. *woruld under wolcnum,* Boet. xx, 57, Gen. 916.

wīs on gewitte, Andr. 470, Gifts of Men 13.

wīs on wordum, Christian Life 4.

wīs ond wordglēaw, Dan. 417.

wlītan in wuldre, Crist and Satan 407. *wlītige in wuldre,* Phnx. 598. *wlīte ond wuldre,* Gen. 36.

wlītig ond wuldorfæst, Dan. 285.

wlītig on wæstmum, Gifts of Men 35. *wlīte ond wæstma,* Gen. 613, Phnx. 332.

H. *wlītig of wāge,* Andr. 732.

H. *wlītig and wynsum,* Crist and Satan 213, The Panther 65, Phnx. 203, 318.

wommum awyrged, Exod. 532, Crist 1561.

wonn and wēste, Gen. 110.

wōp ond wānung, Be Domes Dæge, 201.

wōp ne wracu, Phnx. 51.

H. *word ond weorc* (in various forms), Crist 917, 1236, Crist and Satan 48, 222, Guth. 553, 692, 765, Phnx. 659, The Whale 85.

word awurpan, Elene 770. *wordum toweorpað,* Andr. 65, 191.

word ond wīsdōm, Andr. 65, 569, 1678, Guth. 1104, Phnx. 334.

wordum wīs, Andr. 919 (see under *wis*). Cp. **H.** *wordum wīsfæstum,* A Father's Advice 3.

---

[1] Also in O.S. [2] *Ibid.*

wordcræftes wīs, Elene 592.
word ond gewitt,[1] Gloria, 56.
wordcwide wrītan, Crist 673. *wordum wrītan,* Andr. 13.
wordum sæcgað ond writu cȳpað, Phnx. 425.
H. *wordum wrixlian,* The Lost Soul's Address 115, Bad Character 16.
worhton on worulde, Dan. 296.
wrīdað on wynnum, Phnx. 237.
wuldor ond willa, Paternoster 59.
wuldor ond wurððmynt, Be Domes Dæge 269.
wuldre ond wynne, Crist and Satan 174.
wuldre geweorðed, Phnx. 551.
wuldre gewlītegad, Andr. 543, 69, Azar. 187.
wuldre biwunden, Phnx. 666.
H. *wulf on wealde,* Elene 28.
wuniað and weardiað, Phnx. 172.
wunian in wynnum (in various forms), Crist 622, Crist and Satan 235, 506,
    554, 592. *wunian in wicum,* Gen. 1812, 1890. *wunian in wōcum,*
    Bad Character 46. *wunian in wonge,* Phnx. 363. *wunian in worulde,*
    Crist, 588. *wunian in wuldre,* Crist 347, Dan. 366, Phnx. 386, Rood
    135, 143, 155.
wunian wic, Andr. 1310.
wunde ond wīte, Crist 1207.
gewundod mid wommum, Crist and Satan 156.
wurde on worulde, Gen. 504, 551, Guth. 636. *in worlde geweard,* Crist 40,
    etc.
gewurde on woruldrīce, Exod. 356. *geweorðan on woruldrīce,* Elene 456.
    in woruldrīce weorðan, Elene 1048.
wynnum geweaxen, Phnx. 313.
H. *wyrcean (his) willan,* Gen. 250, Paternoster 17, 81, etc.
wyscað and wēnap, Guth. 47.
yrmpu ne yldo, Phnx. 614. *yldu ne yrmðu,* Phnx. 52.
yrre ond egesful, Exod. 506, Crist, 1528.

THE ALLITERATIVE PHRASES IN OLD ENGLISH PROSE.

In a study of origins it is essential to know whether alliterative phrases are found to any great extent in Old English prose, as well as in the poetry. Accordingly, it seemed especially desirable to collect the phrases from the homiletic prose works, for it is here that we have the most obvious point of contact between Old and Middle English literature. Again, a cursory examination of the Alfredian prose works and of the Anglo-Saxon Chronicle revealed a wealth of alliterative phraseology, and it became apparent that from these sources some evidence might be gleaned concerning the use of stock alliterative phrases in non-homiletic prose and possibly also in daily conversation. Lastly, the wills and laws in Old English were found to be rich in alliterative phraseology, mainly of a dis-

---

[1] Cp. O.S. *so manag uuislik uuord endi giuuit mikil,* Heliand 28.

tinctive type. Hence, there emerge three groups of phrases, each representative of a different tradition ; consequently the bulk of Old English prose comes within our survey.

In the homiletic prose there are 193 phrases, of which over one-fourth occur also in Old English poetry, and concerning which some conclusions have already been drawn. Many of the phrases are essentially religious in association, as for example *gebedum and bletsungum, gewat of worulde,* and *woþ and wanung,* but this does not apply to the majority of the phrases, which are mere everyday expressions, such as *eagan . . . earan, ord and ende, standan stille, wær and wise.*

There are seventy-four cases of pairs of nouns, such as *gebedum and bletsungum,* twenty-two pairs of adjectives, such as *wær and wise,* and twenty-seven pairs of verbs, such as *gewealdan and gewissian, weaxan and wanian.* The majority of the remaining phrases consist of a combination of a noun and verb, such as *forgyfan gyltas, geseon þa gesihþe,* or *weorc to wyrcean.* This last type of phrase, always much more common in prose than in poetry, is naturally of more frequent occurrence in the homiletic prose than in the Old English poetry which we have previously considered. A more important fact, however, is that here we are able to gain some idea of the extent to which alliteration was used in everyday language.

It will be sufficient at this stage to say that the ' homiletic ' phrases survive in considerable numbers in Middle English. These not merely include many everyday expressions which would survive as a matter of course, but also several purely ' homiletic ' phrases, as for example *wurrþshiþe and wullderr,* of so frequent occurrence in *The Ormulum.* A glance at the phrases in the various Middle English sections which are marked *O.E.Pr.* will afford the reader numerous examples. It is interesting to observe that fifty-eight of the 193 ' homiletic ' phrases appear in the early Middle English alliterative prose and minor poetic fragments, and twenty-two in *The Ormulum;* even in the alliterative and non-alliterative romances and satires of a much later period many of the phrases still survive.

In the Alfredian prose there are 420 alliterative phrases, of which about one-eighth occur also in Old English poetry, the proportion being only half as great as in the homiletic prose. The difference is, however, intelligible, for in all probability the majority of the Alfredian phrases were current in everyday language. In support of this we may note that 150 of the phrases consist of a combination of noun and verb, as for example *lif alibban, hauen on hand, sunne scineð,* expressions illustrative of everyday speech rather than of an artificial prose style. There are seventy-four instances of parallel verbs, such as *gleowian and gieddian, habban and healdan,* a type already found both in Old English poetry and in the homiletic prose. Similarly, there are 111 instances of pairs of nouns in apposition, thirty-eight of adjectives and six of adverbs. It is not possible to determine in what proportion of cases these are mere rhetorical expressions—so common in the Alfredian writers both in an alliterative and in a non-alliterative form [1]—yet in many phrases, such as *seocan and sweltenden,* there is no doubt that the writer intended to convey two separate ideas, whereas in the case of the pairs of verbs, a rhetorical repetition seems to be the rule, e.g. *toseðan and tosceadan.*

Concerning the survival of these Alfredian phrases in Middle English, little need be said at this stage ; the statistics in the table clearly indicate that from the early Middle English homilies until Chaucer numerous representatives survive, testifying to the continuity in alliterative phraseology, especially regarding everyday alliterative expressions.

The number of alliterative phrases found in the ' legal ' Old English prose is 137, and the majority of these are entirely confined to this type of literature, if so it may be called. The reader will observe that most of the phrases have no meaning apart from their legal associations, e.g. *borh oþþe bote, wer oþþe wite,* etc. ; nevertheless, the collection as a whole is interesting for its own sake. The small number of phrases which it has in common with other types of Old English prose and poetry and with Middle English generally is due to the use of certain of the usual everyday alliterative expressions which are of little significance ; the ' legal ' phrases remain isolated. One fact is especially worthy of mention : *seel and sibb,* the phrase which occurs alone in the Lindisfarne Gospels in Old English, reappears in Laȝamon's *Brut,* 15154, *sibbe and sæle,* the only other occurrence of the phrase in English.

THE ALLITERATIVE PHRASES IN CERTAIN OLD ENGLISH HOMILETIC PROSE WORKS. [O.E.PR. HOM.]

In this section are gathered together the alliterative phrases found in the Old English homiletic prose works, the writers of which employed much alliteration, involving the use of many stock alliterative phrases. Some of these are also to be found in the poetry, but many others are peculiar to this type of work. The

---

[1] E.g. *alysan and gefreoðian.*

study of these phrases is of considerable importance in tracing the origin of the diction of some of the Middle English poems with which we shall be concerned later. The works from which the following phrases have been extracted are : *The Catholic Homilies of Aelfric*, in two series, edited by B. Thorpe, London, 1844–6 (Abr. *A.H.* 1 and 2—ref. by page and line) ; *Aelfric's Lives of the Saints*, edited by W. Skeat, E.E.T.S. 76, 82, 94, 114—1881–1900 (Abr. *A.L.S.*—ref. by number and line) ; *The Blickling Homilies*, edited by R. Morris, E.E.T.S. 58, 63—1874-7 (Abr. *Blk.*—ref. by page and line) ; *The Homilies of Wulfstan*, edited by A. S. Napier, Berlin, 1883 (Abr. *Wulf.*—ref. by page and line). Phrases found also in Old English poetry are marked *O.E.P.*, and those found also in the Alfredian and ' legal ' prose—*Alf.* and *Leg.* respectively.

anda and yrre, A.L.S. xvii, 25.
Alf. *gebedum and bletsungum*, A.H. 1, 44.17.
benda (sb.) *bite*, Wulf. 209.17.
his bendas toburston, A.H. 2, 358.3, 9, 20, 25.
his bendas tobræce, A.H. 2, 358.11.
O.E.P., Alf. *þas bene ic bidde*, A.L.S. xxxiv, 91.
bersta and bismra, Wulf. 128.3, 157.1.
Leg. *bewarian and bewerian*, Wulf. 191.15.
Hom., Leg. *bidde and beode*, (*bided and beodað*), Wulf. 39.12, etc. (frequently).
bifian and blacian, A.H. 1, 414.11–12.
O.E.P. *blawende byman*, A.H. 1, 312.12. *byman bleowan*, A.H. 2, 196.24.
O.E.P. *blod, ban*, A.H. 1, 236.16. *buton blode and bane*, A.H. 2, 270.22.
  mid blode and mid banum, A.H. 2, 270.19.
O.E.P. *mid. his blode gebohte*, A.H. 1, 374.4.
his bebod tobræce, A.H. 1, 18.12. *bebod tobrecan*, A.H. 1, 18.29, etc.
O.E.P. *gebringað to blisse*, Wulf. 249.27.
bryne oððon blodgyte, Wulf. 170.1, etc. (frequently).
bylde and blysse, A.H. 1, 506.8.
O.E.P., Alf. *caseras and cyningas*, A.H. 1, 576.29, Wulf. 148.28, 263.15.
ciegdon and cwædon, Blk. 245.32, etc.
þæt cild beo acenned, A.H. 1, 202.7, etc.
O.E.P., Alf. *cleopian and ciegan*, Blk. 139.16.
O.E.P., Alf. *clypian and cwepan*, A.H. 1, 50.18, etc., A.H. 2, 38.17, etc., A.L.S. vii, 203, etc., Blk. 147.33, etc., Wulf. 141.4.
O.E.P., Alf. *clypte and cyste* (or *cyste and clypte*), A.L.S. xxx, 272, 336, 381.
on anum cwearterne beclysede, A.H. 1, 402.33.
O.E.P. *cyninga cyning*, A.H. 1, 8.22, etc.
cyðan on his cyððe, A.L.S. xxv, 792.
dæde dydest, A.H. 2, 62.7.
deafe and dumbe, A.L.S. xxi, 190, Wulf. 22.16, 99.3. **O.E.P., Leg.** *dumbe and deafe*, A.H. 1, 292.12, A.H. 2, 436.9. *dumbum . . . deafum*, A.H. 1, 26.12–13.
to deaðe gedydon, A.H. 1, 300.13.

O.E.P., Alf., Leg. *hie demaþ heora domas,* Blk. 63.18.   *mid deoflum and dracum,* Wulf. 241.11.
dimne and deopne, Wulf. 48.2.
dreccan oððe derian, A.H. 1, 272.10–11.
Alf. *drincan drenc,* A.H. 1, 352.6.
Alf. *eagan . . . earan,*[1] A.H. 1, 366.26–7.
O.E.P., Alf. *earmum and eadigum,* A.L.S. xvii, 252, A.H. 1, 64.34.
O.E.P. *his epel and his eard,* A.L.S. xxxi, 146.
Alf. *feallan on gefeohte,* A.L.S. xxvi, 200, 209, xxxii, 66.
O.E.P. *feallan to foldan,* A.H. 2, 508.27.
O.E.P., Alf. *feallan to fotum,* A.H. 1, 62.18, etc., A.H. 2, 152.10, etc., A.L.S. iii, 138, etc.
befeallan on þæt (ece) fyr, A.H. 1, 12.4.
O.E.P. *fell, fex,* A.H. 1, 236.16.
feondræden and geflit, A.L.S. xvii, 25.
Alf. *ferde mid fyrde,* A.L.S. xxv, 601.
Leg. *fett* (from ' fedan ') *and gefrefrað,* A.H. 1, 270.10.
fisceras . . . gefixiað, A.H. 1, 576.25.
O.E.P., Alf. *fixas and fugelas,* A.H. 2, 206.28, 578.6.
O.E.P. *flæsce befangen,* A.H. 1, 36.34, 40.19.
gefrefrige ðe and fultumige, A.H. 1, 560.25 ; cp. **O.E.P.** *frófor ond fultum.*
O.E.P., Alf. *freond . . . feond,* A.H. 1, 522.12.
O.E.P., Alf. *frofer and fultum,* A.H. 2, 22.24.   *frofre and fultum,* A.L.S. xxxi, 1081, Blk. 201.28.   **Alf.** *fultum and frofre,* A.H. 1, 14.19, 196.32, Blk. 203.21 and 26.
fugel ne flyhð, A.H. 1, 464.24.   *fugela eft fleogende,* A.H. 2, 144.24.   **Alf.** *fleogendan fugelas,* A.H. 2, 462.24.
his gast ageaf, A.H. 1, 76.12.   **Alf.** *ageafon heora gastas,* A.L.S. xi, 255.
agifan and agildan, Blk. 55.4.
forgyfan gyltas, A.H. 1, 54.35, etc.   *forgif ure gyltas,* A.H. 2, 596.4.
mid gyfernysse and mid . . . gitsunge, A.H. 1, 176.14–15.   **Leg.** *gitsung and gifernes,* Wulf. 40.9, etc.
þa gifran and þa geornan, Wulf. 190.24.
godas and gydena, A.H. 1, 426.7.
Alf., Leg. *godes gife,* A.H. 1, 2.16, etc.
O.E.P., Alf. *gold and gymmas,* A.L.S. xxvii, 81.   *mid golde . . . mid gymmum,* A.H. 1, 458, 28–9.
Alf. *þæt gold and þa gymstanas,* A.H. 1, 68.21.
Alf. *gold . . . godweb,* A.L.S. xxv, 359.
O.E.P., Alf. *habban and healdan,* Blk. 55.6, etc., Wulf. 47.15, etc.
to hæle and to helpe, Blk. 105.30, Wulf. 252.6.
hatian and hynan, Wulf. 266.29.
Alf. *min heafod ahyldan,* A.L.S. xvi, 159.
here and hungor, Wulf. 129.1, etc. (frequently).
horsum or hundum, A.L.S. xvii, 90.
hundas . . . haran, A.L.S. xxxi, 1057.
huntan . . . huntiað, A.H. 1, 576.25.
Alf. *hynan and hergian,* A.L.S. xi, 353.
gehyrsumian his hæse, A.L.S. xxxi, 1045.

[1] Cp. O.N. *eyrom hlýðir, en augum skóðar.*

idel and æmtig, A.H. 1, 204.11.
O.E.P., Alf. *idel and unnyt*, Blk. 223.2.
O.E.P. *læne lif*, A.H. 2, 508.10, 516.2, Blk. 113.8, Wulf. 113.5, etc.
Alf. *læwed and læred*, A.L.S. xiii, 217, Wulf. 303.21.
Leg. *lare and lage, (larum and lagum)*, Wulf. 65.22, etc. (frequently).
Alf. *geleafan and lufe*, A.H. 1, 98.13, A.H. 2, 468.28. *on hine gelyfað and hine lufiað*, A.H. 1, 288.8.
lecgan his lic, A.L.S. v, 467.
O.E.P. *leof ne lað*, Wulf. 185.2.
O.E.P. *þæs leohtes leoman*, A.H. 1, 76.11.
leornode ic þas lare, A.H. 1, 378.36.
O.E.P., Alf., Leg. *libban* . . . *lif*, A.H. 2, 324.15, 348.24, Blk. 45.19, etc., Wulf. 112.18, etc. *life libban*, A.H. 1, 150.8. *lif leofað*, A.H. 1, 304.15. *leofode his lif*, A.H. 2, 476.16.
Cp. **O.E.P., Alf.** *lichama and leomu*, A.H. 2, 276.19. *lichama and his lyma*, A.H. 2, 386.31.
Alf. *lichoman lustas*, A.L.S. ii, 166, xxiii, 371.
Alf. *lif alætan*, A.H. 2, 104.22, Wulf. 286.24.
O.E.P., Alf. *lif forlætan*, A.H. 2, 508.11, A.L.S. viii, 107, etc. (frequently).
heora lif gelengan, A.H. 1, 100.21. *gelengaþ þin lif*, A.L.S. xiii, 316.
Cp. **O.E.P.** *lifes leoht*, A.H. 1, 530.29.
to lofe na to hlisan, A.L.S. xvi, 365.
þone lyre þe forloren wæs, A.H. 1, 12.24.
mæden and modor,[1] A.H. 1, 354.21, etc.
mærð and myrhð, Wulf. 28.5, etc. (frequently).
Alf., Leg. *magon and moton*, Blk. 95.24, 125.3, Wulf. 50.8, etc. (frequently).
mæg ne mot, Wulf. 305.29.
O.E.P. *man and morðor*, Wulf. 188.14, etc.
Alf. *manigfeald and mislic*, A.L.S. xxiii, 577.
Alf. *manega and mycele*, A.L.S. iv, 404. **Alf.** *mycele and manega*, A.H. 1, 266.27, A.H. 2, 290.21.
manian and myngian. Blk. 161.1, 197.1, Wulf. 303.22.
Leg. *manslagan and manswaran*, Wulf. 114.12, etc.
myrþran and manswaran, Blk. 61.13.
O.E.P., Alf., Leg. *micele and mære*, Blk. 131.8, Wulf. 306.23. *mære and micel*, A.H. 2, 20.35.
mihtig and mære, Wulf. 149.18. *mære and mihtig*, Wulf. 277.22.
O.E.P. *mihta ne mærða*, Wulf. 35.2.
mihte and moste, A.H. 1, 268.31–2 (see *supra*).
O.E.P., Leg. *milde on mode*, Wulf. 74.13.
O.E.P., Hom. *milde and monþwære*, Blk. 71.4.
Leg. *miltse and mildheortnesse*, Wulf. 180.21.
O.E.P., Alf., Leg. *mode and mægene, (mægene and mode)*, Blk. 97.33, 209.24, Wulf. 29.2, etc.
Alf. *munuc and mæssepreost*, A.H. 1, 2.11.
Leg. *muneca and mynecena*, A.H. 2, 518.15.
O.E.P. *mid muþe and mid/on mode*, A.H. 2, 20.33, A.L.S. xvii, 137, xxix, 220.

---

[1] A very common phrase in Middle English religious poetry, especially lyrics.

ord and anginn, A.H. 1, 308.26, etc.
O.E.P., Alf. *ord and ende*, A.H. 2, 220.35, A.L.S. xvi, 308.
ordfruma and ende, A.H. 1, 8.20.
oxena and assan, A.H. 2, 466.12, etc.
rixiað on heofon rice, A.H. 2, 608.13.
ryperas and reaferas, Wulf. 115.2, etc. (frequently).   **Alf.** *rypaþ and reafiaþ*, Wulf. 163.12.
O.E.P., Alf. *sar and sorg*, (*sorh and sar*), A.H. 1, 238.4, A.L.S. xii, 90, Blk. 5.29, Wulf. 139.22, 153.23.
sarig and sorhful, Wulf. 154.4.
sarlic and sorhful, Wulf. 273.6.
sorgung and sargung, Wulf. 114.5, 209.16.
sorhful and sarigmod, Wulf. 133.13.
sorhlic and sar, Wulf. 187.14.
Cp. **O.E.P.** *sar and sace*, Blk. 61.36.
Alf., Leg. *gesceop gesceafta*, A.H. 1, 10.5, etc.
geseah on his gesihðe, A.L.S. xv, 180.
Alf. *geseon þa gesihðe*, A.L.S. xxxiv, 251, Blk. 215.31.
O.E.P., Alf. *secgan soð, secgan to soðe*, etc., A.H. 1, 126.15, etc., A.H. 2, 20.13, etc., A.L.S. vi, 31, etc., Blk. 69.18, etc., Wulf. 45.7, etc.
Leg. *sibbe and some*, Wulf. 73.16, etc.
sierwung and swicdom, A.H. 1, 80.34.
Alf. *singan þisne sang*, A.L.S. xi, 106, 164, xv, 212.
O.E.P. *singan and secgan*, Blk. 105.8, Wulf. 44.26, 75.17.
Leg. *sperum and scyldum*, A.L.S. xxxi, 450.
stalu and steorfa, Wulf. 243.3.
standan stille, A.L.S. v, 402, etc.
stilnysse and sibbe, A.H. 1, 592.6.
Alf. *sunne scinð*, A.H. 2, 446.30.   *læt scinan his sunnan*, A.H. 1, 406.28.
susle and sare, Wulf. 187.18.
swæcc and stenc, A.H. 2, 562.30, 554.35.
O.E.P. *swutol and gesyne*, Blk. 203.36, Wulf. 91.12, etc.
Leg. *sybbie and sehte* (vbs.), Wulf. 266.17.
syllan wiþ sceattum, A.L.S. v, 188.
tæcende and tihtende, A.H. 1, 606.20.
O.E.P. *ne team ne biþ getymed*, A.H. 1, 238.1.
Cp. **O.E.P., Alf.** *ðegnas and ðeowan*, A.H. 2, 584.25.
ðeowum and ðinenum, A.H. 2, 94.16.
þrowian and þolian, Wulf. 122.1, etc.
geþyldig and þolmod, A.L.S. xvi, 335, xvii, 56.
wædlum and wydlum, A.L.S. xxxii, 22.
O.E.P. *wæpna and gewæda*, A.L.S. xxv, 638, xxviii, 84, xxxi, 67.   *wæpna aweorpan*, A.L.S. vi, 240, etc.
mid wæpnum hine werian, A.L.S. xxxi, 621.
mid. wæpnum winnan, A.H. 2, 248.7.
Alf., cp. O.E.P. *wæpmanna and wifmanna*, A.H. 1, 442.1–2.   *wifmann and wæpnedmann*, Blk. 79.19.
on wæstme and on wanunge, A.H. 1, 102.27.
O.E.P., Alf., Leg. *waldend and wyrhta*, Wulf. 21.19, etc.
Alf. *gewat of worulde*, A.H. 2, 150.32, A.L.S. vi, 271, xxxiv, 281.   *of worulde gewat*, A.H. 2, 518.13.   *gewitan of worulde*, A.H. 2, 298.5, etc.

gewealdan and gewissian, A.H. 1, 78.16.

Alf. *weaxan and wanian,* A.H. 1, 154.27, etc. *weaxende and wanigende,* A.H. 2, 214.32.

wedlogan and wærlogan, Wulf. 266.29, 310.5.

to welan and to wiste, Wulf. 132.14, 259.17.

welan and wuldor, A.H. 1, 170.33, A.H. 2, 576.24.

Leg. *weorc (to) wyrcen(ne),* A.H. 1, 160.24, etc., Wulf. 227.13. *he worhte his weorc,* A.H. 2, 356.5.

wepað and waniað, Wulf. 183.2.

O.E.P., Alf. *wer and wif,* A.H. 1, 60.8, etc., A.H. 2, 8.27, etc., A.L.S. xix, 88, etc., Blk. 195.2, etc.

O.E.P., Alf., Leg. *willan wyrcan,* A.H. 1, 264.23, etc., A.H. 2, 412.1, etc., A.L.S. xxxi, 1194, etc., Wulf. 41.1, etc.

Alf. *wilnian and wyscan,* A.L.S. xxxii, 74, xxxvii, 106, Blk. 103.12.

mid his wisdome and mid his willan, A.H. 1, 16.3.

O.E.P. *wise on wordum,* Wulf. 145.34.

wislice and wærlice, Wulf. 167.13, 275.15.

wær and wise, Wulf. 52.29, 55.21.

wislic and weorðlic, Wulf. 168.19.

O.E.P., Alf. *wlite and wuldor, (wuldor and wlite),* A.H. 2, 432.33, Wulf. 185.9, etc.

O.E.P. *wlite and wæstmum,* Blk. 113.16.

O.E.P. *woþ and wanung,* A.H. 1, 592.16, A.L.S. v, 77, Wulf. 139.3.

O.E.P., Alf., Leg. *word and weorc,* A.H. 1, 96.20, etc., A.H. 2, 70.33, etc. A.L.S. xvi, 86, Wulf. 54.3.

O.E.P. *wordum writende,* A.H. 2, 332.12.

worlde wela, Wulf. 149.1, etc.

Alf. *þis gewrit awrat,* A.L.S. xxiv, 102, Wulf. 207.2, etc.

Alf. *of wudum and of wæstenum,* A.L.S. xix, 139.

Leg. *wuldor and weorþung,* Blk. 196.27.

to weorpienne and to wuldrienne, Blk. 197.4.

Alf. *wuldre and wurðscipe,* A.L.S. xxx, 129.

O.E.P., Alf., Leg. *wuldor and wurðmynt,* A.H. 1, 76.23, 470.18, A.H. 2, 116.20, etc. *wuldor and weorþmynt,* A.L.S. x, 293, etc., Blk. 65.25, Wulf. 140.1, etc.

Alf. *wundra gewyrcean* (or *geworhte*),[1] A.H. 1, 4.3, etc., A.H. 2, 132.17, etc., A.L.S. iii, 21, etc., Blk. 19.18, Wulf. 273.24.

wunian on wite, Blk. 61.34, Wulf. 114.7, etc.

wunian on wlite and on wuldre, Wulf. 190.3.

O.E.P. *wunian on wuldre,* A.H. 2, 232.26, A.L.S. xii, 95, xxvii, 156.

wunian on wurþmynte, A.L.S. xxv, 728.

in yrmþum and on earfeðum, Wulf. 188.3.

THE ALLITERATIVE PHRASES IN THE ALFREDIAN PROSE WORKS AND IN THE ANGLO-SAXON CHRONICLE. [O.E.PR. ALF.]

In this section the alliterative phrases occurring in the above-mentioned works are gathered together as affording some evidence

---

[1] Cp. O.S. *uundres geuuarhte.*

of the extent to which alliterative phrases were in everyday use among the Anglo-Saxon people. The collection may also reveal whether poets utilised the common phrases in the making of their verse or preferred more archaic and poetic phrases.

The following editions have been used in the compilation :—[1]

King Alfred's Version of Bede's Ecclesiastical History, edited by T. Miller, E.E.T.S. 95 and 96, 1890–1.
King Alfred's Version of Boethius' Consolations of Philosophy, edited by W. J. Sedgefield, Oxford, 1899.
The Old English Version of the Soliloquies of St. Augustine, edited by W. Endter, 1922.
The Old English Version of Orosius, edited by H. Sweet, E.E.T.S. 79, 1883.
King Alfred's West Saxon Version of Gregory's Pastoral Care, edited by H. Sweet, E.E.T.S. 45, 50, 1871–2. *The Old English Version of the Dialogues of Gregory the Great*, edited in Grein-Wülker, Bibliothek der angelsächsischen-Prosa, vol. 5. *Two of the Saxon Chronicles Parallel*, C. Plummer and J. Earle, 1892.

se æfæsta and se arfulla, Dial. 97.13.
þurh andan and æfæste, Dial. 206.26.
þa æþelan and þa æfæstan, Dial. 111.2.
Leg.   *to are and to iserne*, Past. 266.17, 21.
in hatum baðum heo baðian wolde, Bede 318.16.
mid þy bæðe his blodes geclænsad, Bede 40.15.
gebæron and brohton, Bede 282.9.
Hom.   *his gebede and blætsunge*, Bede 398.26.
gebede and bene, Bede 380.10.   *bene and gebeda*, Bede 194.30 and 432.5.
ðinre bene . . . ðinre bede, Past. 399.30.
O.E.P., Hom.   *mid benum . . . gebiddende*, Dial. 210.19.
on bendum gebunden, Dial. 346.23.
mid beotum bregan, Dial. 237.23.
beran and bringen, Boet. 9.19, Dial. 343.14.
gebiddende and bletsigende, Bede 22.17.   Cp. **Leg., Hom.**   *gebæd heo fore and heo gebletsade and Gode bebead*, Bede 200.1.
ge binnan burh ge buton, Chr. Laud 1052.
gebletsod to biscope, Chr. Laud 1042.
on blostmum and on bledum, Boet. 92.2.
bodode þa bebodu, Dial. 275.8.
oðþe tobræcon, oþþe forbærndon, Chr. Parker 894.
abrecan þa burg, Oros. 158.32, etc.   *seo burg abrocen uæs*, Oros. 74.32.
hie þa burg ne bærndon, Oros. 94.6.
brigges tobrokene, Chr. Laud 1125.
Cp. **O.E.P.**   *bruce blisse*, Dial. 266.14.
burþenas and byrlas, Chr. Laud 1120.
ge þæs ceapes, ge þæs cornes, Chr. Parker 895.
O.E.P., Hom.   *cleopode and cegde*, Bede 190.16, 322.5.

---
[1] The references, except in the case of *The A.S. Chronicle*, are by page and line.

O.E.P., Hom. *cleopode . . . and cwæð,* Bede 392.28. *clypian and cweðan.*
Dial. 28.30, etc. *clypie and cweðe,* Solil. 10.25.
cleopað and cypeð, Dial. 147.4, etc.
wæs cypende and þus cwæð, Bede 228.20. *he cypde me and cwæþ,* Dial.
257.18.
O.E.P., Hom. *clyppan and cyssan,* Dial. 47.3.
cuðe men and creftige, Solil. 3.22.
se cwide þe he cwæð, Boet. 143.14.
O.E.P., Hom. *cyningas and caseras,* Oros. 56.3.
þone cyning and cwene, Bede 140.9.
hi him to cyninge gecuron, Chr. Worc. 905.
he of þæm cynne cuman sceolde, Oros. 264.14.
cystum and cræftum, Boet. 122.3.
O.E.P. *dædbote don,* Oros. 256.13.
O.E.P. *on . . . dælas todælde,* Dial. 87.5.
daro gedon, Bede 158.2.
se deapes dæg, Dial. 291.12.
he þone deað gedigde, Dial. 203.14.
deope bedelfan, Chr. Abing. 1049.
let dician ða dic, Chr. Abing. 1055.
ðære dieglan and ðære diopan (lare), Past. 461.5, 8.
þam dome þæs (ecan) deman, Dial. 221.14, 320.26.
O.E.P., Leg., Hom. *dōmas dēman,* Solil. 8.11.
undom demdon, Chr. Abing. 1052.
ondreden on þam deape, Dial. 337.27.
Hom. *drync drincan,* Dial. 187.25.
drohtian and don, Bede 64.13.
dwellan and dyderian, Boet. 100.5.
dwellan in gedwolan (wander in error), Solil. 13.7.
Hom. *mid eagum, mid earum,* Solil. 6.8, 18.10. *eagan and earan,* Oros.
220.15.
ða þe eardiað ofer eorðan, Past. 128.22.
O.E.P., Leg., Hom. *earme . . . eadige,* Past. 174.14, etc.
ettan oððe erian, Oros. 18.25.
fæder and fruma, Boet. 81.13, etc.
(se arwurða muneca) feder and frouer, Chr. Laud 1089.
O.E.P. *faran to gefeohte,* Oros. 232.4.
farende mid (eallum his) folce, Oros. 170.14.
Leg. *feoh and feorh,*[1] Chr. Laud 755.
gefeohtes and feondscipes, Bede 324.20.
æt (heora forman) gefeohte gefliemde, Oros. 210.18. *him wið gefuhton and hi
geflymdon,* Chr. Worc. 915, etc. (in various forms).
folcgefeoht gefohten, Chr. Laud, 871, 887.
Hom. *on ðæm gefeohte gefeoll,* Oros. 150.24.
O.E.P., Hom. *feoll to his fotum,* Bede 196.29. *feol him to fotum,* Bede
228.17. *to fotum feoll,* Bede 38.21, etc. *feollon . . . to fotum,* Dial.
127.19. *to fotum feallende,* Oros. 66.2.
O.E.P. *þ he moste his feonde afyllan,* Chr. Laud 626.
wið heora fynd feohtan, Bede 48.23. *wið heora feondum gefuhtan,* Bede
44.29–30.

[1] Cp. O.N. *fé eða fjor.*

feorh ge freodom, Oros. 202.28.
Hom. *ferde mid fyrde*, Chr. Laud 1102, 1114.   *mid fierde ferde and him wiþ feaht*, Chr. Parker 835.   *mid firde farende*, Oros. 44.6, etc. (in various forms).
firðrige and fremme, Solil. 33.15.
Cp. **O.E.P.**   *fiscerum and fugelerum*, Oros. 17.25.
hit is fiscwylle and fugolwylle, Bede 30.9.
Hom. *fleogende fuȝelas*, Dial. 261.15.
flod gefleow, Oros. 32.11.
flogettan and fiþercian, Dial. 100.19.
þa folc feollon, Oros. 198.4.
geforðian heora fare, Chr. Laud 1085.
ic þe frasige and ðin fandige, Solil. 35.18.
freondscype and geferræden, Solil. 40.9.
and heora freondscipe þær gefæstnodon, Chr. Laud 1016.   *gefæstnodon . . . freondscipe*, Chr. Abing. 1052.
freoðode and fultomede, Bede 116.5.
Cp. **Leg.**   *his freond and his geferan*, Dial. 181.1.   *friend and geferan*, Boet. 50.2.
O.E.P., Hom.   *freond and feond*, Solil. 69.20 and 21, Boet. 48.8, etc.
swiðe freondlice and swiðe fremsumlice, Past. 22.9.
mid Eadweardes cynges friþe and fultume, Chr. Parker 920.
to frofran and to gefean, Solil. 67.33.
on fugela feðerum, Oros. 18.17.
O.E.P., Hom.   *fugelas and fixas*, Chr. Abing. 1046.
fuglian and fiscian, Solil. 2.5.
his fultume þonan āfōr (went to his help), Oros. 84.2.
Hom. *fultum . . . frofre*, Bede, 358.32.   *min fultum, min frofer*, Boet. 149.24.   **O.E.P., Hom.**   *to heora frofre and fultume*, Dial. 219.27.
fulwihte onfon, Chr. Laud 878.
fylle nu his fætels, Past. 469.9.
þa fyrsas and þa fearn, Boet. 51.29.
gadered gold, Chr. Laud 1137.
ne gafle ne geold, Chr. Laud 675.   *gafol to gieldanne*, Oros. 44.14, etc.   *gafol þe ða Finnas gyldað*, Oros. 18.16 and 17.   *gafol agulde*, Dial. 350.7.   *an gafol guldan*, Oros. 248.21.   *gafol gyldon*, Chr. Laud 1002, 1006.
Hom. *he ageaf his gast*, Dial. 277.7.   *agyfan his gast*, Dial. 324.15.
geaf gislas, Chr. Laud 1052.
geafon and getton, Chr. Laud 675.   *ic . . . geate and gife* (I grant and give), Chr. Laud 963.
na geld na gaule (neither payment nor tax), Chr. Laud 656.
geong and geomerung, Bede 48.5.
þa gersuman þe his fæder ær gegaderode, Chr. Laud 1086.
gersumes him geaf on gold, Chr. Laud 1128.
begietan mid golde, Oros. 48.30.
gifu þ he gifð, Boet. 120.1.
gilpes giernað, Past. 142.22.
(world-)gilpes and gitsunge, Past. 156.2.
gleowian and gieddian, Boet. 26.22.
he swiðe goað and geomrað, Bede 88.15.   *goiende and geomriende*, Bede 88.17.

.godcundum and gastlicum, Dial. 1.10.
godena gumena, Boet. 139.6.
Hom., Leg. *(mid) Godes gife,* Bede 310.20, etc., Past. 320.10, etc.
O.E.P., Hom. *mid golde and mid gimmum,* Boet. 11.27, etc. ; Chr. Laud
   1086. *for golde and for gimmum,* Bede 322.23.
Hom. *mid golde and mid gimstanum,* Oros. 70.26.
Hom. *mid golde and mid godwebbe,* Bede 184.1.
gegyred mid . . . godwebbe, Dial. 310.1.
gripede and gisledon, Chr. of Worc. 1063.
þa geornde se eorl eft griðes and gisla, Chr. Laud 1048.
ða gyrndon hi griðas, Chr. Laud 1087.
O.E.P., Hom. *habban and gehealdan,* Dial. 117.32. *gehabban and gehealdan,*
   Solil. 36.10. *to habbanne and to healdenne,* Bede 450.3. *hæfde and*
   heold, Dial. 340.15. *heold and hæfde,* Bede 154.26, 192.23, Dial. 20.20,
   255.31.
ne hading ne haleging (neither ordination nor consecration), Chr. Laud 675.
(on lichaman) wæs gehæfd and gehyned, Dial. 173.22.
þe eac gehat geheht, Bede 242.31.
(gebigde) hire heafod in þa handa, Dial. 167.21. *his hond on min heafod,*
   Bede 402.17. **O.E.P.** *mid ðy heafde and mid honda,* Bede 400.28.
heo heora heafod and heora eagan to onheldon, Bede 322.30.
heafod upp ahof, Dial. 49.26.
Hom. *his heafod on eorðan hylde,* Bede 178.20.
heah and upp ahafen, Dial. 217.30.
geheaðorade and gehæfte, Boet. 57.5.
helan on horde, Boet. 31.13.
gehele and gehealde (conceal and keep back), Bede 462.21.
(se cyng) heold his hired, Chr. Laud 1085, etc.
heortena heardnes, Dial. 194.6.
þa herehyþa ahreddon, Chr. Parker 894.
Hom. *hergian and hienan,* Oros. 160.9. *hi hendon and hergedon,* Bede 32.27
onhergedon and hleoðedon, Bede 48.24. *hloðedon and hergedon,* Bede 44.32.
hleop on min hors, Bede 404.5.
hlisan and herunge, Boet. 68.31.
fram þam hneccan oþ þone hoh, Dial. 198.10.
gehnescode and gehælede, Past. 182.21.
(beon) holde and gehyrsume, Chr. Laud 1083.
on honda habban, Bede 38.21, etc. *þe þu on þinum handum nu hafast,*
   Dial. 2.10. *on handa hæfde,* Oros. 88.8. *hauen on hand,* Chr. Laud
   1127.
he his eagan mid his hondum to heofonum hofe, Bede 202.16.
upp ahafenum handum, Dial. 65.8.
horsa and hryþra, Dial. 268.18.
of þam hrofe þæs huses, Dial. 62.33.
on huntunge heorta, Bede 30.10.
his hus and his ham, Chr. Laud 1129.
O.E.P. *gehyden and beheligen,* Past. 238.25. *hyt and heleð* (hides and
   conceals), Past. 336.9. *gehyt and oðhielt,* Past. 376.9. *forholena oððe*
   forhydde, Past. 376.7.
Cp. O.E.P. *gehyt his heafod,* Past. 240.12.
onhylde his heafod, Dial. 206.7.
hyrde his hæsum, Dial. 58.7.

hyðde and hergode, Bede 200.30.
O.E.P., Hom.   *idel and unnyt*, Bede 400.4.
gelædde to þam soðan geleafan, Dial. 239.19.
Hom.   *læred and læwed*, Chr. Laud 656, 1125, 1127.
forlætan þone lichaman, Dial. 297.1.
þæs landes lyft, Bede 30.2.
þæs langan lifes,[1] Dial. 339.27.
lare lærde, Bede 230.14, 302.23.
ge ymb lare ge ymb leornunga, Past. 2.9.
(to hyra husum) laðian and lǣdan, Dial. 200.29.
O.E.P.   *lað . . . leof*, Boet. 22.3.
Hom.   *geleafa and lufu*, Solil. 29.11, 30.5.   *lufu and geleafa*, Past. 166.19,
24, etc.
Leg.   *gif he leng moste liuen*, Chr. Laud 1137.
wæs forð on leoht gelæded, Bede 320.15.
leohtran and liþran, Oros. 244.15.
ðære leohtmodnesse and leasmodnesse, Past. 308.6.
leornian and gelyfan, Solil. 68.23.
on leornunge gelæred, Bede 446.8.
mid þære gife þæs cristnan geleafan gelæred wære, Bede 158.5.
men forleten heora land, Chr. Laud 1087.   *hi þa þæt lond forleton*, Oros.
44.22.
oððe þær libban oððe þær licgan, Chr. Parker 901.   **Leg.**   *licgan and libban*,
Chr. Abing. 1052.
libban on lichaman, Dial. 59.23.
his lic ligð, Chr. Laud 796, etc.   *his lichama ligeð*, Dial. 166.4.
þæt him ðæt licede and leof wære, Bede 374.26.
Hom.   *lichoma and limu*, Boet. 90.31, etc.
of lichoman alæded, Bede 212.12, Chr. Worc. 906.   *of lichoman gelæded*,
Bede 290.4, Dial. 53.4.   *alæded of lichoman*, Bede 212.4.   *læded in
lichoman*, Bede 212.11, etc.   *gelæded wæs of lichaman*, Dial. 318.23,
etc.
fram lichoman alesed, Bede 404.30.   *(he his) lichoman tolesed (wære)*, Bede
404.24, Dial. 296.3.
seo halig sawle wæs alysed and geleoðod of þam lichaman, Dial. 282.17,
285.26.   *toleoþed and alysed*, Dial. 349.28.
lichoman luste, Boet. 143.3, Dial. 72.8, etc., Past. 202.22.   *in þæm lichom-
lecan lustfulnesse*, Bede 88.12.
Hom.   *se lust þæs lichaman*, Dial. 32.30, etc.
licige and lustfullige (pleases and delights), Past. 70.24.
lif lædde, Bede 360.22, 464.16.   *his lif gelædde*, Dial. 188.16.   *he gelædde
his lif*, Dial. 52.12.   *lif læden*, Chr. Laud 656.   *lif . . . to lædene*,
Chr. Laud 1093.
Leg.   *æt life and æt lande*, Chr. Worc. 1065.
lif ge lare, Bede 446.7.   *life to lare*, Dial. 2.27.   *his lif oþþe his lar*, Past.
22.8.
þe lifgende wæron in lichaman, Dial. 292.21.   *lifigende on þisum brosniend-
lican lichaman*, Dial. 153.18.
(he þa gyt) lyfde on lichaman, Dial. 314.27, etc.

[1] Cp. O.N. *langt líf*.

O.E.P. *lif forleosan,* Oros. 68.28.
Hom. *heora lif alætan,* Oros. 120.31. *lif alet,* Oros. 224.35. **O.E.P., Hom.** *lif forlætan,* Bede 202.24. *forlætan þis . . . lif,* Dial. 325.13, etc. *lif forlætan,* Oros. 80.35. *he his lif forlet,* Oros. 112.13, etc. *forlet þis lif,* Chr. Laud 988, 992.
O.E.P., Leg., Hom. *lif alibban* Oros. 108.17. *hi hyra lif alyfden,* Oros. 30.6 and 25. *his lif lifde,* Bede 442.13. *his lif . . . lifigan,* Bede 242.31. *lifde he his lif,* Bede 244.16. *lif lifiað,* Dial. 222.17. *lifode in þisum life,* Dial. 299.18. *þises lifes losedan,* Chr. Laud 1120. *lōf and lēan,* Boet. 108.13. *lufan and londleoda,* Oros. 164.6. *gelufedon þæt ece lif,* Dial. 232.16. *lufiendlic and leof,* Bede 324.17. *to þam lustum þæs ecan lifes,* Dial. 230.4. *mæssan onsymbelnesse mærsian,* Bede 112.8. *mid mæssonge mærsode,* Bede 106.9. *mæte and madmas,* Chr. Laud 1006.
Hom. *manig and micel,* Boet. 147.20. *swa monegum and swa miclum,* Bede 476.27. **Hom.** *micla and . . . manega,* Chr. Worc. 1075, Solil. 59.22. *mid miclum and mid monegum* (Godes gifum), Past. 44.16. *micel and manigfeald,* Boet. 118.22. *þæs mannes mod,* Dial. 339.2, etc. *ælces mannes mod,* Past. 445.9. *to manianne ða manðwæran,* Past. 286.22, etc. *(þone) mannoden and metsoden,* Chr. Laud 1087. *ge þa maran ge þa mætran,* Bede 352.25.
Hom., Leg. *meahten and mosten,* Solil. 681.1. *mid medum median,* Dial. 237.23. *gemetlice and medomlice,* Past. 461.30.
O.E.P., Leg., Hom. *micel . . . and mære,* Dial. 340.31. *se micla and se mæra,* Past. 244.4. *mycel mænigo,* Dial. 284.25, etc. *micel menigu,* Past. 403.21.
O.E.P., Hom. *milde mode,* Past. 222.7.
O.E.P., Hom. *milde and monðwære,* Bede 360.30. *miscað and metgað* (apportions and metes out), Boet. 132.19.
Hom. *mistlic and manigfeald,* Boet. 1.5, etc. *mistlice and mænigfealdlice,* Chr. Laud 1104. *mislicra and manigfealdra,* Past. 380.8. *mislicum and monigfaldum,* Past. 6.17. *on hu mislecum and on hu monigfealdum,* Past. 82.25. *missenlice and mænigfealde,* Dial. 254.5. *manigfealdlice and mislice,* Past. 306.5. *on manegum þingum and mislicum,* Chr. Laud 1041.
O.E.P., Leg., Hom. *mod and mægen (monian),* Bede 54.9. *monnum and mægum,* Boet. 71.27.
Hom., Leg. *mot and mæg,* Boet. 93.24.
Hom. *munuc and mæssepreost,* Bede 434.9. *þe munecas of þe mynstre,* Chr. Laud 656, 1131, Dial. 225.18.
O.E.P. *into muntan and moran (ferdon),* Chr. Laud 1095. *þæm muntum and þæm merscum,* Past. 399.13.
O.E.P. *murnende mod,* Boet. 8.17. *næmde (mec mine) noman,* Bede 402.11, etc. *be naman nemnian,* Dial. 312.3, etc. *he hine be naman genemde,* Dial. 311.9. *be noman memnede,* Oros. 72.12.

O.E.P., Hom. *ge ord ge ende, Past.* 385.13.
racode and rǣdde, Boet. 94.13.
racu gerihtan, Dial. 272.9.
pegnas oft rade onridon, Chr. Parker 871.
Cp. **Leg.** *unrǣd rǣddon,* Chr. Abing. 1052.
gerǣdde þone rǣd, Chr. Worc. 1055.
reccan sume race, Boet. 145.26.
ðǣs rices and ðǣs recendomes, Past. 10.1.
rihtan and rǣdan, Boet. 97.12.   *he gerǣdde and gerihte (of gastlicre sop-*
fǣstnan), Dial. 267.13.
rihtlic and rǣdlic, Solil. 33.17.
ryhtlices and gerisenlices, Past. 154.24.
O.E.P. *rode arǣrde,* Bede 154.21.
Hom. *beryptan and bereafodan,* Chr. Abing. 1055.
saca and socne, Chr. Laud 963.
(þǣt us aht)wiþsǣce and wiþstande, Dial. 333.11.
he me sǣde þas sprǣce, Dial. 306.25.
O.E.P., Hom. *sar and sorge,* Dial. 3.22.   *ðurh sar and ðurh sorge,* Past. 34.4.
sorges and sares, Boet. 16.18.
mid hefige sare swiðe swenced, Bede 178.24.   **O.E.P.** *swenced mid (swile)*
and sare, Bede 322.17.
efensargode hire sare, Dial. 215.22, 216.1.
O.E.P. *ðǣre scame and ðǣre scande,* Past. 206.10.
þa scamfǣstan . . . þa scamleasan, Past. 14.9.
(hwa bið)gescended (ðǣt ic eac ðǣs ne)scamige ? Past. 100.5.
gesceadwisnes ne snyttro, Dial. 328.2.
on sceat and on scrud, Chr. Laud 1070.
þa sceat he mid þy spere, Bede 138.8.
sceawedon and gesawon, Dial. 184.12.   *sceawian and geseon,* Bede 386.6,
etc. (in various forms).   (See under *sēon.*)
sceawian and smeagean, Dial. 18.2.
swa beorht scinende steorra, Bede 428.19.
ge in scip astigað, Bede 412.19.   *ða astag he in scip,* Bede 412.19.
se scippend and se stihtere, Past. 391.21.
scipu asǣton, Chr. Parker 897, etc.
Leg., Hom. *gescop ealle gesceafta,* Dial. 253.2.
gescrǣncan and beswican, Dial. 339.23.
scyldan and besecgan (defend and plead), Bede 460.25.
in scynisse synne, Bede 88.5.
sealmas to singenne, Bede 66.5.   *sealmas singan,* Bede 444.11.   *hiora salmas*
sungon, Bede 416.13.   *sangas his sealma,* Dial. 275.13.   *sang his*
sealmas, Dial. 282.12.
in þone seað sette, Bede 154.26.
secggean and smeagean, Past. 66.4.
Leg. *secean and sceawian,* Past. 100.23.
he sendeð his strǣle, Bede 268.28.
to þam seocan and þam sweltendan, Dial. 344.27.
geseon and sceawian, Dial. 173.27.   *to geseonne and to sceawigenne,* Bede
372.11.
geseon and sprecan, Chr. Laud 797.
seonoð gesomnode, Bede 368.2, etc.

he set on his setle, Bede 408.9. *sæt in his stowe on his seðle*, Bede 196.24.
setten him on þes abbotes settle, Chr. Laud 1131. *man sette Hereman
on his setle*, Chr. Worc. 1046.
tosēðan and toscēadan, Solil. 7.11.
sib and ʼsæhte, Chr. Laud 1140.
ge hiora sibbe ge hiora sido, Past. 2.6.
sibbe and smoltnesse, Bede 480.8.
sib and orsorhnes, Bede 356.4.
sibbe and stillnysse, Bede 12.23.
he selfa wære geslægen and beswungcen mid Benedictus swinglan, Dial. 112.14.
sume ofslogon, sume ofswungen, Oros. 154.8.
(singð he) smælor and smicror, Past. 461.3.
smealice and scearplice, Past. 68.6.
scearplicu and smealicu (sharp and searching), Past. 154.1.
smeapancole and spyrigende, Dial. 344.15.
gesnidene and gesmeðde (cut and polished), Past. 252.14.
gesocne and smeunge, Dial. 265.25.
soden and geswenced, Bede 372.26.
he gesomnode his stemne tosomne, Dial. 276.20.
gesomnode in stowe, Bede 278.26.
song þe he sang, Past. 334.23. *þone song, þe heo sungon*, Bede. 284.15.
Hom. *singeð ðone sang*, Past. 409.8, etc.
O.E.P., Hom. *ic eow soð secgu*, Bede 286.17. *soð ic secge*, Bede 354.14.
ic þe soðlice secgo, Bede 266.29. *soð ge sæcgað*, Bede 440.9. *soð
secgan*, Boet. 59.15, etc. *wæs to soðan gesæd*, Chr. Worc. 1066. *to
soðan sædan*, Chr. Laud 1085. *soðes secge*, Past. 216.15. *soðe secgan*,
Dial. 41.20, etc. *to soþum secgan*, Oros. 138.18. *secgan soð*, Solil.
24.10, 47.16, 61.29.
O.E.P. *þa spell þe ic secge*, Oros. 42.2. *ðis spel me sume þara sægdon*,
Bede 330.22. *sægdon sum halig spell*, Bede 344.25.
spel secgað and spreocað, Bede 328.7.
Leg. *to his spere and to his swurde*, Chr. Worc. 1056.
sprecende and sæcgende, Dial. 272.10.
þæs halgan stæres and spelles, Bede 346.1.
gesette and gestaðolade, Bede 232.14, etc. *gestaþelode and gesette*, Dial.
119.19. *gestaðlode and gesette*, Bede 272.31.
him swiðe stiernlice stierde, Past. 196.18.
stilnes and swigung, Dial. 185.1.
unstilre and ungestæððigre, Past. 272.11.
steorra scineð, Boet. 19.3, etc. *steorra . . . scynende*, Chr. Laud 1097.
(See under *scinende*.)
se storm on sæ, Dial. 5.28.
storm gestildon, Bede 14.33. *ðone storm he gesette and gestilde*, Bede 22.7.
in þisse . . . stowe and scire, Dial. 340.32.
on his stowe gesette, Bede 300.5.
mid strængðe and mid staðolfæstnesse, Dial. 349.8.
ðære sunnan sciman, Bede 430.8. *sunnan sciman*, Boet. 89.22, etc.
sunnan scyma, Solil. 67.7.
Hom. *sunne scineð*, Boet. 21.2, etc. *seo sunne scinð*, Solil. 31.18, etc.
he wæs geswenced mid þæs lichaman swinglan, Dial. 274.27.
mid his sweorde sloge, Past. 198.19. *mid sweorde ofslogan*, Bede 416.23.

15

þæs swetan stences, Dial. 282.28, etc.
swincfull and sorhfull, Chr. Laud 1085.
swiðlice and strælice, Past. 150.12.
Hom. *þa gesyhðe geseah*, Dial. 320.3, 322.4.
O.E.P. *tidreð ælc tudor*, Boet. 131.6.
tudres to tilienne, Bede 82.25.
toll and team, Chr. Laud 963.
torras timbredon, Bede 46.7.
totugon and totæron, Oros. 142.24.
geþeaht and þafung, Boet. 11.7, etc.
mid geþohte and geþafunge, Bede 458.1.
Hom., cp. **O.E.P.** *þa ðegnas and eac þa ðeowas*, Past. 14.6.
ðenian þa ðenunga, Past. 26.11.
mid his þenunge and mid his þeawum, Dial. 56.19.
on his mode þohte and þreodode, Bede 148.21.
geðolede on hys þeowdome, Solil. 11.18.
þoncmeotunge and þreodunge, Bede 88.4.
wædlan and wanhale, Past. 322.22.
ða wædlan . . . ða welegan, Past. 180.5. **Leg.** *se welega and se wædla*, Past. 182.10, etc.
wælhreownesse and wedenheortnesse, Dial. 194.17.
ahton wælstowe gewald, Chr. Laud 833 (very frequently).
O.E.P. *wæpnes gewealdan*, Oros. 194.19.
wæpen wyrcean, Bede 46.9. *wæpno worhton*, Bede 46.1.
Cp. **O.E.P.** *gewæpnod and gewæded*, Chr. Laud 992.
wæpmen and wimmen, Chr. Laud 1123. *wæpnedmen ge wimmen*, Bede 162.9, 354.17. **O.E.P.** *wæpned and wif*, Bede 406.17. **Hom.** *wifmen ge wæpnedmen*, Oros. 76.26. *wifmonna and wæpnedmonna*, Oros. 116.30, etc.
wæter and wæta, Boet. 80.13.
gewaniað and gewemmað, Past. 413.2.
gewealc and gewinn, Chr. Laud 1100.
wearm, nalles wlaco, Past. 447.3.
weaxað . . . and widiað, Dial. 315.4.
onweg gewat, Dial. 119.3, etc. *he gewat onweg*, Dial. 222.2.
welan and anwalde, Boet. 77.15, etc.
ge þone welan ge þone wisdom, Past. 4.17.
wela(n) and wyrðmynt, Past. 389.17, 19.
wela and weorþscipe, Boet. 17.18, etc. *welan and wurðscipe*, Solil. 38.4.
welig and weorþ, Boet. 124.26.
wenan and wilnian, Boet. 46.30.
wende west, Chr. Parker 894, etc.
hrægel weofað and wyrcað, Bede 354.23.
þa yða weollon and weddon þæs sæs, Bede 200.11.
weolle an welle (a spring welled up), Bede 418.20.
weorce and gewinne, Dial. 266.3.
on weorce and on worde, Bede, 440.4. *weorcum . . . wordum*, Past. 461.12.
Leg., Hom. *weorc wyrcan*, Boet. 38.4, etc., Oros. 36.27, Solil. 1.3, 5.1. *weorc to wyrceanne*, Past. 10. 14, etc. *wyrc þin weorc*, Dial. 114.18. *wyrceþ (þis) weorc(a)*, Dial. 270.4, etc. *geweorc geworht hæfdon*, Chr. Parker 894.(4), 896.(2), etc. *worhtum*.

weorþan wæter, Dial. 123.31.
weorðfullicost and wunderlicost, Past. 465.1.
O.E.P. *wer and wiif*, Bede 70.15. **Hom.** *weras . . . wif*, Past. 178.14,
    etc. *weras and wif*, Chr. Laud 1011. *ge wera ge wifa*, Dial. 258.17.
Hom. *wexende and waniende*, Chr. Laud 1107. *weoxe and wanode*, Solil.
    58.27, 64.30, 65.22.
wic and wununesse, Bede 366.13.
Leg. *to wife beweddod*, Chr. Laud 1119.
Cp. **O.E.P.** *to wige and to gewinne*, Oros. 154.33.
O.E.P. *ge mid wige ge mid wisdome*, Past. 2.8.
O.E.P., Hom., Leg. *godes willan wyrceað*, Dial. 2.29.
Leg. *hiora willes and hiora gewealdes*, Past. 445.6. **Leg.** *ungewisses oððe
    ungewaldes*, Past. 156.25.
wilna and welena (wilniað), Past. 387.7, 391.18.
wilniende and wenende, Oros. 194.22. *wenan and wilnian*, Boet. 46.30.
windas and gewidera, Bede 412.9.
to gewinne and to wræstlunge lifes and deaðes, Dial. 321.3.
gewinnes waldend, Oros. 36.21.
Hom. *wiscan and willnian*, Solil. 70.18. *ic wysce and wilnige*, Dial. 188.7,
    262.25.
for wisdome and for wærscipe, Past. 148.16. *minne wisdom and minne
    wærscipe*, Past. 272.8.
on wisdome gewrita, Bede 446.21. *mid þy wisdome ælces gewrites*, Dial.
    217.25. *in wisdome gewrito* (in the knowledge of the Scriptures),
    Bede 408.3.
mid wislicum wordum, Dial. 259.22.
Leg. *wist and wæda*, Boet. 77.11.
O.E.P., Hom. *to wlite and to wuldre*, Past. 38.18.
woldon heo amd wendon, Bede 308.11. *woldon heo amd willnadan*, Bede
    232.33. (See under *wilniende*.)
he oferwonn hiera wiþerwinnan, Oros. 280.3.
Leg. *mid worde and mid wædde*, Chr. Laud 1014.[1]
O.E.P., Hom., Leg. *worda oððe weorca*, Past. 30.25. *mid wordum oððe
    mid weorcum*, Past. 156.21. (See under *weorc*.)
O.E.P. *wordum and gewritum*, Past. 356.4.
Cp. **O.E.P.** *þa word þines wisdomes*, Bede 486.3. *ða word wisdomes*,
    Past. 92.23. *wisdomes word*, Dial. 337.32.
Hom. *or worulde gewat*, Bede 444.9.
mid woruldlican wisdomum, Dial. 272.21.
wrecan and wītnian, Boet. 143.22.
ure wregend and wrohtbora, Dial. 221.13.
O.E.P., Leg. *mid writ and mid worde*, Chr. Laud 675. *mid . . . gewrite
    . . . and . . . wordum*, Dial. 175.3.
writ . . . gewriton, Chr. Laud 963. **Hom.** *þam gewritum ðe ic awriten
    gemette*, Bede 4.30.
for wudufæstenne and for wæterfæstenne, Chr. Parker 894.
Hom. *in wuda and in westenum*, Bede 54.5. *on wudum and on westenum*,
    Bede 42.5.
O.E.P. *hi beoð mid . . . wuldre geweorþode*, Dial. 296.13.
Hom. *wuldor and weorðscipe*, Boet. 68.12.

----

[1] The same phrase is found in Old Frisian.

O.E.P., Leg., Hom. *wuldre and wyrðmyndum,* Bede 418.17.
wulfum and wildeorum, Bede 46.23.
wundorlic and wynsum, Boet. 86.11.
wundriende and wafiende, Bede 264.31.
wundrian and weorðian, Boet. 72.27.
mid wundra weorcnesse, Bede 106.13.   *wundra wyrcnisse,* Bede 192.3.
Hom. *wundra wyrcean,* Past. 26.22, etc., Dial. 246.28, etc.   *wundor to wyrcenne,* Oros. 34.5, etc.   *worhte þæt wundor,* Dial. 60.32, etc. (in various forms).   *he worhte (his) wundor,* Past. 102.13, etc.
gewuna and willa, Boet. 17.28, etc.
O.E.P. *wuniende on worulde,* Boet. 21.8, etc.
wyrde and wemde, Bede 382.4.
seo wylle and þæt wæter, Bede 38.34.
in wyrginge and in wanunge, Dial. 289.8.
O.E.P., Leg., Hom. *wyrhta and wealdend,* Boet. 149.11.
wyrhta þe hit worhte, Oros. 54.31.

THE ALLITERATIVE PHRASES IN THE OLD ENGLISH LEGAL PROSE
[O.E.Pr. Leg.].

In this section are gathered together the alliterative phrases found in representative sections of Old English legal prose— particularly the laws and wills.   In these documents a large number of stock alliterative phrases are to be found, many of which are of a purely legal kind.   Alongside these are also found many ordinary alliterative phrases not peculiar to this species of writing.   The following editions have been used :—

Wills : *Anglo-Saxon Wills,* D. Whitelock, Camb. 1930 (abr. *Whitelock*).

Laws : *The Laws of the Earliest English Kings,* F. L. Attenborough, Camb. 1922 (abr. *Attenb.*).

The Laws of the Kings of England from Edmund to Henry I, A. J. Robertson, Camb. 1925 (abr. *Robt.*).

Charters : *Select English Historical Documents of the Ninth and Tenth Centuries,* F. E. Harmer, Camb. 1914 (abr. *Harmer*).

The Crawford Collection of Early Charters and Documents, A. S. Napier and W. H. Stevenson, Oxford, 1895 (abr. *Napier*).

Since the Wills and Laws are of greater importance than the Charters, the collections of the latter by Kemble, de Gray Birch and Thorpe have not been used in the compilation of the following lists, which are only intended to be representative.[1]

---

[1] The references are to page and line, except in the case of the Laws to which reference is made by page and law.

abbod oððe abbodesse, Attenb. 42.23. *abbodas and abbodissan,* Robt. 90.2. *abbode and abbatissan,* Whitelock, 46.11.

hwilum be are, hwilum be æhte (whether landed or personal property [1]), Robt. 106.51. *mine are and mine æhta,* Whitelock, 56.11, 60.29.

we bebeodað Godes bebodum (we enjoin God's commands), Attenb. 170.1.

oððe hine bænde oððe hine beate, Robt. 126.33. *bende ne beate,* Robt. 196.42.

gebete þam byrgean (compensate the trustee of the marriage), Attenb. 46.31. **Hom.,** cp. **Alf.** *ic bidde and bebeode,* Harmer 4.3.

ge binnan . . . ge buton, Harmer 23.3, Robt. 32.3, etc.

to bocan and to bellan, Robt. 106.51.

bodian and bisnian (preach and set an example), Robt. 172.26.

borh oððe bote (debt or compensation), Robt. 84.20, etc.

borg abrece : borges bryce, Attenb. 64.3, etc.

ne bote ne bidde (nor demand compensation), Robt. 58.6.

brede and bigswice (fraud and guile), Attenb. 116.2.

mid calice and on cuppe, Whitelock, 2.12.

ceap ne geceapige, Attenb. 134.12.

ic kithe þe mine quide (I declare to you my will), Whitelock 76.1.

his (mete)-cu and his (mete)-corn, Whitelock 68.4.

gecuran and gecwædon (enacted and agreed upon), Attenb. 102. Introd., Robt. 90, Introd. *habbað gecoren and gecweden,* Robt. 120.6.

biquethen mine quiden (announce my will), Whitelock 2.1

uncwydd and uncrafod, Robt. 70.14.

O.E.P. *to deaðe ne fordeme,* Robt. 80.3.

deofollice dæda, Robt. 86.25.

O.E.P., Alf., Hom. *domas deme(ð),* Robt. 24.1, etc. (very frequently). *undom gedeme,* Robt. 180.15a. *deman swa rihte domas,* Attenb. 114. Introd.

O.E.P., Hom. *dumb oððe deaf,* Attenb. 70.14.

O.E.P., Alf. *ge earm ge eadig,* Robt. 24.1, etc. (frequently).

mid cwice erfe and mid earðe (livestock and produce), Harmer 13.18.

ðæs facnes and ðæs fules (crime and guilt), Attenb. 156.1.

þæt fæsten . . . gefæstan, Robt. 114.5.

fede oððe feormie, Robt. 180.13.

fel and flæsc,[2] Attenb. 50.42.

by felde and be fenne, Whitelock 74.15, 76.7.

man fenge on þe feoh, Whitelock 52.22.

Alf. *æt feo oððe æt feore,* Attenb. 108.12, Robt. 126.33, 196.40.

oððe feo oððe freme (either in property or reputation), Robt. 24.4. *feo oððe freoma,* Robt. 182.16.

feormige fligman : flieman feorme (harbouring a fugitive), Attenb. 46.30, 120.5.

Cp. **Alf.** *geferscipes ge freondscipes,* Robt. 124.27, 160.5.

folce to friðe (public security), Robt. 38.15, etc.

Hom. *(þearfan) frefrian and fedan* (comfort and feed on the poor), Robt. 46.

æt freolse oððe æt fæstene, Attenb. 102.3. *freolsa and fæstena,* Robt. 82.12, etc.

---

[1] The meaning of the more technical phrases is given in brackets.

[2] This phrase occurs frequently in the Old Frisian Laws, and in O.S. *Heliand.*

freond and fultum, Whitelock 46.14 and 26.

to friþe and to freondscipe, Attenb. 102, Introd.   *fri∂ and freondscipe*, Robt. 78.1, etc.

fri∂ and feorh, Robt. 58.3.

fri∂ian ne feormian, Attenb. 120.4.

∂a fri∂mal and ∂a forword, Robt. 56, Introd.

so ful and so forth (so ic it ahte), Whitelock 74.16, 19 and 92.10.

fule and afylede (vile and polluted), Attenb. 108.11.

fyr o∂∂e flod, Robt. 176.5.

gilde . . . -gilde (pay a tax), Robt. 66.4, etc.

Hom. *on gitsungan and on gifernessan* (covetousness), Robt. 86.25, 100.28.

Hom., Alf. *mid Godes gæfe*, Harmer 1.1, etc.   *mid Godes gife*, Attenb. 36, Introd.

buton golde and glæncgum (gold and ornaments), Robt. 114.2.

vnder hande habben, Whitelock 88.23 and 31.

hente mid hearme (pursued with hostility), Attenb. 106.6, Robt. 200.48.

to þam healme and to þam heor∂e (for the estate and the house), Attenb. 56.61.

holdlice hyran (loyally obey), Robt. 90.1.

horsa and hencgestas, Whitelock 50.17.

ne hrieme ne horn blawe, Attenb. 42.20, etc.

husel halga∂ (consecrate the sacrament), Robt. 158.4.

hyde and heafod (the hide and the head), Robt. 68.9.

Alf. *isen o∂∂e æren* (iron or brass), Attenb. 170.1.

Hom. *lara and laga*, Robt. 130.2, 170.21.   *Godes larum and lagum*, Robt. 104.42.

lēaden o∂∂e lǣmen (lead or clay), Attenb. 170.1.

Alf. *gif heo leng libbe*, Attenb. 68.8.   *leng lifede*, Harmer 16.24.   *gif heo leng liui∂*, Whitelock 8.18, etc.

mid leohte and lacum (with candles and offerings), Robt. 104.42.

O.E.P., Alf., Hom. *libban . . . life*, Robt. 30.1.   *life libban*, Robt. 126.31.

Alf. *ne libbende ne licgende*, Robt. 186.24.   *on libbendan and on licgendan*, Whitelock 50.18.

liceteras and leogeras (hypocrites and liars), Robt. 178.7.

Alf. *lif and land*, Robt. 90.35.   *landes and lifes*, Robt. 154.2.

þa hwile þe me lif gelæst, Robt. 38.16.   *swa lange swa me lif gelæst*, Robt. 36.12.

ge on life ge on legere (both during life and after death), Robt. 82.9, 92.5, 124.28.

his lif man aliese (his life shall be redeemed), Attenb. 40.12.

Hom. *gyf he mæg amd mot*, Robt. 184.20.

for mæg and for mundboran (kinsman and protectors), Attenb. 108.12, Robt. 126.33, 196.40.

sio mægbot and sio manbot, Attenb. 60.76.

mansworan o∂∂e mor∂wyrhtan, Attenb. 108.11.   *mor∂wyrhtan o∂∂e mansworan*, Robt. 102.36.

Hom. *mannslagan and manswaran*, Robt. 178.6.

mægslagan and mor∂slagan and mansworan, Robt. 144.15.

medemige be mæþe (mete out in proportion), Robt. 94.10.

mid medwe and mid merisce, Whitelock 70.3.

mid mete and mid mannum (produce and men), Napier 23.3, Whitelock
   32.6, etc.
mete ne munde (food nor shelter), Robt. 8.1.
Hom. *Godes miltse and his mildheortnesse*, Robt. 114, Introd.
O.E.P., Alf., Hom. *on mode and on mægene*, Whitelock 34.2.
on morðweorcan and on manslihtan, Robt. 86.25, 100.28.
to mund and to maldage,[1] Whitelock 82.6.
Hom. *munecas and minicena*, Robt. 80.4. *munecas and mynecena*, Robt.
   90.2, 162.6.
O.E.P., Alf., Hom. *mycel (is) and mære*, Robt. 158.4.
ordel and aðas, Attenb. 1069.
Alf. *ræd aredian* (determine what is advisable), Robt. 102.40, 178.11.
sare and saule (his wounds and his soul), Attenb. 106.10.
Hom. *schelda and spere*, Whitelock 2.9, etc. *scheldes and speren*, Whitelock 6.3. *scyldas and . . . spera*, Napier 23.6. *spæra and scylda,*
   Whitelock 22.20, etc.
Cp. **O.E.P.** *sweord and . . . spæra and . . . scyldas*, Harmer 33.14–15.
   spera and . . . scylda and . . . swyrd, Robt. 208.71. *sweord and
   scyldas and speru*, Whitelock 30.9, etc.
Alf. *swerd and spere*, Whitelock 88.28.
Alf., Hom. *driyten þe alle sheppe shop*, Whitelock, 86.6., 90.27.
swa him his scrift scrife, Attenb. 64.1, 142.26.
seel and sibb (happiness and peace), Harmer 36.19.
Hom. *sibb(e) and som(e)*, Robt. 90.1, 98.25, 168.17. *som and sib*, Robt.
   84.19.
Hom. *sibbiað and sehtað*, Robt. 130.1.
smeagan and geornlice spirian (inquire and diligently search), Robt. 138.40.
   smeagan and spyrian, Robt. 170.21.
Alf. *sæcende and smeagende*, Harmer 7.1–2.
on stalan and on strudungan (thefts and robberies), Robt. 86.25, 100.28.
ge on swynum, ge on sceapum, Harmer 20.21.
tyrian ne tynan (vex nor oppress), Robt. 104.48.
ðeofas and ðeodsceaðan, Robt. 176.4.
uhtsonge and æfensonge, Harmer 23.11–12.
Alf. *to wæde and to wiste* (food and clothing), Robt. 106.51.
wanige his weorðscipe (impair his status), Robt. 92.5.
Hom. *bewarian and bewerian*, Robt. 174.26.
O.E.P., Alf., Hom. *wealdend wyrhta (ealra gesceafta)*, Robt. 104.42, 130,
   Introd.
Alf. *his beweddode wif*, Robt. 162.7.
welan and wædle, Robt. 106.52.
Alf. *welige and wædle*, Robt. 208.68.
gewelegod and gewlenced, Harmer 20.15.
awende oppe gewanude (divert or curtail), Harmer 38.22.
awēodige and awyrtwalie (root up and eradicate), Robt. 174.1.
wer oppe wite (wergeld or fine), Robt. 102.38. *swa wer swa wite*, Robt.
   88.31. *swa be were, swa be wite*, Robt. 200.51. *ge mid were and mid
   wite*, Attenb. 64.2, etc.
werian and weorðiàn, Robt. 104.45.

----

[1] Cp. O.N. *mundr ok maldagi* (quoted by Miss Olszewska).

Alf., Hom. *weorc geweorht(e)*, Robt. 190.5, 212.75. *weorc gewyrce*, Robt. 180.13.

wiccean and wælcyrian, Robt. 144.15.

wiccan oððe wigeleras, Attenb. 108.11, Robt. 92.7, 176.4.

gif he wigie and man gewundie (if he fights and wounds a man), Attenb. 106.6.

ne his gewill ne his geweald (neither his desire nor his authority), Robt. 212.75.

Alf. *unwilles oppe ungewealdes*, Robt. 106.52.   **Alf.** *willes and/ne gewealdes* (willingly and deliberately), Attenb. 120.4, Robt. 106.52.

O.E.P., Alf., Hom. *his willan gewyrcean*, Robt. 170.20.

þeofa gewita and geweorhta (an accessory and accomplice of thieves), Robt. 124.27, 160.5.

witword and gewitnes (asseverations or testimonies), Robt. 64.3.

gif hwa ðonne woh wirce, Robt. 26.6.

Alf. *ge mid worde, ge mid wedd(e)*, Robt. 78.1, 80.5, 90.3.[1]

O.E.P., Alf., Hom. *word and weorc*, Robt. 84.22, etc.   *wordes and/oððe weorces*, Attenb. 102.2, Robt. 100.30, 218.84.

worldlicra weorca (secular employment), Robt. 96.22, 166.15.

gewrit oððe gewitnes, Attenb. 82.41.

Cp. **O.E.P. (2), Alf.** *þa gewritu and þa word* (written and verbal injunctions), Robt. 140.3.

Cp. **O.E.P., Hom.** *to wuldre and to weorðunga*, Harmer 12.23.

O.E.P., Alf., Hom. *wuldor and wurðmynt*, Robt. 174.26, 218.84.

---

[1] This phrase occurs in Old Frisian as *mit wedde end mit worde*.

CHAPTER 10

THE ALLITERATIVE PHRASES IN EARLY MIDDLE ENGLISH WORKS.

WE have already seen that many Old English alliterative phrases of all types survived into Middle English ; at the same time we naturally ask why so many others did not survive. In answer to this, it can be said that numerous Old English words died out before Middle English times ; in this way an alliterative phrase would be broken up and so disappear ; for example, in the phrase *fet ond folme*, the loss of the latter word caused the loss of the phrase altogether. The same fate eventually overtook the phrase *þa seocan ond þa sweltendan.*

The cause of the disappearance of various Old English words is often the ousting of the native word by an Old Norse or Old French word. Thus the O.E. *cyningas ond caseras* is remodelled *kings and kaisers* with the Old Norse cognate form for the second word ; so *bidde (a) ben* is replaced by *bidde a bone*, with the latter word from Old Norse ; in these cases the change is a very minor one, whereas in most cases it was not a cognate but a completely new word that ousted the native one. As interesting examples we may take : O.E. *on blostmum ond on bledum*, replaced by M.E. *blomes ond blossomes ;* O.E. *cleopian and ciegan* (or) *cwepan*, replaced by *clepe and calle ;* O.E. *gold ond gimm* probably replaced by M.E. *gold and gersume ;* O.E. *fedan and frefrian* replaced by *fede and foster*, with the latter word reinforced from Old Norse.

In other phrases a French word ousted the native one : O.E. *Godes gæfe* is replaced by M.E. *Godes grace ;* O.E. *muntas ond moras* by M.E. *mores and mountayns ;* O.E. *beryptan ond bereafian* by M.E. *robbe and reve ;* and O.E. *wig ond gewinn* by M.E. *werre and winne.*

There are also instances in which, for some reason or other, one native word has ousted another native word ; thus *feond* became specialised in meaning and was replaced by *fo* for general purposes. The common O.E. phrase *gefiellan feondas* is replaced by M.E. *felle*

fone ;   O.E. *freondas and feondas* by M.E. *frend and fo.*   In two
other cases we have a peculiar change :   O.E. *mode and mægene*
(very common) and *mod and mihte* (less common) are replaced by
M.E. *might and main ;* O.E. *stið ond stæðfæst* and *strang and stiðmod*
are replaced by M.E. *strong and steadfast.*   But we must always
remember that many Middle English phrases of Old English origin,
though not extant in Old English literature, may nevertheless have
been current in pre-Conquest days.

Hence, in dealing with Middle English phrases, it will always be
of interest to state the number of phrases which have *two* Old
English elements, those which have *one* Old English and *one* Old
Norse or Old French element, and those which have *two* Old Norse
or *two* Old French elements.

THE ALLITERATIVE PHRASES IN THE EARLY MIDDLE ENGLISH
ALLITERATIVE WORKS, EXCLUDING LAȝAMON'S *BRUT.*

The majority of the works included under this heading are, as
we have already seen in the treatment of the poetic compounds,
homiletic in tradition.   This is not merely true of the numerous
alliterative prose-works which in actual bulk are greatly in excess
of the poetry, but also of the poems such as the *Bestiary.*   The fact
that 621 alliterative phrases occur in these works which are of a
popular and homiletic type is not a matter for surprise.   Old
English homiletic literature is rich in alliterative phrases, and from
an examination of the Alfredian prose it seems likely that alliterative
phrases enjoyed great popularity in ordinary speech.

In the case of 482 of these phrases there is a combination of
two native elements, such as *buhan and benden, euer and aa,* or
friȝt ne fer.   Not all such phrases are extant in Old English, but
it is not improbable that vast numbers of them were actually
current.   Fourteen of these phrases are found in Old English
heroic poetry and forty-two in the religious, of which *dimme and
deorc, gleobeames and gome, sake and sinne, treye and tene, wlite and
westum,* are perhaps the most significant.   Nevertheless, it is true
that the majority of these early Middle English phrases which
occur in Old English poetry occur also in Old English prose ; in
short, there is little genuine contact with Old English poetic traditions.   This is also suggested by the fact that fifty-eight of the
phrases are also extant in Old English homiletic prose and fifty-
three in the Alfredian.   Such phrases as *beoden and benen, blod
and bon, drede deþ, lewid and lerid, þuldi and þolemod,* etc., show

the unmistakable homiletic origin of the main body of the phrases in these works, and it is impossible not to believe that the majority of the 482 Old English phrases are genuine survivals.

In fifty-two cases we have interesting phrases consisting of one native element and one Old Norse, such as *ay and oo, blo and blac, meke and milde, þral and þeow ;* they show that new phrases were still being coined, often by the bringing together of two ' semantic cognates '. The same is largely true of the twenty-four phrases of Old English and Old French origin, such as *buffeted and beten, chapele or chirche, lihte oþer lampe, milce and merci, onde and envie.*

In very few cases do we find a phrase consisting of two Old Norse elements or of two Old French elements ; here we have actually only four of the former and six of the latter—e.g. *rap and rac, chaunge chere, preye and preche.* In two cases we have interesting combinations of Old Norse and Old French without any native element—*caste a cri* and *false and frouȝ.*

As we treat of each group of phrases in Middle English, we shall observe how many of these early Middle English phrases recur again and again ; a glance at the table will indicate the survivals right through Laȝamon, Orm, the poems of the Alliterative Revival, Gower, and Chaucer, with the somewhat surprising fact that no less than *one-sixth* survives in Modern English.

THE ALLITERATIVE PHRASES IN THE EARLY MIDDLE ENGLISH FRAGMENTS.

The alliterative phrases found in the first three Middle English Alliterative fragments are given separately, because the poems in question are short, and are also rather distinct from the later works, which are of a more homiletic type.

A Description of Durham.

l. 12, *biscop and breoma bocera :* cp. the O.E. Andr. 607, *bisceopas ond boceras ;* also Laȝamon's *Brut,* 16901–2, etc. (five times), *his biscopes, his bocilærde men.*

l. 8, *in deope dalum,* cp. the O.E. Gen. 305, 421, *on þa deopan dala ;* also *Crist* 1532, *on þæt deope dæl ;* Laȝamon's *Brut,* 26934, *in ane dale deope ;* the phrase also occurs in Middle English alliterative poetry generally.

l. 5, *fisca . . . on floda ;* this phrase occurs in Old English prose (see B.T.), and, as we shall see, is of frequent occurrence in Middle English alliterative poetry ; see page 282, etc.

l. 7, *wuniað in ðem wicum ;* a phrase found in the Old English Genesis, 1812, 1890, as well as in Old English prose ; in Middle English the phrase seems to survive only in the *Cursor Mundi,* 7917.

While these four phrases are obviously traditional, no special significance can be attached to them. The non-alliterative phraseology in a similar manner looks back to Old English times ; cp. *bearnum gecyðed* (9), *domes bideð* (21), *deora ungerim* (8), etc.

In *Wenne, wenne,* the early Middle English charm, there are no examples of alliterative phrases ; the piece is, however, very short. The *1st Worcester Fragment* has one interesting alliterative phrase— l. 16 (nu is þeo leore) *forleten and* (þet folc is) *forloren,* a phrase not apparently found in Old English, but one which is not uncommon in Middle English alliterative poetry ; see page 254.

THE EARLY MIDDLE ENGLISH ALLITERATIVE PHRASES [E.M.E.].

a buten ende, Mar. p. 23. *aa buten ende,* Mar. p. 19.
ay and oo, Deb. l. 268.
bac and brest, Deb. ll. 386, 398.
from bale to eche blisse, Kath. l. 2295.
wið balebondes bitterliche bindest, Mar. p. 13.
Cp. **O.E.P.** *þet bittri bale,* H.M. p. 4. *þu bittre baleful* (beast), Kath. l. 2038.
of alle bales bote, Woh. p. 281. *bale bute bote,* S.W. p. 251. *botneð men of euch bale,* Kath. l. 2488.
to balewe ant to bismere, Kath. l. 552.
wiþ balewsiþ and wiþ bitternesse, Ur. p. 185.
bar þe on my bac, Deb. l. 138.
þou bar in þi brest, Deb. l. 192.
beaten ne binden, Kath. l. 1178. *beaten us ant binden,* Jul. p. 42. *beatest us ant bindest,* Mar. p. 16.
þe wile þou were betin and birst, Deb. l. 180.
beateð þe ant bustep þe, H.M. p. 42.
beateð hire bare bodi, Mar. p. 5.
to bed ibrohte, Jul. p. 7.
O.E.P. & Pr. *þeo bemen blowen,* Dep. l. 443.
O.E.Pr. *i þin eadi beoden ant i þine benen,* Mar. p. 21.
O.E.Pr. *beoden Þ tu biddest,* Mar. p. 11. *heo bed hire beoden,* Mar. p. 8.
me schal beoden and bodien, Kath. l. 1469-70.
beorninde briht, Mar. p. 19.
þet bere ðet blisfule bern, Lef. p. 205.
bere me aboute, Deb. l. 165.
i bidde ant bodie, Mar. p. 17.
Cp. **O.E.P. & Pr.** *bidde(n) . . . bone,*[1] Best. l. 101, Kath. l. 2388, Jul. p. 30, Mar. p. 8. *bede(n) . . . bone,* Deb. l. 309, Kath. l. 2369, Mar. p. 9.
fele biscopes and feole bokelered, Alf. l. 2.
hire bleo bigon to blakien, Mar. p. 9.
briht ant blisful, Lady, l. 19.
blisful ant bliðe, Kath. l. 1857.
bliðe . . . in endelese blisse, Mar. p. 12.
O.E.P. & Pr. *into blisse bringe,* Deb. l. 352. *to blisse brynge,* Hend. l. 312. *us to blisse brynge,* Hend. l. 38.

[1] Cp. O.N. *biðja bónar.*

blo and blac, Deb. l. 144.
O.E.P. & Pr. *blod ant bon*, Best. ll. 495, 636, Kath. l. 908, Jul. p. 62. *blod
ne ban*, Kath. l. 230.
blodles ant banles, Kath. l. 250, Mar. p. 18.
þe blod þat (us) bohte, Woh. p. 283. **O.E.P. & Pr.** *he me wið his blod bohte*,
Woh. p. 285. *bouȝte us with his blod*, Deb. l. 326.
blostme brihtest, Mar. p. 3.
blowen here bellewys, Blc. l. 6.
þer bloweð (inne blisse) blostmen, Lady, l. 37.
i . . . bokes ibreuet, Mar. p. 16.
þi bodi oðer eni of þine ban, Mar. p. 21.
(beren forð) hire bodi (ant) biburieden (hit), Kath. l. 2464.
i bodi ant i breoste, H.M. p. 30.
bold of eche blisse, Woh. p. 273.
bollen as a bite (swollen as a bottle), Deb. l. 68.
iboren ant ibroht forð, Kath. l. 263, Jul. p. 21.
born and bredde, Deb. l. 169.
al here brayn brestes, Blc. l. 6.
ne breoke ne beie, H.M. p. 20.
brekeþ bon, Alf. l. 307.
brec mine bondes, Mar. p. 18.
breke bred, Hend. l. 217.
brihte burde, Mar. p. 17.
briȝt on ble, Deb. l. 121. *brihtest bleo*, Mar. p. 10. *alre bleo brihtest*, Mar.
p. 7.
O.E.P. *so briht blikinde*, Mar. p. 13.
a brond þat were forbrent, Deb. l. 416.
forbroken and forbroiden, Best. l. 108.
O.E.Pr. *bruken blisse*, Mar. p. 19.
buffeted and beten, Woh. p. 281.
buggen ant biȝeoten, Kath. l. 1619.
buh . . . and . . . bei, Mar. p. 7. *buhe ne beie*, Mar. p. 17. *buhe ne beien*,
Jul. p. 13. *to þe buwe and mine kneon ich beie*, Lady, l. 3. *buheð ant
beieð*, Mar. p. 4, etc.
buhsume ant beiesume, Kath. l. 2002.
buhan ant benden, Mar. p. 7, etc.
buh to mine bonen, Lou, p. 211.
bulden a burh, Kath. l. 1642. *buldeð ower boldes*, Jul. p. 72. *ðe wes bold
gebyld*, Gr. l. 1.
O.E.P. *buri (of bale) ant bold (of eauer euch bitternesse)*, S.W. p. 253.
bursten hire banes, Jul. p. 58.
Cp. **O.E.Pr.** *bursten ant breken hire bondes*, Mar. p. 19. *bursten hire bondes
(and breken alle clane)*, Jul. p. 58.
buste ant beate, Jul. p. 24. (See under *beateð*.)
it kaste a cri, Deb. l. 442.
O.E.Pr. *kasten into cwarterne and into cwalmhuse*, Mar. p. 4. *kasten in
cwalmhus*, Kath. l. 1547, Mar. p. 8. *bicluset in cwarterne and i cwalmhuse*, Kath. l. 601. (Cp. *vt of þon quarcerne of þan qualehuse*, Laȝamon's
Brut, ll. 31, 160.)
kene te keoruen, Jul. p. 56.
(i)ken ant icnawen, Kath. ll. 423, 2041, 2222.

we kenniŏ ant cnaweŏ, Kath. ll. 2065–6.
kepeŏ ant copneŏ (expects and longs for), Kath. l. 2424.
changede cher, Mar. p. 3. *chaunged is my chere*, Deb. l. 149.
chapele oŏer chirche, Mar. p. 20.
chit te ant cheoweŏ þe (chides and jaws), H.M. p. 42.
Cp. **O.E.P. & Pr.** *king* . . . *keiser*, Kath. ll. 1909–10. *kinges and keiseres*,
Mar. p. 16, etc., S.W. p. 261.
kynge, keysere and knyght, ABC, l. 20.
þe keiser . . . *ant þe kinge*, Jul. p. 24. *keiser ant king icrunet*, Mar. p. 16.
keiser of kinges, Mar. pp. 4, 10.
þe king of alle kinges, H.M. p. 14. **O.E.P. & Pr.** *kingene king*, Jul. p. 54,
Mar. pp. 11, 18.
king icrunet, Mar. p. 16. *kinges icrunet*, Jul. p. 22.
O.E.Pr. *king ne quene*, M.M. l. 7.
O.E.P. & Pr. *kissen ant cluppen*, Woh. p. 285.
to claterin ant to cleouen (to rattle and cleave asunder), Kath. ll. 2000–1.
cleopien ant callen, Mar. p. 3.
þe clerk and þe knyght, Alf. l. 48. *clerkis and knyghtis*, ABC, l. 4.
on hire cneon to cneolin, Mar. p. 20.
ŏe coc and te capun, Best. l. 300.
ouercom ant akaste ham, Mar. pp. 1, 2, etc.
come to court, Deb. l. 79.
icudd cniht, Kath. l. 2225.
custe ham a cos (of pes), Jul. p. 74.
cuŏ me ant ken me, Mar. p. 16.
cwen icrunet, H.M. p. 8, Kath. l. 1466.
icrunet in his kinedom, Mar. p. 4.
icrunet . . . *wiŏ crune*, H.M. p. 30. *ikruned mid guldene krune*, Lady,
l. 52.
ure cunde ant ure cun, Mar. p. 16.
O.E.Pr. *to deaŏes idon*, Mar. p. 1. *þ me to deaŏe deŏ*, Kath. l. 2405.
O.E.P. *deaŏ drehde*, Kath. l. 1160. *deŏ drehen*, Jul. p. 70, Kath. l. 965.
deŏ drehde, Mar. p. 18. *deŏ dreheŏ*, Mar. p. 1, etc. *drehen na deŏ*,
Kath. l. 1097. *to drehen þis deaŏ*, Kath. l. 1374.
deaŏes dunt, H.M. pp. 22, 38.
deaŏes dute, H.M. p. 50. *dute of deaŏe*, Jul. p. 28.
ded (was) and doluen, Best. ll. 26–7.
of ded and of dult wit, Kath. l. 1262.
Cp. **O.E.P.** *þou þat dedes couþest deme*, Deb. l. 61.
O.E.Pr. ' *alle dedes thou didest*, Deb. l. 71. *þet dede to donne*, H.M. p. 34.
O.E.P. & Pr. *demen me to deaŏe*, Jul. p. 24. *demde hire to deaŏe*, Mar.
p. 19. *to ech deŏ idemet*, Jul. p. 14. *me is deaŏ idemet*, Mar. p. 20. *to
deaŏe fordemest*, Mar. p. 16.
demed for to deien, Woh. p. 283.
O.E.P. & Pr. *demeŏ euchan his dom*, S.W. p. 247. *heo demde feole domes*,
Dep. l. 613.
wyth den of here dyntes, Blc. l. 2.
derf drehen, Kath. l. 2392. *derf drehe*, Mar. p. 5. *þe derf þet tu drehest*,
H.M. p. 24, etc. *þe derf of deaŏ drehen*, Kath. l. 2393.
derueŏ ant drecheŏ (afflict and harass), S.W. p. 251.
Cp. **O.E.P.** *so derne þing ant so derf of Godes dihelnesse*, Mar. p. 16. *ac
æfre diʒelliche þu woldest ham bidernan*, Dep. ll. 490–1.

dihteþ hit ant dealeð, Woh. p. 271.
dihteþ ant demeþ, S.W. p. 267.
O.E.P. *dimme and deorce*, Gr. l. 12.
i . . . diueri ant darie, Mar. p. 16.
diuerin ne dreden (tremble nor dread), Kath. l. 622.
he diueð dun, Best. l. 423.
don out of dahene, Jul. p. 30.
don to deaþe, Jul. p. 18. *don to deaðe*, Kath. l. 2100.
don (opere) dedes, Deb. l. 99.
fordon ant fordemed, Kath. l. 427. *fordude ant fordemde*, Mar. p. 2.
bi doune and dale, Deb. l. 293.
dragan to deaþe, Mar. p. 2. *droh ham to deaþe*, Jul. p. 4.
dream ant drihtfare, Kath. l. 1832.   '
O.E.Pr. (*þæt deouel me*) *ne drecche,* (*ne dweolðe me*), *ne derie*, Lady, l. 148.
dred of deaþ, Kath. l. 165.
O.E.Pr. *ne dred ich na deð*, Mar. p. 5. *dreden deaþ*, Mar. p. 5, etc., Kath.
      l. 125, S.W. p. 255. *dreden na deð*, Kath. l. 1842, etc. *ne dredest na
      deð*, Jul. p. 54. *ne dredeð na deð*, Kath. l. 1215.
drehen ant drahen (endure and suffer), Kath. l. 1891. *idrohen ant idrehen*,
      Jul. p. 34.
dreien ant drehen, Mar. p. 5, etc.
dreori ant drupest alre monne, Kath. ll. 2021–2.
dryve me to deþ, Blc. l. 2.
driven dun, Best. l. 8, H.M. pp. 21, 23, etc. *draf (perto) dunriht*, Kath.
      l. 1997.
duhti oðer dusi (sound or foolish), Kath. l. 781.
dumb and daft, Deb. l. 55.
O.E.P. & Pr. *dumb . . . def*, Deb. l. 118. *dumbe ant deaue*, Kath.
      l. 1062, Mar. p. 6, etc. *þe dumbe ant te deaue*, Mar. p. 6. *def and dumb*,
      Deb. l. 151.
dust oðer deu, Best. l. 7.
to duste hit schal dryuen, Alf. l. 135. *driuen al to duste*, Jul. p. 40.
(*a*)*dusten adun*, H.M. p. 41, etc., Jul. p. 48, etc., Mar. p. 11, etc. *duste him
      dunriht*, Mar. p. 12. *dusten dunewardes*, Kath. l. 1967. *adun . . .
      iduste*, Mar. p. 11.
duste hit swuch dunt, Kath. l. 1999.
eardið in eorðe, Mar. p. 9.
O.E.Pr. *mid eȝen, mid eren*, Ur. l. 189. *et earen, ed ehnen*, S.W. p. 251.
þe eorl and þe epelyng, Alf. l. 44.
to þe engles ant to þe archangels, S.W. p. 259.
þe este ant al þe eise, H.M. p. 40.
euer ant aa, Mar. p. 17.
afal þu mine famen, Jul. p. 32.
false and frouȝ, Deb. l. 300.
swuch farlac ich fele, Mar. p. 16.
for þe farlac offruht, Mar. p. 9.
fecheð hire fode, Best. l. 179.
fedin ant fostrin, Mar. p. 2, etc. *fostrid (fayre) and fedde*, Deb. l. 171.
Cp. **O.E.P.** *þas feye furþ* (the life of a doomed man), Alf. l. 113.
O.E.P. *feir ant freolich*, Jul. p. 6. *feier ant freolich*, Kath. l. 68, S.W.
      p. 257. *freolich . . . ant feir*, Mar. p. 13.
O.E.Pr. *bi feld and fenne*, Deb. l. 115.

O.E.Pr. *fihten wiþ þe feond,* Mar. p. 2.
fist (fiȝt) *ant fle,* Hend. l. 78, etc.
fikel ant fals, Ur. p. 185.
fikele ant frakele, H.M. p. 10.　(Cp. *A Luue Ron,* l. 12.)
þe fisches þat i þe flodes fleoteþ,[1] Mar. p. 9.
O.E.Pr. *flesch ant fel,* Kath. l. 1604.　*fleys and felle,* Deb. l. 359.
flesches fulðe, H.M. p. 28, etc., Lef. p. 205.　*flesches fulðen,* Mar. p. 13.
fleschliche fulðe, H.M. p. 4, etc.　*fleschliche fulþen,* Mar. p. 3, etc.
O.E.Pr. *þet flod þet fleaw* (*of þine wunden*), Lou. p. 211.
to fluttunge ant to fode, H.M. pp. 36, 38.
so forð ant so feor, Mar. p. 15.
to hare freond, ah to hare fan, H.M. p. 42.　Cp. **O.E.P.** *fa, freond,* H.M. p. 17.
famen ant freondes, Mar. p. 8.
fret hire fille, Best. l. 319.
friȝt ne fer, Deb. ll. 343, 476.
for to frourin ant for to fremien, Kath. ll. 284–5.
offruht ant offearet, Kath. ll. 670, 1244.
O.E.Pr. *þe fuheles þe fleon* . . . Mar. p. 9.　*foules flie,* Deb. l. 115.
þe foule fend, Deb. ll. 456, 465.
fule ant fenniliche, Mar. p. 15.
fuleð þi flesch, H.M. p. 48.
þat foule fleys, Deb. l. 45, etc.
fule fulðe, Lady, l. 94.
ifulhet in font, Mar. p. 1.　*fulht of fontstan,* Mar. p. 19.
te gandre and te gos, Best, l. 302.
O.E.Pr. *aȝeuen hire gast,* Jul. p. 58.
glede me wiþ þi gleo, Mar. p. 7.
gleo ant gledunde, Mar. p. 3.
O.E.Pr. *gleobeames amd gome,* Lady, l. 62.
ich gomeni . . . *ant gledie,* Mar. 6.　*me gomeneð ant gledeð,* Mar. p. 11.
gomeful ant glad, Mar. p. 10.
glistinde ant gleaminde, Kath. l. 1653.　*þ glistnede as gleam deð,* Mar. p. 9.
　　glistinde glem, Mar. p. 12.
þei gnawen and gnacchen, Blc. l. 9.
Godes grace, H.M. p. 20, Kath. l. 1248, Mar. p. 16, S.W. p. 257.
Cp. **O.E.Pr.**[2] *gold and gersum,*[2] Kath. l. 797, Woh. p. 269.　*wið gersum ant*
　　wið golde, Mar. p. 3.
Cp. **O.E.Pr.**[2, 3]　*golscipe and giscing, giuernesse,* Best. l. 245.
ðe grace ant þe ȝeoue, Lou. p. 209.
greden ant granin, H.M. p. 64.
igremment ant igabbet, Kath. l. 2273.
to gremien ant o grome gredde, Mar. p. 18.
grennede and ȝenede wide, Deb. l. 403.
greowe as gres doþ, Alf. l. 81.
as gres grenen (as green as grass), H.M. p. 49.
grimful ant grureful, S.W. p. 253.
ha agrisen wes of þ grisliche gra, Mar. p. 9.
grisle ant grure, S.W. p. 251, etc., Mar. p. 15.

---

[1] Cp. O.N. *fiskr flóþi í,* etc.　　　　　　[2] Cp. O.N. *gull ok görsimar.*

of grure ant of granunge, S.W. p. 253.
for þe grure þe graþ þe, Mar. p. 9. *grure graþ euch mon*, Kath. l. 1969.
O.E.P. & Pr. *to habben ant to halden*, Kath. l. 1867. *habben and/ne halden*, Mar. p. 3, etc.
halde ant heie his halewund heastes, Kath. ll. 232-3.
haldeð his heastes, Kath. l. 1788.
þu haldest ant heuest up, Mar. p. 10.
hali ant halewundi, Mar. p. 11.
O.E.Pr. *he halt in his hond*, Kath. l. 1779.
halte ant houerede (hump-backed), Kath. l. 1063. *halt ne houeret*, Mar. p. 20.
halwunde ant halsum, Mar. p. 21.
harde ant hetefeste, Jul. p. 58.
þ tu hauest in heorte, Kath. p. 2301.
heane ant hatele, Kath. l. 1947.
þe heanað ant harmið, Kath. l. 2402. *heaneð us ant hearmeð*, H.M. p. 16.
heani ȝe ant hearmeð, Mar. p. 16.
O.E.Pr. *heaneð ant hateð*, Mar. pp. 8, 17. *henen ant hatien*, Jul. p. 50.
heatel (ham) ant heard (ham), S.W. p. 253.
heaten hit walmhat, Jul. p. 68.
þat þu hefdest on horde, Dep. l. 248.
heh on hire heaued, Mar. p. 10.
Cp. **O.E.Pr.**[2] *heoueð hire on heh up*, Mar. p. 18.
heuen up hare honden, Kath. ll. 1407-8. *on heh iheuen up honden*, Mar. p. 20.
hef (up) hire hond, Mar. pp. 8, 9. *wið honden upaheuene*, Jul. p. 58, etc.
heg is tat hil, Best. l. 18. *in þe hehe hul (hill)*, H.M. p. 28.
O.E.P. *hei and holi*, Lady, l. 70, Lef. p. 207.
help ant hap, Kath. l. 184.
henges dun his heaued, Woh. p. 283.
heren ne hercnin, Kath. l. 1976.
heriede helle, Kath. l. 336, Lef. p. 205. *þu herehedest helle*, Mar. p. 10.
ich heie ant herie, Jul. p. 54. *heien ant/ne herien*, Jul. pp. 18, 40, 56, Kath. ll. 459, 510, 1769, Mar. p. 3, etc. *heiden ant hereden*, Mar. p. 1.
to herien ant to heien, Jul. p. 64. *ihered ant iheied*, Kath. ll. 2380, 2504. *iheret ant iheiet*, Jul. pp. 34, 78.
herien ant hersumin, Kath. ll. 146, 248, etc., Mar. p. 4. *to hersumin ant herien*, Kath. ll. 352-3.
herkeneth and hereth, ABC, l. 10, Kath. l. 1720.
heuy in herte, ABC (2), l. 8.
hirdmen in halle, H.M. p. 43.
hold up min heaved, Lou. p. 213.
hon up ant hongin, Jul. p. 28.
hongeð hire on heh, Mar. p. 5. *hongin on heh*, Mar. p. 6.
hope of heale, Jul. p. 64, Mar. p. 7.
hope and help, Mar. p. 8.
of hude and of hewe, Death Fragment, 20.
O.E.Pr., cp. **O.E.P.**[1] *hudden hare heauet*, Mar. p. 7.
byhud hit on þire heorte, Alf. l. 163.
hitt (hides) hire in hire hole, Best. l. 365.
hule ant huide (cover and hide), Woh. p. 279.
Cp. **O.E.Pr.**[1] *wiþ (against) hunger and wiþ heriunge*, Alf. l. 56.
hunger ant euch hete, Kath. l. 2401.

hus ant hinen, H.M. p. 6.
to huting ant to hokere, Jul. p. 52.
O.E.P. & Pr.   *hut (hȳdan) ant heleð*, Mar. p. 15.
O.E.P. & Pr.   *in and out*, Deb. 1. 108, etc.   *in and ut*, Dep. 1. 268.
his lages luuien, Best. 1. 135.   *lahede hit ant lokede* (ordained and determined it), Kath. 1. 1206.
O.E.P.   *to lahen so lude*, Mar. p. 14.
O.E.Pr.   *þe lare þ ich nu leorni*, Kath. 11. 938–9.   **O.E.Pr.**   *lare . . . lerden*, Kath. 1. 468.   *ilearet in godes lar*, Mar. p. 1.
O.E.P. & Pr.   *þe laðe . . . þe leoue*, H.M. pp. 40, 54.   *loð (hem is ded) ant lef (to liuen)*, Best. 1. 412.
leaf (belief) *ant lare*, Kath. 1. 348, etc.
leafeð ant lest forð (remains and lasts on), H.M. p. 34.
leas and lutiȝ, Dep. 1. 92.   *leas and luti*, Dep. 1. 332.
heo leat (lūtan) lahe, Mar. p. 12.
O.E.Pr.   *leden mi lif*, Lou, p. 211.   *ledeth lyf*, Hend. 1. 270.   *leadeð . . . lif*, S.W. p. 261.   *lif leadað*, H.M. p. 41.   *lyf (to) leden*, Alf. 11. 11, 285, Blc. 1. 20, Lou. p. 211, M.M. 1. 27.
leitede al o leie, Mar. p. 9, Kath. 1. 1651.   *leitinde o leie*, Kath. 1. 671.   *i leitinde leie*, Jul. p. 13.   *seh þene ley leiten*, Jul. p. 66.   *te lei of þi luue leiten*, Mar. p. 18.
leiteð of leome, Mar. p. 13.   *leitinde leome*, Kath. 1. 1681.   *liht leomeð ant leiteð*, Mar. p. 13.
þe leyȝe it lemede, Deb. 1. 404.
of þi leitinde loue, Ur. p. 185.
leiðe ant lodlike, Best. 1. 357.
lenen lif, Kath. 11. 1084–5.   *lif ileanet*, Mar. p. 20.   *lif . . . lent*, Deb. 1. 338.
leof . . . ant . . . licwurðe, H.M. p. 14.
swa leoflic ant swa lufsum, Ur. p. 183.
leoflukest ant lufsumest, Jul. p. 13.
leoflukest . . . to lokin uppon, Mar. p. 4.
leornin ne lustnin, Kath. 1. 110.
þu leosest ant forletest, Mar. p. 6.
leoðebeie limen, Mar. p. 16.
leowsin ant leauen, Jul. p. 38.   *leauen ne leosen*, Mar. p. 5.
leowsin ne leoðien (loosen nor slacken), Kath. 1. 1519.   *leowsede ant leoðede*, Mar. p. 13.   *leowse ant leoðe me*, Mar. p. 14.   *leoðe ant leowse*, Mar. p. 17.
O.E.Pr.   *lewid and lerid*, ABC, 1. 21.
leteð ant leaueð, Mar. p. 21.
O.E.Pr.   *leuestu ant luuest*, Mar. p. 4.   *þeo þ him riht leueð ant luuieð*, Kath. 11. 950–1.   *leueð ant luuieð*, Jul. p. 22, etc.   *luuie and leue*, Jul. p. 16, etc.
O.E.Pr.   *þi luue ant tin bileau*, Mar. p. 16.
leven on ure lore, Deb. 1. 464.
O.E.Pr.   *licomes luste*, Mar. p. 1, etc.   *licomes lust*, H.M. p. 20, etc.   *licomliche lustes*, Ur. p. 189.   *þe lustes of mine licame*, Lou. p. 211.
mi lif ant mi leofmon, Kath. 11. 2348, 2445.   *mi lif ant mi leof*, Kath. 1. 1880.   *mi lif, mi luue, mi leouemon*, Mar. p. 8.   *mi lef, mi lif, mi luue*, Woh. p. 287.   *mi luue, mi lif, mi leof*, Woh. p. 269.   *mi lif ant mi luue*, Kath. 1. 1520.

mi lif, mi leome, Ur. p. 183. *leome ant lif,* Kath. l. 2376. *to lif ant to leomen,*
    Kath. l. 1046, Mar. p. 1.
O.E.Pr. *vre lif leten,* Alf. l. 118.
O.E.P. & Pr. *lif . . . forlete,* Mar. p. 18. *vre oure lyf . . . forleten,* Alf.
    l. 128. *forleten þis lif,* Kath. l. 1376.
O.E.Pr. *þe wile his owe lyf ileste mote,* Alf. l. 149. *Ꝥ lif Ꝥ echliche ilesteð,*
    Mar. p. 1. *ant vre owe lif lutel hwile ileste,* Alf. l. 277. *mi lif hath
    last,* Deb. l. 315.
O.E.Pr. *no lif ne lond,* Deb. l. 233.
lifre and þine lihte, Dep. l. 274.
ligge (so) lowe, Lou. p. 211 (twice). *Ꝥ leið me so lahe,* Mar. p. 16.
lihten swa lah, Mar. p. 14, Jul. p. 8. *lahe iliht,* H.M. p. 32.
ligtlike ge lepeð up, Best. l. 315.
liht oðer lampe, Mar. p. 20.
Cp. **O.E.P. & Pr.** *liht . . . leome,* Mar. p. 8. *liht and . . . leome,* Ur.
    p. 185. *of liht ant of leome,* Mar. p. 20. *leome ant liht,* Kath. ll. 1582,
    1680.
te liht of his leor, S.W. p. 259.
lime and lyþ, Deb. l. 77. *lim ant lið,* Jul. p. 13.
linde and lef, Deb. l. 114.
mei neauer littlin ne aliggen, Mar. p. 5.
lið . . . ant lire (joint and flesh), Jul. p. 58. *tolimit lið ba ant lire,* H.M.
    p. 28.
liðin ant listin, Jul. p. 2. *lusteð me . . . ant liðeð,* Jul. p. 72.
O.E.P. *liuiende in londe,* Mar. p. 2.
þe lives lyȝt, Deb. l. 7.
mines liues leome, Lady, l. 2.
al toloken ant tolimet, Mar. p. 7.
as hit lomp ant lei to, Mar. p. 4.
lonc ant leane, S.W. p. 249.
þat lond to leden, Alf. l. 46.
O.E.Pr. *longes lyues,* Alf. l. 109. *long lyues,* M.M. l. 1. *long lyf,* Hend.
    l. 307.
longe libben, Kath. l. 2275.
O.E.Pr. *such lores ase þou lernest,* Hend. l. 45.
losen lif, Kath. l. 1117.
louerd of lyf, Alf. l. 28. *lauerd of lif,* Kath. l. 2151.
lufsume leor, Jul. p. 21, Kath. l. 1419. *hire lufsum leor,* Mar. p. 3. *lufsum
    on leor,* Woh. p. 269. *þi leor is lufsum,* Kath. l. 313. *þi luueli leor,*
    Woh. p. 269. *hire leofliche leor,* Jul. p. 20.
lufsume lefdi, Kath. l. 104, Mar. p. 13, 16.
mi lufsum leof, Jul. p. 16. *þi lufsume leofmon,* Jul. p. 52, etc., Kath. l. 2305.
lufsum ant lusti, Woh. p. 269.
luken ðe lides, Best. l. 16.
lust of lecherie, H.M. p. 12, etc.
lustneð nu his lare, S.W. p. 267.
mid swuþe luðere lasten, Lady, l. 123.
luuyen hine and lykyen, Alf. l. 28.
O.E.Pr. *manie ant mikle,* Best. l. 536.
matines, masse, Deb. l. 98.
þin mawe and þin milte (maw and melt), Dep. l. 277.
me and mine, Kath. l. 2217.

his medes to mowen, Alf. l. 60.
meies ba ant meken, Mar. p. 16.
men ant meidenes, Mar. p. 17.
men (nou) under mone, Deb. l. 305.
menske ant mildeschipe, Woh. p. 269.
of mesure ant of mete (moderation), S.W. p. 255.
mete ant mel (meat and meal), Kath. l. 1819.
te mihte ant te mot (the might and the reasoning), Kath. l. 1271.
my3t and mayn, Deb. l. 467.
mihti ant meinful, Kath. ll. 1094, 2043, Mar. p. 4, etc.   *meinful ant almihti*,
    Kath. l. 1094.
milce ant merci, H.M. p. 29, Jul. p. 48, Lef. p. 205, Lou. p. 209, Mar. p. 3,
    etc.   *merciable ant milzful*, Jul. p. 52.
purh his milde milce, Kath. l. 1375.   *pi milde milce*, Mar. p. 20.
O.E.P. & Pr.   with milde mod, Deb. l. 477.
milde (ant) meoke, Hend. l. 130, H.M. p. 60, Jul. p. 50, Kath. l. 103, S.W.
    p. 257.   *mildest ant meokest*, Mar. p. 4.
miltschipe ant meokschipe, H.M. p. 62.   *meknesse ant mildschipe*, Woh.
    pp. 273, 275.   *mekelic ant mildschipe*, H.M. pp. 57, 58.
mikel meyne, Deb. l. 280.
that most is of myght, ABC, I, l. 22.
O.E.Pr.   *misliche ant monifald*, Woh. p. 281.
ðe wes molde imynt, Gr. l. 2.
in mot er in market, Best. l. 378.
motede ant mealde (reasoned and discoursed), Kath. l. 1238.
unmuchelin ant melten, Mar. p. 6.
mi murhðe ant mi mede, Jul. p. 30, Kath. l. 2350.   *mi mede ant te murhðe*,
    Jul. p. 18.
pe murhðe ant te menske, H.M. p. 32.
ne mei . . . no muð imelen, Lady, l. 48.   *meale wið muð*, Kath. l. 1722.
mid pine mupe bimænan, Dep. ll. 488-9.
(ma pen alle mon mahten) wið hare mup munnen, Kath. ll. 1698, 2474,
    Mar. p. 5.   *mare pen eni muð hit cuðe munnen*, Mar. p. 23.   *pat ne mei
    hit munne na muð*, S.W. p. 263.
munneð mi nome ant munegeð, Mar. p. 21.
bi . . . ðe necke ant bi ðe nos, Best. l. 303.
in neode ant in nowcin, Kath. l. 2395.
in neodfule ant in nakede, Kath. l. 102.
O.E.Pr.   *his nome nempnede*, Kath. l. 1329.
onde ant envie, Deb. l. 195.
O.E.Pr.   *ordfrume ant ende (ant ord)*, Mar. p. 8.
O.E.P. & Pr.   *ort ant ende*, Jul. p. 24.
patriarke ant prince, Mar. p. 2.
te patriarches ant te prophetes, S.W. p. 261.
wið pel ant wið purpre, Kath. l. 1450.   *purpres ant pelles*, Jul. p. 9.
pile ant pip (peel and pith), Deb. l. 75.
pine oðer passiun, Kath. l. 1157.   *pinen ant passiun*, Jul. p. 62, Kath.
    l. 2390, Mar. p. 1, Woh. p. 275.
pleiferen pleien (in helle), Jul. l. 56.
preye ant preche, Deb. ll. 93, 330.
ragged, roue (O.E. *rūh*), Deb. l. 369.
rap and rac, Deb. l. 140 (= Dan. *rap*, Norw. *rak*).

to ravin reowliche, Jul. p. 48.
aras, ant averde him seoluen from deaðe, Kath. ll. 1111–12.
reauers hit hit robbið, H.M. p. 40.
(þe sunne) reccheð hire rune, Mar. p. 9.
ired ant araht (read and considered), Mar. p. 1.
O.E.Pr. *I rede hem red*, Deb. l. 485.
refde þen riche, Jul. p. 40.
ðanne remen he alle a rem, Best. l. 540.
renneð (ge) rapelike, Best. ll. 178, 368.
reowfulle reames, Jul. p. 7, Kath. l. 162.
rest and ro, Deb. ll. 111, 183, 188. *ro ant rest*, Hend. l. 305. *to ro ant to reste*, Mar. p. 20.
riche of rente (with a large income), Jul. p. 5.
riche robes, Deb. ll. 36, 277.
O.E.Pr. *he hadde riden þat rode*, Deb. l. 417.
O.E.Pr. *riht me ant read me*, Jul. p. 31. *rihte us and reade*, S.W. p. 253.
rondin ant rendin, Mar. p. 6.
rudie ant reade, Kath. l. 1421.
rudi as þe rose, Jul. p. 20. *so read so rose*, Lady, l. 53.
mid here sage ant mid here song, Best. l. 475.
upon þe sadil þer he was set, Deb. l. 418.
O.E.P. *of sake ant of sunne* (guilt and sin), Woh. p. 283.
O.E.P. & Pr. *sar ne sorhe*, Kath. ll. 1164–5. *sorhe ne sar*, Kath. l. 1685. *to sorhe ant to sar*, H.M. p. 38. *sorhe ant . . . sar*, Mar. p. 6. *þurh sar ant þurh sorewe*, Ur. p. 187.
þe sorhful sar, Mar. p. 7.
sarimod ant sorhful, Dep. l. 410, Kath. l. 2327. *wið sari mod ant sorhful*, Kath. l. 2327. **O.E.Pr.** *sorhfule ant sarie*, Mar. p. 17, etc. *seorhful ant sorimod*, Dep. l. 410, Kath. l. 410.
sat or stod, Deb. l. 134.
O.E.Pr. *alle þine schaftes þat tu schop*, Woh. p. 271. *seftes soþ ure seppande*, Best. l. 356. *þes alre schafte schuppent*, Kath. l. 882. *schuppere of alle schaftes*, Woh. p. 281.
schame or sinne, Deb. l. 236. *of scheome ant of sunne*, Kath. l. 91. *in schome ant in sinne*, Woh. p. 277. *to sinne ant schame*, Deb. l. 85.
bi his schome, bi his sor, Lef. p. 207. *scheome . . . sar*, H.M. p. 50. *Pe sar ant te scheome*, Jul. p. 26. *sar ant scheome*, H.M. p. 48.
schame ant sorewe, Deb. l. 304.
scharp sweord, Kath. l. 2334.
schawde him ant sutelede himseolf, Kath. ll. 1834–5.
to schawen hit i schrifte, Mar. p. 15.
schene under schete, Alf. l. 213.
schenre þen þe sunne, H.M. p. 30, etc., Kath. l. 1663, Mar. p. 23, S.W. p. 263. *as schene as schininde sunne*, Mar. p. 19. *tu schinest schenre þen þe sunne*, Mar. p. 13. *schininde as schene as þe sunne*, Jul. p. 54. *schin ease sunne*, H.M. p. 62. **O.E.Pr.** *til ðe sunne haueð sinen*, Best. l. 12.
scendest me mid sunne, Dep. l. 125.
Cp. **O.E.Pr.** *schent ant schomet*, Woh. p. 277. *scheomliche schent te*, H.M. p. 42. *schendlac . . . scheome*, Kath. ll. 1278–9. *to scheome ant to schendlac*, H.M. p. 22. Cp. **O.E.P.** *wið same ant wið sending*, Best. l. 339. **O.E.Pr.** *scheomeð . . . ischend*, Mar. p. 15.

ischild me urom seorwe, Lady, l. 120.
schimmen ant schinen, Mar. p. 9, etc., S.W. p. 257. *schiminde and schan*, Mar. p. 9. *schineð ant schimmeð*, S.W. p. 257.
schininde ant schenre, of ʒimstanes steapre þen is eni steorre, Kath. ll. 1646-8. Cp. **O.E.Pr.** *schineð as doð steorren*, S.W. p. 261.
sipes ge sinkeð, Best. l. 447.
þe schonken ant te schuldren, Jul. l. 48.
schrenchen ant schunchen (deceive and terrify), Jul. p. 34.
þe sea ant te sunne, Kath. l. 1782. *mit see ant mit sunne*, Mar. p. 4.
seggeð hore sunne (confess their sin), Dep. l. 499. *sei ðu scrifte to ðe prest sinnes tine*, Best. l. 159.
sek ant ser (sick and sear), Deb. l. 339.
sec of sorwe, Lou. p. 211.
his sedes to sowen, Alf. l. 59.
(hefden) isehen sihðen of heouene, Kath. ll. 1730-1. **O.E.Pr.** *sihðen þ ich iseo*, Mar. p. 16. *I sauʒ a selly syʒt*, Deb. l. 3.
sely sitte (rest contented), Alf. l. 270.
þ hit ne sem noþðer ne suteli, Mar. p. 5.
þi semli schape, Mar. p. 4.
unsemly for to se, Deb. l. 125.
send me þi sonde, Mar. p. 3, etc. *send . . . sonde*, S.W. p. 249. Cp. **O.E.Pr.** *he set on his domsetle*, Jul. p. 54.
seten stille ase stan, Kath. l. 1253.
sexe and seuen, Best. l. 50.
isi ant iselhðe, Mar. p. 23. *þe sy ant þe selhðe*, Jul. p. 24. *mi sy ant mi selhðe*, Jul. p. 30. *þe selhðe ant te sy*, H.M. p. 54.
O.E.P. & Pr. *siggeð and singeð*, Lady, l. 72.
simple and softe, Best. l. 655.
O.E.Pr. *singen song*, Mar. p. 2. *singinde . . .¹ song*, Mar. p. 19. (a) *song singen*, Mar. p. 1. *hare song . . . heo singen*, S.W. p. 261.
isliket ant ismaket (polished and smoothed), Kath. l. 1660.
sloh ant slec (slough and mud), Kath. l. 1662.
slumeren ant slepen, Best. l. 452.
smecheð ant smealleð, Kath. l. 1526. *smechunge ant smellunge*, H.M. p. 18, S.W. p. 245.
smoke and smoþer, Deb. l. 436.
softe (v̇b.) *mi sar*, Mar. p. 5.
se softe ant se swote, Ur. p. 183. *softe oðer swote*, S.W. p. 263.
sorhin ant siken, H.M. p. 38.
O.E.P. & Pr. *soð . . . segge*, Kath. l. 1090, etc. *soð þat he seide*, S.W. p. 259. *soð is iseid*, Dep. l. 220. *soð beo þ ich segge*, Kath. l. 1008. *seide hire þ soðe*, Kath. l. 153. *soþe isey*, Deb. l. 441. *ich mote soðliche seggen*, Lou. p. 213.
þe sparkes sprongen, Deb. l. 415.
ne spealie na speche, S.W. p. 263.
spec . . . ant seide, Kath. l. 1836. *spec ant seide*, Mar. p. 7.
speche þu maht spillen, Jul. p. 24, cp. A.
spellen many spelles, Blc. l. 8.
with hote speres þorwʒ was stongen, Deb. l. 413.
to spitten ant to speowen, Jul. p. 48.
stalewurðe . . . ant starke, Mar. p. 15.

on stede er on stalle, Best. l. 377. *i stude ant i stalle*, Kath. l. 683.
stertlinde in þe strete, Deb. l. 128.
to astenchen me wið þe stench, Mar. p. 12.
istenet euch strete mid deorewurðe stanes, Kath. ll. 1656–7.
þu steorest te seastream, Mar. p. 9.
steor me ant streng me, Jul. p. 30.
ne stereð ge noght of ðe stede, Best. l. 309.
stireð he nout of slepe, Best. l. 11.
of ðe stoc er of ðe ston, Best. l. 224. *stokes ant ston*, Hend. l. 113. *of stockes ant of stanes*, Mar. p. 1.
O.E.Pr. *stod stille*, Kath. l. 180.
strac ant strahte, Mar. p. 11.
istrahte ant isprad, Ur. p. 185.
strengeð ham stalewardlukest, Mar. p. 14.
strikeð a stream ut, Kath. l. 2479.
strong and stedefast, Best. l. 509.
strong ant starc, Mar. p. 9. *strong ne sterk*, M.M. l. 11. *starcke ant strange*, Jul. p. 78.
strokes þei stryken, Blc. l. 14.
strupeð hire steorcnaket, Mar. pp. 5, 18. *strupen hire steortnaket*, Kath. l. 1537.
stunten ne etstonden, Mar. p. 15.
stute nu ant step (stop), Mar. p. 6.
ne stutteð ne ne studgeð, (cease and stop), Mar. p. 9.
ne suleð þi sawle, H.M. p. 20.
mid sunne isulet, Mar. p. 3.
Cp. **O.E.P. & Pr.** *sutel ant eðsene*, Kath. l. 1033.
hu swart . . . hu suti, Mar. p. 15.
swelten þurh sweord, Mar. p. 7. *mi sweord schal uorswelten ant forswollen þi flesch*, Mar. p. 5.
þe swetnesse of hare song, S.W. p. 261.
wið swepes ant wið schurges, Woh. p. 283.
wið (cnotti) swepes swungen, Woh. p. 281.
swetture ant savurure, H.M. p. 38.
swot sauur, Mar. p. 4.
se swote smel, S.W. p. 261. *swote smeal*, Kath. l. 1588. *smelle . . . swote*, Mar. p. 11. *swotest to smeallen*, Mar. p. 4. *swete for to smelle*, Deb. l. 43. *swote smellinde*, Kath. l. 2195.
swote þu slepest, Dep. l. 425.
swottre ant swettre, Kath. l. 1691. *swotest ant swetest*, Mar. p. 11.
i swinke ant sike, Lady, l. 97.
mi swinc and mi sor, Lady, l. 136.
he suggeden ant sorgeden, Best. l. 559.
talkin ant tauelin (to talk and play at tables), Mar. p. 13.
iteiet ant itunet, Mar. p. 22.
ne tellest na tale, Jul. p. 54. *mi tale tealin*, Mar.ɔ.
italde bi tale, Kath. l. 1286.
tellen . . . tidinges, S.W. p. 253. *to telle þine typinges*, Alf. l. 298.
tellen wiþ tungen, Kath. l. 1700.
ne mei na tunge tellen, S.W. p. 249, etc.
teme and teche, Deb. l. 89.

teone(n) and tintreohe(n), Kath. ll. 403, 623, 1503, 1795, 1888.   *for tene ne for tintreow*, Jul. p. 18.

teth . . . tunge, Dep. ll. 595–6 (cp. *Death*, 170).

te tide ant te time, Mar. p. 18.

O.E.Pr. *þus togged and totorn*, Deb. l. 451.   *tetoggeð ant tetireð hem*, Best. l. 318.

tollið togederes ant toggið, Mar. p. 14.

bi top and tail, Deb. l. 466.

from þe top to þe tan, Jul. 59.

O.E.P. *treye ant tene*, Hend. l. 174, Lady, l. 61.   *to trayen and to teone*, Alf. l. 208.

O.E.Pr. *thuten ant techen* (discipline and instinct), S.W. p. 267.

ne mai . . . no tunge techen, Lady, l. 48.

bitunde us in ane tunne, Mar. p. 17.

twinnen ant tweamen (separate and divide), H.M. p. 38.

O.E.P. *pauieð ant polieð*, Mar. p. 15.   *þeauien ant þolien*, Jul. p. 19.
þicke . . . þosternesse, S.W. p. 251.

his þral ant his þeowe, Mar. p. 12.   *þrel ant . . . þeow*, H.M. p. 42.

þreateð ant þreapeð (threatens and disputes), Kath. l. 1916.

þriven and þro, Deb. ll. 109, 181.

O.E.Pr. *þrowede oðer þolede*, Kath. l. 1156.

ðrowing ðolede, Best. l. 567.

þuldeliche heo hit þolede, Jul. p. 28.

O.E.Pr. *þuldi ant þolemod*, Kath. l. 174.

wa ant weane, Kath. ll. 2104–5.   *þe weane ant te wa*, Kath. ll. 1166–7.
for wa ne for winne, Jul. p. 14.   *ne wa, ne wunne*, S.W. p. 265.

i wunne buten euch wa, Kath. l. 1756.

wa ant wondreðe, Mar. p. 4, etc.

weane . . . ant wondreðe, H.M. p. 10.

wakeneð ant waxeð of þe, Mar. p. 11.

he walkeð and wendeð, Dep. l. 21.

Cp. **O.E.P.** *wanunge ant wepunge*, H.M. p. 50.   *wardi us ant werie*, S.W. p. 253.

O.E.P. *warpen word,*[1] Kath. ll. 643, 1325.

water ne wyn, Deb. l. 158.   *wyn ant water*, Hend. l. 113.

wat awei, Kath. l. 1335.

wecchinde, ham werien, Mar. p. 15.

awei warp, Kath. l. 829.

weile and walawo ! Deb. l. 13.

wel I wot, Deb. l. 382.

weldest ant witest, Mar. p. 11.   *to witen ant to welden*, Mar. p. 2.

O.E.Pr. *þe welt ant wisseð*, Mar. p. 4.   *wisseð ant wealt*, Kath. l. 1780.
wisseð ant weldeð, Jul. p. 4.   *weldinde ant wissinde*, Kath. l. 933.
wissent ant weldent, Mar. p. 20.

he wende his wei, Mar. p. 2.   *wenden me ne wrenchen ut of þe weie*, Mar. p. 4.

O.E.P. *weole after wowe*, Alf. l. 91.   *fra wa to wele*, Woh. p. 285.

wið weole ne wið wunne, Mar. p. 4.   *weole ant wunne*, Mar. p. 20.   *þe weole þe wunne*, H.M. p. 24.   *weole oðer wunne*, H.M. p. 36.   *mi weole, mi wunne*, Ur. p. 183.   *of weole ant of eche wunne*, Ur. p. 187.   *weole . . . wunne*, H.M. p. 50.   *to weolen ant to wunnen*, Mar. p. 7.   *weolen ant*

---

[1] Cp. O.N. *urþusk ð orþum*, etc.

wunne, Jul. p. 10, etc., Kath. l. 1523, Mar. p. 1, S.W. p. 255. *to weolen ant to eche wunnen,* Mar. p. 1. *to þe weolen ant to þe wunnen,* Mar. p. 19. *wunne ant weole,* Kath. ll. 1501, 1695, 2296. *wunne ant weole welden,* Mar. p. 6. *wunne* (adj.) *ant weolefule,* H.M. p. 46.
O.E.Pr. *weopmen ant wummen,* Jul. p. 66, Kath. l. 2323, Mar. pp. 1, 6. *to weorrin ne to wreððen,* Kath. l. 1326.
O.E.Pr. *mine wepnen . . . awarpen,* Mar. p. 16. *were me ant wite,* Mar. p. 3. *to werien ant to witen,* S.W. p. 257. *wite wel ant werien,* S.W. p. 257. *wite ant werie,* Lady, l. 147. *witen þe ant werien,* Jul. p. 56.
werþeð ðus hire web ant weueð, Best. l. 363.
westi ant wrecched, Woh. p. 277.
mit teos ilke wettres weosch me, Mar. p. 19.
widewen mit te weddede, Mar. p. 2.
O.E.P. *wif ant weres (gederunge),* H.M. p. 36. *wif ant weres (sommunge),* H.M. p. 42.
wil ant wunne, H.M. p. 42.
wilde and wod, Deb. l. 16.
wind and watere, Dep. l. 555.
O.E.Pr. *na wind ne na weder,* Jul. p. 72. *þe windes, þe wederes,* Mar. p. 10. *windes ant wederes,* Mar. p. 4, etc.
of wind ant wude ant wettres (wind, woods and rivers), Kath. l. 271.
biwinneð ant biwiteð (win and guard), H.M. pp. 41–2.
O.E.Pr. *wise men and warre,* Best. l. 456. **O.E.Pr.** *wisliche ant warliche,* Kath. l. 82. **O.E.Pr.** *warsiþe and wisedom,* Best. l. 324.
O.E.P. & Pr. *wis on hire wordes,* Kath. l. 547. *wisliche mid worde,* Dep. l. 551. *wis on his word and war on his werke,* Alf. l. 16.
O.E.P. *wise ant witti,* Kath. l. 530. *witti ant wise,* Kath. l. 315. *witti ant wis on hire wordes,* Kath. l. 546.
wit ant wisdom, Alf. ll. 67, 70, etc., Hend. l. 21, Kath. l. 240, etc., Mar. p. 3, etc., Woh. pp. 269, 275. *mi wit ant mi wisdom,* Mar. p. 8. *hare wit ant . . . hare wisdom,* Mar. p. 15. *of wisdom ant of wit,* Kath. l. 452.
þe wisdom of þi wit, H.M. p. 20.
wisdom ne wurschiþe, Lou. p. 211.
wite þu to wisse, Kath. l. 1532.
te witene ant te warden, S.W. p. 267.
þ hefde iwist ant iwenet hire, Mar. p. 2.
witið ham ant wreaðeð, H.M. p. 40.
ne hare wlite, ne hare weden, H.M. p. 24.
O.E.P. & Pr. *wlite ant westum,* Kath. ll. 69, 310, Mar. p. 2.
wlonke ant weolefule, H.M. p. 42.
to wode and water, Deb. l. 101. *þe wudes ant te wettres,* Mar. p. 10.
boðen of wude and of wed (both of trees and plants), Best. l. 181.
bi wode or weyȝe (way), Deb. l. 133.
boðe wone (poverty) *and weole,* Lou. p. 213.
O.E.P. & Pr. *mid worde and mid werke,* Dep. l. 336. *hire wordes ant ec hire werkes,* S.W. p. 249. *wið wil, oðer wið word, oðer wið werc,* S.W. p. 249.
worldes weane, H.M. p. 32.
O.E.Pr. *worldes wele,* Hend. l. 121, Woh. p. 271. *worldes weole,* Alf. l. 103, H.M. p. 360. *wordliche weolen,* H.M. p. 691.

worldes winne, Deb. l. 234. *worldes wunne*, H.M. l. 584. *wunne of þe world*, Mar. p. 8.

worldes wurðschipe, Kath. l. 1502, Mar. p. 15. *to wurðschipe of þe worlde*, Kath. l. 472.

te worldes wealdent, Kath. l. 1723. *þe worldes weldent*, Mar. p. 16. (*þe wealdent ꝥ*) *al þe world wrahte*, Kath. ll. 369, 1765–6, Woh. p. 271. *worldes wruhte*, Mar. p. 21.

O.E.P. *wile ðe we on ðis werld wunen*, Best. l. 201.

worldliche wisdomes, Kath. l. 525, etc.

I wot to wis, Deb. l. 432.

woundes wide, Deb. l. 388. *þat wide wunde*, Woh. p. 283.

þu wrahtest ant weldest, Mar. p. 9.

wraþ . . . wod, Mar. p. 7. *swa wrað ant swa awed þ he o wode wise*, Mar. p. 19.

wrenchen ut of þe weie, Kath. ll. 124–6, Jul. p. 43, Mar. p. 4.

wrynge hond ant wepe, Hend. l. 257.

Cp. **O.E.Pr.** *þeos writeres writes*, Kath. l. 856.

no wrt wexynde a wode, Alf. l. 112.

iwunet ant iwiket (stayed and dwelt), Kath. l. 1740.

wununge of wanunge (abode of woe), S.W. p. 253.

to wurchen al þi wa, Mar. p. 17. *wurcheþ þe wa*, H.M. p. 48. *wa wurchestu*, Jul. p. 50.

O.E.P. & Pr. *wurcheþ . . . wil*, Jul. p. 10, etc., Kath. ll. 371, 2108, Mar. pp. 13, 18. *if we wurcheþ wyllen Cristes*, Alf. l. 283. *ure wil wurche*, Kath. l. 1938. *wrahte þe wil*, Mar. p. 7.

wurch efter mi wil, Mar. p. 4.

wrahte so muche wondreðe, Jul. p. 40.

O.E.Pr. *wurchið summe wundres*, Kath. l. 1053. *wrahte . . . wundres*, Jul. p. 62, Kath. ll. 1071–2, 1133. *wundres ꝥ he wrahte*, Kath. l. 922.

O.E.Pr. *wurches . . . wurkes*, Mar. p. 6. *werkes wurchen*, Kath. l. 171. *werkes iwrahte*, Mar. p. 1.

þe wurmes ant te wildedeor, Mar. p. 10.

wurþen (alle) awei, Kath. l. 1813. (See under *awei warþ*.)

þi wurðli wedes, Deb. l. 25. *worþli wedes for to were*, Deb. l. 393.

wurðschipe ant wurðmunt, Mar. p. 22. *wurðmunt ant wurðschipe*, Kath. ll. 1444–5.

iȝarket ant iȝeue, Mar. p. 18.

ȝeien ant ȝuren, Kath. l. 2014. *to ȝeien ant to ȝuren*, Mar. p. 16. *ȝuren ant ȝeien*, Jul. p. 48, etc. *ȝeinde ant ȝurende*, Kath. l. 160.

(*hymseolue*) *foryemeþ, foryeteþ*, Alf. l. 137.

ȝung of ȝeres, Kath. l. 66. *ȝunge mon of ȝeres*, Jul. p. 5.

N.B.—The poem *Death* (see p. 5) has several noticeable alliterative phrases : *on bolster ne on benche* (l. 90), *his hus and his hom* (l. 44), *þi lyvre and þi lunge* (l. 172), *þi mawe and þi milte* (l. 171), *þi mey and þi mowe* (l. 162), *þi teþ and þi tunge* (l. 170).

THE ALLITERATIVE PHRASES IN LAȜAMON'S *BRUT*. [LAȜ.]

Laȝamon's work is almost as rich in traditional alliterative phrases as in poetic compounds, a fact which bears out our conclusion that the poet was in lineal descent from Old English poetry.

Laȝamon has a total of 250 separate alliterative phrases—a striking number, despite the length of the work. Of these, twenty-three are found in Old English heroic poetry and forty-five in Old English religious poetry. Remembering that many Old English phrases had inevitably disappeared owing to the fact that numerous poetic words had become obsolete, the survivals in Laȝamon are noteworthy. Of very special interest are *drinken and dreomen, lond and leoden, muchel and mære, mid orde and mid egge, seoc and sorhful, bi stiȝen and bi straten, wunien mid wunne,* all of which occur in Old English poetry ; these facts speak abundantly for themselves.

Sixty-eight of Laȝamon's phrases occur in Old English prose, of which the two of greatest interest are *mid sibbe and mid sæle,* occurring as *sele and sibbe* in the Lindisfarne Gospels, and *walc and win,* found also in the Anglo-Saxon Chronicle ; neither of these phrases occurs elsewhere in Middle English. Another noteworthy fact is that with only ten exceptions all the 250 phrases are English in origin, standing in marked contrast to the phrases in the early Middle English alliterative prose and poetry ; Laȝamon is much nearer to Old English and is also less affected by loan-words from Old French and Old Norse. He uses five phrases containing one Old Norse word : *king and kaiser, gold and gersume* (beside *gold and ȝimme*), *halden hustinge, lokede and leitede, tellen tiðinge* (beside the more common *tellen tidinge*). He has also four phrases containing one Old French word : *cacchen and quellen, cnihtes and clærkes, deme and duc, palles and purpres.* There only remains *hulles and heldes,* with the second element of uncertain origin ; these ten exceptions are clearly of little importance.

Laȝamon uses seventy-two alliterative phrases, which also occur in the early Middle English works previously discussed ; a few of these, it will be observed, are homiletic, such as *ilæred and læwed,* but the majority of them are the common stock-in-trade phrases found in all writers, such as *king and quene, fedde and fostredde, wis and war,* etc. The table shows how few of Laȝamon's phrases were destined to survive, which is not surprising, for his work is archaic and representative of an older tradition which has left comparatively few traces in Middle English.

Cp. **O.E.P.** *balde mine beornes,* 21376. *mid balden his beornen,* 19518, 20531. *baldere beornen,* 20208, 31238.
O.E.P. *balu (and) burst* (bale and destruction), 27478–9.
baðieð heore ban, 17189.
O.E.Pr., E.M.E. *þa bed he his bod,* 23407. *heore beoden bideð,* 19722.
O.E.P. & Pr., E.M.E. *bemen (þer) bleowen,* 5107, etc. (42 times).
bemene blæst, 19926.

O.E.P.   *ibide in burʒe,* 30878–9.
O.E.Pr.   *binden mid bende,* 18459.
O.E.P., E.M.E.   *his biscopes, his bocilærde men,* 16901–2, etc. (5 times).
O.E.P., E.M.E.   *bitterest alre baluwen,* 9685, etc. (4 times).
O.E.P.   *blisse . . . in burʒe,* 21667–8.
iboren in (pere) burhe, 292, 17194.
blod and brain, 1468.
E.M.E.   *bulde(n) (. . .) bur(es),* 5982, 29218.
buð (O.E. *būgan) in to bure,* 19036.
cacchen . . . quellen, 31501–2. ˙
kene and custi, 6366.
Cp. **O.E.P. & Pr., E.M.E.**   *king ne kæisere,* 22085, 22657.   *kinge . . .
kæisere,* 9572, etc. (4 times).
king of pessere kineriche, 28754–5.
O.E.Pr., E.M.E.   *king and quene,* 182, 2467, 28141.
þe king and alle his cnihtes, 9858.
his cnihtes, his cheorles, 31249.
E.M.E.   *cnihtes and clærckes,* 31556.
cniht under criste, 25561.   *cnihten under criste,* 27230–1.
ʒeond cludes and ʒeond cliuenen, 32215.
biclused in (ane) castle(n), 12192, 16185.
O.E.Pr. & Pr., E.M.E.   *custen and clupten,* 20557.   *cussede and cluppede,*
5097, 14361–2.   *heo clupten, heo custen,* 18808.   *clupte . . . custe,*
17101–2.
þer we scullen ure daʒes ba driuen to þan ende, 32158–9.
O.E.P. & Pr.   *he a fif dæle dælde his ferde,* 21125–6.
O.E.P.   *ouer/of dales and dunes,* 20860, etc. (5 times).
O.E.P., E.M.E.   *in ane dale deope,* 26934.
ane deope dich, 12422, etc. (3 times).
E.M.E.   *todælen and todihten,* 23627.   *he dihte and delde,* 9192.
O.E.P.   *delen þene dæd* (O.E. dēaþ), 26041–2.
to dæðe idihte, 19671.
O.E.Pr.   *deluen diches,* 9238.   *to deluen dic,* 14225–6.   *dic wes idoluen,*
15472, 15900.
deme and duc, 9634–5.
O.E.P. & Pr., E.M.E.   *demen (. . .) dom(es),* 16867, 22116.
E.M.E.   *idon of (heore) lifdæʒen,* 11295, etc. (25 times).
mid drenche oðer mid dweomerlace, 11326.
O.E.P.   *drinken and dreomen,* 13463, etc. (7 times).
O.E.P. & Pr.   *fallen to (. . .) foten,* 575, etc. (7 times).
ifan and ifeond, 16076–7.
O.E.P.   *fare(n) to fihte,* 17993, etc. (6 times).
O.E.P.   *fare forð,* 19194, etc. (3 times).   *ferden forð,* 18986, etc. (6 times).
forð ferde, 18984, etc. (5 times).
E.M.E.   *fedde and fostredde,* 25857–8, 31751–2.
fehten feondliche, 10414–5, etc. (12 times).
feoh and færde, 4429.
O.E.P.   *feollen þa fæie,* 629, etc. (15 times).
O.E.P.   *ure ifan feollen,* 27617.
O.E.Pr.   *feol þer inne fehte,* 27984.
O.E.P. & Pr.   *feond fallen* (trs. O.E. fiellan), 16106–7, etc. (10 times).
feond fellen (intrs. O.E. feallan), 27687, etc. (5 times).

felden his ferde, 29952.
O.E.P. & Pr. *folc fællen* (trs.), 19492, etc. (6 times).   *feollen þa folckes* (intrs.), 30413, etc. (5 times).
O.E.P. & Pr. *ᶜeollen on/to folden* (trs. and intrs.), 2865, 5390, etc. (8 times).
O.E.P. *lette fleon flan*, 22343–4, 27456–7.
folc. and his ferde, 31341, etc. (7 times).
Cp. **O.E.P.** *feiȝernesse and freoscipe*, 3137.
O.E.Pr. *ferde* (vb.) *with ferde*, 5175.
O.E.P. & Pr. *fisc (and) fuȝel,*[1] 7256, 24265.
flæs na no fisc, 19693.
nu fleð ure ifan, 5894.
O.E.Pr., E.M.E. *fleoð þa fuȝeles*, 21759.
floten bi sæ-flode, 1032.
folc þer wes fæie, 4694.
freoscipe and freondscipe, 10606–7.
fusden feondliche, 23923.
fusen and ferden, 17373–4.   **O.E.P.** *fusen mid/to ferde*, 18886, etc. (9 times). *fusde* (trs.) . . . *ferden*, 16248, etc. (4 times). *his ferde fusde* (intrs.), 18312, etc. (5 times).
O.E.P. *fusde(n) to fihte*, 1735, 22330.
gares gunnen gliden, 19551.
gleomen gon gleowen, 19213.
Cp. **O.E.P.** *gilden to grunde*, 800.
glitene (pp.) *on golde*, 15705.
E.M.E. *mid/for golde and mid/for gersume*, 120, etc. (14 times).   *gold and garisome*, 4064. *gersume and gold*, 883.
O.E.P. & Pr. *mid/of golde and mid/of ȝimme*, 6080, 7624.
heo bigolen mid galdere, 19256–7.
heore ȝelp and heore game, 21007.
O.E.Pr. *ȝirnen grið*, 11860, etc. (7 times).
ȝisles ȝeuen, 6171–2, etc. (4 times).
Cp. **E.M.E.** *for nare ȝitsunge, for nare ȝiuernesse*, 9490–1.
O.E.Pr. *habben in honde*, 3339, etc. (15 times).
O.E.Pr., E.M.E. *heold on honde*, 6824, 8173, 27249.
hæh uppen hulle, 21303.
O.E.P., E.M.E. *heh (heo is) and hali*, 13915.
hælden into hælle, 20539.
E.M.E *ihæuen and ihalden* (elevated and held), 30207.
O.E.P. & Pr. *hafden and heore honden,*[2] 20535.   *moni heaued, moni hond,* 574.
hal and hæil, 12518.
halden hustinge, 5232, etc. (8 times).
whi halst (O.E. *halsian*) *þu þin hafed dun*, 18381.
O.E.P. & Pr. *heortes and hindes*, 1448.
O.E.P. *helm on hæuede*, 23965.   *his helm and his heued*, 21387, etc. (4 times).
in hirede and in halle, 25482.
E.M.E. *his hude and his heowe*, 3071.
ȝeond hulles and ȝeond heldes (= dales).

[1] Cp. O.N. *fisks anda ok fogla mjolk.*
[2] Cp. O.N. *hendr ok hǫfuþ.*

hundes and hauekes, 3299, etc. (8 times).　*hæuekes and hundes,* 3258, etc. (5 times).

mid hornen, mid hunden, 20855.

E.M.E.　*hunger and hete,* 4042, etc. (6 times).

hux and hoker, 28865, cp. 29020–1.

O.E.Pr., E.M.E.　*ilæred, no læwed,* 24625.　*þa lareden . . . þa leouweden,* 31829–30.

ilæsteð þi lif, 9852.　**O.E.Pr., E.M.E.**　*þe while þe ilast his lif,* 6282, 21087–8, 27656–7.

ledan mine leoden, 1203.

O.E.Pr., E.M.E.　*heo leodeð heore lif,* 19720.　*he ledde . . . his lif,* 6291, 7015.　*lif lede,* 1065, 26846.

swa leof swa heore/mi lif, 13441–2, 16561.　*leof alse (his) lif,* 13475–6, etc. (4 times).　*leouere þenne hire/mi lif,* 2978, 3481.

leouede alse his lif, 4954.

O.E.P. & Pr., E.M.E.　*weore him/heom lef, weore him/heom lað,* 3036, 19998.

E.M.E.　*lif and leomen,* 702.　*bi heore liue and bi heore leme,* 19436.　*lif . . . lumen,* 21935.　*lif and lime,* 500.

vppe leome and vppe lif, 2817, etc. (7 times).　*bi heore leomen and bi heore liue(n),* 25167, 26013–4.　*ȝif me leomen and ȝif me lif,* 22376.

libben inne þissere leoden, 29981–2, etc. (4 times).

O.E.P. & Pr.　*libben a þin lif,* 31697.

O.E.P.　*libben on lisse,* 3261.

O.E.P., E.M.E.　*libben/liuede in/on londe,* 3236, etc. (7 times).

O.E.P. & Pr.　*lif libben,* 5959, 15231, 19324.　*libben . . . lif,* 29385–6, 31697.

O.E.P. & Pr.　*lif leosen,* 20112, 25918.

leosen his leoden, 23299, etc. (4 times).　*leosen þis lond ond þas leoden,* 32234–5.　*leosen lond,* 7913.

leomen . . . leosen, 22306, etc. (4 times).

O.E.P. & Pr.　*forleoseden lif,* 25509–10.　*his lif forloren,* 16490.

E.M.E.　*þa lihte and þa liuere,* 6499.

liðen ouer leoden, 20583.　*liðen to/ȝeond/into londen,* 18871, etc. (11 times).　*ut of þissen londen forð he gon liðen ut of þissen leoden,* 11701–3.

liþede þe leode, 1784.

lokede and leitede, 18538–9.

O.E.P.　*(þis) lond ond/ne (þas) leoden,* 4625, etc. (5 times).

heore lif and heore leoden, 31155–6.

O.E.Pr., E.M.E.　*longe libben,* 19263, 19723, 22007.

þe longene and þe liure, 6499.

O.E.P., E.M.E.　*lude loȝen,* 12872.　*lohȝen ludere stevene,* 23987, etc. (4 times).

his marken and his mare (O.E. mǣre), 31220.

E.M.E.　*medewen heo meowen,* 1942.

O.E.P. & Pr.[1]　*meduwen and mores and þa hæȝe muntes,* 4817–8.

O.E.P. & Pr., E.M.E.　*þurh his milde (mihti) mod,* 31390.

O.E.P. & Pr.　*his mod and his main,* 14363.

O.E.P. & Pr.　*muchel and mære,* 1139.　*muchele and mare,* 14230.

muchel . . . and vnimete, 10555, 17866–7, 19408–9.　*vnimete . . . muche,* 11110–1.

---

[1] *muntan and moran.* Chr. Laud 1095 : Sal and Sat. l. 340.

murðe þe þat folc makode, 1794.
his neb and his neose, 8181.
O.E.Pr., E.M.E. *nemnede him his rihte nome,* 29621.
O.E.P. *mid orde and mid egge,* 5202.
Cp. **O.E.P. & Pr.** *ord from þan ende,* 15770, 22983.
E.M.E. *pælles and purþras,* 2368. *þa palles and þa purþres,* 5928.
he pleoȝede his plaȝen, 29219.
radful and rihtwis, 6537.
O.E.Pr., E.M.E. *ræd(eð) me ræd,* 15422, etc. (4 times).
at rede . . . and at rune, 19238–9, 24173.
þa rein bigon to rine, 19745, 28303, 31890.
rixlen a/ouer . . . riche, 23099, 27404–5.
heo rupten, heo ræfden (robbed and plundered), 10584.
sæhte and some, 30039, etc. (4 times). *saht and some,* 2552, 31371.
heore sær and heore sorhsiðes, 11108–9.
O.E.Pr., E.M.E. *særi and sorhful,* 11214–5, etc. (4 times).
O.E.Pr., E.M.E. *særimod and sorhfulle,* 26907. *sarimod and sorful,*
29791–2.
O.E.P. & Pr., E.M.E. *sorȝe and sar* (sb.), 7998. *mid seorwen and mid*
sore, 6885.
Cp. **E.M.E.** *weri of sorȝen and seoc,* 28081.
O.E.P. *seoc and sorhful,* 17644–5.
a saȝe oðer a spelle, 6662.
scæftes and sceldes, 7979, etc. (5 times).
O.E.Pr. *sceld and/ne spere,* 8291, 13694, 18922. **O.E.Pr.** *mid speres and*
mid sceldes, 20517, etc. (4 times). **O.E.Pr.** *mid spere and mid swerde,*
5202. *mid sweorde and mid spere,* 548. **O.E.Pr. & Pr.** *mid sweorden*
and mid schelden, 6699. *sweord . . . scelde,* 7531.
sceldes (gunnen) scenen, 26807, 31236. *sceldes gonnen scanen,* 28554. *sceldes*
þer scenden, 23493, 27756. *sceld . . . to scænde,* 16492.
heo scæken . . . speren, 26481.
scelde him mid his scelde, 8431.
þa sciþen ut scæf, 9366, 20925–6, 23859–60.
O.E.P., E.M.E. *for scome scenden,* 21181, 23681.
secgan saȝe(n), 26345–6, etc. (10 times).
O.E.P. & Pr. *seiden . . . spelles,* 2177–8, 16397–8.
O.E.P. *suggen of sorwen,* 4631–2, 17924–5, 16038–9.
O.E.P. & Pr., E.M.E. *suggen and singen,* 23013.
O.E.P. & Pr., E.M.E. *sugge(n) . . . to soðe,* 8221, etc. (4 times). *to*
soðe ich sugge, 13575, 18952–3. *sugge þurh soðe mine worden,* 25946.
isæid word soðe, 25135. *suggen soððere wordes/spellen,* 13007–8,
20543–4, 28460–1. *suggen soð,* 26384–5. *þa him soð sæide,* 4972.
soð þe to suggen, 28147. *soð seide þe seg,* 8015.
E.M.E. *sende his sonde,* 422, etc. (58 times).
O.E.P. & Pr., E.M.E. *iseon siht,* 5725, 20930.
iset and isemed, 24103, etc. (4 times).
sette(n) sæhtnesse, 9874, 19111.
O.E.Pr. *mid sibbe(n) and mid sahte(n),* 2139, 15149, 16934. *sibba . . .*
seahte, 3670–1. *mid sæhte(n) and mid sibbe(n),* 11308, etc. (8 times).
O.E.Pr. *to sibben and to some,* 9514. *to sæhte, to sibbe and to some,*
4098–9. *sæhte and some,* see supra. **O.E.Pr.** *mid sibbe and mid sæle,*
15154.

sitteð adun stille, 25247, 28172.   **E.M.E.**   *sæt/sat stille*, 3060, etc. (4 times).
Cp. **O.E.Pr.**,[2] **E.M.E.**   *sæt . . . an (his) hæhsetle*, 16645–6, 18526–7.
slæ mid spere, 3943.
E.M.E.   *slepen . . . slumen*, 32057–8.   *slumen and slæpen*, 18408–9.
   slomnen and slepen, 1219–20.
smat hine þurh mid þane spere, 26521, 26549.
on songe ne on spelle, 12093.
speke(n) . . . and spilien, 3816–7, etc.
E.M.E.   *mid spere . . . istunge*, 27597, 27614–5, 27843.   *mid spere him
   ofstong*, 10653, 11364.   *mid spere was ofstungen*, 11441.
on sterren and on sunne, 30495.
O.E.P.   *bi stiȝen and bi straten*, 16366.
stikeden and sloȝen, 20660.
E.M.E.   *(mid)stocken and (mid)stanen*, 626, etc. (4 times).
O.E.Pr., **E.M.E.**   *stod him ful stille*, 18376.
E.M.E.   *strong and sterk*, 17000, etc. (7 times).
O.E.Pr., **E.M.E.**   *sunne scineð*, 31087.   *þa sunne gon to scine*, 31889.
biswak þurh swike, 14864–5.
ich wulle mid swerde his heueð ofswippen, 877–8.
O.E.Pr.   *mid sweorde (al hine) toswungen*, 8025–6, 21069–70, 26469.
   swengeð . . . mid sweorden, 22839–40.
moni swinc, moni swæt, 3281.   Cp. 7488, *He swonc . . . þat he al lauede
   asweote.*
teldes itælded, 17489.
E.M.E.   *tellen tale*, 26217, 26880.
E.M.E.   *tellen tiðinge/tidinge*, 12343, etc. (17 times).
tounes and teldes, 12867.
O.E.P.   *þeinen of (Arðures) þeoden*, 27510–1.
vnhæle and ælde, 11546.
O.E.Pr.   *(moni) walc and (moni) win*, 2542, 6225.
wale and win, 404.
O.E.Pr.   *waxen and wonien*, 981–2, 26990–1.
mid wederen and mid wateren, 18118.
O.E.Pr., **E.M.E.**   *wind and weder*, 12059, etc. (10 times).   *þes wederes,
   wind . . .*, 9734–5.
mid wolcnen and mid wedere, 102.
O.E.P.   *windan mid þa weolcnen*, 25592.
E.M.E.   *(a)wei weorpen*, 15933.
O.E.Pr.   *þa weoleȝen and þa weaðlen*, 427.
O.E.Pr.   *wepen and weinen* (whine), 25827.
O.E.Pr., **E.M.E.**   *wepmon/wapmen and/ne wifmen/wifmon*, 1119, etc. (10
   times).
O.E.P. & Pr.   *his wepnen and his weden*, 23011.
mid wepnen hine wundeden, 1724.
wete weoren his wongen,[1] 30268.
mid winne and mid wurðscipe, 11474.
iwinne wurðscipe, 24707–8, etc. (4 times).   *wurhscipe iwinne*, 20481.
E.M.E.   *he wes wod, he wes wild*, 8593–4, 13741.
O.E.Pr., **E.M.E.**   *wis and war*, 8882, etc. (14 times).
wise men and wihte, 19637.

---

[1] The same phrase occurs in C. Mundi, 18308 ; see Rom. and Rh.A.I.

wys and witfol, 911.
wise me and wite me (guard me and counsel me), 1200.
O.E.P., E.M.E. *heo wes witte, heo wes wis*, 9600.
E.M.E. *alre worulde wunne*, 9072.
O.E.P. & Pr. *(mid) write and (mid) worde*, 3217, 25005, 25291–2. *bi/mid/ þurh worden and bi/mid/þurh writen*, 6675, etc. (6 times).
O.E.Pr. *writen a writ*, 3149.
to wude wenden, 16200, etc. (9 times). *wenden to þan wuden*, 12299.
wenden ouer woldes and ouer wildernes, 21487–8.
in (anne) wude and in (ane) wilderne, 12295–6, 12818, 20226–7. *to ane wilderne, to ane wude*, 18794–5. *þa wuodes and þa wildernes*, 4815–6.
wonien in wansiðe, Cal. MS. 3088. *wonie ine wowe*, Otho MS. 3088.
O.E.P. *wunien . . . mid wunne*, 22089–90, 28620–1.
þe wuneð under weolcne, 28101.
O.E.Pr., E.M.E. *wurchen werk*, 1547, etc. (5 times).
O.E.P. & Pr., E.M.E. *wurchen ic wulle muchel godes wille*, 23743–4. *wurchen after þine willen*, 12167, 18372–3.
þin iwille scal iwurðen, 18932–3, etc. (6 times).
O.E.P. *wurðen a/inne worlde-riche(n)*, 8790–1, 22991–2, 29753–4.
mid wurðscipe wælden, 5985.
[*wurhsipe iwinne*, 20481.]

The Alliterative Phrases in *The Ormulum*, *The Poema Morale* and *The Owl and the Nightingale* (Orm, P.M., O. and N.).

The alliterative phrases occurring in these works have been collected chiefly because the poems concerned are non-alliterative, and are likely to give some indication of the use of alliteration in early Middle English generally.

Orm's long paraphrase yields 109 alliterative phrases, very few of which seem to be of native origin. Fourteen are found in Old English religious poetry and twenty-two in Old English homiletic prose ; this is as we might expect, and on close examination the reader will observe that those traditional phrases which do actually occur in *The Ormulum* are mostly homiletic, such as *lihht and leome*, *shamedd and shendedd, sake and sinne, word and weorrc*.

Orm has a number of phrases of the same type in common with the early Middle English alliterative prose writers, but very few phrases in common with Laȝamon. The chief interest that attaches to Orm's alliterative phrases is his natural fondness for Old Norse words, many of which do not occur elsewhere in Middle English. Occasionally he has a phrase consisting of two Old Norse words— *brodd and blome, to bróddenn and to blomenn ;* but more often he prefers a combination of Old English and Old Norse, such as : *unnbedenn and unnbonedd, full bitterr and full beȝȝse, to greȝȝþenn*

17

and to ȝarrkenn, to ȝemenn and to gætenn, lende and lesske, meoc and milde, shæd and skill, trigg and trowwe. Most of the phrases are of frequent occurrence in *The Ormulum ;* indeed, it is quite noticeable that while Orm's phrases are somewhat few in number, he uses the majority of them over and over again; every student of Orm remembers the painful recurrence of *fullhtned i/att þe flumm, lihht and leome,* and *sake and sinne.*

That few of Orm's phrases occur in later Middle English poetry is not surprising, for quite evidently he coined many new phrases, which, like his work, never became popular.

The Poema Morale was selected as a typical early Middle English non-alliterative religious poem. The reader will see by reference to the list found below how the majority of the phrases have their origin in Old English religious prose and poetry, and occur also in early Middle English alliterative works ; of special interest are : *sciet ne scrud,* occurring in Old English prose, and *sake and sorȝe,* occurring as *sæce ond sorge* in the O.E. *Elene* 1030. A casual examination of similar non-alliterative religious poems of the same period has yielded practically identical results in every case.

The Owl and the Nightingale is typical of early Middle English secular poems ; there are few of the homiletic phrases, but a number of alliterative expressions which must have been widely used.   The majority of them are commonplace and of little interest as such.

THE ALLITERATIVE PHRASES IN *THE ORMULUM.*

aȝȝ occ aȝȝ, 2263, etc.[1]
unbeddenn & unnbonedd, 17081.
O.E.P. & Pr.   *to biddenn hise beness,* 11157.   *bada hise beness,* 11166.
full bitterr & full beȝȝse (bitter and sharp), 6698.
blunnt & blind, 16954.
bracc & brappe (struggle and anger), 1233.
brodd & blome (shoot and bloom), 10773.   *to broddenn & to blomenn,* 10769.
O.E.P. & Pr., E.M.E.   *to brukenn eche blisse,* 2154, etc.
forrbundenn & forrblendedd, 13775.
cherl & child, 14788.
O.E.P. & Pr., E.M.E.   *king of (alle) kingess,* 6709.
cnew & cupe, 15631.   *to cunnen & to cnawenn,* 18849.
cwennkesst wel & cwellesst, 6751.
E.M.E., Laȝ.   *dale & dune,* 9203.
Cp. **O.E.Pr., Alf.**   *þe deope diȝhellnesse,* 5501.

---

[1] O.N. *ei ok ei.*

E.M.E. *deþ & dærne*, 19886.
O.E.P. & Pr., E.M.E., Laȝ. *dom þu best ta demmd*, 17703. *all þurrh rihht dom ben demmde*, 18968.
O.E.Pr., E.M.E. *icc hafe don þiss dede*, (dedication) 122. *dost tuss þise dedess*, 15587.
to dredenn Godess dom, 18174.
wass dreriȝmod & dreofedd (sad and troubled), 6541.
O.E.Pr. *drinnkenn drinnch*, 807, etc.
O.E.P. & Pr., E.M.E. *dumb & dæf*, 9887.
falls and flærd (falsehood and deceit), 15365, etc.
E.M.E., Laȝ. *to fedenn & to fosstrenn*, 1558, etc.
to fedenn ȝuw, to frofreȝnn ȝuw, 11559.
to ferrsenn & to flittenn (remove and carry away), 15653, etc.
æfre fihhtenn ȝæn þe flæsh, 11471.
fillenn all & forþenn, 4137.
Cp. O.E.Pr. *to fisskenn after fisskess*, 13297.
(Crist was) fullhtned i/att þe flumm, 10802, etc.
ȝiff he gillteþþ aniȝ gillt, 6018.
glowende gledess, 1741.
gramm & grill (angry and cruel), 7145, etc. *grill & gramm*, 7196–7.
grimme & grill (angry and cruel), 9881.
to greȝȝþenn & to ȝarrkenn hemm, 9521.
to ȝemenn & to gætenn (to take care and preserve), 3797, etc.
wiþþ hande ne wiþþ herrte, 4445.
wiþþ hæfedd & wiþþ heorrte, 6496.
E.M.E. *hiss hope & all hiss hellþe*, 6889.
O.E.Pr. *hus & ham*, 1608.
O.E.Pr. *wiþþinnenn & wiþþutenn*, 1603, 12156.
kafe & kene, 19962. Cp. Mann. Chr. 66, *kene . . . & kof.*
O.E.Pr., E.M.E., Laȝ. *to læredd & to læwedd*, 967. *fra læredd & fra læwedd follc*, 1680. *læredd follc & læwedd*, 19930. *læwedd follc & læredd*, 1021.
O.E.Pr., E.M.E., Laȝ. *leddenn heore lif*, 125, 435. *leddenn usell lif*, 891. *all hise lif to ledenn*, 2498. *þatt lif þatt ledeþþ men*, 45.
lende & lesske (loin and flank), 4776.
inn haliȝ lif & læfe, 164.
lif & lusst, 1628.
þatt lifeþþ æfre & lassteþþ, 18800.
lifft & land, 3684.
O.E.P. & Pr., E.M.E. *lihht & leome*, 1906, etc.
O.E.Pr. *lufe & (hope) & læfe*, 8318.
lufe & lusst, 2795, etc.
to luten (Crist) & lakenn (to bow down and present gifts to), 6657, 6683. *to lakenn himm & lutenn*, 6633.
to lutenn hire & lefftenn (to bow down and exalt), 2658, etc. *to lefftenn & to lutenn*, 2488.
E.M.E. *meoc & milde*, 667, 1313, etc. *milde & meoc*, 1252, etc.
mett & mæþ (measure and moderation), 2373, 6116, etc.
millce ȝife maht, 14464.
O.E.Pr., E.M.E., Laȝ. *bi name nemmnedd*, 479, etc. *nemmnedd aȝȝ bi name*, 609.

O.E.P. & Pr., E.M.E. *ord & ende*, 6775, 18692, 18722. *wipp ord & buten ende*, 9676.

ræd & run (advice and counsel), 18719.

to reccnenn & to rimenn (to count and number), 11215.

E.M.E. *resste & ro*, 4190, 5208.

O.E.Pr., La3. *to rippenn hemm & ræfenn* (to spoil and plunder), 10212. *rippepp hemm & ræfepp*, 10204.

he wære rowwst & reord (voice and sound), 9569.

O.E.P., E.M.E. *sake & sinne*, 1335, etc. *off sakess & off sinness*, 1127, 13847.

to sahhtlenn hemm & sammnenn, 19286.

sellpe & sel (happiness and prosperity), 17896.

Cp. **E.M.E.** *sennde an sanderrmann*, 18883.

O.E.Pr., E.M.E., La3. *wipp serrhfull (herte) & sari3 (mod)*, 8945.

shæd & skill (discernment and skill), 5534, etc. *skill & shæd*, 1210, 1226.

to shædenn uss fra sinne swa, 7567.

O.E.P. & Pr. *shame & shande*, 11956.

O.E.P., E.M.E., La3. *ne shamedd nass, ne shennd*, 1999. *shamedd himm & shendedd*, 4965. *he shamep pe & shendepp*, 18284.

E.M.E. *shippennd allre shaffte*, 346. *shippennd off alle shaffte*, 11596.

shridd wipp hali3 shrud, 137.

full smepe & soffte, 9664.

soffte & stille, 1307, 4705.

La3. *to spekenn & to spellenn*, 15987.

O.E.Pr. *stanndenn stille & stinntenn pa*, 12845. **E.M.E., La3.** *itt stod all stille*, 6436.

sti3enn upp o strande, 11155. *he stah uppo pe strande*, 10673.

E.M.E. *strang & stedefast*, 4148, 13354, 15072.

to streonenn streon, 323.

Cp. **O.E.Pr., Alf.** *stunnkenn swipe swete*, 8194.

stunnt & stidi3 (foolish and stupid), 9885.

O.E.P. & Pr., E.M.E. *full sutell & full sene*, 18862.

sware & se33denn, 15585.

swinnc & swat, 1616.

O.E.P. *to tiddrenn & to tæmenn* (propagate and bring forth), 18307, 18892.

trigg & trowwe, 6177, 12181.

turrnenn itt & tawwenn itt (see the context), 15903, 15908.

onn unnit & onn idell, (dedication), 82. **O.E.P. & Pr.** *unnitt & idel*, 4921.

E.M.E. *wanndrap & wa*, 4846.

O.E.Pr., E.M.E., La3. *warre & wise*, 18313.

to weddenn patt wifmann, 10407.

to wepenn & to wanenn, 8128.

weppmann & till wifmannkinn, 3058. **O.E.Pr., E.M.E., La3.** *weppmenn & wifmenn*, 3060, etc.

O.E.P. & Pr., E.M.E. *were & wif*, 4614. *forr mann iss were & mann iss wif*, 13890.

patt all pe werelld wrohhte, 18850, 19688. *patt all piss werelld wrohhte*, 16245.

O.E.Pr., E.M.E., La3. *wirrkenn . . . weorc*, 6244, etc.

E.M.E. *wisste itt wel,* 19595. *wisstenn wel,* 15308.
wistenn witerrliȝ, 3446.
witte & wille, 17280, 17572. *wille & witt,* 17577.
O.E.P. *witt & word,* 18503.
O.E.P. & Pr., E.M.E. *word & weorrc,* 2703, etc.
off all hiss woþ & all hiss wa, 5675.
þurrh Godess wraþþe & wrǣche, 909, etc.
O.E.Pr., Laȝ. *þatt tiss Ennglissh writt allrǣresst wrat (& wrohhte),* (dedication), 331–2.
þurrh writess & þurrh werrkess, 14441.
O.E.Pr. *wurrþshipe & wullderr,* 3935, etc.
Laȝ. *wurrshipe winnenn,* 12373.

THE ALLITERATIVE PHRASES IN *THE POEMA MORALE*.
The references are to the Lambeth MS., except where stated.

O.E.P. & Pr., E.M.E. *bohte us mid his blode,* 188.
O.E.P. & Pr., E.M.E. *to deþe idemet,* 106, 115, etc.
E.M.E. *fordon and fordemet,* 270.
O.E.P., cp. **E.M.E.** *gamen and gleo* (Egerton), 288.
O.E.P. & Pr., E.M.E. *forholen and hud,* 77.
ihud in horde, 28.
O.E.P. & Pr., E.M.E., Laȝ. *þe laðe ne þe loue* (foe nor friend), 44.
O.E.Pr., E.M.E., Laȝ., Orm. *lede a lif,* 5, 93, etc.
þin mei, ne þin maȝe, 29.
þenie—þunde, 67.
O.E.P. *sake and sorȝe (and swinc),* 194. **E.M.E.** *sorȝe and swinke,* 204.
O.E.Pr. *sciet ne scrud* (Egerton), 363.
O.E.P. & Pr., E.M.E., Laȝ. *sorewe ne sor* (Egerton), 374.
O.E.Pr., E.M.E., Laȝ. *sunne scinð* (Egerton), 275.
E.M.E. *ne tunge ne can telle* (Egerton), 285.
waning and wow (Lambeth), 231.
O.E.P. & Pr. *woning and woþ* (Trinity), 235.
O.E.P. & Pr., E.M.E., Orm. *werke and worde* (Trinity), 11. *werke and worde,* 27, etc.
in werre and in winne, 246.
O.E.P. & Pr., E.M.E., Orm. *wif—wer,* 31.
O.E.Pr., E.M.E. *worldes wele,* 222. *woruld wele* (Egerton), 315.

THE ALLITERATIVE PHASES IN *THE OWL AND THE NIGHTINGALE*.

at bedde and at borde, 1492. *to bedde and to borde,* 1579.
O.E.P. & Pr., E.M.E. *bringe blisse,* 710.
E.M.E. *to-busteþ and to-beteþ,* 1610.
þar chauling boþ and cheste ȝare, 296 (Cotton MS.). *þar changling beoþ and cheste vare* (Jesus MS.).
mid chauling and mid chatere, 284 (Cotton MS.). *mid changling and myd chatere,* 284 (Jesus MS.).
knarres and cludes, 1001.
O.E.P. & Pr., E.M.E., Laȝ., Orm. *he demeþ (manie riȝte) dom,* 1755.

Cp. O.E.P. & Pr., cp. E.M.E.   *ende of orde*, 1785.
O.E.P., La3.   *forþ hi ferden*, 1789.
heme and hine (masters and servants), 1115.
E.M.E., La3.   *libbe longe*, 1192.
E.M.E., La3.   *lif an(d) lime*, 1098.
O.E.P. & Pr., E.M.E., La3.   *milde mod*, 1032.
sedes springe, 1134.
O.E.Pr., La3.   *sheld and spere*, 1022.
sikeþ sore, 1352.   *sihð wel sore*, 1587.
E.M.E., La3.   *sitte stille*, 282.
E.M.E.   *soweþ his sed*, 1041.   *sedes boþ isowe*, 1129.
springe and sprede, 437.
starc and stor, 1473.
E.M.E., La3.   *starc and strong*, 5.   *starke an(d) stronge*, 524, 1176.
mid staue and stone, 1167.
stif and stronge, 269.
stronge and sure, 1082.
þrusche and þrostle, 1659.
O.E.P., E.M.E.   *warþ a word*, 45.
O.E.Pr., E.M.E., La3., Orm.   *wepmon and wimmane*, 1379.
ac wildernisse hit is and weste, 1000.
Cp. O.E.P. & Pr., E.M.E., La3.   *he is wis an war of worde*, 192.
for ho wel wiste and was iwar, 147.

CHAPTER II

ALLITERATIVE PHRASES IN THE POEMS OF THE REVIVAL [A].

(a) The Non-rhyming Alliterative Poems of the Fourteenth Century.

In the non-rhyming Middle English alliterative poems there occur 1415 distinct alliterative phrases and a total number of instances of roughly 4250. From these facts it is at once evident that the poets in question must have had a very large common stock of such phrases from which to draw. Further, the frequency with which many of the phrases are found is much greater than in the case of the earlier groups already dealt with. Thus the author of *William of Palerne* employs the phrase *man on molde* forty-two times. Some poets naturally make greater use of alliterative phrases than others, but all their works attest the popularity of these expressions which were often of assistance to the author in the mere mechanism of his verse.

The actual number of *distinct* alliterative phrases found in the various poems is here given for the sake of comparison, and the total number of occurrences in brackets :—

Alexander A, 96 (108).
Alexander B, 105 (133).
Joseph of Arimathie, 34 (40).
William of Palerne, 204 (590).
Wynnere and Wastoure, 48 (54).
Parlement of the Thre Ages, 83 (96).
Piers Plowman, 418 (630).
Pierce the Ploughman's Crede, 60 (68).
The Crowned King, 18 (21).
Richard the Redeles, 77 (85).
Mum and Sothsegger, 127 (156).
Chevelere Assigne, 26 (27).
Patience, 68 (70).
Purity, 154 (168).

Sir Gawayn, 187 (229).
St. Erkenwald, 50 (51).
The Destruction of Jerusalem, 137 (155).
The Destruction of Troy, 404 (761).
The Wars of Alexander, 178 (256).
Morte Arthure, 212 (270).
Death and Life, 109 (125).
The Proph. of à Becket, 23 (28).
Scottish Proph. I, 9 (10).
Scottish Proph. II, 7 (7).
Scottish Field, 64 (76).
The Twa Mariit Wemen, 20 (22).

These statistics are illuminating, but would prove definitely misleading unless the varying length of the different poems were

borne in mind.   The number of instances of alliterative phrases in
Piers Plowman, William of Palerne and *The Destruction of Troy* is
in all three cases very high, despite the length of the poems themselves.   On the other hand, the author of the works of the MS.
Cotton Nero A. X. was more restrained in his use of stock phrases,
and did not employ a given phrase repeatedly.   The statistics,
however, show that the alliterative poets had inherited a large
number of these expressions from the past, since so many identical
phrases could not have been coined by various poets writing almost
at the same time.   Moreover, in the majority of the alliterative
poems these phrases are not used artificially, leaving the impression
that they have been put in because of a prevailing fashion ; they
are the alliterative poet's natural manner of writing.   Alone in
such poems as *Death and Life* were they sprinkled about according
to the needs of the alliterative metre.

To discover that of the 1415 phrases, twenty-three alone occur
in old English ' heroic ' poetry and thirty-nine in the ' religious '
is at first sight disappointing, but the bulk of the phrases in question
are of frequent occurrence in these poems, such as *blowe bemes,
kiss and clip, game and gle,* or *lenge in londe ;* and while many of
the phrases are such as also occur in Old English prose (actually
twenty-five in number) it is still evident that there is some slight
but nevertheless real continuity between the two groups.   Thus
londes and ledes, occurring in Old English *Andreas* 1321, and in the
Chronicle poem 1065, l. 25, but not in Old English prose, reappears
in Laȝamon's *Brut, Alexander A, Piers Plowman, Purity* and *William
of Palerne ;* other poetic phrases might similarly be quoted.   Yet
the fact remains that though traces of the Old English poetic
tradition regarding alliterative phraseology are still surviving, they
are much fainter than they were in Laȝamon's *Brut,* a poem in
which we find them marked.

In the case of those phrases which occur also in Old English
prose, there is a total of seventy-four, of which twenty-five occur
also in Old English poetry, and which include for the most part
ordinary expressions such as : *blowe a beme, kiss and clip, def and
dumb, have and holde, live a life,* and *saye sope.*   While there remains
no doubt concerning the genuine survival of many of the older
phrases, it may be useful to point to a few notable examples.   It
should also be remembered that phrases which in Old English were
in ordinary prose usage, though still surviving in the fourteenth
century, may have become definitely archaic by that time.   *Falle
apon folde,* an Old English phrase which survived in Laȝamon's

Brut, reappears in *The Wars of Alexander*, 251, 1641 ; similarly, *hous and home, lered and lewed, londe and lyfe, winde and weder, ware and wise, wodes and wastes*, are all interesting survivals of phrases found in Old English prose.

Roughly one-half of the alliterative phrases occurring in these poems could not have been inherited from Old English, since one or more elements of the phrase in 684 instances is derived from Old French or Old Norse. There are 565 phrases with two native elements, 343 with one Old French and one Old English, ninety-six with one Old Norse and one Old English, twenty with one Old Norse and one Old French, 137 with two Old French elements, and eight with two Old Norse. The remaining phrases containing an element which is Latin or of uncertain origin are here omitted.

It is not unlikely that more of the 565 native phrases are survivals from the past than the hundred which are extant in Old English prose and verse, but on the other hand, since so many new phrases were coined at this time from native and foreign sources in combination, it is probable that some of the purely native phrases are new creations. Sufficient phrases from Old English have survived to demonstrate the connection between the earlier and later groups, but the story is definitely one of " continuity, despite change." This change, as we have already observed in connection with the early Middle English phrases, is frequently due to the ousting of native words by foreign and the consequent replacement of some of the older phrases. By the time of the Alliterative Revival the change is complete, the foreign elements almost outweighing the native.

One hundred and seventy-four of these phrases occur in the early Middle English alliterative works. The number is in itself significant, but some of the individual examples are equally striking. Of special interest are *blo and blac, the Debate between the Body and the Soul*, 144, which reappears in *Purity*, 1017 ; *kenniÒ ant cnaweÒ, Kath.* 2065–6, which is found also in *Piers Plowman* and the *Wars of Alexander*. In both groups there is *freolich* (*frely*) *and faire*, the older form of the more common *faire and fre*, and *liÒin and listin*, both of which reappear in *The Wars of Alexander*. Some of these examples and numerous others indicate that many of the new phrases, consisting of one Old English and one Old French or Old Norse element, must have taken firm root at a very early period.

Thirty-five per cent. of Laȝamon's alliterative phrases survive in the poems of the Alliterative Revival (actually a numerical total of eighty-eight phrases). This high percentage suggests the connection of the later poets with Laȝamon. The most noteworthy phrases which are common to both groups are *falle feiȝe* (*Gaw.* and *W. Alex.*), *falle upon folde* (*W. Alex.*), *hunger and hete* (*Jerus.*), *liue in lisse* (*Will. of Pal.*), *londes and ledes* (see supra), *nose and nebb* (*W. Alex.*), *winne and wirschipe* (*Troy*), *wodes and wildernes* (*Will. of Pal.*). None of these phrases is common in Middle English, and the survival of these older expressions in the works of the Revival alongside the more common stock phrases, suggests that there is an important core of traditional archaic alliterative phraseology.

The interest of the phrases in this group does not lie merely in the testimony they afford to the continuity of the alliterative tradition, but also in the light which they throw upon the poet's methods of workmanship. In Old English poetry the alliterative semantic cognates used are very few and are chiefly confined to adjectives. Alliterative phrases are used with economy and a sense of proportion. In the poems of the Revival there is a larger number of phrases used and more semantic cognates have come into existence owing to the influx of loan words, so that there is a greater temptation to redundancy.

In this group there are 320 phrases consisting of pairs of parallel nouns and in thirteen cases alone does the combination consist of two words representing the same idea ; of such are *faythe and faye*, *fellow and fere*, *licence and leave*, *mariage and matrimony*, *puissance and power*, *residue and remenaunt*. There are similarly eighty-two pairs of parallel adjectives, of which five alone are of identical significance : e.g. *buxsom and bayne*. Of parallel verbs there are 122 examples, including fourteen cases of verbs of identical meaning, such as : *clepe and calle*, *hide and hele*, *kenne and knowe*, *konne and knowe*, *seseþ and stinteþ*, *socour and save*, *wache and wake*, *wilne and wolde*, etc. These facts make it abundantly clear that the temptation to mere repetition was generally avoided.

The Old English poet was, however, much more sparing in his use of alliterative phrases than the Middle English poet. In the older poetry these expressions are more subtly woven into the texture of the verse, whereas in the later poetry they are frequently too self-evident. The more careless poets use them for metrical purposes as much as for the general sense. In the hands of the more skilful metrists such as the author of *Patience*, the phrases are never inserted for their own sake but are used to give weight and dignity to the line as a whole.

There are 218 examples of alliterative phrases, consisting of a verb with a direct object, such as *lache leue ;* 252 examples of a

verb with an " extension," such as *bide in burghe ;* 130 examples
of a noun dependent upon another noun, such as *burne on benche ;*
and thirty-seven of an adjective with noun, such as *fayre of face.*
The phrases are thus for the most part of rigid stock types. Syn-
tactically there is little variety and the meaning is in each case
fairly constant. A phrase can usually be understood apart from
its context, which is only necessary for a more detailed study of the
poet's methods.

Sufficient has already been said to show that many of the
alliterative phrases were inherited from the past. Some of these,
such as *liue in lisse,* are of rare occurrence in Middle English, and
are confined to alliterative poetry. Other phrases are the common
property of all writers, alliterative and non-alliterative. Before
the middle of the fourteenth century such phrases were in common
use, especially in the early lyrics, many of which originated in the
south-western dialect, where the alliterative tradition seems to
have been strongest. Thus, in the following lyric :—

> " Foweles in þe frith,
> þe fisses in þe flod,
> and i mon waxe wod.
> Mulch sorw I walke with
> for beste of bon and blod," [1]

we have five alliterative phrases in the course of six lines. But
the popularity of these expressions must not blind us to the fact
that the alliterative poets used many other phrases which were
largely their exclusive property. The subsequent groups of phrases
will throw further light upon this interesting problem :—

aungells and arcangells, Pierce 690.
auntrus in armes, Troy 537, 3753, etc.
bac or bon, P.Pl. A viii, 77.
E.M.E. *bake and breste,* Gaw. 143, Morte Arthure 1159, 3257, Troy 9125.
bacon and beefe, W. & W. 379.
bayne to my bone, Jerus. 181. *I schal bayþen þy bone,* Gaw. 327.
balȝ/balghe . . . and brode, Gaw. 967, Parl. 112, W. Alex. 4923.
bale be beten, P.Pl. A iv, 80, etc. *ibet al ȝoure bale,* W. of P. 4613. *forto
     bete þy bale,* Mum 453.
to bale were ȝe þanne bore, Alex. B 808.
to byde bale, Gaw. 2041.
bring in bale, Alex. A. 672, W. of P. 134, 4937. *brouȝt (out) of bale,* W.
     of P. 1039, 2037, 3960, 4920, 5506, 5518. *brouȝt vs from bale,* Jerus.
     496. *brought us forth of bale,* Sc. F. 421. **E.M.E.** *fro bale has brouȝt us
     to blis,* Erk. 340. *brought vs out of bale,* D.L. 21.

---

[1] Edited by C. Brown, in *English Lyrics of the Thirteenth Century,*
p. 14.

E.M.E. *bote and/of bale,* P.Pl. B iv, 92, etc., W. of P. 627.[1] *boteles bale,*
M.A. 1014, 3558, 3976.
as bare as a bord, Mum 1070.
baret and/or bale, W. Alex. 4620, Sc. Proph. ii, 4, W. of P. 5517.
bargayned and bou3t, Jerus. 1304, 1317.
a barne in hir barme, W. & W. 418.
E.M.E. *barne was* (*y*)*bor*(*n*), Alex. A 849, D.L. 14, Sc. F. 295, 317, 339,
P.Pl. B xviii, 133, 230, 233.
barons and bachelers, W. Alex. 155, etc., D.L. 78, R.R. iii, 358, Sc. Proph.
i, 95, W. & W. 328. *baronis and knychtis and othir bachilleris,* Twa
Mariit Wemen 476–7. *bachillers . . . barons,* Mum 792.
baroun upon benche, Pur. 1640. *beryns on the benches,* W. & W. 314.
burne of/upon the bench, Gaw. 337, R.R. iv, 69. *þe burnes in benche,*
Mum 806.
barons bolde, Jerus. 229, W. of P. 1436. *barons full bolde,* Pur. 1372,
Troy, 1046. *barouns and bold men,* Jerus. 487.
mony barons full bold and buernes þerin, Troy, 1046. *his baronage bolde
and buernes full noble,* Troy, 324.
barouns and burgeis, P.Pl. A Pro. 96, iii, 150, x, 134, *baroun ne burges ne
burne,* Jerus. 491.
barre bigly . . . (the gates), D.L. 390, Troy, 691, etc. ; cp. Pur. 321.
to-barst and brak, Jos. 384.
batell and baret, Troy 9276.
I am beaten backe, Sc. F. 194.
neuer beaten was in battell, Sc. F. 369.
beawtye and blisse, D.L. 109, 242.
in bedde and at borde, P.Pl. A ii, 55.
beddels and bailyfs, W. Alex. 2294, P.Pl. A iii, 2.
þat bede þe þis buffet, Gaw. 382. *a buffet to beden,* Pierce 636.
oþer bedys or broche, Pierce 323.
beggen his bred, Pierce 626.
beggers and barouns, P.Pl. C vii, 123.
beggers and bedman, P.Pl. C iv, 276.
beggeres and bidderes, P.Pl. B xiii, 241, xv, 199. *bidders and beggers,*
P.Pl. A Pro. 40, A vii, 192, 202, viii, 68. *beggers that beggen,* P.Pl. C
x, 161. *to beggeres that gone and begge an bidden,* P.Pl. B xi, 269.
beggars for heore biddyng biddeth, P.Pl. A iii, 212. *bidde*(*th*) *and begge*(*th*),
P.Pl. A vii, 224, viii, 70, B xv, 251. *bidding as beggeres,* P.Pl. B xv,
221.
beggith and borwith, R.R. iii, 149. *borwynge other begging,* P.Pl. C xviii, 8.
borowe til I begge, Mum 1522.
with bellis and with baners, W. Alex. 1563.
O.E.Pr. *bell oþer book,* Pierce 115.
bachelors on bent, Troy 9718. *bald baratours on bent,* W. Alex. (Dublin)
830, 3502, 5327. *baret on bent,* Troy 8558, 10285. *batell on bent,*
W. Alex. 3557, Troy 91, etc. (13 times). *berne*(*s*) *on bent,* W. Alex.
1328, etc., Troy 6597, etc. *bolde berne on bent,* W. Alex. 3031, Gaw.
1465, Troy 1218. *bold on bent,* Troy 6788, 9866, 10054. *bestis on þe
bent,* W. Alex. 4584. *bodies on bent,* Troy 9685. *britnet on bent,*
Troy 9758, 12883. *brother on bent,* Troy 7633.

---

[1] See N.E.D. under *bale.*

I bent my backe, D.L. 32.
O.E.P. *I bende vp my bowe*, Parl. 43. *bend vp his bow*, Troy 9475.
E.M.E. *bendeth and boweth*, P.Pl. C xi, 37.
in bent and in borwe, Jerus. 308.
E.M.E. *pere a barne*, Alex. A 1020 :. see under *barn was yborn*.
to bere berthen, R.R. ii, 66.
þou berest aboute, Jos. 40.
beren hem bragg (bear themselves boastfully), Pierce 706, W. of P. 2352.
whose body . . . was beriet, Troy 13786. *where my body were buryed*,
 P.Pl. B xi, 74.
bet doun þe burȝ, Pur. 1292.
betyn and brent, Jerus. 1288. *betyn and brent doun vnto bare askes*, Troy
 5007. *betyn doun and brent*, Troy 4777. *brenten and beten*, Jerus.
 657, Troy 11931.
þy buyldyng betyn to þe bare erthe, Troy 2688.
E.M.E. *þe betyng and þe bynding*, Jerus. 494. *ybete and ybounde*, Mum
 172.
bidden þem battle, Alex. A. 122.
O.E.Pr., E.M.E., Laȝ. *bidde (any) bedes*, P.Pl. B v, 407, xii, 29, etc.,
 W. of P. 3024.
byde at þe bay, Gaw. 1582. *bode in his bay*, Gaw. 1564.
(a)byde(n) þe bur, Gaw. 291, 374, Pat. 7.
I bode on the bent, D.L. 149.
byde in blysse, M.A. 8.
Laȝ. *bide in þis burgh*, Becket 104, W. & W. 470.
big and bolde, Will. of Pal. 173.
byg and brode, Jerus. 661.
to bynde bandis, Sc. Proph. ii, 45. Cp. **Laȝ.** *bond him . . . with bondes*,
 P.Pl. C xxii, 57.
bisshop ne baron, Mum 476.
any blast of our breth, W. Alex. 3535.
blee of his body, Erk. 343.
bledden blode, P.Pl. B xvi, 237.
blessed and blype, Alex. B 624.
to bliken of hur ble, Alex. B 411. *blykned þe ble*, Pur. 1759.
E.M.E. *blisse and bale*, P.Pl. B xi, 324. *mi blis and mi bale*, W. of P.
 1539. *thy blisse is my bale*, D.L. 283. Cp. T.M. Wemen 51.
blis and bonchef, Gaw. 1764.
blyth (bearnes) of blee, D.L. 99.
þe blode of thi body, Erk. 290. *brouȝt blod of his bodi*, Pierce 632.
Laȝ. *his blod and his brayn*, Pur. 1788. *the blode and the brayne*, Jerus.
 540, Troy 9584. *his ȝonge blod and his brayn wilde*, Gaw. 89.
þe blode braste owte, Parl. 55, Sc. F. 326. *þe blode out barst*, Jerus. 586.
þe blod out brast, Troy 6924.
O.E.P. & Pr., E.M.E., P.M. *blode that he bouȝte vs with*, P.Pl. B xi, 119,
 W. of P. 2083.
Cp. **O.E.P.**[1] *blody beronen*, D.L. 172, Parl. 62, Troy 7033, etc. (10 times).
 bloudye beronen, Sc. F. 31. *blody beronene*, M.A. 3946 (MS. *be-rouene*).
 blody berowne, M.A. 3971. *blody byrunne*, Jerus. 599, 1119.
E.M.E. *blo . . . blak*, Pur. 1017.

[1] Crist 1176, *beam . . . blodigum tearum birunnen.*

blowen thy blast breemlye, D.L. 364.   *the burlyest blast that euer blowne was*,
   D.L. 145.
breþes con blowe, Pat. 138.
alle that euer ber bugle blowed, Gaw. 1913.   *a bogle . . . be blowen*, Parl. 656.
   bugles and bemes men gun blowe fast, W. of P. 1154.   *bemes blowen*,
   Jerus. 439, 521, 634.   **O.E.P. & Pr., E.M.E., Laȝ.**   *blew bemys*,
   W. Alex. 2616.
ho bluschet to þe burȝe, Pur. 982 (see *Pearl*, 980).
bobaunce and bost, W. of P. 1071, 1129, 3358, Pur. 179, 1712.   *in bost and
   in bobans*, W. Alex. 4252, cp. *for baisting of þi bobance*, W. Alex. 2016.
of body so bolde, Alex. A 1163.   *so bolde of þi bodi*, W. of P. 3231.[1]
E.M.E.   *þe body and þe brest*, W. Alex. 4987.
I may not bot boghe to þi boñe, Erk. 193.
boldist (was) in batell, Troy 4805, 10837, 13079.   *a bolde man in batell*,
   Troy 3754.   *bolde men in batell*, Troy 6943, W. of P. 2428.   *non so
   bold in þat batell*, Troy 6751.   *boldly in batell appon þe bent rydes*,
   M.A. 1450.
bolde and bown, W. & W. 431.
þe bordis and þe benkes, W. Alex. 2927.   *þe benkis and þe bordis*, W. Alex.
   5271.
bores and beres, W. of P. 388.   *my boles and my boreȝ (arn bayted and slayne)*,
   Pur. 55.
to borges and to bacheleres, Pat. 366, M.A. 857.   *bachillier ne bourgoys*,
   Mum 260.
þay borgouneȝ and beres blomes, Pur. 1042.
borly (of brede) and (of) big (strenght), Troy 3769.
borne at a byrthe, Chev. 23.
þay bosked to bedde, Pur. 834.
he bote hymself with his bylle, Chev. 360.
bowne att his bidd(ing), D.L. 216, R.R. iii, 294.   *boun to his bode*, W. Alex.
   2805, Erk. 181, Gaw. 852.   *abowid to his bidding*, Mum 1317.   *bowe(d)
   to his bode*, Pat. 56, 75.
boun me to batell, Troy 9779.   *bowne vnto batell*, Troy 3769.   *boun to batayle*,
   W. of P. 1088.   *bownet vnto batell*, Troy 8185.   *to bataile he bouneȝ
   hym*, M.A. 783.
to bounen his bernes, Jos. 414.   *to boune mo bernes*, Jos. 472.
boweȝ forth fro þe bench, Pur. 854.   *boȝe fro þis benche*, Gaw. 344.
þei bouwe touward þe bente, Jos. 489.
bowis of buskis and of braunches, W. Alex. 2851.
of boweȝ and of breres, W. Alex. 2985.
to bragg and to bost, W. Alex. 4553.   *bragger ne boster*, R.R. ii, 80.   *ffor
   braggynge and ffor bostynge*, R.R. iii, 186.   *bosteth and braggeth*, P.Pl. B
   xiii, 281, Mum 1529.   *bostynge and braggynge*, P.Pl. C vii, 34.
braydeȝ out a (bryȝt) bronde, Gaw. 1584, 1901, M.A. 1172, 2069, 4215, Parl.
   371, Troy, 6407, 10685.
þe brayn out brast, Jerus. 1199.
brawndysche þe blade, M.A. 3359.
þe bred and þe bouf, W. of P. 1849, 1868.
brennen and blasen, P.Pl. B, xvii, 232.   *ne brenne ne blase clere*, P.Pl. B
   xvii, 256.   *ȝe brenne, but ȝe blaseth nouȝte*, P.Pl. B xvii, 262.

---

[1] Cp. *boldnesse of body*, D.L. 7.

to brenne the body, Pierce 667. *the body to bren*, Troy 12288.

E.M.E. *a (bryght) brenninge brond*, Alex. A 683. *(bryȝt) brennande brondeȝ*, Pur. 1012.

alle his breste bledde, Chev. 360.

breuyt in a boke, Troy 65, etc. (5 times). *breued in þe best boke*, Gaw. 2521. *in no boke breved*, Pur. 197. *þat ever wos brevyt in burghe ne in bok(e)*, Erk. 103.

bridis and of bestis, W. Alex. 1532, D.L. 112, P.Pl. B x, 402, xi, 319, xii, 131, etc. *bestis and briddes*, Troy, 11788.

a brid on a boghe, W. Alex. 4982. *birds bradden to the boughes*, Sc.F. 176, 312. *breme birds on the boughs busilye did singe*, D.L. 74. *briddes ful bremely on þe bowes singe*, W. of P. 23. *briddis in þa braunches*, W. Alex. 4782, Alex. B 134.

E.M.E. *bryȝt of (hor) blee*, Alex. A 202, D.L. 65, 87, Erk. 87, Troy 7888. *þe brightest of blee*, Alex. A 578. *bright blased his blee*, Alex. A 729.

bringeth forth barnes, P.Pl. A iii, 147, viii, 76, x, 143. *bring up your bearnes*, D.L. 253.

to bringe abedde, Mum 1210.

E.M.E. *broght (in) to bedde*, Gaw. 1990, P.Pl. C viii, 4, Troy 11892.

to batell brynge of brenyde knyghts, M.A. 316.

O.E.P. & Pr., E.M.E. *bringe vs (in) to blisse*, D.L. 21, 457, Sc.F. 421, Troy 14044. *bringe his soule to blisse*, P.Pl. B xiv, 85. *brought into blisse*, D.L. 268 ; see under *bale*. *brouȝte hire to boure with blisse*, P.Pl. A iii, 97.

bryng (þe) bodworde, W. Alex. 1489, Pur. 473. *bodeworde . . . broght*, W. Alex. 48, 1458, Erk. 105, Jerus. 969, Troy 8315.

bryng out of þe burgh, W. & W. 484.

(þe borȝ) brittened and brent to brondeȝ, Gaw. 2. *brettenede or brynte*, M.A. 3520. *to haue brittenet þat bor*, W. of P. 206, etc.

broad on their bankes, D.L. 25.

brosten the bones and brekyn thaym in sondire, Parl. 231.

brosten and betyn doun, Jerus. 977.

my browes and my berde, Parl. 285. *his berde and browes*, Parl. 156. *with grette browis ybente & a berde*, R.R. iii, 214.

shee burnisht vp her brand, D.L. 175.

brused oþer broken, Pur. 1047.

buffetyn hym, betyn hym, Parl. 224.

he bulde boldus an hih, Alex. B 848. **E.M.E.** *swich a bild bold ybuld*, Pierce, 157. *hie boldus to bulde*, Alex. B 437.

the bilding of þe boures, Mum 1005. *þer watȝ bylded his bour*, Pat. 276. *build þe borowe*, Alex. A 1220. **E.M.E., Laȝ.** *we buldeþ a burwȝ*, Pierce, 118.

(after that Brutus) þis burghe had buggid, Erk. 207. *that biggit the burgh*, Troy 5216.

burde or/ne barne, W. of P. 812, 1971, 2008, 2358. *vuche burde with her barne*, Pur. 378. *þar bridis and þar barnes*, W. Alex. 4046.

to burie in þe burwe, Jerus. 1148, Troy, 13786.

thoru busschis and bromes, R.R. iii, 19.

þe burne and his barneȝ, Pur. 502.

on burne oþer on beste, Jerus. 602. *bernes and bestes*, P.Pl. A iii, 256, etc., Pat. 388. *barnes and birds and bestes*, D.L. 81. *birds and beastes and bearnes*, D.L. 112. *bernys and bridis*, W. Alex. 4125.

Laȝ. *burneȝ (so) bolde,* Gaw. 1574, Mum 144, 165. *beryn be so bolde,*
W. & W. 126, 131. *no buerne was so bolde,* Troy 12887. *euery bearne
full boldlye,* Sc.F. 178. *bolde b(e)urn(e),* Alex. A 9, Gaw. 1631, 2338,
2524, Jerus. 271, 659, Parl. 110, 527, W. of P. 3817.

burn oþur burde, Alex. B 418. *beurdes and bernes,* Alex. A 228, 602. *burneȝ
and burdeȝ,* Pur. 80.

of beryns and of burgeys and bachelors noble, M.A. 857.

O.E.P. *burne of burwe,* Jerus. 1040. *buernes of the burghe,* Troy 11483,
etc. (9 times). *byschop in/of burgh,* W. Alex. 1172, Erk. 3, Troy
4491, 11826.

buske . . . to batell, Alex. A 426, W. Alex. 2908, Jerus. 455, Troy 12877,
W. of P. 1152. *boldly vnto battell busked he,* Sc.F. 261.

(burnes) busken hem out of bedde, Jerus. 739. *busk of hire bed,* W. of P.
1997. *(vche burne) to his bedde busked,* Gaw. 1411. *(þe burd) busked
too bedde,* Alex. A 715, W. of P. 2055. *busk to thy borde bed,* Alex. A
689. *(vche burne) busked him to bedde,* W. of P. 5000. *busked hem
. . . to bedde,* W. of P. 1530, 3021. *to his bed buskes,* Jos. 202, 233.
the burne into bed busket, Troy 9174.

he buskes touward the bent, Jos. 450.

buske and be boun, Troy 2754. *he bad buske him and bowne him,* Sc.F. 113.
he busked and boun was one his beste wyse, W. & W. 110. *y schal buske
me boun,* Jerus. 183. *busked wer boun,* Jerus. 674.

busken out of burwe, Jerus. 369. *busked him into the bour,* P.Pl. A iii, 14.
þer he busked hym a bour, Pat. 437.

buxsom and bayne, W. Alex. 323. *boxum and boun,* P.Pl. A ii, 54, iii, 251.
to be buxome at his bidding, P.Pl. B i, 110, xiv, 221. *buxum ben to his
bidding,* W. of P. 464.

cagged and kaȝt, Pur. 1254.

kagged and knyt, Jerus. 700.

caire   agayn to þi kith, W. Alex. 3562. *cayreȝ bi sum oþer kyth,* Gaw.
2120. *I will not kere out of kythe,* D.L. 47. *keerre yee ffurther of this
kithe,* D.L. 436.

kayred to þe court, Gaw. 43. *that we may kayre till hys courte,* M.A. 6.
kayre to the courte, Parl. 246.

kaire to (his) countre, Troy 13536, W. of P. 2201, 5184, 5190. *kayere to
ȝour cuntreȝ,* M.A. 627.

there called he his councell, Sc.F. 100. *calleþ consail,* Jerus. 964. *calleth to
his councell,* Sc.F. 75.

calle with a hiȝe cry, Pur. 1565.

cares colde, W. of P. 2424, etc., cp. Beow. 2396, *cealdum cearsiðum.*

care and complaint, Troy 3293, 10767.

care or confusion, Troy 2319.

paȝ he be kest into kare, Pur. 234.

kast vp on a clyffe, Pur. 460.

caste on his clothes, P.Pl. A vii, 55. *cast of his clothes,* Troy 12661.

he keste up þe clothe, Chev. 97.

kest vp þe cortyn, Gaw. 1192.

E.M.E. *shee cast vp a crye,* D.L. 212. *kastis vp a kene crie,* W. Alex.
1604, 3996. *kest vp a crie,* W. Alex. 2154, 2345. *loude crye watȝ þer
kest,* Gaw. 64.

he cast vp his croune, Beckett 189. *shee cast of her crowne,* D.L. 348.

catell in cofers, Pierce 283, cp. P.Pl. C vi, 129. *kepe hit in here cofre for catell at hure mede.*

oper catell oper clop, Pierce 116.

katell oper corne, Pierce 397. *of corne and of catell*, Troy 5177. *corne oper catell*, Pierce 322.

she kawȝte out a knyfe, Chev. 62. *þe quen kauȝt a knif*, W. of P. 3199. *he a knyf cauhte*, Jos. 577.

kene and connyng (in armes), W. Alex. 2369.

of kempes and of conquerors, of kynges, Parl. 251.

E.M.E. *to kenne and to knowe*, P.Pl. C xii, 141. *þat knawis wele & ken*, W. Alex. 4678.

kenned crafte, P.Pl. B xix, 229. *kenne me bi somme crafte to knowe*, P.Pl. B ii, 4. *I schal kenne yow by kynde a crafte*, Pur. 865.

comly bykennen to kryst, Gaw. 1307. *I bikenne ȝou to krist*, W. of P. 5424. *bikenned hem to crist*, W. of P. 5454. *bi-kenned him to crist*, W. of P. 350, 371.

kepe counselle, Chev. 50, Troy 11376.

couenaunt(es) to kepe, Troy 705, 9225, 9293.

chalanging ne chydynge, P.Pl. B xi, 15.

chambyrs with chymnes, M.A. 168, 3041, Pierce 209. *a chambre with a chymneye*, P.Pl. B x, 98.

chaplayneȝ to þe chapeles, Gaw. 930.

charite and chastete, Pierce 150.

E.M.E. *chaunged (his) cher(e)*, Alex. A 1039, Gaw. 711, 2169,[1] Jos. 83, Pat. 368, Troy, 7996, 8177, 13805.

colour chaunge, W. of P. 764.

þe chauntre of þe chapel, Gaw. 63.

chauntements or charmes, Jerus. 96. *charmes and Inchauntementes*, Troy 13228. *charmet with enchauntment*, Troy 778.

bi enchaunmens of charmes, W. of P. 137.

þe chekis and þe chauyls, W. Alex. 4984.

by cheeke and by chin, D.L. 122. *his chekes and his chyn*, Pierce 224. *cheekes and chinne*, Alex. A 183. *chynne and cheke*, Gaw. 1204.

alle þat cheffare wolde chepe, Jerus. 1314.

chepen and chose, Gaw. 1271.

to acheue to þe chaunce, Gaw. 1838. *he cheueȝ þat chaunce*, Gaw. 2103. *if hit cheue þe chaunce*, Pur. 1125. *hit is cheuit the a chaunse*, Troy 8113. *hit may chefe hym by chaunce*, Troy 2603.

children and cheorles, P.Pl. A iii, 253. *cherl oper child*, W. of P. 1822. *cherles & children*, P.Pl. B xviii, 104.

E.M.E. *chirches and chapells*, M.A. 3039. *a chirche and a chapaile*, Pierce 119.

kyd(d)e conqueror, M.A. 65, 232, 2261, 2621. *conqueror kid*, Alex. B 26. *conquerors kydde*, M.A. 3407, Parl. 459.

so kynde and so corteys, W. of P. 194. *curtas and kynde*, Troy 3836, Mum 442, P.Pl. A iii, 60.

kynges and captaynes, M.A. 838.

O.E.P. & Pr., E.M.E., Laȝ. *kynge(s) and kaysere*, M.A. 1894, 1959, 2391, P.Pl. C iv, 321, 325, Pur. 1374, R.R. i, 85, W. of P. 483. *" kene kyng "*

---

[1] See *chere* in the glossary to the edition by J. R. Tolkien and E. V. Gordon.

quod þe quene, " kayser of urþe," Pur. 1593.   **E.M.E.** *kynges, knyghtes
and kaysers,* Parl. 605, P.Pl. B ix, 110, x, 100.   *kynge, ne cayser,
ne ʒet no knyʒt,* Erk. 199.   *knyghte, kaysere, or oþer,* M.A. 1651.
E.M.E. *kaysere ne/or kynge,* M.A. 2266, P.Pl. B xix, 134, W. & W. 327.
kyng of ʒour kynde, Jerus. 299.
O.E.P. & Pr., E.M.E., Orm.   *kynge of kynges,* P.Pl. B xviii, 382.
kynge of that/her kyngedom, P.Pl. B xviii, 379, xix, 49.
kyng of þis/that kyth, Alex. A 174, 238, 1146, W. Alex. 843, etc. (5 times),
    Erk. 98, Jerus. 88, M.A. 1929, Parl. 466, P.Pl. B iii, 203, Pur. 1201,
    Sc. Proph. I, 76, Troy 120, etc. (11 times), W. & W. 69, 124.   *king of
    hur kip,* Alex. B 184.   *kynges in/of þe kith,* Troy 12929, 13095.
    kyng in þat kuppe, Jerus. 90.   *hor kyngdomes and hor kyth,* Troy 12849.
a kyng in the cost, þat the kith aght, Troy 12394.
kyng and clerk, Becket, 21.   *clerkis and kynges,* M.A. 3444.
Laʒ. *kyng(es)* . . . *kniʒt(es),* W. Alex. 2473, Gaw. 482, Jerus. 489, 733,
    Parl. 605, P.Pl. A v, 1, etc. (9 times), B ix, 110, x, 100, Troy 4020,
    etc. (18 times), W. of P. 512, 1086, 4630.   *knyghte, king,* M.A. 678.
    kinghed and kniʒthed, P.Pl. A xi, 22, 216.
king under cloude, Troy 3873.
neyther kynge ne conqueror, P.Pl. B xix, 93, M.A. 535.   *knyʒte, kynge,
conqueror,* P.Pl. B xix, 27.
kyng in the coste, Troy 1028, 12394.
kynge vndire Criste, M.A. 2633, W. of P. 1357.   *þe kynge, þat vndir Criste
lifede,* M.A. 3961.   *clerk vnder Crist,* W. of P. 5055, 5344.   *clerkes
vnder Cryst,* P.Pl. B x, 245, xii, 216.   *clergye vnder Cryste,* P.Pl.
B xi, 139.   **Laʒ.** *any kniʒt under Crist,* W. of P. 3671.   *vnder Crist is
no kniʒt,* W. of P. 3305.   *no creature vnder Crist,* P.Pl. B xi, 380.   *al
the Cristendome vnder Crist,* P.Pl. C xiii, 78.
kynge with croune, Gaw. 364, P.Pl. B xix, 463.   *kynges with crounes,* Parl.
    309, P.Pl. A iv, 221, B xix, 463.   *þe kynge crouned of kynges,* W.
    Alex. 4571.   *a kynge crouned with angeles,* P.Pl. B xviii, 369.   *kynge
    crowned with golde,* W. & W. 86.   See *infra* under *crouned* . . . *king.*
the kyng of þe cuntre, Troy 5231, W. Alex. 827.
in all the kyngdome and cuntre, Troy 3932.   *kyngdome and contreeʒ,* M.A.
    27, Parl. 492.
O.E.Pr., E.M.E., Laʒ.   *þe kynge and þe queene,* Chev. 20, P.Pl. B xiii,
    169, W. of P. 4946.   *kings and queens,* D.L. 357, W. of P. 5027.
kissed kyndlye, D.L. 231, M.A. 714, W. of P. 4889.
O.E.P. & Pr., E.M.E., Laʒ.   *to kysse ne clippe,* Troy 871.   *clyp thaym
    and kysse thaym,* Parl. 248.   *clipped and kessed,* W. of P. 859, etc.
    (10 times).   *clupte me and custe,* P.Pl. A xi, 174.   *clippe we in couenant
    and vch of vs cusse other,* P.Pl. B xviii, 417.   *kissyng and clippyng,*
    Troy 2931.   *clipping and kissing,* W. of P. 3659, etc. (12 times).
    with kissing and with clapping, Twa Mariit Wemen, 274.   *sum kissis
    me sum clappis me,* Twa Mariit Wemen, 483.   *kest hit and clipped,*
    W. of P. 63.
her kysttes and her coferes, Pat. 159.
kyte ne krowe, R.R. ii, 178.
kyth and kyn, P.Pl. B xiii, 379, xv, 497.
clad all in clene gold, kirtill and mantill, W. Alex. 4955.   *comliche clade in
    kirtill,* W. & W. 90.   *comelye cladd in kirtle and mantle,* D.L. 83, 445 (?).

clamur and/or crye, Troy 8217, 8720, 11626, 11902.
clatered þe cloudes, W. Alex. 555, Jerus. 54, Pur. 972, Troy 4626, 5787, 12501.
E.M.E. *hit clatered in þe clyff, as hit cleue schulde*, Gaw. 2201, cp. *claterin* and *cleouen*.
clede in a clath, W. Alex. 1086.
E.M.E. *cleped and called*, P.Pl. B xix, 113. *calleʒ and clepes*, Pur. 1345.
to clepe and crie, W. of P. 1977. *cried and clepid*, R.R. iii, 70.
clerkes and knihtes, P.Pl. A iii, 43, iv, 105, B xiii, 437, xv, 325, C viii, 97, xii, 52. *knychtis and clairkis*, T.M. Wemen 435. **E.M.E.**, Laʒ. *of kniʒtes and of clerkis*, P.Pl. B ii, 57.
bothe þe cleweʒ and þe clyfeʒ, M.A. 2013, 2019.
scho has closede him in a cragge, Sc. Proph. i, 139. *in þe crageʒ were closed*, Pur. 449.
icloped in/wiþ cloth(ing), Jos. 295, Pierce 608, W. of P. 294, 2428.
to clucche or to clawe, P.Pl. B xvii, 188.
E.M.E. *knelyde . . . on . . . knee(s)*, Beckett 14, D.L. 76, 119, 353, Gaw. 818, Parl. 229, P.Pl. A ii, 1, 77, xii, 47, Troy 798, W. of P. 1003, 5443, etc.
knelis to þe conqueror, M.A. 2178. *knelyde before þe conqueror*, M.A. 2312.
knyghtes and kene men, M.A. 1895. *knightes full kene*, D.L. 51, Troy 13210.
knychtis and knavys, Sc. Proph. ii, 8. *knyghte or knaffe*, M.A. 2637.
knight oþer clerk, knaue oþer kempe, W. of P. 4029, see under *clerk*.
a knight of that countrie, Sc.F. 156.
knowen and kydde, W. & W. 315. *y-kidde and y-knowe*, Mum 214.
whenne þe kokke can craw, Sc. Proph. i, 73. *bi þat þe coke hade crowe*, Gaw. 1412. *vch kok þat crue*, Gaw. 2008.
cof and quyk, Pur. 624.
þay acolen and kyssen, Gaw. 2472. *acoles . . . and kysses*, Gaw. 1936.
come byfore þe kynge, Chev. 64.
he comeʒ to þe kyng, Gaw. 594.
com to . . . kith, Alex. A. 241, 402, 654. *till I come to my kyth*, Troy 13551. *till þou com to þat kip*, W. of P. 4254. *hou schulde þou com to his kyth*, Pur. 1110. *þat þei may comen in your kip*, Alex. B. 1090. *to quat kyth he be com*, Gaw. 460. *fro what kith bee yee comme*, Alex. A 591.
of what kin he were kome, W. of P. 236. *of what kinne hee comme*, Alex. A. 456. *he were komen of no ken*, W. of P. 513. *komen of hire oune kin*, W. of P. 584. *comen was of gret kin*, W. of P. 4090.
of whate kynde he was comene ?, M.A. 3867.
we come at his commandement, Sc.F. 131.
E.M.E. *com to . . . cort*, Mum 1221, 1238, Pur. 89, 1368, P.Pl. A vi, 75, Troy 2106, W. of P. 330, 507, 1583.
com to þis kuntre, W. of P. 4260.
colde watʒ his cumfort, his care huge, Pat. 264. *all coldes my comford*, Troy 11315. *comfort af all care*, Cr. King 2, W. of P. 1656. *of care and of comfort*, Cr. King 8. *I comfort caughte*, Parl. 170, Troy 9255.
coumfort to keuer, Pat. 223, W. of P. 1521. *keuer . . . comfort*, Gaw. 1221, 1254, Pat. 485.
comly and clene, Pur. 508. *comeleye (castles) and clere (caruen towers)*, D.L. 43.
comand kenely hys knyghtes, W. Alex. 821.

(how he my3t) compas and kast, W. Alex. 415, 1361.   *he cast . . . and compast*, Troy, 12324.   *to compas and kast*, Pur. 1455.
compast in his conscience, Gaw. 1196.
konne and knowe, P.Pl. B xv, 374, xix, 198.
to conne my crede, Pierce 101.   *pou3 pou conne nou3t pi crede*, Pierce 131.
coninge and coynt, W. of P. 653.
coninge of clearkes, D.L. 8.
conquerid cuntre(es), Mum 1415, 1455.   *conquered kyngdomes and contrees*, Parl. 492.   *conquered with conqueste kyngdoms twelue*, Parl. 402.   *conquerede kynges and kyngdomes twelue*, Parl. 440.   *conqueryd that kyngryke*, M.A. 24.
how he may conquere by crafte the kythe, M.A. 2393.   *conqueride pat kyth*, M.A. 2382.
conquirid and ouercome, W. Alex. 174.
coruen pay pe cordes, Pat. 153.
a koste of pis kyth, Pur. 912.   *pe costis and pe kitthis*, W. Alex. 1204.
coundutes . . . and carole3. Gaw. 1655.   *with coundythes and carolles*, Parl. 254.
couerde vp on hire kneese, M.A. 956.   *the knyghte coueride on his knees*, M.A. 2195.   *vpe he coueris one kneys*, M.A. 4274.   *koure doune on hur knees*, Alex. A. 558.
courbed on my knees, P.Pl. B i, 79, ii, 1.
nau per to cout ne to kerve wyth knyf, Pur. 1104.
what I couth and knewe, P.Pl. B xiii, 311.   *what ich knew and couthe*, P.Pl. C vii, 58.
hir craft and hir conyng, Troy, 13252.
crafty and curious, M.A. 211.   *corius and crafty*, Troy 13827.   *corius and craftely grauen*, Troy 8744.   *pat wyth curious crafte coruen wat3 wyly*, Pur. 1452.
craueth ne coueiteth, P.Pl. B xv, 249.
pey crieden alle o cry, Pierce 441.
crispid and kombide, M.A. 1003.
crist . . . on crosse, Erk. 2, Mum 724, P.Pl. A v, 245, ix, 9, W. of P. 1343.
croked and courbed, encrampeschett for elde, Parl. 154.   *croked me, cowrbed me, encrampeschet myn hondes*, Parl. 287.   *crucyfiede one crosse*, M.A. 3428.
E.M.E. *crouned . . . king*, Alex. A 28, 58, Cr. King 35, 51, 141, Jerus. 273, M.A. 3435, Mum, 115, 1632, P.Pl. A ix, 91, 98, R.R. Pro. 24, W. of P. 252, 2580, 4509, 4651.   *crist, crouned king*, D.L. 1, W. of P. 2580, etc.   *pai coronyd pe kidde kynge*, Erk. 254.   *pai coroned hym kyng*, Troy 13088.   *I corouned was in kyth*, M.A. 142.   *he was coroned to kyng in pat kithe*, Troy 13646.   **E.M.E.** *crouned with a croune*, P.Pl. A ii, 10.   *crouned with a croune that kyng*, R.R. i, 33.
crowelle and kene, M.A. 1831, 3086, 3424.
daisshe paym to death, Mum 981.
O.E.Pr., E.M.E., La3. *vche a dale so depe*, Pur. 384.   *a drere dale & a depe*, W. Alex. 4804.   *downe in yhon depe dale*, Becket, 79.
dawed to day, W. of P. 1791, 2218.   *the day did updaw*, T.M. Wemen 512.
tyl the daye dawed, P.Pl. B xviii, 424.   *when pe dawande day*, Pat. 445.
pat pe dayly3t wat3 done, Gaw. 1365.   *pat don was pe day*, Alex. B 118.   *er pis day was done or droghe to pe night*, Troy 8170.   N.B.—See *infra*, under *drive forth pe day*.

whan the day vp drogh, Troy 13366.
all the dale dunned, Sc.F. 329.
E.M.E., La3., Orm. *ouer dales and dounes*, W. of P. 2715, 2903.
all was damped with dew, Sc.F. 310.
now dampnede to þe dede, M.A. 3299.
dampned to the deth, P.Pl. B xviii, 376.
it darkened full dimlie, Sc.F. 302.
dares for dowte, M.A. 3225. *dare(s) for drede*, Gaw. 315, W. of P. 2048.
for drede he wolde not dare, Gaw. 2258.
dartes the Duchemen dalten, M.A. 2101.
in dawngere and dole, M.A. 3067.
daunger (n)or deire, Troy 146, etc.
daunger and drede, Troy 2003, etc. (5 times). *dred and daunger*, Pur.
342.
ded(e) of . . . dynte(s), Gaw. 2664, Jerus. 1200, 1208, M.A. 2178, Parl. 447,
Troy 5731, etc. (20 times).
E.M.E. *ded . . . and doluen*, P.Pl. A vii, 172, W. of P. 2630, 5280.
doluen and ded, Alex. A. 1026, M.A. 975, Parl. 258.
dede and don out of lyue, Alex. A 32, Troy, 5285 ; cp. Alex. A 1147. *dede
and undone*, M.A. 1722, 3778.
ded as a dore nayl, Jerus. 1074, Mum 1646, Parl. 65, P.Pl. A i, 161, W. of P.
628, 3396.
O.E.P. & Pr., E.M.E. *þof it defe were and doumbe*, Troy 4281. *deef or
dum*, Mum 756. **E.M.E., Orm.** *þe dombe aňd þe deue*, Jerus. 126.
dom as a dore-nayl and defe was he bathe, W. Alex. 4747. *as doumbe
as a dore*, P.Pl. A xi, 94.
dele to me my destine, Gaw. 2285.
dele dynttys of dethe, M.A. 332. *to deale dolefull dints*, D.L. 318. *to dele
with dynttis/with dynttis to dele*, W. & W. 103, etc. *deth delt him a
dent*, P.Pl. A xii, 104. *delt Adam such a dint*, D.L. 275. *delt dynttys/
dynttys delt*, Alex. A 143, M.A. 3749, Troy 944, etc. (10 times), W. of
P. 2791, etc. *delingis/dealing of dynt(i)s* W. Alex. 451, Sc.F. 378.
dints that I delt oft, D.L. 332. *the dints that I deale*, D.L. 263. *derfe
dintis and dre3e delt*, W. Alex. 2091. *such a dunt as þou hat3 dalt*,
Gaw. 452. *delte with dynnte3*, M.A. 1277.
to dele . . . þe dome of my wyrdes, Gaw. 1968.
deluen and diggen, Pierce 785. *to digge and to delue*, Mum 977. *I dyke
and delue*, P.Pl. B v, 552. *diken or deluen*, P.Pl. A xi, 184, B vi 143,
193. *þay dy3t and dalfe*, Erk. 45. *idyket and idoluen*, P.Pl. A vi, 36.
dykers and deluers, P.Pl. A vii, 100.
Cp. La3. *to deluen a dyche depe*, P.Pl. B xix, 359. *soe deepe deluen
with diches about*, Sc.F. 82. *depe doluene*, M.A. 975. **O.E.Pr.** *doluen
(þus) depe*, Erk. 99, W. of P. 1564, 4210.
O.E.P. & Pr., E.M.E., P.M. *deemed . . . (to) deth*, D.L. 369, P.Pl. B iii,
305, Troy 5106, 12031, 12251. *þat þe is demed þe deþ*, Alex. B 78.
Cp. **O.E.Pr., E.M.E.** *þat him is demed to deie*, Alex. B. 1061. *when God
demeþ 3ou deie*, Alex. B 589.
demyt hit by dome, Troy 12256. *alle demeden by dome*, Jerus. 267.
O.E.P. & Pr., E.M.E., La3., Orm. *demeden a dom*, Jerus. 1097. *deme
domes*, P.Pl. B xv, 27. *demed be þe dome*, W. Alex. 2164. *þe dom
demed was*, Jerus. 985.

whan alle was demed, and done, Jerus. 1331.
depe in my doungoun, Pur. 158. *dupe as a dunion*, Alex. A 1132.
the derke was done, Parl. 16, Troy 12531.
the derke ouerdrogh, Troy 4664, W. Alex. 1505. *þe derke nyȝt overdrofe*, Erk. 117.
deire with dynt(tes), Alex. A. 1240, Troy 1260, 6752, 7102. *no dynte shal hym dere*, P.Pl. B xviii, 26. *that no dynte of no darte dere them ne schoulde*, M.A. 3611. *the dint of my dart deared*, D.L. 312.
þoȝ ȝe deþ scholde dey, Jerus. 772, Jos. 390. *what deþ by dome þat he dey scholde*, Jerus. 691. *deth deyeden*, P.Pl. B xv, 550.
dethe and deire, Troy 11338, etc. (6 times).
dethe dinges on my dore, Parl. 654.
us bydewen aday þe dewus of heuen, Alex. B 425.
to dyȝe with doel, Pur. 1329.
Laȝ. *diȝt to þe deth*, W. Alex. 744, 1504. *(þi) deth (is) idiȝt*, W. of P. 151, 1643, 3918. *why ne dyȝtteȝ þou me to diȝe*, Pat. 488.
þou wyl diȝt me þe dom, Jos. 429. *þy dom is þe dyȝt*, Pat. 203.
dyn and dole, Troy 6910, 8675.
þat he ne dyngeȝ hym to deþe with dynt of his honde, Gaw. 2105. *dang . . . to dethe*, Troy 7440, etc. (12 times). *dungen to death*, Sc.F. 32, Troy 2086, etc. (8 times). *dingis doun*, W. Alex. 2041. *dyngen hym adoune*, P.Pl. B x, 330. *dungen doun*, Pur. 1266. *dang them with my dints*, D.L. 325, Troy, 302.
no dynte of no darte, M.A. 3611. *the dint of my dart*, D.L. 312.
the dite and the dyn, Troy 1347, 5788, 8680, 11946. *dyn and dyt*, Jerus. 248, 1189.
O.E.Pr., E.M.E., Orm. *do a dede* (in varying forms), Alex. A. 5, Alex. B. 273, etc. (9 times), Erk. 169, Gaw. 1089, Jerus. 179, 1302, M.A. 48, Mum 615, 651, etc., P.Pl. B xix, 129, 177, etc., Pat. 432, Parl. 181, Pur. 110, R.R. iii, 10, Troy, 593, etc., W. of P., 1368, etc.
doer of/in deede(s), Mum 217, 750.
O.E.Pr., E.M.E. *do to dethe* (in varying forms), W. Alex. 3440, D.L. 244, Jerus. 319, Parl. 570, P.Pl. C xxii, 141, Troy 1381, etc. (11 times), W. of P. 4334, etc. (7 times).
E.M.E., Laȝ. *done us of dawe*, Reply of Fr. Daw Thopias, p. 44. *to do . . . of dawe*, Jerus. 184. *don of daweȝ*, M.A. 2056. *of dawe was don*, Jerus. 1299.
do (him no) dispit, Alex. B 958, Jos. 581.
dolefull death, D.L. 220, 232. *dolefully dyen*, D.L. 207.
in dongoun be don, Pur. 1224.
þe donkande dewe, Gaw. 519. *tille eche dale with dewe was donked aboute*, Jerus. 624. *the dew donkit the daill*, T.M. Wemen 10.
doughtie of deede(s), Alex. A 945, Troy 2570, etc. (6 times), W. of P. 3266, etc.
doun þei daschen, Jerus. 1087. *dasschaude doun*, Jerus. 808.
doun fel he . . . ded, Alex. B 130.
doune in a dungion, Troy 12094. *doune in the dongyn*, Troy 12647.
doute no deth, P.Pl. C xi, 197. *dowtyn no dethe*, Troy, 11686. *doutid no deth*, Troy 12121. *we schal doute þe deþ*, Alex. B 326. *adouted as dethe*, Alex. A 247. **E.M.E.** *in doute of the dethe*, Troy, 10664.
doute and dreede, Mum 1334 (sbs.).

with drakes and with dukkes, W. & W. 97.
draweth vp her darts, D.L. 189.
E.M.E. *draweþ to þe depe-warde*, Pierce 411. See N.E.D.
(*þe dor*) *drawen and dit*, Gaw. 1233.
drawen doun, Erk. 6.
dreamed I the dreame, D.L. 455.
he was drechhit in a dream, Troy 13804. *draiht with dreme*, Alex. A 820.
of her . . . dreme þat draihte hur, Alex. A 752. *in dremyng, in
drecchyng*, Cr. King 6.
Cp. **O.E.Pr. Alf., E.M.E.** *drede of . . . deth*, D.L. 198, Mum 127, P.Pl. B
x, 79, xv, 406, C ix, 187, Troy 1359. **E.M.E.** *drede* (vb.) . . . *deth*,
Alex. A. 381, P.Pl. B xi, 259, C x, 17, Troy 11935. *now is dethe at my
dore that I drede most*, Parl. 292.
I dradde to deye, P.Pl. B xiii, 406. *dredeth to be ded*, P.Pl. C xiv, 57, etc.
(*here*) *drede and* (*here*) *doel*, W. of P. 781, 1909.
Orm. *dreden his dom*, Jerus. 366.
drepid and dede, W. Alex. 1233. *drepit with deth*, Troy 9, etc. (6 times).
when it drew too þe derk and þe daie slaked, Alex. A 714. *it droʒe to þe derke*,
W. Alex. 4773. *þe day him wiþdrow into þe derk niʒt*, W. of P. 2993.
the day ouerdrogh and the derk rose, Troy 11917. *it drouʒ to þe dai*, W.
of P. 1914, 2207. *þe dym of þe derkenesse drowe into þe west*, Cr.
King 23.
þay droʒ hem adreʒ, Pur. 71, cp. Gaw. 1031, *he draʒeʒ him ondryʒe*: Troy
10043, M.A. 3968, 4219.
þe day dryueʒ to þe derk, Gaw. 1999, cp. *Quen it is dreuyn to þe derke*, W.
Alex. 687. *þis day . . . þay dryuen*, Gaw. 1468. **Laʒ.** *the day . . .
dryuen to þe end*, Troy 4551. *thus I drife forthe my dayes*, M.A. 3276.
driueth forth the longe day, P.Pl. A Pro. 103. *dryue forth hure daies*,
P.Pl. C i, 225. *dryvon furth þat day*, Troy 4546. *þus driue þei forþ
þe day*, W. of P. 3727, 4998. *sho drof forth hir dayes*, Troy 498.
drof þat day with joy thus to þe derk nyʒt, Gaw. 1176–7. *driuen forth
þe day til þe derke niʒt*, W. of P. 3526, etc.
dryfes ouer þe depe, W. Alex. 64. *dryfande ouer þe deepe*, M.A. 816. *dryuen
purʒ þe depe*, Pat. 263.
E.M.E. *he driueþ to dethe*, W. of P. 3750, etc. *driuen doun to dethe*, W. of
P. 3881, etc. **E.M.E.** *dryuen adoun*, Gaw. 2263. *he sall þame doune
dryff*, Sc. Proph. ii, 37. *þat drof hem dryʒlych adoun*, Pat. 235.
E.M.E. *and never dryʒe no dethe*, Pur. 1032. *drye þe death*, W. Alex. 1069.
to dryʒe a delful dynt, Gaw. 560. *vnder his dyntteʒ dryʒe*, Gaw. 202.
drynke a drauʒte, P.Pl. B xx, 222. *þat with hure drinkinke drawht whan
þei drie þirsten*, Alex. B 529.
dropeden doun, Jerus. 789. *þou droppyd doun dede*, Erk. 320.
bot euer droupe and dare, M.A. 4007.
droupond in drede, Troy 6305.
drouy and dym, Pur. 1016.
dubbed in a dublet, Gaw. 571.
when I dubbed dukkes, M.A. 4198. *ydubbid of a duke*, R.R. iv, 363.
dubbed and dyʒt, Pur. 1688.
all the dukis under dryghtene, Becket, 147.
dukeʒ and dusperes, M.A. 66, etc. (10 times).
uche duk wyth his duthe, Pur. 1367.

douhtie dukes, Alex. A 926.   *dukes that were doughtye*, D.L. 53, 204, Troy
12742.   *a duke douȝty*, R.R. iii, 360.
þei dwelled in duel, W. of P. 2703.
O.E.Pr., E.M.E.   *sum þe eȝen, sum þe eres*, W. Alex. 3151.
in eir and in eorthe, P.Pl. A i, 114.
erthe and eir, P.Pl. A x, 3.
þe erde and þe erthe, W. Alex. 1046.
any erdyng in erthe, Troy 2217.
erle or emperoure, W. Alex. 1612, M.A. 1673.   *emperours and eorles*, P.Pl. A
iii, 206, W. of P. 5269.
ȝe non erþe ne eren, Alex. B 201.
fadeth þe flour, Mum 69.
for I fayled neuer in fight, D.L. 319.
þe fayreste of fegure that fourmede was euer, M.A. 3301.   *one of the fayreste
that fourmed was euere*, M.A. 861.   *the faireste on folde that fygurede
was euer*, M.A. 2151.   *þe fayrest of forme and of face als*, Pur. 253.   *þe
fairest on face*, W. of P. 2034, 2634.
fayr of face, Gaw. 1260, W. Alex. 5476.   *his fayre face*, Gaw. 1758.
fairest of alle fetures, W. of P. 2886, Troy 1018, etc.
þe faireste flour patt on the folde growes, M.A. 315.   *flour feirest of alle*,
Jos. 80.
þe fayrest in felle of flesche, Gaw. 943.
faire other foul, P.Pl. B xi, 386, C xix, 54.
faythe and faye, M.A. 2862.
ffaith and ffellowshipp, D.L. 294.
fallis doun on his face, W. Alex. 3073.
in þe felde fallen, Jerus. 597.
O.E.P., cp. Laȝ., *he fallis doun fey*, W. Alex. 4002.   *to falle fey*, Gaw. 1067.
he falles for fere, Jos. 267.   *for ferd falles*, Jos. 188.
Laȝ.   *þe grekys fellyn in fyght*, Troy 7822.
O.E.P. & Pr., Laȝ.   *falle apon fold*, W. Alex. 251, 1641.
O.E.P. & Pr., Laȝ.   *fallen to fete*,·Jerus. 727.   *fel doun to his fete*, W. of P.
4015, 4239.   *he fell to þe fete*, Troy, 13941.   *ffellyn to fote*, Troy 10178.
See under *fell, fall*, trans.
fals (folk) and feithles, P.Pl. A x, 135.   *fals in hir feiþ*, Pierce 97.
fals and fykel, P.Pl. C vii, 72.   **E.M.E.** *fykel and falce*, Pat. 283.
with falshed and flatery, Troy 12203.
naw þer faltered ne fel, Gaw. 430.
fantome and foly, Parl. 184.
farande and fre, Pur 607.
O.E.P., Laȝ. *fares he furth*, W. Alex. 2116, W. of P. 2730,
fareth he furth, Mum 1166.   *fared him forthe*, Alex. A 62.   *þan
farde hee forthe*, Alex. A 987.   **O.E.P.** *ferd (he) furth*, W. Alex. 2118,
etc., W. of P. 2817, etc.   *whan he is fare so forþ*, Alex. B 939.
O.E.P. *they fared ouer the field*, Sc.F. 167.   *to faren in þe feld*, Alex. B
301, Becket, 75.   *þanne he farus to a feld*, Alex. B 113.
O.E.P. & Pr., Laȝ. *farde to fight*, Alex. A 447, 659.   *þan hee farde in þat
fight*, Alex. A 887.
fare(n) into France, Sc.F. 57, etc. (5 times).   *fared (ferden) into France*,
Parl. 572, 578.
thus ffared I through a ffrith, D.L. 22, 453.

(to make) fatt and full, Pierce 759.

wiþouten faute oþer faus, Jos. 208. *now am I fawty and falce,* Gaw. 2382.

wythouten faut oþer fylþe, Pur. 1122.

fieble and faynt, W. Alex. 1275, P.Pl. B xvii, 116, R.R. ii, 63, Troy 8446, W. of P. 785. *fleuble and/or feynte,* Mum 856, 1042. *faint ne feble,* Troy 5167. *fainttyng and feblenes,* Troy 13936. *febill nor fant,* T.M. Wemen 86.

feble and false, M.A. 2929.

to feche hom som fode, Troy 5176, 9383.

feden vs and festen vs, P.Pl. B xv, 477. *when folk ere fested and fed,* W. Alex. 1.

E.M.E., Laȝ., Orm. *fede and foster,* W. & W. 464. *fed and fostered,* W. of P. 296. **E.M.E.** *fostred and fed,* Alex. A. 1032, D.L. 127, M.A. 4143, W. of P. 243, etc., W. & W. 206. *haue na fostring ne be fed noupire,* W. Alex. 575. *fosterd and fedd,* W. Alex. 3495. *ffostrid and ffodid,* R.R. ii, 135. *ffostrith and ffodeth,* R.R. iii, 52.

there were fey in the fight, Troy 13990.

with fel and with face, P.Pl. B i, 15.

feld full of folke, W. Alex. 3048, P.Pl. A Pro. 17, etc.

feeldes and frithes, Alex. A 15.

fele appon felde, M.A. 2092. *foules on the felde,* P.Pl. B vii, 128. *founden on felde,* M.A. 985. *no freke vpon fel(d)e,* Troy 1187, 9065, W. & W. 287.

a feller in fight, Alex. A 42.

Laȝ. *he wolde felle hem feye,* Jos. 368. *fel hem feiȝe to his feet,* Jos. 569. *forte fallen him feye,* Jos. 558. *if I were fallen fey,* W. Alex. 5371. *falliþ* (tr) *hym fey,* Jerus. 926. *to fell in the feld fay,* Troy 7967. *(wer) fey fallen in þe felde,* Jerus. 610. *there were fellit in the field,* Troy 10090.

O.E.P., cp. **E.M.E., Laȝ.** *he ne felde nat hus foes,* P.Pl. C iv, 240. *þei felden here fon,* W. of P. 3415.

felled þe (falsse) folk, Alex. A 75, 85.

felle and fals, Chev. 239.

felonse and fals, Erk. 231.

felow and fere, Troy 706. *his feloȝe and his fere,* W. Alex. 3282.

they deffended fast the folk, Sc.F. 207.

feng to þe flyȝt, Pur. 377. *he fongeȝ to þe flyȝt,* Pur. 457.

þenne such a ferde on hem fel, Pat. 215.

ferd and a-friȝt, W. Alex. 395.

we ne haue fere of no fou, Alex. B 346.

thenne ferkid I forth, Mum 622. *ferkiþ hym forth,* Jerus. 1042.

ferlyes . . . bifalle, Beckett 25, Gaw. 23, P.Pl. A Pro. 62, Pur. 1563, 1629, Troy 421. *ferly(es) . . . byfelle,* D.L. 49, Jerus. 233, P.Pl. A xii, 58, Pur. 1529, Troy 95. *me bifel a ferly,* P.Pl. A Pro. 6.

ffetis and faire, Troy 3081, W. of P. 4095. *faire and fetyse,* Alex. A. 188, W. of P. 126, etc. (8 times) ; cp. Pur. 174, *fetyse of a fayr forme.*

fettled and forged, Pur. 343.

fewe oþur fale, Alex. B 801.

(of) figour and (of) fourme, W. Alex. 613, 5571.

to no fight in the feld, Troy 11307. *to fyghte in felde,* M.A. 404. *þat was feghtyng in the feld,* Troy 9054. *faughte with hym in the felde,* Parl. 485, 496. *foght in the filde,* Troy 45.

to fy3ten and fenden, P.Pl. B xix, 61.
fight with foon, Parl. 103, W. of P. 3450.   *þou fihtest wiþ þi fon*, Alex. B 341.
   ffight with your foos, Troy 2323, W. Alex. 1034.   *fyghte with . . .*
   foo-men, M.A. 1965, 2021, Troy 12868.   *foughten (for Philiþ) his fone*
   to dustroye, Alex. A 83.
ffoght vppon fote, Troy 6555, 6749.
fyled in a fylor, Gaw. 2225.
E.M.E.   *fylþe of þe flesche*, Pur. 202, 547.
he wat3 funden fautle3, Gaw. 645.
La3.   *fisch ne/nor flesch*, Jerus. 1068, P.Pl. B xiii, 92.   *more fisch than flesh*,
   P.Pl. C vii, 159.   *flesch or/other fisch*, P.Pl. A vii, 298, B xv, 424.
E.M.E.   *fissh(es) in flod*, P.Pl. C vi, 149, B xiv, 42.   *ffishes of (in) the fflod*,
   D.L. 113, 197.   *fisches flete in þe flode*, W. & W. 386.   *vche fysch to þe*
   flod, Pur. 531.   *whenne fissches failen the flode*, P.Pl. B x, 295.
to fihche on þe fom, Alex. B 204.
O.E.P. & Pr., La3.   *fisch and foules*, P.Pl. A x, 168.
fyngres and feet, Jerus. 1027.
flateres and foles, P.Pl. B xiii, 430, 455, C viii, 115.
flee for fere, W. of P. 3121.   *fleigh for fere*, P.Pl. B xx, 168.   *now þou fles for*
   ferde, Gaw. 2272.   *þen fled he for fere*, Troy 13738.   *fled they for feare*,
   Sc.F. 151.   *scho fled for ferd*, W. & W. 416.   *fled (all) in fere*, Troy
   7338, 7549, 9063, 9650.   *fledden for fere*, P.Pl. A ii, 209, Troy 1349,
   3218.   *for fere fleigh*, P.Pl. A ii, 186.   *for fere . . . fle*, W. of P.
   2902.   *flowen for ferde* (fert), Jos. 18, Pat. 183.   *these frekes wold*
   neuer flee for (noe) fere, Sc.F. 349, 362.
flee faste, W. of P. 1272, 3872.   *faste to fle*, P.Pl. A ii, 185.   *fledden faste of*
   the felde, Parl. 382.
fleme out of þe folde, Pur. 287.
O.E.Pr., E.M.E.   *in fleissh, in felle*, R.R. iii, 16.   *in felle and in flesche*,
   Gaw. 943.
flowers flourished in the feild, Sc.F. 311.   *all florisshet with floures þe fildes*
   aboute, Troy 2735.   *faire floryscht filds of floures*, W. Alex. 4379.
   fflowers fflourished in the frith, D.L. 72.   *the frithe3 were floreschte with*
   floure3 fulle many, M.A. 924.   *þe floure in þe fild*, W. Alex. 819.
   floures in feldes, P.Pl. C xiv, 176, Mum 894, 1009, 1039.   *floures in*
   the frithe, P.Pl. B xi, 356, etc., Sc.P. 2.22.
flour and (ne) fruit, P.Pl. A x, 118, B xv, 100.
þe fold and of þe firmament, W. Alex. 30.
þe folde and folk, Pur. 1665.   *folk and folde*, Pur. 1014.
Fader upon folde, Pur. 1175.
fairest on folde, M.A. 2151, W. of P. 5382, Troy 13789.   *fylþe upon folde*,
   Pur. 251.   *no flesch upon folde*, Pur. 356.   *such a fole vpon folde*,
   Gaw. 196.   *no freke vpon folde*, Gaw. 1275.   *freke3 of the folde*, Pur.
   540, P.Pl. C x, 154.   *all þe frutis on þe fold*, W. Alex. 4636.
folowed faste, Jerus. 203, 1143, P.Pl. A iv, 25.   *foloweth . . . faste*, Troy
   5662, P.Pl. B xvii, 80.   *folowes faste*, M.A. 1367.   *following her fast*
   after, D.L. 184.   *fast followed after*, Sc.F. 185.
folweth þe feyþ, Pierce 19.   *folwen nou3t fully þe feiþ*, Pierce 827.
he fonge3 to þe fly3t, Pur. 457.
forge and file, Parl. 212.
my forwarde wyth þe I festen, Pur. 327.

this forward to fille, Troy 602. *forwardis (to) fulfille*, Jerus. 276, Troy
 9278, 9294, 11447. *to folfulle the foreward*, P.Pl. A vii, 38.
so foule and so felle, Gaw. 717.
the ffoulest ffreke that formed was euer, D.L. 157. *the fulsomeste freke that
 fourmede was euere*, M.A. 1061. *the foulleste of fegure that fourmede
 was euer*, M.A. 781.
I founded faste, Parl. 97. *founde3 faste on yor fete*, Pur. 903.
of forme and of face, Pur. 253.
his fourme and his fetoure, W. Alex. 2959. *of feturs and fourme the fairest
 on lyue*, Troy 4002.
O.E.Pr., E.M.E., La3. *foules that fleeghen*, P.Pl. B ix, 139, xii, 239. *fowle
 . . . that flieghes*, M.A. 4002. *feule3 . . . that flye3*, M.A. 926. *fewlis
 flye*, W. & W. 384. *flowen as þe foule dop*, Jerus. 310. *vche fowle to
 þe fly3t*, Pur. 530.
freke(s) vpon fote, Gaw. 329, Troy 356, 9018, W. of P. 2383.
O.E.P., E.M.E. *frely and feyre (faire)*, Chev. 266, 274, M.A. 970, W. Alex.
 785. *faire and free*, W. & W. 434.
frely and fresch, Pur. 173.
frele of hire flesch, P.Pl. A iii, 117.
frend(es) and felow(es), Cr. King 18, Troy 4842, 12374, W. of P. 3806.
 fryndes and ffelowes, Troy 8927. . *as a felaw or a frynde*, W. Alex. 864.
 Cp. **O.E.P.** *be frende with þy foman*, Jerus. 1056. **E.M.E.** *make foos of
 frendes*, P.Pl. C vii, 72, Troy 4844.
as fressche & as fere, W. Alex. 4282. *so faire & so fresche*, W. Alex. 5257.
 faire . . . & . . . fresshe, Mum 959, Troy 13807.
freten þe frute, Pierce 722, 729, P.Pl. B xviii, 194.
in frythes and in forestes, P.Pl. C x, 224. *out of forest and friþes*, W. of P.
 2216.
þe froþe femed at his mouth, Gaw. 1572.
fuerse and fell, Troy 7003, 9648. *felle and fuerse*, Troy 1323. *for þey ben
 felle of defence, ferce men and noble*, Jerus. 867.
ful3ed in font, Pur. 164. *they fologhed hym in a fonte*, Parl. 545. *fullyng
 of fonte*, P.Pl. B xii, 282. **E.M.E.** *fulloght in fonte*, Erk. 299.
furred wyth-inne with felle3, Gaw. 880.
gadred hem alle togideres, P.Pl. B xvi, 80.
gay and ful glad, Pur. 830.
gaye in my gere, Parl. 273. *gered ful gaye*, Pur. 1568.
O.E.P., P.M. *game and gle*, W. of P. 5090. *gle and gomen*, Gaw. 1536.
E.M.E. *quen we gamen suld and glade* (vbs.), W. Alex. 4370. *gamsum and
 glad*, W. of P. 4193.
for gawdis othir gils, Troy 10749. *his gyle and his gawdis*, Troy 12370.
I gedir, I glene, W. & W. 231.
to begele þe gome, Alex. A 882.
gemmes and juellis, W. Alex. 4035, R.R. i, 38, Troy, 1368, etc. *juwèls and
 gemmes*, W. Alex. 4444.
to gete more good, Jos. 94, Mum 413. *þou getest no good*, Alex. B 30.
 goodis to gete, Alex. B 305.
gete grace, Jos. 104, P.Pl. A vi, 126.
to gye and gouerne, M.A. 4, W. Alex. 3387, W. of P. 1105.
gilde al with golde, Pur. 1344.
O,E.Pr. *gird . . . to grounde*, W. Alex. 2278, Troy 1332, etc. (35 times).

giue giftes (in varying forms), Gaw. 288, 1500, M.A. 1503, P.Pl. C iv, 341,
  x, 133, W. of P. 536, 1467, W. & W. 500, Troy 8169, etc.
O.E.Pr. *forgiue gilte* (in varying forms), W. Alex. 2434, Alex. B 386,
  Jerus. 1159, Pat. 404, Pur. 731, P.Pl. A iii, 8, Troy 11581, W. & W. 135.
gyf glory to þy Godde, Pat. 204. *giue no glory vnto God*, D.L. 311.
O.E.Pr., E.M.E. *(hee) gaf up (his) goste*, Alex. A 242, W. Alex. 5458.
  God that me gaffe goste, Parl. 198.
gef . . . goud day, Gaw. 668, 1029, 1290.
gyue . . . grace (in varying forms), Gaw. 920, Jerus. 892, M.A. 4, Pat.
  226, P.Pl. A viii, 184, x, 210, R.R. Pro. 28, W. of P. 2494, 5539.
glam and gle, Gaw. 1652, cp. Gaw. 46, *glaum ande gle*.
glauer ande glam, Gaw. 1426, W. Alex. 5504.
glemered and glent, Gaw. 172. *glemyng of gold*, Twa Mariit Wemen, 202.
  gleterande (in) golde, M.A. 1280, W. Alex. 3346. *glisnande golde*, Erk.
  78, cp. *glisiande as goldwire*, Alex. A 180. *glissenond of gold*, Troy
  5926, 12291, 13794. *glitteringe golde*, D.L. 135, 420. **E.M.E.** *goldin glit-
  terand gleme*, Twa Mariit Wemen, 517. *glimerand gold*, W. of P.
  1427. *gloring gold*, Sc.F. 103. *al þe glowande gold þat he on grounde
  hadde*, Jerus. 908. *alle þe glowande golde upon grounde*, Jerus. 1014.
  al glytered and glent, Gaw. 604.
as the glyssenond glemes þat glenttes on þe sknowe, Troy 10971. *his glorious
  glem þat glent so bryȝt*, Pur. 218.
glose . . . þe godspell, Pierce 345, 709, P.Pl. A Pro. 57.
glowande gledes, P.Pl. B xvii, 217. *glowe as a glede*, P.Pl. B xvii, 223.
  glowande gledfur, Jerus. 1252.
(death) glowed and gran, D.L. 225.
go we on oure gate, W. of P. 2800.
gestes vnder God, W. of P. 4904. *non so glad under God*, Pur. 1077. *glee
  vndire God*, M.A. 489, W. of P. 827. *god vnder God*, W. of P. 4717,
  4732. *gold under God*, D.L. 420. *gome under God*, Alex. A 314, Gaw.
  2470, Mum 182, W. of P. 4902. *no gome under God*, Alex. A 252, W. of
  P. 3761, Troy 572. *any gome that vndyre God leueȝ*, M.A. 1731. *graci-
  oueste gome that vnder God lyffede*, M.A. 3877. *na gref vnder God*,
  W. of P. 2473. *no greuaunce so grete vndur God*, Troy 11776. *þe
  grettest vndir God*, W. Alex. 1904. *gro(o)me vnder God*, D.L. 190,
  M.A. 3489.
godesses and gods, W. Alex. 1874.
  Cp. Laȝ. *nauþer golde ne garyson*, Gaw. 1837. *garysoun oþer golde*, Gaw.
  1255. Cp. **O.E.Pr., Alf., E.M.E.**, Laȝ. *gersoms and golde*, M.A. 1729.
his gold and his godis, Troy 12854.
gorsteȝ and greueȝ, Pur. 99.
my grace and my glorie, W. Alex. 1983. *þi glorie and þi grace*, W. Alex.
  1971.
E.M.E. *grace of God*, Alex. B 84, P.Pl. A x, 48, B ix, 176, W. of P. 1808.
greiþed (of all gere) gaily, W. of P. 2597, 3207, 4186.
graithit hom full graithly, Troy 12290.
al grayþed in grene þis gome, Gaw. 151.
þis gome gered in grene, Gaw. 179, Parl. 122. *þe gome in þe grene*, Gaw. 405.
  gome alle in grene, Parl. 169, 194.
graunte . . . grace, Alex. B 709, D.L. 458, Jerus. 1058, 1160, Jos. 280,
  M.A. 1202, Mum 224, P.Pl. A xi, 291, Troy 39247, W. of P. 984, 3994,
  4789, W. & W. 371, 399.

E.M.E. *green grasse*, D.L. 126, 193, Mum. 879, P.Pl. B xi, 357.   *the gryse was grene growen*, Parl. 8.   *growe grene as þe gres*, Gaw. 235.
þe gretest and þe gloriosest, W. Alex. 1611.
greued . . . God, Pat. 171, 210.
greving and gretyng and gryspyng, Pur. 159.
agrisen of his grym, Alex. B 50.
grisly and great and grim to behold, D.L. 154.
he groned for gref and grame, Gaw. 2502.
gronyng and gref, Troy 10663.
God of þe grounde, Pur. 1324, 1663, Troy 11768.   *gold on ground*, Gaw. 2150, P.Pl. A vii, 216.   *gome vppon grounde*, Jerus. 165, P.Pl. A xi, 170. *gomes of þe ground*, Troy 5481.   *gouernour on the grounde*, R.R. Pro. 42. *grace on the grounde*, D.L. 3, P.Pl. A ix, 53, B v, 264, W. & W. 173. *Greke on þat grounde*, Troy 3764.   *alle the grete upon grounde*, Pur. 1363.   *groome on the ground*, D.L. 86.
grounded in/on God, D.L. 289, Jerus. 513.   *grounded in Gods lawe*, Jacke Upland p. 17, etc. (very frequent).
grounded on þe godspell, Pierce 514.
all þat growus in þe ground, Alex. B 954.
grucche or grone (vbs.), P.Pl. iii, 308.   *withoute grucche oþer groyn* (sbs.), Mum 711.   *any grucche or groyne or grame shuld arise*, Mum 809.
gulty of gyle, Pat. 285.   *I am noȝt gilty of þis gile*, W. Alex. 2574.
þay ȝeȝed and ȝolped, Pur. 846.
þey ȝelden grace to God, Jerus. 254.
ȝeuyn and ȝolden, W. Alex. 2107.
forȝiue and forȝete, P.Pl. B xvii, 242.
a ȝomerly ȝarm of ȝelling, Pur. 971.
ȝomerly ȝaule and ȝelle, Gaw. 1453.
ȝonge and ȝepe, Gaw. 1510, P.Pl. B xi, 17, C xi, 287, xiii, 179.   Parl. 171, Pur. 881, Troy 357, etc. (8 times).   *ȝonge (in my ȝouthe) and ȝape*, 134, 270.   Cp. **E.M.E.** *ȝongeste of ȝeris, and ȝapeste of witt*, W. & W. 119. *a ȝoþ knyght & a ȝonge, of ȝeris but lite*, Troy 6642.   *yonge of ȝeris*, R.R. i, 89.   Cp. T.M. Wemen 79 and 170.
O.E.P. & Pr., E.M.E. *to habben and to holden*, P.Pl. A ii, 70.   *to haue and hold*, Troy 245, 2415, Mum 1439.
O.E.Pr., Laȝ. *he hedde (hit) in honde,*[1] Jos. 270, 591.   *he þat hade all in honde*, Pur. 1704.
hailse . . . hendliche, P.Pl. B. v, 101, B viii, 10, C xi, 10, Pierce 231.
halle ne hous, P.Pl. A ii, 40.   *houses and hallis*, Troy 8683.
hange by the hals, P.Pl. B ii, 195.   *hongen bi the hals*, P.Pl. A ii, 170.   *hangen it vpon the cattes hals*, P.Pl. B Pro. 170.   *hanged on myn hals*, P.Pl. C iv, 227.
hanged in helle, W. & W. 260.
honget on heiȝ, W. of P. 2020.   *hongen an heiȝ*, P.Pl. B i, 172.
happe other hele, Chev. 324, P.Pl. B xx, 383.
hardye and hende, Alex. A 1150.
O.E.Pr. *forto hardien þe hertes*, W. of P. 1156.   *hardynesse of herte*, Pierce 539, P.Pl. B xix, 31.   *how hard were my hert*, Troy 9267.
the hare . . . and þe houndes, Mum 914.

---

[1] Cp. O.N. *hafa þer í hendi*.

Cp. O.E.Pr., Leg. *harmes hent*, Chev. 3, Gaw. 2277, M.A. 3319, R.R. ii, 43, Troy 5778, 9721.   *hent harmes*, Beckett 70, Erk. 232, W. Alex. 2544, W. of P. 2785.
harme and hethyng, Troy 1753, 2216, 3555.   *hethyng and harme*, Troy 1925, 13150.   *hethyng and hate*, Troy 1818.
ne harme nother hurte, R.R. Pro. 74.   *hurt other harme*, Troy 5623, 6789, 6842, W. of P. 4633, W. Alex. 285.
to haunsen and to holden, Jos. 232.
Cp. O.E.P. *hapel vndur heuen*, Alex. B 219, 348, W. Alex. 84, etc. (6 times), Gaw. 1853. *þe hapnest vnder heuen*, Gaw. 56. *hewis under hewin*, Twa Mariit Wemen 32. *oddest vndire heuyn*, W. Alex. 2008, 2321.
Laȝ. *haukes and . . . houndes*,[1] P.Pl. B iv, 125.
his hede and hys hals, M.A. 764.   *his hede and the halse*, Parl. 90, 373.   *to hew þi hede fra þi hals*, W. Alex. 2654.
Orm. *for þy heed ne for þy herte*, Mum 677.
he hef vp his helme, Gaw. 826.
hele of my hurt, Jerus. 199.   Cp. *of that hurte . . . heles he neuer*, M.A. 2209.   *hole of his hurt*, Troy 8857.
helede aȝain hol, Jos. 681.
no helmys ne hewberghes, Troy 6184.   *his helme and his hawberke*, M.A. 2700. *helmes and hamberkes*, Jerus. 845. *helmes . . . hamberkes manye*, Jerus. 640.
Laȝ. *þe helm and þe hed*, Jerus. 1123, W. of P. 3443, 3864. **Laȝ.** *helme of/on . . . hede*, W. Alex. 779, Gaw. 2143, 2197, 2247, Troy 11108, W. & W. 72. *helmes with heads were hewd*, Sc.F. 379.
hendeste in hawle, M.A. 3879.
to hente hele, R.R. i, 96.
hent the helme of his hede, Parl. 373.   *hentes he þe helme*, Gaw. 605.
henten in honde, Troy 3334, W. of P. 4023.   *henntis thaym one honde*, Parl. 236. *by þe hondeȝ hym hent*, Pur. 883. *to hent hit at his honde*, Gaw. 827.
hent harmes : see under *harmes*.
E.M.E. *hered-men in halle*, Gaw. 302.
E.M.E. *heried helle*, Jerus. 153, W. of P. 3725. *þou herghdes helle-hole*, Erk. 291.
herie (þe here God) with herte, Alex. B 358. *herien ful hertely*, Alex. B 731.
hearkneth/herkynes . . . hendly, D.L. 213, M.A. 15, Troy 4895, 9238. *hendely me kerken*, Parl. 267.
E.M.E. *herkned and herde*, Pur. 193.
herken . . . hest, W. of P. 2911.   *þei herden his hest*, W. of P. 4857.
his . . . heire and his hedde, Alex. A 543. *with here on his hedde*, Alex. A 699, Parl. 175, Troy 3820, etc.
þe here of his hed, Gaw. 180, Troy 3021.
herneȝ and havekeȝ, Pur. 537.
O.E.P., Laȝ. *hert(ys) and hynde(s)*, Mum 925, Parl. 5, 17, 195, R.R. ii, 25, 48, W. of P. 389, etc.
Orm. *in þe herte ne in þe hande*, Mum 432. *his hert and his honde*, Gaw. 371.
heueȝ vp his hede, W. Alex. 677, Gaw. 1184.

---

[1] Cp. O.N. *hauka en hunda.*

O.E.Pr., E.M.E. *hewed up his handis,* Beckett 252. *heueþ vp þe honde,* Jerus. 1209. *he heved vp his handis,* Beckett 252. Cp. *myn hondes þat I ne may hefe þam to my hede,* Parl. 288.

hewe of þe heede, Mum 188.

O.E.P. *heven and helle,* Erk. 196, Jerus. 17, Parl. 32, P.Pl. A iii, 125, B iii, 129, xvii, 161, Jacke Upland, p. 17, etc.

heven (sb.) *vpon hyȝe,* Gaw. 2057, Pierce 796.

E.M.E., Laȝ. *hide and hew,* D.L. 158, Troy 3909.

O.E.Pr., E.M.E. *hideth his heede,* Mum 176.

E.M.E. *hid in oure holis,* Alex. B 40. *holus holwe to hiden hem inne,* Alex. B 10. *hid hiȝ in a howle,* Troy 11991. *hyd hom in houles and hyrnys,* Troy 1362. Cp. *þai heȝe þaim to holes & hyrnes & hydis þaim,* W. Alex. 3214. *hudden hem in huirenes,* Jos. 13.

hye king of heauen, D.L. 212, 264, W. of P. 163. *hey heuenkyng,* Jerus. 518. *þe hyȝe heuenkyng,* Pat. 257.

E.M.E. *hyȝe on his hede,* Gaw. 607.

hyȝe in þe heven, Pur. 206.

high on a hill, Crowned King 31. **E.M.E., Laȝ.** *hyȝe hilleȝ,* Gaw. 742, Pur. 380. *hillus ful hie,* Alex. B 435.

hyȝe upon hyȝt, Pur. 458.

hyghes (hym) in haste, Parl. 508, Troy 4608. *hyȝed in haste,* Pat. 217.

hills and hethes, Troy 1350.

neither hill nor holte, D.L. 55. *holtis ne hilles,* W. Alex. 4137.

hittes hym on þe hede, M.A. 2228.

no hode ne no hatte, Parl. 117, 179.

with an hode on his hed, P.Pl. B v, 195.

holde hit euer in his honde, Mum 1692. *haldeȝ in þy honde,* Pur. 734. *quy haldes þou so heghe in honde,* Erk. 223. *held in his hende,* W. & W. 419. *helde in . . . hand,* Alex. A 529, Alex. B 1035, Troy 918.

holde vp myn honde, Jerus. 991. *held I vp myn handes,* P.Pl. A xii, 38.

held hit on hey, Jerus. 226.

E.M.E. *holden alle his hestes,* Pierce 26. *heste(s) to hold,* Jerus. 1003, Troy 11625.

holtis and harewode(s), M.A. 2504, 3544.

holtis and hethe, Gaw. 1320.

(þat hert) honest & hol, Pur. 594.

my hope and my hele, Parl. 117. *the hope of my hele,* M.A. 3958. *in hope of his hele,* P.Pl. B xx, 179. *no hope of þere heale,* Troy 8689.

no hope of no help, Troy 6275.

hoped in herte, W. Alex. 679, Troy 5618, 8880, 8894. *all my hope was on hem & myn herte also,* Pierce 453.

a horse and harnayse, M.A. 2629. *hors and harneys,* Jerus. 438, 510, Troy 1086, W. of P. 2349, 4187, etc. *harnays and hors,* Jerus. 754, cp. *hors with his harnes,* Chev. 278.

of horn ne of hound, W. of P. 210. *wiþ hound and horn,* W. of P. 204.

O.E.Pr. *horse and houndes,* P.Pl. xi, 334. *horse ne hounde,* W. of P. 2198. *horses and howndes,* W. & W. 237.

housed in hirnes, Pierce 182.

O.E.Pr. *my hous and my home,* Gaw. 408. *na houses ne na hames,* W. Alex. 4048. *the houses and the homes,* P.Pl. A iii, 89.

O.E.P. & Pr., E.M.E., P.M. *hudden and heleden,* P.Pl. C xiv, 164.

hunger and hate, Beckett 236.

E.M.E., La3. *hunger and hete*, Jerus. 1064.

huntyd an hare, R.R. i. 55.

hunt we ne hauke, W. Alex. 4271.   *to hauke ne to hunte*, Alex. B 299.
huntynge or haukynge, P.Pl. B iii, 311.

to hunt in holte3, Gaw. 1677.   *I schal hunt in þis holte*, Gaw. 1677.   *forto hunt in the holtes*, Troy 13520.

hunting wiþ hound and horn, W. of P. 204.

hurled on a hepe, D.L. 413, Parl. 57, Pat. 149, Troy 6743, 11048.

O.E.P. & Pr., E.M.E. *(with-)inne & (with-)outen*, W. Alex. 1527, Mum 30, 1243, P.Pl. A vi, 37, Pur. 20 ; —a very common phrase.

jangle as a jaye, W. & W. 26.

to jangle and jape, P.Pl. B ii, 94.   *more jangling of japes*, Troy 2873.

no jargoun no jangle, Alex. B 462.

jocund and joly, Troy 316.

ioy and iolite, W. Alex. 1469.   *jolyte and joy*, W. Alex. 3108.

joy and gentlenesse, D.L. 292.   *gentiliche with Ioye*, P.Pl. A iii, 13.

jolef for joye, Pat. 241.

to joyne wyth hym in justyng, Gaw. 97.

juglers and iapers, Pierce 43.

ne juge ne justice, R.R. iii, 341.   *justice and juge*, Jerus. 82.   *justice and iugges*, M.A. 246, Mum 16.   *bathe juree3 and jugge3 and justice3 of landes*, M.A. 663.

to lachen or lesse, Alex. A 378.

lache . . . his leue, Gaw. 595, 1870, Jerus. 1017, Troy 811, 1024, etc. *laght . . . leue*, Alex. A 250, Troy 9794, 13337.   *lau3te . . . leue*, Jerus. 279, P.Pl. A iii, 26, etc., Troy 5201, 6162, W. of P. 5201, 5413.

lacchit the lond, Troy 5702.   *þat I may lachche no lont*, Pat. 322.

to lachen hem loose, Alex. A 4.

lakkedest and losedest, P.Pl. B xi, 411.

þay la3ed and layked longe, Gaw. 1554.

O.E.P., E.M.E., La3. *la3ed ful loude*, Gaw. 69.   *he la3es so loude*, Gaw. 316. *loude la3ed*, Gaw. 909.   *loude law3eþ þerat*, Jerus. 794.   *lowd thai lewch*, T.M. Wemen 506.

laid law, Beckett 216, 221, 223.   *laye(n) lowe*, Mum 930, W. of P. 484.

lay and leonede, P.Pl. A Pro. 9.

in langour he laye, Chev. 15.   *lay in langour*, Chev. 57.   *liue þer in langour*, W. of P. 2016.   *leave hym in langour*, Alex. A 245.   *leue we þis lady in langour*, Chev. 92.

langour (is) and lisse, P.Pl. B xviii, 225.

large and long, Troy 3855, 3864, etc.   Cp. *lenght ond largenes*, Troy 318. *longe . . . and . . . large*, P.Pl. B xviii, 45, Pur. 1386, Troy 3984, Parl. 115.

E.M.E., La3.   *lasted (his) life*, Alex. A 43, W. of P. 3019.   *lastinge lif*, Alex. B 70.   *laste þy lyf*, Pur. 1594.   *þe lif þat euer schal lesten*, Pierce 850.

O.E.P. & Pr., E.M.E., La3., P.M. *lath or leef*, M.A. 458.   *lef oþur loþ*, Alex. B 867, W. of P. 3624.   *lief or loth*, P.Pl. B ix, 57.

laughyng and louryng, P.Pl. B v, 344.

launce and ly3t, Gaw, 1175.

þe lawe of þe londe, W. of P. 5049.   *no lawe in oure land*, Alex. B 379.

O.E.Pr. *þe lawe and þe lore*, Jerus. 202.   *his lore and his lawe*, Pierce 640.

O.E.Pr., E.M.E., La3., Orm., P.M. *lede(n) . . . lif*, Alex. B 288, 444, 629, 1005, 1011, Cr. King 108, Mum 118, 248, 1378, P.Pl. B ix, 190, iii,

201, R.R. ii, 71, W. of P. 2023. *life lede(n)*, Alex. B 858, Gaw. 2058, Jerus. 892, Jos. 663, M.A. 154, Parl. 256, Twa Mariit Wemen 155. *ladden . . . life*, Alex. A 20, Jos. 16, P.Pl. A viii, 176. *leddyn зoure lyf*, R.R. i, 2.
lede vpon lyfe, Erk. 150, Gaw. 2095, M.A. 430, Troy 4764, etc. (12 times). **E.M.E.** *lede . . . londe*, Alex. A 60, 1199, P.Pl. A iv, 131, C iv, 213, W. of P. 5463. *ladde þe londe*, Alex. A 29. *lederes of my lond*, W. of P. 4158.
leder of þo lordis, Troy 4054.
lede a lortschyp, Gaw. 849. *lede al my/this lordchip*, W. of P. 3159, 3955.
leef vpon lynde, P.Pl. B i, 154.
lelly layne, Gaw. 1863, 2128, 2124.
lelliche louen, Alex. B 622. *lelly lovy þy Lorde*, Pur. 1066. *I schal loue him lelli*, W. of P. 4128.
E.M.E. *þe leme and the light*, Alex. A 774. *na leme of þe lyft, ne liзt of þe sonne*, W. Alex. 4174. **O.E.P., Orm.** *a liзte and a leme*, P.Pl. B xviii, 124, 137. **O.E.P. & Pr.** *lemys of light*, Troy 1684. *þe lem of þe sonne-liht*, Alex. B 520. *the leame of his lyght*, Alex. A 1078. **O.E.P.** *leames full light*, Sc.F. 309. *lemande lyзt*, Jerus. 1256. **E.M.E.** *þe daylyзt lemed*, Gaw. 1180. *light . . . lemyng*, Troy 699. *he leomede as liht al on a lowe*, Jos. 687.
liзtly lasshit þer a leme, Alex. A 334. *þe liзt lemand late laschis fra þe heuyn*, W. Alex. 553.
lendeþ and lihte, Jos. 81.
lenged in lisse, W. of P. 5462.
O.E.P. *lenge(d) in . . . londe*, Alex. A 1, 196, 553, Alex. B 872, Gaw. 411, Jos. 425, Troy 7617, etc. (5 times). *in þe lond . . . lenge*, Jos. 603. *at þat londe lengede*, Jerus. 83. *one this launde lengen*, Parl. 199.
lengged þere longe, Alex. B 1132. *lenged(e) . . . long*, Gaw. 1299, Jos. 16. *whi lengest þou so longe ?*, Jos. 277. *we lengeden full longe*, Pierce 310.
lengthened my life, D.L. 29.
E.M.E. *lente hem hur lif*, Alex. B 413. *þat any lyf myзt be lent*, Pat. 260. *if any liffe were hem lente*, Chev. 112. *lene me lif*, W. of P. 4398.
lent in a londe, W. Alex. 5079, Troy 2341, Pat. 201.
of lenþe and of large, Pur. 314, cp. *large and long*.
þe lenþe of þe londe, Pur. 568.
E.M.E. *lep he vp liзteli*, W. of P. 702. *lepen (vþ) lyзtly*, Gaw. 1131, Mum 510, R.R. iii, 136. *lept vþ full lyghtly*, Troy 8530. *ouer-leep hem lyзtlyche*, P.Pl. C i, 169. *lope he so lihtliche*, P.Pl. A iv, 93. *lepte forth lightly*, Mum 533, 881, 944. *lyзtly lepeз*, Gaw. 328, W. of P. 1973. *liзtly lep he*, W. of P. 1244.
lepe ouer londe, P.Pl. B v, 483. *ouer all þe lond lepeþ*, Pierce 597. *to lepe fro þe lond*, Troy, 5757.
of lere ne of lykame, W. of P. 227. Cp. *lire & lygham*.
lere lettrewre, Crowned King 113. *lered on letrure*, Alex. A 1152.
þe lered men of þe lawe, Jerus. 705. Cp. *lawe to lere*, Alex. B 260.
O.E.Pr., E.M.E., Laз., Orm. *lered . . . lewed*, Crowned King 57, Jacke Upland p. 25, Parl. 46, Pierce 25, P.Pl. A iii, 39, iv, 12, B xv, 140, 388, xix, 110, xx, 101, 246, C vii, 116, xv, 71, xxiii, 266. *lewed and lered*, P.Pl. C xvii, 34. *lewed or lered*, Pierce 18. *for lewede, for lerede*, P.Pl. A ii, 47.

19

lerned on the langage, R.R. Pro. 44.
to lerne þe lawe, Mum 621.   **E.M.E.** *lerned of the lawe*, Pierce 492, Troy
3826.
lerne(th) a lesson, Mum 1477, R.R. i, 9.   *lernde I a lessun*, P.Pl. A v, 125.
O.E.P., E.M.E., La3. *lese . . . lif*, Alex. A 369, Alex. B 322, Gaw. 2142,
P.Pl. B xx, 86, C vii, 315, Mum 167, R.R. iii, 309, W. of P. 2758, W.
Alex. 5.   *leosen his lyf*, P.Pl. A iii, 275.   *þus loste he þe lyf*, Jerus. 946.
his life to be lost, Troy 12276.
La3. *lese here lif, here londes*, W. of P. 2279.   *leosen (heore) lond and
(heore) lyues*, P.Pl. A iii, 131, W. & W. 133.   *lose your lond and your
life*, Alex. A 474.
O.E.P. & Pr., E.M.E. *we schulle forleten oure lif*, Alex. B 329.   **E.M.E.**
lyf leten, P.Pl. C xii, 24.
let hit doun ly3tly, Gaw. 423.
lettred and lewed, P.Pl. B xiii, 287, xv, 347.   *lewed and lettred*, P.Pl. B xii,
98, 158, Mum 652.
leued on his lawe, Pat. 405.   *to leue on her lore*, R.R. i, 93.
leaue here my liffe, Sc.F. 86.   *leuyt here my lyue*, Troy 12375.   *lefte he þe
lif*, Troy 13961.   *I hadde lefte my lyfe*, M.A. 875.   *þus lafte hee his
life*, Alex. A 41.   *whanne he lyf lafte*, Chev. 17.
with the leave of our lord, Sc.F. 85.   *wiþouten leue of þat lord*, Jerus. 1166.
lewte and loue, R.R. i, 43.   *loue and lewte*, P.Pl. B iv, 35, xi, 161, 140, xv,
460.
E.M.E. *licamus lust*, Alex. B 555.
with-oute lycence and leue, Pl.P. C vii, 121.
lyked and loued, P.Pl. B xvi, 201.   *louen and lyken*, W. of P. 162.
likful and lef, Alex. B 498.
liking and lisse, W. of P. 5508.
liking and loue, M.A. 3381, W. of P. 452.
likynge(s) and luste(s), P.Pl. B xvi, 32, R.R. iii, 266.   *lust and lykynge*,
P.Pl. B xv, 51, Troy 9057.   *lusty and liking*, Troy 2201, 13276.
lye in þy loft, Gaw. 1676.
to lye a lesyng, P.Pl. C vii, 209, Pierce 379.
there they lyen and lodged, Sc.F. 255.
E.M.E., La3. *ne lif ne lym*, Erk. 224.   *of life and o lym*, W. Alex. 1918.
lyffe and lyme, M.A. 459, etc. (4 times), P.Pl. B xix, 101.   *lymes . . .
and lyfes*, Mum 1538.   *his lyf and his leome*, P.Pl. A v, 81.
E.M.E. *lyf and loue*, P.Pl. B xvii, 275.   *of lyue and of loue*, Troy 11356.
lift þe lide, Jos. 41.
liftis vp his liddis, W. Alex. 965.   *lift . . . up my liddes*, Cr. King 25.
lyftande up his eghe-lyddes, Erk. 178.   *lift vp þe y3e-lydde3*, Gaw. 446,
Mum 889.
light on . . . lande, Beckett 183, D.L. 219, Troy 2817 (8 times).   *they
lighten doun at þe launde*, W. & W. 209.
lighten downe lowe, D.L. 196.   **E.M.E.** *he lowe liht*, Jos. 145.
þer was no lynde so liht, Jos. 585.   *was neuere leef upon lynde li3ter therafter*,
P.Pl. B i, 154.
his lyndes and his lymes, Gaw. 139.
liones and leopards, W. Alex. 4793, P.Pl. B xv, 272, 293, Pur. 536, Troy
1573.   *lyon and lebard*, W. of P. 2896, 2928, 2935.   *lepards and lions*,
W. Alex. 5084, 5438.

his lire and his lygham, M.A. 3281.

E.M.E. *lithe and lestin*, W. Alex. 3468. *to lere and listen*, Cr. King 13.

O.E.P. & Pr., La3. *lyuen thus heore lyf*, P.Pl. A viii 81. *what lyues thei lyuen*, P.Pl. C xi, 125. *sholde no lyf lyuys*, P.Pl. C vii, 67. *þe lif þat we liue*, Alex. B 270, 579. *that hadde lyued al his lyf*, P.Pl. A xi, 272. *leued his lyff*, R.R. iii, 290.

La3. *liue(d) in lisse*, W. of P. 5103, 5228, 5466. *in lysse to lyue*, P.Pl. C vii, 315. *liued in liking and lisse*, W. of P. 5508. *lenged in lisse*, W. of P. 5462. Cp. *lenge in blisse*, W. of P. 5408, Alex. A 44, Alex. B 628. *liuen in 3oure likinge*, Alex. B 785.

libben in loue, Alex. B 373.

O.E.P., E.M.E., La3. *to libbe in your land*, Alex. B 843. *liue in (their) land*, Sc.F. 41, Alex. A 251, Sc. Proph. I, 62. *lyueth in that londe*, P.Pl. C iv, 423. *lyued in londe*, P.Pl. B xv, 148. *in this lond for to lyue*, Troy 12349.

E.M.E., La3. *þe lyuer and þe ly3te3*, Gaw. 1360. *the lyuer and the lightes*, Troy 10705.

La3. *the lyuer and þe lungge3*, M.A. 2168.

ladde in londe, W. & W. 388. *lady in/of lond*, Alex. A 226, 585, Troy 11327, W. & W. 16, W. of P. 2965. *lede(s) in/of/on the londe*, W. Alex. 4284, Jerus. 98, R.R. ii, 49, Sc.F. 109, Troy 62, etc. (12 times), W. & W. 152, 171, 459. *lude(s) in/of . . . lond*, Alex. A 603, 852, Alex. B 355.

O.E.P., La3. *londes and ledes*, P.Pl. B xv, 520, W. of P. 4001. *lede3 and londe*, Pur. 308. [Cp. Pur. 909.] *londes and leedes and lordships*, Alex. A 12.

my londe and my lycame, P.Pl. C xxi, 94.

O.E.Pr. *the londe and his lyfe*, W. & W. 133. For three other examples of *lond . . . life*, see under *lese lif*. **E.M.E.**

þe londe and the lythe (land and people), Parl. 185, 207. *lande3 and lythes*, M.A. 994.[1]

the lande and the lordshipe, Mum 1454. *with lande3 and lordcheppe3*, M.A. 1727. *in londe and in lordship*, P.Pl. B xiv, 262, 327. Cp. Alex. A 12 *(supra)*. *lond other lordship*, P.Pl. C iv, 318, Mum 1443.

E.M.E. *long and leane*, D.L. 162, Mum 1069, P.Pl. A ix, 110.

as longe as I liue, P.Pl. A iv, 154, 158.

to looke the land over, Sc.F. 60. *lokande on þe londe*, Jerus. 400. *I lokede to a launde*, Parl. 24.

loked alofte, Pat. 447. *the lud looked on loft*, Alex. A 1045. *lookest on loft*, Alex. A 1051. Cp. *lokes vpe to the lyfte*, M.A. 4272.

lord(is) and lad(is), W. Alex. 1602, Gaw. 49, 1115, 2515, Jacke Upland, pp. 22, 34, Mum 46, 462, Rejoinder of Jacke Upland, p. 100, P.Pl. B v, 247, x, 95, xiii, 422, xv, 6, 304, 316, C v. 109, viii, 82, xii, 202, xiii, 219, R.R. iii, 222, Troy 488, 7859, W. of P. 123, etc. (6 times). *lorde (of þis londe)ne lady*, Mum 258. *lordes (in londe) and ladyes*, W. & W. 409.

lord and leiuetenant, Sc.F. 60.

lord and ludes, W. of P. 1439.

lege lord of my lyfe, W. Alex. 3087, Gaw. 545. **E.M.E.** *Lorde of lyf*, P.Pl. B xiii, 120, xviii, 363. *lord of lyf and of liht*, P.Pl. A x, 30, B xviii, 59.

lordschipe of lif, Alex. B 76.

þe Lorde of þe lyfte, Pur. 435, 1356, 1448. *þat ilk lorde þat þe lyfte halde3*, Gaw. 1256.

---

[1] Cp. O.N. *land ok lýðr*.

lorde(s) *in*/*of* . . . *londe*(s), Alex. A 64, 405, 927, 977, 1212, Alex. B
174, Beckett, 99, 223, Gaw. 1133, 1319, Jerus. 354, Mum 96, 194,
1406, Pierce 754, P.Pl. A iii, 196, R.R. ii, 93, iii, 116, 179, Sc.F. 9, 64,
123, 400, Sc. Proph. i, 132, M.A. 1255, 3284, Troy 1618, etc. (15 times),
W. of P. 517, etc. (16 times), W. & W. 20, 409. *lord ouer, þat lond,*
Jerus. 970. *lordship in*/*of londe*(s), M.A. 4276, P.Pl. B xvii, 105
W. of P. 4648.

alosed in lond, Alex. A 139, 577, Alex. B 665, M.A. 3887. *alosed in his lif,*
Alex. B 554.

the losse and the lure, Troy 8691, etc. (8 times). *lure and* . . . *los,* Troy
1440, 2091, 2296.

for (*the*) *loue of oure*/*vr lorde,* Mum 428, Pierce 782, P.Pl. A Pro. 26, 87, C
xiii, 157. *vr lordes loue of heuene,* P.Pl. A vii, 17. *for loue of þe Lord*
þat we leuen inne, Alex. B 597.

louelye to looke vpon, D.L. 97.

E.M.E.   *unloke þe lidde,* Erk. 67. *vn-louked his yȝe-lyddeȝ,* Gaw. 1201.

E.M.E.   *he lowted to me low,* D.L. 179. *they lowted downe lowe,* D.L. 352.
lowely to loute, Mum 1328, W. of P. 3483. *loȝe he louteȝ hem,* Pur. 798.
that lowe louted, P.Pl. B xiii, 26. *with louting full low,* Troy 393, 9253.

he lukkes and laytes, Pat. 277.

þat lufsum vnder lyne, Gaw. 1814.[1]

a lump of led, Pur. 1025.

in lust and in lecherye, Pur. 1350. *lecherye and lustes,* Alex. A 35.   **E.M.E.**
alle leccheries/*lechurus lust,* Alex. B 392, 631, 688.

this made me al madde, Mum 855. *that maketh me so mad,* P.Pl. A v, 106,
Troy 11542.

ᐧ*to make the mariage,* W. of P. 2051, 2098, 3045, etc. *made* . . . *mariage,*
Troy 3461, 13102. *mariage* . . . *made,* P.Pl. A ii, 22, 26, Troy 3468.

melodye made, W. of P. 24.

make amendis, W. of P. 3919, 3996, Mum 1516. *amendes make,* P.Pl. A
v, 75, Mum 1613.

menstracye maked was, W. of P. 1951, 3812.

to make merry, Beckett 160. *maden* (*alle*) *mery,* Troy 2560, etc., W. of P.
1148, 1409, etc. *birds made merry with their mouth,* D.L. 114.

make (*my*) *mone,* Jacke Upland, p. 16, P.Pl. B xv, 534. *made* (*his*) *mone,*
Gaw. 737, W. Alex. 1266. *grete mone she made,* Chev. 83.

mones he made and mournyng, Troy 3562. *make* (*for ȝoure mischief*)
mourninge, Alex. B 1115. *make*(*n*) *mourninge,* Alex. B 472, W. of P.
1049, 1406. *makis mournyng & mane,* W. Alex. 5027.

Laȝ.   *make murþe,* W. of P. 5056, 5224. *to make ony myrthe,* R.R. ii, 12.
makers of myrthes, W. & W. 21. *much merþe con make,* Gaw. 899.
murthes to maken, P.Pl. A Pro. 33. *þe mirþ þat was maked,* W. of P.
4528. *maade him murthe,* P.Pl. A iii, 191. *maden*/*made* . . . *murþe,*
W. of P. 4760, 4851. *this mirth he made,* Alex. A 979. *much mirthe*
he mad, Gaw. 106. *alle þis mirþe þay maden,* Gaw. 71. *murþe* . . .
mad, W. of P. 1470, etc.

maȝty maker of men, Erk. 283. *þou maker of man,* Pat. 482.

makeles of mercy, Sc.F. 46, 292.

almost y madde in mynde, Pierce 280. *as madde of her mynde,* R.R. ii, 184.
mad of þy mynde, Mum 680.

[1] See Gordon and Tolkien, p. 111, note.

(a) *maiden ful meke,* Jos. 79, Pur. 815. *as meke as a mayden,* Troy 130.
3745.
maydenes and (miȝthi) men, W. of P. 153.
maymed and marde, D.L. 141. *marrit and maymyt,* Troy 10456.
haue maistrie of men, Alex. B 433.
maister of þe men, Pierce 269.
ne for maystrie ne for mede, Erk. 34.
maystrie and miht, P.Pl. A v, 85.
to malt so out of memorie, Erk. 158.
to malte my mynde, Pur. 1566.
O.E.P. *man apon mold,* W. Alex. 1130, 3766, D.L. 134, 323, Mum 363,
407, 671, P.Pl. C xv, 168, Pur. 558, 613, 1656, W. of P. 85, etc. (42
times), W. & W. 172. *men vp-on molde,* Alex. B 546, 564, 1108, Erk.
270, Gaw. 914, Pierce 103, P.Pl. A ii, 171, iii, 71, Troy 13222. *man of
þe mold,* W. Alex. 5113. *man of this molde,* P.Pl. B iii, 6. *men of the
mold,* D.L. 290. *men one/of this molde,* Parl. 295, P.Pl. A x, 124, B ii,
37, viii, 14, x, 392, R.R. iii, 316. *men on þat molde,* Troy 1599, 10818.
men that on molde liuen, P.Pl. A ii, 161, B xi, 267. *men that on molde
wandren,* P.Pl. A viii, 80. *he was makeles one molde,* M.A. 3875. *þe
men marred on þe molde,* Pat. 479. *master on molde,* Alex. A 1035.
maistres on molde, P.Pl. B. iii, 290. *þe meruelyousteste man þat on molde
lengeȝ,* M.A. 129. *(alle þe mukel) mayny on molde,* Pur. 514. *medcyn
on molde,* P.Pl. B xvii, 91, Troy 9192. *mensk lady on molde,* Gaw. 964.
meobles on this molde, P.Pl. B ix, 82. *merry maydens on the mold,*
D.L. 205. *mercy on molde,* Alex. B 900, M.A. 977. *mirþe on molde,*
Alex. B 945, 1099, W. of P. 1012, etc. (12 times). *meruellis on mold,*
Troy 11791. *message on molde,* Troy 3577. *no mesure on molde,*
Alex. B 791. *all metals o mold,* W. Alex. 3385. *þei han miht vpon
molde,* Alex. B 739. *mighty on molde,* Troy 159, 2173, 10252. *þe
maȝty on molde,* Pur. 279. *mightiest on molde,* Troy 2408. *myschef on
molde,* P.Pl. A Pro. 64, C xiii. 178, R.R. iii, 9, Pur. 708, W. of P. 917.
moneye on this molde, P.Pl. A i, 42. *mony on mold,* Troy 3434. *þe
multitude . . . on þe molde,* Jerus. 603. *multyplteȝ on þis molde,* Pur. 522.
man and hus make, P.Pl. C xiv, 153.
marchaundise make, Jerus. 1309.
mariage and matrimony, Troy 9223.
to marie the mayden, P.Pl. B ii, 56.
amarride my mynde, R.R. Pro. 16.
martrid and murthrid, Troy 5704.
wythen maskle oþer mote, Pur. 556. Cp. Prl. 899, 923.
masse and matynes, P.Pl. B xi, 275, etc. **E.M.E.** *matins and masse,* P.Pl.
B v, 460, etc., Pierce 592. *messes and matyns,* M.A. 4333.
meblys and money, Troy 11511.
E.M.E., Laȝ. *medues mowen,* Mum 887.
E.M.E., Orm. *me(o)ke and mylde,* P.Pl. A x, 83, Troy 2443. *meke of his
mouth, mylde of his speche,* P.Pl. A ix, 71. *myld and meik,* T.M.
Wemen 513.
mekenesse of minde, Alex. B 614. *so meeke was of moode,* Alex A 1171.
to mele of (a) mater, Troy 209, W. of P. 4009. *to melle in þis mater,* Troy 3185.
E.M.E. *meled þus much with his muthe,* Gaw. 447. *meles with mouthe,*
M.A. 1987. *with mouthe melis,* M.A. 3874. *ne mekills mellis noȝt oure
mouth,* W. Alex. 4310.

melody and musick, W. Alex. 3698.   *musik and melodye*, Parl. 62
þe membrus of a man, Alex. B 696, 707.
þat may mene in his mynde, Erk. 151.
to mene in oure mouth, P.Pl. C iv, 399, A ix, 296.   *menit with mowthe*,
    Troy 2069.
with menske and wyth mete and mynstrasy, Pur. 121.
neþer merked ne made, Jerus. 112.   *merked and made*, M.A. 1304, W. Alex.
    318, 2636.
moch is þi mercy and þi miȝt, þi menske, W. of P. 313.   *mercy and mensk*,
    Pierce 81.
mercy and/ne methe, W. Alex. 816, 4324.
mercy in her mynde, P.Pl. B xvii, 308.   *mercy in my mynd*, Twa Mariit
    Wemen 282.   *mercifull in mynd*, Twa Mariit Wemen 501.   *mercy in*
    thi mynd, P.Pl. B v, 288, 292.
merry in mynde, Gaw. 497, T.M. Wemen 282.   *mirre ben men of mod in*
    minde, Alex. B 927.
alle þis meschef for me is made, Pat. 209.
whenne here mesure is made, Chev. 171.
þe mesure and þe mett, W. Alex. 25.
al in mesure and meþe, Pur. 247.   *in the mesure of his mode and meþe of his*
    wylle, Pur. 565.
Cp. **E.M.E.**   *in mete out of mesure*, P.Pl. C xiv, 189.
E.M.E.   *at mete and at melis*, R.R. iii, 313.
by a metyng (dream) that y met, Cr. King 10.
meved many maters, R.R. iii, 321.   *a matiere be/is y-moeued*, Mum 687, 1504.
    þe more þe matere is meued, Pierce 821.   *the matere that she meued*,
    P.Pl. B xi, 104.   *to meue of þat mater*, Troy 13067.   *of this matere no*
    more meuen ich nelle, P.Pl. C ii, 123.   *ffor mater that my mynde is*
    meued in, R.R. iii, 2.
whanne we meuen our mynde, Alex. B 466.   *whenne his mynde is ymoevid*,
    Mum 1542.   *(noght) meuyt (his) mynd*, Troy 9792, 9951.   *meuyt to/of*
    mynde, Troy 1691, etc.   *euer hit meuyt hym in mynd*, Troy 11242.
    movede in mynde, Sc. Proph. I, 15.   *meuyt out of mynd*, Troy 30.
meuede him mod, P.Pl. C xix, 118.   *why meuestow thi mode*, P.Pl. B x, 263.
    moeued my mode, P.Pl. B xiii, 191.
as michel as y may, Alex. B 285.
mekyll of might, Troy 12994, 13482.   *the might was so mekyll*, Troy 5766.
    that most were of might, Troy 9099.
of whose mykill and might and mayn strenght, Troy 6246.   **E.M.E.**   *noe*
    might, nay no meane/maine, D.L. 433, 443.   *no might, ne no mayn*,
    Troy 10041.   *boþe þe myȝt and þe mayn*, Jerus. 507.   *all the might and*
    þe mayn, Troy 5825.   *lord of myght and mayn*, P.Pl. B xviii, 315, Troy
    9099.   *a God mihtful of main*, Alex. B 663.   *might of his/hur maine*,
    Alex. A 512, 1021.
the myghte and þe maieste, M.A. 1303.
myȝt and maystrye, P.Pl. A iii, 19.
a mighty man, Alex. A 217.   *mightfull menne*, Alex. A 137, 156, etc., Jos.
    508, R.R. ii, 95, iii, 252, W. Alex. 1420.   *men of mekyll myghte*, Parl. 479.
þe miht of a man, Alex. A 666.
mighty and monfull, Troy 2202.
his myȝt and his merci, Pat. 295.   *purȝ myȝt of þy mercy*, Pat. 324.

O.E.P. & Pr., E.M.E., La3., O. & N.[1] *wiþ milde mod*, W. of P. 1985, etc.
in mynde and memory, W. Alex. 1118.
my mynde and my moode, Alex. A 1041.
I wol minge of a mater, W. of P. 1925.
mynned in mynde, W. Alex. 1094.
with mirth and with melodye of mynstralsy, M.A. 242. *with myrthis and melodye*, M.A. 3174. *myrth/myrthes and melody*, Troy 348, 3452. *melodye and mirthes*, Cr. King 21. *melody (and) myrthe*, Troy 11915, Sc.F. 321.
merþ and mynstralsye, Gaw. 1952. *murthe and munstralsye*, P.Pl. A iii, 11. *with myrthe and mynstrasye*, P.Pl. A iii, 98. *with myrthe(s) of mynstralsy*, Troy 3436, W. of P. 1295, 5062. *munstralsye and murthe*, P.Pl. A xi, 35.
musike and myrthes, Troy 3783.
þur3 mony misy and myre, Gaw. 749.
momelyn with here mouthes, Cr. King 88.
þe more and þe mynne,[2] Gaw. 1881, P.Pl. C iv, 399 (see N.E.D.).
mournynge and myrthe, Erk. 350. *murþe and mournyng*, P.Pl. C xviii, 147, W. of P. 4296.
þe mornyng & myschefe, Troy 3566.
morninge and mone, D.L. 186.
neþer money, ne mede, Pierce 346.
monk oþer masseprest, Gaw. 2108.
the mosse and þe marrasse, the mounttez, M.A. 2014.
m(u)kkyde and mynyde, Erk. 43.
munge me in his memorie, P.Pl. A vii, 88.
Cp. O.E.P. & Pr., cp. La3. *ouer mures and muntaynes*, W. of P. 2619. *montayns and mores*, Jerus. 726, Troy 7809.
I mused in mynde, W. Alex. 1629.
E.M.E. *naked and nedefull*, Troy 13321. *the neodi and the nakede*, P.Pl. A vii 14, 212.
naked as a nedle, P.Pl. B xii, 162, xvii, 56, Jerus. 939.
O. E. Pr., E.M.E., La3., Orm. *namede 3ou thaire names*, Parl. 167. *neuen . . . name(s)*, W. Alex. 2187, 4939, 5486, Gaw. 10, Parl. 108, 297, 580, P.Pl. B xix, 18, Pur. 410, Troy 14003. *nem(þ)ne . . . name*, Mum 585, 909, 1418, Pierce 453, 472, W. of P. 368, T.M. Wemen 117.
La3. *3oure nase and 3oure nebb*, W. Alex. 4519.
ne3ed ful neghe, Gaw. 697. *neghen/neyed nere*, Mum 971, 1492, P.Pl. B xx, 231. *then niiged they nighe*, ScF. 171. *3if he nyhed hem ony nere*, R.R. iii, 231.
it ny3e/nied . . . na3t, Alex. A 817, Gaw. 929, M.A. 451, Pat. 465, Pur. 484, Troy 672, 1075, 9585, W. of P. 770, 2599. *it was neghande nyghte*, W. & W. 43. *the night was so neghe*, Troy 6028, 7808. *þe nyght nyied on erthe*, Alex. A 1140.
till that it neighed neere noone, D.L. 137. *it neighed nyeghe the noon*, P.Pl. B xx, 4.
nykked . . . with nay, Chev. 28, Gaw. 706, 2471, Jerus. 89, Sc.F. 53, W. of P. 4145.
þat noble is and namekouþ, Alex. B 823, 1079. *nobill (kyng) and nomekowthe*, Troy 2630.

---

[1] A common M.E. phrase.
[2] Cp. O.N. *meiri ok minni;* not uncommon in M.E. generally.

whyle noye noyet hym, Jerus. 27.
now oper neuer, Gaw. 2216.
þe oke and þe assche, W. & W. 397.
with oile & with ointment, Troy 7526.
old and hor, P.Pl. A vii, 76, C vii, 193.
onest & abill, Troy 5565.
O.E.Pr.   *þe ox and þe asse*, Pur. 1086.
paines and passyons, D.L. 2.   **E.M.E.** *Godes pyne and hus passion*, P.Pl.
   B v, 411.   *passyoun and pyne*, Parl. 555.
pared out of paper, Gaw. 802, Pur. 1408.
parkes and palaces, and pastures, D.L. 44.
passe in pilgremage, M.A. 896.
apas in processione, M.A. 4014.   *pai passyed forthe in processione*, Erk. 351.
all þe pastours & þe playnes, W. Alex. 1198.
patriarkes and prelates, W. of P. 5047.
E.M.E.   *patriarkes and prophetes*, P.Pl. A viii, 12, B x, 340, xii, 138, xiii,
   428, xvi, 198, 251, 256, xviii, 140, 144, 268, C viii, 88.
prophetes and patriarkes, M.A. 3807.
in peryl and payne, Gaw. 733, Troy 12728.   *o payne and o perell*, M.A. 1612.
   fro paines and peril, Alex. A 872.
þe penaunce and payne, Pat. 530.
in penaunce and pouerte, Alex. B 291, Pierce 111.
P.M.   *penyes and poundes*, P.Pl. C i, 161.
appere in his presens, M.A. 94, Troy 1093, 1963, 2581, 11398, 11484.   *peren
   in his presence*, P.Pl. B Pro. 173.   *þou apperit not in presens*, Troy
   8900.
wiþ perrey and pellure, W. of P. 53.   *pelour, pirre, ne perle*, W. Alex. 4036.
aprochen to hys presens, Pur. 8.   *to aproche my presens*, Pur. 147.
peynt and portreyed, Pierce 192.   *portreid and paynt*, Pierce 121.   *peynten
   and purtraye*, P.Pl. B iii, 62, etc.   *peinted and portreide*, W. of P.
   619.
pyneȝ me in a prysoun, Pat. 79.
pypyng and play, Jerus. 253.
for pity and for paine, Sc.F. 290.
(þe peple) pitosly pleyned, Pat. 371.
to plesen the puple, Pierce 74.
plesande and profitabill, M.A. 11.
plucked and pulled, R.R. ii, 126.
pompe and . . . pride, W. Alex. 1767, 2334, 2504, Parl. 187, P.Pl. B xiv,
   192, etc., Troy 2122, W. & W. 422.
poure and penyles, P.Pl. C xiii, 27.   Cp. *þe pore penyles*, Pierce 620.
pouert and payn, Troy 13318.
pouerte and plente, P.Pl. B xi, 323, xii, 9.
prest and parsoun, P.Pl. B v, 422.   *preostes and persones*, P.Pl. A iii, 237,
   309.   *persones and prestes*, P.Pl. B xi, 94, xv, 97, 478.
prestes and prechours, P.Pl. B xv, 433.
prest or prelat or prechour, Mum 624.
with prestis and with prelatis, W. Alex. 1554.   *vche prest and prelates alle*,
   Pat. 389.   *prestes and prelates*, Pur. 1249, Mum 538.   *prelatis and
   prestis*, W. Alex. 1499, P.Pl. C xviii, 244.
prelates and preestes and princis, P.Pl. C xi, 196.

arayed (hym) for to ryde, Parl. 346, P.Pl. A iv, 16.   *all redie araied to ryden*,
    Alex. A 418.   *to ryde alle arayde*, Gaw. 1130.
be arrayes his richemen, Jos. 451, 490.
rascled and remed and routte, P.Pl. C viii, 7.
to reche to such reuerence, Gaw. 1243.   *to reche hym reverens*, Pur. 1369.
I schal reken thaire araye, Parl. 107.   *to reken al þe arai*, W. of P. 1602.
rekens hym þe resons, W. Alex. 1280.   *rekken vp alle þe resounȝ*, Pur. 2.
    rekne hem bi resoun, P.Pl. B i, 22.
rekkenede and renownde, M.A. 3441.
rekenly hym reuerenced, Gaw. 251.   *rekenly wyth reverens*, Pur. 1318.   Cp.
    Pur. 10, *reken wyth reverence*.
þou redeȝ hym ryȝt, Gaw. 373.
also red and so ripe, Pur. 1045.
all redie araied, Alex. A 418.   *redye in araye*, M.A. 311.
redili araiȝed, W. of P. 3563, 4855, M.A. 1453.
radlye in array, Sc.F. 179.
redyng of romaunces, Cr. King 22.   *neuer red in no romanse*, Troy 3896,
    5544.   *ne redde in no romance*, W. & W. 250.   *in romance be redde*,
    M.A. 3440.   *romance to rede*, Parl. 250.
region ne rewme, W. Alex. 992.
þat reigneth in ryght, Alex. A 88.   *too reigne on his ryght as rink in his owne*,
    Alex. A 105.
raigne with royaltie, Sc.F. 37.
resaued (him) with reuerance, W. Alex. 1124, 1182.   *he was resayued as I
    rede with reuerence*, W. Alex. 1646.   *resayues him full rially with reuer-
    ence*, W. Alex. 3210.   *receyued hit myd reuerence*, Jerus. 226.   *receyuit
    . . . with reuerence*, Troy 5297, 8310.
renkys of the rownnde table, M.A. 17, 3612.   *renkes full ryalle of his rownnde
    table*, Parl. 468.
with remyng and rauthe, Troy 8696, 9126.   *ruthe of hor remyng*, Troy 8511.
with renkes in ryotte in reulle in haulle, Parl. 253.
why hatȝ þou rended þy robe ?, Pur. 1595.
to renne and to ride, P.Pl. A iii, 207, etc.   *to ride and renne*, Mum 1480.
    to ride or renne, R.R. ii, 68.   *oþer to ryde, oþer to renne, to rome in his
    ernde*, Pat. 52.   *he ritt or rest or renneth*, P.Pl. B Pro. 171.   *he ryt
    other rest other romyth*, P.Pl. C i, 186.   *to ride and to rayme*, W. Alex.
    2488.
rent vp fro the rygge, Parl. 87.
rent him on the rood, D.L. 377.   *that rent all was on the rood*, D.L. 456.
    on rode rwly to-rent, Pat. 96.
the residue and the remenaunt, P.Pl. A v, 240, vii, 91, B xx, 290.
reson and/or riȝt, W. Alex. 4332, D.L. 260, M.A. 295, 2041, Mum 1479,
    P.Pl. B xi, 364, R.R. iii, 315, Troy 8935, 10715, 12254.   *neither reason
    nor wright*, D.L. 238.   *resoun ne riȝt*, P.Pl. B xii, 209, C iv, 295.   *ritȝe
    and . . . reson*, P.Pl. B iii, 238, xviii, 275, 347, xix, 457, C xx, 3.
    no ryght ne reson, P.Pl. C xii, 29.   *resoun and riȝtwisnesse*, P.Pl. B xix,
    79.
to rest in his rewme, Troy 13061.   *he rested in that realme*, Sc.F. 143.
reste or rome, Mum 573.
to reule alle rewmes, P.Pl. B xvii, 3.   *to reule þis royaume*, Mum 225.
boþe oure reule and our riht, Alex. B 507.

somme were reuled by ryht, Alex. B 916.   *to reule þaym by reason and by
    rightful domes*, Mum 1036.
iche rewme vndir roff, R.R. iii, 248.
ryally . . . arayed, Pur. 812.   *(with mich) riall araie*, Alex. A 267, R.R.
    iii, 361, W. of P. 3782, etc.   *by royal raye*, Mum 644.   *for alle thy
    ryalle arraye*, Parl. 186.
ryal and ryche, Pur. 786.   *riche . . . and reale*, W. of P. 2136, Troy 5361.
royall red blood that ran from thy side, D.L. 4.   *the railinge red blood ran from
    his sides*, D.L. 376.   *þis ryall rede blode ryn appon erthe*, M.A. 3990.
    þat rane (all) on reede blode, M.A. 1526, Mum 1530.   *rynnande on rede
    blode*, M.A. 392, 795.   *he al on rede blode ran*, Jerus. 12.   *of rede blode
    rynnys*, M.A. 2144.
richely rayled, Gaw. 163.   [Cp. D.L. 24, Parl. 119.]   *so richeli al araied*,
    W. of P. 1934, 5333.   *arayet richely*, Troy 9118.
all railme and þe riches, W. Alex. 20.
E.M.E.   *in riche robes*, P.Pl. B xv, 222.   *his ryche robe*, Pat. 379.   *hirs
    robe was ful riche*, P.Pl. B ii, 15.
of richesse and of renoun, Alex. B 581.
now wideȝ (þis renk) purȝ þe ryalme, Gaw. 691.   *ryde in the bares royalme*,
    Beckett 139.
hor renttes, hor riches, Troy 11395, 11456.   *reches ne rent*, Parl. 634.   *ricchesse
    or rentis*, P.Pl. B x, 15.
rigge and rib, Jerus. 1079.
ryȝtwis and rekin, Erk. 245.
þat hit thar ryve ne rote ne no ronke wormes, Erk. 262.
riot and revell, Troy 2936.   *reot and reeuell*, R.R. iv, 20.
rys radly, Pat. 65, 89.   *ryse . . . radly*, Troy 772, W. Alex. 1494.   *riseth
    . . . rudlye*, D.L. 355.   *arises up redely*, Alex. A 746.   *ros . . .
    radly*, Gaw. 1735, Pur. 671, 797, Troy 2698, etc. (10 times), W. of P.
    41, 810.   *radly . . . ros*, Gaw. 367, Pat. 351, 378.   *risen vp raply*,
    P.Pl. A v, 176.   *ros . . . rapely*, R.R. Pro. 13.
whyle you rixlis in this Reame, Troy 221.
robbet my/þaire riches and refte me . . . (godes), Troy 11940, 12388, 13172.
    rafte . . . and robbed, Pur. 1142.   *robberes and . . . reuers*, P.Pl. B
    xiv, 182, C xiv, 58, Reply of Fr. Daw Thopias, p. 85, W. of P. 5478.
to robbe me and to ryfle me, P.Pl. C v, 54.   *robbed or rifled*, P.Pl. B xvii.
    99.   *robbers and riffleris*, R.R. iii, 197.
þe rochereȝ rungen aboute, Gaw. 1427.
bi mony rokkeȝ ful roȝe, Pat. 254.
as rody as a rose, P.Pl. B xiii, 99.   **E.M.E.**   *red as rose*, W. of P. 882.
    rud as þe roose, Troy 3988, etc.   *her rudd redder than the rose*, D.L. 66.
    rose red was hur rode, Alex. A 178.   *the red rayling roses*, D.L. 24,
    Parl. 119, Sc.F. 26, Troy 624.   *riht as the rose that red is*, P.Pl. A x, 119.
all raylede with rede, W. & W. 60.
he romyed and rared, M.A. 784, 1124. Cp. Pur. 1543, *romyes . . . roreȝ*.
ronnen radly in route, Erk. 62.
Cp. **E.M.E.** *roryng and ruth*, Jerus. 303.
rotid and rent, Erk. 260, Pur. 144.
all the route I rent from the round table, D.L. 341.   *with the rout of the round
    table*, Sc.F. 520.   *wyth a reall rowte of þe rounde table*, M.A. 719.   *þe
    ryall rowte of þe rownde table*, M.A. 2919.

he þat rules þe rak, Pat. 176.
ruggis and revys, Sc. Proph. i, 81.
þe rurd schal ryse, Pat. 396.   *per ros (for blasteʒ gode) gret rurd*, Gaw. 1148.
rusches vp in a res, W. Alex. 2978.
þenne ran þay in on a res, Pur. 1782.
sad of his semblaunt, Mum 963, P.Pl. A ix, 112, Troy 3791, W. of P. 228.
     wyth sadde semblaunt, Pur. 640.
alle safe and alle sounde, Chev. 43.   *saaf and sound*, P.Pl. A ix, 29, W. of P.
     868, 2816.   *bothe sound and saf*, Troy 10246.
sailen on þe see, Alex. A 483, 535, Alex. B 203, 297, 451, W. of P. 567.
     sailleʒ/sayled ouer þe see, M.A. 818, Parl. 489.   *sailers on þe see*, W.
     Alex. 4359.   *sailing in þe see*, W. of P. 4938.
with sare (sighingis) and sadd, W. Alex. 5052.
whan þis/þat sawe was said, Alex. B 111, W. Alex. 245, W. of P. 2365.
how his sawle schulde be saued, Gaw. 1879.
sauen hir & saluen hir, P.Pl. B xi, 211–12.
to saue men fram synne, P.Pl. B xviii, 303.
saue from sorwe, W. of P. 1904.
Laʒ. *ne no schafte, ne no schelde*, Gaw. 205.   *now a schaft, now a schild*,
     W. Alex. 1402.
þe schauen schaft schyndered in peceʒ, Gaw. 1458.
(whenne þet) shafte is schyuered, Chev. 301, Troy 1264.
Cp. **O.E.P.**   *shame and shenden*, P.Pl. B xi, 416.   **O.E.Pr., E.M.E., Orm,**
     shamed and shent, D.L. 370.   **E.M.E.**   *schamly be schent*, Alex. B 809.
     Cp. **Laʒ. & Orm.**   *to schenden oþer schamen hem*, Pierce 677.
(no) schame (ne) schenschipe, M.A. 4299, Troy 4176, 8119.   *schenchipe and*
     schame, W. & W. 432, W. of P. 1803.
schelde vs ffro schamesdede, M.A. 3.
schilde us fram schenchip & schame, W. of P. 1803.
O.E.Pr., Laʒ.   *a schelde and a (scharpe) spere*, Gaw. 269.
E.M.E.   *shimered and shone*, D.L. 59, Gaw. 772.
E.M.E.   *schon schene*, Jos. 510.
schynes so schyr, Pur. 1121.   *schon schyrer þen snawe*, Gaw. 956.
schyueryng of scheldes, Jerus. 547.   *scheldes schiuered*, W. of P. 3616.
þe blod schot for scham, Gaw. 318.
he ne schownttes for no schame, M.A. 3715.   *shunt for no shame*, Troy 600,
     13730.   *for shame may þou shunt*, Troy 10377.
shrinke for shame, D.L. 400.   *schrank for schome*, Gaw. 2372.
schupmen and shephurdes, P.Pl. C xviii, 98 = *shipmen and shepherdes*,
     P.Pl. B xv, 354.
the skaith and the skorne, Troy 1874, 13473.   *ne scathe ne scorne*, Mum 73.
     scorne oþer scathe, Mum 170.   *the scorne and the scaith*, T.M. Wemen 358.
scorned and schende, Jerus. 372.
skrykyng and skremyng, Troy 10182.   *skremyt . . . with a skryke*, Troy
     910.
secheth and sercheth, R.R. iii, 20.   *ofserchid . . . and sought*, Mum 771.
see selcothes, D.L. 181.   *whatt selcouthes he see*, Parl. 501.   *there hathe*
     selcouthes bene sene, W. & W. 3.   *selkoupes sen*, Alex. B 1022.   *selkowth*
     to se, Troy 13506.
for fele sellyeʒ had þay sen, Gaw. 239.   *sall sellyes be seyne*, Becket 115.
     a selly þere sene was, Troy 11668.   *I haf sen a selly*, Gaw. 475.

see with sy3t, W. Alex. 4934, Gaw. 197, 226, 1705, Pur. 192, 576, 1710, M.A. 968, etc.

O.E.Pr. *to see in (my) syghte*, W. & W. 455, Troy 7603.

O.E.Pr., E.M.E., La3. *sawe I neuer siche a syghte*, W. & W. 137. *saw a sight*, D.L. 50, 151. *a syghte seene*, M.A. 3985, 4341. *a (seemly) sight to see*, Sc.F. 233, W. of P. 2329. *þe sight3 þat I sawe*, Mum 1292. *the see and the sonde and the sad erthe*, Parl. 333. *þe sege and þe assaut*, Gaw. 1, 2525. Cp. *assegede and sayled it*, Parl. 303. *some segge in this sale*, M.A. 134. *the segges of þe cite*, W. of P. 2223, 3758.

Orm. *seiden and sworen*, P.Pl. B xv, 586. Cp. **La3.** *he said in his saw*, Troy 11505. *whepire it be sele or soro3e*, W. Alex. 249. *semblede in sale*, M.A. 1306. *semblant and solace*, M.A. 75.

E.M.E. *semely to see*, P.Pl. C ii, 55, Pur. 262, Sc.F. 233, Troy 3095, W. of P. 1611. *semly and swete*, Pur. 816. *sende (us) some socoure*, M.A. 3052, W. of P. 2684, 2861. *sokour to sende*, Chev. 111, W. of P. 2671, 2926.

E.M.E., La3. *sende (his) sonde*, Pur. 53, W. of P. 64, etc. *sente sondes*, W. of P. 1078, etc., R.R. iv, 28. *y haue sent þe my sonde*, Alex. B 511. *his sondes into Sodamas wat3 sende*, Pur. 781: *sendeþ sondismen*, Jerus. 342. *sondisman sent*, Jerus. 80. *to seruen in sinne*, Alex. B 761. *seseþ and stinteþ*, Alex. B 91. *the sesone of somere*, Gaw. 516, Parl. 2, Troy 10632, W. Alex. 2895. *a somer seasoun*, Alex. A 999, P.Pl. A Pro. 1, etc., Mum 1080, R.R. iii, 39.

E.M.E. *sett hym vp in his sadill*, Parl. 173. *sett and served*, Alex. A 980. *served and sette*, W. of P. 4906. *seueried and sondrid*, R.R. ii, 14. *sike I and sing*, W. of P. 433, 909.

E.M.E. *to sike and sorwe*, W. of P. 691. *sighe and sorrow*, Sc.F. 289. *siking and sorrow*, Troy 1515, etc. (10 times), W. of P. 5451. *in sorrow and sike*, Erk. 305. *sorow and siking*, Troy 3508, 10587. *sorwes and sikingges*, W. of P. 566. *sorrow and sicknesse and sikinge*, D.L. 187. Cp. **La3.** *sikenesses and sorwes*, P.Pl. B xvii, 334, C xvii, 308. *sobbyng and siking*, Troy 2168. *sobbed and syked*, P.Pl. B xiv, 326. *siked for sorwe þerof sore*, W. of P. 1181. *sike with the sory*, P.Pl. A xi, 190. *nys syke ne sori*, P.Pl. B xvii, 344. *in sorowe . . . to siken*, Alex. A 395. *sikede sore*, P.Pl. A v, 229. *siket full sore*, Troy 1307. *hir that sorest for him syketh*, Parl. 404. *si3ede sore*, Pierce 442. *sykinge for my synnes*, P.Pl. C vi, 107.

E.M.E. *of synne or of shame*, Mum 747. *of synne and of smach*, Pur. 1019.

O.E.P., E.M.E., Orm. *synne and . . . sake*, Pat. 172. *synful and sakles*, Pur. 716. *sakles of syne*, M.A. 3992. *sakles . . . for syne*, M.A. 3986. *synkande in the salt see*, M.A. 3705. *sunkyn in þe se*, Troy 5701. *in þe see sunken*, W. of P. 4044. *synkes in his synne*, Pat. 172. *quen 3e sitt in 3oure sale*, W. Alex. 4432. Cp. *sett in his sale*, W. Alex. 502.

syttes semely in þe sege, Erk. 35. *syttes on segge,* Pat. 93. *to sytt on a sege,*
W. Alex. 236. *syttand so in hire sege,* W. Alex. 548. *satte . . . in/on
a siege,* Mum 359, 596. Cp. *sett hym softe one a sege,* W. & W. 483.
ne we sitte in no sete, Alex. B 988. *sytte in ʒoure sette,* M.A. 1305. *in his
sete . . . sitting,* Troy 9115. *in my seat where I sate,* D.L. 36.
sklaunder and skorne, Troy 5557, etc.
slydes on slepe, Pat. 200. *slydyn vppon shlepe, by slomeryng of age,* Troy 6.
slod . . . aslepe, W. of P. 792. *slydeʒ on a sloumbe,* Pat. 466. *in
slomeryng he slode,* Gaw. 1182.
slippide opon slepe, Erk. 92, Gaw. 244. *sleghly on slepe I slypped,* Troy
2378. *slypped vpon a sloumbe-slepe,* Pat. 186. *slippit vpon slepe,
slomeryng a while,* Troy 8428.
E.M.E., Laʒ. *slomyre ne slepe,* M.A. 4044. *slepeles was slome and slomerde,*
Parl. 101. *slomereres in slepe,* Pierce 91. *as hue slumbered on slepe,*
Alex. A 720. *slumberde in a slepyng,* P.Pl. A Pro. 10. *slombrid and
slepte,* R.R. iv, 62. Cp. *a slomerande slepe,* Becket, 145.
E.M.E. *smellis swete,* Troy 1667.
smoke and smolder [1] (sbs.), P.Pl. B xvii, 321, 323, 341. Cp. Pur. 955,
ai in smolderande smoke smachande full ille.
smoke and smorthre, P.Pl. C xx, 303, 305, 323, Troy 3511. *smorther and
smoke,* [2] Troy 911, 9512, 11796.
smoþely hatʒ smyten, Gaw. 407.
sobbyng and sorow, Troy 8716, 9592, 9609. *sobbyng and sorow, sykyng of
teris,* Troy 8142.
to socour hem and save, W. of P. 2405.
softyng and salue, Jerus. 92.
my solas and socour, Troy 13935.
E.M.E. *the sonne and the see,* P.Pl. B xi, 318.
the sone was sett, Parl. 658.
O.E.Pr., E.M.E., Laʒ., P.M. *sonne schyne(th),* R.R. ii, 134, Sc. Prop. I,
49, W. of P. 1938. *þe schynant sunne,* Mum 1316.
saule vndire son, W. Alex. 4805. *science(s) under sonne,* P.Pl. B xv, 48, C
xiii, 93. *sele vndire son,* W. Alex. 1862. *segge/seggis vnder son,*
W. Alex. 2199, 4935, 5630, Jerus. 680, Pur. 549, W. of P. 1059, 4860,
W. & W. 89, 192. *syn vndire son,* W. Alex. 4262. *cite vnder sonne,*
P.Pl. C iv, 202. *supowell vndire son,* W. Alex. 4300.
O.E.Pr. *þey songen a songe,* Pierce 440. **E.M.E.** *songe I that songe,*
P.Pl. B xix, 206, etc.
E.M.E. *for sorwe and for schame,* W. of P. 2098.
sore and synful, Pur. 1111.
sori for (my) synnes, P.Pl. B v, 608, etc., Mum 93. *sorowe for his synnes,*
Mum 1265.
sorowe and syte, M.A. 1060.
sorow and so(u)rgrem, Troy 3505, 9041.
O.E.Pr., E.M.E., Laʒ. *soth to seyn,* Parl. 78, Mum 283. *soth that ye seyen,*
P.Pl. C xii, 201. *sooth is seyd,* Parl. 574. *I sothe shall saie,* R.R. iii,
170. *be þis sothe at ʒe say,* W. Alex. 4574. **E.M.E.** *soþli forto say,*
W. of P. 1759, etc. (17 times). *soþli to saie,* Alex. B 154. *sothly for
to say,* Parl. 270. *soþli we sen,* Alex. B 490. *say þe sothe,* Erk. 197,

---

[1] See *Body and Soul* (Map's Poems—Camden Soc.), 345.
[2] *Ibid.* 339.

W. & W. 178. *I . . . say . . . as/for sope*, Gaw. 2094, 2110. *say me sekerly sothe*, M.A. 1686. *saye sothe*, Mum 116, 199, etc. *says sope*, Erk. 159. *men saiþ bi ʒow sop þe sawe þet y hirde*, Alex. B 209. *I segge for sothe*, P.Pl. B xi, 289. **O.E.P. & Pr.** *sayde sothly*, Gaw. 673, Pur. 654, Mum 290. *he seyde hem þe sope*, Pierce 658. *we ne sain but sop*, Alex. B 368.

to speke the sothe, W. of P. 5225.

I swere þe for sope, Gaw. 403.

souʒte(n) ouer þe se, Jerus. 291, Parl. 434.

he expouneʒ a speche, Pur. 1058. *expouned his speche*, Pur. 1492. *expowne þe þis speche*, Pur. 1729.

to expoun in spelle, Gaw. 209.

somme soure and somme swete, P.Pl. C xiv, 178. *þe swete, þe soure*, Mum 1050.

souerayngeʒ and senatours, M.A. 2354.

souerayne and seyngnour, M.A. 3313.

souereyn ne soget, Pierce 650. Cp. R.R. Pro. 77.

to sowe (the) seed, Mum 180, 1159, Reply of Fr. Daw Thopìas 41, 45. *ne na sede sawis*, W. Alex. 4268, Troy 178. **E.M.E.** *sede . . . sowe*, Troy 178.

to sowe and to sette, Alex. B 912. *to sowen and to setten*, P.Pl. A vi, 32, vii, 128. *setting and . . . sowing*, P.Pl. B Pro. 21.

a sparthe and a spere, W. Alex. 1403, W. & W. 238.

E.M.E. *speke and seye*, Parl. 382, 650.

O.E.Pr. *as we speke any spech*, W. Alex. 4311. *speche (was) spoken*, Troy 8864, Parl. 366.

Orm. *speke and spelle*, P.Pl. B xv, 600.

Hit is spede-full to speike, Troy 1107. *God is spedfulle in speche*, Alex. B 623. *he that spedeʒ vche speche*, Gaw. 1292. Cp. Troy 7601.

spende no speche, Alex. B 367, W. of P. 4605. *if I spende no spech*, Gaw. 410. *he spendith no speche*, Mum 691.

he sperred þe sted with spurreʒ, Gaw. 670.

to aspye wyth my spelle, Gaw. 1199.

spyed and spured, Gaw. 901. *spied and spuryed*, Gaw. 2093. *to spure and aspye*, P.Pl. C iv, 109.

E.M.E. *to spille any speche*, P.Pl. B ix, 97.

E.M.E. *spitten and spewen*, P.Pl. B x, 40.

spores other spure, P.Pl. B xvii, 12.

spoylles . . . and spillis, M.A. 3159.

O. & N. *spring . . . and sprede*, W. Alex. 1884. *sprynge and sprede*, P.Pl. B xx, 54. *they spryngene and sprede*, M.A. 3158. *springeth and spredeth*, P.Pl. A x, 121. *spryngeth vp and spredeth*, P.Pl. C xiv, 24. *sprange and spred*, Troy 3536. *sprang . . . and spradde*, Pat. 365. *sprong and spradde*, Alex. A 296. *he sprange and sprente and spraddene*, M.A. 3310. *þe tres spradden . . . and sprongen*, Alex. B 123. *the blode sprente owtte and sprede as the horse spryngez*, M.A. 2062.

sprongen with gret sped, Jos. 193.

stablid and stadde, Erk. 274.

so stable and so stedfast, W. Alex. 3381, Troy 8057. *stable and studefast*, P.Pl. A x, 110.

he stakirs, he stumbils, W. Alex. 845.

quen I was stad in þe stoure, W. Alex. 499.

stawed and stoken, Pur. 360.

that euer steed bestrode, Alex. A 10.

steppeȝ in-to stirop, Gaw. 2060.

ho stepped stilly, Gaw. 1191.   *stylle steppen in þe styȝe he styȝtleȝ hym seluen*, Pat. 402.

so sterne . . . and stoute, W. of P. 3534.   *þe stoutest and þe sternest*, W. of P. 2899.

a stuerne man and stalworth, Troy 13169.

steryne in stour, M.A. 377, 2528.   *the sterynneste in stoure*, M.A. 3872.

stiken wiþ þe spere, Jos. 273.

þe styfest, þe stalworþest, Pur. 255.

styf . . . and stour, Jerus. 1180.

stiffe in (þat) stoure, W. Alex. 1322, Parl. 272 (see N.E.D.).

sa stiffe and sa strang, W. Alex. 1149.   *stif and stronge*, Gaw. 34.   *styffnesse and strengthe*, R.R. iii, 251.   *strengest vpon stede and styuest*, P.Pl. B xiii 294, C vii, 43.

stiffe and sturne, Gaw. 2099, W. of P. 3378, etc.

E.M.E.   *stille and softe*, Gaw. 1687.

stille as (þe) ston, Erk. 219, Gaw. 2293, Pur. 1523.   *stont/stoode stille as a stoone*, Mum 755, 826 (see infra *stode*).

I may stinte no stounde, Alex. B 97.   *hee stynted þat stounde and styrred no foote*, Alex. A 1079.

stynt of (our) strif, Jerus. 874, W. of P. 1652.   *he ne stinte of his strife*, Alex. A 951.   *stynte ȝour stryffe*, Parl. 268.

E.M.E.   *þei ne stirred of þe stede*, Alex. B 303.

stire a steppe, M.A. 4133.

a stiþ stede and a strong and straite, Alex. A. 91.

stithe in stoure, Troy 5809.   *sa stithe a steuyn in þe stoure*, W. Alex. 1251.   *stithe men in stoure*, Troy 7, 1179, etc.

E.M.E., Laȝ.   *stockes and stones*, Jerus. 687, Pur. 1343, 1523, 1720.

with ston and with staf, P.Pl. C vii, 106.

stondes in stall, Gaw. 107.

stonde in (a) stede, Alex. A 759, 769, Jerus. 332, 1100, M.A. 1748.   *stode in þe stede*, Jerus. 223, Parl. 21.

stod on an hie stede, Alex. B 114.

O.E.Pr., E.M.E., Laȝ., Orm.   *stode/stoden stille*, Chev. 147, Mum 226, etc., P.Pl. A xii, 61, Troy 2500, W. of P. 2263, etc.

stode astonyed and stared, R.R. ii, 8, Mum 351.   *all astonyt þai stode*, Troy 9488, 11806.

E.M.E.   *stonstill seten*, Gaw. 242.

a store and a styf stede, W. Alex. 745.   *sa store and stithe*, W. Alex. 2050.   *a store man and a stoute, full stithe*, Troy 2886.

a stronge man in stoure and steurnest in fight, Troy 3654.

stoute is he stedefast and stille of his herte, Alex. B 940.

strute and strife, W. & W. 265 (see N.E.D. for early Mn.E. examples).

E.M.E.   *thei striked a strake*, R.R. iv, 80.   *he stryketh a stroke*, Chev. 333. *stifly strike a stroke*, Gaw. 287.   *strike one stroke*, W. & W. 107, 127, 195.

stronge and stalworth, Mum 965.

suffer cowþe syt, Pat. 5.

suffre sorwes, P.Pl. B xx, 46, W. of P. 566, etc. *suffert moche sorow,* Troy
3521.

þat bysulpeȝ manneȝ saule, Pur. 575. *sulped in sawle,* Pur. 1130. *sulp no
more penne in synne þy saule,* Pur. 1135. *sulped in synne,* Pur. 550.

summons he his segges, Sc.F. 128. *hee summoned his seeges,* Sc.F. 204.

to summon the shire, Sc.F. 215.

til þe sunne was neiȝh set, W. of P. 1027.

þe swanne swymmeth, Chev. 362. *swymmen þey swannes,* Chev. 198, 350.

he swenges and swayues, Pat. 253.

sweuene and slepe, Mum 1288.

Orm. *swynke(n) ne swete(n),* P.Pl. A vii, 121, C vi, 57, Pierce 622. *swynken
and sweten,* P.Pl. A vii, 28. **Laȝ.** *swet and/oþur swink,* Alex. B 310,
Cr. King 66. Cp. C.M. 1047, etc.

swingis out his swerde, W. Alex. 806. *he swingis out with a swerd and
swappis him to dethe,* W. Alex. 957. *swinging (out) of swords,* Sc.F.
327, Troy 9668. *with . . . swinge of . . . sworde swappit,* Troy
1271, etc. (6 times). *þe swynge of þe swerde,* M.A. 3676, 4223. *swange
out . . . sword(ys),* Troy 10390, 10430. *þe swerd swiftili swenged,*
W. of P. 3444.

with a swerde swiftly he swappes hym thorowe, M.A. 2981. *with his swerde
swapped of his hed,* W. of P. 3609. *swyftly with swerdes, they swappene
there-after,* M.A. 1464. **Laȝ.** *swyftly with a swerde he swapped of
his hede,* Parl. 551. *thrugh swap of his sword swaltyn belyue,* Troy 5741.
E.M.E. *with a swap of his swerde he swelt in the place,* Troy 7769.
swappede owtte with a swerde, M.A. 1795. *swappon vs with swerdes,*
Troy 9561. *with swappis of her swordes,* Troy 10905. *swappit at
hym swithe a swerd,* Troy 5936. *sweppeȝ in with the swerde,* M.A. 1129.
swappit out his sword swange at þe kyng, Troy 13590.

swouny other swelte, P.Pl. C vii, 129. *swonyng & salt,* Troy 5753. *than
sweltes . . . and in swoune fallis,* M.A. 3969. *cho swounes . . . in a
swounyng, swelte as cho walde,* M.A. 715–16. *swonit in swyne as ho
swelt wold,* Troy 8046. *in a swone & a swogh as he swelt wold,* Troy
8705. *swouned and swelted for sorwe,* P.Pl. B xx, 104. *swoned for
sorwe and swelt,* W. of P. 1494. *swelt for sorwe and swoned,* W. of P.
4268.

take a taste, Alex. B 357.

taken of you tribut, Alex. B 710. *þare tuke he tribute,* W. Alex. 1044.

E.M.E. *þe taile and þe toppe,* M.A. 801. *top ouer tail,* W. of P. 2776.

tary a lytel tyme, Pat. 59. *tarying ouer tyme,* Troy 4596. *wiþoute tariginge
of time,* Alex. B 240.

the taxe and þe trebutte, M.A. 2344. *trebute and/ne taxe,* M.A. 2363, 2350,
2611.

teches and tokenes, Pur. 1049.

I will techen þe þe trewpe, Pierce 794. *to techen me trewli,* Pierce 349.

I schulde tee to þys toun, Pat. 416.

telded vp a tabil, Gaw. 884.

teldis, templis and touris, W. Alex. 552.

E.M.E., Laȝ. *telle a tale,* Jerus. 355, 374, M.A. 16, Mum 773, 1490, Parl.
326, 560, Troy 4295, etc., W. & W. 31, 247. *þan sall I tell ȝou my tale,*
W. Alex. 2145. *telleth the lord a tale,* P.Pl. C xiv, 88. *telle no tales,*
Mum 778. *many tales ȝe tellen,* P.Pl. B x, 374. *heo tolde him a tale,*

P.Pl. A iii, 46. (*whan þis*) *tale was tolde*, Alex. A 605, 997, R.R. iv, 39, W. of P. 1373, 3877, W. Alex. 190. *told was the tale*, Jerus. 1151, Troy 12667. *a tale were ytolde*, R.R. iii, 332. (*tulkes*) *tolden hym þe tale*, Erk. 109.

tolde me bi tulkes, Pur. 1623.

E.M.E., Laȝ. *tellen tidingȝ*, Mum 1389. *told* (*them*) *tydynges*, Alex. A 469, 560, D.L. 391, P.Pl. B xix, 338, W. of P. 2009, etc. (*whanne*) *þe tiding was* (*per*) *told*, Mum 1400, Troy 3254, etc., W. of P. 1478, 2112, etc. *þat þus tipinge tolde*, Alex. B 1077.

P.M. *telle couþ no tonge*, Jerus. 1270. *that no tung might hom telle*, Troy 297. *no tong miȝt telle treuli þe sope*, W. of P. 4558, 4891. *miȝt no tonge telle*, W. of P. 4876. *ne tonge* (*mai*) *telle*, W. of P. 4671, 4910, 5332, 5354. **E.M.E.** *telle . . . with tonge*, Gaw. 31, P.Pl. A xii, 24, B v, 408. *wyth tunge telles*, M.A. 1891.

telle with trawþe, Gaw. 1057. *telle . . . the trewþe*, Pierce 238, Rejoinder of Jacke Upland, p. 43. Sc.F. 193, 354, 389, Troy 1008, etc., W. of P. 5486. *to telle trouthe*, Mum 1271, R.R. ii, 77. *trouthe to telle*, R.R. ii, 41. *þe truth for to telle*, Troy 51, 106, W. of P. 5022. *who-soe truth telleth*, Sc.F. 389.

trewely to telle, P.Pl. A ii, 211. (*who soe*) *truly telleth*, Sc.F. 184, Mum 376. *telle truly*, Gaw. 380, 406, Troy 4080, W. of P. 4245, 5086. *tellest me treuly*, W. of P. 970. *told here treuli al þe sope*, W. of P. 4913, etc. *told here þanne as tit treweli al þe sope*, W. of P. 415. *told he tyt . . . treuli þe sope*, W. of P. 5091. *telle me tiȝtly truly þe sope*, W. of P. 285. *told þei hire tiȝtly al þe trewe sope*, W. of P. 1361. *titli him told al þe trewe sope*, W. of P. 4868. *trewly as tyt he told him þe sope*, W. of P. 292. *I shall tell you full tyte*, Troy 773. *as I shall tell full tite when the tyme askes*, Troy 11622. *as I shall tell you full tite and tary not long*, Troy 12437. *I wol ȝow telle tiȝtly*, W. of P. 2029. *I shall telle the as tite*, P.Pl. B xvi, 61. *I shalle titly ȝow telle*, Parl. 613. *telle me tit*, Jerus. 93, 185. *tell me tidly*, Alex. A 640, etc.

temples þer-inne tulten to þe eorþe, Jos. 100.

in temple and in town (*tour*), Jerus. 1284.

faire tempren his tounge, Alex. B 572.

tendeþ now þis tale, Alex. B 190. *when we tenden any tale*, Alex. B 469. *tale tende we non*, Alex. B 365. *tende treuly my tale*, Mum 996.

tend ye tytely (*to me*), Alex. A 7.

tene for to tell, Sc. Proph. ii, 56. Cp. *tore to tell*.

in tene and in trauaile, P.Pl. A x, 141.

I am in-tent ȝou to telle, Gaw. 624.

Cp. **E.M.E.** *so thester and so thick*, W. Alex. 4173.

he hym thonked þroly, Gaw. 939. *þonket hom þroly*, Troy 2152, 12724. *for to þonk him þroli*, W. of P. 3664. *þroli þonked*, W. of P. 5154.

þrow forth my þro, Pat. 8.

the throstills full throly (*they*) *threpen*, Parl. 14, W. & W. 37. *they threpide wyth the throstilles*, M.A. 930.

O. & N. *þe þrusch and þe þrustele*, W. of P. 819.

hit tydde on a tyme, Jerus. 25. *it bitide þat time*, W. of P. 7. *hit bi-tydde sum tyme*, Pat. 61.

tyffen he(*r*) *takles*, Gaw. 1129.

tild vp . . . tentis, W. Alex. 3860, 4140, Troy 1088. *tild downe ouer tents*, Sc.F. 253. *our tents downe we tilden*, Sc.F. 91.

þat ay wakes and waytes, Pat. 130.
wake or wynke, Parl. 482.
al wakened his wit, Pur. 1422. *awecchen my wit*, Alex. B 96.
wakened his wrath, Pur. 1166.
to wayte on þat won, Pat. 436.
wayue up a window, W. Alex. 945, Gaw. 1743, P.Pl. B v, 611, Pur. 453,
    Troy 676, W. of P. 2978.
þat euer wayued a wynde, Pat. 454.
walkynge in the way, P.Pl. B xviii, 114. *if I walke out of the wey*, R.R. iii, 6.
þou walkis of þe weye, Mum 697.
walk in the world, Jos. 44. *walken fourth in þe worlde*, Mum 386.
walketh and wandreth, P.Pl. B ix, 54.
walwiþ and wyndiþ and waltreþ aboute, Jerus. 735.
E.M.E., Orm. *wandreth and wa/wo*, W. Alex. 528, Troy 11191, 11514.
    wandrynge and woo, D.L. 453, Parl. 257. *wondering and woe*, D.L.
    250, 441. Cp. *forwandreþ in wo*, W. of P. 739.
wandreth he wroghte, M.A. 3157, 3524.
wantoun and wylde, P.Pl. A x, 57.
he waryeþ and wepeþ, Pierce 615.
warpe of hys wedeȝ, M.A. 901. *wedes he warp on hymseluen*, Gaw. 2025.
O.E.P., E.M.E., O. & N. *warpe . . . wordes*, W. Alex. 243, 709, Erk. 321,
    329, Gaw. 224, 1423, Jerus. 779, M.A. 9, 150, Pat. 356, P.Pl. A iv, 142,
    x, 33, B v, 87, 367, Pur. 152, 213, Troy 360, etc. (30 times), Twa
    Mariit Wemen 150.
when þay had waschen worþyly þay wenten to sete, Gaw. 72. *þe wyȝe wesche
    at his wylle, and went to his mete*, Gaw. 887. Cp. Rom.
wasshen or wyped, P.Pl. B xiii, 460. *wesche . . . and wyped*, P.Pl. B xvi,
    228. *wassheth and wypeth*, P.Pl. C x, 250. *thei weshen and wypeden*,
    P.Pl. B xiii, 28. *they wesshen and wyped hym*, P.Pl. B ii, 220.
waschen woundes, Jerus. 847.
wasshen it and wryngen it, P.Pl. B xiv, 18.
be wast and be wildernes, W. Alex. 487. *a wilsom wast and wild*, W. Alex.
    4076, 5565.
be waldis and be wastis, W. Alex. 3792.
wasteth away, D.L. 9.
E.M.E. *water and wyn*, Jerus. 283. *wyn ne water;* Jerus. 1070. *with wyn
    and with watur*, P.Pl. A x, 4.
O.E.Pr., Laȝ. *wax soo and wane*, W. Alex. 4772. *wex and wanyed*, P.Pl. B
    xv. 3. *wanyeth and wexeth*, P.Pl. B viii, 39. *weyne ne waxe*, M.A.
    161.
wax/wex wode, Pur. 204, W. of P. 1974, W. & W. 373.
with weches and warlaws, M.A. 613.
wedde(d) a . . . wyf, Alex. A 19, P.Pl. A iii, 116, xi, 105, Pur. 69, Troy
    635, etc., W. of P. 2012. **O.E.Pr.** *wedd hire to wyfe*, W. Alex. 3452.
O.E.Pr. *þy wedded wyf*, P.Pl. A ii, 123, Pur. 330. *wedded þat wight*,
    Alex. A 225.
Orm. *wedded no wommon*, P.Pl. A viii, 74. *wedde a woman*, P.Pl. A iii,
    113, etc.
wede . . . with worship, Troy 610, 766. *weddit with worship*, Alex. A 225,
    Troy 1379.
þe weder of þe worlde, Gaw. 504.

in wedes and in wysshynges, P.Pl. B ii, 90.
welcometh . . . winlye, D.L. 80.
.*to weld to his wife*, Alex. A 206.
to weld alle þe worchip, Troy 9767, W. of P. 4000.   *my wele and my worschup*
ȝe weldeþ, Jerus. 1011.
welde þis worlde, Pat. 16.
noo wele ne welthe, M.A. 653.
wele and . . . worschip, Gaw. 2432, Jerus, 1011, M.A. 401, 3963, Parl. 175,
    Pur. 651, Troy 3356.   *worchip and wele*, Troy 13967, W. of P. 1325,
    etc. (8 times).
O.E.P., E.M.E.   *wele and/or woo*, Cr. King 112, Gaw. 2134, M.A. 4100,
    R.R. iii, 298, W. Alex. 4621.
O.E.Pr., E.M.E., P.M.   *al the wele in/of the worlde*, Gaw. 1270, Parl. 637,
    W. & W. 268.   *worldliche wele*, Alex. B 32, Pierce 20, 784.
þe welpe of þe world, M.A. 541, 2684, P.Pl. A viii, 172, B x, 24, C xiii, 156,
    W. of P. 3312, 4132, 4758.   *the world full of welth*, D.L. 45.   *þe welthe
    of þe werde*, W. Alex. 5317.
welpe aftur wo, Alex. B 919.
al welwed and wasted, Pat. 475.
weme or wounde, Jerus. 876.
E.M.E.   *wende(n) (on) . . . way*, Beckett 9, 11, D.L. 308, Gaw. 1028,
    Jos. 313, M.A. 2500, Mum 776, Pur. 777, P.Pl. C, xiv, 34, 52, W. of P.
    5165, 5457, W. & W. 104, 460.   *wende of þe waye*, Mum 665,
    735.   *on his wey they wende*, Parl. 668.   *what wey I wende*, P.Pl. C v,
    53.   *went . . . on . . . way*, W. Alex. 428, Gaw. 1557, 2074, P.Pl.
    A Pro. 48, xii, 56, B x, 164, xvii, 47, W. of P. 104, etc.   *thei ne wendeth
    the wey*, P.Pl. C xviii, 190.   *wende by the wey*, P.Pl. C xiv, 42.   *wente
    be þe waie*, Pierce, 420.
wende away, Jerus. 1018, W. Alex. 4066.   *wente(n) . . . away*, Jerus. 1333,
    M.A. 3888.   *awei wendes*, Jos. 546.
wend to (that) warr, Sc.F. 121, W. of P. 3223.
to wende to the watur, Troy 12453.   *they wende ouer the watyre*, M.A. 1299.
    to wende our the wane watter(ys), Beckett 205, 242.
wend at . . . wyll, Alex. A 153, Sc.F. 70.   *wendeȝ at his wylle*, Pat. 339.
wende of þis world, W. of P. 1555, 5537.   *went . . . of this worlde*, Sc.F.
    43, W. of P. 4804.
Laȝ.   *went to the wode*, Parl. 3.   *went bi a wode*, P.Pl. A ix, 54.
wepte . . . water, Jos. 647, P.Pl. A v, 254, B xiv, 324, xvi, 116, C vii, 327.
    water . . . weppit, Troy 8835, etc. (9 times).   *to weope watur*, P.Pl. A
    v, 44, Mum 288.
wepe and weile, P.Pl. A v, 94.   *wepte and weyled*, P.Pl. B xiv, 332, W. of P.
    1515.   *wepyng and weylying*, P.Pl. A v, 261, C vi, 108.   *weping and
    waile*, Troy 9611, etc. (5 times).   *to wailen and to wepyn*, Reply of
    Fr. Daw Thopias, p. 39.   *wailyng and weping*, Troy 3273, 3563.
he wepis on þam for wa, W. Alex. 3153.   *wepyþ for wo*, Jerus. 1201, W. of P.
    1509.   *alle wepyd for woo*, Erk. 310.   *wepte I for wo*, P.Pl. B xi, 3,
    C xii, 166.   *wepande for woo*, M.A. 3561, W. of P. 5424.   *weping and
    wringinge for wo*, W. of P. 5452.   *wepyng and wo*, Jerus. 247, Troy
    499, etc. (9 times), W. of P. 4415.   *þe wo. and þe weping*, W. of P. 378.
E.M.E.   *wepe and wrynge . . . handys*, M.A. 3155, 4287, P.Pl. A ii, 212.
O.E.P. & Pr.   *alle þat weppen myȝt welde*, Pur. 835.   *weppnes to welde*,
    Gaw. 270.

E.M.E. *hit is my wede þat þou were჻,* Gaw. 2358.

werre and/in wo, Alex. A 3, P.Pl. B xviii, 412, W. of P. 2625, 4582.

werre and wrake, Gaw. 16.

a litil wetinge of watur, Alex. B 1033.

La჻. *(I wepte water warm &·) wette my wonges,* Jos. 647. Cp. Rh.A. 1.
alle his wongys were wete for weping of teres, Troy 1521.

ony wikkede werk, Alex. B 378, 387.

wyche჻ and walkyries, Pur. 1577.

wyde as the worlde, Alex. A 1022, P.Pl. B xix, 36, 330.

widwes and widwers, P.Pl. B ix, 174.

wy/wei჻ in/of the werlde, Alex. A 787, Beckett, 95, 217, 234, M.A. 891, etc.
(4 times), Parl. 298, P.Pl. B xvii, 98, Sc.F. 248, Troy 4191, 11706,
W. of P. 1077, 4821, W. & W. 120, 249, 331. *wight in/of þe world,*
Alex. A, 401, 1248, Mum 1727, P.Pl. A x, 71, C xvi, 166, Sc.F. 81,
W. of P. 786, 1797.

wy჻e welcum, Gaw. 814. *þe welcomest wy჻e,* Gaw. 938. *welcum þis ilk wy჻,*
Gaw. 819.

þe wy჻e and his wyf, Pur. 658. *þy wyf and þy wy჻e჻,* Pur. 899.

þe wy჻e þat al wro჻t, Pur. 280. *þe wy჻ that wro჻t alle þinges,* Pur. 5. *þat
wy჻e I worchyþ I wysse þat wro჻t alle þynges,* Pat. 206.

ne so wight in his werkes, Troy 9041.

þe wy჻test and þe worþyest, Gaw. 261. *worthy and wight,* W. Alex. 765.

(with the) wyles of a woman, Parl. 315, Troy 668. *þur჻ wyles of wymmen,*
Gaw. 2415.

wiles and wrenkis, W. Alex. 4365.

thoru the wyles and wronge, R.R. i, 3.

O.E.Pr. *þey wiln and þei wolden,* Pierce 665. *wilne and wolde,* P.Pl. B
xiv, 173, xv, 24. *wilned and wolde,* P.Pl. B xv, 546. *wilnen and wolde,*
P.Pl. C iv, 387. *wilnode and wolde,* P.Pl. C xix, 261.

thorw wyn and thorw women, P.Pl. B i, 32. *bothe women and wyn,* P.Pl. C
xii, 111.

O.E.Pr., E.M.E., La჻. *þe wynde and þe weder,* Pur. 444, 847, Mum 1728,
Troy 2841, W. of P. 5216. *wyndes ne wederes,* P.Pl. C xiii, 189. *þe
wedour and þe wynd,* Jerus. 59, 62, Mum 1024. *wederes and wyndes,*
P.Pl. B. xv, 356.

E.M.E. *wyndes and watres,* P.Pl. A ix, 36. *the wint and the watur,* P.Pl. A
ix, 26, A x, iv. *no wawe of þe wind, no watur of þe rainus,* Alex. B 436.
he may win it in warre, Sc.F. 108. *yet wold it neuer be woone in warr,* Sc.F. 80.
who so wele schal wyn, W. & W. 390.

winne his wille, Jos. 358. *to wynne to my wil,* P.Pl. C vii, 190.

La჻., Orm. *wyn/wynnys . . . wirchipe,* Gaw. 984, M.A. 965, 2444, Pur.
1120, P.Pl. B iii, 348, Troy 810, 9741, W. of P. 3161, 3343, 3371, etc.
won wirschip, W. Alex. 5586, M.A. 3022, Troy 725. *we have wonen in
were þe worchip,* Troy 12199. *wonyn hit in wer, with worship,* Troy
12208. *wynne hym wyth worchyp,* Pur. 1616. *worchip . . . winne(s),*
W. of P. 618, 3808. *worship to win,* Troy 655, etc. (20 times).
wirschip . . . won, W. Alex. 616, etc. (5 times), M.A. 1805, 3342, 3769,
Sc.F. 16, 268 Troy 1488, 3972, 7067.

how thay wirchipe and welthe wanne, Parl. 252.

to winne the world, Alex. B 80, W. of P. 735, 2362, 3099. *he wan al the world,*
Troy 315. *alle the worlde wanne,* Parl. 332. *this world to wynne,*
Parl. 391.

wirchipe and welthe, M.A. 4331, Parl. 252.

La3. *worship and wyn*, Troy 3430, 13346.

E.M.E. *worschipe of wor(l)d*, Alex. B 25. *wirchipe of . . . world*, Parl. 519, Pierce 499, 549, P.Pl. A i, 8. *werldliche worshype*, Pierce 371.

O.E.Pr., **E.M.E.**, **La3.**, **Orm.** *he is wise, pat is war*, Jerus. 1103. *ware and wise*, Mum 1716, M.A. 19. Cp. *wiste . . . war*.

Cp. **O.E.Pr.** *wyse and worthy*, Parl. 395. *wyseste and worthyeste and wyghteste*, M.A. 290. *worthy and wise*, D.L. 125.

wise in his werkes, Troy 3937. *wise in sic werk*, T.M. Wemen 462.

La3. *that weysse was and wyghte*, M.A. 2514.

O.E.P. & Pr., **E.M.E.** *wise in/of his words*, Mum 265, Sc.F. 114, Troy 3807. *swiche wordus of wise*, Alex. B 461.

wise in/of this worlde, P.Pl. B xviii, 232, Troy 9202, 9211.

wissen . . . the . . . wey, P.Pl. A vi, 24, 45, vii 6, Mum 1239.

O. & N. *he wiste, he was war*, W. of P. 1769. *war and wiste*, W. of P. 3594, 3635.

O.E.Pr. *wisshen and willen/wylnen*, P.Pl. B xvii, 346, C xx, 328.

in his wit and ne in his wille, Parl. 573, Mum 231. **Orm.** *þe wit and þe wil*, Alex. B 924, W. & W. 5. *wil ne . . . wit*, P.Pl. C vii, 167.

to witt their wills, Sc.F. 75.

E.M.E. *witte and . . . wisdome*, W. Alex. 898, M.A. 2600, P.Pl. B x, 450, xii, 291, xv, 30, xx, 132, Sc.F. 287. *tourne her witte to wisdome*, P.Pl. B xix, 447. *wisdom and wit*, Alex. B 211, W. Alex. 4240, Cr. King 104, Mum 249, P.Pl. A iv, 62, 68, vii, 47, A xi, 17, B ii, 133, xi, 409, Parl. 601.

E.M.E., **La3.** *witty and wyse*, Mum 213, P.Pl. B xiv, 167, Troy 1463.

O.E.P. *wise . . . and witty*, Alex. B 1121, P.Pl. C x, 51.

wise . . . of wit, Alex. A 1151, Troy 591, 11587. **O.E.P.** *wyseste . . . in/of witt*, Parl. 603, 610.

wiles and wit, P.Pl. C v, 77, Troy 13118, 13127, 13251. *witty and wyly*, Cr. King 81.

witty and wild, Troy 6092.

Orm. *wit wyterly*, Pat. 330.

wyues and widowes, P.Pl. A iii, 120, C vii, 143, ix, 12, Troy 8682. *wyues and wenches*, Pur. 1250. *wyfe, wedowe or wenche*, W. & W. 280. *wedous and wenches and wyues*, W. Alex. 1558.

al the wo of this world, P.Pl. A v, 208, B xiii, 207, xix, 64.

wode of his wit, Troy 5257, etc. (7 times), W. of P. 1771, 2772, etc.

wode in his wrathe, Troy 5924.

O.E.Pr. *wodes and wastes*, D.L. 42, W. of P. 2131. **E.M.E.** *the wodes and þe waters*, Mum 891. **La3.** *wodes and wildernesse*, W. of P. 2605.

3e wonen in þat won, Alex. B 1103. *to wone any quyle in þis won*, Gaw. 257. *he my3te not wonne in the wones*, R.R. iii, 220.

O.E.P. & Pr. *þei were woned in þis word*, Alex. B 551, 557. *wonyed in þe worlde*, Pur. 252, 431. *he so woneth in þis world*, Alex. B 1060. *we woneth in this world*, P.Pl. A viii, 111.

he wonded no wope, Pur. 885. *for wope þat þou ne wonde*, Gaw. 488. Cp. Rh.A. 1 (Pearl 153).

al þe wonder of þe worlde, Gaw. 238.

he wondrid in his wittis, R.R. iii, 216.

O.E.P. & Pr., **E.M.E.**, **Orm.**, **P.M.** *word and/or werk*, Pierce 676, P.Pl. A vii, 214, B v, 372, xiii, 140, xv, 470, Rejoinder of Jacke Upland, p. 45 .

werk(es) and . . . word(es), Mum 357, 548, P.Pl. A v, 69, xi, 261, 267,
B ii, 89, xiii, 145, 312, xiv, 14, C vii, 99, etc., R.R. ii, 68.
O.E.P., Orm. *wordes and wittes*, P.Pl. C 258.
E.M.E. *by my worde ne by my wille*, Mum 468.
O.E.Pr., E.M.E., La3., Orm. *worke such a work*, Mum 1517. *worke þat (y)
wro3t*, Jerus. 178, W. of P. 456, etc. *werkes to wirche/worche*, Alex. B
387, 837, P.Pl. A viii, 185, x, 126. *werk that thei worchen*, P.Pl. A x, 65.
worche it in werke, P.Pl. B x, 252.
O.E.Pr., E.M.E., La3. *worke/worche . . . will*, Alex. A 166, Alex. B 427,
D.L. 313, M.A. 692, P.Pl. A iii, 29, xi, 101, B i, 82, W. of P. 307, etc.
(10 times). *your will for to wirke*, Troy 608, etc.
worche and wynne, P.Pl. B ix, 108.
worche bi (my) wytte, Gaw. 2096, P.Pl. B iii, 7, W. Alex. 2521. *worche by
þy witt*, Jerus. 980. *wyrke aftyre the wytte*, M.A. 149.
wirke now thi wirchipe, M.A. 2187. *wirche him al þe worchip*, W. of P. 5160.
wrou3t . . . worchepe, W. of P. 497, 4040. *worchen al worschipe*,
Alex. B 680.
E.M.E. *werke wo*, Jerus. 294, W. Alex. 2721. *wrought wo*, Troy 9494,
W. of P. 2337, 3589, etc., M.A. 4024.
O.E.Pr. *werke wonderys*, Beckett 108. **E.M.E.** *wro3t wondres*, Jerus. 120,
204, 786, Troy 308.
wirche me no wrong, W. of P. 1173. *þe wronge (þat þey) wro3te*, Jerus. 1234,
Mum 1150, Troy 1735, W. of P. 1545. *the wronge . . . wroghte*,
Parl. 648, R.R. iii, 246.
I ne wot in worlde, Gaw. 1053, Troy 12903, W. of P. 1545.
for wothe, ne wele, ne wrathe, Erk. 233.
woundis full wete, Troy 10087. **E.M.E.** *wyde woundes and wete*, Troy 1329.
O.E.Pr., La3., Orm. *write writtis*, Mum 25. R.R. iv, 26. *to writen him a
writte*, R.R. Pro. 31. *writen is in holi wriht*, Alex. B 139.
his wordes ben wryten, P.Pl. i, 198.
þei wrouhten a wrytte, Alex. B 1136.
wrou3t . . . the/this world, Pierce 798, R.R. iii, 239. **E.M.E., Orm.** *þat
alle þe werlde wrou3te*, Pierce 795.
that wrou3te ony wrake, R.R. i, 43.
wrothe as the wynde, R.R. iii, 153, Troy 13091. *wex wroth as wynde*, Gaw.
319, Pat. 410. *þou art waxen so wroth*, Pat. 497. *waxe I wrothe*,
Mum 841. *þei willn wexen pure wroþ*, Pierce 525. *so wroth . . . to
waxe*, Pat. 491.

(*b*) The Rhyming Romances of the Fourteenth Century
[Rom.].

A study of the alliterative phrases found in the non-alliterative
romances is important for the purposes of comparison. Alliterative
tags are not the exclusive property of alliterative poets, as our study
has already shown. The writers of romance, no less than the early
Middle English authors, had through such poems as *Havelock* and
Horn inherited many traditional alliterative phrases, though it is
not unlikely that the later romance writers often borrowed allite-

rative phrases from the works of the Alliterative Revival. Of the sixty-three rhymed romances here examined, twenty alone antedate the Alliterative Revival, that is to say, were written before 1350, so that the possibility of borrowing in this matter is extremely likely. A list of the romances from which the alliterative phrases have been gathered is given, together with the various editions used ; the abbreviations of the titles in the text are self-explanatory.

NOTE.—PFMS—*The Percy Folio MS.* ; Ritson's, Robson's and Weber's *Metrical Romances* are referred to as *Ritson, Robson, Weber.*

Alisaunder, King—Weber 1.3.
Amadace, Sir—Weber 3.241.
Amis and Amiloun—Weber 2.367.
Arthur—E.E.T.S. 2.
Arthur's Death—PFMS 1.501.
Arthur, Legend of King—PFMS 1.497.
Athelston—E. Stud. 13.331.
Avowynge of Arthur, The—Robson.
Beues of Hamtoun, Sir—E.E.T.S., E.S. 46, 48, 65.
Carle of Carlile, The—PFMS 3.275.
Chronicle of England—Ritson 2.270.
Cleges, Sir—Weber 1.331.
Degare, Sir—PFMS 3.16.
Degrevant, Sir—Thornton Rom. 177.
Eglamour, Sir—Thornton Rom. 88.
Emare—Ritson 2.183.
Erle of Tolous, The—Ritson 3.105.
Firumbras, Sir—E.E.T.S., E.S. 34.
Florence of Rome, Le Bone—Ritson 3.46.
Floris and Blancheflour—Taylor, Oxf.
Gamelyn, The Tale of—Skeat, Oxf.
Green Knight, The—PFMS 2.56.
Guy and Amorant—PFMS 2.136.
Guy and Colebrande—PFMS 2.527.
Guy and Phillis—PFMS 2.201.
Guy of Warwick—E.E.T.S., E.S. 25, 26.
Havelock—Sisam, Oxf.
Horn, King—Hall, Oxf.
Horn Childe and Maiden Rimenhilde—Hall, Oxf.
Ipomydon—Weber 2.279.
Isumbras, Sir—Thornton Rom. 88.
Kyng of Tars, The—Ritson 2.156.

Knight of Curtasy, The—Ritson 3.172.
Lai Le Freine—Weber 1.357.
Lambewell, Sir—PFMS 1.144.
Lamwell, Sir—PFMS 1.522.
Landeval, Sir—A.J. Phil. 10.1.
Laud Troy Book—E.E.T.S. 121–2.
Launcelot du Lake, Sir—PFMS 1.84.
Launfal—Ritson 2.1.
Libeaus Disconus—Ritson 2.1.
Marriage of Gawayne—PFMS 1.105.
Morte Arthur, Le—E.E.T.S., E.S. 88.
Octovian—Weber 3.157.
Octovian, The Emperor—Percy Soc. 1844.
Orfeo, Sir—Ritson 2.248.
Otuel—E.E.T.S., E.S. 39.
Perceval of Galles, Sir—Thornton 1.
Richard Coer de Lion—Weber 2.1.
Rouland and Vernagu — E.E.T.S., E.S. 39.
Rowlande and Sir Ottuell—E.E.T.S., E.S. 35.
Sege of Melayne, The — E.E.T.S., E.S. 35.
Sege of Troy—E.E.T.S. 172.
Seuyn Sages, The—Weber 3.1.
Song of Roland, The—E.E.T.S., E.S. 35.
Sowdane of Babylone, The—E.E.T.S., E.S. 38.
Squire of Lowe Degre, The—Ritson 3.145.
Torrent of Portyngale — E.E.T.S., E.S. 51.
Triamour, Sir—PFMS 2.78.
Tristram, Sir—S.T.S. 1886.
Turke and Gowin, The—PFMS 1.88.
Ywaine and Gawain—Ritson 1.1.

The total number of phrases found in these works is 820 in 138,000 lines of poetry, as compared with 1415 phrases in roughly 50,000 lines of alliterative poetry.   On the other hand, the number of instances of phrases in the former group is 3900, compared with 4250 in the latter.   This suggests that alliterative phrases were extremely popular among the rhyming romance writers, but that the range was much narrower than in the case of the western poets. This is borne out by a detailed comparison of such works as *Sir Gawayn and the Green Knight* and *Le Morte Arthure*.   In the former poem the presence of the alliterative phrases is more difficult to detect because they are woven into the very texture of the work, whereas in *Le Morte Arthure*, which is typical of the rhyming romances, the alliterative phrases are frequently reduced to mere tags introduced as tautological expressions for their own sake. Of such are : *bone and blood, faire and fre, game and gle, londs and ledes, rest and ro, stiff and stronge,* etc.

Of the romance-phrases, fifty-seven are found in Old English poetry (twenty-eight in the *heroic* and forty-one in the *religious*) and eighty-one in Old English prose (forty-four in the homiletic, fifty-six in the *Alfredian* and eighteen in the *legal*).   Thirty-two of these phrases are common to Old English poetry and prose, so that fifteen alone are exclusively poetic in Old English.   One of the most interesting of these is *be doun and den* (Rich. 6636), instead of the more usual *doun and dale ;* this is the genuinely Old English formula, but the romance in question is an early one, so that this example is likely to be a survival.   Two other phrases of special interest are *egge and ord* (*Lib. Dis.*), and *bi stretes and bi stye* (*Emare* 196, 543), the only examples of the phrases in the romances.   Both these expressions survived in Laʒamon's *Brut*, but neither of them was a common Middle English alliterative phrase.   The remaining phrases inherited from Old English are either of the commonplace kind, such as *lede a life* or the stock expressions beloved by the romance writers—*bone and blood, flesh and felle, game and gle, life and londes, ledes and londes, swerd and shelde, wele and wo.*   The conclusion is that the writers of rhymed romance were in direct contact with the main streams of tradition, but that the more exclusive heritage received by the alliterative poets was not shared by the rhyming poets.

One hundred and sixty-two of the phrases are found also in the early Middle English alliterative works, but they are of no special interest in themselves, being largely confined to such as *change chere, body and bones, treye and tene*.   *Ord and ende* is fairly common, and *rest and ro*—a phrase not popular among the alliterative poets, —is of frequent occurrence. As a whole, however, the group is uninteresting, and contains no phrase that would not be expected in any important fourteenth text.

Eighty-seven of the phrases are found in Laȝamon's *Brut*, but for the most part they are not the typically " Laȝamon " phrases, with their heroic associations. They are rather the ordinary phrases of the early Middle English period. A few expressions, however, call for attention : *egge and orde* (one occurrence only), *hete and hongyr* (*Rich.* 1331), and *mode and mayne*, a variant of the more usual *might and mayne*, are significant survivals, though the poems concerned are not late Middle English. Similarly, no specifically " Orm " phrases survive, which is not surprising, seeing that many of the phrases which Orm coined never gained popularity, even with religious writers.

Four hundred and twenty-five of the romance phrases occur also in the poems of the Alliterative Revival. On close examination, it will be seen that most of these are made up of the ordinary commonplace alliterative phrases, which might be found in almost any fourteenth century text, and which have already been discussed. A few are not of this type, but the possibility of borrowing from alliterative poetry need not be ruled out in some cases. Thus, *blo and blac* (*Laud Troy Bk.*), *blode beronnen* (*Laud Troy Bk.*), *drechynge and dremyng* (*The Song of Roland*), *to romy and rowte* (*Avowynge*), *rope and rare* (*Ywaine*) (O.E. *hrōpan and rārian*), are undoubtedly good examples of traditional phrases, surviving in rhymed works, though possibly through the medium of *alliterative* poetry.

Such examples are, however, very rare, and it cannot be too strongly emphasised that the more unusual phrases found in alliterative poetry are absent here ; of such are *harme and hethyng*, *lenge in lisse*, *lenge in londe*, *liue in lisse*, *mesure and meþe*, *smorther and smoke*.

O.E.Pr. *assen and oxen*, Alis. 3407.
A. *backe and bone(s)*, Degare 376, Laud 9058, Sowdane of Babylone 508, 1946, Triam. 985, 1409.
E.M.E., A. *bak and brest(es)*, Laud 6539, 7712, Ywaine 3541, 3611. *his bakke to-braste*, Ipom. 818. *his brakke braste*, Row. & Ot. 834. *brusten bak*, Row. & Ot. 1409.
bake bred, Firum. 577, Rich. 3613.
A. *bakoun and beef*, Oct. 749. *bef and bakouns*, Firum. 2696.
bay and browne, Lib. Dis. 1461.
bayne att my bidding, Carle 303. Cp. **A.** *boun at his bidding*. *att thy bidding bayne*, M. Arthur 1134, Turke 108.

E.M.E., A. *bale and blys*, Triam. 8. *all my bale thou hast turned to blisse,* Carle 418. *ther may no blys fro bale borowe*, Triam. 602.

barley bredd, Florence 2058, Ywaine 1684.

A. *barons and bachelers*, Melayne 809.

A. *barouns . . . burgeys*, Oct. 499, 500, Rich. 4130. *burgeys, baroun,* Alis. 1387, Lib. Dis. 1626.

barons and bonde, Amis. 65, 2473, Oct. 1805.

barre and bolt, Laud 6004.

beaute and bounte, M. Arthur 125, 1739.

beches, birches, Alis. 5242.

bede batelle, Melayne 1464.

beff and broth, Sages 1106.

A. *begge ne/nor borwe*, Athel. 494, Lamb. 27.

A. *to begge my bredd*, Squ. of L. Deg. 137. *to begge brede*, Amis. 1697. *to bid brede,*Amis. 1691.

A. *his bak to bend*, Torrent 2490.

O.E.P., A. *bende a bowe*, Eglam. 294. *he bent his bowe*, Laud 7735. *bende her bowes*, Laud 5545, 5799. *bendis vp bowes*, Melayne 1292. *bowes bende*, Laud 10444, 16627. *bowes bent*, Amis. 506, M. Arthur 2729, 3047, 3074, Oct. 362.

bende his browes, Firum 1954.

A. *berye a body*, Rich. 5141.

A. *bestes and byrdes*, Florence 182, Rich. 3738, Sowd. 131. *byrdus and bestis*, Torrent 2017.

A. *bete my bale*, Amad. 45, Land. 455. *bale(s) . . . bett(e)*, Isum. 764, Lib. Dis. 2088, Melayne 275, Tolous 512, Ywaine 1588, 1806, 3821. *balys bete*, Launfal 971, Oct. 989. See infra under *bote of bale*.

E.M.E., A. *to bete or bynde*, Arthur 238. *they bette and bound*, M. Arthur 13.

E.M.E. *bete þe body*, Beues 1805.

betes on the busshes, Avow. 58.

O.E.Pr., E.M.E., Laȝ., A. *bidde a bede*, Rich. 3592.

E.M.E. *bid a bone*, Firum. 3947. *bidde a boon*, Rich. 2014, 4110. *bede a bone*, Beues 2629, M. Arthur 2803. *a bone he bede*, Avow. 207.

A. *byde bale*, Melayne 1353.

bide þe batayl, Horn Childe 705, 752, etc. *bataile to abide*, Amis. 936. *in batell byde*, Florence 429.

A. *to bide on . . . bente*, Avow. 700, Melayne 1184.

A. *byde in blysse*, M. Arthur 3207. *with blis to abide*, Amis. 1896. *with blisse in borwe to bide*, Amis. 420. Cp. **Laȝ.** *ibide in burȝe*. So **A.** *abide him a buffe*, Avow. 63.

A. *birde on bough*, Land. 430, Melayne 921. *bryd on bowe*, Launfal 931.

bite and beite, Hav. 2440.

E.M.E., A. *blak and blo*, Laud 5640, 16933.

blac and brown, Hav. 1008, 2181. *broun and blake*, Amis. 2461, Hav. 2249, 2694, 2847. *blayke . . . broun*, Sages 121.

A. *blede blod*, Alis. 5863, Sages 1906, 1918. *bled (so mekil) blode,* Ywaine 3609. *the blode þat he had bledde*, Guy 4287. *his blood gan blede*, Oct. 516.

hur blee and hur blode, Triam. 906.

blenkede all his blee, Melayne 1359.

Laჳ., A. *bold bernes,* Amis. 278, 399. *bernus . . . bolde,* Degare 500, etc., Florence 884, Perc. 1524, Rol. 237.

bolde of blood, Turke 181.

bold and breme, M. Arthur 229. *breme and bolde,* Tars 835.

þe boles beyte (bulls to bait), Hav. 2330.

bonayre and benynge, Squ. of L. Deg. 357.

bone and brayn, Florence 1943.

borlich and bolde, Degare 452.

bostus and blawus, Avow. 358.

O. & N., A. *bord and bedde,* Beues 2012, Sages 279, Tolous 606.

bote þe of þi bale, Amis. 2340. *bote of alle bale,* Amad. 202. **E.M.E., A.** *bote of . . . bale,* Gam. 32, 34, Squ. of L. Deg. 112, Ywaine 3062. *boþe bote and bale,* Beues 3676. *after bale cometh bote,* Gam. 631.

wythouten bote or belde, Florence 1721.

O.E.P. & Pr., E.M.E., P.M., A. *bought . . . wiþ hys blod,* Torrent 135, Tolous 1029. *wyth . . . blod us bought,* Lib. Dis. 675, Melayne 432. *bye with blod,* Rol. 377.

E.M.E., A. *bowed and bent,* M. Arthur 3370, Triam. 809.

Cp. **E.M.E.** *bowsom and bayne,* Ywaine, 3101.

A. *boun to batayle,* Horn Childe 691. *in batelle ay full bownn,* Row. and Ot. 90. *to batayle bowne,* M. Arthur 3257, Oct. Emp. 773, 1022, Oct. 1697. *to batayle bayne,* M. Arthur 3315. *to batayle be ye bayne,* M. Arthur 3217.

A. *brag and bost,* Avow. 274, Degare 231, Florence 958.

brayed oute a brand bryჳte, Avow. 214. **A.** *braydede owte with a bryghte brande,* Melayne 326.

breke bake, Sowd. 1201, 1946. *brake . . . back and bonys,* Triam. 985. *brakes backe,* Degare 376. *bakes breake,* Launc. 39.

to brekeþ (hem) bones, Firum. 3328. **E.M.E.** *breke . . . bone(s),* Gam. 142, Guy and Am. 78, Lib. Dis. 1145, Rol. 561, 906. *the bon to-brak,* Gam. 304.

breke hys brayne, Tolous 53.

brekes and bristes, Row. and Ot. 666.

of brede, brawne, Melayne 1599.

E.M.E., A. *brennyng bryჳte,* Amad. 225, Squ. of L. Deg. 829, Lib. Dis. 1785. *brennyng fulle bryჳte,* Avow. 870. *brende bryght,* Lib. Dis. 1767. *brente bryghte,* Launfal 513. See also under *bright brondes.*

brennyng bloo, Oct. Emp. 166.

bresyd and blynde, Triam. 237.

bresyd and all tobrokyn, Florence 103.

to brew thee bale, Sages 2880. *bale(s) to brewe,* Florence 367, 939, 1211.

E.M.E., A. *bryჳte of ble,* Amad. 693, Amis. 2434, Avow. 991, Eglam. 33, 219, 933, Florence 757, 2070, Launfal 849, Lib. Dis. 281, 458, Marr. of Gaw. 4, M. Arthur 3779, 3876, Perc. 2216, Row. and Ot. 393, 521, Tars 368, Tolous 198, 333, 557.

E.M.E. *briჳt on ble,* Orfeo 455. *bryჳter of ble,* Avow. 775. *brighteste of ble,* M. Arthur 3504, Perc. 1829. *the bryghtness of hur blee,* Florence 185. *bryghtened hur blee,* Florence 1157.

O.E.P. *briჳt and bliþe,* Trist. 2970.

Cp. **E.M.E.** *bryght as blome,* Florence 686. *bright as blossome,* Lamb. 83, Tolous 330. *bryჳt as blosme on bouჳ,* Arthur 290. *bryჳt as blosme on* *brere*, Athel. 72, Lamw. 427, Land. 428, Launfal 934, Lib. Dis. 579, M. Arthur 724, 835, Oct. Emp. 41.

bryghte in bour, Alis. 3275, Launfal 629, Row. and Ot. 622. *briʒte in/on boure*, Amis. 66, etc., Firum. 2498, Guy 2674, 5372. *briʒtest in bour*, Trist. 160. *that bride so bright in bower*, Marr. of Gaw. 6. *burdes briʒte on boure*, Firum. 1336. *burde on boure briʒt*, Firum, 4272. *bryght berde yn bour*, Launfal 548. *blysful berde yn bour*, Launfal 750.

A. *bright brond*, Rol. 987. *brand/brond(es) bright*, Green Kn. 22, Guy 2893, etc., Rich. 5457, Row. and Ot. 187, 191. *bryght brondys brennyng*, Florence 98. *brondys brennyng alle bryght*, Oct. Emp. 231. *as brond þat brent*, Roul. and Vern. 145. **E.M.E.** *brond ybrent*, Lib. Dis. 1569. *brondes bright and bare*, Amis. 1347. *brondes, both bryght and broun*, Amis. 2452. *bryght and broune*, Lib. Dis. 552.

by brimes and bankes, Green Kn. 282.

A. *bring out of bale*, Lamb. 534. *broght out of bale*, Florence 2035. *out of bales broght*, Ywaine 2495, 2788. *into such bale was brought*, Green Kn. 216. *yn bale am y broght*, Tolous 621, 638. *broʒt his body on bale*, Firum. 903.

E.M.E., A. *bring to bedd*, Green Kn. 372, Guy 7085, M. Arthur 2989, Tolous 704, Triam. 39, 447, Trist. 159, 1513. *broʒt to bedde*, Guy 10065, Orfeo 93. *in bedde ibroʒt*, Firum. 2411. *to bedd broght*, Oct. Emp. 71.

to bringe out of bende, Lib. Dis. 252, Gam. 457.

O.E.Pr., E.M.E., A. *brynge . . . to blys*, Eglam. 1340, Florence 1681, Guy 10786, Ipom. 2345, Land. 535, Roul. and Vern. 165, Triam. 1717. *to his blysse bringe*, Oct. 1959. *to (heauuens) blisse (our soules) bringe*, Carle 498. *broght the fro thy blysse*, Florence 1495. *of blysse ibroghte*, M. Arthur 1093.

to bring thee out of bondes, Gam. 440.

by brynke and bonke, Laud. 9156. *bank or brynke*, Laud 4227.

broche and beiʒe, Trist. 265, 381, 3020.

broke ne bek, 11283, 12668.

bekke and broke, Laud 14943.

E.M.E., A. *burde bryght*, Avow. 140, etc. (11 times), Firum. 2072, etc., Oct. Emp. 1009, Tars 374, Tolous 843, M. Arthur 3632. See under *brighte in bour*.

A. *burgeys and bachelers*, Rich. 1258, Troy 203.

A. *buskyd in hys bedde*, M. Arthur 1808.

A. *busked . . . boun*, Amis, 279, Lib. Dis. 822, M. Arthur 2151, etc. (5 times), Melayne 774, 1369, 1569, Rol. and Ot. 1209, Trist. 144, Turke 9.

A. *buxum and bayne*, Avow. 768. See under *bowsom and bayne*.

calle and cry, Perc. 2217. *crye and calle*, 3188.

to carke and care, Squ. of L. Deg. 924.

Cp. **O.E.P.** *his care wax alle cold*, Degare 508. *care cold*, Floris & Blan. 970. **A.** *carys cold*, M. Arthur 3905.

A. *cast(e) in care*, Eglam. 118, 150, Firum. 3294, 3395, Tolous 477. *cast out of care*, Roul. and Vern. 109.

E.M.E., A. *cast a cry*, Oct. 13, Row. & Ot. 508, 898. *keste up a cry*, Perc. 1710, Rol. 241, 357, 605, Row. & Ot. 1303. *keste ane heghe cry*, Row. & Ot. 835.

kene and cruel, Laud 15784. **A.** *cruel and kene*, Degare 1060, 1580, 1660, Turke 6.

kepe . . . from care, Oct. Emp. 360, Rol. 13, Sages 2161.

A. *kepe pis counseyle*, Athel. 674.

keuyr þe owte of kare, Amad. 471, 814. *to keuere hym out of care*, Athel. 380. *couere hem of here care*, Athel. 331.

E.M.E., A. *chapel and chyrche*, Horn 1392.

chaste and clene, Florence 2165.

E.M.E., A. *chaunge chere*, Guy 4268. *changet chere*, Amad. 770. *changed . . . cheere*, Degare 540, Firum. 786, Florence 819, Floris & Blan. 1124, Triam. 924, Ywaine 2234. *changy chere*, Launfal 921. *chaungyng of chere*, Squ. of L. Deg. 336.

A. *to chaunge coloure*, Kn. of Curt. 99. *changed hys coloure*, M. Arthur 2998. *hys colour changed*, Firum. 2926.

A. *cheeke and chin*, Guy & Col. 489, M. Arthur 3792.

A. *chepede all her chafare*, Oct. 389–90.

kindle care, Guy & Col. 51, 360. *kyndylde all . . . care*, Florence 2017, Row. & Ot. 60. *kindille cares fulle calde*, Melayne 596.

Cp. **O.E.P. & Pr., E.M.E., Laȝ., A.** *king ne kaiser*, Beues 1595, Hav. 353, 977, 1317, 1725, Laud 6476, 8982. *cayser . . . king*, Alis. 1409, 2632, 4216, 6985, Floris & Blan. 436.

O.E.P. & Pr., E.M.E., Orm., A. *king of kynges*, Roul & Vern. 46, Ywaine 1411.

Laȝ., A. *king(es) and/or knyght(es)*, Alis. 1368, Avow. 144, 1137, Emare 495, Green Kn. 203, Guy 335, etc., Laud 258, etc., M. Arthur 622, etc., Oct. 1945, Oct. Emp. 240, etc., Perc. 1873, Rich. 246, 3582, 5501, Rol. 164, Squ. of L. Deg. 561, Torrent 21, etc., Triam. 1183. *knight and king*, Green Kn. 124, Laud 10650, 10790, Perc. 1528, 1965, Troy 1912.

E.M.E., A. *kyng, knyȝt and kayser*, Laud 8226. *caysere ne knyȝt*, Degare, 1528.

O.E.Pr., E.M.E., Laȝ., A. *kyng and quene*, Alis. 1841, Avow. 802, Florence 2162, Floris & Blan. 249, Green Kn. 223, Guy 11392, Ipom. 1657, Lamb. 452, Laud 461, 4242, Launfal 901, M. Arthur 544, 2289, Oct. 644, 1864, Oct. Emp. 265, Otuel 100, 273, Perc. 1560, Squ. of L. Deg. 271, Tars 313, etc., Triam. 7, 58, 154, Troy 736, Ywaine 3577.

king of this countre, Squ. of L. Deg. 261.

a kyrtell on he caste, Florence 1646.

O.E.P. & Pr., E.M.E., Laȝ., A. *kisse(d) and clyppe(d)*, M. Arthur 1801, Oct. Emp. 443. *klyppe(d) and kysse(d)*, Emare 212, 1020, Floris & Blan. 932, 961, Guy 3080, M. Arthur 3927, Oct. 435, 585, Otuel 605, Sowdane 1935. *clyppyng and kyssyng*, Oct. Emp. 1391, 1685. *cleppen and kissen*, Beues 65, 3943. *hye clepten and hye kuste*, Horn Child 1252. *custen and cle(p)ten*, Horn 1428. *cluppyng and kussyng*, Alis. 7170. *yclupten and kyste*, Horn 1217.

A. *kistes and cofurs*, Amad. 526.

A. *kythe and kynne*, Florence 2045. *keth and kende*, Lib. Dis. 381. Cp. **E.M.E.** *cunde and cun*. *kyn and kyth*, Laud 10218. *ken and kyghth*, Oct. 1822. **E.M.E., A.** *clepe and calle*, Laud 3961. *he cleped and (he) called*, Lamb. 305, 359, Lamw. 299.

cler and colde, Tars 829.

A. *clerk and king,* Troy 584.

E.M.E., La3., A. *clerk and/ne kniht,* Hav. 2083, 2195, 2813, Sages 1922, 2484, 2493, Trist 3128. *knyghtis, clerkis,* Alis. 1371.

A. *in clethynge comly clede,* Row. & Ot. 651. *in (comely) clothyng . . . cledd,* Florence 211.

clongyn in clay, Tolous 494.

clottis of clay, Laud 10602. *as clot of clay,* Laud 17134.

E.M.E., A. *knelutte downe opon thayre kne,* Amad. 826. *he knelyd anon and on hys knees he felle,* Athel. 419. *kneeled on . . . knee(s),* Arthur's Death 145, Avow. 804, Carle 160, Cleges 166, 190, 395, Florence 951, Guy & Col. 100, 136, 564, Isum. 540, M. Arthur 3781, Melayne 643, 787, Oct. Emp. 1047, Perc. 388, Row. & Ot. 637, Squ. of L. Deg. 279, 687, Tolous 1147, Torrent 205, 528. *knelyd downe on hys kne,* Eglam. 909, 1279, 1288. *on here knees he/pey kneleden adoun,* Athel. 501, 549. *on knees they knelyd downe,* M. Arthur 3938. *appon his knees (downn gan) he knele,* Row. & Ot. 488, 725. *on kne knelyd he,* Torrent 133, etc. *vpon his knees can kneele,* Green Kn. 165.

A. *knightes and kempes,* Guy & Col. 5.

A. *kny3te and/ne knaue,* Avow. 737, Hav. 458, 2697, Laud 4873, Rich. 5894, Torrent 1094, Triam. 565. *knaue and/or kny3t,* Laud 8094, Ywaine 1594, 2174, 3564.

A. *pe cok crowe bygan,* Alis. 397. *cokkes crowe,* Freine 148. *cokkes crewe,* Sages 2536.

of coloure cleve, Kn. of Curt. 321.

A. *come of knyges kende,* Launfal 864.

O.E.Pr., A. *com of (Gawenys) kynne,* Lib. Dis. 1646.

comly of kende, Amis. 229, 265.

pat comely vnder kelle, Emare 303. Cp. *lufsum under lyne.*

comforte ne chere (verbs), Kn. of Curt. 323.

crake hure crones, Firum. 2604. *crake . . . crowne(s),* Florence 1478, Hav. 568, Rich. 5423, 5626, 6088. *crakkede (a) croun,* Row. & Ot. 1066. *crakkede . . . many a crowne,* Melayne 261, Tolous 72. *many a crowne yschall gar crake,* Florence 92.

crokyd and crachyd, Florence 2028.

A. *crompylde and crokyd,* Florence 1979. Cp. **A.** *crokyd and crachyd.*

croun and crest, Row. & Ot. 710.

crounede pai (Beues) king, Beues 4253. **E.M.E., A.** *crown(ed) . . . king,* Gam. 694, 695, Guy 10736, 10784, Laud 3400, Melayne 99, Rich. 6183, Rol. 446, Sowdane 2976. *croune him to king,* Floris & Blan. 1301. **E.M.E., A.** *king with . . . croune,* Gam. 671, Guy 10418, Lib. Dis. 794, 975, M. Arthur 3173, etc., Melayne 18, 1280, Oct. Emp. 772, Tolous 897, Triam. 1136, Trist. 5, etc., Turke 48. *pe kyng pat weryd pe coroun,* Athel. 553. *of comely kynges corouned,* Laud. 3249.

E.M.E., A. *crouny wip croune,* Beues 4012.

A. *curtes and kynde,* Triam. 240.

A. *the day dawes,* Laud 10045, 12894, 18279. *day is dawed,* Laud 4192. *day be dawed,* Laud 9938. *peo day dawith,* Alis. 2551. *day dawep,* Tars 396. *the day dawen gan,* Sages 2249. *the day began to dawe,* Avow. 473, Laud 7324. *day can dawe,* Florence 1503. *dawen the day,* Rol. 389, 576. *hyt dawed (ly3th) day,* Degare 597, 1665.

dawning of the day, Carle 459, Oct. Emp. 329.

O.E.P., La3., Orm., A. *dale(s) and doune(s)*, Alis. 3129, 5901, Beues 1829, Guy 8500, 10020, Guy & Col. 10, Horn 161, Kn. of Curt. 213, Laud 1372, Row. & Ot. 744, Triam. 270, 1084. *in dale, in doune*, Alis. 4449, 7542. *ouer dale and ouer doun*, Beues 3755, Laud 10444. *doune and dale*, Alis. 1767, 7026, 7206, Florence 1400, Laud 7354. *bi doune ne dale*, Laud 7605. *ouer doune and dale*, Laud 14049, etc.

the daile and doun dynnyd, Rol. 508.   *the dales dynned*, Perc. 2050.

O.E.P., E.M.E., La3., A. *in a dale depe*, Avow. 269.

A. *dampnyd to dethe*, Rol. 250.

dark and deepe, Alis. 7042.

A. *dare for drede*, Triam. 321.

to dashe him downe, Degare 435.

E.M.E., A. *dede and doluen*, Laud 15895.

E.M.E., La3. *dele and di3te*, Amad. 713, Emare 3, 42, Firum. 3915, Otuel 1561, Rich. 4579, Row. & Ot. 490.   *dighte and dele*, Row. & Ot. 490, 826.

A. *dele . . . dynt(es)*, Alis. 5874, Firum. 900, Lib. Dis. 177, 1365, Rol. 199, Sowdane 2920, Triam. 1215, Ywaine 3538.   *delen dyntes*, Laud 9233, 9606.   *to dely (doghty) dents*, Lib. Dis. 1578.   *dyntes thei deled and dalt*, Laud 7341.   *dyntes to dale*, M. Arthur 1076.

dele a dole, Amad. 42.

O.E.P. & Pr., E.M.E., La3., Orm., O. & N., A. *to deme her dome*, Oct. 226. *þe dom is/was demd*. Hav. 2487, 2488, 2838.   *þe ry3t doom schal I deme*, Athel. 683.   *domes for to deme*, Gam. 826.

deme and dele, Row. & Ot. 1317.

O.E.P. & Pr., E.M.E., P.M., A. *deme to death*, Lamw. 475.

E.M.E., A. *demed to dye*, Triam. 860.

E.M.E. *deme and dighte*, Row. & Ot. 1269.

deere or doe, Degare 275.

dereworth and dere, Sowdane 1512.

dethys dynte, Florence 915.   *dethes dent*, Oct. 1001.

A. *dye a dethe*, Beues 341, Guy 5955.   *(a) deth schall dye*, Oct. 245.

La3., A. *di3t to depe*, Beues 908, Laud 1403, Trist. 208.   *dighte to dede*, Melayne 548, 557, Row. & Ot. 142, etc. (4 times).   *to dethe . . . (y)dyght*, Alis. 2451, Athel. 463, Avow. 56, 136, Oct. 1650, Roul. & Vern. 369, Sages 2306, Torrent 273, 1648, Tolous 489, 507, 846, 1047.

A. *dynge(n) (a)doun*, Eglam. 556, Firum. 717, etc. Guy & Col. 48, 374, Melayne 128, 267, 1255, Row. & Ot. 1058, etc.

A. *to dethe he þame denges*, Degare 324.   *to dede he ne solde hym dynge*, Melayne 234.

of þat dynt was he ded, Athel. 292. Cp. Allit. Troy 1235, *dyed of the dynt*.

E.M.E., La3., A. *do of dawe*, Beues 348.   *done of dawe*, Laud 7800.   *don of dawes*, Tars. 813.   *of dawe don*, Floris & Blan. 1067.   *be don of day*, Firum. 1697.

O.E.Pr., E.M.E., Orm., A. *do a dede*, Amis. 833, Avow. 164, Carle 388, Florence 669, etc., Freine 317, Green Kn. 163, 184, 388, Lib. Dis. 34, 1692, Perc. 1240, 1594, Rich. 695, 926, Rol. 676, Squ. of L. Deg. 173, 368, Tolous 410, 684, Trist. 3073, 3201, Turke 1237, Ywaine 2307, etc.   *do dedes*, Firum. 2151, etc.   *dedus to done*, Emare 4.

O.E.Pr. *do hur to dede*, Avow. 964.   *do to deed*, Floris & Blan. 46, Triam. 206.   **E.M.E., A.** *do to depe*, Firum. 177, Floris & Blan. 306, 1210, Guy

290, etc., Laud 1684, 6713, Lib. Dis. 2022, Rich. 1014, 1128. *done to dede*, Ywaine 2174, 2375. *to dethe don*, Chron. 868, 908, Sages 642.

do you deere, Green Kn. 401.

do oure dute, Sowdane 1024.

O.E.Pr., A. *doluen depe*, Laud 3684.

A. *doughty in/of dede*, Avow. 294, 566, Cleges 8, Degare 12, 300, etc., Eglam. 1257, Firum. 2877, 4444, Florence 882, Green Kn. 144, Isum 273, Lib. Dis. 6, 704, M. Arthur 28, etc., Melayne 3, 626, Oct. Emp. 18, 1438, 1689, Otuel 276, etc., Perc. 18, Rich. 30, etc., Row. & Ot. 1560, Sowdane 207, 1212, Tars 953, Torrent 27, 1725, 2574, Triam. 1422, 1500, Ywaine 866, 3802. *doȝty dedes*, Firum. 2636, Green Kn. 250, 507, Rich. 3729, 6671, Row. & Ot. 904, 1360, 1387. *douhtiest of dede*, Amis 33, etc. (6 times). *doghtines of dede*, Ywaine 29.

O.E.P. *be doun and den*, Rich. 6636.

A. *fel doun ded*, Firum. 2730, etc. *ded doun felle*, Athel. 385. *(falle) dede downe*, Amad. 119. *(fall) ded adoun*, Firum. 891.

A. *dout of dep*, Trist. 2595.

douted to be ded, Ywaine 3236.

A. *drank a draught*, Gam. 608.

E.M.E., A. *drawe to dede*, Beues 4601.

A. *draw down*, The Hare 36.

A. *drechinge and dremyng*, Rol. 80.

A. *(he hede) drede and doute*, Avow. 177.

E.M.E., A. *drede my dethe*, Avow. 143.

adred of deth, Alis. 4267. *drede of deth*, Firum. 5751, Laud 4225, etc., Rol. 211, 551. *of dethe adrade*, M. Arthur 1510.

Orm., A. *dredyd (no wrang) dome*, Florence 153. *þe doome (þey may) drede*, Athel. 565, 575.

Laȝ., A. *day furth þey dryue*, Troy 647. *they droffe the day*, Cleges 158. *day was drif to nyght*, Rol. 1024.

E.M.E., A. *drive to dethe*, Rol. 843.

E.M.E., A. *driuen . . . (a) doun*, Amis 1085, Carle 412, Firum. 2724.

A. *droupe and dare*, Florence 93, M. Arthur 2375, Troy 1413. *y droupe, y dare*, Tolous 553.

A. *dubbed and dyȝt*, Laud 16582, Sages 3233.

A. *the ducke and the drake*, Squ. of L. Deg. 320.

A. *dukes and duchepers*, Melayne 808.

O.E.P. & Pr., E.M.E., Orm., A. *dumb and defe*, Beues 567.

A. *dussched adoun to depe*, Firum. 3068. **E.M.E.** *dust doun (to dede)*, Firum. 854, 998. *to depe þay duste him doun*, Firum. 2011.

O.E.Pr., E.M.E., A. *euen and eghen*, Sages 2141.

for euer and for aye, Guy & Col. 213. Cp. **E.M.E.** *ay and oo ; euer and aa*.

A. *fayr of face*, Emare 373, Firum. 1299, 5205, Florence 566, 1542, Melayne 844, Oct. 1165, Row. & Ot. 614, 1072, Sowdane 226.

fayre of vyys, Lib. Dis. 60. *hys fayr vys*, Lib. Dis. 19.

fayr of fasoun, Lib. Dis. 555, 791. *fayr fassoune*, Lib. Dis. 1467.

A. *fayr of feture*, Cleges 11.

fayre and feate, Guy & Col. 533.

feyre and fyne, Florence 2125, Sages 3012, Ywaine 203.

feir of fleysch, Chron. 598.

A. *fayr of flesh and felle*, Emare 306, Row. & Ot. 8, 81.

fayr so flour, Hav. 1719, 2917.

E.M.E., A. *faire and fre*, Alis. 7585, Arthur's Death 36, Carle 217, Degare 33, 230, 633, Emare 22, 71, 831, 963, Firum. 64, 2823, Florence 480, Guy 726, etc., Hav. 2876, Horn Child 921, Horn 267, Ipom. 2325, Kn. of Curt. 3, Laud 9783, Lib. Dis. 63, M. Arthur 454, 3502, Oct. Emp. 511, etc. (7 times), Perc. 3, 501, Row. & Ot. 238, etc., Squ. of L. Deg. 99, 127, 280, 296, Torrent 782, 2062, Trist. 142. **O.E.P., E.M.E., A.** *frely and fair*, Degare 553, 645. Cp. Laȝ.

A. *falle on þe felde*, Firum. 475. *falle in filde*, Tars 1105. *fallun in the filde*, Avow. 200, 335.

fals of fay, Lib. Dis. 1439.

A. *fals and fel*, Chron. 791. *felle and false*, Guy 9244.

E.M.E., A. *falsse and fykell*, M. Arthur 1178, Rich. 1292, Rol. 147, Sages 2708, Triam. 20.

[*fikil and fel*, Gam. 151.]

falsnes and folye, Gam. 884.

wyth fantasme and fayrye, Lib. Dis. 1432.

O.E.P., A. *fare to felde*, Triam. 1187. *into the feld þei/to fare*, The Hare 95, Lib. Dis. 1544.

fareþ ouer þe fod, Trist. 1304.

O.E.P., A. *forth þei ferden*, Alis. 181.

faste to fyght they founde, Florence 715.

fast he fled, Ywaine 663.

feble and frele, Laud. 12075.

E.M.E., Laȝ., Orm., A. *fed and fostered*, Hav. 1434, 2239. *foster and fede*, M. Arthur 3895.

(*foghte*) *fell and faste*, Lib. Dis. 339.

to fell on the feld, Rol. 496. *feld him in þe feld*, Horn Child 674. **O.E.P.** *fellen in ðe feld*, Otuel 450. *fel doun in the felde*, Ywaine 2602.

O.E.P., A. *in feld hys fon to fell*, Lib. Dis. 1847. **A.** *in felde hym to felle*, Perc. 640.

A. *to fel þe fey*, Horn Child 72, 177, cp. Laȝ. *to felle þam fey*, Row. & Ot. 18.

A. *fellest with to fyght*, Oct. 404.

felle and fere, Row. & Ot. 89.

O.E.P. & Pr. *fellen at hise fet*, Hav. 2185. Laȝ., **A.** *fallet to his fet*, Floris & Blan. 1269. *felde vndir fete*, Melayne 366. *feld vnder fet*, Trist. 635. *fel . . . to his fet*, Trist. 898, Ywaine 2321. *fell to his foote*, Guy & Col. 379. *fellid to his foot*, Rol. 752. **O.E.P.** *falle at his fete*, Rol. 98.

O.E.Pr., E.M.E. *ouer felde and fen*, Oct. 1685. *feldes and forestes*, Squ. of L. Deg. 237. See under *frith*.

A. *byfelle ferly*, M. Arthur 6.

aferd to fyght, Amis. 941.

ferme and fast, Kn. of Curt. 50.

ferse men felle in fighte, Melayne 501.

A. *ferse and felle*, Eglam. 42, 695, Firum. 5284, Florence 427, Melayne 1106, Row. & Ot. 407, 786, Ywaine 2409. *felle and ferse*, Row. & Ot. 41, 862.

fersely fighte, Row. & Ot. 1495. *feȝting furcely*, Avow. 38, 94.

feteryd . . . faste, Athel. 242, Gam. 726, 809..

gape and gren, Carle 213.

gapes and gones, Avow. 180.

O.E.P., E.M.E., P.M., A.   *game and/ne gle,* Emare 474, Floris & Blan. 107, Guy 2492, etc., Ipom. 2245, 2344, M. Arthur 96, 3164, Rol. 188, Tolous 164, Troy 489.   *gamen and/ne gle,* Amis. 540, Degare 3, 1903, Isum. 466, 573, Laud 3016, Row. & Ot. 5, 33.   *gamen and glewe,* Horn Child 275, Trist. 2406.   *gle and game,* Beues 3450, Chron. 456, Freine 17, Horn Child 935, Lib. Dis. 694, 1677, 2126, 2180, Triam. 155. *no game schulde þe glewe,* Triam. 108.   *ther gamyd hur/hym no glewe,* Triam. 462, 1467.

O.E.Pr., E.M.E., A.   *gaue vp the ghost,* Guy & Phil. 38.

O.E.Pr., A.   *giffe giftus,* Amad. 150, Melayne 1412.   *give gifts,* Guy 40, etc., Rol. 931.   *gaf(e) . . . giftus,* Avow. 1087, Rich. 3747.   *gave gifts,* Lamb. 18, Lamw. 15.   *gyffes (he) a gyfte,* Perc. 85, 163.   *gevyth them gyftys,* Florence 305.   *ʒiffe ʒiftys,* Ipom. 338, 2311.   *ʒaue ʒift,* Trist. 627.   *ʒaf ʒeftes,* Land. 21, etc. (4 times).   *yaf gyftes,* Launfal 67.   *ʒeue a ʒift,* Trist. 2921.   *ʒiftes he ʒafe,* M. Arthur 2963, 3045. *ʒeue vs grace,* Oct. 20.

A.   *gete grace,* Tolous 403.

A.   *gif . . . grace,* Amad. 415, Guy 4660, etc., Sowdane 631, 1082, Tolous 4, 1098, Triam. 1491.   *God þat (vs) gaffe (þe) grace,* Melayne 1149, 1571.   *God yeve him/us goode grace,* Gam. 268, 815.   *God ʒif grace,* Laud 3929.

gift ne garison, Rol. 262.

give and ʒeld, Rich. 2339.

gile oþer gynne, Alis. 3991.

A.   *glad and gay,* M. Arthur 302, 2891, 3100.

E.M.E.   *þat glade salle hym no glee,* Melayne 483.   *gladdes þam no glee,* Row. & Ot. 147.   *with alkyn gamyn þam for to glade,* Ywaine 1440.

A.   *glemed golde on the grounde,* Florence 379.   **A.**   *glistered as gold,* Green Kn. 278.   **A.**   *glitteryng all of golde,* Florence 157, cp. Laʒ.   **A.**   *gleteryng with gold,* Rol. 295.

O.E.P. & Pr., Laʒ.   *gold and gemmes,* Laud 15513.   *gold and gymmes,* Alis. 3152.

gold and gerysoun, Firum. 5693.   **E.M.E., Laʒ., A.**   *gold and garsome,* Floris & Blan. 206, 821, 1259.

gold and goules, Squ. of L. Deg. 204.

Cp. **A.**   *the gold in the grounde,* Sages 2103.

go to grounde, Row. & Ot. 1059, Tolous 1116.   *grope to the ground,* Turke 24.

gorgeous and gay, Carle 437.

E.M.E., A.   *grace of God,* Chron. 231, etc., Eglam. 559, etc., Emare 680, etc., Florence 1833, M. Arthur 3588, Rich. 3086, etc., Tars 237, etc., Ywaine 2205.   *Godes/Goddys/Goddus grace,* Amad. 506, etc., Athel. 58, etc., Beues 193, etc., Firum. 829, etc., Guy 1809, etc., Guy & Col. 169, Ipom. 2119, Lib. Dis. 428, etc., Melayne 478, etc., Oct. 1004, 1553, Oct. Emp. 364, Roul. & Vern. 214, 262, 876, Sages 2997, 3585, Sowdane 1134, etc., Tolous 185, Triam. 132, etc.

gracious, gude, Ywaine 3094.

under gras ygrave, Gam. 69.

A.   *graunte grace,* Arthur 637, Firum. 1506, etc., Guy 10724, M. Arthur 3677, Melayne 1056, Rich. 2699, Ywaine 863, etc.   *God graunt þe/vs grace,* Carle 499, Lib. Dis. 166, 250.

gray as any glas, Tolous 340.
graythe in his gere, Avow. 568.
gree and grith, Sowdane 2850.
E.M.E., A. *grene as gras,* Eglam. 776.
A. *great and grim,* Degare 646, Guy & Col. 49.
grete and gud, Melayne 924. *gude and grete,* Melayne 460.
gret and grille, Amis. 1275, 1802.
grym and grylle, Lib. Dis. 1875.
grymme and geyse, Lib. Dis. 597.
(*pelvred*) *wyth grys and gray,* Lib. Dis. 839.
(*pelverd*) *wyth grys and gro,* Launfal 237.
grisly he grones, Avow. 192.
þay grone and grenne, Row. & Ot. 1423.
growen grene, Row. & Ot. 1116.
ʒarket hom ʒare, Avow. 76.
gentyll, jolyf, Launfal 931.
jolly and jocund, Lamb. 512.
hayl and hole, Amis. 2232. *hol and hale,* Sages 2302.
hang aboute his hals, Firum. 249. **A.** *honge be the hals,* Guy 3430.
hangyd hur up be the hare, Florence 2060.
E.M.E. *he hangid his hede full low,* M. Arthur 100. *hingand hir hevyd,*
Ywaine 1036.
E.M.E., A. *hongyd hym ful hyʒe,* Athel. 806.
Cp. **O.E.Pr., Alf., A.** *hard hert,* Amis. 581.
O.E.Pr., A. *harmes hent,* Avow. 280, etc. (4 times), Melayne 1041.
hastelye in hye, Florence 223.
O.E.Pr., Laʒ., A. *have in honde,* Amis. 752, Beues 427, Ywaine 249. *I*
haue hade in honde, Amad. 21. *hadde in honde,* Arthur 311.
O.E.Pr., E.M.E., A. *to haue and . . . hold,* Degare 510, Oct. 1286, Perc. 24,
Sowdane 634, Squ. of L. Deg. 262.
Laʒ., A. *haukes . . . hownds,* Amad. 54, Florence 842, 1525, Guy 845,
Marr. of Gaw. 144-5, Melayne 307, Oct. 890, Squ. of L. Deg. 951.
howndis and haukis, Ipom. 61.
A. *head and hair,* Guy & Col. 398.
A. *her of hed,* Tars 100.
A. *hed and hals,* Laud 7711.
Orm., A. *hed and herte,* Arthur 462, Rich. 2928.
A. *heyghe in hevene,* Rich. 5474. *that heghest was in heuyn,* Avow. 1040.
fro heuen on highte, Malayne 897. *heuen one heghe,* Melayne 360.
E.M.E., Laʒ., A. *heghe appon an hill appon highte,* Melayne 883.
O.E.P. & Pr., E.M.E., P.M., A. *hele and hide,* Horn Child 533, M. Arthur
143, 1473, 3840.
A. *helmes . . . hauberkes,* Firum. 632, etc., Green Kn. 76, Guy 5027,
5054, 9365, Lib. Dis. 1863, Melayne 976, 1565, Oct. 1511, Oct. Emp.
437, etc., Rich. 3287, 5587, Rol. 538, 886, Row. & Ot. 44, Tolous 93.
hauberke and helm, Firum. 4148.
O.E.P., Laʒ., A. *helm on hede,* Amis. 2451, Green Kn. 22, Guy 5514, 10958,
Guy & Col. 8, 146, 152, Hav. 379, etc., Horn Child 64, 98, 143, Kn. of
Curt. 341, Laud 10160, Oct. Emp. 905, Perc. 1358, 1897, Rich. 5810,
Rol. 294, etc., Row. & Ot. 718. *helm and heued,* Firum. 3106, 3704.
helme(s) and hedes, Rol. 698, 747, 948. *helm, heued and hod,* Firum.

3933. *on hys hedde hys helme*, Guy 3619.   *hed and helm*, Rich. 2562,
3132.   *helm and hode*, Firum. 843.   *hefd and hod*, Firum. 5497.

A. *hende in halle*, Athel. 558, Horn Child 381.   *hynde in halle*, Triam. 1206.
henge his harp, Orfeo 344, 500.

A. *hente in honde*, M. Arthur 1037, Tars 1079.   *in hys honde he hent a
spere*, Florence 587.   **A.** *bi the hond hent*, Lib. Dis. 609, Sages 2229.
in hond he hente, Rich. 4027.

E.M.E., A. *herkene and here*, Degare 6, 1443, Rich. 3730.   *herkenyth and
here*, Amis. 24, 517.   *herkeneþ and ȝe mai here*, Beues 738.
here with ere, Orfeo 528.

E.M.E., A. *herwede helle*, Athel. 422, 595, Beues 4469, Ywaine 2874.
harrowed hell, Squ. of L. Deg. 148, Tolous 256.   *harrowes hell*, Green
Kn. 414.
herte and hare, Avow. 27.

O.E.P., Laȝ., A. *hert and hinde*, Beues 2365, Ipom. 389, 668, Squ. of L. Deg.
766, 768, 954, Laud 542, 2410, Oct. 1417.   *hartys . . . hyndys*, Guy
2327, Perc. 218.

E.M.E., A. *my herte is hevy*, Amad. 87.   *his herte was hevy*, M. Arthur 905,
3738.

A. *in hert he hoped*, Sages 2935.

Orm., A. *herte and honde*, M. Arthur 2838, 2943, 3564, Row. & Ot. 1004.

E.M.E., Laȝ., A. *hete and hongyr*, Rich. 1331.

O.E.P., A. *heven and helle*, Alis. 1290, 6025, Firum. 541, Guy & Col. 554,
Oct. 140, 741, Rich. 4940.

O.E.Pr., E.M.E., A. *heues vp his handis to heuen*, Melayne 67.   *hys hond
up haf*, Lib. Dis. 247.

A. *off he hewes his hede*, Melayne 968.
of hewe and here, Rich. 5495.   **A.** *off hide, hewe and here*, Amis. 81.

E.M.E., Laȝ., A. *hide and hewe*, Firum. 4665, Laud 7284, etc., M. Arthur
3735, Rich. 676, Squ. of L. Deg. 388, Tars 752, Triam. 469, Ywaine
868.   *hewe and . . . hide*, Row. & Ot. 65, etc., Tolous 189.

O.E.Pr., E.M.E., A. *to hide his hede*, Rol. 855.   Cp. **O.E.P.** *to huyden his
heved*, Tars 1130.   *his heued to hide*, Amis. 813, Tolous 113.   *your
heddes . . . to hyde*, Lib. Dis. 1113, Row. & Ot. 264.
to hyde in herte, Emare 120, 996.   *in herte ys noght to hyde*, Launfal 57,
Triam. 1629, 1704, Oct. Emp. 1305, 1392.

E.M.E., A. *hyde in holys*, M. Arthur 2571.
hodur and happe, Florence 112.

E.M.E., A. *to holde his heste*, Perc. 127.

O.E.Pr., E.M.E., Laȝ., A. *hold in hond*, Chron. 970.   *holde an honde*, Lib.
Dis. 1277.   **A.** *holde up youre honde*, Tolous 629.   *holdyn vp hys hande*,
Guy 2181.   *held vp her hond*, Amis. 156.   *helde in his hande*, Row. &
Ot. 483.   *helde vp hys hande*, Guy 7478, Marr. of Gaw. 16, Squ. of L.
Deg. 869, Ywaine 3038.   *hys handes he held*, Torrent 210.   *hys/there
handis vpheld*, M. Arthur 926, Melayne 293, Row. & Ot. 489.   *his
hande vp holdes hee*, Row. & Ot. 312.
holtus here, Avow. 684, Land. 50, Launfal 230, M. Arthur 3521, Oct. Emp.
351, etc., Orfeo 214.   *holtes hare*, Trist. 378, etc.   **A.** *to hunt on holtes
hare*, Amis. 507.
bi holtes and bi hille, Trist. 2458.   **A.** *ouer hillis and holtis*, Rol. 279.   *hyllys
and holtys hore*, M. Arthur 3521.

O.E.Pr., La3. *honde and heued,* Firum. 3026.

A. *hors and/nor harnesse* Degare 254, Guy 8547, Kn. of Curt. 166, Rol. 197, 410, Triam. 698.

A. *without hurt or harm,* Rol. 678.

A. *the jay jangled,* Squ. of L. Deg. 51.

A. *they layd hem lowe,* M. Arthur 3127. *that ben leyd so lowe,* Gam. 162. *a lante lone,* Amad. 454.

A. *large and longe,* Laud 531, etc., Row. & Ot. 80, 1308, 1553, Squ. of L. Deg. 1013, Ywaine 2358.

A. *lawe of londe,* Hav. 2815, Horn 1112, Rich. 1024, 1513, Roul. & Vern. 75, Torrent 1178, Triam. 1066. *þe landys lawe,* Athel. 646, Rich. 630, Ywaine 3740.

O.E.Pr., E.M.E., La3., Orm., P.M., A. *lede* (*a*) *lif,* Amad. 830, Amis. 1998, 2482, Degare 726, Emare 77, Firum. 2521, etc., Florence 876, 2173, Freine 303, Melayne 48, Sages 3344, 3999, Triam. 1703, Trist. 2599. *he ledes hys lyff,* Rich. 1115. *he ledeþ his lyf,* Laud 820. *they led theyr lyfe,* Squ. of L. Deg. 1128, Ywaine 4024. *led owre lyffe,* M. Arthur 3685. *leden* (*here*) *lyf,* Gam. 757, 884. *lif to lede,* Floris & Blan. 976, Row. & Ot. 246.

E.M.E., A. *my landes for to lede,* Ywaine 1185.

O.E.Pr. & Pr., E.M.E., La3., P.M., A. *lef/leue . . . lothe,* Amis. 87, Beues 1850, Florence 1492, Guy 7225, Hav. 440, etc., Laud 3120, etc., Sages 1881. *lothe or lefe,* Florence 1246.

A. (*luke now*) *lely that thou layn,* Ywaine 580.

A. *lemede lyght,* Launfal 942. *leomede lihte,* Tars 162. See under *lyght.*

O.E.P., A. *lende in/on londe,* Firum. 5772, Florence 2183. (*that there*) *on londe was lende,* Oct. Emp. 495.

E.M.E., A. *that lenes us life,* Ywaine 3483. *me lyfe hath lente,* Florence 2138. *lyffe . . . lente,* M. Arthur 1323, etc.

lenge and lende, M. Arthur 3276.

A. *lep on lightly,* Rol. 299.

A. *he lepe over lond,* Laud 10528.

lere a lessoun, Firum. 2650.

A. *lerne the lawe,* Tars 480.

lawe to lere, Tars 820.

O.E.P. & Pr., A. *let his lif,* Firum. 1892. *to lete mi liif,* Orfeo 177. **A.** *lif forlete,* Beues 3376, Firum. 1274, Otuel 936.

leevede on . . . lawe, Tars 387, 938.

O.E.Pr., E.M.E., La3., Orm., A. *lewid and lered,* Alis. 2, etc., Beues 4020, Oct. 1715, Rich. 1343, 3100. *lered and/ne . . . lewed,* Laud 6438, 8461.

lewede and lernydd, Florence 1318. *lerned and lewede,* Sowdane 1489.

thi liffe I dar lay, Avow. 291. *my lyfe dar y lay,* Triam. 1464.

(*now may*) *my lyfe no longer last,* Kn. of Curt. 448. *my lyffe laste maye,* M. Arthur 2138. **E.M.E., La3., A.** *whilles me lastithe lyf,* Rol. 195. *last mi liif,* Orfeo 335.

lyff and leme, Rich. 1403, etc. *leme and liif,* Hav. 2555.

E.M.E., La3., O. & N., A. *lyff and lym,* Laud 1223, etc., Melayne 684, 1560, Tars 557, etc. *lyme and lyfe,* Oct. 254.

my life and my likinge, Lamb. 533, Squ. of L. Deg. 1064.

lyff and lyth, Laud 17348. *life and lithe,* Sowdane 1778.

O.E.Pr. *life and . . . londe,* Avow. 593, Rich. 257.   **A.** *land and liffe,*
    Guy & Col. 354.
A. *they lightede appon a lawnde,* Melayne 634.   *on londe is lyght,* Laud 1983.
lyghte als lefe one tree, Row. & Ot 996.
lyght gonne leme, Launfal 888.   **Orm., A.** *lyght . . . leme,* Oct. Emp.
    488–9.   **O.E.P. & Pr.** *light as any leame,* Guy & Col. 546.
lyme and lyþ, Firum. 5092.   See supra *lyff and lym,* etc.   *lim and lithe,*
    Green Kn. 53.   **E.M.E.** *lim and lythe,* Laud 441, 11008, 14560.   (*large
    of*) *lym and lith,* Torrent 2388.   *lyth and lymme,* Guy 10146.
A. *lyons and lebardes,* Guy 3749, Rich. 3586, 5121.
liste and lithe, Amis. 1240, 2402.   **E.M.E., A.** *lystne and lithe,* Alis. 5751,
    Amad. 273, Amis. 471, Oct. Emp. 9, Sowdane 973.   *litheth and
    lesteneth,* Gam. 1, etc.
lythe and lere, Lib. Dis. 1911, 1998.
lythyr and lees, Tolous 1086.
to liue on land, Degare 178.   **O.E.P., E.M.E., La3., A.** *lyue in londe,* Firum.
    2793.   *lived in lande,* Florence 717.   *lyf in londe,* Floris & Blan. 56.
    lived in land, Ywaine 197.
La3. *lyffes nowrewhare in lede,* Isum. 12.
O.E.P. & Pr., La3., A. *live a lif,* Firum. 686, etc., Sages 1667, Sowdane
    2500.   *lyved a lyffe,* M. Arthur 3570.   *libbeth . . . lif,* Sages 227.
E.M.E., La3., O. & N., A. *lyve long,* Rich. 6279.   *liued long,* Orfeo 595.
    longe lybb, Alis. 5892.   **O.E.Pr.** *I may no lenger liven,* Gam. 27.   **A.**
    also longe as I may leve, Athel. 658.
E.M.E., La3., A. *liuer and li3tes,* Trist. 488.
La3., A. *livre and longe,* Alis. 2156, 3728, Firum. 1095, 2984, Lib. Dis. 602.
    longe and livere, Alis. 2727, Rich. 1088
A. *he lokid ouer a lond,* Rol. 99.
O.E.P., La3., A. *londe(s) . . . lede(s),* Beues 1075, Cleges 412, Gam. 61,
    etc., Squ. of L. Deg. 135, Tars 124, Triam. 1269.
A. *londes or lythe,* (O.N. lýðr), Florence 841, 1118, Hav. 2515.   See N.E.D.
A. *lordes and ladies,* Amad. 647, Kn. of Curt. 478, Florence 169, 832,
    Freine 46, Guy & Col. 2, 589, Ipom. 2266, Laud 8574, etc., Lib. Dis.
    1294, M. Arthur 3208, Rich. 154, Turke 8, Ywaine 20, 3287, 4018.
    leuedi and lord, Sages 1810.
A. *lordes of þe londe,* Amad. 858, Athel. 589, 613, 643.   *lord in lond,* Amis.
    1866.   *lordes (that were) in land,* Green. Kn. 204.   *lord of . . . londe,*
    Guy 7064, Laud 131, Perc. 1959, 2135, Torrent 1899, etc., Troy 344.
    A. *ladis in lond,* Amad. 832.
O.E.P. & Pr., E.M.E., La3., A. *lose/lese . . . lif,* Alis. 2842, Amis. 1452,
    1565, Arthur 231, 467, Beues 29, 3163, Florence 29, etc., Land. 283,
    Laud 9077, etc., Rich. 7034, Trist. 2929.   *lesen his lif,* Otuel 148.   *lost
    his lyff,* Laud 9669, 9930.   *our lyues be lost,* Rol. 1046.
life . . . lorne, Lamb. 301, 355, Lamw. 295, M. Arthur 1389, etc., Rol. 388,
    Triam. 538.   **La3., A.** *lif . . . forlorn,* Amis. 1080.   *lyff forlore,* Rich.
    1330.
luf of þe lady, Sages 2994.
A. *thy love and thy lykinge,* Squ. of L. Deg. 1081, cp. **E.M.E.**
lufe . . . as . . . lyfe, Amad. 820, Athel. 74, Degare 17, Lamb. 236,
    Lamw. 224, Land. 198, Launfal 654, Orfeo 123–4, Sages 270, 2566,
    Ywaine 4012.   *loueþ as his lif,* Otuel 251.   *to love myn own lyfe,*
    Tolous 227.   *he loved so his lyf,* Chron. 296.

loved and dlowte, Arthur 116.
that lovely under lace, Florence 1817.
A. *lufsum under lyne,* Emare 864, Row. & Ot. 1279, Trist. 1202, 2816.
E.M.E., A. *lowe lowte,* Lib. Dis. 723, Sowdane 2513. *lowlye (can they) lowte,* Turke 316.
E.M.E., A. *luste of lechery,* Melayne 874.
A. *make melodye,* Oct. 71–2. *melody þai maked,* Orfeo 523.
A. *amendes make,* Firum. 1525, etc.
A. *make . . . merry,* Degare 585, Eglam. 343, Emare 825, Firum. 3416, etc., Rich. 5421, Land. 168, Lib. Dis. 1779, Sowdane 1663, 2083, Trist. 3085. *merry make,* The Hare, 130. *made merry,* Cleges 156, Tolous 1054.
E.M.E., A. *make myrth,* Avow. 1138, Cleges 112, Gam. 783, Otuel 1342, Sages 3784, Sowdane 937, Tars 370, Ywaine 1259, etc. *make murþe and melodie,* Otuel 631. *myrthes make,* Amad. 657. *mechel murthe thei him made,* Laud 10978. *myrthes they made,* Perc. 1031, 1728.
(as the boke) makyth mynde, Florence 2168.
A. *make mone,* Amis. 569, etc., Avow. 1091, Beues 899, Kn. of Curt. 198, 254, 498, Emare 314, Firum. 1196, etc., Florence 1352, Guy 1070, 4612, Guy & Col. 56, Hav. 403, Ipom. 101, Lamb. 24, 519, Lamw. 28, M. Arthur 814, 1406, Marr. of Gaw. 23, Melayne 159, Oct. Emp. 347, 383, Perc. 1081, Sowdane, 944, 2583, Squ. of L. Deg. 21, 106, Tars 437, 491, Tolous 755, Torrent 264, Triam. 182, Ywaine 535, etc. *thei maked moche mone,* Laud 8492. *he made mech mone,* Cleges 84, 107. *made . . . mon,* Athel. 729, Laud 9826, Orfeo 198.
hys mone he mente, M. Arthur 3932.
A. *mournand and made grete mone,* Amad. 390. *mornede and made grete mone,* Melayne 159. **A.** *make mornyng,* Alis. 2905, 4493, 5713, Amis. 284, Green Kn. 215, Guy 4609, etc., Guy & Col. 347, Squ. of L. Deg. 969, Ywaine 666, etc. *mournyng makes,* Amad. 446. *mornyng . . . mas(e),* Tolous 206, 990. *monynge make,* M. Arthur 1384.
A. *made the maryage,* Ywaine 1257.
mad(de) of mode, Amis. 1983, Lib. Dis. 1167.
maine and moode, Guy & Col. 27, Sowdane 2077, Ywaine 1031. **O.E.P. & Pr., Laȝ.** *mode and mayne,* Florence 291.
O.E.Pr. *mayden and modur,* Oct. Emp. 259. *modur, maydyn,* Oct. Emp. 319.
the feirest may on molde, Laud 1534. *maydene one molde,* Perc. 1323.
Cp. **A.** *man of myghte,* Arthur 337, Firum. 2852, etc., Lib. Dis. 659, Oct. 403, Row. & Ot. 885, Sowdane 1200.
men of miȝte, Firum. 1163, etc., Sowdane 496, Triam. 762.
mannys myght, Lib. Dis. 1623.
man most of myghtes, Lib. Dis. 1527, 1590. **A.** *man of mekyl myȝt,* Athel. 413, Row. & Ot. 515, Trist. 2791. *a man of moche myght,* Oct. Emp. 23, 1215. *a man . . . moche of myght,* Tolous 904. *a man of mochel myghte,* Launfal 510. *a man most of myght,* Triam. 1356. *moche man of myght,* Triam. 714.
of mekyll myght, Guy 4087, Rich. 74. *with mekill myghte,* Row. & Ot. 268, 484, 1084. *michel/mickle/mekyl might,* Trist. 2377, Turke 224, Ywaine 2128, etc. **A.** *michel/mekyll of might,* Amis. 868, 1313, Athel. 593, Eglam. 1320, M. Arthur 1560, etc. (15 times), Oct. Emp. 297, Row. & Ot. 143, Roul. & Vern. 427, 739, Torrent 530, 941, Triam. 1576, Tolous 39.

miche/moche/much might, Beues 860, etc., Degare 457, Guy 6532, Lamb. 15, Land. 18, Lamw. 19, M. Arthur 887, Oct. 352, etc., Squ. of L. Deg. 562, 1103. *moche/muche of myght*, Firum. 414, etc., Torrent 1340. *mochel/mychel of myght*, Launfal 521, 588, M. Arthur 1496, etc., Tars 582.

more of myght, Lib. Dis. 1960. **E.M.E.** *most of myght*, Amad. 198, Firum. 381, Florence 1289, Green Kn. 72, 426, Guy 9780, Kn. of Curt. 499, M. Arthur 3943, Sowdane 2546, 3068, Torrent 24, Ywaine 3068, 3505. *of myghtys most*, Athel. 1, Florence 1677, Melayne 550, Sowdane 1635.

mekylle man of mayne, Triam. 740. *men of mickle maine*, Green Kn. 9, 41. *miȝty man/men of mayn*, Firum. 660, 1145. *a man of mayne*, Oct. 1383.

Cp. **A.** *mighty of mayn*, Rol. 738. *of muche mayne*, Chron. 950, Tolous 14. *moche of mayn*, Oct. Emp. 1540, Triam. 957. *mekyll of mayne*, M. Arthur 1690, etc., Melayne 1453, Triam. 1574, Ywaine 871, 2459. *mekylle was hys mayne*, Triam. 1437. **E.M.E.** *of mekyl mayn*, Ywaine 58.

E.M.E., A. *man nor maid*, Turke 93.

man of mold, Cleges 279, Sowdane 136. **O.E.P.** *men of molde*, Horn Childe 966. **A.** *man on molde*, Firum. 361, M. Arthur 1615, Sages 3056. *neuer man that was on molde*, Laud 172. **A.** *men on molde*, M. Arthur 707. *man meryest on molde*, Amis. 1902, 2444. *þe meryeste one molde*, Melayne 843.

E.M.E. *man vndir the mone*, M. Arthur 372, 1798, Hav. 373.

marveld in his mode, Cleges 306.

masse and matins, Guy 1571. **E.M.E., A.** *matyns and/or masse*, Guy 3844, Oct. 692.

Laȝ. *medows and moris*, Rol. 306.

meke of maners, Cleges 21.

E.M.E., Orm., A. *meke and mylde*, Avow. 986, Degare 139, Emare 478, 640, Florence 32, Guy 7243, Perc. 291, Laud 18216, Sowdane 3161, . Triam. 1131. *milde and meke*, Ywaine 1366.

a melys mete, Cleges 347.

mendi . . . þat mis, Trist. 2760.

A. *mercy and myght*, Rol. 33.

A. *to meuen his mood*, Otuel. 1240.

E.M.E., A. *might and main*, Amis. 1970, Beues 1022, 3437, 3444, Firum. 603, etc., Florence 2163, Guy 1823, etc., Lib. Dis. 479, 1389, Laud 6988, 7817, 10371, M. Arthur 606, etc., Melayne 714, etc., Oct. 1445, 1448, Rich. 6952, Row. & Ot. 318, 1338, 1434, 1378, Sowdane 824, 988, Tars 1128, Troy 1435, Ywaine 3, 2499. *mayn . . . and . . . myghte*, Avow. 508, Firum. 659, Gam. 143, Guy 10850, Lib. Dis. 1865, 2078, M. Arthur 854, etc., Melayne 282, 323, Oct. 1221, Row. & Ot. 882, Sowdane 528.

A. *maystry and myghte*, Perc. 1312, 1660, 1736, Tolous 21. *myghtfull in mageste*, Florence 1445. Cp. **A.** *myghte and maieste*.

O.E.P. & Pr. *of mylde mode*, Avow. 978. **E.M.E., Laȝ., O. & N., A.** *with mylde mode*, Amis. 1649, etc., Florence 1512, Ipom. 22, 564, 2304, Lamb. 325, Lamw. 314, M. Arthur 1714, 3245, Oct. 483, 525, Oct. Emp. 1237, 1369, Rich. 3940, Row. & Ot. 875, Tars 58, 331, Tolous 221, Ywaine 483, 525. *myld of mode*, Amad. 792, Amis. 54, Guy 135, Ipom. 68, Marr. of Gaw. 156, Oct. Emp. 817, 1000, Perc. 1826, Rich. 1575, Row. & Ot. 645, Squ. of L. Deg. 149.

with milde mouthe, Sages 2429.
myre ne mos, Athel. 344.
A. *mirthe and melodye*, Amis. 103, 104, Emare 194, Laud 9560, Squ. of
 L. Deg. 1069. **A.** *myrthe of mynstrals*, Florence 2157. **E.M.E., A.**
 with menske and mirthe, Amis. 690.
A. *more and myn*, Emare 915, Florence 549, 2039, Perc. 1608.
Cp. **O.E.Pr., Laʒ., A.** *ouer more and mountayne*, Perc. 1127.
mornynge and menyng, Rol. 369.
O.E.P. *mornyed in hys mode*, M. Arthur 2949, 3443. *mornyd in mode and*
 mayn, Florence 291.
O.E.P. & Pr. *mournyng mode*, Sowdane 2494.
musik and menstrasye, Laud 2993.
O.E.Pr., E.M.E., Laʒ., Orm., A. *bi names neuyn*, Sages 3444.
A. *neʒe/neʒed . . . nere*, Athel. 30, Avow. 831, Degare 524, Firum. 350,
 1911, 2029, Florence 217, Lib. Dis. 572, 1155, M. Arthur 3286, 3444,
 Melayne 1452, Otuel 776, Rol. 688, 797, Triam. 1512, Ywaine, 1311.
 neʒe/nyghe . . . nye, M. Arthur 2832, 3874, Melayne 1234, Row.
 & Ot. 687, 820, Trist. 375. *neghe nere*, Row. & Ot. 285.
it neghed nere the nyght, Ywaine 596. *hyt nyghed the nyʒt fulle nere*, Eglam.
 202. **A.** *the nyght was nyghed nyghe*, M. Arthur 3103.
nick him with no nay, Amis. 2176. **A.** *nykked . . . with nay*, Arthur 503,
 Green Kn. 489. *he nykkes hym with nay*, Perc. 1024.
O.E.P., Laʒ. *of egge and ord*, Lib. Dis. 1923.
O.E.P. & Pr., E.M.E., Orm. *ord and ende*, Beues 1447, Chron. 174, Floris
 and Blan. 47, Guy of Warwick 632, 1030, Launfal 314, Lib. Dis. 384,
 Rich. 7108, Tolous 625, etc.[1]
pert in play, Tars 18.
to pyne or play, Sages 21.
hure disport and hure play, Firum. 2217.
prai for pese, Ywaine 3246.
pres in pryde, Triam. 730, 1623.
A. *prest other persoun*, Amis. 616.
A. *prynces proved in pres*, Triam. 969.
prynce yn pryde, Lib. Dis. 469, 777. *pryncis proude in palle*, M. Arthur
 2712. **A.** *a prowde prynce*, Triam. 755.
proud yn palle, Lib. Dis. 389, 1835. **A.** *prowde in prees*, Oct. Emp. 1641,
 1707. **A.** *prowde in pres*, Melayne 1221, Rich. 1098, 3428, Rol. 141,
 Tars 58, Trist. 57. **A.** *pruddest in prece*, Avow. 782.
prowde of prys, Lib. Dis. 1292.
prowde and precyous, Lib. Dis. 285.
prowde and prest, Triam. 883.
princes prowde yn pryde, Lib. Dis. 816, Lib. Dis. 1234, 1466. *proude in*
 pride, Amis. 120, etc. (7 times), Tars 1069.
putt me to payne, Avow. 528. **A.** *put in/to payne*, M. Arthur 1649, Melayne
 38.
A. *put in prisoun*, Amis. 882, Guy 5590, 7482, Squ. of L. Deg. 394.
queynte and quede, Lib. Dis. 1315.
A. *hys body ranne on blode redde*, Guy 5056.
E.M.E., A. *red as a rose*, Athel. 71.
reed of rust, Oct. 1027.

[1] See M.L.R. 24, p. 392.

O.E.Pr. *rede a red*, Otuel 326.

rede and ryght, M. Arthur 1416, 2311.

A. *reden ariʒt*, Floris & Blan. 554.

A. *thorow hys remes ryde*, Florence 117.

A. *reson and ryght*, Cleges 165. *by resone ne ryʒth*, Degare 1888.

E.M.E., Orm. *rest and/nor ro(e)*, Green Kn. 389, Guy & Col. 606, Oct. Emp. 1192, Rich. 7135. [Cp. Morte Arthure 4304, *we may ryste vs with roo.*]

a rewfull rerd, Florence 1429.

A. *ryally arayed*, Degare 687. **A.** *ryall arraye*, Florence 2147.

ryche aray, Firum. 1338, Florence 1696, Marr. of Gaw. 50, Sowdane 130. *richly raied*, Firum. 2295. *ryche in youre aray*, Squ. of L. Deg. 119.

A. *ryche and reall*, Lib. Dis. 876, Orfeo, 356. *ryche, ryall*, Launfal, 494, 632, Oct. 74.

(he) rides and raykes aboute, Laud 10885.

A. *ride and runne*, Guy & Col. 390, Rich. 3166. *rides and rennes*, Laud 7851. *ryden and ronne*, M. Arthur 1628. *rode . . . ranne*, Florence 126.

A. *rigge and ribe*, Rol. 995.

ryve and rente, M. Arthur 3076.

he riues and russhes, Avow. 59.

robbed and reued, Troy 824., cp. **A.** *robbers and reuers.* **A.** *robbed and reft*, Laud 2883, 12639, 18221, Ywaine, 2253. *robbyng or reuying*, Laud 14537.

Cp. **E.M.E.** *no robber hym to reeve*, Guy 105.

A. *his robe he rente*, Tars 99. *our robes beth torent*, Launfal 140.

A. *in romaunce as we rede*, Oct. 15.

to romy and rowte, Avow. 179., cp. **A.** *romyed and rared.*

rope and rare, Ywaine 242 (O.E. hrōpan & rārian).

rough and rent, Oct. 1790.

E.M.E., A. *as rose (in May) her rude was rede*, Land. 432. *her rode was red as rose on rys*, Launfal 937. *har rode was red*, Launfal 242. *hir rode rede als rose*, Row. & Ot. 620. *hur rudde ys radder then the rose-flour*, Tolous 200.

rufull roun, Lib. Dis. 972.

sadde and sore, Avow. 393. **A.** *sadde and sare*, Row. & Ot. 534, 550, 571, 1456, Torrent 1303. *sadly and sare/sore*, Rol. 921, Torrent 1612.

sadylde hys stede, Florence 1296. *sadle a stede*, Gam. 733. *sadulle (my) stede*, Oct. Emp. 865, 1198.

in his sadul sete, Avow. 209, 403. *in the sadel sat*, Otuel 793.

A. *safe and sownde*, Florence 1918, Melayne 1372, Rol. 478, 816, Squ. of L. Deg. 450. *saue and sound*, Laud 11099, 11947.

saue and sure, Laud 18201.

Laʒ., A. *say a sawe*, Beues 301, 653, Otuel 349.

say in sawe, Amis. 90. *seyde in his sawe*, Tars 39.

saile by the see, Sowdane 741. *saile over the sea*, Turke 120. **A.** *sailing in þe see*, Sowdane 63. *saylen ouer þe see*, Floris & Blan. 187.

asaile þat cite, Alis. 1602, 2788.

save and sayne, Florence 297.

A. *save me of synne*, Degare 705.

saue and spede, Amis. 1247.

save or spyll, Squ. of L. Deg. 130.

A. *to saue my soule,* Guy & Phil. 44.

La3., A. *with schaft and/ne with schelde,* Perc. 52, 126, 1408, 1916. *sheldis and schaftes,* Rol. 328, Tolous. 91.

A. *schaftes . . . schyvered,* Launfal 573, Rol. 766.

schame and skathe, Guy 9118.

O.E.P. & Pr., Orm. *schame and schonde,* Beues 2997, 3095, Chron. 329, 784, Firum. 2426, Floris & Blan. 1118, Sowdane 2222.

O.E.Pr., E.M.E., La3., Orm., A. *schame nor schende* (verbs), Florence 1444.

A. *schenschepe and schame,* Laud 2372. *to schentschepe and schame,* Rich. 4986.

schene vnder schild, Avow. 626.

all toschildurt his schilde, Avow. 333.

A. *schylde fro schame,* Guy 3244, 4714, 5784, 8003, Sages 2530, Sowdane 1122, Tars 537. *schilde þe fro schame,* Gam. 767. *fro schame ye Rowlande schelde,* Row. & Ot. 492.

schylde fro synne, Guy 1340, Triam. 2. *schilde out of syn,* Ywaine 2.

schryuen of hys synne, Athel. 771.

O.E.Pr., E.M.E., La3., A. *see a si3te,* Amad. 86, Athel. 216, Avow. 990, Beues 4523, Firum. 2918, Green Kn. 79, 102, Guy 9093, Lib. Dis. 1186, 1296, Melayne 907, Oct. Emp. 151, Rich. 4976, 5701, Row. & Ot. 1496, Trist. 2944, Ywaine 2609.

see by syght, Oct. Emp. 1029, Otuel 385.

O.E.Pr., A. *see in si3te,* Amad. 435, Tolous 155, 222, 328, Trist. 1262, Ywaine 246, 2314.

A. *see with si3te,* Amad. 285, 476, Beues 4169, Degare 744, Firum. 193, Guy 2168, Ipom. 2151, Launfal 582, 1026, Lib. Dis. 888, 1359, 1587, M. Arthur 400, etc., Melayne 894, Perc. 1290, Roul. & Vern. 1, Trist. 1405, etc.

E.M.E. *that syght for to see,* Tolous 945. *saw þat sighte,* M. Arthur 968.

saw with my sight, Marr. of Gaw. 197.

see and sand, Avow. 4, Ywaine 3657. **A.** *see and sonde,* Emare 15, Tolous 903.

A. *semly to see,* Amis. 426, 534, Athel. 37, Emare 93, etc., Florence 1160, 1487, 2071, Oct. Emp. 90, Row. & Ot. 1210, 1587. *seemely is to see,* Marr. of Gaw. 2. *seemly for to see,* Turke 100. *semelych on to se,* Lib. Dis. 849, Tolous 1212. *semly to sene,* Sowdane 39. *semely on to sene,* Triam. 26. *seemely to be seene,* Marr. of Gaw. 209. **E.M.E.** *vseemly·was to see,* Marr. of Gaw. 127.

a seemly syght, Florence 488, 1543, Oct. Emp. 651, Orfeo 411, Ywaine 365. *semely in syght,* Oct. Emp. 234, Triam. 666. *semelyer yn syght,* Tolous 345. *semely . . . of syght,* Emare 9, 48, 177, Launfal 945. *semelyest of syght,* Oct. Emp. 786.

semely wer sette yn sale, Launfal 497. *semyly sale,* Lib. Dis. 1011, 2111. *semliest in sale,* Amis. 444, 1513.

A. *sende socour,* Firum. 5054, Lib. Dis. 605, Triam. 1486. *sokor send,* Amad. 428, 430. *socour sent,* Ywaine 2318, 2862.

E.M.E., La3., A. *sende his sonde,* Amis. 64, etc. (5 times), Sages 237, 2025. *sende a sonde,* Beues 3305, Guy 10049, 10705, Horn Child 316, M. Arthur 3675. *he sende by sonde,* Chron. 525. *sende sondes,* Rich. 49. *he sent his sonde,* Alis. 2607, Oct. 1585, Tars 939.

serchid and sought, Sowdane 225.

sharpe and share, Guy & Col. 384.

A. *thair sheldes war shivered*, Ywaine 3549, 3553. *scheuyrde scheldes*, Guy 8153.

O.E.Pr., La3., O. & N., A. *shelde and spere*, Alis. 5320, 7261, Amis. 179, 1202, 1220, Avow. 368, 576, Florence 366, 465, 1016, Guy & Col. 147, Hav. 2551, Horn Child 52, 195, Laud 9644, Lib. Dis. 416, 570, Melayne 618, Oct. Emp. 825, 883, Otuel 269, Rich. 254, etc. (5 times), Rol. 445, Row. & Ot. 44, Sages 2793, Torrent 526, 549, etc., Triam. 698, 836, Ywaine 406, etc. *sheld ne spere*, Hav. 489, 624, 1653. *shelds, speres*, Degare 459. **La3.** *spere and schelde*, Beues 3744, Degare 270, etc., Firum 266, 870, Green Kn. 239, Guy 732, etc., Ipom. 536, 910, Isum. 737, Laud 7348, etc., Launfal 576, Lib. Dis. 518, etc., M. Arthur 922, 2135, 2552, Melayne 43, Otuel 118, Oct. 657, 966, 1077, 1527, Row. & Ot. 388, Sowdane 184, etc., Tolous 69, 87.

speres scheveryd, Rich. 5309.

sicur and sure, Laud 5932, 9964. *sure and sekir*, Laud 11427.

A. *syke nor sare* (sb.), Florence 1929.

seke and sare, Perc. 1078.

sekenes sar, Ywaine 2917.

A. *syke and sobbe*, Laud 2676. *sobbing, siking and sor*, Hav. 234.

sykyng sore, Emare 328, 676. *sikynges sore*, Tars 687.

O. & N., A. *syked sore*, Guy 9096. *sore ho sikes*, Amad. 112.

A. *syghe/d sare/sore*, Firum. 5831, Florence 1426, 1703, Isum. 139, M. Arthur 631, etc. (9 times), Oct. Emp. 51, Rich. 3447, Squ. of L. Deg. 22, Tolous 160, 1006, Triam. 1677, Turke 72, Ywaine 2297, etc. *he syghes fulle sore*, Perc. 1064. *syghande fulle sare*, Perc. 1784. *syghynge sare/sore*, Cleges 357, Isum. 183, M. Arthur 802, etc., Squ. of L. Deg. 857. *sighed ful sare*, Sowdane 706. *sore then syghed hee*, Tolous 135. *sore si3te/syghed*, Beues 1312, Kn. of Curt. 69, Floris & Blan. 833, Triam. 30.

many a sore sighe, Rol. 431.

sylke and satyne, Guy 8426.

E.M.E., A. *synne and schame*, Guy 1340. *shame and synne*, Guy 2020, 5910.

O.E.Pr. *synge a songe*, Laud 11753, Sowdane 2109.

E.M.E., A. *synge in songe*, Emare 24, Trist. 1860.

O.E.P. & Pr., E.M.E., La3. *sunge and sayd*, Rich. 215.

sitte at sopere, M. Arthur 153.

sitte one stede, Melayne 6.

E.M.E., La3., O. & N., A. *sitte stille*, Alis. 40, Horn 805, Orfeo 443. *sat stille*, Gam. 849, Orfeo 524, Rich. 3459, Sowdane 1131, Triam. 1650, Ywaine 77. *seten stylle*, Rich. 3471.

A. *sitten in py sete*, Gam. 848. *sittynge uppon a sete*, Sowdane 62. *sate in seate*, Turke 10. *sete in sete*, Amad. 586.

sat there sad and stille, Guy & Col. 168.

E.M.E., A. *sat stane-still*, Sages 3668.

he sat or stode, Amis. 715.

sytole, sautrye, Lib. Dis. 137, 1780.

in slakkes and slade, Row. & Ot. 1418.

La3. *sley and styke*, Rich. 4750.

A. *slidus he on slepe,* Avow. 271.

E.M.E. *for smelle other smekis,* Avow. 236.

smertely and skeet, Gam. 187.

smite wiþ spere, Beues 232. **Laȝ.** *smot(e) him with a/his spere,* Firum. 940, Tolous 1114.

smote a strok, Beues 1885–6, Firum. 588, etc., Guy 10201.

snaw and slete, Ywaine 375.

sober and sound, Carle 2.

Orm., A. *soft and stylle,* Oct. 1238.

assoile hem of here sinne, Gam. 449. *asoylyd of synne,* Rich. 1317.

O.E.Pr., E.M.E., Laȝ., P.M., A. *þe sonne schon,* Beues 3231, Degare 1061, Eglam. 372, Firum. 2475, etc., Laud 9825, Orfeo 152, Squ. of L. Deg. 102. *sonne had schyned,* Laud 13849. *shynning of þe sonne,* Alis. 4941.

E.M.E., A. *of son and see,* Melayne 1054.

A. *the sunne was sette,* Rich. 3155. *to sette bygan the sunn,* Hav. 2671. *sone and suithe,* Chron. 341.

this sorewe save, M. Arthur 2117.

for sorouwe and for scathe, Oct. 303.

E.M.E., A. *sorwe and schame,* Firum. 2862, Lib. Dis. 1449.

A. *sorowe and sikes,* Laud 13508, cp. **E.M.E.**

A. *sorwe and siking save,* Amis. 1200, 1671. *sorow and sighing sore,* Squ. of L. Deg. 857.

A. *sorowe and syte/syght,* Florence 1631, 2109, Guy 2311.

O.E.P. & Pr., E.M.E., Laȝ., P.M. *sorow and sore,* Launfal 229.

O.E.Pr., E.M.E., Laȝ., Orm. *sorful and sori,* Hav. 151, 2541. *sory and sorwful,* Hav. 1248.

sorow and stryffe, M. Arthur 3701.

E.M.E., Laȝ., A. *the sothe to say,* Avow. 160, 585, Carle 379, 433, Cleges 68, 157, 252, Degare 265, etc., Eglam. 736, Firum. 158, etc., Florence 1112, etc., Green Kn. 88, 145, 205, Ipom. 1672, Laud 13119, 17645, etc., M. Arthur 60, etc., Land. 290, Launfal 670, 736, Oct. Emp. 1035, 1697, Perc. 2192, etc., Rich. 942, etc., Sowdane 2275, Torrent 2451, Trist. 1129, etc., Ywaine 15, etc. **O.E.P. & Pr.** *to seye the soothe,* Laud 3165, etc., Ipom. 2078. *soþ to segge,* Otuel 56, 339. *saye soth,* Alis. 3339, Hav. 2008, Sages 1558, 3270, 3939, Tolous 158. *say for/the sothe,* Launfal 453, 784. *says sothe,* Avow. 1050. *sothe say,* Amad. 573. *soþ . . . to say,* Beues 585, etc., Lamb. 331, Lamw. 229, Launfal 815, Rol. 99, etc. *þe sothe gif I schuld say,* Amad. 333. *soth as I you say,* Gam. 556. *for soth . . . y yow say,* Degare 116, etc., Lib. Dis. 78, Tolous 891. *the sothe y wylle yow say,* Oct. Emp. 963. **O.E.P. & Pr., E.M.E., A.** *sothely to say,* Melayne 1567. *sothely to sayne,* Tolous 128. *þe soþe for to sain,* Horn Child 801.

A. *sothe as I spek,* Rol. 926.

O.E.Pr. *spak and sayde,* Firum. 685, Floris & Blan. 139, Hav. 2389. **A.** *speke and segge,* Floris & Blan. 1121, 1172.

O.E.Pr., A. *speche (hast þou) spoken,* Melayne 746.

sparkes gonne out sprynge, Lib. Dis. 1151.

to spare or to spille, Avow. 556.

speech and sight, Guy & Col. 159.

spende and spare not, Land. 131.

A. *to spir and spy,* Ywaine 3013.

22

O. & N., A. (*þe floures*) *sprede and spring*, Orfeo, 67.
stabull and stere (verbs), Florence 1238.
stalworth and starke, Guy 6906.
stedes in the stable, Rich. 6100.   *þe stede out of þe stable*, Beues 2028.   *the stede was broght out of stable*, Oct. 1405.
steedes in my stalle, Gam. 179., cp. **E.M.E.**
A. *the steede he bistrood*, Gam. 189.
stele or stone, M. Arthur 590.
sterne and sterke, Firum. 5558, Guy 10108.
A. *stern/stirrun and stowte*, Avow. 178, 807, Beues 3607, Degare 105, Lib. Dis. 1251, Row. & Ot. 887, Sages 2981.   *stout and sterne*, Beues 2483, Lib. Dis. 402, 1456, Rich. 3826.
to sterte vppon a stede, M. Arthur 3278, etc.
styffe and starke, Guy 8528, Guy & Col. 40.
stiff on stede, M. Arthur 45, 350, 2307, Oct. Emp. 1578, Trist. 3079.   *stipe on stede*, Amad. 577, Horn Child 255, 690, 1095, 1125, Trist. 66, 3014.
A. *styffe and/in stowre*, Florence 573, Green Kn. 46, Ipom. 647, M. Arthur 1811, Marr. of 'Gaw. 8, Perc. 1566, Rol. 143, Squ. of L. Deg. 658, Tolous 1205, Torrent 2649, Triam. 1035, 1207, Turke 151, Ywaine 31.   *styþ on stoure*, Firum. 696.
stiffe and stronge in stoure, M. Arthur 236.
stif and stout, Firum. 875, Guy 6588, 9552, Troy 1840, Laud 8196, etc.
stythe and stowtte, Row. & Ot. 698.   *stoute and stythe*, Tars 1034.
O. & N., A. *stiffe and strong*, Carle 4, Degare 469, Green Kn. 137, Guy 2896, 4684, Guy & Col. 474, Ipom. 9, 115, 1135, 1587, 1904, Laud 7975, etc., Marr. of Gaw. 35, 42, 87, Oct. 1041, Rich. 467, etc. (3 times), Torrent 322, 1491, 2590, Triam. 617.   *strong and stif*, Firum. 794, Laud 3646.
stiffe and stithe, Guy & Col. 357.
O.E.P., A. *stithe and strong*, Amis. 1302.
A. *styff, stalworth and strong*, Laud 3771.
stille so ston, Amis. 1273.   **A.** *stille as* . . . *ston*, Gam. 395, 423, Hav. 928, Otuel 491, 1641, Launfal 357, Oct. 186, Roul & Vern. 525, Sowdane 2537, Tars 549, 603, 636.   *sate stylle as any stone*, Tolous 754.   *ston-styll*, The Hare 42, Perc. 841.
well stylle wythouten stryf, Launfal 660.
A. *stynte strife*, Avow. 137, 288, 528.
A. *stynte of þer stryfe*, Tolous 924.
E.M.E., A. *stirre noghte of this stede*, Melayne 1173.
als he was stoken in that stall, Ywaine 695.
E.M.E., Laȝ., A. *stokkes and stonis*, Avow. 188.   *stones and stokkes*, Rich. 4714.
A. *stonde in stalle*, Amad. 465.
O.E.Pr., E.M.E., Laȝ., Orm., A. *stond/stand stille*, Otuel 313, 493, 583, Torrent 179, Tolous 307, 334, Trist. 359.
stondeth alle stille, Gam. 55.   *stod stille*, Beues 343, Gam 238, 473, 571, Guy 1119, etc., Lamb. 527, M. Arthur 3264, Triam. 74, 279, Ywaine 274.   *stylle he stode*, Florence 908, Oct: Emp. 122, 462.
stande still in a stede, Rol. 817.   *stonde in no stidde*, Amad. 728.   *stode in that stede*, Avow. 972.   *standeth in this stede*, Turke 282.
O. & N. *stones and staue*, Alis. 5843.
stongen wyth a spere, Tolous 645.   **E.M.E., Laȝ.** *with spere ystonge*, Oct. 1, 962.

O. & N. *stor·and stark*, Chron. 464, 538, 796. *stark and store*, Lib. Dis. 1766. *stout and stark*, Lib. Dis. 710.

O.E.P. *by stretes and by stye*, Emare 196. *by stye and strete*, Emare 543. *strike with a sword*, Degare 297.

strong (strokes) and steryn, Row. & Ot. 1407.

E.M.E., Laȝ., O. & N. *strong and stark*, Alis. 5527, Hav. 608, 1271, 2535, Sages 2123. *stark and strong*, Hav. 988.

strange and stowte, Melayne 1531. *strong and stoute*, Rich. 4285, etc. (5 times), Rol. 999, Squ. of L. Deg. 1001, Turke 132.

stronge in stowre, Cleges 492, Florence 2169, Triam. 948, Turke 149.

stub nor ston, Orfeo 346.

A. *suffer sorwe*, Firum. 1084.

sweate and stinke, Carle 112.

Laȝ., A. *swinke and sweat*, Turke 103.

with swerd and staff, Laud 6094.

O.E.P. & Pr., Laȝ. *swerd and shelde*, Alis. 5510, Guy & Col. 349, 366, M. Arthur 85, 2915. *swerdes and scheldes*, Laud 4002. **Laȝ.** *schylde, swyrde*, Guy 11862.

O.E.Pr., Laȝ. *swerde(s) . . . spere(s)*, Alis. 3952, Firum. 1383, Guy 1649, etc., Hav. 2299, Laud 8599, Otuel 840, Perc. 563, Rich. 2547, etc. (6 times), Row. & Ot. 1415. **Laȝ.** *spere(s) . . . swerd(es)*, Alis. 3901, 4201, 7241, 7505, Horn Child 775, Laud 3864, etc., Lib. Dis. 184, M. Arthur 1541, Triam. 1211, Otuel 840.

O.E.Pr. *sworde, schylde or spere*, Tolous 65. *swerdes and speres, scheelds*, Rich. 3886. *scheld, swerd or spere*, Roul. & Vern. 81.

swete of sware, Florence 441.

swiftly and swipe, Trist. 833–4.

Orm. *he swor and seide*, Tars 822.

summe swumme, summe sunke, Otuel 1617.

A. *tabours and trumpes*, Orfeo 301, Rich. 2887, etc., Lib. Dis. 925. *tabourers and trumpours*, Rich. 3750. **A.** *trommpus, tabours*, Emare 389. *trompys, taborus*, Oct. 68, 1190. *trompours and tabourers*, Orfeo 521. *trumpetis and taberers*, Rol. 918.

take tent, Ywaine 1124, etc. (4 times).

talked and tolde, Perc. 1558.

E.M.E., Laȝ., A. *tell a tale*, Alis. 1077, 1138, 3531, Amad. 48, Athel. 153, etc., Beues 666, etc., Degare 2, Emare 948, Firum. 1348, Florence 1129, 1333, Floris & Blan. 788, Guy 5925, etc., Guy & Col. 602, The Hare 1, Hav. 3, Ipom. 1018, Lamb. 502, Laud 2097, 13209, 14564, Lib. Dis. 915, etc. (6 times), M. Arthur 1709, 3291, Melayne 574, 1489, Oct. Emp. 217, 1654, Perc. 1479, 1585, 1971, Rich. 549, etc., Rol. 4, 200, Sages 701, etc., Tars 89, Torrent 407, 734, Triam. 576, 1103, Trist. 99, 3088, Turke 229, Ywaine 90, etc.

(trewely) to telle in tale, Amis. 441, 2337. *telle in tale*, Beues 1540, etc., Launfal 52, Lib. Dis. 2108, Oct. 55, 427, Tars 516. *telle of a tale*, Tolous 7–8. *telle the tale*, Beues 2254 (= count the number). **E.M.E.** *told bi tale*, Beues 245. *tale ytold*, Oct. 1873. *I tell you this tale for true*, Green Kn. 276.

E.M.E., Laȝ., A. *telle tyding(s)*, Arthur 200, Athel. 124, 225, etc., Gam. 703, Guy 2338, etc., Ipom. 1960, Isum. 77, Rich. 800, Sowdane 783, Triam. 156, 670. *telle þis tipeand*, Horn. Child 242.

A. *telle ȝou tyte*, Row. & Ot. 204.

E.M.E., A.　*telle with tong,* Amis. 1886, Triam. 1530, Ywaine 1427.　**E.M.E., P.M., A.**　*telle ne mihte no tonge,* Horn 1269.　*(myghte) no tonge telle,* Perc. 628.　*with tunge telle,* Amad. 818.

A.　*tell the truth,* Green Kn. 330.　*the truth to tell,* Carle 199.

A.　*telle trewly,* Triam. 1522.　*trewly to tell,* Ywaine 329.

tent and/or teld, Laud 11585, 13836.　*tentis and teldis,* Laud 16575.　*no teld ne tent,* Laud 4667.

penche in pouʒt, Orfeo 373.

through thicke and thin, Degare 188.

thryve and/ne thee, Squ. of L. Deg. 1088, Firum. 5841, Guy 5094, Otuel 301.　*þe and thryue,* Amis. 1650, Firum. 4536, Oct. 625.

E.M.E.　*so thryve or thro,* M. Arthur 589.

A.　*tymber and tre,* Laud 3632.

E.M.E.　*tyme and tyde,* Laud 14933.

A.　*toppe ouer tayle,* Row. & Ot. 923.

A.　*tour and town,* Amis 1538, Athel. 42, Degare 732, Emare 804, Firum. 5693, Florence 650, Guy & Col. 11, Horn Child 813, 1134, Lib. Dis. 530, M. Arthur 3263, Row. & Ot. 224, Roul. & Vern. 349, Sowdane 780, etc., Squ. of L. Deg. 264, Trist. 261, Ywaine 1567, etc. (5 times).
A.　*town and toure,* Amad. 497, etc., Amis. 9, etc., Kn. of Curt. 29, 37, Emare 898, Guy 4827, Row. & Ot. 1577.

fro towne to towne, Triam. 590.

to-tused and to-torn, Hav. 1984.

A.　*treason and/or trechery,* Kn. of Curt. 40, Ywaine 1609.　*trecherie, tresoun,* Hav. 2988–9.

O.E.P., E.M.E., A.　*treye and tene,* Amis. 1572, Beues 4588, Laud 11830, Rol. 110, Row. & Ot. 1290, 1518.

A.　*trewe and triste,* Laud 9970.　*trewe and truste,* Laud 17593, Tars 824.
A.　*trusty and trewe,* Rich. 5670.

waken al my wo, Amis. 272.　*wakenyth hur waa,* Florence 1745, 2078.

A.　*walkes in my way,* Avow. 31.

wanne and wete, M. Arthur 1507.

A.　*wanton and wylde,* Guy 8442.

war and wight, Amis. 145.

O.E.Pr.　*war(e) and wis(e),* Amis. 182, Chron. 681, Degare 517, Florence 304, Guy 70, etc., Horn Child 283, Laud 6456, 14812, Sages 1394, 1708, 2870, Trist. 1377, Troy 342, Ywaine 12, etc. (4 times).　**E.M.E., Laʒ., Orm., O. & N., A.**　*wis(e) and war(e),* Alis. 1789, 2129, 2274, Chron. 242, etc., Guy 253, etc., Sages 198, 410, etc., Sowdane, 216.　*so war ne so wys,* Oct. 46.

A.　*er he were war and er he wyst,* Laud 10940.　*wite and war,* Avow. 15.

wayt and wise, Avow. 24.

warn þe waye, Cleges 452, 461.

A.　*they washed all and went to meate,* Carle 305.　*they wessh and wente to mete,* Sowdane 1871.

watur and waweys, Guy 494.

water of the welle, Perc. 7.

E.M.E., A.　*water nor wyne,* Sowdane 2905.　*wyn ne watyr,* Rich. 3048.

E.M.E., A.　*water and wode,* Alis. 1286, 1295.

A.　*wax/wex . . . wod(e),* Beues 1916, Firum. 728, etc., Guy 281, etc., Laud 10739, Oct. Emp. 153, Sowdane 2423, Torrent 73, etc., Troy 1137,

Ywaine 1740. *he wax all wod*, Oct. 1652. *wex al wilde and wode*, Ywaine 1650. *wax wod and wrop*, Firum. 1820. **A.** *wexed wroth*, Arthur 95, Firum. 126, etc., Guy 9365, 9573, Lamb. 293, Lamw. 287, Sowdane 2007. **A.** *wax wrop as wynde*, Athel. 453. *wax ful wroth and wo*, Amis. 1588. *he wex wood and wroth*, Laud 4981. *wax wroth*, Otuel 454. *wrothe wex*, Avow. 229. *for wrathe he wex ner wode*, Amis. 386. *for wraththe he waxeth wood*, Tars 38.

A. *wedde a wife*, Amad. 631, M. Arthur 2987. *wedde wif*, Beues 287. O.E.Pr., **A.** *wedde . . . to wyff*, Firum. 2086, Degare 967, Eglam. 106, 155, Marr. of Gaw. 140, Oct. Emp. 1402, Perc. 1000, Ywaine 3324. *weddyd pat lady to hys wyfe*, Tolous 1207. **O.E.Pr., A.** *hys weddyd wyff*, Athel. 46, Emare 44. *wed no wiffe*, Degare 167. *a wyff to wedde*, Rich. 48.

wedur at wille, Laud 3575.

that weldes both welth and wit, Guy & Col. 518. *to weld all the welth*, Rol. 220. *to welde noður to wynne*, Florence 354.

E.M.E. *wele and wynne*, M. Arthur 3788.

welth and wynne, Squ. of L. Deg. 263.

my wele, my wytt, Tolous 554.

O.E.P., E.M.E., A. *wele and/or wo*, Amis. 11, etc. (7 times), Beues 1964, Degare 88, Isum. 305, 380, 759, Lamb. 318, 615, Laud 306, 785, 2596, Launfal 879, M. Arthur 1823, 1891, Orfeo 5, Squ. of L. Deg. 113, Tars 967, Triam. 57, 177, 382, Ywaine 2015, 2682. *wele ne/nor . . . wo* Degare 1160, 1632, Firum. 2412, Floris & Blan. 88, Hav. 2777, Laud 3060, 4177, 15091, M. Arthur 1823, 1891, Oct. Emp. 359, Oct. 573, 875, Rich. 597, 6521, Sages 3744. *wo and wele*, Emare 573, Guy 5752, M. Arthur 8.

O.E.Pr., A. *wele and worship*, Rol. 225.

A. *all the welthe of pis world*, Rol. 913.

wem and wounde, Amis. 2406. *wemme ne/or wounde*, Rich. 1090, Rol. 685, Squ. of L. Deg. 436, 663. *weme of wounde*, Oct. Emp. 1040.

E.M.E., A. *wende(s) . . . way*, Amad. 229, Athel. 333, 345, Avow. 721, Degare 1709, Firum. 1719, etc., Guy & Col. 449, Isum. 287, etc., Laud 960, Melayne 92, etc., Oct. 350, 377, 680, Rich. 1048, etc., Row. & Ot. 378, Sages 3417, Squ. of L. Deg. 269, 563, 1007, 1124, Torrent 115, 439, etc., Ywaine 236, etc. *wende forp in pi way*, Trist. 3094. **A.** *wende away*, Florence 536, etc., Sages 1630. *he wendith by the way*, Alis. 2909. *away to wend*, Lamb. 578, 604.

went . . . his/her way, Amad. 336, Athel. 333, Beues 3300, Carle 359, Degare 127, etc., Eglam. 334, Emare 186, 542, Gam. 609, Guy & Col. 453, Ipom. 567, etc., Launfal. 1019, M. Arthur 58, etc., Oct. Emp. 588, Perc. 144, 178, 1758, Rol. 88, Roul. & Vern. 401, Sages 2254, 3377, Sowdane 1584, Tolous 407, Triam. 1322. *went away*, Amis. 131, etc. (9 times), Beues 2315, etc., Guy 374, etc., Launfal. 173, M. Arthur 1168, etc., Trist. 796, etc., Tolous 160, 1143, Ywaine 817, etc. *away went*, Green Kn. 211.

Laȝ., A. *wend to the wode*, Guy 7084. *to the wode they went*, Triam. 1121. *to wode he wente*, Lib. Dis. 26. *to the wode y went*, Florence 2062.

where I wende in worlde, M. Arthur 2434.

wepe and wake, M. Arthur 750, etc.

A. *weopyng, waylyng*, Alis. 7883, Rol. 368.

A. *wepynge water*, Sowdane 3226.

A. *wepe and wo*, Orfeo 195, 234. **A.** *wepithe for wo*, Rol. 599. *wepte for wo*, Oct. Emp. 1031. **A.** *wepynge and wo*, Lamw. 360.

E.M.E., A. *shee weeped and wrange her hands*, Degare 68, 132. *wepe and wrong hire hond*, Sages 1950. *wep(e) and . . . hondes wrong*, Amis. 859, Firum. 5117. *weopyng and hondis wryngyng*, Alis. 7977. *wepyd and handys wrange*, M. Arthur 3505, Row. & Ot. 1305. *wepte and wronge her honde*, Emare 639. *wepyd and wrothe hys hande*, Guy 11203. *wrongyn heore hondyn and wepten*, Alis. 7891. *wrungen hondes and wepen*, Hav. 152. *wepe and wrynge*, M. Arthur 3746.

O.E.P. & Pr., A. *wepon(s) welde*, Avow. 222, Beues 4432, Chron. 265, Degare 271, Florence 534, Guy & Col. 107, etc., Hav. 1436, Perc. 20, M. Arthur 1928, Oct. 1311, Rol. 800, Row. & Ot. 372, etc., Sages 2996, Troy 837, Ywaine 1219, 3233. *any wapyn may welde*, Melayne 321.

O.E.Pr., E.M.E., La3., Orm., A. *to werche werke(s)*, Otuel 390, Sages 3183. See also under *wroght*.

O.E.P. & Pr., E.M.E., La3., A. *to werk his wylle*, Arthur 594, Emare 227. *wirke 3our wille*, Melayne 795. *his wil to wirk*, Sages 3354.

E.M.E., A. *werche . . . wo*, Firum. 1545, Florence 1199, Perc. 1896, Rich. 2535, Rol. 318, Roul. & Vern. 48, Sowdane 148, 2209.

E.M.E., A. *he wered swiche a wede*, Trist. 653. *wedes to wer*, Ywaine 3107. *in wer and wo*, Amis. 236, Troy 364.

wery and woo, Triam. 418.

A. *werre and wrake*, M. Arthur 1695, 3666.

La3., A. *wete . . . wonges*, Trist. 732.

wyght in wede, Rich. 4438.

wyght in were, Tolous 96.

A. *wighte and worthy*, Melayne 549. *worthy and wyghte*, Melayne 495. 609, 627.

E.M.E., La3. *wilde and wod*, Amis. 1015, Firum. 2307, Lib. Dis. 507, Tolous 108. See also under *wax*. *wode and wylde*, Guy 10630, Sages 1462. *wilde and wrope*, Firum. 672.

E.M.E., A. *wind and water*, Hav. 1360, Horn Child 746, Rol. 832. *watyr and wynde*, Torrent 3.

O.E.Pr., E.M.E., La3., A. *winde and weder*, Beues 3860, Floris & Blan. 456, Oct. 1237, Rol. 582, Tolous 238, Torrent 1843.

La3., Orm., A. *winne worschepe*, Laud 8427, 12337, 13097, Perc. 11, Rich. 2311, Rol. 213, 225, Tolous 837. *worship wynne*, M. Arthur 35, 2596, Laud 16494, Melayne 1529, Sowdane 1149. *much worshipp wan*, Carle 8.

A. *wyse of werkys*, Florence 1366.

wise and wi3t, Amis. 437, 1910, 1574, Horn Child 30, Lib. Dis. 349, 2092, Oct. 1808, Roul. & Vern. 450, Trist. 90.

La3., A. *wys of wytte and wyght*, Lib. Dis. 5.

O.E.P., E.M.E., La3. *wis, witti*, Laud 7137. **O.E.P.** *witti and wis*, Laud 12154.

A. *wit and wisdam*, Laud 638, 2471. *wisdom and wit*, Sages 49.

Cp. **O.E.P. & Pr., A.** *wyse wordys*, M. Arthur 3132.

y wis and nou3t at wene, Trist. 17. *wist withouten wene*, Land. 292. *to wytt wythouten wene*, Florence 2156. *to wite and nou3t at wene*, Trist. 1207, etc. *wot and wene*, Torrent 1559. *wel ich wot and nou3t ne wene*,

Beues 3374. *wot wythouten wene*, Florence 1086, Oct. Emp. 1230, Trist. 2100.

Orm., O. & N. *weel I wot*, Athel. 468.

wite and ward, Beues 2934.

wlonkest on wede, Degare 576.   Cp. *worthy in wede*.

wough and wrong, Amis. 2102.

in wo to welde and wende, Lib. Dis. 2028.

woo and wrake, M. Arthur 1451, 2654, Sowdane 2446.

A. *wod of wit*, Alis. 1831, Sages 495.

wodes and wonges, Hav. 397, 1444.

Cp. **O.E.Pr., Alf., A.** *to wonye in (worldly) wone*, Launfal 933.

O.E.P. & Pr., E.M.E., Orm., P.M., A. *in word and werk*, Rol. 209. *in word, in werk, in wille*, Amis. 152.

O.E.Pr., E.M.E., P.M., A. *werldes wele*, Isum. 53.

A. *out of world iwent*, Tars 1143.

A. *all the/thys world to wynne*, Florence 1691, Launfal 148, Lib. Dis. 1953.

E.M.E., La3. *worldes winne* (sb.), Amis. 604, 2244.

thys worlde wroght and wan, M. Arthur 2439. **E.M.E., A.** *by Him that al this world hath wrou3t*, Laud 2030, M. Arthur 373.

that worthy was to welde, Florence 1718.

worthy wyght, Florence 800.

that worthy ys yn wone, Florence 1346.

worthy in wede, Amis. 30, Green Kn. 135, Melayne 867, etc., M. Arthur 2709. *worþy vnder wede*, Emare 250, 612, 988, Row. & Ot. 861. *worthli in wede*, Amis. 1430. *worthily in wede*, Roul. & Ot. 714. *worthliest in wede*, Amis. 138, etc. *worthiest in wede*, Torrent 33, cp. *lufsum under lyne*. *worthly in wede*, Degare 1892. *in worthli wede*, Tars 125.

E.M.E., A. *woundes wyde*, Firum. 887, etc., Guy 1084, etc., Row. & Ot. 1175, Tolous 126, Trist. 3332, Ywaine 2630. **A.** *woundes wyde and wete*, Row. & Ot. 940, 1462. *woundys wanne and wete*, Florence 1994.

A. *to wrynge and wessche*, Oct. 1212.

to wring and writhe, Guy & Col. 15.

O.E.Pr. *wrought with curyous werke*, Carle 368. **A.** *for werkes that he wroughte*, Gam. 309. *werkis wroght*, M. Arthur 16. *he these werkys hath wroght*, Oct. 756. *soche werkys new sche wroght*, Tolous 1021.

A. *wroght . . . wo*, Amis. 1068, 1575, 2130, Guy 11094, M. Arthur 2391, Row. & Ot. 114, Squ. of L. Deg. 988, Triam. 1344, 1415, Trist. 3271, Tolous 1119.

O.E.Pr. *wrou3t þat wonder*, Trist. 1506. *wroughten wonders*, Sowdane 987. **E.M.E., A.** *thys wonder hath wroght*, Triam. 1104.

wrought such wrake, M. Arthur 1181. *wurche wrake*, Avow. 323.

A. *wroght wrong*, Guy 5052, Trist. 2666.

E.M.E. *wrothe and wode*, Amis. 1357, Floris & Blan. 1111, 1183, M. Arthur 3062, Sowdane 1734. See also under *wax*.

wurche him no woundes, Avow. 44.

(*c*) The Alliterative Works with End-rhyme (Rh.A. 1).

Under this heading are included not merely the works in the alliterative long line with the simple addition of end-rhyme (Chapter 4, vol. 1), but also *all* Minot's poems, *The Pearl* and *The*

Enemies of Man, owing to the excessive amount of alliteration found in these poems.

This group is relatively unimportant, for the works are of a miscellaneous character and are of widely differing dates. The interest, however, lies in the list itself and the parallels indicated in the margin. There are 261 phrases in the group, of which ninety-four occur in *Pearl* and sixty-nine in *Minot*. Those in the former poem are inevitably more closely connected with the phrases in the *A*-group, to which they properly belong, while Minot's phrases are more stereotyped, though they make it abundantly clear that he was in some way connected with the northern school of alliterative poetry, whose works are discussed in the next section. Similarly, the short lyric—*The Enemies of Man*—employs no less than eighteen alliterative phrases, many of which are striking : *now fals now frouȝ, now min now mare, woŋges wete*, etc.

The table of phrases will indicate the number of the phrases that occur also in Old English prose and poetry, and in the successive groups. An important Old English poetic phrase survives in *Pearl* 736, *folde and flode*, and the more common Old English phrase *main and mode* appears in Minot. Of the notable phrases which occur also in the poems of the Alliterative Revival, the following may be mentioned : *del and daunger, dynge on a dore, droupe and dare, gader and glene, happe and hele, hele and hide, more and min, sorȝ and site, swete and swinke*. Such expressions show that these alliterative rhyming poets in some measure shared the alliterative traditions.

Rom. *baroun and bonde*, Husb. 30.
Rom. *bataile to bede*, Minot 11.35.
A., Rom. *bende bowes*, Minot 6.23.
Laȝ., A., Rom. *þe beornes þat were bolde*, On Serving Crist 58.
E.M.E., A. *ber a barne*, Pearl 426.
oure bales to bere, Pearl 807.
A., Rom. *bete(n)* . . . *bale*, Harley Lyric 4.21, Minot 2.28 & 29, 1st Rolle Lyric 20.
E.M.E., A., Rom. *bute of all my bale*, Minot 1.4.
abiden þat bone, Pearl 1090.
E.M.E., Rom. *bid a bone*, Minot 1.3. *bid* (sb. = asking for) *to þe bon*, Husb. 7.
blysned þe borȝ al bryȝt, Pearl 1048.
in blysse to brede, Pearl 415.
O.E.P. & Pr., E.M.E., A., Rom. *bryng me to blysse*, 1st Rolle Lyric 28. *to blisse he is broht*, Harley Lyric 4.19. *þat hatȝ me broȝt þys blysse ner*, Pearl 286.
E.M.E., A., Rom. *my blisse, my bale*, Pearl 373, 478.
blo and blynde, Pearl 83.

blith als brid on brere, Minot 7.128.

A. *blusched on þe burghe*, Pearl 980.

E.M.E., Rom. *þe body and þe bon*, On Serving Crist 72.

my breste in bale bot bolne and bele, Pearl 18.

ani breste for bale aȝt haf forbrent, Pearl 1139.

A., Rom. *(þat barn þat) broht vs of bale*, Rawl. Luke 48.

E.M.E., P.M., A., Rom. *þe blod vs boȝt fro bale*, Pearl 651.

bowsom his bodword to bede, Rawl. Luke 12.

þe brokeȝ brym, Pearl 1074.

by broke and by brynke, Husb. 70.

A. *his burthen he bereth*, Harley Lyric 1.2.

E.M.E., A., Rom. *cayser ant knyght*, Harley Lyric 4.7.

oure care is kest, Pearl 861. **Rom.** *cast in care*, Minot 5.7, 6.18, 9.60.

care ful colde, Pearl 50, cp. Beow. 2396, *cealdum cearsiðum.* **A., Rom.**
   cares colde, Husb. 61, Minot 4.67, 7.87, Pearl 808.

keruen and caggen, Pearl 512.

E.M.E., A., Rom. *changed chere*, Minot 4.45.

Rom. *kindel . . . care*, Minot 2.10, 2.19, 10.23, 11.26.

E.M.E., A., Rom. *king with croune*, Minot 7.170.

O.E.Pr., E.M.E., Laȝ., A., Rom. *kyng and quene*, Pearl 468. *quen oþer
   kyng*, Pearl 448.

clene and clere, Pearl 227, 737.

E.M.E., Laȝ., Rom. *clerc and knight*, Husb. 30.

O.E.P. & Pr., E.M.E., Laȝ., A., Rom. *clip and kys*, Minot 6.29.

E.M.E., A. *come to corte*, Pearl 701.

conig ne cat, Minot 8.75.

corne is coruen, Pearl 40.

E.M.E., A., Rom. *corounde me quene*, Pearl 415. **E.M.E., A., Rom.**
   corounde þe kyng, Pearl 480.

our corses in clotteȝ clynge, Pearl 857. [See **Rom.** under *clynge* and *clot*.]

for crafte ne for cunninge, 1st Chester Play 47.

Rom. *crak (a) crowne*, Minot 1.59, 2.10 & 11.

A., Rom. *er þe day dawe*, Harley Lyric 1.40.

A., Rom. *dareand all for drede*, Minot 1.39.

E.M.E., A., Rom. *dedes* (Death's) *dint*, Minot 1.26.

A. *del and (gret) daunger*, Pearl 250.

A., Rom. *delid a dint*, Minot 7.141.

E.M.E. *demed of heore dedes*, On Serving Christ 24.

A. *(deþ) dinges o þi dore*, The Enemies of Man 89.

of dintes ȝe may ȝow dowt, Minot 6.34.

E.M.E., Rom. *dyȝt and deme*, Pearl 360.

O.E.Pr., E.M.E., Orm., A., Rom. *do (a) dede*, Rawl. Matt. 43.

O.E.Pr., A., Rom. *doghty in dede*, Minot 3.92, 9.39, Harley Lyric 4.45.

with dole er dight, Minot 1.80.

E.M.E., Laȝ., A., Rom. *don out of daweȝ*, Pearl 282.

A., Rom. *dongen doun*, Minot 7.74.

E.M.E., Laȝ., Orm., A., Rom. *doun and dale*, Pearl 121, Rawl. Luke 46.

E.M.E. *driuen to dale*, Minot 10.3.

E.M.E., A., Rom. *doun drof*, Pearl 30. *dryue al doun*, Pearl 1094.

A., Rom. *droupe and dare*, Minot 1.9.

Cp. **O.E.P., E.M.E., A., Rom.** *fa and frende*, Rawl. Mark 9. *þi fas . . .
   þi frendes*, The Enemies of Man 111-2

A., Rom.   *fayre face*, Pearl 169.   *face þat watȝ so fayr*, Pearl 809–10.

O.E.P., E.M.E., A., Rom.   *fair and fre*, Rawl. Luke 4.

A., Rom.   *fals and fel*, Minot 1.74, 5.23, 11.24.

E.M.E.   *now fals, now frouȝ*, The Enemies of Man 42.

Cp. **E.M.E., A., Rom.**   *in feld, in frith and in fen*, Minot 3.29.

O.E.P., E.M.E., Laȝ., A., Rom.   *felles our fase*, Rawl. Mark 30.

Rom.   *felles him in fyȝt*, Enemies of Man 51.

A., Rom.   *ferlyes befall*, Rawl. Luke 21.

A., Rom.   *fers and fell*, Minot 8.33, 9.7.

O.E.P. & Pr., A., Rom.   *to his fete pay felle*, Pearl 1120.

A., Rom.   *fled for ferde*, Minot 4.27 & 93.

our flesche is fouled wiþ þe fende, The Enemies of Man 9.

A.   *flor and fryte*, Pearl 29.

þe flowres are fallen, Minot 9.6 & 7.

folde vp hyr face, Pearl 434.

O.E.P.   *folde and flode*, Pearl 736.

E.M.E., A.   *at þe font fulluht*, On Serving Christ 2.

the forst freseth, Harley Lyric 1.5.

O.E.Pr., E.M.E., Laȝ., A., Rom.   *fowleȝ per flowen*, Pearl 89.

frek to fare, Minot 1.13.

Rom.   *frek to fight*, Minot 4.54 & 84.

O.E.P., Laȝ., O. & N., A., Rom.   *ffurth he ferd*, Minot 4.19.

A.   *gadered and yglened*, The Enemies of Man 81.

galle oper glet, Pearl 1060.

A.   *gaudes and gile*, Minot 2.18 & 30.

get (O.N. gǽta) *for paire gile*, Minot 2.36.

glory and gle, Pearl 1123.

glowed and glyȝt, Pearl 114.

A.   *where we go bi ani gate*, Enemies of Man 19.

E.M.E., A., Rom.   *Godes grace*, Pearl 63, etc.

A., Rom.   *gif him* (or *þe*) *grace*, Minot 7.29, 2nd Love-Scrap 15.   **A., Rom.** *graunt* (*him*) *grace*, Minot 4.8, 6.80, 8.46.

E.M.E., A., Rom.   *gras þat is green*, Husb. 46.

E.M.E., A.   *vch gresse mot grow*, Pearl 31.

greme ne gryste, Pearl 465.

E.M.E.   *gronynge and grure*, On Serving Christ 28.

A.   *happe and hele*, Pearl 16, 713.

as harporeȝ harpen in her harpe, Pearl 881.

O.E.P. & Pr., E.M.E., P.M., A., Rom.   *hele and hide*, Minot 6.16 & 17.

A., Rom.   *held vp paire hend*, Minot 3.32.

Cp. **O.E.Pr., E.M.E., A., Rom.**   *heuen vp her hende*, The Enemies of Man 11.

Cp. **O.E.P., Laȝ., A., Rom.**   *helm and heuyd*, Minot 7.59.

heued þe on hight, 1st Rolle Lyric 15.

A.   (*in heuen ouer*) *hyȝ þou heue*, Pearl 473.

Cp. **O.E.Pr. Leg., A., Rom.**   *hent harmes*, Minot 6.15, Pearl 388.

(*man*) *of happe more hente*, Pearl 1195.

E.M.E., A., Rom.   *heried hell*, Minot 7.34.

Orm., A., Rom.   *with hert and hand*, Minot 1.21.

O.E.Pr., E.M.E., A., Rom.   *þaire heuiddes for to hide*, Minot 4.72.   *en hod his hede for te hude*, Husb. 22.

Cp. **O.E.P., Alf., E.M.E., A., Rom.**   *hide in hole*, Minot 10.10 & 11.

hunted from hale to hurne, Husb. 35.
hunt als hund dose hare, Minot 8.21. Cp. **O.E.Pr.** *honteth ase hound doth the hare*, Husb. 56.
O.E.Pr., E.M.E., A., Rom. *yӡe and ere*, Pearl 1153.
paire laykes lett (prevented), Minot 3.64.
laste and lade, Pearl 1146 (O.E. hlæstan & hladan).
A., Rom. *bi law of land*, Minot 8.63.
O.E.P. & Pr., E.M.E., A., Rom. *leme with* (*of*) *lyght*, Harley Lyric 4.3, Pearl 119. **E.M.E., A., Rom.** *such lyӡt per lemed*, Pearl 1043.
lenge and loute, Pearl 933.
O.E.Pr., E.M.E., Laӡ., O. & N., A., Rom. *mai ich no lengore lyve*, Husb. 6.
O.E.Pr., Rom. *lere* (vb.) . . . *lare*, Minot 10.28.
E.M.E., A., Rom. *to leue on his lare*, Minot 5.9.
O.E.Pr., E.M.E., Laӡ., Orm., P.M., A., Rom. *lyf* (*ӡe*) *lede*, Pearl 392, 409, 774, Minot 11.39 (variant forms).
O.E.P., Laӡ., A., Rom. *londes and leodes*, Husb. 27.
A., Rom. *loute lowe*, Minot 7.97, 9.65. *law gan pai lout*, Minot 9.64.
Cp. **E.M.E., cp. Rom.** *lufsoum of lyth and lere*, Pearl 398.
luf and lyste, Pearl 467.
A., Rom. *make mone*, Minot 2.27, 3.35, 9.45, 11.5, Husb. 1, On Serving Christ 74.
Laӡ., A., Rom. *make mirthe*, Minot 4.81, Pearl 1149. *mirpe make*, The Enemies of Man 62.
O.E.P. & Pr., Laӡ., Rom. *main and mode*, Minot 6.77.
Rom. *mekill might*, Minot 7.12.
E.M.E., Rom. *mekil of maine*, Minot 1.85.
E.M.E., Orm., Rom. *meke and mylde*, Pearl 961.
A. *meued my mynde*, Pearl 156.
A., Rom. *now min, now mare*, The Enemies of Man 22.
mys ne mornyng, Pearl 262.
pe mo pe myryer, Pearl 850.
mokke and mul, Pearl 905.
mold : **O.E.P., A., Rom.** *men upon mold*, Husb. 1. *men on pis mold*, Rawl. John 18. **A.** *mirth on mold*, Minot 8.4. *mirth of pis mold*, The Lament of the Monk 8.
morne and mype, Pearl 359.
A. *withouten mote oper/ne mascle*, Pearl 726, 843 [cp. 899 & 923].
hys prese, hys prys, Pearl 419.
prickes and prokes, The Enemies of Man 58.
pride in prese, Minot 7.109.
A. *proud in prese*, Minot 1.90.
Rom. *prowd in pall*, Minot 7.110.
rasch and ronk, Pearl 1167.
raweӡ and randeӡ, Pearl 105.
remen for raupe, Pearl 858 [cp. **E.M.E.** *reowfulle reames*].
A. *rent on rode*, Pearl 806.
A., Rom. *reson and right*, Minot 10.27. *resoun . . . ryӡt*, Pearl 665.
A., Rom. *araye ryalle*, Pearl 191.
of rych renoun, Pearl 1182.
ryche and ryf, Pearl 770.
rycheis ne ro, Husb. 18.

ronk and ryf, Pearl 844.
A., Rom. *robbed and reued,* Minot 9.24.
on rode wes raught, On Serving Christ 5.   See supra.
(blod) ran on rode, Pearl 646.
a rownande rourde, Pearl 112.
A. *semblaunt sade,* Pearl 211.   Cp. *sad of semblaunt.*
to saue and to socoure, Minot 3.22.
O.E.Pr., La3., O. & N., A., Rom. *scheld and spere,* Minot 1.14.   **La3., Rom.**
    spere and scheld, Minot 4.50, 7.105.
O.E.P. *schyre and schene,* Pearl 42.
A., Rom. *se and sand,* Minot 3.1.
A., Rom. *see with sight,* Pearl 985.
E.M.E., A., Rom. *semely to se,* 1st Burlesque 18.   *semely on to sene,* Pearl
    45.
Rom. *semly on syght,* Harley Lyric 4.2.
for seolk ne for cendal, On Serving Christ 23.
A., Rom. *fro all sins vs saue,* Minot 6.81.
E.M.E., Rom. *fro sin and schame,* Minot 5.16.
Cp. **E.M.E.** *syng no sawe ne no song,* Husb. 4.   **O.E.Pr., E.M.E., A., Rom.**
    syng . . . song, Pearl 882, 888, 891.
A., Rom. *syken sare,* The Lament of the Monk 3.   *sore sighed,* Minot
    7.157.
by slente oper slade, Pearl 141.
I slode vpon a slepyng sla3te, Pearl 59 [cp. **A.**] & [cp. **Rom.**].
now snelle, now slawe, The Enemies of Man 40.
with sobre soun, Pearl 532.
Rom. *assoyl of sin,* Minot 3.115, 7.33, 9.30.
solace . . . oper sore, Pearl 130.
now song, now sites (lamentations), The Enemies of Man 24.
A., Rom. *sor3 and syt,* Pearl 663.
E.M.E., A., Rom. *sorow and schame,* Minot 1.64.   *fro sorow and schame and*
    syn, Minot 4.12.
mi sorow slake, Minot 5.4.
O.E.P. & Pr. *sope who so seys,* The Enemies of Man 1.   **E.M.E., La3., A.,**
    Rom. *pe suth to sai(ne),* Minot 1.81, 3.71, 9.15.   *saye soth,* Pearl 482.
in speche I spelle, Pearl 793.   Cp. **A.**
expoun in speche, Pearl 37.   Cp. **A.**
stareand on pe sternes, Minot 3.67.
A., Rom. *ster(e)n and stout,* Minot 2.13.
Rom. *stif on stede,* Minot 7.50.   *stout on stede,* Minot 1.54.
E.M.E., La3., A., Rom. *by stok oper ston,* Pearl 380.
O.E.Pr, E.M.E., La3., Orm., A., Rom. *I stod ful stylle,* Pearl 182, 1085.
A., Rom. *stont fulle iðe stude,* Husb. 33.
stote and stare, Pearl 149.
Rom. *stout and styf,* Pearl 779.
strot ne stryf, Pearl 848.
O.E.Pr., E.M.E., La3., P.M., A., Rom. *sunne . . . schon,* Pearl 1057.
    per schyne3 ful schyr agayn pe sunne, Pearl 28.   **A.** *with schymeryng*
    schene (full schrylle) pay schynde, Pearl 80.   *schon pat schene,* Pearl 166
    [cp. **E.M.E.**].   **A.** *(as schorne golde) schyr (her fax penne) schon,* Pearl
    213.   *pat schyrrer pen sunne wyth schafte3 schon,* Pearl 982.

[1] For the O.N. origin of this phrase see Miss Olszewska, *op. cit.,* p. 84.

wordes wroght, Minot 1.45.
A., Rom. *worschyp and wele*, Pearl 394.
Rom. *worthy wyȝte*, Pearl 494.
Rom. *worthly in wede*, Minot 5.38, 10.2.
Rom. *I wot and wene*, Pearl 47, 201.
E.M.E., A., Rom.[1] *a wounde ful wyde [and wete]*, Pearl 1135.
O.E.Pr., Laȝ., Orm., A. *writen y my writ*, Husb. 39.
wroȝten woghe, Pearl 622.
A., Rom. *worȝt wrang*, Pearl 631.
wrypen and worchen, Pearl 511.

(d) The Alliterative Works in Rhymed Stanzas (Rh.A. 2)

These northern alliterative works in rhymed stanzas contain 470 distinct alliterative phrases, a number sufficient to indicate that the authors in question made as much use of stock expressions as did the northern poets. Fifty-four Old English alliterative phrases are represented, twenty of which are found exclusively in Old English poetry, twenty-one in the prose, and thirteen jointly in prose and poetry. Among these there are few of any special interest ; *wlonkest in wedys* (*Awntyrs of Arthure* 9, 347, and *Pistill of Susan* 26, 186) is perhaps the most valuable survival in the group. The remaining are such as survive in the unrhymed alliterative works.

The table of phrases together with the marginal notes will indicate the historical continuity of the alliterative phraseology in these poems. It must be sufficient here to point to one or two notable details. The early Middle English phrases *mele with mouthe, mene with mouthe, munne with mouthe* are the only notable survivals from the early group, though the actual number of survivals is ninety-three. Similarly, none of Laȝamon's distinctive phrases is found in these poems. From the unryhmed alliterative poems 280 phrases survive, most of which are of a commonplace kind. The connection of *Morte Arthure* with *The Awntyrs of Arthure* accounts for such parallels as *danger and doel*, while other interesting phrases are *dukes and dusperes, felawe and fere, landes and ledes, londes and lithes, mare and minne, swelte and swoune, wrenke and wile*. Nevertheless, the phrases are for the most part such as might be found in any rhymed romance of the fourteenth century ; thus 218 of the phrases are found also in the romance group. These facts speak abundantly for themselves, and a closer study of the phrases suggests that these northern writers were on the whole less in contact with tradition than were the western writers.

[1] The whole phrase.

A. *owr the air and the erd*, Houlate 9.
angir and ire, Gol. 944.
A., Rom., Rh.A. 1. *balis . . . bete*, Quatr. 46, 119, Awntyrs 103.
E.M.E., A., Rom., Rh.A. 1. *for baill or for blis*, Gol. 293.
fra bale may vs borowe (O.E. beorgan), Quatr. 468.
E.M.E. *in bale me bound*, Fortune 58.
That bocht yow from baillis, Pleas. Satire 4.
A., Rom. *to bale was broghte*, St. John 184.
A., Rom., Rh.A. 1. *broghte out of bale*, Quatr. 246, 262.
my bales to breven, Con. Courts 23.
A. *baret and bale*, Awntyrs (Douce) 290.
Cp. **O.E.Pr., E.M.E.** *þe bandis breke*, Quatr. 259.
O.E.P. & Pr., E.M.E., Rom. *of bane nor of blude*, Gol. 6, 384. *his body,
his bone and his blode*, Quatr. 509. **E.M.E., Rom., Rh.A. 1.** *body and
bane*, Quatr. 198.
E.M.E., A., Rom., Rh.A. 1. *a barne was borne*, Quatr. 149. *þe barne . . .
scho bare*, St. John 72.
a barne in þat burghe, St. John 183.
A., Rom. *barrounis and bacheleiris*, Rauf 11.
A. *baronis and beirnis*, Gol. 5, 522.
A. *byschopis and baroinnis*, Quatr. 446.
A., Rom. *baronis and burowis*, Gol. 1170. *burges nor baroun*, Prol. to the
8th Bk. Aeneid 116.
bere . . . bodworde, Quatr. 110.
Laȝ., A., Rom., Rh.A. 1. *beryns . . . balde*, Awntyrs 40, 242, Gol. 733.
A. *beryns and byrdes*, Awntyrs 174.
A. *beirnys on bent*, Gol. 637, 687, Rauf 730.
bide in bale, Quatr. 332.
A. *to bide in blysse*, St. John 9.
A., Rom. *on the bent bides*, Awntyrs (Douce) 330.
A., Rom. *birdis one bewes*, Awntyrs 127, Quatr. 5.
with birny and brand, Gol. 199, 679, Rauf 764, 806.
birny and breistplait, Gol. 567, 964, 977.
A., Rom. *bled he his blud*, Houlate 536. *of his blude bled*, Gol. 608.
A., Rom. *blow a blaste*, Gol. 534, 592.
blauing of bemys, Gol. 467. **O.E.P. & Pr., E.M.E., Laȝ., A., Rom.** *bemys
salle blawe*, Quatr. 393.
A., Rom. *the king his bugle has blowene*, Awntyrs (Douce) 330.
Rom. *blenke(de) of his ble*, Quatr. 180, 212.
blys and blythnes, Prol. to 8th Bk. Aeneid 18, cp. **E.M.E.**
blith and bousum, Gol. 351.
O.E.P., Rom. *blyth and bricht*, Gol. 378, Houlate 556.
A. *blythest of ble*, Houlate 3, 17, 409.
blomes and blossomes, Quatr. 2.
O.E.P. & Pr., E.M.E., P.M., A., Rom. *with his blude boghte*, Quatr. 245.
E.M.E., Laȝ., Rom., Rh.A. 1. *bone þat þou bede*, Pride of Ladies 4.
A., Rom. *thair bodeis wes beryit*, Gol. 650.
borne of a byrde bryghte, St. John 7.
A. *borlich and bigge*, Pistill 226.
A., Rom. *boun to the battale*, Gol. 813.
A. *boune at (your) bidding*, Gol. 330, 1209, Rauf 124. *at his bidding full
bane*, Gol. 1209. *to his byddyng bowand*, St. John 98.

A. *bowsum and boun,* Gol. 445.
A., Rom. *bouxsom and bayne,* St. John 98.
A. *braunche and beugh,* Houlate 607,
A. *braid with his brand,* Rauf 858. **A., Rom.** *braide out brandis,* Awntyrs (Douce) 122, Gol. 757.
brawndeche owte his brande, Awntyrs 122, Pistill 319.
E.M.E., A., Rom. *brennynde so briȝt,* Pistill 319.
A. *bretnet and brent* (in baret to byde), Pistill 147.
E.M.E., A., Rom. *bright(est) of ble,* Gol. 134, 212, 316, 1146, Quatr. 46.
E.M.E., Rom. *bryȝt as the blostme,* Fortune 68.
E.M.E., A., Rom. *till he was in bed brocht,* Rauf 269.
Cp. **O.E.P. & Pr., E.M.E., A., Rom., Rh.A. 1.** *bringe (vs) to blysse,* Awntyrs 200, Quartr. 156, 268, St. John 8, 98, 105. *to þe blisse bringe,* Awntyrs (Douce) 249.
broght . . . boidword of blis, Gol. 171. **A.** *bodword haue I brocht,* Rauf 902.
the broun and the black, Prol. to the 8th Bk. Aeneid 57.
O.E.Pr., A., Rom. *with buke and with belle,* Awntyrs 30, Quatr. 33, Rauf 533.
burgh and bour, Gol. 330, 406.
burly and bold, Houlate 406 (cp. Degare 452, *borlich and bolde*).
burly and braid, Gol. 934.
A. *busket hym to battell,* Gol. 548.
Cp. **O.E.P., A., Rom., Rh.A. 1.** *in cares so colde,* Awntyrs 151.
Rh.A. 1. *casten in care,* Quatr. 221.
E.M.E., A., Rom. *cast a cri,* Pistill 153. *kest vp ane cry,* Gol. 953.
kene and cruell, Gol. 46, 1109. **A., Rom.** *cruell and kene,* Awntyrs 601, Gol. 92, 597, 694, 846, 1030.
kenneth us care, Con. Courts 85.
heo keuered vp on hir kneos, Pistill 252.
A., Rom. *chaffare y chepe,* Con. Courts 73.
E.M.E., A., Rom., Rh.A. 1. *changis my cheir,* Rauf 721. *vnchangide of chere,* St. John 62.
A., Rom. *kynd and courtese,* Gol. 363.
Rom., Rh.A. 1. *kyndyls my kare,* Awntyrs 90.
Cp. **O.E.P. & Pr., E.M.E., Laȝ., A., Rom.** *kyng and (ne) kayser,* Quatr. 353, 445. *kaysere or kynge,* Awntyrs 410. *czsar nor king,* Gol. 1120.
Laȝ., A., Rom. *kyng and his knightes,* Gol. 582, 834, 1230.
E.M.E., A., Rom., Rh.A. 1. *king with croune* (or *crouned*), Fortune 86, Gol. 12, etc., Houlate 294. *crouned king in kith,* Awntyrs (Douce) 360, Fortune 113, cp. **A.**
O.E.Pr., E.M.E., Laȝ., A., Rom., Rh.A. 1. *king and quene,* Awntyrs 10, 686, 694, Rauf 250.
A., Rom. *ne kythe ne no kyne,* Quatr. 467.
A., Rom. *cledde in clethyng,* Rauf 705, St. John 168.
closede in clay, Quatr. 234, 337.
E.M.E., A. *knawen and kende,* Gol. 1211, 1325, St. John 209.
A., Rom. *kneilit on his kne,* Rauf 337.
E.M.E., Laȝ., A., Rom., Rh.A. 1. *knyght, clerk,* Prol. to the 8th Bk. Aeneid 115.
knicht of the court, Rauf 30.
E.M.E., A., Rom., Rh.A. 1. *I cum to the court,* Rauf 260, 299.

comaunded hem kenely, Pistill 214.

A. *comly (cumly) and clere*, Gol. 178, 366, etc., Houlate 338, Quatr. 118, Rauf 194.

A. *conqueror and kyng*, Gol. 1321.

A. *crucyfiede one croyse*, Awntyrs 134, 223.

by crosse and by crede, Awntyrs (Douce) 97.

A. *kud and knewe*, Pride of Ladies 34 (cp. **Orm.** *cnew and cupe*).

curtase and clere, Gol. 53, Quatr. 84.   *courtes and cleir*, Rauf 716.

with daggaris thay dang, Gol. 711.

Laȝ., Orm., A., Rom., Rh.A. 1. *dale and downe*, Fortune 14.   *dalis and doun*, Gol. 226, Rauf 414.   *dovnis and dellis*, Gol. 29.

A., Rom., Rh.A. 1. *day dawis*, Rauf 924.   *day daweth*, Fortune 3, Gol. 609, 732, Rauf 924.

A. *danger and dreid*, Gol. 948.

A., Rh.A. 1. *danger and doel*, Awntyrs (Douce) 184.

the dout and the danger, Gol. 302.

darkys and darys, Awntyrs 52.

E.M.E., A., Rom. *dede and dolvene*, Quatr. 235.

dede hire in a dungon, Pistill 174.

O.E.P., E.M.E., Laȝ., A., Rom. *deip dalis*, Gol. 29.

A., Rom., Rh.A. 1. *dele dyntes* (in various forms), Gol. 67, 542, etc., Rauf 512.

Cp. **O.E.Pr., E.M.E., A., Rom.** *deme (him) for to dye*, Quatr. 189, St. John 112.

Laȝ., A., Rom. *to deþ be diht*, Pistill 246, 267.   *þus dethe wil ȝou diȝte*, Awntyrs 170.

A. Rom. *I schal diȝte þe a Duke & dubbe þe with honde*, Awntyrs 672.

A., Rom. *dyng me to deid*, Houlate 65.

A., Rom., Rh.A. 1. *ding pame doun*, Rauf 915.

O.E.Pr., E.M.E., Orm., A., Rom., Rh.A. 1. *do dedes*, Houlate 505, Rauf 513, St. John 125.

A. *domes to dele*, Pistill 292.

E.M.E., Laȝ., A., Rom., Rh.A. 1. *don out of dawen*, Pistill 242.

dottit or daft, Pract. Med. 11.

A., Rom., Rh.A. 1. *doughty of/in deid*, Gol. 329, 405.

A., Rom. *downe dede gun pay falle*, St. John 225.

for drede of þe dethe, Awntyrs (Douce) 54.

drefling and dremis, Aeneid 1.

Cp. **Laȝ., A.** *dryve for the þe day (to þe derke nighte)*, Awntyrs (Douce) 564. **A.** *quhen it drew to the dirk nycht*, Gol. 228.

droupun and daren, Awntyrs (Ireland) 52. **A., Rom.** *drouping and dare*, Fortune 123, Houlate 188.

A., Rom. *dukis and duchepeiris*, Awntyrs 4, Gol. 1334, Rauf 10.

O.E.Pr., E.M.E., A., Rom., Rh.A. 1. *er ouper eȝè*, Pride of Ladies 29.

empreouris and erlis, Rauf 3.   **A.** *erelles and emperours*, Quatr. 447.

O.E.P., A. *fairand ouir þe feildis*, Rauf 8, 443, 589.

O.E.P., E.M.E., A., Rom., Rh.A. 1. *faire and free*, Quatr. 24.

fair farrand and fre, Houlate 153 (cp. *farande and fre*, Pur. 607).

A., Rom., Rh.A. 1. *fair of face*, Fortune 56, St. John 32.   **A.** *farest of face*, Gol. 1060, Awntyrs (Douce) 137.   *fayr of fell and of face*, Gol. 352.

A., Rom. *that fallis on þe feild*, Rauf 74.

falowe and falle, Quatr. 208.

A.   *febill and faynt*, Gol. 122.

A., Rom.   *to fecht on (Goddis) fais*, Rauf 751.

E.M.E., La3., Orm., A., Rom.   *fedd and fosterde*, St. John 32.

O.E.P., A., Rom.   *fel fey to þe grund*, Gol. 640.   Cp. **La3.** *feollen þæ fæie*.

A., Rom.   *feye to be fellit*, Houlate 495.

A.   *felawe and fere*, Quatr. 80.

fellit þe freke, Gol. 106.

O.E.P., La3., O. & N., A., Rom., Rh.A. 1.   *ferde forth (in þat frith)*, Fortune 28.

A., Rom., Rh.A. 1.   *a ferly bifell* (in various forms), Awntyrs 716, (Douce) 72, 299, 709, Pistill 129, 361, Rauf 2.

figur and face, Awntyrs 137, Houlate 106.

of figure so fre, Gol. 379.

A., Rom.   *fi3te one a felde*, Awntyrs (Douce) 430.

A., Rom.   *þei feght one fote*, Awntyrs (Douce) 573.   *thai faucht on fute*, Gol. 635.

with na fylthe filede, St. John 59.

Rom.   *firth and fell*, Gol. 27, 1293.   *by frythis and fellis*, Awntyrs 8, 50.

A., Rom., Rh.A. 1.   *in frythe and in felde*, St John 256.

A., Rom.   *frythes and forestes*, Awntyrs 682.

firth, forest and fell, Gol. 193, 1318, 1357.

A.   *fledde faste*, Awntyrs 80.

O.E.Pr., E.M.E., La3., A., Rom.   *flesche and felle*, Quatr. 281, 410.

A., Rh.A. 1.   *flowrus and fruit*, Pistill 43, 98.

faught vpone fold, Gol. 570, 961.   *formed on fold*, Houlate 321.   *ferly on fold*, Houlate 46.   *forest on fold*, Houlate 15.   *formyt on fold*, Houlate 355.   **A.** *freke on fold*, Gol. 56, 1007, 1079, Awntyrs (Douce) 431, 476, 500.   *fundun on fold*, Gol. 16.

E.M.E., A., Rh.A. 1.   *folowed in fontestone*, Awntyrs (Douce) 225.

Rom.   *to fote hem falle*, Con. Courts 66, etc.

foundis to þe feght, Gol. 660.

foundis in feir, Gol. 751, Rauf 702.

fowlis of the firth, Houlate 906, Rauf 680.

E.M.E., A., Rom.   *frely and faire*, Awntyrs 682, Houlate 308.   **O.E.P.** *frelich and feire*, Pistill 17.

fremmyt nor freyndis, Gol. 909, 1079.

Cp. **O.E.P., E.M.E., A., Rom., Rh.A. 1.**   *frend and (nor) fo (fa)*, Fortune 40, Gol. 56, 1187.

O.E.P., cp. **E.M.E., P.M., A., Rom.**   *gamyn and gle*, Rauf 953, 1144, Awntyrs (Douce) 146.   *gamen and glewe*, Quatr. 307.

garbed in grene, Awntyrs (Douce) 508.

of garsomes and of golde, Awntyrs 147.   **E.M.E., La3., A., Rom.** *gersome and golde*, Awntyrs (Douce) 664.

gyftis and gersomes, Awntyrs 697.

gladen and glees, Pistill 84, 354.

A., Rom.   *glemyt as gold*, Gol. 21.

A. Rom.   *gleterande golde*, Awntyrs (Douce) 27, 496.

glitterande full gay, Rauf 667.

I gloppyne and I grete,[1] Awntyrs 91.

_____

[1] For the O.N. origin of this phrase, see Miss Olszewska, *op. cit.*, p. 80.

gloryous and gaye, Awntyrs 366.

A. *glowe as a glede*, Awntyrs 117, 393 (cp. **Orm.** *glowende gledes*).

glowand on gleid, Gol. 558.

A. *graithit in grene*, Gol. 603.

A., Rom., Rh.A. 1. *(God) graunt þe grace*, St John 30, 247, Gol. 514, 792.

    A., Rom., Rh.A. 1. *gyffe (þe) grace*, Awntyrs 228, St John 139. *grete grace was þe gyffen and grauntede also*, St John 139.

Rom. *gracious and gude*, Quatr. 342, 515, Gol. 118, 1124. *gude and gracius*, Gol. 389.

A., Rom. *growing so grene*, Pistill 67, 87.

þe gayest on grund, Gol. 8, 472, Rauf 482. *gedling on ground*, Rauf 619.

    O.E.P., A., Rom. *gold on ground*, Rauf 499. **A.** *grumys on grund*, Gol. 8.

A. *þat on þe grownde growes*, Awntyrs 146.

gudly and gay, Houlate 398.

O.E.Pr., Laȝ., A., Rom. *hadde in hande*, Quatr. 455.

O.E.P. & Pr., E.M.E., A., Rom. *to hafe and to holde*, Awntyrs (Douce) 668.

Orm., A., Rom., Rh.A. 1. *with hart and with hand*, Gol. 872.

O.E.Pr., E.M.E., A., Rom. *heef hir hondus on hiȝ*, Pistill 262.

A., Rom., Rh.A. 1. *þei held vp here hondes*, Awntyrs (Douce) 663.

O.E.P. & Pr., E.M.E., P.M., A., Rom., Rh.A. 1. *hele and hyde*, Quatr. 476–7.

A., Rom. *hendeste in haulle*, Awntyrs 131. *hendeste in halle*, St John 229.

E.M.E., A., Rom., Rh.A. 1. *heried helle*, Quatr. 261.

E.M.E., A., Rom. *herkene and here*, Quatr. 28.

O.E.P., Laȝ., A., Rom. *hert ne hynde*, Fortune 30.

E.M.E., Laȝ., A., Rom. *in hyde and in hewe*, Quatr. 303. *on hide ne on huwe*, Awntyrs (Douce) 108.

A., Rom. *of hair and of hyde*, Houlate 950.

Cp. **O.E.Pr., A., Rom., Rh.A. 1.** *hynt grete harmys*, Gol. 703.

A., Rom. *holtis hare*, Awntyrs (Douce) 43, Houlate 773, Gol. 470.

A., Rom. *holtis and hillys*, Awntyrs 57, Gol. 234.

A. *honest and habill*, Gol. 739.

E.M.E., Orm. *our hope and our helpe*, Houlate 735.

A., Rom. *thy hors and harnes*, Rauf 393.

A. *with hounde and with horne*, Awntyrs (Douce) 435.

A. *in hous and in hall*, Houlate 142.

A., Rom. *huntynge . . . in holtis so hare*, Awntyrs (Douce) 43, Houlate 773.

in hurstes and huwes (O.N. haugr), Awntyrs (Douce) 57.

A., Rom. *the jangland ja(y)*, Houlate 789.

Rom. *joly and gentill*, Gol. 391.

A. *lacched his leue*, Pistill 237.

A., Rom. *laid is full law*, Gol. 726.

O.E.P., A., Rom., Rh.A. 1. *þe lande and þat lede*, St John 211.

A., Rom. *alle þe landes and þe lythes*, Awntyrs 678.

A., Rom. *yone landis suld leid*, Gol. 48.

A., Rom. *(languor) lent is in land*, Prol. to the 8th Bk. Aeneid 14. *þe lande . . . þat he gun in lende*, St John 211.

E.M.E., A., Rom., Rh.A. 1. *law lout* (vb.), Gol. 991.

O.E.Pr., A. *of lawe and of lare*, Quatr. 449. *wiþ his lawes and his lare*, St John 212.

O.E.Pr., E.M.E., La3., Orm., A., Rom. *lawit nor lerd* (O.E. lǣwed . . . lǣred), Gol. 1080.
A. *leidis in land*, Gol. 1163, Prol. to the 8th Bk. Aeneid 27, 59.132. *leid of þis land*, Gol. 430. *leidis on þe land*, Gol. 622, 667, 908.
A. *na leid on lyfe*, Rauf 591.
O.E.Pr., E.M.E., La3., Orm., P.M., A., Rom., Rh.A. 1. *I leid my life*, Rauf 47.
E.M.E., A., Rom., Rh.A. 1. *lemand ful light*, Gol. 485. *lemyt so light*, Gol. 615.
E.M.E., A., Rom. *Lord þat lenest us lyf*, Pride of Ladies 1. (he) þat vs *lyf lent*, St John 19, Pistill 353.
A., Rom. *lent in land*, Rauf 591 (O.E. lendan).
O.E.P. & Pr., E.M.E., La3., A., Rom. *leose my lyf*, Con. Courts 65. *lossit . . . his life*, Gol. 726.
Rom. *this lessen ye lere*, St. John 244.
A. *lerne me ane lessoun*, Prol. to the 8th Bk. Aeneid.
E.M.E. *in whame vs awe for to leue and loue hym [and lowtte]*, Quatr. 73. [Cp. Arthur 116, *loved and alowte*.]
O.E.P., E.M.E., La3., A., Rom. *libben in londe*, Con. Courts 1.
A. *lichtit on the land*, Gol. 622, 677.
with lyking and lyst, Houlate 755. Cp. **A.**
A., Rom. *with lyking and luf*, Houlate 18.
(quhil you) likis and list, Gol. 186.
A. *my lyfe dar I layd*, Rauf 374.
A. *to life ay in lykynge*, St. John 6.
thus thow lyffede in the lande, St. John 257. See under *libben in londe*.
he lift vp þe lach, Pistill 229.
lyghte and lenge, Awntyrs. 214.
A., Rom. *lord of land*, Gol. 257, 1323. *lord in þat land*, Awntyrs 279.
A., Rom. *lordis and ladyis*, Quatr. 469, Awntyrs (Douce) 538, Gol. 179, 1253, Houlate 461. *lordingis and ladyis*, Gol. 1051.
(with) loss and (with) lyking, Houlate 385, 528. *with loving and loiss*, Houlate 568.
lufsum of lait, Gol. 746, 1271. *lufly of lyre*, Gol. 614, 1003, 1145. **E.M.E., Rh.A. 1.** *(þat lady) louesum of lere*, Pistill 275. *(a lady) louesum of lote*, Awntyrs (Douce) 344.
E.M.E., A., Rom., Rh.A. 1. *he lowtit full lawe*, Houlate 460.
A. *lusty and likand*, Gol. 258.
þou makis me alle mad, Quatr. 254.
A., Rom., Rh.A. 1. *made thay thayre mane* (moan), St. John 186.
A., Rom. *makis he mery*, Gol. 771.
La3., A., Rom. *make myrthe*, Fortune 15, Houlate 2, Quatr. 168, etc.
A., Rom. *make mournyng*, Quatr. 7, 10.
E.M.E., A., Rom. *mayne and myght*, Gol. 514.
A., Rom., Rh.A. 1. *of mare and of myne* (less), Quatr. 45. *the mare and the myn*, Gol. 1159.
E.M.E., A., Rom. *matynes or messes*, Awntyrs 198. *messes and matynes*, Awntyrs 229.
E.M.E., Orm., Rom., Rh.A. 1. *meke and mylde*, Quatr. 339, St. John 57.
E.M.E., A. *mel with mouth*, Gol. 354.
E.M.E., A. *mene with mouthe*, St. John 28.
E.M.E. *that I ne mai no3t munne (non murthis) with muthe*, Old Age 22–3.

menskful of myght, Gol. 481.

menstralis and musicianis, Houlate 756.

E.M.E., La3., O. & N., A., Rom. *with a mylde mode,* Awntyrs, 642. **O.E.P. & Pr.** *a mylde mode,* Quatr. 511. *myldeste of mode,* Awntyrs 226, St. John 33.

paire mysse for to mende, St. John 215.

mold : **A.** *maid on mold,* Gol. 350, Houlate 13. **O.E.P., A., Rom.** *man on molde,* Fortune 73. **A., Rom., Rh.A. 1.** *men vpone mold,* Gol. 512, 682. *manlyest on mold,* Gol. 457. *marrit on þe mold,* Gol. 965. *mellit* (spoke) *on mold,* Gol. 572. *to mensk on mold,* Gol. 446. **A., Rom.** *meryest on mold,* Gol. 1160, 1171 : cp. *a meriere man of molde,* Fortune 73. *mobil* (*meble*) *one molde,* Awntyrs 199, Gol. 807.

moost in his mi3te, Awntyrs 267. **E.M.E., Rom.** *þat maste es of myghte,* St. John 1.

O.E.Pr., Rom. *the mother and the maydin,* Rauf 510. *maydene . . . modyr,* Quatr. 318.

A. *to moue of a mater,* Quatr. 41.

A. *mouit in his mude,* Gol. 300.

A. *murnyng and myrth,* Gol. 1148.

A. *murnyng and mone,* Gol. 646.

murnis in his mynd, Prol. to the 8th Bk. Aeneid 54. *murnand in mude,* Gol. 1128.

O.E.Pr., E.M.E., La3., Orm., A., Rom. *names to nevyn,* Houlate 33.

E.M.E., A. *nedfulle and nakede,* Awntyrs 185.

A., Rom. *nei3ed wel nere,* Pistill 27. *nei3es wel nere,* Pistill 318. *nechit him neir,* Houlate 682. *nyghit hym ner,* Gol. 1017.

A., Rom. *nikke* (. . .) *with nay,* Gol. 115, 332, Old Age 2, Pistill 148.

O.E.Pr., A., Rom. *an oxe and an asse,* Quatr. 148.

A. *thai passit in thare pilgramage,* Gol. 235.

payand þe price, Gol. 143.

E.M.E., A. *patriarkis and prophetis,* Houlate 122.

preciousse and pure, Houlate 81, 109, etc.

A. *prelatis and princis,* Rauf 6.

A., Rom. *prestys and parsones,* Quatr. 448.

proud as a þo (peacock), Con. Courts 87.

Rom., Rh.A. 1. *proudeste in palle,* Awntyrs 66, 335. *proudest in pall,* Gol. 235. *prouddeste in palle,* St John 223.

A., Rom., Rh.A. 1. *proudest in preis,* Rauf 624.

puneschede in pyne, St John 224.

with purfelle and peloure, Quatr. 473.

A., Rom. *we are putt in þat payne,* Quatr. 380.

putt in a pytt, Quatr. 362.

A. *put into prison,* Pistill 327.

A., Rom. *real and riche,* Pistill 29.

E.M.E., A., Rom. *reddere in rode pan rose in þe rayne,* Awntyrs 161.

all reddy to ryde, Gol. 906.

A., Rom., Rh.A. 1. (*in*) *riall array,* Awntyrs (Douce) 691, Gol. 15, Rauf 478, etc. *rial of array,* Gol. 1347. *ryke of array,* Houlate 368, 669. Cp. **A.** *in riche robus arayed,* Pistill 212. *arayede in robys,* Quatr. 456.

A., Rom. *richely arrayede,* Awntyrs 172.

E.M.E., A., Rom. *red as þe rose,* Pistill 212.

A.   *rekkenys by resonne*, Quatr. 486.
A., Rh.A. 1.   *rent one rude*, Awntyrs 317.
A.   *ressaue with reuerence*, Houlate 146, 869.
A., Rom., Rh.A. 1.   *ressoun and rycht*, Awntyrs (Douce) 350, 362, 597, Gol. 189, Houlate 968, Prol. to the 8th Bk. Aeneid 7.
A., Rom.   *to ryn and to ryde*, Quatr. 450.
ryse on a rawe, Quatr. 395.
Rom.   *sadly and sare*, Gol. 574.
sakeles of syn, Pistill 240 (cp. **E.M.E.** *sake and sinne*).
A.   *to saue and to salf*, Gol. 793.
Laȝ., A., Rom.   *say . . . sawes*, Pistill, 34, 287, Pride of Ladies 9.
Laȝ., A., Rom.   *schaft and scheild*, Gol. 544.
A., Rom.   *fro schame me schyld*, 2nd Burlesque 29.
O.E.Pr., Laȝ., O. & N., A., Rom., Rh.A. 1.   *schelde and spere*, Awntyrs (Douce) 428, Gol. 907.
Rom.   *scheilde from sinne*, Pleas Satire 9, Pride of Ladies 7.
Rom.   *schene vndir scheild*, Gol. 639, 777.
þat schynede and schane, Quatr. 150.
Cp. **O.E.P., A., Rh.A. 1.**   *schynyng so schir*, Gol. 610.
skremes and skrykis, Awntyrs 619.   **A.**   *biginneth to skryke and scremeth*, Con. Courts 61.
scrilles and scrykes, Awntyrs 536.   *skirles and skirkes*, Awntyrs 536.
A.   *schrenkis for na schame*, Gol. 1077.   *schrynketh for shome*, Con. Courts 59.
heo ne schunte for no schame, Pistill 231.
A., Rom., Rh.A. 1.   *bi se nor bi sande*, Pistill 254.
A.   *selcoup(es) to se(e)ne*, Awntyrs (Douce) 333, Pistill 69.
A., Rom.   *see with syghte*, Fortune 64, Gol. 1106.   *sey (I nevere) with syȝth*, Fortune 64, Rauf. 848.   *sene was with syghte*, Awntyrs 359.
O.E.Pr., E.M.E., Laȝ., A., Rom.   *(þat) syghte for to see*, Quatr. 99, Gol. 255.
A.   *sege vndir son*, Gol. 1042.
to seke socoure, Quatr. 496.
A.   *to seik our the sey*, Gol. 3, Houlate 303.
seiknes nor sairnes, Sum Practysis 19.
Rom.   *sekerly and sure*, Houlate 22, 85.
semly and schene, Awntyrs 696.
Rom.   *semely in sale*, Gol. 1092.   *seymly in sale*, Gol. 1156.
E.M.E., A., Rom., Rh.A, 1.   *semely to se*, Gol. 381, etc.   *semely to sene*, Rauf 677.
E.M.E., Rom.   *(a) semely syght*, Gol. 255, 1257.
semely and sure, Houlate 569.
send and saynd, Gol. 47, 367.
A.   *ane sayndis-man ye send*, Gol. 326.
with serwe biset, Pistill 145.
A.   *þe seson of somere*, Pistill 66.
A.   *set in þi sete*, Awntyrs (Douce) 180.
O & N., A., Rom., Rh.A. 1.   *siked wel sare*, Pistill 222.   *syghande fulle sare*, Awntyrs 88.   *syghe sare*, Quatr. 26, 237.
the sone in the sky wes schynyng so schir, Gol. 610.   *schene schane the son*, Gol. 242.   **O.E.Pr., E.M.E., Laȝ., P.M., A., Rom., Rh.A. 1.** *the schynyng of the son*, Gol. 41.

Rom. *þi sare syghynge,* Quatr. 54. *sikande and syghande,* Quatr. 8.

E.M.E. *syexe other sevene,* Con. Courts 37.

signete or sele, Gol. 1105.

I slaid on a swevynnyng, slummerande a lite, Prol. to the 8th Bk. Aeneid 3

A. *in a slommuryng of slepe,* 2nd Burlesque 3.   Cp. **E.M.E., Laȝ.**

þe slete and þe snawe, Awntyrs 82.

sonken y þe see, Con. Courts 80.

A. *soukene in syn,* Quatr. 331.

E.M.E., Rom. *þe sonne and þe see,* Pistill 264.

sorowfull and sad, Houlate 187.

O.E.P. & Pr., E.M.E., Laȝ., A., Rom., Rh.A. 1. *sothe for to saye,* Quatr. 300, St. John 158.   *sothe forto seyn,* Fortune 65.   *sothe to saye,* Fortune 66.

suth sall I say, Gol. 535, etc.   *I sall say thee the suith,* Rauf 248.   *the suith gif I sall say,* Rauf 378.

O.E.P. & Pr., E.M.E., A., Rom. *sothely to saye,* Awntyrs 21, etc., Pistill 13, etc.   *suthly to sane/say,* Gol. 4, etc., Houlate 671.

sotil and sage, Pistill 14.

speche and spelle, Quatr. 27.   [Cp. **A.** *to speke and spelle.*]

þay spetede þame one speris, Quatr. 162.

A. *stable and steidfast,* Houlate 174.   *stedfaste and stabille,* Quatr. 340.

stabille and stille, Quatr. 304.

stalwart and stabill, Gol. 741.

A. *staluart and strang,* Gol. 89, 353, 710.

þat standis bi þi syde, Quatr. 225.

A., Rom., Rh.A. 1. *stande in . . . stede,* Quatr. 14, 291.

A. *stiflie and sture,* Rauf 16.

stok stille as ane stane, Gol. 108.

O.E.Pr., E.M.E., Laȝ., Orm., A., Rom., Rh.A. 1. *stondis stone stille,* Awntyrs 580.

stotin and stynt, Gol. 767.

Rom. *stout and strang and stalwart,* Rauf 875.

Cp. **A., Rom.** *stout (countenaunce) and sture,* Gol. 87.

he strikes ful sare, Awntyrs (Douce) 581.

sufferede for our syne, Quatr. 176.

A. *withe a swap of a swerde,* Awntyrs (Douce) 581.

þe swerd swapped one his swange, Awntyrs (Douce) 617.

A. *he swapped him (yne at þe swyre) with a swerde,* Awntyrs (Douce) 514.

Laȝ., A. *out with swerdis þai swang,* Gol. 562.

swart ant forswat, Con. Courts 70.

A. *we swelte and we swoune,* Quatr. 357.

Rom., Rh.A. 1. *swiftly and swith,* Gol. 380, St. John 164.

Rom., Rh.A. 1. *take tent,* Gol. 149, Rauf 314.

E.M.E., Laȝ., A., Rom., Rh.A. 1. *telle a tale,* Awntyrs 314, Quatr. 190, Gol. 149.

E.M.E., A., Rom., Rh.A. 1. *telle with tonge,* Gol. 415, 780, 1094.

A. *it were teir to telle* (etc.), Awntyrs 121, Gol. 213, 760, 898, 1341, Houlate 421, 578, Rauf 474.

E.M.E., Laȝ., A., Rom. *tell tythynges,* Awntyrs (Douce) 314, Quatr. 157, 288.

A. Rom. *trewly to tell* (or *to tell trewly*), Awntyrs 34, Gol. 659, etc., Houlate 501, Pistill 314, 340.

tender and trewe, Houlate 286, 403.

tendir and tryde, Houlate 992.

E.M.E., Rom. *tyde and tyme*, Rauf 48.

A. *wiþ tonge and wiþ top*, Pistill 221.

A., Rom. *of townnes, of towris*, Awntyrs 149. **Rom.** *towris and townis*, Houlate 550.

toret and teone, Pistill 149.

A., Rom., Rh.A. 1. *trayste and trewe* (or *trewe and trayste*), Gol. 756, 913, 1174, Houlate 287, Pistill 187, Sum Practysis 54, St. John 89.

Rh.A. 1. *trewe for to trayste*, Quatr. 133.

a treuthe for to trye, Quatr. 185.

A. *tresone and tray*, Quatr. 64.

A. *we trinet a trot*, Pistill 225.

A., Rom., Rh.A. 1. *the trumpe & the ta(l)burn*, Houlate 760.

A. *þat waye þou vs wysse*, St. John 13.

A., Rom., Rh.A. 1. *walke one my wey*, Awntyrs (Douce) 315.

Rom. *now wakneþ heor wo*, Pistill 297.

O.E.P. & Pr., A., Rom. *wapinnis to wald* (or *weild*), Awntyrs (Douce), 575, Gol. 7, 820.

A. *warp on* (or *of*) *wedes*, Fortune 4, Pistill 124.

O.E.Pr., A., Rom., Rh.A. 1. *wedded his* (or *to*) *wif*, Awntyrs (Douce), 696, Pistill 186.

wed . . . to wyfe and weild, Rauf 925. *wedde and welde to wif*, Con. Courts, 64. Cp. **A.**

O.E.P., E.M.E., A., Rom., Rh.A. 1. *to wele or to wa*, Quatr. 505.

O.E.Pr., E.M.E., P.M., A., Rom., Rh.A. 1. *alle þe wele of þis werlde*, Quatr. 19. **A., Rom.** *alle þe welthe of þe werlde*, Awntyrs 215, 425, Gol. 1132, Quatr. 72, 236, St. John 196.

A. *þat weldis alle þis werlde*, Quatr. 69 (cp. **E.M.E.**).

E.M.E., A., Rom., Rh.A. 1. *wende* (*on*) . . . *way* (in variant forms), Awntyrs, 315, Gol. 114, etc., Quatr. 254, 518, Rauf 691.

wepus for wo, Awntyrs 560. *wrong handes . . . and wepten*, Pistill 171. **A., Rom.** *wrange scho hir handis* (*and*) *wepe þane for wa*, Quatr. 210. *heo wepte for wo*, Pistill 201.

Rom. *paire werke and paire wyll*, St. John 195. *be werk and be will*, Gol. 1244.

Cp. **O.E.P. & Pr., E.M.E., Laȝ., Orm., O & N.** *wepmon ant wyf*, Pride of Ladies 3.

A. *wy in þis warld*, Awntyrs 639, Gol. 1342. **A., Rh.A. 1.** *wyghte in þis werlde*, Quatr. 352, 367, St. John 21.

Laȝ., Orm., A., Rom., Rh.A. 1. *winne worschipe*, Awntyrs 264, Gol. 1046, Rauf 460.

A. *(wynnes) wirchippis and welthis*, Awntyrs 264.

E.M.E., A., Rom. *wynde and water*, Quatr. 89.

O.E.Pr., E.M.E., Laȝ., A., Rom. *the wynde and the wedyrs*, Awntyrs 328.

wirchipe to welde, Awntyrs 341, Rauf 965, St. John 252.

A., Rom., Rh.A. 1. *worschipe and wele*, Awntyrs (Douce) 340, Gol. 73, Houlate 252.

O.E.P., E.M.E., Laȝ., A., Rom. *wyse and witty*, St. John 251. **A., Rom.** *witty and wyse*, St. John 55.

Cp. **O.E.Pr., A.** *wys and worthy*, Gol. 1235, Houlate 175. **A.** *wourthy and wyse*, Gol. 325, 1097, 1288, Rauf 356.

witlese and wode, Gol. 573, 972, 1014.

O.E.P., Rom. *wlonkest in wedys*, Awntyrs 9, 347, Pistill 26, 186.

E.M.E., Orm., A. *wo and wandrepe*, Quatr. 30. **Rh.A. 1.** *wandreth or wough*, Gol. 199.

O.E.P., E.M.E., A. *word . . . warp*, Fortune 112, Pistill 134.

E.M.E., A., Rom., Rh.A. 1. *worche (hire) wo*, Awntyrs (Douce) 56, Con. Courts 89, Pistill 65.

O.E.P. & Pr., E.M.E., Orm., P.M., A., Rom. *neiper in word ne in werk*, Pistill 251.

E.M.E., Laȝ., Rom. *worldes wynne*, Con. Courts 78.

Rom. *wourthy in wedis*, Gol. 365, 414, 563 (cp. **E.M.E.**).

Rom. *worthy and wight*, Gol. 198, 656, Houlate 513, Rauf 965. **A., Rom.** *wicht and wourthy*, Gol. 1248.

E.M.E., A., Rom., Rh.A. 1. *woundis . . . wyde*, Gol. 634, 701.

A., Rom. *wox wonder wraith*, Rauf 100.

Cp. **A.** *wod wraith as the wynd*, Gol. 770.

A., Rom. *ne wrenke ne no wyle*, Quatr. 420.

O.E.P. & Pr., E.M.E., Laȝ., A., Rom. *wroghte paire will*, St. John 171.

wrocht in pis worlde, Prol. to the 8th Bk. Aeneid 6, St. John 4.

Cp. **E.M.E., A.** *ȝaipe, thocht he ȝong was*, Houlate 602.

A. *ȝauland and ȝomerand with many loude ȝelles*, Awntyrs (Douce) 86.

to ȝowt and to ȝowle, Houlate 102.

(e) ALLITERATIVE PHRASES IN THE NORTHERN ALLITERATIVE PROSE WORKS.

In this section are included the alliterative phrases from *A Talkyng of the Love of God*,[1] *The Form of Perfect Living*,[2] and *On Prayer*.[3] The other prose works of the School of Rolle are not so thoroughly alliterated, and since a cursory examination of them revealed that the scattered phrases were usually found in these three works, it seemed unnecessary to record them.

E.M.E., A., Rom., Rh.A. 1. *of alle bales bote*, Talk. p. 359, l. 7. *boote of alle bale*, Talk. p. 362, l. 19.

A., Rom., Rh.A. 1 & 2. *beete alle bales*, Talk. p. 346, l. 33.

Cp. **E.M.E., O. & N.** *wip betyng and bustyng*, p. 359, l. 37.

so bleyk and so blo, Talk. p. 359, l. 36. Cp. *blak and blo*, A., etc.

O.E.P. & Pr., E.M.E., P.M., A., Rom., Rh.A. 1 & 2. *bouȝte wip (. . .) blod*, Talk. p. 346, l. 8, p. 349, l. 19, p. 365, l. 9.

O.E.P. & Pr., E.M.E., O & N., A., Rom., Rh.A. 1 & 2. *bringep (endeles) blisse*, Talk. p. 350, l. 9.

E.M.E., A., Rom., Rh.A. 1 & 2. *pe chaungyng of his cheere*, Talk. p. 362, l. 6.

clop or clout, Talk. p. 359, l. 2.

---

[1] Edit. *Yorkshire Writers*, C. Horstmann, vol. 2, pp. 345–66.

[2] *Ibid.*, vol. 1, pp. 3–49 (Camb. Dd.).

[5] *Ibid.*, vol. 1, pp. 295–300.

O.E.P. & Pr., E.M.E., La3., A., Rom., Rh.A. 1.   *cluppe and cusse*, Talk. p. 347, l. 8. p. 352, l. 5, p. 356, l. 19, p. 366, l. 23.   *cusse and cluppe*, Talk. p. 364, ll. 10, 14, 17.

A.   *cumfort and care*, Talk. p. 348, l. 23.

Rom.   *dempned to dep*, Talk. p. 358, l. 29, p. 360, l. 9.

E.M.E., La3., A., Rom., Rh.A. 1.   *to don him pere o dawe*, Talk. p. 360, l. 14.

O.E.Pr., E.M.E., A., Rom., Rh.A. 2.   *e3en and eren*, Talk. p. 348, l. 9.

O.E.P., E.M.E., A., Rom.   *feir and freoly*, Talk. p. 350, l. 15, p. 360 l. 28.

E.M.E., A., Rom.   *fikel and fals*, Talk. p. 346, ll. 28, 39.

E.M.E., A., Rom.   *fissches in pe flod*, Talk. p. 358, l. 7.

A.   *fylth of paire flesch*, Perf. Liv. p. 4, l. 19.   **E.M.E.** *flesches fulpe*, Talk. p. 349, l. 17.

flytand and feghtand, Perf. Liv. p. 44, l. 30.

Cp. O.E.Pr., A., Rom.   *foules in pe flyht*, Talk. p. 358, l. 6.

A.   *pe freelte of our flesch*, Perf. Liv. p. 47, l. 12.

gleteryng and glemyng, On Prayer, p. 295, l. 15.

E.M.E., A., Rom., Rh.A. 1 & 2.   *pe grace of god*, Perf. Liv. p. 18, l. 12, etc., On Prayer, p. 296, l. 3, etc.

A., Rom., Rh.A. 1 & 2.   *gyf me grace*, Perf. Liv. p. 30, l. 19.

E.M.E.   *hei3ed and heried*, Talk. p. 356, l. 36.

Cp. O.E.P., etc.   *heuene for helle*, Talk. p. 350, l. 18.

O.E.Pr., E.M.E., La3., Orm., P.M., A., Rom., Rh.A. 1 & 2.   *lede a lyf*, Talk. p. 358, ll. 2, 7, Perf. Liv. p. 5, l. 32.

E.M.E., A.   *longe and lene*, Talk. p. 360, l. 16.

E.M.E., Rh.A. 1 & 2.   *louesum leor*, Talk. p. 353, ll. 17, 20, etc.

O.E.P.   *loue . . . lisse*, Talk. p. 366, l. 25.

louelich and louesum, Talk. p. 346, l. 12.

pe lufe and pe louyng (O.E. lōfung) *of god*, Perf. Liv. p. 30, l. 11, etc.

A.   *lust and letchery*, Perf. Liv. p. 20, l. 17.

A., cp. Rh.A. 2.   *luste and lykynge*, Perf. Liv. p. 4, l. 7, p. 33, l. 7, On Prayer, p. 299, ll. 28, 36, etc.

E.M.E.   *mekenesse and myldeschupe*, Talk. p. 356, l. 9.   **E.M.E., Orm. A., Rom., Rh.A. 1 & 2.** *mylde and meke*, Talk. p. 360, l. 44.   *mylde mekenes*, On Prayer, p. 300, l. 7.   *mylde and mekenesse*, Talk. p. 353, l. 25.

meseyse and mischeef, Talk. p. 358, l. 19.

La3., A., Rom., Rh. 1 & 2.   *myrthe for to make*, On Prayer, p. 299, l. 6.

A., Rom.   *myrthe and melodye*, On Prayer, p. 295, l. 15.

O.E.Pr., E.M.E., La3., Orm., A., Rom., Rh.A. 2.   *to nempnen his nome*, Talk. p. 349, l. 12.   *to neuen his nome*, Perf. Liv. p. 22, l. 22.   *pat name be neuend*, Perf. Liv. p. 35, l. 9.

A.   *peyne and passion*, Talk. p. 354, l. 19, p. 357, l. 4, p. 362, l. 6.

A.   *pouert and pyne*, Talk. p. 358, l. 19.

Rom.   *toriuen and torent*, Talk. p. 360, l. 1.

O.E.P., E.M.E., Orm., A.   *of sake and of synne*, Talk. p. 361, l. 32.

Cp. O.E.P. & Pr., cp. E.M.E., A., Rom.   *schome and schenschupe*, Talk. p. 347, l. 22, p. 349, l. 32, p. 357, l. 9.   *schendfuliche and schomeliche*, Talk. p. 357, l. 37.

E.M.E., Rom., Rh.A. 1.   *schome and sunne*, Talk. p. 356, l. 13.

A.   *serwe and sikyng*, Talk. p. 351, l. 14.

O.E.P. & Pr., E.M.E., La3., P.M., Rom.   *serwe and sore*,   Talk. p. 360, l. 11.

A., Rom.   *sike and sobbe*, Talk. p. 362, l. 8.

O. & N., A., Rom., Rh.A. 1 & 2. *sike sore,* Talk. p. 349, l. 29, p. 360, l. 12.

sygheand and sorowande, On Prayer, p. 300, l. 14. *sorowynge and syghynge,* On Prayer, p. 296, l. 36.

O.E.Pr., E.M.E., Laȝ., A. *syt in a setel,* Perf. Liv. p. 41, l. 32.

E.M.E., Laȝ., A. *slomerande and slepande,* On Prayer, p. 297, l. 5.

E.M.E. *softe and swete,* Talk. p. 364, l. 17.

O.E.Pr., E.M.E., Laȝ., Rom. *sori and serwhfol,* Talk. p. 360, l. 22.

O.E.P. & Pr., E.M.E., Laȝ., Rom. *sore and sorwe,* Talk. p. 347, l. 21.

A. *sorow or sekenes,* Perf. Liv. p. 24, l. 35. Cp. **Laȝ.**

spittyng and spoutyng, Talk. p. 359, l. 37.

E.M.E., P.M., A., Rom., Rh.A. 1 & 2. *may no tonge telle,* Perf. Liv. p. 28, l. 26, On Prayer, p. 295, l. 10, Talk. p. 347, l. 32, p. 359, l. 27.

A. *wakande and wynkande,* On Prayer, p. 297, l. 8.

warnyng and wissyng, Talk. p. 349, l. 14.

E.M.E. *welde and wrouȝte,* Talk. p. 362, l. 26.

O.E.P., E.M.E., A., Rom., Rh.A. 1 & 2. *wele and wo,* Perf. Liv. p. 9, l. 13, p. 46, l. 17.

A., Rom., Rh.A. 2. *welth of þe worlde,* Perf. Liv. p. 44, l. 32.

O.E.Pr., E.M.E., P.M., A., Rom., Rh.A. 1 & 2. *werldes wele,* On Prayer, p. 297, l. 3.

E.M.E., Laȝ., Rom., Rh.A. 2. *worldes wynne,* Talk. p. 358, l. 15.

E.M.E., Rom., Rh.A. 1. *weole and wynne,* Talk. p. 346, l. 11, p. 347, l. 23.

E.M.E., Rom., Rh.A. 2. *in wille and in werk,* Talk. p. 349, l 38.

O.E.P. & Pr., E.M.E., Laȝ., Orm., O. & N., A., Rom. *wyse and war,* Perf. Liv. p. 13, l. 4.

E.M.E., A., Rom. *wit and wisdam,* Talk. p. 353, l. 22, etc. (very frequent).

E.M.E. *to wite me and were* (O.E. *werian*) *me,* Talk. p. 357, l. 1.

þi worþ and þi worschupe, Talk. p. 347, l. 32.

The phrases occurring in the other Rolle prose works are mostly to be found in the above list, but such as the following also are found :—

E.M.E., A., Rh.A. 2. *herken and here.*

E.M.E. *to leve and to lese.*

Rom., Rh.A. 2. *loue and lykyng* (cp. **A.**).

E.M.E., A., Rom., Rh.A. 2. *masse and matins.*

perish and pass.

prayer and petition.

A. *vice and vertue.*

A. *welth and wo.*

O.E.P. & Pr., E.M.E., Orm., P.M., A., Rom., Rh.A. 2. *word and werk.*

CHAPTER 12

THE ALLITERATIVE PHRASES IN NON–ALLITERATIVE MIDDLE ENGLISH WORKS OF THE FOURTEENTH CENTURY.

HANDLYNG SYNNE, GOWER AND CHAUCER.[1]

THESE alliterative phrases from typical fourteenth-century non-alliterative works are only relevant in so far as a study of them enables us to realise to what extent such phrases were at this time common in other than purely alliterative works.

HANDLYNG SYNNE is a typical religious work with its 103 alliterative phrases, of which none of any real significance go back to Old English prose or poetry. Almost half of them, however, are found in the early Middle English alliterative homiletic works and two-thirds of them are found in either the alliterative or non-alliterative romances. The explanation of this fact is that Mannyng along with many other fourteenth-century writers utilised that common stock of alliterative phrases which was not the exclusive possession of the alliterative poets ; consequently his phrases are not of special interest. Two phrases, however, are remarkable : *fals or frow*, found also in *The Debate between the Body and the Soul* and in *The Enemies of Man,* and *gryl ne grym,* first found in *The Ormulum.*

A total of 190 separate alliterative phrases in the works of Gower is not surprising, for we have already seen that many alliterative expressions were the unconscious stock-in-trade of practically all writers ; the list shows that nearly all Gower's phrases are of this type. 116/190 are to be found in the works of the Alliterative Revival and 118 in the non-alliterative romances, while 105 survive in Modern English. Gower's phrases are therefore of little interest, save to attest the popularity of alliteration in the south-east in the fourteenth century. Naturally, however,

---

[1] The last reference on the right is *Rh.A.* 2. *Rolle, Gower,* etc., need not, for obvious reasons, be recorded.

there are one or two survivals of interest, such as *hap and hele*, found also in *Piers Plowman, Pearl*, and Chaucer, and *knowe and kid*, occurring in the *Satire on the Pride of Ladies*.

Considering the bulk of Chaucer's work, the number of alliterative phrases used by him is small ; allowing for omissions, the total is not more than 350, but many of these phrases naturally occur several times in the course of his work. A study of the phrases and of the marginal qualifications attached will indicate to the reader the origin and previous history of the alliterative phrases in question. Very few are traceable in Old English prose or poetry, and such as are found there are phrases common in Middle English works, both alliterative and non-alliterative. Some few are of interest, such as *hyde and hele* and *londes and ledes*, the presence of which in Chaucer's writings is remarkable.

Two hundred and ten of Chaucer's phrases are also to be found in the poems of the Alliterative School, but this is of little moment; for on closer examination it will be discovered that they are ordinary phrases which might occur in any representative Middle English work, though there are indeed a few phrases to which this does not apply, of which the most noticeable are *cost and care, holte and heethe*, and *rome or ryde*, all found elsewhere only in the alliterative writers.

The clue to the understanding of Chaucer's phrases is perhaps to be found in the fact that 195 out of a total of 315 actually survive in Modern English. Similarly, it seems evident that the majority of the phrases used by Chaucer in the fourteenth century were at that time in everyday use among the people, while the remaining phrases were handed down through literary usage, though these are such as might be found in the works of almost any fourteenth-century writer of importance.

THE ALLITERATIVE PHRASES IN HANDLYNG SYNNE.

O.E.Pr., E.M.E., La3., A., Rom. *badde hys bedys*, 12174.
E.M.E. *þy self beryst þan on þy bak*, 11553.
to bete or bayte, 5988.
to bye or to borowe, 364.
Rom. *byryed . . . here body*, 11745.
Rom. *bledde neuer blode*, 9106.
A., Rom. *bobaunce and bost*, 4576.
E.M.E., Rom., Rh.A. 1 & 2. *body and bone*, 5388.
A. *3yue my body for to brenne*, 7140.
brenned þat . . . body, 9769.
E.M.E. *þe bondes to-braste*, 10672.
E.M.E., Rh.A. 2. *his bondes dyd breke*, 10610.

Rom. *brewed hys bale,* 6000. *breweþ moche bale,* 2354, 10934.

O.E.P. & Pr., E.M.E., A., Rom., Rh.A. 1 &· 2. *to brynge vs echone to blys,* 9974. *to brynge hym to blys,* 6276. *bringe þe to blys,* 6453. *me to blys brynge,* 8018.

Rom. *to brynge hym oute of . . . bonde,* 11998.

A., Rom., Rh.A. 2. *broȝt to bale,* 8741.

E.M.E., A., Rom., Rh.A. 2. *broȝt to bedde,* 11228. *to bedde are broȝt,* 7563.

Rom. *kalle and crye,* 7944.

Rom. *chaste and clene,* 7686.

Cp. A., Rom. *cumforte yn alle hys care,* 10698.

O.E.Pr., E.M.E., Orm., A., Rom., Rh.A. 1 & 2. *þe dede to do,* 8932. *þey dedyn þat almes dede,* 6622.

O.E.P. & Pr., E.M.E., Orm., A., Rom. *def and doumbe,* 5905.

Laȝ., A., Rom., Rh.A. 2. *to þe depe were dyght,* 1355.

Laȝ., A., Rom., Rh.A. 1 & 2. *to do swyche men a dawe,* 2172. *for to do so men to dawe,* 2124. *doun o dawe,* 1070.

Cp. O.E.Pr. Alf., E.M.E., A., Rom., Rh.A. 2. *for drede of deþ,* 10551.

A., Rom. *for drede and doute,* 9134.

E.M.E., Rom. *euere and oo,* 3697.

falle or fayle, 7912.

fals and feynte, 11766.

E.M.E., A., Rom. *fals and fykyl,* 2684. *so fals ne so fykyl,* 5222.

E.M.E., Rh.A. 1. *fals or frow,* 2305.

A. *feyre as flours,* 3502.

fonde and fare, 2939.

A., Rh.A. 1. *frute and floures,* 1414.

O.E.Pr., A., Rom. *to ȝyue hym a ȝyft,* 5600, etc.

A., Rom., Rh.A. 1 & 2. *God ȝyue vs grace,* 12053.

A. *gleteryng glemys,* 380.

Laȝ., A., Rom., Rh.A. 2. *gletryng golde,* 1408.

Rh.A. 1. *goun many a gate,* 6855.

A., Rom., Rh.A. 1 & 2. *graunteþ hym grace,* 11927.

A., Rom. *grete and grym,* 2800.

Orm., Rom. *gryl ne grym,* 5598.

handlyng with honde, 83.

Laȝ., A., Rom. *haukys or (yn) houndes,* 3084.

O.E.P., E.M.E., A., Rom. *heuene and helle,* 8247.

A., Rh.A. 2. *hors and harnyse,* 4596.

A., Rom., Rh.A. 1. *lawe of londe,* 2206.

O.E.Pr., E.M.E., Orm., Laȝ., A., Rom., Rh.A. 1 & 2. *ledde hys lyfe,* 6732. *swyche a lyfe þan shal he lede,* 4313. *sykyr lyfe shalt þou noun lede,* 6107. *how þat ȝe ȝoure lyuys lede,* 1950.

O.E.P. & Pr., Laȝ., A., Rom. *lyfe to lyue,* 1608. *leuyd yn hys lyfe,* 1439. *lyuyng here a lyue,* 1415. *lyued a synful lyfe,* 8027.

O.E.P. & Pr., E.M.E., Laȝ., A., Rom. *lefe ne loth,* 4378. *lefe no loth,* 3018. *for lefe no for lope,* 2711. *boþe lefe and lope,* 2789.

O.E.Pr., E.M.E., Orm., Laȝ., A., Rom., Rh.A. 2. *lered and lewed,* 8818.

E.M.E. *lestene and lerne,* 118.

E.M.E., A. *þe lust of lecchery,* 7577.

A., Rom., Rh.A. 1. *he made hys mone,* 7740.

E.M.E., A., Rom., Rh.A. 2. *at matyns or at messe,* 8811. *matyns or messe song,* 4541.

E.M.E., Orm., Rom., Rh.A. 1 & 2. *meke and mylde,* 3874. *meke or mylde,* 1136. **E.M.E., Orm., Rom.** *mylde and meke,* 259. *so mylde and so meke,* 5823.

Rom. *a melys mete,* 1330.

E.M.E., A., Rom., Rh.A. 2. *myght and mayn,* 5022.

O.E.P. & Pr., E.M.E., Laȝ., A., Rom., Rh.A. 2. *mylde of mode,* 5838.

A., Rom., Rh.A. 2. *(hys passyun) neyghed nye,* 9905.

O.E.Pr., E.M.E., Orm., Laȝ., A., Rom., Rh.A. 2. *to nemme hys name,* 6783.

A., Rom., Rh.A. 2. *of parsone or prest,* 8792. *persones, prestes,* 6073.

E.M.E., A. *with payne and . . . passyoun,* 5293.

A. *pouert and peyne,* 6676.

prys and pru, 2854.

O.E.Pr., E.M.E., Laȝ., A., Rom., Rh.A. 2. *he sagh a syght,* 5256.

E.M.E. *sate and stode,* 5589.

Rom. *to saue or spyl,* 12368.

O.E.P. & Pr., E.M.E., Laȝ., Rom. *seyde and sunge,* 4192.

E.M.E., A., Rom., Rh.A. 1. *so semely by syȝt,* 8172.

E.M.E., Laȝ., A., Rom. *sendeþ hys sondys,* 1990.

Cp. **O.E.Pr, E.M.E., A., Rom.** *our shenshyp and oure shame,* 8250.

Rom. *shryue þe of a synne,* 5173.

synke for synne, 1108.

E.M.E., Rom., Rh.A. 1. *synne and shame,* 3652, 4420. **Rom., Rh.A. 1.** *shame ne synne,* 4383.

to synne and hemself shende, 10146.

Cp. **Laȝ., A., Rom., Rh.A. 2.** *to sorowe and to sykenesse,* 7200.

sorow or smerte, 3964.

E.M.E., Laȝ., A., Rom., Rh.A. 1 & 2. *þe sope to seye,* 8739. **O.E.P. & Pr.** *þe sope y seye,* 3304. *sope to sey,* 11755. *sey me þe sope,* 10647.

speke with sawe, 8932.

O.E.Pr., E.M.E., A., Rom. *spak and seyde,* 5904.

A., Rom., Rh.A. 2. *stylle as a stone,* 6186. **A., Rom., Rh.A. 2.** *stode þe dede, stylle as stone,* 2288. **O.E.Pr., E.M.E., Orm., Laȝ., A., Rom., Rh.A. 1 & 2.** *stode stylle,* 5603.

Rom. *stoute and stark,* 4987.

Rom., Rh.A. 2. *strong and stout,* 4957.

O.E.P. & Pr., E.M.E., Laȝ., A., Rom., Rh.A. 1. *þere þe sunne ys more shynyngge,* 2301.

O.E.Pr., E.M.E., Rom., Rh.A. 1. *sungge þat songge,* 9155.

E.M.E. *swete of sauoure,* 1398. *swete of al sauoure,* 5000.

saueryd swete as spycerye, 1396.

E.M.E., Laȝ., A., Rom., Rh.A. 1 & 2. *þerby wyl y telle a tale,* 8742. *þys tale y tolde,* 8881, 10249.

telleþ and techeþ, 8100.

E.M.E., Rom., Rh.A. 2. *tyde or tyme,* 2381.

E.M.E., A., Rom. *top and tayle,* 5416, 8884.

E.M.E., A., Rom., Rh.A. 2. *ne tunge telle,* 7024.

A., Rom. *wax nygh wode,* 4458. *wox wode,* 8046.

A., Rom. *wax ful (of ire and) of wrap,* 1266.

O.E.P., E.M.E., A., Rom., Rh.A. 1 & 2. *wele no wo,* 3263, 5086.

A. *welþe to wynne,* 1410.

A., Rom. *with-oute wem or wounde,* 10764.

E.M.E., A., Rom., Rh.A. 1 & 2. *y wente my weye,* 12230.
wykked and wylde, 714.
E.M.E. *wyndes, watrys, wodes,* 9892.
Rom. *wrap and wo,* 3800.

The Alliterative Phrases in the Works of Gower.

The following alliterative phrases from the English works of Gower are merely collected from Paul Hofer's *Alliteration bei Gower,* 1890. This excellent dissertation contains lists of phrases all of which have been gathered together for the purpose of comparative study.

E.M.E., A., Rom., Rh.A. 2. *to bedde brought.*
bere blame.
O.E.Pr, E.M.E., Laȝ., A., Rom. *to bid (a) bede.*
A., Rom. *birde and beste.*
A., Rom., Rh.A. 2. *blast bloweth.*
F.M.E., A., Rom., Rh.A. 1 & 2. *bliss and bale.*
O.E.P. & Pr., E.M.E., Rom., Rh.A. 2. *blood and bone.*
A., Rom., Rh.A. 1. *bowe bende.*
A., Rom. Rh.A. 1 & 2. *cares cold.*
chalk for chese.
A., Rom. *chin and cheke.*
E.M.E., A., Rom. *clepe and call.*
A. *clepe and crie.*
A., Rom., Rh.A. 2. *in clothes clad.*
cloudy and clere.
E.M.E., A., Rom., Rh.A. 1 & 2. *come to court.*
A., Rom., Rh.A. 1 & 2. *day bedaweth.*
day of drede.
delve and diche. **A.** *dike and delve.*
A., Rom., Rh.A. 2. *to deth dight.*
Laȝ., A., Rom. *diches depe.*
A., Rom. *die deth.*
O.E.Pr., E.M.E., Orm., A., Rom., Rh.A. 1 & 2. *do dedes.*
O.E.P. & Pr., E.M.E., Orm., A., Rom. *doumbe and defe.*
E.M.E., Orm., A., Rom., Rh.A. 1 & 2. *downes and deles. downes (and) dales.*
Rom. *drinke draught.*
O.E.Pr., Orm. *drinke drinke.*
Laȝ., A., Rom., Rh.A. 2. *drive (forth the) day.*
O.E.Pr., E.M.E., A., Rom., Rh.A. 1 & 2. *ere and eye.*
A., Rom., Rh.A. 1 & 2. *faire face.*
A. *faire (and) foule.*
A. *faire fresshe (floures).*
fat and full.
O.E.P. & Pr. *fende (and) frende.*
fire and flame.
O.E.P. & Pr., Laȝ., A., Rom. *fissh and fowl.*

E.M.E., Rom., Rh.A. 2. *frende and fo.*
A. *fressh and faire.*
fresshe and fre.
Rom. *go to grounde.*
A. *god and godesse.*
E.M.E., A., Rom., Rh.A. 1 & 2. *þe grace of God. Goddes grace.*
gras and grein.
a grave begrave.
E.M.E., A., Rom., Rh.A. 1. *grene gras.*
O.E.Pr., E.M.E., A., Rom. *ʒive (yaf) ʒiftes.*
Rh.A. 1. *hap and hele.*
Cp. **O.E.Pr., Alf., A., Rom.** *harde herte.*
O.E.Pr., Rh.A. 1. *hare and hounde.*
O.E.Pr. *have on honde.*
Orm., A., Rom. *hede and herte.*
O.E.Pr., E.M.E., A., Rom. *helde in honde.*
O.E.P., Laʒ., A., Rom., Rh.A. 2. *hert and hinde.*
Laʒ., Orm., A., Rom., Rh.A. 1 & 2. *herte and honde.*
O.E.P., A., Rom. *heven and helle.*
E.M.E., Laʒ., Rom., Rh.A. 2. *hide and hewe.*
E.M.E., A., Rom. *hilles high.*
E.M.E. *holden behest.*
A., Rom. *by honde hente.*
O.E.Pr., E.M.E., A., Rom., Rh.A. 1. *hondes heven.*
Laʒ. *houndes and hornes.*
O.E.Pr., E.M.E., Orm., Rom. *in and oute.*
O.E.Pr., E.M.E., Orm., A., Rom. *king of kinges.*
A., Rom., Rh.A. 2. *knelend upon kne.*
E.M.E., Laʒ., A., Rom., Rh.A. 2. *king and knight. knight and king.*
A., Rom., Rh.A. 2. *kith and kinne.*
Rh.A. 2. *knowe and kid.*
Rom. *laste longe.*
E.M.E., Laʒ., A., Rom. *lasteth life.*
to laugh or loure.
law of love.
A., Rom., Rh.A. 1. *lawes of/in londe.*
O.E.Pr., E.M.E., Laʒ., Orm., A., Rom., Rh.A. 1 & 2. *lede (a) life.*
O.E.P. & Pr., E.M.E., Laʒ., A., Rom. *lef or loth.*
leges of the londe.
A., Rom., Rh.A. 2. *lord(es) of londe.*
O.E.Pr., E.M.E., A., Rom., Rh.A. 1. *lenger live.*
O.E.P. & Pr., Laʒ., A., Rom., Rh.A. 2. *to lese (a) life.*
light lampes.
O.E.P. & Pr., E.M.E., Laʒ., A., Rom. *to live (a) life.*
O.E.Pr., E.M.E., Laʒ., A., Rom. *(to) live longe.*
O.E.Pr., E.M.E. *lives longe.*
long and late.
A., Rom., Rh.A. 2. *lord and lady.*
Cp. **E.M.E., Orm.** *love and lust. loves lust.*
lustes of life.
Cp. **E.M.E., A., Rh.A. 2.** *lust and liking.*

24

E.M.E., A., Rom. *lust of lecherie.*
A., Rom. *make melodie.*
make mencion.
La3., A., Rom., Rh.A. 1 & 2. *make merth.*
A., Rom., Rh.A. 1 & 2. *make mone.*
A., Rom. *mannes might.*
E.M.E., A., Rom., Rh.A. 2. *matins and masse.*
E.M.E., Orm., A., Rom., Rh.A. 1 & 2. *meke and milde.*
A., Rom. *merthe and melody.*
A., Rom., Rh.A. 1. *mochel might.*
odde or even.
pouer people.
E.M.E., A. *preche and preie.*
profit, ne prise.
pruneth and piketh.
E.M.E., A., Rom., Rh.A. 2. *red roses.*
A., Rom., Rh.A. 2. *richelly arraied.*
roote and rinde. rinde and roote.
O.E.P. & Pr., E.M.E., La3., A., Rom., Rh.A. 1 & 2. *say sothe.*
Rom. *save and/or spille.*
A., Rom. *sauf and sound.*
E.M.E., La3., A., Rom., Rh.A. 2. *sende a sonde.*
O.E.Pr., E.M.E., La3., A., Rom., Rh.A. 2. *se(ne) a sight.*
A. *set and serued.*
sharpe spere.
sharpe swerd.
O.E.Pr., La3., A., Rom., Rh.A. 1 & 2. *shield and spere.*
Cp. O.E.Pr., E.M.E., La3., A., Rom., Rh.A, 1 & 2. *shinen .as the sonne.*
ship on the see.
A., Rom. *sighen and sobbe.*
A., Rom., Rh.A. 1 & 2. *sighe sore.*
A. *singe, and . . . sike.*
O.E.Pr., E.M.E., A., Rom., Rh.A. 1. *singe a songe.*
E.M.E., La3., Rom. *sitte stille.*
sleighte and subtilte.
slepe softe.
smock and sherte.
Cp. A. *sobbing and sory.*
sobre and softe.
softe or sharpe.
E.M.E. *softe and swete.*
O.E.P. & Pr., E.M.E., La3., A., Rom., Rh.A. 1. *sonne shineth.*
E.M.E., A., Rom. *sorwe and sike.*
Rom. *sorwe and strife.*
O.E.Pr, E.M.E., Rom. *sorweth sore.*
O.E.P. & Pr., E.M.E., A., Rom., Rh.A. 2. *sothly saie.*
A., Rom. *soule save.*
A. *soure, swete.*
O.E.P. *spake and sunge.*
spede and/or spille.
E.M.E., A., Rom. *speke and say. spake and said.*

speke softe.
speke and sounen.
A., Rom. (*flowers*) *sprede and springe.*
stalketh stille.
stere (*a*) *ship.*
A., Rom., Rh.A. 1. *sterne and stoute.*
Orm., A. *still and softe.*
E.M.E., A., Rom., Rh.A. 2. *stille as ston.*
A., Rom. *suffre sorwe.*
O.E.Pr., La3., A., Rom., Rh.A. 1. *swerd and spere.*
swere and sain. **Orm., Rom.** *swore and said.*
swithe and smarte.
teche and telle.
E.M.E., La3., A., Rom., Rh.A. 1 & 2. *telle a tale.*
E.M.E., La3., A., Rom., Rh.A. 2. *telle tiding(es).*
A., Rom. *telle trouthe.*
E.M.E., A., Rom., Rh.A. 2. *tethe . . . tunge.*
E.M.E., Rom., Rh.A. 2. *time and tide.*
E.M.E., A., Rom., Rh.A. 2. *tunge telle.*
A. *vice and virtue.*
waite and wacche.
warde and wacche.
O.E.Pr., E.M.E., La3., Orm., A., Rom. *ware and wise. wise and ware.*
Cp. O.E.Pr., Alf., Rom. *water . . . welle.*
Orm., A., Rom., Rh.A. 1 & 2. *wedde* (*a*) *wife.*
O.E.P., E.M.E., A., Rom., Rh.A. 1 & 2. *wele and wo.*
A. *welth and wo.*
E.M.E., A., Rom., Rh.A. 1 & 2. *went away.*
A., Rom. *wepe and weile.*
wepend (*and*) *wofull.*
A., Rom. *wepinge and wo.*
O.E.Pr., E.M.E., A., Rom., Rh.A. 1. *werkes wrought.*
O.E.Pr., La3., A. *wexe and wane.*
A. *wide world.*
E.M.E., A., Rom., Rh.A. 2. *winde and water.*
O.E.Pr., E.M.E., La3., A., Rom., Rh.A. 2. *wind* (*and*) *weder.*
O.E.Pr., A. *wishe and wolde.*
Rom., Rh.A. 1. *wit and wene.*
Orm., Rom. *witen wel.*
E.M.E., Rom. *wode and/for wroth.*
E.M.E., A., Rom., Rh.A. 2. *worche wo.*
O.E.Pr., E.M.E., Rom. *worchen wonder. wonder wrought.*
A., Rom. *wordes wise.*
A., Rom., Rh.A. 2. *worldes welthe.*
worldes welthe winne.
O.E.Pr. *worldes werke.*
A., Rom. *worlde winne.*
E.M.E., A. *worldes worship.*
Rom., Rh.A. 1. *worship and wele.*
A., Rom., Rh.A. 2. *worthy and wise.*
A., Rom. *wroughten wronge.*

ALLITERATIVE PHRASES IN CHAUCER'S WORKS.

The alliterative phrases occurring in Chaucer's works have been ably collected by C. F. McClumpha.[1] His important dissertation is not, however, generally accessible, and for convenience' sake an alphabetical list of the phrases in question is here appended, derived chiefly from McClumpha's work ; the references are not given, since these can be found in the latter.

McClumpha's plan of classifying the phrases into groups according to construction and meaning is not followed, and some of his phrases are not included, since they are not true alliterative phrases but merely alliterative combinations. It should be clearly understood that no credit is claimed for the following lists, which are merely included for the light which McClumpha's work can throw on the many problems which we are trying to solve.

A., Rom. *bacoun or beef.*
baker and botiler.
Rom. *barley bread.*
beaute and bounte.
A., Rom. *begge or borwe.*
O.E.P. & Pr., E.M.E., La3., A., Rom., Rh.A. 2. *bemys blowe.*
bemes brighte.
A., Rom., Rh.A. 1. *bende bowe.*
bere blame.
A., Rh.A. 1. *bere burthene.*
beres or boles (bulls).
A., Rom. *beestes and briddes.*
A., Rom. *briddes and bestes.*
O.E.Pr., E.M.E., La3., A., Rom. *bidde bedes.*
E.M.E., A., Rom. *blak and bloo.*
blis, bitternesse.
O.E.P. & Pr., E.M.E., A., Rom., Rh.A. 2. *blood and bones.*
Rom., Rh.A. 1 & 2. *body and bones.*
A., Rom. *bold baroun.*
bore and bere. bere and bore.
E.M.E., A., Rom., Rh.A. 1. *bote ne bale.*
O.E.P. & Pr., E.M.E., A., Rom., Rh.A. 1 & 2. *bought with blood.*
E.M.E., A., Rom. *bowe and bende.*
braunche and blome.
E.M.E., Rom. *breke bone (and bak).*
A. *brennyng and blasyng.*
E.M.E., A. *brennynge bronde.*
A., Rom., Rh.A. 2. *brenne bright.*
briddes of boures.
Rom. *bright in bour.*

[1] C. F. McClumpha, *The Alliteration of Chaucer*, Leipzig (not dated).

Cp. O.E.P., O.E.Pr., E.M.E., A., Rom., Rh.A. 1 & 2.   *brynge to blysse.*
broun as bery.
broun and bryght.
Orm.   *buddes and blomes.*
busy as bees.
E.M.E., A., Rom.   *calle and clepe.*
Cp. O.E.P., A., Rom., Rh.A. 1 & 2.   *cares colde.*
Cp. **A.** *charitable and chaste.*
A., Rom.   *chaunge colour.*
chaunge countenance.
Rom., Rh.A. 2.   *clad in clothes.*
Rh.A. 1.   *clene and cler.*
A.   *clepe ne crye.*
Rom.   *crie and calle.*
Rom.   *cok croweth.*
cost and care.
A., Rom.   *croys of crist.*
E.M.E., A., Rom., Rh.A. 1 & 2.   *crowned . . . kynge.*
A., Rom., Rh.A. 2.   *curteise and kynde.*
A., Rom., Rh.A. 1 & 2.   *day daweth.*
A., Rom.   *damned to dethe.*
O.E.Pr., A., Rom.   *day of doom.*
Laʒ., Orm., A., Rom., Rh.A. 2.   *dale and doune.*   **E.M.E., Rom., Rh.A.
1 & 2.**   *doune and dale.*
derknes of deth.
A., Rom.   *deth to dyen.*
Laʒ.   *diche deepe.*
A.   *dyke and delve.*
O.E.P. & Pr., Laʒ., Orm., A., Rom.   *domes to deme.*
O.E.P. & Pr., E.M.E., Orm., A., Rom.   *doumbe (and) defe.*
Cp. **O.E.Pr., E.M.E., A., Rom., Rh.A. 2.**   *drede of dethe.*
A., Rom.   *drynke draughte.*
O.E.Pr., Orm.   *drinken drynke.*
A., Rom., Rh.A. 1 & 2.   *fair of face.*
O.E.P., E.M.E., (cp. A.), Rom., Rh.A. 1 & 2.   *faire and fre. faire, fresh,
fre.*   **A.** *fressh and feire.*   Cp. **A.** *fresshe and fre.*
A.   *faire, fetys.*
Rom.   *fyne, faire.*
O.E.P. & Pr., Laʒ., A., Rom., Rh.A. 1 & 2.   *falleth to foote.*
A., Rh.A. 2. *feble and feynt.*   **A.** *feynt and feble.*
ferm and feithfull.
A., Rom., Rh.A. 1.   *fers and felle.*
fier of flynt.
A., Rom., Rh.A. 2.   *fight in felde.*
A., Rom.   *fight with fone.*
fykil and felle.
fir and flambe.
A., Rom.   *fyssh in floode.*
A., Rom., Rh.A. 1.   *fledden for fere.*
Laʒ., A., Rom.   *fleissche and fissch.*   **A., Rom.** *fisch and fleische.*
A., Rom.   *folowe fast.*

Laȝ., Orm., A., Rom., Rh.A. 2.   *fostered and ifedde.*
A.   *foule or faire.*
O.E.Pr., A., Rom.   *fowel in flight.*
fredom and fraunchise.
frendly, faithfully.
A., Rom.   *freend ne felawe.*
Cp. O.E.P., E.M.E., A., Rom., Rh.A. 1 & 2.   *freend, foe.*
A., Rom.   *gaderud togider.*
O.E.Pr., A., Rom.   *gaf giftes.*
O.E.P., A., Rom., Rh.A. 2.   *game and gle.*
Cp. O.E.Pr., Alf.   *gemmes in gold.*
A., Rom., Rh.A. 1 & 2.   *give grace.*
O.E.Pr., A., Rom.   *gilt forgive.*
gold ne gere.
A.   *governe and gye.*
E.M.E., A., Rom., Rh.A. 1.   *grace of God.*
A., Rom., Rh.A. 1 & 2.   *graunt grace.*
E.M.E., A., Rom.   *grene gras.*
grone and grete.
O.E.Pr., E.M.E., A.   *yaf up gost.*
halke and herne.
halle and home.
A.   *halle and hous.*
A., Rh.A. 1.   *happe, hele.*
A., Rom.   *harde hertis.*
O.E.Pr., A.   *hardnes of herte.*
harde and hevy.
E.M.E., A., Rom., Rh.A. 1 & 2.   *harwed helle.*
A.   *hauke and hunte.*
O.E.Pr., Laȝ., A., Rom.   *have in honde.*
heedes in hode.
heel and honour.
hele and hewe.
A.   *heer of heed.*
helpe and hyndre.
A., Rom.   *hente in honde.*
O.E.Pr., A., Rom.   *here and hownd.*
Orm., A., Rom., Rh.A. 1 & 2.   *herte and hand.*
herte nor hele.
O.E.P., Laȝ., A., Rom., Rh.A. 2.   *herte, hynde.*
O.E.P., A., Rom.   *hevene or helle.*
O.E.P. & Pr., E.M.E., A., Rom., Rh.A. 1 & 2.   *hyde and hele.*
Cp. O.E.Pr., E.M.E., A., Rom., Rh.A. 1.   *hide in hole.*
O.E.Pr., E.M.E., Laȝ., A., Rom.   *hold in hande.*
A.   *holte and heeth.*
A., Rom.   *honged by hals.*
hope and herte.
A., Rom., Rh.A. 2.   *hors and hernoyse.*
O.E.Pr., A.   *hors, houndes.*
Cp. Laȝ., Orm.   *horsemen, haukes, houndes.*
O.E.Pr., Orm., A.   *hous and home.*

La3., A. *hulles hye.*
A., Rom. *jangle as a jay.*
kene and cold.
kepe counseil.
kerve with knif.
O.E.P. & Pr., E.M.E., La3., A., Rom., Rh.A. 1. *kissith, clippith.*
E.M.E., A., Rom., Rh.A. 2. *knele on knees.*
La3., A., Rom., Rh.A. 2. *knights and kynges.*
knotty and knarry.
kutte and kerven.
A., Rom. *large and long.*
Rom. *lasten long.*
late and longe.
O.E.Pr., E.M.E., La3., Orm., A., Rom., Rh.A. 1 & 2. *lede lif.*
A. *lef on lynde.*
O.E.P., E.M.E., La3., A., Rom. *leigh loude.*
O E.Pr., E.M.E., La3., Orm., A., Rom., Rh.A. 2. *lered and lewed.*
A. *lerned in lawe.*
lerned in lore.
O.E.Pr., E.M.E., La3., A., Rom., Rh.A. 2. *lif (is) lost.*
E.M.E., La3., A., Rom. *lymes or lif.*
A., Rom. *lyoun and lepart.*
O.E.P. & Pr., La3., A., Rom. *lyve lyf.*
E.M.E. *lyves lyght.*
Cp. O.E.Pr., E.M.E., La3., A., Rom., Rh.A. 1. *live long.*
O.E.P., La3., A., Rom., Rh.A. 1 & 2. *lond and lede.*
A., Rom., Rh.A. 2. *lord or lady.*
A. *lordship, or lond.*
O.E.P. & Pr., E.M.E., Laz., A., Rom. *loth or leef.*
Rom. *love lif.*
lust and likerousnesse.
O.E.Pr. *mayde and moder.*
E.M.E., A., Rom., Rh.A. 2. *mayn and might.*
A., Rom. *make melodye.*
A., Rom. *make amend.*
La3., A., Rom., Rh.A. 1 & 2. *make mirth.*
A., Rom., Rh.A. 1 & 2. *make mone.*
manhode and myght.
by mette or by mesure.
O.E.P. & Pr., E.M.E., A., Rom., Rh.A. 1 & 2. *mylde mode.*
A. *mynde and memory.*
A., Rom. *myrth and melody.*
A. *musyke and melodye.*
O.E.Pr., E.M.E., La3., Orm., A., Rh.A. 2. *names neven.*
A., Rom., Rh.A. 2. *nighen ner.*
A., Rom. *nighe nighte.*
A. *now or neuere.*
A. *peny ne pound.*
A. *peril and payne.*
A. *pite, peyne.*
plat and playn.

A. *portray or peynte.*
A. *prest ne prelate.*
A. *presumption and pride.*
prince and page.
prys and profyt.
prive and pert.
proud and pert.
A., Rom., Rh.A. 2. *putte in prison.*
rape and renne.
E.M.E., A., Rom., Rh.A. 1 & 2. *red as rose.*
A., Rom., Rh.A. 2. *renne and ryde.* **A.** *rome or ryde.*
A., Rom., Rh.A. 2. *riche array.*
A., Rom., Rh.A. 1 & 2. *right and resoun.*
Laȝ., A., Rom., Rh.A. 2. *saye sawes.*
A., Rom. *sayle in see.*
save or sley.
Rom. *save or spille.*
schame and sorwe.
A., Rom., Rh.A. 1. *sorwe and schame.*
O.E.Pr., Laȝ., A., Rom., Rh.A. 1 & 2. *scheeld, spere.* **O.E Pr., A., Rom., Rh.A. 1.** *spere and scheeld.*
A., Rom., Rh.A. 2. *scheld fro schame.* *sheld fro shonde.*
schepperd and schepe.
Cp. O.E.P., E M.E., A. *shine sheene.*
O.E.Pr., E.M.E. *shinen starres.*
A., Rom. *schyveren schaftes.*
O.E.Pr., E.M.E., Laȝ., A., Rom. *see a sighte.*
E.M.E., A., Rom., Rh.A. 1 & 2. *seemly to see.*
O.E.P. & Pr., E.M.E., Laȝ., A., Rom., Rh.A. 1 & 2. *seye sothe.*
O.E.Pr., E.M.E., Laȝ., A., Rom. *seyn and synge.* **O.E.P. & Pr., A., Rom.** *synge and seye.*
A., Rom. *sende socour.*
E.M.E., Laȝ., A., Rom. *send (a) sonde.*
A., Rom. *sigh and sobbe.*
A., Rom., Rh.A. 1 & 2. *sighte soore.*
sighte and seyde.
E.M.E., A., Rom. *sik and sore.* **A., Rom.** *sobbes and sikes.*
Cp. Laȝ., A. *siknes and sorwe.* **A., Rom.** *sorwe and sykes.*
O.E.Pr., E.M.E., A., Rom., Rh.A. 1. *sing a song.*
E.M.E., Laȝ., A., Rom. *sitte stille.*
O.E.Pr., E.M.E., Laȝ., Orm., A., Rom., Rh.A. 1. *stand stille.*
skornes and skoffes.
slepen softe.
E.M.E., Laȝ., A. *slomber, sleep.*
Rom., Rh.A. 2. *snow or slete.*
E.M.E., Rh.A. 2. *sonne and see.*
O.E.Pr., E.M.E., Laȝ., A., Rom., Rh.A. 1 & 2. *sonne shyneth.*
sore aschamed.
sory and sad.
Cp. O.E.Pr., E.M.E., A., Rom. *sorwes sore.*
O.E.P. & Pr., E.M.E., A., Rom., Rh.A. 2. *sothly seye.*

A., Rom. *soule save.*
E.M.E., A. *sowe seed.*
O.E.Pr., E.M.E., A., Rom. *spake and seyde.*
A., Rom. *speche spoken.*
Rom. *stedes in stalle.*
A., Rh.A. 2. *stedfast and stable.*
A., Rom., Rh.A. 1. *stern and stoute.*
Cp. E.M.E. *sterte out of sleepe.*
Orm., A., Rom. *stille and soft.*
A., Rom., Rh.A. 2. *stille as ston.*
A., Rom. *stynte strife.*
E.M.E., Laȝ., A., Rom., Rh.A. 1. *stokkes and stones.*
A., Rom. *suffer sorwe.*
A., Rh.A. 2. *swelte and swouned.*
swete or soure.
Orm., A., Rom. *swor and sayde.*
swote, smothe, softe.
E.M.E., Laȝ., A., Rom., Rh.A. 1 & 2. *telle tale.*
E.M.E., Laȝ., A., Rom., Rh.A. 2. *telle tidynges.*
A., Rom. *telle trauthe.*
A., Rom., Rh.A. 2. *telle trewely.*
told and taught.
A., Rom., Rh.A. 1 & 2. *tonge telle.*
E.M.E., Rom. *toppe and taylle.*
A., Rom., Rh.A. 2. *toun and tour.*
A., Rom. *trewe tale.*
A., Rom. *trow truly.*
A. *vertue, vices.*
A. *vileny or vice.*
devynen or devyse.
A. *wake or wynke.*
O.E.Pr., E.M.E., Laȝ., Orm., A., Rom. *war and wys.*
Rom. *water at/fro well.*
wawes of water.
O.E.Pr., Laȝ., A., Rom. *waxe and wane.*
wax wery.
A., Rom., Rh.A. 1 & 2. *wed wyf.*
O.E.Pr., A., Rom. *weddyd wyf.*
Orm., A., Rom. *wed woman.*
O.E.P., E.M.E., A.,ʾRom., Rh.A. 1 & 2. *wele and/or woo.*
E.M.E., A., Rom., Rh.A. 1 & 2. *went away.*
A., Rom. *wepe and waile.*
wepe and biwayle.
A., Rom. *wepe, wryng, wayle.*
A., Rom. *wepe water.*
A., Rom. *wepyng and wo.*
A., Rom. *wept and wrong.*
widewe or wyf.
E.M.E., Laȝ., Rom. *wilde and wood.*
wynde and wrappe.
wily and wys.

A. *wyn and wymmen.*
E.M.E., A., Rom., Rh.A. 2. *wynd and water.*
O.E.Pr., E.M.E., Laʒ., A., Rom., Rh.A. 2. *wynde, weder.*
A., Rh.A. 2. *wys and worthi.* **A., Rh.A. 2.** *worthi and wys.*
Orm., Rom. *wite wel.*
Orm., A. *wytte and wille.*
O.E.Pr., E.M.E., A., Rom. *wonders wroughte.*
A., Rom. *wood of witt.*
wood and/or wooth.
E.M.E., Rom., Rh.A. 1. *woode and water.*
O.E.P. & Pr., E.M.E., Laʒ., Orm., A., Rom., Rh.A. 2. *worche wille.*
E.M.E., A., Rom., Rh.A. 1 & 2. *worche woo.*
O.E.Pr., E.M.E., Laʒ., Orm., A., Rom., Rh.A. 1. *worche workes.*
A., Rom., Rh.A. 1. *worche wronge.*
O.E.P. & Pr., E.M.E., Orm., A., Rom., Rh.A. 2. *word, werk.*
E.M.E., A., Rom. *word or wille.*
O.E.P., Orm., A. *word and witte.*
A., Rom. *world wynne.*
E.M.E., A., Rom. *the world wrought.*
Rh.A. 1. *worth the while.*
E.M.E., A., Rom., Rh.A. 1 & 2. *woundes wyde.*

NOTE.—*worde and ende :* see *ord and ende,* **O.E.P. & Pr., E.M.E., A., Rom.,** etc.

	No.	O.E.P., H.	O.E.P., R.	O.E.Pr., Hom.	O.E.Pr., Alf.	O.E.Pr., Leg.	E.M.E.	Laʒ.	Orm.	P.M.	O. & N.	A.	Rom.	Rh.A. 1.	Rh.A. 2.	Rolle.	H.S.	Gower.	Chaucer.	Modern.
O.E.P., H. .	174	—	66	18	21	2	14	23	5	5	1	23	28	8	19	4	3	7	11	13
O.E.P., R. .	346	66	—	48	49	13	42	45	14	9	5	39	41	17	21	12	10	12	24	30
O.E.Pr., Hom.	193	18	48	—	67	23	58	28	22	7	6	43	44	17	19	10	13	21	30	37
O.E.Pr., Alf.	420	21	49	67	—	26	53	51	21	7	5	52	56	17	18	8	14	30	32	32
O.E.Pr., Leg.	137	2	13	23	26	—	13	15	3	2	2	14	18	7	6	1	2	6	9	13
E.M.E. .	621	14	42	58	53	13	—	72	28	14	12	174	162	72	93	38	45	63	75	103
Laʒ. . .	250	23	45	28	51	15	72	—	14	4	10	88	87	25	40	12	19	29	47	42
Orm. . .	109	5	14	22	21	3	28	14	—	3	2	30	25	11	14	6	7	15	22	16
P.M. . .	21	5	9	7	7	2	14	4	3	—	0	11	12	6	6	6	4	4	6	5
O. & N. .	30	1	5	6	5	2	12	10	2	0	—	14	13	3	6	4	2	6	11	13
A. . .	1415	23	39	43	52	14	174	88	30	11	14	—	425	129	280	45	60	116	210	280
Rom. . .	820	28	41	44	56	18	162	87	25	12	13	425	—	138	218	41	73	118	181	249
Rh.A. 1 .	261	8	17	17	17	7	72	25	11	6	3	129	138	—	82	19	24	37	53	69
Rh.A. 2 .	470	19	21	19	18	6	93	40	14	6	6	280	218	82	—	25	31	56	76	115
Rolle. .	70	4	12	10	8	1	38	12	6	6	4	45	41	19	25	—	18	19	25	24
H.S. . .	103	3	10	13	14	2	45	19	7	4	2	60	73	24	31	18	—	29	43	59
Gower .	190	7	12	21	30	6	63	29	15	4	6	116	118	37	56	19	29	—	103	105
Chaucer .	315	11	24	30	32	9	75	47	22	6	11	210	181	53	76	25	43	103	—	195
Modern .	2112	13	30	37	32	13	103	42	16	5	13	280	249	69	115	24	59	105	195	—

The long list of alliterative phrases occurring in modern English, to which reference has already been made, had to be deleted on account of expense.   It was thought wiser, however, to leave the statistics in the final column as they might be useful in making comparisons.   This list of modern phrases, while laying no claim to absolute completeness, contained all survivals from the earlier groups, so that the illustrations of continuity which it would have afforded are not altogether lost.

PART IV.

STYLE.

CHAPTER 13

THE USE OF "TAGS" IN MIDDLE ENGLISH ALLITERATIVE POETRY.

BEFORE proceeding to deal with the style of alliterative poetry in general, it seemed desirable to gather together in a preliminary chapter the various types of "tag" so frequently found in much of Middle English alliterative verse.

It will be readily admitted that the "bob and wheel" structure almost inevitably calls for the use of tag-like expressions, though the author of *The Pistill of Susan* generally manages to avoid them. Thus, in *The Quatrefoil of Love*, out of forty instances of the "bob" there are fourteen cases of meaningless expressions, e.g. :—

> (450–1), *þat now are fulle ryalle to ryne and to ryde*
> *In lande.*

Similarly, in *Sir Gawain and the Green Knight*, at least thirty out of the 102 examples are quite irrelevant, e.g. :—

> (485–6), *Wyth wele walt þay þat day, til worþed an ende,*
> *In londe.*

Whatever excuse may be made for such tags as these, no legitimate one can be adduced to explain the use of tags within the alliterative long line itself. The requirements of the alliteration are not so exacting as to account for the habitual employment of unnecessary tags which only serve to throw into greater prominence the general diffuseness in style of Middle English alliterative poetry. The second half-line is frequently devoid of any real significance, and the majority of the poets seem to have resorted to these tags " to fill out their verses ". It will be seen from a study of the devices employed which poets were most negligent, and how different poets overcame their metrical difficulties in different ways.

(1) THE USE OF AN INFINITIVE IN THE SECOND HALF-LINE, PRECEDED BY A WORD BEGINNING WITH THE REQUIRED ALLITERATIVE SOUND.

This is a device employed most frequently in *Alexander A*, in which there are eight examples of an adverb, such as *seemly* with *to knowe*, and four of an adjective, such as *grim* with *to beholde*, in every case the word being varied to suit the alliteration. The following list is reasonably complete, though it is not impossible that an odd example may have been missed.

Alex. A. *brem too beholde*, 533. *choice too beholde*, 183.
grym to beholde, 77. *stoute too beholde*, 734.
prestly too here, 171. *faitly too knowe*, 804.
lelli too knowe, 127. *seemely too knowe*, 118, 545.
so true is too knowe, 198. *wisly to knowe*, 144, 372, 571.
soothely to lere, 624. *lovely to seene*, 192.

Alex. B. *worpi to haue*, 25. *nedli to knowe*, 149.
ful ӡare to kenne, 241. *trysty to leue*, 829.

W. Alex. *ware mervaile to here* (Ash.) 1164.
wer mervell to telle (Dub.) 1164.
þat reuthe was to here, 1280. *wer mervelle to rekyn*, 1245.
was mervale to see, 1061.

Troy. *clene to beholde*, 13827. *dole to beholde*, 11116.
faire to beholde, 1386. *fresshe to behold*, 13182.
fuerse to behold, 12009. *pyne to behold*, 933, 12509.
ruthe to beholde, 8044. *shene to beholde*, 330.
wyn to beholde, 4265. *wo to beholde*, 13735.
dole for to se, 11498. *ferly to se*, 1357, etc.

Death & Life.
(*soe grislye & gret &*) *grim to behold*, 154.
(*a sight was*) *sorrowful to behold*, 151.
winlye to behold, 45. *winne to behold*, 139.
lodlye to see, 162. *kindlye to showe*, 111.

Jerus. (*was*) *deil to byholde*, 641. (*was*) *pite to byholde*, 1243.
þat deil was to hure, 1097.

Morte Arthure. *dredfulle to beholde*, 760.

Pat. *gret selly to here*, 140.

Mum. (*bablid with his bile*) *þat blisse was to hire*, 938.

Gaw. *glorious to here*, 46.

Pierce. *þat sorwe was to heren*, 440.

Parl. *as dole es to here*, 400, 452. *lele for to schewe*, 115.

Quatr. *es wonder to here*, 53. *so trewe for to trayste*, 133.
grete dole for to see, 162, 179, 231.
gret reuth was to see, 205.

Cp. Pur. *blo, blubrande, and blak, vnblype to neӡe*, 1017.

and Alex. A. *Than, shortly to showe, þei scharplich went*, 82.

(2) —— MEN OF ARMES.

An alliterative tag used by a number of Middle English alliterative poets is of a similar kind, and is likewise employed for the sake of alliteration.   It is confined to the second half-line, and consists of the phrase *men of armes*, preceded by an adjective which alliterates with the stressed words of the first half-line.   For the most part the adjective is vague and colourless in meaning.   The accompanying list contains all the examples that have been found.

alle mene of armes, M.A. 273.
big men of armes, W. Alex. 1295, Troy 6311.
bold men of armys, Troy 6866, W. Alex. 1594.
kant men of armes, Troy 8999, 9647.
kene men of armys, Troy 6460, 6486, 7773, W. Alex. 90, W. of P. 2288,
    2638, 3544.
chief men of armys, Cr. King 94.
kyd men of armys, Troy 1741, etc. (9 times).
clene men of arme3, Jos. 408, M.A. 1603, etc. (6 times), W. of P. 4693.
clere men of armes, M.A. 4265.
derfe men in armys, Troy 2570.
fele men of armes, W. Alex. 803 *, Troy 5467.
ferse/furse men of armys, M.A. 1537, 1710, 1897, Parl. 349, Troy 1132, etc.
    (7 times).
fyue hondred men of armes, Jos. 476.
fresche men of armes, M.A. 364, 2501.
gude men of armes, M.A. 563, etc. (6 times), Parl. 351, W. of P. 1348, Troy
    1506.
joly mane of armes, M.A. 3415.
light men of armys, Troy 6208.
prise men of armys, M.A. 2755, 3005, Troy 3685, 9414, 12570.
proud men of armys, Troy 1693, 6294, 6363.
sad men of armys, Troy 7108, W. & W. 193.   Cp. Troy 5903, *a sad mon o*
    armys.
sekyre men of arme3, M.A. 2659.   Cp. Jerus 434, *a siker man of armys*.
sharp men of armys, Troy 4055, 5780.
shene men of armys, Troy 2805.
sleghe men of armes, M.A. 2979.
styffe mene of armes, M.A. 3623.
strong men of armys, Troy 1193.
sure men of armys, Troy 2327, 10029.
thro men of armes, W. Alex. 1246.
wale men of armys, Troy 4716.
wight men in armys, Troy 2215.
wyse men of armes, M.A. 19, 2681, 2746, 3036.

It will be seen that, apart from scattered examples, this tag is found chiefly in *Morte Arthure* and in *The Destruction of Troy*. The use of such phrases is illustrative of the diffuseness in style of much of M.E. alliterative poetry.

The same phrase is occasionally found without the word *man :*

e.g. *that feirce were in armes,* Sc.F. 56, 110, 124.
happye(ste) in armes, M.A. 2974, 3879.
so proude in his armes, Gaw. 2104.
thryftye in armes, M.A. 317.

Such phrases are quite rare, and *The Parlement of the Thre Ages* and *The Destruction of Troy* are in fact the only poems to show an extensive use of this tag. ·The former poem has

doghety in armes, 181 ; *preued in armes,* 328 ; *full lusty in armes,* 474 ; *bolde beryn in armes,* 527 ; *full priste in his armes,* 618 ; *full euerous in armes,* 622. *The Destruction of Troy* has numerous examples, of which the following are mere representatives : *biggest in armes,* 1032 ; *stithest in armys,* 10812 ; *strongest in armes,* 7, etc.

(3) —— OF DEEDS.

Another tag of the same type as the last occurs repeatedly in *Scottish Field, The Parlement of the Thre Ages* and *The Destruction of Troy*, but only occasionally in a few other poems. A colourless adjective precedes the phrase *of deeds,* and is similarly varied to suit the alliteration.

Sc. Field has nine examples :

that epe was of deeds, 220, 340.	*that eke was of deeds,* 282.
that proued was of deeds, 20, 272.	*that keene is of deeds,* 359.
and wyttye of deeds, 162.	*that sterne was of deeds,* 226, 294.

Parl. has six examples :

and ʒape of my dedys, 270.	*full gracyous of dedis,* 528.
kiluarde of dedis, 516.	*and kyd of his dedis,* 477.
and wyse of his dedis, 455.	*full sauage of his dedys,* 616.

Troy has many examples, of which the following are representative : *haithill of dedis,* 38 ; *wise of his dedis,* 3919, 3949, etc. ; *ʒeuerus of dedis,* 3933 ; *pert of his dedis,* 4119 ; *a prise mon of dedis,* 5449 ; *abill of dedys,* 6108, 9415, 10612 ; *wight of hor dedys,* 10036.
There are in addition three examples in *Mum and Sothsegger :*

witti and wise, worthy of deedis, 213.
But sum ben so courtoys and kinde of paire deedis, 442.
The moste merciful among paym and meukest of deedes, 1031.

Cp. *Death and Life,* 103 : *that courteous were of deeds.*

It would appear that a simple phrase such as *sterne of deeds* was varied by careless poets to suit the needs of the alliteration, thus reducing a reasonable phrase to a valueless tag.

TAGS IN MIDDLE ENGLISH ALLITERATIVE POETRY 385

(4) þAT . . . IN ERTHE.

A fourth tag is similarly varied in accordance with the alliteration required. The verb represented by the dots conveys the
idea of *live*, and is usually one of the following : *dwellede, lyffede,
lengede, regnede* or *wonnede*. *Morte Arthure* has more examples
than any other alliterative poem :

> (þe doughtyeste) *þat duellyde in erthe*, 219, 3322.
> (þe doughtyeste) *þat ever was duelland in erthe*, 3444.
> (na Romayne) *þat regnes in erthe*, 310.
> (þe rycheste) *that regneʒ in erthe*, 865.
> (þe richeste blode) *þat regnys in erthe*, 3027.
> (alle) *that regnede in erthe*, 2035.
> (was never roye so riche) *þat regnede in erthe*, 3274.
> (no lede) *þat lyffes in erthe*, 2326.
> (alle froyteʒ) *þat floreschede in erthe*, 3247.
> (alle ledis . . .) *þat lengede in erthe*, 3286.
> (ne rayne-dere) *þat rynnes appone erthe*, 4001, cp. 3342 and 3496.

There are only scattered examples in the other poems :

> (alle þe bestes) *þat breden uppon erthe*, Mum 987, cp. Mum 181, 212.
> (he was þe wiseste in witt) *þat euer wonnede in erthe*, Parl. 603.
> (no lud) *þat liueþ in erþe*, W. of P. 4144.
> (þe gladdest gome) *þat miʒt go on erþe*, W. of P. 1263.
> (of alle lordis þe lord) *þat leues in erthe*, W. Alex. 1722.
> (Alle þat glydeʒ & gotʒ, & gost of lyf habbeʒ,
> I schal wast with my wrath) *þat wons vpon vrþe*, Pur. 326.
> (For ther is neither lered ne lewed) *þat lyveth vpon erthe*, Cr. King 57.

Individual poets evolve similar tags to complete the alliteration
and fill out the line. Thus the author of *Sc.F.* has

> . . . *that are soe feirce holden*, 342, 374 ;

and   . . . *he was soe keene holden*, 102.

Similarly, the author of *Alexander A* relied upon a whole stock of
colourless adjectives, as we have already noted [1] ; so he writes *careful
dintes, lopelike dintes* and *selcoupe dintes*, etc. Perhaps this particular poet is more careless than others in this respect, but it is a
general weakness of much alliterative verse in Middle English that
the second half-line is so often devoid of any real significance.

(5) To . . . þE soþE.

This is a tag found almost exclusively in *William of Palerne*,
and belongs to a whole group of tags in which the poet vouches for

[1] P. 27.

the accuracy of his statements.   Its constant recurrence in *William of Palerne* becomes wearisome to the reader.

The starting-point for this tag was undoubtedly the common alliterative phrase *to say soth*.   The examples of this phrase are not given here, because in itself the phrase is not a tag.

> *to carpe þe sope*, W. of P. 503, etc. (8 times).
> *to karpe þee soothe*, Alex. A. 683.
> *to kiþe þe sope*, W. of P. 4086.
> *to deme þe sope*, W. of P. 151, etc. (8 times).
> *to mene þe sope*, M.A. 3556, W. of P. 4618, etc. (5 times).
> *to minge þe sope*, W. of P. 1937, 4327.
> *to munge þe sope*, W. of P. 2735, 4968, 5341.
> *to neuen þe sope*, W. of P. 2453, 2517.
> *to nymphe þe sope*, W. of P. 2179.
> *to proue þe sope*, W. of P. 681, 750, 4287, 4765, W. Alex. 261.
> *to rekene þe sope*, W. of P. 1954, 5057.
> *to seie al þe sope*, W. of P. 4606, etc.
> *to speke þe sope*, W. of P. 5225.
> *to talke þe sope*, W. of P. 1018, 1322, 1721.
> *to telle þe sope*, W. of P. 437, etc. (14 times).

Similar phrases of various kinds are of frequent occurrence in alliterative poetry.   Of such are *wer mervell to tell*, W. Alex. 771,[*] 1164 ; *wer wonder to tell*, W. Alex. 811 ; *feiþely (for) to telle*, W. of P. 201, 209, 1151 ; *pertly to telle*, W. of P. 180 ; *redeliche to telle*, W. of P. 5467 ; *schortly (for) to telle*, M.A. 1716, Pierce 634, W. of P. 1160.   *Soþli to saie*, Alex. B. 154, W. of P. 1759, etc. (very frequently).   *Wite ȝe/witow for sope*, W. of P. 105, etc. (very frequently), *(þe) sope for to telle*, Alex. A. 290, 1000, Parl. 650, Prl. 653, R.R. ii, 116, W. of P. 34, etc. (nineteen times), W. & W. 221.   Such phrases of assurance are thus common in Middle English alliterative poetry, and examples could be multiplied without difficulty.[1]

Another group of still more personal phrases is found, of which the following will serve as illustrations :—

> *as I here telle*, Alex. A. 102.
> *as I may tell*, Alex. A. 848.
> *as I might tell*, Alex. A. 22.
> *as I aboue told*, Troy 11826.
> *as I fore tolde*, Alex. A. 1245.
> *as I tel after*, Alex. A. 1154.
> *as I shall tell*, Alex. A. 1148.
> *as I haf herde telle*, Gaw. 26, 1144.
> *as I haue herde saye*, Chev. 213.

[1] See *The Gestes of Alexander*, F. P. Magoun, Jr., introductory note on style.

as I beforen seide, Jos. 124.
þat I er said, Troy 126, 9110, cp. Bestiary 191, etc.
as I er sayde, Pat. 28.
as I tofore saide, Alex. A. 876.
as I trowe, Pierce 837, R.R. ii, 99, etc.
as I hope, Erk. 4, Troy 1100.
as I wene, R.R, ii. 100, Sc.F. 270, 341.

(6) " As the book says ", etc.

This tag has likewise originally resulted from the poet's desire to vouch for the accuracy of his statements. Phrases of this type are particularly common in Middle English alliterative poetry, but are by no means confined to it. Cp. Sir Cleges 242, *so seyth the boke*, or Wulfstan's Old English Homilies, 79.7, 89.23, etc., *þæs þe bec seggað*. The examples in Middle English alliterative poetry are here listed :—

as auctors alegges, M.A. 4342.
as awlde men telles, M.A. 279.
as the bible telleth, P.Pl. A iii, 259.
as the booke recordeth, D.L. 271.
as þe boke says, Troy 4333, etc. (11 times).   *as þe buke sais*, W. Alex. 881, etc. (5 times), Beckett 167.
as þe buke/boke telles/telleth, W. Alex. 17, etc. (33 times), Beckett 12, 164, 207, Chev. 7, 270, P.Pl. B Pro. 101, xi, 134, xix, 67, C ii, 28, Troy 167.
as þe buke witnes, W. Alex. 916.
as demys the boke, Troy 12164.
sais þe buke, W. Alex. 1080, etc. (6 times).   *seith the boke*, P.Pl. B xii, 59, 281, C xx, 234.
as tellen oure bokes, W. of P. 7, 198.
as þe Bruytte tellys, M.A. 4346.
þe clause me recordis, W. Alex. 3361.
as þe clause tellus, W. Alex. 278, etc. (5 times), Troy 4305, etc. (5 times).
sais þe clause, W. Alex. 3908, 4820, 5432.
as þe crede tellis, Gaw. 643.
as cronecle tellith, R.R. iii, 93.   *as cronicles telles*, M.A. 274, 3218.   *þe cronaclis tellis*, W. Alex. 938.   *as cronycles me tolde*, P.Pl. C vi, 179.
as doctourȝ us tellith, R.R. iii, 289.
as Duchemen telles, M.A. 1251.
as eldres vs tellen, Jerus. 106.
as the gest tellus, Troy 286, etc. (5 times).   *as gestes vs telles*, M.A. 2876.
as tellep þe gest, W. of P. 5033.
as þe godspelles tellep, Pierce 257, 275.
as hathell men me telles, M.A. 3501.
as holywryt telleth, P.Pl. B iii, 332.
as ledes me telles, M.A. 2399.
sais me þe lettur, Troy 10750, 11481, 12880.
þe letterure & þe line þus it calles, W. Alex. 2170.
þe lyne me recordis, W. Alex. 2060.

sais me the lyne, Troy 8401, etc. (5 times), W. Alex. 2047.   *as þe lyne says*,
    Troy 7194.
as þe lyne tellis, W. Alex. 1439.   *tellis the lyne*, Troy 12268.
as me mynd tellis, W. Alex. 3389.
as þe prose tellis, W. Alex. 2397, 3328, 5425, Troy 9087, 11624.
þe prose þus it callis, W. Alex. 5080.
sais þe prose, W. Alex. 2062.
as þe roll saide, Troy 12621.
þe romance it calles, W. Alex. 1077.
as romawns vs tellis, M.A. 3200.   *þe romance it tellis*, W. Alex. 4920.
þe romance it witnes, W. Alex. 488, 2900.
said þe romance, W. Alex. 3350.
þe scripture it callis, W. Alex. 2119.
as saith vs the story, Troy 1619, 7826.
tellis the story, Troy 11081.   *þe store me tellis*, W. Alex. 3854, 4828.   *as the
    story tellis*, Parl. 423, Troy 922, 8652.   *as þe storys telleþ*, Jerus. 826.
    þe story me tellis, W. Alex. 2050, 3854.
as the tale saise, Troy 13381.
as the tale shewes, Troy 11945, 12447, 13449.
here tellus þe tale, Troy 665.
þe text me recordis, W. Alex. 214.
as þe text sayse, Troy 1027, etc. (4 times).
for so þe text tellis, W. Alex. 1592, Mum 376.
as demys þe textis, W. Alex. 1231.
as says me þe text, W. Alex. 741 (Dublin).
as tellis þe textis, W. Alex. 2997, Troy 11738.
þe titill recordis, W. Alex. 1044.
as the trety sais, Troy 154, etc. (15 times).
as wyse men tellis, W. Alex. 725.
as wittnesse tellis, M.A. 3552.
as it þe writte callis, W. Alex. 2152.
no writ me declaris, Troy 11378.
þe writt me recordis, W. Alex. 709, 3986.
as the writte sayes, Troy 4432, etc. (6 times).   *thus þe write sais*, Troy 4432,
    etc. (6 times).   *sais þe writt*, W. Alex. 1376.
as the writ shewes, W. Alex. 4895, Troy 5432.
as þe writt tellis, W. Alex. 3131, Troy 5550.
as holy wryt telles, Pat. 60.
as mynes vs þe writtis, W. Alex. 1249.
as says þe wryt, Pur. 657.
as tellis me þe writtis, W. Alex. 1485.
as I in writt fynd, W. Alex. 24.
as I fynd wreten, W. Alex. 643, 2045, 3922.
as I am infourmede, W. Alex. 1531, 2893, 3341.

    Such tags are similarly found in the early Middle English
alliterative verse ; cp. *Departing Soul's Address to the Body*, 548,
643 : *so þe bec seggeþ* ; 684, *so þe bec mæneþ*.   *The Wohunge of Ure
Lauerde*, p. 271 : *as þe bok witnesses*.   *The Bestiary* 38, also *ic it
o boke rede*.   *Juliana*, p. 4, *as redegunge telleþ*.   *A Description of*

Dur̗ham 20, *ðes ðe writ seggeð* . . . etc. In the later rhymed alliterative verse the same phrases recur quite frequently : *as the buik sayis, Rauf* 353 : *als the huke tellis, Awntyrs* 2 : *as witnese the buke, St. John* 54 : *Quhar the trete tellis, Houlate* 307 : *as tellis the writ, Houlate* 507, etc.

(7) " ON BENT," ETC.

The vocabulary of the Middle English alliterative poets was rich in words for *warrior, knight*, etc:, and in connection with each of these words there developed an alliterative phrase or tag, such as : *freke appon folde, lede in londe, segge under sonne*. It is difficult to decide whether these expressions are genuine phrases or mere tags, and hence for the sake of convenience they will be found listed as alliterative phrases ; often, however, we find such phrases as *renke appon folde*, or even *in erthe*, as a mere tag. These are listed below with references to the alliterative phrases which have already been given. It should be noted that such phrases as *man appon molde* served as a starting point for phrases consisting of any word beginning with *m*, followed by *on molde*. In like manner we find interesting developments in connection with the other tags.

on bent, Gaw. 353, M.A. 1067, W. & W. 156, etc.   *on þe bent*, D.L. 149, 223, Jerus. 540, M.A. 915, 1431, W. & W. 105, 143. *vpon the bent*, D.L. 63. *appon þe bente*, M.A. 1380, 2010. N.B.—Quite often *on bent* is not a tag but has a definite meaning, as in *on bent whare he standes*, M.A. 1054. The usual alliterative phrase is *berne on bent*, see supra.

vnder Criste, M.A. 405, etc. (6 times), Troy 309, Twa Mariit Wemen 454, W. of P. 501.   The usual alliterative phrases are *king* . . ., *kniʒt* . . ., *clerk vnder criste ;* see supra, *vnder Krystes seluen*, Gaw. 51.

abouen erþe, Alex. B. 1000.   *in erthe*, M.A. 527.   *on erthe*, D.L. 11, M.A. 469, Pierce 611. *vpon erþe*, Alex. B. 39, D.L. 8. *(no gome) in þis erþe*, Jerus. 165.[1]   *(gomus) vpon erþe*, Alex. B. 796. *(lede) appon erthe*, M.A. 1721. *(noe leed) vpon earth*, D.L. 315. *(no man) vpon erþe*, Jerus. 166. *(wy) vppon erthe*, R.R. iii, 288.

in erde, Gaw. 2416, Pur. 601.   *on erd*, Pur. 892.

on felde, M.A. 1345, 1537.   *on þe felde*, D.L. 64, M.A. 1442, 1496. *appon þe felde*, M.A. 2143. The usual alliterative phrase is *freke on felde*, see supra.

one foulde, M.A. 1071, 3302. *appon þe folde*, W. & W. 174. *vpon folde*, Gaw. 396, etc. (4 times), Pur. 1147. The usual alliterative phrase is *freke on fold*, see supra.

vndir God, M.A. 1201, 2412, W. & W. 173. The usual alliterative phrases are *gome* . . . , *grome vnder God*, see supra.

[1] Miss Day rightly reads *grounde* from A.D. MSS.

appon grounde, W. & W. 173. *vpon grounde,* Gaw. 417, 1070. *on the grounde,* D.L. 3. The usual alliterative phrases are *gome . . . grome appon grounde,* see supra.

vnder heuen, W. Alex. 713, etc., Cr. King 124, D.L. 284, Erk. 166, Gaw. 56, 352, M.A. 2613, Parl. 320. (*þe gaiest*) *vndire heuen,* W. Alex. 5144. (*kyng*) *vnder heuene,* R.R. i, 33. (*ne renke*) *vnder heuen,* W. Alex. 992. (*no sege*) *vndir heuen,* W. Alex. 2390, W. of P. 4278. *vndire heuenriche,* M.A. 3879. The usual alliterative phrase is *hapel vnder heuen,* see supra.

in londe, Beckett 168, Gaw. 679. *on* (*the*) *londe,* D.L. 92, 97, 286, M.A. 2220, 3712, Sc.F. 380. *vpon londe,* D.L. 350, Pur. 1207, R.R. ii, 143. The usual alliterative phrase is *lede in londe,* see supra.

on molde, Alex. B 752, 839, Gaw. 964, 1795, M.A. 952, etc. *on the molde,* Gaw. 137, M.A. 1397. *upon molde,* Alex. B 101, Gaw. 1795. The usual alliterative phrase is *man on molde,* see supra.

vndir sonne, W. Alex. 34, 736, M.A. 4035. The usual alliterative phrase is *segge vnder sonne,* see supra.

The phrase *under sunne* is reminiscent of the French phrase *sous ciel ; under sunnan* is found in Old English in the *Metra* of Boethius, xiv, 7, and in the form *vnder sonne* is very common in Middle English poetry and prose of every type. For *wy of þis werlde* and *wight of þis werlde* see supra. Similar tags occur in the early M.E. alliterative works :

under criste, Alf. 38, Laȝ. 27230, etc.[1]

on dugeðe, Laȝ. 19754.

buuen eorþe, Alf. 315. *in eorðe,* Lou. p. 209. *on eorðe,* H.M. 360, Laȝ. 1150, etc. (common). *ouer erðe,* Woh. p. 284. *uppen eorðe,* Alf. 123, 177.

on folde, Laȝ. 15730.

vndir gode seolue, Laȝ. 27233.

on leoden, Laȝ. 1, etc.

in londe, Laȝ. 1 (Otho MS.), etc. *o londe,* Best. 392, 617.

(*no man*) *vndir lufte,* Laȝ. 10104, 18767, 27237.

vnder sunnen, Laȝ. 108, 11973, etc. *under sunne,* Mar. p. 15, Woh. p. 273, etc.

on þeode, Alf. 263, Laȝ. 11144, 20056.

o(*n*) *werlde,* Alf. 122, Best. 106, 356, 493, 597, H.M. 104, etc., Jul. 4, etc., Lou. p. 211. *on worlde,* Laȝ. 22069, etc.

The use of these tags is not a marked characteristic of Old English poetry, despite the occasional use of such phrases as *man on moldan,* etc.[2] Such otiose expressions are much more frequent

---

[1] For references see p. 114.

[2] See also the following occasional phrases listed in the O.E. heroic and religious alliterative phrases : *b . . . in burgum, golde on grunde, h . . . under heofonum, r . . . under roderum, w . . . under wolcnum, w . . . under weorulde.* The total number of such phrases is, however, small.

in the later verse, possibly because the poets were more lax and relied upon devices of this type more frequently.[1]

It is clear that alliterative poets frequently made use of loose expressions, sometimes for metrical reasons, sometimes ostensibly to give assurance of the historicity of the details mentioned, but frequently for no apparent reason.   The austerity of the older alliterative style under the influence of popular prose and verse has given place to a looser and more discursive manner of expression.

---

[1] The O.E. phrase *oft and gelome*, which occurs so frequently in the *Chronicle* and in the homiletic prose, survives both in *Sawles Warde* and in other early M.E. homilies.

CHAPTER 14

THE STYLE OF MIDDLE ENGLISH ALLITERATIVE POETRY.

WHILE most of the alliterative poets of the fourteenth century have some distinctive features of style, the common stylistic characteristic of almost all their poetry is its " looseness ".   One has but to think of the tags, mere selections of which have been collected in the last chapter.   Some writers make so extensive a use of these expressions, especially to fill out the second half-line, that their poetry loses all freshness and feeling of originality.   The same is true of the use made of stock alliterative phrases, and even so accomplished a writer as the author of *Sir Gawain and the Green Knight* is not free from these faults.   Perhaps the worst poems in this respect are *Alexander A* and *Death and Life ;* at the opposite extreme, however, there are *The Destruction of Jerusalem* and *St. Erkenwald*, both distinguished in different ways for their concentrated style and vigorous writing.

Closely allied to this use of tags and phrases is the employment of " otiose " adjectives for the purposes of alliteration.   This has already been noticed in connection with *Alexander A*,[1] in which all sorts of absurdities are found.   While no other alliterative poets display so inexperienced a hand as the author of *Alexander A*, too many of them are content to fall back on such colourless adjectives as *blisful, bright, dere*, etc., according to the needs of the alliteration.

The limits of space do not allow further discussion and illustration of these shortcomings of the alliterative poets.   Nor is it possible to give full details of the stylistic mannerisms of the various poets, and only the more important features can be touched upon.   Four points which have already been mentioned in previous writings are briefly outlined as showing the limits and possibilities of work to be done in this direction.   Thereafter follows a detailed

---

[1] P. 27.

historical treatment of the absolute use of the adjective, which is largely an additional way of increasing the number of synonyms for *man, person, warrior*. The chapter closes with a historical account of the use of the simile in Old and Middle English alliterative poetry.

Two other specific points of less importance have been discussed by Mr. Savage—*the use of the pleonastic pronoun*,[1] which he finds rarely in the " Gawain " works, and in *The Wars of Alexander*, and *the use of the historical present*, which he finds is rare in *St. Erkenwald* and *Pearl*, slightly more marked in *Gawain* and *Purity*, and abundant in *Patience* and *The Wars of Alexander*. Metrical stylistic points, such as alliterative grouping and the quatrain arrangement,[2] have already been discussed in the earlier volume.

(*a*) *The Fondness for beginning a line with " For "*.—The fondness for beginning a line with *for* has been noted by Mr. Savage [3] as being a characteristic of the style of the *Gawain*-poet, but it is doubtful whether the point is of any value in determining a common authorship of the poems in question. *For* at the beginning of a line may be used in very differing senses, and as in the early lines of *Patience* the number of examples may often be unnaturally increased by the nature of the work translated. *Purity*, ll. 181–4 and 185–6, form such a remarkable succession of examples of the feature that one naturally feels that it must represent a definite mannerism on the part of the poet, though even there the element of chance must be reckoned with. The following statistics, on the whole, militate against the idea that the feature is of a distinctive nature:

(*a*) The *Gawain*-group : *Pat.* 34/531 lines ; *Pur.* 67/1812 ; *Prl.* 43/1212 ; *Gaw.* 84/2530 ; *Erken.* 8/352.

(*b*) Works with high percentages : *Mum* 178/1751 ; *Alex. B* 100/1139 ; *Alex. A* 54/1249 ; *Pierce* 30/855.

(*c*) Works with the normal percentage : *Jerus.* 18/1334 ; *Parl.* 11/665 ; *W. & W.* 23/503 ; *Joseph* 22/709 ; *Chev.* 10/370 ; *Quatr.* 14/520 ; *D.L.* 6/458 ; *Sc.F.* 9/422 ; *M.A.* 83/4346.

The feature is most prominent in *Mum and Sothsegger*, but no inference can be drawn from that fact.

---

[1] *St. Erkenwald*, p. lxi.

[2] See the important article by Miss Mabel Day, *Strophic Division in Middle English Alliterative Verse*, ENGLISCHE STUDIEN, vol. 66, p. 245, 1932.

[3] See H. L. Savage, *St. Erkenwald*, p. lx.

(*b*) *The device of beginning and ending the poem with approximately the same words* is found in *Patience*, *Pearl* and *Sir Gawain*, but not in any other alliterative work.

(*c*) *The use of an absolute construction attached to the sentence by means of* " *and*," first described by R. J. Menner, in his edition of *Purity*, p. xviii, is found only in the works of the *Gawain*-poet, except in *Death and Life*, whose author borrowed so freely from *Purity*. A typical example quoted by Professor Menner is (*Gaw.* 53) :—

> " & ho þe comlokest kyng þat þe court haldes."

(*d*) *The Periphrases for* '*God*'.—Professor Menner,[1] in his thorough treatment of these periphrases occurring in alliterative poetry, observes that this is a distinctive feature of the works of the *Gawain*-poet. He gives a complete list of the examples in *Purity*, *Patience* and *Gawain*, to which should be added Mr. Savage's five examples from *St. Erkenwald*.[2] Of these elaborate periphrases three alone are found outside the *Gawain* group : *W. & W.* 296, ' It es plesynge to the prynce þat paradyse wroghte ' ; *W. Alex.* 4518, ' þat hathill at on hiȝe sittis ' ; *Death and Life* 13, ' the prince that paradice weldeth '. Professor Menner rightly explains the two latter examples as borrowings from the *Gawain* group, including *St. Erkenwald*, which has in 161 the very phrase, " þe prince þat paradis weldes ". He might also have added that the author of *Sc.F.* uses the same phrase in line 203, and probably also in the defective line 87. The author of *Death and Life* may have borrowed the phrase from *Purity* 195, which in turn passed into *Sc.F.* *W. & W.* most certainly preceded *Purity* in time of composition, so that the *Gawain*-poet may have first met the feature in that poem.[3] He, however, extended its use widely, and it can be said of him that " the wonder of the creation is still vividly before the mind of the medieval poet ".

A DISTINCTIVE FEATURE OF MIDDLE ENGLISH ALLITERATIVE POETRY—THE ABSOLUTE USE OF THE ADJECTIVE.

The substantival use of the adjective is a marked characteristic of Middle English alliterative poetry, and many of the examples of this usage in fifteenth and sixteenth century works, especially in

---

[1] R. J. Menner, *Purity*, pp. xvi-xviii.

[2] *Op. cit.* p. lxiii.

[3] Cp. " *the prince that paradise made*," *Richard the Redeles*, Pro. 33, and *Mum & Sothsegger*, 185.

Early Scottish verse, are undoubtedly due to the popularity of alliterative verse in the fourteenth century.   In Old English poetry *laÐ*, adj. ' hateful,' came to be used as a noun meaning ' foe,' and *se goda* and *gomele* ' ancients ' are fairly common.   The Old Saxon usage of the neuter adj. *frī* in the sense of ' lady ' found its way into the O.E. *Genesis* 457, *freo fægroste*, a type which survived into Middle English poetry.   There are also in Old English a few examples of the substantival use of the adjective for concrete things as opposed to persons ; *hringmǣl*, an adj., is used as a noun in *Beowulf* 1521, 1564, but probably as an adj. in 2037.   Similarly, some scholars have thought that *heard* 1566 is used for a ' sword,' though the case is admittedly doubtful.   In M.E. *þe scharpe* is found exclusively in alliterative poetry for ' a sharp weapon '— *Gawain* 424, 1593, 1902, 2313, 2332 : *M.A.* 3842 : *Joseph of Arimathie* 513, *schrindringe of sharpe* (sharp weapons) : *Chevelere Assigne* 307 (the sharp edge).   *þe schene Gaw* 2268 stands for ' the bright blade,' and in *Patience* 440 for ' the bright sun '.   The author of *Gawain* has in addition the following examples of the absolute use of the adj. for concrete things : *þe broun* 1162, ' brown hide of deer ' ; *on coolde* 2475, ' the cold snowy ground ' ; *þe forme* 499, ' the beginning ' ; *þe fresche* 122, ' fresh meats ' ; *þe fayre grene* 189, ' green hair ' ; *þe hyʒe* 1152, 1169, 2004, ' the high ground ' ; *þe naked* 423, ' the naked flesh ' ; *þe sylueren* 124, ' the silver dishes '. Further examples in alliterative poetry are very rare ; cp. *þe playn*, *Erkenwald* 138, ' the level floor ' ; *þe dede*, *Erkenwald* 116, ' the dead body ' ; *þe grene*, *Alexander B* 502, ' green things ' ; *þe nakid*, *The Wars of Alexander* 4182, *The Destruction of Troy* 6403, ' the naked flesh ' : *breme of the birds*, *Death and Life* 34, ' noise of birds ' ; cp. 74, *breme birds*, ' noisy birds ' ; *a blee of a blewe noble*, *M.A.* 3332, ' a distinguished blue colour ' ; *uch hidde*, *Purity* 1628, ' each hidden thing ' ; *alle hende*, *Purity* 1083, ' all pleasant things ' ; *for roʒ*, *Patience* 144, ' on account of the rough weather ' ; *þo derworth depe*, *Pearl* 109, ' deep places ' ; *þe fyrst*, *Gawain* 1072, ' the first day of the year ' ; *the gayes*, R.R., ii, 94, ' gay clothes ' ; *my body & my beste*, *R. R. Pro.* 47, ' the best part of me ' ; *the ripen*, *Piers Plowman*, C, xix, 107, ' the ripe fruits '.   It will be observed that this peculiar use of the adjective, definitely derived from older sources, is most prominent in the works of the *Gawain*-poet, though it is by no means confined to them.   There are no examples of this type in non-alliterative verse.

The second type, in which the adjective is applied to a person, is much more common, though it is almost confined to alliterative works. *þat hende* (that gracious one) is not uncommon in northern verse from 1300 onwards, while *þat semely* and *þat faire* are common poetic forms in the fourteenth century. But *þat gaye, þat gentil, þat schene*, etc., seem to be confined to alliterative verse. Many of these, such as *þat brighte, þat wlonke*, survived from northern alliterative poetry into Scottish verse.

It is not generally realised how extensive was the use of this feature in Middle English alliterative poetry. The following collection is reasonably complete, though it is not impossible that some examples have escaped notice :—

(*a*) The earlier works :

Alexander A. þat cumly 783, 989. *þat douhtie* 962. *þat louely* 750. *þat menskfull* 651. *þat seemelich* 768, 1012.
Alexander B. þe noble, ' the noble one,' 73.
William of Palerne. þat komli, ' fair one,' 873, 3058. *þe fre*, ' the noble boy,' 505. *þat gode*, ' that gracious lady,' 1334. *þe hende* 863. *þe lef*, ' the dear one,' 1645. *loueli lef* (voc.), ' dear one,' 2314. *þat schene*, ' the beautiful girl,' 733, 3299. *þat semly*, ' that fair one,' 732, 853, etc. *swete* (voc.), 904.
Wynnere & Wastoure. þat hend, ' gracious one,' 419.
The Parlement of the Thre Ages. that doughty, ' that doughty one,' 344.
Chevelere Assigne. þat febulle 76.

No examples are found in *Joseph of Arimathie*, so that in this group of early works the feature is on the whole rare.

(*b*) The ' Piers Plowman ' group :

Piers Plowman. this sike, ' this sick man,' C xx, 61. Cp. *Alfred Boethius* 38.7, " se sioca ". The singular used as sb. is much rarer than the plural: *Siuyle* ' Civil Law' (personified), A ii, 57, etc. *soleyne*, ' a solitary person,' B xii, 205. *sory*, ' miserable man,' B xvii, 344. *surquydous*, ' an arrogant man,' B xix, 335. *my deore*, ' my dear one,' A vii, 241.
Richard the Redeles. that steddefaste iii, 209.

There are no examples in *Pierce the Ploughman's Crede* or *The Crowned King*.

(*c*) The ' Gawain ' group :

Patience. þo wery for-wro3t, ' that weary one exhausted with toil,' 163.
Purity. þat fre, ' that noble one,' 929. *þy meke*, ' thy meek servant,' 776.
Gawain. an auncian, ' an old lady,' 948. *þe clere*, ' the fair lady,' 1489. *þat comly*, ' fair knight or lady,' 674, 1755. *þat cortays*, ' gracious lady,' 2411. *3onder dere*, ' yon noble one,' 678. *fayr* (voc.), ' fair lady,' 1213. *þe felle*, ' the wild beast,' 1585. *my fre* 1545. *þat fre* 1549, 1783, ' noble lady '. *þat gay* 970, 2035. *my gay* 1822, ' fair lady or knight '. *þat gentyle*, ' noble knight,' 542. *þat grene*, ' green man,' 464. *þe grete*, ' great one,' 2490. *þis grymme*, ' fierce beast,' 1442. *þe 3onge*, ' the

O.E.P., La3., Orm., A. *dale(s) and doune(s)*, Alis. 3129, 5901, Beues 1829, Guy 8500, 10020, Guy & Col. 10, Horn 161, Kn. of Curt. 213, Laud 1372, Row. & Ot. 744, Triam. 270, 1084. *in dale, in doune*, Alis. 4449, 7542. *ouer dale and ouer doun*, Beues 3755, Laud 10444. *doune and dale*, Alis. 1767, 7026, 7206, Florence 1400, Laud 7354. *bi doune ne dale*, Laud 7605. *ouer doune and dale*, Laud 14049, etc.
the daile and doun dynnyd, Rol. 508. *the dales dynned*, Perc. 2050.
O.E.P., E.M.E., La3., A. *in a dale depe*, Avow. 269.
A. *dampnyd to dethe*, Rol. 250.
dark and deepe, Alis. 7042.
A. *dare for drede*, Triam. 321.
to dashe him downe, Degare 435.
E.M.E., A. *dede and doluen*, Laud 15895.
E.M.E., La3. *dele and di3te*, Amad. 713, Emare 3, 42, Firum. 3915, Otuel 1561, Rich. 4579, Row. & Ot. 490. *dighte and dele*, Row. & Ot. 490, 826.
A. *dele . . . dynt(es)*, Alis. 5874, Firum. 900, Lib. Dis. 177, 1365, Rol. 199, Sowdane 2920, Triam. 1215, Ywaine 3538. *delen dyntes*, Laud 9233, 9606. *to dely (doghty) dents*, Lib. Dis. 1578. *dyntes thei deled and dalt*, Laud 7341. *dyntes to dale*, M. Arthur 1076.
dele a dole, Amad. 42.
O.E.P. & Pr., E.M.E., La3., Orm., O. & N., A. *to deme her dome*, Oct. 226. *þe dom is/was demd.* Hav. 2487, 2488, 2838. *þe ry3t doom schal I deme*, Athel. 683. *domes for to deme*, Gam. 826.
deme and dele, Row. & Ot. 1317.
O.E.P. & Pr., E.M.E., P.M., A. *deme to death*, Lamw. 475.
E.M.E., A. *demed to dye*, Triam. 860.
E.M.E. *deme and dighte*, Row. & Ot. 1269.
deere or doe, Degare 275.
dereworth and dere, Sowdane 1512.
dethys dynte, Florence 915. *dethes dent*, Oct. 1001.
A. *dye a dethe*, Beues 341, Guy 5955. *(a) deth schall dye*, Oct. 245.
La3., A. *di3t to depe*, Beues 908, Laud 1403, Trist. 208. *dighte to dede*, Melayne 548, 557, Row. & Ot. 142, etc. (4 times). *to dethe . . . (y)dyght*, Alis. 2451, Athel. 463, Avow. 56, 136, Oct. 1650, Roul. & Vern. 369, Sages 2306, Torrent 273, 1648, Tolous 489, 507, 846, 1047.
A. *dynge(n) (a)doun*, Eglam. 556, Firum. 717, etc. Guy & Col. 48, 374, Melayne 128, 267, 1255, Row. & Ot. 1058, etc.
A. *to dethe he þame denges*, Degare 324. *to dede he ne solde hym dynge*, Melayne 234.
of þat dynt was he ded, Athel. 292. Cp. Allit. Troy 1235, *dyed of the dynt.*
E.M.E., La3., A. *do of dawe*, Beues 348. *done of dawe*, Laud 7800. *don of dawes*, Tars. 813. *of dawe don*, Floris & Blan. 1067. *be don of day*, Firum. 1697.
O.E.Pr., E.M.E., Orm., A. *do a dede*, Amis. 833, Avow. 164, Carle 388, Florence 669, etc., Freine 317, Green Kn. 163, 184, 388, Lib. Dis. 34, 1692, Perc. 1240, 1594, Rich. 695, 926, Rol. 676, Squ. of L. Deg. 173, 368, Tolous 410, 684, Trist. 3073, 3201, Turke 1237, Ywaine 2307, etc. *do dedes*, Firum. 2151, etc. *dedus to done*, Emare 4.
O.E.Pr. *do hur to dede*, Avow. 964. *do to deed*, Floris & Blan. 46, Triam. 206. **E.M.E., A.** *do to depe*, Firum. 177, Floris & Blan. 306, 1210, Guy

A. *clerk and king*, Troy 584.
E.M.E., Laȝ., A. *clerk and/ne kniht*, Hav. 2083, 2195, 2813, Sages 1922, 2484, 2493, Trist 3128. *knyghtis, clerkis*, Alis. 1371.
A. *in clethynge comly clede*, Row. & Ot. 651. *in (comely) clothyng . . . cledd*, Florence 211.
clongyn in clay, Tolous 494.
clottis of clay, Laud 10602. *as clot of clay*, Laud 17134.
E.M.E., A. *knelutte downe opon thayre kne*, Amad. 826. *he knelyd anon and on hys knees he felle*, Athel. 419. *kneeled on . . . knee(s)*, Arthur's Death 145, Avow. 804, Carle 160, Cleges 166, 190, 395, Florence 951, Guy & Col. 100, 136, 564, Isum. 540, M. Arthur 3781, Melayne 643, 787, Oct. Emp. 1047, Perc. 388, Row. & Ot. 637, Squ. of L. Deg. 279, 687, Tolous 1147, Torrent 205, 528. *knelyd downe on hys kne*, Eglam. 909, 1279, 1288. *on here knees he/pey kneleden adoun*, Athel. 501, 549. *on knees they knelyd downe*, M. Arthur 3938. *appon his knees (downn gan) he knele*, Row. & Ot. 488, 725. *on kne knelyd he*, Torrent 133, etc. *vpon his knees can kneele*, Green Kn. 165.
A. *knightes and kempes*, Guy & Col. 5.
A. *knyȝte and/ne knaue*, Avow. 737, Hav. 458, 2697, Laud 4873, Rich. 5894, Torrent 1094, Triam. 565. *knaue and/or knyȝt*, Laud 8094, Ywaine 1594, 2174, 3564.
A. *pe cok crowe bygan*, Alis. 397. *cokkes crowe*, Freine 148. *cokkes crewe*, Sages 2536.
of coloure clere, Kn. of Curt. 321.
A. *come of knyges kende*, Launfal 864.
O.E.Pr., A. *com of (Gawenys) kynne*, Lib. Dis. 1646.
comly of kende, Amis. 229, 265.
pat comly vnder kelle, Emare 303. Cp. *lufsum under lyne*.
comforte ne chere (verbs), Kn. of Curt. 323.
crake hure crones, Firum. 2604. *crake . . . crowne(s)*, Florence 1478, Hav. 568, Rich. 5423, 5626, 6088. *crakkede (a) croun*, Row. & Ot. 1066. *crakkede . . . many a crowne*, Melayne 261, Tolous 72. *many a crowne yschall gar crake*, Florence 92.
crokyd and crachyd, Florence 2028.
A. *crompylde and crokyd*, Florence 1979. Cp. **A.** *crokyd and crachyd*.
croun and crest, Row. & Ot. 710.
crounede pai (Beues) king, Beues 4253. **E.M.E., A.** *crown(ed) . . . king*, Gam. 694, 695, Guy 10736, 10784, Laud 3400, Melayne 99, Rich. 6183, Rol. 446, Sowdane 2976. *croune him to king*, Floris & Blan. 1301. **E.M.E., A.** *king with . . . croune*, Gam. 671, Guy 10418, Lib. Dis. 794, 975, M. Arthur 3173, etc., Melayne 18, 1280, Oct. Emp. 772, Tolous 897, Triam. 1136, Trist. 5, etc., Turke 48. *pe kyng pat weryd pe coroun*, Athel. 553. *of comely kynges corouned*, Laud 3249.
E.M.E., A. *crouny wip croune*, Beues 4012.
A. *curtes and kynde*, Triam. 240.
A. *the day dawes*, Laud 10045, 12894, 18279. *day is dawed*, Laud 4192. *day be dawed*, Laud 9938. *peo day dawith*, Alis. 2551. *day dawep*, Tars 396. *the day dawen gan*, Sages 2249. *the day began to dawe*, Avow. 473, Laud 7324. *day can dawe*, Florence 1503. *dawen the day*, Rol. 389, 576. *hyt dawed (lyȝth) day*, Degare 597, 1665.
dawning of the day, Carle 459, Oct. Emp. 329.

21

young one,' 951. *þe hende*, ' gracious knight,' 827, 1104.   *hende* (voc.),
' gracious knight,' 1252, 1813, 2330.   *þat hende*, ' gracious one,' 946.
þat ientyle, ' noble knight,' 542.   *þat lufsum under lyne*, ' fair one,' 1814.
þe menskful, ' gracious lady,' 1268.   *þat noble*, ' that noble knight,' 1750.
his riche, ' noble steed,' 2177.   *þat semly*, ' fair knight,' 672.   *þe sturne*,
' stern knight,' 214.   *þat swete*, ' sweet lady,' 1222.   *þat wlonk*, ' noble
one,' 1988.   *þat worþy* 1508.   *worþy* (voc.) 1276, ' noble lady '.

Pearl.   *my blysfol beste*, ' my happy best one,' 279.   *my dere endorde* 369.
þat frech as flor-de-lys 195.   *my frely*, ' my fair one,' 1155.   *þat gracios
gay* 189.   *þat gaye* 433.   *þat gentyl* 602.   *now hynde þat* . . ., ' gracious
one,' 909.   *(þe) innocente* 625, etc.   *þat lufsoum of lyth & lere* 398.
þat schene, ' that fair one,' 166, 965.   *þat swete* 240.   *my swete* 325.   *þat
worþyly* 47.

There are no examples in *St. Erkenwald*.

(*d*) The later alliterative group :

Morte Arthure.   *þat bolde* 1012.   *þat hende* 1135.   *þat ryall* 53.   *no skathell*,
' no hurtful one,' 1642.   *þat steryn* 1229, 2528.   stiȝttelys *steryn* one
steryne with styffe men of armes 3622.   *þat wlonke*, ' that proud woman,'
3338.
The Wars of Alexander.   *þis athill*, ' this noble one,' 681, 837, 964.   *þis
briȝt* 5204.   *þat dere* 265.   *þat hend* 264, 4757, 5162.   *þat mild* 5098,
5218.   *þat schene*, ' fair maid,' 4759.   *þat semely* 2003, 5264.   *my
swete* 2826.
The Destruction of Troy.   *þat abill* 11840.   *the bolde*, ' the bold knight,' 507,
etc.   *þat bold* 11024.   *þat bright* 1405, 3183, etc.   *þat choise* 13851.   *þat
clene*, ' fair lady,' 1914.   *þat comly* 552, etc.   *þat dere* 9225.   *þe derfe*,
' the bold dragon,' 176.   *þat doughty* 5284, etc.   *the doghty* 10851, 11016.
þat faire 525, 8040, 13028.   *þat fre* 466, etc.   *a fre*, ' a woman,' 1386.
þat fuerse, ' that fierce knight,' 8011.   *þat gay* 13668.   *a gay*, ' a fair
lady,' 2697.   *þat gentill* 128.   *this gentill* 437, 756.   *þat gret* 1858.   *a
grete* 7018.   *þe hend*, ' the gracious knight,' 8380.   *þat hynd*, ' gracious
lady,' 1396, etc.   *þat loodly*, ' horrible dragon,' 934.   *þat louely* (used of
either sex) 2909, 3104, 3125, 12131.   *þat mighty* 767, 1952, 10879.
the mighty 9155.   *this mylde* 449, 13860.   *þat noble* 12271.   *þat orribill*
13260.   *þis proud* 13721.   *þat pure* 3341, 10775.   *þat rioll*, ' that
prince,' 7157.   *þat sem(e)ly* 390, etc.   *þat shene*, ' fair lady,' 6477, 6668,
8144.   *þat slegh*, ' that cunning one,' 3849.   *þat speciall* 13196.   *no
stuerne*, ' no enemy,' 567.   *þat swete* 579, 10567.   *þat worthy* 513, etc.
þat yeþe, ' that virago,' 13231.
Death and Life.   *þat fayre* 64, 450.   *Sir Hind* 101, cp. lines 107 and 340.

(*e*) The Northern rhymed works :

St. John the Evangelist.   *þat hende* 80.   *þat hendest in halle* 229.   *þat semly*
99.
The Quatrefoil of Love.   *þat bryghte* 147.   *þat comly* 32.   *þat semely* 108,
186, 300.
The Pistill of Susan.   *þat hende* 133.   *an innocent* 323.   *innocentis blode*,
' the blood of an innocent one,' 284.   *þat worly* 54.   *þat worliche* 134.
þat worthi (Ireland MS.).

The Awntyrs of Arthure. þat burly 645. *þat comly* 288. *þat frely* 376. *þat gay* 530. *þat hende* 698. *þat lufly* 397. *þe sturne* 532.

Golagros and Gawain. that auenand, ' courteous one,' 1283. *this auenand & honest* 1194. *the deir* 600, 1284. *yone deir* 785. *yone douchty* 329. *that doughty* 730, 947, 967. *the gay,* 'the fair one,' 988. *the gentill* 1201. *that heynd* 183, 1103. *the heynd* 219, 265. *that lordly* 1276. *that lufly of lyre* 614. *that lufly* 991. *that myld,* ' gentle knight,' 354. *our nobill* 410. *the nobill* 1017. *the sterne* 108, 987. *yone sterne* 276, 349. *yon trew,* ' true man,' 356.

The Houlate. the deir 136. *that deir* 170. *my deir* 482. *that gud* 86, 666. *that vnsufferable* 926.

Rauf Coilȝear. that bald 407, 712. *no douchtie* 588. *ony douchtie* 796. *that gay* 783. *that hardy,* 'that bold man,' 642. *that hende* 697. *that ryall* 14. *that teneful* 458. *ane worthie* 765. *worthy* (voc.) 925.

It is interesting to note that in *The Wars of Alexander,* ' þis athill ' is distinct from the noun ' hathel,' so that it would seem doubtful whether ' hathel ' is in any sense an adjective used as a noun.

The number of examples in (*a*) and (*b*) is negligible, and in (*d*) and (*e*) the instances are in the main due to imitation of those in (*c*)—the *Gawain* group, to which it is known that the poets in question were indebted directly or indirectly. The *Gawain*-poet thus made extensive use of the adjective for a personal noun (chiefly representing ' a knight '); he thereby increased his vocabulary considerably and added another twelve synonyms for " knight, warrior " to the ten which he already possessed (such as *renke, segge,* etc.). In so doing, he avoided the monotonous recurrence of stock words, a temptation which most alliterative poets naturally found very hard to resist. The northern rhyming poets were more indiscriminate in their use of these new stock synonyms, and their verse is not enhanced by the mechanical employment of such tag-like expressions.

In dealing with the absolute use of the adjective in the plural, care has to be taken to distinguish between vague inclusive plurals, such as *þe qwik and þe dede, þe neodi and þe nakid,* and the plural which is merely an extension of the singular usage already mentioned. The most usual example of the latter type is *mony* + adj. absolute, e.g. *mony bolde, Troy* 1210; *mony boldes, Troy* 1405; *mony noble, Troy* 284; *mony sterne, Golagros and Gawain* 19; *mony cumly, Rauf Coilȝear* 574. The *Gawain*-poet prefers the adjective used by itself: *bolde,* ' bold men,' 21; *þe dere,* ' noble company, ' 928; *riche,* ' noble ones, ' 66, 361; *menskful,* 'honourable men,' 555. Other interesting examples are *þe fuerse,* ' the fierce bulls,' *Troy* 888, and *the grym,* ' the fierce animals '. Examples in the plural are rarer than in the singular, but the principle involved is the same in both cases.

The absolute use of the adjective with an abstract meaning is of rarer occurrence, but precedents are found from Old English times, as in the case of *woghe* (*Pearl* 622), an adjective used with the meaning of " evil ".   Similarly, *presente* adj., ' presence,' *Pearl* 389, 1193 is not uncommon.   Stranger examples are, however, *hys blyþe*,' compassion,' *Pearl* 354; *þi bliþe*, *Troy* 2196 ; *cler*, 'clearness,' *Pearl* 1050 ; *þurȝ ronk of his wylle*, ' strength of his will,' *Patience* 298 ; *þe graiþ*, ' the truth,' *Pierce the Ploughman's Crede* 34 ; *uncoupes*, ' unfamiliar events,' *Joseph of Arimathie* 187, a form which survives in modern dialect (see E.D.D.) ; *selcouthes* is, however, of frequent occurrence.

To sum up, in all three types—the concrete, the personal and the abstract, precedents were certainly not lacking, but some alliterative writers, notable the *Gawain*-poet, faced with the somewhat exacting demands of alliterative verse, seized the opportunity of surmounting some of their difficulties by the extension of the absolute use of the adjective, this affording them a richer vocabulary to meet their needs.

The Use of Simile.

The meagreness of similes in Old English poetry is in marked contrast with the extensive use made of comparison in Middle English poetry.   In this matter there is little continuity, though reasons for the change are not far to seek.   The early alliterative works are for the most part devoid of simile, but the charm *Wenne Wenne* has an example of the ' clustered ' simile :   9–12, " Shrivel as the coal upon the hearth, shrink as the dirt in the stream and dwindle even as water in a pail.   May you become as little as a linseed grain and much smaller, likewise, than a handworm's hip-bone."

In the pre-fourteenth century alliterative poetry, however, it is Laȝamon's *Brut* that affords the most notable example of the use of the simile.   It is scarcely true to say that Laȝamon uses the fully developed epic simile ; he makes a simple comparison, and is then carried away by the opportunity thus afforded for description.   But he excels both in the longer and shorter simile, which is always spontaneous, never studied or deliberate.   Professor Wyld, in the article already referred to, has gathered together the chief of Laȝamon's similes which in freshness and poetic worth are finer

than anything in the later alliterative poetry, where there is
nothing to compare with the simile in which the hunting down of
Childric is likened to a fox pursued by hounds (Vol. II, pp. 445–54).
Among other similes mentioned by Professor Wyld, the most
outstanding are : Arthur seeing his dead knights lying like great
steel fish below the waters of the stream, their scales gleaming as it
were gold-plated shields and their fins afloat, as it were spears
(Vol. II, pp. 471–2) ; a host of fugitives is like a lofty wood when
the wild wind shakes it violently (Vol. II, p. 421) ; Arthur rushing
impetuously upon his enemies is like the fleet wolf when he sallies
from the wood bedecked with snow, purposing to devour such
beasts as he fancies (Vol. II, p. 412). Laȝamon gets the most he
can out of simile ; he uses it effectively and with a true sense of the
fitting.

The later alliterative poets are not merely less successful in
their use of simile ; for the most part they make little or no attempt
to get away from conventional forms. Something is ' as dead as
a door-nail ' or ' as red as a rose ' or ' as naked as a needle '. All
the alliterative poets make use of some of these expressions, though
the majority can on occasion write something more vivid and
original. So the author of *Pierce the Ploughman's Crede* gives us a
vivid sketch of a friar by piling up effective similes (see p. 59) ; cp.
Morte Arthure 1090, " his berde was brothy and blake that tille his
brest rechede, Grassede as a mereswyne with corkesfulle huge " ;
or *The Wars of Alexander* 3894–5, " With backis . . . bigger and
hardere þan ony comon cogill-stane or cocatryse scales " ; or *The
Quatrefoil of Love* 331, " When þay ar sounkene in syne as fercost
in flode ".

The similes of the *Gawain*-poet are invariably short, occasionally
conventional, but frequently striking. A number of them are
drawn from animal life, even in *Pearl* (see lines 184, 345, 1085, etc.).
St. Erkenwald 343 (quoted on p. 77) is, however, the most apt
example to be found in this group of five poems so frequently
considered together. Much has been written concerning the
clustering of similes in the *Gawain* poems, and it is undoubtedly
true that there is, as Miss Thomas, Professor Menner and others,
have pointed out, more of this grouping of similes in these poems
than in any other alliterative work (e.g. 14/24 in *Purity* are thus
grouped) ; but other poems have examples of clustered similes,
such as *The Destruction of Troy* 3019–84, containing an elaborate
description of Helen. So there is the group of similes in *Pierce
the Ploughman's Crede*, already alluded to, and a group of three

in *The Destruction of Jerusalem* 525–33.   On the whole, the use of simile in the alliterative works is disappointing, and definitely unworthy of the tradition set by Laȝamon.

The alliterative poetry is often at its lowest stylistically.   Its frequent lack of concentration, and its general looseness are regrettable, but viewed as a complete whole its contributions to our early literature are of permanent value.   In its pages the heroic spirit of our forefathers is still aglow with poetic fire, though it had to accommodate itself to a new age with new interests and new tastes.   That it triumphed over so many of its difficulties is remarkable.   It quickly reached maturity and almost as quickly faded into oblivion, though its spirit was destined to remain.

INDEX.

403